FLORA SIMLENSIS
A HANDBOOK OF THE FLOWERING PLANTS OF SIMLA
AND THE NEIGHBOURHOOD

FLORA SIMLENSIS
A HANDBOOK OF THE FLOWERING PLANTS OF SIMLA
AND THE NEIGHBOURHOOD

BY THE LATE

COL. SIR HENRY COLLETT, K.C.B., F.L.S.

BENGAL ARMY

WITH AN INTRODUCTION

BY

W. BOTTING HEMSLEY, F.R.S. F.L.S.

KEEPER OF THE HERBARIUM AND LIBRARY, ROYAL BOTANIC GARDENS, KEW

AND 200 ILLUSTRATIONS IN THE TEXT

DRAWN BY MISS M. SMITH

Artist at the Herbarium, Royal Botanic Gardens, Kew

AND A MAP

GYAN

Published by

GYAN

Gyan Publishing House
5, Ansari Road
Daryaganj, New Delhi-110002
Phone: 011-47034999, 9811692060
E-mail: books@gyanbooks.com

Distribution Network
gyanbooks.com
India, USA, Canada, UK, Australia, France

ISBN : 978-81-212-9990-9 (PB)
First Published, 1902

2nd Impression 2021

Printed at: Gyan Press, Delhi.

Flora Simlensis A Handbook of the Flowering Plants of Simla
Author: Col. Sir Henry Collett

FLORA SIMLENSIS

A Handbook

OF THE

FLOWERING PLANTS OF SIMLA

AND THE NEIGHBOURHOOD

BY THE LATE

COL. SIR HENRY COLLETT, K.C.B., F.L.S.

BENGAL ARMY

WITH AN INTRODUCTION

BY

W. BOTTING HEMSLEY, F.R.S., F.L.S.

KEEPER OF THE HERBARIUM AND LIBRARY, ROYAL BOTANIC GARDENS, KEW

AND 200 ILLUSTRATIONS IN THE TEXT

DRAWN BY MISS M. SMITH

Artist at the Herbarium, Royal Botanic Gardens, Kew

AND A MAP

CALCUTTA AND SIMLA

THACKER, SPINK & CO.

LONDON: W. THACKER & CO., 2 CREED LANE, E.C.

1902

LILIUM POLYPHYLLUM

TO

SIR JOSEPH D. HOOKER

G.C.S.I., F.R.S., D.C.L., &c.

It was the desire of my dear Brother to dedicate this 'Handbook' to the illustrious and venerable Author of the 'Flora of British India,' to which work he was greatly indebted, and I am happy in being permitted to give effect to this wish.

ELLEN A. COLLETT.

LONDON, 1902.

CONTENTS

PREFACE

It has been my endeavour to produce a book which shall supply to residents at Simla, interested in botany and acquainted with the rudiments of that science, the means of identifying the trees, shrubs and herbs they see in their walks about the station roads and paths, in the neighbouring valleys or on excursions to Mushobra, Mahasu, Shali Peak, Fagoo, Narkunda, Huttoo, Baghi Forest and the Sutlej valley down to the hot springs near Suni. I have assigned no strictly defined limits to the 'Flora,' believing that this would answer the requirements of students better than if I were to confine it, for instance, to the territorial limits of the Simla Municipality or any other arbitrarily fixed boundaries. It is based on my own collection, made under ordinary conditions during a residence at Simla of about four years; and, judging from my own experience, a book is much needed containing descriptions of the plants found in the district roughly defined above. The area thus covered is extensive, ranging from about 2,000 to 10,000 feet of altitude, and including portions both of the outer arid regions and of the inner subalpine summits of the N.W. Himalaya. The number of species described is therefore proportionately large, and amounts to more than 1,300.

A short summary of the characters and distribution is given under each Natural Order followed by a key to the Genera. In a similar manner a short summary of generic characters and distribution is followed by a key to the Species. A short description is then given of each species, with its approximate local, Himalayan and general distribution, and period of flowering. The author's name is given after the name of each species, followed by a reference to the volume and page of the 'Flora of British India' which contains the description of the species, with further references and synonymy. An asterisk before a name signifies that I have seen no specimen of the species in question collected in or near Simla; but, judging from its known range, it may be expected to occur within the limits of the 'Flora.' For example, if a species has been collected at Murree on the West and in Kumaon on the East, it will probably be found within the Simla district.

In the distribution 'Simla' signifies that the species has been found in Simla or in the immediate neighbourhood, while 'Mushobra,' 'Mahasu,' etc., indicate that I have seen specimens from one or more of these places. 'Temperate Himalaya' signifies that the species extends along the Himalaya from Sikkim to Cashmere. 'Western Himalaya' indicates the region from Kumaon to Cashmere.

The derivation of the generic names is given as nearly as possible without any pretension to original research in this direction.

The illustrations are all from original drawings by Miss M. SMITH, made from dried specimens, except in a few instances where the species happened to be in cultivation at Kew. All the figures are approximately half the natural size, and the dissections are enlarged. Students will, I am sure, find the task of identifying plants much facilitated by these beautiful and characteristic illustrations, and I cannot sufficiently express my gratitude to Miss SMITH for the great pains she has taken to produce artistic and accurate representations. Miss SMITH derived much assistance in her work from collections of beautiful water-colour drawings of Simla flowers kindly lent to me by Major C. E. GUBBINS and by the late Colonel W. C. MACKINNON. The plants figured are all common Simla species, but British plants or their close allies are purposely omitted, as figures of these are already available in many works on British botany.[1] A considerable number of Simla plants also occur in Britain, and this is noted at the end of the description, together with the common English name.

Thanks to the kindness of Sir WILLIAM THISELTON-DYER, Director of the Royal Botanic Gardens, Kew, I have enjoyed the great advantage of preparing this work in the Herbarium, being thus enabled to supplement my own imperfect collection of Simla plants by the largest and best-named collection of Indian and Himalayan plants in existence. Working in the Herbarium has also given me free access to the numerous rare and beautifully illustrated works in the Library, and has placed me in communication with the officers of the Herbarium Staff, for whose unfailing courtesy and readiness to afford me the advice and assistance for which I was perpetually asking I beg to offer my hearty thanks and acknowledgments. I am under obligations of this nature to the whole of the staff, but it is to Mr. W. BOTTING HEMSLEY, F.R.S., the Keeper, that I am most deeply indebted; indeed, if my book should be found to possess any merit, it is to him that credit is due. He kindly read the whole of the manuscript while the work was in progress, and the drawings were all made under his supervision. To Mr. N. E. BROWN I owe the determination of many critical specimens, while Mr. C. B. CLARKE, F.R.S., was never weary of giving me the benefit of his wide knowledge of Indian plants and accurate botanical judgment. I am also under many and deep obligations to the undermentioned:—Sir DIETRICH BRANDIS, K.C.I.E., F.R.S., etc., late Inspector General of Forests to the Government of India; Mr. J. S. GAMBLE, C.I.E., F.R.S., late Conservator of Forests, and Director of the Imperial Forest School, Dehra Dun; F. J. DUTHIE, B.A., F.L.S., Director of the Botanical Department, Northern India; Sir GEORGE KING,

[1] Excellent figures of all the British species of Flowering Plants and Ferns, as understood by Bentham, will be found in 'Illustrations of the British Flora,' by W. H. Fitch and W. G. Smith, published by Messrs. Reeve & Co., London.

K.C.I.E., F.R.S., LL.D., etc., late Superintendent of the Royal Botanic Gardens, Calcutta ; Major D. Prain, M.B., F.R.S.E., etc., the present Superintendent ; and to Dr. G. Watt, C.I.E., F.L.S., Reporter on Economic Products to the Government of India.

I am further indebted to Lady Elisabeth Bruce [now Lady Babington Smith] and Mr. H. Babington Smith, authors of a privately printed list of Simla plants containing notes on the colours of their flowers, localities and seasons of flowering, which has most kindly been placed at my disposal.

HENRY COLLETT.

[*June* 1900.]

IN MEMORIAM

I HAVE watched the progress of this work with sympathy and interest. I had not thought that the death of its distinguished author would impose on me the sad task of writing these words to his memory.

Sir Henry Collett was born in 1836 and entered the Bengal Army when he was only nineteen. His military career was one of great distinction. The Commander-in-Chief, Field-Marshal Earl Roberts, K.G., V.C., etc., has with great kindness given me the following account of it.

March 1, 1902.

Dear Sir William Thiselton-Dyer, — I was indeed well acquainted with the late Sir Henry Collett, and had a great regard for him. Throughout his military life he was as persevering and thorough as you describe him to be in the preparation of his book on the indigenous plants of Simla.

Sir Henry Collett took a prominent part in several campaigns. As quite a boy he served during the Indian Mutiny. The following year, 1858, he took part in the Sittana Expedition on the N.W. Frontier of India.

Five years later (1862–63) he was with a force employed in the Cossya and Jyntea hills on the S.E. Frontier of India, and received a severe wound in the ankle, which lamed him for life.

In 1867–68 he took part in the Abyssinian Expedition, and it was then, I think, I first made his acquaintance.

When the second Afghan war broke out in 1878, I applied for Major (as he then was) Collett to be attached to my column as Assistant Quarter-Master-General. He remained with me during the two years the war lasted, and afforded me very valuable assistance. It was from information gained by Major Collett, by means of a personal reconnaissance he made, that I was enabled to adopt the Spingawi route and thus turn the strong position held by the Afghans on the Peiwar Kotal.

Between the years 1886–90, Colonel Collett served first as Quarter-Master-General in India, then in command of a brigade in Burma, and subsequently in command of the Eastern Frontier District during the Chin-Lushai Expedition. In 1891, Major-General Collett commanded the expedition to Manipur, and acted as Chief Commissioner of Assam.

General Collett was frequently mentioned in despatches, he was thanked by the Government of India for his services in Assam, and before he retired from the Army in 1893, he had the honour of being made a Knight Commander of the Bath.

No one who was acquainted with Sir Henry Collett could fail to appreciate his kindly disposition and charm of manner, as well as his many soldierly qualities. He was one of the few officers in the Army I have met with who was as devoted to science as to his professional duties.

Sir Henry Collett's retirement was a serious loss to the Indian Army, but I rejoice to think that the last years of his life were spent in pursuits which were thoroughly congenial to him, with a result which confirms my high estimate of his application, resolution, and ability.

Believe me,
Yours very truly,
ROBERTS.

For nearly forty years Collett was actively employed in military duties, and mostly in India. From his youth he had a strong taste for scientific studies. It is remarkable that he was able, practically unaided, to prosecute them with such success. Our common friend, Mr. J. S. Gamble, C.I.E., F.R.S., late Director of the Forest School, Dehra Dun, has given me some interesting particulars. He 'used to say of himself, that his wound, obtained at an early period of his service, incapacitated him for the games which most soldiers, at any rate young men, delight in.' He first took up astronomy and physics. Mr. Gamble continues: 'I always used to envy him his power of application and his wonderful capacity of concentrating his attention on a new subject and not resting till he had got to understand it. . . . He had a wonderfully clear power of explaining. . . . When the discoveries of the telephone and microphone etc. were made, he was much interested; and he amused himself by constructing a microphone and sending messages from one end of his house to the other. Often I have spent some hours over it with him, and he was delightfully pleased when he could induce a fly to walk on the drum and listen to its footsteps.'

Collett seems to have first become interested in botany in 1878 during the Kuram Valley expedition, perhaps influenced by the late Brigade-Surgeon Aitchison, C.I.E., F.R.S.

The latter wrote: 'Early in 1879, I proposed to the Quarter-Master-General, Major Collett, that it might prove advantageous to science if some one were appointed to accompany the column in the contemplated advance on Kabul. General Roberts at once recommended the proposal to superior authority, which ultimately resulted in my being attached to the force as botanist.' The result was embodied in the important paper published in the 'Journal of the Linnean Society' (Botany, xviii. pp. 1–113).

Late in 1879 Collett paid a brief visit to England. He wrote to Sir Joseph Hooker on September 16, apologising for his inability to deliver a letter from Aitchison in person, having 'to return immediately in consequence of the news which has been received from Kabul.' He adds: 'I had not much time when in Kuram for botanical pursuits, but I collected most of the plants which were new to me, and some of them will be forwarded to you.'

It was, however, about 1885 that Collett's attention was seriously turned to botanical work. In the summer of that year the Simla Naturalists' Society was founded. Sir Courtenay Ilbert, K.C.S.I., was President, and Collett was an original member. The present work is the fulfilment of a hope expressed by the President in the preface to the first number of the journal that one outcome of its work would be 'a handbook such as may be worthy of a district singularly rich in objects of interest to the naturalist, and as may furnish information to be sought in vain in the arid pages of a district manual.' The society has been described as 'a small band of ardent naturalists.' They no doubt confirmed Collett in his permanent devotion to botany. He contributed his first botanical papers to its journal and is also reported to have delivered to it a lecture on polarised light.

Collett collected assiduously the plants of Simla and formed a herbarium which he used in the preparation of this book. After his death it was given by his family to Kew. In 1887–88 he was in command of a brigade in Burma, and in the Southern Shan States on the little-explored frontier of Upper Burma he found an opportunity of breaking new ground. In A. H. Hildebrand, C.I.E., the superintendent of the Southern Shan States, he found a colleague of tastes sympathetic with his own. Collett says: 'I began collecting plants in this region partly to gratify my own love of botany, and partly in response to the request of my friend Dr. (now Sir George) King, K.C.I.E., F.R.S.' The results were published in 1890 in the 'Journal of the Linnean Society' (Botany, xxviii. pp. 1–150). No fewer than 725 species of flowering plants were enumerated. These were worked out at Kew and published under the joint names of Collett and W. B. Hemsley. The collection included two of the most remarkable plants ever introduced into European gardens. Both are remarkable for the size of their flowers: *Rosa gigantea* is the largest single-flowered rose known, it is described as having flowers 5–6 inches in diameter; it climbs to the top of the tallest trees, and Collett is said to have detected it at the distance of two miles by means of a field-glass; *Lonicera hildebrandiana* is a honeysuckle with flowers seven inches long; it was named in honour of his friend who 'kindly gave much assistance in collecting,' and who, after an infinity of trouble, ultimately succeeded in transmitting living seeds to Kew. In 1889 Collett had himself sent to Kew living plants of two extremely remarkable orchids which he had discovered, *Bulbophyllum racemosum* and *Cirrhopetalum Collettii.*

After 1889 Collett's hands were pretty full of serious military and administrative duties. I heard nothing from him till after his retirement in 1893. Even then it is an open secret that high professional advancement was still within his reach. But he had begun to be afflicted with deafness, and as he told me in after years he thought no one with that infirmity was justified in assuming high military command.

He eventually settled in London, and it must have been early in 1895 that he came to consult me about his projected 'Flora of Simla.' He had a good practical knowledge of it in the field, and his first idea was that he might make a sort of rough draft and that some member of my staff might put it into a proper technical shape. I pointed out to him that such a collaboration would be in no way satisfactory, that the merit of the book would be the personal impress that he would give to it himself, and that I should not be inclined to aid the undertaking unless he undertook it single-handed. Collett pleaded his want of technical knowledge, but the real obstacle was only his excessive modesty. He was a little shy of coming to work amongst us with only the equipment of the amateur, and though possessed of indomitable pluck was diffident as to the result. I assured him that it was merely a question of learning the grammar of an unfamiliar language; that it might be an irksome task for a few weeks, but that he would soon acquire the necessary facility and that he would then feel a new interest in the prosecution of his work. I promised him that his path should be smoothed by the willing assistance of my staff, and he agreed with some demur to make the attempt. I call to mind no similar case of a man late in life, after a course of exceptional distinction, quietly taking the position of a pupil in another field. But the wisdom of my advice was abundantly justified. Collett stuck to his task with bulldog tenacity occasionally relieved by a groan. But he soon mastered his difficulties and became the severest critic of his own work, the early portions of which he entirely rewrote. For several succeeding years he worked at Kew with the greatest regularity, spending the best part of the day in the Herbarium and ending with a walk in the gardens, where I was often amused to find that the habit of the old Quarter-Master-General had not been lost and that nothing escaped his observant eye.

Some failure of his health probably took place, though so imperceptibly as to escape observation. The old military fire was roused by the outbreak of the South African war, which he followed with absorbing attention. His first estimates of its course were extravagantly optimistic, to be followed by others equally pessimistic. With no military knowledge but some conception of the conditions, I ventured to differ from him in both respects. But the war weighed heavily on him, and he told me he could not sleep at night for thinking of it and its consequences. He had, however, almost completed the manuscript of his book, and commenced printing. He then took a holiday in Ireland with Mr. Gamble. It is possible that he over-fatigued himself. On his return he had some kind of sudden seizure, and for some time he was in a precarious state but slowly recovered. He then came to see me at Kew, and though he was obviously very much broken I did not feel any immediate anxiety about him. But he had repeated failure of the heart's action, and to this he eventually succumbed. He spent his life strenuously and with distinction in the service of his country and in the interests of science, and the end came with the simple exhaustion of his physical powers.

Almost his last enquiry was as to the progress of his book. This fortunately had been left in a state which enabled Mr. W. B. Hemsley, F.R.S., the Keeper of the Herbarium, to see it through the press with little difficulty. I think Collett felt no real anxiety as to its fate. He hoped that it would stimulate an interest in a subject which he himself had found a pleasant recreation in the midst of official duties. Those who use it will speedily discover that it is no mere compilation but the outcome of conscientious and independent work. Collett had the true scientific temperament. He had no respect for scientific authority and distrusted textbooks. He was never content without verifying the facts for himself. He described his plants fresh from the field and at once entered in his notebooks copious memoranda and excellent drawings, and these he constantly used in working up his material at Kew.

At first sight there may seem something anomalous in a distinguished soldier devoting his years of retirement to botanical studies, still more perhaps in prosecuting them in the midst of his professional duties. As a matter of fact, the obligations of botanical science to the Army are very great: it is sufficient to recall the names so familiar to botanists of the late General Munro, C.B.; of the late Colonel Grant, C.B., C.S.I., and of Lieutenant-General Sir Richard Strachey, G.C.S.I. The flora of Tibet would be hardly known to us but for the collections made by military officers, of whom Captain Deasy, the late Captain Wellby and Captain Malcolm, D.S.O., may more particularly be mentioned. Nor is it easy to estimate the position our knowledge of the Indian flora would occupy without the labours of a long series of officers of the Indian Medical Department. And among Russian officers the name of General Przewalski will always stand out pre-eminent for his botanical work in Western Asia. The fact is that the qualities that make for success both in the soldier and the botanist are largely identical: they are quick observation and the power of rapidly drawing correct observations from minute facts. When Collett discovered his giant rose through his field-glass he was using his eyes and his reasoning powers precisely as he would have done in a military reconnaissance.

Collett's personality had something wholly out of the common. Rather below the average height he had a spare, erect and well-knit figure. A bright, frank and alert expression was accompanied by a singular charm of manner. In many ways he constantly reminded me of the late General Gordon. And as with him a keen glance would sometimes flash from the eyes which showed that stern resolution would not be wanting on occasion. There was nothing about him of the *beau sabreur*, but he had all the impress of a man destined to lead and command. As with most distinguished soldiers, his address was singularly modest and simple; at the same time he held decided views on most subjects and with extreme tenacity, though rarely caring to give expression to them. Nor did he ever refer to his past career. In fact, I never induced him to talk about it except in the case of the Manipur expedition, on which on merely geographical grounds I asked for information. He was not a copious correspondent, and his letters were always strictly to the point and expressed with soldierly terseness.

Mr. Gamble, himself a botanist of distinction, who had long worked with him in India, sums up his estimate of Collett's powers in words with which from my own experience I entirely concur:—

'I am convinced that if Collett had been a professional botanist he would have made a great name for himself; and it is possible that had he been spared, his work, supported by his knowledge of the world, his wide reading and by his distrust of anything he could not personally verify, would have been more original and so perhaps more valuable. He was quite undaunted ; he talked of taking up the Simla mosses when his Phanerogamic Flora should be published !'

I devote these words to the memory of my friend. I will but add this : no one who has ever come to work amongst us at Kew has more completely won the affectionate regard of everyone with whom he has come in contact.

W. T. Thiselton-Dyer.

Kew, 1902.

INTRODUCTION

(BY W. BOTTING HEMSLEY)

IN the foregoing biographical sketch Sir William Thiselton-Dyer has expressed feelings shared by myself and others who were more or less associated with the Author in connection with this work, and I need go no further into personal matters than to explain the extent of my responsibility. Sir Henry's Preface is much too modest concerning himself, and much too lavish in acknowledgment of assistance from others. As a matter of fact, although he consulted me on many points from the beginning, and I made considerable alterations in his manuscript of the early Orders, I have in no instance referred back to the plants themselves in connection with the descriptions.

The first serious attack of illness overtook Sir Henry just after the first sheet was set up in type, and while the questions of style and typography were still under consideration. When sufficiently recovered, towards the end of the year 1900, to discuss the matter, he arranged with my daughter to correct the proofs, under my supervision. The body of the work was then practically completed, but it was the Author's wish to revise some portions of it, more especially that relating to the Grasses and the Preface. His health improved so much that we all hoped he would be able to carry out his intentions; but although his interest in the work was unabated to the very last, he was unable to do any more than settle points of detail as the printing progressed. The Preface was written before his illness; hence the absence of any mention of the arrangement made with Miss Hemsley. I think it important to put this fact on record, because I could not undertake to read the proofs through myself; and this may explain errors overlooked that I might or ought to have detected had I read them all critically.[1]

[1] It is unfortunate that a few synonyms were not included by the Author, because it sometimes happens that they have been more used in previous publications than the names adopted in the present work; for instance, *Picea Morinda* is comparatively familiar in English gardens under the synonym of

The question of what should be included in the Introduction was never discussed. I only know that it was Sir Henry's intention to compile a Glossary, and I undertook to prepare a Synopsis of the Natural Orders. I am wholly responsible for this part of the book, except that I am indebted to my friends Mr. C. W. Hope, late of the Engineering Department, Government of India, for a list of the Ferns, and Mr. J. S. Gamble, C.I.E., F.R.S., formerly Conservator of Forests to the Government of India, and Director of the School of Forestry at Dehra Dun, for some notes on the Vegetation. He and Sir Henry were old friends, and they botanised together the district of Simla.

POSITION, AREA AND CLIMATE

The area is defined or rather described in the Preface, and the Map supplies further information.

The town of Simla, the centre of the district whose Flora is described in the following pages, is situated in about 31° 6′ N. latitude, and 77° 10′ E. longitude, at an altitude of 7,230 ft., and exactly on the watershed of the two great river-systems, the Ganges and the Indus. The rivulets flowing northward and westward are feeders of the Sutlej, which rises in Western Tibet and forms the most easterly of the five principal tributaries of the Indus, which flows into the Arabian Sea; whilst the Giri river and its affluents to the east flow into the Jumna, one of the great tributaries of the Ganges, which debouches into the Bay of Bengal.

The climate of the district exhibits considerable variations at different elevations and exposures. In round numbers there is a total difference of 8,000 ft. in elevation; and then there is the factor of aspect, whether northern or southern, to be taken into account. From observations near Simla at about 7,000 ft. the mean temperature of January, the coldest month, is 40°·6 Fahr., and of June, the warmest month, 67°·1; whilst for the year it is 54°·86. The lowest temperature recorded, 26°·6, occurred on two days in February 1882, and the highest, 86°, on three days in May

Abies Smithiana. Full synonymy, however, is given in the *Flora of British India*, to which the inquirer is referred.

One more explanation I may give here. It has been represented to me that amateurs generally are puzzled by the 'authors,' that is, the names or abbreviations of names, cited after the names of the plants. Briefly the 'author' is the person who described the plant under the genus in question, or referred it to that genus, even without description, the plant having been already adequately described though, inferentially, referred to the wrong genus.

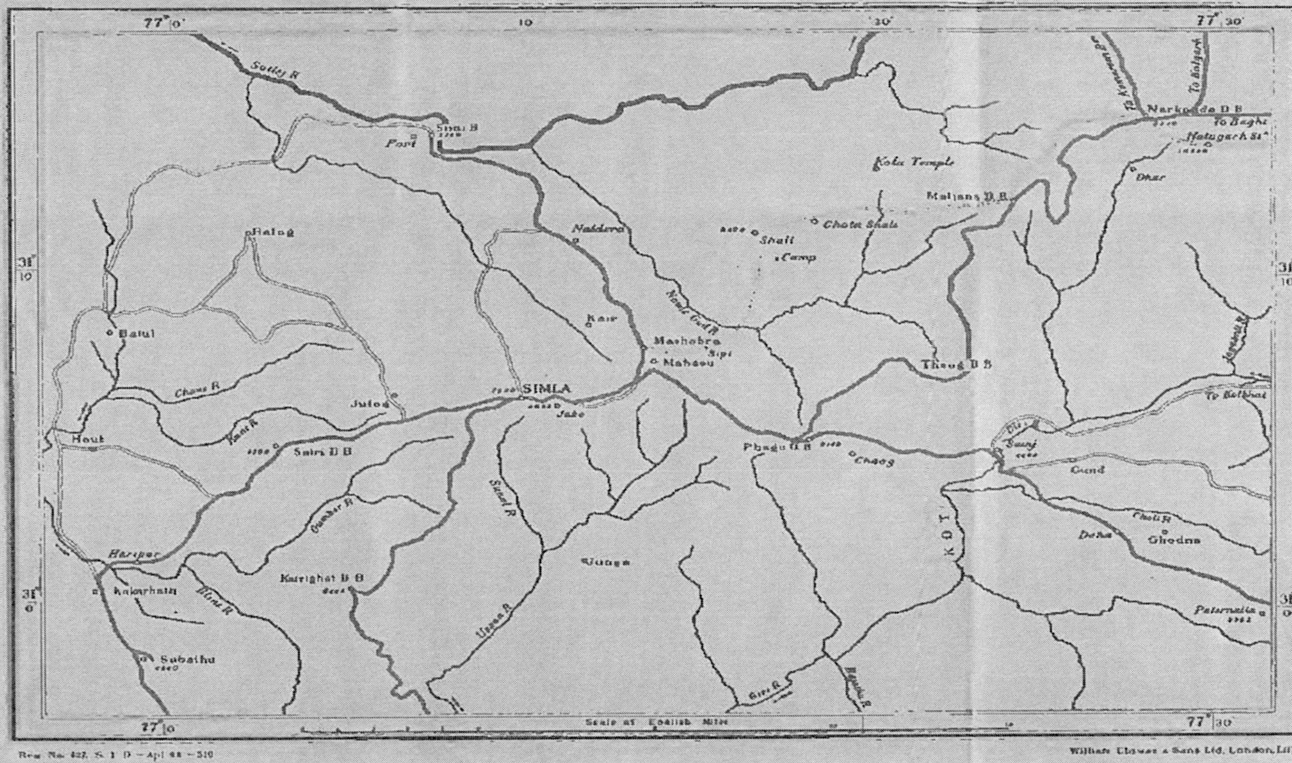

SIMLA
Sutlej R
Fort
Narkanda D B
To Baghi
Hatugarh St.
To Kotgarh
Dhar
Kota Temple
Matiana D.B.
Chota Shali
Shali
Camp
Naldera
Nauti Gad R
Kair
Mashobra
Sipi
Mahasu
Theog D B
Jako
Phagu D B
Chaog
To Kotkhai
Giri R
Gund
Choli R
Deha
Ghodna
Paternalla
K O T
Junga
Sanol R
Giri R
Kasighat D B
Gumbar R
Haripur
Kakarhatti
Subathu
Balal R
Hout
Sairi D B
Jutog
Chamb R
Batul
Balog
Scale of English Miles
Rew. No. 427, S. I. D. – Apl 88 – 510
William Clowes & Sons Ltd, London, Lith.

and one in June. Snow falls from December to March, and not infrequently lies for several weeks.

The period of greatest rain is from June to September, with an average of 52 inches; whilst the fall for the whole year is 70 inches. There is a considerable decrease in the rainfall northward; at Kotgarh, for example, it is little more than half that of Simla.

DESCRIPTION OF THE MAP

The map is on a scale of four miles to the inch, and it bears the names of the principal localities mentioned in the body of the work, with their respective elevations. The rivers and streams are coloured blue, and the main roads yellow. Unfortunately the spelling of Indian geographical names is anything but uniform, and the spelling throughout this book of several of the localities is so different from that on the map as to be unrecognisable to persons unversed in the vagaries of geographers and officials. The orthography of the map is, I believe, official at the present day; whilst that of the book has long been current, and is more familiar. In other works quoted or cited several other variants occur. Perhaps placing the different spellings side by side is the most useful way of presenting them.

Book	Map	Other Works
Baggi	Baghi	Bargi
Baghi	—	—
Bhagi	—	—
Boileaugunge	—	Boileauganj
Charaog	Chaog	—
Chor	—	Choor, Chur
Fagoo	Phagu	Fargoo
Fagu	—	—
Giri	Giri	Giree
—	Gumber	Gambar
Huttoo	Hatugarh	Hattoo
—	—	Hattou, Hatu
—	—	Whattoo
Jako	Jako	Jacka, Chaka, Jakko
Jutogh	Jutog	—
Kairi	Kair	—
Kotgurh	Kotgarh	Kotgerh, Kotgorh
Matiana	Matiana	Matteana
Mahasu	Mahasu	Mahassoo
Mushobra	Mashobra	—

Book	Map	Other Works
Naldera	Naldera	Nahl Dehra
Nal Dehra	—	—
Narkunda	Narkanda	Nagkunda
Patarnala	Paternalla	—
Sainj	Sainj	—
Synj	—	—
Subathoo	Subathu	Sabathu
—	—	Soobathoo
—	—	Subbathoo
Sungree	—	Soongri
Syree	Sairi	—

The Chor, frequently mentioned in the body of the work, is a peak just without the limits of the map to the south-east. It is nearly 12,000 ft. high, and is situated in about 30° 52′ and 77° 32′. This and Hatugarh are the only elevations in the district on which there is a subalpine vegetation.

COLLECTORS

As long ago as 1855 Hooker and Thomson ('Flora Indica,' Introduction, p. 203) stated that the flora of Simla might be considered as exceedingly well known, and at p. 69 of the same work the collections are summarised, but the number of persons named as having collected in Simla is not large. This is perhaps due to the fact, that when the great Indian botanists Wallich, Royle and Falconer successively botanised in the North-West, Simla was in an early stage of its history. The earliest noteworthy collection in the Kew Herbarium labelled as coming from Simla was made by the Countess of Dalhousie, who evidently was no mere collector but a keen botanist; for in a letter dated Dalhousie Castle, February 4, 1833, to Sir William Hooker, announcing the despatch of 600 duplicates of her Simla plants, she gives some interesting particulars. At the date when the plants were collected (1830) the Earl of Dalhousie was Commander-in-Chief in India, and subsequently he was appointed Governor-General. Referring to their journeys Lady Dalhousie says: 'At Simla we remained nearly seven months. This station is 7,500 ft. above the level of the sea, in the region of the *Pinus Deodara* and *Rhododendron arboreum*. Subbathoo, where several of the plants were gathered, is on a lower range at 4,000 ft. Mahassoo is 9,000 ft., and the greatest elevation I reached was Whattoo Mountain, 10,763 ft.

At Simla I found five species of *Pinus*; at Mahassoo four of oak —all evergreen.' From the foregoing it appears that she saw and distinguished all the species of pine and oak observed by later botanists. Colonel (Lieutenant-General) Munro, Major (Lieutenant-Colonel) Madden, Captain (General Sir Richard) Strachey, Mr. Winterbottom, Captain Simpson, General and Mrs. Walker, Major Vicary and Mr. M. P. Edgeworth were also among the early amateurs who contributed to Sir William Hooker's herbarium, now forming part of the National Herbarium at Kew. Among botanists of that period the collections of Griffith, Jacquemont and Thomson are at Kew. Later contributors are Sir Dietrich Brandis, Mr. J. S. Gamble and Dr. G. Watt; and Sir Henry Collett's collection has been presented to Kew since his decease. The titles of their published works, containing more or less information concerning the flora of Simla, are included in the 'Bibliography,' p. lxvii. Extracts of passages relating to the vegetation of Simla have been made from the writings of several of the travellers named.

VEGETATION

Only a very imperfect idea of the composition of the Vegetation of a country can be gained from an enumeration of the plants constituting its flora, even when some explanation is given under each species of its relative prevalence. A species may be common and generally dispersed, and yet not constitute a conspicuous feature in the landscape, by the roadside, in pastures or in woods. Fifty per cent. probably of the species have to be sought for, and not more than twenty-five per cent. enter into the physiognomies of the vegetation. Some trees and shrubs are conspicuous as individuals; others only from growing gregariously. Some herbs have large and brightly coloured flowers; yet others having smaller flowers, but growing in masses, give greater character to the vegetation. Had the Author been spared to complete his work, he would doubtless have pictured in words the appearance of the country at different seasons. This want I shall attempt to meet in some measure. Following the Author, I shall introduce some further comparisons with the flora of the British Islands, beginning with the ordinal composition of the Simla flora, premising that the Simla district has a smaller area than the county of Sussex, in which about 1,000 species of flowering plants grow wild.

Table showing the number of Genera and Species of each Natural Order in the Flora of Simla, and the number of these Genera and Species common to Simla and the British Islands.

Orders	Genera		Species	
	Simla District	British Islands	Simla District	British Islands
Ranunculaceæ	12	7	33	4
Magnoliaceæ	1	0	1	0
Menispermaceæ	3	0	6	0
Berberidaceæ	2	1	6	1
Papaveraceæ	2	1	2	1
Fumariaceæ	3	2	6	1
Cruciferæ	11	9	23	11
Capparidaceæ	2	0	2	0
Violaceæ	1	1	4	0
Bixaceæ	2	0	2	0
Polygalaceæ	1	1	5	0
Caryophyllaceæ	12	9	25	7
Hypericaceæ	1	1	5	1
Malvaceæ	4	1	10	2
Tiliaceæ	3	0	8	0
Linaceæ	2	1	2	0
Malpighiaceæ	1	0	1	0
Geraniaceæ	4	4	20	5
Rutaceæ	7	0	7	0
Simarubaceæ	1	0	1	0
Meliaceæ	2	0	4	0
Aquifoliaceæ	1	1	2	0
Celastraceæ	4	1	8	0
Rhamnaceæ	5	1	11	0
Vitaceæ	2	0	6	0
Sapindaceæ	6	1	10	0
Sabiaceæ	2	0	3	0
Anacardiaceæ	3	0	8	0
Coriariaceæ	1	0	1	0
Leguminosæ	45	8	114	12
Rosaceæ	12	10	42	7
Saxifragaceæ	9	4	16	2
Crassulaceæ	6	3	11	0
Droseraceæ	1	1	1	0
Halorrhagidaceæ	2	2	3	3
Myrtaceæ	1	0	1	0
Melastomaceæ	1	0	1	0
Lythraceæ	2	0	2	0
Onagraceæ	2	2	9	4
Samydaceæ	1	0	1	0
Cucurbitaceæ	4	0	4	0
Begoniaceæ	1	0	2	0
Datiscaceæ	1	0	1	0
Ficoideæ	1	0	1	0
Umbelliferæ	14	12	26	3
Araliaceæ	2	1	2	1
Cornaceæ	2	1	4	0
Caprifoliaceæ	4	2	13	0
Rubiaceæ	13	2	23	2

Orders	Genera		Species	
	Simla District	British Islands	Simla District	British Islands
Valerianaceæ	1	1	2	0
Dipsaceæ	3	2	5	0
Compositæ	59	27	109	19
Campanulaceæ	4	3	6	0
Ericaceæ	4	0	5	0
Monotropaceæ	1	1	1	0
Plumbaginaceæ	1	0	1	0
Primulaceæ	6	5	14	2
Myrsinaceæ	1	0	2	0
Styracaceæ	1	0	1	0
Oleaceæ	6	2	10	0
Apocynaceæ	5	0	5	0
Asclepiadaceæ	10	0	14	0
Loganiaceæ	1	0	2	0
Gentianaceæ	5	1	16	0
Boraginaceæ	8	3	12	1
Convolvulaceæ	5	2	10	2
Solanaceæ	7	3	11	4
Scrophulariaceæ	24	8	40	8
Orobanchaceæ	1	1	1	0
Lentibulariaceæ	1	1	1	0
Gesneraceæ	3	0	4	0
Bignoniaceæ	2	0	3	0
Acanthaceæ	10	0	15	0
Verbenaceæ	8	1	8	1
Labiatæ	29	13	59	7
Plantaginaceæ	1	1	3	2
Nyctaginaceæ	2	0	2	0
Illecebraceæ	1	0	1	0
Amarantaceæ	7	0	9	0
Chenopodiaceæ	3	2	5	2
Phytolaccaceæ	1	0	1	0
Polygonaceæ	3	2	23	3
Piperaceæ	3	0	3	0
Lauraceæ	4	0	7	0
Thymelæaceæ	2	1	3	0
Elæagnaceæ	2	1	2	0
Loranthaceæ	2	1	7	1
Santalaceæ	2	1	2	0
Balanophoraceæ	1	0	1	0
Euphorbiaceæ	12	2	22	3
Urticaceæ	16	3	35	1
Juglandaceæ	1	0	1	0
Myricaceæ	1	1	1	0
Cupuliferæ	5	5	10	0
Salicaceæ	2	2	9	1
Gnetaceæ	1	0	1	0
Coniferæ	7	3	9	2
Orchidaceæ	18	10	38	5
Scitamineæ	4	0	5	0
Hæmodoraceæ	2	0	2	0
Iridaceæ	1	1	2	0
Hypoxidaceæ	1	0	1	0
Dioscoreaceæ	1	0	4	0
Liliaceæ	18	8	32	3

Orders		Genera		Species	
		Simla District	British Islands	Simla District	British Islands
Commelinaceæ		3	0	6	0
Juncaceæ		2	2	7	4
Araceæ		6	1	11	1
Lemnaceæ		2	2	4	4
Alismaceæ		1	1	1	1
Naiadaceæ		3	3	8	6
Eriocaulaceæ		1	1	3	0
Cyperaceæ		12	5	56	2
Gramineæ		58	21	133	21
Totals . . .	113	639	244	1326	173

Summary

		Genera		Species	
Dicotyledones . .		498 or 78·0 per cent.		1003 or 75·8 per cent.	
Monocotyledones					
Petaloideæ . .	62	133 or 20·8	,,	121	313 or 23·3 ,,
Glumaceæ . . .	71			192	
Gymnospermæ . . .		8 or 1·2	,,		10 or 0·9 ,,
		639 100			1326 100

The proportion of species of Dicotyledones and Monocotyledones in the flora of the world is about 81·30 and 18·70 per cent., and the 23·3 per cent. of Monocotyledones in Simla is very high. It is due in this instance to the large number of grasses in this comparatively small area. For the whole of India the percentage is 23·43, and for other large areas that I have calculated it varies from 17·30 in Europe; 18·50, Australia; 19·38, North America; to 21·50 in Mexico.

From the foregoing comparison of the floras of the Simla District and the British Islands it will be understood that a person having some knowledge of the latter will be well prepared to take up the study of the former. It is true that only about 13 per cent. of the species are the same; but nearly 40 per cent. of the genera are common to the two countries. Incidentally it may be mentioned that in higher latitudes the resemblances become stronger. Thus in a collection of about 500 species from the neighbourhood of Kirin, in about 126° E. long. and 44° N. lat., 160 were British, or just 32 per cent. of the whole.

On the other hand, it is somewhat surprising to find that thirty-eight Natural Orders are represented in the small district of Simla which are not included in the flora of the British Islands. This is partly accounted for by the fact that a small portion of the former comes within the subtropical zone. Apart from this, the British flora is very poor as compared with the Japanese, for example, even after eliminating the subtropical element found in the warmer part of Japan. Again, comparing the list of Orders not represented in Britain with the list of Orders represented in Simla by only one genus and one species it will be seen that sixteen out of twenty-three are the same. Among Orders which do not occur in Britain several which are not wholly tropical or subtropical are somewhat numerous in Simla. Thus of the Rutaceæ there are seven genera and seven species, of the Asclepiadaceæ ten and fourteen, and of the Acanthaceæ ten and fifteen, respectively.

Against this, twelve Natural Orders are represented in the British flora but not in that of Simla. About half of these, however, are aquatic or marsh plants, which accounts for their absence from Simla. The rest are small Orders, except the Amaryllidaceæ, of which the Hæmodoraceæ and Hypoxidaceæ are regarded as Suborders by some botanists.

Natural Orders represented in the Simla District but not in the British Islands.

Magnoliaceæ
Menispermaceæ
Capparidaceæ
Bixaceæ
Malpighiaceæ
Rutaceæ
Simarubaceæ
Meliaceæ
Vitaceæ
Sabiaceæ
Anacardiaceæ
Coriariaceæ
Myrtaceæ
Melastomaceæ
Samydaceæ
Begoniaceæ
Datiscaceæ
Ficoideæ
Myrsinaceæ
Styracaceæ
Asclepiadaceæ
Loganiaceæ
Gesneraceæ
Bignoniaceæ
Acanthaceæ
Nyctaginaceæ
Amarantaceæ
Phytolaccaceæ
Piperaceæ
Lauraceæ
Balanophoraceæ
Juglandaceæ
Gnetaceæ
Scitamineæ
Hæmodoraceæ
Hypoxidaceæ
Dioscoreaceæ
Commelinaceæ

Natural Orders represented in the British Islands but not in the Simla District.

Nymphæaceæ
Resedaceæ
Cistaceæ
Frankeniaceæ
Portulacaceæ
Elatinaceæ
Empetraceæ
Polemoniaceæ
Ceratophyllaceæ
Hydrocharidaceæ
Amaryllidaceæ
Typhaceæ

A glance at the table, pp. xxviii.–xxx., showing the number of genera and species of each Natural Order in the flora of Simla is sufficient to enable one to realise that certain Orders constitute a prominent feature in the aspect of the vegetation, or if not in its aspect at least in its composition, whilst others form no appreciable part of the vegetation. Thus thirty-five, or nearly a third, of the Orders are represented by only one genus, and twenty-three of these Orders by only one genus and one species each. The following lists bring them all under the eye at once, and by referring to the remarks under the descriptions one can gain an idea of their respective positions in the formation of the vegetation. For example, *Balanophora involucrata* (p. 443) has been collected only once in the Simla District, and that more than half a century ago; and many others are very rare or inconspicuous. On the other hand *Ilex dipyrena* appears to be a common tree at elevations of 5000 to 8000 ft.

Natural Orders of which there is only one Genus and only one Species in the Flora of Simla.

Magnoliaceæ	Datiscaceæ	Phytolaccaceæ
Malpighiaceæ	Ficoideæ	Balanophoraceæ
Simarubaceæ	Monotropaceæ	Juglandaceæ
Coriariaceæ	Plumbaginaceæ	Myricaceæ
Droseraceæ	Styracaceæ	Gnetaceæ
Myrtaceæ	Orobanchaceæ	Hypoxidaceæ
Melastomaceæ	Lentibulariaceæ	Alismaceæ
Samydaceæ	Illecebraceæ	

Natural Orders of which there is only one Genus, but more than one Species in the Flora of Simla.

Violaceæ	Begoniaceæ	Plantaginaceæ
Polygalaceæ	Valerianaceæ	Iridaceæ
Hypericaceæ	Myrsinaceæ	Dioscoreaceæ
Aquifoliaceæ	Loganiaceæ	Eriocaulaceæ

The next table shows that a large proportion of the genera and species belong to a few Natural Orders. Eighteen out of 113 Orders comprise 372 out of the 639 genera, and 853 out of the 1326 species. Further, it will be seen that the three Orders, Gramineæ, Leguminosæ and Compositæ, furnish more than a quarter of both genera and species. In the flora of the world the position of these Orders in relation to each other is just reversed.

Natural Orders of twenty Species and upwards in the Flora of Simla.

Orders	Genera	Per cent.	Species	Per cent.
Ranunculaceæ . .	12	1·9	33	2·5
Cruciferæ . . .	11	1·7	23	1·7
Caryophyllaceæ . .	12	1·9	25	1·8
Geraniaceæ . . .	4	0·6	20	1·5
Leguminosæ . . .	45	7·0	114	8·6
Rosaceæ	12	1·9	42	3·2
Umbelliferæ . . .	14	2·2	26	2·0
Rubiaceæ . . .	13	2·0	23	1·7
Compositæ . . .	59	9·2	109	8·2
Scrophulariaceæ . .	24	3·7	40	3·0
Labiatæ	29	4·5	59	4·4
Polygonaceæ . . .	3	0·5	23	1·7
Euphorbiaceæ . .	12	1·9	22	1·7
Urticaceæ . . .	16	2·5	35	2·6
Orchidaceæ . . .	18	2·8	38	2·9
Liliaceæ	18	2·8	32	2·4
Cyperaceæ . . .	12	1·9	56	4·2
Gramineæ . . .	58	9·1	133	10·0
Totals:—18 orders, or 16·0 per cent. . .	372	58·2	853	64·3

I will conclude these comparisons with some figures relating to species and genera. Some years ago I compiled[1] a series of calculations of the relative generic and specific composition of the floras of different areas, a few of which may be reproduced here for comparison with the Flora of Simla. Of course these figures are only rough approximations for the world and the larger areas, but for the smaller areas they are almost exact.

Regions	Average number of Genera to an Order	Average number of Species to a Genus
World	37·50	12·65
India.	13·0	6·0
Mexico	11·0	6·4
N. America	9·6	6·2
Australia	8·7	6·4
Simla	5·6	2·0
St. Helena	1·4	1·0

[1] *Biologia Centrali-Americana, Botany*, vol. i. Introd. (1888), p. xxiii.

It will be seen that in large areas, such as India, Mexico and Australia, the number of species to a genus is approximately half of what it is in the whole world; whereas in the small area of Simla it is less than a sixth, and in the remote St. Helena it is only a twelfth. This is in accord with the general law that the floras of small areas and of remote islands are relatively richer in Orders and Genera than in Species. But the average number of species to a genus is unusually low in Simla for a continental area having a luxuriant vegetation.

In my recent paper on the Flora of Tibet[1] I obtained the following figures:—

Regions	Orders	Genera	Species
Himalaya, from 15,000 ft. and upwards . . .	38	149	470
Tibet	41	119	283

THE TREES OF SIMLA

The woody element largely predominates in the vegetation of Simla, and the following species attain the dimensions and character of trees, though some of them are shrubby in certain localities:—

Bixaceæ

Flacourtia sapida.
Xylosma longifolia.

Malvaceæ

Bombax malabaricum.

Tiliaceæ

Grewia oppositifolia.
    vestita.

Rutaceæ

Murraya Koenigii.
Limonia acidissima.
Ægle Marmelos.

Meliaceæ

Melia Azedarach.
    indica.
Cedrela serrata.
    Toona.

Aquifoliaceæ

Ilex dipyrena.
    odorata.

Celastraceæ

Euonymus Hamiltonianus.
    lacerus.
    pendulus.
    tingens.
Elæodendron glaucum.

[1] *Journal of the Linnean Society*, xxxv. p. 230.

Rhamnaceæ

Zizyphus Jujuba.
oxyphylla.
Rhamnus triqueter.
virgatus.

Sapindaceæ

Æsculus indica.
Sapindus Mukorossi.
Acer cæsium.
caudatum.
cultratum.
oblongum.
villosum.
Staphylea Emodi.

Sabiaceæ

Meliosma dilleniæfolia.
pungens.

Anacardiaceæ

Rhus Cotinus.
punjabensis.
semialata.
succedanea.
Wallichii.
Pistacia integerrima.
Odina Wodier.

Leguminosæ

Erythrina suberosa.
Butea frondosa.
Dalbergia Sissoo.
Cassia Fistula.
Bauhinia purpurea.
retusa.
variegata.
Acacia arabica.
Catechu.
modesta.
Albizzia Lebbek.
mollis.
Albizzia odoratissima.
stipulata.

Rosaceæ

Prunus Puddum.
Padus.
Pyrus Aucuparia.
baccata.
foliolosa.
lanata.

Saxifragaceæ

Itea nutans.

Myrtaceæ

Eugenia Jambolana.

Samydaceæ

Casearia tomentosa.

Cornaceæ

Marlea begoniæfolia.
Cornus capitata.
oblonga.

Caprifoliaceæ

Viburnum coriaceum.
stellulatum.

Rubiaceæ

Stephegyne parvifolia.
Hymenodictyon excelsum.
Wendlandia exserta.

Ericaceæ

Pieris ovalifolia.
Rhododendron arboreum.

Myrsinaceæ

Myrsine semiserrata.

Styracaceæ

Symplocos cratægoides.

Oleaceæ

Nyctanthes Arbor-tristis.
Fraxinus floribunda.
Olea cuspidata.
  glandulifera.
Ligustrum compactum.

Apocynaceæ

Holarrhena antidysenterica.

Boraginaceæ

Cordia Myxa.
Ehretia lævis.

Bignoniaceæ

Oroxylum indicum.

Verbenaceæ

Vitex Negundo.

Lauraceæ

Cinnamomum Tamala.
Machilus Duthiei.
  odoratissima.
Phœbe lanceolata.
Litsea consimilis.
  lanuginosa.
  polyantha.

Euphorbiaceæ

Buxus sempervirens.
Bridelia montana.
Phyllanthus Emblica.
Glochidion velutinum.
Putranjiva Roxburghii.
Mallotus philippinensis.

Urticaceæ

Ulmus Wallichiana.
Celtis australis.
Trema politoria.
Morus indica.
Ficus bengalensis.
  Cunia.
  hispida.
  nemoralis.
  palmata.
  religiosa.
  Roxburghii.
  Rumphii.

Juglandaceæ

Juglans Regia.

Myricaceæ

Myrica Nagi.

Cupuliferæ

Betula alnoides.
  utilis.
Alnus nepalensis.
  nitida.
Quercus dilatata.
  glauca.
  incana.
  semecarpifolia.
Carpinus viminea.

Salicaceæ

Salix alba.
  babylonica.
  daphnoides.
  elegans.
  oxycarpa.
  tetrasperma.
  Wallichiana.
Populus ciliata.

Coniferæ

Pinus excelsa.
  longifolia.

Cedrus Deodara.
Picea Morinda.
Abies Pindrow.
Taxus baccata.
Cupressus torulosa.

Gramineæ

Dendrocalamus strictus.

Totals :—One hundred and thirty-seven Species belonging to eighty-three Genera and thirty-six Orders.

All the earlier travellers were struck by the variety of trees of the different altitudinal zones of vegetation. I have quoted Lady Dalhousie at p. xxvi. William Griffith during his short visit noted that *Pinus longifolia, P. excelsa, Cedrus Deodara* and *Picea Morinda* characterised successive zones. Mr. (now Sir Edward) Buck's paper on twenty trees of the Simla neighbourhood is extremely interesting, and it embodies the impressions of an amateur rather than those of a professional botanist; but he frequently cites Dr. G. Watt as his authority. However, I have not been able to ascertain whether the latter published anything on this subject. Divested of the glowing language of the lecturer his main facts merit reproduction. The twenty trees are: seven conifers, three oaks, a *Rhododendron*, an *Andromeda* [*Pieris*], four maples, two species of *Cornus* and two laurels. One of the characteristic features of the neighbourhood is the rapid transition from one region or belt of vegetation to another in ascending or descending the precipitous sides of the great Himalayan ranges. The most prominent elements in each climatic belt are its conifers. It must not be understood from this that the characteristic trees of the successive zones do not intermingle. Approaching Simla from Kalka by way of Subathu, *Pinus longifolia* begins to appear at elevations between 2,000 and 3,000 ft.; and this thinly clad, inelegant conifer and the prickly *Euphorbia Royleana* constitute the only conspicuous vegetation on the scorching, arid, southern slopes for some forty or fifty miles of the upward journey. But the southern and western slopes generally are bare or very scantily clothed with vegetation, so that we are indebted to this by no means always ornamental pine for relieving the barren monotony of the scenery. Standing on the summit of Huttoo or one of the other peaks north of Simla, and facing southward the scene is just the reverse, the whole country appearing as if covered with forest, in consequence of seeing only northern slopes. *Pinus longifolia* is the prevailing conifer up to 6,000 ft.; but near Simla, at elevations of 5,000 to 6,000 ft., it is gradually replaced by *Pinus excelsa*. *Cedrus Deodara* is the next distinguishing conifer. It has almost the same range as

Pinus excelsa, though occurring at both lower and higher elevations; but it is very capricious in its distribution. For instance, after passing the seventh mile from Simla, on the way to Huttoo, a distance of forty miles, it is conspicuous by its absence. Under favourable conditions it attains a large size, and the trunk of one at Kotgurh was twenty feet in girth. Passing from Simla to Mashobra *Abies Smithiana* [*Picea Morinda*] is first encountered, and it ranges from 7,500 to 9,500 ft., forming a belt distinctly above the cedar. Ascending Huttoo the lofty *Abies Webbiana* [*Abies Pindrow*] is met with at about 8,000 ft. Thus there are five conifer steps. The cheer pine (*Pinus longifolia*), from 2,000 to 6,000 ft.; the blue pine (*Pinus excelsa*), from 5,000 to 7,000 ft.; the deodar, up to 8,000 ft.; the spruce fir (*Picea Morinda*), from 7,000 to 9,000 ft.; and the silver fir (*Abies Pindrow*), at 8,000 to 10,000 ft. Each of the three upper coniferous belts has its characteristic oak. In the lowest the white oak (*Quercus incana*) is associated with the deodar; in the middle the green oak (*Q. dilatata*) intermingles with *Picea Morinda*; and in the upper, along with *Abies Pindrow*, the brown oak (*Q. semecarpifolia*) is the prevailing species. The yew (*Taxus baccata*) is most abundant in the silver fir belt; and the cypress (*Cupressus torulosa*) is found only on the north slopes of Shali at 8,000 to 9,000 ft. Of the two hollies in the Simla district *Ilex dipyrena* is much the commoner, occurring in all three of the upper belts. The showy *Rhododendron arboreum* ranges between 5,000 and 8,000 ft., with a preference for the lower elevations on the north side. *Andromeda ovalifolia* [*Pieris ovalifolia*], a member of the same Natural Order, is often associated with this Rhododendron. *Cornus capitata*, along with the barberry, the white rose and the pomegranate, constitutes in June a blaze of yellow, white and red flowering bushes between Simla and Mashobra. *Cornus macrophylla* belongs more especially to the belt characterised by *Pinus excelsa*. The two laurels included by Mr. Buck in his twenty trees are not clearly identifiable on account of an evident confusion of names, but most probably *Machilus Duthiei* and *Litsea consimilis* were intended. His four species of maple—*Acer cæsium, A. caudatum, A. cultratum* and *A. villosum*—are mostly at home in the forests of Narkunda and Huttoo. Mr. Buck in his concluding remarks refers to the folly of destroying the forests to grow potatoes for a decade or so, by which time the rains had denuded the rocky substratum of its soil and produced a permanent barren.

CLIMBING SHRUBS

Shrubs are also proportionately much more numerous than in the British Islands, and the genera, of which there are climbing species, number upwards of thirty :—

Schizandra	Sabia	Trachelospermum
Cocculus	Cæsalpinia	Cryptolepis
Stephania	Bauhinia	Dæmia
Cissampelos	Mimosa	Holostemma
Capparis	Acacia	Cynanchum
Hiptage	Rubus	Marsdenia
Euonymus	Rosa	Pergularia
Berchemia	Hydrangea	Tylophora
Sageretia	Hedera	Hoya
Helinus	Jasminum	Porana
Vitis	Vallaris	Ficus

THE HERBACEOUS ELEMENT

Always continuing the comparisons with the British Flora, the herbaceous element demands little comment. Generally speaking, the herbaceous plants of Simla are showier than the British species. The principal and most striking diversity in the herbaceous vegetation of the two countries is due to the presence in Simla of a number of genera of the leading Natural Orders—Leguminosæ, Compositæ and Gramineæ—which are altogether unrepresented in Britain. The same may be said of the Scrophulariaceæ, Acanthaceæ, Labiatæ, Amarantaceæ, Urticaceæ and Araceæ. On the whole, the petaloid monocotyledons of Simla are more conspicuous than those of Britain ; yet none probably is so effective as the bluebell (*Scilla nutans*) of British woods and meadows. Prominent among them is *Lilium polyphyllum*, the subject of the Frontispiece.

THE FERNS OF SIMLA

The ferns of Simla are so numerous that the late Sir Henry Collett never intended to include them in the present work, but he contemplated publishing an account of them in a separate volume. He collected material for this purpose, and I have before me a list of seventy-one species collected by him during one season. As may be seen from the Bibliography at p. lxvii several other persons have made a special study of this class of plants, and Colonel

Beddome's 'Handbook' may be mentioned as the best available work for naming the ferns of Simla. Although descriptions could not be given, I have considered it desirable to append a complete list of the species hitherto discovered in the District of Simla. I am indebted to Mr. C. W. Hope for this list, and I present it entirely on his authority. In addition to his own very rich collection, it embodies the results of several collectors whose names are not mentioned in connection with the flowering plants. Among them General Blair, Mr. T. Bliss, Mr. E. W. Trotter and the late H. F. Blanford, F.R.S.

Trichomanes Filicula, *Bory*
Woodsia elongata, *Hook.*
Dicksonia scabra, *Wall.*
Davallia immersa, *Wall.*
  pseudocystopteris, *Kze.*
  Beddomei, *Hope*
  Clarkei, *Baker*
  tenuifolia, *Sw.*
Cystopteris fragilis, *Bernh.*
Adiantum lunulatum, *Burm.*
  caudatum, *L.*
  Edgeworthii, *Hook.*
  Capillus-Veneris, *L.*
  venustum, *Don*
  pedatum, *L.*
Cheilanthes subvillosa, *Hook.*
  Dalhousiæ, *Hook.*
  albomarginata, *Clarke*
  farinosa, *Kaulf.*
  anceps, *Blanford*
  grisea, *Blanford*
Onychium auratum, *Kaulf.*
  japonicum, *Kze.*
  contiguum, *Hope*
Cryptogramme crispa, *R. Br.*
Pellæa nitidula, *Baker*
  calomelanos, *Link*
Pteris longifolia, *L.*
  cretica, *L.*
  digitata, *Wall.*
  quadriaurita, *Retz.*
  excelsa, *Gaud.*
  aquilina, *L.*
Ceratopteris thalictroides, *Brongn.*
Woodwardia radicans, *J. Sm.*
Asplenium ensiforme, *Wall.*
  Trichomanes, *L.*
  septentrionale, *Hoffm.*
  unilaterale, *Lam.*
  planicaule, *Wall.*
  Adiantum-nigrum, *L.*
  fontanum, *Bernh.*
  exiguum, *Bedd.*
  varians, *Hk. & Gr.*
  thelypteroides, *Michx.*
  macrocarpum, *Bl.*
  nigripes, *Mett.*
  tenellum, *Hope*
  tenuifrons, *Wall.*
  Mackinnoni, *Hope*
  Filix-fœmina, *Bernh.*, var. dentigera, *Clarke*
  rupicola, *Hope*
  Schimperi, *A. Br.*
  pectinatum, *Wall.*
  fimbriatum, *Hook.*
  foliosum, *Wall.*
  longifolium, *Don*
  japonicum, *Thb.*
  polypodioides, *Don*
  multicaudatum, *Wall.*
Aspidium marginatum, *Wall.*
  obliquum, *Don*
  ilicifolium, *Don*
  acanthophyllum, *Franchet*

Aspidium Thomsoni, *Hook.*
lobatum, *Sw.*
angulare, *Willd.*
squarrosum, *Don*
Prescottianum, *Hook.*
Bakerianum, *Atkinson*
falcatum, *Sw.*
Nephrodium Gamblei, *Hope*
repens, *Hope*
Thelypteris, *Desv.*
Filix-mas, *Rich.*
parallelogrammum, *Kze.*
Kingii, *Hope*
barbigerum, *Hook.*
Schimperianum, *Hochst.*
cochleatum, *Don*
Blanfordi, *Hope*
ramosum, *Hope*
odontoloma, *Moore*
marginatum, *Wall.*
crenatum, *Baker*
Boryanum, *Baker*
molle, *Desv.*
Papilio, *Hope*
cicutarium, *Baker*
Oleandra Wallichii, *Presl*
Polypodium erubescens, *Wall.*
distans, *Don*
laterepens, *Hope*
Polypodium Dryopteris, *L.*
Polypodium punctatum, *Thb.*
lineatum, *Colebr.*
multilineatum, *Wall.*
amœnum, *Wall.*
lachnopus, *Wall.*
microrrhizoma, *Clarke*
argutum, *Wall.*
fissum, *Baker*
rivale, *Mett.*
lineare, *Thb.*
simplex, *Sw.*
clathratum, *Clarke*
membranaceum, *Don*
oxylobum, *Wall.*
malacodon, *Hook.*
Stewartii, *Clarke*
ebenipes, *Hook.*
juglandifolium, *Don*
Nothochlæna Marantæ, *R. Br.*
Gymnogramme Totta, *Schlecht.*
Levingei, *Baker*
vestita, *Hook.*
javanica, *Bl.*
involuta, *Hook.*
Osmunda Claytoniana, *L.*
regalis, *L.*
Ophioglossum vulgatum, *L.*
Botrychium Lunaria, *Sw.*
ternatum, *Sw.*
lanuginosum, *Wall.*

This gives a total of 124 species belonging to twenty-three genera, as against sixteen genera and thirty-seven species in the British Islands, and twenty-five species in the county of Sussex, which has a larger area than Simla, as here understood—a rich fern flora indeed! With the exception of the Gramineæ (133 species), ferns are more numerous than any Natural Order of flowering plants in the Flora of Simla.

ASPECTS OF THE VEGETATION OF SIMLA

From Dr. T. Thomson's 'Western Himalaya and Tibet' the following observations, made in 1847–1848, are extracted :—

In consequence of the sudden elevation of the mountain range at the place where Simla has been built, there is a most complete and surprising change in the vegetation and general appearance of the scenery. During the last ascent on the road from the plains this is sufficiently perceptible, although from the great ravages which the proximity of so large a population has made in the oak woods, only a few stunted bushes are now left on the southern exposure. Between the plains and Simla the hills are totally devoid of trees, but immediately on gaining the top of the ridge on which the station is built, we enter a fine forest, which covers all the broader parts of the range, especially the slopes which have a northern aspect.

The nature of the forest varies a good deal with the exposure and with the quality of the soil. By far the greater part consists of an oak [*Quercus incana*] and a rhododendron [*Rhododendron arboreum*], both small evergreen trees, rarely exceeding thirty or forty feet, with wide-spreading arms and rugged twisted branches. A species of *Andromeda* [*Pieris ovalifolia*] is also very common, and a holly [*Ilex dipyrena*], *Euonymus*, *Rhamnus*, and *Benthamia* [*Cornus*] are the other more common trees, if we except the *Coniferæ*, of which four species occur. Of these *Pinus longifolia* is common at the western or lower extremity of the station, and prevails, to the exclusion of any other tree, on the dry sunny spurs which run towards the south, at elevations from 2,000 to 5,000 ft. This species is, of all the Indian pines known to me, except its near ally *P. Khasyana*, that which is capable of enduring the most heat, and at the same time the greatest variation in amount of moisture, as it is found at elevations of not more than 1,000 feet above the level of the sea, equally in the hot humid valleys of Sikkim, where it enjoys a perpetual vapour-bath, and on the dry sandstone hills of the Upper Punjab, on which rain hardly ever falls. It is only, however, at low elevations, where the mean temperature is high, that it is capable of supporting a great amount of humidity, for in the damp climates of the Himalaya it is entirely wanting, except in the deepest valleys; and even in the drier districts it is always observed to select the sunnier, and therefore warmer exposures. Its upper limit is usually about 7,000 feet above the level of the sea, though on Jako at Simla a few stunted trees rise as high as 7,700 feet.

Pinus excelsa is also a very common species at Simla, particularly on the southern face of Mount Jako, which is the highest part of the ridge. *Abies Smithiana* [*Picea Morinda*], the third coniferous tree, is exceedingly rare, a few trees only occurring in a shady ravine facing the west; while the deodar, the fourth species, is common on the southern and western slopes of Jako, above 7,000 feet; and again in shady groves at the bottom of the valleys on both sides of the ridge, as low as 5,000 feet. This beautiful tree, the cedar of the Indian mountains, seems limited to the western half of the Himalayan range, extending from the most westerly part of Nipal, as far as the mountains of Afghanistan.

The forest extends in parts close up to the peak of Jako, which has an elevation of 8,053 feet. The very summit, however, which is a short flat ridge, and a considerable part of the east and south face are bare [of trees] and grassy, or covered with scattered shrubs. The more common shrubby forms of the vegetation of the temperate zone are *Salix*, *Rosa*, *Rubus*, *Lonicera*, *Viburnum*, *Berberis*, *Indigofera*, and *Prinsepia*, all, except the two last, quite European. *Indigofera* forms a remarkable exception, and one well worthy of note, as the genus is a very tropical one, although its shrubby species are particularly abundant throughout the whole of the Western Himalaya.

The herbaceous vegetation of the spring months quite corresponds, in the temperate nature of its forms, with what has been found to be the case with the trees and shrubs; but during the rainy season, as has been well pointed out by Dr. Royle in his valuable essay on the distribution of Himalayan plants, this is much less markedly the case. At the commencement of spring, in April—for March is still too cold for much vegetation—the weather being generally bright, though with occasional heavy showers, the earliest flowers are species of *Viola*, *Fragaria*, *Geranium*, *Veronica*, *Valeriana*, and dandelion. From April, as summer advances, the temperature gradually rises, till towards the end of June, when the rainy season commences. These months are generally dry, and if no rain falls the heat is sometimes considerable, the thermometer rising as high as 80° in the shade. Still the flora is almost entirely temperate, the early spring plants being succeeded by many others of European families, principally *Ranunculaceæ*, *Rosaceæ*, *Labiatæ*, *Stellatæ*, *Polygonaceæ*, *Epilobiaceæ*, *Primulaceæ*, &c. I can hardly enumerate a single spring flowering plant which does not belong to an European family. Few species are, however, identical with those of Europe, except *Stellaria media*, *Cerastium vulgatum*,

Taraxacum officinale, *Verbascum Thapsus*, *Thymus Serpyllum*, and *Poa annua*.

The commencement of the rainy season [in June] is the signal in the mountains, as it is very universally throughout India, wherever that season is well marked, for the appearance of a very vigorous and luxuriant growth of plants of annual growth, the seeds or rootstocks of which had been lying dormant in the soil awaiting the access of heavy rain. At Simla, as elsewhere in the temperate region of the Himalaya, we find at this season numerous species of *Impatiens*, *Acanthaceæ*, *Orchideæ*, and *Labiatæ*, several Gentians and *Cichoriaceæ*, a great many grasses and *Cyperaceæ*, and species of *Parnassia*, *Drosera*, *Pedicularis*, *Roscoea*, *Dipsacus* *Thalictrum*, *Urtica*, &c. The *Labiatæ* of the rainy season are mostly species of *Plectranthus* and *Elsholtzia*, both quite Indian genera, and very extensively distributed in mountainous districts. The *Orchideæ* of Simla are entirely terrestrial, the dryness and cold of the winter months being greater than are compatible with the occurrence of epiphytical species of this Natural Order, and for the same reason, I presume, *Melastomaceæ*, so abundant in the Eastern Himalaya, are quite wanting.

The view from the peak of Jako is one of the most agreeable and diversified which occur in any part of the Himalaya, although from the rather too level top of the mountain, and the intrusion of the forest almost to the very summit, the whole panorama cannot be embraced at once. Immediately under the eye are the numerous spurs and ridges covered with scattered houses, and the deep ravines which terminate the steep slopes below the station; towards the plains the whole valley of the Gambar is seen and the station of Sabathu. To the north a valley stretches from Simla as far as the Sutlej River, distant about fifteen miles, so direct that the greater part of it is seen, though the river itself is concealed. East of north a long partially wooded ridge, about four miles distant at its nearest point, running parallel to the valley just mentioned, excludes the view of the nearer part of the Sutlej valley; but the lofty ranges north of that river, covered with dense forest and backed by masses of brilliant snow, close in the view in that direction. Due east lies the Mahasu ridge, covered on the Simla slopes with a dense forest of deodar; and to the south, across the valley of the Giri, towards which numerous rugged ridges run, is the mountain called the Chor, the highest peak of the range which separates the Giri from the Tons, the crest of which is upwards of 12,000 feet in height.

The geological structure of the Himalaya between Simla and the plains is not easily discovered by the cursory observer. The general basis of the mountains is clay-slate, occasionally very micaceous, passing into a coarse sandstone, but here and there limestone occurs interstratified. The dip is extremely variable, and the rocks, whatever their age, are evidently highly metamorphosed. The tertiary formations, so well illustrated by Falconer and Cautley, extend all along the base of the mountains, and penetrate in some places far into the valleys, for certain rocks in the neighbourhood of Sabathu have been indicated by Major Vicary which appear to be of the same age, or perhaps of a still older tertiary epoch.

From Simla to Fagu, a distance of fourteen miles, the road follows throughout the course of the main range, not always on the very crest of the ridge, but seldom at any great distance from it. After passing round the peak of Jako it turns northward and descends abruptly about 500 feet to a low part of the ridge, elevated about 6,800 feet, and quite bare of trees. The ridge continues in a north-east direction for nearly four miles. On the slope of the hill below the road there is a small cluster of trees of *Cupressus torulosa*, a species of cypress, one of the rarer conifers of the Himalaya, the most favourite situation of which seems to be on very steep mountains in the interior, at elevations of from seven to nine thousand feet. It was found abundantly by Major Madden on Shali, a [limestone] peak twenty miles east of Simla, and it appears to extend thence west as far as Simla, where it occurs in several places on hot, dry, and very bare rocky hills as low as six thousand feet.

About four miles from Simla a sudden increase in the elevation of the range takes place. The road ascends the steep face of the ridge with a deep ravine on either hand, that to the right bare, while on the left there is first a thicket of rose and willow bushes, and further on an oak-wood of a species, *Quercus floribunda* [*Q. dilatata*], different from that common at Simla and indicative of greater elevation, though here growing with *Rhododendron* and *Andromeda* [*Pieris*], common Simla trees. At an elevation of about 8,000 feet forest commences, and the road runs for a mile through fine trees of deodar and spruce, *Abies Smithiana* [*Picea Morinda*], generally on the very crest of the ridge, looking down towards the east into a deep and broad valley.

From an elevation of about 8,000 feet the Mahasu ridge rises to at least 9,000 feet, and as it is throughout well wooded, the road along it is extremely beautiful. On the earlier part of the ridge the forest consists chiefly of pine, *Pinus excelsa* and *Abies Smithiana* being abundant, and more especially the deodar, which, on the slope facing the west, may be seen in the greatest profusion, thousands of trees springing up in dense masses on the slopes which have been bared by the axe, or still more destructively by the fires of the hillmen.

After about five miles the road enters a dense forest of large massive pines, intermixed with two species of sycamore, and a fine cherry, which relieve the otherwise too gloomy foliage of the coniferous trees. A magnificent climbing vine, which attaches itself to the tallest trees, rising in light green coils round their trunks, and falling in graceful festoons from the branches high overhead, adds much to the elegance of the scene, and renders it, in the expressive words of Griffith, who was familiar with the rich vegetation of the humid forests of the Eastern Himalaya, the only true Himalayan forest of the western mountains.

On this ascent the road rises to about 9,000 feet, the crest of the Mahasu ridge being 9,200 feet. The large size and dense shade of the trees, and the abundance of *Abies Smithiana* [*Picea Morinda*], of the sycamore, and of the gigantic vine, give the forest a totally different appearance from that of Simla, and the undergrowth presents also a considerable amount of novelty; a species of currant, a fine *Spiræa*, *Indigofera atropurpurea*, and fine species of *Rosa* and *Rubus* forming thickets under the tall trees. This forest, indeed, from its dense shade and great humidity exhibits a much greater contrast to the ordinary temperate vegetation of the Himalaya than is usually observed below 9,000 feet, at which elevation the upper temperate or subalpine vegetation begins fairly to predominate over that which is prevalent from 5,000 to 9,000 feet.

On the very summit of the Mahasu ridge there are a few trees of *Quercus semecarpifolia*, the alpine oak of the Western Himalaya, an European-looking and partially deciduous species, and of *Picea Webbiana*, or *Pindrow*, the silver fir of the Indian mountains, a dark sombre-looking pine, abundant in the forests of the interior. These trees may be adopted as the characteristics of the subalpine zone, in every part of which, from 9,000 to about 12,000 feet, which is the highest limit of tree vegetation in the Western Himalaya, they abound. On Mahasu they are entirely confined to the crest of the ridge, and form no part of the forest below.

Fagu is situated immediately above the valley of the river Giri. The mountains to the right, which dip into the valley of the Giri, are bare of forest, with a good deal of cultivation in small terraced fields on the steep sunny slopes. On the left hand, again, the deep valley which runs towards the Sutlej is full of forest, not rising, however, to the ridge, which is bare, or lined only with scattered jungle of *Indigofera*, *Desmodium*, *Spiræa*, roses, and brambles. It seems to be a constant rule that the depressions of the ridges are bare and open, while the more elevated portions are covered with forest. Probably the cause of this is the greater humidity of the higher slopes, which attract the rain clouds, while the lower ranges are dry. The currents of air which sweep up the valleys may also in part be the cause of the bareness of the ridges opposite their summits.

At Theog, nearly eight miles from Fagu, the cultivation is principally of barley, which is sown in early spring, and reaped in the beginning or middle of June, according to the season. Beyond Theog the road is covered with brushwood on the left hand, but bare on the right. The highest part of the road is about two miles beyond Theog, and has an elevation of about 9,000 feet. The northern face of this hill is prettily wooded with the holly-leaved oak.

The ravine immediately below Mattiana is crossed at an elevation probably a little above 6,000 feet, as the trees of the temperate region, such as the holly-leaved oak [*Quercus dilatata*] and woolly oak [*Q. incana*], *Andromeda*, and *Rhododendron*, continue to the very bottom of the descent; and *Pinus excelsa* is common on the eastern slope, a little way above the stream. On the banks of this there were a few trees of an *Acacia* [*Albizzia mollis*] common in the lower forests. I observed also a laurel, an olive, *Rhus*, and the common Toon, *Cedrela Toona* [more likely *C. serrata*], all indicative of the commencement of a subtropical vegetation, which no doubt must be abundant on its banks a very few miles further down. Few of the plants observed in the valley were different from those common around Simla; a species of *Caragana*, a leguminous genus abundant in Siberia and in the interior and more dry parts of the Himalaya, was perhaps the most interesting.

The ascent from the ravine was well wooded in its lowest part with oak and pine. A few trees of a very handsome poplar, *Populus ciliata*, a tall, widely branching, large-leaved tree, occurred in its lower part, as did also *Benthamia fragifera* [*Cornus capitata*] and a yew, apparently undistinguishable from the common European species.

The ripening of the apricot in a valley, among forest, at an elevation of 7,000 feet indicates an undoubted diminution of the rainfall. Very little change, however, is observable in the wild vegetation till the upper part of the last steep ascent, when a number of species make their appearance which are strangers to the more external ranges. A species of hazel [*Corylus Colurna*], as a tree, and *Lappa*, *Achillea*, *Leonurus*, *Cheiranthus*, and *Rumex acetosa*, as herbaceous plants, may be mentioned as instances, as also a *Polygonum*, with elegant panicles of white honey-scented flowers.

Nagkanda Bungalow, elevated 9,300 feet above the level of the sea, is situated on a depression of the main range, where it has a direction from west to east. The ridge to the west, towards Mattiana, is elevated little more than 10,000 feet, while to the east rises the peak of Hattu to a height of 10,456 feet.

The top of Hattu is only about 1,500 feet above the Nagkanda Bungalow, and the distance is nearly five miles. The first mile is bare of wood on the ridge, though the forest on both sides rises within a few feet of the crest, which is bordered by brushwood. As soon as the ascent commences the ridge becomes covered with forest, at first principally pine, spruce, and silver fir (*Picea*) being the principal species. Yew is also very common, forming a fine tall tree, and the few non-coniferous trees are chiefly the alpine oak, sycamore, and cherry.

On the top of Hattu the grassy slopes are covered with a luxuriant herbage of *Potentillæ*, *Labiatæ*, *Gentianaceæ*, *Epilobium*, *Polygonum* and *Anemone*, while a few stunted bushes of *Quercus semecarpifolia*, a simple-leaved *Pyrus*, and a willow are the only shrubby vegetation. The forest, however, rises close to the base of the cliffs on the western face, and contains all the species common on the ascent of the mountain, the vegetation of the summit being in no respect peculiar, not even in early spring exhibiting any truly alpine plant. The mountain bamboo, a graceful small species of *Arundinaria* [*A. spathiflora*], which is extremely abundant in the woods of the upper temperate and subalpine zones, adorns the rocky hollows close to the summit.

In looking back from the summit of Hattu towards Simla and the plains it may be observed that the country is well wooded, though when viewed from Simla or the heights of Mahasu the same mountains had appeared almost bare. This diversity in the aspect of the country, according to the direction from which it is seen, is due to the ridges being well wooded on one face and bare of trees on the other.

The shrubby and herbaceous vegetation of Hattu is exceedingly luxuriant. The more open glades of the forest are filled with an undergrowth of tall balsams, annual-stemmed *Acanthaceæ*, *Dipsacus*, *Compositæ*, among which the beautiful *Calimeris* [probably *Erigeron multiradiatus*] is very abundant, while in the drier pine-forest a graceful little bamboo occurs, often to the exclusion of every other plant. It grows in dense tufts, eight or ten or even twelve feet high, the diameter of the stem not exceeding a quarter of an inch. The currant of the Mahasu ridge is also common, with many of the same shrubs which are there abundant. The ridge close to Nagkanda is much drier, and has fewer peculiar plants, the resemblance to the Simla flora being there very remarkable.

Since Thomson wrote the foregoing, upwards of fifty years ago, considerable changes have taken place, mainly due to the felling of timber trees and the clearing of large areas for the cultivation of the potato and other crops.

Mr. J. S. Gamble has kindly supplied the following notes descriptive of the conditions a few years ago :—

The town of Simla occupies the slopes of the peak of Jako, 8,053 feet, from which radiate three principal spurs : to the west the long spur which runs out to the village (bazár) of Boileauganj, beyond which is the outlying hill of Jatogh ; to the north the Elysium Hill spur, covered with houses, in a forest of white oak and rhododendron ; and to the south the spur of Chota Simla. Eastwards the slope is precipitous, falling to the village of Sinjoli on the main ridge along which, though first through a tunnel, passes the chief road into the interior of the mountains.

The whole of the slopes of these spurs down to a level of 6,000 feet, and in some valleys still lower, has been acquired by the Government from the rulers of the Native States to which the land originally belonged, Patiála, Kuenthal, and Koti, and is managed by a Municipal Committee who have taken great pains to preserve the forest vegetation so that the station of Simla presents a marked contrast to the country outside, which is characterised by bare grassy slopes with occasional villages and patches of cultivation wherever the slope is sufficiently easy to admit of terracing, and with patches of forest in ravines and on the steeper hillsides. In recent years a considerable improvement has been effected, and under the enlightened advice of the Punjab Government, the rulers of the adjoining States, and especially the Raja of Patiála, have introduced measures of forest conservancy, so that much of the formerly destroyed forest is now in process of reconstitution.

The forest of Simla is now managed under a special working plan which aims first at its preservation. The Jako peak and its nearer spurs are covered to the north and east chiefly with forests of white oak, *Quercus incana*, through which self-sown deodars are constantly endeavouring, if not checked, to push their way. The lower slopes and those of the Elysium spur have mixed with the oak much *Rhododendron arboreum* of large size and beautiful appearance when in flower, and many specimens of the pretty white-flowered *Pieris ovalifolia*. The western slopes of the Jako peak and the Chota Simla spur are covered with an almost unbroken mass of deodar, occasionally mixed with blue pine, *Pinus excelsa*. The south slopes of the main ridge and the dry sunny spurs which take off from it are covered with forest of the long-leaved pine, *Pinus longifolia*, which here reaches the elevation of 7,000 ft., at least 2,000 ft. higher than it usually does in the great Himalayan valleys. The northern slopes of this same ridge are covered with mixed forest chiefly, the ravines like those of Annandale and the Glen having many such evergreen trees as the holly, *Ilex dipyrena*, *Euonymus tingens* and *E. pendulus*, the laurel, *Machilus Duthiei* and *Litsœa umbrosa*, hornbeam, hazel, *Cornus capitata*, with bushes of *Rhamnus*, *Lonicera*, *Viburnum*, and others. In the forests of oak and deodar there is little or no shrubby vegetation, though here and there, especially on dry exposures, wherever blanks occur, *Indigofera heterantha*, *Desmodium tiliæfolium*, *Berberis aristata*, and *B. Lycium*, *Spiræa canescens*, *Elsholtzia polystachya*, *Buddleia paniculata*, *Plectranthus rugosus* and *Lonicera quinquelocularis* are characteristic. On the cooler and damper slopes *Salix elegans*, *Viburnum*, brambles, and some of the above-mentioned are the chief shrubs, while in the undergrowth of the ravines *Indigofera hebepetala*, *Myrsine africana*, *Sarcococca pruniformis*, *Rosa macrophylla*, and *Prinsepia* are the most prominent. The herbaceous vegetation of Simla is remarkable for containing many species of great beauty, and wherever it is undisturbed by grazing animals it shows, almost the whole year round, except during the months of winter, the aspect of a wild garden which it would be the despair of a garden lover to imitate. Spring begins in April and brings with it the violets, the strawberry, *Primula denticulata*, *Geranium*, and *Anemone*. Then by degrees, as the weather gets warmer and drier, other plants appear, chiefly *Acanthaceæ*, *Labiatæ* and *Compositæ*. About the middle of June the first burst of the monsoon is felt, and with it comes the curious *Arisæmata* and *Sauromatum*, *Cautleya* and *Roscoea*, ground orchids such as *Satyrium*, *Habenaria*, *Hemipilia*, and *Spiranthes*, *Lilium polyphyllum*, *Polygona* and *Gentiana*, while the rocks are bright with the flowers of *Saxifraga ligulata*. Down in the Glen and in the waterfall valley *Platystemma violoides*, *Chirita*, *Begonia*, and ferns appear on the wet rocks, and the trees are draped with epiphytic ferns, especially of the genus *Davallia*, as well as with such plants as *Peperomia* and *Elatostemma*. But, perhaps, of all seasons, the autumn is the finest in general colouring, for it is then that we find on the hillsides the everlasting *Anaphalis* and *Gnaphalium*, many other Compositæ and Labiatæ, Gentianaceæ, the tall spikes of *Morina* and the spiny heads of *Echinops*, while the woods are gay with *Strobilanthes*. In fact all seasons in Simla, except extreme winter, have their show. At Fagu there are few trees except some pollarded *Quercus dilatata*, but on the peak above are still to be found a few specimens of the brown-leaved oak, *Quercus semecarpifolia*, and many plants of beauty and interest may be collected on the grassy slopes towards Cheog if the grazing has not been too severe.

It is at Fagu that the road to the Giri valley branches off and goes on over the Paternála range with a path leading to the conspicuous and interesting Chor Mountain, which rises to 12,000 ft. and possesses a few interesting alpine plants.

The road to the Upper Sutlej valley passes for most of the way on a level path cut out of the rock or winding round the hill-sides to Theog, Matiána and Nagkanda, forty miles from Simla, the whole road possessing great interest to the lover of scenery and the botanist. Most of the road lies either through cultivated lands or round bare slopes, but in the ravines there are oak and rhododendron forest. From Matiána an interesting excursion can be made to the limestone peak of Shali, where the Himalayan cypress, *Cupressus torulosa*, grows; and from Nagkanda the favourite excursion is that to the top of Hattu, whence there is a magnificent panorama of the snowy range, with the valley of the Sutlej on one side and that of the Pábar, a tributary of the Jumna, on the other. The forest on Hattu consists of the firs *Picea Morinda* and *Abies Pindrow* below, with *Quercus semecarpifolia* around the peak and on the slopes to the north. In the Bhagi forest many trees of European genera occur, such as walnut, elm, hazel, birch, alder, maple, poplar, willow, hornbeam, holly; the whole mixed with shade-loving shrubs, small bamboos (*Arundinaria spathiflora*), ferns and herbaceous plants. Among the latter balsams are conspicuous, the curious *Podophyllum Emodi* and the tall spikes of *Lilium giganteum*. On the grassy slopes to the south there is, in early autumn, quite a blaze of colour, the most conspicuous plants being *Erigeron multiradiatus, Corydalis Govaniana, Potentilla atrosanguinea, Anaphalis, Delphinium, Aconitum* and *Pedicularis*, while various species of *Saxifraga* and *Sedum* adorn the crevices of the rocks.

In recent years much has been done in the way of planting trees and making gardens in Simla, and the excellent and very successful works undertaken by the municipality for the regulation of ravines have completely changed the aspect of the slopes and done away with the many unsightly landslips that used to disfigure them. The work has been done by letting the water go down in ladder-like stone-built troughs, the sides of which have been carefully planted with willows, poplars and other trees, and more especially with the false acacia, *Robinia Pseud-acacia.*

CONCLUDING REMARKS ON THE FLORA OF SIMLA

The comparisons made with the British flora will prepare the student for even greater affinities when the whole of Europe is considered, and such is indeed the case. But, taking the data on distribution given in this book, which possibly are susceptible of some emendation and augmentation, just one third (432) of the species are restricted to the Himalaya; yet such characteristic Himalayan genera as *Meconopsis*, *Cathcartia* and *Stylophorum* (*Papaveraceæ*); *Codonopsis*, *Leptocodon* and *Cyananthus* (*Campanulaceæ*); *Rhododendron* (*Ericaceæ*); *Primula* (*Primulaceæ*); *Gentiana* (*Gentianaceæ*), and *Pedicularis* (*Scrophulariaceæ*) are either not represented at all or only by very few species. But the paucity of essentially Himalayan types is partly due to the fact that absolutely alpine elevations are not reached in Simla. That it is not so altogether is proved by the fact that *Meconopsis robusta* ranges from Nepal to Kumaon at 8,000 to 10,000 ft., *Codonopsis rotundifolia* from Kumaon to Kashmir at 7,000 to 11,000 ft., and many of the species of *Rhododendron* grow much below 10,000 ft. On the other hand many of the characteristic Simla plants extend westward into the Mediterranean region, and nearly all of the Coniferæ extend to Afghanistan, whilst a variety of *Pinus excelsa* is found in Rumelia and Montenegro. There are no quite local species in the Flora of Simla, but probably about half of the 432 species peculiar to the Himalaya are only found west of Simla. The entire absence of epiphytic and rock orchids is remarkable, especially as the climatic conditions do not seem to be altogether unfavourable. Ferns are abundant, and many of them are epiphytic. In Sikkim epiphytic orchids are common between 5,000 and 6,000 ft., and various species of *Dendrobium*, *Bulbophyllum*, *Cœlogyne*, &c. are recorded from altitudes of 7,000 to 8,000 ft. Among palms *Plectocomia himalayana* ascends to 7,000 ft., and *Calamus montanus* to 6,000 ft.

CLASSIFICATION OF THE NATURAL ORDERS OF FLOWERING PLANTS REPRESENTED IN THE FLORA OF SIMLA

It was originally intended to construct a key to the Natural Orders, in concordance with the keys to the Genera and Species, but after due consideration it has been decided to explain their classification rather than enter into structural details. The reason is that only a very elaborate key would be sufficient, and an elaborate one would be deterrent to the amateur, who gains his knowledge largely from external characters, and would therefore be bewildered by the intricacies of a long series of alternatives encumbered with numerous exceptions.

The sequence of the Natural Orders in this work is adopted from Bentham and Hooker's 'Genera Plantarum.'

Flowering Plants are primarily divided into three Classes of very unequal proportions, namely :—

I. Dicotyledones, comprising the orders Ranunculaceæ to Salicaceæ, pp. 1–481.

II. Gymnospermæ, comprising the orders Gnetaceæ and Coniferæ, pp. 481–488.[1]

III. Monocotyledones, comprising the orders Orchidaceæ to Gramineæ, pp. 489–636.

Definitions of the Classes and Divisions

I. Dicotyledones : Herbs, shrubs or trees of the most varied habit. Stem, when perennial, consisting of a central pith, concentric layers of wood and a separable bark, increasing in size by additional layers immediately beneath the bark. Leaves net-veined, commonly disarticulating from the branches freely. Parts

[1] Dicotyledones were formerly divided into Angiospermæ (having the ovules enclosed in an ovary) and Gymnospermæ (having the ovules on open carpels), but they are now almost universally regarded as constituting distinct Classes, and the Gymnospermæ are placed after the Monocotyledones.

of the flower free or united, usually in fives or some multiple of this number. Ovule or ovules enclosed in an ovary. Embryo having two cotyledons or seed-leaves, usually distinguishable before germination, and appearing above ground in germination.

Division 1. POLYPETALÆ: Petals free from each other or sometimes slightly united.

Subdivision 1. THALAMIFLORÆ. Calyx free from the ovary. Petals in one or more series. Stamens usually numerous. Ovary or ovaries usually superior. *Ranunculaceæ* to *Tiliaceæ*.

Subdivision 2. DISCIFLORÆ. Calyx usually free from the ovary. Stamens usually definite, inserted within, upon or around a disk. Ovary superior or immersed in the disk. *Linaceæ* to *Coriariaceæ*.

Subdivision 3. CALYCIFLORÆ. Sepals more or less united and more or less enclosing or adnate to the ovary. Petals and stamens inserted on the tube of the calyx or around the top of the ovary. *Leguminosæ* to *Cornaceæ*.

Division 2. GAMOPETALÆ. Petals combined, forming a variously shaped corolla. Stamens usually few and attached to the corolla.

Subdivision 1. INFERÆ. Ovary inferior. Stamens of the same number as the lobes of the corolla or rarely fewer. *Caprifoliaceæ* to *Campanulaceæ*.

Subdivision 2. HETEROMERÆ. Ovary almost always superior. Stamens free or inserted on the corolla. Carpels of the pistil more than two. *Ericaceæ* to *Styracaceæ*.

Subdivision 3. BICARPELLATÆ. Ovary almost always superior. Stamens alternate with the lobes of the corolla and of the same number or fewer. Carpels of the pistil usually two. *Oleaceæ* to *Plantaginaceæ*.

Division 3. MONOCHLAMYDEÆ. Flowers usually small and green. Perianth not differentiated into calyx and corolla or none. *Nyctaginaceæ* to *Salicaceæ*.

II. GYMNOSPERMÆ: Shrubs or trees, usually resinous. Stem consisting of a central pith, concentric layers of wood and a separate bark, increasing in size by additional layers immediately beneath the bark. Leaves usually needle-shaped or scale-like. Flowers in cones, spikes or clusters, the sexes separate. Perianth none. Ovule or ovules not enclosed in an ovary, but attached to the scales of the cone. Embryo having two or several cotyledons, distinguishable before germination and appearing above ground in germination. *Gnetaceæ* and *Coniferæ*.

III. MONOCOTYLEDONES: Herbs, more rarely shrubby as in *Dioscorea* and *Smilax* or arboreous as in *Palmæ*, *Cordyline*, *Dracæna* and some *Bambusæ*. Stem destitute of central pith, not increasing in diameter by concentric layers of new tissues. Leaves usually parallel-veined, but net-veined in *Smilax*, *Araceæ* and some others, usually not disarticulating freely from the branches. Parts of the perianth free or united, usually in threes or reduced to rudimentary organs and enclosed in chaff-like scales, as in the *Cyperaceæ* and *Gramineæ*. Ovule or ovules enclosed in an ovary. Embryo usually very small and embedded in abundant albumen; cotyledon one, not easily distinguished before germination, and usually not appearing above ground in germination.

Division 1. PETALOIDEÆ. Perianth usually consisting of six coloured segments in two series.

Subdivision 1. INFERÆ. Ovary inferior. *Orchidaceæ* to *Dioscoreaceæ*.

Subdivision 2. SUPERÆ. Ovary superior. *Liliaceæ* to *Naiadaceæ*.

Division 2. GLUMIFERÆ. Perianth reduced to rudimentary organs enclosed in chaff-like bracts. *Eriocaulaceæ* to *Gramineæ*.

Briefly summarised the Classification of Plants is into Classes, Divisions or Subclasses, Natural Orders, Genera, Species and Varieties. For example, the Marsh Marigold, p. 11, belongs to—

Class: *Dicotyledones*.
Division: *Polypetalæ*.
Subdivision: *Thalamifloræ*.
Natural Order: *Ranunculaceæ*.
Genus: *Caltha*.
Species: *palustris*.

Varieties are distinguished by differences in the colour of the flowers and other minor characters.

Exceptional Floral Structures

It has been explained that a key to the Natural Orders to be useful must be elaborate. This is because there are so many exceptions to the general characters of some Orders; and it is a key to the exceptions that is most needed by the beginner. I shall not attempt this, but a few words on the subject may be helpful. In the first place it should be understood that it is the sum of the characters that determines the place of a plant in the natural system, and not a conspicuous character that strikes the eye more than all the rest. Taking the Ranunculaceæ, for example, the genera here associated present a great variety in appearance and in structure, and the untrained observer might wonder on what grounds they were brought together, especially when compared with such Orders as the Cruciferæ, the Umbelliferæ and others. Thus the genera *Clematis, Anemone* and *Caltha* have a calyx and no corolla; but the sepals are usually brightly coloured and are commonly called petals. Their true nature is deduced from analogies, the occasional presence of rudimentary petals and other circumstances. In *Delphinium* and *Aconitum* the sepals and petals are so peculiarly formed that it is difficult to decide which belong to the former and which to the latter series. *Actæa*, again, differs from all the other genera in having a berry fruit. In this connection it must be conceded that a *Ranunculus* is much more like a *Potentilla* than any of the genera named; but the essential difference is that the stamens are inserted on the calyx in *Potentilla*, whereas in *Ranunculus* the sepals may be pulled away leaving the stamens on the receptacle.

A few other examples of unusual structures or developments in flower and fruit may be useful.

In *Schizandra* (Magnoliaceæ) the receptacle or axis on which the carpels are seated elongates in the fruiting condition to six or nine inches, and has the appearance of being the axis of a raceme of flowers, each containing a single carpel.

In the Papaveraceæ the sepals fall so early that the expanded flower consists of petals only, enclosing the stamens and pistil.

In the Polygalaceæ two of the sepals are like petals and the lowest of the three petals is much enlarged and crested.

In the Malvaceæ the petals are often slightly connate at the base and adnate to the staminal column.

In *Impatiens* the lower sepal (or three combined) is the largest and most conspicuous part of the flower.

In *Helinus* (Rhamnaceæ) the ovary is inferior.

In *Coriaria* the petals are persistent, become fleshy and enclose the carpels.

In *Bryophyllum* and *Kalanchoë* (Crassulaceæ) the petals are united, forming a gamopetalous corolla.

The same thing occurs in the Cucurbitaceæ.

In *Cornus capitata* the white bracts of the involucre, enclosing a cluster of small flowers, resemble the sepals of a *Clematis*.

In the Asclepiadaceæ the structure of the stamens is very peculiar, and the pollen coheres in masses similar to the condition in orchids.

In *Euphorbia* several male flowers surround one female flower, without separate envelopes, the whole having the appearance of a single flower.

In *Ficus* numerous minute flowers are enclosed in the receptacle or fig.

In *Iris* the stigmatic divisions of the style are like petals.

These few deviations from the usual structure are given as a caution to students not to be misled by external resemblances.

GLOSSARY

Comparatively few technical terms are used in the descriptions in this work, but some familiar words have a definite signification in botanical language which requires explanation. Even the term petal has a more restricted meaning than it has in common parlance. Therefore it seems desirable to give a glossary, if only a very limited one. In addition to the names of organs and qualifying terms, a number of the commoner specific names are included. Illustrative examples have been selected as far as possible from the plants figured.

A, as a prefix, denotes absence of an organ or organs: *apetalous, acotyledonous*.

Accumbent.—Applied to the embryo, especially of the Cruciferæ, when the radicle is turned up and applied to the edges of the cotyledons, thus o=. See *Arabis alpina*, p. 81.

Achene.—A dry, one-seeded, indehiscent fruit, as in the Compositæ, or one carpel in a cluster, as in the fruit of the Buttercup.

Aculeatus.—Armed with prickles, which arise in the epidermal tissue.

Acuminate.—Having a tapering tip, as the leaves of *Pilea umbrosa*, p. 464.

Acute.—Having a sharp-pointed tip.

Adherent.—Employed to denote union of the parts of different whorls or series in flowers, as calyx and ovary in all inferior ovaries, and stamens and corolla in most of the Gamopetalæ.

Adnate.—Organs of different series united, as the stamens to the corolla in *Primula*, p. 298.

Adventitious.—Roots, tubers or buds produced on any other than the ordinary part of the plant are termed adventitious.

Æstivation.—The disposition of the sepals or petals with regard to each other in the flower-bud.

Alatus.—See *Winged*.

Albumen.—The substance found in many seeds in addition to the embryo; in some orders (Gramineæ) it forms the bulk of the seed, in others (Leguminosæ), it is almost always entirely absent.

Albus.—White.

Alternate.—One above the other at different levels, as the leaves of the Oak, or between each other, as the sepals and petals of most plants.

Amplexicaulis.—Clasping the stem, as the leaves of *Parnassia*, p. 177, *Chirita*, p. 366, and *Platystemma*, p. 367.

Androgynous.—When male and female flowers are intermixed or associated in the same head or spike.

Anemophilous.— Fertilised by the wind conveying the pollen from flower to flower, as most plants having inconspicuous flowers, such as the Sedges and Grasses.

Annual.—Plants that flower only once and the same year or season as they spring from seeds. See *Monocarpic*.

Anther.—The part of a stamen in which the pollen is generated. They mostly open or dehisce to allow the pollen to escape by longitudinal slits; sometimes by valves, as in *Berberis* and *Machilus*, p. 432; sometimes by pores, as in *Rhododendron*.

Arborescens.—Growing into a tree.

Arenarius.—Growing in sandy soil.

Argenteus.—Silvery.

Aril.—A pulpy or fleshy appendage to the coat or testa of a seed, as in *Euonymus*.

Aristatus.—Armed or bearing bristles, as the glumes of Grasses and the anthers of *Pieris*.

Arvensis. — Growing in cultivated ground.

Auriculatus.—Having ear-like appendages or lobes, as the leaves of *Meriandra*, p. 393.

Awn.—A stiff or flexible bristle.

Axil.—The angle formed by a branch with the attached leaf, or by any axis with the attached organ.

Axillary.—Produced in the axils of the leaves or other organs.

Axis.—The root, stem and branches which bear leaves, the parts of the flower, etc.

Azureus.—Sky-blue.

Baccate.—Having a more or less fleshy fruit.

Barbatus.—Bearded.

Berry.—Botanically a berry is an indehiscent fruit, fleshy or pulpy throughout with immersed seeds, as in the Grape and Gooseberry.

Bi, in compounds, signifies twice or two. *Bilabiate*, two-lipped, as the corolla of *Salvia*, *Dicliptera* and *Justicia*, and most of the Acanthaceæ, Labiatæ and allied natural orders. *Bifid*, as the petals of *Stellaria*, p. 51.

Blade.—The lamina or flat part of a leaf.

Bracts.—The more or less leaf-like or scale-like organs on the inflorescence and immediately beneath the flowers. They constitute the involucre in the Compositæ, etc. In *Flemingia*, p. 145, they completely enclose the flowers.

Bracteole.—The bracts immediately beneath or next to the flower.

Bulb.—A stock consisting of an axis and leaf-formations with buds in their axils, as in the Onion and Hyacinth.

Bulb, Naked.—Having loose scales like the Lily.

Bulb, Solid.—See *Corm*.

Bulb, Tunicated.—Having the outer scales membranous, as the Tulip.

Bullatus.—Blistered in appearance.

Cæsius.—Ash-grey.

Calcaratus.—Spurred, as the petals of *Aquilegia*, and the corolla of *Halenia*, p. 328.

Calyx.—The outer floral envelope, where there are two dissimilar envelopes, as in the Buttercup and Primrose; the sepals composing it are free in the former and combined in the latter.

Campestris.—Growing in fields or open country.

Candidus.—Pure white.

Canescens.—Becoming grey or hoary.

Capitate.—Terminating in a knob, as the pistil of many plants; clustered in heads, as the flowers of the Compositæ and *Primula denticulata*, p. 298.

Capitulum.—A dense head of flowers.

Capsule.—A dry, dehiscent seed-vessel.

Carneus.—Flesh-colour.

Carpel.—One of the component parts of a fruit or seed-vessel. A seed-vessel consists of one or more carpels. They are separate, as in the Buttercup, or combined, as in the Flax. The pod of the Leguminosæ consists of a single carpel, p. 132.

Caryopsis.—The grain of Grasses.

Catkin.—A deciduous spike of flowers, as in the Willow, p. 479, and Poplar.

Cernuus.—Drooping, pendent.

Character.—The features by which species, genera and orders are distinguished from each other are termed their characters.

Ciliate.—Having marginal hairs; minutely fringed.

Claw.—The stalk of a petal, etc., as in many Cruciferæ and Caryophyllaceæ, *Gypsophila cerastoides*, p. 46.

Cleistogamic.—Fertilisation in closed flowers. Many plants, besides their ordinary flowers, produce others which never expand, yet they yield good seed, as the Violet.

Coccineus.—Scarlet.

Cœruleus.—Pale blue.

Coherent.—Employed to denote union of parts of the same whorl, as the stamens of the Papilionaceæ and the petals of the Gamopetalæ.

Column.—The name given to the combined style and stamen or stamens in Orchids, and the combined stamens in *Malva*, p. 58.

Comose.—Bearing a tuft of hairs, as the seeds of *Epilobium*, p. 195, and *Trachelospermum*, p. 312. In *Amphicome*, p. 368, the seeds are comose at both ends. It is not usual to describe the pappose achenes of the Compositæ as comose

Compound.—Of several parts, as a pinnate leaf, *Cassia*, p. 148; as a bipinnate leaf, *Albizzia*, p. 154.

Cone.—The name given to the compound fruit of *Pinus*, and of other genera of the Coniferæ, pp. 485–488. Also applied to other frutescences and to male inflorescences of similar shape.

Connate.—Parts of the same whorl combined, as the petals of the Primrose and the stamens of the Mallow.

Cordata.—Heart-shaped; *cordate*, as the leaves of *Marsdenia*, p. 318.

Coriaceous.—Leathery in texture, as the leaves of the common Laurel.

Corm.—A fleshy, underground, bulb-like stock, as in Crocus.

Cornutus. — Horned. Used in very much the same sense as *calcaratus*, and sometimes as *aristatus*; as the appendages of the anthers of the Melastomaceæ, p. 190, Vacciniaceæ and Ericaceæ, p. 294.

Corolla.—The inner floral envelope where there are two, and usually the most showy part of the flower. It may consist of separate petals, as in the Buttercup, or of united petals, as in the Primrose.

Corymb.—An inflorescence in which the lower flower-stalks are longer than the upper, thus bringing the flowers nearly to a level, as in Candytuft and *Spiræa canescens*, p. 158.

Cotyledon.—A seed-leaf or embryonal leaf. In dicotyledons the embryo has two cotyledons; in monocotyledons the embryo has only one cotyledon.

Crenate.—Having rounded teeth, as the leaves of *Potentilla*, p. 166.

Crested.—As the petals of *Grewia*, p. 62; the lowest petal of *Polygala*, p. 48.

Cucullatus.—Hood-shaped.

Cuneatus.—Wedge-shaped.

Cuspidatus.—Having a hard point.

Cyme.—An irregular clustered inflorescence, as in *Viburnum*, p. 221. A scorpioid cyme, as in Forget-me-not.

Deciduous.—Falling early or the same season, as the leaves of many trees. Used in contradistinction to *evergreen* in the case of leaves, and to *persistent* in the case of sepals and other organs.

Decumbent.—Plants having trailing barren and ascending flower-stems.

Decurrent.—Running down, as the blade of the leaves on the stems of many Thistles.

Decussate.—Applied to leaves arranged in alternating pairs forming four vertical rows, as in *Pycreus nitens*, p. 553, and *Cyperus niveus*, p. 556.

Dehiscence.—The opening or splitting of seed-vessels and anthers.

Dentate.—Toothed, having the margin notched with small, triangular lobes, as the leaves of the Dead-nettle and *Nepeta leucophylla*, p. 398.

Dicotyledon.—Having two seed-leaves usually distinguishable in the embryo or plantlet while still in the seed.

Didynamous.—Having four stamens, two shorter than the others, as in *Micromeria biflora*, p. 392.

Digitate.—Divided into leaflets in a radiate manner, as the leaves of the Horse Chestnut and *Potentilla nepalensis*, p. 166.

Dimorphic.—Of two forms, as the leaves of *Aconitum heterophyllum*, p. 14, and of *Pimpinella diversifolia*, p. 210.

Diœcious.—Bearing male and female flowers on different individuals.

Disk.—Applied to an organ usually between the stamens and the ovary, sometimes between the petals and stamens, and often in the form of a ring, as in *Zizyphus*, p. 89, and *Sageretia*, p. 92.

Dissepiments.—The partitions of an ovary or fruit.

Distichous.—Arranged in two opposite vertical rows.

Dorsal.—Appertaining to the back. As applied to carpels and stamens, it is the outside or that part next to the observer, as opposed to *ventral* or the side next the axis or centre of the flower.

Drupe.—A fleshy fruit having a hard endocarp or stone enclosing the seed, as the Cherry.

Drupelet.—A fleshy fruit composed of a number of carpels with hard endocarps, as in most species of *Rubus*, p. 161.

E, Ex, denotes absence, as *ebracteate*, *eglandular*, *exalbuminous*.

Echinate.—Clothed with prickles, as the shell of the fruit of the Sweet Chestnut.

Elliptical.—Oval, similar to ovate, but both ends equal.

Emarginate.—Notched at the tip, as the petals of *Stellaria crispata*, p. 51.

Embryo.—The plantlet or germ of a plant found in the seed.

Ensiform.—Sword-shaped, as the leaves of *Iris*, p. 515.

Entire.—Having an unbroken margin.

Entomophilous.—Fertilised by insects conveying the pollen from flower to flower, as most plants having showy flowers.

Epi, signifies upon in compounds, *Epipetalous*, as the stamens of *Salvia*, p. 395, *Torenia*, p. 353, and *Scrophularia*, p. 349, stamens on the corolla.

Epicalyx.—The name given to the accessory lobes of the calyx of *Potentilla*, p. 166, and other genera.

Epiphyte.—A plant that grows upon another but does not draw its nourishment therefrom.

Ex, in composition means without, as *exalbuminous*; or outside, as *exogenous*.

Exserted.—Projecting, as the stamens and style from the corolla of *Elsholtzia*, p. 389, and *Caryopteris*, p. 381.

Extrorse.—Applied to anthers which open outwards or away from the pistil.

Fascicled.—Clustered.

Filament.—The stalk of a stamen bearing the anther.

Filiform.—Slender, thread-like.
Fimbriate.—Fringed on the margin, as the labellum of *Habenaria intermedia*, p. 502.
Flavus.—Pale yellow.
Floret.—Often applied to the individual flowers of the Compositæ and other plants, of which the inflorescence is popularly termed a flower.
Folium.—A leaf.
Follicle.—A several-seeded carpel dehiscing along the inner or ventral suture, as in *Delphinium denudatum*, p. 12.
Free.—Not joined together or with other organs, as all the parts of the flower of a Buttercup.
Frond.—Applied to the leaves of ferns and some other groups of plants.
Fruit.—The seed-vessel of any plant, whether edible or otherwise.
Fugacious.—Falling very early, as the sepals of Poppies.
Fulvus.—Dull yellow.
Fuscus.—Brown.

Gamopetalous.—Petals united and forming a corolla which falls away as a whole, as in the Labiatæ.
Genus.—See under the heading 'Classification,' p. lv.
Glabrous.—Having no hairs; smooth.
Glandular.—Furnished with glands or secretory organs, as the leaves of *Drosera*, p. 187. The variously formed and situated honey-secreting organs of flowers are termed glands.
Glaucous.—Of the peculiar pale blue-green seen in the leaves of the common Pea.
Glume.—The bracts enclosing the flowers of the Gramineæ and Cyperaceæ.
Graveolens.—Of a strong odour.
Gymnos, signifies naked in compounds.

Habit.—The general aspect of a plant, due to its mode of growth, stature, branching, foliage and other characteristics.
Helmet-shaped.—As the upper sepal of *Aconitum heterophyllum*, p. 14.
Herbaceous.—Applied to all green parts that are not woody, and to stems that flower and then die.
Hermaphrodite.—Having both sexes, stamens and pistil, in the same flower.
Heterogamous.—Flower-heads are heterogamous when they contain more than one kind of flower, as male and female, or neuter and hermaphrodite, as in some Compositæ.
Hirsutus.—Clothed with rather long, soft hairs.
Hispidus.—Clothed with rather long, stiff hairs.
Homogamous.—Flower-heads are homogamous when all the flowers are alike, that is, male, female or hermaphrodite, as in some Compositæ.
Humilis.—Dwarf, used in comparison.
Hypo, used in compounds to denote below, under; as hypogynous petals and stamens below the ovary in *Anemone*, p. 5.

Imbricate.—Used more especially to denote that sepals or petals overlap each other in bud instead of their edges just meeting.
Incumbent.—Applied to the embryo, especially of the Cruciferæ, when the radicle is turned against the back of one of the cotyledons; thus, o ‖. See *Sisymbrium strictum*, p. 34.
Inferior.—This term is employed to designate the relative positions of the different parts of a flower, but more especially it means, with regard to the ovary, that the calyx is adherent to it, so that the ovary is situated below the flower proper, as in *Epilobium*, p. 195, *Aralia*, p. 217, and *Viburnum*, p. 221.
Inflorescence.—The arrangement of the flowers when they are not solitary in the axils of the leaves, as the raceme in *Sisymbrium*, p. 34, the panicle in *Meliosma*, p. 102, the umbel in *Heracleum*, p. 215, and the catkin in *Salix*, p. 479. Spikes, racemes, corymbs, etc., may be simple (unbranched) or paniculate (branched).
Involucel.—A secondary involucre enclosing the separate flowers, as in the Dipsaceæ; see *Morina*, p. 239.
Involucre.—The name given to one or more series of bracts surrounding a head of flowers, as in all the Compositæ. In *Cornus capitata*, p. 219, the involucre is the conspicuous part of the inflorescence.
Irregular.—Sepals or petals unequal in size or different in shape in the same flower, as in *Aconitum*, p. 14.

Keel.—The two lower more or less combined petals of the flowers of the Papilionaceæ constitute the keel or carina. An organ is keeled when it has a ridge like the keel of a boat, as the carpels of *Delphinium*, p. 12.

Labellum.—See *Lip*.
Labiate.—Lipped, as the corolla of most of the Labiatæ, Verbenaceæ, Acanthaceæ and Scrophulariaceæ.
Laciniate.—Irregularly cut or divided.
Lacustris.—Growing in lakes.
Lanceolate.—Of leaves, etc., nearly ovate but tapering to both ends and broadest

below the middle. See *Swertia*, p. 327, *Schizandra*, p. 16, *Impatiens*, p. 74, and *Ilex*, p. 84.

Lateral.—Employed to designate the two side petals or wings between the standard and keel in Leguminosæ, and the side lobes of the lip of an Orchid and other similar relative positions of organs.

Leaflet.—The ultimate articulated divisions of compound leaves, as in *Thalictrum*, p. 7, *Cedrela*, p. 82, *Vitis*, p. 94, *Astragalus*, p. 126, *Cassia*, p. 148, and *Albizzia*. p. 154. In many compoundly divided leaves the ultimate segments are not jointed to the rhachis, and do not eventually separate from it, and are properly designated lobes or segments.

Legume.—The pod or seed-vessel of the Leguminosæ, etc.

Ligulate.—Strap-shaped, as the ray-flowers of the Compositæ; all the flowers are ligulate in the suborder to which the Dandelion and *Lactuca*, p. 285, belong.

Linear—Narrow, with almost parallel edges, as the leaves of Grasses and Sedges.

Lip.—The name given to one of the divisions of the perianth of Orchid flowers. This is usually different in shape and larger than the rest of the segments. See *Bilabiate.*

Littoralis.—Inhabiting the sea-shore.

Lobe.—A division of a leaf, leaflet or petal.

Lucidus.—Shining.

Luteus.—Yellow.

Macro, in composition long but sometimes used instead of *mega* to indicate large.

Membranous.—Employed to designate the texture of leaves, etc., when they are thin and limp, as opposed to coriaceous or leathery.

Midrib.—The central rib-like thickening of a leaf. Where there are similar lateral thickenings proceeding from the base towards the apex of the leaf they are commonly termed nerves. Some authors call the primary veins, which proceed from the midrib towards the margin, nerves. *Coriaria nepalensis*, p. 107, has three-nerved leaves; in *Osbeckia stellata*, p. 190, they are five-nerved. The net-like vascular system of a leaf is termed the venation.

Mono, in composition signifies one, as *monocotyledon.*

Monocarpic.—Flowering and fruiting only once, whether the same season that the plant springs from seed or the season after or many years after, as the Talipot Palm and many kinds of Bamboo, which flower once and then die.

Monocotyledon.—Having only one seed-leaf.

Monœcious.—Sexes, stamens and pistil, in separate flowers, but on the same plant.

Mucronate.—Terminating in a short, hard point.

Natans.—Of swimming or floating habit.

Natural Order.—See under the heading 'Classification,' p. lv.

Nerves.—See *Midrib.*

Nivalis.—From snowy regions.

Niveus.—Snowy-white.

Nudus.—Naked, that is, a surface without scales, hairs or other appendages, as leaves and other organs.

Numerous.—When organs exceed from twelve to twenty, as the stamens of *Albizzia mollis*, p. 154.

Nut.—Variously applied both in popular and botanical writings. The Hazel nut and the Acorn, without the involucre or cup, are true nuts. See *Quercus*, p. 474. The seed-vessel or grain of the Cyperaceæ is also designated a nut.

Nutans.—Drooping, nodding, as the flowers of the Snowdrop.

Nutlet.—Applied to small one-seeded fruits and the divisions of the fruits of the Boraginaceæ and Labiatæ. See *Cynoglossum furcatum*, p. 332.

Ob, a prefix denoting inversion, as *oblanceolate, obovate, obcordate*, etc.

Obtuse.—Having a rounded or blunt tip.

-oides.—An affix denoting resemblance.

Orbicular.—Circular in outline.

Oval.—The same as elliptical.

Ovary.—That part of the pistil containing the ovules or young seeds There may be several or many ovaries in the same flower, each having a single cavity or cell, as Larkspur and Buttercup; or there may be only one ovary and that one-celled, as in the Leguminosæ and Compositæ, or more than one-celled, as in the Umbelliferæ and Scrophulariaceæ.

Ovate.—Egg-shaped, as the leaves of *Lychnis*, p. 49, and *Grewia*, p. 62.

Ovule.—A young seed.

Pale.—The name given to the inner flowering glume of Grasses differing from the others in being two-nerved or two-ribbed.

Palmate.—Lobed in the form of a hand, as the leaves of *Malva*, p. 58, and *Zehneria*, p. 200.

Palustris.—Growing in marshes.

Panicle.—A general name for loosely branched inflorescences, such as that of the Horse Chestnut and many Grasses, as *Panicum plicatum*, p. 583. More strictly, a panicle is a compound inflorescence, which may be spicate, racemose, corymbose or cymose in composition.

Papilionaceous.—Shaped like a butterfly. Applied more especially to the flowers of the Pea family. In such flowers the upper petal is the standard, the lateral petals the wings, and the lower petals combined the keel.

Pappus.—The calyx-limb of the Compositæ, usually composed of hairs or bristles, less frequently of scales. See *Aster*, p. 250, *Serratula*, p. 275, *Ainsliæa*, p. 277.

Parasite.—A plant that grows upon and roots into the tissues of another from which it obtains its nourishment, as *Cuscuta*, p. 340, and *Viscum*, p. 440.

Pedicel.—A flower-stalk; properly the ultimate branchlets of a compound inflorescence, each bearing one flower; but often employed instead of peduncle.

Peduncle.—When flowers are solitary, as in the axils of the leaves, the stalk is termed a peduncle. It is also employed to designate the stalk of a cluster or head of flowers, as in the Compositæ.

Peltatus.—Produced from within the margin, as the leaf-stalks of *Cissampelos*, p. 19.

Perennial.—Flowering more than once from the same root or root-stock, more especially applied to herbs that die down annually.

Perianth.—The floral envelopes collectively; but employed more especially where there is only one series or where there is no distinct differentiation into calyx and corolla.

Pericarp.—The shell of a fruit or seed-vessel. It consists of distinct parts in some fruits; thus in the Peach there is the skin or epicarp, the flesh or mesocarp, and the stone or endocarp.

Perigynous.—Growing on the tube or throat of the calyx, as the petals and stamens in most of the Rosaceæ.

Persistent.—Of more than ordinary duration, as the calyx of the Strawberry, the style in many Cruciferæ, and the leaves of evergreens.

Petals.—The separate or united parts of the floral envelope. See *Corolla*.

Petaloid.—Resembling petals in colour and texture, commonly applied to the perianth of the Lilies and other monocotyledonous orders.

Petiolate.—Having a stalk.

Petiole.—A leaf-stalk.

Petiolule.—The stalk of a leaflet.

Phænogamous or *Phanerogamous.*—Having manifest flowers in contradistinction to ferns, which are designated *Cryptogamous*.

Pinnate.—A compound leaf divided into leaflets. There are simply pinnate leaves, *Cedrela*, p. 82, *Indigofera*, p. 122, and bipinnate leaves, *Albizzia*, p. 154, and others of greater degrees of division. There are no buds in the axils of a leaflet.

Pinnatifid.—As applied to leaves and other organs, signifies that they are lobed or divided, but not quite to the midrib.

Pinnule.—Pinnules are the primary divisions of a bipinnate leaf; leaflets are the primary divisions of a pinnate leaf and the secondary divisions of a bipinnate leaf.

Pistil.—The female organs of a flower collectively. It consists of one carpel, as in Leguminosæ; of several free carpels, as in the Buttercup; or of several combined carpels, as in Flax. The simplest form of pistil consists of an ovary and stigma, but the latter usually has a stalk or style. Some authors call the carpels of a fruit pistils when they are free, as in the Buttercup.

Placenta.—The process or body which bears the ovules in the ovary.

Plumose.—Feathery, as the pappus of *Ainsliæa*, p. 277, and the ripe achenes of *Clematis*, p. 3.

Plumule.—The primary bud of an embryo.

Pollen.—The powdery substance formed in the anthers. It consists of minute, unicellular bodies whose function is to fertilise the ovules, and it is thus regarded as the male element in sexual reproduction.

Polygamous.—When male, female and hermaphrodite flowers are intermixed on the same individual plant.

Polypetalous.—Petals free, as in the Buttercup.

Præcox.—Flowering early.

Pratensis.—Growing in meadows.

Procumbent.—Applied to stems that lie on the ground but do not form roots at the joints.

Pubescent.—Clothed with short, soft hairs.

Putamen.—The stone of a fruit such as the Peach.

Raceme.—A kind of inflorescence in which the flowers are nearly equally stalked and arranged singly on a common axis or peduncle, as in *Astragalus chlorostachys*, p. 126.

Rachis, Rachilla.—See *Rhachis*.

Radical.—Proceeding from the crown of the root or root-stock, as the leaves of the Dandelion and Primrose.

Radicle.—The first root of a plant growing from a seed.

Receptacle.—The top of the axis bearing the parts of the flower, as in the Buttercup; or bearing the flowers, as in the Compositæ and in *Ficus.*

Recurved.—Curled or turned backwards, as the perianth-segments of *Lilium polyphyllum*, see frontispiece.

Regular.—When all the parts of each series of organs in a flower are alike, as the sepals and petals of the Buttercup.

Reniform.—Kidney-shaped in outline or form.

Repens.—Creeping.

Rhachis.—Used to designate the axis of a fern-frond, the principal axis of a compound leaf or of an inflorescence. The diminutive *rhachilla* is more especially used as the name of the axis of the flower-spikelet in Grasses.

Rhizome.—A creeping, usually underground stem, producing erect stems at intervals.

Riparius.—Growing on the banks of streams and lakes.

Rotate.—In the form of a wheel, as the corolla of *Androsace.*

Ruber.—Red.

Ruderalis.—Growing in waste places.

Rugosus.—Wrinkled.

Rupestris.—Growing on rocks.

Sabulosus.—Growing in gravelly or sandy places.

Sagittate.—Shaped in the form of an arrow-head.

Salver-shaped.—Applied to the corolla, as in *Syringa*, p. 308, and many species of *Primula*, p. 298.

Sarmentose.—Climbing by means of long, flexible branches and resting on other shrubs rather than attaching themselves, as the Blackberry and many Roses.

Saxatilis.—Growing on rocks or stones.

Scabrous.—Furnished with rigid, prickly hairs or bristles.

Scandens.—Climbing.

Scape.—A flower-stalk or stem, usually leafless, springing direct from the root or root-stock, as in *Ophiopogon*, p. 513, and *Eriocaulon*, p. 550.

Scarious.—Thin, dry and membranous, as the glumes of most Grasses.

Seed-vessel.—Fruit, whether edible or otherwise.

Semi, denotes half or partial.

Sempervirens.—Evergreen.

Septum.—A partition in an ovary or fruit.

Sericeus.—Silky.

Serotinus.—Late.

Serrate.—Saw-toothed, as the edges of the leaves of *Pilea umbrosa*, p. 464.

Sessile.—Stalkless.

Setaceus.—Bristly.

Sheathing.—Enveloping some other part, as the base of the leaves of Grasses and the stipules of *Polygonum*, p. 424.

Simple.—Applied to leaves and other organs in contradistinction to *compound.* For example a leaf is simple when the division does not extend to the midrib.

Sinus.—A recess of a lobed organ.

Spadix.—A spicate inflorescence enclosed in a leafy bract or spathe, as in *Arisæma*, p. 541.

Spathe.—A leafy bract enclosing the inflorescence as in *Arisæma*, p. 541.

Spathulate.—Oblong and tapering downwards into a stalk, as the leaf of the Daisy.

Spike.—An inflorescence having the flowers sessile on a common axis, which may be simple or branched. *Plantago*, p. 408.

Spine.—A sharp, woody outgrowth having its seat below the skin or epidermis, as in *Flacourtia*, p. 41.

Spurred.—Having a hollow, tubular projection, as the upper sepal of *Delphinium*, p. 12, the upper petal of *Corydalis*, p. 26, the corolla of *Halenia*, p. 328, the labellum of *Habenaria*, p. 502, and the anthers of *Pieris*, p. 294. The last are more correctly described as *aristate.*

Squamatus.—Clothed with scales, as the leaves of *Elæagnus*, p. 436.

Stamen.—The organ in a flower which produces the pollen or male element. It usually consists of filament and anther.

Staminode.—A rudimentary organ in a series next to the stamens.

Standard.—The name given to the upper petal of the flowers of the Papilionaceæ, *Flemingia*, p. 145, and *Impatiens*, p. 74.

Stellate.—Radiating, as hairs and other organs.

Stigma.—The viscous part of a style which receives the pollen, which then grows down into the ovary and fertilises the ovules.

Stipitate.—Stalked, as applied to ovaries, carpels and pods. *Bœnninghausenia*, p. 77.

Stipules.—Bract-like appendages at the base of the leaf-stalks of many plants. They are toothed or pinnatifid in the Violet, spine-like in *Zizyphus*, p. 89, in many species of *Astragalus*, p. 126, and in the False Acacia *Robinia*, and leaf-like in *Lathyrus Aphaca.*

Stolon.—An offset or runner producing roots at intervals and forming independent plants, as in *Viola*, p. 40.

Strictus.—Of narrow, stiff, erect habit of growth.

Style.—The usually slender termination

of a carpel or ovary bearing the stigma.

Subulate.—Awl-shaped.

Sulcate.—Furrowed.

Superior.—As an ovary or pistil when it is free from the calyx and other parts of the flower.

Sylvestris, *Sylvaticus.* — Inhabiting woods. Sometimes used in the sense of wild as opposed to cultivated.

Symmetrical.—When all the whorls of a flower—sepals, petals, stamens and carpels—are the same in number.

Syn, signifies union, as *syncarpous* when the carpels are consolidated, as in Flax and *Hypericum*; or *syngenesious* when the anthers are united, as in the Compositæ.

Tendril.—A twining organ by means of which a plant climbs. In *Zehneria*, p. 200, it is a modified branch; in *Vicia* and *Lathyrus* it is a modified leaflet.

Tenuis.—Slender, thin.

Teres.—Cylindrical.

Testa.—The skin of a seed.

Thalamus. — The apex of the axis on which the parts of the flower are seated. See *Receptacle.*

Tomentose.—Clothed with a dense, short down. Almost the same as *pubescent*, but hairy in a stronger degree.

Toothed.—The same as *dentate.* Notched on the margin, as the leaves of many plants. When the teeth are rounded the term *crenate* is employed; when the points of the teeth are directed towards the tip of the leaf the term *serrate* is employed. See *Craniotome*, p. 401, and *Quercus dilatata*, p. 474.

Torus.—See *Receptacle.*

Tri, in compounds means three, as *trifoliolate*, the leaves of *Rhynchosia himalensis*, p. 144.

Truncate.—When the end or tip of an organ is more or less square as if cut off.

Tube.—The united part of a calyx or corolla is termed the tube, whatever its shape, as distinguished from the lobes or limb.

Tuber.—An underground, fleshy stem or stock like the Potato. Tuberous-rooted, as *Dahlia.*

Tuberculate.—Furnished with excrescences on the surface.

Uliginosus.—Growing in swampy places.

Umbel.—An inflorescence in which the flower-stalks radiate from one point, as in the Ivy. In *Heracleum*, p. 215 and most of the Umbelliferæ the umbels are compound, that is, having branches of the second order.

Umbrosus.—Growing in shady places.

Unarmed. — Destitute of spines or prickles.

Undulate.—Having a wavy margin.

Unisexual.—Flowers or plants bearing only male or female organs.

Urens.—Stinging.

Utricle.—The name given to the bladder-like envelope of the nut of *Carex* p. 567.

Valvate.—Applied to sepals and petals when their edges meet in the flower-bud but do not overlap.

Valve.—The pieces into which a seed-vessel divides or splits, as the pods of Cruciferæ, *Sisymbrium*, p. 34, and Leguminosæ, *Astragalus*, p. 126; and the trap-door-like covers of the anthers of the Berberidaceæ and Lauraceæ, *Machilus Duthiei*, p. 432.

Veins.—See *Midrib.*

Velutinus.—Velvety, as the surface of some leaves.

Ventral.—The part of an organ facing the centre of a flower.

Verrucosus.—Warty.

Versatile.—Affixed by the middle, as the anthers of grasses.

Verticillate.—When several leaves spring from the same horizontal plane, as in *Galium*, p. 235.

Virens.—Becoming green.

Virgatus.—Having long, slender, stiff stems or branches.

Viridis.—Green.

Viviparous.—Forming buds in the inflorescences which eventually fall off and grow into independent plants, as some Lilies and Rushes.

Volubilis.—Twisting, twining, as *Ipomœa*, p. 337, and *Cuscuta*, p. 340.

Whorl.—A ring of organs on the same plane, as the leaves of *Galium*, p. 235, and the carpels of *Malva*, p. 58. This term is also used to designate the two opposite clusters or cymes of flowers of most Labiatæ.

Winged.—Furnished with a membranous or leafy expansion, as the seeds of many Coniferæ, the fruit of *Acer*, p. 99, and *Begonia*, p. 202.

Wings.—The lateral petals of the Papilionaceæ and the sepals of Polygalaceæ.

LIST OF THE PLANTS FIGURED

All the figures are approximately half the natural size of the plants represented. The separate flowers, parts of flowers, seed-vessels, seeds, etc., are mostly enlarged to show their structure more distinctly.

BIBLIOGRAPHY

The following list of books and articles includes the principal ones consulted and cited, and also a few others that may be useful to the student of the Flora and Vegetable Products of Simla and the surrounding country.

Beddome, R. H. Handbook to the Ferns of British India, with 300 figures, chiefly in the text. 1883. Supplement, 1892.

Bentham, G. Outlines of Elementary Botany, as Introductory to Local Floras. New Edition.

Blanford, H. F. An annotated List of the Ferns of Simla between the Elevations of 4,500 and 10,500 ft. Printed for private distribution only. No date, but from internal evidence it must have appeared since 1883.

Blanford, H. F. The Silver Ferns of Simla and their Allies. 'Journal of the Simla Naturalists' Society,' ii. pp. 13–22. 1886.

Blanford, H. F. A List of the Ferns of Simla in the N.W. Himalaya, between Levels of 4,500 and 10,500 ft. 'Journal of the Asiatic Society of Bengal,' lvii. 2, pp. 294–315, tt. 16–21. 1888.

Brandis, D., and J. Lindsay Stewart. The Forest Flora of North-West and Central India. 1874.

Brandis, D., and J. Lindsay Stewart. Illustrations of the Forest Flora of North-West and Central India, with 70 quarto uncoloured plates. 1874.

Brandis, D. Vegetation and Country from Narkanda to Pangi. Simla, 1879.

Brandis, D. Der Wald des äusseren Nordwestlichen Himalaya. 'Verhandlungen des naturhistorischen Vereins der preussischen Rheinlande und Westphalens,' xxxxii. pp. 153–180. About 1885–6.

Bruce, Lady Elisabeth, assisted by *H. Babington Smith* and others. An annotated List of Flowers collected in the neighbourhood of Simla and Mashobra. Simla, 1897.

Buck, E. C. Twenty Trees of the Simla Neighbourhood. 'Journal of the Simla Naturalists' Society,' i. pp. 27–43. 1885.

Clarke, C. B. A Review of the Ferns of Northern India. 'Transactions of the Linnean Society,' 2nd Series, Botany, i. pp. 425–611, plates 49–84. 1880.

Coldstream, W. Grasses of the Southern Punjab. Photo-lithographs of some of the Principal Grasses found at Hissar. 1889.

Collett, H. Two Simla Plants. 'Journal of the Simla Naturalists' Society,' ii. pp. 1–11. 1886.

Collett, H. Some Simla Grasses. 'Journal of the Simla Naturalists' Society,' ii. pp. 55–58. 1886.

Duthie, J. F., and J. B. Fuller. Field and Garden Crops of the North-western Provinces and Oudh, with 100 uncoloured plates. 1882–1893.

Gamble, J. S. A Manual of Indian Timbers. 1881. A new edition is passing through the press.

Gamble, J. S. The Hill Route from Mussoorie to Simla. 'Indian Forester,' xxiv. (1898), pp. 105–111, with a map.

Griffith, W. Journals of Travels. 1847. Loodianah to Simla, pp. 506–516.

Hoffmeister, W. Travels in Ceylon and Continental India. 1848. Simla, pp. 474–480.

Hooker, J. D., and T. Thomson. Flora Indica, with an Introductory Essay. 1855. Simla, Introduction, p. 202.

Hooker, J. D. The Flora of British India. Seven vols. 1875–1897.

Hope, C. W. The Ferns of North-western India, illustrated. 'Journal of the Bombay Natural History Society,' xii.–xiv. 1899–1902.

Jacquemont, V. Voyage dans l'Inde pendant les années 1828–1832. Tome iv., Botanique, containing 180 uncoloured plates. 1844.

Royle, J. Forbes. Illustrations of the Botany . . . of the Himalaya Mountains, containing 97 coloured plates. 1839.

Sunder, Lall Pathak, Pundit. Reafforestation of the Mahasu-Fagu Ridge. 'Indian Forester,' xxii. (1896), pp. 44–49.

Thomson, T. Western Himalaya and Tibet: A Narrative of a Journey through the Mountains of Northern India during the years 1847–8. 1852.

Watt, G. Dictionary of the Economic Products of India. Six volumes. 1889 to 1893.

Wight, R. Icones Plantarum Indiæ Orientalis, containing 2,101 uncoloured plates. 1840–1853.

I. RANUNCULACEÆ

HERBS of various habit or climbing shrubs (*Clematis*). Leaves radical, alternate or opposite (*Clematis*). Flowers usually 2-sexual, regular or irregular, presenting a great variety of form in the different genera. Sepals usually 5, free; petal-like, when the petals are wanting or rudimentary; falling off after flowering; imbricate or valvate (*Clematis*); all alike or sometimes differing much in shape. Petals variously formed, the same in number as the sepals or more, sometimes wanting or reduced, flat or spurred, imbricate. Stamens usually numerous, free. Carpels several or many, rarely only one or two, distinct, 1-celled, one- or many-ovuled, style simple. Fruit of one or more, usually numerous, achenes or follicles; or a many-seeded berry (*Actæa*).—Abundant in cold and temperate regions, rare in the tropics.

In *Ranunculaceæ* the sepals and petals present almost as great a variety of form as all the other orders of the *Thalamifloreæ*, but the great majority can be recognised by their numerous free stamens and free carpels.

SHRUBS. LEAVES OPPOSITE. Sepals large, petal-like . . . 1. *Clematis*.
HERBS. LEAVES ALTERNATE or RADICAL.
  Carpels 1-ovuled. Flowers regular.
    Petals none. Sepals 4–8, petal-like.
      Flowers in an umbelliform cyme, with ear-like involucres . . . . 2. *Anemone*.
      Flowers in panicles, involucres none . . . . 3. *Thalictrum*.
    Petals 5–8, more conspicuous than the sepals.
      Petals scarlet, without a basal gland . . . . 4. *Adonis*.
      Petals yellow, with a basal gland . . . . 5. *Ranunculus*.
  Carpels many-ovuled.
    Flowers very irregular.
      Sepals flat, regular. Petals spurred . . . . 7. *Aquilegia*.
      Upper sepal produced at the base in the form of a spur . . . . 8. *Delphinium*.
      Upper sepal helmet-shaped, base not produced . 9. *Aconitum*.
    Flowers regular or nearly regular.
      Flowers 1–2 in. diam., yellow . . . . . . 6. *Caltha*.
      Flowers 3–4 in. diam., red or white . . . . 12. *Pæonia*.
      Flowers hardly ¼ in. diam., white.
        Carpels 2–5. Follicles flat . . . . . 11. *Cimicifuga*.
        Carpel solitary. Berry ovoid . . . . . 10. *Actæa*.

1. CLEMATIS. The Greek name.—Temperate regions, rare in the tropics.

Shrubs climbing by means of their leaf-stalks. Leaves of 3 leaflets or pinnate, opposite, or clustered at the nodes; leaflets often lobed, usually irregularly toothed. Flowers solitary on axillary stalks, or in loose axillary panicles. Sepals 4, rarely more, large, petal-like, spreading or erect, valvate in bud. Petals none. Stamens numerous, filaments glabrous or hairy. Fruit a head of nearly sessile achenes conspicuous by the persistent styles which grow out into long feathery tails.

Leaves with 3 leaflets. Flowers solitary on long stalks.
- Flowers white . . . . 1. *C. montana.*
- Flowers dull purple . . . . 2. *C. barbellata.*

Leaves pinnate. Flowers in panicles.
- Sepals spreading.
  - Flowers $\frac{1}{3}$–$\frac{1}{2}$ in. diam. . . . . 4. *C. Gouriana.*
  - Flowers $\frac{3}{4}$–1 in. diam.
    - Leaflets hairy . . . . 3. *C. grata.*
    - Leaflets downy . . . . 5. *C. puberula.*
- Sepals erect, tips recurved.
  - Filaments hairy only on the lower half . . . 6. *C. nutans.*
  - Filaments hairy throughout.
    - Stem and leaflets glabrous . . . . . 7. *C. connata.*
    - Stem and leaflets hairy . . . . . . 8. *C. Buchananiana.*

1. **Clematis montana,** *Buch.-Ham.*; *Fl. Br. Ind.* i. 2. Glabrous or pubescent. Stems terete. Leaves of 3 leaflets, stalked, clustered at the nodes; leaflets narrowly ovate, acute, margins more or less toothed, especially towards the tip. Flowers 2–3 in. diam., white, solitary on axillary stalks longer than the leaves. Sepals oblong, flat, spreading, tip rounded. Anthers and achenes glabrous.

Simla, common on open hill-sides; April.—Temperate Himalaya, 4000–12,000 ft.

This species is widely cultivated in England on account of its early flowering season.

2. **Clematis barbellata,** *Edgew.*; *Fl. Br. Ind.* i. 3. Glabrous or nearly so. Stems terete. Leaves of 3 leaflets, stalked, clustered at the nodes; leaflets ovate-lanceolate, often lobed, irregularly sharply toothed. Buds ovoid, acute. Flowers dull purple, solitary on axillary stalks at first shorter than the leaves, lengthening in fruit. Sepals $\frac{3}{4}$–1 in. long, pubescent, lanceolate, long-pointed, spreading. Filaments usually fringed with long hairs. Anthers hairy on the back. Achenes glabrous.

Mushobra, Mahasu, in forest; May, June.—W. Himalaya, 5000–12,000 ft.

3. **Clematis grata,** *Wall.*; *Fl. Br. Ind.* i. 3. More or less hairy. Stems deeply furrowed. Leaves pinnate; leaflets rarely only 3, hairy on both surfaces, ovate-lanceolate, often cordate, usually lobed, pointed, irregularly sharply toothed. Flowers $\frac{3}{4}$–1 in. diam., cream-coloured, fragrant, in panicles often longer than

the leaves. Sepals oblong-ovate, tomentose outside, spreading. Filaments glabrous. Achenes densely pubescent.

Simla, Mushobra, common; August.—W. Himalaya, 2000–8000 ft.—China, Africa.

4. **Clematis Gouriana,** *Roxb.*; *Fl. Br. Ind.* i. 4. Glabrous or nearly so. Stems furrowed. Leaves pinnate or 2-pinnate; leaflets thin, smooth, ovate-lanceolate, cordate, long-pointed, entire. Flowers $\frac{1}{3}$–$\frac{1}{2}$ in. diam., pale yellow, crowded in panicles. Sepals densely pubescent, oblong, tip rounded, spreading. Filaments glabrous. Achenes hairy.

Valleys below Simla; June, July.—Hilly districts throughout India, 1000–3000 ft.—Java, Philippines.

5. **Clematis puberula,** *Hook. f. & Thoms.*; *Fl. Br. Ind.* i. 4. Downy. Stems furrowed. Leaves pinnate; leaflets thin, nearly

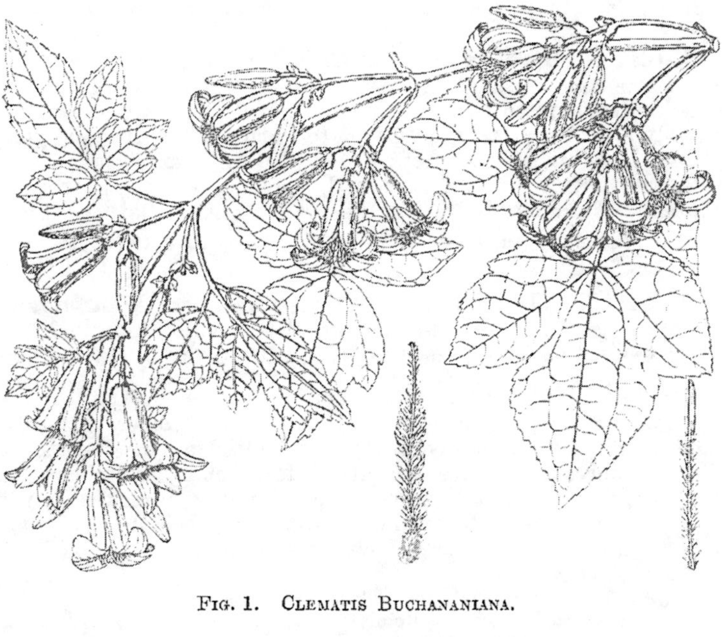

FIG. 1. CLEMATIS BUCHANANIANA.

glabrous, ovate or narrowly lanceolate, long-pointed, often 3-lobed, margins irregularly sharply toothed, rarely entire. Flowers few, in leafy panicles, pale yellow, 1 in. diam. Sepals silky-pubescent outside, narrowly oblong, spreading, tip rounded. Filaments glabrous. Achenes hairy.

Simla, Mushobra; August.—W. Himalaya, 4000–7000 ft.

6. **Clematis nutans,** *Royle*; *Fl. Br. Ind.* i. 5. Silky-pubescent. Stems slender, furrowed. Leaves pinnate; leaflets ovate-oblong or lanceolate, undivided or 3–5-lobed, margins entire or sharply and irregularly toothed. Flowers drooping, pale yellow, in panicles. Sepals ¾–1 in. long, densely silky-pubescent outside, not ribbed, oblong, erect, tip recurved, pointed. Filaments hairy only on the lower half, tapering upwards. Achenes densely hairy.

Valleys below Simla; September, October.—W. Himalaya, 2000–5000 ft.

7. **Clematis connata,** *DC.*; *Fl. Br. Ind.* i. 6. Glabrous except the flowers, stems faintly grooved. Leaves pinnate, the bases of the opposite stalks more or less united, sometimes forming a broad flat expansion; leaflets ovate-lanceolate, cordate, sometimes lobed, sharply irregularly toothed. Flowers yellow-white, in panicles. Sepals ¾–1 in. long, tomentose on both surfaces, not ribbed, oblong, erect, tip recurved, obtuse. Filaments hairy throughout. Achenes densely hairy.

Simla, Mushobra; July–September.—Temperate Himalaya, 4000–10,000 ft.

8. **Clematis Buchananiana,** *DC.*; *Fl. Br. Ind.* i. 6. Shortly hairy. Stems grooved. Leaves pinnate, the bases of the opposite stalks more or less united; leaflets broadly ovate, cordate, often lobed, coarsely and irregularly crenately toothed. Flowers pale yellow, in long leafy panicles. Sepals ¾–1 in. long, tomentose outside, pubescent within, ribbed, narrowly oblong, erect, tip recurved, pointed. Filaments hairy throughout. Achenes hairy. (Fig. 1.)

Simla, common; August.—Temperate Himalaya, 5000–10,000 ft.

2. **ANEMONE.** From the Greek *anemos*, wind, referring perhaps to some species appearing in the windy months of early spring.—Cold and temperate regions, rare in the S. Hemisphere.

Perennial herbs. Stems erect, usually branched. Leaves radical, long-stalked, deeply lobed, margins toothed. Flowers rather large, regular, in a simple or compound, umbelliform cyme bearing leaf-like involucres at its base and at the forks of its branches; cymes few- or many-flowered. Sepals 5–8, petal-like, imbricate, spreading. Petals none. Stamens numerous. Carpels many, 1-ovuled, styles short. Fruit a head of sessile achenes.

Radical leaves 5–7-lobed.
- Leaves glabrous on the upper, white-tomentose on lower surface. Achenes woolly . . . . . 1. *A. vitifolia.*
- Leaves silky on both surfaces. Achenes glabrous . 4. *A. polyanthes.*

Radical leaves 3-parted.
- Leaves crenate. Achenes hairy . . . . . . 2. *A. obtusiloba.*
- Leaves sharply toothed. Achenes glabrous . . . 3. *A. rivularis.*

1. **Anemone vitifolia,** *Buch.-Ham.*; *Fl. Br. Ind.* i. 8. Stem 1-3 ft., white-pubescent, robust. Radical leaves orbicular, 4–8 in. across, cordate, deeply 5-lobed, sharply toothed, upper surface glabrous,

lower white-tomentose. Involucral leaves similar but smaller and shortly stalked. Flowers $1\frac{1}{2}$–2 in. diam., white. Sepals 5–8, silky outside. Ovaries pubescent. Achenes densely white-woolly, crowded in globose heads.

Simla ; June–September.—Temperate Himalaya, 5000–10,000 ft.
Habit of the garden *A. japonica*, but the radical leaves of the latter are 3-foliolate.

2. **Anemone obtusiloba,** *D. Don* ; *Fl. Br. Ind.* i. 8. Stems 6–12 in., tufted, hairy. Radical leaves orbicular, 2 in. across, 3-parted, softly hairy on both surfaces, lobed and crenately toothed.

FIG. 2. ANEMONE RIVULARIS.

Involucral leaves less than 1 in. long, sessile, 3-lobed. Flowers $1\frac{1}{2}$–2 in. diam., white or tinged with blue near the base. Sepals 5–7, silky outside. Ovaries and achenes coarsely hairy.

Fagoo, Huttoo, on open pastures ; May, June.—Temperate and alpine Himalaya, 8000–15,000 ft.

3. **Anemone rivularis,** *Buch.-Ham.*; *Fl. Br. Ind.* i. 9. Stem 1–3 ft., silky pubescent. Radical leaves orbicular, 3–6 in. across, 3-parted, silky pubescent on both surfaces, deeply lobed and sharply toothed. Involucral leaves 3–4 in. long, 3-parted, segments lobed, narrow, pointed, sharply toothed. Flowers 1–1½ in. diam., white, lower surface tinged with purple. Sepals 5–8, silky outside. Ovaries and achenes glabrous, styles hooked. (Fig. 2.)

Simla; May, June.—Throughout India on hills above 5000 ft.

4. **Anemone polyanthes,** *D. Don*; *Fl. Br. Ind.* i. 9. Densely silky. Stem 1–2 ft. Radical leaves orbicular, 2–4 in. across, cordate, 5–7-lobed, segments wedge-shaped, 3-lobed, crenate. Involucral leaves 1–2 in., sessile, oblong, 3-lobed, crenate. Umbels many-flowered, usually compound. Flowers 1–1½ in. diam., white. Sepals about 6. Ovaries and achenes glabrous, flattened, oval; styles straight or hooked.

Huttoo; August.—Temperate Himalaya, 10,000–12,000 ft.

3. **THALICTRUM.** The classical name.—Temperate and cold northern regions (Britain, Meadow Rue); very rare in the Southern Hemisphere.

Perennial, glabrous herbs. Stems erect, rarely partially decumbent, branched. Leaves alternate, base of stalk sheathing, pinnate or 2-pinnate, some or all of the pinnules with 3 leaflets; leaflets stalked, orbicular or ovate, more or less distinctly 3-lobed, crenate or bluntly toothed, the crenatures often with a minute point, rarely entire, lower surface paler than the upper. Flowers small, regular, often polygamous, in panicles; floral leaves alternate, not involucrate. Sepals 4–5, imbricate, petal-like, soon falling off. Petals none. Stamens numerous, sometimes coloured and projecting beyond the calyx. Carpels several or many, sessile or shortly stalked, 1-ovuled, style short. Fruit a small head of usually ribbed and more or less flattened, rarely terete, achenes; style persistent, curved or nearly straight, tip hooked.

Thalictrum elegans, *Wall.*; *Fl. Br. Ind.* i. 10, occurs on the Chor and possibly on Huttoo. It is an alpine species, rarely growing below 10,000 ft., and is easily recognised by its *long-stalked* achenes, and very small 3-*lobed* leaflets, *scarcely* $\frac{1}{5}$ *in. long.*

Carpels shortly stalked.
  Sepals green. Anthers $\frac{1}{5}$ in. acute. Leaflets up to 2½ in. across . . . . 1. *T. neurocarpum.*
  Sepals white. Anthers $\frac{1}{20}$ in.
    Flowers large. Sepals $\frac{4}{10}$ in. Anthers blunt . 2. *T. pedunculatum.*
    Flowers small. Sepals $\frac{1}{10}$ in. Anthers acute . 3. *T. rostellatum.*
Carpels sessile.
  Sepals white. Anthers $\frac{1}{20}$ in.
    Panicle branches few, long. Flowers solitary.
      Sepals $\frac{2}{10}$ in. Anthers acute . . . . . 4. *T. saniculæforme.*
    Panicle branches many, short. Flowers clustered.
      Sepals $\frac{1}{10}$ in. Anthers blunt . . . . . 5. *T. javanicum.*
  Sepals green. Anthers $\frac{1}{5}$ in., acute . . . . . 6. *T. foliolosum.*

1. **Thalictrum neurocarpum,** *Royle*; *Fl. Br. Ind.* i. 11, *under T. reniforme.* Stems 3–8 ft., hollow. Leaves 6–12 in. or more, the lower pinnules often with 3 leaflets; leaflets mostly orbicular, ½–2½ in., cordate, coarsely crenate or bluntly toothed, upper surface covered with bloom. Sepals $\frac{3}{10}$ in., narrowly oblong, obtuse, pale green. Stamens as long as the sepals, filaments tinged with purple, anthers nearly ⅕ in. long, acute. Carpels shortly stalked.

FIG. 3. THALICTRUM JAVANICUM.

Achenes $\frac{3}{10}$ in., including the nearly straight style, pubescent, ribs prominent.

Mushobra, Narkunda; June–August.—Temperate Himalaya, 8000–10,000 ft.

2. **Thalictrum pedunculatum,** *Edgew.*; *Fl. Br. Ind.* i. 12. Stem 1–2 ft., weak, sometimes half-trailing. Leaves 3–10 in., long-stalked, pinnules very long, with 3 leaflets; leaflets ⅓–1 in., orbicular or obovate, usually 3-lobed, coarsely crenate. Flowers long-stalked. Sepals $\frac{4}{10}$ in., ovate, white. Stamens shorter than the sepals, anthers $\frac{1}{20}$ in., blunt. Carpels shortly stalked.

Achenes nearly $\frac{1}{2}$ in., including the style, terete, spindle-shaped, ribs prominent.

Simla, Mahasu, Narkunda ; April.—W. Himalaya, 6000–9000 ft.

3. **Thalictrum rostellatum,** *Hook. f. & Thoms.* ; *Fl. Br. Ind.* i. 12. Stems 1–3 ft., rather rigid. Leaves 2–6 in., lower pinnules often with 3 leaflets ; leaflets $\frac{1}{4}$–$\frac{1}{2}$ in., orbicular, more or less 3-lobed, crenate. Sepals $\frac{1}{10}$ in., ovate, white. Stamens shorter than the sepals, anthers $\frac{1}{20}$ in., acute. Ovaries shortly stalked. Achenes nearly $\frac{1}{10}$ in., including the nearly straight needle-like style.

Mahasu, Fagoo, Narkunda ; August.—Temperate Himalaya, 7000–10,000 ft.

4. **Thalictrum saniculæforme,** *DC.* ; *Fl. Br. Ind.* i. 13. Stem 6–12 in. Leaf nearly as long, usually only one, radical, sometimes a few smaller stem-leaves ; pinnules with 3 leaflets ; leaflets $\frac{1}{2}$–1 in., orbicular or obovate, 3-lobed, entire or coarsely crenate. Panicle-branches few, long, spreading. Flowers few, mostly solitary. Sepals $\frac{1}{5}$ in., ovate, white. Stamens shorter than the sepals, anthers $\frac{1}{20}$ in., pointed. Ovaries sessile. Achenes $\frac{1}{8}$ in., including the slender nearly straight style.

Simla, on trees and rocks, not common ; frequent at Mussoorie ; July.—Temperate Himalaya, 7000–8000 ft.

5. **Thalictrum javanicum,** *Blume* ; *Fl. Br. Ind.* i. 13. Stems 2–3 ft., pale coloured. Leaves 4–12 in., pinnules usually with 3 leaflets ; leaflets $\frac{1}{2}$–$1\frac{1}{4}$ in., orbicular or ovate-oblong, 3-lobed, entire or coarsely crenate. Panicle-branches many, short. Flowers clustered. Sepals $\frac{1}{10}$ in., ovate, white. Stamens longer than the sepals, filaments thickened upwards, anthers $\frac{1}{20}$ in., blunt. Ovaries numerous, sessile. Achenes $\frac{1}{5}$ in., including the slender style. (Fig. 3.)

Simla, common ; July.—Temperate Himalaya, 6000–12,000 ft.—Mountains of Western India, Java.

6. **Thalictrum foliolosum,** *DC.* ; *Fl. Br. Ind.* i. 14. Stems 4–8 ft. Leaves 6–18 in., pinnules often with 3 leaflets ; leaflets $\frac{2}{5}$ – $\frac{4}{5}$ in., oblong-ovate, 3-lobed, crenate or almost sharply toothed. Sepals $\frac{1}{5}$ in., ovate, green. Stamens longer than the sepals, filaments thread-like, anthers $\frac{1}{5}$ in., acute. Ovaries sessile. Achenes $\frac{1}{5}$ in., including the style, ribs prominent.

Simla, common ; July.—Throughout the Himalaya, 5000–8000 ft.—Africa, Europe.

4. **ADONIS.** The classical name.—N. temperate regions of the Old World.

Adonis æstivalis, *Linn.* ; *Fl. Br. Ind.* i. 15. An annual, nearly glabrous herb. Stems 1–2 ft., leafy, erect, branched. Leaves alternate, sessile, pinnately divided into thread-like segments. Flowers regular, about ½ in. diam., solitary at the end of branches. Sepals 5, ovate, green or slightly coloured, soon falling off. Petals 5–8, rather longer, scarlet with a dark purple spot at the base, spreading, basal gland none. Stamens numerous. Carpels many, 1-ovuled, style short. Fruit an ovoid or oblong head of many small, wrinkled, pitted achenes tipped with the persistent styles. The head lengthens as the fruit ripens.

Kotgurh, in cornfields; March, April.—W. Himalaya, up to 6000 ft.—Temperate Asia, Europe.

Closely allied to the British *A. autumnalis* (Pheasant's Eye).

5. **RANUNCULUS.** From the Latin *rana*, a frog, referring to the damp situations in which some species grow.—All temperate, alpine and subarctic regions (Britain, Buttercup).

Annual or perennial herbs. Radical leaves long-stalked, usually deeply lobed. Stem-leaves alternate, smaller, usually lobed. Flowers regular, panicled. Sepals 5, green, imbricate, soon falling off. Petals 5, yellow, shining, imbricate, each with a thickened glandular spot at the base covered, in some species, with a minute scale. Stamens numerous. Carpels several or many, 1-ovuled, in a globose or oblong head, style short. Fruit a head of small achenes sometimes flattened, the tip of the persistent styles often hooked.

The gland at the base of the petals secretes honey and thus renders the flowers attractive to insects.

The flowers of *Ranunculus* resemble in some points those of *Rubus*, *Potentilla*, *Fragaria* and *Geum*, genera belonging to *Rosaceæ*. The sepals and petals are similar in number, colour and shape, the stamens in all are numerous and free, and the fruit is composed of small distinct achenes. But in *Ranunculaceæ* the sepals and petals are inserted on the receptacle, in *Rosaceæ* on the calyx. This constitutes the difference between *Thalamifloral* and *Calycifloral* flowers.

Radical leaves deeply 3-lobed. Achenes glabrous or hairy.
- Stem and leaves glabrous Achenes in oblong or cylindric heads . . . . 2. *R. sceleratus.*
- Stem and leaves hairy. Achenes in globose heads.
  - Flowers ½ in. diam. Achenes hairy . . . . . 1. *R. hirtellus.*
  - Flowers ½–1 in. diam. Achenes glabrous.
    - Stems decumbent, producing runners. Leaves of an ovate outline, mid-lobe longer than the others. Achenes minutely dotted . . . . 3. *R. diffusus.*
    - Stems erect, without runners. Leaves of a rounded outline, mid-lobe not longer than the others. Achenes not dotted . . . . 4. *R. lætus.*

Radical leaves wedge-shaped, not lobed. Achenes spinous . 5. *R. arvensis.*

1. **Ranunculus hirtellus**, *Royle*; *Fl. Br. Ind.* i. 18. Perennial, more or less covered with adpressed hairs. Stems 6–18 in., often tufted, erect or almost decumbent. Radical leaves 1¼–2 in. across, long-stalked, cordate, deeply 3-lobed, segments coarsely toothed,

often lobed. Stem-leaves digitately 3–5-parted, segments narrow, entire or toothed near the tip. Flowers $\frac{1}{2}$ in. diam., bright yellow. Achenes hairy, in globose heads.

Mahasu, Narkunda, in forest; April–June.—W. Himalaya, 6000–10,000 ft. Closely allied to the British *R. auricomus* (Goldilocks).

2. **Ranunculus sceleratus,** *Linn.*; *Fl. Br. Ind.* i. 19. Annual, glabrous, yellow-green. Stem usually 6–12 in., sometimes 1–3 ft., erect, succulent, hollow. Radical leaves $\frac{1}{2}$–$1\frac{3}{4}$ in. across, long-stalked, deeply 3-lobed, segments lobed, obtusely toothed near the top. Stem-leaves shortly stalked, 3-parted, segments narrow, lobed and toothed. Flowers $\frac{1}{3}$ in. diam., numerous, petals pale yellow. Sepals reflexed. Achenes glabrous, in oblong heads, ultimately becoming cylindrical and longer.

River bed below Paniah, Simla; Sutlej valley; April–June.—Throughout N. India and Bengal, ascending to 5000 ft.—N. temperate regions (Britain, Celery-leaved Buttercup).

3. **Ranunculus diffusus,** *DC.*; *Fl. Br. Ind.* i. 19. Perennial, covered with soft spreading hairs. Stems decumbent, 6–12 in., producing runners from among the radical leaves rooting and forming fresh plants at the joints. Radical leaves 2–3 in. across, long-stalked, cordate, deeply 3-lobed; segments lobed, sharply toothed, mid-lobe the longest giving the leaf an ovate outline. Stem-leaves similar but smaller and shortly stalked. Flowers $\frac{1}{2}$–$\frac{3}{4}$ in. diam., long-stalked, bright yellow. Achenes in globose heads, glabrous, flattened, minutely dotted, margins thickened.

Simla, common; May–September.—Temperate Himalaya, 6000–10,000 ft.—Java.
Closely allied to the British *R. repens.*

4. **Ranunculus lætus,** *Wall.*; *Fl. Br. Ind.* i. 19. Perennial, covered with long closely adpressed hairs. Stems 1–2 ft., erect, without runners, usually much branched. Radical leaves 2–4 in. across, sometimes larger, long-stalked, deeply 3-lobed; segments deeply lobed, sharply toothed, nearly equal in length giving the leaf a rounded outline. Stem-leaves similar but smaller and shortly stalked. Flowers 1 in. diam., long-stalked, bright yellow. Achenes in globose heads, glabrous, flattened, not dotted, margins thickened.

Simla, Sutlej valley; May–September.—Temperate Himalaya, 4000–8000 ft.—Tibet.
Closely allied to the British *R. acris.*

5. **Ranunculus arvensis,** *Linn.*; *Fl. Br. Ind.* i. 20. Annual, pale green, slightly hairy on the upper parts, otherwise glabrous. Stem 6–24 in., erect, branching. Radical leaves 1–3 in., long-stalked, spathulate or wedge-shaped, 3–5-toothed at the tip, otherwise entire. Stem-leaves shortly stalked, deeply divided into

2 or 3 narrow segments, entire, or the tip lobed or toothed. Flowers ½ in. diam., petals pale yellow. Achenes in globose heads, flattened, spinous.

Simla, in cornfields; March, April.—W. Himalaya, 4000–7000 ft.—N. Asia, Europe (Britain, Corn Buttercup).

6. CALTHA. From the Greek *calathos*, a cup, referring to the shape of the flower in the common species.—N. and S. temperate regions.

Caltha palustris, *Linn.*; *Fl. Br. Ind.* i. 21. A glabrous, perennial herb. Rootstock thick, creeping. Stems 6–18 in., often tufted, erect, robust. Leaves shining, chiefly radical, 2–5 in. across, long-stalked, orbicular or kidney-shaped, deeply cordate; teeth small, close, regular. Stem-leaves alternate, smaller, the upper sessile, embracing the stem like an involucre. Flowers regular, few, 1–2 in. diam., terminal. Sepals 5 or 6, petal-like, bright yellow, oval or oblong-obtuse, imbricate. Petals none. Stamens many. Carpels many, sessile, many-ovuled, style short, curved. Fruit a head of narrow, flattened, many-seeded follicles beaked with the persistent styles.

The Chor on marshy ground, perhaps on Huttoo; June.—W. Himalaya, 8000–10,000 ft.—N. Asia, N. America, Europe (Britain, Marsh Marigold).

7. AQUILEGIA. From the Latin *aquila*, an eagle, referring to the claw-like spurs.—N. temperate regions.

Aquilegia pubiflora, *Wall.*; *Fl. Br. Ind.* i. 24, *under A. vulgaris.* A perennial, thinly hairy or pubescent herb. Stems leafy, 1–2 ft., sometimes taller, erect, branched. Leaves glaucous; lower long-stalked, pinnate, pinnules with 3 leaflets; upper alternate, shortly stalked, leaflets 3, deeply 3-lobed, segments coarsely crenate. Flowers drooping, nearly 1 in. diam., in a loose panicle bearing at the forks a few sessile leaves much less divided than the lower ones. Sepals 5, flat, ovate-lanceolate, soon falling off. Petals 5, yellow-green, nearly white or pale purple, the base of each produced into an obtuse, hooked spur projecting between the calyx-lobes. Stamens numerous, inner ones reduced to scales. Carpels 5, sessile, style long thread-like, ovules many. Follicles tipped with the persistent styles, many-seeded.

Simla, common; May, June.—W. Himalaya, 5000–10,000 ft.—Afghanistan. Closely allied to the British Columbine (*A. vulgaris*).

Honey is secreted in the point of the spurs; the flowers are visited by humble bees.

8. DELPHINIUM. From the Greek *delphin*, a dolphin, referring to the form of the flowers.—N. temperate regions including Britain (Larkspur).

Erect herbs. Leaves deeply lobed. Flowers irregular, racemed. Sepals 5, petal-like, free, the upper one produced at the base in the form of a spur, the others flat. Petals 4, the two upper each produced at the base into a tubular spur enclosed within the spur of the sepal, limb small; the two lateral petals flat, clawed, limb smaller than the sepals. Stamens many, filaments flattened at the base, tapering upwards. Ovaries 3, sessile, many-ovuled, style short, curved. Follicles many-seeded, tipped with the persistent styles.

Honey is secreted in the spurs of the two upper petals, and can be obtained only by insects having a long proboscis, such as humble bees. In young flowers the stamens are so placed that a bee's head rubs against the anthers; in older flowers the stamens have withered and the stigmas then stand in the way of the bee's head.

Nearly glabrous. Sepals spreading. Spur straight, cylindric . . . . 1. *D. denudatum.*
Very hairy. Sepals erect. Spur curved, conical . . . 2. *D. vestitum.*

1. **Delphinium denudatum,** *Wall.*; *Fl. Br. Ind.* i. 25. Glabrous or slightly downy. Stems 2–3 ft., branched. Radical leaves

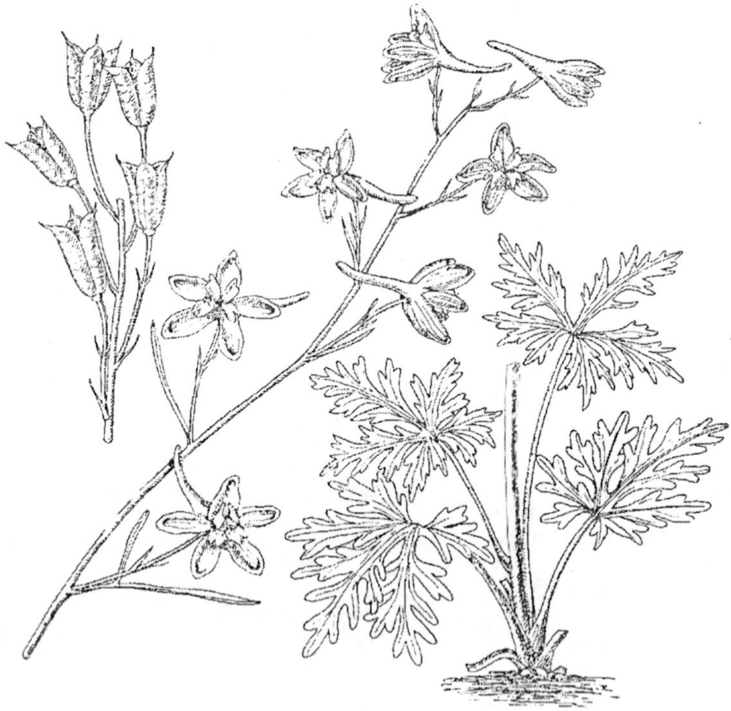

FIG. 4. DELPHINIUM DENUDATUM.

2–6 in. across, orbicular, long-stalked, divided nearly to the base, segments 5–9, narrow, pinnately lobed, often toothed. Stem-leaves few, shortly stalked, upper sessile, more or less deeply 3-lobed, lobes narrow, mostly entire. Flowers few, scattered, 1–1½ in. long, spur cylindric, nearly straight. Sepals spreading, varying from deep blue to faded grey. Petals blue, the lateral ones 2-lobed, hairy. (Fig. 4.)

Simla; April–June.—W. Himalaya, 5000–10,000 ft.

2. **Delphinium vestitum,** *Wall.*; *Fl. Br. Ind.* i. 26. Very hairy. Stems 1½–3 ft., usually simple. Radical leaves orbicular, 6–12 in. across, long-stalked, deeply 5–7-lobed, segments lobed, sharply toothed at the end. Stem-leaves similar but smaller. Flowers numerous, crowded, 1–1¼ in. long, spur conical, curved. Sepals dark blue, erect, tips converging. Petals dull blue, the lateral ones ovate, entire.

Fagoo, Narkunda; July.—W. Himalaya, 8000–12,000 ft.

9. **ACONITUM.** Etymology obscure, perhaps from the Greek *akontion*, a dart, referring to some species being used to poison arrows.—Mountains of the N. Hemisphere (Britain, Monkshood).

Perennial erect herbs. Leaves alternate, simple, sometimes lobed. Flowers irregular, racemed. Sepals 5, petal-like, free, erect, the upper one helmet-shaped, the others flat, the two lateral broader than the 2 lower. Petals 2 or 4, concealed within the calyx, the 2 upper enclosed in the helmet, long-clawed with a short, concave, spurred limb; the 2 lower very small or wanting. Stamens many, filaments flat, wide at the base, tapering upwards. Ovaries 3 or 5, sessile, many-ovuled, style short, straight. Follicles many-seeded.

The roots of some species (though not of the two described) are poisonous. Honey is secreted in the spurred limb of the long-clawed upper petals. The manner of the cross fertilisation by humble bees is the same as in *Delphinium*.

Stem-leaves stalked, deeply lobed. Flowers pale yellow . . . . 1. *A. Lycoctonum*.
Stem-leaves sessile, not lobed. Flowers dull green-blue . . . . 2. *A. heterophyllum*.

1. **Aconitum Lycoctonum,** *Linn.*; *Fl. Br. Ind.* i. 28. Pubescent, at least on the upper parts. Stem 3–6 ft., branched. Leaves orbicular, 6–12 in. diam., lobed nearly to the base, segments 5–9, lobed and sharply toothed; lower leaves long-stalked, upper nearly sessile. Flowers 1 in. long, pale yellow. Helmet pointed in front and produced upwards in a high obtuse peak. Lateral sepals much shorter than the helmet. Follicles 3.

Baghi forest; June.—W. Himalaya, 8000–10,000 ft.—N. Asia, Europe.

2. **Aconitum heterophyllum,** *Wall.*; *Fl. Br. Ind.* i. 29. Glabrous or the upper parts downy. Stems 1–3 ft., leafy, rarely branched. Lower leaves stalked, orbicular or broadly ovate, cordate, more or

less 5-lobed, teeth obtuse or acute: upper leaves stem-clasping, lanceolate, not lobed, sharply toothed. Flowers 1 in. long, dull

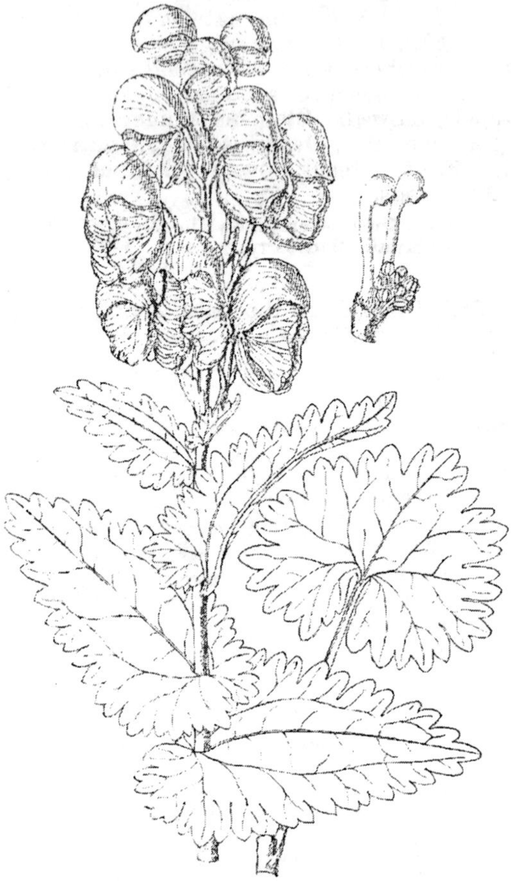

FIG. 5. ACONITUM HETEROPHYLLUM.
Petals and stamens, sepals removed.

green-blue with purple veins. Helmet pointed in front, top rounded. Lateral sepals as long as the helmet. Follicles 5. (Fig. 5.)

Fagoo, Narkunda; September.—W. Himalaya, 8000–12,000 ft.
Root used in medicine, native name *Atees*.

10. ACTÆA. From *akte*, the Greek name of the Elder, referring to a resemblance in foliage and fruit.—Temperate and cold regions of the N. Hemisphere.

Actæa spicata, *Linn.*; *Fl. Br. Ind.* i. 29. A perennial, more or less pubescent herb. Stems 2–3 ft., erect, usually branched. Leaves 6–12 in., alternate, pinnately compound, the pinnules often with 3 leaflets; leaflets ovate-lanceolate, pointed, often lobed, deeply and sharply toothed. Flowers regular, scarcely ¼ in. diam., white, crowded in short terminal racemes lengthening in fruit. Sepals 4, petal-like, concave, soon falling off. Petals 4, shorter than the sepals, clawed. Stamens numerous, longer than the sepals, anthers small. Ovary solitary, many-ovuled, stigma sessile, flat. Fruit a black, ovoid, glabrous berry, containing numerous small seeds.

Narkunda in forest; June.—Temperate Himalaya, 6000–10,000 ft.—N. Asia, N. America, Europe (Britain, Baneberry).

11. CIMICIFUGA. From the Latin *cimex*, a bug, and *fugare*, to drive away.—Europe, N. Asia, N. America.

Cimicifuga fœtida, *Linn.*; *Fl. Br. Ind.* i. 30. A perennial, more or less pubescent herb. Stems 3–6 ft., erect, leafy, branched. Leaves 6–18 in., pinnately compound; leaflets 1–3 in., rarely more, ovate or lanceolate, deeply and sharply toothed, terminal leaflet 3-lobed. Flowers nearly regular, hardly ¼ in. diam., white, crowded in short or long racemes, solitary in the axils of the upper leaves, and combined in a terminal, sometimes large and spreading, panicle. Sepals and petals 5–7 (no clear distinction between them), imbricate, ovate, concave; one or two of the inner ones deeply 2-lobed, the tips white, broad, notched. Stamens numerous, ultimately longer than the sepals. Ovaries 2–5, rarely more, many-ovuled, style short, stigma pointed. Follicles ½ in. long, flat, tipped with the persistent styles. Seeds 6–8.

Patarnala in forest, and probably Baghi; September.—Temperate Himalaya, 7000–12,000 ft.—E. Europe, Siberia.

12. PÆONIA. The Greek name.—N. temperate regions (Britain, Pæony).

***Pæonia Emodi,** *Wall.*; *Fl. Br. Ind.* i. 30. A glabrous, perennial herb. Stems 1–2 ft., leafy, erect. Leaves alternate, 6–12 in. long; leaflets 3, usually 3-parted, segments lanceolate, pointed, entire. Flowers few, showy, 3–4 in. across, long-stalked, usually solitary in the axils of the upper leaves. Buds globose. Sepals 5, orbicular, concave, green, persistent, the outer ones ending in a leaf-like point. Petals 5–10, broadly ovate, concave, red or white. Stamens many. Ovaries 1–3, densely hairy, many-ovuled, seated on a fleshy disk; style short, broad, recurved. Follicles ovoid, 1 in. Seeds few, large.

Kumaon, Hazara; May, June.—W. Himalaya, 5000–10,000 ft.

II. MAGNOLIACEÆ

A SMALL Order, chiefly American and Asiatic, represented in the N.W. Himalaya only by a single species.—Named in honour of Pierre Magnol, a French botanist of the seventeenth century.

SCHIZANDRA. From the Greek *schizo*, to cleave, and *aner, andros*, a man; referring to the separated anther cells.—Mountains of India and Java, N. America.

Schizandra grandiflora, *Hook. f. & Thoms.*; *Fl. Br. Ind.* i. 44. A glabrous, climbing shrub with long, slender branches. Leaves alternate or clustered, ovate or oblong-lanceolate, entire or with small

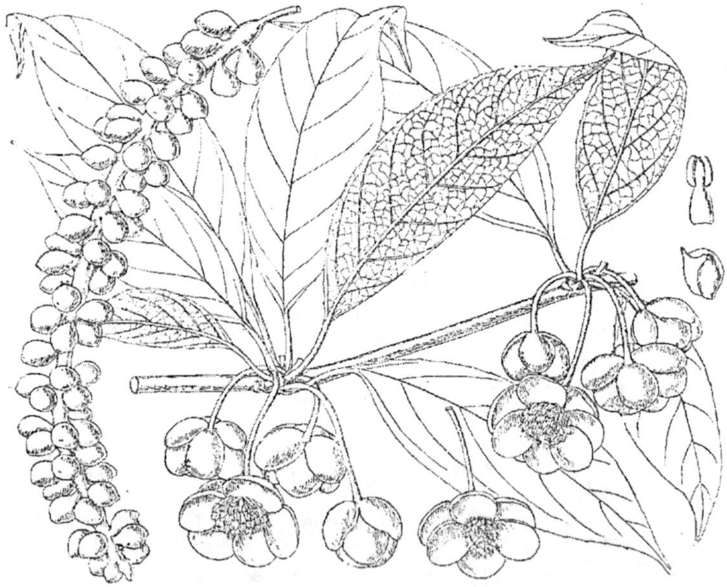

FIG. 6. SCHIZANDRA GRANDIFLORA.

distant teeth, stalks and veins on the lower surface red. Flowers fragrant, 1-sexual, globose, 1 in. diam., on drooping axillary stalks. Sepals and petals 9, similar, waxy-white often tinged with pink, ovate, concave, outer ones smaller. Male flowers: stamens about 40, small, crowded on an ovoid, fleshy column, filaments thick, anther-cells separated. Female flowers rather larger than the male, outer sepals more highly coloured: ovaries numerous, distinct, minute, sessile, crowded on an oblong, fleshy column, 1-celled, stigma sessile, ovules 2. In fruit the column lengthens to 6–9 in., bearing numerous sessile, globose, red, 2-seeded berries, nearly $\frac{1}{2}$ in. diam. (Fig. 6.)

Simla (Jako), Matiana, Narkunda, in forest; May, June.—Simla to Bhotan 6000–10,000 ft.

III. MENISPERMACEÆ

Climbing or sometimes erect shrubs, rarely small trees. Leaves alternate, stalked, simple, entire or sinuate, rarely lobed, sometimes peltate. Inflorescence various. Flowers small or minute, 1-sexual; the male and female on different plants. Sepals 6 or 4 (only one in the female flowers of *Cissampelos*), free, usually imbricate in 2 series, the outer shorter than the inner. Petals 6 or 3 (only one in the female flowers of *Cissampelos*), much smaller than the sepals, free or 4 united in a shallow cup. Stamens in the male flowers usually as many as the petals, opposite to them, filaments free or united in a column, anthers 2-celled, bursting transversely, free or forming a ring round the peltate top of the staminal column; in the female flowers the stamens, or at least the anthers, are wanting. Ovaries 3 or 1, distinct, 1-celled, 1-ovuled; style terminal, simple or 3-fid. Drupe small, the enclosed stone horse-shoe-shaped, grooved and ridged on the edges, variously sculptured on the faces, often perforate in the centre. Seed one, curved.—A large tropical Order.—Name from the Greek *mene*, the moon, and *sperma*, a seed, referring to the crescent-shaped seeds.

Stamens free. Leaves not peltate or cordate. Flowers in panicles . . . . 1. *Cocculus*.
Stamens united in a column. Leaves peltate or cordate.
  Glabrous. Flowers in umbels . . . . 2. *Stephania*.
  Pubescent or tomentose. Flowers in cymes or clustered in the axils of orbicular bracts . . . . . . 3. *Cissampelos*.

1. COCCULUS. From the Greek *kokkos*, a berry.—All warm regions.

Erect or climbing shrubs or small trees. Leaves stalked, lanceolate or ovate, not peltate nor cordate. Flowers minute, male in axillary panicles or sessile clusters; female solitary or in small, stalked clusters. Sepals 6. Petals 6. Male: stamens 6, free, anthers 4-lobed. Female: staminodes 6, ovaries 3, style simple. Drupe globose, about $\frac{1}{6}$ in. diam.

The berries known as *Cocculus indicus*, used to poison fish and formerly to adulterate malt liquors, are the fruit of an *Anamirta*, a tropical genus of this Order.

An erect shrub or small tree. Glabrous . . . . . 1. *C. laurifolius.*
Climbing shrubs. Tomentose or pubescent.
  Tomentose or hairy. Male flowers in axillary panicles 2. *C. villosus.*
  Pubescent. Male flowers in sessile, axillary clusters . 3. *C. Leæba.*

1. **Cocculus laurifolius,** *DC.*; *Fl. Br. Ind.* i. 101. An erect shrub or small tree. Leaves 3–5 in., glabrous, shining, shortly stalked, dark green, lanceolate, 3-nerved, entire. Flowers numerous, in narrow, axillary panicles shorter than the leaves. Drupe black.

Sutlej valley; April.—Outer Himalaya up to 5000 ft.—Japan.

2. **Cocculus villosus,** *DC.*; *Fl. Br. Ind.* i. 101. A climbing, grey-tomentose, more or less hairy shrub. Leaves ovate or ovate-oblong, 1–3 in. Male flowers few, in narrow, axillary panicles 1–1½ in. long. Female flowers 1–3, sessile at the end of short axillary stalks, sometimes racemed. Drupe dark purple, stone beautifully moulded.

Giri valley; September.—Throughout India, ascending to 3000 ft.—Africa.

3. **Cocculus Leæba,** *DC.*; *Fl. Br. Ind.* i. 102. A grey-pubescent, climbing shrub. Leaves ½–1½ in., variable in shape, narrowly oblong or ovate, sometimes lobed. Male flowers crowded in small, sessile, axillary clusters. Female 1–3, sessile at the end of short axillary stalks. Drupe dark purple.

Valleys below Simla; August, September.—Plains of India, ascending to 3000 ft.—W. Asia, Africa.

2. **STEPHANIA.** From the Greek *stephanos*, a crown, referring to the ring of anthers on the top of the staminal column.—Tropics of the Old World.

Glabrous, climbing shrubs. Leaves peltate, orbicular or triangular. Flowers small, umbellate. Male flowers: sepals 6; petals 3, thick, fleshy; stamens 6, the filaments united in a column, top dilated, peltate, the anthers forming a ring round the margin. Female flowers: sepals 3; petals 3, thick, fleshy; ovary single, style 3-parted. Drupe small, globose.

Leaves triangular. Flowers purple . . . . 1. *S. elegans.*
Leaves orbicular. Flowers yellow . . . . 2. *S. rotunda.*

1. **Stephania elegans,** *Hook. f. & Thoms.*; *Fl. Br. Ind.* i. 103. Leaves about 4×2½ in., varying much in size, triangular-ovate, entire, acute, base rounded, lower surface pale. Umbels axillary, solitary or several in a long-stalked cyme. Flowers $\frac{1}{10}$ in. diam., red-purple, sepals obovate. Drupe red.

Valleys below Simla; September.—Sikkim to Simla, 6000 ft.

2. **Stephania rotunda,** *Lour.*; *Fl. Br. Ind.* i. 103. Leaves broadly ovate or orbicular, 3–7 in. across, sinuate, lower surface pale. Umbels axillary, solitary or several in a long-stalked cyme. Flowers $\frac{1}{6}$–$\frac{1}{4}$ in. diam., green-yellow; sepals narrowly wedge-shaped. Drupe red.

Valleys below Simla; July, August.—Hilly districts throughout India, ascending to 6000 ft.—Siam, Cochin-China.

3. **CISSAMPELOS.** From the Greek *cissus*, ivy, and *ampelos*, a vine, referring to the habit of the plants.—All hot regions.

Cissampelos Pareira, *Linn.*; *Fl. Br. Ind.* i. 103. A climbing, softly pubescent or tomentose shrub. Leaves orbicular or broadly ovate, 1–4 in. across, peltate or cordate. Flowers small. Male

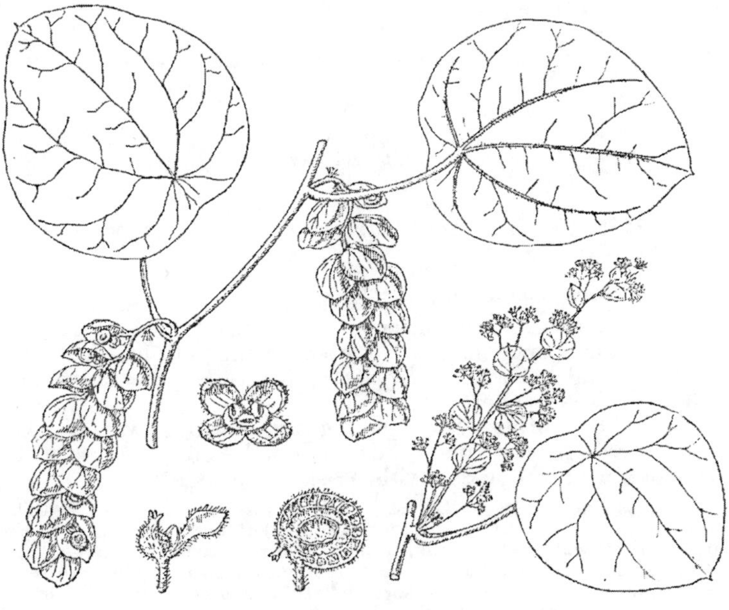

FIG. 7. CISSAMPELOS PAREIRA.

flowers in stalked, branched cymes, clustered in the leaf-axils or borne on long, axillary, raceme-like shoots, each cyme in the axil of a small leaf-like bract; sepals 4, hairy, ovate, spreading; petals united in a shallow, 4-lobed cup; stamens 4, filaments united in a very short column, top dilated, peltate, anthers sessile round the margin. Female flowers clustered in the axils of orbicular bracts crowded in long, axillary racemes; sepal 1, pubescent, broadly ovate; petal 1, opposite the sepal, similar but smaller and deeply lobed; ovary 1, hairy, style shortly 3-fid. Drupe hairy, globose, scarlet. (Fig. 7.)

Common in valleys below Simla; May–August.—Throughout India, ascending to 6000 ft.—All warm regions.

Ropes are manufactured from the strong fibres of the stems.

IV. BERBERIDACEÆ

Erect shrubs or herbs. Leaves alternate or tufted, simple, sometimes deeply lobed. Flowers regular, 2-sexual, racemed or solitary. Sepals 3 or 6, free, imbricate, petal-like. Petals 6, similar to the sepals. Stamens 6, free, opposite the petals, anthers 2-celled, opening by upturned valves or lateral slits. Ovary 1-celled, ovules few or many; style terminal, short or none, stigma large. Fruit a berry.—A small Order inhabiting chiefly temperate and mountainous regions.

Shrubs. Flowers small, yellow, racemed . . . . . 1. *Berberis.*
Herbs. Flowers large, pink or white, solitary . . . . 2. *Podophyllum.*

1. BERBERIS. The Arabic name.—N. temperate regions including Britain (Barberry) S. America.

Shrubs; wood yellow. Leaves in tufts of ten having 3–5-branched spines at the base, simple, spiny-toothed, rarely entire. Flowers less than ½ in. diam., globose, yellow, in bracteate, simple or compound racemes. Sepals 6, petal-like, the outer smaller. Petals 6, usually shorter than the sepals, 2-glandular at the base. Stamens 6, anther-cells opening by upturned valves. Ovules few. Style short or none, stigma broad, peltate. Berry globose or ovoid, usually covered with bloom. Seeds few.

The mature stamens of Barberry flowers possess a curious irritability; if touched by an insect they spring forward and jerk out the pollen.—The small, orange or red, raised spots often seen on barberry leaves are a stage in the life of the parasitic fungus that produces 'rust' in wheat and other grasses. The connection between barberry bushes and 'rust' had been suspected by farmers long before it was scientifically ascertained to exist.—The wood furnishes a yellow dye used by natives for colouring leather; the fruit is eaten.—Several species of *Berberis* having pinnate leaves (Sect. *Mahonia*) are cultivated in gardens, and one (*B. nepalensis*) occurs wild in the Himalaya but not near Simla.

Style none, stigma sessile.
  Leaves 1½–2½ in.; teeth numerous, close-set . . . 1. *B. vulgaris.*
  Leaves ½–¾ in.; teeth few . . . . . . 2. *B. brachybotrys.*
Style short but distinct.
  Flowers in compound, long-stalked racemes, much longer than the leaves . . . . 3. *B. aristata.*

Flowers in simple, short-stalked racemes, hardly longer than the leaves.
  Leaves thin, broadly lanceolate, $1\frac{3}{4}$–$3\frac{1}{2}$ in. Flower-stalks thick, $\frac{1}{4}$ in. . . . . 4. *B. coriaria.*
  Leaves tough, narrowly lanceolate, $1\frac{1}{2}$ in. Flower-stalks slender, $\frac{1}{2}$ in. . . . . 5. *B. Lycium.*

1. **Berberis vulgaris,** *Linn.*; *Fl. Br. Ind.* i. 109. Bark brown. Leaves stalked, thin, ovate, $1\frac{1}{2}$–$2\frac{1}{2}$ in., teeth small, equal, numer-

FIG. 8. BERBERIS ARISTATA.

ous, close-set. Racemes shortly stalked, simple, drooping, much longer than the leaves. Stigma sessile. Berry oblong-ovoid, red.

Narkunda; June.—Temperate Himalaya, 8000–12,000 ft.—N. temperate regions (Britain).

2. **Berberis brachybotrys,** *Edgew.*; *Fl. Br. Ind.* i. 109, *under B. vulgaris.* A low, rigid shrub. Leaves sessile, hard, lanceolate, $\frac{1}{2}$–$\frac{3}{4}$ in., teeth few, sharp. Racemes simple, sessile, shorter than the leaves. Flowers crowded. Stigma sessile. Berry ovoid, red.

The Shali, 9000 ft.; June.—Sikkim to Simla, 6000–12,000 ft.

3. **Berberis aristata,** *DC.*; *Fl. Br. Ind.* i. 110. Young branches red. Leaves sessile, broadly lanceolate, $1\frac{1}{2}$–2 in., teeth

few, distant. Racemes long-stalked, compound, corymbose or umbellate, drooping, much longer than the leaves. Style short but distinct. Young fruit cylindric; berry oblong-ovoid, red. (Fig. 8.)

Simla, common; May, June.—Temperate Himalaya, 6000–7000 ft.—S. India.

4. **Berberis coriaria,** *Royle*; *Fl. Br. Ind.* i. 110, *under B. aristata.* Bark white. Leaves nearly sessile, broadly lanceolate, $1\frac{3}{4}$–$3\frac{1}{2}$ × $\frac{3}{4}$–1 in., entire or the teeth few and distant. Racemes shortly stalked, simple, barely longer than the leaves; flower-stalks thick, $\frac{1}{4}$ in. long. Style short but distinct. Berry globose, purple-blue, covered with bloom.

Narkunda; May, June.—Kumaon to Simla, 7000–10,000 ft.

5. **Berberis Lycium,** *Royle*; *Fl. Br. Ind.* i. 110. Bark pale grey. Branches angular. Leaves sessile, tough, narrowly lanceolate, $1\frac{1}{2}$ × $\frac{1}{2}$ in., acute, entire or the teeth few and small; upper surface bright green, lower paler. Racemes shortly stalked, simple, barely longer than the leaves. Flowers pale yellow, stalks slender, $\frac{1}{2}$ in. Style short but distinct. Berry ovoid, violet, covered with bloom.

Simla, common; April.—W. Himalaya, 3000–9000 ft.

2. **PODOPHYLLUM.** From the Greek *pous, podos*, a foot, and *phyllum*, a leaf, referring to the shape of the leaves.—N. Asia, N. America.

Podophyllum Emodi, *Wall.*; *Fl. Br. Ind.* i. 112. A glabrous, succulent; erect herb. Scape 6–18 in., leafy at the top. Leaves 2, often purple-spotted, alternate, peltate, orbicular, 6–10 in. across, 3-parted, segments lobed, sharply toothed. Flower solitary, rarely 2, cup-shaped, $1\frac{1}{2}$ in. diam., white, sometimes pink. Sepals 3, petal-like, soon falling off. Petals 6. Stamens 6, anthers opening by lateral slits. Ovules many. Style short, stigma crest-like, ridged. Berry ovoid, 1–2 in., scarlet. Seeds many, small, enveloped in pulp.

Matiana, Narkunda, rare; April–June.—Temperate Himalaya, 8000–14,000 ft.

V. PAPAVERACEÆ

ERECT, glabrous or nearly glabrous herbs; juice coloured. Leaves alternate, pinnatifid. Flowers 2-sexual, regular, terminal, solitary. Sepals 2 or 3, free, falling off as the flower expands. Petals 4 or 6, in 2 series, hypogynous, free, soon falling off. Stamens numerous, free, anthers 2-celled. Ovary superior, 1-celled; stigma sessile, ovules numerous. Capsule dehiscing by pores or valves.—Temperate and subtropical regions of the N. Hemisphere; very few within the tropics or in the S. Hemisphere. Some species have spread as weeds of cultivation over nearly the whole world.

Meconopsis aculeata, *Royle*; *Fl. Br. Ind.* i. 118, occurs on the Chor, but is not found below 11,000 ft. A prickly herb, 1–2 ft. high, with pinnatifid leaves and blue-purple flowers 2–3 in. across.

Leaves not spinous. Flowers red with a dark centre . . 1. *Papaver*.
Leaves spinous, thistle-like. Flowers yellow. . . . . 2. *Argemone*.

1. PAPAVER. The classical (Latin) name of the Poppy; etymology obscure.—Temperate and subtropical Asia, N. Africa, Europe, rare in the S. Hemisphere.

Papaver dubium, *Linn.*; *Fl. Br. Ind.* i. 117. Nearly glabrous; stems 1–2 ft.; juice milky. Leaves sessile, 3-6 in., pinnatifid, segments lobed, acute. Buds ovoid, nodding. Flowers 1–2 in. diam., terminal on long bristly stalks. Sepals 2, ovate. Petals 4, in unequal pairs, crumpled in bud, red with a dark spot at the base, soon falling off. Ovary more or less divided by about 6 ovule-bearing partitions projecting inwards nearly to the centre of the cavity; style none; stigmas as many as the partitions, linear, adnate to the convex top of the ovary and radiating from its centre; ovules numerous. Capsule glabrous, narrowly oblong, $\frac{3}{4}$–1 in., opening by pores close under the projecting rim of the stigmatic disk. Seeds numerous, small, kidney-shaped, minutely netted.

Simla, in fields; March, April.—W. Himalaya, 4000–7000 ft.—W. Asia, Europe (Britain, Poppy).

P. Rhœas, *Linn.*; *Fl. Br. Ind.* i. 117; the Field Poppy of Britain, extends to Kashmir and may perhaps occur in fields as far west as Simla; it differs from the above in having flowers 3–4 in. diam., 8–12 stigmatic rays, and a globose capsule.

The Opium Poppy, *P. somniferum*, is sometimes cultivated in the Simla district.

2. ARGEMONE. From the Greek *argema*, a white spot in the eye; the juice of the plant was used as a remedy in diseases of the eye.—America; naturalised elsewhere.

Argemone mexicana, *Linn.*; *Fl. Br. Ind.* i. 117. Glabrous, glaucous. Stems 1–4 ft., prickly, branching. Juice yellow. Leaves thistle-like, stem-clasping, oblong, 3–7 in., sinuately pinnatifid, spinous veins white. Flowers yellow, 1–2 in. diam., terminal on short, leafy branches. Sepals 3, prickly, ovate, produced just below the tip in a short, horn-like excrescence. Petals 6. Ovary prickly, 1-celled; stigma sessile, 4–6-lobed; ovules numerous, borne on the walls of the cavity. Capsule prickly, oblong-ovoid, 1–1½ in., opening by 4–6 valves. Seeds numerous, globose, netted.

Badherighat, below Jutogh; May, June.—Throughout India, common in fields and on roadsides, ascending to 5000 ft.—An introduced weed, widely naturalised in nearly all tropical countries.

VI. FUMARIACEÆ

GLABROUS herbs; rootstock usually perennial. Leaves alternate, rarely opposite, glaucous, pinnately divided; leaflets small, thin, more or less lobed; stipules none. Flowers irregular, corymbose or racemed. Sepals 2, small, scale-like. Petals 4, erect, tips converging; the two outer larger than the two inner, united at the base, and the upper one spurred in *Corydalis* and *Fumaria*; inner pair narrow, their crested tips united over the stigma. Stamens 6, united in 2 sets of 3 each, the middle anther of each set 2-celled, lateral anthers 1-celled. Ovary 1-celled; ovules several or only one; style thread-like, stigma dilated, often 2-lobed. Fruit a 2-valved, several-seeded capsule, or a 1-seeded nutlet. Seeds small, black.—Temperate and warm regions of the N. Hemisphere; S. Africa.

Petals not spurred. Leaf-stalks ending in a tendril . . . 1. *Dicentra.*
Upper petal spurred. Tendrils none.
  Fruit a flat capsule. Spur half the length of the petal . 2. *Corydalis.*
  Fruit a globose nutlet. Spur less than one-third the length of the petal . . . . 3. *Fumaria.*

1. DICENTRA. From the Greek *dis*, twice, and *kentron*, a spur, referring to the spurred petals of some species.—Temperate regions of N. Asia and N. America.

Dicentra Roylei, *Hook. f. & Thoms.*; *Fl. Br. Ind.* i. 121. A slender herb climbing by its leaf-tendrils. Stems 2-3 ft. Leaves irregularly pinnate, 2–4 in., the stalk often ending in a branching tendril; leaflets few, stalked, ovate, $\frac{1}{3}$–$\frac{3}{4}$ in., entire, acute. Flowers 2–4, corymbose, yellow, heart-shaped, $\frac{3}{4}$–1 in. long; bracts narrowly lanceolate, toothed. Sepals soon falling off. Outer petals similar, oblong, concave, base dilated, tip hooded; inner petals narrow, clawed, keeled. Style long. Capsule narrowly oblong, nearly $1\frac{1}{2}$ in. including the persistent style. Seeds many.

Simla below 6000 ft., rare; September.—Temperate Himalaya, 5000–6000 ft. Several species of *Dicentra* (often written *Dielytra* or *Diclytra*) are cultivated, notably *D. spectabilis* from China with large, drooping, rose-crimson flowers.

2. CORYDALIS. The classical name.—Temperate regions of the N. Hemisphere; S. Africa.

Erect or procumbent herbs. Leaves pale green, pinnately divided; leaflets deeply lobed, segments usually entire. Flowers in racemes. Outer petals dissimilar; upper one broad, concave, produced at the base into a hollow spur about half as long as the petal; lower one flat, narrow. Inner petals narrow, clawed, keeled. Lower set of stamens spurred at the base, the spur projecting inside the petal-spur. Capsule ovate-oblong or ovate, 2-valved. Seeds several.

Petals purple . . . . 1. *C. rutæfolia.*
Petals wholly yellow.
  Flowers 1 in. long. Stems erect . . . . . . 2. *C. Govaniana.*
  Flowers $\frac{1}{2}$ in. long. Stems procumbent . . . . 3. *C. ramosa.*
Petals yellow, tipped with dark purple . . . . . 4. *C. cornuta.*

1. **Corydalis rutæfolia,** *DC.*; *Fl. Br. Ind.* i. 122. Stems 4–8 in., erect or nearly so. Leaves 2 or 3, nearly opposite, pinnules with 3 leaflets; leaflets ovate or oblong, variable in size, entire. Raceme usually only one, 3–10-flowered; bracts ovate, leaf-like. Flowers purple, $\frac{3}{4}$–1 in. long; spur obtuse. Capsule ovate-oblong, $\frac{1}{3}$ in.

Simla in woods, not common; April.—W. Himalaya, 6000–10,000 ft.—W. Asia, China.

2. **Corydalis Govaniana,** *Wall.*; *Fl. Br. Ind.* i. 124. Rootstock thick, crowned with withered leaf-sheaths. Stems often tufted, 8–18 in., erect. Radical leaves nearly as long as the stem, long-stalked, 2-pinnate; leaflets wedge-shaped, deeply lobed, segments narrow, obtuse or acute. Stem-leaves similar but smaller, few, sometimes none. Racemes long-stalked; bracts long, broadly wedge-shaped, deeply lobed. Flowers bright yellow, numerous, crowded, 1 in. long; spur conical. Capsule ovate, $\frac{1}{2}$–$\frac{2}{3}$ in.

Huttoo; June.—W. Himalaya, 8000–12,000 ft.

3. **Corydalis ramosa,** *Wall.*; *Fl. Br. Ind.* i. 125. Stem procumbent, 6–24 in., leafy, branches usually long and straggling. Leaves pinnately divided; leaflets deeply lobed, segments small, ovate-oblong, entire, acute or obtuse. Racemes many; bracts leaf-like, deeply lobed. Flowers yellow, $\frac{1}{2}$ in. long; spur obtuse. Capsule ovate, $\frac{1}{3}$ in.

Simla, Matiana; May–August.—Temperate Himalaya, 4000–8000 ft.
In the *Fl. Br. Ind.* the range is erroneously given as 'Alpine Himalaya, alt. 12–15,000 ft.'

4. **Corydalis cornuta,** *Royle*; *Fl. Br. Ind.* i. 126. Stems procumbent, 6–24 in., leafy, branches usually long and straggling. Leaves pinnately divided; leaflets deeply lobed, segments small,

FIG. 9. CORYDALIS CORNUTA.

ovate, entire or sometimes lobed, obtuse. Racemes many; bracts small, lobed or entire. Flowers yellow, tipped with dark purple, $\frac{1}{2}$–$\frac{3}{4}$ in. long; spur curved, obtuse. Capsule ovate, $\frac{1}{2}$ in. (Fig. 9.)

Simla; July–October.—Temperate Himalaya, 7000–10,000 ft.

3. **FUMARIA.** From the Latin *fumus*, smoke, but the application is obscure.—Temperate regions of the Old World.

Fumaria parviflora, *Lam.*; *Fl. Br. Ind.* i. 128. Annual. Stems diffuse, 4–24 in., much branched. Leaves pale green, pinnately divided; leaflets deeply lobed, segments very narrow, lobed or entire. Flowers pale pink or white, $\frac{1}{4}$–$\frac{1}{3}$ in. long, in numerous, short racemes; bracts lanceolate. Outer petals dissimilar; upper one broad, concave, produced at the base in a short rounded spur, less than $\frac{1}{3}$ the length of the petal; lower one flat, narrow. Inner petals narrow, clawed, keeled. Lower set of stamens spurred at the base, the spur projecting inside the petal-spur. Fruit a very small, globose, 1-seeded nutlet.

Simla, in fields, common; May, June.—N. India, ascending to 6000 ft.—Temperate regions of the N. Hemisphere; rare in Britain, but closely allied to the Common Fumitory (*F. officinalis*).

VII. CRUCIFERÆ

Annual or perennial herbs. Stems usually erect; scapose only in *Eutrema*. Leaves simple or compound; radical stalked, spreading in a rosette; stem-leaves alternate; stipules none. Flowers almost always without bracts, in terminal racemes or corymbs, usually short and crowded when flowering commences, lengthening as it advances, and becoming much elongated in fruit. Sepals 4, free, the 2 lateral often larger than the others and dilated or saccate. Petals 4, free, entire, placed cross-wise, usually equal. Stamens 6, free, 2 short, opposite the lateral sepals, 4 longer in pairs, opposite the other two sepals; anthers basifixed, 2-celled; two, four or six green, fleshy glands are placed near the base of the stamens. Ovary sessile, 2-celled; ovules several or many in each cell (only one in *Lepidium*); style short or none; stigma capitate or 2-lobed. Pods long or short, stalked, divided into 2 cells by a membranous partition from which the 2 valves usually fall away at maturity leaving the seeds on its edges; in *Raphanus* the pod is indehiscent. Seeds small, attached in each cell alternately to its right and left edge; if all lie along the centre of the cell they are said to be in one row, if along the sides of the cell in two rows. The radicle of the embryo is said to be accumbent when placed against the edges of the cotyledons, if against the back of one of them it is incumbent; if the cotyledons are folded over the radicle they are conduplicate: these characters are of much systematic value in *Cruciferæ*.—A very large Order ranging over all temperate and cold regions, but most abundant in the Old World.—The name *Cruciferæ* is from the Latin *crux, crucis*, a cross, and refers to the arrangement of the petals.

The staminal glands usually secrete honey which collects about the base of the pistil or in the saccate sepals and serves to attract insects.

This Order contains a number of useful cultivated plants; the following sometimes occur as escapes near villages and are the modified descendants of wild species indigenous in Europe or temperate Asia.

Brassica.[1] Erect, usually annual herbs. Flowers bright yellow, in corymbs, elongating in fruit into erect racemes. Pods usually erect or spreading, normally 2-valved, more or less constricted between the seeds, prolonged beyond the valves in a seedless beak. The following species are cultivated in Upper India.

1. **Brassica rugosa**, *Prain*, var. typica, *Prain*; *Fl. Br. Ind.* i. 157, *under B. juncea*, in part.—Stem short at first, when in flower 4–6 ft., branched. Basal leaves persistent, numerous, crowded, obovate, 12-15 × 8-9 in., stalk 3-4 in.; stem-leaves similar but smaller, sessile, not stem-clasping. Flowers ½ in. diam. Pods 1¼–1½ in. long including the beak; beak narrowly conical, ¼ in. Seeds 14–20 in a pod.—A cold weather crop in the W. (at least as far as Kumaon), Central and E. Himalaya.—Cabbage Mustard. Native name *Pahari rai*.

2. **Brassica juncea**, *Hook. f. & Thoms.*; *Fl. Br. Ind.* i. 157, in part.—Stem 3–6 ft., much branched. Leaves large, pinnatifid, without basal lobes, terminal lobe much the largest: blade of the basal leaves 6–8 × 2–4 in., toothed; upper leaves 2-2½ × ½ in., entire. Flowers ½ in. diam. Pods 2¼–2½ in. including the beak; beak narrowly conical, nearly ½ in. Seeds about 40 in a pod.—A cold weather crop in the plains and lower Himalaya.—Indian Mustard. Native name *Asl rai*.

3. **Brassica campestris**, *Linn.* var. Sarson, *Prain*; *Fl. Br. Ind.* i. 156, *under B. campestris*, sub-sp. Napus, in part.—Stem 4–5 ft., unbranched or branching only near the top. Leaves glaucous, all (except the lowest 2 or 3) with stem-clasping, basal lobes: lower leaves pinnatipartite, 6–8 × 2–3 in., terminal lobe much the largest; upper leaves oblong or lanceolate, 2½–3 in., more or less sinuately pinnatifid. Flowers nearly ½ in. diam. Pods various, erect or pendent, sometimes 3- or 4-valved; erect pods 2 in., pendent pods 3–3¼ in. long including the beak; beak conical, up to 1 in. Seeds 30–80 in a pod.—A cold weather crop in the plains, and hills up to 6000 ft.—Indian Colza. Native name *Sarson*.

4. **Brassica Napus**, *Linn.*, var. dichotoma, *Prain*; *Fl. Br. Ind.* i. 156, *under B. campestris*, sub-sp. Napus, in part.—Stem 1–4 ft., much branched. Leaves small, all (except the lowest 2 or 3) with stem-clasping, basal lobes: basal leaves not more than 4 × 2 in., more or less pinnatifid, terminal lobe much the largest; upper leaves triangular-lanceolate, 1–2 × ½–¾ in., entire. Flowers about ½ in. diam. Pods 2-2¼ in. long including the beak; beak conical, rather more than ½ in. Seeds about 20 in a pod.—A cold weather crop in the plains, a spring crop in the Himalaya.—Indian Rape. Native name *Tori* or *Lahi*.

The common 'drum head cabbage' with its varieties of cauliflower, broccoli, Brussels sprouts, kohl-rabi, knol-khol, etc. is believed to be derived from *B. oleracea* indigenous on the S.W. coasts of Europe including Britain.

The Radish, *Raphanus sativus*, Linn.; *Fl. Br. Ind.* i. 166 is also cultivated. Leaves pinnate or pinnatifid, terminal leaflet or lobe very broad. Flowers

---

[1] The descriptions in this genus have been compiled from a valuable paper by Surgeon-Major D. Prain, Superintendent of the Royal Botanic Gardens, Calcutta, entitled *A Note on the Mustards cultivated in Bengal*. Bengal Secretariat Press, 1898.

rather large, usually white or lilac, with purple veins. Pods indehiscent, terete, thick, $1\frac{1}{4}$ in., more or less constricted between the seeds, prolonged beyond the valves in a pointed beak about half the length of the pod. Seeds separated by pith.—As cultivated in native gardens, the Radish has a very long, coarse, thick, white root. Native name *Moollee*.

Pod prolonged beyond the valves in a pointed beak . . . 8. *Eruca*.
Pod not prolonged beyond the valves.
  Pod linear, long.
    Leaves, at least the lower ones, pinnatifid or pinnatisect.
      Seeds in two rows . . . . 1. *Nasturtium*.[1]
      Seeds in one row.
        Flowers yellow.
          Leaves simply pinnatifid; segments oblong . 2. *Barbarea*.
          Leaves 2- or 3-pinnatisect; segments linear . 5. *Sisymbrium*.[2]
        Flowers white or tinged with violet. Leaves simply pinnatifid . . . . 4. *Cardamine*.
    Leaves simple.
      Stems $\frac{1}{2}$–4 ft. Flowers racemose.
        Flowers white, straw-colour or pale pink.
          Leaves with 2 basal lobes, stem-clasping . 3. *Arabis*.
          Leaves without basal lobes, not stem-clasping 5. *Sisymbrium*.[3]
        Flowers orange-yellow . . . . 7. *Erysimum*.
      Stemless. Scapes 2–3 in. Flowers corymbose, white 6. *Eutrema*.
  Pod oblong, $\frac{1}{4}$–$\frac{1}{3}$ in. Leaves pinnatifid. Flowers yellow 1. *Nasturtium*.[4]
  Pod triangular, ovate or orbicular, short, flattened. Flowers white.
    Seeds, one in each cell . . . . 10. *Lepidium*.
    Seeds, several or many in each cell.
      Leaves pinnatifid. Pod triangular . . . . 9. *Capsella*.
      Leaves simple. Pod orbicular or ovate . . 11. *Thlaspi*.

1. **NASTURTIUM**. The classical name for some kind of Cress; etymology obscure.—Temperate regions, rare in tropical.

Glabrous, perennial or annual herbs. Stem creeping, floating or erect. Leaves pinnate or pinnatifid or the upper ones nearly entire. Flowers small white or yellow, in racemes. Sepals equal, similar, spreading. Petals shortly clawed. Stigma nearly sessile, capitate. Pods linear (oblong in *N. palustre*), usually curved, spreading, valves convex. Seeds in 2 rows; radicle accumbent.

Flowers white. Leaves pinnate . . . . 1. *N. officinale*.
Flowers yellow. Leaves pinnatifid.
  Pods oblong, $\frac{1}{4}$–$\frac{1}{3}$ in. . . . . 2. *N. palustre*.
  Pods linear, 1–$1\frac{1}{2}$ in. . . . . 3. *N. montanum*.

1. **Nasturtium officinale**, *R. Br.*; *Fl. Br. Ind.* i. 133. Glabrous. Stem short or long, creeping or floating, sometimes much branched. Leaves pinnate, 2–4 in.; leaflets sessile, ovate,

[1] Except *N. palustre*, which has an oblong pod.
[2] *S. Sophia* only.
[3] Except *S. Sophia*, which has pinnatisect leaves.
[4] *N. palustre* only.

½ in., entire or sinuate. Racemes short. Flowers white. Petals longer than the sepals. Pods linear, ½–1 in.

Simla, in ditches; April-September.—N. India, ascending to 7000 ft.—Temperate Asia, Europe, including Britain (Common Watercress). Often cultivated.

2. **Nasturtium palustre,** *DC.*; *Fl. Br. Ind.* i. 133. Glabrous. Stems 6–12 in., erect or nearly so, branched. Radical leaves numerous, stalked, 2–6 in., deeply pinnatifid, lobes toothed, lower ones distinct, narrow, terminal one large, broad. Stem-leaves similar or ovate-lanceolate, sessile, toothed. Racemes long. Flowers yellow. Petals and sepals nearly equal. Pods oblong, ¼–⅓ in.

Simla; April–September.—N.W. India, ascending to 10,000 ft.—Europe (Britain, Marsh Watercress).

3. **Nasturtium montanum,** *Wall.*; *Fl. Br. Ind.* i. 134. Glabrous or nearly so. Stem erect, grooved, 6–18 in., branched. Lower leaves stalked, 2–4 in., pinnatifid at least near the base, toothed, gradually passing into the sessile, sinuate-toothed, ovate upper leaves. Racemes long. Flowers yellow. Petals and sepals nearly equal. Pods linear, 1–1½ in.

Simla; April–September.—N. India, ascending to 7000 ft.—Burmah.—China, Japan.

2. **BARBAREA.** From 'Herb of St. Barbara,' the old name for *B. vulgaris.*—Most temperate regions.

Barbarea vulgaris, *R. Br.*; *Fl. Br. Ind.* i. 134. A glabrous, perennial herb. Stem leafy, stiff, erect, 6–18 in.; branches few, short. Leaves 2–4 in., lower stalked, upper sessile, mostly pinnately lobed, lower lobes usually few, small and narrow, terminal lobe large, broadly ovate; sometimes all narrow, or the leaves oblong and deeply toothed towards the base. Flowers small, bright yellow, racemed. Sepals erect, equal, similar. Petals clawed. Style short, stigma capitate. Pods linear, ¾–1½ in., erect or slightly spreading, 4-angled. Seeds in one row; radicle accumbent.

Simla; June.—Temperate Himalaya, 6000–10,000 ft.—W. Asia, Africa, Australia, Europe (Britain, Winter Cress, Yellow Rocket).

3. **ARABIS.** Etymology uncertain.—N. temperate and cold regions, rare in the S. Hemisphere.

Annual or perennial herbs, usually more or less covered with forked or stellate hairs. Stems erect, leafy, simple or with a few short branches. Leaves simple: radical stalked; upper stem-clasping, the base prolonged downwards in two short lobes. Flowers white or pale yellow, in racemes. Sepals short, erect, lateral ones slightly saccate. Petals clawed. Stigma nearly sessile. Pods linear, long, flat. Seeds in one row or in two; radicle accumbent.

Basal lobes of stem-leaves pointed. Seeds in two rows . 1. *A. glabra.*
Basal lobes of stem-leaves obtuse. Seeds in one row.
Leaves stellately hairy, lower surface green . . 2. *A. alpina.*
Leaves glabrous or nearly so, lower surface white . 3. *A. amplexicaulis.*

FIG. 10. ARABIS ALPINA.

1. **Arabis glabra**, *Bernh.*; *Fl. Br. Ind.* i. 135. Glabrous except the radical leaves, glaucous. Stem stiff, 2–4 ft. Leaves oblong-lanceolate: radical stellately hairy, 3–4 in., sinuate-toothed, soon disappearing; stem-leaves glabrous, entire, basal lobes pointed, lower leaves 3–6 in., upper gradually smaller. Flowers small, white or pale yellow. Pods erect, 2–3½ in. Seeds in two rows.

Narkunda; May–July.—W. Himalaya, 6000–10,000 ft.—Australia, N. temperate regions; closely allied to the British *A. perfoliata*, Tower Mustard.

2. **Arabis alpina**, *Linn.*; *Fl. Br. Ind.* i. 135. More or less covered with forked or stellate hairs. Stems 6–18 in. Leaves oblong-lanceolate, obtuse, toothed rarely entire: radical 1–4 in., crowded, spreading; stem-leaves smaller, basal lobes obtuse. Flowers white, $\frac{1}{3}$ in. diam. Pods 1½–2 in., erect, ultimately spreading. Seeds in one row. (Fig. 10.)

Simla; March, April.—W. Himalaya, 5000–12,000 ft.—N. arctic regions and high mountains.

3. **Arabis amplexicaulis,** *Edgew.*; *Fl. Br. Ind.* i. 136. Glabrous or slightly stellately hairy. Stem 6–18 in. Leaves with a white bloom on the lower surface: radical obovate-oblong, $1\frac{1}{2}$–4 in., coarsely toothed; stem-leaves smaller, toothed, usually pointed, basal lobes obtuse. Flowers white, $\frac{1}{3}$ in. diam. Pods $1\frac{1}{2}$–3 in., spreading. Seeds in one row.

Narkunda; April–June.—W. Himalaya, 5000–9000 ft.

4. **CARDAMINE.** From *cardamon*, a Greek name for some kind of Cress (*Lepidium*).—Temperate regions.

Annual or perennial herbs; glabrous or with a few simple scattered hairs. Stems leafy, erect, sometimes weak and half decumbent, usually branched. Leaves stalked, pinnately lobed, radical ones sometimes numerous and spreading; in *C. impatiens* the stem-leaves have two long narrow lobes at the base of the stalk, these are absent in the other species. Flowers usually white or tinged with violet, racemed. Sepals equal at the base. Petals clawed. Style usually short, stigma simple or 2-lobed. Pods linear, long, flat, sometimes bursting elastically. Seeds in one row; radicle accumbent.

Flowers $\frac{1}{10}$ in. long. Petals nearly erect.
  Stem-leaves not lobed at the base.
    Segments broadly ovate with a few large, lobe-like teeth, terminal one broad, very obtuse. Pods obtuse . . . . 1. *C. sylvatica.*
    Segments oblong-ovate, crenate, terminal one lanceolate, tapering. Pods pointed . . . . 2. *C. oxycarpa.*
  Stem-leaves lobed at the base . . . . . . 3. *C. impatiens.*
Flowers nearly $\frac{1}{2}$ in. long. Petals spreading . . . . 4. *C. macrophylla.*

1. **Cardamine sylvatica,** *Link*; *Fl. Br. Ind.* i. 138, *under C. hirsuta.* Stem 6–12 in., weak. Leaves 2–6 in., radical few, stem-leaves not lobed at the base; segments about 7, of the lower leaves broadly ovate or orbicular, with a few large, lobe-like teeth, of the uppermost often narrowly oblong, terminal segment largest, obtuse or rounded. Flowers white, $\frac{1}{10}$ in. long. Petals longer than the sepals, nearly erect. Stigma almost sessile. Pods $\frac{1}{2}$–1 in., obtuse, erect.

Simla, Chadwick falls; March.—All temperate regions (Britain).

2. **Cardamine oxycarpa,** *Hook. f. & Anders.*; *Fl. Br. Ind.* i. 138, *under C. hirsuta.* Stem 6–18 in., erect. Leaves 2–3 in., radical few; stem-leaves not lobed at the base; segments about 7, oblong-ovate, crenate, the terminal one much the longest, tapering. Flowers white, $\frac{1}{10}$ in. long. Petals longer than the sepals, nearly erect. Style distinct. Pods 1–$1\frac{1}{4}$ in., pointed, erect at first, ultimately spreading.

Simla, Narkunda; July.—Hilly districts throughout India, ascending to 9000 ft.

3. **Cardamine impatiens,** *Linn.*; *Fl. Br. Ind.* i. 138. Stem erect, 6–18 in., stiff. Leaves 3–4 in., radical few or many; base of the stem-leaves dilated and furnished with two long, stem-clasping lobes; segments 7–15, sometimes alternate, those of the radical leaves ovate, obtusely lobed, of the stem-leaves longer, lanceolate, entire. Flowers white, $\frac{1}{10}$ in. long, crowded. Petals shorter than the sepals, nearly erect. Pods $\frac{3}{4}$–1 in., pointed, erect.

Simla, common; March–May.—Temperate Himalaya, 5000–12,000 ft.—Temperate Asia, Europe (Britain).

The ripe pods explode elastically, jerking out the seeds and curling up the valves.

4. **Cardamine macrophylla,** *Willd.*; *Fl. Br. Ind.* i. 139. Perennial; rootstock creeping. Stems erect, 1–2$\frac{1}{2}$ ft., robust. Leaves 6 in.: radical few, soon disappearing, segments usually 9, 1$\frac{1}{2}$–3 in., irregularly sharply and deeply toothed, ending in a long, nearly entire, tail-like point; segments of the stem-leaves smaller and more numerous. Flowers white or tinged with violet, nearly $\frac{1}{2}$ in. long, crowded. Petals more than twice as long as the sepals, spreading. Pods $\frac{3}{4}$–1 in., erect at first, ultimately spreading.

Sungri, near Narkunda; June.—Temperate Himalaya, 7000–12,000 ft.—N. Asia, Japan.

5. **SISYMBRIUM.** A Greek name for some kind of Watercress.—Temperate regions in most parts of the world.

Annual or biennial herbs, glabrous, or slightly hairy. Stems erect. Leaves simple or pinnately lobed, 2–3-pinnatisect: radical, rosulate, often soon disappearing; stem-leaves sessile or stalked. Flowers $\frac{1}{4}$ in. or less diam., white, pale pink or yellow, in racemes. Sepals erect, bases equal or the lateral slightly saccate. Petals clawed. Stigma nearly sessile, obscurely 2-lobed. Pods linear, long, terete or slightly flattened. Seeds in one row; radicle incumbent except in *S. Thalianum*.

Leaves undivided, toothed, sinuate or nearly entire.	
Stem-leaves stalked. Flowers white	5. *S. Alliaria.*
Stem-leaves sessile.	
Flowers white. Pods $\frac{1}{2}$–1 in.	1. *S. Thalianum.*
Flowers pink. Pods 1–2 in.	2. *S. strictum.*
Leaves pinnately lobed; lobes broad. Flowers white or pink	3. *S. Wallichii.*
Leaves 2–3-pinnatisect; segments thread-like. Flowers yellow	4. *S. Sophia.*

1. **Sisymbrium Thalianum,** *J. Gay*; *Fl. Br. Ind.* i. 148. Slightly hairy, hairs scattered, spreading, simple, forked or stellate. Stems 6–12 in., slender, branching. Leaves undivided; radical ovate, 1–2 in., toothed or nearly entire, obtuse; stem-leaves few, distant, narrowly oblong, 1 in. or less, sessile, base not lobed.

Flowers white. Pods very slender, $\frac{1}{2}$–1 in., glabrous, erect, curved, nearly terete. Cotyledons placed obliquely so that the radicle is not quite incumbent.

Simla; March-July.—Plains of the Punjab, ascending to 6000 ft.—Temperate Asia, Europe (Britain, *Arabis Thaliana* of Bentham and some other authors).

2. **Sisymbrium strictum**, *Hook. f. & Thoms.*; *Fl. Br. Ind.* i. 149. Whole plant rough with stellate pubescence. Stem 1–2 ft., un-

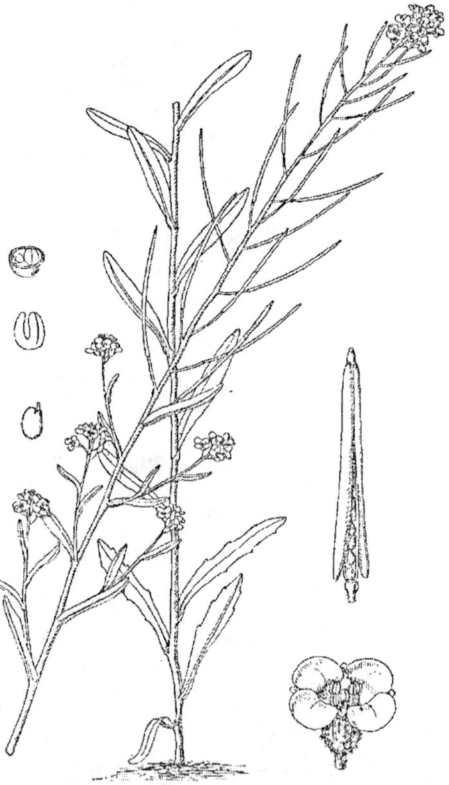

FIG. 11. SISYMBRIUM STRICTUM.

branched, stiff. Leaves undivided: radical few, soon disappearing; stem-leaves sessile, narrowly oblong, sinuate or obscurely toothed, acute, lower ones 1–1$\frac{1}{2}$ in., upper gradually diminishing in size. Flowers pale pink. Pods very slender, 1–2 in., glabrous, terete, curved, nearly erect. (Fig. 11.)

Narkunda; June, July.—W. Himalaya, 5000–10,000 ft.—Tibet.

3. **Sisymbrium Wallichii**, *Hook. f. & Thoms.*; *Fl. Br. Ind.* i. 149. Rough with simple, forked and stellate hairs. Stems slender, 6–18 in., erect. Leaves pinnately lobed: radical 1–3 in., lobes broad, obtuse, usually pointing downwards, terminal lobe largest; stem-leaves few, sessile, smaller, sometimes nearly entire. Flowers white, changing to pale pink. Pods very slender, 2–3½ in., glabrous, spreading, curved.

Kumaon to Kashmir, 5000–7000 ft.; April, May.

4. **Sisymbrium Sophia**, *Linn.*; *Fl. Br. Ind.* i. 150. Finely pubescent. Stems 1–2 ft. Leaves numerous, 1½–2 in., sessile, twice or thrice pinnatisect; segments short, thread-like. Flowers pale yellow. Pods glabrous, slender, 1 in., slightly flattened, curved, erect or spreading.

Simla; April–July.—Temperate Himalaya, 5000–7000 ft.—N. Africa, America, Europe (Britain, Flixweed).

5. **Sisymbrium Alliaria**, *Scop.*; *Fl. Br. Ind.* i. 151. Glabrous or nearly so, dull green. Stem 1–3 ft., usually unbranched. Lower leaves long-stalked, ovate or orbicular, 1½–3 in. across, cordate, sinuate or crenate; upper on shorter stalks, ovate or triangular, 1–2 in. across, cordate, coarsely toothed. Flowers white, ¼ in. diam. Pods glabrous, 1½–2 in., nearly terete, erect.

Simla, Matiana; April–June.—W. Himalaya, 6000–10,000 ft.—W. Asia, Europe (Britain, Hedge Garlic).

The crushed leaves smell strongly of garlic.

6. **EUTREMA**. From the Greek *eu*, completely, decidedly, and *trema*, a hole; the partition dividing the cells of the pod is in some species incomplete near the middle.—Himalaya. Arctic Siberia.

Eutrema primulæfolium, *Hook. f. & Thoms.*; *Fl. Br. Ind.* i. 152. A glabrous, perennial herb; root thick, cylindric; stem none. Scapes several, slender, erect, 2–3 in., leafless but bearing a few small sessile bracts. Flowers small, white, in short corymbs. Sepals erect, base equal. Petals clawed. Stigma sessile, 2-lobed. Pods ½–1 in., nearly terete, curved. Seeds in two irregular rows; radicle incumbent.

Huttoo, on rocks; May, June.—W. Himalaya, 6000–11,000 ft.

7. **ERYSIMUM**. A classical plant-name; probably of *E. officinale*, the Hedge Mustard.—N. temperate and cold regions.

Erysimum hieracifolium, *Linn.*; *Fl. Br. Ind.* i. 153. A perennial herb, covered with short, adpressed, forked, stellate and simple hairs. Stems erect, robust, 6–24 in., angled. Stem-leaves sessile, oblong, 1–4 in., sinuate-toothed or nearly entire. Flowers orange-yellow, $\frac{1}{4}$–$\frac{1}{3}$ in. diam., racemed, crowded. Sepals erect, lateral slightly saccate. Petals long-clawed. Style distinct, stigma 2-lobed. Pods linear, $1\frac{1}{4}$–2 in., nearly square, erect. Seeds in one row; radicle incumbent.

Matiana, Narkunda; May, June.—W. Himalaya, 6000–12,000 ft.—N. Asia, N. Europe.

8. ERUCA. The classical name of *Brassica Eruca*.—Mediterranean region. W. Asia.

Eruca sativa, *Mill*; *Fl. Br. Ind.* i. 158. An annual or biennial herb, glabrous or slightly hairy, glaucous. Stem 6–18 in., erect, branching. Leaves sessile, 1–4 in., pinnatifid; segments coarsely toothed, terminal one broad; upper leaves smaller, sometimes nearly entire. Flowers pale yellow or white, $\frac{3}{4}$–1 in. across, in racemes; veins dark. Sepals erect, lateral slightly saccate. Petals clawed. Stigma capitate. Pods erect, pressed against the stem, oblong-ovoid, $\frac{1}{2}$–1 in., nearly terete, prolonged in a flat, pointed, seedless beak half the length of the valves. Seeds in two rows; cotyledons folded longitudinally over the radicle.

Mushobra; August.—N. India, ascending to 10,000 ft.—N. Africa, S. Europe.

Cultivated as a field crop in the N.W.P. for the oil expressed from the seeds. An escape. Native name *Duan*.

9. CAPSELLA. Diminutive of the Latin *capsa*, a box, referring to the pod.—N. and S. temperate regions.

Capsella Bursa-pastoris, *Medic.*; *Fl. Br. Ind.* i. 159. An annual herb, more or less covered with forked hairs; root long, tapering. Stems erect, 6–18 in., branched. Radical leaves variable, usually pinnatifid, sometimes lanceolate, terminal lobe broadly triangular, segments nearly entire; upper leaves pinnatifid, lobed at the base, stem-clasping; uppermost lanceolate. Flowers small, white, racemed. Sepals spreading, equal at the base. Pods nearly flat, triangular, about $\frac{1}{4}$ in. broad. Seeds many, in two rows; radicle incumbent.

Simla; April–October.—A cosmopolitan weed. Shepherd's Purse of Britain.

10. LEPIDIUM. The classical name for the Garden Cress, *Lepidium sativum*.—Chiefly Europe and Asia.

Lepidium sativum, *Linn.*; *Fl. Br. Ind.* i. 159. An annual, glabrous herb. Stems erect, 6–18 in., branched. Radical leaves twice pinnatisect; stem-leaves sessile, pinnatifid or lanceolate. Flowers small, white, in long racemes. Sepals erect, equal at the base. Pods ovate, ⅕ in., notched at the tip, margins winged. Seeds one in each cell; radicle incumbent.

Simla, in fields; April, May.—Cultivated in all temperate regions.

Cress is commonly cultivated in gardens, and often occurs as an escape. Native name *halim*.

11. THLASPI. The Greek name for Cress.—N. temperate regions and the Andes.

Annual or perennial, glabrous herbs. Stems erect. Leaves simple; upper stem-clasping, base 2-lobed. Flowers small, white, racemed. Sepals erect, base equal. Petals clawed. Pods spreading horizontally, orbicular or ovate, flattened, margins winged, top notched; style persistent in the notch. Seeds 1–8 in each cell; radicle accumbent.

Stem-leaves toothed. Pod orbicular, ½ in. broad. Style very short . . . . 1. *T. arvense*.
Stem-leaves entire. Pod oblong-ovate, scarcely ¼ in. broad. Style long . . . . 2. *T. alpestre*.

1. **Thlaspi arvense,** *Linn.*; *Fl. Br. Ind.* i. 162. Annual. Stems 6–18 in., simple or branched. Radical leaves soon withering; stem-leaves oblong or lanceolate, 1–4 in., coarsely toothed, the upper ones prolonged at the base in two long, pointed, stem-clasping lobes. Pods ovate-orbicular, about ½ in. broad including the wing, deeply notched; style very short. Seeds 5 or 6 in each cell.

Simla, in cultivated or waste ground, not common; April–July.—Temperate Himalaya, 1000–10,000 ft.—Asia, Europe (Britain).

A weed of cultivation.

2. **Thlaspi alpestre,** *Linn.*; *Fl. Br. Ind.* i. 162. Perennial. Stems usually tufted, 6–12 in., stiff, rarely branched. Radical leaves ovate, orbicular or oblong, often toothed near the base; stem-leaves oblong or ovate, ¼–1 in., entire, base prolonged in two short, obtuse lobes. Pods oblong-ovate, scarcely ¼ in. broad including the wing, narrowed towards the base, notch broad; style long. Seeds 4–8 in each cell.

Simla, Mahasu, Narkunda; April–June.—Temperate Himalaya, 7000–12,000 ft.—N. temperate regions (Britain); the Andes.

VIII. CAPPARIDACEÆ

HERBS or shrubs. Leaves alternate, simple or digitately compound. Flowers regular, 2-sexual, solitary or racemed. Sepals 4, free. Petals 4, imbricate. Stamens numerous, free. Ovary sessile or stalked, 1-celled, ovules many. Capsule linear or ovoid. Seeds small, in 2 or more perpendicular rows.—Chiefly tropical regions.

Leaves digitately compound. Ovary sessile . . . . . 1. *Polanisia.*
Leaves orbicular. Ovary stalked . . . . 2. *Capparis.*

1. POLANISIA. From the Greek *polus*, many, and *anisos*, unequal; anthers numerous but variable in numbers, some of the stamens being imperfect.—Most tropical and subtropical regions.

Polanisia viscosa, *DC.*; *Fl. Br. Ind.* i. 170, *under Cleome viscosa.* An annual, viscidly pubescent herb. Stems 1–3 ft., erect. Leaves digitately compound; leaflets 3–5, unequal, the largest about 1 in., nearly sessile, ovate, entire. Flowers racemed, long-stalked, yellow, ½ in. long. Sepals 4, lanceolate. Petals 4, clawed, limb ovate, reflexed. Stamens 12–20, some without anthers. Ovary sessile; style short. Capsule linear, 2–3 in., glandular. Seeds wrinkled.

Simla, waste ground, rubbish heaps; June–September.—Throughout India, ascending to 5000 ft.—A common tropical weed.

2. CAPPARIS. From *kabar*, the Arabic name of a species of the genus.—Most warm regions.

Capparis leucophylla, *DC.*; *Fl. Br. Ind.* i. 173, *under C. spinosa.* A trailing, long-branched shrub, more or less covered with white pubescence. Leaves pale green, orbicular, about 1 in. across; a pair of recurved prickles (stipules) at the base of the short stalk. Flowers globose in bud, solitary, axillary, about 1 in. diam. Sepals 4, green, concave. Petals 4, obovate, not clawed, white at first, turning pink as they fade. Stamens numerous, filaments purple, longer than the petals. Ovary stalked, overtopping the stamens; stigma sessile. Capsule ovoid, nearly 1 in., bent downwards, 6-ribbed, opening irregularly, valves crimson inside. Seeds embedded in pulp.

Sutlej valley below 5000 ft., usually growing on hot dry rocks; June–October.—Lower Himalaya.—Persia.

Closely allied to *C. spinosa*, a shrub of S. Europe, the pickled flower-buds of which are known as Capers. The flower-buds and unripe fruit of *C. aphylla*, a leafless shrub common on the Punjab plains, are also eaten. Native name *karil.*

IX. VIOLACEÆ

An Order spread over nearly the whole world; some of the species are shrubs or small trees. In the W. Himalaya *Viola* is the only genus.

VIOLA. The old Latin name of the Violet.—Nearly all temperate regions.

Small herbs. Stem usually short or none. Leaves radical or alternate, simple, stalked; stipules persistent. Flowers irregular, 2-sexual, on axillary stalks, usually solitary. Sepals 5, persistent, nearly equal, prolonged downwards in a short, flat, obtuse blade. Petals 5, spreading, the lowest one usually the largest, its base produced in a hollow spur, the other 4 flat, nearly equal. Stamens 5, anthers sessile, erect, 2-celled, united in a ring encircling the ovary, each tipped with a small triangular lobe, the 2 lower produced at the base in short spurs enclosed within the petal-spur. Ovary sessile, 1-celled, style thickened upwards; stigma dilated; ovules several, disposed in 3 lines on the walls of the cavity. Capsule ovoid, opening horizontally by 3 boat-shaped valves, the sides of which pressing on the smooth ovoid seeds eject them successively with considerable force.

Honey is secreted within the spur; the details of the cross-fertilisation effected by insects vary in the several species.—In the autumn on most plants minute closed (*cleistogamic*) flowers may be found near the ground which produce abundant seed. See Darwin's *Forms of Flowers*, chap. viii.

Flowers yellow . . . . 1. *V. biflora.*
Flowers lilac or pale blue.
  Leaves narrowly triangular. Stigma 3-lobed, hollowed at the top . . . . 2. *V. Patrinii.*
  Leaves ovate.
    Stipules entire or toothed. Stigma 3-lobed, beaked . 3. *V. serpens.*
    Stipules fringed. Stigma truncate, not beaked . 4. *V. canescens.*

1. **Viola biflora,** *Linn.*; *Fl. Br. Ind.* i. 182. Glabrous or pubescent. Stems usually erect, 3–10 in. Leaves 2 or 3, kidney-shaped, $\frac{3}{4}$–1 in. across, crenate; stipules ovate or oblong. Flowers 1 or 2 on the same stalk, pale yellow, the lower petal streaked with black; spur very short; stigma 2-lobed.

Huttoo; June.—Temperate Himalaya.—N. temperate regions.
A very hairy form with larger leaves and flowers occurs on the Chor; it is *V. reniformis*, Wall., included under *V. biflora* in the *Fl. Br. Ind.*

2. **Viola Patrinii,** *Ging.*; *Fl. Br. Ind.* i. 183. Glabrous or pubescent. Stems very short or none. Leaves tufted, triangular, usually narrowly elongate, $1\frac{1}{3}$–$2\frac{1}{2} \times \frac{1}{2}$–$1\frac{1}{2}$ in., base cordate or

truncate, margins crenate; upper part of stalk usually winged; stipules entire or nearly so, adnate for more than half their length. Flowers usually dark lilac, often scented, stalks sometimes 6 in. long. Stigma 3-lobed, hollowed at the top.

Simla (the Downs), common; April–June.—Temperate Himalaya.—China, Japan.

3. **Viola serpens,** *Wall.*; *Fl. Br. Ind.* i. 184. Glabrous or with scattered, white hairs. Stems short but distinct, covered with withered scales, often producing runners. Leaves broadly ovate, 1–2 in., deeply cordate, crenate or sharply toothed, acute; stipules entire or toothed. Flowers lilac. Stigma 3-lobed, produced laterally in a hooked beak.

Simla, Mahasu, Narkunda, in woods above 7000 ft.; April–July.—Hilly districts throughout India.—China, Java.

4. **Viola canescens,** *Wall.*; *Fl. Br. Ind.* i. 184, *under V. serpens.* Softly densely pubescent. Stems none or very short,

FIG. 12. VIOLA CANESCENS.

nearly always producing long, leafy runners. Leaves tufted, ovate, $\frac{3}{4}$–2 in., deeply cordate, crenate; stipules fringed. Flowers lilac. Stigma terminal, truncate, not beaked. (Fig. 12.)

Simla, common; April–November.—Hilly districts throughout India, 3000–7000 ft.

X. BIXACEÆ

Trees or shrubs, often spinous. Leaves alternate, simple, shortly stalked. Flowers small, axillary, usually crowded in short, densely clustered racemes or sometimes scattered along the branches, 1-sexual, the male and female on different plants. Sepals 5, imbricate. Petals none. Stamens numerous, filaments thread-like, anthers versatile. Ovary 1- or 4–5-celled, girt at the base by a ring-shaped disk; ovules few in each cell, attached to the walls, not to the axis. Styles 1 or 4–5. Berry globose. Seeds 2 or 6–12.—Chiefly tropical regions.—*Bixa* is an altered form of the native name of a species common in Brazil.

Leaves pubescent, ovate, 1–2½ in. Styles 4 or 5 . . . 1. *Flacourtia.*
Leaves glabrous, oblong-lanceolate, 2–6 in. Style 1. . . . 2. *Xylosma.*

Fig. 13. Flacourtia sapida.

1. FLACOURTIA. In honour of Etienne de Flacourt, French Governor of Madagascar, author of a history of that island.—Warm regions of Asia and Africa.

Flacourtia sapida, *Roxb.*; *Fl. Br. Ind.* i. 193, *under F. Ramoutchi.* A shrub or small tree, pubescent, usually spinous. Leaves ovate, 1–2½ in., toothed. Flowers green-yellow. Sepals ovate. Male flowers solitary or in small clusters or in short, sometimes compound racemes; stamens numerous, much longer than the sepals. Female flowers solitary or in pairs; ovary globose, 4- or 5-celled, seated in a notched, cup-like disk; styles 4 or 5, free, spreading, stigmas dilated 2-lobed. Berry $\frac{1}{3}$ in. diam., red. Seeds 8–10. (Fig. 13.)

Suni, Sutlej valley; March, April.—Low hills throughout India, up to 3000 ft.

The fine-grained wood is used in turnery, for combs &c. The fruit is eaten.

2. XYLOSMA. From the Greek *xylon*, wood, and *osme*, scent, odour; the wood is aromatic.—Most tropical and subtropical regions.

Xylosma longifolium, *Clos*; *Fl. Br. Ind.* i. 194. A tree, glabrous, sometimes spinous. Leaves thick, shining, oblong-lanceolate, 2–6 in., long-pointed, toothed. Flowers yellow. Sepals ovate. Male flowers numerous, in short, densely clustered, often compound racemes, sometimes forming a continuous inflorescence nearly a foot long; stamens much longer than the sepals. Female flowers crowded in short, densely clustered racemes or sometimes nearly sessile and scattered along the branches; ovary ovoid, 1-celled, seated on a narrow, ring-shaped disk; style 1, short, erect, stigma capitate. Berry $\frac{1}{4}$ in. diam., red or black. Seeds 2.

Suni, Sutlej valley; January–March.—Low hills throughout India, up to 5000 ft.

XI. POLYGALACEÆ

An Order consisting of herbs, shrubs and small trees spread over nearly all warm and temperate regions, but represented in the N.W. Himalaya only by *Polygala*.

POLYGALA. From the Greek *polus*, much, and *gala*, milk; the herbs grow in pastures and were supposed to increase the yield of milk in cows.—Nearly all temperate and warm regions.

Annual or perennial herbs. Leaves alternate, simple, entire; stipules none. Flowers small, irregular, 2-sexual, in racemes. Sepals 5, free, unequal, in 2 series: 3 outer, small, green; 2 inner (the *wings*), ovate or oblong, much larger, coloured, finely veined. Petals 3 unequal, united at the base: 2 upper small; the lowest (the *keel*), longest, concave, tip lobed and often crested with a finely divided fringe. Stamens 8, united in 2 sets of 4 each, adnate to the petals; anthers opening by pores at the top. Ovary 2-celled; style long incurved, stigma dilated. Capsule membranous, flattened, opening at the margins, usually enclosed in the persistent calyx. Seeds appendaged at the base, one in each cell.

The British 'Milkwort' (*P. vulgaris*) is closely allied to the Himalayan speies.

Flowers purple or pink.	
Keel 2-lobed at the tip, not crested	1. *P. triphylla.*
Keel with a fringed crest at the tip.	
Stem and leaves densely hairy	2. *P. crotalarioides.*
Stem and leaves glabrous or nearly so.	
Perennial. Rootstock woody. Leaves linear, ½–1 in.	3. *P. abyssinica.*
Annual. Root fibrous. Leaves lanceolate, 1–2 in.	4. *P. persicariæfolia.*
Flowers yellow	5. *P. chinensis.*

1. **Polygala triphylla,** *Buch.-Ham.*; *Fl. Br. Ind.* i. 201. Annual, glabrous. Stems weak, nearly erect, 2–4 in., branched. Leaves orbicular or spathulate, ½–1 in.; stalk often winged. Flowers deep pink, in slender, erect, terminal racemes 1–1½ in. Calyx falling off after flowering. Keel-petal 2-lobed at the tip, not crested. Capsule orbicular, narrowly winged.

Simla, Chadwick Falls, Syree; August–October.—Temperate Himalaya, 4000–8000 ft.—Malaya.

FIG. 14. POLYGALA CROTALARIOIDES.

2. **Polygala crotalarioides,** *Buch.-Ham.*; *Fl. Br. Ind.* i. 201. Perennial, densely hairy. Rootstock woody, often tuberous. Stems short, thick, decumbent, branches long spreading. Leaves nearly sessile, ovate or oblong-ovate, ½–2 in. Flowers purple, crowded in axillary racemes. Calyx persistent. Keel-petal crested. Capsule heart-shaped, fringed. (Fig. 14.)

Simla, in crevices of rocks, common; April–October.—Temperate Himalaya, 4000–7000 ft.

Royle (*Illustr. Pl. Himal.* 76) mentions that the root is used by the hill people as a cure for snakebite.

3. **Polygala abyssinica,** *R. Br.*; *Fl. Br. Ind.* i. 202. Perennial, glabrous or pubescent. Rootstock woody. Stems short; branches numerous, 6–18 in., slender, ascending. Leaves sessile, linear, ½–1 in. Flowers in long, terminal racemes. Calyx persistent, wing-sepals pale grey. Corolla purple, keel-petal crested. Capsule ovate, notched, narrowly winged.

Simla, on open, grassy hill-sides, common; August, September.—W. Himalaya, 3000–8000 ft.—W. Asia, Africa.

4. **Polygala persicariæfolia,** *DC.*; *Fl. Br. Ind.* i. 202. Annual, pubescent. Root fibrous. Stems erect, 6–18 in., branched. Leaves nearly sessile, lanceolate, 1–2 in. Flowers in stalked, erect, usually terminal racemes. Calyx persistent, wing-sepals pale yellow-grey. Corolla pink, keel-petal crested. Capsule ovate, notched, minutely fringed, narrowly winged near the top.

Valleys below Simla; September.—Himalaya, 5000–9000 ft.—Tropical Africa and Australia.

5. **Polygala chinensis,** *Linn.*; *Fl. Br. Ind.* i. 204. Annual, pubescent. Stems erect or diffuse, 2–6 in. Leaves sessile, narrowly oblong, ½–1½ in., obtuse. Flowers yellow, crowded in axillary racemes. Calyx persistent. Keel-petal minutely crested. Capsule ovate, notched, fringed, narrowly winged.

Simla, in valleys; August, September.—Throughout India, ascending to 5000 ft.—Tropical Asia, Australia.

XII. CARYOPHYLLACEÆ

Annual or perennial herbs. Stems erect or partially decumbent, rarely climbing, usually thickened at the joints. Leaves opposite or in opposite clusters, flat or terete, simple, entire, bases often more or less united; stipules none or scarious. Flowers regular, 2- rarely 1-sexual, in forking cymes or panicles, rarely solitary. Sepals 4 or 5, persistent, free or united. Petals as many as the sepals, usually clawed, sometimes very small or none. Stamens free, twice as many as the petals, rarely 5 or fewer. Ovary free; styles linear, 3–5 (in *Polycarpæa* only 1). Capsule membranous, fleshy and berry-like only in *Cucubalus*, 1-celled (or 3–5-celled near the base), opening at the top in as many or twice as many teeth or valves as there are styles; in *Cucubalus* only the fruit breaks up irregularly. Seeds small, usually many, rarely only 1 or 2, attached to a central column.—Cosmopolitan, but most abundant in the temperate and cold regions of the N. Hemisphere.—Name from *Caryophyllus aromaticus*, a tree whose dried flower-buds are cloves; referring to the scent of the cultivated 'Clove pink,' *Dianthus caryophyllus*.

Sepals united in a 5-toothed calyx

Calyx clasped at the base by imbricate bracts . . . . 1. *Dianthus*.
Calyx without basal bracts.
  Styles 2.
    Calyx bell-shaped. Petals nearly white, notched . 2. *Gypsophila*.
    Calyx cylindric. Petals pink, margins jagged . . 3. *Saponaria*.
  Styles 3.
    Calyx cylindric, or ovoid and inflated. Fruit a membranous capsule . . . . 4. *Silene*.
    Calyx bell-shaped. Fruit fleshy, berry-like . . 5. *Cucubalus*.
  Styles 5. Petals fringed . . . . 6. *Lychnis*.

Sepals free

Leaves opposite; stipules none.
  Petals 2-lobed.
    Petals shortly lobed. (See also *Stellaria bulbosa*) . 7. *Cerastium*.
    Petals deeply lobed (except *S. bulbosa*) . . . . 8. *Stellaria*.
  Petals entire, sometimes none.
    Leaves flat, bases not united . . . . . . 9. *Arenaria*.
    Leaves terete, bases united in a scarious sheath . . 10. *Sagina*.
Leaves in opposite clusters; stipules small, scarious.
  Sepals green, obtuse. Styles 5 . . . . . . 11. *Spergula*.
  Sepals shining white, acute. Style 1 . . . . . 12. *Polycarpæa*.

1. DIANTHUS. From the Greek *dios*, divine, and *anthos*, a flower; the flower of the gods.—N. temperate regions.

* **Dianthus angulatus,** *Royle*; *Fl. Br. Ind.* i. 215. A perennial, glabrous herb. Stems stiff, slender, 6–12 in., nearly erect. Leaves linear, acute, radical 3–6 in., upper $\frac{1}{2}$–$1\frac{1}{2}$ in. Flowers solitary, terminal. Calyx tubular, $\frac{1}{2}$–$\frac{2}{3}$ in., clasped at the base by about 4 imbricate, pointed bracts. Petals 5, pink, clawed, limb fringed. Stamens 10. Ovary stalked; styles 2. Capsule opening at the top by 4 teeth.

Kunawar, 7000–13,000 ft.; June.—W. Himalaya.
A plant of the inner dry ranges.

2. GYPSOPHILA. From the Greek *gypsos*, chalk, and *philo*, I love, referring to the habitat of some species.—Northern Asia, Europe.

Gypsophila cerastioides, *D. Don*; *Fl. Br. Ind.* i. 217. A perennial, pubescent herb. Stems several, 4–8 in., slender, spreading. Leaves obovate or spathulate, $\frac{1}{3}$–$1\frac{1}{2}$ in., lower ones stalked, upper nearly sessile. Flowers numerous, small, in panicled cymes. Calyx bell-shaped. Petals nearly white, streaked with purple, clawed,

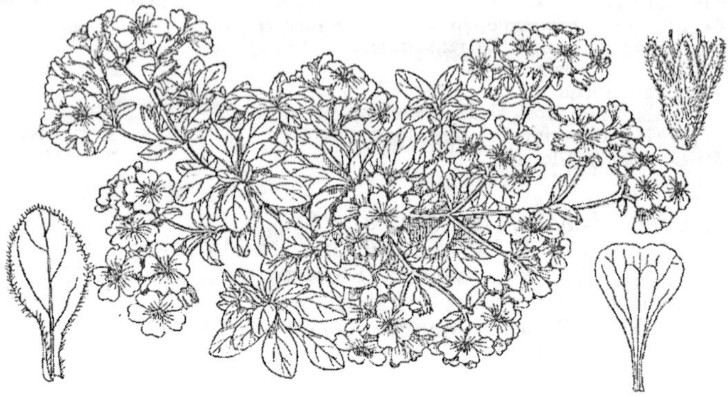

FIG. 15. GYPSOPHILA CERASTIOIDES.

limb slightly notched. Stamens 10. Ovary nearly sessile; styles 2. Capsule opening to about the middle by 4 valves. (Fig. 15.)

Mushobra, Matiana, Narkunda; May, June.—W. Himalaya, 6000–12,000 ft.

3. SAPONARIA. From the Latin *sapo*, soap; the leaves and roots of some species are boiled and used as soap.—N. Asia, Europe, N. Africa.

Saponaria Vaccaria, *Linn.*; *Fl. Br. Ind.* i. 217. An annual, glabrous herb. Stems erect, 1–2 ft. Leaves sessile, oblong, $1\text{–}2\frac{1}{2} \times \frac{1}{4}\text{–}\frac{1}{2}$ in., acute; stem-leaves cordate, united at the base. Flowers in terminal, forked cymes. Calyx cylindric, $\frac{1}{2}$ in., becoming ovoid in fruit, nerves 5, broad, green. Petals 5, pink, clawed, limb obovate, jagged. Stamens 10. Ovary nearly sessile; styles 2. Capsule opening at the top by 5 teeth.

Simla, in cornfields; April, May.—Throughout India.—W. Europe, N. Africa, N. Asia.
A weed of cultivation.

4. SILENE. From Silenus, the attendant of Bacchus, referring to the viscid glands of most species.—Europe, Asia, N. America, S. Africa; a very large genus.

Annual or perennial, usually viscid, herbs. Stems often tufted, erect or ascending. Radical leaves stalked; upper sessile, more or less united at the base. Calyx tubular or ovoid and inflated, usually narrowed towards the mouth. Petals 5, clawed, limb entire or 2-lobed, sometimes with 2 minute scales at its base. Stamens 10. Ovary usually stalked; styles 3. Capsule opening at the top in 6 teeth or short valves. Seeds many.

Flowers white.
  Glabrous. Calyx ovoid, inflated. Petals not fringed . 1. *S. inflata.*
  Viscidly pubescent. Calyx tubular. Petals fringed . 5. *S. Griffithii.*
Flowers pink or brown-purple.
  Petals not lobed.
    Petals pink; limb short, obovate . . . . . 2. *S. conoidea.*
    Petals brown-purple; limb long, narrow . . 4. *S. Falconeriana.*
  Petals deeply 2-lobed . . . . 3. *S. tenuis.*

1. **Silene inflata,** *Smith*; *Fl. Br. Ind.* i. 218. Perennial, glabrous. Stems 1–3 ft., ascending, rarely erect. Leaves pale green, ovate, 1–2 in., acute. Flowers few, drooping, in loose, terminal panicles. Calyx inflated, ovoid, $\frac{3}{4}$ in. long, net-veined. Petals white, blade 2-lobed. Ovary broadly ovoid. Capsule globose.

Simla, Mushobra, Narkunda; June, July.—Temperate Himalaya.—N. Asia, N. Africa, Europe, including Britain (Bladder Campion).

2. **Silene conoidea,** *Linn.*; *Fl. Br. Ind.* i. 218. Annual, glandular-pubescent. Stems ascending or erect, 6–18 in. Leaves narrowly lanceolate, 1–3 in., acute. Flowers few, erect, in terminal panicles. Calyx tubular, finely grooved, 1 in., narrowed upwards, teeth long, linear. Petals pink, limb short, obovate. Ovary oblong-ovoid. Capsule ovoid, pointed, hard, shining, enclosed in the globosely inflated calyx.

Simla, in cornfields; April, May.—Plains of the Punjab, ascending to 8000 ft.—N. temperate Asia, N. Africa, S.E. Europe.

*3. **Silene tenuis,** *Willd.*; *Fl. Br. Ind.* i. 219. Perennial, lower parts glabrous, more or less pubescent upwards. Stems several, 6–18 in., erect or ascending. Leaves chiefly basal, narrowly lanceolate, 1–3 in. Flowers crowded in short, terminal racemes or narrow cymes. Calyx tubular, $\frac{1}{3}$–$\frac{1}{2}$ in., thin, pubescent. Petals brown-purple, limb deeply 2-lobed. Ovary oblong. Capsule ovoid.

Kunawar to Kashmir, 8000–12,000 ft.; July, August.—Northern and Arctic Asia.

4. **Silene Falconeriana,** *Royle*; *Fl. Br. Ind.* i. 220. Perennial. Stems erect, 1–4 ft., viscidly pubescent on the lower parts, becoming glabrous upwards. Leaves linear-lanceolate, 1–3 in. Flowers in short, opposite, axillary cymes. Calyx tubular, $\frac{1}{2}$ in., nerves green. Petals brown-purple, limb long, narrow, obtuse. Ovary oblong. Capsule ovoid.

Simla, on grassy hill-sides, 4000 ft.; September.—W. Himalaya, 3000–9000 ft.

* 5. **Silene Griffithii,** *Boiss.*; *Fl. Br. Ind.* i. 220. Perennial, densely viscid-pubescent. Stems ascending or erect, robust, 12–18 in. Leaves ovate-lanceolate, $2\text{–}4 \times \frac{3}{4}\text{–}1\frac{1}{4}$ in. Flowers in opposite, axillary, usually 3-flowered cymes. Calyx tubular, $\frac{3}{4}$–1 in. Petals white, deeply 2-lobed, lobes fringed. Ovary and capsule oblong.

W. Himalaya, Garhwal to Kashmir; June–August.—W. and Central Asia.

5. **CUCUBALUS.** A name of classical origin; derivation uncertain.—Europe, Asia. Only one species.

***Cucubalus baccifer,** *Linn.*; *Fl. Br. Ind.* i. 222. A rambling, half-climbing, pubescent herb. Stems 2–3 ft., weak, diffusely branched. Leaves ovate-lanceolate, $1\text{–}3 \times \frac{1}{3}\text{–}1\frac{1}{2}$ in., acute, lower ones shortly stalked, upper sessile. Flowers nodding, in forked cymes, forming lax, leafy panicles. Calyx bell-shaped, $\frac{1}{2}$ in. Petals 5, white, tinged with yellow-green, clawed, limb 2-lobed, with 2 minute scales at its base. Stamens 10. Ovary shortly stalked, globose; styles 3. Capsule berry-like, blue-black, globose, nearly $\frac{1}{2}$ in. diam., 3-celled at the base, fleshy at first, becoming dry and breaking up irregularly when mature. Seeds numerous.

Temperate Himalaya, 5000–12,000 ft.; June, July.—Central Asia, Europe.

6. **LYCHNIS.** From the Greek *lychnos*, a lamp: the flowers of some species are very brilliant.—N. temperate regions, Andes.

Perennial herbs. Stems weak, nearly erect. Lower leaves usually stalked, upper sessile. Calyx tubular, inflated. Petals 5, clawed, limb fringed, usually with 2 scales at its base. Stamens 10. Ovary shortly stalked; styles 5. Capsule ovoid, sometimes 5-celled at the base, opening at the top by 5 teeth or short valves often split into double the number. Seeds many.

Petals much longer than the calyx; fringe long; segments 2-lobed . . . . 1. *L. fimbriata.*
Petals hardly longer than the calyx; fringe short; segments entire . . . . 2. *L. nutans.*

1. **Lychnis fimbriata,** *Wall.*; *Fl. Br. Ind.* i. 225, *under L. indica.* Pubescent, often viscidly glandular, especially the inflorescence. Stems 2–4 ft., diffusely branched. Leaves very variable in shape and size, ovate, ovate-lanceolate or narrowly lanceolate, acute, the smaller forms $1\text{–}2\frac{1}{2} \times \frac{1}{3}\text{–}1$ in., the larger $5 \times 1\frac{1}{2}$ in. Flowers erect or nodding, in cymes forming terminal panicles. Calyx bell-shaped, $\frac{1}{2}\text{–}\frac{3}{4}$ in. Petals much longer than the calyx, purple or cream-white, flowers of both colours often on the same plant, limb long-fringed, segments usually 4, divided into 2 lobes.

Simla, common; September, October.—Temperate Himalaya, 5000–10,000 ft.

2. **Lychnis nutans,** *Benth.*; *Fl. Br. Ind.* i. 225. Perennial, pubescent, often viscidly glandular, especially the inflorescence.

Stems 2–3 ft., weak, diffusely branched. Lower leaves lanceolate, about 3×1 in.; upper broadly ovate, pointed, about $1\frac{1}{2}$–$2\frac{1}{2}$×1–$1\frac{3}{4}$

FIG. 16. LYCHNIS NUTANS.

in. Flowers nodding, in cymes, forming terminal panicles. Calyx $\frac{1}{2}$ in., globose. Petals hardly longer than the calyx, purple, limb shortly fringed, segments 4–6, undivided. (Fig. 16.)

Huttoo; July–October.—Temperate Himalaya, 9000–10,000 ft.

7. CERASTIUM. From the Greek *keras*, a horn, referring to the horn-shaped capsules, which protrude from the calyx.—Temperate and cold regions.

Annual or perennial herbs. Leaves ovate or oblong. Flowers white, in terminal, forked cymes. Sepals 5, free, margins and tip scarious. Petals 5, shortly lobed. Stamens 10, occasionally fewer. Ovary sessile, ovoid; styles 5. Capsule cylindric, twice as long as the calyx, opening by 10 teeth. Seeds many.

Glabrous. Petals twice as long as the sepals . . . 1. *C. dahuricum.*
Pubescent. Petals not longer than the sepals . . . 2. *C. vulgatum.*

1. **Cerastium dahuricum,** *Fisch.*; *Fl. Br. Ind.* i. 227. Perennial, glabrous. Stems shining, long, straggling over bushes or long grass. Leaves sessile, ovate $1\frac{1}{2} \times 1$ in., or oblong $2\frac{1}{2} \times \frac{3}{4}$ in., bases united. Cymes repeatedly forked; flowers long-stalked. Sepals ovate-lanceolate, $\frac{2}{5}$ in., margins narrow. Petals nearly twice as long as the sepals. Capsule-teeth recurved.

Matiana, Huttoo; May, June.—W. Himalaya, 9000–11,000 ft.—Caucasus to Siberia.

2. **Cerastium vulgatum,** *Linn.*; *Fl. Br. Ind.* i. 228. Annual, pubescent, usually more or less viscid. Stems often numerous, 6–12 in., spreading from the base or nearly erect, usually much branched. Lower leaves stalked, ovate or spathulate; upper sessile, varying from broadly ovate to narrowly oblong, $\frac{1}{2}$–1 in. Cymes variable, their branches spreading or umbellate or reduced to a compact head. Sepals lanceolate, about $\frac{1}{5}$ in., margins broad. Petals about as long as the sepals. Stamens sometimes 5 or even fewer. Capsule-teeth straight.

Simla, very common; April–October.—Hilly regions throughout India, ascending to 15,000 ft.—Temperate N. Asia, N. Africa, Europe; widely diffused as a weed of cultivation (Britain, Mouse-ear Chickweed).

The numerous forms of this variable plant have been regarded by some botanists as species. Three varieties are common at Simla: (1) that with open spreading cymes, frequent on road sides and dry situations; (2) that with the flowers in an umbel-like cluster; (3) that with the stalks so reduced that the flowers form a head. The two latter are usually found in shady, moist places.

8. **STELLARIA.** From the Latin *stella*, a star, referring to the form of the flowers.—Nearly all cold and temperate regions.

Annual or perennial herbs, glabrous or partially pubescent, rarely hairy. Stems angled, slender, weak, often diffuse, sometimes matted, a line of hairs usually running down between the joints. Leaves, at least the upper ones, sessile or nearly so, rarely long-stalked. Flowers white, in cymes, sometimes in panicles, seldom solitary. Sepals 5 or 4, free, often viscidly pubescent. Petals as many as the sepals, rarely none, deeply 2-lobed, except *S. bulbosa*. Stamens 10, sometimes fewer. Ovary sessile; styles usually 3, rarely 2 or 5. Capsule sometimes 3–5-celled at the base, opening by as many valves as there are styles, the valves sometimes split at the tip. Seeds usually numerous and small, rarely 1 or 2 or few and larger.

Petals not longer than the sepals.
  Leaves 2–8 in.
    Leaves all sessile . . . . 1. *S. crispata.*
    Lower leaves stalked . . . . 2. *S. paniculata.*
  Leaves $\frac{1}{2}$–1 in.
    Lower leaves stalked. Petals shorter than the sepals or none . . . . 4. *S. media.*
    Leaves all sessile. Petals as long as the sepals . 7. *S. longissima.*

Petals longer than the sepals.
Styles 3. Leaves sessile, 3–8 in. . . . . 1. *S. crispata.*[1]
Styles 5. Lower stem-leaves long-stalked . . . 3. *S. aquatica.*
Styles 2.
Stems decumbent, 6–12 in. Petals 2-parted nearly to the base . . . . 5. *S. latifolia.*
Stems erect, 2–4 in. Petals shortly 2-lobed . . 6. *S. bulbosa.*

1. **Stellaria crispata,** *Wall.*; *Fl. Br. Ind.* i. 229. Stems shining, nearly erect, 2–4 ft., hairy at the joints and with a line of hairs running down between them, otherwise glabrous. Leaves glabrous, oblong or lanceolate, 3–8 in., sessile, usually cordate,

FIG. 17. STELLARIA CRISPATA.

long-pointed, margins often crisped. Cymes pubescent. Sepals lanceolate, nearly $\frac{1}{5}$ in., acute, pubescent, often viscid. Petals shorter or longer than the sepals, 2-lobed. Styles 3. Seeds 1 or 2, large. (Fig. 17.)

Simla, in shady places; July, August.—Temperate Himalaya, 5000–10,000 ft.

2. **Stellaria paniculata,** *Edgew.*; *Fl. Br. Ind.* i. 229. Stems shining, decumbent or nearly erect, 2–4 ft., hairy at the joints and with a line of hairs running down between them, otherwise glabrous. Leaves glabrous or minutely pubescent, ovate-lanceolate, long-pointed, 2–4 in.: lower ones narrowed into a winged stalk;

[1] *S. crispata* has two forms of flowers—petals minute or petals much longer than the sepals.

upper nearly sessile. Cymes viscidly pubescent, forming terminal or axillary, many-flowered panicles. Sepals viscid, lanceolate, $\frac{1}{7}$ in. Petals shorter than the sepals, 2-lobed. Styles 3. Seed only one, large.

Fagoo, Narkunda, in forests; July–September.—W. Himalaya, 7000–9000 ft.—Nilghiris.

3. **Stellaria aquatica,** *Scop.*; *Fl. Br. Ind.* i. 229. Pubescent, upper parts viscid. Stems decumbent, 1–3 ft. Leaves ovate, cordate, $\frac{1}{2}$–2 in., acute: lower ones long-stalked; upper shortly stalked or sessile. Flowers in leafy, axillary or terminal cymes. Sepals viscid, lanceolate, about $\frac{1}{6}$ in. at the time of flowering, enlarged in fruit. Petals narrow, deeply 2-lobed, about $1\frac{1}{2}$ times as long as the calyx. Styles 5.

Simla, Narkunda, in wet places and along streams; May-October.—Temperate Himalaya, 4000–8000 ft.—N. and Central Asia, N. Africa, Europe, including Britain.

4. **Stellaria media,** *Linn.*; *Fl. Br. Ind.* i. 230. Glabrous or pubescent. Stems nearly erect or procumbent, 6–24 in., a line of hairs running down between the joints, much branched. Leaves ovate, acute, $\frac{1}{2}$–1 in., usually cordate: lower ones stalked; upper sessile, often narrower. Flowers in axillary or terminal cymes. Sepals hairy, often viscid, $\frac{1}{7}$ in. Petals shorter than the sepals, deeply 2-lobed, sometimes wanting. Stamens often reduced in number. Styles 3.

Simla, common; April-October.—N. India, ascending to 14,000 ft.—N. arctic and temperate regions (Britain, Common Chickweed).
A very variable and widely colonised plant.

5. **Stellaria latifolia,** *Benth.*; *Fl. Br. Ind.* i. 231. Stems shining, much branched, 6–12 in., mostly decumbent, often matted, glabrous or the upper parts pubescent. Leaves nearly sessile: lower ones broadly ovate, almost orbicular, $\frac{2}{5}$ in., abruptly narrowed in an acute point; upper lanceolate, acute. Flowers solitary, long-stalked. Sepals 4, lanceolate, $\frac{1}{4}$ in., finely pointed. Petals 4, twice as long as the sepals, 2-parted nearly to the base. Stamens 8. Styles 2.

Huttoo, on rocks; June.—W. Himalaya, 6000–8000 ft.

*6. **Stellaria bulbosa,** *Wulf.*; *Fl. Br. Ind.* i. 231. Glabrous or nearly so. Rootstock creeping, bearing small, globose tubers. Stems simple, erect, 2–4 in. Leaves ovate-lanceolate, $\frac{3}{4}$–$1\frac{3}{4}$ in., narrowed into a short stalk. Flowers 1 or 2, long-stalked. Sepals 4 or 5, broadly lanceolate, $\frac{1}{5}$ in. Petals 4 or 5, ovate-oblong, much longer than the sepals, shortly 2-lobed. Styles 2. Seeds few, large.

In damp, shady forests from Bhotan to Kashmir, 6000–12,000 ft.; April–July.—Siberia, Carinthia, Transylvania.

A curious little plant as regards both structure and distribution, occurring probably near Narkunda. Minute cleistogamic flowers are frequently produced in the axils of the lower leaves and from the top of the rootstock.

7. **Stellaria longissima,** *Wall.*; *Fl. Br. Ind.* i. 232. Lower parts glabrous or pubescent, becoming densely hairy or almost woolly near the flowers. Stems shining, much branched, 6–18 in., mostly decumbent, usually matted. Leaves sessile, narrowly oblong or lanceolate, $\frac{1}{2}$–1 in., acute. Flowers solitary or in small cymes. Sepals narrowly lanceolate, $\frac{1}{5}$ in. Petals as long as the sepals, deeply 2-lobed. Styles 3.

Huttoo; June, July.—Temperate Himalaya, 8000–12,000 ft.

9. **ARENARIA.** From the Latin *arena*, sand; many species grow in sandy places.—Nearly all temperate and cold regions.

Annual or perennial herbs. Stems tufted, slender, much branched, ascending or decumbent. Leaves nearly sessile, small, flat. Flowers small, white, in terminal cymes. Sepals 5, free, lanceolate, acute. Petals 5, shorter than the sepals, entire. Stamens 10. Ovary ovoid; styles 3 or 5. Capsule globose, opening by 6 or 10 valves. Seeds numerous.

Leaves ovate-lanceolate. Styles 3. Seeds rough . . 1. *A. serpyllifolia.*
Leaves orbicular. Styles 5. Seeds smooth . . . . 2. *A. orbiculata.*

1. **Arenaria serpyllifolia,** *Linn.*; *Fl. Br. Ind.* i. 239. Often more or less viscid. Stems 4–12 in. Leaves ovate-lanceolate, $\frac{1}{8}$–$\frac{1}{2}$ in., acute. Flowers numerous. Petals obovate. Styles 3. Capsule opening by 6 valves. Seeds rough.

Simla, Mushobra, common; April–July.—N. India, ascending to 12,000 ft.—Temperate Asia, Europe (Britain).

*2. **Arenaria orbiculata,** *Royle*; *Fl. Br. Ind.* i. 240. Stems very slender, 4–12 in. Leaves orbicular, less than $\frac{1}{4}$ in. diam. Flowers sometimes solitary. Petals ovate. Styles 5. Capsule opening by 10 valves. Seeds smooth.

Bhotan to Kashmir, on damp rocks in shady places, 5000–8000 ft.; May–August.

10. **SAGINA.** The Latin for nourishing food; the application is obscure.—Most temperate regions.

Sagina procumbens, *Linn.*; *Fl. Br. Ind.* i. 242. A very small, glabrous herb. Stems tufted, slender, 2–6 in., spreading. Leaves terete, acute, $\frac{1}{4}$–$\frac{1}{3}$ in., united at the base in a scarious sheath. Flowers very small, white, solitary on axillary or terminal stalks much longer than the leaves. Sepals 4 or 5, free. Petals 4 or 5, shorter than the sepals, entire, sometimes wanting. Stamens

4 or 5. Styles 4 or 5. Capsules opening to the base by 4 or 5 valves. Seeds many.

Simla, Theog, Narkunda, on gravel walks and roadsides; May–September.—Temperate Himalaya.—Most temperate regions (Britain, Pearlwort).

11. SPERGULA. From the Latin *spargere*, to scatter; referring to the numerous seeds produced.—Cosmopolitan in temperate regions; most common on cultivated ground.

Spergula arvensis, *Linn.*; *Fl. Br. Ind.* i. 243. A pubescent, often viscid, annual herb. Stems tufted, slender, 6–18 in., erect or ascending. Leaves linear, $\frac{1}{2}$–2 in., in opposite clusters; stipules scarious. Flowers small, white, in terminal, forked cymes, on long stalks reflexed after flowering. Sepals 5, free, green, obtuse. Petals 5, entire, obtuse, slightly longer than the sepals. Stamens 10. Styles 5. Capsule longer than the calyx, opening by 5 valves. Seeds many.

Simla, in cornfields.—N. India.—N. Hemisphere (Britain, Corn-Spurrey); widely colonised.

12. POLYCARPÆA. From the Greek *polus*, many, and *carpos*, fruit, referring to the numerous capsules.—Most warm countries; rare in America.

Polycarpæa corymbosa, *Lamk.*; *Fl. Br. Ind.* i. 245. A pubescent herb. Stems erect or ascending, 6–12 in., much branched. Leaves linear, $\frac{1}{3}$–1 in., in opposite clusters; stipules scarious. Flowers crowded in conspicuous, silvery cymes. Sepals 5, free, scarious, shining white, narrowly lanceolate, $\frac{1}{10}$ in., acute. Petals 5, white, much shorter than the sepals, entire. Stamens 5. Style 1, tip 3-toothed. Capsule much shorter than the calyx, opening by 3 valves. Seeds numerous, small.

Giri valley, 4000 ft.; July, August.—Throughout India, ascending to 7000 ft.—Most tropical regions, rare in America.

XIII. HYPERICACEÆ

A SMALL Order, widely spread in temperate and warm regions, but rare in the tropics; represented in the N.W. Himalaya by the single genus *Hypericum*.

HYPERICUM. From *Hypericum*, the classical name of some species of the genus.—Chiefly N. temperate regions.

Shrubs or perennial herbs, glabrous, usually glandular. Stems erect. Leaves opposite, sessile or nearly so, simple, entire; stipules none. Flowers regular, 2-sexual, yellow, in cymes or corymbs, usually terminal, sometimes combined in panicles. Sepals and petals 5 each, free, imbricate. Stamens numerous, united at the base in 3 or 5 distinct bundles, anthers 2-celled, versatile. Ovary 3- or 5-celled; ovules many; styles 3 or 5, simple, distinct. Capsule opening from the top by 3 or 5 valves. Seeds numerous, small.

Shrubs. Stamens in 5 bundles. Styles 5.
  Petals rather longer than the stamens. Styles twice as long as the ovary.
    Branches terete. Flowers 2 in. diam. Sepals ovate . . . 1. *H. cernuum.*
    Branches 4-angled. Flowers 1–1½ in. diam. Sepals lanceolate . . . . 2. *H. lysimachioides.*
  Petals twice as long as the stamens. Styles not longer than the ovary . . . . . . 3. *H. patulum.*
Perennial herbs. Stamens in 3 sets. Styles 3.
  Stems 2-angled. Sepals entire . . . . . 4. *H. perforatum.*
  Stems terete. Sepals fringed with stalked glands . 5. *H. elodeoides.*

1. **Hypericum cernuum,** *Roxb.*; *Fl. Br. Ind.* i. 253. A shrub, 3–6 ft., branches terete. Leaves ovate about 3 × 1¼ in., or oblong-

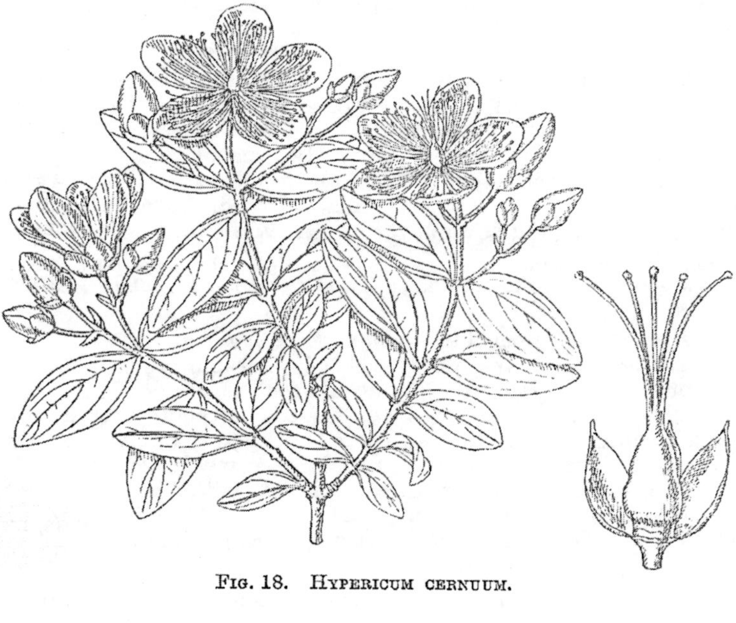

FIG. 18. HYPERICUM CERNUUM.

lanceolate 1¼–3 × ½–1 in., each pair of leaves placed at right angles to the next pair above or below it. Flowers 2 in. diam., in terminal cymes. Sepals ovate, $\frac{1}{4}$ in. Petals rather longer than the stamens. Stamens in 5 bundles. Ovary 5-celled; styles 5, twice as long as the ovary. Capsule $\frac{1}{2}$ in. (Fig. 18.)

Simla; March–May.—W. Himalaya, 5000–7000 ft.

2. **Hypericum lysimachioides,** *Wall*; *Fl. Br. Ind.* i. 254. A shrub, 1–3 ft. Branches 4-sided, at least towards the end. Leaves ovate, about $1\frac{1}{4} \times \frac{1}{2}$ in.; lower surface pale, black-dotted. Flowers $1–1\frac{1}{2}$ in. diam., in terminal, leafy, forked cymes. Sepals narrowly lanceolate, $\frac{1}{3}$ in. Petals rather longer than the stamens. Stamens in 5 bundles. Ovary 5-celled; styles 5, nearly twice as long as the ovary. Capsule $\frac{1}{4}$ in.

Simla, Mushobra; April–July.—W. Himalaya, 5000–8000 ft.

3. **Hypericum patulum,** *Thunb.*; *Fl. Br. Ind.* i. 254. A shrub, 1–3 ft. Branches 2-ridged. Leaves ovate $1\frac{1}{2} \times \frac{3}{4}$ in., or oblong-lanceolate $1\frac{1}{4}–2 \times \frac{1}{3}–\frac{3}{4}$ in., each pair placed at right angles to the next pair above or below it; lower surface pale, black-dotted. Flowers 1 in. diam., in terminal cymes. Sepals ovate, $\frac{1}{4}$ in. Petals twice as long as the stamens. Stamens in 5 bundles. Ovary 5-celled; styles 5, as long as the ovary. Capsule $\frac{1}{3}$ in.

Simla, on Summer Hill; August, September.—Temperate Himalaya, 3000–7000 ft.—China.

4. **Hypericum perforatum,** *Linn.*; *Fl. Br. Ind.* i. 255. A perennial herb. Stems 1–2 ft., 2-angled. Leaves oblong, $\frac{1}{3}$–1 in., obtuse, veins pellucid, lower surface pale. Flowers 1 in. diam., in terminal corymbs. Sepals narrowly lanceolate, acute, $\frac{1}{4}$ in., margins often black-dotted. Petals black-dotted on the margins. Stamens in 3 bundles, anthers black-dotted. Ovary 3-celled; styles 3, twice as long as the ovary. Capsule $\frac{1}{3}$ in.

Simla, in shady, damp forest; April–October.—W. Himalaya, 3000–8000 ft.—N. temperate Asia, N. Africa, Europe (Britain, Common St. John's Wort).

5. **Hypericum elodeoides,** *Choisy*; *Fl. Br. Ind.* i. 255. A perennial herb. Stems terete, 1–2 ft., stoloniferous. Leaves ovate, obtuse, $1 \times \frac{2}{3}$ in.; or broadly lanceolate, acute, $1\frac{1}{2} \times \frac{3}{4}$ in.; lower surface pale, margins black-dotted. Bracts fringed with stalked glands. Flowers $\frac{3}{4}$ in. diam., in cymes, often numerous and forming terminal panicles. Sepals narrowly lanceolate, acute, $\frac{1}{4}$ in., black-dotted and streaked, fringed with stalked glands. Petals black-dotted and streaked. Stamens in 3 bundles; anthers black-dotted. Ovary 3-celled; styles 3, twice as long as the ovary. Capsule $\frac{1}{4}$ in.

Simla, Narkunda, in shady, damp forest; July, August.—Temperate Himalaya, 6000–12,000 ft.
Closely allied to the British *H. montanum*.

XIV. MALVACEÆ

Herbs, low shrubs or trees, commonly furnished with stellate hairs. Leaves alternate, simple and often deeply lobed or digitately compound. Flowers 2-sexual, regular, axillary, solitary or in small cymes. Calyx 5-lobed, rarely a spathe, persistent, except in *Bombax*, sometimes furnished with a whorl of bracteoles. Petals 5, twisted in bud, base adhering to the staminal tube. Stamens numerous; filaments united in a staminal tube enclosing the pistil, except in *Bombax*; anthers 1-celled, borne on the tube itself or on short free filaments into which the upper part of the tube divides. Ovary sessile, 5–12-celled; styles as many as the carpels, united for about half their length or more, stigmatic along their free ends or terminating in capitate stigmas; ovules one or several in each cell. Fruit of 5–12 dry, 1-seeded carpels ultimately separating from the axis, or a many-seeded capsule splitting from the top in 5 valves. Seeds usually small, sometimes enveloped in a covering of long, silky hairs.—A large Order, most abundant in warm countries, but inhabiting nearly all regions except the coldest.

Cotton is obtained from the covering of the seeds of various species of *Gossypium*, a genus of this Order. Several kinds are cultivated in India, all having large yellow flowers with a purple centre.

- Herbs or shrubs. Leaves simple. Filaments united in a tube.
  - Staminal tube dividing into short, free, anther-bearing filaments. Carpels 1-seeded.
    - Bracteoles 3. Styles stigmatic along their free ends . . . 1. *Malva*.
    - Bracteoles none. Stigmas capitate . . . . . . 2. *Sida*.
  - Staminal tube bearing the anthers on its surface. Carpels several-seeded . . . . 3. *Hibiscus*.
- Trees. Leaves compound. Filaments united only at the base . 4. *Bombax*.

1. MALVA. The classical name of some member of the Order, probably the Hollyhock, *Althæa rosea*.—Temperate regions of the Old World.

Hairy or pubescent herbs. Leaves long-stalked, orbicular, cordate, more or less lobed, crenate or sharply toothed. Flowers stalked or nearly sessile, in axillary clusters. Bracteoles 3. Calyx bell-shaped, 5-lobed. Petals longer than the calyx, notched. Stamens united in a tube separating at the top into short, free, anther-bearing filaments. Ovary 10–12-celled, carpels arranged in a ring round a central axis; styles united for about half their length, stigmatic along their free ends; ovule solitary in each cell. Fruit enclosed in the persistent calyx; carpels indehiscent, 1-seeded, ultimately separating from the axis.

Stems erect.
Flowers nearly sessile. Bracteoles lanceolate . . 1. *M. verticillata.*
Flowers distinctly stalked. Bracteoles ovate . . 2. *M. silvestris.*
Stems decumbent, spreading.
Flowers long-stalked. Petals 2–3 times as long as the calyx . . . . 3. *M. rotundifolia.*
Flowers shortly stalked or sessile. Petals hardly longer than the calyx . . . . 4. *M. parviflora.*

1. **Malva verticillata,** *Linn.*; *Fl. Br. Ind.* i. 320. Stellately hairy. Stems erect, 1–4 ft. Leaves 2–6 in. across, lobes shallow

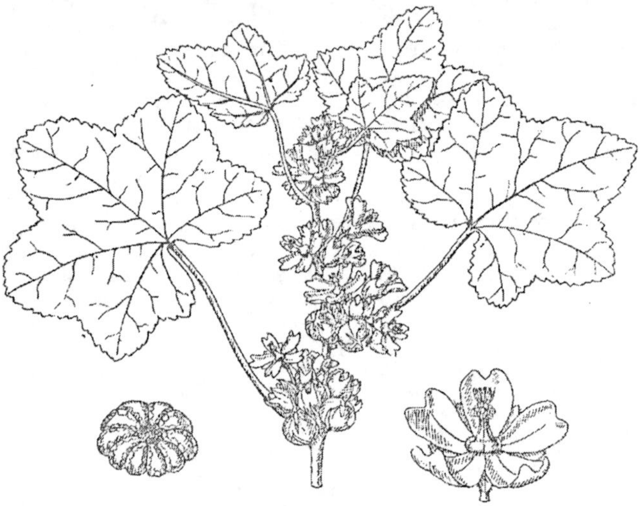

FIG. 19. MALVA VERTICILLATA.

Flowers small, crowded in nearly sessile clusters. Bracteoles narrowly lanceolate, acute. Petals pale pink, nearly twice as long as the calyx. (Fig. 19.)

Simla, Matiana; May–August.—Temperate Himalaya, up to 12,000 ft.—Northern Asia, N. Africa, Europe.

2. **Malva silvestris,** *Linn.*; *Fl. Br. Ind.* i. 320. More or less covered with spreading hairs. Stems erect, 1–3 ft. Leaves 1–3 in. across, lobes shallow or deep, the middle one usually the longest. Flowers large, stalked. Bracteoles ovate. Petals pale purple, darker-streaked at the base, 2–3 times as long as the calyx.

Theog; June.—W. Himalaya, 2000–8000 ft.—North temperate regions of the Old World (Britain, Common Mallow).

3. **Malva rotundifolia,** *Linn.*; *Fl. Br. Ind.* i. 320. Stellately pubescent. Stems decumbent, spreading, the central ones usually

ascending. Leaves 1–3 in. across, lobes shallow, broad. Flowers small, long-stalked. Bracteoles narrowly oblong, acute. Petals pale lilac, darker-streaked, 2–3 times as long as the calyx.

Matiana, Narkunda; June.—Plains of N. India, ascending to 10,000 ft.—W. Asia, Europe (Britain, Dwarf Mallow).
A weed of cultivation.

4. **Malva parviflora,** *Linn.*; *Fl. Br. Ind.* i. 321. Pubescent. Stems decumbent, 6–12 in., spreading. Leaves $\frac{1}{2}$–2 in. across, lobes usually obscure. Flowers small, shortly stalked or sessile. Bracteoles linear. Petals pale pink, hardly longer than the calyx.

Mushobra; May, June.—Plains of N. India.—W. Asia, W. Africa, Europe.

2. **SIDA.** A name adopted by Linnæus from classical authors. —Tropical and subtropical regions.

Low shrubs, more or less covered with stellate hairs or pubescence. Stems erect or nearly so. Leaves simple, not lobed. Calyx bell-shaped, 5-lobed, lobes triangular, acute. Bracteoles none. Petals pale yellow, slightly longer than the calyx. Stamens united in a tube separating at the top into short, free, anther-bearing filaments. Ovary 5–10-celled, carpels 1-ovuled, arranged round a central axis; styles united for about half their length; stigmas minute, capitate. Fruit enclosed in the persistent calyx; carpels shortly pointed, ultimately separating from the axis, 1-seeded, opening irregularly.

Leaves cordate; stalks 1–2 in.; lower surface green . . . 1. *S. humilis.*
Leaves wedge-shaped at base; stalks $\frac{1}{4}$ in. or less; lower surface grey-pubescent . . . . 2. *S. obovata.*

1. **Sida humilis,** *Willd.*; *Fl. Br. Ind.* i. 322. Stellately hairy. Leaves ovate, about $2\frac{1}{2} \times 1\frac{1}{2}$ in., cordate, long-pointed, toothed; lower surface green, bearing a few scattered, stellate hairs; stalks 1–2 in. Flowers about $\frac{1}{3}$ in. diam., solitary or in pairs or small cymes. Carpels 5.

Valleys below Simla; September.—Throughout India, ascending to 5000 ft.—Tropical Africa and America.

2. **Sida obovata,** *Wall.*; *Fl. Br. Ind.* i. 323, *under S. rhombifolia.* Stellately pubescent. Leaves variable, obovate about $1\frac{1}{2} \times 1$ in., or ovate about $2 \times 1\frac{1}{2}$ in., or orbicular about $\frac{3}{4} \times \frac{3}{4}$ in., base wedge-shaped, margins toothed at least on the upper half; lower surface grey with dense pubescence; stalks $\frac{1}{4}$ in. or less. Flowers about $\frac{1}{3}$ in. diam., in clusters. Carpels 7–10.

Syree, Sutlej valley; September, October.—Throughout India, ascending to 6000 ft.—Tropics of both Hemispheres.

3. HIBISCUS. The classical name of *Althæa officinalis*, the Marsh Mallow.—Tropical and sub-tropical regions of the Old World.

Pubescent or hairy herbs. Stems erect. Leaves simple, usually deeply lobed. Flowers axillary, solitary, usually large and showy, sometimes forming a terminal raceme. Calyx bell-shaped, 5-lobed or in *H. cancellatus* a spathe. Bracteoles numerous or in *H. Solandra* none. Stamens united in a tube bearing on its surface numerous nearly sessile anthers, tip truncate or lobed. Ovary 5-celled; styles united for about half their length, stigmas capitate; ovules several in each cell. Fruit a 5-celled, many-seeded capsule, enclosed in the persistent calyx and splitting from the top in 5 valves.

Hibiscus Sabdariffa, *Linn.*; *Fl. Br. Ind.* i. 340. The Rozelle or Red Sorrel of the West Indies is cultivated throughout India for its succulent, acid, red or green calyces which make excellent jelly and tarts. Native name *Pitwa*.

Calyx bell-shaped, 5-lobed. Flowers ½–1½ in. diam.
  Bracteoles numerous. Flowers pale yellow with dark purple centre . . . . 1. *H. Trionum*.
  Bracteoles none. Flowers pale yellow or white . . 2. *H. Solandra*.
Calyx a spathe. Flowers 4–5 in. diam., pale yellow with dark purple centre . . . . 3. *H. cancellatus*.

1. **Hibiscus Trionum,** *Linn.*; *Fl. Br. Ind.* i. 334. Annual, pubescent or hairy. Stems 1–2 ft. Lower leaves orbicular, 1–2 in. diam.; upper deeply 3–5-lobed, lobes oblong, 1–2 in., obtuse, coarsely toothed, central one longest. Flowers about 1½ in. diam., pale yellow with dark purple centre. Calyx bell-shaped, inflated, 5-lobed about half way down, lobes broad, acute. Bracteoles numerous, linear.

Sutlej valley; July–October.—Throughout India, ascending to 6000 ft.—Warm regions of the Old World.

A widely spread weed of cultivation.

2. **Hibiscus Solandra,** *L'Hérit.*; *Fl. Br. Ind.* i. 336. Annual, pubescent or hairy. Stems 1–3 ft. Lower leaves cordate, orbicular or ovate and long-pointed, 1–2½ in. across, more or less 3-lobed, crenate or sharply toothed; upper deeply 3-lobed, lobes narrowly oblong, toothed. Flowers pale yellow or white, ½–¾ in. diam. Calyx bell-shaped, 5-lobed nearly to its base, lobes narrow, pointed.

Simla, Sutlej valley; July–October.—Throughout India, ascending to 5000 ft.—Tropical Africa.

3. **Hibiscus cancellatus,** *Roxb.*; *Fl. Br. Ind.* i. 342. Annual, very bristly. Stems 2–3 ft. Leaves cordate, coarsely toothed or crenate: lower ones long-stalked, orbicular or ovate, up to 6×5 in., more or less 3- or 5-lobed; upper arrow-head shaped, lobes long,

narrow, tapering. Flowers few, 4–5 in. diam., pale yellow with dark purple centre. Calyx an ovate, folded spathe, tip obscurely 5-toothed. Bracteoles numerous, linear, 1½ in., bristly, curved, the tips meeting over the top of the buds.

Simla, Syree; July, August.—Throughout India, ascending to 6000 ft.—Burmah.

4. **BOMBAX.** From the Greek *bombyx*, silk, referring to the fine silky wool enveloping the seeds.—Most tropical regions.

Bombax malabaricum, *De Cand.*; *Fl. Br. Ind.* i. 349. A tall tree, the lower part of the trunk usually buttressed; branches whorled, spreading horizontally; young stem covered with conical prickles. Leaves glabrous, digitately compound; leaflets 5–7, shortly stalked, lanceolate, 4–8 in., entire, long-pointed. Flowers large, red, occasionally white, in the axils of fallen leaves, crowded towards the end of branches, appearing before the young leaves. Calyx falling off with the corolla, cup-shaped, thick, leathery, irregularly lobed, silky white inside. Bracteoles none. Petals thick, oblong, 3–6 in., tomentose outside, pubescent or glabrous within. Stamens numerous, in three series about half as long as the petals; outer ones united near the base in 5 bundles, 10 intermediate shorter, 5 innermost forked near the top. Ovary 5-celled; styles united to near the top, stigmatic along their free ends. Capsule woody, oblong, 4–5 in., splitting by 5 valves from the top. Seeds numerous, enveloped in fine silky wool.

Simla; February, March.—Throughout India, ascending to 6000 ft.—Java, Sumatra, Australia.

The *Semel* or Cotton tree. The calyces of the flower-buds are eaten; and the silky wool of the seeds is used to stuff pillows and quilts.

XV. TILIACEÆ

Trees, shrubs or herbs. Leaves alternate, simple, sometimes lobed, crenate or sharply toothed; stipules free. Flowers regular, 2-sexual, yellow or orange, in cymes or small clusters, rarely solitary. Sepals usually 5, free, valvate in bud. Petals usually 5, free, base glandular or naked. Receptacle more or less elevated, bearing the sepals and petals at its base, the stamens and ovary at its top. Stamens numerous or about 10, free, anthers 2-celled. Ovary sessile, 2–5-celled; ovules few or many in each cell; style columnar, tip lobed or toothed. Fruit a globose drupe or a capsule either globose and covered with hooked spines or long, narrow and glabrous. Seeds few or many, usually pendulous.—

A small Order, widely though thinly spread over most parts of the world except very cold climates; most abundant in tropical regions.

The Lime trees of Britain belong to a genus (*Tilia*) of this Order not represented in India, though it reappears in China and Japan.

Petals glandular at the base. Fruit globose or ovoid.
  Stamens numerous. Fruit a smooth drupe . . . 1. *Grewia.*
  Stamens about 10. Fruit a prickly capsule . . . 2. *Triumfetta.*
Petals not glandular at the base. Fruit a long, narrow, glabrous capsule . . . . 3. *Corchorus.*

1. GREWIA. In honour of N. Grew, an English botanist, the earliest English writer on vegetable anatomy.—Warm regions of the Old World.

Small trees, young parts more or less covered with rough, stellate pubescence. Leaves shortly stalked, ovate, toothed, long-

FIG. 20. GREWIA OPPOSITIFOLIA.

pointed, sides usually unequal. Flowers in leaf-opposed or axillary cymes. Sepals 5, thick, tomentose outside, nearly glabrous and coloured within. Petals 5, much shorter than the sepals, base with a large, thick, fringed gland on the inside. Receptacle elevated, hairy. Stamens numerous. Ovary 2–4-celled; ovules 1 or 2 in each cell; stigma 2–4-lobed. Drupe globose, usually lobed, containing 1–4 stones, each with 1 or sometimes 2 seeds.

Cymes leaf-opposed. Sepals $\frac{1}{2}$–$\frac{3}{4}$ in. Petals pale yellow . 1. *G. oppositifolia.*
Cymes axillary. Sepals $\frac{1}{3}$–$\frac{1}{2}$ in. Petals orange . . 2. *G. vestita.*

1. **Grewia oppositifolia**, *Roxb.*; *Fl. Br. Ind.* i. 384. A tree, 20–40 ft. Leaves rough, 2–4 in., toothed, base rounded, lower surface pale, pubescent. Flowers in stalked, 3–5-flowered cymes placed nearly or quite opposite a leaf; buds cylindric. Sepals narrowly oblong, $\frac{1}{2}$–$\frac{3}{4}$ in. Petals half as long as the sepals, pale yellow. Drupe about $\frac{1}{2}$ in. diam., olive-green, covered with scattered, stellate hairs, black and glabrous when ripe. (Fig. 20.)

Simla, valleys below 6000 ft.; May.—N.W. Himalaya.

Frequently planted. The wood is used for oar-shafts, banghy poles, spears, bows, &c.; the foliage is lopped for fodder and may often be seen stored between the branches; the fibres of the inner bark are manufactured into ropes and nets; and the fruit is eaten. Native name *Bèòl.*

*2. **Grewia vestita**, *Wall.*; *Fl. Br. Ind.* i. 387, *under G. asiatica.* A tree, 20–25 ft. Leaves rough, 2–4 in., obscurely lobed, base rounded, wedge-shaped or cordate; lower surface densely gray-tomentose. Flowers numerous, in axillary, shortly stalked, crowded cymes. Sepals yellow, narrowly lanceolate, $\frac{1}{3}$–$\frac{1}{2}$ in. Petals orange, hardly $\frac{1}{3}$ the length of the sepals. Drupe about $\frac{1}{4}$ in. diam., black and glabrous when ripe.

Outer hills from Kumaon to the Indus, ascending to 4000 ft.; February–May.—Bengal, Central Provinces.

The wood &c. is put to similar uses as that of *G. oppositifolia.* Native name *Dhaman.*

2. TRIUMFETTA. In honour of G. B. Triumfetti, an Italian botanical author of the 17th century.—Tropical regions.

Erect herbs or shrubs, usually more or less rough with stellate hairs or pubescence. Leaves long-stalked, ovate or ovate-lanceolate, sometimes lobed, toothed, long-pointed, base rounded or slightly cordate. Flowers usually numerous and crowded in nearly sessile, axillary clusters often forming long, interrupted, leafy spikes, rarely few or leaf-opposed. Sepals 5, oblong, hairy outside, abruptly pointed. Petals 5, yellow or orange, nearly as long as the sepals, a hairy gland at the base. Receptacle elevated, fleshy, lobed. Stamens about 10. Ovary prickly, 3–5-celled; stigma toothed. Capsule small, globose or ovoid, densely covered with hooked prickles, opening by 3–5 valves. Seeds 1 or 2 in each cell.

Stems and leaves densely pubescent or bristly. Flowers yellow. Capsule woolly or hairy.
- Bristly. Flowers $\frac{1}{2}$–$\frac{3}{4}$ in. long. Prickles of capsule $\frac{1}{4}$ in. . . . 1. *T. pilosa.*
- Pubescent. Flowers $\frac{1}{4}$ in. long. Prickles of capsule $\frac{1}{10}$ in. . . . . 2. *T. rhomboidea.*

Stems and leaves nearly glabrous. Flowers orange. Capsule glabrous . . . . 3. *T. annua.*

1. **Triumfetta pilosa**, *Roth*; *Fl. Br. Ind.* i. 394. Perennial, rough with long bristles. Stems 1–3 ft. Leaves ovate-lanceolate,

3–5 × 1–2 in., lowest leaves more or less lobed. Flowers yellow, $\frac{1}{2}$–$\frac{3}{4}$ in. long. Capsule $\frac{1}{3}$ in. diam., densely pubescent, prickles $\frac{1}{4}$ in., bristly.

Simla; June–October.—Throughout India, ascending to 5000 ft.—Tropical Asia and Africa.

2. **Triumfetta rhomboidea,** *Jacq.*; *Fl. Br. Ind.* i. 395. Perennial, densely pubescent. Stems 1–3 ft. Leaves broadly ovate, 2–3$\frac{1}{2}$ × 1$\frac{1}{2}$–3 in., 3- or 5-lobed, lobes long-pointed; uppermost leaves usually not lobed. Flowers yellow, $\frac{1}{4}$ in. long or less. Capsule $\frac{1}{5}$ in. diam., densely white woolly, prickles $\frac{1}{16}$ in., bristly.

Simla; June–October.—Throughout India, ascending to 5000 ft.—Tropical regions of Asia, Africa and America.

3. **Triumfetta annua,** *Linn.*; *Fl. Br. Ind.* i. 396. Annual, nearly glabrous, the stem with a line of hairs along one side, shifting at each joint. Leaves ovate, 1$\frac{1}{2}$–3$\frac{1}{2}$ × $\frac{3}{4}$–2 in., with a few scattered hairs. Flowers orange, $\frac{1}{4}$ in. long or less; clusters sometimes leaf-opposed. Capsule glabrous, $\frac{1}{4}$ in. diam., prickles $\frac{1}{4}$ in., glabrous.

Simla; June–October.—Throughout India, ascending to 5000 ft.—Malay archipelago, Tropical Africa.

3. **CORCHORUS.** A name adopted by Linnæus from classical authors.—Most tropical regions.

Herbs, usually annual, or small shrubs. Leaves shortly stalked, not lobed, crenate or sharply toothed; stipules long, bristle-like. Flowers small, yellow, 1–3 on short, thick, axillary or leaf-opposed stalks. Sepals usually 5, sometimes 4. Petals 5 or 4, usually longer than the sepals, not glandular at the base. Receptacle slightly elevated. Stamens numerous. Ovary 3–5-celled; style short, stigma shortly lobed. Capsule glabrous, long, narrow, erect, cylindric or angled, tipped with a short beak. Seeds numerous.

The valuable fibre Jute is derived from the inner bark of *C. capsularis*, *C. olitorius* and some other species of this genus. It is used in the manufacture of rope, string and the gunny bags in which grain is packed for export.

Capsule cylindric; beak entire.
  Stems erect. Leaves 2–4 in. Capsule 2 in. . . . 1. *C. olitorius.*
  Stems prostrate. Leaves $\frac{1}{2}$–$\frac{3}{4}$ in. Capsule 1–1$\frac{1}{2}$ in. . 2. *C. Antichorus.*
Capsule 6-angled; beak 3-fid; divisions spreading . . 3. *C. acutangulus.*

1. **Corchorus olitorius,** *Linn.*; *Fl. Br. Ind.* i. 397. Annual, nearly glabrous. Stems 1–4 ft., erect, branching. Leaves ovate, lanceolate, 2–4 × 1–2 in.; the lowest tooth on each side running out in a long, curved bristle; stalk and veins on the lower surface hairy. Capsule cylindric, 2 in., 5-valved, beak entire.

Simla, below 4000 ft.; July–September.—Cultivated throughout India and in most tropical countries.

The 'Jew's Mallow.' Most frequently met with as an escape; the leaves are eaten as a vegetable, and the bark yields jute.

2. **Corchorus Antichorus,** *Ræusch.*; *Fl. Br. Ind.* i. 398. Perennial, nearly glabrous. Rootstock thick, woody, dividing at the top into several prostrate, twisted, interlacing branches, 6–12 in. long. Leaves broadly ovate or oblong, $\frac{1}{2}$–$\frac{3}{4}$ in., crenate. Petals often shorter than the sepals. Capsule cylindric, 1–$1\frac{1}{2}$ in., 4-valved, beak entire.

Simla, below 5000 ft.; July–September.—Throughout India on dry arid soil.—Asia, tropical Africa.

3. **Corchorus acutangulus,** *Lam.*; *Fl. Br. Ind.* i. 398. Annual. Stems hairy, prostrate or ascending, 1–3 ft. Leaves ovate, acute, 1–2 × $\frac{1}{2}$–1 in., the lowest tooth on each side sometimes ending in a bristle; stalks hairy. Capsule 3-celled, 6-angled, $\frac{3}{4}$–$1\frac{1}{2}$ in., beak 3-fid, the divisions toothed, spreading.

Simla, below 5000 ft.; July–September.—Throughout India.—Australia, tropical Africa, W. Indies.

XVI. LINACEÆ

Herbs or small shrubs. Leaves alternate, simple, usually entire; stipules minute or none. Flowers regular, 2-sexual. Sepals 5, free, imbricate. Petals 5, free, imbricate, twisted in bud, soon falling off. Stamens 5, alternate with 5 small staminodes, united at the base, anthers 2-celled, versatile. Ovary free, 3–5-celled, ovules 2 in each cell separated by an imperfect partition; styles 3–5, or sometimes more in *Reinwardtia*, united at the base, stigmas capitate. Capsule globose, separating into 5 or 10 valves. Seeds small, 2 or 1 in each cell.—A small, widely dispersed Order.

A herb, 4–10 in. Styles 5 . . . . 1. *Linum.*
A shrub, 2–3 ft. Styles usually 3 . . . . 2. *Reinwardtia.*

1. **LINUM.** The classical name of the Flax.—Temperate and warm regions.

***Linum mysorense,** *Heyne*; *Fl. Br. Ind.* i. 411. An annual, glabrous herb. Stems slender, erect, 4–10 in., branching near the top. Leaves sessile, oblong, about $\frac{1}{2}$ in., acute. Flowers $\frac{1}{4}$ in. diam., in terminal, corymbose racemes, lengthening in fruit. Sepals ovate, acute. Petals yellow, longer than the sepals. Ovary

5-celled; styles 5, united near the base. Capsule $\frac{1}{8}$ in. diam., separating into 5 two-seeded or 10 one-seeded valves.

W. Himalaya, 3000–5000 ft.; July–November.—Hilly districts throughout India.

The common flax, *L. usitatissimum*, with sky-blue flowers varying to white, is cultivated throughout the plains and up to 6000 ft. in the hills, for the sake of the oil (linseed or *alsi ki tel*) expressed from the seeds, no use being made of the fibre contained in the stems. The plant has been cultivated from remote antiquity.

2. REINWARDTIA. In honour of K. Reinwardt, a Dutch botanist.—Hilly districts throughout India, ascending to 6000 ft.

Reinwardtia trigyna, *Planch.*; *Fl. Br. Ind.* i. 412. A glabrous shrub. Stems 2–3 ft., erect or ascending. Leaves entire, ovate-lanceolate, 2–4 in., narrowed into a slender stalk, tip obtuse or

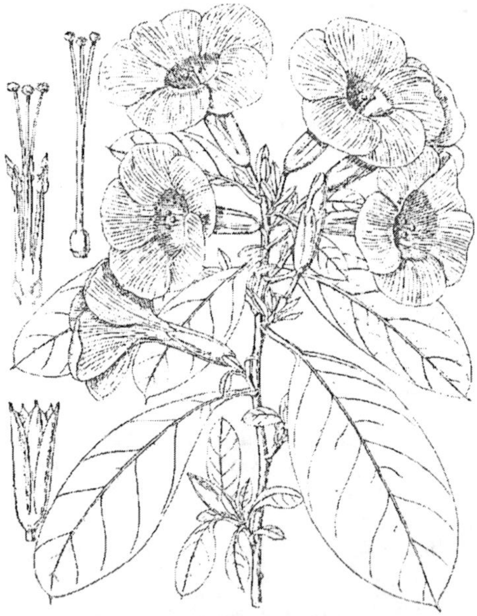

FIG. 21. REINWARDTIA TRIGYNA.

acute, minutely mucronate, lower surface pale. Flowers about 1 in. diam., axillary, solitary or in small clusters, sometimes combined in a terminal corymb. Sepals lanceolate, acute. Petals primrose-yellow, much longer than the calyx. Stamens usually in 2 sets, 3 long, 2 shorter. Ovary 3–5-celled; styles usually 3, sometimes 4–7, longer or shorter than the stamens, more or less united, rarely free. Capsule globose, $\frac{1}{4}$ in. diam., separating into as many valves as there are styles. (Fig. 21.)

Simla, the Glen; April, May.

This plant presents great differences in the number of styles, and in the relative length of the styles and stamens. See Darwin's *Forms of Flowers*, chapter vii., regarding similar differences in *Linum*.

XVII. MALPIGHIACEÆ

A small Order of trees and shrubs, chiefly American; a few genera in Africa and Asia, rare in Polynesia and Australia; represented in the N.W. Himalaya by only one species.—Named in honour of Marcello Malpighi, an Italian botanical author of the 17th century, one of the first to investigate vegetable anatomy.

HIPTAGE. From the Greek *hiptamai*, to fly, referring to the winged seeds.—Tropical Asia.

Hiptage Madablota, *Gærtn.*; *Fl. Br. Ind.* i. 418. A tall, climbing shrub. Leaves opposite, glabrous, thick, shortly stalked, ovate-lanceolate, 4–6 in., entire; stipules none. Flowers $\frac{3}{4}$ in. across, fragrant, showy, in axillary, pubescent racemes forming a terminal, leafy panicle; stalks 2-bracteate near the middle. Calyx tomentose, 5-parted, a large, smooth, oblong, brown gland on the outer surface. Petals 5, free, reflexed, silky, clawed, unequal, much longer than the calyx, uppermost with a large yellow spot, the others white, margins wavy, fringed. Stamens 10, curved, united at the base, lowest one twice as long as the others, all anther-bearing. Ovary 3-lobed, 3-celled, one ovule in each cell; style long, curved, stigma terminal. Fruit of 1–3 globose, 3-winged nuts or samaras about $\frac{1}{3}$ in. diam.; wings unequal, narrowly oblong, up to 2 in.; a 4th much shorter wing usually present.

Sutlej valley, near Basantpur; April.—Throughout India, in ravines and moist places, ascending to 3000 ft.—China, Java.

XVIII. GERANIACEÆ

Annual or perennial herbs. Leaves opposite or alternate, simple or compound, stipulate except in *Impatiens*. Flowers often showy, 2-sexual, regular or irregular, axillary, solitary, in pairs, racemose or in umbel-like clusters. Sepals 5, free; in *Impatiens* 3, the lower one petal-like and spurred. Stamens 10 or 5, the alternate ones antherless in *Erodium*, filaments free or united at the base; anthers 2-celled, versatile, in *Impatiens* cohering round the pistil. Ovary free, 5-lobed or in *Impatiens* oblong; styles 5 or in *Impatiens* none, adnate to a central axis or partially united; stigmas terminal, linear or capitate, in *Impatiens* sessile and minutely 5-toothed; ovules in each cell solitary, several or numerous. Fruit capsular, breaking up when ripe into 5 distinct carpels or opening by 5 valves. Seeds few or numerous, attached to the central axis of the capsule.—An Order dispersed through nearly all temperate and subtropical regions; rare in Australia.

Flowers regular.
  Stamens 10, all anther-bearing.
    Leaves simple or pinnately lobed . . . . . . 1. *Geranium.*
    Leaves with 3 leaflets . . . . 3. *Oxalis.*
  Stamens 10, only 5 anther-bearing . . . . . . 2. *Erodium.*
Flowers irregular. Stamens 5 . . . . 4. *Impatiens.*

1. GERANIUM. From the Greek *geranos*, a crane, referring to the long-beaked fruit (Crane's Bill).—Chiefly cold and temperate regions in the N. Hemisphere.

Erect, diffuse or procumbent herbs; joints swollen. Leaves opposite, stalked, orbicular and palmately lobed or of triangular outline and divided to the base into 3 or 5 pinnatifid segments. Flowers 2-sexual, regular, in pairs on axillary stalks. Sepals 5, free, ending in a short pointed tip. Petals 5, free, clawed, alternate with 5 glands. Stamens 10, all anther-bearing, 5 longer alternate with 5 shorter; filaments flattened, united at the base. Receptacle prolonged upwards in a persistent, 5-grooved, tapering column. Ovary of 5 nearly distinct, 1-celled carpels, whorled round and adnate to the base of the column. Styles 5, adnate to the column; stigmas terminal, simple, linear, ultimately diverging. As the fruit develops, the column and styles elongate; when ripe the carpels and the lower part of the styles separate from the column, the styles coiling upwards with a jerk and ejecting the seeds; styles glabrous on the inner surface. After the seeds have been scattered, the persistent calyx, the column, and the curled up styles carrying the empty carpels, somewhat resemble a miniature chandelier. Seeds, one in each carpel, small, smooth.

See Kerner's *Nat. Hist. of Plants*, ii. 836, for a description of the dispersal of the seeds.

Flowers $1\frac{1}{2}$–2 in. diam., blue-purple . . . . . . 1. *G. Wallichianum.*
Flowers $\frac{3}{4}$ in. diam. or less.
  Petals purple or pink.
    Leaves orbicular, palmately lobed; segments toothed.
      Leaves hairy or pubescent.
        Leaf-segments equal . . . . . . 2. *G. nepalense.*
        Leaf-segments very unequal . . . . . 3. *G. divaricatum.*
      Leaves glabrous, shining . . . . . . 5. *G. lucidum.*
    Leaves triangular, 3–5-parted; segments pinnately divided . . . . 4. *G. Robertianum.*
  Petals pink with dark purple base . . . . . 6. *G. ocellatum.*

1. **Geranium Wallichianum,** *Sweet*; *Fl. Br. Ind.* i. 430. Perennial, hairy; rootstock thick. Stems robust, 1–4 ft., erect. Leaves orbicular, 2–5 in. across, palmately 3–5-lobed; segments wedge-shaped, pointed, acutely and irregularly toothed; stipules oblong-ovate, ½–1 in. Flowers blue-purple, 1½–2 in. diam. Sepals abruptly long-pointed. Petals slightly notched, claw hairy.

Simla, common; July–September.—Temperate Himalaya, 7000–11,000 ft.

Resembles the British *G. pratense* which occurs on the Chor and higher ranges; distinguished from it by the 7–9-lobed leaves and linear-lanceolate stipules.

2. **Geranium nepalense,** *Sweet*; *Fl. Br. Ind.* i. 430. Perennial, pubescent or softly hairy. Stems prostrate, diffuse, 6–18 in., branches rooting at the joints. Leaves orbicular, 1½–3 in. across,

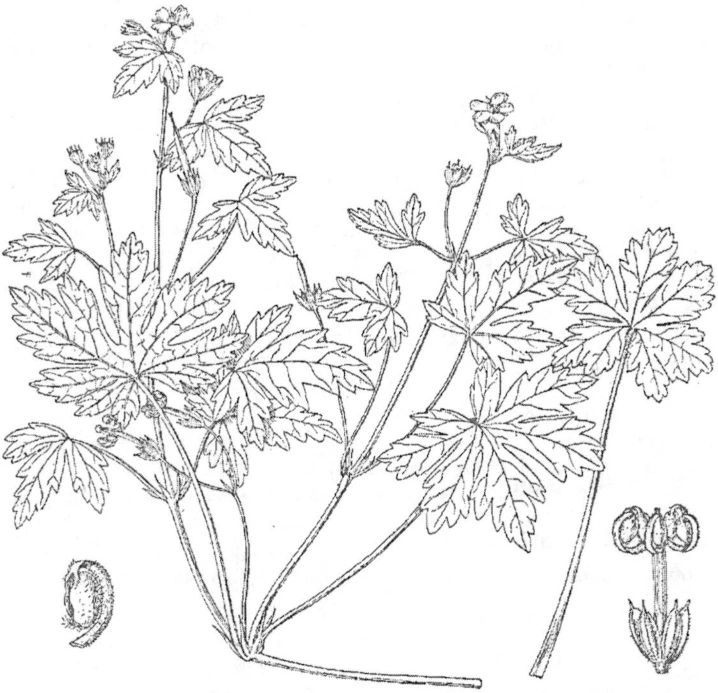

FIG. 22. GERANIUM NEPALENSE.

palmately 3–5-lobed; segments equal or nearly so, irregularly lobed and toothed; stipules narrowly lanceolate, ½ in. Flowers pale purple, ⅓–⅔ in. diam. Sepals acute, shortly pointed. Petals slightly notched. (Fig. 22.)

Simla, common; May–September.—Temperate Himalaya, 5000–9000 ft.—China, Japan.

3. **Geranium divaricatum,** *Ehrh. Beitr.* vii. 164, *included under G. molle, Linn.*; *Fl. Br. Ind.* i. 432. Annual, softly hairy. Stems nearly prostrate, 6–24 in., diffusely branched. Leaves orbicular, about 2 in. across, palmately 3–5-lobed; segments unequal, central one much the longest, teeth obtuse; stipules very narrow, ¼ in., acute. Flowers pale purple, pink-veined, ⅓ in. diam. Sepals acute, minutely pointed. Petals notched. Capsules deflexed, diverging.

Simla, on rocks, not common; June–September.—W. Himalaya, 5000–8000 ft.

4. **Geranium Robertianum,** *Linn.*; *Fl. Br. Ind.* i. 432. Annual or biennial, softly hairy, usually glandular and strongly scented, often turning red. Stems erect, 12–24 in. Leaves triangular, 1–3 in. broad, divided to the base in 3–5 pinnately lobed segments, central segment longest, lobes acute; stipules lanceolate, ¼ in. Flowers red-pink, streaked with white, ½ in. diam. Sepals acute, long-awned. Petals entire.

Narkunda, in shady valleys; August.—W. Himalaya, 6000–8000 ft.—W. Asia, Europe, including Britain (Herb Robert).

5. **Geranium lucidum,** *Linn.*; *Fl. Br. Ind.* i. 433. Annual, nearly glabrous, often turning bright red. Stems slender, erect or diffuse, 6–12 in. Leaves shining, orbicular, 1–2 in. across, palmately 5–7-lobed; segments bluntly toothed; stipules acute, ⅕ in. Flowers pink, hardly ⅓ in. diam. Calyx 5-angled, sepals erect, acute, minutely pointed, tips converging. Petals entire.

Simla, on old walls, common; April, May.—W. Himalaya, 6000–9000 ft.—N. Asia, N. Africa, Europe, including Britain (Crane's Bill).

6. **Geranium ocellatum,** *Camb.*; *Fl. Br. Ind.* i. 433. Annual, hoary pubescent. Stems prostrate or diffuse, 12–18 in. Leaves orbicular, ½–2 in. across, palmately 5–7-lobed; segments 3-lobed, toothed. Petals pink, with dark purple base, forming an almost black spot in the centre of the flower. Sepals acute, minutely awned. Petals broad, entire.

Simla, Annandale Wad; March–May.—Hilly districts in N. India, 1000–6000 ft.

2. **ERODIUM.** From the Greek *erodios*, a heron, referring to the long-beaked fruit.—N. Temperate regions of the Old World; South Africa, Australia.

Erodium cicutarium, *L'Hérit.*; *Fl. Br. Ind.* i. 434. Annual, hairy, more or less viscidly glandular. Stems tufted, branches prostrate, from a few inches to 2 ft. long; joints swollen. Leaves opposite, mostly radical, 1½–4 in., pinnately divided, pinnules 14–22, pinnatifid; segments acute, often lobed; stipules scarious, broadly lanceolate, acute. Flowers small, purple, often spotted, in stalked, axillary, erect, 2–10-flowered umbels. Sepals 5, acute, minutely awned. Petals 5, unequal, entire, alternate, with 5 glands. Stamens as in *Geranium* except that the 5 shorter ones are without anthers. Receptacle, ovary, styles, seeds and manner of dehiscence as in *Geranium*, except that the ripe carpels are pitted at the top and the styles silky on the inner surface.

Simla, not common; April–June.—W. India, ascending to 8000 ft.—N. Asia, N. Africa, Europe, including Britain.

3. OXALIS. From the Greek *oxus*, sharp, acid, referring to the taste of the leaves.—Most temperate and warm regions.

Annual or perennial herbs. Leaves with 3 sessile leaflets, alternate or all radical, long-stalked; stipules small, adnate to the stalks. Flowers regular, 2-sexual, solitary on radical stalks or in small umbels. Sepals 5, free. Petals 5, twisted in bud, free, without glands. Stamens 10, 5 long, 5 shorter, all anther-bearing, filaments united at the base. Ovary 5-lobed, 5-celled; styles 5, more or less united, stigmas capitate. Capsule ovoid or cylindric, 5-angled, opening in 5 valves. Seeds small, 2, 3 or several in each cell.

The flowers vary in the number and length of the stamens and styles. See Darwin's *Forms of Flowers*, chapter iv.

Flowers yellow, in small umbels. Leaves alternate . . 1. *O. corniculata.*
Flowers white or pale pink, solitary. Leaves all radical . 2. *O. Acetosella.*

1. **Oxalis corniculata,** *Linn.*; *Fl. Br. Ind.* i. 436. Annual or perennial, hairy. Stems procumbent, 6–18 in., much branched, rooting at the joints. Leaves alternate, $\frac{1}{2}$–1 in. across; leaflets pale green, obcordate. Flowers in small, long-stalked umbels. Petals yellow, twice as long as the calyx. Capsule tomentose, cylindric, $\frac{1}{2}$–1 in., tipped with the persistent styles. Seeds several in each cell.

Simla, roadsides, common; April–November.—Throughout India, ascending to 8000 ft.—Nearly all regions; Britain.

2. **Oxalis Acetosella,** *Linn.*; *Fl. Br. Ind.* i. 436. Perennial, pubescent; rootstock scaly. Stem none. Leaves all radical, 1–2 in. across; leaflets obovate, faintly notched, lower surface often purple. Flowers solitary on long, radical stalks, 2-bracteate about the middle. Petals white or pale pink, veined with purple, 3–4 times as long as the calyx. Capsule glabrous, ovoid, $\frac{1}{3}$ in. Seeds 2 or 3 in each cell.

Baghi forest, in damp, shady places; June, July.—Temperate Himalaya, 8000–12,000 ft.—N. temperate regions (Britain, Wood Sorrel).

The seeds are expelled through the fissures of the opening capsule by a curious action dependent on a difference of tension between the outer and the inner seed-coats. See Kerner's *Nat. Hist. of Plants*, ii. 835.

The leaves of cultivated plants are sometimes worn as Shamrock but wild plants are hardly above ground on March 17.

4. IMPATIENS. Name refers to the sudden bursting of the ripe capsule.—Chiefly mountainous regions in tropical Asia and Africa; a few in Europe and N. America.

Erect, succulent, usually glabrous herbs; stems branching, usually hollow, joints more or less swollen. Leaves simple, alternate or opposite, sometimes whorled, sharply toothed or crenate, often glandular on the margins and at the base of the stalk; stipules none. Flowers borne on slender stalks, irregular, in racemes or umbel-like clusters, sometimes solitary on axillary stalks. Sepals 3 (or 5); the 2 upper small, flat, usually green; the lower (or 3 combined) forming the lip, much larger, petal-like, more or less tubular, produced at the base in a hollow spur. Petals 3 (or 5); the upper one, the standard, broad and somewhat concave, often crested; the 2 lower (each of 2 combined) forming the wings, smaller, deeply 2-lobed. Glands none. Stamens 5; filaments short, thick, flattened; anthers cohering round the pistil. Ovary oblong, 5-celled; stigma sessile, 5-toothed when mature; ovules numerous in each cell. Capsule ovoid, club-shaped, linear or narrowly oblong, often irregularly swollen, bursting asunder when ripe by 5 valves which separate from the seed-bearing axis and rolling up with a jerk scatter the numerous small seeds.

* Flowers pink, purple or crimson

Flowers solitary on axillary stalks. Capsule tomentose	1. *I. Balsamina.*
Flowers in racemes or umbel-like clusters, often paniculate. Capsule glabrous.	
Leaves stalked.	
Flowers 1–1½ in. long, excluding the spur.	
Capsule club-shaped, thick at the tip, gradually narrowed to the base	2. *I. Roylei.*
Capsule linear.	
Stems 4–10 ft. Leaves opposite or whorled, rarely alternate	4. *I. gigantea.*
Stems 1–3 ft. Leaves alternate . .	7. *I. amphorata.*
Flowers ½–¾ in. long, excluding the spur . .	3. *I. Thomsoni.*
Leaves sessile, stem-clasping	5. *I. amplexicaulis.*

* * Flowers yellow

Flowers 1¼–1½ in. long, excluding the spur. Lip abruptly contracted into a strongly curved spur .	6. *I. scabrida.*
Flowers not more than 1 in. long, including the spur.	
Lip gradually narrowed into a nearly straight spur.	
Flowers ½ in. long	8. *I. racemosa.*
Flowers 1 in. long	9. *I. laxiflora.*

* * * Flowers white, lip sometimes spotted

Flowers ½ in. long, including the spur. Spur ¼ in. long	10. *I. micranthemum.*
Flowers ¼ in. long. Spur minute or none . . .	11. *I. brachycentra.*

1. Impatiens Balsamina, *Linn.*; *Fl. Br. Ind.* i. 453. Pubescent. Stems 6–18 in. Leaves alternate, sessile or shortly stalked, narrowly lanceolate, 1½–2½ in., tapering to the base, sharply toothed. Flowers pink or nearly white, ½ in. long excluding the spur, solitary on axillary, usually clustered stalks. Standard tipped with a small, green point. Spur ½ in. long, slender, cylindric, curved. Capsule tomentose, ovoid, ⅓–½ in. long, acute.

Valleys below Simla; August, September.—Throughout India, ascending to 5000 ft.—China, Malaya.
Widely cultivated; common on the borders of rice fields.

2. **Impatiens Roylei,** *Walp.*; *Fl. Br. Ind.* i. 468. Glabrous. Stems 3–6 ft. Leaves opposite or whorled, rarely alternate, stalked, lanceolate, 2½–6 in., usually sharply and regularly toothed, long-pointed, teeth gland-tipped. Flowers pale pink, 1¼–1½ in. long excluding the spur, in terminal racemes or umbel-like clusters, sometimes paniculate. Lip spotted with yellow, broadly bell-shaped, abruptly contracted into a cylindric, curved, rather thick, yellow spur hardly ¼ in. long. Capsule club-shaped, about 1 × ¼ in., thickest near the tip, narrowed to the base.

Mahasu, common; July–September.—Temperate Himalaya, 7000–9000 t.

*3. **Impatiens Thomsoni,** *Hook. f.*; *Fl. Br. Ind.* i. 469. Glabrous. Stems 1–4 ft. Leaves opposite or whorled, stalked, lanceolate, 2–6 in., sharply toothed or crenate, long-pointed; a small bristle-like gland between the teeth or crenatures. Flowers pale pink, ½–¾ in. long excluding the spur, in terminal, umbel-like clusters, sometimes paniculate. Lip spotted with brown or yellow, funnel-shaped, gradually narrowed into a slender, tapering spur nearly ½ in. long. Capsule club-shaped, about ¾ × ⅓ in., irregularly swollen, tapering to the base.

Temperate Himalaya, 6000–12,000 ft.; July–September.

4. **Impatiens gigantea,** *Edgew.*; *Fl. Br. Ind.* i. 469, *under I. sulcata.* Glabrous. Stems 4–10 ft. Leaves usually opposite or whorled, stalked, ovate-lanceolate, 3–7 in., crenate, long-pointed; a small bristle-like gland on the upper side of each crenature. Flowers pink purple or dark crimson, 1–1¼ in. long excluding the spur, in terminal, umbel-like, often paniculate clusters. Lip darker spotted, broadly funnel-shaped, abruptly contracted into a nearly cylindric, curved spur about ⅓ in. long. Standard keeled at the back. Wings orange-streaked. Capsule linear, 1¼ in. long, terete or nearly so, acute.

Simla, Mahasu, common; July–September.—Temperate Himalaya, 7000–12,000 ft.

5. **Impatiens amplexicaulis,** *Edgew.*; *Fl. Br. Ind.* i. 469. Glabrous. Stems 1–3 ft. Leaves sessile, stem-clasping, lower ones opposite, upper alternate, oblong or oblong-lanceolate, 3–7 in., long-pointed, crenate; crenatures gland-tipped. Flowers purple, ¾–1 in. long excluding the spur, in axillary, umbel-like clusters or

racemes. Lip funnel-shaped, abruptly narrowed into a cylindric, usually nearly straight spur about $\frac{1}{3}$ in. long. Capsule oblong, $\frac{3}{4}$–1 in., terete, acute.

Simla; July–September.—W. Himalaya, 5000–12,000 ft.

6. **Impatiens scabrida,** *DC.*; *Fl. Br. Ind.* i. 472. Pubescent. Stems 2–4 ft. Leaves alternate, sessile or nearly so, ovate or lanceolate, 2–6 in., sharply toothed, teeth gland-tipped. Flowers yellow, spotted with brown, $1\frac{1}{4}$–$1\frac{1}{2}$ in. long excluding the spur,

FIG. 23. IMPATIENS SCABRIDA.

single on axillary, usually paired stalks. Lip broadly funnel-shaped, abruptly contracted into a slender, cylindric, incurved spur $\frac{1}{2}$ in. long. Standard with a green, horn-like outgrowth on the back, especially conspicuous in bud. Capsule linear, $1\frac{1}{2}$–2 in., terete, acute. (Fig. 23.)

Simla, more common at Mahasu; July–September.—Simla to Bhotan, 7000–10,000 ft.

7. **Impatiens amphorata,** *Edgew.*; *Fl. Br. Ind.* i. 475. Glabrous. Stems 1–3 ft. Leaves usually alternate, stalked, lanceolate, 3–6 in., crenate; a small bristle-like gland on the upper side

of each crenature. Flowers purple, 1–1¼ in. long excluding the spur, in racemes or umbel-like clusters, often paniculate. Lip darker spotted, broadly funnel-shaped, narrowed into a slender, cylindric, incurved spur ⅓ in. long. Standard keeled at the back, tip crested. Wings usually white on the lower half. Capsule linear, 1–1¼ in., terete, acute.

Simla, in woods, common; September, October.—W. Himalaya, 5000–8000 ft.

8. **Impatiens racemosa,** *DC.*; *Fl. Br. Ind.* i. 479. Glabrous. Stems 2–3 ft. Leaves alternate, stalked, lanceolate or oblong-lanceolate, 3–9 in., crenate; crenatures gland-tipped. Flowers yellow, ½ in. long, including the spur, in racemes or umbel-like clusters. Lip boat-shaped, gradually narrowed into a slender, nearly straight, tapering spur ⅓ in. long. Wings darker spotted, produced in a long, linear tail descending into the spur. Capsule linear, ½–¾ in., terete, acute.

Simla, Fagu, Narkunda, in shady, damp ravines; August, September.—Simla to Sikkim, 5000–8000 ft.

9. **Impatiens laxiflora,** *Edgew.*; *Fl. Br. Ind.* i. 479. Glabrous. Stems 2–4 ft. Leaves alternate, stalked, lanceolate or ovate-lanceolate, 3–5 in., long-pointed, crenate; a small, bristle-like gland in the angle between the crenatures. Flowers yellow, 1 in. long including the spur, in axillary racemes or umbel-like clusters. Lip boat-shaped, gradually narrowed into a slender, nearly straight, tapering spur ½–¾ in. long. Capsule linear, terete, ¾ in.

Simla, Huttoo; August, September.—Simla to Sikkim, 5000–10,000 ft.

10. **Impatiens micranthemum,** *Edgew.*; *Fl. Br. Ind.* i. 481. Glabrous. Stems 1–4 ft. Leaves usually alternate, stalked, ovate-lanceolate, 3–4 in., crenate; crenatures gland-tipped. Flowers white, the lip spotted with pink and yellow, ½ in. long including the spur, in racemes or umbel-like clusters usually in the axils of the upper leaves. Lip boat-shaped, gradually narrowed into a slender, straight, tapering spur ¼ in. long. Capsule narrowly oblong, ½ in., nearly terete, acute.

Huttoo; July, August.—W. Himalaya, 6000–10,000 ft.

*11. **Impatiens brachycentra,** *Kar. & Kir.*; *Fl. Br. Ind.* i. 481. Glabrous. Stems ½–2 ft. Leaves alternate, stalked, ovate-lanceolate, 2–5 in., crenate; the crenatures gland-tipped. Flowers white, ¼ in. long including the spur, in racemes or umbel-like clusters usually in the axils of the upper leaves. Lip boat-shaped; spur minute or none. Capsule narrowly oblong, ½ in., nearly terete, acute.

Mussoorie to Kashmir, 8000–12,000 ft.; August, September.

XIX. RUTACEÆ

Herbs, shrubs or small trees, often spinous, all parts more or less charged with aromatic glands. Leaves alternate, pinnate or simple; stipules none. Flowers regular, usually 2-sexual, in panicles or racemes. Calyx small, 4- or 5-lobed. Petals 4 or 5, none in *Zanthoxylum*, free, usually imbricate. Stamens 5–10, numerous in *Ægle*, free, anthers 2-celled. Disk cup-shaped or a fleshy, cushion-like ring or inconspicuous. Ovary ovoid, 2–5-celled, many-celled in *Ægle*; ovules 1–8, many in *Ægle*, in each cell. Styles usually united, stigmas terminal. Fruit a capsule, berry or drupe, or the carpels separating when ripe. Seeds small.—A large Order containing among other useful plants the Orange, Lime, Citron, Shaddock and Pummeloe; the name is taken from the typical genus *Ruta*, Rue.

Herbs.
  Flowers ¼ in. long. Leaflets ¼–¾ in., entire . . 1. *Bœnninghausenia.*
  Flowers 1–1½ in. long. Leaflets 2–4 in., toothed . 2. *Dictamnus.*
Shrubs or small trees.
  Leaves oblong-lanceolate . . . . . . 4. *Skimmia.*
  Leaves pinnate. Leaflets 3–21.
    Leaf-stalks winged.
      Flowers yellow. Petals none . . . . 3. *Zanthoxylum.*
      Flowers white. Petals 4 . . . . . 6. *Limonia.*
    Leaf-stalks not winged.
      Leaflets 11–21. Stamens 10 . . . 5. *Murraya.*
      Leaflets 3–5. Stamens numerous . . 7. *Ægle.*

1. BŒNNINGHAUSENIA. In honour of Freiherr von Bœnninghausen, a German botanist.—Mountains of N. India to China and Japan. Only the following species.

Bœnninghausenia albiflora, *Reichenb.*; *Fl. Br. Ind.* i. 486. A perennial, nearly glabrous herb. Stems erect, 1–2 ft., branching. Leaves gland-dotted, 2-pinnate; leaflets ovate, ¼–¾ in., entire. Flowers 2-sexual, white, about ¼ in. long, in a terminal, leafy panicle. Calyx short, 4-lobed, persistent. Petals 4, much longer than the calyx, oblong, soon falling off. Stamens 6–8, unequal, inserted outside the base of a cup-shaped disk. Ovary 3–5-celled, stalked, lobed; styles 3–5, united, stigmas minute; ovules 6–8 in each cell. When ripe the carpels separate as small, several-seeded, distinct fruits. (Fig. 24.)

Simla, common in woods; July–September.—Temperate Himalaya, 4000–8000 ft.—Japan.

The crushed leaves have a strong, disagreeable smell. The plant is known among the hillmen as *pissu mar*, the flea killer.

2. DICTAMNUS. The classical name of *D. albus.*—S. Europe to China.

***Dictamnus albus,** *Linn.*; *Fl. Br. Ind.* i. 487. A perennial, heavy-scented herb, covered with small, raised glands. Stems robust, erect, 12–24 in., branched. Leaves gland-dotted, odd-pinnate, 6–12 in.; leaflets 9–15, opposite, sessile, ovate-lanceolate, 2–4 in., toothed. Flowers 2-sexual, showy, 1–1½ in. long, pink or white, in an erect, terminal raceme 6–12 in. long. Sepals 5,

FIG. 24. BŒNNINGHAUSENIA ALBIFLORA.

narrowly lanceolate, persistent. Petals 5, much longer than the sepals, lanceolate, nearly equal, spreading. Stamens 10, as long as the petals, hairy, glandular, bristle-tipped. Ovary nearly sessile, ovoid, rough with glandular hairs, 5-celled; ovules 3 or 4 in each cell; style long, simple. When ripe the carpels separate as 2–3-seeded, tomentose, beaked, distinct fruits ½ in. long. Seeds black, shining.

W. Himalaya, 6000–8000 ft.—Asia, S. Europe.
Frequently cultivated in gardens in England.

3. ZANTHOXYLUM. From the Greek *xanthos*, yellow, and *xylon*, wood.—Most tropical and warm regions.

Zanthoxylum alatum, *Roxb.*; *Fl. Br. Ind.* i. 493. A shrub or small tree, nearly glabrous; stem and branches armed with long, sharp prickles, those on young stems conical, thick, rising from a corky base. Leaves odd-pinnate, 2–6 in., stalk winged, 2 stipular spines at the base; leaflets 5–9, opposite, sessile, lanceolate, 2–4 in., gland-dotted, entire or with a few small teeth; midrib often prickly. Flowers small, yellow, 1- or 2-sexual, crowded in pubescent, short, lateral panicles. Calyx 6–8-lobed. Petals none. Stamens 6–8 (in the female flowers none), much longer than the calyx. Carpels 1–3, rarely 4 or 5 (rudimentary in the male flowers), distinct; styles lateral, free, stigma capitate; ovules 2 in each carpel. Fruit of 1–3 small, pale red, globose drupes ultimately splitting in 2 valves. Seed solitary, black, shining.

Simla; April–June.—Himalaya, below 5000 ft.
Walking sticks and clubs are made from the stems; the fragrant twigs are used as tooth brushes.

4. SKIMMIA. An adaptation of the Japanese name.—Temperate Himalaya, 6000–10,000 ft., Afghanistan, China, Japan.

Skimmia Laureola, *Sieb. & Zucc.*; *Fl. Br. Ind.* i. 499. A glabrous shrub, 3–8 ft. Leaves gland-dotted, oblong-lanceolate, 3–6 in.,

FIG. 25. SKIMMIA LAUREOLA.

entire, crowded near the end of branches. Flowers about $\frac{1}{2}$ in. diam., yellow or white, 1- or 2-sexual, in compact, erect, terminal panicles $1\frac{1}{2}$–2 in. long. Calyx 5-lobed, persistent. Petals oblong, much longer than the calyx. Stamens 5 (none in the female flowers), filaments as long as the petals. Ovary ovoid (rudimentary in the male flowers), 3-celled, ovule 1 in each cell; style divided at the top in 3 short, stigmatic branches. Drupe ovoid, red, $\frac{1}{2}$–$\frac{3}{4}$ in. long, containing 2, sometimes 1 or 3 seeds. (Fig. 25.)

Simla, Mahasu, common; April, May, often flowering again in the autumn. —Temperate Himalaya, 6000–10,000 ft.

The leaves have a strong orange-like smell when crushed.

5. **MURRAYA.** In honour of J. A. Murray, a botanical author of the seventeenth century, born at Stockholm.—Tropical Asia.

Murraya Kœnigii, *Spreng.*; *Fl. Br. Ind.* i. 503. A small, pubescent tree. Leaves gland-dotted, odd-pinnate, 6–12 in., often crowded towards the end of branches, stalk not winged; leaflets 11–21, alternate, shortly stalked, lanceolate, 1–2 in., entire or with a few small teeth near the tip. Flowers white, $\frac{1}{3}$ in. long, 2-sexual, in terminal panicles. Calyx 5-parted, persistent. Petals 5, nearly erect, much longer than the calyx, dotted with green glands. Stamens 10, free, 5 long, 5 shorter. Ovary ovoid, 2-celled, sessile on a fleshy disk; ovules 1 or 2 in each cell; style terminal, short, stigma capitate. Berry ovoid, $\frac{1}{3}$ in. diam., black, wrinkled, seeds 1 or 2.

Sutlej valley; May, June.—Throughout India, ascending to 5000 ft.

Often cultivated; the aromatic leaves are used to flavour curries.

6. **LIMONIA.** From *Limuna*, the Persian name of the citron. —Tropical Asia.

Limonia acidissima, *Linn.*; *Fl. Br. Ind.* i. 507. A glabrous shrub or small tree, armed with long, straight spines. Leaves gland-dotted, odd-pinnate, 1–4 in., stalk broadly winged; leaflets 5–9, opposite, sessile, ovate, $\frac{3}{4}$–$1\frac{1}{2}$ in., crenate or sharply toothed. Flowers 2-sexual, white, $\frac{1}{3}$ in. diam., in short, axillary, often leafy racemes. Calyx 4-lobed, persistent. Petals 4, gland-dotted, much longer than the calyx. Stamens 8, nearly equal, shorter than the petals. Ovary 4-celled, sessile on a ring-shaped disk; ovule 1 in each cell; style terminal, short, stigma capitate. Berry globose, $\frac{1}{3}$ in. diam., acid, yellow, turning to dark purple, smooth, containing 2–4 seeds.

Valleys below Simla; April, May.—Hilly districts throughout India, ascending to 4000 ft.

The hard, yellow wood is used for the axles of oil-presses, rice-pounders, etc.

7. **ÆGLE.** Classical name of one of the Hesperides; derived from the Greek *aigle*, splendour.—Tropical Asia and Africa.

Ægle Marmelos, *Correa*; *Fl. Br. Ind.* i. 516. A small tree, attaining 35 ft. in cultivation, armed with long, straight spines. Leaves glabrous, odd-pinnate, 2–3 in., stalks not winged; leaflets 3, rarely 5, ovate-lanceolate, 2–3 in., crenate, lateral ones opposite, nearly sessile, terminal long-stalked. Flowers 2-sexual, white, 1¼ in. diam., in short panicles. Calyx 5-lobed, soon falling off. Petals 5, thick, oblong, much longer than the calyx, gland-dotted, spreading. Stamens numerous, filaments short, anthers narrow, very long, erect. Ovary ovoid, 10–20-celled; style terminal, short, stigma capitate; ovules many in each cell. Berry grey or yellow, globose, 2–5 in. diam., rind woody, cells 8–16. Seeds numerous, flat, oblong, woolly, embedded in orange-coloured, sweet, aromatic pulp.

Valleys below Simla, often planted near villages; May.—Throughout India, ascending to 4000 ft.

The *Bēl* tree. Wood very hard, used for naves of cart-wheels, etc.; the pulp of the fruit is a valuable medicine.

XX. SIMARUBACEÆ

A SMALL Order of trees or shrubs growing in most tropical or subtropical regions. The characters are those of Rutaceæ except that the leaves are not gland-dotted.—*Simarouba* is the Carib name for a tree, *Simaruba amara*, whose bark is used medicinally by the natives of S. America.

PICRASMA. From the Greek *picrasmos*, bitterness, referring to the intensely bitter bark.—Tropical Asia, W. Indies, Brazil.

* **Picrasma quassioides**, *Benn.*; *Fl. Br. Ind.* i. 520. A tall shrub; all parts very bitter; inflorescence and young parts pubescent, otherwise glabrous. Leaves alternate, odd-pinnate, 10–18 in.; leaflets opposite, sessile, ovate-lanceolate, 2–4 in., toothed, long-pointed, the lowest pair much smaller than the others. Flowers regular, polygamous, small, green, in axillary panicles. Sepals 5, imbricate, persistent. Petals 5, much longer than the sepals, ovate, acute, valvate, enlarged and persistent in fruit. Stamens 5 (none in the female flowers), as long as the petals, hairy at the base; anthers 2-celled. Ovary free (none in the male flowers), sessile on a thick, cushion-like disk, lobed, 3–5-celled; ovule 1 in each cell; styles 3–5, free at the base and tips, cohering near the middle, stigmas terminal. Fruit of 1–5 nearly dry, black, globose, 1-seeded drupes about ¼ in. diam.

Outer Himalaya, from the Chenab to Nepal, between 3000 and 5000 ft.; April–June.—S. China.

XXI. MELIACEÆ

Trees; young parts and inflorescence pubescent, otherwise glabrous. Leaves alternate, pinnate or 2-pinnate; leaflets opposite or nearly so, shortly stalked, unequal-sided, not gland-dotted. Flowers numerous, small, regular, 2-sexual, usually sweet-scented, in panicles. Calyx 5- or 6-parted. Petals 5 or 6, much longer than the calyx, free, imbricate. Stamens 10 or 5, filaments united or free, anthers 2-celled. Ovary ovoid, 3–5-celled, sessile on a fleshy disk; style terminal, simple; stigma peltate, lobed; ovules 2 or several in each cell. Fruit a drupe or capsule; seeds 1, 5 or many.

Stamens 10–12, united in a tube. Ovules 1 or 2 in each cell . 1. *Melia.*
Stamens 5, free. Ovules 8–12 in each cell . . . . . . 2. *Cedrela.*

The Mahogany tree, *Swietenia Mahagoni*, a native of Central America, is often planted in India; there are several good specimens in the Saharunpore Botanical Gardens and a fine avenue at the Hoogly railway station.

1. MELIA. The Greek name of the Ash, *Fraxinus.*—Asia, Australia.

Trees, 20–40 ft. Leaves pinnate or 2-pinnate; leaflets nearly opposite, toothed, long-pointed. Flowers honey-scented, in large, axillary panicles. Calyx 5- or 6-parted. Petals 5–6, narrowly spathulate. Stamens 10–12, filaments united in a tube, toothed at the top, anthers sessile within and below the top of the tube. Ovary 3- or 5-celled, disk ring-shaped; stigma 3- or 5-lobed; ovules 2 in each cell. Drupe ovoid or globose; stone 1- or 5-celled; seeds one in each cell, small, smooth.

Leaves pinnate. Flowers white . . . . 1. *M. indica.*
Leaves 2-pinnate. Flowers lilac . . . . 2. *M. Azedarach.*

1. **Melia indica,** *Brandis*; *Fl. Br. Ind.* i. 544, *under M. Azadirachta,* Linn. Leaves odd-pinnate, 9–15 in., crowded near the end of branches; leaflets 9–13, lanceolate, 1–3 in. Flowers white, $\frac{1}{5}$ in. long. Calyx-segments 5, rounded. Petals 5. Anthers 10. Ovary usually 3-celled. Drupe ovoid-oblong, $\frac{1}{2}$–$\frac{3}{4}$ in., smooth, dark purple when ripe; stone 1-celled, 1-seeded.

° Simla, in valleys; March–May.—Throughout India, ascending to 5000 ft.
The *Neem* tree, though not truly wild in India, is often planted and furnishes excellent timber. The bitter bark and leaves are used medicinally and an oil is expressed from the fruit. Held sacred by the Hindus; wood used for making idols.

2. **Melia Azedarach,** *Linn.*; *Fl. Br. Ind.* i. 544. Leaves 2-pinnate, 9–18 in.; leaflets 3–7, ovate-lanceolate, $\frac{1}{2}$–$1\frac{1}{2}$ in. Flowers lilac, $\frac{1}{4}$–$\frac{1}{3}$ in. long. Calyx-segments 5 or 6, acute. Petals 5 or 6.

Staminal-tube purple, anthers 10 or 12. Ovary usually 5-celled. Drupe ovoid or globose, $\frac{1}{2}$–$\frac{3}{4}$ in. diam., yellow and wrinkled when ripe; stone 5-celled, 5-seeded.

Valleys below Simla, Sainj in the Giri valley; March-May.—Planted throughout India; wild in the N.W. Himalaya up to 5000 ft.—Persia, China.

The *Bukain* or Persian lilac, though not probably truly wild in India, is commonly planted in the plains. Wood used for furniture. The bitter bark and leaves are used in native medicine and an oil is extracted from the fruit.

FIG. 26. CEDRELA SERRATA.

2. CEDRELA. Diminutive of the Latin *cedrus*, a cedar, referring to the aromatic wood.—Tropical Asia, Australia and America.

Trees attaining 60–70 ft. Leaves pinnate; leaflets lanceolate or ovate-lanceolate, long-pointed, entire or toothed. Flowers white or pink, about $\frac{1}{4}$ in. long, in terminal, pendulous panicles. Calyx small, 5-parted. Petals 5, oblong, erect. Stamens 5, free, inserted on the disk; disk thick, orange-coloured, lobed. Ovary

5-celled; stigma 5-lobed; ovules 8–12 in each cell. Capsule opening from the top by 5 valves which ultimately fall away and leave the axis and cell-partitions as a pentagonal column of soft wood; seeds numerous, winged.

Leaflets entire. Panicles shorter than the leaves. Ovary hairy . 1. *C. Toona.*
Leaflets toothed. Panicles longer than the leaves. Ovary glabrous . . . . 2. *C. serrata.*

1. **Cedrela Toona,** *Roxb.*; *Fl. Br. Ind.* i. 568. Leaves even-pinnate, 12–18 in.; leaflets 10–20, nearly opposite or sometimes alternate, 2–5 in., entire. Panicles shorter than the leaves. Flowers honey-scented. Calyx-segments obtuse or acute, ciliate. Petals ciliate. Ovary hairy. Capsule oblong, $\frac{3}{4}$–1 in. long; seeds winged at both ends.

Sutlej valley; April, May.—Throughout India, ascending to 3000 ft.—Java, Australia.

The *Toon* tree; timber highly valued for furniture, door-panels, carving, etc.

2. **Cedrela serrata,** *Royle*; *Fl. Br. Ind.* i. 568, *under C. Toona.* Leaves usually odd-pinnate, 15–20 in.; leaflets 15–25, opposite, 3–6 in., toothed. Panicles longer than the leaves. Flowers usually pink, rather fœtid. Calyx-segments obtuse, glabrous. Petals glabrous. Ovary glabrous. Capsule ovoid, acute, $1\frac{1}{4}$–$1\frac{1}{2}$ in. long; seeds winged only at the upper end. (Fig. 26.)

Matiana, Sainj in the Giri valley; May, June.—W. Himalaya, 3000–8000 ft., in moist, shady places.

The Hill *Toon.* Native name *Tooni.*

XXII. AQUIFOLIACEÆ

A SMALL, widely spread Order, represented in India by a single genus.—*Aquifolium,* pointed leaf, was the classical name of the Holly.

ILEX. The classical name of the holm or evergreen oak. which often has prickly, holly-like leaves.—Widely spread in tropical and temperate regions, most numerous in S. America.

Evergreen shrubs or small trees. Leaves alternate, simple, shortly stalked, hard, shining, usually toothed; stipules small, soon falling off. Flowers small, white, 1- or 2-sexual, regular, crowded in axillary clusters. Calyx 4-parted, persistent. Petals 4, broadly ovate, obtuse, united at the base. Stamens 4, about as long as the petals and adhering to their base, anthers 2-celled. Ovary globose, sessile, 2–4-celled; stigma broad, sessile, lobed;

ovules solitary in each cell. Drupe globose, containing 2–4 one-seeded stones.

The British holly is *Ilex Aquifolium*.

Leaves 2–4 in., spinous-toothed or entire. Drupe usually of 2 stones . . . . 1. *I. dipyrena*.
Leaves 4–8 in.; teeth small, close, regular. Drupe of 4 stones 2. *I. odorata*.

1. **Ilex dipyrena**, *Wall.*; *Fl. Br. Ind.* i. 599. Leaves ovate or ovate-lanceolate, 2–4 in., spinous-toothed or entire. Flowers

FIG. 27. ILEX DIPYRENA.

usually 2-sexual. Ovary 2-, rarely 3- or 4-celled. Drupe scarlet, globose, $\frac{1}{3}$ in. diam., containing 2, rarely 3 or 4 stones. (Fig. 27.)

Simla, frequent; April–June.—Temperate Himalaya, 5000–8000 ft.

2. **Ilex odorata**, *Buch.-Ham.*; *Fl. Br. Ind.* i. 599. Leaves oblong-lanceolate, 4–8 in., long-pointed; teeth numerous, small, close-set, regular. Flowers 1-sexual. Ovary 4-celled. Drupe black, ovoid, $\frac{1}{4}$ in. long, usually containing 4 stones.

Valleys below Simla; April, May.—Temperate Himalaya, 3000–6000 ft.

XXIII. CELASTRACEÆ

SHRUBS or small trees. Leaves opposite or alternate, stalked, simple, not lobed or gland-dotted; stipules small, soon falling off. Flowers small, regular, usually 2-sexual, sometimes polygamous, in loose, forking cymes or panicles. Calyx 4- or 5-parted, persistent, lobes imbricate. Petals 4 or 5, free, spreading, longer than the sepals, imbricate, inserted on or beneath the margin of the disk. Stamens 4 or 5, inserted on or beneath the margin of the disk, alternate with the petals, filaments short, awl-shaped, anthers 2-celled. Disk broad, fleshy, occupying the bottom of the calyx, often lobed. Ovary sessile on the disk or partially immersed in it, usually lobed, 3–5-celled, ovules 2 in each cell; style short, erect, sometimes divided at the top in stigmatic arms. Fruit a capsule or a drupe. Seeds 1, rarely 2 in each cell, usually enveloped in a red, fleshy, outer coat (aril or arillode).—A small Order scattered over the tropical and temperate regions of the whole world.

Leaves opposite.
- Stamens inserted on the margin of the disk. Fruit a winged, angled or prickly capsule . . . . . 1. *Euonymus.*
- Stamens inserted under the edge of the disk. Fruit an ovoid drupe . . . . 4. *Elæodendron.*

Leaves alternate.
- A climbing shrub. Flowers in terminal panicles. Capsule globose . . . . 2. *Celastrus.*
- An erect shrub. Flowers in axillary cymes. Capsule 3-angled . . . . 3. *Gymnosporia.*

1. EUONYMUS. The classical name for plants of this genus; derived from the Greek *eu*, good, and *onoma*, a name.—Asia, N. America, Europe (Britain, Spindle tree, *E. europæus*).

Trees or shrubs, glabrous. Leaves opposite, shortly stalked, toothed. Flowers 2-sexual, in axillary cymes. Calyx flat, 4- or 5-parted, lobes obtuse. Petals 4 or 5, often toothed or fringed. Stamens 4 or 5, inserted with the petals on the margin of the nearly flat disk. Ovary immersed in the disk, 3–5-celled; style sometimes minute. Capsule 4- or 5-lobed, lobes angled or winged, globose and prickly in *E. echinatus*; cells 4 or 5, opening down the middle; seeds 1, rarely 2 in each cell, enveloped in a fleshy, red coat or arillode, and remaining exposed after the capsule has opened.

Leaves thick, leathery. Petals crenate, fringed or toothed.
- Erect trees. Capsule smooth.
  - Petals purple-veined, crenate. Capsule 4- or 5-angled, not winged . . . . 1. *E. tingens.*
  - Petals white, fringed. Capsule with 4 broad, rounded wings . . . . 4. *E. pendulus.*
- Climbing shrubs. Capsule prickly. Petals toothed . 3. *E. echinatus.*

Leaves thin, membranous. Petals entire.
Style minute. Capsule with 4 long, tapering wings 2. *E. lacerus.*
Style short, distinct. Capsule 4-lobed, not winged 5. *E. Hamiltonianus.*

1. **Euonymus tingens,** *Wall.*; *Fl. Br. Ind.* i. 610. A small tree. Leaves thick, leathery, ovate or ovate-lanceolate, 1–3 in.; upper surface dark green, wrinkled, lower pale; margins crenate or sharply toothed. Flowers $\frac{1}{2}$ in. diam., the parts in 5's, rarely in 4's. Petals orbicular, yellow-white, purple-veined, margins minutely crenate. Style as long as the stamens. Capsule obscurely 4- or 5- angled, not winged. (Fig. 28.)

FIG. 28. EUONYMUS TINGENS.

Simla, common; May.—W. Himalaya, 6000–10,000 ft.

2. **Euonymus lacerus,** *Buch.-Ham. in D. Don, Prodr.* 191; *Fl. Br. Ind.* i. 611, *under E. fimbriatus.* A shrub or small tree. Leaves thin, membranous, ovate or orbicular, 2–3 in.; teeth acute, small and regular or deep and somewhat irregular. Flowers $\frac{1}{4}$ in. diam., the parts in 4's. Petals broadly ovate, white, entire. Stamens very short. Style minute. Capsule with 4 long, tapering wings.

Narkunda, Shali; May, June.—Temperate Himalaya, 8000–10,000 ft.

* 3. **Euonymus echinatus,** *Wall.*; *Fl. Br. Ind.* i. 611. A large, climbing shrub; stems attached to trees or rocks by tufts of aerial rootlets. Leaves leathery, ovate-lanceolate, 2–3 in.; upper surface dark green, lower paler; margins crenate or bluntly toothed. Flowers $\frac{1}{4}$ in. diam., the parts in 4's. Petals orbicular, white,

minutely toothed. Style distinct. Capsule prickly, globose, $\frac{1}{3}$ in. diam.

Himalaya, 7000–12,000 ft.; March, April.—China, Luchu archipelago.

4. **Euonymus pendulus,** *Wall.*; *Fl. Br. Ind.* i. 612. A small tree; branches drooping. Leaves thick, leathery, oblong-lanceolate, $2\frac{1}{2}$–5 in.; upper surface dark green, shining, lower pale; margins sharply toothed. Flowers $\frac{1}{3}$ in. diam., the parts in 4's, rarely in 5's. Petals ovate-oblong, white, minutely fringed. Style short but distinct. Capsule with 4 broad, rounded wings.

Simla, the Glen, Shali; May, June.—Temperate Himalaya, 3000–8000 ft.

5. **Euonymus Hamiltonianus,** *Wall.*; *Fl. Br. Ind.* i. 612. A shrub or small tree. Leaves thin, membranous, ovate or oblong-lanceolate, $2\frac{1}{2}$–4 in., minutely toothed. Flowers $\frac{1}{3}$ in. diam., the parts in 4's. Petals oblong-lanceolate, green-white, entire. Style short but distinct. Capsule deeply 4-lobed, not winged.

Narkunda; June.—W. Himalaya, 4000–9000 ft.

2. **CELASTRUS.** The Greek name of the Privet, *Ligustrum vulgare*.—Tropical Asia, Australia, N. America.

* **Celastrus paniculata,** *Willd.*; *Fl. Br. Ind.* i. 617. A climbing shrub; branches covered with small, white, wart-like excrescences. Leaves alternate, glabrous, membranous, ovate or orbicular, $2\frac{1}{2}$–$4\frac{1}{2} \times 2$–$3\frac{1}{2}$ in., toothed, abruptly pointed. Flowers polygamous, pale yellow-green, in terminal, pendulous panicles. Calyx 5-parted, lobes rounded. Petals 5, inserted under the disk. Stamens 5, inserted on the margin of the disk. Ovary 3-lobed, sessile on the concave disk, 3-celled; ovules 2 in each cell; style acute. Capsule globose, $\frac{1}{4}$ in. diam., cells 3, opening down the middle; seeds 3 or 6, each enveloped in a red, fleshy coat or aril and remaining exposed after the capsule has opened.

Throughout India, ascending to 4000 ft.; April–June.—Malay archipelago.

3. **GYMNOSPORIA.** From the Greek *gymnos*, naked, and *spora*, a seed.—Many warm regions of the Old World.—This genus is merged in *Celastrus* in *Benth. & Hook. f. Gen. Plant.* i. 997.

Gymnosporia Royleana, *Wall.*; *Fl. Br. Ind.* i. 620. A stiff, erect, much-branched, spinous shrub, 8–12 ft. Leaves alternate, glabrous, ovate or orbicular, $\frac{3}{4}$–$1\frac{1}{2}$ in., crenate or sharply toothed. Flowers numerous, 2-sexual, white, in short, axillary cymes. Calyx 5-parted, lobes obtuse, ciliate. Petals 5, oblong. Stamens 5, inserted under the margins of the 5-lobed disk. Ovary half immersed in the disk, 3-lobed, 3-celled; style 3-lobed at the top.

Capsule 3-angled, $\frac{1}{4}$ in. diam., cells 3, opening down the middle. Seeds 3, half enveloped in a red, fleshy, outer coat or aril.

Sutlej valley; March–October.—N.W. India, ascending to 4000 ft., usually on hot, dry, rugged slopes.

4. **ELÆODENDRON.** From the Greek *elaia*, an olive, and *dendron*, a tree, referring to the shape of the fruit and to its oily seeds.—S. Africa, Asia, America, Australia.

* **Elæodendron glaucum,** *Pers.*; *Fl. Br. Ind.* i. 623. A tree. Leaves opposite, glabrous, hard, leathery, very variable in shape and size, ovate, orbicular or oblong, 2–4 × 1–2$\frac{1}{2}$ in., crenate, sharply toothed or nearly entire; stalks $\frac{1}{2}$–1 in. Flowers yellow-brown, usually 2-sexual, in large, axillary cymes. Calyx 5-parted, lobes obtuse. Petals 5, oblong. Stamens 5, inserted under the margin of the disk, filaments recurved. Ovary conical, 3-lobed, half immersed in the disk, 3-celled; style entire. Drupe ovoid, $\frac{1}{2}$ in. long, yellow-green; stone 1- or 2-celled, cells 1-seeded.

Throughout India, ascending to 6000 ft.; February–June.

XXIV. RHAMNACEÆ

Shrubs or small trees, usually erect, often spinous, tendril-bearing only in *Helinus*. Leaves simple, alternate or nearly opposite, entire or toothed, with 3–5 prominent, basal nerves or feather-veined; stipules small, soon falling off, spinous and persistent in *Zizyphus*. Flowers very small, yellow-green, regular, usually 2-sexual, in axillary clusters, cymes or panicles, rarely solitary, umbellate in *Helinus*. Calyx-tube cup-shaped, persistent, free or in *Helinus* adherent to the ovary; limb 4- or 5-lobed, segments valvate, erect or spreading, triangular, acute, keeled on the inner surface, usually falling off after flowering. Petals 4 or 5, rarely none, inserted on the mouth of the calyx-tube or on the margin of the disk, smaller than the calyx-lobes, hood-like or the margins infolded. Stamens 4 or 5, inserted with and opposite to the petals, more or less enclosed by them at least at first. Disk usually thick; in *Rhamnus* thin, lining or filling up the calyx-tube; in *Helinus* ring-shaped and lying on the top of the ovary. Ovary sessile, superior, except in *Helinus*, sometimes more or less immersed in the disk, 2–4-celled; style erect, simple, usually short, stigma terminal, 3-branched or 3-lobed. Fruit drupaceous, containing 1–4 one-seeded stones, the base, except in *Helinus*, enclosed in the persistent calyx-tube.—An Order inhabiting tropical and temperate regions.

Leaves prominently 3–5-nerved from the base . . . . . 1. *Zizyphus.*
Leaves feather-veined.
  Leaves toothed.
    Leaves alternate (except *R. virgatus*). Disk very thin. Ovary quite free . . . . 3. *Rhamnus.*
    Leaves opposite or nearly so (see also *Rhamnus virgatus*). Disk thick, surrounding the ovary . 4. *Sageretia.*
  Leaves entire.
    Branches without tendrils. Ovary 2-celled, free . 2. *Berchemia.*
    Branches with terminal tendrils. Ovary 3-celled, adherent to the calyx . . . . 5. *Helinus.*

1. ZIZYPHUS. From *zizouf*, the Arabic name of the Lotus, *Z. vulgaris.*—Tropical and temperate regions.

Erect shrubs or small trees. Leaves alternate, usually shortly stalked, prominently 3–5-nerved from the base; stipules persistent, spinous, sharp, usually unequal, sometimes only one. Flowers

FIG. 29. ZIZYPHUS OXYPHYLLA.

unequally stalked, crowded in small, axillary cymes or clusters. Calyx 5-parted, tube short. Petals 5, deflexed; disk thick, flat, filling up the calyx-tube. Stamens 5. Ovary immersed in the disk, 2-celled; style 2-branched. Drupe fleshy; stone 1–2-celled.

Flowers and lower surface of leaves tomentose . . . . 1. *Z. Jujuba.*
Flowers and lower surface of leaves glabrous . . . . 2. *Z. oxyphylla.*

1. **Zizyphus Jujuba,** *Lamk.*; *Fl. Br. Ind.* i. 632. Usually a small tree, sometimes a shrub; trunk short, branches spreading, drooping at the ends; young shoots tomentose. Leaves sometimes sessile, oblong-ovate or nearly orbicular, 1–3 in., entire or with small, close-set teeth; upper surface dark green, glabrous, lower grey or tawny tomentose. Flowers tomentose outside, crowded in small, stalked or sessile, axillary cymes. Drupe sweet, globose on wild trees, ovoid on cultivated, $\frac{1}{2}$–$\frac{3}{4}$ in., dark brown, orange or red; stone wrinkled, usually 2-celled.

Simla; July, August.—Cultivated and self-sown throughout India, ascending to 6000 ft.—Asia, Australia, tropical Africa; widely spread.

The *Bêr* tree, cultivated for its edible fruit, is exceedingly variable in the shape of the leaves, the density of the tomentum, and also in the shape and size of the fruit. May be found in flower or fruit at almost any season.

2. **Zizyphus oxyphylla,** *Edgew.*; *Fl. Br. Ind.* i. 634. Quite glabrous; branches purple. Leaves unequal-sided, ovate, $1\frac{1}{2}$–$2\frac{1}{2}$ in., crenate or sharply toothed, long-pointed, acute. Flowers glabrous, in small, axillary clusters, sometimes solitary. Drupe orange, ovoid, $\frac{1}{3}$ in.; stone 1-celled. (Fig. 29.)

Simla, Mahasu; July–September.—Temperate Himalaya, 1000–7000 ft.

2. **BERCHEMIA.** Probably in honour of Van Bergheim (French, Berchem), a Dutch painter of the seventeenth century.—Tropical regions of Asia, Africa and America.

Erect or climbing, glabrous shrubs, without spines. Leaves alternate, shortly stalked or nearly sessile, entire, ovate, feather-veined; veins 5–15 pairs, parallel, straight. Flowers on short, unequal stalks in small, axillary or terminal clusters or cymes, sometimes panicled. Calyx 5-parted, tube cup-shaped. Petals 5. Stamens 5. Disk thick, lining the calyx-tube. Ovary surrounded by the disk, 2-celled, ovoid, narrowed upwards in a straight, simple style as long as the petals; stigma 2-lobed. Drupe cylindric or ovoid; stone 2-celled.

Leaves 2–3 in. Flowers in terminal panicles . . . 1. *B. floribunda.*
Leaves $\frac{1}{4}$–1 in. Flowers in small, axillary or terminal clusters 2. *B. lineata.*

*1. **Berchemia floribunda,** *Wall.*; *Fl. Br. Ind.* i. 637. A climbing shrub. Leaves 2–3 in., acute, lower surface pale; veins 10–15 pairs. Flowers clustered in large, terminal panicles. Drupe oblong, flattened, $\frac{2}{3}$ in., purple.

Temperate Himalaya, Sikkim to the Jhelam, 3000–6000 ft.; June, July.

*2. **Berchemia lineata,** *DC.*; *Fl. Br. Ind.* i. 638. A small, diffuse shrub. Leaves sometimes nearly sessile, $\frac{1}{4}$–1 in., obtuse;

veins 5–7 pairs. Flowers in small, axillary or terminal clusters. Drupe ovoid, $\frac{1}{4}$ in., purple-blue.

Temperate Himalaya, Sikkim to the Indus, 4000–10,000 ft., usually on rocks; May–July.

3. RHAMNUS. The classical name of some spinous shrub, perhaps a *Rhamnus* or *Lycium*.—Most warm and temperate regions except Australia.

Shrubs or small trees, usually erect, spinous or unarmed. Leaves alternate, nearly opposite in *R. virgatus*, stalked, toothed, feather-veined, veins nearly parallel. Flowers sometimes polygamous, on short, unequal stalks in axillary clusters or panicles, rarely solitary. Calyx 4- or 5-parted, tube cup-shaped. Petals 4–5 or none. Stamens 4–5. Disk thin, lining the calyx-tube. Ovary at the bottom of the calyx-tube, quite free, 3–4-celled, narrowed upwards into a short, 2–4-branched style. Drupe small, berry-like, obovoid or globose, black when ripe, containing 2–4 stones.

Spinous. Leaves nearly or quite opposite . . . . 1. *R. virgatus.*
Unarmed. Leaves alternate.
  Erect shrubs or trees. Leaves $2\frac{1}{2}$–5 in.
    Flower-clusters axillary. Petals none . . . 2. *R. purpureus.*
    Flower-clusters in axillary panicles. Petals 5 . . 3. *R. triqueter.*
  A procumbent shrub. Leaves $\frac{1}{2}$–$1\frac{1}{2}$ in. . . . 4. *R. procumbens.*

1. **Rhamnus virgatus,** *Roxb.*; *Fl. Br. Ind.* i. 639, *under R. dahuricus.* A spinous shrub or small tree, nearly or quite glabrous. Leaves opposite or nearly so, sometimes in clusters or crowded near the end of short, thick, opposite branches, lanceolate or ovate, 1–4 in., often long-pointed, sometimes crenate. Flowers crowded in the axils of the clustered leaves or at the base of branches. Drupe obovoid, $\frac{1}{4}$ in. long.

Simla, Mahasu, common; April–June.—Hilly districts throughout India, ascending to 9000 ft.—N. China, E. Siberia, Manchuria.

Closely allied to the common Buckthorn of Britain (*R. catharticus*).

2. **Rhamnus purpureus,** *Edgw.*; *Fl. Br. Ind.* i. 639. An unarmed shrub, glabrous or nearly so; young branches purple. Leaves alternate, rarely nearly opposite, ovate-lanceolate, $2\frac{1}{2}$–5 in., often abruptly pointed. Flowers in small, axillary clusters. Petals none. Drupe obovoid, $\frac{1}{4}$ in. long.

Simla, Jako, Narkunda; May, June.—W. Himalaya, 5000–10,000 ft.

3. **Rhamnus triqueter,** *Wall.*; *Fl. Br. Ind.* i. 639. An unarmed, pubescent shrub or small tree. Leaves alternate, oblong-ovate, acute, 3–5 in. Flowers in small clusters on long branches of axillary panicles. Drupe ovoid, $\frac{1}{4}$ in.

Valleys below Simla; May–August.—W. Himalaya, 3000–5000 ft.

4. **Rhamnus procumbens,** *Edgew.*; *Fl. Br. Ind.* i. 640. A small, procumbent, unarmed, nearly glabrous shrub. Leaves alternate, leathery, shining, lanceolate, $\frac{1}{2}$–$1\frac{1}{2}$ in., acute. Flowers on rather long stalks, solitary or in pairs. Petals none. Drupe globose, $\frac{1}{6}$ in. diam.

Shali, Naldera, on rocks; May, June.—Simla to Kumaon, 7000–8000 ft.

4. **SAGERETIA.** In honour of A. Sageret, a French botanist of the nineteenth century.—Asia, N. America.

Shrubs or small trees; branches long, drooping, half climbing, usually spinous. Leaves opposite or nearly so, shortly stalked, ovate or ovate-lanceolate, toothed, feather-veined; veins 3–7 pairs, nearly parallel. Flowers in axillary and terminal panicles. Calyx 5-parted, tube cup-shaped, lobes persistent. Petals 5. Stamens 5. Disk thick, lining the calyx-tube, margin 5-lobed. Ovary ovoid, surrounded by the disk, 3-celled; style very short, 3-lobed. Drupe small, globose, containing 3 stones.

Leaves 2–4 in.; veins about 7 pairs . . . . 1. *S. oppositifolia.*
Leaves $\frac{3}{4}$–$1\frac{1}{2}$ in.; veins about 3 pairs . . . . 2. *S. theezans.*

1. **Sageretia oppositifolia,** *Brongn.*; *Fl. Br. Ind.* i. 641. A straggling, half-climbing shrub; young leaves and shoots tomentose. Leaves ovate-lanceolate, 2–4 in., acute or long-pointed, veins about 7 pairs. Flowers in long, terminal, pubescent, often leafy panicles. Drupe $\frac{1}{4}$ in. diam., black.

Valleys below Simla; June–October.—W. Himalaya, 2000–6000 ft.

FIG. 30. SAGERETIA THEEZANS.

2. **Sageretia theezans,** *Brongn.*; *Fl. Br. Ind.* i. 641. A shrub; young leaves and shoots pubescent. Leaves ovate, $\frac{3}{4}$–$1\frac{1}{2}$ in., veins about 3 pairs. Flowers in short, axillary panicles often combined in long, leafy, terminal panicles. Drupe $\frac{1}{6}$ in. diam., dark brown. (Fig. 30.)

Naldera, valleys below Simla, Suni in the Sutlej valley; July–October.—W. Himalaya, 3000–8000 ft., and hilly districts in the Punjab.—China.
The fruit is eaten. In China the leaves are used by the poorer classes as tea.

5. **HELINUS.** From the Greek *helinos*, a tendril.—Africa, India.

Helinus lanceolatus, *Brandis*; *Fl. Br. Ind.* i. 644. An unarmed, glabrous, climbing shrub; branches slender, grooved, bearing terminal, woody, simple coiling tendrils. Leaves alternate, shortly stalked, ovate or ovate-lanceolate, 1–2½ in., entire, feather-veined, veins nearly parallel. Flowers in small, umbellate clusters at the end of long, axillary stalks. Calyx-tube cup-shaped, adherent to the ovary, 5-lobed. Petals 5, inserted with the 5 stamens on the margin of the disk. Disk ring-shaped, on the top of the inferior, 3-celled ovary. Style short, 3-branched. Fruit globose, ¼ in. diam., consisting of the ovary enclosed in the calyx-tube and containing 3 flattened, leathery seeds.

Valley below Sipi; May–September.—N. India, ascending to 5000 ft.

XXV. VITACEÆ

Erect or climbing shrubs. Leaves alternate, stalked, simple or compound; stipules membranous, often conspicuous. Flowers small, 2-sexual, regular, in panicles, racemes or cymes. Calyx small, cup-shaped. Petals 4 or 5, free or united at the base, valvate, recurved, soon falling off. Stamens 4 or 5, opposite the petals, free or partially united, anthers 2-celled. Ovary free, ovoid, 2–6-celled; style short, simple, stigma terminal; ovules 2 or 1 in each cell. Fruit a globose, succulent berry containing 1–6 seeds.—A large Order inhabiting the tropical and temperate regions of nearly the whole world.

Climbing shrubs. Stamens free. Two ovules in each cell . . . 1. *Vitis.*
Erect shrubs. Stamens inserted in a 5-cleft tube. One ovule in each cell . . . . 2. *Leea.*

1. VITIS. The Latin name of the Vine.—Tropical and subtropical regions of Asia and Africa, Pacific Islands, America.

Shrubs, climbing by means of tendrils. Leaves simple or digitately or pedately compound. Tendrils leaf-opposed, simple or branched. Flowers in leaf-opposed, rarely axillary, often tendril-bearing panicles, racemes or cymes. Calyx obscurely 4- or 5-lobed. Petals 4 or 5, free or cohering at the tips and falling off as a cap. Disk of 4 or 5 small glands alternate with the petals. Stamens 4 or 5, free. Ovary 2-celled, narrowed upwards in a short, thick style; stigma circular, flat; ovules 2 in each cell. Berry globose, succulent, 1- or 2-celled, containing 1–4 seeds.

The Grape vine, *V. vinifera*, was formerly cultivated in Kunawar, but the vine disease appeared in 1855–60 and since then the cultivation has almost disappeared. Excellent grapes are grown in Kashmir and many parts of India, notably Peshawar.

Leaves simple.
Leaves tomentose on lower surface. Flowers in panicles . . . 1. *V. lanata.*
Leaves glabrous. Flowers in racemes . . . . 2. *V. parvifolia.*
Leaves compound.
Leaflets 3.
Leaves glabrous. Flowers yellow-green . . . 3. *V. himalayana.*
Leaves pubescent. Flowers red-brown . . . 4. *V. divaricata.*
Leaflets 5 . . . . 5. *V. capreolata.*

1. **Vitis lanata,** *Roxb.*; *Fl. Br. Ind.* i. 651. All parts more or less covered with red-brown wool or tomentum. Stem and branches woody, climbing over high trees. Leaves simple, cordate-ovate, about $4\frac{1}{2} \times 4$ in., sometimes obscurely lobed, sharply toothed, pointed; upper surface woolly, becoming nearly glabrous

FIG. 31. VITIS HIMALAYANA.

with age, lower densely tomentose. Flowers yellow-green, in large panicles. Petals 5, cohering at the tips. Stamens 5. Berry $\frac{1}{3}$ in. diam., purple.

Valleys below Simla; April, May.—Throughout India in hilly districts, ascending to 6000 ft.—China, Formosa, Luchu archipelago.

2. **Vitis parvifolia,** *Roxb.*; *Fl. Br. Ind.* i. 652. Glabrous. Stem and branches slender, trailing. Leaves simple, ovate, 1–3 × $\frac{3}{4}$–2 in., cordate or truncate, sharply toothed, acute, sometimes deeply 3–5-lobed. Flowers green, in short, erect, simple or branched racemes. Petals 5, cohering at the tips. Stamens 5. Berry $\frac{1}{4}$ in. diam., black.

Simla, Mahasu; April, May.—W. Himalaya, 3000–6000 ft.

3. **Vitis himalayana,** *Brandis*; *Fl. Br. Ind.* i. 655. Glabrous, climbing over tall trees. Leaves digitately compound; leaflets 3, shortly stalked, ovate, $1\frac{1}{2}$–5 × 1–$2\frac{1}{4}$ in., sharply toothed, long-pointed, upper surface dark green, shining, lower pale; lateral leaflets unequal-sided. Flowers yellow-green, in spreading cymes. Petals 4 or 5. Stamens 4 or 5. Berry $\frac{1}{3}$ in. diam., black. (Fig. 31.)

Simla, common; April, May.—W. Himalaya, 6000–11,000 ft.—China. In autumn the leaves turn bright red or ruddy brown.

4. **Vitis divaricata,** *Wall.*; *Fl. Br. Ind.* i. 657. Pubescent. Stems slender, sometimes very long. Leaves digitately compound; leaflets 3, stalked, ovate-lanceolate, 6–10 × 3–4 in., toothed, long-pointed; lateral leaflets unequal-sided, often cordate and lobed. Flowers red-brown, in small, umbellate cymes. Petals 5. Stamens 5. Berry $\frac{1}{3}$ in. diam., black.

Simla; July.—Temperate Himalaya, 4000–7000 ft.

5. **Vitis capreolata,** *D. Don*; *Fl. Br. Ind.* i. 659. Glabrous. Stems creeping, wiry. Leaves pedately compound; leaflets 5, shortly stalked, ovate-lanceolate, toothed, long-pointed, unequal, the terminal one largest, 1–$2\frac{1}{2}$ in. long. Flowers yellow-green, in small, umbellate cymes. Petals 4. Stamens 4. Berry $\frac{1}{4}$ in. diam., black.

Simla, the Glen, Mushobra, on rocks and tree trunks; July–September.—Temperate Himalaya, 4000–7000 ft.

2. **LEEA.** In honour of James Lee, a noted nurseryman and botanist of the eighteenth century.—Tropical regions of Asia and Africa, rare in Australia.

Leea aspera, *Edgew.*; *Fl. Br. Ind.* i. 665, *under L. aspera. Wall.* A robust, spreading shrub, 2–10 ft.; stems and branches grooved. Uppermost leaves usually simply pinnate or the lower pinnæ with 3 leaflets; lower leaves 2-pinnate; leaflets 5–7 in each main division, shortly stalked, cordate-ovate, 5–6 × 2–3 in., abruptly tapering into a long point; principal veins about 14 pairs, prominent, parallel; margins coarsely toothed; both surfaces minutely bristly, rough Flowers yellow-green, in spreading, leaf-opposed, nearly glabrous cymes. Calyx 5-lobed. Petals 5, oblong, bases united and adnate to the staminal tube. Stamens 5, lower part of filaments united in a 5-lobed tube adnate to the petals. Ovary 3–6-celled; style short, simple, stigma terminal; ovule one in each cell. Berry $\frac{1}{3}$ in. diam., black when ripe.

Simla; August, September.—Throughout India, ascending to 5000 ft.

Mr. C. B. Clarke in *Trimen's Journ. Bot.* 1881, p. 136, has shown that the *Leea* of the N.W. Himalaya is *L. aspera*, as described by Edgeworth in *Trans. Linn. Soc.* xx. 36, and is not the plant referred to under that name by Wallich in *Roxb. Fl. Ind.* ed. Carey, ii. 468, which is *L. robusta*, *Roxb. Fl. Ind.* i. 655.

XXVI. SAPINDACEÆ

ERECT trees or shrubs, rarely climbing herbs. Leaves alternate or opposite, stalked, simple and frequently lobed or compound; stipules usually small and soon falling off. Flowers usually small and regular, in cymes or panicles, 2- or 1-sexual, the male and female sometimes on different plants. Calyx of 4 or 5 sepals, free or united in a tube. Petals 4 or 5, rarely none, alternate with the sepals, often unequal, sometimes bearing a small scale on the inner face. Disk fleshy, complete as an entire or lobed ring, or incomplete (the posterior half wanting), or reduced to glands, or altogether absent. Stamens normally 8, sometimes fewer, inserted within the disk, filaments usually long, anthers oblong, 2-celled, versatile or erect. Ovary sessile, free, 3- or 2-celled; styles 1–3; ovules 1 or 2, rarely several in each cell. Fruit various, capsular or samaroid. Seeds 1–3, rarely numerous.—An Order dispersed throughout nearly the whole world; most abundant in tropical, absent in very cold regions.

Leaves alternate

Leaves compound.
- A climbing herb. Leaves ternately pinnate, 3 leaflets on division. Capsule membranous, inflated . 1. *Cardiospermum*.
- A tree. Leaves simply pinnate, leaflets about 15. Drupe yellow, fleshy . . . . 3. *Sapindus*.

Leaves simple. Valves of the capsule winged on the back 5. *Dodonæa*.

Leaves opposite

Leaves simple, usually lobed. Fruit of 2 samaras joined to a short axis . . . . 4. *Acer*.

Leaves compound.
- Leaves digitate; leaflets 5–9. Capsule thick, leathery. Seeds 1–3, large . . . . 2. *Æsculus*.
- Leaves pinnate; leaflets 3. Capsule membranous, inflated. Seeds several, small . . . . . 6. *Staphylea*.

1. CARDIOSPERMUM. From the Greek *cardia*, a heart, and *sperma*, a seed, referring to the heart-shaped excrescence on the seeds.—Chiefly tropical America; only 3 or 4 species in Asia and Africa, two of those being also found in America.

Cardiospermum Halicacabum, *Linn.*; *Fl. Br. Ind.* i. 670. An annual, climbing, nearly glabrous herb; branches long, slender, grooved. Leaves alternate, ternately pinnate, 2½–3 in.; each division with 3 coarsely toothed, 3-lobed, pointed leaflets, the centre one the longest. Flowers few, small, white, irregular, in axillary, long-stalked corymbs having a pair of simple coiled tendrils near the base. Sepals 4, free, concave, the 2 outer very small. Petals 4, in unequal pairs, each with a small scale on the inner face. Disk reduced to 2 glands. Stamens 8, unequal, inserted at the base of the ovary. Ovary 3-celled; style short, 3-parted; ovule 1 in each cell. Capsule globose, membranous, veined, 3-cornered. Seeds 3, spherical, black, bearing a conspicuous, white, heart-shaped excrescence.

Valleys below Simla; August, September.—Throughout India, ascending to 4000 ft.—Most tropical and subtropical countries.

2. ÆSCULUS. The Latin name of an Oak having edible acorns; derived from *esca*, food, nourishment.—Temperate regions of Asia and America.

Æsculus indica, *Colebr.*; *Fl. Br. Ind.* i. 675. A tree; buds sticky. Leaves glabrous, opposite, long-stalked, digitately compound; leaflets 5–9, oblong-lanceolate, long-pointed, toothed, central ones 6–9 in., outer ones shorter. Flowers irregular, about 1 in. long, in numerous, small, pubescent cymes disposed in terminal, erect, narrow, pyramidal panicles 12–15 in. long; the upper flowers in each cyme usually male. Calyx tubular, splitting as the flower opens, 5-toothed. Petals 4, clawed, white and yellow, base often streaked with red; 2 petals narrower than the others. Disk incomplete, the posterior half wanting, lobed. Stamens 7, longer than the petals, inserted at the base of the ovary within the disk. Ovary tomentose, narrowly oblong, 3-celled; style simple, as long as the stamens; ovules 2 in each cell. Capsule smooth, brown, ovoid, 1–2 in., containing 1–3 large, globose, dark brown, shining seeds.

Simla (planted), Narkunda forests (wild); April, May.—W. Himalaya, 4000–10,000 ft.—Afghanistan.

The Horse Chestnut of Europe, *Æ. Hippocastanum*, has larger leaflets and prickly capsules.

3. SAPINDUS. From the Latin *sapo*, soap, and *indicus*, Indian; the drupes of *S. Saponaria* and other species contain a pulp which lathers with hot water and is used for washing.—Nearly all tropical countries.

Sapindus Mukorossi, *Gærtn.*; *Fl. Br. Ind.* i. 683. A tree. Leaves glabrous, alternate, usually even-, sometimes odd-pinnate; leaflets 8–15, alternate or the upper ones nearly opposite, lanceolate, about $4\frac{1}{2} \times 1\frac{1}{4}$ in., entire. Flowers numerous, small, polygamous, purple, in terminal, pubescent, pyramidal panicles 4–8 in. long. Sepals 5, free, in 2 series, imbricate. Petals 5, clawed; a minute, hairy scale projecting on each side at the base of the fringed blade. Disk complete, flat, 5-angled. Stamens 8, inserted at the base of the ovary within the disk, filaments hairy. Ovary 3-lobed,

3-celled; style short, simple; ovule 1 in each cell. Drupe yellow, smooth, globose, $\frac{3}{4}$ in. diam.

Sutlej valley, a tree on the left bank above the Komarsen bridge; cultivated throughout N. India, ascending to 5000 ft.—China, Japan.

The drupes are used in medicine; also as soap for washing clothes and the hair. Native name *Keetha*.

4. ACER. The classical name of the Maple.—Europe, N. America, Asia.

Trees. Leaves opposite, long-stalked, simple, usually lobed. Flowers small, regular, polygamous, white or tinged with green, in corymbs or racemes. Calyx 5- or 4-parted, segments imbricate in bud. Petals 5 or 4, imbricate. Disk thick, ring-shaped, lobed. Stamens usually 8, inserted on the disk. Ovary 2-lobed, 2-celled; styles 2, linear, incurved, more or less united; ovules 2 in each cell. Fruit of 2 conjoined samaras, ultimately separating from the short axis; wings large, membranous, net-veined, more or less diverging, thickened along the lower edge. Seed one or rarely two in each samara.

In the *Fl. Br. Ind.* i. 693, Simla is recorded as a locality for *A. lævigatum, Wall.*, but I have seen no specimen. Brandis (*For. Fl.* 110) and Gamble (*Man. Ind. Timb.* 99) both give the Jumna as the western limit of the species. It has oblong, entire leaves $2\frac{1}{2}$–6×1–2 in., green on the lower surface.

Acer campestre, Common Maple, is wild in Britain; *A. Pseudoplatanus*, the Sycamore or Great Maple (called the Plane in Scotland), is naturalised.

Leaves not lobed, oblong, entire; lower surface white . . 1. *A. oblongum.*
Leaves lobed.
  Leaves 5-lobed; margins toothed.
    Lobes pointed, but not produced in tail-like tips.
      Margins of leaves not fringed; lower surface white 2. *A. cæsium.*
      Margins of leaves minutely fringed; lower surface green . . . . 3. *A. villosum.*
    Lobes narrowed into long, linear, tail-like tips . . 4. *A. caudatum.*
  Leaves 5–7-lobed; margins entire . . . . . . 5. *A. cultratum.*

1. **Acer oblongum,** *Wall.*; *Fl. Br. Ind.* i. 693. Evergreen. Leaves glabrous, not lobed, oblong, 3–6×1–2 in., entire, long-pointed, upper surface dark green, lower white. Flowers in hairy corymbs.

Simla, the Glen; February–April.—Temperate Himalaya, 2000–6000 ft.—China, Luchu archipelago.

2. **Acer cæsium,** *Wall.*; *Fl. Br. Ind.* i. 695. Glabrous or nearly so. Leaves cordate, 5-lobed, 3–7 in., closely and sharply toothed; lower surface covered with a pale bloom; lobes pointed, the 2 basal smaller, sometimes obscure. Flowers in corymbs, appearing with the young leaves.

Simla, Mahasu, Narkunda; March, April.—Temperate Himalaya, 7000–10,000 ft.

3. **Acer villosum,** *Wall.*; *Fl. Br. Ind.* i. 695. Leaves glabrous or nearly so on the surface; margins minutely fringed, cordate, 5-lobed, 4–10 in.; teeth few, irregular, distant; lobes pointed, the 2 basal smaller, sometimes obscure. Flowers in long, often branched, hairy, clustered racemes, appearing before the leaves.

Narkunda; March, April.—Temperate Himalaya, 7000–9000 ft.

4. **Acer caudatum,** *Wall.*; *Fl. Br. Ind.* i. 695. Leaves glabrous or nearly so, slightly cordate, 5-lobed, 2–5 in., closely and

FIG. 32. ACER CAUDATUM.

sharply, irregularly toothed; lobes narrowed into a long, linear, tail-like tip, the 2 basal smaller, sometimes obscure. Flowers in short, glabrous racemes, appearing with the leaves. (Fig. 32.)

Simla, Mahasu, Matiana, Narkunda; March, April.—Temperate Himalaya, 7000–11,000 ft.

5. **Acer cultratum,** *Wall.*; *Fl. Br. Ind.* i. 696, *under A. pictum, Thunb.* Glabrous. Leaves usually cordate, 5–7-lobed, 3–6 in.,

entire; lobes pointed, the 2 basal smaller, sometimes obscure. Flowers long-stalked, in corymbs, appearing with the leaves. Wings of fruit widely divergent, forming a nearly straight line.

Narkunda; May.—Temperate Himalaya, 6000–9000 ft.

The wings of the fruit of the Japanese *A. pictum*, *Thunb.*, are erect and almost touching.

5. **DODONÆA.** In honour of R. Dodoens, a Dutch herbalist of the sixteenth century.—Mostly in Australia.

Dodonæa viscosa, *Linn.*; *Fl. Br. Ind.* i. 697. An evergreen shrub; leaves and young shoots viscid with yellow, resinous dots. Leaves alternate, sessile, simple, glabrous, varying from oblong-lanceolate acute to oblanceolate obtuse, 2–4 in., entire or sinuate, tapering downwards; stipules none. Flowers small, yellow, 1- and 2-sexual, often on different plants, in short, terminal panicles or racemes. Sepals 5, ovate, free. Petals and disk none. Stamens usually 8, filaments very short, anthers nearly as long as the sepals. Ovary usually 3-, sometimes 2- or 4-lobed and celled; styles as many as the cells, long, united nearly to the top; ovules 2 in each cell. Capsule 3- (or 2- or 4-)celled; valves winged on the back, ultimately separating from the axis, wings membranous broadly orbicular. Seeds 1–3.

Valleys below Simla; June–September.—Throughout India, ascending to 4500 ft.—Most warm countries.

Native name *Sanatta*; commonly planted for hedges.

6. **STAPHYLEA.** From the Greek *staphyle*, a cluster, referring to the inflorescence.—N. America, Europe, Asia.

Staphylea Emodi, *Wall.*; *Fl. Br. Ind.* i. 698. A shrub or small tree, glabrous; bark spotted. Leaves opposite, long-stalked, pinnately compound; leaflets 3, nearly equal, 2 lateral sessile, terminal stalked, ovate, 2–6 × 1–3 in., finely toothed, long-pointed, lower surface pale; stipules long, linear, soon falling off. Flowers white, nearly ½ in. long, in short panicles, appearing with the young leaves. Bracts stipule-like. Calyx white, 5-parted, segments ovate-oblong, obtuse, erect. Petals 5, oblong, erect, as long as the calyx. Disk complete, nearly filling up the calyx-tube, 5-lobed. Stamens 5, erect, as long as the petals, inserted with them outside the edge of the disk. Ovary 3-lobed and 3-celled; styles 3, as long as the petals, erect, free or united near the top, stigmas capitate; ovules 6–8 in each cell. Capsule membranous, inflated, broadly ovoid, 2–3 in., yellow-white, narrowed to the base, shortly 3-pointed at the top. Seeds several, globose.

Narkunda, in forest; April, May.—W. Himalaya, 6000–8000 ft.

Natives think that walking sticks made of the wood keep off snakes; probably on account of the spotted bark. The Afghan name is *Marchob*, serpent-stick.

XXVII. SABIACEÆ

TREES or climbing shrubs. Leaves alternate, simple; stipules none. Flowers $\frac{3}{4}$ in. diam. or minute, usually 2-sexual, single on axillary stalks or panicled. Calyx 5-parted, lobes nearly equal, imbricate. Petals 5, equal or unequal, opposite the sepals, imbricate. Stamens 5, opposite the petals, filaments rather thick, all or only 2 anther-bearing. Disk ring- or cup-shaped. Ovary sessile, 2-lobed, 2-celled; styles 2, simple, erect, more or less cohering, tips ultimately recurved; ovules 2 in each cell. Drupe solitary or in pairs; stone 1-celled, 1-seeded.—A small Order, chiefly Asiatic.

Climbing shrubs. Leaves entire. Flowers $\frac{3}{4}$ in. diam. . . . 1. *Sabia.*
Erect trees. Leaves toothed. Flowers minute . . . . . 2. *Meliosma.*

1. SABIA. From *Soobja*, the Bengali name of *Sabia lanceolata.*—India, China, Japan, Malayan peninsula and archipelago.

Sabia campanulata, *Wall.*; *Fl. Br. Ind.* ii. 1. A glabrous, climbing shrub. Leaves shortly stalked, oblong-lanceolate, 2–4 in., entire, long-pointed. Flowers regular, 2-sexual, brown-purple, $\frac{3}{4}$ in. diam., single on axillary, usually solitary stalks. Calyx very short. Petals $\frac{1}{3}$–$\frac{1}{2}$ in. long, ovate, concave, obtuse. Stamens all anther-bearing. Disk ring-shaped, 5-lobed. Drupe orbicular, flattened, wrinkled, $\frac{1}{4}$ in. diam., solitary or in pairs.

Mushobra, in the woods above the Waterworks road, Narkunda, not common; April, May.—Temperate Himalaya, 5000–9000 ft.

2. MELIOSMA. From the Greek *meli*, honey, and *osma*, odour, referring to the flowers.—Himalaya, China, Corea, Japan, S. and Central America.

Small trees. Leaves simple; lateral nerves prominent on the lower surface, running out into sharp teeth. Flowers minute, irregular, 2- rarely 1-sexual, in panicles. Bracts none or 1–2. Sepals as long as the outer petals, concave. Petals unequal, the 3 outer orbicular, concave, the 2 inner much smaller, 2-lobed. Disk cup-shaped, membranous, toothed, surrounding the base of the ovary. Filaments 5; two bearing large, globose anthers, connective much dilated; three without anthers. Drupe globose, containing a 1-seeded stone.

Leaves ovate; lateral nerves straight; teeth numerous, close-set . . . . 1. *M. dilleniæfolia.*
Leaves lanceolate; lateral nerves curved; teeth few, distant 2. *M. pungens.*

1. **Meliosma dilleniæfolia,** *Wall.*; *Fl. Br. Ind.* ii. 4. Leaves rusty-pubescent, shortly stalked, ovate, 6–10 × 3–5 in., abruptly pointed; lateral nerves straight, parallel; teeth numerous, small,

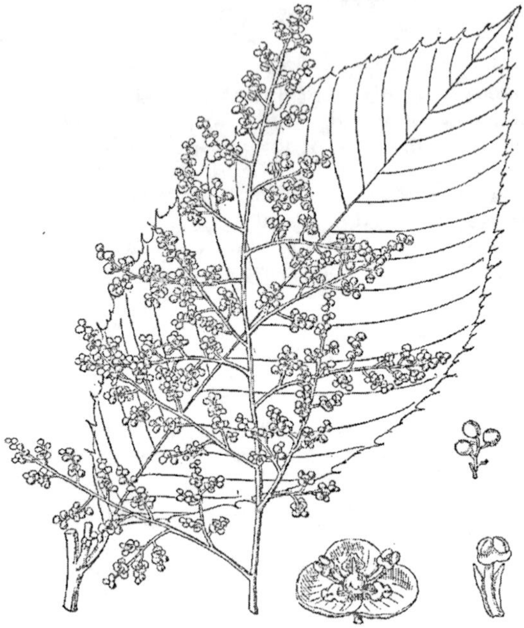

FIG. 33. MELIOSMA DILLENIÆFOLIA.

close-set, regular; lower surface pale. Panicle 6–12 in. Flowers 2-sexual, shortly stalked. Bracts none. (Fig. 33.)

Simla, not common; June, July.—Himalaya, Simla to Sikkim, 4000–8000 ft.

2. **Meliosma pungens,** *Wall.*; *Fl. Br. Ind.* ii. 4. Leaves nearly glabrous, shortly stalked, lanceolate, 6–8 × $1\frac{1}{2}$–2 in., long-pointed; lateral nerves curved; teeth few, large, distant. Panicle 6–12 in. Flowers 2- or 1-sexual, sessile. Bracts 2 or 1.

Narkunda, not common; May, June.—Temperate Himalaya, 3000–7000 ft. Common about Mussoorie.

XXVIII. ANACARDIACEÆ

SHRUBS or trees; the bark often abounding in gum or acrid juice. Leaves alternate, pinnate or simple, crowded towards the end of branches; stipules none. Flowers small, regular, 2- or 1-sexual, sometimes polygamous, in panicles or racemes. Calyx 4- or 5-parted, persistent. Petals 4, 5 or none, longer than the calyx, free, imbricate. Disk ring-shaped, often lobed, sometimes wanting in the female flowers. Stamens 5–8, none or rudimentary in the female flowers; filaments free, sometimes very short; anthers 2-celled, usually versatile. Ovary sessile, ovoid, rudimentary in the male flowers, 1-celled; styles usually 3 or 4; ovule solitary. Drupe nearly dry; stones hard, 1-seeded.—Name from the Greek *ana*, similar, and *cardia*, a heart; referring to the thick heart-shaped stalk of the Cashew nut, *Anacardium occidentàle*.

The Mango tree belongs to this Order; it is cultivated in the lower hills up to 3000 ft.

Petals pale purple or yellow-green.
  Petals 5. Stamens 5 . . . . 1. *Rhus*.
  Petals 4. Stamens 8 . . . . 3. *Odina*.
Petals none. Anthers large, deep red . . . . 2. *Pistacïa*.

1. RHUS. From *rous*, the classical name of *R. Cotinus*.—Temperate regions, rarer in the tropics.

Trees or shrubs; juice usually acrid. Leaves simple or odd-pinnate, turning red in the autumn before they fall; leaflets opposite, entire or toothed. Flowers polygamous, usually very small, but conspicuous by their number, forming large, dense panicles; male and female often on different trees. Calyx 5-parted, much shorter than the petals. Petals 5, equal, spreading. Stamens 5. Styles 3, short. Drupe small, more or less flattened; seed often oily.

Leaves simple . . . . 1. *R. Cotinus*.
Leaves compound.
  Leaves of 3 leaflets . . . . 2. *R. parviflora*.
  Leaves pinnate; leaflets 7–18.
    Leaflets toothed; leafstalk winged . . . . . 3. *R. semialata*.
    Leaflets entire[1]; leafstalk not winged.
      Leaves glabrous.
        Leaflets sessile. Drupes tomentose . . . 4. *R. punjabensis*.
        Leaflets stalked. Drupes glabrous . . . 6. *R. succedanea*.
      Leaves tomentose . . . . 5. *R. Wallichii*.

[1] In *R. punjabensis* the leaflets sometimes have a few irregular, distant teeth.

1. **Rhus Cotinus,** *Linn.*; *Fl. Br. Ind.* ii. 9. A shrub or small tree. Leaves undivided, long-stalked, obovate or ovate, 2–4 in., entire, stalks and lower surface pubescent. Flowers pale purple, in drooping, hairy panicles 3–6 in. long; fertile flowers few. Drupe

FIG. 34. RHUS COTINUS.

hairy, cordate, about $\frac{1}{4}$ in. long, unequally lobed. After flowering the stalks of the numerous, sterile flowers become elongated and covered with long, silky hairs, forming a spreading panicle of slender, feathery branches. (Fig. 34.)

Valleys below Simla, common, the Glen; March–August.—W. Himalaya, 3000–5000 ft.—E. Asia, S. Europe; and a very closely allied species in N. America.

Bark and leaves used for tanning. Wood bright yellow.

*2. **Rhus parviflora,** *Roxb.*; *Fl. Br. Ind.* ii. 9. A shrub, covered with soft, red-brown tomentum. Leaves stalked; leaflets

3, ovate, irregularly crenate, lateral ones sessile, central one shortly stalked, largest 2–3 in. Flowers pale yellow-green, in hairy, terminal panicles up to 12 in. long. Drupe brown, glabrous, shining, ovoid, $\frac{1}{6}$ in.

N.W. Himalaya from the Sutlej to Nepal, 2000–5000 ft.; May, June.—Pachmarhi, Central India.

3. **Rhus semialata,** *Murray*; *Fl. Br. Ind.* ii. 10. A tree; young parts, leaf stalks and inflorescence pubescent. Leaves odd-pinnate, 12–18 in., the upper part of the rachis narrowly winged; leaflets 9–13, lateral sessile, end one on a winged stalk, ovate-lanceolate, 2–5 in., closely and sharply toothed, lower surface tomentose. Flowers pale yellow-green, in large panicles nearly as long as the leaves. Drupe tomentose, red-brown, nearly $\frac{1}{4}$ in. diam.

Simla, the Glen, Mahasu; April–June.—Temperate Himalaya, 3000–7000 ft.—China, Japan.

Galls of various shapes, caused by insects, frequently occur on the branches; they are used in the manufacture of ink and in native medicine.

4. **Rhus punjabensis,** *Stewart*; *Fl. Br. Ind.* ii. 10. A tree; young parts pubescent. Leaves glabrous, odd-pinnate, 12–18 in.; leaflets 11–13, lateral sessile, end one stalked, ovate-oblong $2\frac{1}{2}$–5 in., acute, entire, rarely with a few irregular, distant teeth. Flowers white or pale yellow-green, in large, broad panicles about half the length of the leaves. Drupe red-tomentose, $\frac{1}{6}$ in. diam.

Simla, Jako, the Glen; May–July.—W. Himalaya, 3000–8000 ft.

The juice raises blisters and makes black stains on paper.

5. **Rhus Wallichii,** *Hook. f.*; *Fl. Br. Ind.* ii. 11. A tree; all parts rusty tomentose. Leaves odd-pinnate, 12–18 in., resembling those of a walnut; leaflets 7–11, lateral sessile or nearly so, end one long-stalked, ovate or ovate-oblong, 3–9 in., abruptly pointed, entire. Flowers in axillary panicles much shorter than the leaves. Petals green-yellow, with dark veins. Drupe ovoid or globose, $\frac{1}{3}$ in. long, brown-tomentose at first, ultimately nearly glabrous.

Simla, the Glen; May, June.—Temperate Himalaya, 6000–7000 ft.

The juice is highly corrosive. In Japan lacquer is in part prepared from the juice of the closely allied *R. vernicifera*.

6. **Rhus succedanea,** *Linn.*; *Fl. Br. Ind.* ii. 12. A tree. Leaves glabrous, odd-pinnate, 6–12 in.; leaflets 7–13, lateral shortly stalked, end one long-stalked, ovate-oblong, 3–6 in., acute or long-pointed, entire, shining. Flowers green-yellow, in drooping panicles shorter than the leaves. Drupe globose, $\frac{1}{4}$ in. diam., glabrous, pale yellow.

Valleys near Simla; May, June.—Temperate Himalaya, 3000–6000 ft., Assam.—Japan, China, Java.

The Simla tree is the variety *himalaica* of the *Fl. Br. Ind.*

2. PISTACIA. The classical name of the Pistachio Nut, *P. vera*.—Mediterranean region, E. Asia, Mexico.

Pistacia integerrima, *Stewart*; *Fl. Br. Ind.* ii. 13. A tree; glabrous or nearly so. Leaves odd- or even-pinnate, 6–9 in.; leaflets 7–11 or 8–10, nearly opposite, shortly stalked, lanceolate, 2½–5 in., long-pointed, entire, base unequal, young foliage red. Flowers red, 1-sexual, the male and female on different trees, in lateral panicles, appearing with the young leaves. Petals none. Male flowers: calyx very small, 5-parted, stamens 5–7, anthers large oblong, deep red, nearly sessile. Female flowers: calyx 4-parted, lobes narrow acute, soon falling off, disk and stamens none, style 3-parted, tips broad, recurved. Drupe glabrous, wrinkled, globose, ¼ in. diam., grey when ripe.

Simla, near the road between Annandale and the Glen; April, May.—W. Himalaya, 1500–8000 ft.—Cultivated in the plains.

Large crooked galls, often 6–7 in. long, form on the leaves in the autumn; they are sold in bazaars under the name of *Kakri singi* and are used in native medicine. The heartwood is hard and durable and is highly esteemed for carving, furniture and all kinds of ornamental carpentry.

3. ODINA. Origin of name uncertain.—A small genus; chiefly African.

Odina Wodier, *Roxb.*; *Fl. Br. Ind.* ii. 29. A tree. Leaves few, stellately tomentose when young, becoming glabrous afterwards, odd-pinnate; leaflets 7–9, opposite, lateral shortly stalked, end one long-stalked, ovate, 3–6 in., entire, abruptly long-pointed. Flowers appearing before the young leaves, 1-sexual, male and female on different branches or on different trees, in small clusters arranged along simple or branched, stellately tomentose, racemose panicles 3–6 in. long, in the axils of fallen leaves or at the end of the thick, naked branches. Calyx 4-lobed, persistent. Petals 4, yellow-green, much longer than the calyx, spreading. Male flowers: stamens 8, nearly as long as the petals, ovary rudimentary, 4-cleft. Female flowers: stamens rudimentary, styles 4, short, thick. Drupe oblong, about ½ in., flattened, glabrous, red when ripe.

Valleys below Simla; February–April.—Throughout India, ascending to 5000 ft.—Burmah.

As seen in the arid valleys near Simla, this tree, especially when its branches have been lopped for fodder and its trunk hacked for gum, presents a singularly ungainly appearance, but in the moist forests, at the foot of the hills, it grows into a handsome spreading tree, and it is only in such situations that its valuable, hard, heavy heartwood is developed in sufficient thickness to be useful. The yellow gum obtained from the bark is used for calico-printing.

XXIX. CORIARIACEÆ

A SMALL Order of doubtful affinity, consisting of a single genus, of which the few species are widely distributed. The structure of the pistil and fruit resembles that of *Phytolacca* in some respects.

CORIARIA. From the Latin *coriarius*, pertaining to leather; the leaves are used for tanning.—Mediterranean region to China and Japan; New Zealand and the Andes.

Coriaria nepalensis, *Wall.*; *Fl. Br. Ind.* ii. 44. A glabrous shrub; branches 4-angled, arching; bark red. Leaves opposite, nearly sessile, ovate, 1–3 × $\frac{3}{4}$–2 in., shortly pointed, entire; basal

FIG. 35. CORIARIA NEPALENSIS.

nerves prominent, curved, 1 or 2 on each side of the midrib. Flowers small, 2-sexual, regular, in lateral, clustered racemes 2–6 in. long. Sepals 5, imbricate, spreading, persistent. Petals 5, green, smaller than the sepals at first, soon enlarging and becoming fleshy and keeled on the inner face, persistent. Stamens 10, free, anthers large, oblong, coral-red, protruding, conspicuous. Carpels 5, distinct, 1-celled, whorled round and attached to a short, central axis; styles 5, simple, long, thick; ovule solitary. Fruit of 5 small, distinct, one-seeded, prominently ridged carpels, enclosed within the much enlarged, purple, succulent petals and separated from one another by the projecting petal-keels. (Fig. 35.)

Simla, common; March, April.—Temperate Himalaya, 3000–7000 ft.—China.

Native name *Masuri*; this shrub is said to have been abundant on the site of Mussoorie, and to have given its name to the station.

XXX. LEGUMINOSÆ

HERBS, shrubs or trees, of extremely varied habit and appearance. Leaves simple or compound, alternate, rarely opposite or whorled, stipulate. Flowers usually 2-sexual. Sepals 5, rarely fewer, often unequal, usually combined in a 5-toothed calyx. Petals 5, rarely fewer, dissimilar or nearly alike, free or more or less united, usually longer than the calyx and inserted at the bottom of its tube. Stamens 10, rarely fewer, numerous only in *Acacia* and *Albizzia*, free or variously united, commonly hypogynous; filaments thread-like, sometimes dilated towards the tip; anthers 2-celled, usually uniform. Ovary free, 1-celled; style simple, slender, continuous with the ovary; stigma usually small and terminal; ovules several or many, rarely only 1 or 2. Fruit a pod, usually dry and opening by 2 similar valves, in a few genera ultimately breaking up into indehiscent, one-seeded joints; seeds attached alternately along the upper margin of the valves, sometimes separated from one another by partitions or by constrictions of the pod.—Leguminous plants constitute a vast Order spread over nearly the whole globe, Papilionaceæ being generally dispersed, Cæsalpinieæ and Mimoseæ most abundant in the warmer regions.

Many species are cultivated, either for their flowers or as forage plants or for their seeds which are used as food by both man and beast; among the last the two following species are cultivated near Simla in addition to those subsequently mentioned.

Cicer arietinum. A herb. Leaves pinnate; leaflets about 13. Flowers pea-like, blue-purple or white. Pod 1 in.; seeds 2. The common *gram*.

Cajanus indicus. A shrub. Leaves of 3 sessile leaflets. Flowers pea-like, yellow, veined with red. Pod 2–3 in.; seeds 3–5. The *arhardhal*.

The False Acacia, *Robinia Pseud-acacia*, a N. American tree, common in Britain, is often planted at Simla. Leaves odd-pinnate; leaflets entire. Flowers white, fragrant, in pendulous racemes.

Leguminosæ are divided into three Sub-orders :

Corolla pea-shaped. Petals dissimilar . . . . . . I. *Papilionaceæ.*
Corolla regular. Petals similar or nearly so.
 Flowers large, in clusters, racemes or panicles. Petals free. Stamens shorter or only slightly longer than the corolla . . . . II. *Cæsalpinieæ.*
 Flowers small, in heads or spikes. Petals united. Stamens much longer than the corolla . . . III. *Mimoseæ.*

I. PAPILIONACEÆ. Flowers pea-like. Calyx usually bell-shaped and 5-toothed. Petals usually clawed, dissimilar, consisting of an upper one called the standard and two lower pairs, the wings and keel respectively: standard outermost, covering the others, usually broadly ovate, free or slightly adherent to the stamens; wing-petals usually oblong, free or adherent to the inner petals; keel-petals innermost, usually ovate, their tips more or less incurved and their lower margins more or less united. Stamens 10, in *Dalbergia* only 9; all free, all united or united in two bundles of 5 each, or the upper stamen free and the others united; the stamens if united sheathing the ovary and more or less free above the middle; filaments usually thread-like, sometimes the alternate ones thickened towards the tip; anthers usually uniform, sometimes alternately large and small.—The name *Papilionaceæ* is derived from the Latin *papilio* from the resemblance of the corolla to a butterfly.

Papilionaceous flowers are all specialised in structure for fertilisation by insects; the details varying in the different genera.

A. Leaves simple

Stamens all free. Leaves apparently whorled . . . . 2. *Thermopsis.*
Stamens all united. Leaves alternate . . . . . . 4. *Crotalaria.*[1]
Upper stamen free, others united
 Pod jointed. Flowers not enclosed within bracts.
  Petals shorter than the calyx . . . . . 21. *Alysicarpus.*
  Petals longer than the calyx . . . . . . 23. *Desmodium.*[2]
 Pod not jointed. Flowers enclosed within bracts . . 37. *Flemingia.*[3]

B. Leaves compound

* Leaflets two

Stamens all united. Style glabrous . . . . . . 17. *Zornia.*
Upper stamen free, others united. Style bearded . . 25. *Lathyrus.*[4]

* * Leaflets three

† Terminal leaflet stalked. (See also *Trifolium minus.*)

Trees.
 Flowers white, pale pink or yellow-white.
  Stamens 10, upper one free, others united. Pod jointed . . . . 22. *Ougeinia.*
  Stamens 9, all united. Pod not jointed . . . 38. *Dalbergia.*[5]

[1] All species except *C. medicaginea.* [2] *D. gangeticum* only has simple leaves. [3] *F. fruticulosa* only. [4] Species 2, 3 and 4. [5] *Dalbergia* usually has 5, sometimes 3 leaflets.

Flowers red or orange red.
Calyx 2-lipped. Pod glabrous, cylindric . . . 29. *Erythrina.*
Calyx tubular. Pod tomentose, flat . . . 30. *Butea.*
Shrubs or herbs.
Leaflets toothed. Flowers small.
Flowers yellow.
Pod straight or nearly so . . . . . . 7. *Trigonella.*
Pod spirally twisted or strongly curved . . 9. *Medicago.*
Flowers white. Pod ovoid. Seeds only 1 or 2 . 8. *Melilotus.*
Leaflets entire.
Pod jointed, or constricted between the seeds.
Stems twining.
Flowers yellow . . . . 28. *Dumasia.*
Flowers purple-blue . . . . . . 31. *Pueraria.*
Stems erect or prostrate.
Racemes cylindric. Pod folded within the calyx . . . . 20. *Uraria.*
Racemes simple. Pod straight, protruding . 23. *Desmodium.*[1]
Pod neither jointed nor constricted between the seeds.
Stems erect. Pod 1-seeded . . . . . 16. *Lespedeza.*
Stems twining or trailing.[2] Pod more than 1-seeded, except sometimes in *Rhynchosia.*
Flowers $\frac{1}{2}$ in., pale lilac, solitary, in pairs or in short racemes . . . . . . 26. *Amphicarpæa.*
Flowers $\frac{1}{2}$ in., pink-white, racemed. Lower bracts large, involucrate . . . . . 27. *Shuteria.*
Flowers 1–$1\frac{1}{2}$ in., pink or red, clustered at the end of long, naked stalks . . . . . 33. *Vigna.*
Flowers $\frac{1}{4}$–$\frac{1}{2}$ in., yellow. Keel and style spirally twisted . . . . 32. *Phaseolus.*
Flowers $\frac{1}{2}$–$\frac{3}{4}$ in., pale yellow. Standard with 2 small pouches in the middle . . . . 34. *Dolichos.*
Flowers $\frac{1}{3}$–$1\frac{1}{4}$ in., yellow. Pod with transverse, parallel grooves between the seeds . 35. *Atylosia.*[3]
Flowers $\frac{1}{4}$–$\frac{3}{4}$ in., yellow or red. Pod $\frac{1}{2}$–$1\frac{1}{4}$ in. . 36. *Rhynchosia.*

† † Terminal leaflet sessile. (See also *Atylosia* and *Trifolium minus.*)

Stamens all free. A shrub. Flowers yellow. Anthers uniform . . . . 1. *Piptanthus.*
Stamens all united. Anthers dissimilar.
Pod flat, $\frac{3}{4}$–1 in. Seeds 1–15 . . . . . . 3. *Argyrolobium.*
Pod globose, $\frac{1}{7}$ in. Seeds 2 . . . . . . 4. *Crotalaria.*[4]
Upper stamen free, others united.
Flowers numerous, in heads or racemes.
Flowers in terminal heads . . . . . . 5. *Trifolium.*[5]
Flowers in axillary racemes . . . . . . 11. *Indigofera.*[6]
Flowers few, in small clusters or solitary.
Flowers red, in terminal, head-like clusters . . 37. *Flemingia.*[7]
Flowers blue, solitary or in pairs . . . . . 6. *Parochetus.*

* * * Leaflets 5 or more

† Leaves with a terminal leaflet

Stamens all free. A shrub. Leaflets 21–41. Flowers yellow 39. *Sophora.*

[1] *D. gangeticum* only has simple leaves. [2] *F. fruticulosa* only. [3] *A. scarabæoides* has the terminal leaflet very shortly stalked. [4] *C. medicaginea* only. [5] *T. minus* has the terminal leaflet shortly stalked. [6] *I. trifoliata* only. [7] *F. vestita* only.

Stamens united at the base, ultimately dividing into two bundles of 5 each. A herb. Leaflets 41–61. Flowers yellow . . . . 19. *Æschynomene.*
Stamens 9, all united. A tree. Leaflets 5 or 3. Flowers yellow-white . . . . 38. *Dalbergia.*[1]
Upper stamen free, others united.
Leaflets 5, 2 at the base of the leaf-stalk, 3 at the end. Flowers yellow, in umbels. Five longer stamens thickened upwards . . . . 10. *Lotus.*
Leaves covered with short hairs fixed by the centre. Flowers red, pink or purple, in racemes . . . 11. *Indigofera.*[2]
Flowers yellow, in racemes. Ovary stalked. Style bearded. Pod inflated . . . . 12. *Colutea.*
Flowers red, in leaf-opposed racemes. . . . . 13. *Tephrosia.*
Flowers pink, yellow or yellow-green, in axillary racemes or heads, rarely solitary or in pairs . . 15. *Astragalus.*

† † Leaves terminating in a spine, bristle or tendril

Stamens united in two bundles of 5 each. Flowers pale blue. Pod jointed . . . . 18. *Smithia.*
Upper stamen free, others united. Pod not jointed.
Leaves terminating in a spine. A shrub. Flowers yellow . . . . 14. *Caragana.*
Leaves terminating in a bristle or tendril. Herbs
Style cylindric, nearly glabrous . . . . . 24. *Vicia.*
Style flattened, bearded along the inner side . . 25. *Lathyrus.*[3]

* * * * Leaflets none

Stipules leaf-like. Leaves terminating in a tendril. Flowers yellow . . . . 25. *Lathyrus.*[4]

II. CÆSALPINIEÆ. Calyx 5-parted, spathe-like and undivided or spathe-like and splitting into 2 or 3 unequal segments. Petals free, imbricate, nearly equal and similar, the upper one innermost. Stamens 10 or fewer, free or united close to the base, shorter or only slightly longer than the corolla.

Calyx 5-parted. Leaves pinnately divided.
Shrubs prickly. Leaves 2-pinnate . . . . . . 40. *Cæsalpinia.*
Trees or herbs, not prickly. Leaves simply pinnate . 41. *Cassia.*
Calyx spathe-like and undivided or splitting into 2 or 3 segments. Leaves simple, notched or 2-lobed . . . 42. *Bauhinia.*

III. MIMOSEÆ. Flowers usually very small, crowded in globose heads or cylindric spikes. Calyx bell-shaped or tubular, teeth 4 or 5. Petals 4 or 5, united in a tubular or bell-shaped corolla. Stamens 8 or numerous, much longer than the corolla, free or more or less united.

Stamens 8, free. Pod jointed . . . . 43. *Mimosa.*
Stamens numerous. Pod not jointed.
Stamens free or united only at the base . . . . 44. *Acacia.*
Stamens united up to the top of the corolla . . . 45. *Albizzia.*

[1] *Dalbergia* usually has 5, sometimes 3 leaflets. [2] All species except *I. trifoliata.* [3] *L. luteus* only. [4] *L. Aphaca* only.

1. **PIPTANTHUS.** From the Greek *pipto*, to fall, and *anthos*, a flower; referring to the early falling of the flowers.—Temperate Himalaya, China, Central Asia.

Piptanthus nepalensis, *Don*; *Fl. Br. Ind.* ii. 62. An erect shrub. Leaves with three leaflets, nearly glabrous; leaflets sessile, lanceolate, 3–5 in., entire. Flowers yellow, 1–$1\frac{1}{4}$ in. long, crowded in short, hairy racemes. Bracts ovate, tomentose, soon falling off. Calyx tomentose, bell-shaped; 2 upper teeth broad, united to above the middle; 3 lower narrow, divided nearly to the base, equal. Petals clawed: standard erect, notched, margins reflexed; wings nearly as long as the curved, obtuse keel. Stamens all free; anthers uniform. Ovary stalked, nearly glabrous; style incurved, glabrous; stigma minute. Pod stalked, flat, $3\text{–}5 \times \frac{1}{2}\text{–}\frac{3}{4}$ in. Seeds 4–10.

Upper road from Matiana to Narkunda; April, May.—Temperate Himalaya, 7000–9000 ft.—China.

2. **THERMOPSIS.** From the Greek *thermos*, a lupin, and *opsis*, resemblance.—Himalaya, Central and E. Asia, N. America.

Thermopsis barbata, *Royle*; *Fl. Br. Ind.* ii. 62. A perennial herb. Stems tufted, erect, 6–18 in. Leaves of 3 sessile leaflets with leaf-like stipules at the base thus having the appearance of 3–7 whorled leaves, glabrous or hairy, lanceolate, 1–2 in., entire. Flowers dark violet-purple, 1 in. long, crowded in short, axillary racemes forming a long, terminal panicle. Bracts leaf-like, shaggy, united at the base. Calyx shaggy, bell-shaped; teeth 5, lanceolate, 2 upper more or less united. Petals glabrous, long-clawed: standard orbicular, 2-lobed, margins reflexed; wings shorter than the oblong keel. Stamens all free. Ovary hairy; style incurved; stigma minute. Pod hairy, broadly oblong, 1–2 in., acute. Seeds 2–6.

Patarnala; May, June.—Temperate Himalaya, 8000–12,000 ft.

3. **ARGYROLOBIUM.** From the Greek *argyros*, silver, and *lobos*, a pod.—Mediterranean region to India; Africa, chiefly South.

Small shrubs or perennial herbs. Branches long, slender, diffuse or procumbent. Leaves of 3 leaflets; leaflets sessile, nearly equal. Flowers small, in stalked racemes or clusters. Calyx deeply 2-lipped, upper lip 2-toothed, lower 3-toothed; teeth narrowly lanceolate. Petals glabrous, hardly longer than the calyx: standard oblong-orbicular, notched; wings oblong; keel broadly-oblong, obtuse, shorter than the standard. Stamens all united in a closed tube, 5 longer with large, basi-fixed anthers, 5 shorter with smaller, versatile anthers. Ovary sessile; style incurved; stigma minute. Pod $\frac{3}{4}$–1 in., erect, straight, narrow, flattened; seeds 6–15.

Densely silky. Leaflets lanceolate, acute. Flowers yellow . 1. *A. flaccidum.*
Thinly silky or glabrous. Leaflets obovate, obtuse. Flowers pink . . . . 2. *A. roseum.*

1. **Argyrolobium flaccidum,** *Jaub. & Spach*; *Fl. Br. Ind.* ii. 63. A small, erect shrub densely covered with short, adpressed, silky hairs; branches 12–18 in., sometimes dwarfed to less than 6 in. Leaflets oblong-lanceolate, $\frac{1}{2}$–$\frac{3}{4}$ in., acute. Flowers yellow, few, in short racemes. Pod $\frac{3}{4}$–1 in.; seeds 6–8.

Sutlej valley; May–July.—N.W. India, ascending to 9000 ft.

*2. **Argyrolobium roseum,** *Jaub. & Spach*; *Fl. Br. Ind.* ii. 64. A perennial, thinly silky herb; branches 6–12 in. Leaflets broadly obovate, $\frac{1}{3}$ in., base wedge-shaped, tip rounded. Flowers pink, few, clustered. Pod $\frac{3}{4}$ in.; seeds 10–15.

N.W. India, ascending to 7000 ft.; May–July.—Persia, Beloochistan.

4. CROTALARIA. From the Greek *krotalon*, a rattle, referring to the rattling of the seeds in the inflated pods.—Widely dispersed in tropical and warm regions.

Herbs or shrubs. Leaves alternate, simple or of 3 leaflets, entire; stipules usually small or none, in *C. alata* conspicuous as decurrent wings. Flowers yellow, rarely blue, in terminal or leaf-opposed racemes. Calyx 2-lipped; teeth 5, long, linear, the 2 upper more or less united. Petals about as long as the calyx or much longer: standard orbicular, notched, often with a small, hard knob just above the short claw; wings shorter than the standard; keel strongly incurved, pointed. Stamens all united in a tube split along the upper side, 5 shorter with long, basi-fixed anthers, 5 longer with smaller, versatile anthers. Ovary sessile or nearly so; style strongly curved or abruptly inflexed, bearded on the inner side below the minute stigma. Pod oblong or globose, inflated; seeds 2 or more, often numerous.

Leaves simple. Pod oblong, 6- to many-seeded.
  Flowers yellow.
    Petals never much longer than the calyx.
      Pod $\frac{1}{2}$ in. or less.
        Stems prostrate. Calyx and lower surface of leaves densely red-hairy. Flowers $\frac{1}{6}$ in. or less.
          Pod $\frac{1}{2}$ in. . . . . 1. *C. prostrata.*
          Pod $\frac{1}{4}$ in. or less . . . . 2. *C. humifusa.*
        Stems erect or diffuse. Calyx and lower surface of leaves white-pubescent. Flowers $\frac{1}{3}$ in. . 6. *C. albida.*
      Pod 1–1$\frac{1}{4}$ in.
        Stipules large, decurrent as conspicuous wings on the stem and branches . . . . . 4. *C. alata.*
        Stipules small, not decurrent . . . . . 5. *C. mysorensis.*

Petals $1\frac{1}{2}$–2 times as long as the calyx.
Leaves 1–2 in. Pod $\frac{3}{4}$ in., densely hairy . . 3. *C. hirsuta.*
Leaves 2–6 in. Pod $1\frac{1}{2}$–2 in., nearly glabrous . 8. *C. sericea.*
Flowers pale blue . . . . 7. *C. sessiliflora.*
Leaves with 3 leaflets. Pod globose, 2-seeded . . . 9. *C. medicaginea.*

1. **Crotalaria prostrata,** *Roxb.*; *Fl. Br. Ind.* ii. 67. A perennial, diffuse, hairy herb; stems slender, prostrate or trailing, 6–12 in. Leaves simple, nearly sessile, oblong-ovate, $\frac{1}{2}$–$1\frac{1}{2}$ in., obtuse, lower surface densely red-hairy; stipules small. Flowers $\frac{1}{5}$ in. long, few, racemose. Calyx densely red-hairy. Petals yellow, hardly longer than the calyx; standard red-streaked. Pod oblong, $\frac{1}{2}$ in., glabrous; seeds 12–18.

Sutlej valley, Suni; April.—Throughout India, ascending to 5000 ft.—Java.

2. **Crotalaria humifusa,** *Grah.*; *Fl. Br. Ind.* ii. 67. A perennial, diffuse, hairy herb; stems slender, prostrate, 6–12 in. Leaves simple, nearly sessile, orbicular-ovate, $\frac{1}{2}$–1 in., lower surface densely red-hairy; stipules small. Flowers few, $\frac{1}{8}$ in. long, racemose. Calyx densely red-hairy. Petals yellow, hardly longer than the calyx. Pod oblong, glabrous, not more than $\frac{1}{4}$ in. long; seeds 6–8.

Simla; July–September.—Temperate Himalaya, 4000–6000 ft.

3. **Crotalaria hirsuta,** *Willd.*; *Fl. Br. Ind.* ii. 68. A perennial, diffuse, hairy herb; stems prostrate or climbing over brushwood, much branched, one to several feet long. Leaves simple, sessile, ovate, 1–2 in., acute; stipules small. Flowers $\frac{1}{2}$ in. long, 2–3 in a raceme. Calyx hairy. Petals yellow, $1\frac{1}{2}$ times as long as the calyx; the standard and sometimes the wings spotted with purple. Pod oblong, $\frac{3}{4}$ in., densely hairy; seeds 8–10.

Simla; July–September.—Throughout India, ascending to 4000 ft.

*4. **Crotalaria alata,** *Buch.-Ham.*; *Fl. Br. Ind.* ii. 69. A densely hairy, erect undershrub, 1–2 ft. Leaves simple, nearly sessile, oblong, 1–3 in., tip rounded; stipules large, pointed, persistent, decurrent as conspicuous wings on the stem and branches. Flowers $\frac{1}{3}$ in. long, few, racemed. Calyx densely hairy. Petals pale yellow, hardly longer than the calyx. Pod oblong, 1–$1\frac{1}{2}$ in., glabrous; seeds 30–40.

N.W. India, ascending to 5000 ft.; July–September.—Assam.—Java.

*5. **Crotalaria mysorensis,** *Roth.*; *Fl. Br. Ind.* ii. 70. A densely hairy, erect undershrub, 1–2 ft. Leaves simple, nearly sessile, narrowly oblong, 1–3 in., obtuse or acute; stipules small. Flowers $\frac{1}{2}$–$\frac{3}{4}$ in. long, racemed. Calyx densely hairy. Petals yellow, hardly longer than the calyx. Pod oblong, 1–$1\frac{1}{4}$ in., glabrous; seeds 20–30.

Throughout India, ascending to 4000 ft.; July–September.

6. **Crotalaria albida,** *Heyne*; *Fl. Br. Ind.* ii. 71. An erect or diffuse, much-branched, silvery-pubescent undershrub, 1–2 ft. Leaves simple, nearly sessile, narrowly oblong, 1-2 in., obtuse, upper surface minutely dotted, lower white-pubescent; stipules none. Flowers $\frac{1}{3}$ in. long, racemed. Calyx white-pubescent. Petals pale yellow, not longer than the calyx. Pod oblong, $\frac{1}{2}$ in., glabrous; seeds 6–12.

Simla; July-September.—Throughout India, ascending to 7000 ft.—China, Malay Islands.

7. **Crotalaria sessiliflora,** *Linn.*; *Fl. Br. Ind.* ii. 73. An erect, hairy herb, 6–24 in. Leaves simple, shortly stalked, narrowly oblong-lanceolate, 1–4 × $\frac{1}{5}$–$\frac{1}{3}$ in., acute, upper surface glabrous or thinly hairy; stipules minute. Flowers $\frac{1}{3}$ in. long, nearly sessile, upper ones racemed, lower often axillary. Calyx densely covered with long hairs. Petals pale blue, not longer than the calyx. Pod oblong, $\frac{1}{2}$ in., glabrous; seeds 10–15.

Simla, Chadwick Falls, Waterworks Road; August, September.—Throughout N. India, ascending to 6000 ft.—China, Japan, Malay Islands.

8. **Crotalaria sericea,** *Retz.*; *Fl. Br. Ind.* ii. 75. An erect, silky-pubescent shrub, 3–6 ft.; stems robust, grooved. Leaves simple, nearly sessile, obovate, narrowed to the base, 2–6 × 1–3 in., tipped with a minute bristle; uppermost leaves lanceolate, acute; upper surface glabrous, lower finely pubescent; stipules small. Flowers $\frac{3}{4}$–1 in. long, in long, terminal racemes. Calyx pubescent. Petals yellow, nearly twice as long as the calyx. Pod oblong, 1$\frac{1}{2}$–2 in., nearly glabrous; seeds many.

Valleys below Simla; August–October.—Throughout India, ascending to 4000 ft.—Tropical Asia.

9. **Crotalaria medicaginea,** *Lam.*; *Fl. Br. Ind.* ii. 81. A perennial, silky-pubescent herb; branches 6–12 in., prostrate, spreading. Leaflets 3, nearly sessile, broadly wedge-shaped or narrowly obovate, $\frac{1}{4}$–$\frac{3}{4}$ in.; stipules minute. Flowers $\frac{1}{4}$ in. long, racemed. Calyx pubescent. Petals yellow, twice as long as the calyx. Pod globose, $\frac{1}{7}$ in. diam., pubescent; seeds 2.

Valleys below Simla, Sutlej valley, Suni; April–October.—Throughout India, ascending to 5000 ft.—Tropical Asia, Australia.

5. **TRIFOLIUM.** The Latin name of Clover, signifying three-leaved.—Most temperate regions except Australasia.

Erect or procumbent herbs. Leaves of 3 leaflets; leaflets nearly sessile or the terminal one stalked, usually toothed; stipules united to the leaf-stalk. Flowers small, numerous, crowded in long-stalked, ovoid or globose heads. Bracts small or none. Calyx bell-shaped; teeth 5, nearly equal or the 3 lower longer. Petals narrow, persistent; the claws united to the staminal tube; keel obtuse. Upper stamen free, others united. Style slightly curved, glabrous; stigma minute. Pod very small, indehiscent, enclosed within the brown, deflexed, withered corolla; seeds 1 or 3–4.

Heads $\frac{3}{4}$–$1\frac{1}{2}$ in. diam. Terminal leaflet sessile.
  Flowers red-purple. Pod 1-seeded . . . . . . 1. *T. pratense.*
  Flowers white or tinged with pink. Pod 3-4-seeded . 2. *T. repens.*
Heads $\frac{1}{4}$ in. diam. or less. Terminal leaflet stalked. Flowers very small, yellow . . . . 3. *T. minus.*

1. **Trifolium pratense,** *Linn.*; *Fl. Br. Ind.* ii. 86. Perennial, hairy; stems decumbent or nearly erect. Leaflets ovate or oblong, entire or toothed, tip obtuse or notched; terminal leaflet sessile. Stipules large, broadly ovate, veined, long-pointed, much shorter than the leaf-stalks. Heads ovoid or globose, $\frac{3}{4}$–$1\frac{1}{2}$ in. diam., with 1 or 2 leaves near the base. Flowers red-purple, nearly sessile. Calyx-teeth nearly equal, narrow, longer than the tube. Pod 1-seeded.

Simla, common; April–July.—W. Himalaya, 4000–8000 ft.—Temperate Asia, Europe (Britain, Purple Clover).—Widely colonised.

2. **Trifolium repens,** *Linn.*; *Fl. Br. Ind.* ii. 86. Perennial, glabrous or slightly hairy; stems slender, procumbent, rooting at the joints. Leaflets obovate, toothed, veins prominent, tip notched; terminal leaflet sessile. Stipules narrowly oblong, much shorter than the leaf-stalk. Heads globose, $\frac{3}{4}$–$1\frac{1}{4}$ in. diam. Flowers white or tinged with pink, shortly stalked. Calyx-teeth lanceolate, nearly equal, shorter than the tube. Pod 3–4-seeded.

Simla, common; April–July.—Temperate Himalaya.—Asia, Europe (Britain, Dutch Clover).—Widely colonised.

3. **Trifolium minus,** *Smith*; *Fl. Br. Ind.* ii. 86. Annual, nearly glabrous; stems trailing. Leaflets obovate, finely toothed; terminal leaflet shortly stalked. Stipules broadly lanceolate, nearly or quite as long as the leaf-stalk. Heads ovoid, $\frac{1}{4}$ in. diam., or less. Flowers yellow, shortly stalked. Calyx-teeth narrow, acute, the 2 upper much shorter than the tube, the 3 lower longer. Pod obovoid, 1-seeded.

Simla, common; an introduced weed, now naturalised; April, May.—Europe (Britain, Lesser Clover).—Commonly called the Shamrock.

6. **PAROCHETUS.** From the Greek *para*, near, and *ochetos*, a stream, referring to the usual habitat.—A genus of only one species.

Parochetus communis, *Buch.-Ham.*; *Fl. Br. Ind.* ii. 86. A hairy herb; stems long, thread-like, prostrate, rooting at the joints. Leaflets 3, nearly sessile, obcordate, entire or minutely toothed. Stipules lanceolate, acute, nearly free. Flowers deep violet-blue,

$\frac{1}{2}$–$\frac{3}{4}$ in. long, solitary or in pairs at the end of a stalk longer than the leaves. Calyx bell-shaped; teeth 5, acute, the 2 upper united to near the tips. Petals free from the staminal tube: standard erect, clawed; keel shorter than the wings. Upper stamen free, others united, filaments not dilated, anthers nearly uniform. Style glabrous, inflexed; stigma minute. Pod glabrous, $\frac{3}{4}$–1 in., straight, tipped with the persistent style; seeds many.

Matiana, in damp grass, not common; April–September.—Himalaya from Simla eastwards, 4000–13,000 ft.—Nilghiris, Burmah, Java, Africa.

7. **TRIGONELLA.** From the Greek *treis*, three, and *gonia*, an angle; referring to the triangular form of the flowers.—Asia, Mediterranean region, South Africa, Australia.

Annual, fragrant herbs; stems usually several, much branched, diffuse, procumbent, or erect. Leaves of 3 leaflets; leaflets small, obovate, upper half toothed, lower entire, wedge-shaped, lateral leaflets nearly sessile, terminal one stalked, veins prominent, parallel, running out into small, sharp teeth; stipules united to the leaf-stalk, lanceolate, entire or toothed, long-pointed. Flowers small, few, pale yellow, in umbels or short racemes at the end of axillary stalks often tipped with an awn-like point. Calyx bell-shaped; teeth 5, distinct, nearly equal, very narrow, acute. Petals narrow: standard and wings nearly equal; keel shorter, obtuse. Upper stamen nearly or quite free, others united. Style glabrous, slightly incurved; stigma minute. Pod much longer than the calyx, flat or nearly so, straight or curved; seeds several or many.

Trigonella Fœnum-græcum, *Linn.*, an erect, strongly-scented herb, is grown during the cold season throughout N. India as a pot-herb and occasionally as a fodder-crop. The seeds are used medicinally and as a spice. The plant was in high repute in ancient times both as food and medicine. Pod 2–3 in. long. The *Fenugreek* of old authors. Native name *methi* from the Sanskrit.

Flowers 1–4 in an umbel. Petals slightly longer than the calyx.
- Umbel-stalk tipped with a bristle-like awn . . . . 2. *T. gracilis.*
- Umbel-stalk not tipped with an awn.
  - Calyx-teeth shorter than the tube. Pod 1–2 in. long, net-veined . . . . 1. *T. polycerata.*
  - Calyx-teeth much longer than the tube. Pod $\frac{1}{2}$ in. long, parallel-veined . . . . 3. *T. pubescens.*

Flowers 6–12 in a raceme. Petals 2 or 3 times as long as the calyx.
- Pod straight, breadth about $\frac{1}{3}$ of length . . . . 4. *T. Emodi.*
- Pod curved, breadth about $\frac{1}{6}$ of length . . . . 5. *T. corniculata.*

1. **Trigonella polycerata,** *Linn.*; *Fl. Br. Ind.* ii. 87. Glabrous or slightly hairy; stems slender, 6–12 in., diffuse or procumbent. Leaflets $\frac{1}{4}$–$\frac{1}{2}$ in. Flowers 2–4, umbellate; umbel-stalk not awned.

Calyx hairy; teeth shorter than the tube. Petals rather longer than the calyx. Pod glabrous, 1–2 × $\frac{1}{10}$ in., slightly flattened and curved, net-veined.

Simla; June–September.—Plains of N. India, ascending to 6000 ft.—W. Asia, S. Europe, N. Africa.

2. **Trigonella gracilis,** *Benth.*; *Fl. Br. Ind.* ii. 88. Glabrous or nearly so; stems slender, 6–18 in., diffuse or procumbent. Leaflets $\frac{1}{5}$–$\frac{1}{2}$ in. Flowers 1–3, umbellate; umbel-stalk tipped with a bristle-like awn. Calyx slightly hairy; teeth about as long as the tube. Petals a little longer than the calyx. Pod pubescent, about $\frac{1}{2} \times \frac{1}{5}$ in., flat, straight, transversely veined.

Naldera; October.—W. Himalaya, 5000–9000 ft.

*3. **Trigonella pubescens,** *Edgew.*; *Fl. Br. Ind.* ii. 88. Nearly glabrous or hairy; stems slender, 6–18 in., diffuse or procumbent. Leaflets $\frac{1}{4}$–$\frac{1}{2}$ in. Flowers 1–3, umbellate; umbel stalk not awned. Calyx hairy; teeth much longer than the tube. Petals slightly longer than the calyx. Pod hairy, about $\frac{1}{2} \times \frac{1}{5}$ in., flat, straight, transversely veined.

W. Himalaya, 7000–10,000 ft.; June–September.

*4. **Trigonella Emodi,** *Benth.*; *Fl. Br. Ind.* ii. 88. Glabrous or pubescent; stems erect or nearly so, 12–24 in., often robust. Leaflets $\frac{1}{3}$–$\frac{3}{4}$ in. Flowers 6–12, racemose; stalk prolonged in a short point. Calyx hairy; teeth about as long as the tube. Petals 2–3 times as long as the calyx. Pod glabrous, about $\frac{3}{4} \times \frac{1}{5}$ in., flat, straight, transversely veined.

W. Himalaya, 4000–10,000 ft.; June–September.

5. **Trigonella corniculata,** *Linn.*; *Fl. Br. Ind.* ii. 88. Glabrous; stems erect or nearly so, 12–24 in., often robust. Leaflets $\frac{1}{4}$–$\frac{3}{4}$ in. Flowers 6–12, racemose; stalk produced beyond the flowers in an awn-like point. Calyx nearly glabrous; teeth about as long as the tube. Petals 2–3 times as long as the calyx. Pod glabrous, deflexed, about $\frac{3}{4} \times \frac{1}{10}$ in., flat, slightly curved, transversely veined.

Simla; June–September.—W. Himalaya, 5000–12,000 ft.—W. Asia, S. Europe.

8. MELILOTUS. From the Greek *meli*, honey, and lotus; the flowers are much frequented by bees.—Temperate regions of the Old World; widely colonised.

Melilotus alba, *Lam.*; *Fl. Br. Ind.* ii. 89. A pubescent or nearly glabrous herb; stems erect, 1–3 ft. Leaves of 3 leaflets; leaflets ovate or oblong, $\frac{1}{2}$–1 in., upper part toothed, base entire, lateral leaflets nearly sessile, terminal one stalked, veins parallel, running out into small sharp teeth; stipules narrowly lanceolate, long-pointed, united to the leaf-stalk. Flowers nearly $\frac{1}{5}$ in. long, white, in long, axillary racemes. Calyx bell-shaped; teeth 5, distinct, lanceolate, nearly equal, acute. Standard not clawed; wings and keel nearly equal, shorter than the standard; keel obtuse. Upper stamen free, others united. Style glabrous, incurved; stigma minute. Pod indehiscent, ovoid, about $\frac{1}{7}$ in. longer than the calyx, tipped with the persistent style; seeds 1 or 2.

Simla; June-September.—Plains of N. India, ascending to 12,000 ft.—W. Asia, Europe (Britain).

Melilotus parviflora, *Desf.*, is common in fields in the plains and may occur below 3000 ft. Flowers pale yellow, hardly $\frac{1}{12}$ in. long.

9. MEDICAGO. The classical name of the Lucern, *M. sativa.* —Asia, Europe, N. Africa; widely colonised.

Herbs; stems erect or procumbent. Leaves of 3 leaflets; leaflets upper part toothed, lower entire, lateral leaflets nearly sessile, terminal one stalked, veins parallel, running out into small sharp teeth. Stipules narrowly lanceolate, long-pointed, united to the leaf-stalk. Flowers bright yellow, blue in the cultivated *M. sativa*, in stalked, axillary racemes, heads or clusters. Calyx bell-shaped; teeth 5, distinct, nearly equal, acute. Petals twice as long as the cályx: standard not clawed; keel shorter than the wing-petals, obtuse. Upper stamen free, others united. Style glabrous, incurved; stigma minute. Pod strongly curved or spirally twisted, smooth or prickly; seeds solitary, several or many.

Stems erect. Leaflets oblong. Flowers $\frac{1}{3}$ in. long, in racemes . . . . 1. *M. falcata.*
Stems procumbent. Leaflets obovate. Flowers less than $\frac{1}{4}$ in. long, in heads or clusters.
  Flowers numerous, in globose heads. Pod smooth . 2. *M. lupulina.*
  Flowers 2–6, clustered. Pod prickly . . . . 3. *M. denticulata.*

* 1. **Medicago falcata,** *Linn.*; *Fl. Br. Ind.* ii. 90. Perennial, glabrous or nearly so; stems nearly erect, 1–2 ft., much branched. Leaflets narowly oblong, $\frac{1}{3}$–1 in. Flowers $\frac{1}{3}$ in. long, in racemes. Pod glabrous, strongly curved but not forming a complete spire, $\frac{1}{2}$–$\frac{3}{4}$ in.; seeds 5–10.

Orchard below the Retreat, Mushobra; June–September; W. Himalaya, 5000–12,000 ft.—W. Asia, Europe (Britain).

Lucern, *M. sativa*, closely allied to this species, has purple or blue flowers and spirally twisted pods. Cultivated for fodder throughout N. India.

* 2. **Medicago lupulina,** *Linn.*; *Fl. Br. Ind.* ii. 90. Annual, pubescent; stems numerous, slender, 1–2 ft., diffuse or procumbent. Leaflets obovate, $\frac{1}{4}$–$\frac{1}{2}$ in. Flowers very small, numerous, crowded in globose or ovoid heads about $\frac{1}{4}$ in. diam. Pod

smooth, minute, strongly curved, black when ripe, tip coiled; seed solitary.

Plains of N. India, ascending to 10,000 ft.; March–October.—W. Asia, N. Africa, Europe (Britain).

3. **Medicago denticulata,** *Willd.*; *Fl. Br. Ind.* ii. 90. Annual, nearly glabrous; stems several, 4–24 in., procumbent. Leaflets obovate, $\frac{1}{4}$ to nearly 1 in. Flowers about $\frac{1}{6}$ in., in 2–6-flowered clusters. Pod net-veined, flat, spirally twisted in 2 or 3 coils and bearing two rows of hooked spines along the outer margin; seeds several.

Valleys below Simla; March–October.—Plains of N. India, ascending to 5000 ft.—Asia, N. Africa, Europe (Britain).

10. **LOTUS.** A classical name applied by the ancients to several species.—Most temperate regions.

Lotus corniculatus, *Linn.*; *Fl. Br. Ind.* ii. 91. A perennial, glabrous herb; stems slender, decumbent or ascending, very short or more than a foot long. Leaves of 5 leaflets; leaflets ovate, obovate or oblong, $\frac{1}{4}$–$\frac{3}{4}$ in., nearly sessile, entire, 2 at the base of the leaf-stalk, 3 at the tip, occasionally there is only one leaflet at the base and 4 at the tip or 3 at the tip and one intermediate; stipules none or reduced to minute glands. Flowers about $\frac{1}{2}$ in. long, yellow, often streaked with crimson, 5–10 in a long-stalked, axillary umbel with a leaf of 3 leaflets close under it. Calyx bell-shaped; teeth 5, distinct, nearly equal, acute. Petals about twice as long as the calyx: standard longer than the wings, clawed, erect; keel abruptly incurved, pointed. Upper stamen free, others united, 5 alternate ones longer than the others and thickened upwards; anthers uniform. Style abruptly incurved just above the ovary, glabrous; stigma minute. Pod cylindric, straight, 1–1$\frac{1}{2}$ in.; seeds several, separated by a pith-like substance which nearly fills the pod.

Simla, Matiana, Huttoo; April–September.—Asia, Africa, Australia, Europe (Britain, Bird's-foot Trefoil).

11. **INDIGOFERA.** From the Latin *indicum*, signifying a blue pigment believed to be the same as the modern indigo, derived from the word India, whence it was procured, and *fero*, I bear. —A large genus spread through nearly all tropical, and extending into some temperate regions.

Herbs or shrubs more or less covered with white, adpressed hairs fixed by the centre, often mixed with ordinary hairs or tomentum. Leaves odd-pinnate; leaflets 5 or more, rarely only 3, entire, usually opposite; stipules usually small, shortly united to the leaf-stalk. Flowers red, pink or purple, in axillary, often erect racemes, rarely in ovoid heads. Bracts minute or long and more or less enclosing the flower-buds, falling off as the flowers expand. Calyx small, bell-shaped; teeth 5, nearly equal or the lowest longer. Petals soon falling off, except sometimes the standard; keel straight, obtuse. Upper stamen free, others united; anthers tipped with a minute point. Ovary sessile; ovules usually many; style glabrous, incurved; stigma small, capitate, often minutely hairy. Pod cylindric or nearly so, straight or slightly curved, often deflexed; seeds 6–12, rarely only 2, separated by pith-like partitions.

The indigo dye of commerce is chiefly obtained from *I. tinctoria*, doubtfully wild in India.

Leaflets 3. Flowers crowded in short, sessile racemes . . 2. *I. trifoliata.*
Leaflets 5 or more.
  Flowers in ovoid heads. Pod $\frac{1}{7}$ in., 2-seeded . . . 1. *I. enneaphylla.*
  Flowers in racemes. Pod $\frac{3}{4}$ in. or more, many-seeded.
    Bracts minute.
      Calyx-teeth bristle-like, much longer than the tube . . . . 3. *I. hirsuta.*
      Calyx-teeth triangular, not longer than the tube 4. *I. Gerardiana.*
    Bracts long, more or less enclosing the flower-buds.
      Leaflets 9–11, ovate or ovate-oblong, thinly hairy or glabrous. Pod glabrous.
        Bracts boat-shaped, abruptly narrowed in a long, tail-like point . . . . 6. *I. hebepetala.*
        Bracts lanceolate, gradually narrowed to the point.
          Flowers very dark purple-red . . . . 5. *I. atropurpurea.*
          Flowers bright pink . . . . . . 7. *I. pulchella.*
      Leaflets 19–35, oblong, densely hairy or tomentose. Pod tomentose . . . . . . 8. *I. Dosua.*

*1. **Indigofera enneaphylla,** *Linn.*; *Fl. Br. Ind.* ii. 94. Perennial, silvery pubescent; stems numerous, tufted, procumbent, 12–18 in., much branched. Leaves $\frac{1}{2}$–$1\frac{1}{2}$ in.; leaflets 7–11, usually alternate, obovate, $\frac{1}{4}$–$\frac{1}{2}$ in. Flowers very small, bright red, crowded in nearly sessile, ovoid heads $\frac{1}{4}$–$\frac{1}{2}$ in. long. Calyx-teeth long, bristle-like. Pod pubescent, about $\frac{1}{7}$ in.; seeds 2.

Throughout India, ascending to 4000 ft.; January–December.—Malay Islands, N. Australia.

*2. **Indigofera trifoliata,** *Linn.*; *Fl. Br. Ind.* ii. 96. Perennial, pubescent or hairy; branches numerous, long, spreading from the base, procumbent or ascending. Leaflets 3, sessile, oblong, $\frac{1}{2}$–1 in., gland-dotted. Flowers small, red, crowded in short, sessile racemes. Calyx-teeth long, bristle-like. Pod pubescent, about $\frac{1}{2}$ in.

Throughout India, ascending to 4000 ft.; June–December.—Asia to Tropical Australia.

*3. **Indigofera hirsuta,** *Linn.*; *Fl. Br. Ind.* ii. 98. Annual or biennial, herbaceous, densely hairy; stems 2–4 ft., erect. Leaves 2–6 in.; leaflets 5–11, opposite, obovate, 1–2 in.; stipules long, bristle-like, fringed. Flowers small, red, crowded in slender, hairy racemes 2–6 in. long. Bracts minute. Calyx-teeth much longer than the tube, bristle-like, fringed. Pod hairy, about $\frac{3}{4}$ in.

Throughout India, ascending to 4000 ft.; June–January.—Nearly all tropical regions.

4. **Indigofera Gerardiana,** *Wall.*; *Fl. Br. Ind.* ii. 100, including var. *heterantha*. A silvery pubescent or tomentose shrub. Leaves $1\frac{1}{2}$–3 in.; leaflets 7–23, opposite, ovate or oblong-ovate, $\frac{1}{4}$–$\frac{3}{4}$ in.,

Fig. 36. Indigofera Gerardiana.

both surfaces hairy. Racemes 2–4 in. Bracts minute. Flowers $\frac{1}{4}$–$\frac{1}{2}$ in. long, pale red or purple. Calyx-teeth triangular, not longer than the tube. Pod pubescent, 1–2 in. (Fig. 36.)

Simla, common; May–July.—Temperate Himalaya, 5000–8000 ft.

5. **Indigofera atropurpurea,** *Buch.-Ham.*; *Fl. Br. Ind.* ii. 101. A tall, nearly glabrous shrub; branches erect. Leaves 6–12 in.; leaflets 11–17, opposite, ovate-oblong, 1–$1\frac{1}{2}$ in., both surfaces thinly pubescent. Racemes 6–12 in. Bracts lanceolate, gradually narrowed to the point. Flowers very dark purple-red, $\frac{1}{4}$–$\frac{1}{3}$ in. long. Pod glabrous, 1–$1\frac{1}{2}$ in.

Sutlej valley, near Rampore; June, July.—Temperate Himalaya, 4000–9000 ft.—China.

6. **Indigofera hebepetala,** *Benth.*; *Fl. Br. Ind.* ii. 101. A tall shrub, thinly hairy or glabrous; branches erect. Leaves 4–8 in.; leaflets 9–17, opposite, ovate or ovate-oblong, $\frac{3}{4}$–$1\frac{3}{4}$ in. Racemes 2–6 in. Bracts boat-shaped, abruptly narrowed in a long, tail-like point, quite enclosing the flower-buds. Flowers crimson-red, $\frac{1}{3}$ in. long. Pod glabrous, $1\frac{1}{2}$–$2\frac{1}{4}$ in.

Mahasu, Theog, Narkunda; May, June.—Temperate Himalaya, 6000–15,000 ft.

7. **Indigofera pulchella,** *Roxb.*; *Fl. Br. Ind.* ii. 101. A thinly hairy or glabrous shrub. Leaves 2–6 in.; leaflets 11–19, opposite, ovate or oblong-ovate, $\frac{3}{4}$–1 in. Racemes 2–6 in. Bracts lanceolate, gradually narrowed in a long point. Flowers bright pink, fading to violet, $\frac{1}{3}$ in. long. Pod glabrous, 1–$1\frac{1}{2}$ in.

Valleys below Simla; March–May.—Plains of N. India, ascending to 5000 ft.—Nilghiris.

8. **Indigofera Dosua,** *Buch.-Ham.*; *Fl. Br. Ind.* ii. 102. A densely hairy or tomentose shrub. Leaves $2\frac{1}{2}$–$4\frac{1}{2}$ in.; leaflets 19–35, opposite, narrowly oblong, $\frac{1}{4}$–$\frac{1}{3}$ in., both surfaces hairy, lower paler. Racemes 2–4 in. Bracts hairy, narrowly lanceolate, long-pointed, much longer than the flower-buds. Flowers bright red, nearly $\frac{1}{2}$ in. long. Pod tomentose, $\frac{3}{4}$–$1\frac{1}{4}$ in.

Simla, Mushobra; May, June.—Temperate Himalaya, Assam to Simla, 6000–8000 ft.

12. COLUTEA. The classical name of some plant of this affinity; etymology obscure.—Temperate Asia, S. Europe.

Colutea nepalensis, *Sims*; *Fl. Br. Ind.* ii. 103, *under C. arborescens, Linn.* An erect, nearly glabrous shrub. Leaves odd-pinnate, 2–6 in.; leaflets 9–13, pale green, obovate, $\frac{1}{4}$–$\frac{1}{2}$ in. Flowers yellow, often tinged with red, $\frac{3}{4}$ in. long, in axillary racemes. Calyx bell-shaped; teeth 5, short, nearly equal, the lowest longest. Standard orbicular, spreading, having 2 small folds just above the short claw; wings oblong; keel broad, curved, obtuse, the long claws united. Upper stamen free, others united. Ovary stalked, pubescent; style strongly curved, bearded along the inner side, tip inflexed; stigma thick, dilated. Pod bladder-like, ovoid, $1\frac{1}{2}$–2 in. long, splitting at the top when mature; seeds many, kidney-shaped.

Simla, Mahasu, Matiana; July, August.—Temperate Himalaya, 8000–11,000 ft.

Closely allied to the S. European *C. arborescens*, Bladder Senna, so called from the inflated pods and the purgative properties of the leaflets.

13. TEPHROSIA. From the Greek *tephros*, ash-coloured, referring to the pubescence of most species.—Most tropical regions.

Tephrosia purpurea, *Pers.*; *Fl. Br. Ind.* ii. 112. A perennial, pubescent herb; stems erect, 1–2 ft., woody. Leaves odd-pinnate, 2–5 in.; leaflets 9–21, oblong-lanceolate, $\frac{1}{2}$–1 × $\frac{1}{5}$–$\frac{1}{3}$ in., entire, obtuse, bristle-tipped, upper surface nearly glabrous, lower silky, veins straight, parallel. Flowers red, $\frac{1}{4}$–$\frac{1}{3}$ in. long, in leaf-opposed racemes. Calyx silky, bell-shaped; the 3 lower teeth about as long as the tube, 2 upper longer. Standard orbicular, silky outside; keel incurved, obtuse. Upper stamen free, others united. Style strongly curved, glabrous; stigma capitate. Pod sessile, pubescent, flat, 1$\frac{1}{2}$–2 × $\frac{1}{5}$ in.; seeds 6–10.

Simla, in meadows, July–September.—Throughout India, ascending to 6000 ft.—Widely spread throughout the tropics.

14. CARAGANA. The Mongolian name for *C. arborescens.*—Central and Eastern China, Japan.

Caragana brevispina, *Royle*; *Fl. Br. Ind.* ii. 116. A tall, erect shrub, more or less hairy or pubescent. Leaves equally pinnate, 2–3 in., clustered on short, thick branchlets; leaflets 8–16, opposite, ovate, obovate or oblong-ovate, $\frac{1}{4}$–1 in., entire, upper surface glabrous, lower silky-pubescent, paler; leaf-rachises usually persisting as long, thick spines, naked or bearing 1 or 2 leaflets; stipules spinescent. Flowers bright yellow, nearly 1 in. long, in stalked few-flowered umbels shorter than the leaves. Calyx pubescent, oblique, tubular; teeth 5, nearly equal, shorter than the tube, spine-tipped. Standard orbicular, erect, shortly clawed, sides reflexed; keel straight, obtuse. Upper stamen free, others united. Ovary hairy; style short, hairy, nearly straight; stigma minute. Pod flattened, pubescent, 1$\frac{1}{2}$–2 × $\frac{1}{5}$ in., woolly inside; seeds 3 or 4.

Matiana, Narkunda; June–August.—W. Himalaya, 6000–9000 ft.—Chinese Tartary, Afghanistan.

15. ASTRAGALUS. The classical name of a shrub supposed to be of this affinity.—A very large genus, widely distributed over the temperate regions of the northern Hemisphere; one species in S. America and one in S.E. Africa.

Herbs or shrubs. Leaves odd-pinnate; leaflets many, usually opposite, entire. Flowers in stalked, axillary racemes or heads. Calyx bell-shaped or tubular; teeth 5, nearly equal. Petals narrow, clawed: standard erect; wings about equal to the incurved, obtuse keel. Upper stamen free, others united. Ovary sessile or stalked; style incurved, glabrous; stigma small, capitate. Pod usually more or less divided length-wise by the infolding of the lower suture; seeds 3–12.

Densely hairy or tomentose. Stems trailing.
- Flowers in racemes. Leaflets 13–17 . . . . 1. *A. Amherstianus.*
- Flowers in heads. Leaflets 21–31 . . . . . 4. *A. leucocephalus.*

Glabrous or thinly hairy. Stems erect or nearly so.
Flowers many in a raceme.
Leaflets 31–41. Flowers pink or lilac, hardly $\frac{1}{2}$ in. long . . . . 2. *A. trichocarpus.*
Leaflets 13–17. Flowers pale yellow-green, $\frac{1}{2}$–$\frac{3}{4}$ in. long . . . . 5. *A. chlorostachys.*
Flowers solitary or in pairs . . . . . . 3. *A. hosackioides.*

1. **Astragalus Amherstianus,** *Benth.*; *Fl. Br. Ind.* ii. 119. An annual herb, densely covered with shining, white hairs; stems tufted, slender, 6–18 in., trailing. Leaves 1–1$\frac{1}{2}$ in.; leaflets 13–17, narrowly oblong, $\frac{1}{4}$ in. Flowers pale yellow or pink, $\frac{1}{4}$ in. long, in racemes $\frac{1}{2}$–$\frac{3}{4}$ in. long. Calyx nearly as long as the corolla; teeth linear, as long as the tube. Pod sessile, curved, $\frac{1}{2}$ in., incompletely 2-celled; seeds 10–12.

Simla; May, June.—W. Himalaya, 6000–10,000 ft.

2. **Astragalus trichocarpus,** *Grah.*; *Fl. Br. Ind.* ii. 121. A tall, erect, nearly glabrous shrub; branches straight, grooved. Leaves 3–6 in.; leaflets 31–41, oblong, $\frac{1}{4}$–$\frac{1}{2}$ in., upper surface pale green, lower silvery hairy. Flowers numerous, pink or lilac, hardly $\frac{1}{2}$ in. long, crowded in racemes 3–4 in. long. Calyx bell-shaped, much shorter than the corolla; teeth shorter than the tube. Pod stalked, pubescent, oblong, $\frac{3}{4}$–1 in., incompletely 2-celled; seeds 4–6.

Simla, the Glen, &c., common; April, May.—Central Himalaya, Simla to Kumaon, 5000–8000 ft.

3. **Astragalus hosackioides,** *Benth.*; *Fl. Br. Ind.* ii. 123. A perennial, nearly glabrous herb; stems tufted, slender, 1–2$\frac{1}{2}$ ft., nearly erect, often zigzag, much branched. Leaves 1–2 in.; leaflets 13–15, ovate-oblong, about $\frac{1}{3}$ in., obtuse. Flowers yellow, $\frac{1}{4}$ in. long, solitary or in pairs. Calyx half as long as the corolla; teeth much shorter than the tube. Pod stalked, straight, $\frac{3}{4} \times \frac{1}{5}$ in.; when ripe the membranous lining separates from the outer coat and is constricted between the seeds; seeds 5–6.

Shali, 8000 ft.; September.—W. Himalaya.

4. **Astragalus leucocephalus,** *Grah.*; *Fl. Br. Ind.* ii. 128. A perennial herb, densely covered with silvery white hairs; stems tufted, 4–12 in., ascending. Leaves 1–3 in.; leaflets 21–31, crowded, oblong, $\frac{1}{4}$ in. Flowers pale yellow, $\frac{1}{3}$ in. long, in ovoid heads $\frac{1}{2}$–$\frac{3}{4}$ in. long. Calyx nearly as long as the corolla; teeth linear, as long as the tube. Pod 1-celled, sessile, oblong, $\frac{1}{6}$ in., included within the calyx; seeds 3 or 4.

Simla, Naldera; April, May.—W. Himalaya, 1000–7000 ft.—Afghanistan.

5. **Astragalus chlorostachys,** *Lindl.*; *Fl. Br. Ind.* ii. 128. A tall, erect shrub; stems glabrous or pubescent, grooved. Leaves 4–6 in.; leaflets 13–17, oblong, $\frac{3}{4}$–1 in., obtuse, both surfaces

thinly hairy, lower paler. Flowers numerous, pale yellow-green, often tinged with lilac, $\frac{1}{2}$–$\frac{3}{4}$ in. long, crowded in racemes 3–6 in. long. Calyx pubescent, tubular, about half as long as the corolla,

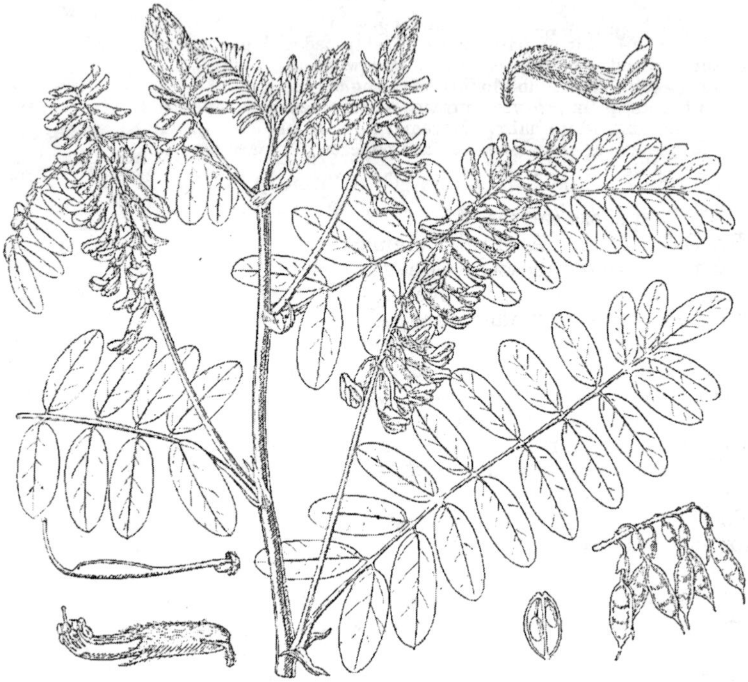

FIG. 37. ASTRAGALUS CHLOROSTACHYS.

mouth oblique; teeth very short. Pod glabrous, oblong, pointed, $\frac{1}{2}$ in., narrowed into a stalk twice as long as the calyx, 2-celled; seeds 6–10. (Fig. 37.)

Simla, Mahasu; August, September.—W. Himalaya, 5000–14,000 ft.

16. LESPEDEZA. In honour of D. Lespedez, Governor of Florida in the eighteenth century and a patron of botany.—N. Asia, N. America.

Erect, pubescent or hairy undershrubs. Leaflets 3, entire, lateral sessile, terminal one stalked, largest. Stipules soon falling off. Flowers numerous, in axillary clusters or racemes. Bracts small. Calyx bell-shaped; teeth 5, long, narrow, nearly equal. Standard broad, erect, clawed; keel slightly curved and obtuse, or strongly curved and acute. Upper stamen free, others united. Ovary 1-ovuled; style glabrous, long, incurved; stigma minute. Pod ovate, flat, indehiscent; seed solitary.

Leaflets at least three times longer than broad. Flowers in sessile clusters. Keel obtuse. Pod hardly longer than the calyx.
Flowers $\frac{1}{4}$ in. long or less.
Flowers pale yellow or white, tinged with purple. Leaflets $\frac{1}{2}$–$\frac{3}{4}$ in. . . . . 1. *L. sericea.*
Flowers pale purple. Leaflets $\frac{1}{4}$–$\frac{1}{2}$ in. . . . . 2. *L. juncea.*
Flowers $\frac{1}{2}$ in. long, pale yellow. Keel tipped with purple 3. *L. Gerardiana.*
Leaflets about as long as broad. Flowers in racemes. Keel acute. Pod much longer than the calyx.
Leaflets $\frac{1}{2}$ in.; lower surface densely covered with shining, white hairs. Racemes 1 in. or less . . 4. *L. stenocarpa.*
Leaflets 1–1$\frac{1}{4}$ in.; lower surface pubescent. Racemes 3–6 in. . . . . 5. *L. eriocarpa.*

1. **Lespedeza sericea,** *Miq.*; *Fl. Br. Ind.* ii. 142. A shrub; stems 2–3 ft., densely pubescent. Leaves nearly sessile, crowded, overlapping; leaflets wedge-shaped, $\frac{1}{2}$–$\frac{2}{3}$ × $\frac{1}{10}$ in., upper surface nearly glabrous, lower densely white-silky. Flowers nearly sessile, $\frac{1}{4}$ in. long, pale yellow or white, tinged with purple, in numerous, small, axillary clusters. Calyx white-silky. Keel slightly curved, obtuse. Pod $\frac{1}{8}$ in., thinly silky, hardly longer than the calyx.

Simla; July, August.—Throughout the Himalaya, 3000–8000 ft.—China, Japan, N. Australia.

2. **Lespedeza juncea,** *Pers.*; *Fl. Br. Ind.* ii. 142. A small shrub, rarely more than 6–12 in. high; stems densely pubescent, sometimes decumbent near the base. Leaves shortly stalked, crowded, overlapping; leaflets oblanceolate, $\frac{1}{4}$–$\frac{1}{2}$ in., upper surface nearly glabrous, lower densely grey-silky. Flowers nearly sessile, hardly $\frac{1}{4}$ in. long, pale purple, in numerous, small, axillary clusters. Calyx grey-silky. Keel slightly curved, obtuse. Pod $\frac{1}{8}$ in., thinly silky, hardly longer than the calyx.

Simla; August.—W. Himalaya, up to 7000 ft.—N. and Eastern Asia.

3. **Lespedeza Gerardiana,** *Grah.*; *Fl. Br. Ind.* ii. 142. A shrub;

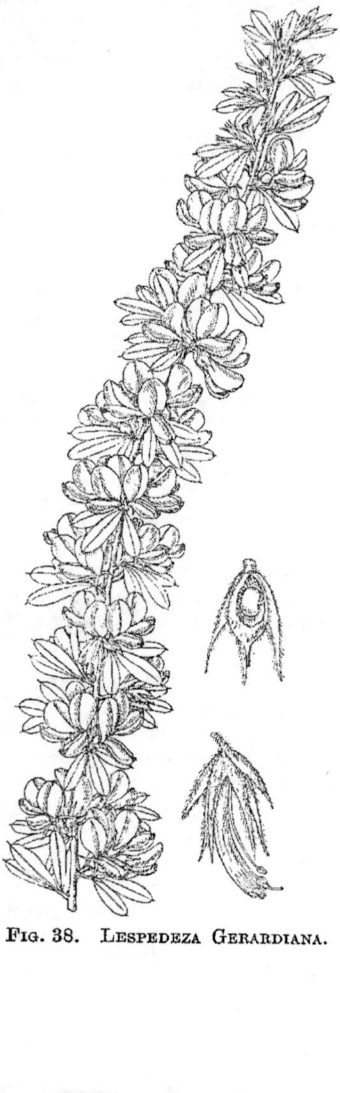

FIG. 38. LESPEDEZA GERARDIANA.

stems 1–3 ft., densely pubescent. Leaves shortly stalked, not crowded, slightly over-lapping; leaflets oblanceolate, $\frac{1}{2}$–$\frac{3}{4}\times\frac{1}{5}$ in., upper surface glabrous, lower densely grey-silky. Flowers nearly sessile, $\frac{1}{2}$ in. long, pale yellow, in numerous, small, axillary clusters. Calyx grey-silky. Keel slightly curved, obtuse, tipped with brown-purple. Pod $\frac{1}{10}$ in., silky, concealed in the calyx. (Fig. 38.)

Simla; August.—Throughout the Himalaya, 5000–10,000 ft.

4. **Lespedeza stenocarpa,** *Maxim.*; *Fl. Br. Ind.* ii. 143, *under L. macrostyla, Baker.* A shrub; stems 3–4 ft., densely pubescent. Leaves shortly stalked; leaflets obovate, about $\frac{1}{2}$ in. long and nearly as broad, upper surface nearly glabrous, lower densely covered with shining, white-silky hairs. Flowers nearly $\frac{1}{2}$ in. long, deep red, crowded in racemes hardly $\frac{1}{2}$ in. long; buds hidden by the ovate, silky bracts. Calyx white-silky. Keel strongly curved, acute. Fruiting racemes 1–2 in. Pod $\frac{1}{2}$ in., grey-silky, narrowly oblong, much longer than the calyx, tapering upwards to the base of the long, hairy, persistent style.

Sutlej and Giri valleys; July–December.—Plains of N. India, ascending to 5000 ft.

5. **Lespedeza eriocarpa,** *DC.*; *Fl. Br. Ind.* ii. 144. A shrub; stems 3–4 ft., pubescent. Leaves stalked; leaflets ovate or obovate, about $1\times\frac{3}{4}$ in., upper surface glabrous, dark green, lower pubescent, paler. Flowers nearly $\frac{1}{3}$ in. long, deep purple-red, in stalked racemes 3–6 in. long. Calyx brown-silky. Keel strongly curved, acute. Pod ovate, $\frac{1}{4}$ in., hairy, acute, much longer than the calyx.

Simla, Mushobra, Matiana, not common, Shali, abundant; September.—Throughout the Himalaya, 4000–9000 ft.

17. ZORNIA. In honour of J. Zorn, a Bavarian botanical author of the eighteenth century.—A small American genus, one species being also widely diffused in the tropics.

Zornia diphylla, *Pers.*; *Fl. Br. Ind.* ii. 147. A hairy or pubescent, nearly erect herb; stems several, tufted, 6–12 in., slender. Leaves of 2 leaflets; leaflets nearly sessile, lanceolate, $\frac{1}{2}$–1 in., entire, acute, lower surface black-dotted; stipules leaf-like, produced downwards. Flowers nearly sessile, yellow, $\frac{1}{4}$ in. long, in erect, axillary racemes 1–3 in.; each flower almost hidden in a pair of leaf-like, fringed bracts. Calyx membranous, half as long as the petals; teeth 5, the 2 upper united, 2 lateral very short, lowest as long as the upper. Standard orbicular; keel incurved, obtuse. Stamens united in a closed tube, 5 longer bearing globose anthers, alternate with 5 shorter, bearing oblong anthers. Style incurved, glabrous; stigma minute. Pod protruding from between the bracts, flattened, minutely prickly; upper margin nearly straight, lower deeply indented, dividing the pod into 2–5 indehiscent, 1-seeded joints.

Valleys below Simla; July–September.—Throughout India, ascending to 5000 ft.—Nearly all tropical regions.

18. SMITHIA. In honour of Sir J. E. Smith, founder of the Linnean Society, who died in 1828.—Tropical regions of the Old World.

Smithia ciliata, *Royle*; *Fl. Br. Ind.* ii. 150. An erect, annual herb; stems glabrous, 6–18 in. Leaves pinnate, $\frac{1}{2}$–$\frac{3}{4}$ in.; rachis ending in a bristle; stipules scarious, persistent; leaflets 6–12, narrowly oblong, $\frac{1}{3}$ in., obtuse, hairy, sensitive. Flowers pale blue or nearly white, $\frac{1}{3}$ in. long, crowded in stalked, axillary, 1-sided racemes $\frac{1}{4}$–$\frac{1}{2}$ in. long. Bracts scarious, persistent. Bracteoles fringed, half the length of the calyx. Calyx membranous, nearly as long as the corolla, divided almost to the base in two entire, fringed lips, the upper the larger. Standard orbicular; keel incurved, obtuse. Stamens all united at first, ultimately splitting into two bundles of 5 each. Ovary many-ovuled; style incurved; stigma minute. Pod rough, flattened, upper margin nearly straight, lower deeply indented, forming 6–8 indehiscent, 1-seeded joints folded face to face within the calyx.

Simla, Naldera, often on grassy slopes; July–September.—Himalaya, Simla to Assam, 3000–6000 ft.

19. ÆSCHYNOMENE. From the Greek *aischuno*, to make ashamed, referring to the sensitive leaves collapsing when touched. —Tropical and subtropical regions.

Æschynomene indica, *Linn.*; *Fl. Br. Ind.* ii. 151. An annual, shrubby, glabrous herb; stems 1–3 ft., erect, much branched. Leaves odd-pinnate, 2–3 in., stalk glandular; leaflets 41–61, sensitive, alternate, crowded, narrowly oblong, obtuse, diminishing in size towards the end of the leaves. Flowers yellow, often streaked with purple, $\frac{1}{3}$ in. long, in numerous, axillary, glandular racemes. Bracts and bracteoles small, lanceolate. Calyx half as long as the petals, divided nearly to the base in 2 nearly equal, entire or obscurely toothed lips. Standard orbicular, erect; keel nearly straight, obtuse. Stamens all united near the base, ultimately dividing into two bundles of five each. Style incurved, glabrous; stigma minute. Pod stalked, flattened, smooth, 1–1$\frac{1}{2}$ in., upper margin nearly straight, lower indented, dividing the pod into 7–9 indehiscent, 1-seeded joints.

Valleys below Simla; common on the borders of ricefields; July–September. —Throughout India, ascending to 5000 ft.—All tropical regions of the Old World.

Æ. aspera, a large, thick-stemmed, perennial plant, is common in marshes in Bengal and S. India; the light, white pith is made into toys, solah hats, &c.

20. URARIA. From the Greek *oura*, a tail, referring to the inflorescence.—Tropical regions of Asia, Africa and Australia.

Uraria neglecta, *Prain*; *Journ. As. Soc. Bengal*, lxvi. ii. 382; *Fl. Br. Ind.* ii. 156; *U. lagopus* in part. An erect shrub, 3–10 ft.; stems and branches densely pubescent. Leaves of 3 leaflets; leaflets ovate-oblong, 2–3 in., net-veined, entire, base rounded, upper surface nearly glabrous, lower pubescent, lateral nearly sessile, terminal one largest, stalked. Flowers very numerous, purple, $\frac{1}{4}$–$\frac{1}{3}$ in. long, on long, hairy stalks crowded in cylindric, terminal racemes 3–6 in. long and about 1 in. diam. Bracts hairy, ovate, $\frac{1}{3}$ in., pointed. Calyx hairy, nearly as long as the petals, tube short; teeth 5, very narrow, nearly equal, the 2 upper partially united. Standard orbicular, erect; keel incurved, obtuse. Upper stamen free, the others united. Style glabrous, inflexed; stigma minute. Pod sessile, constricted between the seeds; joints 6–8, glabrous, flattened, folded face to face within the calyx, indehiscent.

Valleys below Simla; August, September.—Throughout the Himalaya, 2000–6000 ft.—Assam.

21. ALYSICARPUS. From the Greek *alusis*, a chain, and *carpos*, fruit; referring to the jointed pod.—Tropical regions of the Old World.

Alysicarpus rugosus, *DC.*; *Fl. Br. Ind.* ii. 159. A diffuse, nearly glabrous herb; stems 6–24 in. Leaves ovate or oblong, about 1 × $\frac{1}{2}$ in., entire; stipules scarious, lanceolate, $\frac{1}{4}$–$\frac{1}{2}$ in., acute. Flowers crowded in terminal racemes 1–4 in. long. Calyx $\frac{1}{4}$–$\frac{1}{3}$ in., 4-lobed nearly to the base; lobes fringed, overlapping, upper one broad, 2-toothed, 3 lower narrowly lanceolate, acute. Petals pale pink, shorter than the calyx; keel slightly curved, obtuse. Upper stamen free, others united. Style-tip incurved; stigma capitate. Pod sessile, about $\frac{1}{4}$ in., composed of 3–5 glabrous, wrinkled, 1-seeded, indehiscent joints, enclosed within the calyx.

Valleys below Simla; July–September.—Throughout India, ascending to 4500 ft.—Tropics of the Old World, Cape, W. Indies.

A. vaginalis, *DC.*, is common in the plains and may occur below 4000 ft. Leaves oblong $\frac{1}{2}$–2 in., or orbicular $\frac{1}{4}$–$\frac{1}{2}$ in. Calyx $\frac{1}{5}$ in., shorter than the petals. Pod $\frac{3}{4}$–1 in., much longer than the calyx; joints 4–6, smooth.

22. OUGEINIA. From Ujjain, a town in Central India whence seeds of *O. dalbergioides* were sent in 1795 to Dr. Roxburgh, Calcutta Botanic Gardens. Only one species.

Ougeinia dalbergioides, *Benth.*; *Fl. Br. Ind.* ii. 161. A tree, 20–40 ft. Leaves of 3 leaflets; stipules soon falling off; leaflets pubescent, broadly ovate, sinuate or crenate, lateral nearly sessile, $1\frac{1}{2}$–3 in., terminal one stalked, 2–6 in. Flowers numerous, appearing with the young leaves, nearly $\frac{1}{2}$ in. long, in short racemes crowded at the joints of the old branches; stalks pubescent, thread-like, often clustered. Calyx pubescent, bell-shaped; teeth 5, short, blunt, nearly equal, the 2 upper united. Petals white or pale pink, much longer than the calyx: standard broad, erect, notched; keel slightly curved, obtuse, nearly as long as the wings. Upper stamens free, others united. Style incurved, glabrous; stigma small. Pod glabrous, flat, $1\frac{1}{2}$–3 in., composed of 2–5 oblong, 1-seeded, indehiscent joints.

Sutlej valley; March–May.—Central and N. India, ascending to 4000 ft.

23. DESMODIUM. From the Greek *desmos*, a chain, referring to the jointed pod.—Most tropical regions; Cape of Good Hope, N. America, extra-tropical Australia.

Shrubs, sometimes herblike; stems erect or prostrate. Leaves of 3 leaflets, except *D. gangeticum*; leaflets entire or sinuate, lateral nearly sessile, terminal one stalked, larger. Flowers small, in terminal or axillary, simple or branched racemes, except *D. triflorum*, often combined in panicles. Calyx bell-shaped; teeth 5, the 2 upper more or less united, 3 lower, distinct, equal. Petals longer than the calyx: standard broad, erect; keel nearly straight, obtuse. Upper stamen nearly or quite free, others united. Ovary usually sessile; ovules several or many; *D. podocarpum* has a stalked ovary and only 2 ovules; style incurved, glabrous; stigma minute. Pod flat, much longer than the calyx, more or less divided by constrictions into several, rarely only 2, one-seeded, indehiscent joints; in *D. gyrans* the pod is dehiscent along the lower margin and does not break up into joints.

Leaves compound.
  Flowers $\frac{1}{2}$ in. long.
    Lateral leaflets nearly as long as the terminal one.
      Pod $\frac{1}{2}$–1 in.; joints $\frac{1}{7}$ in. long . . . . . 2. *D. floribundum.*
      Pod 2–$2\frac{1}{2}$ in.; joints nearly $\frac{1}{2}$ in. long . . . 3. *D. tiliæfolium.*
    Lateral leaflets less than $\frac{1}{4}$ the length of the terminal one . . . . 10. *D. gyrans.*
  Flowers $\frac{1}{4}$ in. long or less.
    Stems erect or nearly so. Terminal leaflet 1 in. or more.
      Pod stalked. Flowers $\frac{1}{8}$ in. long . . . . 1. *D. podocarpum.*
      Pod sessile. Flowers $\frac{1}{4}$ in. long.
        Leaflets lanceolate, long-pointed, sinuate . 5. *D. sequax.*
        Leaflets ovate or ovate-oblong, entire.
          Leaflets ovate-oblong; terminal one 2–3 in. Upper margin of pod wavy, lower deeply indented . . . . 6. *D. concinnum.*
          Leaflets ovate; terminal one 1–2 in. Upper margin of pod straight, lower slightly indented . . . . 7. *D. polycarpum.*
    Stems prostrate or trailing. Terminal leaflet $\frac{1}{2}$ in. or less.
      Flowers in leaf-opposed clusters, not racemed. Upper margin of pod not indented . . . 8. *D. triflorum.*
      Flowers in racemes. Upper margin of pod deeply indented . . . . 9. *D. parvifolium.*
Leaves simple . . . . 4. *D. gangeticum.*

1. **Desmodium podocarpum,** *DC.*; *Fl. Br. Ind.* ii. 165. An erect, pubescent, small shrub. Leaflets entire, broadly obovate, usually acute, lower surface pale; terminal one $1\frac{1}{2}$–$2\frac{1}{2}$ × $1\frac{1}{4}$–$2\frac{1}{4}$ in. Racemes up to 12–18 in. long, drooping. Flowers pink, $\frac{1}{8}$ in. long. Pod $\frac{1}{2}$ in., stalked; stalk 3-4 times as long as the calyx; upper margin straight, lower deeply indented; joints 2.

Simla, common; July, August.—W. Himalaya, 4000–7000 ft.—China, Japan, Mandchuria.

2. **Desmodium floribundum,** *G. Don*; *Fl. Br. Ind.* ii. 167. A large, erect shrub; stems hairy. Leaflets entire, ovate, obtuse or acute; both surfaces hairy, lower pale; terminal one 2–3 × 1–$1\frac{1}{2}$ in.

FIG. 39. DESMODIUM FLORIBUNDUM.

Racemes numerous. Flowers crowded, pink-purple, nearly $\frac{1}{2}$ in. long. Pod sessile, densely hairy, $\frac{1}{2}$–1 × $\frac{1}{10}$ in.; upper margin slightly, lower deeply indented; joints 3–8, $\frac{1}{7}$ in. long. (Fig. 39.)

Simla, common; June–September.—Throughout the Himalaya, 2000–7000 ft.—China.

3. **Desmodium tiliæfolium,** *Don*; *Fl. Br. Ind.* ii. 168. A tall, erect shrub; stems tomentose or nearly glabrous. Leaflets broadly ovate, entire or sinuate, obtuse or acute; upper surface thinly hairy or pubescent, lower usually grey-tomentose or nearly

glabrous and pale; terminal leaflet 2–4 × $1\frac{1}{3}$–$2\frac{3}{4}$ in. Racemes numerous, up to 12 in. long. Flowers pale pink, $\frac{1}{2}$ in. long. Pod sessile, pubescent or densely hairy, 2–$2\frac{1}{2}$ × $\frac{1}{4}$ in.; upper margin slightly, lower deeply indented; joints 6–9, nearly $\frac{1}{2}$ in. long.

Simla, Mushobra, common; July–October.—Throughout the Himalaya, 2000–9000 ft.

4. **Desmodium gangeticum**, *DC.*; *Fl. Br. Ind.* ii. 168. A nearly erect undershrub; stems pubescent. Leaves simple, ovate $1\frac{1}{2}$ × 1 in., or oblong-ovate 4 × $1\frac{3}{4}$ in., entire, obtuse or acute; upper surface nearly glabrous, lower tomentose or thinly hairy. Racemes numerous, up to 12 in. long. Flowers pink, hardly $\frac{1}{4}$ in. long. Pod sessile, pubescent, curved, $\frac{1}{2}$–$\frac{3}{4}$ in.; upper margin slightly, lower deeply indented; joints 6–8.

Sutlej valley; March.—Throughout India, ascending to 5000 ft.—Tropical Asia and Africa.

5. **Desmodium sequax**, *Wall.*; *Fl. Br. Ind.* ii. 170. A tall, erect shrub; stems tomentose or pubescent. Leaflets lanceolate or ovate-lanceolate, sinuate, long-pointed, both surfaces pubescent, lower much the paler; terminal leaflet $2\frac{1}{2}$–4 × $1\frac{1}{2}$–$2\frac{1}{2}$ in. Racemes numerous. Flowers pink, $\frac{1}{4}$ in. long. Pod sessile, $\frac{1}{2}$–$\frac{3}{4}$ in., tomentose, hairs minutely hooked; upper margin slightly, lower deeply indented; joints 6–8.

Simla; August, September.—Himalaya, Simla to Sikkim, 4000–7000 ft.

6. **Desmodium concinnum**, *DC.*; *Fl. Br. Ind.* ii. 170. A tall, erect, pubescent shrub; branches drooping. Leaflets ovate-oblong, entire, both surfaces thinly hairy; terminal leaflet 2–3 × $\frac{3}{4}$–1 in. Racemes numerous, up to 10 in. long. Flowers dark blue, $\frac{1}{4}$ in. long. Pod sessile, pubescent, curved, $\frac{1}{2}$–$\frac{3}{4}$ in.; upper margin wavy, lower deeply indented; joints 4–6, upper margin of each concave.

Simla; August, September.—Throughout the Himalaya, 1000–7000 ft.

7. **Desmodium polycarpum**, *DC.*; *Fl. Br. Ind.* ii. 171. An erect or nearly erect, hairy undershrub. Leaflets broadly ovate, entire; upper surface nearly glabrous, lower hairy, paler; terminal leaflet 1–2 × $\frac{1}{2}$–1 in. Racemes $1\frac{1}{2}$–3 in. Flowers purple, sometimes white, hardly $\frac{1}{4}$ in. long. Pods sessile, crowded, straight, hairy, $\frac{3}{4}$–1 in.; upper margin straight, lower slightly indented; joints 5–7.

Valleys below Simla; July, August.—Throughout India, ascending to 5500 ft.—Tropical and temperate Asia, Pacific Islands, Zanzibar.

8. **Desmodium triflorum**, *DC.*; *Fl. Br. Ind.* ii. 173. A small shrub; stems tufted, prostrate, sometimes rooting at the joints, 6–18 in., very slender, hairy, much branched. Leaflets obovate,

entire, about $\frac{1}{4}$–$\frac{1}{3}$ in. across; upper surface glabrous, lower thinly hairy, paler. Flowers bright blue, hardly $\frac{1}{6}$ in. long, solitary on hairy, drooping, thread-like stalks, in leaf-opposed clusters of 2–6. Calyx densely hairy; teeth very long. Pod sessile, $\frac{1}{3}$–$\frac{1}{2}$ in., pubescent or glabrous, slightly curved, net-veined; upper margin straight, lower slightly indented; joints 3–5.

Giri valley, usually in grass; September, October.—Common in pastures throughout India, ascending to 4000 ft.—Most tropical regions.

9. **Desmodium parvifolium,** *DC.*; *Fl. Br. Ind.* ii. 174. A small shrub; stems tufted, trailing, 6–24 in., glabrous or thinly hairy, much branched. Leaflets ovate or oblong-ovate, $\frac{1}{5}$–$\frac{1}{2}$ in. long, entire; upper surface glabrous, lower thinly hairy. Racemes numerous, $\frac{1}{2}$–1 in., hairy. Flowers purple-blue, hardly $\frac{1}{5}$ in. long. Calyx densely hairy; teeth long. Pod sessile, $\frac{1}{4}$–$\frac{1}{2}$ in., straight, pubescent, both margins deeply indented; joints 3–5.

Simla, common round Summer Hill; August-October.—Throughout India, ascending to 6000 ft.—Tropical Asia, extending to Japan.

10. **Desmodium gyrans,** *DC.*; *Fl. Br. Ind.* ii. 174. An erect, nearly glabrous undershrub. Leaflets oblong-lanceolate, entire, obtuse; upper surface glabrous, lower thinly hairy, pale; lateral leaflets very small, about $\frac{1}{2}$ in., one or both often wanting; terminal one 2–5 × $\frac{3}{4}$–1 in. Racemes numerous, 3–8 in. Flowers nearly $\frac{1}{2}$ in. long, pale yellow, the wing-petals tinged with pink or blue; buds in pairs, enveloped in the bracts. Pod dehiscent, opening along the lower margin, sessile, 1–1$\frac{1}{2}$ in., curved, glabrous; upper margin continuous, lower slightly indented between the 6–8 seeds.

Valleys below Simla; August, September.—Throughout India, ascending to 5000 ft.—Tropical Asia.

The Telegraph or Semaphore plant; so named from the jerky vertical movements of the lateral leaflets, especially when exposed to full sunshine.

24. VICIA. The classical name of some kind of Vetch, probably *Vicia sativa.*—N. temperate regions and S. America.

Annual or perennial herbs; stems weak, often climbing. Leaves pinnate, the rachis ending in a tendril; leaflets usually many, opposite or nearly so, entire, midrib running out in the form of a minute bristle; stipules large, pointed, often toothed, base prolonged below the attachment in a pointed lobe. Flowers few or numerous, in stalked, axillary racemes, sometimes solitary or in pairs. Calyx bell-shaped; teeth 5, the 3 lower longer than the upper. Petals longer than the calyx: standard broad, erect; keel nearly straight, obtuse, shorter than the wings. Upper stamen nearly or quite free, others united. Style incurved, cylindric, nearly glabrous or pubescent all round or minutely bearded on the outer face close under the small stigma. Pod flat; seeds few or several.

An acclimatised form of the Broad or Field bean, *Vicia Faba*, is common in gardens throughout N.W. India, and is occasionally cultivated up to 8000 ft. It has smaller leaves, flowers and seeds than the European plant.

Vicia sativa, *L.* (probably introduced), is common in the N.W.P., and may occasionally be found up to 6000 ft. (Almora, Naini Tal). Leaflets 8–12, $\frac{3}{4}$–1 in. long. Flowers red-blue, $\frac{2}{3}$ in., usually solitary, sometimes in pairs, sessile in the leaf-axils. Pod glabrous, 1$\frac{1}{2}$–2 in.; seeds 8–10. Cultivated as a fodder plant in Britain from the time of the Romans. Tare or Common Vetch.

Flowers few or solitary, white, tinged with pale blue, $\frac{1}{5}$–$\frac{1}{4}$ in. long.
  Leaves $\frac{1}{2}$–1 in. Leaflets 6–12. Pod glabrous . . 1. *V. tetrasperma.*
  Leaves 1$\frac{1}{2}$–3 in. Leaflets 12–20. Pod hairy . . 2. *V. hirsuta.*
Flowers numerous, pink or purple, $\frac{1}{3}$–$\frac{2}{3}$ in. long.
  Leaflets 8–16, narrowly oblong, $\frac{1}{10}$ in. broad . . . 3. *V. tenera.*
  Leaflets 16–32, ovate, $\frac{1}{4}$–$\frac{1}{3}$ in. broad . . . . 4. *V. rigidula.*

*1. **Vicia tetrasperma,** *Moench*; *Fl. Br. Ind.* ii. 177. Annual, nearly glabrous. Leaves $\frac{1}{2}$–1 in.; leaflets 6–12, narrowly oblong, $\frac{1}{3}$–$\frac{3}{4}$ in., obtuse. Flowers solitary or in pairs, $\frac{1}{4}$ in. long, pale blue. Pod oblong, $\frac{1}{2}$ in., glabrous; seeds 3 or 4.

N.W. Himalaya (Naini Tal, Almora), in woods, not common; April, May. —Temperate Asia, N. Africa, Europe (Britain).

2. **Vicia hirsuta,** *Koch*; *Fl. Br. Ind.* ii. 177. Annual, more or less hairy; stems 1–3 ft. Leaves 1$\frac{1}{2}$–3 in.; leaflets 12–20, oblong, narrowed to the base, $\frac{1}{4}$–$\frac{3}{4}$ in., tip notched. Flowers six or less in a raceme, $\frac{1}{5}$ in. long, white, tinged with pale blue. Pod oblong, acute, $\frac{1}{4}$–$\frac{1}{2}$ in., hairy; seeds 2.

Simla, in hedges and fields, common; March, April.—N. India, ascending to 6000 ft., Nilghiris.—Temperate Asia, N. Africa, Europe (Britain, Hairy Vetch or Tare).

3. **Vicia tenera,** *Grah.*; *Fl. Br. Ind.* ii. 177. Perennial, nearly glabrous; stems 1–4 ft. Leaves 2–4 in.; leaflets 8–16, narrowly oblong, $\frac{1}{2}$–1 × $\frac{1}{10}$ in., acute. Flowers many in a raceme, $\frac{1}{3}$ in., pale pink. Pod thin, obliquely oblong, glabrous, acute, 1–1$\frac{1}{4}$ in.; seeds 6–8.

Simla; April, May.—Kumaon to Simla, 6000–8000 ft.

4. **Vicia rigidula,** *Royle*; *Fl. Br. Ind.* ii. 178, including *V. pallida, Turcz.* Perennial, glabrous; stems 2–5 ft. Leaves 2–6 in.; leaflets 16–32, ovate, $\frac{1}{2}$–1 × $\frac{1}{4}$–$\frac{1}{3}$ in., obtuse. Flowers many in a raceme, $\frac{1}{3}$–$\frac{2}{3}$ in. long, pink or purple-blue. Pod thin, obliquely oblong, acute, 1$\frac{1}{4}$–1$\frac{1}{2}$ in., glabrous; seeds 5–8.

Simla; August, September.—W. Himalaya, 4000–9000 ft.

25. LATHYRUS. The Greek name of some kind of Vetch, probably *L. sativus*.—N. temperate regions and S. America.

Annual or perennial herbs; stems weak, sometimes climbing, usually angular, winged only in *L. sativus*. Leaflets 2–8 or in

L. Aphaca none; rachis ending in a long tendril or in a short bristle. Stipules large, acute, in *L. Aphaca* very large and leaf-like, usually produced below the attachment in 2 long, pointed lobes. Flowers axillary, stalked, solitary or in pairs or racemed. Calyx-tube bell-shaped; teeth 5, nearly equal or the 3 lower longer. Petals longer than the calyx: standard broad, erect, notched; keel nearly straight, obtuse, shorter than the wings. Upper stamen free, others united. Style incurved, flattened below the stigma, bearded along the inner face; stigma small. Pod oblong, flat, tipped with the persistent style; seeds several or many.

L. sativus, *Linn.*, is cultivated throughout India, and occasionally up to 4000 ft. in the hills. The seeds (*Khesari dhal*) are eaten, but are poisonous if used habitually or in large quantities. Stems 4-angled, 2 of the angles broadly winged. Rachis ending in a long, 3-branched tendril. Leaflets 2. Flowers $\frac{3}{4}$ in. long, solitary. Standard and wings blue-purple; keel pale pink. Pod 1 in.; upper margin 2-winged; seeds 4 or 5. Cultivated in S. Europe from very early times for fodder and for the seeds.

Rachis ending in a long tendril.
  Leaflets none. Stipules leaf-like. Flowers yellow . 1. *L. Aphaca.*
  Leaflets two.
    Flowers red, solitary . . . . 2. *L. sphæricus.*
    Flowers yellow, racemed . . . . . . 3. *L. pratensis.*
Rachis ending in a short bristle.
  Leaflets 2. Flowers red, $\frac{1}{3}$ in. . . . . . . 4. *L. inconspicuus.*
  Leaflets 6–8. Flowers yellow, tinged with orange, 1 in. . . . . 5. *L. luteus.*

1. **Lathyrus Aphaca,** *Linn.*; *Fl. Br. Ind.* ii. 179. Annual, glabrous; stems trailing, about 1 ft. Rachis ending in a tendril. Leaflets none. Stipules leaf-like, cordate, triangular, about $1 \times \frac{1}{2}$ in., entire. Flowers yellow, $\frac{1}{3}$ in. long, solitary, rarely two, at the end of long, axillary stalks. Pod 1–1$\frac{1}{4}$ in.; seeds 4–6.

Simla, Mushobra, on waste ground or in fields; April, May.—Throughout N. India, ascending to 7000 ft.—W. Asia, N. Africa, Europe (Britain).

2. **Lathyrus sphæricus,** *Retz.*; *Fl. Br. Ind.* ii. 180. Annual, glabrous; stems trailing, 6–18 in. Rachis ending in a tendril. Leaflets 2, narrowly lanceolate, 2–3 in. Stipules narrow, base 2-lobed. Flowers red, $\frac{1}{3}$ in., solitary, shortly stalked. Pod 1–2$\frac{1}{2}$ in.; seeds 10–12.

Simla, Boileaugunge; April, May.—Throughout N. India, ascending to 5500 ft.—W. Asia, N. Africa, Europe.

3. **Lathyrus pratensis,** *Linn.*; *Fl. Br. Ind.* ii. 180. Annual, hairy; stems trailing, 1–3 ft. Rachis ending in a tendril. Leaflets 2, lanceolate, 1–2 in. Stipules large, leaf-like, base 2-lobed. Flowers yellow, $\frac{1}{3}$–$\frac{1}{2}$ in. long, in long, stalked racemes. Staminal tube nearly abruptly truncate. Pod glabrous, 1$\frac{1}{2}$ in.; seeds numerous.

Mahasu, Fagu; June–September.—W. Himalaya, 6000–8000 ft.—W. Asia, N. Africa Europe (Britain).

4. **Lathyrus inconspicuus,** *Linn.*; *Fl. Br. Ind.* ii. 180. Annual, glabrous; stems trailing, 6–18 in. Rachis ending in a bristle. Leaflets 2, narrowly lanceolate, 1–3 in. Stipules narrow, base 2-lobed. Flowers bright red, $\frac{1}{3}$ in., solitary. Pod 1–1$\frac{1}{2}$ in.; seeds 10–12.

Simla; April, May.—Punjab, ascending to 6000 ft.

5. **Lathyrus luteus,** *Baker*; *Fl. Br. Ind.* ii. 180. Perennial, glabrous; stems nearly erect, 2–3 ft. Leaves 3–5 in.; rachis ending in a bristle; leaflets 6–8, ovate-lanceolate, about 3 × 1$\frac{1}{2}$ in., acute; stipules large, leaf-like, base 2-lobed. Flowers bright yellow, tinged with orange, 1 in. long, in stalked racemes. Pod 2–3 in.; seeds numerous.

Mushobra, woods above the Waterworks Road, Mahasu, Matiana; May, June.—W. Himalaya, 8000–10,000 ft.—Temperate Asia, Europe.

26. AMPHICARPÆA. From the Greek *amphi*, both, and *carpos*, fruit, referring to the two kinds of pod borne by *A. monoica*. —Himalaya, China, Japan, N. America.

Amphicarpæa Edgeworthii, *Benth.*; *Fl. Br. Ind.* ii. 181. A pubescent herb; stems very slender, twining. Leaves of 3 leaflets; leaflets thin, broadly ovate, nearly equal, about 1$\frac{1}{4}$ × 1 in., entire, acute, terminal one stalked, lateral nearly sessile. Flowers axillary, about $\frac{1}{2}$ in. long, pale lilac, sometimes 1-sexual or without petals (cleistogamic), solitary or in pairs or short racemes. Calyx tubular; teeth 5, distinct, the two upper ones the shorter. Petals much longer than the calyx: standard obovate, erect, spurred at the base; keel slightly incurved, obtuse, nearly as long as the wings. Upper stamen free, others united. Style incurved, glabrous; stigma small. Pod flat, hairy, about 1 in., acute; seeds 2–4.

Simla, in woods, 5000–6000 ft.; August, September.—China, Japan.

Closely allied to the N. American *A. monoica*, Elliott, which bears two kinds of pod: (1) as above described, and (2) one-seeded, orbicular pods about $\frac{1}{3}$ in. diam., which are produced near the base of the stem or on plants with prostrate stems, and bury themselves in the ground. See Darwin's *Forms of Flowers*, p. 327. The Simla species probably produces both kinds of pod, though there is no record of it.

27. SHUTERIA. In honour of D. Shuter, medical officer, Madras Presidency, at the end of the eighteenth century and beginning of the nineteenth.—India, China, tropical Africa.

Shuteria involucrata, *Wight & Arn. Prodr.* 207; *Fl. Br. Ind.* ii. 181, *under S. vestita*. A more or less hairy herb; stems slender, twining. Leaves of 3 leaflets; leaflets nearly equal, ovate, 1–2¼ × ⅓–1¼ in., entire, obtuse, upper surface glabrous, lateral nearly sessile, terminal 1-stalked; stipules lanceolate, acute. Flowers white, tinged with pink, ½ in. long, in clusters of 2 or 3, crowded in axillary, bracteate racemes; the orbicular, leaf-like bracts of the lowest 1 or 2 clusters forming involucres round the flowers. Calyx tubular; teeth 5, short, acute, the 2 upper nearly or quite united, the lowest tooth the longest. Petals longer than the calyx: standard obovate, erect; keel nearly straight, obtuse, shorter than the wings. Upper stamen free, others united. Style incurved, glabrous; stigma small, capitate. Pod flat, narrow, 1–1¼ in., tipped with the persistent style-base; seeds 5 or 6.

Simla, Dhami, North of Jutogh; November.—Himalaya, Simla to Assam, 3000–7000 ft.—Nilghiris.

28. DUMASIA. In honour of J. B. Dumas, a French botanical author of the nineteenth century.—Tropical regions of Asia and Africa.

Dumasia villosa, *DC.*; *Fl. Br. Ind.* ii. 183. A densely hairy, perennial herb; stems slender, twining. Leaves of 3 leaflets; leaflets nearly equal, ovate, 1½–3 × ¾–1¾ in., entire, obtuse or acute, lateral nearly sessile, terminal one stalked. Flowers yellow, ½–¾ in. long, in axillary, bracteate racemes. Calyx tubular, mouth obliquely truncate; teeth obscure. Petals twice as long as the calyx: standard obovate, erect; keel slightly incurved, obtuse, nearly as long as the wings. Upper stamen free, others united. Style long, straight and pubescent for about half its length, then flattened and abruptly incurved, terminal portion awl-shaped, glabrous; stigma capitate. Pod flat, yellow-tomentose, 1–1½ in., constricted between the seeds; seeds 3 or 4.

Simla, Annandale, Shali; August, September.—Himalaya, Simla to Assam, 3000–7000 ft.; Nilghiris.—Africa.

29. ERYTHRINA. From the Greek *erythros*, red, referring to the colour of the flowers.—Most tropical and subtropical regions; Cape of Good Hope.

Erythrina suberosa, *Roxb.*; *Fl. Br. Ind.* ii. 189. A tree, 30–50 ft.; branches prickly. Leaves of 3 leaflets; leaflets broadly ovate, entire, upper surface glabrous, lower pale or red-brown tomentose or pubescent, lateral 3½ × 3 in., nearly sessile, terminal one 5 × 4½ in., long-stalked. Flowers red, appearing shortly after the young leaves, 1½–2 in. long, in small clusters crowded in short, terminal racemes. Calyx ⅓ in., 2-lipped; teeth obsolete. Standard oblong; wings minute, curved; keel-petals united, hardly half the length of the standard. Upper stamen free except at the base, others united. Ovary tomentose; style short, glabrous, incurved; stigma small. Pod stalked, glabrous, cylindric, 5–6 in., contracted between the seeds, long-pointed; seeds 2–5, dark purple.

Sutlej valley; March, April.—Throughout India, ascending to 4000 ft.

The wood is white, soft and light, yet fibrous and tough. It is used for making scabbards, sieve-frames, &c. *E. indica*, the 'Coral tree,' is often planted in N. India.

30. BUTEA. In honour of John, Earl of Bute, a botanical author and patron of botany in the eighteenth century.—Tropical Asia.

Butea frondosa, *Roxb.*; *Fl. Br. Ind.* ii. 194. A tree, 30–50 ft. Leaves of 3 leaflets; leaflets hard, stiff, broadly ovate, entire, upper surface nearly glabrous, lower tomentose, lateral about $3\frac{1}{2} \times 2\frac{1}{2}$ in., nearly sessile, terminal one about $4\frac{1}{2} \times 3\frac{1}{2}$ in., long-stalked. Flowers deep red, tinged with orange, appearing before the leaves, about $2\frac{1}{2}$ in. long, in small clusters crowded on axillary or terminal racemes. Calyx brown-tomentose, tubular, $\frac{1}{2}$ in.; teeth 5, short, the 2 upper united. Petals strongly curved, nearly equal, silvery-tomentose outside; keel acute. Upper stamen free, others united. Style long, curved, glabrous; stigma capitate. Pod stalked, tomentose, oblong, about $6 \times 1\frac{1}{2}$ in.; lower portion flat, empty, not opening; tip swollen, splitting round the single seed.

Sutlej valley, Kalka; March, April.—Throughout India, ascending to 4000 ft.

The *Dhak*. The leaves are used as fodder, as plates and as wrapping for parcels. A yellow dye prepared from the flowers is in great request during the Holi festivities.

31. PUERARIA. In honour of M. N. Puerari, Professor of Botany at Copenhagen in the eighteenth century.—Tropical Asia, China, Japan.

Pueraria tuberosa, *DC.*; *Fl. Br. Ind.* ii. 197. A shrub; root tuberous; stems very long, pubescent, twining. Leaves of 3 leaflets; leaflets broadly ovate, entire or sinuate, pointed, upper surface nearly glabrous, lower densely hairy, terminal one long-stalked, 4–9 in., lateral shortly stalked, smaller, unequally sided. Flowers purple-blue, appearing before the leaves, $\frac{2}{3}$ in. long, in small clusters crowded in long, panicled racemes. Calyx $\frac{1}{3}$ in., densely covered with red-brown hairs; teeth short, acute, 2 upper nearly or quite united. Standard orbicular; keel nearly straight, obtuse, slightly shorter than the wings. Upper stamen free at both ends but connected at the middle with the sheath formed by the others. Ovary hairy; style glabrous, abruptly incurved at the base; stigma small, capitate. Pod flat, densely grey-hairy, 2–3 in., deeply constricted between the seeds, tipped with the persistent style-base; seeds 2–6, separated by partitions.

Basantpur, Sutlej valley; April.—Throughout India, ascending to 4000 ft. The tuberous roots are eaten and used medicinally. They are also given as fodder to the ponies in Simla.

32. PHASEOLUS. The Greek name of the Kidney-bean, *P. vulgaris*.—Warm regions of both Hemispheres; widely cultivated.

Herbs; stems slender, trailing, twining or erect. Leaves of 3 leaflets; leaflets nearly equal, usually lobed, margins entire, lateral nearly sessile, terminal one long-stalked. Flowers yellow, in short, head-like, axillary racemes. Calyx bell-shaped; teeth 5, the 2 upper more or less united, lowest tooth the longest. Petals much longer than the calyx: standard orbicular, spreading; keel narrow, long, obtuse, twisted in a complete spire. Upper stamen free, others united. Style spirally twisted, bearded below the obliquely placed stigma. Pod cylindric or flat; seeds 6–12, separated by pith-like partitions.

The following species are cultivated throughout India:—the 'Mùng,' *P. Mungo*; the 'Mòth,' *P. aconitifolius*; the Urd or Màsh, *P. radiatus*; the Scarlet-runner, *P. multiflorus*; the Kidney-bean, *P. vulgaris*. All may be recognised by the spirally twisted keel and bearded style.

Leaflets oblong. Flowers hardly ¼ in. long. Pod cylindric 1. *P. trilobus*.
Leaflets broadly ovate. Flowers ½ in. long. Pod flat . . 2. *P. calcaratus*.

*1. **Phaseolus trilobus,** *Ait.*; *Fl. Br. Ind.* ii. 201. Stems trailing or twining, 1–2 ft., hairy. Leaflets nearly glabrous, oblong, 1–2 in., more or less deeply 3-lobed. Flowers pale yellow, hardly ¼ in. long. Pod glabrous, cylindric, 1–2 in., curved; seeds 6–12.

Himalaya to Ceylon and Burmah, ascending to 7000 ft. in the N.W.P.; August.—W. and tropical Asia, Africa.

On a sheet of this species in the Kew Herbarium has been written by Mr. Bentham, 'Simla to Almora, 4000–7000 ft., Madden.' This is probably the authority for the distribution given in the *Fl. Br. Ind.* I have seen no Simla specimen.

2. **Phaseolus calcaratus,** *Roxb.*; *Fl. Br. Ind.* ii. 203. Stems trailing or twining, 1–3 ft., hairy. Leaflets nearly glabrous, broadly ovate, acute, 1½–3 in., sometimes lobed. Flowers yellow, ½ in. long. Pod glabrous, flat, 2–3 in., straight or curved; seeds 8–12.

Valleys below Simla; August.—Throughout India, wild and cultivated. Native name *Mùng*.

33. VIGNA. In honour of Domenic Vigna, a professor at Padua in the seventeenth century.—Tropical and subtropical regions, Cape of Good Hope, Australia.

Vigna vexillata, *Benth.*; *Fl. Br. Ind.* ii. 206. A perennial, roughly hairy herb; rootstock thick, woody; stems twining or trailing, 3–5 ft., hairy. Leaflets 3, nearly equal, not lobed, entire, long-pointed, variable in shape, ovate-lanceolate about $2\frac{1}{2} \times 1\frac{1}{2}$ in., or narrowly lanceolate about $3 \times \frac{1}{2}$ in.; lateral nearly sessile, terminal one stalked. Flowers pink or red, turning blue-purple as they fade, 1–$1\frac{1}{2}$ in. long, in a cluster of 2–4 at the end of naked, axillary stalks 6–18 in. long. Calyx-tube bell-shaped; teeth 5, long, lanceolate, nearly equal, distinct. Petals much longer than the calyx: standard orbicular, spreading; keel strongly incurved but not spirally twisted, obtuse. Upper stamen free, others united. Style incurved, bearded below the obliquely placed stigma. Pod densely hairy, flat, 2–3 in., acute; seeds 10–15, separated by pith-like partitions.

Simla, on grassy slopes; August, September.—Hilly districts throughout India, ascending to 8000 ft.—Nearly all tropical regions, S. Africa, Australia.

34. **DOLICHOS.** From the Greek *dolichos*, long, probably referring to the long, twining stems of some species.—Tropical regions.

Dolichos biflorus, *Linn.*; *Fl. Br. Ind.* ii. 210. An annual, hairy herb; stems nearly erect; branches climbing. Leaves of 3 leaflets; leaflets nearly equal, often lobed, entire, ovate-lanceolate, 1–2 in., acute, lateral nearly sessile, terminal one stalked. Flowers yellow, $\frac{1}{2}$–$\frac{3}{4}$ in. long, solitary or in small, axillary, nearly sessile clusters. Calyx-tube very short; teeth 5, long, nearly equal, very narrow, the two upper partially united. Petals longer than the calyx: standard ovate, spreading, with 2 small, membranous, fringed, dark brown pouches in the centre; keel slightly incurved, obtuse. Upper stamen free, others united. Style slender, incurved, glabrous except a ring of minute hairs just below the terminal stigma. Pod flat, curved, $1\frac{1}{2}$–$2 \times \frac{1}{4}$ in., hairy, tipped with the persistent, hook-like style-base; seeds 5–7.

Valleys below Simla; August, September.—Throughout India, ascending to 5000 ft.—Tropical regions of the Old World.

Widely cultivated for fodder; native name *Khulti.*

Dolichos Lablab is cultivated throughout India and up to 6000 ft. A twining, perennial herb; roots tuberous. Leaflets broadly ovate, 2–3 in., long-pointed. Flowers $\frac{1}{2}$–$\frac{3}{4}$ in. long, white or pale purple, racemed. Style thickened upwards, bearded along the inner side. Pod glabrous, oblong, $1\frac{1}{2}$–$2 \times \frac{1}{2}$–$\frac{3}{4}$ in., tipped with the persistent style-base. Native name *Sèm* or *Sèmbi.*

35. **ATYLOSIA.** From the Greek *a*, without, and *tylos*, a callosity; the standard is without the hard, basal protuberances characteristic of some genera.—Tropical Asia, Madagascar, Australia.

Tomentose or hairy shrubs; stems twining or trailing. Leaves of 3 leaflets, lower surface more or less covered with minute, resinous dots ; leaflets nearly equal, not lobed, entire, acute, lateral nearly sessile, terminal one stalked, rarely nearly sessile. Flowers yellow, in axillary racemes or clusters. Calyx-tube short ; teeth 5, nearly equal, acute, the 2 upper partially united, lowest the longest. Petals longer than the calyx : standard orbicular, spreading ; keel slightly incurved, obtuse. Upper stamen free, others united. Style thread-like, incurved, glabrous ; stigma small, capitate. Pod oblong, flat, marked with transverse, parallel grooves between the seeds, tipped with the persistent style-base ; seeds 4–10, separated by partitions.

Flowers $\frac{3}{4}$–$1\frac{1}{4}$ in. long. Pod $1\frac{1}{2}$–2 in.
  Leaflets longer than broad. Corolla persistent. Pod $\frac{1}{3}$ in. broad, grey-pubescent . . . . . . 1. *A. mollis.*
  Leaflets as long as broad. Corolla soon falling off. Pod $\frac{1}{2}$ in. broad, thinly hairy . . . . . . 3. *A. platycarpa.*
Flowers scarcely $\frac{1}{3}$ in. long. Pod $\frac{3}{4}$–1 in. . . . . . 2. *A. scarabæoides.*

1. **Atylosia mollis,** *Benth.*; *Fl. Br. Ind.* ii. 213. Densely pubescent or tomentose ; stems long, twining. Leaflets ovate, longer than broad ; terminal one about 2 × 1 in. Flowers yellow, 1–$1\frac{1}{4}$ in. long, racemed. Corolla persisting until the pod is fully developed. Pod $1\frac{1}{2}$–2 × $\frac{1}{3}$ in., grey-pubescent ; seeds 8–10.

Valleys below Simla, Haripur ; July–September.—Himalaya, Chamba to Sikkim, 2000–6000 ft.

2. **Atylosia scarabæoides,** *Benth.* ; *Fl. Br. Ind.* ii. 215. Pubescent or hairy ; stems long, twining or trailing. Leaflets ovate or oblong ; terminal one about $\frac{3}{4}$ × $\frac{1}{3}$ in. or $1\frac{1}{4}$ × $\frac{1}{2}$ in., sometimes very shortly stalked. Flowers yellow, scarcely $\frac{1}{3}$ in. long, in axillary clusters of 2–6. Corolla soon falling off. Pod $\frac{3}{4}$–1 × $\frac{1}{4}$ in., densely hairy ; seeds 4–6.

Simla, Naldera, on grassy slopes ; July–September.—Throughout India, ascending to 6000 ft.—Tropical Asia, Madagascar, Mauritius.

3. **Atylosia platycarpa,** *Benth.* ; *Fl. Br. Ind.* ii. 216. Pubescent or hairy ; stems long, trailing or twining. Leaflets orbicular, as long as broad, end one 1–3 in. across. Flowers yellow, $\frac{3}{4}$ in. long, in racemes, or one or two together at the end of a short stalk. Corolla soon falling off. Pod $1\frac{1}{2}$ × $\frac{1}{2}$ in., thinly hairy ; seeds 5 or 6.

Simla ; August, September.—W. Himalaya, 1000–8000 ft.

36. **RHYNCHOSIA.** From the Greek *rhynchos,* a beak, referring to the incurved keel-petals.—Most warm regions ; a few species in S. Africa and N. America.

Shrubs or perennial herbs, more or less hairy ; stems trailing or twining, rarely erect. Lower surface of leaves dotted with minute, resinous glands. Leaflets 3, nearly equal, rarely lobed, entire; lateral nearly sessile, terminal one stalked. Flowers usually yellow, in axillary racemes. Calyx-tube short; teeth 5, acute, nearly equal or the lowest much the longest, the 2 upper partially united. Standard broadly obovate, spreading; keel incurved, obtuse. Upper stamen free, others united. Style long, incurved, pubescent or glabrous, not bearded; stigma small. Pod oblong, flat, acute or tipped with the persistent style; seeds 2 or 1.

Stems erect. Lower surface of leaves white-tomentose. Flowers yellow . . . . 1. *R. Pseudo-cajan.*
Stems trailing or climbing.
 Flowers yellow, or yellow streaked with purple.
  Flowers scarcely $\frac{1}{4}$ in. long. Terminal leaflet $\frac{1}{4}$–$\frac{3}{4}$ in. long . . . . 2. *R. minima.*
  Flowers $\frac{1}{2}$–$\frac{3}{4}$ in. long. Terminal leaflet 1–2$\frac{1}{2}$ in. long.
   Leaflets obtuse. Lowest calyx-tooth much shorter than corolla. Standard hairy . . 3. *R. Falconeri.*
   Leaflets long-pointed. Lowest calyx-tooth as long as corolla. Standard glabrous . . 4. *R. himalensis.*
 Flowers dark red . . . . 5. *R. sericea.*

1. **Rhynchosia Pseudo-cajan,** *Camb.*; *Fl. Br. Ind.* ii. 223. An erect shrub, 4–6 ft.; stem and branches white-tomentose. Leaflets ovate; terminal one 1$\frac{1}{2}$–2 × $\frac{3}{4}$–1 in.; upper surface green, pubescent; lower white, tomentose. Flowers yellow, $\frac{1}{2}$ in. long. Calyx white-tomentose. Standard and style pubescent. Pod 1 in., white-tomentose.

Sutlej valley; August, September.—W. Himalaya, Murree to Kumaon, 3000–9000 ft.

2. **Rhynchosia minima,** *DC.*; *Fl. Br. Ind.* ii. 223. Pubescent; stems long, slender, trailing or climbing. Leaflets orbicular; terminal one $\frac{1}{4}$–$\frac{3}{4}$ in. across. Flowers yellow, scarcely $\frac{1}{4}$ in. long. Style nearly glabrous. Pod $\frac{1}{2}$ in., pubescent.

Sutlej valley; September–January.—Throughout India, ascending to 4000 ft.—Nearly all tropical and sub-tropical countries; temperate N. America and S. Africa.

3. **Rhynchosia Falconeri,** *Baker*; *Fl. Br. Ind.* ii. 224. More or less hairy; stems long, trailing or climbing. Leaflets ovate, obtuse; terminal one 1–1$\frac{1}{2}$ × $\frac{3}{4}$–1$\frac{1}{4}$ in. Flowers yellow, $\frac{1}{2}$ in. long. Calyx densely hairy; lowest tooth much shorter than the corolla. Standard hairy. Style glabrous. Pod 1–1$\frac{1}{4}$ in., hairy.

Shali, 7500 ft.; August, September.—Garhwal.

4. **Rhynchosia himalensis,** *Benth.*; *Fl. Br. Ind.* ii. 225. More or less hairy, viscidly glandular; stems long, trailing or

climbing. Leaflets ovate, long-pointed, base rounded; terminal one $1\frac{1}{2}$–$2\frac{1}{2}\times1\frac{1}{4}$–$1\frac{1}{2}$ in. Flowers yellow, veined with purple, nearly

FIG. 40. RHYNCHOSIA HIMALENSIS.

$\frac{2}{3}$ in. long. Calyx pubescent; lowest tooth as long as the corolla. Standard and style glabrous. Pod 1–$1\frac{1}{4}$ in., pubescent. (Fig. 40.)

Simla; July, August.—W. Himalaya, Murree to Kumaon, 3000–6000 ft.

5. **Rhynchosia sericea,** *Span.*; *Fl. Br. Ind.* ii. 225. Softly pubescent, viscidly glandular; stems thick, long, trailing or climbing. Leaflets broadly ovate, acute, base rounded; terminal one 2–$3\times1\frac{3}{4}$–$2\frac{3}{4}$ in. Flowers dark red, $\frac{3}{4}$ in. long. Calyx and standard hairy. Pod $1\frac{1}{4}$ in., tipped with the glabrous, persistent style.

Simla, Mushobra, common on grassy banks; July–September.—N. India, ascending to 7000 ft.

37. FLEMINGIA. In honour of Dr. J. Fleming, Bengal Army, who died in 1815.—Tropical Asia, Australia, Africa.

Procumbent or trailing shrubs. Leaves simple or of 3 nearly sessile leaflets, entire, lower surface gland-dotted. Flowers in small clusters, racemose, each cluster hidden within a large folded bract, or terminal, on long, axillary stalks without enveloping bracts. Calyx-tube short; teeth 5, narrow, long-pointed, the lowest the longest. Petals nearly equal, longer than the calyx: standard broadly ovate, spreading; keel incurved, obtuse or acute. Upper stamen free, others united. Style incurved, thickened near the middle, tip glabrous or hairy; stigma small. Pod short, oblong, turgid; seeds 1 or 2.

Leaves simple. Flower-clusters racemose, each enclosed by a large, folded bract . . . . 1. *F. fruticulosa.*
Leaves of 3 leaflets. Flower-clusters terminal on long, axillary stalks without enveloping bracts . . . . . 2. *F. vestita.*

1. **Flemingia fruticulosa,** *Wall.*; *Fl. Br. Ind.* ii. 227, *under F. strobilifera.* Branches procumbent, 6–18 in., spreading from the base. Leaves simple, cordate, ovate or nearly orbicular,

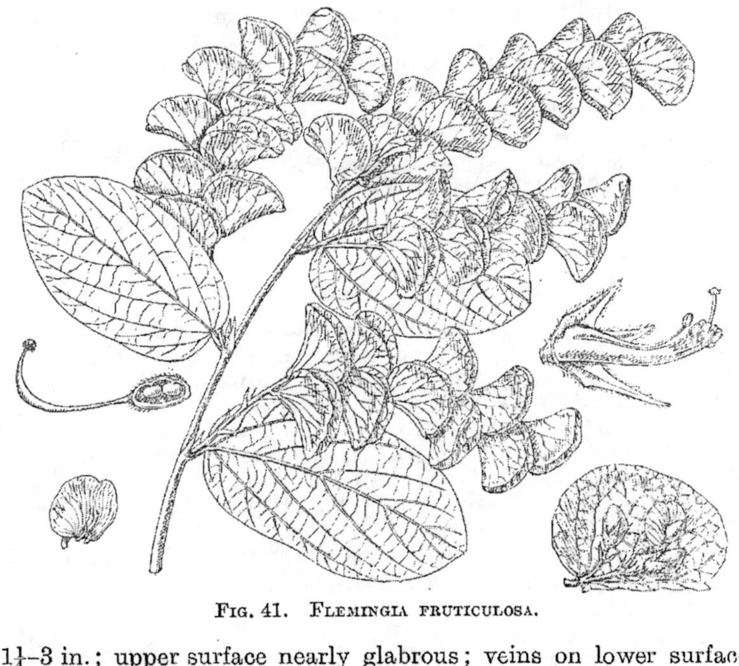

FIG. 41. FLEMINGIA FRUTICULOSA.

$1\frac{1}{4}$–3 in.; upper surface nearly glabrous; veins on lower surface prominent. Flowers pink or white, $\frac{1}{3}$ in. long, in small clusters enclosed by folded, membranous, orbicular bracts nearly $\frac{3}{4}$ in. long and arranged in two rows in short racemes. Keel slightly incurved, obtuse. Style-tip glabrous. Pod $\frac{1}{4}$ in.; seeds 2. (Fig. 41.)

Simla, on banks; August–October.—W. Himalaya, Dalhousie to Kumaon, 4000–9000 ft.

2. **Flemingia vestita,** *Benth.*; *Fl. Br. Ind.* ii. 230. Pubescent or hairy; root tuberous; stems trailing, 1–2 ft. Leaves of 3 nearly sessile leaflets; leaflets ovate, $1\frac{1}{4} \times 1$ in. Flowers bright red, $\frac{3}{4}$ in. long, in small clusters at the end of long, axillary stalks. Calyx and corolla hairy. Keel strongly incurved, acute. Style-tip hairy. Pod $\frac{1}{4}$ in., enclosed in the calyx; seed solitary.

Simla, on grassy slopes; August, September.—Himalaya, Simla to Assam. The root is edible.

38. DALBERGIA. In honour of Nicholas Dalberg, a Swedish botanist, who died in 1820.—Widely spread in tropical regions.

Dalbergia Sissoo, *Roxb.*; *Fl. Br. Ind.* ii. 231. A tree; young parts pubescent. Leaves pale green, odd-pinnate; leaflets 3 or 5, alternate, broadly ovate, $1\text{–}3 \times \frac{3}{4}\text{–}2\frac{1}{4}$ in., entire, abruptly pointed, terminal one stalked. Flowers sessile, yellow-white, $\frac{1}{3}$ in. long, in short, axillary panicles. Calyx bell-shaped; teeth 5, short, the 2 upper united, lowest the longest. Petals much longer than the calyx; standard ovate; keel nearly straight, obtuse. Stamens 9, all united, tube split along the upper side. Ovary hairy; style short, thick, glabrous; stigma capitate. Pod long-stalked, thin, glabrous, strap-shaped, $1\frac{1}{2}\text{–}4 \times \frac{1}{4}\text{–}\frac{1}{2}$ in.; seeds 2–4.

Sutlej valley; March–June.—Throughout India, ascending to 4000 ft.

A valuable timber tree; widely planted. Wood suitable for nearly all purposes. Native name, *Shisham* or *Sissoo.*

39. SOPHORA. Origin of name obscure.—Most warm and temperate regions.

Sophora mollis, *Grah.*; *Fl. Br. Ind.* ii. 251. An erect shrub, 3–4 ft. Leaves pale green, odd-pinnate, 5–10 in.; leaflets 21–41, ovate, $\frac{1}{2}\text{–}\frac{3}{4}$ in., nearly sessile, entire. Flowers yellow, appearing with the young leaves, nearly $\frac{3}{4}$ in. long, crowded in short, axillary racemes. Calyx tubular, $\frac{1}{4}$ in.; teeth 5, short, blunt, the 2 upper united, often obscure. Petals nearly equal; standard broadly obovate, spreading. Stamens all free; anthers versatile. Style incurved, glabrous; stigma minute. Pod stalked, glabrous, 3–4 in., consisting of 4–6 one-seeded, 4-winged joints contiguous or separated by linear constrictions sometimes nearly an inch long.

Sutlej valley; March, April.—N. India, ascending to 6000 ft.

40. CÆSALPINIA. In honour of Andreas Cesalpini, professor of medicine at Pisa in the sixteenth century. He was the first botanist to classify plants by the flowers and seeds.—Most warm regions.

Cæsalpinia Sepiaria, *Roxb.*; *Fl. Br. Ind.* ii. 256. A prickly, climbing shrub. Leaves 2-pinnate, 10–18 in.; leaflets 16–24, opposite, nearly sessile, oblong, $\frac{1}{2}\text{–}1$ in., obtuse. Flowers yellow,

½ in. long, wing-stalked, in erect racemes 6–12 in. long. Calyx 5-parted; lobes oblong, overlapping, the lowest concave and largest. Petals 5, orbicular, spreading, the upper one the smallest and innermost. Stamens 10, all free, longer than the petals; lower half of filament dilated, woolly; anthers uniform. Ovary sessile; style glabrous; stigma small. Pod glabrous, nearly flat, oblong, 2–3 × 1 in., tipped with the hard, persistent style-base; seeds 4–8, mottled.

Sutlej valley, Basantpur, Subathoo; February–April.—Throughout India and Burmah, ascending to 4000 ft.—China.

41. CASSIA. The classical name of some tree with aromatic bark.—Nearly all tropical and subtropical regions; N. temperate Asia and America.

Trees or herbs, not prickly. Leaves even-pinnate; rachis often gland-bearing; leaflets few or numerous, opposite, entire. Flowers yellow, in racemes or solitary or in clusters of 2 or 3. Calyx 5-parted; lobes overlapping. Petals 5, nearly equal, spreading, the upper one the innermost. Stamens all free, 10, rarely all perfect or 5 or 4; perfect anthers uniform, usually dehiscing by a terminal pore. Ovary nearly sessile; style incurved; stigma small. Pod flat, cylindric or 4-angled; seeds numerous, rarely few.

In the *Fl. Br. Ind.* ii. 266, it is stated that *C. pumila*, Lam. ascends to 7000 ft.; I have seen no specimen from above 1000 ft. The statement was perhaps founded on a wrongly named specimen of *C. dimidiata* (230, Edgeworth) in the Kew Herbarium.

Leaflets 4–16, ovate, 1–5 in.
  A tree. Leaflets 8–16. Flowers numerous, in long racemes. Pod cylindric . . . . . . 1. *C. Fistula*.
  Herbs. Leaflets 4 or 6. Flowers few, in pairs or short racemes.
    Leaflets 6. Perfect stamens 7. Pod 4-angled . . 2. *C. obtusifolia*.
    Leaflets 4. Perfect stamens 5. Pod flat . . . 3. *C. Absus*.
Leaflets 40–100, narrowly oblong, ¼ in. or less.
  Stems procumbent. Stamens 10 . . . . . . 4. *C. mimosoides*.
  Stems erect. Stamens 5 or 4 . . . . . . 5. *C. dimidiata*.

1. **Cassia Fistula**, *Linn.*; *Fl. Br. Ind.* ii. 261. A small tree. Leaves glabrous, 12–18 in.; leaflets 8–16, ovate, 2–5 in., acute or obtuse. Flowers yellow, long-stalked, in drooping racemes 1–2 ft. long. Sepals ⅓ in., obtuse, soon falling off. Petals obovate, ¾–1 in., clawed. Stamens unequal; 3 lowest much the longest, curved, perfect; 4–6 intermediate in length, perfect; remaining 1–3 very short, abortive. Pod cylindric, 1 in. diam., 1–2 ft. long, filled with a soft pulp separating the numerous, flat seeds.

Sutlej valley; March, April.—Throughout India, ascending to 4000 ft.—Tropical Asia, Africa.—Native name, *Amaltás*.

This is an exceedingly showy tree when in flower, and Grant-Duff in his *Notes of an Indian Journey*, p. 122, speaks of it as 'that infinitely glorified cousin of the Laburnum.'

2. **Cassia obtusifolia,** *Linn.*; *Fl. Br. Ind.* ii. 263, *under C. Tora.* An annual, erect, shrub-like herb, 3–6 ft. Leaves 2–3 in.; leaflets 6, hairy, ovate, 1–2 in., acute, an awl-shaped, yellow gland between the lowest pair. Flowers yellow, $\frac{1}{2}$–$\frac{3}{4}$ in. diam., in pairs on short, axillary stalks. Stamens 10; lower 7 nearly equal, perfect; 3 upper minute, abortive. Pod linear, 6–9 in., 4-angled; seeds numerous.

Naldera, Sutlej valley; September, October.—Throughout India, ascending to 5000 ft.—Most tropical regions.

3. **Cassia Absus,** *Linn.*; *Fl. Br. Ind.* ii. 265. An erect, branched, viscidly glandular, biennial herb, 6–18 in. Leaves 1$\frac{1}{2}$–3 in.; leaflets 4, ovate, 1–1$\frac{1}{2}$ in., obtuse, a small, awl-shaped gland between each pair. Flowers few, red-yellow, $\frac{1}{4}$ in. diam., in short racemes. Stamens 5, equal, perfect. Pod hairy, flat, 1–2 × $\frac{1}{4}$ in.; seeds 6.

Valleys below Simla; August, September.—Throughout India, ascending to 5000 ft.—Most tropical regions.

4. **Cassia mimosoides,** *Linn.*; *Fl. Br. Ind.* ii. 266. Perennial; stems several, hairy, spreading, 12–18 in., procumbent or ascending. Leaves 1–2 in.; leaflets 40–100, narrowly oblong, $\frac{1}{4}$ in.,

FIG. 42. CASSIA MIMOSOIDES.

acute, midrib close to the upper margin, a small, circular, sessile gland between or just below the lowest pair. Flowers yellow, $\frac{1}{4}$ in. diam., axillary, solitary or in clusters of 2–3. Stamens 10, nearly equal, all perfect. Pod flat, hairy, 1$\frac{1}{2}$ × $\frac{1}{6}$ in.; seeds 15–20. (Fig. 42.)

Valleys below Simla, on grassy slopes; August, September.—Throughout India, ascending to 5000 ft.—Nearly all tropical regions.

5. **Cassia dimidiata,** *Baker*; *Fl. Br. Ind.* ii. 266, *under C. mimosoides*. An annual, nearly glabrous herb; stems erect, $1\frac{1}{2}$–3 ft. Leaves 2–3 in.; leaflets 50–100, narrowly oblong, $\frac{1}{3}$ in., acute, midrib close to the upper margin, a small, circular, sessile gland between or just below the lowest pair. Flowers yellow, hardly $\frac{1}{4}$ in. diam., axillary, usually solitary. Stamens 4 or 5, nearly equal, perfect. Pod flat, thinly hairy, $1\frac{1}{2} \times \frac{1}{6}$ in.; seeds 10–15.

Valleys below Simla, in fields; August, September.—Throughout India, ascending to 5000 ft.—Most tropical regions.

42. **BAUHINIA.** In memory of John and Caspar Bauhin, German botanists of the sixteenth century.—Widely spread in tropical and subtropical regions.

Erect trees or tendril-bearing climbers. Leaves simple, notched or 2-lobed, entire. Flowers large, showy, in racemes, corymbs or panicles. Calyx-tube short; limb long, spathe-like and undivided or splitting as the flower opens into 2 or 3 often reflexed segments. Petals 5, slightly unequal, clawed, erect or spreading, the upper one the innermost. Stamens 3–5, free, anthers versatile. Ovary stalked; style cylindric; stigma terminal. Pod flat, oblong; seeds 6–15.

Trees.
- Leaves notched at the top. Petals $\frac{1}{3}$ in., pale yellow . 1. *B. retusa.*
- Leaves deeply 2-lobed. Petals 1–2 in., pink or purple.
  - Calyx splitting to the base in 2 ultimately reflexed segments. Perfect stamens 3, rarely 4 . . . . 3. *B. purpurea.*
  - Calyx spathe-like, not splitting. Perfect stamens 5 . 4. *B. variegata.*

A climbing shrub. Petals 1 in., white, changing to cream-yellow . . . . 2. *B. Vahlii.*

1. **Bauhinia retusa,** *Buch.-Ham.*; *Fl. Br. Ind.* ii. 279. A small tree. Leaves glabrous, cordate, orbicular, 4–6 in., notched at the tip. Flowers in large, terminal panicles. Calyx pubescent; limb splitting to the base in 2 or 3 segments. Petals pubescent outside, oblong, $\frac{1}{4}$–$\frac{1}{3}$ in., pale yellow, with purple streaks or spots. Stamens 3. Pod glabrous, 5×1 in.

Valleys below Simla; September, October.—Central and N. India, W. Himalaya from Kumaon to the Beeas up to 4000 ft.

2. **Bauhinia Vahlii,** *Wight & Arn.*; *Fl. Br. Ind.* ii. 279. A large climber, sometimes 100 ft. long, covered with red-brown tomentum; branches frequently terminating in a pair of opposite tendrils. Leaves cordate, orbicular, 6–18 in., 2-lobed nearly to the middle. Flowers in large, terminal corymbs. Calyx-limb splitting into 2 ultimately reflexed segments. Petals hairy outside, obovate, 1 in., white, turning to cream-yellow. Stamens 3. Pod tomentose, thick, $6\text{–}18 \times 2\text{-}3$ in.

Sutlej valley, Kalka; April–June.—Throughout Central and Northern India, ascending to 5000 ft.

This species is put to more uses than almost any other forest plant except the bamboo. The large flat leaves are sewn together and used as plates, cups, rough table-cloths, umbrellas, cloaks and rain-caps; the seeds are roasted and eaten; the fibres of the bark are made into ropes, and from the trunk exudes a copious gum. Native name *Taur.*

3. **Bauhinia purpurea,** *Linn.*; *Fl. Br. Ind.* ii. 284. A tree. Leaves glabrous, cordate, ovate or orbicular, 4–6 in., 2-lobed nearly to the middle, lobes sometimes pointed. Flowers in pubescent racemes, often combined in panicles. Calyx-limb splitting to the base in 2 ultimately reflexed segments. Petals oblong-lanceolate, 1–2 in., pink; margins waved. Stamens 3, occasionally 4. Pod glabrous, $6–12 \times \frac{1}{2}–\frac{3}{4}$ in.

Valleys below Simla; September–November.—Throughout India, ascending to 5000 ft. Often planted.

4. **Bauhinia variegata,** *Linn.*; *Fl. Br. Ind.* ii. 284. A tree. Leaves glabrous, cordate, orbicular, 2–4 in., 2-lobed to about $\frac{1}{3}$ of their length. Flowers in small, pubescent corymbs. Calyx-limb spathe-like, not splitting into segments, tip 5-toothed. Petals oblong, 2 in., light red-purple, upper one darker and often tinged with cream and red; margins waved. Stamens 5. Pod glabrous, $6–18 \times \frac{3}{4}$ in.

Sutlej valley; February–April.—Throughout India, ascending to 4000 ft.-Burmah, China.

The *Kuchnár* or Geranium tree. Often planted.

43. MIMOSA. Supposed to be derived from the Greek *mimos*, a mimic; referring to the highly sensitive leaves of some of the species imitating animal movement.—Warm regions of America, Africa and Asia; chiefly America.

Mimosa rubicaulis, *Lam.*; *Fl. Br. Ind.* ii. 291. A prickly, pubescent, erect or half-climbing shrub. Leaves 2-pinnate, 3–6 in.; pinnules 3–10 pairs; leaflets 12–30, sensitive, narrowly oblong, $\frac{1}{4}$ in., acute, mid-rib close to the upper margin. Flowers minute, purple at first, afterwards changing to white, crowded in globose heads $\frac{1}{3}–\frac{1}{2}$ in. diam., and forming terminal racemes. Calyx and corolla tubular, 4-toothed. Stamens 8, free, 2–3 times as long as the corolla. Style slightly longer than the stamens; stigma minute. Pod stalked, glabrous, thin, flat, slightly curved, $3–5 \times \frac{1}{2}$ in., the 6–10 square, 1-seeded joints separating when ripe from between the persistent, marginal frame.

Valleys below Simla; August, September.—Throughout India, ascending to 4000 ft.—Afghanistan.

44. ACACIA. The classical name of some species of *Acacia*, probably *A. vera.*—Most warm regions. Species with the leaves reduced to flattened stalks are abundant in Australia.

Trees or shrubs, erect or climbing, spinous or prickly. Leaves 2-pinnate; rachises often glandular; pinnules opposite; leaflets usually numerous, small, $\frac{1}{10}$–$\frac{1}{4}$ in., opposite, entire. Flowers small, barely $\frac{1}{4}$ in. long, usually yellow, in globose heads or cylindric spikes, axillary or paniculate at the end of branches. Calyx bell-shaped, 4- or 5-toothed or lobed. Petals 4 or 5, more or less united. Stamens very many, usually more than 50, much longer than the corolla, free or united close to the base; anthers minute. Style thread-like; stigma minute. Pod nearly cylindric or flat, 2-valved or indehiscent; seeds 3-12.

Flowers in globose heads.
  Trees or shrubs. Heads axillary.
    Heads with a whorl of small bracts at the base. Pod glabrous, irregularly cylindric . . . . . 1. *A. Farnesiana.*
    Heads with a whorl of small bracts about the middle of the stalk. Pod tomentose, flat, contracted between the seeds . . . . . 2. *A. arabica.*
  Climbing shrub. Heads panicled . . . . 5. *A. cæsia.*
Flowers in cylindric spikes.
  Leaves 3–6 in. Pinnules 10–20 pairs. Leaflets narrowly oblong . . . . 3. *A. Catechu.*
  Leaves 1–2 in. Pinnules 2–3 pairs. Leaflets obovate 4. *A. modesta.*

1. **Acacia Farnesiana,** *Willd.*; *Fl. Br. Ind.* ii. 292. An erect shrub; branches zigzag, covered with minute, raised, grey dots. Leaves $1\frac{1}{2}$–2 in.; stipules spinescent; pinnules 4–8 pairs; leaflets 20–40 on a pinnule, narrowly oblong. Flowers deep yellow, fragrant, crowded in long-stalked, globose heads $\frac{1}{3}$–$\frac{1}{2}$ in. diam., forming axillary clusters of 2–5; heads with a whorl of small bracts at the base. Pod glabrous, thick, irregularly cylindric, often curved, 2–3 in.; seeds separated by dry, spongy tissue, and arranged obliquely in 2 rows.

Sutlej valley, Suni; January–March.—Throughout India, ascending to 3000 ft. Often planted.—Nearly all hot countries.

The pods and bark are used in native medicine and for tanning; the flowers in perfumery. Native name *Kikar.* Cultivated in S. Europe.

2. **Acacia arabica,** *Willd.*; *Fl. Br. Ind.* ii. 293. A tree attaining 50 ft. in the plains but usually stunted in the hills; branches zigzag, pubescent. Leaves 1–2 in.; stipules spinescent, white and very long on old branches; pinnules 3–6 pairs; leaflets 20–40 on a pinnule, narrowly oblong. Flowers yellow, fragrant, crowded in long-stalked, globose heads $\frac{1}{2}$ in. diam., forming axillary clusters of 2–5; stalks bearing just above the middle a whorl of small bracts. Pod stalked, grey-tomentose, flat, 3–6 in., contracted between the circular seeds.

Sutlej valley; July–September.—Throughout India, ascending to 3000 ft. —Arabia, Africa.

The hard, tough and very durable wood is widely used in the construction of agricultural implements, boats, tent-pegs, &c. The gum procured by incisions made in the branches is used in native medicine, and by dyers and cloth-printers; it forms part of the various gums exported as East Indian gum arabic. The bark is used for tanning and dyeing, and that of the roots in the preparation of native spirits. The green pods and young leaves make excellent fodder and the trees are in consequence often much lopped and mutilated. Native name *Kikar* or *Babul*.

3. **Acacia Catechu,** *Willd.*; *Fl. Br. Ind.* ii. 295. A tree, 30–40 ft. Leaves pubescent, 3–6 in.; stipules soon falling off; a pair of flattened, recurved prickles inserted below the leaf-base; pinnules 10–20 pairs; leaflets 60–100 on a pinnule, narrowly oblong. Flowers pale yellow, crowded in stalked, cylindric spikes 2–4 in. long, solitary or forming small, axillary clusters. Pod stalked, glabrous, flat, thin, oblong, $2–3 \times \frac{1}{2}–\frac{3}{4}$ in., acute.

Valleys below Simla; May–July.—Throughout N. India, ascending to 3000 ft.

The hard wood is put to the same uses as that of *A. arabica*. The 'Cutch' of commerce (native name *Katha*) is the heart-wood cut into chips and boiled down; in the East it is eaten with Betel leaf, *Piper Betle*, Linn., and is exported to Europe for dyeing and tanning. Native name *Khair*.

4. **Acacia modesta,** *Wall.*; *Fl. Br. Ind.* ii. 296. A small tree. Leaves glabrous, grey-green, 1–2 in.; stipules soon falling off; a pair of flattened, recurved prickles inserted below the leaf-base; pinnules 2–3 pairs; leaflets 6–10 on a pinnule, obovate. Flowers white or pale yellow, in stalked, cylindric, drooping spikes 1–2 in. long, solitary or forming small, axillary clusters. Pod stalked, glabrous, flat, oblong, $2–3 \times \frac{1}{4}–\frac{1}{2}$ in.

Sutlej valley, Suni; April, May.—Common throughout N.W. India and the Punjab, ascending to 4000 ft.—Afghanistan.

The wood is hard and durable and is used for agricultural implements; the leaves are used as fodder.

5. **Acacia cæsia,** *Wight & Arn.*; *Fl. Br. Ind.* ii. 297, *under A. Intsia*. A climbing, pubescent shrub; branches covered with small prickles. Leaves 3–12 in.; stipules soon falling off; pinnules 4–15 pairs; leaflets 20–60 on a pinnule, narrowly oblong, obliquely acute. Flowers pale yellow, crowded in stalked, globose heads $\frac{1}{3}–\frac{1}{2}$ in. diam., forming large, terminal panicles. Pod stalked, tomentose or ultimately glabrous, flat, oblong, $4–6 \times 1$ in.

Throughout India, ascending to 4000 ft. in Kumaon; April–August.—Burmah.

45. ALBIZZIA. In honour of Albizzi, an Italian naturalist of the eighteenth century.—Warm regions of Asia, Africa and Australia.

Unarmed trees. Leaves 2-pinnate; rachises usually bearing a gland near the base and between one or more pairs of the leaflets; stipules usually small and soon falling off, large and more persistent in *A. stipulata*; pinnules opposite or nearly so; leaflets sessile, opposite, entire, unequal-sided. Flowers $\frac{1}{2}–1\frac{1}{2}$ in.

long including the stamens, crowded in globose, axillary, stalked heads forming terminal racemes or panicles. Calyx bell-shaped or tubular, 5-toothed. Corolla tubular, 5-lobed. Stamens numerous, far protruding, filaments often coloured, more or less united, the staminal tube about as long as the corolla; anthers minute. Style thread-like; stigma small. Pod broadly oblong, flat, thin, 2-valved or indehiscent; seeds 4–15.

Leaflets obtuse.
  Flowers $1\frac{1}{2}$ in., shortly stalked. Corolla glabrous.
    Leaflets 6–18; lower surface nearly glabrous . . 1. *A. Lebbek.*
  Flowers 1 in., sessile. Corolla hairy. Leaflets 20–50; lower surface tomentose . . . . . . 2. *A. odoratissima.*
Leaflets acute.
  Flowers pink, 1–$1\frac{1}{2}$ in. Stipules linear . . . 3. *A. mollis.*
  Flowers yellow, $\frac{1}{2}$–1 in. Stipules broad, cordate . 4. *A. stipulata.*

1. **Albizzia Lebbek,** *Benth.*; *Fl. Br. Ind.* ii. 298. A tree. Leaves nearly glabrous, 3–12 in.; pinnules 2–4 pairs; leaflets 6–18 on a pinnule, oblong, 1–$1\frac{1}{2}\times\frac{1}{2}$ in., obtuse. Heads long-stalked, in clusters of 2–4, forming short, terminal racemes or panicles. Flowers white, $1\frac{1}{2}$ in. long; stalks $\frac{1}{6}$ in. Calyx pubescent. Corolla glabrous. Pod glabrous, 6–$12\times1\frac{1}{2}$–2 in.

Valleys below Simla; April, May.—Throughout India ascending to 5000 ft.—Tropical Asia; Africa; N. Australia.
The *Siris*; frequently planted.

2. **Albizzia odoratissima,** *Benth.*; *Fl. Br. Ind.* ii. 299. A tree. Leaves pubescent, 6–12 in.; pinnules 3–8 pairs; leaflets 20–50 on a pinuule, oblong, $\frac{3}{4}$–$1\times\frac{1}{4}$ in., obtuse, upper surface pubescent, lower brown-tomentose. Heads shortly stalked, in small clusters forming terminal panicles. Flowers pale yellow, 1 in. long, sessile. Calyx and corolla hairy. Pod 6–8×1 in., brown-tomentose, ultimately glabrous.

Throughout India, ascending to 3000 ft.—April–June.—Tropical Asia.

3. **Albizzia mollis,** *Boiv.*; *Encyc.* xix. *Siècle*, ii. 33 (*Prain in Journ. As. Soc. Bengal*, lxvi. Part II. No. 2. 514), *Fl. Br. Ind.* ii. 300, *under A. Julibrissin.* A small tree. Leaves softly hairy, 6–12 in.; stipules linear, soon falling off; pinnules 6–12 pairs; leaflets 20–50 on a pinnule, obliquely oblong, $\frac{3}{4}\times\frac{1}{4}$ in., acute. Heads long-stalked, in clusters of 2–3, forming short, terminal racemes. Flowers pink, 1–$1\frac{1}{2}$ in. long. Calyx and corolla silky pubescent. Stamens pink-tipped. Pod pubescent, 4–$6\times\frac{3}{4}$–1 in. (Fig. 43.)

Sutlej valley, Suni, below Matiana; April–June.—Outer Himalaya, from the Indus to Assam, usually near water.

4. **Albizzia stipulata,** *Boiv.*; *Fl. Br. Ind.* ii. 300. A tree. Leaves pubescent or hairy, 6–12 in.; stipules pink, very large, broad, cordate, not persistent; pinnules 6–15 pairs; leaflets 40–80 on a pinnule, obliquely oblong, $\frac{1}{3}$–$\frac{1}{2}$ in., acute. Heads

shortly stalked, in clusters of 2–3, forming bracteate racemes. Bracts ovate, acute, brown-tomentose, soon falling off. Flowers

FIG. 43. ALBIZZIA MOLLIS.

yellow, $\frac{1}{2}$–1 in. long. Calyx and corolla silky pubescent. Stamens tinged with red. Pod pubescent, ultimately glabrous, $6 \times \frac{3}{4}$ in.

Below Sipi on the road to Shali; April–June.—Throughout India, ascending to 4000 ft.—Tropical Asia.

XXXI. ROSACEÆ

HERBS, shrubs or trees. Leaves alternate; stipules free or adnate to the stalk, sometimes soon falling off. Flowers regular, usually 2-sexual. Calyx-tube free from or adnate to the ovary;

limb divided into 5, rarely 4, usually equal lobes, in some genera alternating with a similar number of bracteoles. Petals 5, rarely 4, equal. Stamens usually numerous, inserted with the petals around the mouth of the calyx-tube, filaments free, anthers 2-celled. Carpels several or numerous, rarely only one, superior or inferior, distinct or combined into a several-celled ovary; ovules 1 or 2 in each ovary or cell, rarely more (*Spiræa*). Styles as many as the carpels or cells, usually simple and free; stigmas terminal. Fruit various, the ovaries either remaining free or becoming combined with each other or with the calyx; seeds small, 1 or 2 in each ovary or cell, rarely more.—A very large Order spread over nearly the whole globe, but most abundant in N. temperate regions.

See remarks on p. 9 regarding the resemblance of the flowers of *Rubus*, *Potentilla*, *Fragaria* and *Geum* to those of *Ranunculus*.

A. Carpel or carpels superior. Fruit not enclosed in the calyx-tube.

Calyx without bracteoles.
  Carpel only one.
    Unarmed trees. Calyx falling early . . . . . 1. *Prunus*.
    Spring shrubs. Calyx persistent in fruit . . . 2. *Prinsepia*.
  Carpels more than one.
    Unarmed shrubs. Carpels on the base of the calyx. Fruit of 3–5 small follicles . . . . . . 3. *Spiræa*.
    Prickly shrubs. Carpels on a conical or oblong receptacle. Fruit of numerous, small, succulent drupelets 4. *Rubus*.
Calyx with 5 bracteoles alternate with its lobes.
  Fruit dry, consisting of a head of numerous, small achenes.
    Achenes hairy. Style terminal, long . . . . . 5. *Geum*.
    Achenes glabrous (except *P. fruticosa*). Style lateral, very short . . . . 7. *Potentilla*.
  Fruit succulent, consisting of the enlarged receptacle bearing the minute, glabrous achenes . . . . 6. *Fragaria*.

B. Carpels superior or inferior. Fruit adnate to the calyx-tube or wholly enclosed within it.

Herbs. Flowers yellow. Calyx with a ring of small, hooked bristles outside the mouth . . . . 8. *Agrimonia*.
Trees or shrubs. Flowers white or pink.
  Carpels free from the calyx-tube, but wholly enclosed within it . . . . 9. *Rosa*.
  Carpels adnate to the calyx-tube.
    Fruit fleshy, with 2–5 parchment-like cells in the centre, each containing 1 or 2 seeds . . . . 10. *Pyrus*.
    Fruit drupe-like, enclosing 2–5 bony, 1-seeded nutlets.
      Spinous shrubs. Leaves crenate. Nutlets 5 . . 11. *Cratægus*.
      Unarmed shrubs. Leaves entire. Nutlets usually 2 12. *Cotoneaster*.

1. PRUNUS. The classical name of the Plum tree.—N. temperate regions.

Unarmed, glabrous trees. Leaves simple, toothed, usually provided with a pair of glands at the base. Flowers white or pink. Calyx without bracteoles, free, falling off early; tube bell-shaped, limb 5-lobed. Petals 5. Stamens numerous. Carpel solitary, at the base of the calyx-tube; style terminal; ovules 2. Drupe fleshy, juicy, enclosing a hard, 1-seeded stone.

The following fruit trees of this genus are cultivated in or near Simla. The almond, *P. Amygdalus*, flowers pink, appearing before the leaves, drupe velvety, stone slightly flattened, covered with shallow wrinkles and minute holes; native name *badám*. The peach, *P. persica*, flowers pink, appearing before or with the leaves, drupe downy, stone deeply and irregularly furrowed; native name *arú*. The nectarine, a variety of *P. persica*, drupe glabrous. The apricot, *P. armeniaca*, flowers white, appearing before or with the leaves, drupe downy or glabrous, stone smooth, margins thickened and grooved; native name *Zardálu*; the most common fruit tree about the hill villages. The plum, *P. communis*, and its varieties, such as the damson, bullace, &c., flowers white, appearing with the leaves, drupe glabrous, often covered with bloom, stone smooth. The sweet cherry, *P. Avium*, flowers white, clustered, appearing in April or May, leaf-stalks 2-glandular, drupe smooth, stone smooth. The wild cherry, *P. cerasus*, leaf-stalks without glands, drupe smooth, acid.

Flowers 1 in. diam., pale pink, solitary or in small, sessile clusters . . . . 1. *P. Puddum.*
Flowers $\frac{1}{3}$ in. diam., white, in racemes . . . . . . 2. *P. Padus.*

1. **Prunus Puddum,** *Roxb.*; *Fl. Br. Ind.* ii. 314. Leaves ovate, $2\frac{1}{2}$–5 in., long-pointed, teeth glandular; stalks glandular; stipules long, 3–5-parted, glandular-fringed. Flowers 1 in. diam., pink, solitary or in small clusters, crowded towards the end of branches. Calyx-tube $\frac{1}{3}$ in. long, lobes acute. Petals oblong, obtuse. Style long; stigmatic lobes usually 3, spreading. Drupe ovoid, red and yellow, acid; stone wrinkled and furrowed.

Valleys below Simla; October, November.—Himalaya, Simla to Bhootan, 3000–6000 ft.—Native name *Pajja*; often cultivated.

2. **Prunus Padus,** *Linn.*; *Fl. Br. Ind.* ii. 315. Leaves ovate or ovate-lanceolate, 4–6 in., minutely toothed, long-pointed; stipules linear, soon falling off. Flowers $\frac{1}{3}$ in. diam., white, in drooping racemes 3–8 in. long. Stigma peltate, lobed. Drupe globose, red, turning to dark purple or black, acid.

Simla, common; April–June.—Himalaya, Murree to Sikkim, 6000–10,000 ft. —N. Africa, Siberia, &c. (Britain, Bird Cherry).

The young fruit is sometimes attacked by insects, causing it to swell out into a curved, horn-like excrescence.

2. **PRINSEPIA.** In honour of James Prinsep, formerly Secretary of the Asiatic Society, Bengal.—Himalaya, N. China.

Prinsepia utilis, *Royle*; *Fl. Br. Ind.* ii. 323. A glabrous, spiny shrub; spines often leaf-bearing. Leaves lanceolate, 1–3 in., minutely toothed, long-pointed. Flowers white, $\frac{1}{4}$ in. diam., in short, axillary racemes. Calyx without bracteoles, free, persistent; tube cup-shaped, shallow; limb 5-lobed, segments unequal, orbicular, imbricate. Petals 5, orbicular. Stamens numerous, filaments short. Carpel solitary, superior, inserted at the base of the calyx-tube; style terminal, short, thick; stigma large, capitate;

ovules 2. Drupe purple, $\frac{1}{2}$–$\frac{2}{3}$ in., obliquely oblong, the style almost basal in consequence of one-sided growth; stone smooth, 1-seeded by abortion.

Simla, Mushobra; April, and again during the winter.—Temperate Himalaya, 4000-8000 ft.

3. SPIRÆA. The classical name of the Meadow-Sweet, *S. Ulmaria*.—N. temperate and cold regions.

Erect, unarmed shrubs or perennial herbs. Leaves simple or compound; stipules usually small and soon falling off. Flowers numerous, $\frac{1}{6}$–$\frac{1}{4}$ in. diam., usually 2-sexual, crowded in racemes, corymbs or panicles. Calyx without bracteoles, persistent; tube cup-shaped, limb 5-lobed. Petals 5, orbicular. Stamens about 20, filaments sometimes united at the base. Carpels 3–5, rarely more or fewer, superior, inserted at the base of the calyx-tube, free or united at the base; style short; stigma terminal; ovules 2–several. Fruit of 3–5 small, 2- to several-seeded, dry follicles opening along one or both sutures.

Spiræa cantoniensis, a glabrous shrub from China, is frequently cultivated in Simla. Leaves lanceolate, deeply toothed. Flowers white, showy, in numerous, small umbels.

Leaves irregularly pinnatisect; lateral lobes unequal, mostly small; terminal lobe 2–6 in. diam., 3–5-parted . 1. *S. vestita*.
Leaves pinnately compound.
  Leaves 2- or 3-pinnate. Leaflets ovate, usually in threes . . . . 2. *S. Aruncus*.
  Leaves simply pinnate. Leaflets narrowly lanceolate 3. *S. sorbifolia*.
Leaves simple, toothed.
  Flowers pink . . . . 4. *S. bella*.
  Flowers white.
    Leaves $\frac{1}{4}$–$\frac{3}{4}$ in., nearly sessile. Flowers in small corymbs clustered at the end of numerous, short, lateral, leafy branchlets . . . . . . 5. *S. canescens*.
    Leaves 1–$1\frac{1}{2}$ in., stalked. Flowers in large corymbs terminating the stem or main branches . . 6. *S. vaccinifolia*.

1. **Spiræa vestita,** *Wall.*; *Fl. Br. Ind.* ii. 323. A shrub-like herb; rootstock perennial; stems 1–2 ft., pubescent. Leaves irregularly pinnatisect, 2–12 in.; upper surface glabrous, lower pubescent, pale; lateral lobes few or many, very unequal, acutely toothed, all small or 1 or 2 pairs up to about $1\frac{1}{2}$ in. long; terminal lobe 2-6 in. diam., deeply divided into 3-5 sharply toothed, long-pointed segments; stipules persistent, large, semi-orbicular, acutely and irregularly toothed. Flowers white, in large, compound, corymbose, terminal cymes. Follicles hairy.

Huttoo; May, June.—W. Himalaya, 7000–10,000 ft.—Kamtschatka. Resembling and closely allied to the British Meadow-Sweet, *S. Ulmaria*.

2. **Spiræa Aruncus,** *Linn.*; *Fl. Br. Ind.* ii. 323. A shrub-like herb; rootstock perennial; stems 2–4 ft., nearly glabrous.

Leaves 2- or 3-pinnate, 6–12 in.; upper surface glabrous, lower pubescent, pale; leaflets usually in threes, ovate, 1–3 in., sharply and irregularly toothed, narrowed upwards into a tail-like tip. Flowers white, 1-sexual, the male and female on different plants, in long, slender, panicled, pubescent racemes. Follicles glabrous, shining.

Huttoo; June, July.—W. Himalaya, 8000–10,000 ft.—N. Asia, W. Europe, N.W. America.

Superficially resembles *Astilbe rivularis*, but the flowers have petals and 6–8 ovaries.

Fig. 44. Spiræa canescens.

3. **Spiræa sorbifolia,** *Linn.*; *Fl. Br. Ind.* ii. 324. A tall, nearly glabrous shrub. Leaves simply pinnate, 8–12 in.; leaflets 13–19, narrowly lanceolate, 2–4 in., sharply toothed, long-pointed. Flowers white, in terminal panicles 6–12 in. long. Follicles glabrous.

Simla, Mushobra, common; May–July.—W. Himalaya, 7000–10,000 ft.—N. Asia.

4. **Spiræa bella,** *Sims*; *Fl. Br. Ind.* ii. 324. A shrub; stems 2–4 ft., nearly glabrous. Leaves simple, glabrous, ovate, 1–2 in., sharply and irregularly toothed except near the base; lower surface covered with a pale bloom. Flowers pink, often polygamous, in

broad, terminal, compound, pubescent corymbs. Follicles pubescent.

Simla, Mahasu, common; April–July. — Temperate Himalaya, 6000–12,000 ft.

5. **Spiræa canescens,** *Don*; *Fl. Br. Ind.* ii. 325. A shrub, softly tomentose or pubescent, 3–6 ft.; branches arching. Leaves simple, ovate, $\frac{1}{4}$–$\frac{3}{4}$ in., nearly sessile, entire or toothed towards the tip. Flowers white, in small, compound corymbs clustered at the end of numerous, short, leafy, lateral branchlets often all turned to one side. Follicles hairy. (Fig. 44.)

Simla, Mushobra, common; May, June. — Temperate Himalaya, 6000–12,000 ft.

6. **Spiræa vaccinifolia,** *Don*; *Fl. Br. Ind.* ii. 325. A shrub, softly tomentose or pubescent, 1–3 ft. Leaves simple, ovate, 1–1$\frac{1}{2}$ in., stalked, usually sharply toothed or crenate towards the tip, sometimes almost entire; lower surface covered with pale bloom. Flowers white, in broad, terminal, compound, tomentose corymbs. Follicles glabrous.

Simla, Elysium hill, Naldera, Shali, always on limestone; May, June.—W. Himalaya, 6000–8000 ft.

4. **RUBUS.** The Latin name for the Bramble, derived from *ruber*, red, referring to the colour of the fruit in some species.—This genus is found in nearly all parts of the globe and includes the Brambles, Blackberry and Raspberry of Britain.

Prickly shrubs; stems and branches usually weak, trailing or climbing. Leaves simple or compound; stipules narrow, inconspicuous; leaflets sharply, often irregularly toothed, lateral nearly sessile, terminal one stalked. Flowers white or pink, in corymbose panicles, sometimes solitary or in small clusters. Calyx without bracteoles, persistent; tube spreading; limb 5-lobed. Petals 5. Stamens numerous. Carpels numerous, superior, crowded on a conical or shortly oblong receptacle; style thread-like; stigma terminal; ovules 2. Fruit globose, formed by the combination of numerous, succulent, 1-seeded drupelets.

R. nutans was introduced from Kumaon by Sir Edward Buck, about 1883, at the Retreat, Mushobra. It is now common in Simla gardens and appears to be running wild. Stems prostrate, slender, hairy. Leaves compound; leaflets 3. Flowers white, drooping, 1$\frac{1}{2}$ in. diam. Drupelets red.

Flowers white.
  Leaves simple, lobed . . . . 1. *R. paniculatus.*
  Leaves compound.
    Lower surface of leaflets glabrous, green . . . 3. *R. macilentus.*
    Lower surface of leaflets grey- or white-tomentose
      Stem and branches shaggy, with long, tawny bristles . . . . 4. *R. ellipticus.*
      Stem and branches glabrous, covered with white bloom . . . . 5. *R. biflorus.*

Flowers pink. Leaves compound.
Leaflets 3, rarely 5. Calyx-lobes long-pointed. Drupelets pink . . . . 2. *R. niveus.*
Leaflets 5–11. Calyx-lobes acute. Drupelets black . 6. *R. lasiocarpus.*

1. **Rubus paniculatus,** *Smith*; *Fl. Br. Ind.* ii. 329. A rambling climber; prickles few, very small; branches tomentose. Leaves simple, broadly ovate, 3–5 in., usually cordate, long-pointed, more or less lobed, upper surface nearly glabrous, lower white-tomentose. Flowers white, in spreading, tomentose, terminal panicles. Calyx white-tomentose; lobes narrowly pointed, longer than the petals. Drupelets black or dark purple.

Simla, the Glen, below Mahasu; April–June.—Temperate Himalaya, 3000–7000 ft.

2. **Rubus niveus,** *Wall.*; *Fl. Br. Ind.* ii. 335. A large, rambling shrub; stems and branches glabrous or pubescent, purple; prickles small. Leaves compound; leaflets 3, rarely 5, often long-pointed, lateral leaflets lanceolate or broadly ovate, 1–2½ in., terminal one lanceolate, oblong or ovate, 1½–3 in., often lobed, upper surface green, pubescent, at least along the nerves, lower white-tomentose or pale green and pubescent. Flowers pink, ¼–1 in. diam., solitary or in small clusters. Calyx-lobes tomentose inside and out, long-pointed, usually much longer than the petals, rarely shorter. Drupelets pink, like those of a Raspberry.

Simla, Mahasu, common; May–July. — Temperate Himalaya, 6000–10,000 ft.

There are two distinct varieties of this plant: one, having the lower surface of the leaflets white-tomentose, is *R. hypargyrus*, Edgeworth; the other, having both surfaces green, is *R. concolor*, Wallich. Both varieties occur at Simla, the latter usually in shady forest.

3. **Rubus macilentus,** *Camb.*; *Fl. Br. Ind.* ii. 336. A trailing shrub; stems and branches glabrous, shining, red-brown; prickles numerous, curved, up to ¼ in. long. Leaves compound; leaflets 3, glabrous or nearly so, midrib often prickly, both surfaces green; lateral leaflets ovate, about 1 in., sometimes wanting, terminal one ovate-lanceolate or oblong, 1½–2½ in. Flowers white, about ⅓ in. diam., solitary or in clusters of 2 or 3. Calyx hairy inside and out; lobes long-pointed, as long as the petals, rarely longer. Drupelets yellow or orange.

Simla, Mushobra; April, May.—Temperate Himalaya, 5000–9000 ft.

A variety with small leaflets hardly ½ in. long occurs at Simla, usually in forest.

4. **Rubus ellipticus,** *Smith*; *Fl. Br. Ind.* ii. 336. A large, grey-tomentose shrub; stems and branches trailing, shaggy with long, tawny bristles; prickles numerous, curved. Leaves compound; leaflets 3, orbicular-ovate, lateral leaflets 1–1½ in., sometimes wanting, terminal one 1½–4 in., upper surface green, pubescent, lower grey-tomentose. Flowers white, ½–⅓ in. diam.,

crowded in axillary and terminal panicles. Calyx-lobes tomentose inside and out, ovate, acute, shorter than the petals. Drupelets yellow.

Simla, Mushobra; March, April, sometimes flowering again during the cold season.—Throughout the Himalaya, 2000–7000 ft.—Burmah, S. China.

The fruit has the flavour of Raspberry and is very good to eat.

5. **Rubus biflorus,** *Buch.-Ham.*; *Fl. Br. Ind.* ii. 338. A large, spreading, nearly erect shrub; stems and branches glabrous, covered with white bloom or powder as if whitewashed; prickles numerous, small, recurved. Leaves compound; leaflets 3 or 5, ovate-lanceolate, lateral leaflets 1–1½ in., terminal one rather

FIG. 45. RUBUS BIFLORUS.

larger, often lobed; upper surface green, pubescent, lower white-tomentose. Flowers white, ½–¾ in. diam., long-stalked, solitary or in small clusters. Calyx-lobes tomentose inside, acute, usually shorter than, rarely as long as the petals. Drupelets yellow or orange. (Fig. 45.)

Simla; April, May.—Temperate Himalaya, 7000–9000 ft.

6. **Rubus lasiocarpus,** *Smith*; *Fl. Br. Ind.* ii. 339. A large, spreading shrub; stems and branches glabrous, purple, pendulous and often rooting at the tips; prickles small, usually few.

Leaves compound; leaflets 5–11, ovate or ovate-lanceolate, lateral leaflets $1\frac{1}{2}$–$2\frac{1}{2}$ in., terminal one rather larger, often lobed; upper surface green, glabrous, lower white-tomentose. Flowers dark pink, $\frac{1}{3}$–$\frac{2}{3}$ in. diam., crowded in small, tomentose panicles. Calyx-lobes tomentose inside and out, lanceolate, acute, longer than the petals. Drupelets black, hoary.

Simla, Mahasu, common; March-May.—Throughout the Himalaya, 4000–10,000 ft.—Burmah, Java.

A prostrate variety with 3–7 much smaller leaflets is distinguished in the *Fl. Br. Ind.* as *R. foliolosus*, Don; it occurs in the Mahasu forests.

5. GEUM. From the Greek *geuo*, to stimulate; referring to the aromatic roots.—Nearly all temperate and cold regions.

Soft, hairy herbs; rootstock perennial; stems several, erect. Leaves pinnately compound; lateral segments or leaflets in unequal pairs, terminal one largest. Radical leaves numerous, crowded; stem-leaves few. Stipules broad, toothed, often lobed, adnate to the base of the leaf-stalk. Flowers yellow, few, long-stalked, in terminal cymes. Calyx persistent; tube bowl- or cup-shaped, bearing on its outer margin 5 small bracteoles alternate with the 5 lobes of the limb. Petals 5, broadly obovate. Stamens numerous. Carpels numerous, superior, densely hairy, crowded on a dry, convex receptacle; style terminal; stigma minute; ovule solitary. Fruit a globose head of densely hairy achenes always dry; achenes each tipped with the elongated, persistent style.

Radical leaves 4–6 in. Flowers $\frac{1}{2}$–$\frac{3}{4}$ in. diam. Calyx-lobes reflexed. Style jointed in the middle . . . . . 1. *G. urbanum.*
Radical leaves 6–12 in. Flowers 1–$1\frac{1}{2}$ in. diam. Calyx-lobes spreading. Style simple, not jointed . . . . . 2. *G. elatum.*

1. **Geum urbanum,** *Linn.*; *Fl. Br. Ind.* ii. 342. Stems 1–3 ft. Leaves pinnate; leaflets acutely and irregularly toothed. Radical leaves 4–6 in.; lateral leaflets 6–12, nearly sessile, uppermost pair large, others all small but the alternate pairs larger; terminal leaflet stalked, nearly orbicular, 1–3 in. diam., often lobed. Upper stem-leaves usually of 3 leaflets; the lateral leaflets sometimes merged in the terminal one and forming a 3-lobed leaf. Lower stem-leaves similar to the radical but shorter. Flowers pale yellow, $\frac{1}{2}$–$\frac{3}{4}$ in. diam. Calyx lobes reflexed. Style sharply incurved and jointed near the middle, lower portion glabrous, persistent, becoming elongated and hooked in fruit, terminal portion hairy, ultimately breaking off.

Simla, common; May–July.—W. Himalaya, 6000–11,000 ft.—W. Asia, Europe (Britain, Herb-Bennet).

2. **Geum elatum,** *Wall.*; *Fl. Br. Ind.* ii. 343. Stems 12–18 in. Radical leaves pinnatisect, 6–12 in.; segments crenate or sharply toothed, often lobed; lateral segments numerous, nearly or quite distinct, broad-based, sessile, ovate or oblong, up to 1 in. long,

pairs alternately large and small, gradually diminishing in size from the uppermost downwards; terminal segment much larger, 3-lobed. Stem-leaves few, small, pinnately lobed. Flowers bright yellow, 1–1½ in. diam. Calyx-lobes spreading. Style glabrous, nearly straight, simple, not jointed or hooked in fruit.

Huttoo; September, October.—W. Himalaya, 9000–12,000 ft.

6. **FRAGARIA.** From the Latin *fragrans*, fragrant, referring to the fruit.—N. temperate regions including Britain (Strawberry); S. America; Sandwich Islands.

Soft, silky herbs; rootstock perennial, producing long runners rooting at the joints; stems nearly erect. Leaves mostly radical, tufted, long stalked, digitately compound. Leaflets 3, sessile, ovate, toothed. Stem-leaves few, sometimes undivided. Stipules adnate to the base of the leaf-stalk. Flowers yellow or white, nodding, often polygamous, axillary or few in terminal cymes. Calyx persistent; tube spreading, bearing on its outer margin 5 bracteoles alternate with the 5 lobes of its limb. Petals 5, broadly obovate. Stamens numerous. Carpels numerous, very small, distinct, superior, crowded on a convex receptacle; style lateral, short, persistent; stigma minute; ovule solitary. Fruit insipid, usually red, consisting of the globose, much enlarged, succulent receptacle, its surface dotted with the numerous seed-like, minute, glabrous achenes.

Flowers yellow. Bracteoles 3-toothed . . . . . . 1. *F. indica.*
Flowers white. Bracteoles entire . . . . 2. *F. vesca.*

1. **Fragaria indica,** *Andr.*; *Fl. Br. Ind.* ii. 343. Leaflets ½–1½ in.; teeth small, often blunt. Stipules broad, toothed. Flowers yellow, ½–1 in. diam. Calyx-bracts large, 3-lobed.

Simla, Mushobra, common; April, May. — Throughout the Himalaya, ascending to 8000 ft.—Asia, mountainous regions.

2. **Fragaria vesca,** *Linn.*; *Fl. Br. Ind.* ii. 344. Leafstalks sometimes bearing an additional minute pair of leaflets. Leaflets 1–1½ in., deeply and acutely toothed; teeth tipped with tufts of silky hairs. Stipules narrow, entire. Flowers white, ¾–1 in. diam. Bracteoles small, entire.

Simla, Mahasu, common; April-June. — Temperate Himalaya, 5000-10,000 ft.—N. temperate regions. (Britain, Wild Strawberry.)

7. **POTENTILLA.** From the Latin *potens*, powerful; referring to the reputed medicinal properties of some species.—N. temperate, arctic and mountainous regions.

Shrubs or herbs, rarely annual, usually softly hairy. Leaves stalked, digitately compound with 3 or 5 leaflets or pinnately compound with from 3 to numerous leaflets; leaflets usually toothed; stipules adnate to the base of the leafstalk. Flowers usually yellow, sometimes white, red or purple, in corymbose cymes, rarely axillary and solitary. Calyx persistent; tube shallow, bowl-shaped, bearing on its outer margin 5 bracteoles alternate with the 5 lobes of the limb. Petals 5, usually obcordate, sometimes obovate or narrowly oblong. Stamens numerous, rarely 5–10. Carpels numerous, very small, distinct, superior, crowded on a small, dry receptacle; styles lateral, short, persistent; stigma minute; ovule solitary. Fruit a head of numerous, hard, glabrous (except *P. fruticosa*) achenes, covered by the inflexed calyx-lobes.

In using the following key regard must be had to the basal leaves; the upper leaves in Nos. 3, 5 and 10 often have only three leaflets, and might be mistaken for digitately compound leaves.

A. Leaves digitately compound.

Leaflets 3.	
Flowers yellow.	
Flowers $\frac{1}{4}$ in. or less diam.	
Stamens 5–10	1. *P. Sibbaldi.*
Stamens numerous	9. *P. Kleiniana.**
Flowers $\frac{3}{4}$–1 in. diam.	7. *P. argyrophylla.*
Flowers dark crimson	8. *P. atrosanguinea.*
Leaflets 5.	
Flowers dark crimson, $\frac{3}{4}$–1 in. diam. . . .	6. *P. nepalensis.*
Flowers yellow, $\frac{1}{4}$ in. diam.	9. *P. Kleiniana.**

B. Leaves pinnately compound.

Stamens 5. Flowers yellow, $\frac{1}{4}$ in. diam.	2. *P. albifolia.*
Stamens numerous.	
Leaflets entire. A shrub	3. *P. fruticosa.*
Leaflets toothed. Herbs.	
Leaflets numerous, pairs alternately large and small	4. *P. fulgens.*
Leaflets 3–9, pairs not alternately large and small.	
Petals twice as long as the calyx . . .	5. *P. fragarioides.*
Petals shorter than the calyx	10. *P. supina.*

1. **Potentilla Sibbaldi,** *Haller*; *Fl. Br. Ind.* ii. 345. A perennial herb, covered with long, silky hairs; stems tufted, 2–12 in., procumbent or ascending. Leaves digitately compound; leaflets 3, wedge-shaped, tip sharply 3–5-toothed, otherwise entire. Flowers pale yellow, $\frac{1}{4}$ in. or less diam., in terminal, corymbose cymes. Petals as long as the calyx. Stamens 5, alternate with the petals and sometimes 1–5, opposite to them. Achenes glabrous.

Huttoo, Bhagi; July.—Alpine Himalayas, 9000–15,000 ft.—Lofty mountains in the N. temperate zone (Scotch Highlands); Arctic regions.

2. **Potentilla albifolia,** *Wall.*; *Fl. Br. Ind.* ii. 347. A perennial herb; stems several, slender, pubescent, 6–12 in., diffusely spreading. Leaves pinnately compound; leaflets 5–9, ovate, $\frac{1}{4}$–1

* *P. Kleiniana* has leaves of 3 and of 5 leaflets.

in., deeply and sharply toothed, lateral leaflets gradually or irregularly diminishing in size fiom the uppermost pair downwards; upper surface green, pubescent, lower white-tomentose. Flowers yellow, $\frac{1}{4}$ in. diam., solitary on slender, axillary stalks. Petals oblong, shorter than the calyx. Stamens 5. Achenes glabrous.

Huttoo, Bhagi; June, July.—W. Himalaya, 8000–10,000 ft.

I have retained the name for this species adopted in the *Fl. Br. Ind.*, but D. Don's *micropetala*, 1825, has priority over Wallich's published in 1828.

3. **Potentilla fruticosa,** *Linn.*; *Fl. Br. Ind.* ii. 347. An erect shrub, 1–4 ft. Leaves pinnately compound, crowded; leaflets 3–7, ovate-lanceolate, $\frac{1}{3}$–$\frac{2}{3}$ in., entire, acute; upper surface densely silky, hairy, lower glabrous. Flowers numerous, bright yellow, 1–1$\frac{1}{2}$ in. diam., solitary, terminal; stalks silky. Petals much longer than the calyx. Stamens numerous. Achenes hairy.

Huttoo; July–September.—Temperate Himalaya, 8000–12,000 ft.—N. Asia, Europe. (England, rare.)

4. **Potentilla fulgens,** *Wall.*; *Fl. Br. Ind.* ii. 349. A perennial herb; stems robust, erect, 6–24 in., hairy. Leaves pinnately compound, 2–8 in.; leaflets numerous, pairs alternately large and small, diminishing in size from the uppermost downwards, ovate, closely and sharply toothed, terminal leaflet 1–1$\frac{1}{2}$ in.; upper surface green, hairy, lower silvery tomentose. Flowers yellow or orange-yellow, $\frac{1}{2}$ in. diam., crowded in terminal corymbs. Petals scarcely longer than the calyx. Stamens numerous. Achenes glabrous.

Simla, Mushobra; common; August–October.—Temperate Himalaya, 6000–9000 ft.

5. **Potentilla fragarioides,** *Linn.*; *Fl. Br. Ind.* ii. 350. A perennial herb; stems 4–12 in., erect or nearly so, pubescent or hairy. Leaves pinnately compound; leaflets 5–9, often only 3 in the upper leaves, ovate or oblong-ovate, lateral leaflets gradually diminishing in size from the uppermost pair downwards, terminal leaflet $\frac{1}{2}$–1$\frac{1}{2}$ in., teeth large, blunt or acute; upper surface green, hairy, lower densely covered with long, pale or white hairs. Flowers long-stalked, yellow or white, $\frac{1}{2}$ in. diam., in open, terminal corymbs. Petals twice as long as the calyx. Stamens numerous. Achenes glabrous.

Simla, common; June–August.—Temperate Himalaya, 4000–7000 ft.

I am unable to distinguish *P. Leschenaultiana* and its variety *P. bannehalensis* (*Fl. Br. Ind.* ii. 350) from the species described above.

6. **Potentilla nepalensis,** *Hook.*; *Fl. Br. Ind.* ii. 355. A perennial herb; stems erect, 1–3 ft., hairy. Leaves digitately compound; leaflets 5, often only 3 in the upper leaves, ovate or

oblong-ovate, unequal, the largest 1–2 in., teeth large, blunt or acute; both surfaces thinly hairy. Flowers dark crimson, $\frac{3}{4}$–1 in.

FIG. 46. POTENTILLA NEPALENSIS.

diam., in terminal, spreading panicles. Petals obcordate, longer than the calyx. Stamens numerous. Achenes glabrous. (Fig. 46.)

Simla, common; July, August.—W. Himalaya, 5000–9000 ft.

7. **Potentilla argyrophylla,** *Wall.*; *Fl. Br. Ind.* ii. 356. A perennial herb; stems erect, robust, 2–3 ft., pale-tomentose. Leaves digitately compound; leaflets 3, ovate, 2–3 in., coarsely and acutely toothed; upper surface green, finely hairy, lower white-tomentose. Flowers long-stalked, yellow, $\frac{3}{4}$–$1\frac{1}{4}$ in. diam., in terminal panicles. Stamens numerous. Achenes glabrous.

Matiana Narkunda; July, August.—Temperate Himalaya, 8000–12,000 ft.

8. **Potentilla atrosanguinea,** *Lodd.; Fl. Br. Ind.* ii. 357, *under P. argyrophylla.* A perennial herb, not differing from *P. argyrophylla* except that the flowers are dark crimson.

Mahasu, Huttoo; June–October.—Temperate Himalaya, 8000–12,000 ft.

9. **Potentilla Kleiniana,** *Wight & Arn.*; *Fl. Br. Ind.* ii. 359. An annual herb; stems several or many, diffusely spreading, 6–24 in., slender, thinly hairy. Leaves digitately compound; leaflets 3 or 5, ovate or narrowly oblong, unequal, the longest ½–1½ in., teeth blunt or acute. Flowers stalked, yellow, ¼ in. diam., in terminal, corymbose cymes. Stamens numerous. Achenes glabrous.

Valleys below Simla, Annandale; May-October.—Temperate Himalaya, 3000–7000 ft.—Nilghiris.—China, Japan.

10. **Potentilla supina,** *Linn.*; *Fl. Br. Ind.* ii. 359. An annual herb; stems several or many, prostrate or diffusely spreading, 6–18 in., pubescent or hairy. Leaves pinnately compound, 1–3 in.; leaflets 5–9, in the upper leaves often only 3, oblong, ¼–1 in., crenate or sharply toothed, sometimes lobed, lateral leaflets nearly equal; both surfaces thinly hairy. Flowers yellow, ¼ in. diam., solitary, axillary. Petals shorter than the calyx. Achenes glabrous.

Sutlej valley.—Throughout India, ascending to 8000 ft.—Asia, Africa.

8. **AGRIMONIA.** Etymology obscure.—N. temperate regions; S. America.

Agrimonia Eupatorium, *Linn.*; *Fl. Br. Ind.* ii. 361. A perennial, hairy herb; stems erect, 2–3 ft. Leaves pinnately compound. Lower leaves 4–7 in.; leaflets coarsely toothed, very unequal, larger ones 5–9, ovate, ½–1½ in., intermixed with a number of much smaller ones. Upper leaves gradually smaller and with fewer leaflets. Stipules adnate to the base of the leaf-stalk. Flowers yellow, ⅓ in. diam., in terminal, spike-like racemes, each flower in the axil of a small, 3-cleft bract and with 2 smaller, 3-toothed bracteoles at the top of its stalk. Calyx-tube top-shaped, grooved, bearing outside its mouth a ring of small, hooked bristles; limb 5-lobed. Petals 5, oblong. Stamens 15. Carpels 2, free, enclosed within the calyx-tube; styles thread-like, protruding; stigmas terminal, dilated; ovule solitary. Achenes 1 or 2, enclosed in the hardened, bristly calyx crowned with a ring of hooked bristles.

Simla, common; July, August.—Temperate Himalaya, 3000–10,000 ft.—N. Asia; Europe (Britain, Common Agrimony).

9. **ROSA.** The classical name.—N. temperate and subtropical regions (Britain, Rose).

Erect or climbing shrubs, usually prickly. Leaves pinnately compound; leaflets toothed; stipules large, adnate to and sheathing the base of the leaf-stalk. Flowers solitary or corymbose, large, white or pink. Calyx-tube ovoid, hairy or silky within, mouth contracted; lobes 5 or 4, spreading in flower, erect or reflexed in fruit. Petals usually 5, rarely 4. Stamens numerous. Carpels numerous, small, usually silky, distinct, sessile at the base of the calyx-tube and wholly enclosed within it. Styles lateral, hairy, more or less protruding above the calyx-mouth, free or united in a column; stigma terminal; ovule solitary. Fruit of several hard, hairy achenes enclosed within the succulent calyx-tube.

Erect shrubs. Styles free.
  Flowers pink. Petals 5, shorter than the sepals . 1. *R. macrophylla.*
  Flowers white. Petals 4, longer than the sepals . 2. *R. sericea.*
Climbing shrubs. Styles united in a column. Flowers white . . . . 3. *R. moschata.*

1. **Rosa macrophylla,** *Lindl.*; *Fl. Br. Ind.* ii. 366. Erect, prickly or smooth; stipules, flower-stalks and calyx more or less glandular. Leaves 2–7 in.; stalks tomentose; leaflets 7–11, nearly glabrous, ovate, acute, teeth small, regular, lateral leaflets gradually diminishing in size from the uppermost pair downwards, terminal one $\frac{3}{4}$–3 in. Flowers pink, solitary or corymbose, 1–2$\frac{1}{2}$ in. diam. Calyx-lobes 5, narrow, longer than the petals, tip dilated, toothed. Petals 5. Styles free, hardly protruding above the calyx-mouth. Fruit ovoid, red; calyx-lobes erect.

Simla, Mushobra, Matiana, Narkunda; April, May.—Temperate Himalaya, 4000–10,000 ft.—China.

There are two distinct varieties of this species. At Simla and Mushobra the stems are prickly, the leaves about 3 in., and the end leaflet rarely more than 1 in. At Matiana and Narkunda, in forest undergrowth, prickles are usually wanting, the leaves are 6–7 in., and the end leaflet 1$\frac{1}{2}$–3 in.

2. **Rosa sericea,** *Lindl.*; *Fl. Br. Ind.* ii. 367. Erect, pubescent, sometimes glandular, prickly or smooth. Leaves 1–3 in., clustered; leaflets 5–11, narrowly oblong, sharply toothed near the tip, otherwise entire, lateral leaflets gradually diminishing in size from the uppermost pair downwards, terminal one $\frac{1}{3}$–1 in. Flowers white, solitary, 2–2$\frac{1}{2}$ in. diam., on short, lateral shoots. Calyx-lobes 4, ovate-lanceolate, shorter than the petals, long-pointed. Petals 4. Styles free, protruding far above the calyx-mouth. Fruit bright red, pear-shaped; calyx-lobes erect.

Huttoo, Baghi; June.—Temperate Himalaya, 9000–13,000 ft.—China.

There are two varieties of this species. When growing in shady forest the stems are usually without prickles, and the leaves 2–3 in.; on open, dry hillsides the prickles are numerous, and the leaves only 1–1$\frac{1}{2}$ in.

3. **Rosa moschata,** *Mill.*; *Fl. Br. Ind.* ii. 367. Climbing, glabrous or nearly so, prickly. Leaves 3–6 in.; leaflets 3–7, ovate, nearly equal, 1–3 in., toothed, acute. Flowers white, 1$\frac{1}{2}$ in.

diam., in terminal corymbs. Calyx-lobes 5, narrowly lanceolate, shorter than the petals, long-pointed. Petals 5. Styles united in a column protruding far above the calyx-mouth. Fruit globose; calyx-lobes reflexed.

Simla, common; April–June. — Temperate Himalaya, 4000–8000 ft.— Afghanistan, Europe and Abyssinia, eastward to China.

10. PYRUS. The classical name of the Pear tree.—N. temperate regions.

Trees or shrubs. Leaves stalked, simple or pinnate, toothed; stipules soon falling off. Flowers in simple or compound, terminal corymbs. Calyx-tube bell-shaped, adnate to the ovary, becoming enlarged and fleshy in fruit; lobes 5, reflexed, persistent or falling off after flowering. Petals 5, orbicular, shortly clawed. Stamens numerous. Carpels enclosed within and adnate to the calyx-tube; styles 2–5, free to the base or nearly so; stigma terminal, small. Fruit globose, fleshy, having 2–5 parchment-like cells at the centre, each containing 1 or 2 seeds or pips.

The Apple, *P. Malus*, bearing pink flowers $1\frac{1}{2}$–2 in. diam., and the common Pear, *P. communis*, bearing white flowers $1\frac{1}{3}$ in. diam., are both planted at Simla and flower during March and April. The Quince, *Cydonia vulgaris*, with white or pale red flowers is also cultivated in the N.W. Himalaya.

Leaves simple, sometimes lobed. Calyx-lobes fallen off in fruit.
  Leaves usually glabrous. Flowers few, in simple corymbs. Fruit apple-shaped.
    Leaves sharply toothed. Fruit red, smooth . . . 1. *P. baccata.*
    Leaves crenate, rarely sharply toothed. Fruit yellow-brown, rough . . . . 2. *P. Pashia.*
  Leaves usually white-tomentose on lower surface. Flowers numerous, in compound corymbs. Fruit pear-shaped . . . . 3. *P. lanata.*
Leaves pinnately compound. Calyx-lobes persisting on the fruit.
  Corymb-branches and lower surface of leaves glabrous 4. *P. Aucuparia.*
  Corymb-branches and lower surface of leaves red-tomentose . . . . 5. *P. foliolosa.*

1. **Pyrus baccata**, *Linn.*; *Fl. Br. Ind.* ii. 373. A small, more or less pubescent tree. Leaves simple, ovate, 2–3 in., sharply toothed, sometimes long-pointed. Flowers about 10 or fewer, in simple corymbs, long-stalked, white, $1\frac{1}{2}$ in. diam.; buds pink. Calyx-lobes falling off. Styles 5, nearly free, base woolly. Fruit apple-shaped, $\frac{1}{3}$–$\frac{1}{2}$ in. diam., red, smooth, shining.

Deoti; April, May.—W. Himalaya, 6000–10,000 ft.—Siberia, China, Japan. Often planted in Britain (Siberian Crab).

2. **Pyrus Pashia**, *Buch.-Ham.*; *Fl. Br. Ind.* ii. 374. A small tree; barren branchlets usually ending in a spine. Leaves simple, ovate or ovate-lanceolate, 2–4 in., crenate or long-pointed,

tomentose or woolly when young, ultimately glabrous; on young trees the leaves are sometimes deeply 3-lobed and sharply toothed. Flowers about ten or fewer, in simple corymbs, white, tinged with

FIG. 47. PYRUS PASHIA.

pink, 1 in. diam. Calyx tomentose; lobes falling off. Styles 3–5, free, base woolly. Fruit apple-shaped, ½–1 in. diam., yellow-brown, rough, with small, white spots. (Fig. 47.)

Simla, common; April, May.—Temperate Himalaya, 3000–8000 ft.—Burmah, N. China.

3. **Pyrus lanata**, *Don*; *Fl. Br. Ind.* ii. 375. A tree, more or less white-tomentose. Leaves woolly when young, simple, ovate or oblong-ovate, 3–6 in., upper surface glabrous, lower white-tomentose, margins sharply toothed, more or less lobed. Flowers numerous, white, ½ in. diam., in tomentose, compound corymbs. Calyx tomentose; lobes falling off. Styles 2 or 3, densely woolly. Fruit pear-shaped, ½–1 in. long, red, smooth.

Simla, Jako, Narkunda; April, May.—W. Himalaya, 8000–10,000 ft. Closely allied to the British *P. Aria* (White Beam).

4. **Pyrus Aucuparia**, *Gaertn.*; *Fl. Br. Ind.* ii. 375. A small tree or tall shrub; leaves and inflorescence nearly or quite glabrous. Leaves pinnate, 4–6 in.; rachis glabrous; leaflets 15–25, opposite, oblong-lanceolate, ½–2 in., sharply toothed; upper surface green, glabrous, lower pale, almost white, glabrous except on the nerves. Flowers numerous, pink, ⅓ in. diam., crowded in glabrous or slightly hairy, compound corymbs. Calyx glabrous;

lobes persistent. Styles 2–5, base woolly. Fruit red or nearly white, globose, $\frac{1}{3}$–$\frac{1}{2}$ in. diam.

Huttoo; June, July.—Temperate Himalaya, 9000–13,000 ft.—Europe to China and Japan (Britain, Rowan tree or Mountain Ash).

5. **Pyrus foliolosa,** *Wall.*; *Fl. Br. Ind.* ii. 376. A shrub or small tree; leaves and inflorescence more or less covered with red-brown tomentum. Leaves pinnate, 4–6 in.; rachis tomentose; leaflets 11–31, opposite, oblong-lanceolate, 1–1$\frac{1}{2}$ in., sharply toothed, acute; upper surface green, hairy, lower paler, hairy, midrib and nerves tomentose. Flowers numerous, white or tinged with green, $\frac{1}{4}$ in. diam., crowded in tomentose, compound corymbs. Calyx pubescent; lobes persistent. Styles 2–5, free, base pubescent. Fruit red or covered with blue bloom.

Huttoo; May, June.—Temperate Himalaya from Kumaon to Sikkim, 9000–12,000 ft.

11. **CRATÆGUS.** From the Greek *kratos*, strength, referring to the wood.—N. temperate regions, most numerous in N. America.

***Cratægus crenulata,** *Roxb.*; *Fl. Br. Ind.* ii. 384. A large, glabrous, spiny shrub. Leaves usually crowded on short, lateral branchlets, narrowly oblong, 1–2 in., shortly stalked, crenate, obtuse. Flowers white, $\frac{1}{4}$ in. diam., in numerous, terminal, compound corymbs. Calyx-tube bell-shaped, adnate to the ovary; lobes 5, obtuse, persistent. Petals 5, orbicular. Stamens numerous. Carpels 5, distinct, 1-celled, enclosed within and adnate to the calyx-tube, only the tips free; styles 5; stigma capitate; ovules 2 in each ovary. Fruit drupe-like, globose, $\frac{1}{4}$ in. diam., orange-red, containing 5 bony, free, triangular, 1-seeded nutlets, the tips protruding between the calyx-lobes.

The Sutlej to Bhootan, 2500–8000 ft.; April, May.

Closely allied to *C. Pyracantha* which is often trained against walls in Britain. The bright red fruit remains on the tree nearly all the winter.

The British Hawthorn, *C. Oxyacantha*, occurs in Kashmir and at Murree, but does not extend east of Kishtwar. The leaves are deeply lobed, and the fruit contains a single, 1- or 2-celled stone.

12. **COTONEASTER.** From the Latin *Cotonia* (*Cydonia*), the Quince, and *aster* (*ad instar*), similar.—Temperate Asia, Europe, N. Africa, Mexico.

Shrubs, sometimes procumbent. Leaves shortly stalked, simple, entire; stipules soon falling off. Flowers small, in terminal and axillary cymes, sometimes solitary. Calyx-tube bell-shaped, adnate to the ovary; lobes 5, short, persistent. Petals 5, orbicular. Stamens numerous. Carpels 2–5, 1-celled, enclosed within and adnate to the calyx-tube, only the tips free;

styles 2–5; stigmas capitate; ovules 2 in each ovary. Fruit drupe-like, containing 2–5 bony, 1-seeded nutlets, the upper part of each free from the calyx-tube.

C. multiflora, *Bunge*, is recorded in the *Fl. Br. Ind.* ii. 386, from Kashmir and Garhwal. Further material received since the publication of that work has, however, proved that this species does not extend to the Himalaya.

Leaves 1–3 in.; margins flat.
  Leaves ovate or ovate-lanceolate; upper surface glabrous or nearly so. Cymes stalked, many-flowered. Fruit globose, nearly black when ripe . . . . 1. *C. bacillaris.*
  Leaves narrowly lanceolate; upper surface hairy. Cymes nearly sessile, few-flowered. Fruit oblong, red when ripe . . . . 2. *C. acuminata.*
Leaves $\frac{1}{4}$–$\frac{1}{2}$ in.; margins recurved . . . . . . 3. *C. microphylla.*

1. **Cotoneaster bacillaris**, *Wall.*; *Fl. Br. Ind.* ii. 384. A large shrub with long, slender branches. Leaves ovate or ovate-lanceolate, 1–3 in., obtuse or acute, both surfaces glabrous or nearly so,

FIG. 48. COTONEASTER BACILLARIS.

lower often hairy along the nerves, margins flat. Flowers white, $\frac{1}{3}$ in. diam., in large, hairy or pubescent, stalked, loosely branched cymes on short, lateral, leafy branchlets. Fruit globose, $\frac{1}{4}$ in. diam., red at first, nearly black when ripe. (Fig. 48.)

Simla, Mushobra; May, June.—Temperate Himalaya, 4000–8000 ft.
The wood is used for walking sticks, whence the name (Latin, *bacillum*).

C. rosea, *Edgeworth*, occurs on the Chor and on Marali; it differs from the above, to which it has been reduced as var. *affinis* in the *Fl. Br. Ind.*, in the leaves being more or less hairy on the upper surface and tomentose on the lower, especially when young, in its tomentose calyx, smaller pink flowers and red fruit. This species was formerly, in part, referred to *C. multiflora.*

2. **Cotoneaster acuminata,** *Lindl.*; *Fl. Br. Ind.* ii. 385. A shrub with long, slender branches. Leaves crowded, lanceolate, 1–2 in., long-pointed, both surfaces hairy, margins flat. Flowers white, $\frac{1}{4}$ in. diam., in hairy, small, nearly sessile cymes on very short, lateral, leafy branchlets. Fruit oblong, $\frac{1}{3}$ in. long, red when ripe.

Huttoo; May–July.—Temperate Himalaya, 5000–12,000 ft.

3. **Cotoneaster microphylla,** *Wall.*; *Fl. Br. Ind.* ii. 387. A dwarf, dense, usually procumbent, much branched shrub. Leaves hard, ovate, $\frac{1}{4}$–$\frac{1}{2}$ in., acute or obtuse, upper surface dark green, shining, lower pubescent or tomentose, margins recurved. Flowers white, $\frac{1}{3}$ in. diam., usually solitary. Fruit globose, $\frac{1}{4}$ in. diam., bright red.

Simla; May, June.—Temperate Himalaya, 4000–10,000 ft.—China.

XXXII. SAXIFRAGACEÆ

Shrubs or herbs of various habit. Leaves alternate or opposite, sometimes rosulate; stipules usually none. Flowers usually regular, 2-sexual; inflorescence various. Calyx-tube more or less adnate to the ovary; limb usually 5- or 4-lobed. Petals 5 or 4, rarely none. Stamens usually 5 or 10, rarely numerous, inserted with the petals on the mouth of the calyx-tube or on the margin of the ovary; filaments free, thread-like, or, in *Deutzia*, flattened and 3-pointed; anthers 2-celled. Ovary more or less adnate to the calyx-tube, usually 1- or 2-celled, sometimes 3–5-celled; styles as many as the ovary-cells except in *Chrysosplenium* and *Ribes*, free or more or less united; stigmas terminal, small; ovules usually numerous. Fruit a capsule, often 2-beaked or, in *Ribes*, a berry; seeds usually minute, inserted on the inner angle of the cells except in *Parnassia*.—A large Order ranging over nearly the whole world; most abundant in cold and temperate regions.

Stamens 5.
- Leaves compound, 2-pinnate. Petals none. Herbs . 1. *Astilbe.*
- Leaves simple, sometimes lobed. Petals 5.
  - Herbs. Flowers solitary, terminal, on erect scapes 4. *Parnassia.*
  - Shrubs or small trees. Flowers racemed.
    - Leaves not lobed. Fruit a capsule . . . . 8. *Itea.*
    - Leaves 3- or 5-lobed. Fruit a berry . . . . 9. *Ribes.*

Stamens more than 5, usually 10.
- Herbs. Leaves alternate or rosulate.
  - Flowers $\frac{1}{4}$–$1\frac{1}{4}$ in. diam. Petals 5 . . . . . 2. *Saxifraga.*
  - Flowers minute. Petals none . . . . . 3. *Chrysosplenium.*

Shrubs. Leaves opposite.
  Flowers in compound corymbs, some of the outer ones much larger than the others. Filaments thread-like . . . . 5. *Hydrangea.*
  Flowers in spreading panicles, all alike. Filaments flattened, 3-pointed . . . . 6. *Deutzia.*
Stamens 20–40. Petals 4. Shrubs . . . . . . 7. *Philadelphus.*

1. **ASTILBE.** From the Greek *a,* without, and *stilbe,* brilliancy; referring to the small, apetalous flowers.—N. Asia, N. America.

Astilbe rivularis, *Buch.-Ham.*; *Fl. Br. Ind.* ii. 389. An erect, hairy herb, 3–4 ft. high; rootstock perennial. Leaves alternate, 6–18 in., irregularly 2-pinnate, lower pinnules usually with 3 leaflets; stipules large, membranous, sheathing; base of leaf-

FIG. 49. ASTILBE RIVULARIS.

stalks dilated, hairy; leaflets ovate, sometimes lobed, 1–4 in., cordate, sharply and unequally toothed, long-pointed, upper surface glabrous, lower minutely bristly along the midrib and nerves. Flowers very small, sometimes 1-sexual, green-yellow, in a terminal panicle 1–2 ft. long. Calyx-tube bell-shaped, adnate to the base of the ovary; limb deeply 5-lobed, persistent. Petals none. Stamens 5, opposite the sepals. Ovary nearly free, 2-celled; styles 2. Capsule small, 2-beaked; seeds numerous, minute. (Fig. 49.)

Simla, Mushobra, in forest undergrowth; July, August. — Temperate Himalaya, 4000–7000 ft.

Habit of *Spiræa Aruncus* from which the apetalous flowers and fewer stamens at once distinguish it.

2. SAXIFRAGA. From the Latin *saxum*, a stone, and *frango*, to break; referring to the former repute of some species as a remedy for stone; an idea derived from their growing among rocks.—North temperate, alpine and Arctic regions; Andes of S. America.

Herbs; rootstock perennial; stems erect or decumbent, often densely tufted. Leaves simple, lower often rosulate or crowded, upper alternate. Flowers in terminal panicles or corymbs, rarely solitary. Calyx adnate to the base of the ovary; tube short; limb deeply 5-lobed. Petals 5. Stamens 10. Ovary 2-celled, lower half adnate to the calyx; styles 2, distinct, usually divergent; ovules numerous. Capsule 2-beaked; seeds many, minute.

Small, slender herbs. Flowers yellow.
- Leaves ovate, 1–2 in., entire, lower stalked, upper sessile . . . . 1. *S. diversifolia.*
- Leaves linear or narrowly lanceolate, $\frac{1}{4}$–$\frac{1}{2}$ in., glandular-fringed or bristly on the margins, all sessile.
  - Leaves uniformly scattered. Sepals glandular. Runners none . . . . 2. *S. filicaulis.*
  - Lower leaves crowded, densely imbricate. Sepals glabrous. Runners numerous . . . . . 3. *S. Brunoniana.*

Large, thick-stemmed herbs. Flowers white or pink.
- Leaves hairy, entire, fringed; stalk sheathing at the base only . . . . 4. *S. ciliata.*
- Leaves glabrous, toothed; stalk sheathing nearly throughout its length . . . . 5. *S. Stracheyi.*

1. **Saxifraga diversifolia,** *Wall.*; *Fl. Br. Ind.* ii. 393. Stems erect, 6–12 in., more or less glandular-hairy. Lower leaves crowded, long-stalked, ovate, 1–2 in., entire; stem-leaves distant, sessile. Flowers yellow, $\frac{1}{2}$ in. diam., in terminal corymbs. Base of petals glandular. Sepals glandular, reflexed in fruit. (Fig. 50.)

Simla, rare, Mushobra, Mahasu, common; August, September.—Temperate Himalaya, 8000–17,000 ft.

The plant described above is typical *S. parnassifolia*, Wall. *S. Moorcroftiana*, Wall., which occurs on the Chor, is a much taller and more robust herb with lanceolate or oblong leaves 2–4 in. long. In the *Fl. Br. Ind.* both forms are included under *S. diversifolia.*

2. **Saxifraga filicaulis,** *Wall.*; *Fl. Br. Ind.* ii. 396. Stems very slender, wiry, tufted, 3–8 in., leafy, procumbent, much branched, roughly glandular, pubescent. Leaves usually scattered,

rarely crowded, sessile, rigid, linear, $\frac{1}{4}$–$\frac{1}{2}$ in., glandular-fringed, acute, the upper ones often bearing bulbils in the axils. Runners none. Flowers yellow, solitary, terminal, $\frac{1}{4}$–$\frac{1}{2}$ in. diam. Sepals glandular, erect in fruit.

Matiana, **Huttoo**, on rocks September, October.—W. Himalaya, 9000–12,000 ft.

FIG. 50. SAXIFRAGA DIVERSIFOLIA.

3. **Saxifraga Brunoniana,** *Wall.*; *Fl. Br. Ind.* ii. 397. Stems very slender, wiry, tufted, 3–8 in., erect, usually forking, glabrous or slightly glandular. Lower leaves crowded, densely imbricate, sessile, narrowly lanceolate, $\frac{1}{4}$–$\frac{1}{2}$ in., glabrous, margins bristly, acute, having numerous, long, leafless, thread-like runners with terminal buds issuing from between them; upper leaves few, distant, smaller. Flowers yellow, terminal, 2–4 on a stem, $\frac{1}{2}$ in. diam. Sepals glabrous, erect in fruit.

Huttoo, on rocks, not common; September, October.—Abundant on the Chor.—Temperate Himalaya, 10,000–16,000 ft.

4. **Saxifraga ciliata,** *Royle*; *Fl. Br. Ind.* ii. 398, *under S. ligulata, Wall.* Rootstock very thick; stems short, thick, fleshy, procumbent. Leaves ovate or orbicular, 2–6 in. long at the time of flowering, in the autumn attaining a foot or more across and turning bright red, cordate, margins entire, fringed with short, close, stiff hairs, both surfaces hairy, becoming nearly glabrous in age; stalk stem-sheathing at the base. Flowers white, pink or

purple, 1¼ in. diam., in a spreading, cymose panicle terminating a flexible scape 4–10 in. long ; styles long.

Simla, common on rocks ; March, April.—Temperate Himalaya, 7000–10,000 ft.

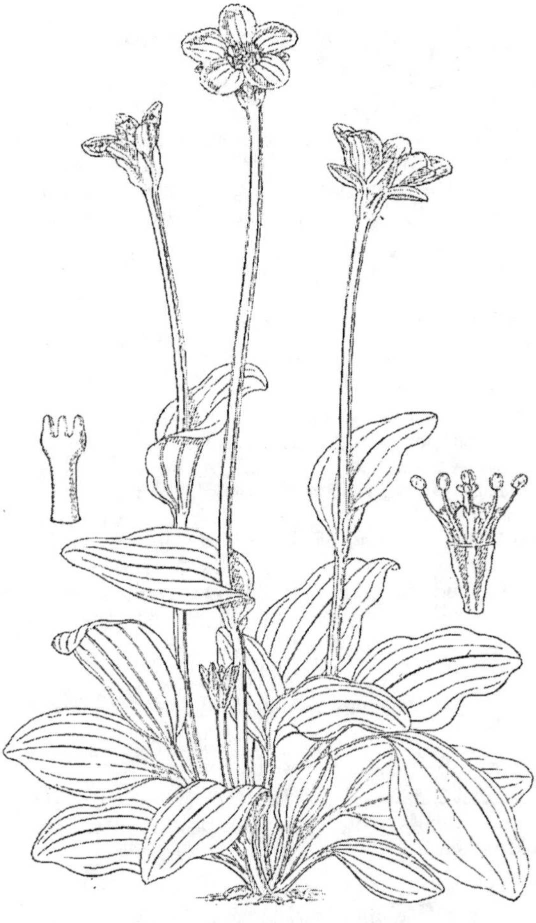

FIG. 51. PARNASSIA NUBICOLA.

5. **Saxifraga Stracheyi,** *Hook. f. & Thoms.* ; *Fl. Br. Ind.* ii. 398. Habit and flowers of *S. ciliata*. Leaves ovate or obovate, 2–4 in. at the time of flowering, afterwards attaining 8–12 in., rarely cordate, margins toothed, both surfaces glabrous ; stalk stem-sheathing nearly throughout its length.

Huttoo ; June.—Common on the Chor.—W. Himalaya, 8000–14,000 ft.

3. CHRYSOSPLENIUM. From the Greek *chrysos*, gold, and *splen*, the spleen; referring to the yellow flowers of some species and their supposed remedial properties.—N. temperate and Arctic regions; S. America; most numerous in China and Japan.

Chrysosplenium tenellum, *Hook. f. & Thoms.*; *Fl. Br. Ind.* ii. 401. A delicate, annual, glabrous herb; stems thread-like, procumbent, 1–3 in., leafy, often matted. Leaves stalked, alternate, kidney-shaped, hardly $\frac{1}{4}$ in. broad; marginal lobes 4–6, shallow, rounded. Flowers $\frac{1}{10}$ in. diam., green-yellow, stalked, solitary, scattered. Calyx-tube adnate to the ovary; lobes 4, obtuse. Petals none. Stamens about 8. Ovary 1-celled; styles 2; ovules numerous. Capsule half-superior, 2-beaked; seeds few or many.

Baghi, Marali, on wet rocks; June.—W. Himalaya, 9000–10,000 ft.

4. PARNASSIA. From Parnassus, a mountain in Greece, the abode of the Muses.—N. temperate and cold regions.

Parnassia nubicola, *Wall.*; *Fl. Br. Ind.* ii. 402. A glabrous herb; rootstock perennial. Leaves radical, long-stalked, ovate or oblong-ovate, 1–2 in., cordate, entire, acute. Scapes erect, slender, angular, 6–12 in., bearing a sessile leaf about the middle and a solitary, terminal, white flower about 1 in. diam. Calyx-tube short, adnate to the base of the ovary; lobes 5, obtuse. Petals 5, entire or slightly jagged. Stamens 5, alternate with 5 fleshy, flattened, 3-lobed staminodes. Ovary ovoid, base adnate to the calyx-tube, 1-celled; style very short; stigma capitate, 3-lobed; ovules numerous. Capsule obovoid, $\frac{1}{2}$ in. long, opening by 3 valves; seeds inserted on the valves. (Fig. 51.)

Simla, the Glen, common; August, September.—Temperate Himalaya, 6000–12,000 ft.

5. HYDRANGEA. From the Greek *hydor*, water, and *aggeion*, a vase or cup; referring to the cup-shaped capsule.—Himalaya, E. Asia, America.

Hydrangea altissima, *Wall.*; *Fl. Br. Ind.* ii. 404. A climbing shrub. Leaves opposite, ovate or lanceolate, 3–6 in., sharply toothed, long-pointed, glabrous except along the nerves and in the nerve-axils on the lower surface; stalks pubescent. Flowers in rounded, compound, hairy cymes, 3–6 in. across; some of the outer sterile flowers conspicuous from the enlarged, coloured calyx; others all small and fertile. Sterile flowers: calyx-limb petal-like, white, spreading, 4-lobed, $1\frac{1}{4}$ in. across; petals none. Fertile flowers $\frac{1}{10}$ in. long: calyx-tube adnate to the ovary, limb very short, 4-toothed; petals 4, white, cohering, falling off like a cap;

stamens 10 ; ovary inferior, 2-celled, styles 2, diverging. Capsule crowned with the persistent calyx-limb and styles.

Narkunda, in forest ; July.—Himalaya, Simla to Bhotan, 4000–10,000 ft.
In the common garden Hydrangea, *H. Hortensia*, a native of China and Japan, all the flowers have become sterile.

6. DEUTZIA. In honour of Johann Deutz, a Dutch naturalist of the eighteenth century and a friend and patron of the botanical traveller, Thunberg.—Himalaya, China, Japan and a doubtful species in Mexico.

Erect shrubs, more or less stellately hairy ; branches opposite. Leaves simple, finely toothed. Flowers white, in spreading, terminal panicles. Calyx-tube bell-shaped, adnate to the ovary ;

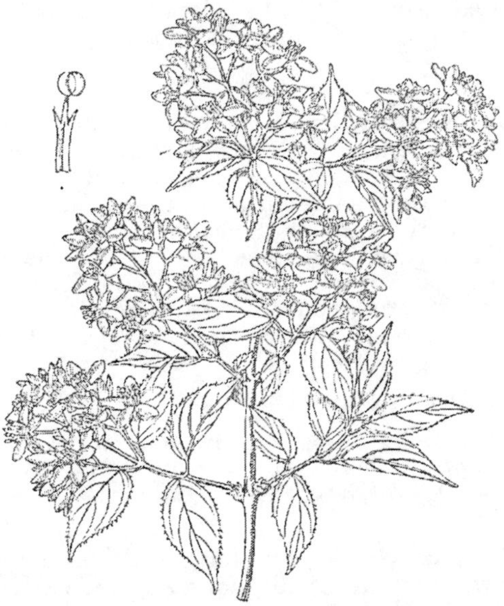

FIG. 52. DEUTZIA STAMINEA.

lobes 5, persistent. Petals 5. Stamens 10, the alternate ones longer, filaments flattened, 3-pointed, central point anther-bearing. Ovary inferior, usually 3-celled ; styles 3–5, long, free or nearly so ; ovules numerous. Capsule inferior, globose, ultimately opening by 3–5 valves ; seeds numerous, minute.

Leaves 2–5 in.; lower surface green. Calyx-teeth obtuse . 1. *D. corymbosa.*
Leaves 1–2 in.; lower surface grey-tomentose. Calyx-teeth acute . . . . 2. *D. staminea.*

1. **Deutzia corymbosa,** *R. Brown* ; *Fl. Br. Ind.* ii. 406. Bark thin, peeling off in flakes. Leaves nearly sessile, ovate-lanceolate,

2–5 in., long-pointed, covered with scattered, stellate hairs; lower surface green. Flowers $\frac{1}{2}$ in. diam., in a few corymbose panicles. Stalks and calyx stellately pubescent. Calyx-teeth ovate, obtuse.

Mushobra, Shali, Narkunda, in forest; May, June.—Temperate Himalaya, 6000–10,000 ft.—N. Asia.

2. **Deutzia staminea,** *R. Brown*; *Fl. Br. Ind.* ii. 407. Leaves shortly stalked, ovate-lanceolate, 1–2 in., long-pointed; upper surface rough with stellate pubescence, lower grey, stellately tomentose. Flowers $\frac{3}{4}$ in. diam., in numerous panicles. Stalks and calyx stellately tomentose. Calyx-teeth triangular, acute. (Fig. 52.)

Simla, Prospect hill; April, May.—W. Himalaya, 5000–9000 ft.—China.

7. **PHILADELPHUS.** The classical name of a shrub not identified by modern botanists.—Himalaya, Japan, N. America, Europe.

Philadelphus coronarius, *Linn.*; *Fl. Br. Ind.* ii. 407. An erect shrub, nearly or quite glabrous; branches opposite. Leaves opposite, shortly stalked, ovate-lanceolate, 2–3 in., long-pointed; teeth small, distant, sometimes wanting; margins often hairy. Flowers white, orange-scented, about 1 in. diam., in short, terminal racemes. Calyx-tube bell-shaped, adnate to the ovary; lobes 4, broadly triangular, acute, persistent, inner surface pubescent. Petals 4, ovate. Stamens 20–40. Ovary inferior, 4-celled; styles 4, united for about one third of their length. Capsule inferior, obconical, opening by 4 valves.

Matiana, Narkunda; June.—Temperate Himalaya, 5000–9000 ft.—Eastern Europe, Japan.

This plant is typical *P. coronarius*, Linn., not the variety *tomentosus* described in the *Fl. Br. Ind.* Commonly cultivated in Britain and often called Seringat (French) or the Mock Orange.

8. **ITEA.** The Greek name for the Willow; most species are of quick growth and are usually found on the banks of streams.—Himalaya, China, N. America.

Itea nutans, *Royle*; *Fl. Br. Ind.* ii. 408. A shrub or small tree. Leaves alternate, stalked, ovate-oblong, 3–6 in., sharply toothed, usually long-pointed; upper surface glabrous, lower pubescent. Flowers white, $\frac{1}{10}$ in. long, in clusters of 3–7 forming pubescent, drooping racemes 4–8 in. long. Calyx pubescent; tube bell-shaped, adnate to the lower half of the ovary; lobes 5, persistent. Petals 5, tips inflexed. Stamens 5. Ovary 2-celled; style undivided, grooved, persistent; stigma capitate; ovules several. Capsule half-superior, separating into 2 valves through the cell-partition and the style; seeds several.

Sutlej valley near Suni; April.—Simla to Kumaon, 3000–5000 ft.

9. RIBES. Origin of name obscure.—Asia, America, Europe (Britain, Gooseberry, Currant).

Erect shrubs. Leaves stalked, at first clustered, ultimately alternate, triangular-ovate, cordate, 3- or 5-lobed; lobes acute, sometimes long-pointed, sharply and irregularly toothed. Flowers small, 2- or 1-sexual, in bracteate racemes. Calyx-tube ovoid, lower half adnate to the ovary; lobes 5, much larger than the 5 small petals. Stamens 5, filaments short. Ovary inferior, 1-celled; styles 2, partially united, tips recurved; stigmas capitate. Berry succulent, globose, 1-celled, crowned with the persistent calyx-lobes and stamens; seeds few or numerous, small, immersed in pulp.

Racemes glandular. Bracts longer than the flower-stalks. Flowers mostly 1-sexual . . . . 1. *R. glaciale.*
Racemes pubescent, not glandular. Bracts shorter than the flower-stalks. Flowers 2-sexual.
  Leaves scented. Racemes 2–3 in. Lower flower-stalks longer than the upper. Berry black . . . . . 2. *R. nigrum.*
  Leaves inodorous. Racemes 3–6 in. Flower-stalks equal. Berry red . . . . 3. *R. rubrum.*

1. **Ribes glaciale,** *Wall.*; *Fl. Br. Ind.* ii. 410. Glabrous or slightly pubescent. Leaves 1–3 in. across; lobes usually 3, acute, often long-pointed, mid-lobe largest; lower surface pale. Racemes glandular, 1–2 in., erect in flower, nodding in fruit. Bracts narrowly lanceolate, much longer than the flower-stalks. Flowers usually 1-sexual, male and female on different shrubs, green or dull brown, $\frac{1}{4}$ in. diam. Berry $\frac{1}{4}$ in. diam., red, sour.

Huttoo; June.—Temperate Himalaya, 7000–12,000 ft.

*2. **Ribes nigrum,** *Linn.*; *Fl. Br. Ind.* ii. 411. Pubescent. Leaves scented, long-stalked, 2–4 in. across; lobes 3 or 5; upper surface glabrous, lower dotted with minute, yellow glands. Racemes not glandular, drooping, 2–3 in.; stalks of the lower flowers longer than those of the upper. Bracts shorter than the flower-stalks. Flowers 2-sexual, green, often tinged with dull purple, $\frac{1}{3}$ in. diam. Calyx gland-dotted. Berry $\frac{1}{3}$ in. diam., purple-black.

W. Himalaya, Kumaon to Kashmir, 7000–12,000 ft.; June. — China, N. Europe (Britain, Black Currant).

3. **Ribes rubrum,** *Linn.*; *Fl. Br. Ind.* ii. 411. Pubescent or nearly glabrous. Leaves long-stalked, 2–3 in. across; lobes 3 or 5. Racemes not glandular, pendulous, 3–6 in.; flower-stalks short, nearly equal. Bracts shorter than the flower-stalks. Flowers 2 sexual, green-yellow, $\frac{1}{3}$ in. diam. Berry $\frac{1}{4}$ in. diam., red.

Mahasu, Narkunda; April, May.—W. Himalaya, 8000–12,000 ft.—N. Asia, Europe (Britain, Red Currant).

XXXIII. CRASSULACEÆ

SUCCULENT herbs, sometimes with a woody base. Leaves usually fleshy, undivided or rarely lobed; stipules none. Flowers 2-sexual, regular, in terminal cymes or panicles, rarely axillary. Calyx free, persistent, 4–8-parted, tubular in *Bryophyllum*. Petals as many as the sepals, free or united for the greater part of their length, sometimes persistent. Stamens as many or twice as many as the petals, free and inserted with the petals at the base of the calyx or more or less adnate to the corolla; anthers 2-celled, attached to the filaments at their back. Carpels as many as the petals, superior, distinct or nearly so, each with a small, flat scale at its base, 1-celled, narrowed upwards in a slender style; stigma terminal, small; ovules many, rarely few or only one. Follicles distinct, each containing many or few small seeds, rarely only one, attached to the inner angle.—A widely diffused genus, rare in tropical regions and in the Southern Hemisphere.

Stamens as many as the petals.
  Stems procumbent. Leaves opposite. Flowers minute, axillary . . . . 1. *Tillæa.*
  Stems erect. Leaves alternate. Flowers relatively conspicuous, in terminal panicles . . . . . 2. *Crassula.*
Stamens twice as many as the petals. Flowers usually conspicuous.
  Petals united for the greater part of their length.
    Calyx tubular, 4-toothed . . . . . . 3. *Bryophyllum.*
    Calyx 4-lobed nearly to the base . . . . . 4. *Kalanchoe.*
  Petals quite free.
    Calyx of 4 or 5 sepals . . . . 5. *Sedum.*
    Calyx of 8 sepals . . . . 6. *Sempervivum.*

1. **TILLÆA.** In honour of M. A. Tilli, an Italian botanist of the seventeenth century.—A small, widely distributed genus.

Tillæa pentandra, *Royle*; *Fl. Br. Ind.* ii. 412. A very small, glabrous, annual herb; stems usually several, slender, procumbent, leafy, 2–4 in. Leaves opposite, crowded, bases united, narrowly lanceolate, $\frac{1}{4}$ in., entire, acute. Flowers minute, pink or white, axillary, sessile, solitary or in small clusters. Calyx 4- or 5-parted. Petals 4 or 5, nearly as long as the sepals. Stamens 4 or 5. Carpels 4 or 5. Follicles 4 or 5, 1- or 2-seeded.

Simla, common on rocks and old walls; July–September.—W. Himalaya, 3000–6000 ft.—S. India, Africa.

2. **CRASSULA.** From the Latin *crassus*, thick, referring to the leaves.—Himalaya, one species; Africa, abundant at the Cape of Good Hope.

Crassula indica, *Decaisne* ; *Fl. Br. Ind.* ii. 413. A glabrous, fleshy herb; stem erect, 4–12 in. Leaves thick, entire, acute: radical rosulate, spathulate, $\frac{1}{2}$–1 in.; stem-leaves alternate, sessile, oblong, $\frac{1}{2}$–1 in. Flowers dull pink, $\frac{1}{3}$ in. long, in a terminal panicle. Calyx 5-parted. Petals 5, much longer than the sepals. Stamens 5. Carpels 5. Follicles 5, many-seeded.

Simla, Theog, on rocks; August, September.—Himalaya, Simla to Bhotan, 3000–8000 ft.

3. **BRYOPHYLLUM.** From the Greek *bruein*, to sprout, and *phyllon*, a leaf; detached leaves lying on damp earth produce buds in their marginal notches.—Tropical Africa, and now generally spread in tropical and subtropical countries.

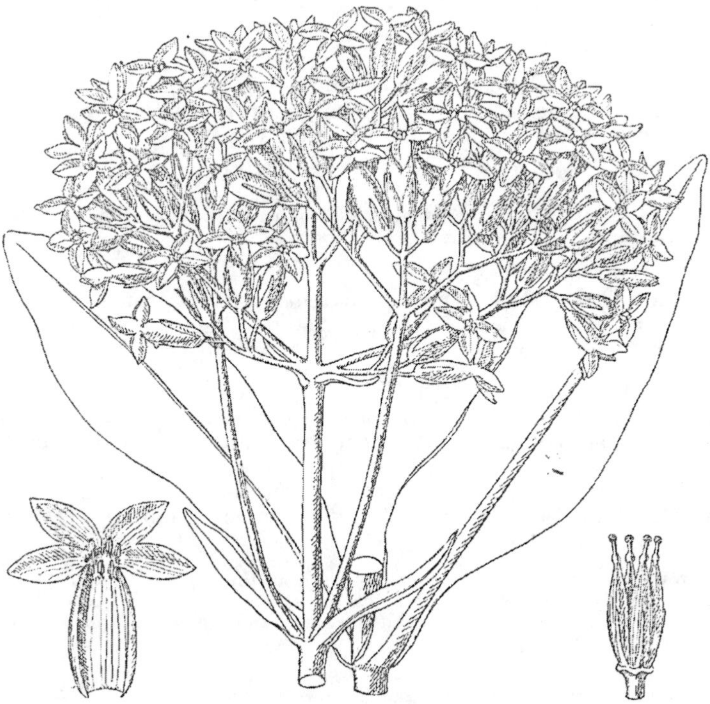

Fig. 53. Kalanchoe spathulata.

Bryophyllum calycinum, *Salisb.*; *Fl. Br. Ind.* ii. 413. A perennial, glabrous herb; stem erect, hollow, 1–4 ft. Leaves usually simple, rarely compound with 3 leaflets, opposite, stalked, fleshy, ovate or oblong, 3–6 in., crenate, obtuse. Flowers pendulous, cylindric, 2 in. long, in a large, terminal panicle. Calyx tubular, inflated, green, tinged with red and spotted with white, 4-toothed. Corolla tubular, twice as long as the calyx; tube cylindric, green; lobes 4, tinged with red, acute, spreading. Stamens 8, in two series inserted about the middle of the corolla-tube. Carpels 4. Follicles 4, many-seeded, enclosed within the dry, persistent calyx and corolla.

Sutlej valley; May, June.—Throughout India, ascending to 3000 ft.; an introduced plant, spread throughout nearly all tropical regions; often cultivated.

4. **KALANCHOE.** The Chinese name of one of the species.—Tropical Asia, tropical and South Africa, Brazil.

Kalanchoe spathulata, *DC.*; *Fl. Br. Ind.* ii. 414. A perennial, glabrous herb; stem erect, 1–4 ft. Leaves fleshy, opposite, crenate or nearly entire; lower crowded, stalked, oblong-spathulate, 4–8 in.; upper distant, nearly sessile, oblong, 3–4 in. Flowers yellow, $\frac{3}{4}$–1 in. long, in a large, terminal corymb. Calyx divided nearly to the base; segments 4, triangular, acute. Corolla tubular, twice as long as the calyx; tube inflated, narrowed to the mouth; lobes 4, spreading, acute. Stamens 8, in two series inserted at the mouth of the corolla-tube, filaments very short. Carpels 4. Follicles 4, many-seeded, enclosed in the dry, persistent calyx and corolla. (Fig. 53.)

Valleys below Simla; September–November. — Lower Himalaya, 1000–5000 ft.—Burmah, China, Java.

5. **SEDUM.** From the Latin *sedere*, to sit, referring to the broad, spreading, radical leaves of some species.—N. temperate regions including Britain (Stonecrop); one species in the Andes.

Succulent herbs; stems erect or ascending. Leaves thick, usually undivided, entire or rarely toothed, alternate or rarely opposite; radical leaves often rosulate. Flowers small, 2-sexual, regular, in terminal, usually compound cymes. Calyx 4- or 5-lobed nearly to the base. Petals 4 or 5, free. Stamens twice as many as the petals. Carpels 4 or 5; ovules numerous. Follicles few- or several-seeded.

Sedum asiaticum, *DC.*, grows on rocks near the top of the Chor but has not been found nearer Simla. It has a thick, woody rootstock; several stems 3–12 in. high; small, narrow, toothed leaves; and numerous, yellow flowers crowded in terminal cymes.

Flowers white.
- Leaves narrowly oblong; radical few or none; stem-leaves numerous . . . . 1. *S. linearifolium.*
- Leaves spathulate; radical numerous, rosulate; stem-leaves few, distant . . . . . . 3. *S. rosulatum.*

Flowers white, striped with pink. Leaves oblong or obovate . . . . 4. *S. adenotrichum.*

Flowers pink or pink-purple.
- Leaves strap-shaped, 3–5-lobed . . . . . 2. *S. trifidum.*
- Leaves ovate or orbicular, undivided . . . . 5. *S. Ewersii.*

Flowers yellow. Leaves cylindric . . . . . . 6. *S. multicaule.*

1. **Sedum linearifolium**, *Royle*; *Fl. Br. Ind.* ii. 420. Nearly or quite glabrous; stems tufted, erect, 2–6 in. Leaves sessile, narrowly oblong, $\frac{1}{2}$–$\frac{3}{4}$ in., entire or with a few small teeth, obtuse: radical few or none; stem-leaves usually numerous. Flowers white, nearly $\frac{1}{3}$ in. long, crowded.

Matiana, on rocks; July.—The Chor.—W. Himalaya, 7000–10,000 ft.

2. **Sedum trifidum**, *Wall.*; *Fl. Br. Ind.* ii. 420. Glabrous; stems erect, 4–12 in. Leaves strap-shaped, 1–4 in., tapering to a sessile base, 3–5-lobed; lobes divergent, unequal, $\frac{1}{4}$–1 in., entire or sometimes toothed, obtuse. Flowers pale pink, $\frac{1}{4}$ in. long in bud, crowded in leafy cymes. The whole plant turns crimson when withering.

Simla, common on trees and rocks; August, September. — Temperate Himalaya, 6000–12,000 ft.

FIG. 54. SEDUM ADENOTRICHUM.

3. **Sedum rosulatum**, *Edgew.*; *Fl. Br. Ind.* ii. 420. Glandular-pubescent or glabrous; stems nearly erect, 2–4 in. Leaves spathulate, narrowed into a sessile base: radical numerous, rosulate, $\frac{1}{4}$–1 in.; stem-leaves few, distant, $\frac{1}{10}$ in. Flowers white, long-stalked, $\frac{1}{5}$ in. long, in open, loose cymes.

Simla, on rocks and walls; April–June.—W. Himalaya, 5000–9000 ft.—Afghanistan.

4. **Sedum adenotrichum,** *Wall.*; *Fl. Br. Ind.* ii. 420. Glandular-pubescent; stems nearly erect, 3–10 in. Leaves sessile, oblong or obovate: radical rosulate, ½–1½ in.; stem-leaves few, distant, ¼ in. Flowers white, striped with pink, nearly ⅓ in. long, in open, loose cymes. (Fig. 54.)

Simla, common on rocks and walls; April, May.—W. Himalaya, 3000–8000 ft.

5. **Sedum Ewersii,** *Ledeb.*; *Fl. Br. Ind.* ii. 421. Glabrous; stems often numerous, nearly erect, 6–12 in. Leaves glaucous, nearly sessile, occasionally opposite, ovate or orbicular, ½–1 in. across, sometimes sinuate: radical few or none; stem-leaves numerous. Flowers pink-purple, ¼ in. long in bud, crowded in broad cymes.

Matiana, Narkunda; July, August. — W. Himalaya, 8000–15,000 ft.—N. Asia.

6. **Sedum multicaule,** *Wall.*; *Fl. Br. Ind.* ii. 422. Glabrous; stems usually several, nearly erect, 4–8 in., branched. Leaves nearly sessile, cylindric, ½–1 in., acute; both radical and stem-leaves usually numerous. Flowers yellow, ¼ in. long in bud; cyme-branches long, racemose, leafy.

Simla, on rocks; July, August.—Temperate Himalaya, 4000–7000 ft.—China, Japan.

6. **SEMPERVIVUM.** From the Latin *semper*, always, and *vivere*, to live; some species exhibit a remarkable tenacity of life. —Europe (Britain, Houseleek); W. Asia; N. and tropical Africa; Canary Islands.

Sempervivum sedoides, *Decaisne*; *Fl. Br. Ind.* ii. 423. A succulent herb; rootstock perennial; stems annual, erect, 2–3 in., leafy. Leaves fleshy, nearly glabrous, sessile, oblong-ovate, entire, obtuse: radical rosulate, closely imbricate, ½–¾ in.; stem-leaves alternate, ⅓–½ in., overlapping. Flowers pubescent, white, ⅓ in. long, crowded in a terminal cyme. Calyx 8-lobed to the base; lobes acute. Petals 8, nearly twice as long as the sepals. Stamens 16. Carpels 8, pubescent; ovules numerous. Follicles many-seeded.

Simla, Theog, on rocks, not common; July, August.—W. Himalaya, 7000–8000 ft.

XXXIV. DROSERACEÆ

A SMALL Order distributed over nearly all temperate and tropical regions, but most numerous and diversified in Australia; limited in the Himalaya to the genus *Drosera*.

DROSERA. From the Greek *droseros*, covered with dew; referring to the shining, glandular hairs.—Nearly all regions; most numerous in W. Australia (Britain, Sundew).

Drosera lunata, *Buch.-Ham.*; *Fl. Br. Ind.* ii. 424, *under D. peltata.* Erect herb; stems erect, slender, minutely glandular, leafy, 4–12 in., often branching. Leaves alternate, half-moon shaped,

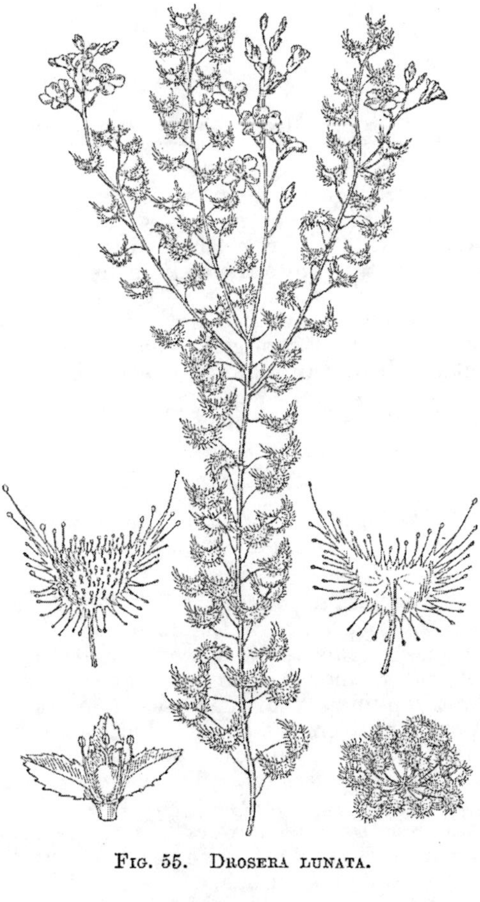

FIG. 55. DROSERA LUNATA.

about $\frac{1}{4}$ in. across, peltate, upper surface and margins beset with viscid, glandular hairs; radical leaves smaller, rosulate, soon disappearing. Flowers 2-sexual, regular, white, $\frac{1}{4}$ in. diam., in terminal, branching racemes. Calyx 5-parted; segments glandular, minutely toothed. Petals 5, entire. Stamens 5. Ovary free, ovoid, 1-celled; styles 3; stigmas terminal, minutely fringed; ovules numerous. Capsule enclosed within the persistent calyx and corolla, 3-valved; seeds minute, attached to the valves. (Fig. 55.)

Simla, common on pasture lands and banks; August, September.—Temperate Himalaya, 4000–8000 ft.—Hilly regions throughout India.

Darwin by the publication of his *Insectivorous Plants* (1875) has added greatly to the interest of the Sundews. At Simla it is impossible to find a plant without some captured insects or their remains entangled on the leaves.

XXXV. HALORRHAGIDACEÆ

WEAK, flaccid herbs, growing in water or on mud. Leaves opposite or whorled, simple or pinnately divided; stipules none. Flowers minute, 1-sexual, regular or incomplete, spicate or axillary. Calyx-tube adnate to the ovary; limb usually 4-toothed. Petals 4 or none. Stamens 8 or only one; anthers 2-celled. Ovary inferior, 4-celled; ovule solitary in each cell. Fruit a minute, oblong or orbicular capsule, dividing when ripe into 4 one-seeded nuts.—Nearly all regions.—Origin of name obscure.

Leaves whorled, pinnately divided. Flowers in a terminal spike . . . . 1. *Myriophyllum.*
Leaves opposite, undivided. Flowers axillary . . . 2. *Callitriche.*

1. MYRIOPHYLLUM. From the Greek *murion*, many, and *phyllon*, a leaf.—Nearly all regions; most numerous in Australia.

Myriophyllum spicatum, *Linn.*; *Fl. Br. Ind.* ii. 433. A glabrous, nearly submerged herb, the flower-spikes only appearing above the surface; stems leafy, varying in length according to the depth of water, more or less branched. Leaves whorled, usually in fours, pinnately divided; segments simple, distinct, hair-like, $\frac{1}{4}$–$\frac{1}{2}$ in. Flowers sessile, in whorls of about 4 forming slender, terminal spikes; each flower surrounded by 1 large and 2 minute bracts; upper flowers male, lower female. Male flowers: calyx 4-toothed; petals 4, concave; stamens 8, filaments short; ovary rudimentary. Female flowers: calyx 4-grooved, teeth 4, minute; petals minute or none; stigmas 4, nearly sessile. Fruit oblong, dividing into 2 or 4 nutlets.

Simla, the Glen; June–August.—W. Himalaya, 1000–6000 ft.—Afghanistan.—N. temperate and cold regions. (Britain, Water Milfoil.)

2. CALLITRICHE. From the Greek *kalos*, beautiful, and *thrix*, *trichos*, hair; referring to the stems.—Nearly all regions (Britain, Water Starwort).

Glabrous herbs, growing in water or on mud; stems slender, brittle, intricately branched, rooting at the joints. Leaves undivided, entire, lower opposite, uppermost crowded in little, flat rosettes. Flowers axillary, usually solitary, each between two minute bracts (sometimes wanting). Calyx and corolla none. Male flowers: a solitary stamen, filament long. Female flowers: a 4-lobed ovary; styles 2, long, thread-like. Fruit orbicular, flattened, sessile or nearly sessile.

Margins of fruit winged, acute . . . . 1. *C. stagnalis.*
Margins of fruit not winged, blunt . . . . . . 2. *C. verna.*

1. **Callitriche stagnalis,** *Scop.*; *Fl. Br. Ind.* ii. 434. Leaves ovate or spathulate, sometimes very narrow, about $\frac{1}{4}$ in. long. Margins of fruit winged, acute.

Sipi, below Mushobra; August, September.—Mountainous regions throughout India, 5000–10,000 ft.—Cosmopolitan (Britain).

*2. **Callitriche verna,** *Linn.*; *Fl. Br. Ind.* ii. 434. Leaves oblong or spathulate, $\frac{1}{4}$–$\frac{1}{2}$ in. Margins of fruit not winged, blunt.

W. Himalaya, 5000–8000 ft.—Nearly all temperate and cold climates, including Britain.

XXXVI. MYRTACEÆ

A very large Order inhabiting nearly all tropical and most subtropical regions. Abundant throughout India, but only a single species extends into the outer valleys of the N.W. Himalaya.—*Myrtus* is the classical name of the common Myrtle.

The Australian Gum trees, *Eucalyptus*, belong to this Order; *E. Globulus* and *E. obliqua* have been planted at Simla several times, but they usually succumbed to the winter frosts.

EUGENIA. In honour of Prince Eugene of Savoy of the seventeenth century, a patron of botany.—Most tropical regions.

Eugenia Jambolana, *Lam.*; *Fl. Br. Ind.* ii. 499. A glabrous tree. Leaves firm, shining, covered with minute, transparent dots, opposite, stalked, ovate or ovate-lanceolate, 3–6 in., entire, usually long-pointed; lateral veins numerous, parallel, uniting to form a single vein running just within the margin; stipules none. Flowers 2-sexual, regular, pale green, $\frac{1}{4}$–$\frac{1}{3}$ in. long to the tips of the stamens, nearly sessile, crowded in small, rounded clusters terminal on the branches of lateral panicles 2–4 in. long. Calyx-tube adnate to the ovary, funnel-shaped; limb shortly 4-lobed. Petals 4, rounded, concave, cohering, carried upwards by the unfolding of the stamens and falling off as the flower expands. Stamens numerous, in several series, much longer than the petals, inserted with them around the mouth of the calyx-tube, folded in bud. Ovary inferior, 2-celled; style simple, linear; stigma terminal, small; ovules many in each cell. Berry succulent, globose or oblong, $\frac{1}{2}$–$1\frac{1}{4}$ in., dark purple, crowned with the rim of the calyx-tube; seed usually solitary.

Sutlej valley; May, June.—Throughout India, ascending to 5000 ft. Frequently planted; fruit eaten. Native name *Jamun.*

XXXVII. MELASTOMACEÆ

A large Order inhabiting nearly all tropical regions; abundant in America and E. Asia. Only one species extends to the lower

Fig. 56. Osbeckia stellata.

valleys of the N.W. Himalaya.—Name from the Greek *melas,* black, and *stoma,* the mouth, said to be given on account of the edible fruit of some species staining the lips.

OSBECKIA. In honour of Peter Osbeck, a Swedish botanist and traveller, who visited China in the eighteenth century.—Asia, chiefly India; Australia.

Osbeckia stellata, *Wall.*; *Fl. Br. Ind.* ii. 517. An erect shrub; branches 4-sided, bristly. Leaves opposite, minutely bristly, shortly stalked, lanceolate, 3–6 in., entire, tapering to a fine point; longitudinal nerves 5, prominent; stipules none. Flowers 2-sexual, regular, pink-purple, 2–2½ in. diam., in small, terminal clusters. Calyx clothed with soft, matted, white, stellate bristles; tube bell-shaped, partially adnate to the ovary, persistent; lobes 4 or 5, lanceolate, nearly as long as the tube, alternate with 5 much shorter lobes, all falling off after flowering. Petals 4 or 5, twisted in bud. Stamens 8 or 10, inserted with the petals on the mouth of the calyx-tube; filaments yellow, curved; anthers yellow, 2-celled, longer than the filaments, strongly curved, dehiscing by terminal pores. Ovary ovoid, 4- or 5-celled, enclosed within and partially adnate to the calyx-tube, crowned with 4 or 5 hairy, erect lobes at the base of the long, curved style; stigma terminal, small; ovules numerous. Capsule nearly free, oblong-ovoid, $\frac{1}{2}$–$\frac{3}{4}$ in., opening at the top by pores; calyx-tube narrowed at the throat and produced in a short, spreading limb; seeds numerous, minute. (Fig. 56.)

Simla, Lansdowne Falls, not common; September. — From Simla to Bhootan up to 5000 ft.—China, Malaya.

XXXVIII. LYTHRACEÆ

ERECT shrubs or herbs. Leaves opposite, rarely whorled, simple, entire; stipules none. Flowers 2-sexual, regular, in axillary clusters. Calyx free, bell-shaped or tubular, toothed. Petals as many as the calyx-teeth, small, sometimes soon falling off, inserted at the top of the calyx-tube. Stamens as many or twice as many as the petals, inserted on the calyx-tube. Ovary free, at the bottom of the calyx-tube, 2- or 4-celled; style simple, thread-like; stigma terminal, small; ovules numerous. Capsule partially or entirely enclosed within the persistent calyx-tube; seeds numerous, small.—Nearly all tropical and temperate regions; most abundant in America.—Name from the Greek *lythron*, gore, referring to the colour of the flowers.

The Pomegranate, *Punica Granatum*, occurs in the valleys below Simla, probably as an escape; a shrub with large, red flowers and hard, globose fruit. Native name *andr.*

A herb. Calyx green, $\frac{1}{10}$ in. long. Stamens 8 . . . 1. *Ammannia.*
A shrub. Calyx red, $\frac{1}{3}$–$\frac{1}{2}$ in. long. Stamens 12 . . . 2. *Woodfordia.*

1. AMMANNIA. In honour of Johann Ammann, a Swiss botanical author of the eighteenth century.—Tropical and warm regions.

Ammannia senegalensis, *Lam.*; *Fl. Br. Ind.* ii. 570. An annual, glabrous herb, 6–24 in.; branches opposite, 4-angled. Leaves sessile, lanceolate, 1–2 in. Flowers very small, in small, shortly stalked clusters. Calyx bell-shaped, green, obscurely 4-toothed. Petals 4, pink, soon falling off. Stamens 8, inserted about the middle of the calyx-tube. Ovary globose, enclosed within the calyx-tube, 4-celled; stigma capitate. Capsule more or less protruding from the calyx-tube, bursting irregularly.

Valleys below Simla; March, April.—Throughout N. India, ascending to 5000 ft., common in rice fields.—Asia, Africa, Australia and America.

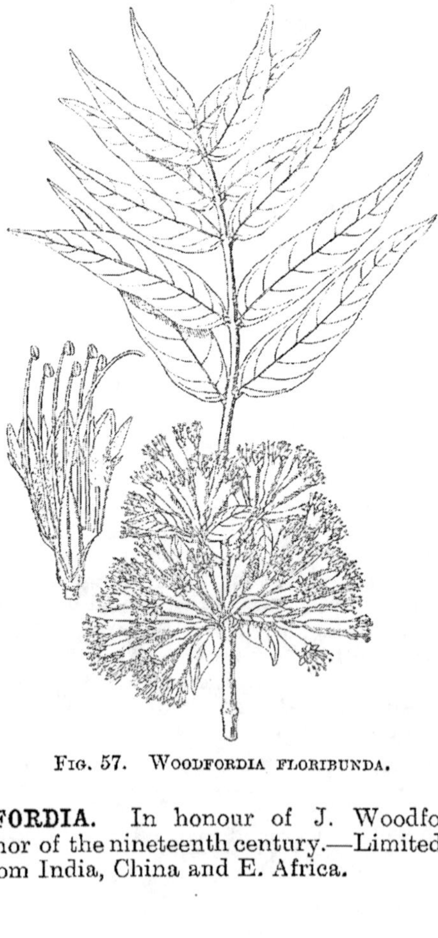

Fig. 57. Woodfordia floribunda.

2. WOODFORDIA. In honour of J. Woodford, a British botanical author of the nineteenth century.—Limited to the following species from India, China and E. Africa.

Woodfordia floribunda, *Salisb.*; *Fl. Br. Ind.* ii. 572. A pubescent shrub; branches long, spreading. Leaves opposite, sometimes in whorls of three, sessile, lanceolate, 2–4 in., tapering to a fine point; upper surface green, lower white, black-dotted. Flowers clustered, numerous, shortly stalked. Calyx tubular, $\frac{1}{3}$–$\frac{1}{2}$ in., bright red; teeth 6, short, alternating with 6 minute, accessory teeth. Petals 6, red, hardly longer than the calyx-teeth. Stamens 12; filaments long, red, far protruding, inserted below the middle of the calyx-tube. Ovary oblong, 2-celled; style far protruding. Capsule enclosed within the calyx-tube, opening by 2 valves. (Fig. 57.)

Valleys below Simla; flowers during the cold season.—Throughout India, ascending to 5000 ft.—China, Africa, Madagascar.

This plant varies in the relative length of the stamens and styles as described by Darwin in the case of *Lythrum Salicaria* (*Forms of Flowers*, p. 137), a species omitted from the *Fl. Br. Ind.*, but which occurs, undoubtedly wild, near Sultanpur in the Kulu Valley and in Kashmir. The flowers of *Woodfordia floribunda* are used for dyeing silk.

XXXIX. ONAGRACEÆ

Annual or perennial herbs; stems erect or ascending. Leaves opposite and alternate, simple, usually toothed; stipules none. Flowers 2-sexual, regular, in racemes. Calyx-tube adnate to the ovary; limb 2- or 4-parted, lobes valvate. Petals 2 or 4. Stamens 8 or 2, inserted with the petals on the top of the ovary, filaments thread-like, anthers 2-celled. Ovary inferior, 1-, 2- or 4-celled; style thread-like; stigma capitate or 4-lobed, lobes distinct or combined; ovules numerous or only one in each cell. Capsule long, linear and opening by 4 valves or short, ovoid and indehiscent; seeds small, numerous or only 1 or 2, tipped with a tuft of long hairs or naked.—Temperate regions; rare in the tropics.

Several species of Evening Primrose, *Œnothera,* have become naturalised about Simla.

Petals 4. Stamens 8. Capsule many-seeded, opening by 4 valves 1. *Epilobium.*
Petals 2. Stamens 2. Capsule 1- or 2-seeded, indehiscent . . 2. *Circæa.*

1. EPILOBIUM. From the Greek *epi,* upon, and *lobos,* a pod; referring to the position of the corolla.—Very widely spread in temperate and cold regions and particularly abundant in New Zealand (Britain, Willowherb).

Herbs; stems leafy. Leaves opposite and alternate, usually toothed. Flowers axillary, pink or purple, rarely white, forming long or short, leafy racemes towards the end of the stems or branches. Calyx-tube linear, 4-angled or nearly cylindric; limb

4-parted, lobes acute, falling off after flowering. Petals 4, erect or spreading, notched. Stamens 8, the alternate ones slightly shorter. Ovary 4-celled; stigmas 4, distinct and spreading or erect and combined in a club-shaped body; ovules numerous. Capsule elongate, 4-angled, 4-celled, the valves separating from the 4-sided, seed-bearing, central column; seeds numerous, small, tipped with a tuft of long hairs.

Haussknecht's *Monographie der Gattung Epilobium*, 1884, has been followed in this genus instead of the *Fl. Br. Ind.*

Stigmas distinct, spreading or recurved. Flowers $\frac{1}{2}$ in. long.
- Densely hairy. Leaves all stem-clasping . . . . 1. *E. hirsutum.*
- Pubescent. Leaves nearly sessile, not stem-clasping, lower ones stalked . . . . 2. *E. parviflorum.*

Stigmas combined, club like. Flowers less than $\frac{1}{3}$ in. long.
- Leaves linear-lanceolate, not more than $\frac{1}{4}$ in. broad, tapering to a fine point . . . . 3. *E. cylindricum.*
- Leaves lanceolate or ovate, $\frac{1}{2}$–$1\frac{1}{4}$ in. broad.
  - Stems pubescent all round.
    - Leaves thin, lanceolate, tapering to the base. Racemes numerous, axillary . . . . . 4. *E. Royleanum.*
    - Leaves thick, ovate, abruptly narrowed at the base. Racemes few, terminal . . . . . 5. *E. brevifolium.*
  - Stems glabrous, shining, except vertical lines of crisp pubescence. . . . . 6. *E. lætum.*

1. **Epilobium hirsutum,** *Linn.*; *Fl. Br. Ind.* ii. 583. Densely clothed with soft, white hairs; stems erect, robust, 2–5 ft., cylindric except near the base, usually branched. Leaves lanceolate, $1–3 \times \frac{1}{4}–\frac{1}{2}$ in., stem-clasping; teeth small, sharp. Flowers pink-purple, $\frac{1}{2}$ in. long. Stigmas distinct, at first erect, ultimately recurved. Capsule $1\frac{1}{2}–3\frac{1}{2}$ in.

Kotgurh, Sutlej and Giri valleys, in wet places; August–September.—W. Himalaya, 5000–7000 ft.—N. Asia, Africa, Europe (Britain).

2. **Epilobium parviflorum,** *Schreb.*; *Fl. Br. Ind.* ii. 584. Pubescent; stems erect or ascending, slender, 1–3 ft., cylindric, usually branched. Leaves shortly stalked or nearly sessile, not stem-clasping, ovate-lanceolate, $1–2 \times \frac{1}{2}–\frac{3}{4}$ in.; teeth small, sharp. Flowers pale pink-purple, $\frac{1}{2}$ in. long. Stigmas distinct, at first erect, ultimately spreading. Capsule 2–3 in.

Simla, Sutlej valley; May–August.—W. Himalaya, 5000–7000 ft.—W. Asia, N. Africa, Europe (Britain).

3. **Epilobium cylindricum,** *Don*; *Fl. Br. Ind.* ii. 585, *under E. roseum,* var. *cylindricum.* Pubescent; stems erect or ascending, cylindric or obscurely angular, 1–3 ft. Leaves sessile or shortly stalked, linear-lanceolate, $1–2\frac{1}{2} \times \frac{1}{4}$ in., tapering to a fine point; teeth, small sharp; both surfaces nearly glabrous, lower paler.

Racemes numerous, axillary. Flowers pale pink, less than $\frac{1}{4}$ in. long. Stigmas combined, club-like. Capsule $1\frac{1}{2}$–$2\frac{1}{2}$ in.

Simla; August, September.—Temperate Himalaya, 6000–10,000 ft.

4. **Epilobium Royleanum,** *Hausskn. Monogr. Epilob.* 205; *Fl. Br. Ind.* ii. 584, *under E. roseum*, var. *Dalhousianum.* Pubescent; stems erect or ascending, pubescent all round, 1–3 ft., branched. Leaves thin, flaccid, sessile or the lower ones shortly stalked,

FIG. 58. EPILOBIUM ROYLEANUM.

lanceolate, $1\frac{1}{2}$–$3 \times \frac{1}{2}$–1 in., tapering to both ends, acute; teeth small, sharp; lower surface paler. Racemes numerous, axillary. Flowers pale pink, hardly $\frac{1}{4}$ in. long. Stigmas combined, club-like. Capsule $1\frac{1}{2}$–2 in. (Fig. 58.)

Simla, common; July, August.—Temperate Himalaya, 7000–12,000 ft.

5. **Epilobium brevifolium,** *Don*; *Fl. Br. Ind.* ii. 584, *under E. roseum.* Pubescent; stems erect, cylindric, pubescent all round, 1–3 ft., usually unbranched. Leaves rather thick, sessile or nearly so, ovate, obtuse, 1–$2 \times \frac{1}{2}$–$1\frac{1}{4}$ in., abruptly narrowed at the base;

teeth small, sharp or lower leaves often nearly entire; lower surface paler. Racemes few, terminal. Flowers purple-pink, hardly $\frac{1}{3}$ in. long. Stigmas combined, club-like. Capsule 2–3 in.

Simla, common; June–September.—W. Himalaya, 6000–12,000 ft.

6. **Epilobium lætum,** *Wall. No.* 6329, in part, *i.e. Hausskn. Monogr. Epilob.* 218; *Fl. Br. Ind.* ii. 584, *under E. hirsutum,* var. *lætum,* in part. Stems erect, slender, 6–24 in., angled, usually unbranched, glabrous and shining except lines of crisp pubescence running down from the leaf-bases. Leaves sessile or nearly so, lanceolate, $1–1\frac{3}{4} \times \frac{1}{2}$ in.; teeth small, sharp. Racemes short, terminal. Flowers white or pale pink, $\frac{1}{4}$ in. long. Stigmas combined, club-like. Capsule 2–3 in.

Narkunda; July.—Simla to Sikkim, 6000–12,000 ft.

2. CIRCÆA. After Circe, the enchantress of classical mythology.—A small genus, inhabiting N. temperate and cold regions.

Perennial herbs; stems usually unbranched. Leaves opposite, long-stalked, thin, ovate, sinuately toothed. Flowers less than $\frac{1}{4}$ in. diam., in terminal and lateral racemes. Calyx-tube ovoid; limb 2-parted, lobes reflexed, falling off after flowering. Petals 2, notched. Stamens 2. Ovary 1- or 2-celled; style filiform; stigma capitate; ovule 1 in each cell. Capsule nut-like, indehiscent, 1- or 2-celled, rough with hooked bristles; seeds naked, 1 in each cell.

Ovary 2-celled. Seeds 2.
  Leaves ovate, narrowed to the base . . . . . 1. *C. lutetiana.*
  Leaves ovate-lanceolate, cordate . . . . . . 2. *C. cordata.*
Ovary 1-celled. Seed solitary . . . . 3. *C. alpina.*

1. **Circæa lutetiana,** *Linn.*; *Fl. Br. Ind.* ii. 589. Pubescent; stems erect or ascending, 1–2 ft. Leaves ovate, $2–3 \times 1–1\frac{3}{4}$ in., narrowed to the base, acute. Flowers white or tinged with pink. Ovary 2-celled. Capsule obovoid, $\frac{1}{8}$ in.; seeds 2.

Mushobra, in woods; August, September.—Temperate Himalaya, 7000–10,000 ft.—N. Hemisphere, southward to N. Africa. (Britain, Enchanter's Nightshade.)

2. **Circæa cordata,** *Royle*; *Fl. Br. Ind.* ii. 589. Pubescent or hairy; stems erect, 1–2 ft. Leaves ovate-lanceolate, $3–4 \times 1\frac{1}{2}–2$ in., cordate, long-pointed. Flowers white. Ovary 2-celled. Capsule ovoid, $\frac{1}{8}$ in.; seeds 2.

Simla, in woods; August, September.—W. Himalaya, 7000–9000 ft.—N. China, Japan.

3. **Circæa alpina,** *Linn.*; *Fl. Br. Ind.* ii. 589. Glabrous or slightly pubescent; stems erect, 4–8 in. Leaves broadly ovate,

$\frac{1}{2}$–1 in. across, obtuse or acute. Flowers white or tinged with pink. Ovary 1-celled. Capsule very small; seed one.

Mushobra, Mahasu, in woods; August, September.—Temperate Himalaya, 7000–11,000 ft.—Temperate regions of the N. Hemisphere including Britain.

XL. SAMYDACEÆ

A SMALL Order inhabiting nearly all tropical regions; represented in the N.W. Himalaya by only one genus.—*Semyda* is the Greek name of some tree, probably the Birch.

CASEARIA. In honour of Johann Casearius, a Dutch missionary in Cochin China, and a botanical author of the seventeenth century.—Widely spread in tropical regions, most abundant in America.

Casearia tomentosa, *Roxb.*; *Fl. Br. Ind.* ii. 593. A small, tomentose tree. Leaves alternate, shortly stalked, with trans-

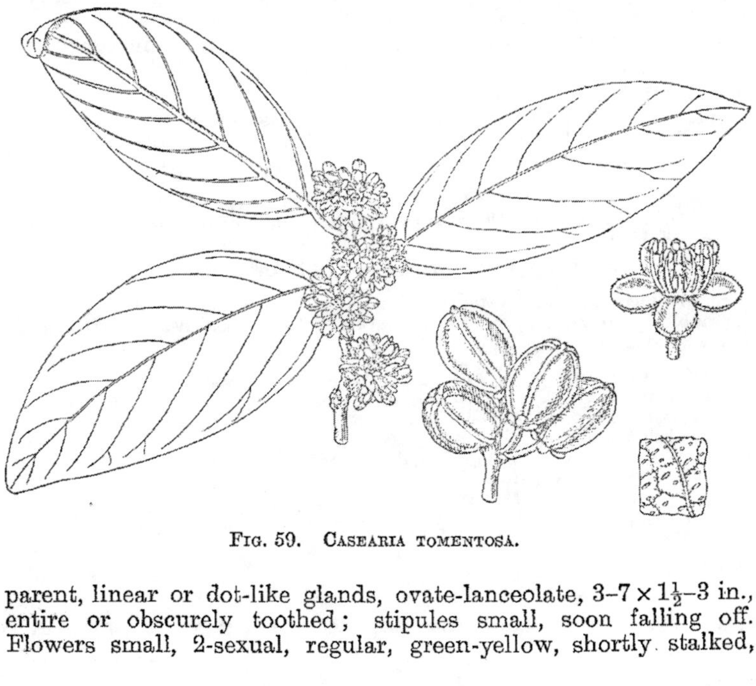

FIG. 59. CASEARIA TOMENTOSA.

parent, linear or dot-like glands, ovate-lanceolate, 3–7 × 1$\frac{1}{2}$–3 in., entire or obscurely toothed; stipules small, soon falling off. Flowers small, 2-sexual, regular, green-yellow, shortly stalked, crowded in axillary clusters. Calyx free, persistent, tomentose, 5-parted; lobes orbicular, concave. Petals none. Stamens 8, inserted at the base of the calyx, alternate with 8 hairy staminodes, filaments free, anthers 2-celled. Ovary superior, 1-celled; style very short; stigma capitate; ovules numerous. Capsule more or less succulent, ovoid, $\frac{3}{4}$ in. long, 6-ribbed, opening by 3 valves; seeds about 8 on each valve, ovoid, enveloped in a fleshy, red aril. (Fig. 59.)

Sutlej valley, Suni; April, May.—Throughout India, ascending to 3000 ft. —Malay islands, N. Australia.

XLI. CUCURBITACEÆ

PERENNIAL or annual herbs, often rough, juice watery; stems usually long, climbing by means of spirally twining, lateral tendrils. Leaves alternate, stalked, undivided or lobed, usually cordate; principal nerves basal. Flowers axillary, 1-sexual, male and female on the same or on different plants. Calyx-tube adnate to the ovary; limb 5-lobed or toothed. Corolla 5-lobed nearly to the base, inserted on the calyx-limb. Stamens 3, inserted on the calyx-tube; filaments free, usually short; anthers included, free or united, one anther 1-celled, the others 2-celled, cells linear, folded, curved or straight. Ovary inferior, 3-celled; style single; stigma 3-branched or 3-lobed; ovules usually numerous, inserted on projections or placentas issuing from the cell-walls. Fruit capsular or berry-like, opening by 3 valves or indehiscent; seeds many or few, small, usually flattened.—A large Order, chiefly tropical, rare in temperate regions, most abundant in Africa.—Name derived from the Latin *cucumis*, a cucumber, and *orbis*, a sphere, globe; referring to the shape of some Gourds.

Many species are cultivated, such as Cucumbers, Melons, Gourds, Pumpkins, Vegetable Marrows, etc., most of them of very ancient cultivation, but unknown in a wild state.

Flowers more than 1 in. diam.
- Flowers white. Petals fringed . . . . . 1. *Trichosanthes.*
- Flowers yellow. Petals entire . . . . . 2. *Herpetospermum.*

Flowers less than $\frac{1}{4}$ in. diam.
- Stems and leaves rough, bristly or covered with minute, sharp points . . . . 3. *Mukia.*
- Stems and leaves smooth, glabrous or slightly pubescent . . . . 4. *Zehneria.*

1. **TRICHOSANTHES.** From the Greek *thrix*, *trichos*, hair, and *anthos*, a flower; referring to the fringed petals.—Asia, N. Australia.

Trichosanthes palmata, *Roxb.*; *Fl. Br. Ind.* ii. 606. A large, perennial, climbing herb; stem angular. Leaves roughly pubescent, cordate, 2–6 in. diam., more or less deeply 3–7-lobed, toothed. Tendrils branched. Flowers white, 1½–3 in. diam., male and female usually on different plants. Male flowers on two axillary stalks, one bearing a solitary flower and soon falling off (sometimes wanting), the other a bracteate raceme, short and head-like at first, afterwards lengthening to 6–10 in.; bracts broadly obovate, margins jagged; calyx-tube funnel-shaped, 1½ in., lobes lanceolate, irregularly toothed; corolla-margins long-fringed; filaments very short. Female flowers solitary, axillary, shortly stalked; calyx and corolla nearly as in the male; ovary ovoid, narrowed upwards; style 1 in., tip 3-cleft; ovules numerous. Fruit smooth, globose, 1¼–2 in. diam., indehiscent, red, striped with orange; seeds flattened, immersed in dark green pulp.

Valleys below Simla, 5th Waterfall; June-September.—Throughout India, ascending to 5000 ft.—Asia, N. Australia.

2. HERPETOSPERMUM. From the Greek *herpetos*, creeping, and *sperma*, a seed: the seeds somewhat resemble a small beetle.—Temperate Himalaya.

Herpetospermum caudigerum, *Wall.*; *Fl. Br. Ind.* ii. 613. A large, nearly glabrous, climbing herb. Leaves slightly rough-pubescent, long-stalked, broadly cordate-ovate, 2–6 in. across, toothed, often lobed, long-pointed. Tendrils branched. Flowers bright yellow, 1½–2 in. diam., male and female on different plants. Male flowers racemed; calyx-tube funnel-shaped, ¾–1 in. long, lobes linear; corolla-margins entire; filaments very short, anthers united. Female flowers solitary, shortly stalked; calyx and corolla nearly as in the male; ovary ovoid, narrowed upwards; style ½ in., tip 3-cleft, stigmas 2-lobed; ovules 4 in each cell. Capsule ovoid, 3 × 1½ in., narrowed to both ends, opening by 3 valves; seeds 12, flattened, oblong, ½ in. long, minutely pointed at one end, embedded in a fibrous, nearly dry pulp.

Valleys below Simla; August, September.—Bhotan to Simla, 5000–8000 ft.

3. MUKIA. Adapted from *Mucca*, the name given to *M. scabrella* in Rheede's *Hort. Mal.* viii. t. 13.—Asia, Africa, Australia.

Mukia scabrella, *Arn.*; *Fl. Br. Ind.* ii. 623. An annual, climbing herb; stems and leaves very rough, bristly or covered with minute, sharp points. Leaves broadly cordate-ovate, 1½–3 in. across, toothed, more or less 3-lobed or -angled, long-pointed. Tendrils unbranched. Flowers yellow, less than ¼ in. diam., nearly sessile, solitary or in small clusters, male and female on the same plant. Male flowers: calyx bell-shaped, toothed; corolla-segments acute; filaments very short, anthers free. Female flowers: calyx and corolla nearly as in the male; ovary bristly, ovoid; style club-shaped, stigma 3-lobed; ovules few in each cell. Fruit nearly smooth, berry-like, globose, ½ in. diam., bright red, indehiscent; seeds few, rough.

Mushobra, in orchards; June.—Common throughout India, ascending to 6000 ft.—Malaya, Africa, Australia.

4. ZEHNERIA. In honour of Joseph Zehner, an Austrian botanical artist.—Asia, Africa, Australia, S. America.

Zehneria umbellata, *Thwaites*; *Fl. Br. Ind.* ii. 625. A climbing herb; stems and leaves smooth, glabrous or slightly pubescent.

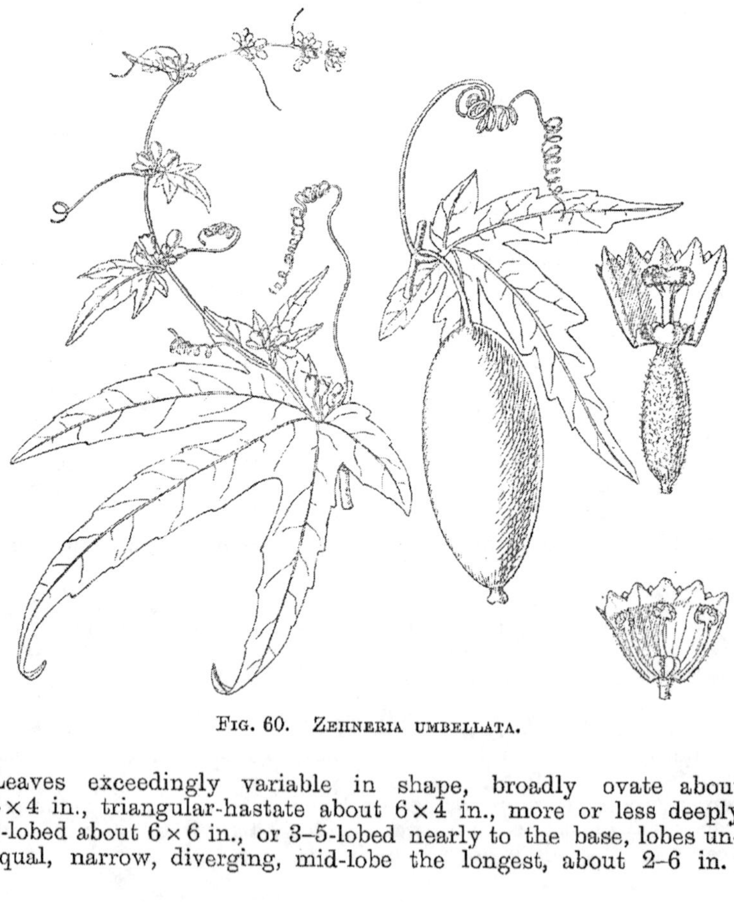

FIG. 60. ZEHNERIA UMBELLATA.

Leaves exceedingly variable in shape, broadly ovate about 6×4 in., triangular-hastate about 6×4 in., more or less deeply 3-lobed about 6×6 in., or 3–5-lobed nearly to the base, lobes unequal, narrow, diverging, mid-lobe the longest, about 2–6 in.;

two or more forms, with intermediate forms, being sometimes borne on one plant. Tendrils usually branched, sometimes flower-bearing. Flowers pale yellow or white, $\frac{1}{4}$ in. diam. or less, male and female on the same or on different plants. Male flowers umbellate; calyx glabrous or pubescent, bell-shaped, toothed; corolla hairy within; filaments rather long. Female flowers solitary or in pairs; calyx and corolla nearly as in the male; ovary glabrous, pubescent or tomentose, narrowly oblong; style 3-lobed at the top; ovules numerous. Fruit glabrous, pubescent or tomentose, berry-like, ovoid, $\frac{3}{4}$–$1\frac{1}{2}$ in. long, bright red, indehiscent; seeds 6–12, smooth. (Fig. 60.)

Simla, Mushobra, common; July, August.—Throughout India, ascending to 7000 ft.—Asia, N. Australia.

The form having tomentose ovary and fruit is distinguished as var. *nepalensis* in the *Fl. Br. Ind.*

XLII. BEGONIACEÆ

A LARGE Order chiefly inhabiting moist tropical regions and consisting almost entirely of species belonging to the genus *Begonia*. Abundant in the hot damp valleys of Burmah and the E. Himalaya; only two species extending their range to the N. West.

BEGONIA. In honour of Michel Begon, French Governor of San Domingo and a patron of botany in the seventeenth century.—Nearly all tropical regions in moist shady places; apparently absent from Australia.

Succulent herbs; rootstock tuberous; stems slender, weak, nearly erect. Leaves mostly radical (those on the stem alternate), long-stalked, undivided, more or less unequally sided, irregularly sinuate and toothed; stipules free, ovate, soon falling off. Flowers pale pink, 1-sexual, male and female on the same plant, in axillary, stalked, bracteate cymes. Sepals 3–5, in two series, free, unequal, imbricate, coloured. Petals none. Male flowers: sepals 4, the two outer larger; stamens numerous, nearly free, inserted with the sepals on the receptacle, anthers 2-celled. Female flowers: sepals 3 or 5, the two outer larger; ovary inferior, 3-celled, 3-angled; style-branches 3, each ending in 2 spirally rolled stigmas; ovules numerous, inserted on axile placentas. Capsule 3-sided, the angles produced in thin, flat wings, opening by 3 valves; seeds numerous, minute.

Leaves roughly hairy on the upper surface, pubescent on the lower. Wings of capsule very unequal . . . . . . 1. *B. picta*.
Leaves glabrous on both surfaces. Wings of capsule nearly equal . . . . 2. *B. amœna*.

1. **Begonia picta,** *Smith*; *Fl. Br. Ind.* ii. 638. Stems pubescent, 6–15 in. Leaves ovate, 3–5 × 2–3 in., cordate, acute, sometimes long-pointed, basal lobes nearly equal; upper surface roughly hairy, green, blotched and variegated with pink; lower pubescent, blotched with purple; veins prominent. Flowers 1–1½ in. diam.

FIG. 61. BEGONIA PICTA.

Male flowers: outer sepals orbicular, inner oblong. Female flowers: sepals 5, outer broadly ovate, inner narrower; style persistent. Capsule pubescent, about ½ in. broad, one of the wings much longer than the others, up to 1 in. (Fig. 61.)

Simla, on damp rocks, common; July, August.—Bhotan to Simla, 2000–6000 ft.

2. **Begonia amœna,** *Wall.*; *Fl. Br. Ind.* ii. 642. Glabrous; stems 6–12 in., often producing runners from the base. Leaves ovate, 2–4 × 1½–3 in., cordate, long-pointed, basal lobes nearly equal. Flowers ¾–1 in. diam. Male flowers: outer sepals ovate, inner much narrower. Female flowers: sepals 3, outer ovate, inner smaller. Capsule about ½ in. broad, crowned by the persistent style and enlarged sepals; wings nearly equal, about ¼ in. long.

Simla, on damp rocks, common; July, August.—Dalhousie to Sikkim, 5000–7000 ft.

XLIII. DATISCACEÆ

A VERY small Order inhabiting Asia, N. America and S.E. Europe; represented in the N.W. Himalaya by a single species.

DATISCA. Origin of name unknown.—W. Asia, California, Mexico.

***Datisca cannabina,** *Linn.*; *Fl. Br. Ind.* ii. 656. A glabrous herb; stem erect, robust, 2–6 ft.; branches flower-bearing, long. Stem-leaves alternate, pinnate (lower ones the larger), 6–12 in.; leaflets 5–11, shortly stalked, lanceolate, 6 × 1½ in., coarsely toothed, tip long pointed, entire. Leaves of the branches alternate, linear-lanceolate, 1–3 in., toothed or entire; stipules none. Flowers 1-sexual, regular, male and female on different plants, yellow, small, shortly stalked, in numerous, axillary clusters. Male flowers: calyx-tube very short, limb 5-lobed; petals none; stamens 11–13, inserted on the calyx, anthers linear-oblong, 2-celled, nearly sessile. Female flowers: calyx-tube ovoid, obscurely 3-angled, adnate to the ovary, limb 3-toothed; petals none; ovary inferior, 1-celled; styles 3, each divided nearly to the base in 2 linear stigmas; ovules numerous, attached to 3 placentas on the cell-wall. Capsule oblong, ⅓ in., opening at the top; seeds numerous, minute.

Temperate Himalaya, Kashmir to Nepal, 1000–6000 ft.—W. Asia.
Not yet recorded from the Simla region, but it may occur in the Sutlej or Giri valley.

XLIV. FICOIDEÆ

A SMALL Order, chiefly African, but scattered through most tropical and subtropical regions; represented in the N.W. Himalaya by a single species.—Name derived from the Latin *ficus*, a pustular swelling, referring to the numerous, shining vesicles on the leaves of some species of *Mesembryanthemum* and *Aizoon*.

MOLLUGO. The specific name of *Galium Mollugo* transferred to this genus on account of the general resemblance between the plants.—Tropical and subtropical regions.

Mollugo stricta, *Linn.*; *Fl. Br. Ind.* ii. 663. An annual, erect, glabrous, usually much branched herb, 4–12 in. high. Leaves opposite or whorled, often unequal, nearly sessile, narrowly lanceolate, $\frac{1}{2}$–$1\frac{1}{2}$ in., entire, acute; stipules membranous, soon falling off. Flowers 2-sexual, regular, orange or pink, hardly $\frac{1}{10}$ in. long, in numerous, terminal, compound cymes. Sepals 5, distinct. Petals

FIG. 62. MOLLUGO STRICTA.

none. Stamens 3–5, hypogynous. Ovary superior, ovoid, 3-celled; styles 3, short, free, stigmas terminal; ovules numerous, attached to axile placentas. Capsule globose, enclosed within the persistent calyx; seeds many, rough with minute points. (Fig. 62.)

Valleys below Simla; July–September.—Throughout India, ascending to 5000 ft.

XLV. UMBELLIFERÆ

ERECT, rarely decumbent herbs. Leaves alternate, undivided or divided; base of stalks often dilated and sheathing the stem. Flowers small, usually less than $\frac{1}{4}$ in. diam., regular or nearly so, 2-sexual or polygamous, in umbels, rarely in heads. Umbels compound or simple, with or without bracts and bracteoles at the base of the primary and secondary rays respectively. Calyx-tube adnate to the ovary; limb obsolete or 5-toothed. Petals 5, inserted on the margin of the calyx, equal or the outer ones of the umbel larger, tip usually acute and abruptly inflexed. Stamens 5, anthers versatile. Ovary 2-celled, crowned with a fleshy, 2-lobed disk; styles 2, stigmas terminal, small; ovules solitary in each cell. Fruit inferior, dry, consisting of two 1-seeded, indehiscent carpels which separate from a very slender, simple or forked, central axis and are traversed longitudinally by usually 5 ridges or wings, the central ridge being called the dorsal, the two marginal the lateral, and the remaining two the intermediate ridges. The carpels are also often furnished with internal, longitudinal oil-canals or vittæ, which are best seen in cross sections. Seed pendulous from the top of the cell, inner face flat or grooved in the centre.—A numerous Order represented in nearly all cold and temperate regions, rare in the tropics. Name from the Latin *umbella*, a parasol or umbrella, referring to the inflorescence.

Besides the species here described the two following are cultivated throughout India and may occasionally be found as escapes near houses.

Fœniculum vulgare or Fennel. A tall, glabrous herb emitting a powerful odour when rubbed. Leaves pinnately dissected; segments linear. Umbels compound, usually without bracts. Flowers yellow. Fruit small, oblong.—Native name, *Sonf*.

Coriandrum sativum or Coriander. A glabrous herb, 6–18 in. high, emitting a very disagreeable odour when rubbed. Leaves pinnately divided; segments of the lower leaves broadly ovate, lobed and toothed; of the upper thread-like. Umbels compound. Flowers white. Calyx-teeth unequal, acute. Fruit small, ovoid.—Native name *Dhanya*.

The following species is common on the Chor during September and October, but does not occur below 11,000 ft.

Pleurospermum Brunonis, *Benth.*; *Fl. Br. Ind.* ii. 706. Stem erect, 6–18 in. Leaves pinnately divided; segments thread-like. Umbels compound. Bracts large and conspicuous, white-margined. Flowers purple. Fruit black, oblong, nearly $\frac{1}{4}$ in.

A. Leaves undivided

Leaves orbicular or kidney-shaped, crenate . . . . 1. *Hydrocotyle.*
Leaves ovate, lanceolate or linear, entire . . . . . 4. *Bupleurum.*

B. Leaves divided

Leaves palmately divided; segments 3–5 . . . . . 2. *Sanicula.*
Leaves pinnately divided.
  Fruit flattened; lateral ridges winged.
    Dorsal and intermediate ridges also winged; lateral wings narrow.
      Calyx-teeth none . . . . 10. *Ligusticum.*
      Calyx-teeth lanceolate . . . . 11. *Selinum.*
    Dorsal and intermediate ridges not winged; lateral wings broad.
      Lateral wings of the 2 half-fruits free . . . 12. *Angelica.*
      Lateral wings of the 2 half-fruits cohering until separation on ripening . . . . 13. *Heracleum.*
  Fruit not flattened; lateral ridges not winged.
    Fruit smooth (see also 8. *Anthriscus*).
      Calyx-teeth lanceolate, acute . . . . . 9. *Œnanthe.*

Calyx-teeth none.
  Fruit ovoid or oblong, about $\frac{1}{10}$ in.
    Flowers red. Leaf-segments linear . . 3. *Vicatia.*
    Flowers white or yellow-green. Leaf-segments lanceolate . . . . . . 5. *Pimpinella.*
  Fruit cylindric, $\frac{1}{4}$–$\frac{1}{2}$ in. long . . . . 7. *Chærophyllum.*
Fruit bristly (see also 8. *Anthriscus*).
  Bristles scattered, minute. Fruit $\frac{1}{2}$–$\frac{3}{4}$ in. long 6. *Osmorhiza.*
  Bristles dense, long, curved. Fruit $\frac{1}{10}$ in. long 14. *Caucalis.*
Fruit smooth or minutely bristly, cylindric, $\frac{1}{3}$–$\frac{1}{2}$ in. Ridges obscure . . . . 8. *Anthriscus.*

1. **HYDROCOTYLE.** From the Greek *hydor*, water, and *cotyle*, a cup, referring to the cup-shaped leaves of *H. vulgaris* (Britain, Marsh Pennywort), sometimes containing water.—Temperate and tropical regions.

Small herbs growing in wet or marshy places ; stems prostrate, rooting at the joints. Leaves orbicular or kidney-shaped, crenate, often lobed, usually long-stalked ; stipules small, scarious. Umbels axillary, simple, small, head-like, stalked or nearly sessile. Bracts few or none. Flowers minute. Calyx-teeth none. Fruit orbicular or oblong, flattened, very small.

Leaves rough, bristly. Flowers 30–40 in a head . . 1. *H. javanica.*
Leaves smooth, glabrous. Flowers 10 or fewer in a head.
  Leaves orbicular, $\frac{1}{4}$–1 in. across, 5–7-lobed . . 2. *H. rotundifolia.*
  Leaves kidney-shaped, $\frac{3}{4}$–2 in. across, not lobed . 3. *H. asiatica.*

1. **Hydrocotyle javanica,** *Thunb.*; *Fl. Br. Ind.* ii. 667. Leaves rough, bristly, orbicular, 1–3 in. across, deeply cordate, 7-lobed, crenate. Umbels globose. Bracts none. Flowers 30–40 in an umbel, yellow-green, crowded.

Valleys below Simla ; July.—Temperate Himalaya, 2000–8000 ft.—Tropical Asia, Australia.

2. **Hydrocotyle rotundifolia,** *Roxb.*; *Fl. Br. Ind.* ii. 668. Leaves glabrous, shining, orbicular, $\frac{1}{4}$–1 in. across, deeply cordate or peltate, 5–7-lobed, crenate. Umbels small. Bracts few, small. Flowers about 10 in an umbel, green-white, crowded.

Valleys below Simla ; April–July.—Throughout India, ascending to 7000 ft. —Tropical Asia.

3. **Hydrocotyle asiatica,** *Linn.*; *Fl. Br. Ind.* ii. 669. Leaves glabrous, kidney-shaped, $\frac{3}{4}$–2 in. across, crenate, not lobed. Umbels small, sometimes clustered. Bracts few, small. Flowers 3 or 4 in an umbel, purple-white.

Sutlej valley, Suni ; April, May.—Throughout India, ascending to 3000 ft. —Tropical and subtropical regions.

2. SANICULA. Etymology obscure; perhaps from the Latin *sano*, to heal, as during the Middle Ages the plant was believed to possess curative properties.—A small genus; most temperate regions.

Sanicula europæa, *Linn.*; *Fl. Br. Ind.* ii. 670. Glabrous; stem erect, 1–3 ft. Leaves palmately divided, segments 3–5, ovate, toothed, often lobed, teeth finely pointed: radical leaves long-stalked, 2–6 in. across; stem-leaves few, smaller. Umbels irregularly compound. Bracts few, leaf-like. Rays unequal, repeatedly forking. Branches ending in a very small head of flowers surrounded by small, linear bracteoles. Flowers minute, white, mostly 1-sexual. Calyx-teeth lanceolate, acute. Fruit ovoid, $\frac{1}{10}$ in., covered with hooked prickles.

Simla, Mahasu, in forest; June–August.—Temperate Himalaya, 4000–12,000 ft.—Mountains of S. India.—Asia, Africa, Europe (Britain).

3. VICATIA. In honour of P. R. Vicat, a Swiss physician and botanical author of the eighteenth century.—Himalaya.

Vicatia coniifolia, *DC.*; *Fl. Br. Ind.* ii. 671. Glabrous; stem erect, 1–2 ft. Leaves finely divided, 2–3-pinnate; leaflets pinnatifid, segments linear, acute. Umbels compound. Bracts linear, usually reduced to one. Rays 6–12, unequal, Bracteoles several, linear, much longer than their umbels. Flowers minute, dark red. Calyx-teeth none. Fruit smooth, oblong, about $\frac{1}{10}$ in.; ridges slender, distinct, not winged.

Huttoo; July, August.—Temperate Himalaya, 6000–12,000 ft.

4. BUPLEURUM. Origin of name obscure.—Temperate Asia, Africa, N.W. America, Europe (Britain, Hare's Ear).

Perennial, glabrous, erect herbs. Leaves undivided, ovate, lanceolate or linear, entire, usually sessile; longitudinal nerves prominent. Umbels compound, numerous, usually paniculate. Rays 3–8, unequal. Flowers yellow, except *B. longicaule*. Calyx-teeth none. Fruit smooth, ovoid or oblong, less than $\frac{1}{4}$ in.; ridges usually slender, distinct.

Bupleurum longicaule, *Wall.*, occurs on rocks near the top of the Chor and is common near Dalhousie and Dharmsala above 8000 ft. Stems several. Bracteoles 5–8, ovate-lanceolate, much longer than their umbels. Petals and disk nearly black.

In the following key the foliage-leaves of the stem are referred to, not the floral leaves of the panicle branches.

Leaves at least $\frac{1}{2}$ in. broad, usually more.
- Leaves ovate or lanceolate, lower ones stalked. Bracteoles none or only one, linear . . . . . 1. *B. lanceolatum*
- Leaves oblong or ovate-oblong, all sessile. Bracteoles 2–4, broadly ovate, leaf-like . . . . . 2. *B. Candollii.*

Leaves at most $\frac{1}{3}$ in. broad, usually less.
 Leaves 4–10 in. long ; margins thick . . . . 3. *B. falcatum.*
 Leaves 1–3 in. long ; margins thin.
  Leaves obtuse, bristle-tipped ; nerves 5–7, prominent 4. *B. tenue.*
  Leaves finely acute ; nerves about 11, not prominent 5. *B. Maddeni.*

1. **Bupleurum lanceolatum,** *Wall.* ; *Fl. Br. Ind.* ii. 674. Stems 1–5 ft. Leaves ovate up to 3 × 2 in., ovate-lanceolate up to 5 × 2½ in. or narrowly lanceolate up to 4 × 1 in., usually tapering

FIG. 63. BUPLEURUM TENUE.

to a fine point ; lower leaves stalked, upper nearly sessile. Bracts none or only one, linear, up to $\frac{1}{4}$ in. long. Bracteoles 2–6, narrowly lanceolate, much shorter than their umbels, falling off after flowering. Fruit ovoid, hardly $\frac{1}{5}$ in. long ; ridges obscure.

Fagu ; August, September.—Temperate Himalaya, 4000–9000 ft.

2. **Bupleurum Candollii,** *Wall.* ; *Fl. Br. Ind.* ii. 674. Stems 1–3 ft. Leaves sessile, more or less stem-clasping, oblong up to 5 × 1 in. or ovate-oblong up to 2 × $\frac{3}{4}$ in., usually finely pointed.

Bracts 2–4, broadly ovate, $\frac{1}{2}$–1 in. long, leaf-like, acute. Bracteoles 4–5, ovate, about as long as their umbels. Fruit ovoid, hardly $\frac{1}{5}$ in. long; ridges distinct.

Simla, Mahasu, Matiana; July–September.—Temperate Himalaya, 7000–12,000 ft.

3. **Bupleurum falcatum,** *Linn.*; *Fl. Br. Ind.* ii. 676. Stems glaucous, 1–4 ft. Leaves sessile, linear, 4–10 × $\frac{1}{4}$–$\frac{1}{3}$ in., usually curved like a scythe; nerves 5–7, prominent, margins thick. Bracts 2–5, linear-lanceolate, acute, up to $\frac{1}{4}$ in. long. Bracteoles 4–5, lanceolate, shorter than their umbels. Fruit oblong, hardly $\frac{1}{5}$ in. long; ridges distinct.

Simla, Mushobra, common; Temperate Himalaya, 3000–10,000 ft.—W. Asia, Europe (Britain).

4. **Bupleurum tenue,** *Don*; *Fl. Br. Ind.* ii. 677. Stems flexuous, 1–3 ft. Leaves sessile, narrowly oblong, 1–3 × $\frac{1}{4}$ in.; nerves 5–7, prominent, margins thin, tip obtuse, bristle-tipped. Umbels often borne on short, lateral branches. Bracts 1–4, lanceolate, $\frac{1}{4}$ in. or less, acute. Bracteoles 4–5, obovate-lanceolate, longer than their umbels. Fruit oblong, $\frac{1}{10}$ in.; ridges distinct. (Fig. 63.)

Simla, Mushobra, common; July–September.—Plains of N. Punjab; Temperate Himalaya, up to 9000 ft.

5. **Bupleurum Maddeni,** *C. B. Clarke*; *Fl. Br. Ind.* ii. 678. Aspect and characters of *B. tenue*, except that the finely acute leaves have about 11 slender nerves, and the bracteoles are about equal to their umbels.

Simla; July, August.—Simla to Mussoorie, 6000–8000 ft.

5. **PIMPINELLA.** Supposed to be derived from *bipinnula*, 2-pinnate.—N. temperate regions, S. Africa, rare in S. America.

Perennial, erect herbs. Leaves pinnate or 2-pinnate; leaflets lanceolate, pinnatifid or toothed; radical leaves sometimes undivided. Umbels compound. Bracts none or 1–5, linear. Rays unequal. Bracteoles 3–8, linear, less than $\frac{1}{4}$ in., sometimes none. Flowers yellow-green or white; stalks unequal, usually long. Calyx-teeth none. Fruit glabrous or pubescent, ovoid, about $\frac{1}{10}$ in. long; ridges slender, distinct.

Leaves 2-pinnate. Rays 5–10. Fruit glabrous . . . 1. *P. acuminata.*
Leaves 1-pinnate. Rays 10–20. Fruit roughly pubescent 2. *P. diversifolia.*

1. **Pimpinella acuminata,** *C. B. Clarke*; *Fl. Br. Ind.* ii. 686. Glabrous, except the leaves; stems 2–5 ft. Leaves pubescent on both surfaces, 2-pinnate; leaflets 3–5 on each pinnule, 1–2 × $\frac{1}{2}$–$\frac{3}{4}$ in., irregularly lobed and toothed, long-pointed. Bracts 1–5. Rays 5–10. Bracteoles 3–5. Flowers yellow-green, 6–12 in an

umbel; stalks in fruit much elongated, drooping. Petals soon falling off. Fruit smooth.

Simla, common in woods; July–September.—W. Himalaya, 4000–8000 ft.

2. **Pimpinella diversifolia,** *DC.*; *Fl. Br. Ind.* ii. 688. Hairy or pubescent; stems 2–5 ft. Leaves 1-pinnate; leaflets 3 or 5, rarely reduced to only 1, very variable in shape, lanceolate $1\frac{1}{2}$–5×1–2 in., or sometimes, in the radical leaves, broadly ovate

FIG. 64. PIMPINELLA DIVERSIFOLIA.

and about 1 in. across, coarsely or finely, irregularly toothed, usually cordate, often long-pointed. Bracts none or 1–2. Rays 10–20. Bracteoles 3–8 or none. Flowers white, 8–16 in an umbel; stalks in fruit elongated. Fruit roughly pubescent. (Fig. 64.)

Simla, common; July–September.—Temperate Himalaya, 4000–10,000 ft.—China.

6. **OSMORHIZA.** From the Greek *osme*, odour, and *rhiza*, a root; the root smells like Aniseed.—N. Asia, N. America and the Andes.

Osmorhiza Claytoni, *C. B. Clarke*; *Fl. Br. Ind.* ii. 690. A perennial, erect herb, 2–5 ft. Leaves large, 2-pinnate; leaflets in threes, bristly-pubescent, ovate or lanceolate, 1–2 in., irregularly and coarsely toothed, sometimes lobed. Umbels compound. Bracts 1–5, linear, $\frac{1}{3}$ in. Rays 3–6, slender, more or less drooping, 1–4 in. Bracteoles about 6, lanceolate, $\frac{1}{4}$ in. Flowers white, 3–6 in an umbel; stalks unequal, bristly towards the top, elongated in fruit. Calyx-teeth none. Fruit nearly cylindric, $\frac{1}{2}$–$\frac{3}{4}$ in. long, covered with minute, scattered bristles; ridges slender, distinct.

Narkunda; May–July. — Western Himalaya, 5000–8000 ft.—N.E. Asia, N. America.

7. CHÆROPHYLLUM. From the Greek *chairo*, to rejoice, and *phyllon*, a leaf; referring to the beauty, and, in some species, fragrance of the leaves.—N. temperate regions.

Perennial, erect herbs; root sometimes tuberous or spindle-shaped. Leaves 1–3-pinnate; leaflets regularly or irregularly lobed and toothed. Umbels compound. Bracts none. Rays unequal. Bracteoles 2–5, linear, up to $\frac{1}{3}$ in. long, soon reflexed. Flowers white or red, polygamous, 10–15 in an umbel; stalks slender, unequal, elongated in fruit. Calyx-teeth none. Fruit glabrous, nearly cylindric, $\frac{1}{4}$–$\frac{1}{2}$ in., narrowed to both ends; ridges equal, distinct, blunt.

Leaves 2- or 3-pinnate; segments irregularly lobed and toothed.
  Stem and leaves hairy. Base of stem clothed with long, stiff hairs pointing downwards . . . . 1. *C. villosum.*
  Stem and leaves glabrous or only slightly hairy . 2. *C. reflexum.*
Leaves 1- or 2-pinnate; segments closely and regularly toothed. If pinnatifid the lobes nearly similar and the teeth regular . . . . 3. *C. acuminatum.*

1. **Chærophyllum villosum,** *Wall.*; *Fl. Br. Ind.* ii. 690. Root thick, fleshy, spindle-shaped; stem 1–4 ft., more or less hairy, and clothed, at least towards the base, with long, stiff hairs pointing downwards. Leaves large, varying much in size and cutting, hairy or pubescent, 2- or 3-pinnate; leaflets pinnatifid; segments irregularly and acutely lobed and toothed. Rays 3–6. Fruit $\frac{1}{3}$ in.

Simla, Fagoo, Huttoo; June–August.—Temperate Himalaya, 5000–12,000 ft. The root is eaten and called 'Wild Carrot' by the hill people; it is a favourite food of bears.

2. **Chærophyllum reflexum,** *Lindl.*; *Fl. Br. Ind.* ii. 691. Aspect and characters of *C. villosum*, except that the stem and leaves are glabrous or only slightly hairy, the fruit is $\frac{1}{3}$–$\frac{1}{2}$ in. long and the barren flowers are nearly always reflexed after flowering.

Simla, Fagoo; June–August.—W. Himalaya, 5000–9000 ft.

3. **Chærophyllum acuminatum,** *Lindl.*; *Fl. Br. Ind.* ii. 691. Stem 2–4 ft., more or less hairy. Leaves hairy or pubescent, 1- or-

2-pinnate; leaflets triangular or nearly oblong, up to 2 × ¼ in., closely and regularly toothed, or, if pinnatifid, the lobes nearly similar and the teeth regular. Rays 4–12. Fruit ¼ in.

Mahasu, Fagoo, Huttoo; June–August.—W. Himalaya, 5000–9000 ft.

8. ANTHRISCUS. The classical name of *Scandix australis*, Southern Chervil.—N. temperate regions; rare in America.

***Anthriscus nemorosa,** *Spreng.*; *Fl. Br. Ind.* ii. 692. A perennial, nearly glabrous, erect herb, 5–8 ft. Leaves large, 2- or 3-pinnate; leaflets broad, pinnatifid; segments toothed or entire. Umbels compound. Bracts none. Rays 10–15. Bracteoles several, lanceolate, ¼–⅓ in., entire. Flowers white, often polygamous, many in an umbel; stalks long, slender, unequal. Calyx-teeth none. Fruit black, glabrous or rough with minute, scattered bristles, nearly cylindric, ⅓–½ in.; ridges obscure.

Garhwal to Kashmir, 7000–11,000 ft.; May, June.

9. ŒNANTHE. From the Greek *oinos*, wine, and *anthos*, a flower; some species have a slight vinous scent.—N. Hemisphere, S. Africa.

Œnanthe stolonifera, *Wall.*; *Fl. Br. Ind.* ii. 696. A nearly glabrous herb, growing in water or marshy places; stem 2–4 ft., succulent, thick, decumbent or ascending, often floating, rooting at the lower joints and producing stolons at its base. Leaves 1- or the lower 2-pinnate, uppermost often reduced to 3 leaflets; leaflets lanceolate, 1–2 × ½–1 in., toothed, sometimes lobed. Umbels leaf-opposed, long-stalked, compound. Bracts none or 1–3. Rays 15–30, nearly equal. Bracteoles several, linear, up to ¼ in. Flowers white, many in an umbel, often polygamous. Calyx-teeth lanceolate, acute. Fruit glabrous, obovoid, ⅛ in. long; ridges distinct, but not elevated.

Valleys below Simla; June–August.—Throughout N. India, ascending to 5000 ft.—Malaya, China, Japan.

10. LIGUSTICUM. The classical name of *L. Levisticum*, Lovage, a plant growing abundantly in the Ligurian Alps, Piedmont.—N. Hemisphere.

Ligusticum elatum, *C. B. Clarke*; *Fl. Br. Ind.* ii. 698, including *L. marginatum*. A perennial, erect, glabrous or nearly glabrous herb, 2–4 ft. Leaves minutely bristly, 1- or 2-pinnate, sometimes very large; leaflets ovate-lanceolate, pinnatifid, acutely and irregularly toothed, often lobed. Umbels compound, long-stalked. Bracts 1–5, linear, ¼ in. Rays many, minutely bristly, nearly equal. Bracteoles 6–12, linear, ¼ in. Flowers white, many in an umbel, polygamous. Calyx-teeth none. Fruit glabrous, ovate, flattened, hardly $\frac{1}{5}$ in. long; ridges all winged, the wings of the lateral broader than those of the dorsal and intermediate ridges.

Simla, Mahasu, Huttoo, in open, grassy places; July–October.—Simla to Naini Tal, 7000–9000 ft.

11. SELINUM. From *selinon*, the Greek name for Celery; referring to the resemblance of the leaves.—Chiefly N. temperate regions.

Perennial, nearly glabrous herbs; stems erect, finely grooved, hollow. Leaves pinnately divided. Umbels compound, pubescent, long-stalked. Bracts 1–8, linear, up to $1\frac{1}{2}$ in. long, entire or lobed and toothed near the tip, usually fallen off in fruit. Rays numerous, thick, angular, nearly equal, hairy or minutely bristly. Bracteoles 5–12, linear, usually longer than their umbels, entire or lobed and toothed near the tip, persistent. Flowers white, polygamous, many in an umbel; stalks slender, unequal. Calyx-teeth narrowly lanceolate. Fruit glabrous, ovate or oblong, flattened, up to $\frac{3}{10}$ in. long; ridges all winged, the wings of the lateral broader than those of the closely contiguous, dorsal and intermediate ridges.

Leaves 3–5-pinnate. Leaflets divided into numerous, linear segments . . . . 1. *S. tenuifolium.*
Leaves 1–2-pinnate. Leaflets lanceolate, lobed and sharply toothed . . . . 2. *S. vaginatum.*

1. **Selinum tenuifolium,** *Wall.*; *Fl. Br. Ind.* ii. 700. Stems 2–8 ft. Leaves large, finely divided, lower long-stalked, 4- or 5-pinnate, upper 3-pinnate; leaflets pinnatisect; segments linear, acute, entire or toothed. Fruit ovate, $\frac{3}{10}$ in. long.

Mahasu, Matiana, Shali, Huttoo; July–October.—Temperate Himalaya, 6000–13,000 ft.

Aromatic; highly esteemed as sheep fodder by the hill shepherds. Native name *Khès havò*, referring to the leaves.

2. **Selinum vaginatum,** *C. B. Clarke*; *Fl. Br. Ind.* ii. 700. Stems 2–4 ft. Leaves 1- or 2-pinnate; leaflets lanceolate, pinnatifid; segments sharply and irregularly toothed, often lobed. Fruit oblong, $\frac{2}{10}$ in. long.

Mahasu, Huttoo; July–October.—W. Himalaya, 6000–12,000 ft.

12. ANGELICA. From the Latin *angelus*, a divine messenger; some species were once believed to be efficacious against poison, witchcraft &c.—Chiefly N. temperate and arctic regions.

Angelica glauca, *Edgew.*; *Fl. Br. Ind.* ii. 706. A glabrous herb; stem erect, hollow, 4–12 ft., finely grooved. Leaves usually large, 1–3-pinnate; leaflets often in threes or reduced to 3, sometimes to 1, ovate or lanceolate, undivided or lobed, irregularly and sharply toothed; upper surface dark green, lower glaucous. Umbels compound, long-stalked. Bracts several, linear, up to 1 in. Rays many, nearly equal. Bracteoles many, linear, $\frac{1}{4}$ in. Flowers white or purple, many in an umbel. Calyx-teeth none. Fruit glabrous, flattened, oblong, $\frac{1}{2} \times \frac{1}{4}$ in.; dorsal and intermediate ridges not winged, lateral ridges expanded into membranous, broad, free wings so that the fruit is surrounded by a double or two-leaved border.

Narkunda, Huttoo; July–September.—W. Himalaya, 8000–10,000 ft.
The aromatic root is used medicinally and as a spice by the hill men. Kashmiri name *Chohóre.*

13. HERACLEUM. Heracleon, derived from *Herakles* the Greek form of Hercules, was the classical name of some plant that cannot now be identified.—N. temperate regions.

Perennial herbs; stems erect, grooved, hollow. Leaves pinnately divided. Umbels compound, long-stalked. Bracts few, linear, $\frac{1}{4}$–$\frac{1}{2}$ in., often falling off after the flowering season. Rays unequal. Bracteoles 4–8, linear, up to $\frac{1}{4}$ in. long. Flowers white, usually polygamous, many in an umbel; stalks unequal. Calyx-teeth none or very small. Fruit flattened, ovate or obovate, $\frac{2}{5}$–$\frac{1}{2}$ in. long; dorsal and intermediate ridges not winged, lateral ridges expanded into membranous, broad, cohering wings so that the fruit, before the ripe carpels separate, is surrounded by a single border. Vittæ conspicuous as 4 dark, nearly parallel lines on each carpel.

Glabrous or nearly so. Leaflets narrowly lanceolate or strap-shaped, entire, rarely lobed or toothed. Calyx-teeth none . . . . 1. *H. cachemiricum.*
Hairy or densely pubescent. Leaflets oblong or ovate, toothed, usually lobed. Calyx-teeth small.
  Stems slender, 1–3 ft. Leaflets $\frac{1}{4}$–3 in. long; both surfaces covered with scattered, short, white hairs . . . . 2. *H. canescens.*
  Leaflets 4–12 in. long; upper surface nearly glabrous, lower densely pubescent, paler . . 3. *H. candicans.*

1. **Heracleum cachemiricum,** *C. B. Clarke*; *Fl. Br. Ind.* ii. 712. Glabrous or nearly so; stems slender, 1–3 ft., nearly leafless. Leaves mostly radical, pinnate, long-stalked; leaflets few, often in threes, sessile, narrowly lanceolate or strap-shaped, 1–4 × $\frac{1}{4}$–$\frac{3}{4}$ in., entire, rarely lobed or with a few distant teeth. Rays 5–10. Calyx-teeth none. Fruit glabrous or minutely pubescent, ovate, $\frac{4}{10} \times \frac{3}{10}$ in.

Mushobra; May, June.—Garhwal to Kashmir, 5000–8000 ft.
This species hardly differs from that described as *Peucedanum Dhana,* Buch.-Ham., in the *Fl. Br. Ind.* ii. 709.

2. **Heracleum canescens,** *Lindl.*; *Fl. Br. Ind.* ii. 713. Stems slender, 1–3 ft., hairy, nearly leafless. Leaves up to 12 in. long, 1- or 2-pinnate; leaflets sessile, oblong or ovate, $\frac{1}{4}$–3 in., undi-

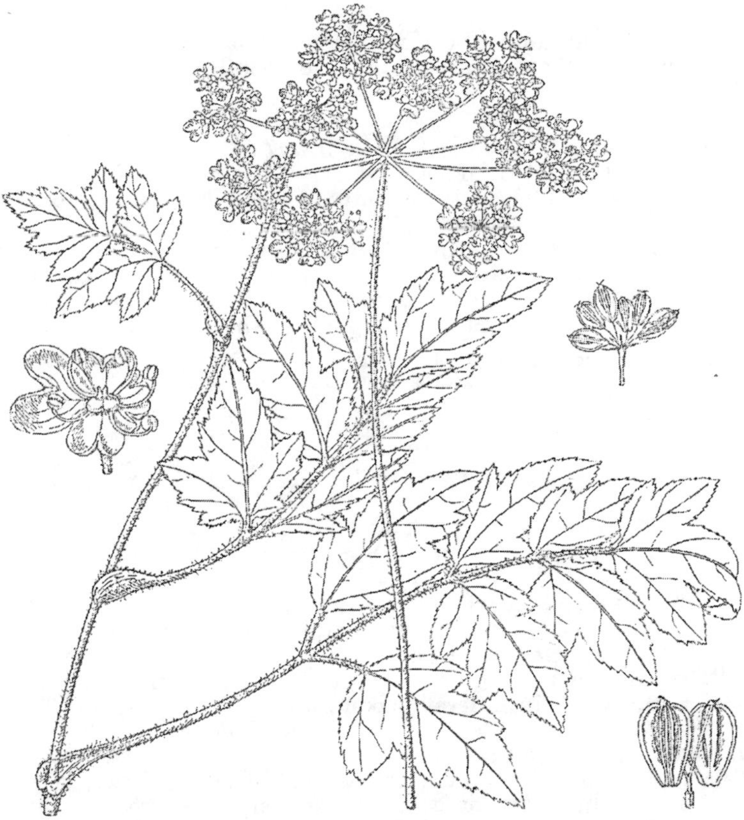

FIG. 65. HERACLEUM CANESCENS.

vided or 3-lobed, irregularly toothed; both surfaces covered with scattered, short, white hairs. Rays 5–20, up to 3 in. long in fruit. Calyx-teeth small, linear, acute. Fruit pubescent, obovate, $\frac{1}{3}$–$\frac{1}{2} \times \frac{1}{4}$ in. (Fig. 65.)

Simla, Mahasu, common in woods; July–September.—W. Himalaya, 6000–8000 ft.

3. **Heracleum candicans,** *Wall.*; *Fl. Br. Ind.* ii. 714. Stem robust, 2–6 ft., densely pubescent. Leaves 6–18 in., pinnate or pinnatifid, rarely 2-pinnate; leaflets oblong, 6–12 in., pinnately lobed, irregularly toothed; upper surface dark green, nearly

glabrous, lower densely pubescent, paler. Rays 10–40, up to 6 in. long in fruit. Calyx-teeth small, linear, acute. Fruit pubescent, obovate, $\frac{1}{3}$–$\frac{1}{2}$ × $\frac{1}{4}$–$\frac{1}{3}$ in.

Simla, Mahasu, common; May–August.—W. Himalaya, 6000–12,000 ft.

14. **CAUCALIS.** The classical name of some umbelliferous plant, perhaps *Caucalis orientalis.*—Temperate regions of the Old World.

Caucalis Anthriscus, *Scop.*; *Fl. Br. Ind.* ii. 718. An annual, erect, roughly hairy or pubescent herb, 1–3 ft. Leaves 1- or 2-pinnate; leaflets lanceolate, pinnatifid; segments entire or toothed, acute. Umbels compound, long-stalked. Bracts 1–5, linear, $\frac{1}{5}$–$\frac{1}{2}$ in. Rays 5–12, very unequal. Bracteoles several, linear, sometimes longer than their umbels. Flowers pale pink, many in an umbel. Calyx-teeth none. Fruit ovoid, $\frac{1}{10}$ in. long, covered with short, rough, curved and usually minutely hooked bristles.

Simla, Mushobra; June, July.—Temperate Himalaya, 3000–9000 ft.—N. Asia, N. Africa, Europe (Britain, Hedge Parsley).

XLVI. ARALIACEÆ

Erect or climbing shrubs. Leaves alternate, simple or pinnately compound; stipules none or soon falling off. Flowers numerous, small, regular, 2-sexual or polygamous, in simple, globose umbels, solitary, racemed or panicled. Bracts small, at the base of the flower-stalks, not involucrate, soon falling off. Calyx-tube adnate to the ovary; limb 5-toothed or obsolete. Petals 5, imbricate or valvate in bud, reflexed in flower. Stamens 5, inserted with the petals on the margin of the calyx-tube. Ovary inferior, 5-celled, surmounted by a flat or conical disk; styles 5, free or united; stigmas terminal; ovules solitary in each cell, pendulous. Fruit a small, succulent, berry-like drupe, containing 5 bony, 1-seeded nuts.—Mostly tropical; a few species in N. temperate regions.

Erect shrubs. Leaves compound. Calyx-limb 5-toothed. Styles free . . . . 1. *Aralia.*
Climbing shrubs. Leaves simple. Calyx-limb obsolete. Styles united . . . . 2. *Hedera.*

1. **ARALIA.** Origin of name unknown.—Asia, N. America.

Aralia cachemirica, *Decaisne*; *Fl. Br. Ind.* ii. 722. An erect, roughly pubescent shrub, 5–10 ft. Leaves large, pinnately compound; leaflets 5–9, stalked or sessile, oblong-ovate, 3–6 × $1\frac{1}{2}$–3 in., toothed, sometimes lobed, abruptly pointed, lower surface pale. Umbels numerous, panicled or racemed. Flowers white. Calyx

FIG. 66. ARALIA CACHEMIRICA.

5-toothed. Petals imbricate. Disk flat. Styles free. Fruit black, globose, $\frac{1}{10}$ in. diam., 5-ribbed. (Fig. 66.)

Theog, Narkunda, in forest; August, September.—Temperate Himalaya, 8000–12,000 ft.

2. HEDERA. The classical name for the Ivy.—Temperate regions of the Old World, Australia.

Hedera Helix, *Linn.*; *Fl. Br. Ind.* ii. 739. A shrub, climbing by aerial, adhesive rootlets. Leaves simple, thick, shining, ovate, angular or 3–5-lobed, very variable in size, those of the barren stems usually more deeply lobed than of the flowering shoots. Umbels stellately hairy, solitary or in clusters of 2 or 3, sometimes panicled. Flowers yellow-green, polygamous. Calyx-limb obsolete. Petals valvate. Disk conical. Styles united in a very short column. Fruit black or yellow, sometimes red, smooth, globose, $\frac{1}{4}$ in. diam.

Simla; September, October.—Himalaya, 6000–10,000 ft.—N. Asia, Europe (Britain, Common Ivy).

XLVII. CORNACEÆ

Trees or shrubs. Leaves alternate or opposite, stalked, simple, entire or angularly lobed; stipules none. Flowers small, white, regular, 2-sexual, in cymes or involucrate heads. Calyx-tube adnate to the ovary; limb 6- or 4-toothed. Petals 6 or 4, valvate in bud, usually free, inserted on the margin of the ovary. Stamens as many as the petals, inserted with them. Ovary inferior, 2 celled; style short or long; stigma terminal; ovules solitary in each cell. Fruit succulent, drupe-like, usually free and $\frac{1}{4}$–$\frac{1}{3}$ in. long, containing a small, 2-celled, 2-seeded stone; in *C. capitata* very small and coalescing in a globose head.—Chiefly N. temperate regions.

Leaves alternate. Petals 6, long, strap-shaped. Stamens 6 . 1. *Marlea.*
Leaves opposite. Petals 4, short, oblong. Stamens 4 . . . 2. *Cornus.*

1. MARLEA. The native name in Sylhet of *M. begoniæfolia.*—Asia, Australia, Polynesia.

Marlea begoniæfolia, *Roxb.*; *Fl. Br. Ind.* ii. 743. A nearly glabrous tree. Leaves alternate, broadly ovate, unequally sided, 3–6 × 2$\frac{1}{2}$–6 in., usually angularly lobed, sometimes entire, long-pointed. Flowers $\frac{3}{4}$ in. long, in axillary cymes. Calyx minutely 6-toothed. Petals 6, long, white, strap-shaped, reflexed, sometimes cohering near the base. Stamens 6, filaments short, hairy, anthers long, linear, yellow, cohering. Style long, slender, hairy, tip 4-lobed. Drupes free, dark purple, ovoid, $\frac{1}{3}$ in., crowned with the calyx-limb; stone enveloped in pulp, sometimes, by abortion, 1-celled and 1-seeded.

Simla, the Glen, not common; March–May.—Throughout N. India, ascending to 6000 ft.—China, Japan.

2. CORNUS. The Latin name of the Dogwood tree, *Cornus Mas,* Linn., derived from *cornu,* horn; referring to the hard wood.—Chiefly N. temperate regions.

Trees or shrubs. Leaves opposite, entire; upper surface green, lower pale, nearly white. Flowers white, in terminal, compound cymes or in involucrate heads. Calyx 4-toothed. Petals 4, oblong, spreading. Stamens 4, filaments long, glabrous, anthers free. Style short; stigma capitate. Drupes globose or ovoid, usually free and about $\frac{1}{4}$ in. long; in *C. capitata* very small and coalescing in a succulent, globose head 1–2 in. diam.

Flowers $\frac{1}{3}$–$\frac{1}{2}$ in. diam., in compound cymes.
  Leaves ovate, 2–3 in. broad. Petals hairy outside . 1. *C. macrophylla.*
  Leaves oblong, 1–1$\frac{1}{2}$ in. broad. Petals glabrous . 2. *C. oblonga.*
Flowers very small, crowded in heads with an involucre of 4 yellow, petal-like bracts . . . . 3. *C. capitata.*

FIG. 67. CORNUS CAPITATA.

1. **Cornus macrophylla,** *Wall.*; *Fl. Br. Ind.* ii. 744. A large tree. Leaves broadly ovate, 4–6 × 2–3 in.; upper surface glabrous, lower minutely hairy. Cymes terminal, compound, hairy, 2–4 in. across. Flowers nearly $\frac{1}{2}$ in. diam. Calyx hairy. Petals oblong, hairy outside. Drupe pubescent, globose, $\frac{1}{5}$ in. diam.

Simla, Mushobra; April–June.—Himalaya, 4000–8000 ft.—China, Japan.

2. **Cornus oblonga**, *Wall.*; *Fl. Br. Ind.* ii. 744. A shrub or small tree. Leaves oblong, $3-6 \times 1-1\frac{1}{2}$ in., long-pointed; upper surface glabrous, lower minutely hairy. Cymes terminal, compound, pubescent, $1-2\frac{1}{2}$ in. across. Flowers nearly $\frac{1}{3}$ in. diam. Calyx pubescent. Petals oblong, glabrous. Stamens pink, longer than the petals. Drupe glabrous, ovoid, $\frac{1}{4}$ in. long.

Simla; August–October.—Temperate Himalaya, 4000–7000 ft.—Burmah.

3. **Cornus capitata**, *Wall.*; *Fl. Br. Ind.* ii. 745. A small tree. Leaves oblong or ovate, 2–3 in., densely, minutely hairy; stalks short. Flowers very small, crowded in hemispheric, terminal heads $\frac{1}{2}$ in. diam., with a conspicuous involucre of 4, rarely 5, pale yellow, petal-like, ovate bracts $1-1\frac{1}{4}$ in. broad. Drupes very small, coalescing in a succulent, globose head 1–2 in. diam., yellow or when ripe tinged with red. (Fig. 67.)

Simla, common; May–July.—Himalaya, from the Beeas to Bhotan, 3500–7000 ft.

Often called the Strawberry tree; fruit edible.

XLVIII. CAPRIFOLIACEÆ

Shrubs, rarely small trees. Leaves opposite, simple, usually entire; stipules none. Flowers 2-sexual, regular or irregular. Calyx-tube adnate to the ovary; limb 5-lobed or toothed, sometimes obsolete. Corolla gamopetalous; tube long or short, often unsymmetrically dilated near the base; limb 5-lobed or 5-toothed, sometimes 2-lipped. Stamens 5, rarely 4, inserted on the corolla-tube; anthers oblong or linear, versatile. Ovary inferior, 1–5-celled; style short or long, stigma capitate; ovules solitary and pendulous or several and inserted at the inner angle in each cell. Fruit baccate or drupaceous, rarely dry, 1–5-celled; seeds one to many.—Chiefly N. temperate regions; absent from Africa.—Name from the Latin *capra*, a goat, and *folia*, leaves; referring to the climbing habit of some species.

Flowers numerous, in terminal cymes.
  Cymes many-flowered. Calyx-teeth short or none. Stamens 5 . . . . 1. *Viburnum.*
  Cymes 3-flowered, in head-like clusters. Calyx lobes long, linear. Stamens 4 . . . . 2. *Abelia.*
Flowers axillary, in pairs. Ovary 2- or 3-celled . . . . 3. *Lonicera.*
Flowers in whorls, combined in drooping, axillary spikes. Ovary 5-celled . . . . 4. *Leycesteria.*

1. **VIBURNUM**. The Latin name of the Wayfaring Tree, *V. Lantana.*—Chiefly N. temperate regions.

Shrubs or small trees. Leaves stalked, entire, sharply toothed or crenate. Flowers small, regular, white or pink, crowded in terminal, compound cymes. Calyx-limb shortly toothed, obsolete only in *V. coriaceum*, persistent. Corolla funnel-shaped, tubular or rotate; limb 5-lobed, lobes equal spreading, erect only in *V. coriaceum*. Stamens 5. Ovary 1-celled; style short, stigma small; ovule solitary. Drupe glabrous, oblong or ovoid, usually flattened and grooved, 1-seeded.

Leaves entire or crenate.
 Leaves ovate or orbicular; lower surface tomentose. Calyx-limb 5-toothed . . . . 1. *V. cotinifolium.*
 Leaves oblong-lanceolate, glabrous. Calyx-limb obsolete . . . . 3. *V. coriaceum.*
Leaves sharply toothed.
 Flowers hardly $\frac{1}{5}$ in. long. Corolla rotate. Stamens in one series . . . . 2. *V. stellulatum.*
 Flowers $\frac{3}{4}$ in. long. Corolla funnel-shaped. Stamens in two series . . . . 4. *V. fœtens.*

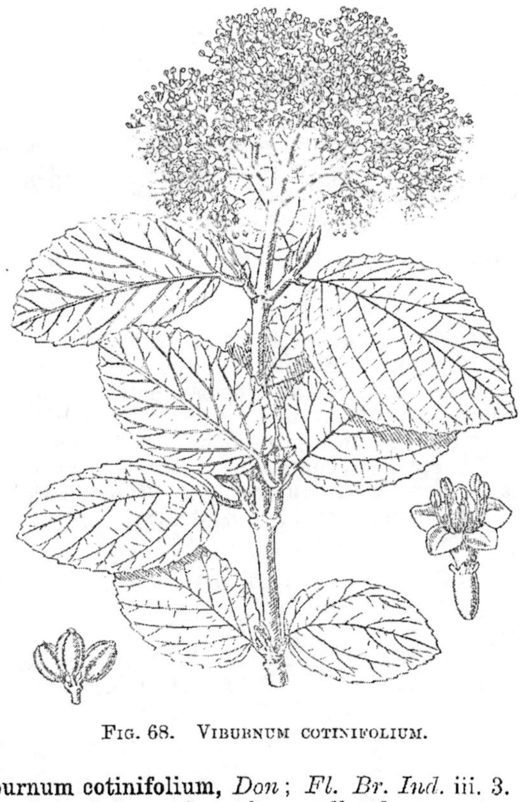

FIG. 68. VIBURNUM COTINIFOLIUM.

1. **Viburnum cotinifolium,** *Don*; *Fl. Br. Ind.* iii. 3. A shrub; young shoots and cyme-branches stellately tomentose. Leaves

thick, ovate or orbicular, 2–5 in., cordate, crenate or nearly entire; upper surface green, softly pubescent or nearly glabrous, lower grey, stellately tomentose, sometimes glabrous when old. Cymes round-topped, 2–3 in. across. Flowers numerous, white or tinged with pink, $\frac{1}{3}$ in. long. Calyx glabrous. Corolla funnel-shaped. Drupe red, turning black when ripe, oblong, $\frac{1}{3}$ in. (Fig. 68.)

Simla, common; April, May.—Temperate Himalaya, 6000–11,000 ft. Nearly allied to the British Wayfaring Tree, *V. Lantana*. Fruit edible.

2. **Viburnum stellulatum,** *Wall*; *Fl. Br. Ind.* iii. 4. A shrub or small tree; young shoots and cyme-branches stellately hairy. Leaves ovate or lanceolate, $2\frac{1}{2}$–6 in., sharply toothed; upper surface glabrous, lower stellately hairy, especially on the nerves. Cymes almost spherical, 3–5 in. diam. Flowers numerous, white, hardly $\frac{1}{5}$ in. long. Calyx stellately hairy. Corolla rotate, stellately hairy outside. Drupe bright red, shining, oblong, $\frac{1}{3}$ in.

Simla, Mahasu; May–July.—Temperate Himalaya, 6000–11,000 ft.

3. **Viburnum coriaceum,** *Blume*; *Fl. Br. Ind.* iii. 5. A shrub or small tree; young shoots and cyme-branches pubescent. Leaves glabrous, thick, oblong-lanceolate, 3–7 in., entire. Cymes flat-topped, 3–5 in. across. Flowers numerous, white, nearly $\frac{1}{4}$ in. long. Calyx glabrous, limb obsolete. Corolla tubular, lobes erect. Anthers purple. Drupe black, ovoid, $\frac{1}{5}$ in.

Simla, Summer hill; July–September. — Temperate Himalaya, 4000–8000 ft.

4. **Viburnum fœtens,** *Decaisne*; *Fl. Br. Ind.* iii. 8. A shrub; young shoots and cyme-branches pubescent or tomentose. Leaves fetid when crushed, ovate or oblong-lanceolate, 2–5 in., sharply toothed; upper surface glabrous or nearly so, lower hairy, especially on the nerves. Cymes numerous, 1–3 in. across. Flowers white or pink, $\frac{3}{4}$ in. long, appearing before or with the leaves. Calyx glabrous. Corolla funnel-shaped. Stamens in two series, 2 near the mouth of the corolla-tube, 3 lower down. Drupe red, oblong, $\frac{1}{2}$ in.

Narkunda; April–June.—W. Himalaya, 7000–10,000 ft.

2. **ABELIA.** In honour of Dr. Clarke Abel, physician to Lord Amherst's Embassy to China in 1817.—N. Asia.

Abelia triflora, *R. Brown*; *Fl. Br. Ind.* iii. 9. A shrub, 3–6 ft. Leaves glabrous or nearly so, lanceolate, $1\frac{1}{2}$–3 in., entire, minutely fringed, long-pointed; stalks short, dilated at the base. Flowers pale pink or white, $\frac{3}{4}$ in. long, in small, bracteate, 3-flowered cymes (central flower sessile), crowded in head-like clusters at the end of branches. Calyx hairy; tube oblong, 5-ribbed; lobes long, linear, fringed, persistent. Corolla funnel-shaped, pubescent; tube slender, nearly cylindric; lobes equal, spreading. Stamens 4, at the mouth of the corolla-tube. Ovary 3-celled; 2 cells containing several abortive ovules, the third one perfect ovule; style long. Fruit dry, narrowly oblong, crowned with the elongated calyx-lobes, 1-seeded.

Naldera, Shali, on limestone; May, June.—W. Himalaya, 5000–10,000 ft.

3. LONICERA. In honour of Adam Lonicer, a German botanist of the sixteenth century.—N. temperate regions, rare in the tropics.

Erect shrubs; branches prostrate in *L. parvifolia*. Leaves entire. Flowers almost regular or irregular, in pairs, each pair borne on a single axillary stalk or sessile in a leaf-axil; rarely in sessile, axillary clusters of 3 or 4 flowers. Bracts 2, linear, spreading, in *L. hispida* boat-shaped and erect. Bracteoles 2, small, ovate, sometimes wanting. Calyx-tube ovoid; limb short, toothed, persistent, teeth often unequal. Corolla tubular and 5-toothed or 2-lipped and the tube very short, upper lip erect, 4-toothed, lower reflexed, entire. Stamens 5. Ovaries sometimes united in pairs, 2- or 3-celled; style long, slender, stigma capitate; ovules several in each cell. Berries small, distinct or sometimes united in pairs, 2- or 3-celled, crowned with the small calyx-limb; seeds 1 or very few.

The common Honeysuckle of Britain, *L. Periclymenum*, belongs to this genus, but the Fly Honeysuckle, *L. Xylosteum*, often planted in shrubberies, is more nearly allied to the species here described.

Corolla almost regular, tubular, 5-toothed.
- Bracts broad, boat-shaped, erect, half concealing the flowers . . . . 1. *L. hispida.*
- Bracts narrow, flat, spreading.
  - Flowers purple. Berry black . . . . . 2. *L. purpurascens.*
  - Flowers white or pink. Berry red.
    - Leaves 1–$2\frac{1}{2}$ in. long . . . . . . 3. *L. angustifolia.*
    - Leaves $\frac{1}{3}$–$\frac{1}{2}$ in. long . . . . . . 4. *L. parvifolia.*

Corolla irregular, 2-lipped, tube short.
- Each pair of flowers (rarely 3 or 4) sessile in a leaf-axil . . . . 5. *L. quinquelocularis.*
- Each pair of flowers borne on a single axillary stalk.
  - Corolla glabrous. Ovaries united. Berry black . . . . 6. *L. orientalis.*
  - Corolla hairy. Ovaries free. Berries red . 7. *L. alpigena.*

1. Lonicera hispida, *Pall.*; *Fl. Br. Ind.* iii. 11. An erect shrub. Leaves roughly hairy, nearly sessile, ovate or oblong-lanceolate, 1–4 in., acute. Flowers $\frac{3}{4}$ in. long, each pair borne on a single axillary stalk. Bracts large, hairy, broadly boat-shaped, erect, overlapping, half concealing the flowers. Bracteoles none.

Corolla almost regular, tubular, pale green, often hairy. Berries red, ovoid, $\frac{1}{3}$ in., distinct.

Marali beyond Baghi; June.—Temperate Himalaya, 9000–13,000 ft.—Central Asia, Siberia.

This species probably occurs on Huttoo.

2. **Lonicera purpurascens,** *Hook. f. & Thoms.*; *Fl. Br. Ind.* iii. 12. An erect shrub. Leaves shortly stalked, hairy, oblong, $\frac{3}{4}$–$1\frac{1}{2}$ in., obtuse or acute, lower surface often tomentose. Flowers $\frac{1}{2}$ in. long, each pair borne on a single axillary stalk. Bracts narrow, $\frac{1}{4}$ in., spreading. Bracteoles short. Corolla almost regular, tubular, purple, hairy. Berries coalescing in a black, globose fruit, $\frac{1}{4}$ in. diam.

Huttoo, common; June.—Temperate Himalaya, 9000–12,000 ft.

FIG. 69. LONICERA QUINQUELOCULARIS.

3. **Lonicera angustifolia,** *Wall.*; *Fl. Br. Ind.* iii. 13. An erect shrub, glabrous or nearly so; young shoots hairy. Leaves shortly stalked, lanceolate, 1–$2\frac{1}{2} \times \frac{1}{4}$–$\frac{3}{4}$ in., acute, lower surface pale. Flowers $\frac{1}{3}$–$\frac{1}{2}$ in. long, each pair borne on a single, slender, axillary stalk. Bracts narrow, $\frac{1}{3}$ in., spreading. Bracteoles united, enclosing the ovaries. Corolla almost regular, tubular, white or tinged with pink, pubescent. Berries coalescing in a red, globose fruit, $\frac{1}{4}$ in. diam.

Simla, common; May, June.—Temperate Himalaya, 7000–12,000 ft.

4. **Lonicera parvifolia,** *Edgew.*; *Fl. Br. Ind.* iii. 13. A glabrous shrub; branches prostrate. Leaves shortly stalked, oblong-ovate or obovate, $\frac{1}{3}$–$\frac{1}{2}$ in.; lower surface pale. Flowers $\frac{1}{3}$–$\frac{1}{2}$ in. long, each pair borne on a single axillary stalk. Bracts narrow, twice as long as the ovaries, spreading. Bracteoles united, half enclosing the ovaries. Corolla almost regular, tubular, white or tinged with pink. Berries coalescing in a red, globose fruit $\frac{1}{4}$ in. diam.

Simla, Jako, Huttoo, the Chor, on rocks; June.—Temperate Himalaya, 8000–12,000 ft.

5. **Lonicera quinquelocularis,** *Hardw.*; *Fl. Br. Ind.* iii. 14. An erect, pubescent shrub. Leaves shortly stalked, ovate, 1–2 in. Flowers $\frac{1}{2}$–$\frac{3}{4}$ in. long, each pair sessile in a leaf-axil, rarely in clusters of 3 or 4. Bracts linear, short. Bracteoles united at the base, half enclosing the ovaries. Corolla irregular, 2-lipped, yellow, hairy. Berries distinct, ovoid, $\frac{1}{4}$ in. long, white, translucent. (Fig. 69.)

Simla, common; April–June.—Temperate Himalaya, 5000–12,000 ft.

6. **Lonicera orientalis,** *Lamk.*; *Fl. Br. Ind.* iii. 15. An erect, nearly glabrous shrub. Leaves stalked, ovate, $1\frac{1}{2}$–3×1–$1\frac{3}{4}$ in., acute; lower surface pale. Flowers $\frac{1}{2}$ in. long, each pair borne on a single axillary stalk. Bracts linear, shorter than the ovaries. Bracteoles none. Corolla irregular, 2-lipped, pink. Ovaries united. Berries coalescing in a black, globose fruit $\frac{1}{4}$ in. diam.

Narkunda; May, June.—W. Himalaya, 7000–10,000 ft.—W. Asia.

7. **Lonicera alpigena,** *Linn.*; *Fl. Br. Ind.* iii. 15. An erect shrub. Leaves shortly stalked, lanceolate, 2–$4 \times \frac{3}{4}$–$1\frac{1}{2}$ in., long-pointed, acute, more or less glandular-hairy. Flowers $\frac{3}{4}$ in. long, each pair borne on a single axillary stalk. Bracts linear, nearly twice as long as the ovaries. Bracteoles very small. Corolla irregular, 2-lipped, hairy, yellow at first, turning to red. Ovaries free. Berries distinct, red, globose, $\frac{1}{4}$ in. diam.

Huttoo; May, June.—W. Himalaya, 9000–12,000 ft.

4. **LEYCESTERIA.** In honour of W. Leycester, a friend of Dr. Wallich and at one time Chief Justice in Bengal.—Himalaya and Western China.

Leycesteria formosa, *Wall.*; *Fl. Br. Ind.* iii. 16. A nearly glabrous, erect shrub; stems several, herbaceous, hollow. Leaves ovate or ovate-lanceolate, 2–5×1–3 in., entire, sometimes toothed, narrowed to a long, slender point; stalks short, united at the base. Flowers white, often tinged with purple, in bracteate whorls of 5 or 6 combined in axillary, drooping spikes. Bracts leaf-like, cordate, purple-tinged. Bracteoles similar but smaller. Calyx-tube ovoid; limb 5-lobed, 1 or 2 lobes much longer than the others. Corolla funnel-shaped, $\frac{1}{2}$–1 in., 5-lobed. Stamens 5. Ovary 5-celled; style long, slender; ovules numerous in each cell. Berry glandular-hairy, dark purple, globose, $\frac{1}{4}$ in. diam., crowned with the persistent calyx-limb; seeds numerous.

Simla, Mahasu, in forest; June, July.—Simla to Bhotan, 5000–10,000 ft.

XLIX. RUBIACEÆ

Trees, shrubs or herbs of various habit. Leaves simple, opposite or whorled, entire; stipules usually persistent, attached to the stem between the bases of the leaves, minute or absent only when the leaves are whorled. Inflorescence various. Flowers 2-sexual, usually regular and symmetric. Calyx-tube adnate to the ovary; limb 4- or 5-toothed or 4- or 5-lobed, sometimes wanting. Corolla gamopetalous; limb 4- or 5-lobed, usually spreading. Stamens as many as the corolla-lobes, inserted at the mouth or on the tube of the corolla; filaments short or long; anthers 2-celled. Ovary inferior, 2- or 5-celled; style short or long, simple or branched; stigma usually linear or capitate; ovules many or solitary in each cell. Fruit usually capsular, rarely succulent; seeds small or minute, few or many.—A very large Order, abundant in most tropical and subtropical regions.

Among species of great economic importance are:—The Coffee shrub, *Coffea arabica*, a native of E. tropical Africa, now widely cultivated; the *Cinchonae*, shrubs or trees from whose bark Quinine is extracted, natives of the Peruvian Andes and now cultivated in India, Java and elsewhere; *Cephaëlis Ipecacuanha*, a native of Brazil, from the roots of which the drug Ipecacuanha is obtained; *Rubia tinctorum*, indigenous in S. Europe, and cultivated in India and elsewhere, from whose roots the red dye, Madder, is obtained.

A. Ovules many in each cell

Trees or shrubs.
  Flowers small, numerous, in heads or panicles.
    Flowers in globose heads . . . . . . 1. *Stephegyne*.
    Flowers in panicles.
      Panicle-branches spike-like, erect. Stigma entire . . . . 2. *Hymenodictyon*.
      Panicle-branches spreading. Stigma 2-branched 3. *Wendlandia*.
  Flowers $\frac{3}{4}$ in. long, solitary, axillary . . . . 8. *Randia*.
Herbs.
  Leaves whorled. Corolla 5-lobed . . . . . 4. *Argostemma*.
  Leaves opposite. Corolla 4-lobed.
    Calyx-teeth contiguous in fruit . . . . . 5. *Hedyotis*.
    Calyx-teeth distant in fruit.
      Leaves sessile, not more than $\frac{1}{5}$ in. broad . 6. *Oldenlandia*.
      Leaves stalked, $\frac{1}{3}$–$\frac{1}{2}$ in. broad . . . . . 7. *Anotis*.

B. Ovule solitary in each cell

Shrubs. Ovary 5-celled.
  Flowers each half-enclosed in a tubular involucre formed of 2 partially united bracts . . . . . 10. *Leptodermis.*
  Flowers not enclosed in an involucre . . . . . 9. *Hamiltonia.*
Herbs. Ovary 2-celled.
  Leaves opposite. Calyx-teeth 4 . . . . . . 11. *Spermacoce.*
  Leaves whorled. Calyx-teeth none.
    Corolla 5-lobed. Fruit succulent . . . . . 12. *Rubia.*
    Corolla 4-lobed. Fruit dry . . . . . . 13. *Galium.*

1. STEPHEGYNE. From the Greek *stephos* (poetical for *stephanos*), a crown, and *gyne*, a woman; referring to the structure of the stigma.—Tropical Asia and Africa.

Stephegyne parvifolia, *Korth.*; *Fl. Br. Ind.* iii. 25. A pubescent or nearly glabrous tree. Leaves opposite, shortly stalked, ovate or orbicular, 2–6 in. broad; stipules large, obovate, soon falling off. Flowers small, numerous, pale yellow, crowded in globose heads 1 in. diam. Calyces coherent; tube short; limb none or minute. Corolla glabrous, funnel-shaped; tube long; lobes 5, short, acute. Stamens 5, inserted at the mouth of the corolla-tube, filaments very short. Ovary 2-celled; style long, slender, far-protruding; stigma cylindric, cap-like; ovules many in each cell. Capsule ovoid, nearly $\frac{1}{5}$ in. long, ultimately opening by 2 valves; seeds numerous, minute.

Sutlej valley; May–July.—Throughout India, ascending to 4000 ft.—Burmah.

2. HYMENODICTYON. From the Greek *hymen*, skin or membrane, and *dictyon*, a net; referring to the membranous, net-veined wing of the seeds.—Tropical Asia and Africa.

***Hymenodictyon excelsum,** *Wall.*; *Fl. Br. Ind.* iii. 35. A tree, all parts more or less pubescent. Leaves opposite, stalked, ovate or orbicular, 4–10 in.; stipules large, oblong, soon falling off. Flowers very numerous, small, fragrant, white, sometimes tinged with green, crowded on the spike-like, erect branches of terminal panicles. Calyx 5-toothed. Corolla funnel-shaped; tube long; lobes 5. Stamens 5, inserted at the mouth of the corolla-tube, filaments very short. Ovary 2-celled; style slender, long, far-protruding; stigma ovoid; ovules many in each cell. Capsule stalked, recurved, oblong-ovoid, $\frac{3}{4}$ in., ultimately opening by 2 valves; seeds numerous, small, the seed-coat extended outwards in a membranous wing deeply split at the base.

Throughout India as far west as the Ravi, ascending to 5000 ft.; June, July.—Java.

3. WENDLANDIA. In honour of J. C. Wendland, a German botanical author, at the beginning of the 19th century.—Tropical Asia.

Wendlandia exserta, *DC.*; *Fl. Br. Ind.* iii. 37. A small tree; young shoots grey-tomentose. Leaves opposite, stalked, lanceolate or ovate-lanceolate, 5–9 in.; upper surface pubescent, lower grey-tomentose; stipules ovate, recurved, persistent. Flowers numerous, small, fragrant, white, in large, tomentose, spreading, terminal panicles. Calyx 5-lobed. Corolla salver-shaped, 5-lobed; lobes long, reflexed. Stamens 5, filaments protruding. Ovary 2-celled; style protruding, stigma 2-branched; ovules numerous in each cell. Capsule tomentose, globose, 2-valved; seeds many, minute.

Sutlej valley, Subathoo; March, April.—Throughout India as far west as the Chenab, ascending to 4000 ft.

FIG. 70. ARGOSTEMMA VERTICILLATUM.

4. ARGOSTEMMA. From the Greek *argos*, white, and *stemma*, a wreath; referring to the inflorescence.—Warm valleys in mountainous regions of Asia.

Argostemma verticillatum, *Wall.*; *Fl. Br. Ind.* iii. 43. A delicate, nearly glabrous herb; stems slender, erect, 2-6 in. Leaves 4, sessile in a terminal whorl, unequal, lanceolate or ovate-lanceolate, 1–4 in., lower surface pale; stipules minute. Flowers $\frac{1}{3}$ in. diam., shining, white, in terminal umbels. Calyx 5-toothed. Corolla rotate, 5-parted; segments acute, spreading. Stamens 5, anthers oblong, erect, dehiscing by terminal pores. Ovary 2-celled; style slender, stigma capitate; ovules many in each cell.

Capsule 2-celled, opening irregularly at the top; seeds many, minute. (Fig. 70.)

Simla, the Glen, on wet rocks; July, August.—Simla to Sikkim, 2000–6000 ft.—Burmah.

Argostemma sarmentosum, *Wall.*, *Fl. Br. Ind.* iii. 42, occurs at Mussoorie and as far west as Garhwal. It is distinguished from the above by its long, thread-like runners, broader leaves, and by the flowers having their parts in fours.

5. **HEDYOTIS.** From the Greek *hedus*, sweet, and *ous*, *otos*, an ear; referring to the fragrant and sometimes ear-shaped leaves of *H. Auricularia*.—Chiefly tropical Asia.

Decumbent herbs; stems 1–2 ft., usually rooting at the lower joints. Leaves opposite, smooth or rough, sessile or shortly stalked; stipules fringed with long bristles. Flowers small, white, in axillary, sessile or shortly stalked cymes. Calyx-tube ovoid; teeth 4, acute, contiguous in fruit. Corolla bell-shaped; lobes 4, spreading. Stamens 4, included. Ovary 2-celled; style short, stigma deeply 2-lobed; ovules many in each cell. Capsule ovoid or globose, 2-celled, indehiscent or opening irregularly at the top; seeds numerous, minute.

Rough, with minute bristles. Leaves sessile, narrowly lanceolate. Calyx bristly . . . . 1. *H. hispida.*
Smooth, glabrous. Leaves stalked, ovate. Calyx smooth . 2. *H. stipulata.*

1. **Hedyotis hispida,** *Retz*; *Fl. Br. Ind.* iii. 60. Stems angular, roughly pubescent. Leaves sessile or nearly so, narrowly lanceolate, $1\frac{1}{2}$–$2\frac{1}{2}$ in., acute; upper surface roughly pubescent, lower bristly. Flowers usually numerous, crowded in axillary, sessile, rounded cymes. Calyx roughly bristly.

Valleys below Simla; July–October.—N. India, ascending to 5000 ft.—China.

2. **Hedyotis stipulata,** *R. Br.*; *Fl. Br. Ind.* iii. 63. Stems terete, smooth. Leaves shortly stalked, smooth, glabrous or with a few scattered hairs, ovate, $\frac{1}{2}$–2 in., acute. Flowers usually few, in small, sessile or shortly stalked, axillary cymes. Calyx smooth, glabrous; teeth long.

Valleys below Simla; July–October.—Temperate Himalaya, 4000-5000 ft.—Japan.

6. **OLDENLANDIA.** In honour of H. B. Oldenland, a Danish botanist of the seventeenth century.—Most tropical and subtropical regions; chiefly Asiatic.

Slender herbs, erect or procumbent, usually minutely bristly. Leaves opposite, sessile, not more than $\frac{1}{5}$ in. broad; stipules small, membranous, fringed with unequal bristles. Flowers small, white or red, stalked, axillary or terminal, solitary or 2–4 in each cyme. Calyx-tube ovoid; teeth 4, distant in fruit. Corolla salver-shaped; tube short or long, lobes 4. Stamens 4, included. Ovary 2-celled; style short, stigma 2-lobed; ovules many in each cell. Capsule 2-celled, opening at the top; seeds numerous, minute.

Flowers white.
  Stems erect. Capsule globose, not ribbed . . . 1. *O. corymbosa.*
  Stems procumbent. Capsule bell-shaped, prominently ribbed . . . . 2. *O. crystallina.*
Flowers red . . . . 3. *O. coccinea.*

1. **Oldenlandia corymbosa,** *Linn.*; *Fl. Br. Ind.* iii. 64. Minutely bristly; stems slender, erect, 3–12 in., simple or much branched. Leaves linear-lanceolate, $\frac{1}{2}$–2 in., acute. Flowers white, solitary on long, slender, axillary stalks or 2–4 in a small cyme. Corolla-tube short. Capsule globose, not ribbed.

Valleys below Simla, Naldera; August–October.—Throughout India, ascending to 6000 ft.—Tropical Asia, Africa, America.

2. **Oldenlandia crystallina,** *Roxb.*; *Fl. Br. Ind.* iii. 65. Minutely bristly or nearly glabrous; stems tufted, procumbent, much branched. Leaves lanceolate or ovate-lanceolate, $\frac{1}{2}$–$\frac{2}{3}$ in., acute. Flowers white, solitary on long, slender, axillary stalks or 2–4 in a small cyme. Corolla-tube short. Capsule bell-shaped, prominently ribbed.

Annandale, on gravel walks; September, October.—Throughout India, ascending to 6000 ft.—Java.

3. **Oldenlandia coccinea,** *Royle*; *Fl. Br. Ind.* iii. 69. Minutely bristly; stems slender, rigid, erect, 4–12 in. Leaves distant, narrowly lanceolate, $\frac{1}{2}$–$1\frac{1}{2}$ in. Flowers bright red, $\frac{1}{4}$ in. diam., axillary or terminal, solitary or 2–4 in a small cyme; stalks short, elongating in fruit. Calyx-lobes long, linear. Corolla-tube long. Capsule oblong or globose.

Simla, common on grassy slopes; August, September.—W. Himalaya, 3000–8000 ft.

7. **ANOTIS.** From the Greek *aneu*, without, and *ous, otos*, an ear; referring to the absence of intermediate teeth between the calyx-lobes.—Tropical Asia and Australia.

Anotis calycina, *Wall.*; *Fl. Br. Ind.* iii. 73. An annual, slender herb; stems tufted, erect, shining, 2–8 in., 4-angled. Leaves opposite, ovate or ovate-lanceolate, $\frac{1}{4}$–$1 \times \frac{1}{3}$–$\frac{1}{2}$ in., shortly stalked; upper surface minutely hairy, lower nearly glabrous, pale; stipules membranous, margins bristly. Flowers small, white or pale lilac, solitary on slender, axillary stalks or 2–4 in a small cyme. Calyx-tube ovoid; teeth 4, minute, distant in fruit. Corolla tubular, 4-lobed. Stamens 4, anthers nearly sessile at the mouth of the corolla-tube. Ovary 2-celled; style slender, protruding, 2-branched; ovules many in each cell. Capsule hemispheric, opening at the top by 2 valves; seeds many, minute.

Simla, Mushobra; August, September. — Temperate Himalaya, 3000–7000 ft.

8. RANDIA. In honour of Isaac Rand, a British botanical author of the eighteenth century.—All tropical regions; most abundant in Asia and Africa.

Randia tetrasperma, *Roxb.*; *Fl. Br. Ind.* iii. 109. A small, glabrous, rigid shrub; branchlets short, usually ending in a spine. Leaves opposite, crowded towards the end of branchlets, ovate or oblanceolate, $\frac{1}{2}$–2 in., narrowed into a short stalk; stipules broadly lanceolate, long-pointed. Flowers solitary, axillary, sessile, $\frac{3}{4}$ in. long, white, tinged with green. Calyx-tube ovoid; lobes 5, long, narrow. Corolla tubular; lobes 5, long, acute, reflexed. Stamens 5, at the mouth of the corolla-tube; anthers long, linear, nearly sessile. Ovary 2-celled; styles slender, far-protruding, stigma spindle-shaped; ovules many in each cell. Berry purple, globose, $\frac{1}{3}$ in. diam.; seeds small, about 6 in each cell, immersed in pulp.

Simla; April–June.—Temperate Himalaya, 4000–6000 ft.

Randia dumetorum, *Lamk.*, is a common shrub throughout N. India, and may occasionally be found in the hills up to 3000 ft. It differs from the above in having long, axillary spines, densely hairy calyx and corolla, and yellow fruit.

9. HAMILTONIA. In honour of Dr. Francis Hamilton (previously Buchanan), of the Bengal Medical Service and Superintendent of the Botanic Garden, Calcutta, at the end of the eighteenth and beginning of the nineteenth centuries.—India, China.

Hamiltonia suaveolens, *Roxb.*; *Fl. Br. Ind.* iii. 197. An erect shrub, 4–10 ft.; branches spreading. Leaves fetid when crushed, opposite, stalked, roughly pubescent, ovate-lanceolate, 3–9 in.; stipules short, broad, acute, persistent. Flowers $\frac{1}{2}$ in. long, blue-lilac, sometimes white, in small, bracteate, head-like clusters at the end of short, forking branches forming terminal, pubescent panicles. Calyx hairy, short; limb 5-parted, persistent. Corolla pubescent, funnel-shaped; lobes 5, short, spreading. Stamens 5, filaments short, anthers linear. Ovary 5-celled, the partitions more or less disappearing in fruit; style long, slender, 5-branched at the top; ovules solitary in each cell. Capsule small, ovoid, opening from the top in three valves; seeds 5, oblong, 3-angled, outer coat loose, net-like. (Fig. 71.)

Tara Devi, and valleys below Simla, common; September-November.—Throughout India, ascending to 6,500 ft.—China.

10. LEPTODERMIS. From the Greek *leptos*, thin, delicate, and *derma*, skin; referring to the thin, membranous involucre surrounding each flower.—India, Burmah, China.

FIG. 71. HAMILTONIA SUAVEOLENS.

Leptodermis lanceolata, *Wall.*; *Fl. Br. Ind.* iii. 198. A rigid, erect, nearly glabrous shrub, 4–8 ft.; branches spreading. Leaves fetid when crushed, opposite, shortly stalked, lanceolate, 1–3 in., finely pointed; both surfaces, margins and nerves beset with scattered, minute, white hairs; stipules short, broad, acute, persistent. Flowers often 1-sexual, nearly $\frac{1}{2}$ in. long, white, sometimes tinged with purple, in small, bracteate heads terminal on short branchlets and forming a large, paniculate inflorescence, each flower half-enclosed in a tubular involucre formed of two partially united, thin, membranous, pointed bracts. Calyx small; lobes 5, obtuse, fringed, persistent. Corolla funnel-shaped; tube hairy within; lobes 5, short, spreading. Stamens 5, filaments short, anthers linear. Ovary 5-celled; style long, slender, 5-branched at the top; ovules solitary in each cell. Capsule cylindric, $\frac{1}{3}$ in., splitting from the top in 5 valves; seeds 5, each enveloped in a loose, fibrous, netted covering.

Simla; June–September.—Temperate Himalaya, 4000–10,000 ft.

11. SPERMACOCE. From the Greek *sperma*, a seed, and *acoce*, a point; probably referring to the sharp, persistent teeth of the calyx.—Tropical and subtropical regions.

Erect or procumbent herbs; stems and branches 4-angled. Leaves opposite, sessile; stipules short, broad, united to the leaf-bases, fringed with long bristles. Flowers small, sessile in axillary, bracteate clusters. Calyx ovoid; teeth usually 4, linear, persistent. Corolla funnel-shaped, 4-lobed. Stamens 4. Ovary 2-celled; style slender, stigma capitate or 2-lobed; ovules solitary in each cell. Capsule dividing when ripe into two one-seeded, half-fruits, each ultimately dehiscent.

Stems erect, prickly. Clusters usually globose, many-flowered 1. *S. stricta.*
Stems procumbent, hairy. Clusters 4–6-flowered . . . 2. *S. hispida.*

1. **Spermacoce stricta,** *Linn.*; *Fl. Br. Ind.* iii. 200. Stems erect, 6–12 in., angles minutely prickly. Leaves narrowly lanceolate, 1–2 in., acute; both surfaces rough with minute prickles. Flowers white; clusters many-flowered, usually globose. Corolla hardly $\frac{1}{3}$ in. long. Stigma capitate.

Valleys below Simla; June–October. — Throughout India, ascending to 6000 ft.—Tropical Asia and Africa.

*2. **Spermacoce hispida,** *Linn.*; *Fl. Br. Ind.* iii. 200. Stems procumbent, 6–12 in., angles hairy. Leaves ovate or obovate, $\frac{1}{2}$–$1\frac{1}{2}$ in., acute or obtuse; both surfaces rough with minute bristles. Flowers blue or white; clusters 4–6-flowered. Corolla $\frac{1}{5}$–$\frac{1}{2}$ in. long. Stigma 2-lobed.

Throughout India, ascending to 3000 ft.; June–October.

12. RUBIA. The Latin name of Dyers' Madder, *R. tinctorum*; derived from *ruber*, red.—Most tropical and temperate regions.

Rubia cordifolia, *Linn.*; *Fl. Br. Ind.* iii. 202. A climbing herb; rootstock perennial; stems and branches elongate, rather rigid, 4-angled, angles minutely prickly. Leaves in whorls of 4, long-stalked, cordate-ovate, 2–4 in., long-pointed; nerves and margins prickly, otherwise nearly glabrous, basal nerves prominent; stipules none. Flowers small, dark red, in numerous, small cymes forming large, bracteate panicles. Calyx-tube globose; limb obsolete. Corolla rotate; lobes 5, tips incurved. Stamens 5. Ovary

2-celled; style 2-branched, stigmas capitate; ovules solitary in each cell. Fruit succulent, globose or slightly 2-lobed, $\frac{1}{5}$ in. diam., black, 2-celled or by abortion 1-celled; juice red; seeds 2, small.

Simla, Mushobra; July–October.—Hilly districts throughout India, ascending to 8000 ft.—N.E. Asia, tropical Africa.
Native name *Manjeet*. A red dye is obtained from the roots.

13. GALIUM. From *galion*, the Greek name of the Yellow Bed-Straw, *G. verum*; probably derived from *gala*, milk, the flowers having formerly been used to curdle milk.—Nearly all regions, most abundant in temperate climates.

Herbs; stems and branches slender, weak, 4-angled, usually trailing or climbing. Leaves whorled, sessile, rarely stalked; nerves lateral and sometimes obscure or basal and prominent. Flowers small or minute, usually numerous, in axillary and terminal cymes often forming large panicles, rarely solitary. Calyx-tube ovoid or globose; limb obsolete. Corolla rotate; lobes 4, spreading. Stamens 4, filaments short, anthers protruding. Ovary 2-celled; styles 2, short, stigmas capitate; ovules solitary in each cell. Fruit small, dry, globose, slightly 2-lobed, smooth or covered with hooked bristles; seeds 2, small.

G. vestitum, *Don*, *Fl. Br. Ind.* iii. 206, has been collected on the Rogi cliffs near Chini, and may occur nearer Narkunda. It is distinguished by its short, oblong, obtuse, laterally nerved, densely hairy leaves in whorls of 4 or 6 and the fruit covered with hooked bristles.

A. Fruit covered with hooked bristles

Leaves 3-nerved from the base . . . . . . 1. *G. rotundifolium*.
Leaves laterally nerved.
Leaves 6 or 8 in a whorl.
Stems smooth, glabrous . . . . . . 2. *G. triflorum*.
Stems prickly along the angles . . . . 3. *G. Aparine*.
Leaves 4 in a whorl. Stems hairy or bristly . . 4. *G. hirtiflorum*.

B. Fruit smooth

Leaves 6 or 8 in a whorl, laterally nerved.
Leaves bristly or minutely prickly, $\frac{1}{2}$–1 in. long . 5. *G. asperifolium*.
Leaves glabrous, less than $\frac{1}{4}$ in. long . . . 6. *G. acutum*.
Leaves 4 in a whorl, 3-nerved from the base . . . 7. *G. cryptanthum*.

1. **Galium rotundifolium**, *Linn.*; *Fl. Br. Ind.* iii. 204. Stems and branches trailing, angles hairy. Leaves in whorls of 4, ovate, $\frac{1}{2}$–1 in.; upper surface hairy or pubescent, lower minutely prickly on the nerves and margins, otherwise nearly glabrous; basal nerves 3, prominent. Flowers white, often tinged with green or yellow. Fruit covered with hooked bristles. (Fig. 72.)

Simla, common; July, August.—Throughout the Himalaya, 4000–10,000 ft.—W. Asia, N. Africa, Europe.

2. **Galium triflorum,** *Michx.*; *Fl. Br. Ind.* iii. 205. Stems smooth, glabrous, erect or ascending, 6–12 in. Leaves in whorls of 6 or 8, nearly glabrous, lanceolate, narrowed to the stalk-like base; upper leaves 1–2½ in., lower smaller; nerves lateral. Flowers white or tinged with yellow. Fruit covered with hooked bristles.

Mushobra, Mahasu, Narkunda, in forest; May, June.—Temperate Himalay 6000–10,000 ft.—Asia, N. Europe, America.

This species has the habit and odour of the British Sweet Woodruff, *Asperula odorata.*

A variety occurs at Simla (*Hoffmeisteri* of the *Fl. Br. Ind.*) having distinctly stalked, ovate leaves ½ in. long, sometimes only 4 in a whorl.

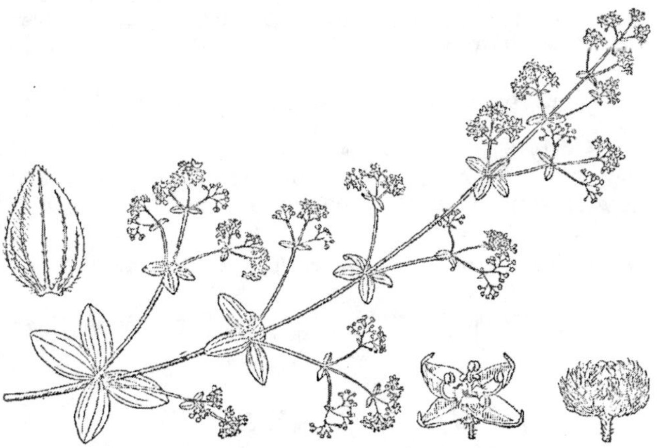

FIG. 72. GALIUM ROTUNDIFOLIUM.

3. **Galium Aparine,** *Linn.*; *Fl. Br. Ind.* iii. 205. Stems and branches trailing or climbing, angles beset with minute, recurved prickles, otherwise glabrous. Leaves in whorls of 6 or 8, linear or narrowly lanceolate, ½–1½ in.; midrib and margins minutely prickly; nerves lateral. Flowers white, tinged with green. Fruit covered with hooked bristles.

Huttoo; July, August.—Temperate Himalaya, 8000–12,000 ft.—W. Asia, N. Africa, Europe (Britain, Goosegrass, Cleavers).

*4. **Galium hirtiflorum,** *Req.*; *Fl. Br. Ind.* iii. 206. Stems trailing or ascending, more or less covered with hairs or bristles. Leaves in whorls of 4, hairy or bristly, linear, ½–1 in.; nerves lateral. Flowers minute, red. Corolla fringed. Fruit covered with hooked bristles.

Garhwal, Almora; July, August.—Sirmore to Sikkim, 4000–10,000 ft.

5. **Galium asperifolium,** *Wall.*; *Fl. Br. Ind.* iii. 207, *under G. Mollugo.* Stems trailing, diffuse, angles minutely prickly,

otherwise glabrous. Leaves in whorls of 6 or 8, bristly or minutely prickly especially on the margins and nerves, linear or narrowly lanceolate, $\frac{1}{2}$–1 in., tip spinescent; nerves lateral. Flowers red. Fruit smooth.

Simla, common; June–August.—Temperate Himalaya, 5000–12,000 ft. Habit of the British *G. Mollugo.*

*6. **Galium acutum,** *Edgew.*; *Fl. Br. Ind.* iii. 208. Stems prostrate, interlaced, glabrous, shining. Leaves in whorls of 6, crowded, glabrous, ovate-lanceolate, less than $\frac{1}{4}$ in., tip spinescent; nerves lateral, obscure. Flowers white. Fruit smooth.

The Chor to Sikkim, on rocks, 7000–12,000 ft.; September, October. This species may have been overlooked on Huttoo.

7. **Galium cryptanthum,** *Hemsl.*; *Hook. Icon. Plant.* t. 1469; *Fl. Br. Ind.* iii. 209, *under G. verum, Scop.* Stems trailing or ascending, softly hairy. Leaves in whorls of 4, shortly stalked, hairy, ovate, $\frac{1}{2}$–$\frac{3}{4}$ in., acute; basal nerves 3, prominent. Flowers few, yellow or white, usually produced in only the upper whorls. Fruit smooth.

Narkunda; July, August.—Kumaon to Chamba, 7000–11,000 ft.

L. VALERIANACEÆ

A SMALL Order widely diffused over nearly all temperate regions except Australia.

The Spikenard of the ancients, Indian Nard of modern times, *Nardostachys Jatamansi*, belongs to this Order. It is a perennial herb inhabiting the Alpine Himalaya at an altitude of 11,000–15,000 ft., and is esteemed on account of its aroma and stimulating properties.

VALERIANA. Origin of name uncertain.—All temperate regions except Australia.

Perennial, erect herbs. Leaves opposite, undivided or pinnate, mostly radical or crowded near the base of the stem; stipules none. Flowers numerous, 2- or 1-sexual, the male and female sometimes on different plants, $\frac{1}{10}$ in. diam. or less, the smaller being 1-sexual, in bracteate cymes forming a terminal corymb or panicle. Calyx-tube adnate to the ovary; limb at flowering time scarcely perceptible, unrolling afterwards in about 12 linear, hairy lobes. Corolla funnel-shaped; limb 5-lobed, spreading. Stamens 3, inserted on the corolla-tube, protruding. Ovary inferior, cells 3, one containing a solitary, pendulous ovule, the others empty;

style slender, undivided, stigma terminal. Fruit small, 1-celled, 1-seeded, crowned with the pappus-like calyx-limb.

Stems 6–18 in. Leaves undivided. Corymb terminal . 1. *V. Wallichii.*
Stems 1–5 ft. Leaves pinnate. Corymbs axillary . . 2. *V. Hardwickii.*

1. **Valeriana Wallichii,** *DC.*; *Fl. Br. Ind.* iii. 213. Pubescent; rootstock thick, horizontal; stems 6–18 in., usually tufted. Radical leaves persistent, stalked, cordate-ovate, 1–3 × 1–2½ in., toothed or sinuate, acute. Stem-leaves shortly stalked, smaller. Flowers white or tinged with pink, in a terminal corymb 1–3 in. across, often 1-sexual, the male and female on different plants.

Simla, Mushobra; March–May.—Temperate Himalaya, 7000–10,000 ft.—Afghanistan.

V. pyrolæfolia, *Decaisne, Fl. Br. Ind.* iii. 212, is closely allied to the above, differing only in its broadly ovate or orbicular, obtuse radical leaves and sessile stem-leaves. It occurs on the Chor and perhaps on Huttoo.

FIG. 73. VALERIANA HARDWICKII.

2. **Valeriana Hardwickii,** *Wall.*; *Fl. Br. Ind.* iii. 213. Pubescent; rootstock descending. Radical leaves few, soon disappearing, stalked, ovate, 2–4 × 1½–3 in. Stem-leaves pinnate, 3–6 in., lower ones stalked, crowded, upper sessile; leaflets 3–7, lanceolate,

usually entire, long-pointed, end one largest. Flowers white, in numerous, axillary, stalked, compound corymbs forming a long, terminal panicle, often 1-sexual. (Fig. 73.)

Simla, Mushobra, common; July–September.—Temperate Himalaya, 4000–12,000 ft.

The root is exported to the plains partly for medicinal use, but mainly as a perfume.

LI. DIPSACEÆ

Erect, usually perennial herbs. Leaves opposite, rarely whorled, entire, toothed or pinnatifid, prickly in *Morina*; stipules none. Flowers 2-sexual, crowded in axillary clusters or in long-stalked, terminal, involucrate heads. Receptacle of the heads covered with scales or hairs. Base of each flower enclosed in a tubular sheath or involucel free from or united with the calyx-tube. Calyx-tube adnate to the ovary; limb free. Corolla superior, tubular; limb 4- or 5-lobed, lobes spreading, usually unequal. Stamens 2 or 4, inserted at the mouth of the corolla-tube; filaments free, usually protruding; anthers 2-celled, versatile. Ovary inferior, 1-celled; style long, slender, undivided, stigma terminal; ovules solitary, pendulous. Achene enclosed within the persistent involucel, tip free, usually crowned with the persistent calyx-limb.—A small Order inhabiting nearly all regions in the Old World except Australia.

Leaves prickly. Flowers in axillary clusters . . . . . 1. *Morina*.
Leaves unarmed. Flowers in terminal heads.
  Flowers white. Corolla 4-lobed . . . . 2. *Dipsacus*.
  Flowers purple. Corolla 5-lobed . . . . 3. *Scabiosa*.

1. MORINA. In honour of Louis Morin, a French botanical author of the seventeenth century.—W. Asia, S. Europe.

Glabrous or softly pubescent. Leaves sometimes whorled, narrowly oblong, sinuately pinnatifid, prickly, thistle-like; upper ones shorter, sessile, united at the base. Flowers sessile, crowded in the axils of the upper leaves forming a terminal, interrupted spike. Involucel funnel-shaped, unequally spinous-toothed. Calyx-limb 2-lobed, soon falling off, lobes entire, notched or bifid. Corolla-tube long, slender; limb obscurely 2-lipped, 5-lobed, lobes unequal, ultimately spreading. Perfect stamens 2, rudimentary stamens usually 2. Stigma broad, disk-like. Achene small, free within the involucel.

For an interesting description of the method of fertilisation in the flowers of this genus, see Kerner's *Natural History of Plants*, ii. 352.

Flowers white or pink.
Calyx-lobes entire. Corolla white or faintly tinged with pink . . . . 1. *M. persica.*
Calyx-lobes notched. Corolla deep pink . . . . 2. *M. longifolia.*
Flowers yellow . . . . 3. *M. Coulteriana.*

FIG. 74. MORINA LONGIFOLIA.

1. **Morina persica,** *Linn.*; *Fl. Br. Ind.* iii. 216. Stems $1\frac{1}{2}$–3 ft. Leaves up to 9 in., hard, very prickly. Flowers white or faintly tinged with pink. Calyx-lobes obovate, entire. Corolla-tube 1–$1\frac{1}{2}$ in. Filaments longer than the corolla-lobes.

Simla; May, June.—W. Himalaya, 6000–9000 ft.—W. Asia, S. Europe. The typical *M. persica* of S. Europe has notched calyx-lobes.

2. **Morina longifolia,** *Wall.*; *Fl. Br. Ind.* iii. 216. Stems 2–4 ft. Leaves up to 15 in. Flowers deep pink. Calyx-lobes notched. Corolla-tube 1 in. Filaments much shorter than the corolla-lobes. (Fig. 74.)

Mahasu, Theog, Huttoo; July–September.—Temperate Himalaya, 9000–14,000 ft.

3. **Morina Coulteriana,** *Royle*; *Fl. Br. Ind.* iii. 216. Stems 1–2 ft. Leaves up to 6 in. Flowers yellow. Calyx-lobes bifid; segments spinous. Corolla-tube $\frac{1}{2}$–$\frac{3}{4}$ in. Filaments shorter than the corolla-lobes.

Patarnala; September.—W. Himalaya, 9000–13,000 ft.—Kashgar.

2. **DIPSACUS.** The classical name of the Fuller's Teasel, *D. fullonum*; derived from the Greek *dipsaein*, to be thirsty, referring probably to the united leaf-bases holding water.—Asia, N. Africa, Europe.

Dipsacus inermis, *Wall.*; *Fl. Br. Ind.* iii. 217 including *D. strictus, Don.* More or less rough with stiff hairs or bristles; stems robust, 4–10 ft. Leaves ovate or lanceolate, 3–12 in., coarsely toothed, long-pointed; lower leaves pinnatifid, terminal lobe much the largest; upper leaves sometimes 3-parted; stalks dilated and united at the base. Flowers numerous, white, crowded in hemispheric, terminal heads 1 in. diam., surrounded by an involucre of 6–8 spreading, leaf-like bracts. Receptacle covered with broad, concave scales abruptly narrowed in long, fringed, spine-like points overtopping the flowers when in bud. Involucel small, 4-toothed, adnate to the calyx-tube. Calyx-limb cup-shaped, hairy, 4-angled, 4-lobed, overtopping the involucel. Corolla pubescent; limb unequally 4-lobed. Stamens 4, anthers protruding. Stigma linear. Achene enclosed in the 8-ribbed involucel, crowned with the calyx-limb or ultimately naked.

Simla, Mushobra; July–October.—Temperate Himalaya, 6000–12,000 ft. Closely allied to the British Small Teasel, *D. pilosus*.

3. **SCABIOSA.** From the Latin *scabies*, mange or itch; referring to the former use of the plants as a remedy for skin diseases. —W. Asia, Africa, Europe.

***Scabiosa Candolliana,** *Wall.*; *Fl. Br. Ind.* iii. 219. Rootstock perennial; stems tufted, 12–18 in. Leaves chiefly basal, pubescent, narrowly oblong, 1–1$\frac{1}{2}$ in., entire. Flowers purple, in hemispheric, terminal heads $\frac{1}{2}$ in. diam., surrounded with an involucre of short, imbricate, ovate bracts. Receptacle covered with short, soft hairs. Involucel-base adnate to the calyx-tube;

limb scarious, pubescent, funnel-shaped, 16–20-ribbed. Calyx-limb consisting of 5 long, spreading, rough bristles. Corolla pubescent, 5-lobed, that of the outer flowers larger and more unequally lobed than of the inner. Stamens 4. Stigma capitate. Achenes minute, enclosed within the base of the spreading, disk-like involucel and crowned by the persistent calyx-limb.

W. Himalaya, 3000–5000 ft.; May–July.
Allied to the British Small Scabious, *S. Columbaria.*

LII. COMPOSITÆ

Herbs or shrubs. Leaves alternate or opposite, rarely whorled, simple or compound; stipules none. Flowers usually numerous and small, crowded in a simple head on the dilated summit of the stalk or receptacle, surrounded by an involucre of bracts; or in a compound head, having the appearance of a simple head, but composed of a number of small, involucrate or component heads, containing one or about 12 flowers each. Simple heads are of three kinds:—(1) discoid heads, all the flowers tubular and alike, the outer flowers sometimes more slender than the inner; (2) radiate heads, the outer or ray-flowers ligulate, i.e. having the lobes of the corolla united in a strap-shaped ligule and the inner or disk-flowers tubular; (3) ligulate heads, all the flowers ligulate. Involucral bracts in one or several series. Receptacle naked, bristly or bearing scales or floral bracts, one for each flower, the base usually enclosing the ovary. Flowers of a head all 2-sexual; or the outer flowers female or neuter and the inner ones 2-sexual or male; or, rarely, the heads or the whole plant bearing 1-sexual flowers. Calyx-tube adnate to the ovary; limb wanting or appearing as a pappus of hairs, bristles or scales. Corolla tubular or ligulate, inserted on the ovary; limb toothed or lobed. Stamens 5, rarely 4, attached to the corolla-tube; filaments usually free; anthers cohering in a tube sheathing the style, rarely free, 2-celled, base of each cell sometimes tailed or prolonged downwards in a minute bristle. Ovary 1-celled; style linear, usually divided at the top in two stigmatic arms; ovule solitary. Fruit a small, dry, 1-seeded nut or achene, usually crowned with the pappus, sometimes prolonged upwards in a beak.—A very large Order inhabiting all parts of the world; more than a thousand genera have been described.—Name from the Latin *compositus*, compound, referring to the heads.

The flowers of most *Compositæ* are adapted for cross-fertilisation by insects. See Müller's *Fertilisation of Flowers*, pp. 315–364; Kerner's *Natural History of Plants*, ii. 318, &c.; Lubbock's *British Wild Flowers in Relation to Insects*, p. 111.

The naming of a composite plant will be facilitated if attention is paid to the following points :—

1. Whether the heads are simple or compound.
2. Whether the heads are discoid, radiate or ligulate.
3. The character of the pappus or its absence.
4. The colour of the flowers.
5. The character of the achenes.
6. The character of the leaves and involucral bracts.
7. The characters of the receptacle, whether flat or not, whether naked or not, and the nature of the bristles or scales if present.

Abstract of the Key to the Genera

A. Simple heads, subdivided into
  I. Discoid heads; flowers all tubular.
  II. Radiate heads; ray-flowers ligulate, disk-flowers tubular.
  III. Ligulate heads; flowers all ligulate.

B. Compound heads, includes only 3 genera.

A. Simple heads

I. Discoid heads

* Pappus of hairs

Flowers purple or red (white in *Eupatorium*).
  Involucral bracts not spiny. Leaves not prickly.
    Receptacle naked.
      Leaves alternate.
        Involucral bracts in several series, unequal.
          Stems naked . . . . 1. *Vernonia.*
          Stems winged . . . . 14. *Laggera.*
        Involucral bracts in one series, equal . . . 37. *Emilia.*
      Leaves opposite or whorled. Flowers white . . 4. *Eupatorium.*
    Receptacle bristly.
      Pappus feathery . . . . 43. *Saussurea.*
      Pappus minutely barbed . . . . . . 44. *Serratula.*
  Involucral bracts spiny.
    Leaves not prickly or spiny . . . . . . 40. *Arctium.*
    Leaves prickly.
      Stems winged. Pappus not feathery . . . . 41. *Carduus.*
      Stems not winged. Pappus feathery . . . . 42. *Cnicus.*[1]
Flowers yellow (sometimes white in *Cnicus*).
  Involucral bracts spine-tipped.
    Spines short. Pappus feathery . . . . . . 42. *Cnicus.*[2]
    Spines long, needle-like. Pappus not feathery . . 45. *Tricholepis.*
  Involucral bracts not spine-tipped.
    Involucral bracts green.
      Style-arms short.
        Herbs.
          Anther-cells tailed . . . . 13. *Blumea.*
          Anther-cells not tailed . . . . 12. *Conyza.*[3]

[1] *C. arvensis* only. [2] *C. argyracanthus* and *C. Wallichii*, former sometimes has white flowers. [3] Except *C. stricta*, which has minutely radiate heads.

Shrubs . . . . 21. *Inula*.[1]
Style-arms very long, thread-like . . . . . 36. *Gynura*.
Involucral bracts scarious.
Clusters of heads enclosed by leaf-like bracts . 16. *Filago*.
Clusters of heads not enclosed by bracts . . 19. *Gnaphalium*.
Flowers white (see also *Eupatorium* and *Cnicus*).
Woolly herbs. Heads many-flowered.
Heads in a terminal cluster . . . . . . 17. *Leontopodium*.
Heads in corymbs . . . . 18. *Anaphalis*.
Nearly glabrous herbs. Heads 1–4-flowered . . . 47. *Ainsliea*.

* * Pappus of distinct or united scales or of barbed bristles

Pappus of 3–4 short, club-like scales. Flowers white . 2. *Adenostemma*.
Pappus a toothed ring. Flowers pale blue. . . . 3. *Ageratum*.
Pappus of 2 barbed bristles. Flowers yellow . . . 31. *Bidens*.[2]

* * * Pappus none

Leaves pinnately lobed or divided.
Heads globose. Outer flowers white, inner yellow . 6. *Dichrocephala*.
Heads very small, shining, numerous, in large, terminal panicles . . . . 35. *Artemisia*.[3]
Heads in flat corymbs. Flowers yellow. Leaves finely divided . . . . 34. *Tanacetum*.
Heads in small, panicled clusters. Flowers rose-purple. Leaves finely divided . . . . . 7. *Cyathocline*.
Leaves usually lanceolate, never pinnately lobed or divided.
Flowers yellow. Achenes long, ending in a short, glandular beak . . . . 23. *Carpesium*.
Flowers white or pale yellow. Achenes long, club-shaped, covered with stalked glands . . 24. *Adenocaulon*.
Heads 1-sexual. Involucre of female heads covered with hooked bristles . . . . . . 25. *Xanthium*.
Heads conical. Leaves opposite. Flowers white or yellow . . . . 30. *Spilanthes*.
Heads very small, shining, numerous, in terminal panicles. Leaves wedge-shaped . . . . . 35. *Artemisia*.[4]
Flowers orange-red. Involucre and leaves prickly . 46. *Carthamus*.

II. Radiate heads (ligules minute in *Myriactis* and *Conyza*)

* Pappus of hairs

Ray-flowers yellow. Disk-flowers yellow.
Involucral bracts in several series, unequal.
Leaves stalked.
Ligules minute . . . . 12. *Conyza*.[5]
Ligules conspicuous.
Ray-flowers 10–12 in a head . . . . . 5. *Solidago*.
Ray-flowers more than 20 in a head . . . 21. *Inula*.[6]
Leaves sessile. Heads long-stalked . . . . 22. *Vicoa*.
Involucral bracts in one series, equal, a few smaller at the base . . . . 38. *Senecio*.

[1] *I. Cappa* only; the others have radiate heads. [2] *B. tripartita* only; the others have radiate heads. [3] Except *A. parviflora*, which has wedge shaped leaves. [4] *A. parviflora* only; the others have pinnately divided leaves. [5] *C. stricta* only; the others have discoid heads. [6] Except *I. Cappa*, which has discoid heads.

Ray-flowers lilac or purple. Disk-flowers yellow.
- Ray-flowers in 1 or 2 series . . . . . . 10. *Aster.*
- Ray-flowers in more than 2 series . . . 11. *Erigeron.*

Ray-flowers white. Disk-flowers white. Heads solitary 48. *Gerbera.*

* * Pappus of bristles or scales

(sometimes none in *Rhynchospermum* and *Spilanthes*)

Receptacle naked. Pappus of 3–8 bristles, sometimes none. Achenes beaked . . . . 9. *Rhynchospermum.*

Receptacle covered with broad, folded scales each enclosing several flowers. Pappus of 2–5 minute teeth . . . . 27. *Eclipta.*

Receptacle covered with concave scales each partially enclosing a single flower.
- Heads flat, $\frac{1}{3}$–$\frac{1}{2}$ in. diam. . . . . . . 29. *Blainvillea.*
- Heads conical, $\frac{1}{3}$–$\frac{3}{4}$ in. long. Pappus sometimes wanting . . . . 30. *Spilanthes.*

Receptacle covered with narrow, flat scales nearly as long as the flowers. Pappus of 2–3 stiff-barbed bristles . . . . 31. *Bidens.*[1]

Receptacle covered with small, 3-toothed scales. Pappus of several fringed scales . . . . . 32. *Galinsoga.*

* * * Pappus none (see also *Rhynchospermum* and *Spilanthes*)

Leaves ovate, lanceolate or triangular.
- Involucral bracts glandular . . . . . . 26. *Siegesbeckia.*
- Involucral bracts not glandular.
  - Heads hemispheric. Ligules minute. Receptacle naked . . . . 8. *Myriactis.*
  - Heads flat. Ligules broad. Receptacle scaly . 28. *Sclerocarpus.*

Leaves pinnatisect; segments linear . . . . . 33. *Achillea.*

III. Ligulate heads

* Pappus of simple hairs

Achenes beaked.
- Beak of achenes dilated at the tip . . . . 55. *Lactuca.*
- Beak of achenes not dilated at the tip.
  - Heads corymbose. Stems leafy . . . . 51. *Crepis.*[2]
  - Heads solitary. Leaves all radical . . . . 54. *Taraxacum.*

Achenes not beaked.
- Receptacle hairy or bristly.
  - Stems naked. Receptacle covered with long hairs . . . . 52. *Pterotheca.*
  - Stems leafy. Receptacle covered with short bristles . . . . 53. *Hieracium.*
- Receptacle naked.
  - Flowers purple or white . . . . . . 56. *Prenanthes.*
  - Flowers yellow.
    - Juice white, milky.
      - Stem-leaves none or few, small and stalked 51. *Crepis.*[3]
      - Stem-leaves numerous, large, stem-clasping 57. *Sonchus.*
    - Juice yellow. Margins of leaves beset with minute, white teeth . . . . . . 58. *Launæa.*

[1] Except *B. tripartita*, which has discoid heads. [2] Except *C. japonica*, which has achenes without beaks. [3] *C. japonica* only; the others have beaked achenes.

* * Pappus of feathery hairs

Flowers yellow.
  Heads numerous, corymbose. Leaves sinuate-toothed . . 50. *Picris.*
  Heads solitary, terminal. Leaves entire . . . . 59. *Tragopogon.*

* * * Pappus of short, blunt scales

Heads sessile. Flowers blue . . . . 49. *Cichorium.*

B. Compound heads

Component heads, each containing a single flower.
  Heads terminal. Leaves prickly . . . . . 39. *Echinops.*
  Heads axillary. Leaves not prickly . . . . . 20. *Cæsulia.*
Component heads, each containing about 12 flowers . . 15. *Sphæranthus.*

1. VERNONIA. In honour of W. Vernon, botanist and traveller in N. America in the seventeenth century.—Chiefly tropical regions; abundant in America and Africa.

Erect herbs. Leaves alternate. Heads discoid, corymbose. Involucral bracts in several series; receptacle naked; flowers tubular, all similar, purple; pappus long, copious; corolla-tube slender, 5-lobed; style-arms long, acute, hairy all round. Achenes pubescent.

Outer involucral bracts shorter than the inner; tips acute . . . . 1. *V. cinerea.*
Outer involucral bracts longer than the inner; tips dilated . . . . 2. *V. anthelmintica.*

1. **Vernonia cinerea,** *Less.*; *Fl. Br. Ind.* iii. 233. Pubescent; stems 6–12 in., sometimes decumbent at the base, grooved. Leaves nearly sessile, lanceolate or ovate, $\frac{1}{2}$–$1\frac{1}{2}$ in.; teeth few, coarse. Heads numerous, $\frac{1}{4}$ in. diam. Involucral bracts narrowly lanceolate, acute, outer ones smaller than the inner; pappus white. Achenes $\frac{1}{16}$ in., terete.

Simla; August, September.—Throughout India, ascending to 8000 ft.—Tropical Asia, Africa, Australia.

2. **Vernonia anthelmintica,** *Willd.*; *Fl. Br. Ind.* iii. 236. Stems robust, erect, 4–6 ft., glandular-pubescent near the top. Leaves rough, ovate-lanceolate, 3–5 in., coarsely toothed, long-pointed, narrowed into a short stalk. Heads $\frac{1}{2}$–$\frac{3}{4}$ in. diam. Involucral bracts narrowly oblong, tips dilated, outer bracts longer than the inner; pappus tawny; corollas often unequal. Achenes $\frac{1}{5}$ in., ribbed.

Valleys below Simla; August.—Throughout India, ascending to 5000 ft.—Afghanistan.
Usually seen near villages. The seeds are used in native medicine.

2. ADENOSTEMMA. From the Greek *aden*, a gland, and *stemma*, a wreath, referring to the glandular achenes.—All tropical regions.

Adenostemma viscosum, *Forst.*; *Fl. Br. Ind.* iii. 242. An erect herb, 1–3 ft., glandular-pubescent or nearly glabrous. Leaves opposite, lanceolate or ovate, 6 × 3 in., coarsely toothed, narrowed into the stalk; uppermost sessile. Heads discoid, corymbose, ¼ in. diam. Involucral bracts herbaceous, spathulate, in 2 series; flowers tubular, white, all similar; pappus of 3 or 4 short, club-like scales; corolla ⅛ in., dilated upwards, 5-lobed; style-arms long, thick. Achenes ⅛ in., 3- or 4-angled, glandular.

Sutlej valley; August.—Throughout India, ascending to 5000 ft.—All tropical regions.

3. AGERATUM. From the Greek *a*, without, and *geras*, old age; the plants continue in flower for a long time.—America. The following species is naturalised in nearly all tropical regions.

Ageratum conyzoides, *Linn.*; *Fl. Br. Ind.* iii. 243. An erect, softly hairy herb, 1–3 ft. Leaves opposite, stalked, lanceolate or ovate, 3 × 1½ in., crenate. Heads numerous, discoid, ¼ in. diam., in dense, rounded corymbs. Involucral bracts narrow, nearly equal, ribbed, acute, in 2 series; flowers tubular, pale blue or white, all similar; pappus of 3–5 linear, acute, minutely barbed scales, united in a toothed, cup-like ring; corolla-tube dilated upwards, lobes 5, short; style-arms short. Achenes $\frac{1}{16}$ in., angled, black, viscid.

Sutlej valley; May–September.—Throughout India, ascending to 5000 ft.

4. EUPATORIUM. The classical name of some plant of this affinity, probably of *E. cannabinum*.—Most warm and temperate regions.

Tall, erect shrubs. Leaves opposite or whorled. Heads numerous, discoid, in spreading panicles or compact corymbs. Involucral bracts few, unequal; receptacle naked; flowers tubular, pale purple or white, all similar; pappus rigid, rough; corolla-tube dilated upwards, lobes 5, short; style-arms long, threadlike, pubescent all round, blunt. Achenes ⅛ in., angled.

Inner involucral bracts obtuse. Heads panicled . . 1. *E. Reevesii.*
Inner involucral bracts acute. Heads corymbose . . 2. *E. cannabinum.*

1. **Eupatorium Reevesii**, *Wall.*; *Fl. Br. Ind.* iii. 243. Hoary-pubescent; stems 4–5 ft., much branched. Leaves shortly stalked, lanceolate or ovate, 3 × ½ in., coarsely toothed; upper smaller, often entire and alternate. Heads ¼ in. long, in large, spreading

panicles. Outer involucral bracts short, inner obtuse; flowers pale purple.

Valleys below Simla; September, October.—Simla to Bhotan, 2000-6000 ft. —China, Japan.

2. **Eupatorium cannabinum,** *Linn.*; *Fl. Br. Ind.* iii. 243. Pubescent; stems 4–6 ft. Leaves sessile in distant pairs, sometimes whorled, lanceolate, $4 \times 1\frac{1}{2}$ in., coarsely toothed. Heads $\frac{1}{3}$ in. long, in compact, rounded corymbs. Involucral bracts very unequal, outer short, inner acute; flowers nearly white.

Sutlej valley; July, August.—Temperate Himalaya, 3000–11,000 ft.—W. Asia, Europe (Britain, Hemp Agrimony).

5. **SOLIDAGO.** From the Latin *solidare*, to make whole or sound; referring to the reputed healing properties of some species. —N. temperate regions; abundant in America.

Solidago Virga-aurea, *Linn.*; *Fl. Br. Ind.* iii. 245. An erect, pubescent herb; stems 6–24 in., rarely branched. Leaves alternate, lanceolate; lower 4–5 in., stalked, toothed; upper smaller, sessile, entire. Heads radiate, $\frac{3}{8}$ in. long, numerous, crowded in a long, leafy, terminal panicle. Involucral bracts unequal, narrow, acute; receptacle naked; flowers yellow; pappus long, rough; ray-flowers not more than 10 or 12; corolla of inner flowers 5-lobed; style-arms of inner flowers flattened, acute. Achenes ribbed.

Simla, common; June–September.—Temperate Himalaya, 5000–9000 ft.—Temperate Asia, America, Europe (Britain, Golden Rod).

6. **DICHROCEPHALA.** From the Greek *dichros*, two-coloured, and *cephale*, a head.—Asia, Africa, Polynesia.

Pubescent or roughly hairy herbs; stems 6–24 in., usually erect, sometimes diffuse. Leaves alternate, more or less pinnatifid. Heads discoid, globose, $\frac{1}{6}$–$\frac{1}{4}$ in. diam. Involucral bracts few; receptacle elevated, flat; flowers minute; corolla of the outer series white, very slender, 2- or 3-toothed, of the inner yellow, 4- or 5-lobed; pappus none or in the outer flowers of 2 minute bristles. Achenes smooth, flat.

Leaves stalked. Heads $\frac{1}{6}$ in. diam. . . . . . 1. *D. latifolia.*
Leaves sessile. Heads $\frac{1}{4}$ in. diam. . . . . . 2. *D. chrysanthemifolia.*

1. **Dichrocephala latifolia,** *DC.*; *Fl. Br. Ind.* iii. 245. Stems sometimes diffuse and branching from the base. Leaves $1\frac{1}{2}$–4 in., stalked; lobes irregularly and coarsely toothed, end lobe often broadly ovate. Heads $\frac{1}{6}$ in. diam., on slender stalks, panicled.

Simla, common; June-September.—Simla to Sikkim, 1000-9000 ft.—Hilly districts in S. India.—Tropical and subtropical Asia and Africa.

2. **Dichrocephala chrysanthemifolia,** *DC.*; *Fl. Br. Ind.* iii. 245. Stems erect. Leaves 1–2½ in., sessile, stem-clasping; lobes toothed or entire, end lobe broad or narrow, lateral lobes usually acute. Heads ¼ in. diam., usually solitary; stalks thick, diverging. Corollas turning a uniform dull purple when in fruit. (Fig. 75.)

Simla; July–October.—W. Himalaya, 6000–7000 ft.—Nilghiris, tropical Asia and Africa.

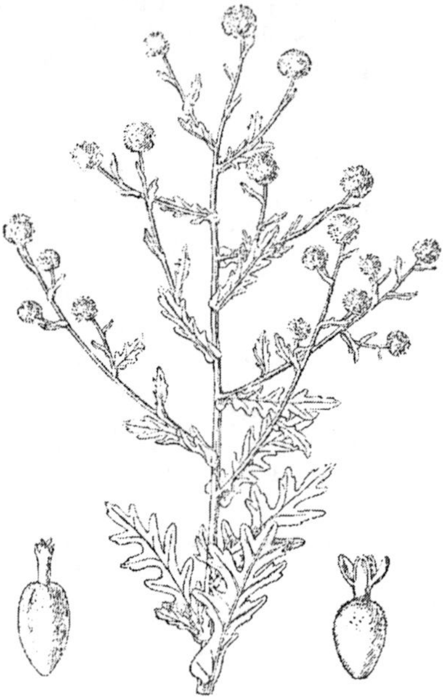

Fig. 75. Dichrocephala chrysanthemifolia.

7. CYATHOCLINE. From the Greek *cyathos*, a cup, and *cline*, a bed; referring to the cup-shaped receptacle.—India.

Cyathocline lyrata, *Cass.*; *Fl. Br. Ind.* iii. 246. An erect, pubescent, sweet-scented herb, 10–24 in. Leaves alternate, sessile, 1–5 in., pinnatisect; lobes narrow, sharply toothed. Heads discoid, hemispheric, ⅙ in. diam., in small, rounded, panicled clusters. Involucral bracts rather broad, acute; receptacle elevated, cup-shaped; pappus none; corollas rose-purple, those of the outer flowers very slender, 2-toothed, of the inner larger, 5-lobed. Achenes minute, smooth.

Sutlej valley, borders of ricefields, &c.; March–May.—Throughout India, ascending to 5000 ft.—Burmah.

8. MYRIACTIS. From the Greek *murios*, a thousand or many, and *actis*, a ray; referring to the numerous, diverging heads.—Asia, Africa.

Myriactis Wallichii, *Less.*; *Fl. Br. Ind.* iii. 247, including *M. nepalensis*, Less. An erect, much branched, pubescent or roughly hairy herb, 1–3 ft. Leaves alternate, ovate or lanceolate, 1–4 in.; teeth coarse and irregular, contiguous or distant; stalks winged. Heads minutely radiate, hemispheric, varying from $\frac{1}{8}$–$\frac{1}{2}$ in. diam., paniculate on diverging stalks. Involucral bracts 3–4-seriate; receptacle convex, naked; ray-flowers white; disk-flowers yellow, turning dull purple in fruit; pappus none; ligules entire; corollas of disk-flowers 4–5-lobed. Achenes flat, smooth.

Simla, common; June–September.—Temperate Himalaya, 4000–10,000 ft. —Central Asia.

9. RHYNCHOSPERMUM. From the Greek *rhynchos*, a beak, and *sperma*, a seed; referring to the achenes.—E. Asia.

Rhynchospermum verticillatum, *Reinw.*; *Fl. Br. Ind.* iii. 248. A pubescent herb, 2–3 ft.; branches slender, spreading. Leaves alternate, shortly stalked, lanceolate, 1–3 in., entire or faintly toothed, long-pointed. Heads radiate, hemispheric, $\frac{1}{5}$ in. diam., on short, thick stalks, often one in every axil along the branches. Involucral bracts in few series, lanceolate, margins scarious; receptacle flat, naked; flowers all white or those of the disk pale yellow; pappus of 3–8 bristles or none; ligules entire or notched; corollas of disk-flowers 4–5-lobed. Achenes flat, beaked.

Valleys below Simla; July–October.—Temperate Himalaya, 5000–6000 ft. —E. Asia.

10. ASTER. The classical name for some composite plant, derived from the Greek *aster*, a star; referring to the radiate heads. —Most temperate and cold regions; abundant in N. America.

Erect, branched herbs. Leaves alternate. Heads radiate, large. Involucral bracts in few series; receptacle flat or slightly convex, naked; ray-flowers in one or two series, lilac or purple; ligules long, entire or minutely toothed; disk-flowers yellow, tubular, 5-toothed; pappus copious, rough. Achenes flattened.

Stems straight. Heads $\frac{1}{2}$–$\frac{3}{4}$ in. diam. . . . . . 1. *A. molliusculus.*
Stems zigzag. Heads $1\frac{1}{2}$–2 in. diam.
  Leaves nearly sessile . . . . 2. *A. Thomsoni.*
  Leaves on winged stalks . . . . 3. *A. asperulus.*

1. **Aster molliusculus,** *Wall.*; *Fl. Br. Ind.* iii. 251. Pubescent or hairy; stems usually tufted, 12–24 in., slender, leafy, often

tinged with red. Leaves narrowly lanceolate, 1 in., entire or obscurely toothed. Heads long-stalked, $\frac{1}{2}$–$\frac{3}{4}$ in. diam.; ray-flowers lilac; ligules short, often recurved; outer hairs of the pappus much shorter than the inner. Achenes hairy. (Fig. 76.)

Simla, on dry banks, common; May–September.—W. Himalaya, 5000–8000 ft.—Tibet.

FIG. 76. ASTER MOLLIUSCULUS.

2. **Aster Thomsoni,** *C. B. Clarke*; *Fl. Br. Ind.* iii. 252. Hairy; stems 1–3 ft., bending at the joints. Leaves nearly sessile, ovate, 2–4 × 1–2$\frac{1}{2}$ in., coarsely and sharply toothed, long-pointed. Heads 1$\frac{1}{2}$–2 in. diam. Involucral bracts herbaceous; ray-flowers purple; ligules long, spreading; pappus of disk-flowers short. Achenes pubescent.

Simla, common in woods; July–September.—Temperate Himalaya, 7000–10,000 ft.

A form with leaves about 1$\frac{1}{2}$ × $\frac{3}{4}$ in. and smaller flowers occurs at Mahasu.

3. **Aster asperulus,** *Nees*; *Fl. Br. Ind.* iii. 252. Similar in aspect to *A. Thomsoni*, but the stem is nearly glabrous, the leaves have winged stalks, and the pappus is as long as the corollas.

Simla; July–October.—W. Himalaya, 4000–9000 ft.

11. ERIGERON. The classical name of a plant allied to the Groundsel, *Senecio vulgaris*, derived from the Greek *eri*, early, and *geron*, an old man; some species are covered with hoary down when young.—N. temperate regions.

Erect herbs. Leaves alternate. Heads radiate, small or large. Involucral bracts in few series; receptacle flat or slightly convex, naked; ray-flowers in more than two series, lilac or purple; ligules short or long, entire or minutely toothed; disk-flowers yellow, tubular, 5-toothed; pappus copious or scanty, rough. Achenes flattened.

Heads not more than ½ in. diam. Ligules slightly exceeding the pappus.
  Heads ¼ in. diam. Leaves crowded, linear, 1½–4 in. long . . . . 1. *E. linifolius.*
  Heads ½ in. diam. Leaves distant, lanceolate or obovate, 1–2½ in. long . . . . 2. *E. multicaulis.*
Heads 1–2 in. diam. Ligules far exceeding the pappus . 3. *E. multiradiatus.*

1. **Erigeron linifolius,** *Willd.*; *Fl. Br. Ind.* iii. 254. More or less hairy; stems 1–3 ft., often much branched. Leaves crowded, all sessile, linear, 1½–4 in. and entire, or sometimes the lower ones stalked, ½ in. broad and coarsely toothed. Heads numerous, about ¼ in. diam., on slender stalks, forming a leafy, corymbose panicle. Ray-flowers pale purple or white; ligules slightly exceeding the pappus.

Simla, roadsides; May–August.—A garden escape.

2. **Erigeron multicaulis,** *DC.*; *Fl. Br. Ind.* iii. 255, *under E. alpinus.* More or less hairy or pubescent; stems 6–24 in., often tufted. Radical leaves stalked, oblong, spreading. Stem-leaves lanceolate, narrowed to a sessile base, 1–2½ × ⅕–⅓ in., or obovate, about 2 × ¾ in., entire or obscurely toothed, acute or obtuse. Heads solitary, long-stalked, about ½ in. diam., in terminal, corymbose panicles. Involucral bracts linear, outer shorter, inner long-pointed; ray-flowers pale purple; ligules slightly exceeding the pappus. Achenes hairy.

Simla, common; May–October.—Temperate Himalaya, 3000–10,000 ft.
The two extreme forms of this species, (*a*) with narrowly lanceolate, almost linear leaves, and (*b*) with broadly obovate leaves, look very different; the latter might for convenience be distinguished as var. *obovatus*; but the two are connected by intermediates.

3. **Erigeron multiradiatus,** *Benth.*; *Fl. Br. Ind.* iii. 256. Hairy; stems 8–24 in. Leaves sessile, ovate-lanceolate, 1½ × ¾ in.,

entire or coarsely toothed, acute. Heads long-stalked, solitary or corymbose, 1–2 in. diam. Involucral bracts narrow, acute; pappus scanty; ray-flowers dark purple; ligules spreading, far exceeding the pappus.

Huttoo, abundant; August, September.—Temperate Himalaya, 7000–12,000 ft.

12. CONYZA. A classical plant-name, applied to both *Inula viscosa* and *Pulicaria vulgaris*; origin obscure.—Chiefly tropical regions.

Erect herbs. Leaves alternate. Heads discoid, in *C. stricta* minutely radiate, corymbose. Involucral bracts many, narrow, outer smaller; receptacle flat or convex, usually naked; flowers pale yellow; pappus in one series; corolla of outer flowers slender, 2–3-toothed, minutely radiate in *C. stricta*, of the inner larger, 5-lobed; anther-bases obtuse, not tailed. Achenes minute, flattened, pubescent.

Heads discoid, $\frac{1}{3}$ in. diam.
Softly hairy. Stems 6–15 in. Heads few, in close corymbs . . . . 1. *C. japonica.*
Pubescent and glandular. Stems 2–4 ft. Heads numerous, in spreading corymbs . . . . . 2. *C. viscidula.*
Heads minutely radiate, very numerous, $\frac{1}{6}$ in. diam., in large corymbs . . . . 3. *C. stricta.*

1. **Conyza japonica,** *Less.*; *Fl. Br. Ind.* iii. 258. Softly hairy; stems 6–15 in., often tufted, simple or branched. Leaves sessile, often crowded, obovate-spathulate, oblong or lanceolate, 1–3 in., coarsely toothed, base of upper leaves sometimes dilated. Heads globose, $\frac{1}{3}$ in. diam., in terminal, close corymbs. Involucral bracts acute. Variable in shape and cutting of leaves and in hairiness.

Simla, common; April–September.—Simla to Burmah, 1000–7000 ft.—China, Japan.

2. **Conyza viscidula,** *Wall.*; *Fl. Br. Ind.* iii. 258. Pubescent and glandular; stems 2–4 ft., leafy, much branched. Leaves lanceolate, 2–4 in., narrowed to both ends, entire or toothed. Heads numerous, $\frac{1}{3}$ in. diam., in large, spreading corymbs.

Waterworks Road, Mushobra; September.—Simla to Burmah, 1000–7000 ft.—E. Asia, Australia.

3. **Conyza stricta,** *Willd.*; *Fl. Br. Ind.* iii. 258. Hoary-pubescent or rough; stems 1–2$\frac{1}{2}$ ft., leafy, much branched. Leaves pinnately lobed and toothed or linear and entire, 1–2 in.; upper ones smaller. Heads very numerous, minutely radiate, $\frac{1}{6}$ in. diam.,

on slender stalks forming large, terminal and axillary corymbs. Ligules very short, notched; corolla of inner flowers 5-lobed.

Simla, common; August, September.—Temperate Himalaya, 1000–6000 ft. —S. India, Burmah.—E. Africa.

13. BLUMEA. In honour of Dr. C. L. Blume, a Dutch botanist of the nineteenth century.—Tropical regions of Asia, Africa, and Australia.

Blumea Wightiana, *DC.*; *Fl. Br. Ind.* iii. 261. An erect herb densely covered with soft, often glandular hairs; stems 10–24 in., simple or branched. Leaves alternate, toothed; lower ovate, $1\frac{1}{2}$–$2 \times \frac{3}{4}$–1 in., stalked or nearly sessile; upper lanceolate or linear, smaller, sessile. Heads discoid, $\frac{1}{4}$ in. diam. or rather less, crowded in stalked, terminal or axillary cymes. Outer involucral bracts few, short, inner many, narrow, acute, slightly exceeding the flowers; receptacle flat, naked; flowers pale yellow, often a few purple ones in the centre; pappus scanty; corollas of outer flowers very slender, minutely 2–3-toothed, of inner larger, 4–5-lobed; anther-cells tailed; style-arms short. Achenes minute, angled, slightly pubescent.

Valleys below Simla; April–June.—Throughout India, ascending to 4000 ft. —Tropical Asia, Africa, Australia.

14. LAGGERA. In honour of Dr. Lagger, a Swiss botanist of the nineteenth century.—Tropical regions of Asia and Africa.

Laggera alata, *Schultz-Bip.*; *Fl. Br. Ind.* iii. 271. An erect, glandular-pubescent herb; stems robust, 2–4 ft., leafy, winged with the decurrent leaf-bases. Leaves alternate, oblong, 4×1 in., acute; teeth numerous, small, sharp. Heads many, discoid, $\frac{1}{2}$ in. diam., in axillary racemes often forming a large, terminal, leafy panicle. Involucral bracts many, narrow, rigid, acute, the outer shorter, the inner equalling the flowers; receptacle flat, naked; pappus white; flowers purple; corollas of the outer very slender, minutely toothed, of the inner larger, 5-lobed; style pubescent. Achenes small, hairy.

Sutlej and Giri valleys; September, October.—Hilly districts throughout India, 1000–6000 ft.—Tropical Asia and Africa.

L. flava, *Benth.*, is common in the plains and may occur in the hills below 3000 ft.; it differs from *L. alata* in its slender, naked, glabrous stem and yellow flowers.

15. SPHÆRANTHUS. From the Greek *sphaira*, a globe, and *anthos*, a flower, referring to the shape of the inflorescence.—Tropical regions of the Old World.

***Sphæranthus indicus,** *Linn.*; *Fl. Br. Ind.* iii. 275. A nearly erect, softly hairy, shrub-like herb; stems 6–18 in.; branches long, spreading, winged with the decurrent leaf-bases. Leaves alternate, sessile, obovate-oblong, $\frac{1}{2}$–$1\frac{1}{2}$ in., narrowed to the base, toothed. Heads compound, globose, about $\frac{1}{3}$ in. diam., solitary, terminal; component heads numerous, very small, crowded, each containing about 12 pink or purple flowers. Involucral bracts nearly as long as the flowers, linear, hairy at the tip; receptacle naked; pappus none; outer flowers 10–12, female, corolla-tube dilated in the middle, 4- or 5-toothed; innermost flowers 2 or 3, 2-sexual, corolla-tube slender, straight, 2–3-toothed. Achenes minute.

Throughout India, common on dry ricefields, ascending to 5000 ft.; December–March.—Tropical regions of the Old World.

16. FILAGO. From the Latin *filum*, a thread; referring to the cottony leaves and stems.—Temperate regions of the Old World.

Filago germanica, *Linn.*; *Fl. Br. Ind.* iii. 277. A nearly erect or prostrate, cottony herb; stems 1–6 in., branched from the base. Leaves alternate, obovate-oblong, $\frac{1}{2}$ in., stalked or sessile. Heads numerous, discoid, $\frac{1}{8}$ in. long, crowded in sessile clusters in the forks of the branches, the clusters enclosed by leaf-like bracts. Involucral bracts pale yellow, scarious, shining, acute; pappus rough; corollas of the outer flowers very slender, of the inner larger but scarcely dilated at the top, 4–5-toothed. Achenes minute, rough.

Suni, in the Sutlej valley, on dry, rocky ground; April–June.—N. India, ascending to 3000 ft.—W. Asia, Europe (Britain, Cudweed).

17. LEONTOPODIUM. From the Greek *leon*, a lion, and *pous, podos*, a foot; referring to the clustered heads.—Mountains of Europe and Asia.

Leontopodium alpinum, *Cass.*; *Fl. Br. Ind.* iii. 279. A perennial, woolly herb; flowering-stems tufted, 2–6 in., slender, leafy, erect or nearly so. Leaves sessile, $\frac{1}{2}$–1 in., entire; basal spathulate, rosulate; stem-leaves linear, alternate. Heads discoid, 1-sexual, $\frac{1}{4}$ in. long, 3–5, sessile in a terminal cluster with a few spreading, densely woolly, leaf-like bracts at its base. Involucral bracts in many series, scarious, oblong-lanceolate, purple-tipped, the outer ones woolly; receptacle convex, naked, pitted; pappus in one series, longer than the corolla, minutely barbed; corollas white, tubular, of two kinds, those of the female flowers linear, minutely 5-toothed, those of the male flowers dilated in the upper half, deeply 5-toothed. Perfect achenes ovoid, rough; those of the male flowers linear, smooth.

Theog, in pastures, Narkunda; May, June.—Alpine Himalaya, 9000–18,000 ft.—Central Asia, Europe (the Edel-Weiss of the Alps).

18. ANAPHALIS. An alteration of the Greek *gnaphalion*, a lock of wool.—Asia, chiefly in temperate and mountainous regions.

Herbs, more or less densely covered with woolly or cottony tomentum; stems erect, leafy. Leaves alternate, entire, stem-clasping, often lobed at the base. Heads discoid, small, clustered in terminal or axillary corymbs. Involucral bracts in many series, scarious, shining, the outermost short and woolly, the inner longer; receptacle naked; flowers numerous, white or pale yellow; pappus free; corolla of the outer flowers very slender, 2–4-toothed, of the inner slightly larger, 5-lobed. Achenes minute, oblong, glabrous.

Involucral bracts acute, spreading in flower.
  Leaves narrowly lanceolate, $\frac{1}{2}$–1 in. Heads 2–7 in a corymb . . . . 1. *A. nubigena.*
  Leaves broadly ovate, 2–4 in. Numerous heads in a corymb . . . . 2. *A. triplinervis.*
Involucral bracts obtuse, erect in flower.
  Leaves lanceolate.
    Leaves thin; lower surface cinnamon-red or grey . 3. *A. cinnamomea.*
    Leaves thick; lower surface white . . . . . 4. *A. adnata.*
  Leaves linear.
    Leaves $1\frac{1}{2}$–2 in.; basal lobes long, decurrent . . 5. *A. araneosa.*
    Leaves $\frac{1}{2}$–1 in.; basal lobes short . . . . . 6. *A. contorta.*

1. **Anaphalis nubigena,** *DC.*; *Fl. Br. Ind.* iii. 279 *under* var. *intermedia.* Stems tufted, slender, 6–12 in., unbranched. Leaves usually few and scattered, sometimes crowded towards the base of the stem, narrowly lanceolate or spathulate, $\frac{1}{2}$–1 in., tipped with a small, black, naked point. Heads 2–7, $\frac{1}{2}$ in. diam., in a terminal corymb. Involucral bracts acute, spreading in flower.

Theog, Huttoo; July, August.—Alpine Himalaya, 9000–16,000 ft.

*2. **Anaphalis triplinervis,** *C. B. Clarke*; *Fl. Br. Ind.* iii. 281. Stems robust, 1–2 ft., usually unbranched, often flexuous. Leaves 3–5-nerved, broadly ovate, 2–4 × 1–2 in., acute or obtuse, tipped with a small, black, naked point. Heads $\frac{1}{2}$ in. diam., numerous, in terminal corymbs. Involucral bracts acute, spreading in flower.

Temperate Himalaya, 6000–10,000 ft.; July, August.—Abundant on the Jalowri Pass.

3. **Anaphalis cinnamomea,** *C. B. Clarke*; *Fl. Br. Ind.* iii. 281. Stems 1–2 ft. Leaves 1–3-nerved, narrowly lanceolate, 2–5 × $\frac{1}{2}$–$\frac{3}{4}$ in., acute, usually shortly lobed at the base; upper surface dark green, lower cinnamon-red or grey-tomentose. Heads $\frac{1}{3}$ in. diam., numerous, in terminal, compound corymbs. Involucral bracts broad, obtuse, erect in flower, spreading in fruit. (Fig. 77.)

Simla, Shali; September.—Temperate Himalaya, 5000–9000 ft.—E. Asia.

4. **Anaphalis adnata,** *DC.*; *Fl. Br. Ind.* iii. 282. Stems robust, 2–4 ft. Leaves thick, broadly lanceolate or oblong, often spathulate, $3 \times \frac{3}{4}$ in., acute; basal lobes, if present, short. Heads $\frac{1}{4}$ in. diam., numerous, in dense, rounded, terminal and axillary corymbs. Involucral bracts broad, obtuse, erect in flower, spreading in fruit, outer ones usually pale yellow.

Simla, Shali; September.—Simla to Bhotan, 6000–8000 ft.—Burmah.

FIG. 77. ANAPHALIS CINNAMOMEA.

5. **Anaphalis araneosa,** *DC.*; *Fl. Br. Ind.* iii. 283. Stems 1–3 ft., more or less winged by the decurrent leaf-bases. Radical leaves oblanceolate. Stem-leaves linear, $1\frac{1}{2}–2 \times \frac{1}{8}–\frac{1}{4}$ in., acute, margins often recurved, basal lobes usually long, acute and decurrent. Heads $\frac{1}{6}$ in. diam., very numerous, forming a broad, terminal corymb 3–6 in. across. Involucral bracts broad, obtuse, erect in flower, spreading in fruit.

Simla, common; September.—Temperate Himalaya, 5000–8000 ft.

6. **Anaphalis contorta,** *Hook. f.*; *Fl. Br. Ind.* iii. 284. Stems 6–18 in., usually branched from the base; branches often decum-

bent. Leaves usually crowded, linear, $\frac{1}{2}$–1 × $\frac{1}{8}$ in., acute or obtuse, shortly lobed at the base, margins sometimes recurved. Heads $\frac{1}{6}$ in. diam., in dense, terminal corymbs. Involucral bracts broad, obtuse, erect in flower, spreading in fruit, outer ones often pale purple.

Simla, common; August, September. — Temperate Himalaya, 7000–10,000 ft.

19. GNAPHALIUM. The Greek name of a woolly plant, probably *G. germanicum*, the Cudweed of Britain; derived from *gnaphalion*, a lock of wool.—Temperate and subtropical regions.

Erect, more or less softly woolly herbs. Leaves alternate, entire. Heads discoid, numerous, $\frac{1}{8}$ in. diam., in irregularly globose clusters at the end of corymbose branches. Involucral bracts many, erect, scarious, shining, inner as long as the flowers, outer shorter; receptacle flat, naked; flowers bright yellow; pappus scanty, hairs free at the base; corolla of the outer flowers slender, 3–4-toothed, of the inner larger, 5-toothed. Achenes oblong, slender, rough.

Leaves spathulate; both surfaces woolly . . . . 1. *G. luteo-album.*
Leaves linear; upper surface green, glabrous, lower woolly 2. *G. hypoleucum.*

1. **Gnaphalium luteo-album,** *Linn.*; *Fl. Br. Ind.* iii. 288, *under* var. *multiceps*. Stems often tufted, 6–18 in., simple or branched. Leaves crowded or distant, sessile, basal lobes sometimes decurrent, spathulate, 1–3 × $\frac{1}{4}$–$\frac{1}{3}$ in., both surfaces woolly; uppermost leaves lanceolate, acute.

Simla, common; June–August.—Throughout India, ascending to 10,000 ft.—Most warm and temperate regions (Britain, Jersey Cudweed).

Var. 2, *pallidum*, differs only in the heads being pale brown instead of bright yellow; it is common in the plains and may occur in the Sutlej valley.—In the British form of this species the heads are pale yellow.

2. **Gnaphalium hypoleucum,** *DC.*; *Fl. Br. Ind.* iii. 288. Stems robust, 12–24 in., pubescent near the base, woolly on the upper parts, usually much branched. Leaves sessile, linear, 1$\frac{1}{2}$–2$\frac{1}{2}$ × $\frac{1}{8}$ in., long pointed; upper surface green and rough, lower white and woolly; basal lobes blunt.

Simla, common; September, October.—Temperate Himalaya, 3000–7000 ft.—Nilghiris.—E. Asia, N. Africa.

20. CÆSULIA. From the Latin *cæsullæ*, having blue eyes; referring to the flowers.—India.

Cæsulia axillaris, *Roxb.*; *Fl. Br. Ind.* iii. 291. A glabrous, erect herb, 6–12 in. Leaves alternate, sessile, dilated at the base, narrowly lanceolate, 2–4 × $\frac{1}{4}$–$\frac{1}{2}$ in., long-pointed; teeth small, rather far apart. Heads compound, axillary, sessile, globose, $\frac{1}{2}$–$\frac{3}{4}$ in. diam., involucrate; component heads numerous, crowded on a flat receptacle, each containing a single, blue-purple or white flower. Involucral bracts 2, opposite, embracing the flower, keeled and winged at the back, tips erect, free, acute; pappus none; corolla tubular, 5-lobed. Achenes flattened, margined, enclosed within and adnate to the involucral bracts.

Sutlej valley, common in ricefields and marshy ground; July–October.—N. India, ascending to 3000 ft.

21. INULA. The classical name of the Elecampane, *I. Helenium.*—Asia, Africa, Europe.

Shrubs. Leaves alternate, toothed. Heads large and solitary, or small and in corymbs, radiate except *I. Cappa.* Involucral bracts unequal, narrow, rigid, leaf-like in *I. grandiflora*; receptacle naked; flowers yellow; ray-flowers more than 20; pappus scanty, rough; corolla of outer flowers ligulate, except *I. Cappa,* of inner tubular, 5-toothed. Achenes small, cylindric, silky.

Heads radiate.
  Heads 2–2$\frac{1}{2}$ in. diam. Ligules narrow. $\frac{3}{4}$–1 in. long . 1. *I. grandiflora.*
  Heads $\frac{1}{3}$ in. diam. Ligules broad, short . . . . 3. *I. cuspidata.*
Heads discoid, $\frac{1}{3}$ in. diam., sometimes with a few very short ligules . . . . 2. *I. Cappa.*

1. **Inula grandiflora,** *Willd.*; *Fl. Br. Ind.* iii. 294. Bristly hairy; stems leafy, 12–18 in., simple or branched. Leaves sessile, dilated at the base, lanceolate, 2–3 × $\frac{3}{4}$ in., glandular-toothed, fringed with long hairs. Heads 2–2$\frac{1}{2}$ in. diam., solitary. Involucral bracts toothed, outer ones long, leaf-like, inner shorter, narrow; ligules narrow, $\frac{3}{4}$–1 in. long, 3-toothed.

Matiana; September.—Temperate Himalaya, 8000–12,000 ft.—W. Asia. Abundant on the Jalowri Pass.

2. **Inula Cappa,** *DC.*; *Fl. Br. Ind.* iii. 295. Aromatic; stems robust, 4–8 ft.; branches and inflorescence tomentose. Leaves thick, shortly stalked, oblong-lanceolate, 3–6 × $\frac{3}{4}$–1$\frac{1}{2}$ in.; upper surface hairy, lower softly and densely silky; teeth close-set, short. Heads very many, $\frac{1}{3}$ in. diam., in numerous, crowded, rounded corymbs, not radiate or with few and very short ligules. Involucral bracts linear, rigid, acute, inner ones as long as the flowers, outer gradually shorter.

Valleys below Simla; September, October.—Simla to Bhotan, 4000–6000 ft. —E. Asia.

3. **Inula cuspidata,** *C. B. Clarke*; *Fl. Br. Ind.* iii. 296. Stems 4–8 ft.; branches slender, nearly glabrous. Leaves thin, stalked, ovate-lanceolate, 5 × 2 in., long-pointed; upper surface rough,

lower thinly pubescent; teeth numerous, small, sharp. Heads many, radiate, $\frac{1}{3}$ in. diam., on slender stalks crowded in broad, terminal corymbs. Involucral bracts linear, rigid, acute, inner ones as long as the flowers, outer shorter; ligules short, broad, 2- or 3-toothed. (Fig. 78.)

Simla, common; September, October.—W. Himalaya, 4000–7000 ft.

FIG. 78. INULA CUSPIDATA.

22. VICOA. In honour of G. B. Vico, an Italian scientific author of the end of the seventeenth and beginning of the eighteenth centuries.—Asia, Africa.

Rough or softly hairy, erect herbs; stems leafy, branched. Leaves alternate, stem-clasping, lobed at the base. Heads radiate, long-stalked. Involucral bracts many, inner ones as long as the disk-flowers, outer shorter; receptacle flat, naked; flowers yellow; pappus scanty; ligules 1- or 2-toothed; corolla of disk-flowers 5-lobed. Achenes small, cylindric, silky-pubescent.

Roughly pubescent. Flowers orange-yellow. Ligules short, broad, recurved . . . . 1. *V. auriculata*
Densely and softly hairy. Flowers bright yellow. Ligules long, narrow, spreading . . . . 2. *V. vestita.*

1. **Vicoa auriculata,** *Cass.*; *Fl. Br. Ind.* iii. 297. Roughly pubescent; stems rigid, slender, 1–3 ft., usually red. Leaves narrowly lanceolate, $2 \times \frac{1}{5}$ in., toothed or entire, acute; basal lobes blunt. Heads orange-yellow, $\frac{1}{4}$–$\frac{1}{2}$ in. diam. Involucral bracts narrow, acute, tips erect or recurved; ligules short, broad, recurved.

Simla; September, October.—Throughout India, ascending to 6000 ft.

2. **Vicoa vestita,** *Benth.*; *Fl. Br. Ind.* iii. 297. Densely and softly hairy; stems 10–18 in. Leaves thin, oblong-lanceolate, $1\text{–}2 \times \frac{1}{2}\text{–}1$ in., toothed; basal lobes short, obtuse. Heads bright yellow, $\frac{3}{4}$–1 in. diam. Involucral bracts long, linear, fringed, tips recurved; ligules long, narrow, spreading.

Sutlej valley, in cornfields; April.—Throughout India, ascending to 4000 ft. —Afghanistan.

23. CARPESIUM.

23. CARPESIUM. From *carpesion*, the Greek name of some aromatic plant.—Asia, Europe.

Erect, branched herbs. Leaves alternate, lanceolate. Heads discoid. Involucral bracts many, outer ones green, more or less leaf-like, inner much shorter, dry, broad, oblong, obtuse; receptacle flat, naked; flowers yellow; pappus none; corolla of outer flowers 3-toothed, of the inner slightly larger, 5-toothed. Achenes long, smooth, ribbed, tip shortly beaked, glandular.

Heads $\frac{1}{2}$–1 in. diam., solitary, terminal, nodding . . 1. *C. cernuum.*
Heads not more than $\frac{1}{4}$ in. diam.
  Heads few, solitary or in small clusters at the end of long, axillary stalks. Leaves broadly lanceolate 2. *C. trachelifolium.*
  Heads numerous, axillary, nearly sessile or in axillary racemes. Leaves narrowly lanceolate . 3. *C. abrotanoides.*

1. **Carpesium cernuum,** *Linn.*; *Fl. Br. Ind.* iii. 300. Pubescent or shortly hairy; stems 1–3 ft. Leaves lanceolate, $2\text{–}5 \times \frac{3}{4}\text{–}1\frac{1}{2}$ in., toothed, acute; lower ones narrowed into a short, winged stalk, upper sessile. Heads $\frac{1}{2}$–1 in. diam., terminal, solitary, nodding; several of the outer involucral bracts large, leaf-like.

Simla, common in woods; August–October.—Temperate Himalaya, 6000–8000 ft.—Asia, Europe.

The Simla plant is *cernuum proprium* of the *Fl. Br. Ind.* Var. *pedunculosum* occurs at Mahasu; it is distinguished by its large, ovate leaves all with winged stalks, and the long, stiff, leafless stalks of the heads.

2. **Carpesium trachelifolium,** *Less.*; *Fl. Br. Ind.* iii. 301. More or less covered with long, soft hairs; stems 10–18 in. Lower leaves long-stalked, broadly lanceolate, $3 \times 1\frac{1}{2}$ in., cordate, sinuate-toothed; upper smaller, sessile, nearly entire. Heads few, not more than $\frac{1}{4}$ in. diam., solitary or in small clusters at the end of long, axillary stalks.

Valleys below Simla; August.—Temperate Himalaya, 4000–6000 ft.

3. **Carpesium abrotanoides,** *Linn.*; *Fl. Br. Ind.* iii. 301. Pubescent or nearly glabrous; stems 2–4 ft.; branches long, slender, leafy. Leaves sessile, lanceolate, 4–8 × $\frac{1}{2}$–$1\frac{1}{4}$ in., narrowed to both ends, entire. Heads numerous, inserted along the whole length of the branches, not more than $\frac{1}{4}$ in. diam., axillary, sessile or shortly stalked or crowded in short, erect, axillary racemes.

Valleys below Simla, not common; August, September.—Temperate Himalaya, 4000–6000 ft.—Asia, Europe.

The flowers, which have a powerful odour, are used in Kashmir to dye silk.

24. **ADENOCAULON.** From the Greek *aden*, a gland, and *caulos*, a stem or stalk.—Himalaya, Japan, N. America.

Adenocaulon bicolor, *Hook. f.*; *Fl. Br. Ind.* iii. 302. An erect herb, 1–3 ft.; stems and branches covered with grey, cottony hairs. Leaves alternate, thin, orbicular, 2–4 in. across, cordate, sinuately angled and toothed, upper surface glabrous, lower white-tomentose: lower leaves on long, more or less winged stalks; upper smaller, sessile. Heads discoid, $\frac{1}{4}$ in. diam., in a loose panicle; branches slender, viscidly glandular towards the end. Involucral bracts 5, green, spreading, reflexed in fruit; receptacle flat, naked; flowers about 10, white or pale yellow, outer ones only fertile; pappus none; corolla 4- or 5-lobed. Achenes long, club-shaped, covered with stalked glands.

Narkunda, in forest; August.—Simla to Sikkim, 6000–9000 ft.—W. Asia, N.W. America.

25. **XANTHIUM.** From *Xanthion*, the Greek name of *Xanthium Strumarium*, derived from *xanthos*, yellow; the ancients extracted a dye from the plant.—Native country uncertain; now widely dispersed throughout tropical and temperate regions. A casual weed in S. England.

Xanthium Strumarium, *Linn.*; *Fl. Br. Ind.* iii. 303. An erect, coarse herb, $1\frac{1}{2}$–3 ft., sometimes more. Leaves alternate, rough, long-stalked, cordate, lobed and toothed, triangular and about 2 × 1 in., or orbicular and 4 in. across. Heads 1-sexual, male and female on the same plant, combined in axillary or terminal clusters. Male heads uppermost, globose, $\frac{1}{3}$ in. diam.; involucral bracts few, short, narrow, in one series; receptacle cylindric; flowers numerous, crowded, each enclosed in a translucent scale; pappus none; corolla white or green, tubular, 5-toothed; filaments united, anthers free; ovary and style rudimentary or wanting. Female heads ovoid, $\frac{1}{2}$ in. long; outer involucral bracts few, short, inner many, in one series, narrow, united, covered with hooked bristles and terminating in two strong, hooked beaks; flowers 2; pappus and corolla none; style-branches long, thread-like, protruding from between the beaks. Achenes obovoid, thick, enclosed in the hardened, involucral bracts.

Valleys below Simla, common near villages and roadsides; April–November.—Common throughout India, ascending to 5000 ft.—Most tropical and temperate regions.

A plant of anomalous structure. Native name *chota datura*.

This species is naturalised in Australia, where it has become a troublesome weed, and the Government of Queensland has spent considerable sums in its attempted extirpation.

26. SIEGESBECKIA. In honour of Dr. J. G. Siegesbeck, a German botanist of the eighteenth century.—Tropical and subtropical regions.

Siegesbeckia orientalis, *Linn.*; *Fl. Br. Ind.* iii. 304. An erect herb, 1–3 ft., clothed with crisped hairs; branches opposite, spreading. Leaves opposite, ovate or broadly triangular, 2–5 × $1\frac{1}{2}$–4 in., coarsely toothed, acute or obtuse; stalks winged. Heads radiate, $\frac{1}{4}$ in. diam., in leafy panicles. Involucral bracts in two series, the outer five bracts spathulate, long, narrow, spreading, glandular-pubescent, inner ones shorter, erect; receptacle flat, covered with small, concave scales; flowers yellow, sometimes white; pappus none; ligules 2- or 3-lobed; corolla of the inner flowers 3–5-lobed. Achenes curved, angled, blunt at the base.

Simla, common; September, October.—Throughout India, ascending to 6000 ft.—All warm regions.

27. ECLIPTA. From the Greek *ecleipo*, to omit or leave out; referring to the absence of the pappus.—Most tropical regions.

Eclipta alba, *Hassk.*; *Fl. Br. Ind.* iii. 304. A slender, usually erect, roughly pubescent herb, 1–2 ft. Leaves very variable, opposite, sessile, narrowly lanceolate, 2-3 × $\frac{1}{4}$–$\frac{1}{3}$ in., toothed or nearly entire. Heads radiate, $\frac{1}{4}$–$\frac{1}{3}$ in. diam., terminal on erect stalks. Involucral bracts leaf-like, outer larger; receptacle flat, covered with broad, folded scales each enclosing several flowers; flowers white; pappus of 2–5 minute teeth; ligules 2-toothed or entire; corolla of the inner flowers 4–5-lobed. Achenes narrowly oblong, ribbed, tipped with the pappus teeth.

Valleys below Simla, in ricefields or marshy ground; August, September.—Throughout India, ascending to 5000 ft.—All warm regions.

28. SCLEROCARPUS. From the Greek *scleros*, hard, and *carpos*, fruit.—Asia, Africa, tropical America.

Sclerocarpus africanus, *Jacq.*; *Fl. Br. Ind.* iii. 305. An erect, roughly pubescent herb, 1–2 ft. Leaves lower usually opposite, upper alternate, ovate, $2\frac{1}{2} \times 1\frac{1}{4}$ in., narrowed into a short stalk, acutely toothed. Heads radiate, $\frac{1}{3}$–$\frac{1}{2}$ in. diam., at the ends or in the forks of the branches. Involucral bracts few, leaf-like, outer spreading; receptacle convex, covered with large, ribbed scales enfolding the lower half of the fertile disk-flowers; flowers yellow; pappus none; ligules broad, spreading, notched; corolla of the disk-flowers 3-5-toothed. Achenes curved, ribbed, enclosed in the hardened, pointed scales.

Valleys below Simla, in cornfields; July, August.—Throughout India, ascending to 5000 ft.—Tropical Africa.

29. BLAINVILLEA. In honour of D. de Blainville, a French zoologist of the nineteenth century.—Nearly all tropical regions.

Blainvillea latifolia, *DC.*; *Fl. Br. Ind.* iii. 305. A stiff, roughly pubescent, erect herb, 1–2 ft. Leaves lower opposite, upper alternate, ovate or triangular, $3 \times 2\frac{1}{4}$ in., toothed. Heads radiate, $\frac{1}{3}$–$\frac{1}{2}$ in. diam., terminal at the end of branches or axillary and nearly sessile. Involucral bracts few, outer ones broad, leaf-like, inner gradually passing into scales; receptacle covered with rigid, concave scales each embracing a flower; flowers yellow or white; pappus of 2–5 unequal bristles united in a short ring; ligules small, 2- or 3-toothed; corolla of the disk-flowers 5-lobed. Achenes 3-angled, inner ones often flattened, each enclosed in a scale.

Below Sipi, usually in cornfields, not common; August.—Throughout India, ascending to 5000 ft.—All tropical regions.

30. SPILANTHES. From the Greek *spilos*, a spot or stain, and *anthos*, a flower; referring to the dark-coloured pollen.—Most tropical regions, chiefly America.

***Spilanthes Acmella,** *Linn.*; *Fl. Br. Ind.* iii. 307. An annual herb, more or less pubescent, sometimes hairy; stems 1–2 ft., usually decumbent near the base. Leaves opposite, stalked, ovate-lanceolate, about $2 \times 1\frac{1}{4}$ in., toothed or entire. Heads discoid or radiate, conical, $\frac{1}{3}$–$\frac{3}{4}$ in. long, solitary on long stalks. Involucral bracts green, lanceolate, in 2 series; receptacle narrowly conical, covered with concave scales each enclosing the lower part of a flower; flowers white or yellow, mostly 2-sexual or the outer female and shortly rayed; pappus none or 1 or 2 bristles; corolla bell-shaped, lobes 4, spreading. Achenes flattened, each enclosed in a scale.

Throughout India, ascending to 5000 ft.; May–October.—All warm regions.

31. BIDENS. The Latin for 2-toothed; referring to the pappus.—Nearly all temperate and warm regions; most abundant in America.

Erect herbs; stems robust, ½–3 ft., usually glabrous near the base, pubescent upwards. Leaves opposite, stalked. Heads radiate, except *B. tripartita*, corymbose. Involucral bracts in 2 or 3 series, united near the base, outer ones green, inner membranous; receptacle covered with narrow, flat scales nearly as long as the yellow flowers; pappus of 2 or 3 erect, stiff, barbed bristles; ligules white or yellow, 2–3-toothed, spreading; corolla-tube of disk-flowers narrow, dilated at the top, 5-toothed. Achenes wedge-shaped or linear, ½ in. long including the pappus.

Heads discoid. Leaves digitately 3-lobed . . . . . 1. *B. tripartita.*
Heads radiate.
 Leaves 1-pinnate. Ligules white . . . . . 2. *B. pilosa.*
 Leaves 2-pinnate. Ligules yellow . . . . . 3. *B. Wallichii.*

*1. **Bidens tripartita,** *Linn.*; *Fl. Br. Ind.* iii. 309. Leaves 2½–4 in., digitately 3–5-lobed; lobes lanceolate, toothed, end one longest. Heads discoid, ⅔ in. diam., on short, erect stalks. Outer involucral bracts leaf-like, longer than the flowers, tips dilated. Achenes wedge-shaped, barbed along the ribs, pappus of usually two bristles.

Temperate Himalaya, in marshes, 3000–5000 ft.; August–October.—N. Africa, N. America, Europe (Britain, Bur-Marigold).

2. **Bidens pilosa,** *Linn.*; *Fl. Br. Ind.* iii. 309, *under* var. 1, *pilosa proper.* Leaves 3–5 in., 1-pinnate; leaflets 3–5, ovate, toothed. Heads radiate, ¼–½ in. diam., on long, thick, diverging stalks; ligules white; pappus of usually three barbed bristles. Achenes linear, rough.

Valleys below Simla; September, October.—Throughout India, ascending to 6000 ft.—All warm countries.

3. **Bidens Wallichii,** *DC.*; *Fl. Br. Ind.* iii. 309, *under* var. 2, *bipinnata* of *B. pilosa.* Leaves 3–6 in., 2-pinnate; segments variously cut and lobed. Heads radiate, ¼–⅓ in. diam., on long, slender, diverging stalks; ligules yellow; pappus of usually 3 bristles. Achenes linear, rough.

Simla, common; August, September.—Throughout India, ascending to 8000 ft.—Burmah, China.

32. **GALINSOGA.** In honour of M. M. de Galinsoga, a Spanish botanist of the eighteenth century.—Tropical America; introduced in India.

Galinsoga parviflora, *Cav.*; *Fl. Br. Ind.* iii. 311. An erect herb; stems weak, 6–18 in., usually smooth towards the base, roughly hairy upwards. Leaves opposite, stalked, ovate-lanceolate, 1–2½ in., more or less toothed. Heads radiate, ¼ in. diam., on slender stalks. Involucral bracts few, broad, green, smooth;

receptacle conical, covered with small, lanceolate, 3-toothed scales; pappus of about 15 spathulate, fringed scales; ligules few, white, very short, notched; disk-flowers yellow; corolla 5-toothed. Achenes angled, roughly pubescent, crowned with the pappus scales.

Simla, common near houses; January-December.—Himalaya, 4000–8000 ft.; introduced from America.

Naturalised in a few localities in England.

33. ACHILLEA. From *Achilleos*, the classical name of *A. Millefolium*; in honour of the mythical hero Achilles.—N. temperate regions.

Achillea Millefolium, *Linn.*; *Fl. Br. Ind.* iii. 312. An erect, pubescent herb; stems 6–24 in., leafy, grooved. Leaves alternate, oblong-lanceolate, $2\text{–}4 \times \frac{1}{4}\text{–}\frac{3}{4}$ in., 3-pinnatisect; segments linear, acute; radical leaves stalked, upper sessile. Heads radiate, $\frac{1}{4}$ in. diam., crowded in compound corymbs. Involucral bracts few, erect, outer ones shorter; receptacle flat, covered with thin, oblong scales nearly as long as the flowers; flowers white or pale pink; pappus none; ligules rounded, reflexed; corolla of disk-flowers 5-lobed. Achenes oblong, flattened, shining.

Mahasu, Huttoo; August-October.—W. Himalaya, 6000–9000 ft.—N. Asia, N. America, Europe (Britain, Milfoil).

34. TANACETUM. Origin of name doubtful; said to be altered from the Greek *athanasia*, immortality, referring to the persistent flowers.—N. temperate regions.

Strong-scented, erect herbs. Leaves alternate, pinnatisect; segments linear. Heads discoid, numerous, in terminal corymbs. Involucral bracts many, erect, margins coloured, outermost linear; receptacle convex, naked; flowers yellow; pappus none; corolla 5-toothed. Achenes smooth, 5-ribbed.

Leaves $\frac{1}{4}\text{–}\frac{3}{4}$ in. Involucral bracts woolly. Flowers orange-yellow . . . . 1. *T. nubigenum.*
Leaves (radical) 6–18 in. Involucral bracts hairy. Flowers bright yellow . . . . 2. *T. longifolium.*

1. **Tanacetum nubigenum,** *Wall.*; *Fl. Br. Ind.* iii. 318. Hoary; stems tufted, 12 in., densely leafy in the upper part. Leaves $\frac{1}{4}\text{–}\frac{3}{4}$ in., sessile. Heads nearly $\frac{1}{4}$ in. diam., orange-yellow. Involucral bracts woolly.

Shali; September, October.—Simla to Sikkim, 9000–12,000 ft.

2. **Tanacetum longifolium,** *Wall.*; *Fl. Br. Ind.* iii. 320. Hairy; stems 6–18 in., leafy and densely hairy towards the top. Leaves 6–18 in., mostly radical, far overtopping the flowers. Heads

several, $\frac{1}{3}$ in. diam., corymbs crowded. Involucral bracts hairy; flowers bright yellow.

Huttoo, the Chor; September, October.—W. Himalaya, 10,000-13,000 ft.

35. ARTEMISIA. The classical name of some species of the genus; *Artemis* was the Greek Diana.—N. temperate regions.

Erect, more or less aromatic, shrub-like herbs; stems grooved, usually much-branched. Leaves stalked or sessile, alternate, wedge-shaped or pinnately lobed or divided, bearing at the base close to the stem a pair of small, leaf-like lobes. Heads numerous, discoid, very small, globose, $\frac{1}{6}$ in. diam. or less, in simple or compound racemes forming long, terminal, leafy panicles. Involucral bracts few, hairy or pubescent, scarious or with scarious margins, shining, outer ones shorter than the inner; receptacle naked or hairy; flowers few, tinged with green, yellow or purple; pappus none; corolla of the outer flowers very slender, 2- or 3-toothed, of the inner larger, 5-toothed. Achenes minute.

A. maritima, *Linn.*; *Fl. Br. Ind.* iii. 323 (a British species), is common on the arid, inner ranges and in Afghanistan, but does not occur near Simla. It is distinguished by its short, white-tomentose, 2-pinnatisect leaves with linear segments.

The 'Wormwood' of Britain, *A. Absinthium*, extends to N. Asia but not to the east of Kashmir.

Leaves wedge-shaped; tip toothed or lobed . . . . . 1. *A. parviflora.*
Leaves pinnately lobed or divided.
  Leaf-segments thread-like . . . . 2. *A. scoparia.*
  Leaf-segments broad or narrow, never thread-like.
    Ultimate leaf-segments and wing of rachis entire or nearly so . . . . 3. *A. vulgaris.*
    Ultimate leaf-segments and wing of rachis closely pinnatifid . . . . 4. *A. vestita.*

1. **Artemisia parviflora,** *Roxb.*; *Fl. Br. Ind.* iii. 322. Hairy or nearly glabrous; stems 1–3 ft. Lower leaves sessile, wedge-shaped or obovate-oblong, 1–3 in., lateral margins usually entire, tip broad, toothed or lobed. Floral leaves similar, smaller, often lobed nearly to the base, sometimes lanceolate.

Simla, common; September, October.—Hilly districts throughout India, 3000–10,000 ft.

2. **Artemisia scoparia,** *Waldst.*; *Fl. Br. Ind.* iii. 323. Glabrous or nearly so; stems slender, 1–2 ft., much branched. Leaves stalked or nearly sessile, 2–3-pinnatisect, 1–3 in. long; segments thread-like. Floral leaves simple, linear, short. Heads very numerous, minute, nodding.

Valleys below Simla; September, October.—N. India, ascending to 5000 ft.

3. **Artemisia vulgaris,** *Linn.*; *Fl. Br. Ind.* iii. 325, including *A. glauca*, *Pall.*, and *A. Roxburghiana*, *Besser*; *Fl. Br. Ind.* iii. 322 and 326. Hairy or tomentose; stems shrub-like, much

branched, 3–6 ft. Lower leaves 1–3-pinnately lobed or 1–3-pinnatifid, 1-3 in. long; ultimate segments narrow or rather broad, entire or nearly so, acute or obtuse; upper surface pubescent or hairy, lower tomentose or densely hairy, white-grey or brown; leaf-rachis winged, wings entire or nearly so. Floral leaves 3-lobed nearly to the base or lanceolate.

Simla, common; August-October.—Throughout India, ascending to 12,000 ft. —Temperate Asia, Europe (Britain, Mugwort).

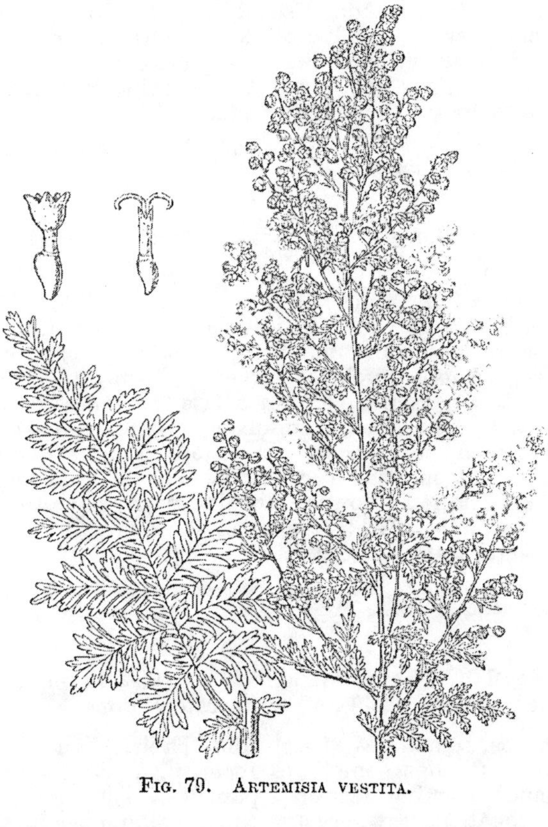

FIG. 79. ARTEMISIA VESTITA.

4. **Artemisia vestita,** *Wall.*; *Fl. Br. Ind.* iii. 326. Hoary-pubescent; stems 1–4 ft.; branches usually few and short. Leaves fern-like, 2-pinnate, 1–3 in. long; ultimate segments narrowly oblong, closely pinnatifid, lobes acute; upper surface dark green, pubescent, lower white-tomentose; leaf-rachis winged, wings closely pinnatifid, segments uniform, acute, comb-like. Floral leaves similar, smaller. (Fig. 79.)

Simla, common on the Downs; September, October.—Temperate Himalaya, 4000–10,000 ft.—Afghanistan, N. China.

36. GYNURA. From the Greek *gyne*, a woman, and *ouros*, a tail; referring to the long style-arms.—Warm regions of Asia, Africa and Australia.

Gynura angulosa, *DC.*; *Fl. Br. Ind.* iii. 334. A robust, succulent, glabrous herb; stems erect, branched, 3–10 ft. Leaves alternate, sessile, lanceolate or oblong, 6–12 in.; lower sometimes 2 ft., irregularly toothed, long-pointed; upper ones broadly lobed at the base. Heads discoid, $\frac{1}{2}$–$\frac{3}{4}$ in. long, in terminal, bracteate corymbs. Involucral bracts 10–12, in one series, narrow, equal, margins scarious; receptacle flat, naked; flowers orange-yellow; pappus white, copious; corolla slender, 5-toothed; style-arms very long. Achenes ribbed.

Valleys below Simla, not common; September, October.—Hilly districts throughout India, ascending to 7000 ft.

37. EMILIA. Origin of name unknown.—India, tropical Africa.

Emilia sonchifolia, *DC.*; *Fl. Br. Ind.* iii. 336. An erect, glabrous herb, 10–24 in. Radical leaves spreading, usually stalked, more or less pinnatifid, 2-4 in.; lobes entire or coarsely toothed, terminal lobe much the largest. Stem-leaves few, alternate, similar to the radical or lanceolate or ovate, 1–4 in., sessile or stalked, base often lobed, stem-clasping. Heads discoid, $\frac{1}{3}$–$\frac{1}{2}$ in. long, long-stalked, corymbose. Involucral bracts in one series, narrow, equal, edges often more or less united, reflexed in fruit; receptacle flat, naked; flowers purple; pappus white, copious; corolla slender, 5-toothed; tips of style-arms minutely conical. Achenes 5-angled, angles bristly.

Valleys below Simla; August, September.—Throughout India, ascending to 6000 ft.—Asia, Africa.

38. SENECIO. From the Latin *senex*, an old man, referring to the white pappus.—Cold and temperate regions.

Erect herbs, sometimes of a shrubby habit. Leaves alternate. Heads radiate (ligules sometimes inconspicuous), in corymbs or short racemes forming terminal panicles. Involucral bracts in one series, equal, narrow, erect, a few smaller ones at the base; receptacle flat, naked; flowers yellow; pappus white, soft, copious; ligules short or long, entire or toothed; corolla of disk-flowers 5-toothed; style-arms obtuse, tips minutely hairy. Achenes nearly cylindric, ribbed.

The two following species are common on the Chor at about 11,000 ft.:

S. amplexicaulis, *Wall.*; *Fl. Br. Ind.* iii. 348. Glabrous; stems 2-5 ft., very thick. Leaves large, kidney- or halberd-shaped, regularly toothed; stalks of the upper leaves with a broad, stem-sheathing wing. Heads many-flowered, crowded in racemes; ligules very long.

S. Kunthianus, *Wall.*; *Fl. Br. Ind.* iii. 354. Stems slender, leafy, 18–24 in. Leaves lanceolate, toothed; lower surface white-tomentose. Heads many-flowered, in broad, terminal corymbs.

Heads 4–10-flowered.
  Leaves pinnately lobed . . . . . . 1. *S. graciliflorus.*
  Leaves ovate.
    Leaf-stalks winged . . . . 4. *S. alatus.*
    Leaf-stalks naked . . . . 5. *S. rufinervis.*
Heads many-flowered.
  Leaves pinnately lobed . . . . . . 2. *S. chrysanthemoides.*
  Leaves ovate or spathulate . . . . . 3. *S. nudicaulis.*

1. **Senecio graciliflorus**, *DC.*; *Fl. Br. Ind.* iii. 338. Glabrous; stems 2–6 ft., grooved. Leaves thin, stalked, not lobed at the base, long-pointed, 4–6 × 2–4 in., pinnately divided into oblong, acute, coarsely toothed segments; uppermost leaves narrow or linear, sessile. Heads numerous, often drooping, narrowly cylindric, $\frac{1}{3}$ in. long, 5–8-flowered, in small clusters forming terminal corymbs. Involucral bracts 5–7, linear; ray-flowers 2–5, inconspicuous; ligules deeply toothed.

Mahasu, Narkunda, in forest; August, September.—Temperate Himalaya, 8000–13,000 ft.

2. **Senecio chrysanthemoides**, *DC.*; *Fl. Br. Ind.* iii. 339. Glabrous or nearly so towards the base, pubescent upwards; stems 2–6 ft., robust, finely grooved. Lower leaves 6–9 × 3–4 in., pinnately divided into broad, toothed lobes; terminal lobe much the largest, ovate, irregularly lobed and toothed; basal lobes lobed and toothed, stem-clasping. Upper leaves sessile, usually smaller and narrower; lobes more numerous. Leaves often purple on the lower surface. Heads numerous, $\frac{1}{2}$ in. diam., many-flowered, in large, spreading, terminal corymbs. Involucral bracts 10–12, oblong, acute; ray-flowers 8–12, conspicuous; ligules 3-toothed.

Simla, Mahasu, common; August, September.—Temperate Himalaya, 7000–13,000 ft.

3. **Senecio nudicaulis**, *Buch.-Ham.*; *Fl. Br. Ind.* iii. 340. Stems glabrous, 12–24 in., grooved. Leaves nearly smooth on the upper surface, white- or purple-tomentose on the lower, obovate or spathulate, 2–3 in., crenate or sharply toothed; radical leaves spreading, narrowed into a winged stalk; stem-leaves few, distant, sessile, basal lobes stem-clasping. Heads $\frac{1}{3}$ in. diam., many-flowered, in terminal corymbs. Involucral bracts 10–14, ovate, pointed, 3-nerved along the centre, margins broad, scarious; ligules conspicuous, long, narrow, 3-toothed.

Simla, common, on dry slopes; May, June.—Temperate Himalaya, 5000–10,000 ft.

4. **Senecio alatus**, *Wall.*; *Fl. Br. Ind.* iii. 358. Stems thick and hairy, often shaggy towards the base, 1–4 ft. Leaves pubes-

cent, ovate, 6–12 × 4–6 in., long-pointed, cordate, irregularly sinuate-toothed, long-pointed; stalks broadly winged. Heads slender, cylindric, shortly stalked, $\frac{1}{3}$–$\frac{1}{2}$ in. long, 4–6-flowered, in short racemes forming large, terminal panicles. Involucral bracts 4–7, linear, obtuse, pubescent; ray-flowers 1–2; ligules very short, entire, inconspicuous.

Narkunda, common; August, September.—Simla to Sikkim, 7000–9000 ft.

5. **Senecio rufinervis,** *DC.*; *Fl. Br. Ind.* iii. 355. Tall, shrublike; stems, branches and inflorescence tomentose. Leaves shortly stalked, ovate, 5–8 × 2–4 in., long-pointed, sharply toothed; lower surface white-tomentose except the red nerves. Heads numerous, slender, $\frac{1}{3}$ in. long, 6–10-flowered, in small, rounded corymbs. Involucral bracts 5–8, much shorter than the flowers; ray-flowers 2–5; ligules broad, conspicuous, minutely 3-toothed.

Simla, Mahasu, common in forest; August, September.—Simla to Kumaon, 6000–8000 ft.

39. ECHINOPS. From the Greek *echinos*, a hedgehog, and *opsis*, appearance; referring to the spinous involucral bracts.—Asia, Africa, S. Europe.

Tall, erect, thistle-like herbs; stems, branches and lower surface of leaves densely white-cottony. Leaves alternate, pinnatifid, spiny. Heads compound, terminal, solitary, globose, $1\frac{1}{2}$–3 in. diam.; component heads numerous, crowded, each containing a single pale blue or white flower. Involucral bracts in several series, outermost of coarse hairs or of narrow, spine-tipped bracts, intermediate of spathulate, spine-tipped bracts, one of the spines often prolonged beyond the flowers, innermost of united bracts enclosing the ovary and lower part of the corolla-tube; pappus a ring of short bristles; corolla tubular, deeply lobed. Achenes long, hairy, crowned with the pappus.

E. echinatus, *DC.*; *Fl. Br. Ind.* iii. 358, is common in the plains and may occur in the hills below 3000 ft.; the leaves and outer involucral bracts resemble those of *E. cornigerus*, but the heads are only 1–$1\frac{1}{2}$ in. diam., always white, and with several long, projecting spines.

Several species of *Echinops* are in cultivation and are known as Globe Thistles.

Outer involucral bracts numerous, soft, hair-like. Leaf-lobes broad . . . . 1. *E. cornigerus.*
Outer involucral bracts few, spathulate, spine-tipped. Leaf-lobes linear . . . . 2. *E. niveus.*

1. **Echinops cornigerus,** *DC.*; *Fl. Br. Ind.* iii. 358. Leaves 4–8 in., pinnately divided into broad, flat, lobed and toothed, spiny segments; upper surface cobwebby. Heads $2\frac{1}{2}$–3 in. diam., with or without projecting spines. Outer involucral bracts numerous, soft, coarse, hair-like, about $\frac{3}{4}$ in. long.

Simla, common; August, September.—W. Himalaya 6000–9000 ft.

2. **Echinops niveus,** *Wall.*; *Fl. Br. Ind.* iii. 359. Leaves 3–8 in., pinnately divided into numerous, linear, spiny segments, margins recurved. Heads 1½–3 in. diam., usually without projecting spines. Outer involucral bracts few, narrow, spathulate, spine-tipped. (Fig. 80.)

Simla, common; August, September.—W. Himalaya, 4000–8000 ft.

FIG. 80. ECHINOPS NIVEUS.

40. ARCTIUM. From the Greek *arctos*, a bear; referring to the rough, coarse appearance of the plants.—Asia, Europe.

Arctium Lappa, *Linn.*; *Fl. Br. Ind.* iii. 359. An erect, coarse, rough herb, 2–4 ft. Leaves radical and alternate, stalked, broadly ovate, 3–12 in. across, cordate, sinuate-toothed; lower surface hoary or white-cottony. Heads discoid, globose, ¾–1½ in. diam., in terminal clusters. Involucral bracts many, upper half spreading, tips rigid, hooked; receptacle flat, densely bristly; flowers purple; pappus copious, short, minutely barbed; corolla-tube long, 5-lobed; style white, arms united. Achenes large, glabrous, angled, finely ribbed.

Narkunda; September.—W. Himalaya, 6000–9000 ft.—W. Asia, Europe (Britain, Burdock).

41. CARDUUS. The classical name of a Thistle or thistle-like plant; etymology doubtful.—Asia, N. Africa, Europe.

Carduus nutans, *Linn.*; *Fl. Br. Ind.* iii. 361. An erect, robust, rough herb; stems 1–4 ft., winged, grooved. Leaves alternate, oblong, 6–12 in., sessile, continued down the stem in interrupted, spinous wings, pinnately lobed; margins sinuate, spiny. Heads discoid, $\frac{3}{4}$–$1\frac{1}{2}$ in. diam., ovoid or globose, solitary or clustered, drooping. Involucral bracts many, tips spinous, spreading or reflexed; receptacle flat, densely bristly; flowers crimson; pappus copious, long, rough, united at the base into a ring; corolla-tube long, deeply 5-lobed. Achenes glabrous, obtusely 4-angled; pappus soon falling off.

Simla, Narkunda, in fields; July–October.—W. Himalaya, 6000–12,000 ft. —W. Asia, N. Africa, Europe (Britain, Musk Thistle).

42. CNICUS. From *knekos*, the Greek name of various kinds of Thistle and thistle-like plants.—N. temperate regions.

Erect, rough herbs; stems robust, not winged. Leaves alternate, prickly or spiny. Heads discoid. Involucral bracts many, spine-tipped, the outer ones leaf-like; receptacle flat, densely bristly; flowers dingy purple or yellow, varying to white; pappus long, copious, feathery, united at the base; corolla deeply 5-lobed, tube long. Achenes glabrous, obtusely 4-angled, pappus soon falling off.

Flowers dingy purple . . . . 1. *C. arvensis.*
Flowers pale yellow or white.
  Leaf-margins uniformly beset with long, rigid spines.
    Tips of inner involucral bracts not dilated . . 2. *C. argyracanthus.*
  Leaf-margins spiny, but the long spines confined to the end of the lobes. Tips of inner involucral bracts dilated . . . . 3. *C. Wallichii.*

1. **Cnicus arvensis,** *Hoffm.*; *Fl. Br. Ind.* iii. 362. Rootstock creeping; stems numerous, 2–4 ft., upper parts cobwebby-tomentose. Leaves sessile, oblong, 3–6 × $\frac{3}{4}$–1 in., sinuate or pinnatifid, spinous; upper surface pale, rough, lower white-tomentose. Heads 1-sexual, male and female on different plants, solitary or clustered or corymbose. Male heads globose, $\frac{1}{2}$–1 in. diam.;

female ovoid, longer. Involucral bracts many; outer ones ovate or triangular, shortly spine-tipped; inner longer, tips undulate, recurved; innermost linear-lanceolate; flowers dingy purple; pappus brown.

Valleys below Simla, in fields; March–May.—N. India, ascending to 5000 ft. —W. Asia, Europe (Britain).

2. **Cnicus argyracanthus,** *DC.*; *Fl. Br. Ind.* iii. 362. Stems robust, branched, grooved, 3–6 ft., rough or cottony. Leaves green and nearly glabrous on both surfaces, irregularly pinnately lobed, margins densely beset with long, rigid spines: radical leaves stalked, 10–24 × 1–1½ in.; stem-leaves shorter, sessile, basal lobes broad. Heads numerous, globose, ¾–1 in. diam., sessile or shortly stalked, crowded in terminal clusters. Outer involucral bracts ending in long, rigid, erect or spreading spines; innermost linear, long-pointed; flowers pale yellow or white; pappus nearly white.

Simla, Fagoo, common; July–September.—Temperate Himalaya, 6000–9000 ft.

3. **Cnicus Wallichii,** *DC.*; *Fl. Br. Ind.* iii. 363. Stems robust, branched, grooved, roughly hairy or glabrous, 4–10 ft. Leaves glabrous or the lower surface white-cottony, sessile, more or less lobed at the base, 4–6 × ¾–1½ in., irregularly pinnately lobed; margins spiny, the longer spines few and confined to the ends of the lobes. Heads ½–1¼ in. diam. Outer involucral bracts narrow, ending in long, rigid, spreading spines; tips of the inner bracts dilated; flowers dull yellow; pappus brown or dirty white.

Simla, in fields; July–October.—Temperate Himalaya, 5000–9000 ft.

Two of the six varieties into which this species has been divided in the *Fl. Br. Ind.* occur in or near Simla, viz.:

Var. 2, *cernuus.* Leaves white-cottony on the lower surface. Heads ½–¾ in. diam., on long, nearly leafless stalks.

Var. 3, *glabratus.* Leaves nearly glabrous on the lower surface. Heads 1–1¼ in. diam., sessile or shortly stalked, clustered.

43. SAUSSUREA. In honour of H. B. and T. de Saussure, father and son, the former a botanist, celebrated for his investigations of the Flora of the Alps; the latter equally celebrated as a chemist and physicist.—Mountains in N. temperate regions.

Erect herbs. Leaves radical and alternate, not prickly, usually more or less pinnately lobed; upper surface glabrous, rough, lower white-tomentose. Heads discoid. Involucral bracts many, erect, not spiny but the tips usually rigid and sharp, inner ones narrower and longer than the outer; receptacle densely bristly; flowers dark purple or pale red; pappus in one series, feathery, flattened and united at the base; corolla slender, deeply 5-lobed. Achenes oblong, 4-ribbed, wrinkled, pappus soon falling off leaving a shallow cup surrounding the base of the style.

Flowers dark purple.
Stems 1-6 in. Heads flat, ½–1 in. diam. . . . 1. *S. taraxacifolia.*
Stems 2-5 ft. Heads globose, 1½–2 in. diam. . . 4. *S. hypoleuca.*
Flowers pale red.
Heads broad, ¾–1½ in. diam., many-flowered . . 2. *S. candicans.*
Heads narrow, ¼ in. diam., 5- or 6-flowered . . 3. *S. albescens.*

1. **Saussurea taraxacifolia,** *Wall.*; *Fl. Br. Ind.* iii. 368. Stems cottony, erect, 1–6 in., base covered with the withered remains of old leaf-stalks. Leaves mostly radical, spreading, shortly stalked, 4–8 × ½–1 in., pinnatifid; lobes triangular, acute, all pointing downwards like the lobes of a Dandelion leaf; upper surface green, glabrous, lower white-tomentose. Heads solitary, ½–1 in. diam. Involucral bracts not spine-tipped; flowers dark purple.

Huttoo; August–October.—Simla to Sikkim, 10,000–15,000 ft.

2. **Saussurea candicans,** *C. B. Clarke*; *Fl. Br. Ind.* iii. 373. Stems cottony, erect, 1–5 ft., often branching near the top. Radical leaves oblong or obovate, narrowed into a short stalk, 1–6 × ½–1½ in., entire or sinuate, pinnately lobed near the base; upper surface rough, lower white-tomentose. Stem-leaves usually few, sessile, lanceolate, usually smaller than the radical leaves. Heads ¾–1½ in. diam., long-stalked, solitary or corymbose. Involucral bracts rigid, sharp; flowers pale red.

Simla, common; April–June.—N. India, ascending to 7000 ft.—Afghanistan.

3. **Saussurea albescens,** *Hook. f. & Thoms.*; *Fl. Br. Ind.* iii. 374. Stems cottony, slender, erect, leafy, 6–10 ft., branching near the top. Leaves narrowly lanceolate, 4–12 in., entire, toothed or more or less pinnately lobed; upper surface rough, lower white-tomentose. Heads erect, narrow, ½–¾ in. long, 5- or 6-flowered in long-stalked corymbs. Involucral bracts rigid, tinged with purple; flowers pale red.

Fagoo, Matiana, Shali; September, October.—Temperate Himalaya, 6000–10,000 ft.

4. **Saussurea hypoleuca,** *Spreng.*; *Fl. Br. Ind.* iii. 374. Stems pubescent or glabrous, erect, leafy, 2–5 ft., simple or branching near the top. Radical leaves narrow, 6–10 in., pinnatifid; lateral lobes pointing downwards, terminal lobe much larger, oblong. Stem-leaves 3–8 in., pinnately lobed; lateral lobes 2–4 pairs, oblong, less than 1 in. long, terminal lobe triangular, acute, 2–4 × 1–3 in., toothed or sinuate; upper surface rough, lower white-tomentose. Heads solitary, globose, 1½–2 in. diam., nodding. Involucral bracts rigid, purple; flowers dark purple.

Huttoo; August-October.—Temperate Himalaya, 7000–13,000 ft.

44. SERRATULA. From the Latin *serrula*, a small saw; referring to the toothed leaves of some species.—N. temperate regions, Africa.

Serratula pallida, *DC.*; *Fl. Br. Ind.* iii. 379. A rough, erect, perennial herb; stems 1–3 ft., simple or branched. Leaves chiefly radical, stalked, variable in shape and size, broadly ovate or oblong, 3–12 × 2–6 in. and toothed, or 1–6 in. long and deeply pinnately lobed; stem-leaves few or none. Heads discoid, 1–1½ in. diam., solitary on a long, thick stalk. Involucral bracts many, erect, glabrous, acute but not spine-tipped; inner ones long, narrow, outer

FIG. 81. SERRATULA PALLIDA.

shorter and broader; receptacle bristly; flowers purple; pappus in several series, rigid, minutely barbed, innermost series longer than the corolla-tube, outer very short; corolla deeply 5-lobed. Achenes oblong, smooth, flattened, obscurely ribbed. (Fig. 81.)

Simla, common; May, June.—W. Himalaya, 6000–8000 ft.

45. TRICHOLEPIS. From the Greek *thrix, trichos*, a hair, and *lepis*, a scale; referring to the finely pointed involucral bracts.—India, Afghanistan.

Tricholepis elongata, *DC.*; *Fl. Br. Ind.* iii. 380. A rough, perennial herb; stems erect, 2–5 ft., diverging in several long, straight branches nearly leafless towards the end. Leaves alternate, variable in shape and size, lanceolate or oblong, 2–4 × $\frac{3}{4}$–2 in., and toothed, or ovate and pinnately lobed near the base, 4 × 1$\frac{1}{2}$ in., or pinnately divided throughout into long or short, entire or toothed lobes; the different forms being sometimes seen on the same plant. Heads discoid, $\frac{1}{2}$–1$\frac{1}{4}$ in. diam., solitary at the end of branches. Involucral bracts many, erect, very narrow, with a long, recurved or twisted, needle- or hair-like point; receptacle densely bristly; flowers pale yellow; pappus copious, rigid, minutely barbed, inner series nearly as long as the corolla, outer very short; corolla-tube slender, 5-lobed. Achenes smooth.

Simla, common; August, September.—W. Himalaya, 4000–8000 ft.

46. CARTHAMUS. Derived from the Arabic *qurtom*, to paint; a red dye is obtained from the flowers.—S. Europe, W. Asia.

Carthamus tinctorius, *Linn.*; *Fl. Br. Ind.* iii. 386. A glabrous, erect, thistle-like herb, 1$\frac{1}{2}$ ft. Leaves alternate, stiff, sessile, lanceolate, 1$\frac{3}{4}$–3 × $\frac{1}{2}$–1$\frac{1}{4}$ in.; teeth spinous. Heads discoid, $\frac{1}{2}$–1 in. diam., terminal. Involucral bracts many, spinous, erect, outer ones leaf-like, inner narrow; receptacle flat, densely bristly; flowers orange-red; pappus none; corolla-tube slender, deeply 5-lobed. Achenes glabrous, 4-angled.

Cultivated throughout India for the dye obtained from the flowers and the oil from the seeds. Occasionally found as an escape near villages. June–September.—Native name *Kusumbh.* The Safflower or Bastard Saffron; not known in a wild state.

47. AINSLIÆA. In honour of Dr. Whitelaw Ainslie, author of 'Materia Indica,' 1826.—Himalaya, China, Japan.

Erect, perennial herbs of singular habit. Leaves alternate, chiefly radical. Heads discoid, sessile or nearly so, narrow, $\frac{3}{4}$–1$\frac{1}{2}$ in. long, in clusters or spikes. Involucral bracts many, erect, glabrous, rigid, acute, inner ones long, outer shorter; flowers 1–4, usually 3 in a head, white or tinged with pink; pappus feathery; corolla-tube slender, limb slightly 2-lipped, lobes 5, long, narrow, unequal. Achenes hairy.

Leaf-stalks not winged. Heads in small clusters . . . 1. *A. aptera.*
Leaf-stalks winged. Heads in spikes . . . . . . 2. *A. pteropoda.*

1. **Ainsliæa aptera,** *DC.*; *Fl. Br. Ind.* iii. 388. In March and April the slender, leafless stems, 1–4 ft. high, bear numerous heads in small clusters; after fruiting the stems decay and in most cases disappear. In June the rootstock produces several long-stalked, broadly triangular, ovate or orbicular leaves about 4 × 4$\frac{1}{2}$ in.

cordate, sinuate-toothed and roughly pubescent or silky. During the rains, July to September, a new stem is thrown up bearing leaves, numerous closed heads and small buds. Towards the end of October most or all of the heads open out and shed an abundance of seeds, but without having exhibited flowers as in the spring.

FIG. 82. AINSLIÆA APTERA.

During the winter the leaves drop off, and in the spring the buds produce perfect flowers. The plant is an example of cleistogamy, see *Violaceæ*, p. 39. The cleistogamic flowers of the October heads have small, closed corollas concealed in the pappus and containing the anthers and style. (Fig. 82.)

Simla, Mahasu, in woods, common; March, April.—Temperate Himalaya, 6000–8000 ft.

Sometimes called Aaron's Rod.

2. **Ainsliæa pteropoda,** *DC.*; *Fl. Br. Ind.* iii. 388. Habit and characters of *A. aptera* except that the stems are only 1–2 ft., the radical leaves are usually present on winged stalks, silky,

ovate, $2 \times 1\frac{1}{2}$ in., finely toothed; and the heads are in spikes, rarely clustered.

Valleys below Simla; March, April.—Simla to Bhotan, 5000–6000 ft.—Burmah.

48. GERBERA. In honour of T. Gerber, a German naturalist and traveller of the eighteenth century.—Asia, Africa.

Herbs. Leaves all radical, glabrous on the upper surface, white-tomentose on the lower. Heads radiate, solitary on long, erect, leafless stalks. Involucral bracts many, erect, the inner-

FIG. 83. GERBERA LANUGINOSA.

most slightly onger than the pappus, the outer gradually shorter; receptacle flat, naked; flowers white; pappus copious; corolla-tube slender, limb 2-lipped; lobes of the ray-flowers very unequal, outer ones long, spreading, 3-toothed, inner much shorter, bifid; lobes of the disk-flowers nearly equal, outer ones 3–4-toothed, inner bifid or entire; style-arms obtuse. Achenes rough, flattened, ribbed, narrowed at the tip.

Involucral bracts woolly outside. Pappus rough . . 1. *G. lanuginosa.*
Involucral bracts glabrous outside. Pappus smooth . . 2. *G. Kunzeana.*

1. **Gerbera lanuginosa,** *Benth.*; *Fl. Br. Ind.* iii. 390. Leaves lanceolate, $2\frac{1}{2}$–$6 \times \frac{3}{4}$–3 in., often pinnately lobed near the base, entire, minutely toothed or sinuately lobed, sessile or stalked; stalks winged at the top, silky at the base. Heads 1–2 in. diam.; stalks 6–12 in., cottony or naked or with a few minute, scattered bracts. Involucral bracts narrowly lanceolate, acute, white-woolly outside; flowers often tinged with pink; pappus white, rough with minute barbs. Achenes slightly hairy. (Fig. 83.)

Simla, common on dry slopes; May–October.—W. Himalaya, 4000–8000 ft.
The white coating on the leaves is used for making cloth, also as tinder, and to staunch wounds, etc. by the natives.

2. **Gerbera Kunzeana,** *Braun*; *Fl. Br. Ind.* iii. 390. Habit of the preceding species, but the heads are cylindric and only $\frac{1}{2}$–$\frac{3}{4}$ in. diam., and their stalks bear numerous long, thread-like bracts. Involucral bracts broadly lanceolate, glabrous; pappus brown, smooth; corolla of disk-flowers sometimes 5-toothed instead of 2-tipped. Achenes hairy.

Huttoo, not common; July–September.—Temperate Himalaya, 7000–12,000 ft.

49. CICHORIUM. The classical name of the Succory or Endive, *C. Endivia*; etymology obscure.—Temperate regions of the Old World.

Cichorium Intybus, *Linn.*; *Fl. Br. Ind.* iii. 391. An erect, usually rough and more or less glandular, perennial herb; juice milky; stems 1–3 ft., angled or grooved; branches tough, rigid, spreading. Radical and lower leaves 3–6 in., pinnatifid, lobes toothed, pointing downwards; upper leaves alternate, small, entire. Heads ligulate, 1–$1\frac{1}{2}$ in. diam., terminal and solitary or axillary and clustered, sessile or on short, thick stalks. Involucre of about 8 inner bracts and a few outer smaller ones, all leaf-like with concave bases; receptacle flat, usually bristly; flowers bright blue; pappus of 1 or 2 series of short, blunt, erect scales; ligules very long, spreading, 5-toothed; style-arms long. Achenes smooth, angled, crowned with the ring of pappus scales.

Simla, Boileaugunge, in fields; August, September.—N.W. India, ascending to 6000 ft.—W. Asia, Europe (Britain, Wild Chicory).
The Endive is supposed to be a cultivated form of this species.

50. PICRIS. From the Greek *picros*, bitter, referring to its qualities.—N. Asia, N. Africa, Europe.

***Picris hieracioides,** *Linn.*; *Fl. Br. Ind.* iii. 393. A herb, rough with stiff, hooked hairs; stems erect, 1–4 ft., robust, branched; juice milky. Leaves alternate, narrowly lanceolate, 3–8 in.: lower ones stalked, sinuate-toothed; upper smaller, stem-clasping, usually entire. Heads numerous, corymbose or paniculate, ligulate, $\frac{1}{2}$–$\frac{3}{4}$ in. diam., on bracteate stalks. Involucral bracts narrow, black-hairy, inner ones equal, in one series, outer many, shorter, spreading; receptacle flat, naked; flowers yellow; pappus copious, white, feathery, in one series with a few short hairs at the base; ligules long, spreading, 5-toothed. Achenes terete, smooth, narrowed to both ends, ribbed, transversely wrinkled, brown when ripe.

Murree to Bhotan; April–September.—Temperate Himalaya, 6000–8000 ft. —W. Asia, N. Africa, Europe (Britain).

51. CREPIS. The classical name of a plant of this affinity, probably the Ox-tongue, *Picris echioides*.—N. temperate regions, rare in the tropics.

Erect or nearly erect herbs. Leaves chiefly radical, usually pinnatifid; upper ones alternate. Heads ligulate, in terminal corymbs. Involucral bracts usually many, with a few erect, smaller ones at the base; receptacle flat, naked; flowers yellow; pappus white, soft, not feathery; ligules long, spreading, 5-toothed. Achenes oblong, slender, finely ribbed, beaked except in *C. japonica*.

Heads $\frac{1}{2}$–1 in. diam. Involucral bracts many. Achenes beaked.
  Outer involucral bracts rough with hooked hairs. Hardened and keeled in fruit . . . . . . 1. *C. fœtida.*
  Outer involucral bracts softly pubescent, fringed . . . 2. *C. sibirica.*
Heads $\frac{1}{6}$–$\frac{1}{4}$ in. diam. Involucral bracts 6–8. Achenes not beaked . . . . 3. *C. japonica.*

*1. **Crepis fœtida,** *Linn.*; *Fl. Br. Ind.* iii. 393. Rough, branched from near the base; branches 6–18 in., nearly erect or spreading. Lower leaves 2–6 in., pinnatifid, toothed, end lobe the largest; upper leaves smaller, stem-clasping, toothed or entire. Heads long-stalked, $\frac{1}{2}$ in. diam. Involucral bracts many, outer ones rough with hooked hairs and becoming hardened and keeled in fruit; flowers bright yellow. Outer achenes $\frac{1}{4}$ in., curved; inner $\frac{1}{3}$–$\frac{1}{2}$ in., straight, finely ribbed; beak long, very slender.

W. Himalaya, in fields, 6000–8000 ft.; April–September.—W. Asia, Europe (Britain).

*2. **Crepis sibirica,** *Linn.*; *Fl. Br. Ind.* iii. 394. More or less rough; stems robust, erect, 6–18 in. Lower leaves 6–12 in., stalked, pinnatifid, lobes rounded and finely toothed, end one the largest; upper leaves smaller, narrowly lanceolate, stem-clasping. Heads few, long-stalked, 1 in. diam. Involucral bracts many, pubescent, obtuse, fringed, inner ones long, linear, outer shorter, broadly ovate; pappus scanty. Achenes $\frac{1}{2}$ in., slender, glabrous, finely ribbed, tapering into a short beak.

W. Himalaya, 6000–10,000 ft.; July-October.--N. Asia, Europe.

3. **Crepis japonica**, *Benth.*; *Fl. Br. Ind.* iii. 395. Glabrous or nearly so, smooth; stems often tufted, erect, slender, 6–24 in.; branches spreading. Leaves nearly all radical, in a rosette, soft, thin, 1-4 in., usually pinnatifid, lobes toothed, end one the largest,

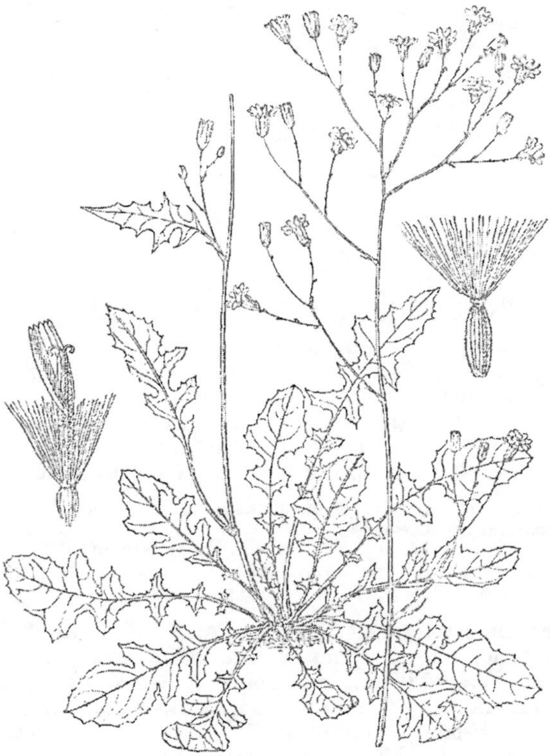

FIG. 84. CREPIS JAPONICA.

or sometimes obovate and sinuate-toothed. Heads many, $\frac{1}{6}$–$\frac{1}{4}$ in. diam., in terminal corymbs. Involucral bracts 6–8, narrowly oblong, green, erect; flowers pale yellow. Achenes flattened, finely ribbed, $\frac{1}{12}$ in., not beaked. (Fig. 84.)

Simla, common in shady places; March–July.—Throughout India, ascending to 10,000 ft.—E. Asia.

52. PTEROTHECA. From the Greek *pteron*, a wing, and *thece*, a sheath or case, referring to the prominent ribs of the achenes.—W. Asia, S. Europe.

Pterotheca Falconeri, *Hook. f.*; *Fl. Br. Ind.* iii. 399. An erect herb; stems many, slender, 6–18 in., branched, nearly glabrous towards the base, glandular upwards. Leaves all radical, 4–6 in., spathulate and pinnatifid, or 1–2 in. and obovate with a few small teeth. Heads ligulate, $\frac{1}{2}$–$\frac{3}{4}$ in. diam., on slender stalks. Involucre cylindric; bracts pubescent, inner ones 8–10, equal, linear, acute, outer few and small, usually spreading; receptacle flat, covered with long hairs; flowers yellow; pappus very short, soft, white, not feathery; ligules long, broad, spreading, 5-toothed. Achenes linear, prominently ribbed, minutely wrinkled, narrowed to both ends, not beaked, red when ripe; outer achenes often flattened and sterile.

Matiana, Baghi, in cornfields; June–August.—W. Himalaya, 5000–9000 ft. —Afghanistan.

53. HIERACIUM. From the Greek *ierax*, a hawk; application obscure.—N. temperate regions, S. Africa, the Andes.

Perennial, erect herbs; juice milky; stems robust, 1–3 ft., branched. Leaves alternate, lanceolate, toothed. Heads ligulate, $\frac{1}{2}$–$\frac{3}{4}$ in. diam., stalked. Involucral bracts many, black-hairy or pubescent, narrow, acute, inner ones nearly equal, outer smaller; receptacle flat, bristly; flowers yellow; pappus copious, rough, rigid, brittle, tawny; ligules long, spreading, 5-toothed; base of anther-cells not tailed; style-arms slender. Achenes glabrous, terete, ribbed, narrowed to the base, not beaked, black when ripe.

Leaves broadly lanceolate; radical persistent. Tips of outer involucral bracts erect . . . . 1. *H. vulgatum.*
Leaves narrowly lanceolate; radical soon disappearing. Tips of outer involucral bracts recurved . . . . 2. *H. umbellatum.*

1. **Hieracium vulgatum,** *Koch*; *Fl. Br. Ind.* iii. 399. Hairy. Leaves glabrous on the upper surface, hairy on the lower, broadly lanceolate, 3–6 × $\frac{3}{4}$–1$\frac{1}{2}$ in., long-pointed, irregularly and coarsely toothed: radical leaves many, persistent or long-stalked; upper few, sessile. Heads on glandular-hairy stalks. Involucral bracts often cottony in bud, black-hairy, usually glandular.

Simla, Mahasu; June–September.—W. Himalaya, 6000–10,000 ft.—W. Asia, Europe (Britain, Hawkweed).

Included under *H. murorum*, Linn., in Bentham's *British Flora.*

2. **Hieracium umbellatum,** *Linn.*; *Fl. Br. Ind.* iii. 400. Nearly glabrous, not glandular; base of stem sometimes hairy. Leaves sessile, narrowly lanceolate, 3 × $\frac{1}{2}$ in.; teeth few, small; radical leaves soon disappearing. Heads usually numerous, irregularly

umbelled; stalks pubescent. Involucral bracts black-downy with a few interspersed hairs; tips of the outer bracts recurved.

Matiana, in woods; August, September.—W. Himalaya, 5000–10,000 ft.—W. Asia, N. America, Europe (Britain, Hawkweed).

54. TARAXACUM. From the Greek *tarasso*, to stir up; referring to its medicinal effects.—Temperate and cold regions.

Taraxacum officinale, *Wigg.*; *Fl. Br. Ind.* iii. 401. A perennial herb; juice milky. Leaves all radical, sessile, usually glabrous, variable in shape, narrowly oblong, 2–8 in., irregularly pinnatifid, lobes linear or triangular, acute, toothed, pointing downwards, or rarely oblanceolate and nearly entire. Heads ligulate, $\frac{1}{3}$–2 in. diam., glabrous, solitary on a hollow, leafless stalk 2–8 in. long. Inner involucral bracts linear, erect, nearly equal, margins often white, tips usually thickened or hooked; outer bracts short, ovate, erect or recurved; receptacle flat, naked; flowers yellow; pappus copious, white, not feathery, soft; ligules long, spreading, 3–5-toothed, often brown on the back; style-arms long. Achenes glabrous, flattened, ribbed, narrowed to the base, minutely spiny on the upper half, abruptly contracted into a long, slender beak crowned by the pappus.

Simla, common; March–November.—Himalaya, 1000–18,000 ft.—Temperate and cold regions.

Closely allied to the British Dandelion, *T. Dens-leonis.*

T. Wattii, *Hook. f.*, *Fl. Br. Ind.* iii. 402, occurs on the top of Shali; it differs from the above in the short, thick beak of the achenes.

55. LACTUCA. The Latin name of the Lettuce, *L. sativa*, derived from *lac, lactis*, milk; referring to its juice.—N. temperate regions, S. Africa.

Erect or decumbent, leafy herbs; juice milky. Leaves alternate, usually provided with a pair of basal lobes close to the stem. Heads ligulate, few-flowered. Involucre narrowly cylindric; bracts in few series, thin, green, margins often membranous, inner ones long, narrow, nearly equal; outer lanceolate or ovate, usually much shorter; receptacle flat, naked; flowers yellow or blue; pappus copious, silvery white, soft, not feathery; ligules long, spreading, 3–5-toothed; style-arms long. Achenes flattened, more or less rough, ribbed, beaked, tip of the beak dilated in a pappus-bearing disk.—Ripe achenes are necessary to distinguish this genus from *Prenanthes*.

Flowers yellow.
- Stems leafy. Leaves pinnatifid . . . . . 1. *L. Scariola.*
- Stems naked. Radical leaves triangular . . 6. *L. sagittarioides.*

Flowers blue or blue-purple.
- Stems erect.
  - Stems 6–18 in. Beak twice as long as its achene 2. *L. dissecta.*
  - Stems 3–7 ft. Beak not longer than its achene.
    - Leaves entire . . . . 3. *L. longifolia.*

Leaves more or less lobed and toothed. Stems sometimes dwarfed	4. *L. hastata.*
Stems prostrate or pendulous. Leaves pinnatifid. Heads racemose, drooping	5. *L. macrorhiza.*

1. **Lactuca Scariola,** *Linn.*; *Fl. Br. Ind.* iii. 404. Glabrous or nearly so; stems erect, 2–5 ft., leafy, branched, usually prickly towards the base. Leaves sessile, 5–7 in., pinnatifid, segments toothed, pointing downwards; lower surface usually prickly on the midrib and nerves; stem-leaves lobed at the base. Heads $\frac{1}{2}$ in. long, erect; flowers yellow. Achenes brown; beak very slender, about as long as the body.

Mushobra, Sutlej valley; March–November.—W. Himalaya, 6000–11,000 ft. —W. Asia, Europe (Britain).

2. **Lactuca dissecta,** *Don*; *Fl. Br. Ind.* iii. 405. Glabrous or nearly so; stems often tufted, erect, 6–18 in., leafy and much branched or naked and nearly simple. Leaves 1–4 in., pinnatifid, lobes varying much in size and cutting: radical leaves usually many, sessile; lower stem-leaves stalked; upper ones sessile, lobed at the base; uppermost linear. Heads many, $\frac{1}{4}$–$\frac{1}{2}$ in. long, corymbose; stalks slender, erect; flowers pale blue. Achenes 3-ribbed on each face, margins thickened; beak very slender, twice as long as the body.

Simla, common; April–September.—Temperate Himalaya, 4000–8000 ft.—Afghanistan.

3. **Lactuca longifolia,** *DC.*; *Fl. Br. Ind.* iii. 405. Glabrous; stems erect, 3–6 ft., branched. Leaves 4–7 × $\frac{1}{4}$–$\frac{1}{2}$ in., long-pointed, entire, stem-clasping; basal lobes narrow, acute, appressed to the stem. Heads $\frac{1}{2}$ in. long; stalks slender, erect; flowers blue-purple. Achenes thickened on the margins; beak very slender, not longer than the body.

Shali, Daha in the Giri valley; September.—Temperate Himalaya, 4000–9000 ft.

4. **Lactuca hastata,** *DC.*; *Fl. Br. Ind.* iii. 407. Stems robust, erect, 4–7 ft., sometimes dwarfed and slender, glabrous towards the base, more or less glandular upwards especially on the branches of the inflorescence. Leaves variable, smooth or rough; stalks naked or winged, base dilated or 2-lobed; blade 6–12 × 1$\frac{1}{2}$–4 in., pinnately lobed, terminal lobe broad, coarsely toothed, lower lobes many or few or none. Heads $\frac{3}{4}$ in. long, in branched racemes forming a terminal panicle. Involucral bracts bristly hairy, the outer about half as long as the inner; flowers 10–30, dark blue. Ripe achenes black, margins thickened; beak about half as long as the body.

Simla, Theog, in forest; July–October. — Temperate Himalaya, 4000–12,000 ft.—Mountains in S. India.

This species has the aspect of *Prenanthes Brunoniana*, but the heads contain 10–30 flowers instead of 3–5, and the achenes are distinctly beaked.

5. **Lactuca macrorhiza,** *Hook. f.*; *Fl. Br. Ind.* iii. 408. Glabrous or nearly so; root thick, woody; stems tufted, prostrate or pendulous, much branched. Leaves thin, variable in size and shape, usually pinnately lobed, sometimes cordately orbicular or ovate; margins sinuate; stalks naked or winged, dilated or lobed at the base. Heads $\frac{1}{2}$–$\frac{3}{4}$ in. long, in terminal, drooping, corymbose

FIG. 85. LACTUCA MACRORHIZA.

racemes; flowers grey-blue. Achenes black when ripe; beak slender, about half as long as the body. (Fig. 85.)

Simla, Mahasu, common on rocks and banks; August, September.—Temperate Himalaya, 6000–12,000 ft.

6. **Lactuca sagittarioides,** *C. B. Clarke*; *Fl. Br. Ind.* iii. 410. Glabrous; stems usually tufted, slender, erect, 6–18 in., branching. Leaves all radical, arrow-head shaped, rarely 1 or 2 lanceolate, 2–3 in. long, entire or toothed, lobes acute; stalks long, narrowly winged at the top. Heads $\frac{1}{3}$ in. long, in terminal, erect corymbs; stalks slender; flowers yellow. Achenes brown when ripe; beak much shorter than the body.

Daha, in the Giri valley; May, June.—Temperate Himalaya, 5000–6000 ft.

56. PRENANTHES. From the Greek *prenes*, drooping, and *anthos*, a flower; referring to the heads.—N. temperate regions.

Erect herbs; juice milky. Leaves alternate. Heads ligulate, slender, pendulous. Involucre narrowly cylindric; bracts in few series, thin, green, inner ones long, narrow, nearly equal; outer few, much smaller; receptacle flat, naked; flowers 3–8 in a head, purple or white; pappus white or pale brown, not feathery; ligules long, spreading, 5-toothed; style-arms long. Achenes oblong, glabrous, angled, crowned with a pappus-bearing disk, not beaked.—Ripe achenes are necessary to distinguish this genus from *Lactuca*.

Stems 1–6 ft. Heads numerous, panicled. Leaves of various shapes . . . . 1. *P. Brunoniana*.
Stems 12–18 in. Heads few, solitary, long-stalked. Leaves always triangular . . . . 2. *P. violæfolia*.

1. **Prenanthes Brunoniana,** *Wall.*; *Fl. Br. Ind.* iii. **411.** Smooth or rough, sometimes glandular especially on the inflor-

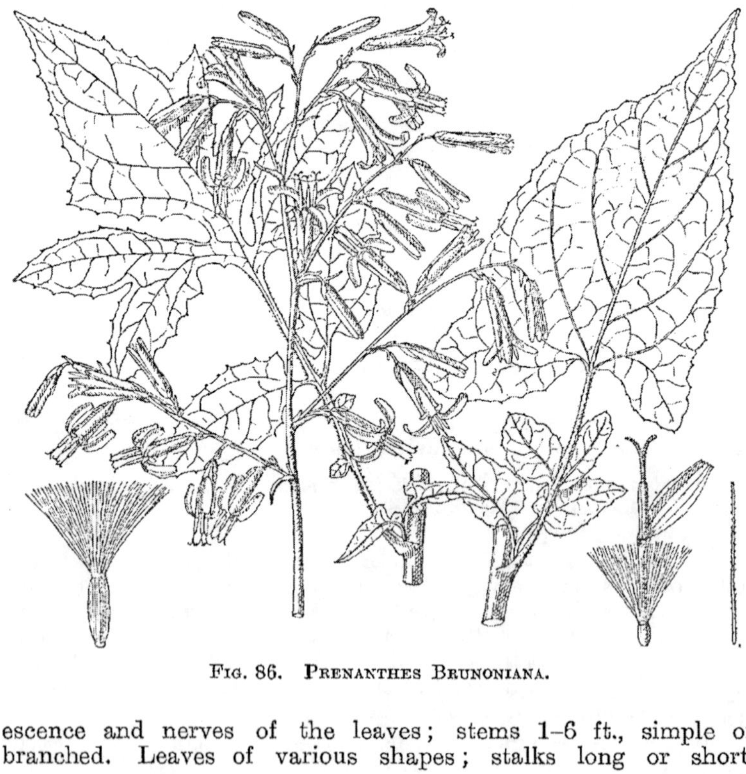

Fig. 86. Prenanthes Brunoniana.

escence and nerves of the leaves; stems 1–6 ft., simple or branched. Leaves of various shapes; stalks long or short, slender, naked or winged, their bases sometimes dilated or lobed; blade 4–8 in. or more, lanceolate or triangular, cordate or truncate, toothed or sinuate, often pinnatifid with large or small, variously cut and toothed lobes. Heads $\frac{1}{2}$–$\frac{3}{4}$ in. long, in a terminal panicle; flowers 3–5 in a head, purple or white. (Fig. 86.)

Simla, common in woods; August, September.—W. Himalaya, 6000–9000 ft.

This species has the aspect of *Lactuca hastata*, but the heads are 3–5- instead of 10–30-flowered, and the achenes are without a beak.

2. **Prenanthes violæfolia,** *Decaisne*; *Fl. Br. Ind.* iii. 412. Glabrous except a few hairs on the summit of the leaf-stalks; stems slender, 12–18 in. Leaves triangular, 1–2 in. each way, entire or obscurely sinuate-toothed, cordate or the basal lobes acute; stalks of the lower leaves with dilated base or a rounded, leaf-like, stem-clasping lobe. Heads $\frac{1}{2}$–$\frac{3}{4}$ in. long, few, solitary, long-stalked; flowers 3–8 in a head, purple.

Huttoo, rare; September, October.—Kashmir to Kumaon, 9000–12,000 ft.

57. SONCHUS. The classical name of *Sonchus oleraceus.*—Temperate regions.

Succulent, erect herbs; juice milky; stems hollow, grooved or angled. Leaves usually pinnately lobed or coarsely toothed: radical stalked; upper alternate, stem-clasping, base lobed. Heads ligulate, many-flowered, in terminal panicles. Involucre ovoid; bracts many, overlapping, green, outer ones smaller; receptacle flat, naked; flowers yellow; pappus copious, white, not feathery; ligules long, spreading, 5-toothed. Achenes flattened, oval, 3–5-ribbed on each face, minutely transversely wrinkled, not beaked.

Leaves hard; teeth long, unequal, spinous . . . . . 1. *S. asper.*
Leaves thin; teeth small, prickly, not spinous.
  Basal lobes of stem-leaves acute . . . . . . 2. *S. oleraceus.*
  Basal lobes of stem-leaves rounded . . . . . 3. *S. arvensis.*

1. **Sonchus asper,** *Vill.*; *Fl. Br. Ind.* iii. 414. Glabrous or slightly glandular on the upper parts; stems 2–3 ft., branched. Leaves hard, lanceolate or pinnatifid, 6–10 × 2–3 in., waved; teeth numerous, long, unequal, divergent, spinous; basal lobes recurved, rounded. Heads $\frac{3}{4}$–1 in. diam.

Simla, in fields; August.—Throughout India, ascending to 12,000 ft.—All temperate and many tropical regions; Britain.

Included under *S. oleraceus* in Bentham's *British Flora.*

2. **Sonchus oleraceus,** *Linn.*; *Fl. Br. Ind.* iii. 414. Glabrous or slightly glandular on the upper parts; stems 2–3 ft., branched. Leaves thin, lanceolate or pinnatifid, 3–6 in.; terminal lobe large,

lateral lobes pointing downwards, sometimes only one pair; teeth small; basal lobes acute, entire or pinnatifid. Heads $\frac{3}{4}$–1 in. diam.

Simla, in fields, common; July–October.—Throughout India, ascending to 8000 ft.—All temperate and many tropical regions (Britain, Sowthistle).

3. **Sonchus arvensis,** *Linn.*; *Fl. Br. Ind.* iii. 414. Glabrous towards the base, glandular-hairy upwards; stems 2–4 ft. Leaves mostly radical, pinnatifid, 4–6 in.; lobes pointing downwards; teeth small; basal lobes rounded, appressed to the stem. Heads 1–2 in. diam.

Simla, roadsides, common; July–October.—Throughout India, ascending to 8000 ft.—All temperate and many tropical regions (Britain, Corn Sowthistle).

58. LAUNÆA. In honour of M. de Launay, a French botanical author of the eighteenth century.—W. Asia, Africa, Europe.

Glabrous, perennial herbs; stems or branches erect or decumbent; juice yellow. Radical leaves numerous, spreading, sessile, oblong, 4–8 × 1–3 in., pinnately lobed or pinnatifid; segments entire or coarsely toothed, obtuse or acute, margins at least of the older leaves beset with minute, hard, sharp, white teeth. Stem-leaves few or none, similar but smaller. Heads ligulate, narrow, $\frac{1}{3}$–$\frac{2}{3}$ in. long, shortly stalked, solitary or in clusters usually forming more or less interrupted racemes. Involucral bracts many, green, margins white, membranous, inner ones long, equal, narrow, outer shorter; receptacle flat, naked; flowers yellow; pappus copious, soft, white, not feathery, united at the base; ligules long, spreading, 5-toothed. Achenes narrowly oblong, smooth, ribs thick, rounded; pappus soon falling off.

Stems erect. Achenes as long as the pappus . . . 1. *L. secunda.*
Stems decumbent. Achenes much shorter than the pappus 2. *L. nudicaulis.*

1. **Launæa secunda,** *C. B. Clarke*; *Fl. Br. Ind.* iii. 416. Stems erect, 1–3 ft., nearly or quite leafless except near the base; branches long, slender. Heads $\frac{1}{3}$ in. long, solitary or in small clusters of 2 or 3, forming long, one-sided racemes. Achenes as long as the pappus.

Sutlej valley; July–October.—N.W. India, ascending to 5000 ft.

2. **Launæa nudicaulis,** *Less.*; *Fl. Br. Ind.* iii. 416. Stems tufted, usually numerous, decumbent, branching, 6–24 in., naked or with a few small leaves below the flower-clusters. Heads $\frac{1}{2}$–$\frac{2}{3}$ in. long, in clusters of 2–5 or about 10, rarely solitary, forming much interrupted racemes or crowded together at the end of branches. Achenes much shorter than the pappus.

Valleys below Simla, in fields; April–June.—Throughou India, ascending to 8000 ft.

59. TRAGOPOGON. From the Greek *tragos*, a goat, and *pogon*, a beard; referring to the long, coarse pappus.—Asia, W. Africa, Europe.

Tragopogon gracile, *Don*; *Fl. Br. Ind.* iii. 417. A glabrous or sometimes slightly cottony herb; stems often tufted, 6–18 in., erect, simple or branched from near the base; juice milky. Leaves alternate, narrow, entire, 3–8 in., acute, base stem-sheathing; radical leaves sometimes as long as the stem. Heads ligulate, 1–2 in. diam., solitary, terminal. Involucral bracts 5–8, $\frac{1}{2}$–$1\frac{1}{2}$ in. long, in one series, green, acute; receptacle flat, naked; flowers yellow; pappus in one series, feathery, united at the base, a few naked-tipped hairs usually projecting beyond the others; ligules long, spreading, 5-toothed. Achenes slender, ribbed, minutely prickly on the upper half, tapering into a short beak.

Simla, on grassy slopes, common; May–October.—Temperate Himalaya, 6000–10,000 ft.

LIII. CAMPANULACEÆ

Erect or decumbent herbs. Leaves undivided, alternate or rarely opposite, toothed or crenate; stipules none. Flowers 2-sexual, purple or blue, axillary or terminal, solitary or in panicles or racemes. Calyx-tube adnate to the ovary; limb free, 5-lobed, persistent. Corolla regular or irregular, usually persistent, 5-lobed; lobes valvate in bud. Stamens 5, alternate with the corolla-lobes and inserted with the corolla on the top of the ovary; anthers united or free. Ovary 2–5-celled; style linear, stigma when mature divided into 2–5 spreading lobes. Capsule 2- or 3-valved; seeds many, minute.—All regions, but most abundant in temperate climates.

Corolla irregular, 2-lipped. Anthers united . . . . 1. *Lobelia*.
Corolla regular. Anthers free
  Corolla lobed nearly to the base.
    Segments spreading, star-like . . . . . . 2. *Cephalostigma*.
    Segments not spreading, bell-shaped . . . . 3. *Wahlenbergia*.
  Corolla lobed half-way down or less, bell-shaped . 4. *Campanula*.

1. LOBELIA. In honour of Mathias Lobel, a Flemish botanist of the sixteenth century.—Most tropical and temperate regions.

Lobelia trialata, *Buch.-Ham.*; *Fl. Br. Ind.* iii. 425. Glabrous; stems 4–12 in., nearly erect, branched, 3-sided, angles winged. Leaves sessile, ovate or lanceolate, $\frac{1}{4}$–1 in., sharply toothed in the upper half, base wedge-shaped, entire. Flowers pale blue or white; stalks 1-flowered, slender, axillary. Calyx-teeth linear, acute. Corolla 2-lipped, $\frac{1}{6}$ in. long, upper lip 2-parted, lower

3-lobed. Anthers united, tipped with bristles. Stigma 2-lobed. Capsule 2-valved.

Naldera; August–October.—N. India, common in the plains, ascending 5000 ft.—Burmah, Abyssinia.

2. CEPHALOSTIGMA. From the Greek *cephalos*, a head, and *stigma*.—India, Africa, South America.

Cephalostigma hirsutum, *Edgew.*; *Fl. Br. Ind.* iii. 429. Roughly hairy; stems 2–5 in., erect, much branched. Leaves nearly sessile, broadly lanceolate, $\frac{1}{2}$–$\frac{3}{4}$ in., crenate; margins wavy and crisped. Flowers blue, in panicles. Calyx-teeth acute. Corolla $\frac{1}{8}$ in., deeply divided; segments narrow, stellately spreading. Anthers free or nearly so. Stigma shortly 3-lobed. Capsule globose, 3-valved.

Common on banks; August, September.—W. Himalaya, 2000–5000 ft.

3. WAHLENBERGIA. In honour of G. Wahlenberg, a Swedish botanist of the eighteenth century.—Widely spread in subtropical and temperate regions.

Wahlenbergia gracilis, *DC.*; *Fl. Br. Ind.* iii. 429. Glabrous or hairy; stems 4–24 in., erect or decumbent, usually branched from the base. Leaves sometimes opposite, sessile, linear or narrowly oblong, $\frac{1}{2}$–2 in., more or less toothed. Flowers pale blue, long-stalked, solitary or in panicles. Calyx-teeth triangular, acute. Corolla bell-shaped, $\frac{1}{6}$–$\frac{2}{3}$ in. long, deeply divided; lobes oblong. Anthers free. Stigma 3-lobed. Capsule 3-valved, tapering to the base.

Simla, Boileaugunge, in fields; May–October—Common throughout India, ascending to 7000 ft.—E. Asia, Australia, S. Africa.

4. CAMPANULA. From the Latin *campanula*, a bell.—N. temperate regions.

Flowers in spikes or racemes. Calyx-tube ovoid or globose. Corolla bell-shaped; lobes not extending below the middle. Filaments dilated at the base, anthers free. Ovary 3-celled; stigma 3-lobed. Capsule 3-valved from the base.

Stems erect.
- Corolla $1\frac{1}{2}$ in. long, dark purple . . . . . . 1. *C. latifolia.*
- Corolla $\frac{1}{4}$–$\frac{1}{2}$ in. long, pale lilac . . . . . . 2. *C. colorata.*

Stems procumbent, thread-like. Corolla $\frac{1}{2}$ in. long, blue . 3. *C. argyrotricha.*

1. **Campanula latifolia,** *Linn.*; *Fl. Br. Ind.* iii. 439. Stems 2–6 ft., glabrous, erect, robust, furrowed, branched. Leaves roughly pubescent on the lower surface, broadly lanceolate or ovate, $2\frac{1}{2}$–5×2–3 in., base wedge-shaped or cordate, margins coarsely toothed or crenate, lower leaves stalked, upper sessile.

Flowers large, dark purple, racemed, lower ones long-stalked. Calyx-teeth lanceolate, $\frac{1}{2}$–$\frac{3}{4}$ in. Corolla 1–1$\frac{1}{2}$ in.; lobes acute. Capsule $\frac{1}{2} \times \frac{1}{3}$ in.

Huttoo, in woods; July, August.—W. Himalaya, 8000-11,000 ft.—W. Asia, Europe (Britain).

2. **Campanula colorata,** *Wall.*; *Fl. Br. Ind.* iii. 440; including *C. canescens* and *C. cana.* Roughly hairy or tomentose; stems 6–24 in., erect, slender, simple or branched. Leaves broadly or narrowly lanceolate, 1–1$\frac{1}{2}$ in., sessile, crenate or toothed. Flowers

FIG. 87. CAMPANULA COLORATA.

numerous, pale lilac, in clusters or panicles. Calyx-teeth lanceolate, $\frac{1}{4}$ in., entire or toothed. Corolla $\frac{1}{4}$–$\frac{1}{2}$ in. long, hairy outside; lobes short. Varies much in size and hairiness according to situation; often produces small cleistogamic flowers. (Fig. 87.)

Simla, common; May-October.—Plains of N. India, ascending to 10,000 ft.

3. **Campanula argyrotricha,** *Wall.*; *Fl. Br. Ind.* iii. 441. Stems numerous, procumbent, thread-like, hairy. Leaves nearly sessile, thin, ovate, $\frac{3}{4} \times \frac{1}{2}$ in., often smaller, toothed or nearly entire, softly silvery-hairy with a few long hairs interspersed. Flowers blue, long-stalked, solitary or racemed. Calyx-teeth $\frac{1}{5}$ in., usually

entire. Corolla $\frac{1}{2}$-$\frac{3}{4}$ in. long, hairy outside. Often produces small, cleistogamic flowers. (Fig. 88.)

Huttoo, common on rocks; August, September.—W. Himalaya, 8000–11,000 ft.

Fig. 88. Campanula argyrotricha.

LIV. ERICACEÆ

Trees or shrubs usually erect, sometimes decumbent. Leaves alternate, undivided, usually entire, very small and closely overlapping in *Cassiope*. Flowers regular, 2-sexual, in racemes or terminal corymbs, or axillary and usually solitary. Calyx free, 5-lobed. Corolla hypogynous, bell-shaped, tubular or salver-shaped, 5-toothed or 5-lobed. Stamens 10, rarely 8, inserted with the corolla, sometimes slightly attached to its base; filaments free; anthers oblong, opening by terminal pores, sometimes provided with spur-like processes. Ovary 5- or 10-celled; style simple, cylindric; stigma terminal, capitate in *Rhododendron*. Capsule opening by 5 or 10 valves, berry-like in *Gaultheria*; seeds numerous, minute.—All regions; chiefly temperate and cold.

Flowers axillary, usually solitary. Decumbent shrubs.
  Leaves $\frac{1}{2}$ in. long, thin, spreading . . . . . 1. *Gaultheria*
  Leaves less than $\frac{1}{4}$ in. long, thick, closely appressed overlapping . . . . 2. *Cassiope*.
Flowers in long racemes. A tree . . . . . . 3. *Pieris*.
Flowers in terminal corymbs. Trees or erect shrubs . . 4. *Rhododendron*.

1. GAULTHERIA. In honour of Gaulthier, a French-Canadian physician and botanist of the eighteenth century.—Chiefly America; a few species in Asia and Australia.

Gaultheria nummularioides, *Don*; *Fl. Br. Ind.* iii. 457. A small shrub; stems prostrate; branches hairy, ascending. Leaves thin, nearly sessile, spreading, ovate, $\frac{1}{2} \times \frac{1}{3}$ in., acute, upper surface glabrous, lower hairy; margins toothed, fringed. Flowers solitary, axillary, $\frac{1}{4}$ in. long, pink or white. Calyx ovoid; teeth lanceolate. Corolla tubular; teeth minute, recurved. Stamens 10, filaments dilated, anther-cells 2-spurred. Fruit berry-like, dark blue, the 5-celled capsule being enclosed in the persistent, enlarged, succulent calyx.

The Chor, Marali, covering banks; June, July.—Himalaya, 8000–12,000 ft. —Java.

This species ought to occur on Huttoo; but no specimens are on record.

2. **CASSIOPE.** Of classical origin; Cassiope was the mother of Andromeda; also the name of an allied genus.—Cold N. regions.

Cassiope fastigiata, *D. Don*; *Fl. Br. Ind.* iii. 459. A small shrub; stems tufted, 4–12 in., decumbent, much branched. Leaves thick, sessile, erect, closely appressed, overlapping, ovate-oblong, less than $\frac{1}{4}$ in., acute; margins membranous. Flowers axillary, drooping, solitary or in clusters of 2 or 3, white; stalks hairy, curved. Calyx glabrous. Corolla bell-shaped, $\frac{1}{3}$ in. long; lobes short, recurved. Stamens 10, anther-cells 1-spurred. Capsule erect, globose, 5-valved.

Huttoo, on rocks; June, July.—Temperate Himalaya, 10,000–14,000 ft.

3. **PIERIS.** From *Pieria*, a district of Macedonia; the abode of the Muses.—Himalaya, Burmah, Japan, N.E. America.

Pieris ovalifolia, *D. Don*; *Fl. Br. Ind.* iii. 460. A small, glabrous tree. Leaves shortly stalked, ovate or oblong, 4×2 in., entire, acute. Flowers white, in racemes 4–8 in. long. Calyx-segments lanceolate. Corolla pubescent, tubular, $\frac{1}{3}$ in. long, narrowed to the mouth; teeth small, spreading or recurved. Stamens 10, filaments 2-spurred at the top. Capsule globose, 5-valved. (Fig. 89.)

Simla, common in forest; May.—Temperate Himalaya, 5000–8000 ft.

4. **RHODODENDRON.** From the Greek *rhodon*, a rose, and *dendron*, a tree.—Mountains of Asia, Europe, N. America, Australia, New Guinea.

Trees or erect shrubs. Leaves crowded towards the end of branches, shortly stalked, leathery, entire. Flowers in terminal corymbs. Corolla-tube long or very short; limb spreading. Stamens 8 or 10. Stigma capitate. Capsule cylindric, woody, 5- or 10-valved.

The two following species occur on the Chor, flowering in June:—

R. campanulatum *Don*: *Fl. Br. Ind.* iii. 466. A shrub. 6–12 ft. Leaves ovate, 4 × 2 in.; lower surface cinnamon-coloured, tomentose. Flowers pale pink, often spotted. Corolla bell-shaped, 1 in.; lobes spreading.

R. Anthopogon, *D. Don*; *Fl. Br. Ind.* iii. 472. A shrub, 1 ft., highly aromatic. Leaves ovate, 1 × ½ in.; lower surface covered with red-brown scales. Flowers sulphur-coloured. Corolla salver-shaped, ¾ in. long. Occurs also on Marali.

A tree. Leaves 2½–5 in. Flowers 1–2 in. long . . . 1. *R. arboreum.*
A small shrub. Leaves ¾–1 in. Flowers less than ½ in. long. 2. *R. lepidotum.*

FIG. 89. PIERIS OVALIFOLIA.

1. **Rhododendron arboreum,** *Smith*; *Fl. Br. Ind.* iii. 465. A tree. Leaves oblong-lanceolate, 2½–5 × 1–1½ in.; upper surface glabrous, lower silvery-scaly. Flowers red or pink, sometimes spotted, rarely white, crowded in large, head-like corymbs. Calyx small, persistent; teeth unequal. Corolla bell-shaped, 1–2 in. long. Stamens 10, alternate ones longer. Capsule scaly, 1 in., curved, 10-valved.

Simla, common; March–May, occasionally again in July and August if the spring flowering has been checked by drought, hailstorms, &c.—Temperate Himalaya, 6000–8000 ft.—Burmah.

2. **Rhododendron lepidotum,** *Wall.*; *Fl. Br. Ind.* iii. 471. An erect, aromatic shrub, 1–4 ft.; inflorescence and young parts covered with minute, circular, silvery or brown scales. Leaves oblong or obovate, ¾–1 in.; upper surface silvery-scaly, lower brown-scaly. Flowers dingy yellow or pale pink-purple, in small

corymbs, sometimes reduced to a single flower. Calyx-lobes obtuse. Corolla-tube very short, globose; lobes rounded, spreading, $\frac{1}{2}$ in. across. Stamens 8. Capsule scaly, $\frac{1}{3}$ in., 5-valved.

Simla, Jako, Huttoo; June.—Temperate Himalaya, 8000–15,000 ft.

LV. MONOTROPACEÆ

SUCCULENT, waxy white or pale yellow-brown herbs growing under trees on decaying vegetable matter; root fibrous, densely interlaced; stems tufted, rarely solitary, erect, covered with alternate, appressed scales. Leaves none. Flowers regular, 2-sexual. Sepals free, scale-like, usually 4, nearly as long as the petals. Petals free, hypogynous, 4 or 5, imbricate, base slightly dilated. Stamens 8 or 10, nearly as long as the petals. Anthers broadly kidney-shaped, 1-celled, opening by two transverse slits. Ovary superior, ovoid, 4- or 5-celled, 8- or 10-grooved; style thick, short, elongating in fruit; stigma terminal, broad, nearly on a level with the anthers. Capsule 4- or 5-celled, opening by slits opposite the middle of the cells; seeds very numerous, minute.—A small Order inhabiting North temperate forest regions.

Flowers waxy white, solitary, terminal . . . . . 1. *Monotropa.*
Flowers pale yellow brown, several, racemed . . . 2. *Hypopitys.*

1. **MONOTROPA.** From the Greek *monos*, one, and *trepein*, to turn; the flowers of some species are all turned to one side.—Himalaya, Japan, N. America.

Monotropa uniflora, *Linn.*; *Fl. Br. Ind.* iii. 476. Glabrous, waxy white; stems 6–12 in.; scales broadly lanceolate, $\frac{3}{4}$ in. Flowers waxy white, solitary, terminal, drooping. Petals 5, $\frac{3}{4}$ in. long. Stamens 10. Capsule 5-celled, erect. (Fig. 90.)

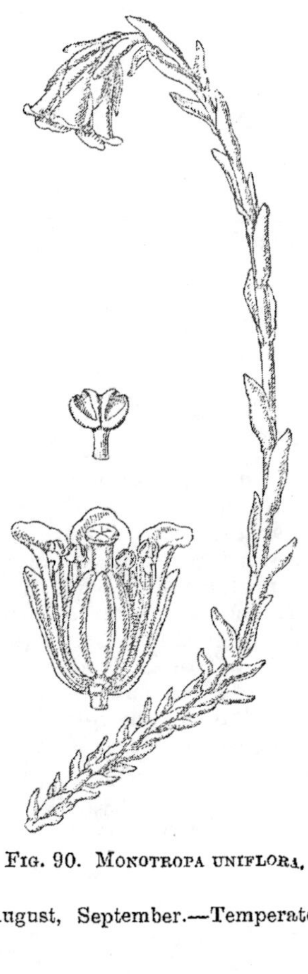

FIG. 90. MONOTROPA UNIFLORA.

Simla, the Glen, Narkunda, in forest; August, September.—Temperate Himalaya, 6000–8000 ft.—Japan, N. America.

2. HYPOPITYS. From the Greek *hypo*, under, and *pitys*, a pine; the plants usually grow in pine forests.—Northern forest regions.

Hypopitys lanuginosa, *Nutt.*; *Fl. Br. Ind.* iii. 476. Hairy or pubescent, pale yellow-brown; stems 6–18 in.; scales ovate-oblong, ¾ in. Flowers pale yellow-brown, several in a terminal, bracteate raceme; terminal flower with 5 petals and 10 stamens, the others with 4 petals and 8 stamens. Petals ½ in. long, inner surface densely hairy. Capsules 5- or 4-celled, erect.

Mushobra, Narkunda, in pine forest.—Temperate Himalaya, 8000–10,000 ft. —N. Asia, N. America.

Closely allied to the British Bird's Nest, *Monotropa Hypopithys* of most authors.

LVI. PLUMBAGINACEÆ

A SMALL Order extending over most parts of the world, chiefly near the sea and in salt marshes.—There are several genera in India, but it is restricted to the following species in the N.W. Himalaya.

The Thrift, *Armeria*, and Sea Lavender, *Statice*, of the British coasts both belong to this Order.

PLUMBAGO. The Latin name of *P. europæa*, derived from *plumbum*, lead; the plant was used medicinally.—All warm regions.

Plumbago zeylanica, *Linn.*; *Fl. Br. Ind.* iii. 480. A diffuse, rambling undershrub; stems several, 2–4 ft. Leaves alternate, glabrous, ovate, 2–3 in., entire, acute; stalks short, stem-clasping. Flowers 2-sexual, regular, white, in bracteate, often branched, glandular spikes 4–12 in. long. Calyx inferior, tubular, glandular, 5-ribbed, 5-toothed. Corolla hypogynous, salver-shaped; tube ¾ in.; lobes 5, nearly equal, rounded, spreading. Stamens 5, free from the corolla, opposite its lobes, dilated at the base; anthers protruded, 2-celled. Ovary superior, 1-celled, narrowed into a long, linear style 5-branched at the top; ovule solitary. Capsule enclosed in the persistent calyx, opening transversely near the base; seed oblong.

Giri and Sutlej valleys; June, July.—Cultivated throughout India; often seen as an escape near villages below 5000 ft.—Tropical regions of the Old World.

LVII. PRIMULACEÆ

HERBS of various habit; rootstock usually perennial. Leaves undivided, usually entire; stipules none. Flowers 2-sexual, regular. Calyx free, except in *Samolus*, 5- rarely 4-lobed or toothed, persistent. Corolla hypogynous, gamopetalous; tube cylindric and distinct or very short, the corolla being lobed nearly to its base; limb 5- rarely 4-lobed, spreading or erect. Stamens 5, rarely 4, inserted in the tube or at the base of the corolla, opposite to the lobes; filaments short or long, usually free; anthers 2-celled. Ovary free, except in *Samolus*, ovoid or globose, 1-celled; style short or long; stigma simple; ovules usually many, attached to a free central column. Capsule 1-celled, opening from the top by 5 valves, except in *Anagallis*; seeds minute, usually numerous.—A widely spread Order, chiefly inhabiting N. temperate and alpine regions.

Flowers in heads, umbels or whorls, or solitary on radical stalks. Corolla-tube distinct
- Corolla-tube longer than the calyx . . . . . . 1. *Primula.*
- Corolla-tube shorter than the calyx. . . . . . 2. *Androsace.*

Flowers racemed or axillary. Corolla lobed nearly to the base.
- Flowers borne in the axils of leaves or bracts; stalks naked. Ovary superior.
  - Corolla $\frac{1}{4}$ or $\frac{1}{3}$ in. diam. Leaves $\frac{1}{2}$ in. or more long.
    - Filaments glabrous. Capsule opening from the top in 5 valves . . . . 3. *Lysimachia.*
    - Filaments hairy. Capsule opening by a circular fissure round the middle . . . . . . 4. *Anagallis.*
  - Corolla minute. Leaves less than $\frac{1}{4}$ in. long . . 5. *Centunculus.*
- Flowers not axillary; stalks bearing a small bract near the middle. Ovary half-inferior . . . . . . 6. *Samolus.*

1. PRIMULA. From the Latin *primus*, first; referring to the early flowering of many species.—Chiefly N. temperate and alpine regions; S. America.

Herbs; stems very short or none. Leaves all radical, sessile or stalked, spathulate, oblong or ovate, toothed. Flowers $\frac{1}{2}$ to nearly 1 in. diam., crowded in a terminal, head-like umbel or solitary on distinct radical stalks or whorled. Calyx tubular, 5-lobed. Corolla funnel- or salver-shaped; tube longer than the calyx, cylindric; limb spreading, 5-lobed. Stamens 5, included, inserted near the base or at the throat of the corolla-tube; filaments very short. Ovary globose; style as long as the corolla-tube or much shorter; stigma capitate; ovules numerous. Capsule globose, splitting from the top in 5 valves; seeds many, minute.

The flowers of the common Primrose and other species of *Primula* present two forms in the same species: long-styled, with the stamens deep in the corolla-tube; and short-styled, with the stamens at its mouth. These forms are important in connection with cross-fertilisation by insects. See Darwin's *Forms of Flowers*, chap. i.

Flowers usually purple or lilac, sometimes white.
 Flowers crowded in a terminal, head-like umbel . . 1. *P. denticulata.*
 Flowers solitary on distinct, radical stalks . . . 2. *P. petiolaris.*
Flowers yellow, whorled . . . . 3. *P. floribunda.*

1. **Primula denticulata,** *Smith*; *Fl. Br. Ind.* iii. 485. Slightly mealy. Leaves waved and wrinkled, sessile or narrowed into short, broad stalks, oblong-spathulate, 2–4 in., enlarging after

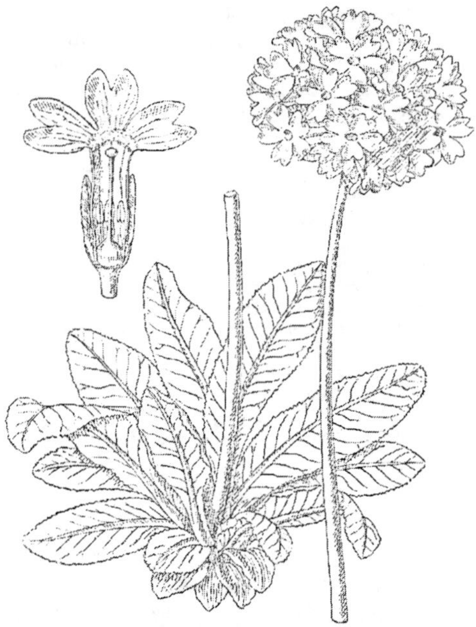

FIG. 91. PRIMULA DENTICULATA.

flowering; teeth very small, sharp, unequal. Flowers varying from dark purple to pale lilac, crowded in a globose, head-like umbel terminal on a single, naked, radical stalk 4–12 in. long. Corolla salver-shaped, about ½ in. diam.; lobes notched. (Fig. 91.)

Simla, common on Jako; March, April.—Temperate Himalaya, 7000–13,000 ft.—Afghanistan, Burmah.

2. **Primula petiolaris,** *Wall.*; *Fl. Br. Ind.* iii. 493. More or less mealy at least on the buds. Leaves thin, membranous, sessile or narrowed into a winged stalk, oblong or ovate, 2–6 in., sharply and

irregularly toothed. Flowers usually purple, sometimes varying to white, solitary on slender, distinct, radical stalks. Corolla funnel-shaped, $\frac{3}{4}$–1 in. diam.; lobes toothed or acute, sometimes rounded. (Fig. 92.)

Mahasu, Matiana, Narkunda, on rocks and grassy slopes above 8000 ft.; April, May.—Simla to Bhotan, 4000–12,000 ft.

3. **Primula floribunda,** *Wall.*; *Fl. Br. Ind.* iii. 495. Glandular-pubescent. Leaves thin, narrowed into a broad, winged stalk, ovate, $1\frac{1}{2}$–$4 \times \frac{1}{2}$–$1\frac{1}{2}$ in., coarsely and irregularly toothed. Flowers yellow, unequally stalked, in one or several superposed whorls borne on slender, erect, solitary or tufted scapes 4–8 in. high. Corolla salver-shaped, about $\frac{1}{2}$ in. diam.; lobes notched.

Simla, near water or under damp rocks; January–December.—W. Himalaya, 3000–6000 ft.

FIG. 92. PRIMULA PETIOLARIS.

2. **ANDROSACE.** From the Greek *aner, andros,* a man, and *sacos,* a shield; the application is variously explained, but probably the shape of the leaves of the common species suggested the name.—N. temperate, alpine and arctic regions.

Small herbs; stems none or very short. Leaves alternate or crowded in rosettes, stalked or sessile, lobed and toothed or entire. Flowers small, in involucrate umbels terminal on slender, erect scapes. Calyx tubular, 5-lobed. Corolla salver-shaped, $\frac{1}{4}$–$\frac{1}{2}$ in. diam.; tube shorter than the calyx, narrowed and wrinkled at the mouth; lobes 5, spreading, entire or slightly indented.

Stamens 5, inserted on and included in the corolla-tube, filaments very short. Ovary top-shaped; style short, stigma capitate; ovules few. Capsule ovoid, splitting from the top in 5 valves; seeds few, usually only 2.

Leaves long-stalked, orbicular. Involucral bracts toothed 1. *A. rotundifolia.*
Leaves sessile, lanceolate. Involucral bracts entire.
  Runners rooting, naked between the rosettes of leaves . 2. *A. sarmentosa.*
  Runner-like branches not rooting, leafy throughout . 3. *A. lanuginosa.*

1. **Androsace rotundifolia,** *Hardw.*; *Fl. Br. Ind.* iii. 496. More or less hairy, sometimes glandular. Runners none. Leaves all radical, long-stalked, orbicular, $\frac{1}{2}$–$1\frac{1}{2}$ in. across, cordate; margins lobed, lobes shallow, toothed or crenate, rarely entire. Scapes several, tufted, 1–6 in. Involucral bracts wedge-shaped, toothed. Calyx-lobes acute, enlarged and spreading in fruit. Corolla deep pink, varying to nearly white, larger or smaller than the calyx.

Simla, Mushobra, on rocks and banks; April–June.—W. Himalaya, 5000–11,000 ft.

A very hairy variety with brighter and smaller flowers than the Simla plant occurs on the limestone rocks at Naldera and on Shali.

FIG. 93. ANDROSACE LANUGINOSA.

2. **Androsace sarmentosa,** *Wall.*; *Fl. Br. Ind.* iii. 498. More or less softly hairy. Runners long, rooting and forming rosettes of leaves at the ends, otherwise leafless. Leaves all radical or in rosettes, sessile or nearly so, lanceolate, $\frac{1}{2}$–1 in., entire. Scapes solitary, 3–6 in. Involucral bracts short, narrowly lanceolate, entire. Calyx-lobes acute or obtuse. Corolla pale pink-purple, darker towards the centre, mouth of tube yellow.

Narkunda, Marali, on rocks; June, July.—Temperate Himalaya, 9000–14,000 ft.

3. **Androsace lanuginosa,** *Wall.*; *Fl. Br. Ind.* iii. 498. Whole plant densely covered with long, almost silvery, white, silky hairs. Runner-like branches trailing, leafy and forming at intervals rosettes of leaves but not rooting. Leaves radical or alternate or crowded in rosettes, sessile, lanceolate, $\frac{1}{2}$–$\frac{3}{4}$ in., entire. Scapes solitary, 3–4 in. Involucral bracts short, narrowly lanceolate, entire. Calyx-lobes acute or obtuse. Corolla pale or dark purple, usually tinged with blue, yellow in the centre. (Fig. 93.)

Simla, common on rocks and banks; April–July.—W. Himalaya, 6000–10,000 ft.

3. LYSIMACHIA. The classical name signifying Loosestrife and perhaps more correctly applied to *Lythrum Salicaria*, the Purple Loosestrife of Britain.—Chiefly N. temperate and subtropical regions.

Erect, decumbent or prostrate, gland-dotted herbs. Leaves alternate or opposite, usually stalked, entire. Flowers solitary, rarely in pairs, in the axils of the upper leaves or of bracts, stalked, rarely sessile, forming terminal racemes or raceme-like spikes. Calyx 5-parted; segments lanceolate. Corolla bell-shaped or rotate, 5-lobed nearly to the base; lobes entire, twisted in bud. Stamens 5, inserted at the base of the corolla, filaments glabrous, distinct or connected at the base by a membrane or ridge. Ovary globose; style slender, persistent, stigma terminal, simple; ovules many. Capsule small, globose, splitting from the top by 5 valves; seeds numerous, minute.

- Corolla bell-shaped, pale purple or white.
  - Flowers stalked.
    - Leaves ovate lanceolate. Flower-stalks much longer than their bracts . . . . . . 1. *L. lobelioides.*
    - Leaves narrowly lanceolate. Flower-stalks much shorter than their bracts . . . . . . 2. *L. pyramidalis.*
  - Flowers sessile or nearly sessile . . . . . 3. *L. chenopodioides.*
- Corolla rotate, yellow.
  - Leaves alternate. Flower-stalks slender, as long as the leaves . . . . 4. *L. alternifolia.*
  - Leaves opposite. Flower-stalks thick, shorter than the leaf stalks . . . . 5. *L. japonica.*

1. **Lysimachia lobelioides,** *Wall.*; *Fl. Br. Ind.* iii. 502. Glabrous; stems angular, ascending, 1–2 ft., branching from the base. Leaves alternate, ovate-lanceolate, 1–2 × $\frac{1}{4}$–$\frac{3}{4}$ in., tapering into a short stalk, acute. Flowers pale purple or white, in terminal racemes 3–6 in. long, elongated in fruit; stalks much longer than their bracts. Calyx nearly as long as the corolla, margins of lobes membranous. Corolla bell-shaped, $\frac{1}{4}$ in. diam. Filaments not united at the base; anthers protruding.

Simla; May–July.—Temperate Himalaya, 4000–8000 ft.

2. **Lysimachia pyramidalis,** *Wall.*; *Fl. Br. Ind.* iii. 503. Glabrous; stems erect, $\frac{1}{2}$–2 ft., usually much branched. Leaves alternate, sessile or nearly so, narrowly lanceolate, $\frac{1}{2}$–3 × $\frac{1}{8}$–$\frac{1}{2}$ in., upper ones smaller. Flowers pale purple, in terminal racemes 3–9 in. long; stalks much shorter than their bracts. Calyx as long as the corolla. Corolla bell-shaped, $\frac{1}{4}$ in. diam. Filaments not united at the base; anthers included.

Simla; June–October.—Simla to Nepal, 5000–8000 ft.

3. **Lysimachia chenopodioides,** *Watt*; *Fl. Br. Ind.* iii. 503. Glabrous; stems ascending, $\frac{1}{2}$–1$\frac{1}{2}$ ft., usually much branched. Leaves alternate, ovate-lanceolate, $\frac{1}{2}$–1$\frac{1}{2}$ × $\frac{1}{3}$–$\frac{3}{4}$ in., tapering into a rather long stalk, acute. Flowers pale purple, solitary, axillary, sessile or nearly so. Calyx as long as the corolla. Corolla bell-shaped, $\frac{1}{4}$ in. diam. Filaments not united at the base; anthers included.

Valleys below Simla; May–July. Kashmir to Bhotan, 5000–9000 ft.

4. **Lysimachia alternifolia,** *Wall.*; *Fl. Br. Ind.* iii. 504. Pubescent or slightly hairy; stems decumbent, 6–12 in., branching from the base. Leaves alternate, ovate-lanceolate, 1–1$\frac{1}{2}$ × $\frac{1}{2}$–$\frac{3}{4}$ in., stalked or the upper ones nearly sessile, acute. Flowers yellow, solitary, axillary; stalks slender, as long or nearly as long as the leaves. Calyx longer than the corolla. Corolla rotate, $\frac{1}{4}$ in. diam. Filaments united at the base; anthers included.

Valleys below Simla; June–September.—Simla to Bhotan, 2000–6000 ft.

5. **Lysimachia japonica,** *Thunb.*; *Fl. Br. Ind.* iii. 505. Hairy and densely pubescent; stems prostrate, rooting at the lower joints, 6–12 in. Leaves opposite, stalked, ovate, 1–1$\frac{1}{2}$ × $\frac{3}{4}$–1 in., acute. Flowers yellow, solitary or in pairs, axillary; stalks thick, shorter than the leaf-stalks. Calyx longer than the corolla. Corolla rotate, $\frac{1}{4}$–$\frac{1}{2}$ in. diam. Filaments united at the base; anthers included.

Valleys below Simla, the Glen; June–August.—Kashmir to Bhotan, 3000–8000 ft.—China and Japan.

4. **ANAGALLIS.** The classical name of the Pimpernel, *A. arvensis*; etymology doubtful.—Chiefly N. temperate regions.

Anagallis arvensis, *Linn.*; *Fl. Br. Ind.* iii. 506. A glabrous, gland-dotted herb; stems slender, erect or decumbent, 6–12 in., branching from the base; branches 4-angled. Leaves opposite, sessile, broadly ovate, $\frac{1}{2}$–1 in., entire, acute. Flowers closing in dull weather, bright blue, solitary, axillary; stalks slender, longer than the leaves. Calyx 5-parted; segments narrowly lanceolate, acute. Corolla rotate, $\frac{1}{3}$ in. diam., 5-lobed nearly to the base; lobes glandular-fringed, entire, twisted in bud. Stamens 5, inserted at the base of the corolla, filaments hairy. Ovary globose; style slender, stigma terminal, simple: ovules many. Capsule small, globose, opening by a circular fissure round the middle; seeds numerous, minute.

Simla, common in fields; May–October.—Throughout India, ascending to 7000 ft.—W. Asia, Europe (Britain, Pimpernel); the flowers are usually red in N. Europe. Widely colonised in other countries.

5. CENTUNCULUS. Etymology doubtful.—Europe, Asia, America.

***Centunculus tenellus,** *Duby*; *Fl. Br. Ind.* iii. 506. An annual herb; stems erect, 2–6 in., simple or branched. Leaves alternate, sessile, ovate, less than 1/4 in. long, entire, acute. Flowers minute, white or pink, solitary, axillary; stalks usually shorter than the leaves, elongating in fruit. Calyx 4- or 5-lobed. Corolla rotate, 4- or 5-lobed. Stamens 4 or 5, inserted at the base of the corolla. Ovary globose; style thread-like, stigma simple; ovules many. Capsule globose, opening by a circular fissure round the middle; seeds numerous.

Hilly districts throughout India, ascending to 6000 ft.; usually on damp, grassy places; April–October.—Tropical America and Australia.

6. SAMOLUS. Etymology obscure.—Chiefly temperate regions of the S. Hemisphere, and the following widely diffused species.

Samolus Valerandi, *Linn.*; *Fl. Br. Ind.* iii. 506. A glabrous herb; stems ascending or erect, 6–18 in., usually branched. Leaves obovate or spathulate, 1–4 in., entire; lower crowded, spreading, stalked; upper alternate, smaller, nearly sessile. Flowers small, white, not axillary, in terminal racemes corymbose at first, ultimately elongating; stalks bracteate about the middle. Calyx-tube hemispheric, half adnate to the ovary; limb 5-toothed. Corolla bell-shaped, deeply 5-lobed, 1/8 in. diam.; limb spreading. Stamens 5, inserted at the base of the corolla, filaments very short, alternate with 5 minute scales. Ovary globose, lower half adnate to the calyx-tube; style short, stigma capitate; ovules many. Capsule globose, small, crowned with the calyx-teeth, splitting from the top in 5 valves; seeds numerous, minute.

Sutlej valley, on marshy ground near Suni; April.—W. Himalaya, 3000–4000 ft.—Nearly all regions (Britain, Brookweed).

LVIII. MYRSINACEÆ

An Order inhabiting nearly all tropical and subtropical regions; largely represented throughout India, but having only two species in the Simla neighbourhood.

MYRSINE. The Greek name of the Myrtle, *Myrtus communis*; both genera have gland-dotted leaves.—Nearly all tropical regions, chiefly Asiatic.

Shrubs or small trees. Leaves alternate, undivided, dotted with pellucid glands, usually toothed; stipules none. Flowers glandular, very small, regular, polygamous, in axillary clusters, sometimes apparently crowded along the branches owing to the leaves having fallen off. Calyx free, persistent, 4- or 5-lobed, much shorter than the corolla. Corolla rotate, hypogynous, 4- or 5-lobed. Stamens 4 or 5, inserted on the base of the corolla opposite its lobes, filaments very short, anthers 2-celled. Ovary superior, ovoid, 1-celled, narrowed upwards in a short style; stigma large, terminal, capitate or 3-lobed; ovules several, attached to a free central column. Fruit berry-like, indehiscent, globose, hardly $\frac{1}{5}$ in. diam., smooth, red; seed large, solitary.

Fig. 94. Myrsine africana.

A shrub. Leaves $\frac{1}{2}$–1 in. Flowers nearly sessile . . 1. *M. africana.*
A small tree. Leaves 3–5 in. Flowers stalked . . . 2. *M. semiserrata.*

1. **Myrsine africana,** *Linn.*; *Fl. Br. Ind.* iii. 511. A small, erect, pubescent shrub. Leaves nearly sessile, lanceolate, $\frac{1}{2}$–1 in., sharply toothed. Flowers nearly sessile. Calyx and corolla 4-lobed. Stamens 4. Stigma capitate, covered with minute protuberances. Berry dotted with red glands. (Fig. 94.)

Simla, the Glen; March–May.—Temperate Himalaya, 2000–9000 ft.—S. Africa.

2. **Myrsine semiserrata,** *Wall.*; *Fl. Br. Ind.* iii. 511. A small, glabrous tree. Leaves shortly stalked, lanceolate, 3–5 in., sharply toothed towards the tip, rarely entire, margins gland-dotted. Flowers stalked. Calyx and

corolla 4- rarely 5-lobed. Stamens 4, rarely 5. Stigma of 3 spreading lobes.

Simla, the Glen; January–May.—Bhotan to the Beeas, 3000–9000 ft.—Burmah.

LIX. STYRACACEÆ

A SMALL Order inhabiting most warm regions except Africa. Seventy species are found in India but only one extends to the N.W. Himalaya.—*Styrax* was the classical name of the S. European tree, *S. officinale*, whose bark produces the resinous substance known as *storax*. The Moluccan tree *S. Benzoin* yields the resin called *benzoin*. Both substances are used in medicine and perfumery.

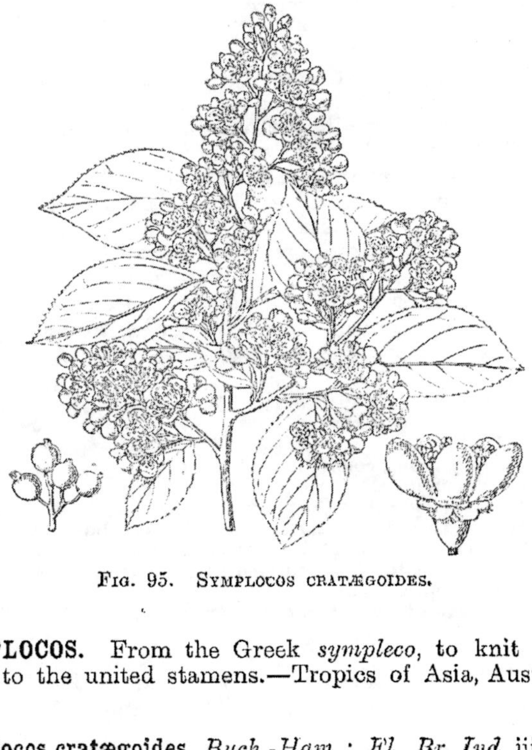

FIG. 95. SYMPLOCOS CRATÆGOIDES.

SYMPLOCOS. From the Greek *sympleco*, to knit together; referring to the united stamens.—Tropics of Asia, Australia and America.

Symplocos cratægoides, *Buch.-Ham.*; *Fl. Br. Ind.* iii. 573. A shrub or small tree; young parts and inflorescence hairy, otherwise glabrous. Leaves shortly stalked, ovate, 2–4 in., toothed, acute or obtuse, turning yellow in drying; stipules none. Flowers regular, 2-sexual, fragrant, white, $\frac{1}{3}$ in. diam., in terminal panicles 2–6 in. long. Calyx-tube adnate to the ovary; lobes 5, short, obtuse, minutely fringed. Petals 5, nearly free. Stamens numerous, filaments united at the base in 5 sets, inserted at the base of the corolla. Ovary inferior, 2-celled; style long, linear, stigma capitate; ovules 2 or 3 in each cell, pendulous. Drupe globose or ovoid, about $\frac{1}{4}$ in. diam., crowned with the persistent calyx-limb, black when ripe; seed solitary. (Fig. 95.)

Simla, Narkunda; April–June.—Temperate Himalaya, 3000–8000 ft.—Burmah, Japan.

The inflorescence resembles that of the Hawthorn; hence the specific name. The leaves and bark are used in dyeing, yielding a yellow colour.

LX. OLEACEÆ

Trees or shrubs. Leaves opposite, except in *Jasminum humile*, undivided or pinnate; stipules none. Flowers 2-sexual, rarely polygamous, regular, in cymes or panicles. Calyx free, bell-shaped or tubular, usually small, toothed or nearly entire, persistent. Corolla salver- or funnel-shaped or rotate, usually 4-lobed or in *Fraxinus* of 4 petals united at the base in two pairs. Stamens 2, inserted on the corolla-tube or at the base of the petals; filaments usually short, anthers 2-celled. Ovary superior, 2-celled; style usually short, stigma terminal, simple or 2-lobed; ovules 2 in each cell, rarely solitary. Fruit drupe-like, berry-like or capsular; seeds 1 or 2 in each cell, sometimes solitary through the suppression of one cell.—A small Order inhabiting all warm and temperate regions.

Leaves pinnate.
  Shrubs. Corolla salver-shaped, lobes 5 . . . . . 1. *Jasminum.*
  Trees. Corolla-lobes 4, nearly free . . . . . . 4. *Fraxinus.*
Leaves undivided.
  Bracts 2, conspicuous, concealing the calyx . . . 2. *Nyctanthes.*
  Bracts none or minute.
    Corolla-tube longer than the calyx.
      Leaves ovate; lower surface white. Corolla-tube cylindric, $\frac{3}{10}$ in. . . . . 3. *Syringa.*
      Leaves lanceolate; lower surface green. Corolla-tube funnel-shaped, $\frac{1}{10}$ in. . . . . 6. *Ligustrum.*
    Corolla-tube not longer than the calyx . . . . 5. *Olea.*

1. JASMINUM. Derived from *jâsemîn*, the Persian name, signifying fragrant.—Tropical and temperate regions of the Old World.

Climbing, sometimes erect, glabrous shrubs; branches long. Leaves opposite, rarely alternate, odd-pinnate; leaflets opposite, nearly sessile, entire, end one the longest. Flowers white or yellow, in terminal clusters. Calyx-tube short; teeth 5, short or long. Corolla salver-shaped; tube cylindric; lobes 5. Stamens included in the corolla-tube, filaments short. Style slender, simple; stigma capitate, obscurely 2-lobed. Berry deeply 2-lobed or globose through the suppression of one cell; seeds solitary in each cell.

Calyx-teeth much shorter than the tube.
Flowers white . . . . 1. *J. dispermum.*
Flowers yellow . . . . 2. *J. humile.*
Calyx-teeth much longer than the tube.
Leaflets 3–7. Corolla-tube $\frac{1}{3}$ in. . . . . . 3. *J. officinale.*
Leaflets 7–11. Corolla-tube $\frac{3}{4}$ in. . . . . . 4. *J. grandiflorum.*

1. **Jasminum dispermum,** *Wall.*; *Fl. Br. Ind.* iii. 602. A climbing shrub. Leaves opposite, 4–6 in.; leaflets 3-5, lanceolate or ovate-lanceolate, long-pointed, end one 2–4 in. Flowers numerous, crowded, white, sometimes tinged with pink, $\frac{3}{4}$–1 in. long. Calyx-teeth much shorter than the tube.

Simla, Lansdowne Falls; April.—Temperate Himalaya, 2000–8000 ft.

2. **Jasminum humile,** *Linn.*; *Fl. Br. Ind.* iii. 602. An erect shrub. Leaves alternate, 2–4 in.; leaflets 3–7, oblong or ovate, end one 1–2 in. Flowers yellow, $\frac{1}{2}$–$\frac{3}{4}$ in. long. Calyx-teeth much shorter than the tube.

Simla, common; May–October.—Temperate Himalaya, 2000–9000 ft.

3. **Jasminum officinale,** *Linn.*; *Fl. Br. Ind.* iii. 603. A climbing or half erect shrub. Leaves opposite, 2–4 in.; leaflets 3–7, ovate or ovate-lanceolate, long-pointed, end one 1–2 in. Flowers white, numerous, crowded. Calyx-teeth linear, more than half the length of the corolla-tube. Corolla-tube $\frac{1}{3}$ in.; lobes $\frac{1}{3}$ in. long.

Fagoo, Narkunda; May–July.—W. Himalaya, 3000–9000 ft.
The common white Jessamine cultivated in Britain.

4. **Jasminum grandiflorum,** *Linn.*; *Fl. Br. Ind.* iii. 603. A climbing shrub. Leaves opposite, 3–4 in.; leaflets 7–11, ovate, end one $\frac{1}{2}$–1 in., often partially united with the uppermost pair. Flowers white, often tinged with purple outside. Calyx-teeth linear, less than half the length of the corolla-tube. Corolla-tube $\frac{3}{4}$ in.; lobes $\frac{1}{2}$ in. long.

Simla, common; May–September.—Simla to Nepal, 2000–7000 ft.
Cultivated throughout India.—Native name *Chambel.*

2. **NYCTANTHES.** From the Greek *nyx, nyctos,* night, and *anthos,* a flower; the flowers open in the evening and fall off the following morning.—India.

Nyctanthes Arbor-tristis, *Linn.*; *Fl. Br. Ind.* iii. 603. A rough, hairy shrub or small tree; branches 4-angled. Leaves shortly stalked, ovate, 3–4 in., entire or toothed, long-pointed. Flowers fragrant, sessile, in clusters of three, forming terminal cymes. Calyx tubular, entire or minutely toothed, almost concealed by 2 broad, ovate bracts. Corolla salver-shaped; tube cylindric, orange, $\frac{1}{4}$ in.; lobes usually 6, white, 2-lobed, margins jagged. Stamens included, filaments very short. Style cylindric; stigma entire; ovules solitary in each cell. Capsule flat, orbicular, $\frac{1}{2}$–$\frac{3}{4}$ in. across, splitting into two 1-seeded carpels.

Valleys below Simla; July–September.—N. India, ascending to 4000 ft. Cultivated throughout India.

FIG. 96. SYRINGA EMODI.

3. SYRINGA. From the Greek *syrinx, syringos*, a musical pipe, reed; referring to the long, straight branches from which the pith is easily removed to make a flute or whistle.—Temperate Asia, E. Europe.

Syringa Emodi, *Wall.*; *Fl. Br. Ind.* iii. 604. A large shrub; young parts and inflorescence pubescent, otherwise glabrous. Leaves stalked, ovate, $2\frac{1}{2}$–5×1–2 in., entire, acute; lower surface pale or white. Flowers small, white, in terminal panicles 3–6 in. long. Calyx short, obscurely 4-toothed. Corolla salver-shaped;

tube $\frac{3}{10}$ in., cylindric, much longer than the calyx; lobes 4, long-pointed, tips inflexed. Filaments short, anthers protruding. Style short; stigma 2-lobed. Capsule cylindric, $\frac{3}{4}$ in. long, 2-valved; seeds 2 in each cell, flat, winged. (Fig. 96.)

Narkunda, Baghi; May.—W. Himalaya, 9000–12,000 ft.
Cultivated in Britain under the name of Himalaya Lilac; the flowers have a heavy, rather disagreeable smell.

4. FRAXINUS. The classical name of the Common Ash, *F. excelsior*.—N. temperate regions.

***Fraxinus floribunda,** *Wall.*; *Fl. Br. Ind.* iii. 605. A large tree. Leaves odd-pinnate; leaflets 7–9, opposite, stalked, ovate-oblong, $5 \times 1\frac{3}{4}$ in., toothed, long-pointed. Flowers small, polygamous, mostly 2-sexual, in terminal panicles 6–8 in. long. Calyx short, 4-toothed. Petals 4, white, narrowly oblong, much longer than the calyx, cohering at the base in pairs. Stamens longer than the petals, attached to their base. Ovary minute; style short, stigma very long, fleshy, erect. Fruit a narrow, winged, 1-seeded nut $1–1\frac{1}{2}$ in. long.

Temperate Himalaya, not common, 5000–9000 ft.; April, May.
Closely allied to the Flowering or Manna Ash, *F. Ornus*, a native of S. Europe, cultivated in Britain.

5. OLEA. The Latin name of the Olive, *O. europæa*.—N. temperate regions and New Zealand.

Trees or shrubs. Leaves leathery, stalked, ovate or lanceolate, entire. Flowers small, in panicles. Calyx short, 4-toothed. Corolla rotate; tube not longer than the calyx; lobes 4. Filaments short, anthers protruding. Style short; stigma 2-lobed. Drupe ovoid; seed solitary, oily.

Leaves densely scaly on the lower surface, not glandular. . 1. *O. cuspidata.*
Leaves glabrous on the lower surface; nerve-axils glandular . . . . 2. *O. glandulifera.*

***1. Olea cuspidata,** *Wall.*; *Fl. Br. Ind.* iii. 611. A tree; branches and inflorescence scaly. Leaves oblong-lanceolate, $2–4 \times \frac{1}{3}–\frac{3}{4}$ in.; tip hard, acute; upper surface glabrous, shining, lower densely covered with minute, red-brown scales. Flowers white, in numerous, short, axillary panicles. Drupe $\frac{1}{4}–\frac{1}{3}$ in. long, black when ripe.

Hilly regions in N.W. India, ascending to 6000 ft.; April, May.
Closely allied to the Olive tree of S. Europe, *O. europæa*.

2. **Olea glandulifera,** *Wall.*; *Fl. Br. Ind.* iii. 612. A small, glabrous tree. Leaves ovate, $4–5 \times 1\frac{1}{2}$ in., long-pointed; the axils of the principal nerves on the lower surface glandular. Flowers

white, in terminal or lateral panicles 2–3 in. long. Drupe $\frac{1}{3}$–$\frac{1}{2}$ in. long, black when ripe.

Sutlej valley, Basantpur; March–May.—Temperate Himalaya, 2000–6000 ft. —Mountains of S. India.

6. LIGUSTRUM. The Latin name of a shrub, probably the Privet, *L. vulgare*, derived from *ligare*, to bind; referring to the use made of the flexible branches.—Asia, Australia, Europe.

Ligustrum compactum, *Hook. f. & Thoms.*; *Fl. Br. Ind.* iii. 616. A glabrous shrub or small tree. Leaves stalked, lanceolate, 3–5 × $\frac{3}{4}$–1$\frac{1}{2}$ in., entire, long-pointed. Flowers small, white, in terminal panicles 4–6 in. long. Calyx short, obscurely 4-toothed. Corolla-tube funnel-shaped, $\frac{1}{10}$ in. longer than the calyx; lobes 4. Filaments short, anthers protruding. Style short; stigma 2-lobed. Drupe ovoid, $\frac{1}{4}$–$\frac{1}{3}$ in. long; seeds 1–3.

Valleys below Simla, not common, Koti, Khogua on the road to the Chor; May, June.—W. Himalaya, 3500–6000 ft.

Allied to the Privet, *L. vulgare*, of Britain.

LXI. APOCYNACEÆ

TREES or shrubs. Leaves opposite, in threes in *Nerium*, simple, entire; stipules none. Flowers 2-sexual, regular, in terminal or axillary cymes. Calyx free, usually small, often glandular at the base within, deeply 5-lobed. Corolla salver-shaped; tube long or short, usually dilated round the stamens; limb spreading, 5-lobed. Stamens 5, inserted on the corolla-tube; filaments short; anthers distinct but more or less cohering in a cone, free from or adherent to the stigma, cell-bases obtuse or produced downwards in short, curved, pointed tails. Ovary superior, 2-celled, cells distinct or united; style simple, linear, stigma terminal; ovules few or many in each cell. Fruit a berry or two distinct or more or less united follicles; seeds few or many, naked or crowned with a tuft of hairs.—Nearly all tropical and subtropical regions.

Plumeria acutifolia, the Frangipani tree, is cultivated throughout India, and sometimes planted in the lower hills. A small tree with thick branches and copious, milky juice. Leaves lanceolate, 6–15 in., crowded at the end of branches. Flowers fragrant. Corolla salver-shaped, white, pale yellow in the centre, 2–3 in. across.

Vinca rosea, the Periwinkle, a West Indian plant, is cultivated throughout India, and sometimes seen as an escape. Leaves obovate. Flowers axillary, pink, 1$\frac{1}{2}$–2 in. diam.

Anthers free from the stigma; cell-bases obtuse.
- A spinous shrub. Leaves 1–1$\frac{1}{2}$ in. Fruit a berry . . 1. *Carissa.*
- An unarmed tree. Leaves 6 in. Fruit two long follicles . . . . 2. *Holarrhena.*

Anthers adherent to the stigma; cell-bases produced in short, curved, pointed tails.
- Calyx-lobes as long as the corolla-tube. . . 3. *Vallaris.*
- Calyx-lobes much shorter than the corolla-tube.
  - Flowers red or pink. Leaves in threes . . 4. *Nerium.*
  - Flowers white. Leaves opposite. . . . 5. *Trachelospermum.*

1. CARISSA. Probably a modification of the native name.—Asia, Africa, Australia.

Carissa Carandas, *Linn.*; *Fl. Br. Ind.* iii. 630. An erect, spinous shrub; branches forking, rigid; inflorescence pubescent, otherwise glabrous. Leaves leathery, nearly sessile, ovate, $1–1\frac{1}{2} \times \frac{1}{2}–\frac{3}{4}$ in., usually obtuse. Flowers white, in small, terminal cymes. Calyx-segments acute. Corolla-tube $\frac{1}{2}–\frac{3}{4}$ in., lower portion cylindric, upper dilated; lobes acute. Stamens included, inserted near the top of the tube; anthers free from the stigma, cell-bases obtuse. Ovary-cells united; style short, stigma spindle-shaped; ovules 4 in each cell. Fruit an ovoid berry $\frac{1}{2}$ in. long, green at first, then red, nearly black when ripe; seeds 2–4, naked.

Valleys below Simla on open hill-sides; September–April.—Throughout India, ascending to 5000 ft.

'The fruit is used for making preserves. When ripe it may be used for tarts and puddings, for which purpose no fruit of the country is preferable; it has when cooked much of the flavour of the green gooseberry.'—Firminger's *Manual of Gardening*, p. 256.—The ripe fruit is sold in bazars, and the shrub is occasionally cultivated.—Native name *Kurónda.*

2. HOLARRHENA. From the Greek *holos*, whole, and *arren*, male; the anthers are free from the stigma.—Tropical Asia and Africa.

Holarrhena antidysenterica, *Wall.*; *Fl. Br. Ind.* iii. 644. A glabrous or pubescent tree. Leaves nearly sessile, ovate-oblong, about 6×3 in., acute. Flowers white, in terminal, corymbose cymes. Calyx-segments acute. Corolla pubescent; tube $\frac{1}{2}$ in., cylindric; lobes oblong, obtuse. Stamens inserted near the base of the tube, included; anthers free from the stigma, cell-bases obtuse. Ovary-cells nearly distinct; style short, stigma spindle-shaped; ovules numerous in each cell. Follicles glabrous, slender, terete, 8–15 in. long, distinct from the base, usually curved and touching at the tips; seeds numerous, crowned with a tuft of long, silky hairs.

Valleys below Simla, Subathoo; April–June.—Throughout India, ascending to 3500 ft.

3. VALLARIS. Etymology doubtful.—India.

Vallaris Heynei, *Spreng.*; *Fl. Br. Ind.* iii. 650. A climbing shrub; inflorescence pubescent, otherwise nearly glabrous. Leaves shortly stalked, ovate-oblong, 2–3 × $\frac{3}{4}$–1 in., acute. Flowers white, fragrant, in axillary, drooping cymes. Calyx-lobes as long as the corolla-tube, obtuse. Corolla-tube $\frac{1}{10}$ in., cylindric; limb spreading, $\frac{3}{4}$ in. across, lobes rounded. Stamens inserted near the mouth of the tube, filaments hairy, anthers cohering in a cone round the stigma, adherent to it, a smooth, white gland on the back of each, cells produced downwards in short, curved tails. Disk 5-lobed. Ovary-cells united; style hairy, stigma capitate; ovules many in each cell. Fruit oblong, pointed, about 6 × 2 in., ultimately separating into 2 follicles; seeds numerous, crowned with a tuft of hairs.

Sutlej valley; December–April.—Throughout India, ascending to 5000 ft. Often cultivated in gardens.

FIG. 97. TRACHELOSPERMUM FRAGRANS.

4. NERIUM. From *nerion*, the Greek name of the Oleander, *N. Oleander*; derived from *neros*, damp, humid, referring to the habitat of the plants.—N. Asia, S. Europe.

Nerium odorum, *Soland.*; *Fl. Br. Ind.* iii. 655. An erect, glabrous shrub; juice milky. Leaves in threes, leathery, shortly stalked, narrowly lanceolate, 4–6 in., acute. Flowers red or pink, fragrant, in terminal cymes. Calyx-lobes lanceolate. Corolla-tube $\frac{3}{4}$ in., lower portion cylindric, upper dilated; 5 fringed scales on the throat; limb spreading, $1\frac{1}{2}$ in. diam., lobes rounded. Stamens inserted near the mouth of the tube; filaments hairy; anthers cohering in a cone round the stigma, adherent to it, each prolonged upwards in a long, thread-like, hairy appendage, cells produced downwards in short, curved tails. Ovary-cells nearly distinct; style long, stigma conical, flat-topped; ovules many in each cell. Follicles narrow, straight, 6–9 in., united at first, ultimately separating; seeds numerous, crowned with a tuft of short hairs.

Sutlej valley, in ravines; April-October.—Throughout N. India, ascending to 5000 ft.

Cultivated throughout India; closely allied to the Oleander of S. Europe.

5. **TRACHELOSPERMUM.** From the Greek *trachelos*, the neck, and *sperma*, a seed; referring to the long, narrow seeds.—E. Asia.

Trachelospermum fragrans, *Hook. f.*; *Fl. Br. Ind.* iii. 667. A climbing, nearly glabrous shrub; branches pendulous. Leaves shortly stalked, ovate-lanceolate, $3–5 \times 1–1\frac{1}{2}$ in. Flowers white, fragrant, in terminal or axillary cymes. Calyx-lobes lanceolate. Corolla-tube cylindric, $\frac{1}{3}–\frac{1}{2}$ in., dilated near the mouth; limb spreading, $\frac{1}{2}$ in. diam., lobes oblong. Stamens inserted near the top of the tube; anthers cohering in a cone round the stigma, adherent to it, tips acute, cells produced downwards in short, curved tails. Disk of 5 small, erect glands. Ovary-cells distinct; style cup-shaped at the top, stigma oblong; ovules many in each cell. Follicles slender, terete, 4–8 in., distinct from the base, usually curved and nearly touching at the tips; seeds numerous, crowned with a tuft of long hairs. (Fig. 97.)

Valleys below Simla, Lansdowne Falls; April-July.—Simla to Burmah 2000–6000 ft.

LXII. ASCLEPIADACEÆ

Shrubs or herbs; stems erect, twining or climbing; juice often milky and acrid. Leaves opposite, usually stalked, simple, entire; stipules none. Flowers regular, 2-sexual, usually in axillary, umbellate cymes. Calyx free, small, 5-lobed nearly to the base. Corolla hypogynous; tube usually short; limb 5-lobed, spreading.

Corona composed of usually 5 distinct or united, variously shaped scales attached to the staminal tube or in *Cryptolepis* only to the corolla-tube. Stamens 5, inserted near the base of the corolla; filaments flat, united in a short tube enclosing the pistils or in *Cryptolepis* only free; anthers 2-celled, coherent round the stigma, the pollen of each cell agglutinated in a small, ovoid, pollen mass of wax-like consistency, granular only in *Cryptolepis*; anther-tips membranous, produced, except in *Ceropegia*, usually inflexed over the stigma. Carpels 2, free at least near the base; styles short, more or less cohering; stigmas terminal, united in a 5-angled disk bearing at each corner a small, hard, dark-coloured gland or corpuscle attached to the pollen mass on each side of it; the ten pollen masses being thus united in five pairs, the members of each pair derived from different but contiguous anthers; ovules numerous in each carpel. Fruit of two distinct follicles usually diverging from their base, one occasionally abortive; seeds numerous, small, crowned with a tuft of long hairs.—A large Order chiefly inhabiting tropical and subtropical regions.—*Asclepias* was the classical name of *Cynanchum Vincetoxicum*; derived from *Asclepiades*, the Greek form of the Latin *Æsculapius*, a famous physician.

The flowers are curiously adapted to facilitate cross-fertilisation by insects; see Müller's *Fertilisation of Flowers*, p. 396.

The structure of the flowers of this Order is difficult to understand from a description, and most of the hill species have flowers too small for easy dissection. The flowers of the Mudár, *Calotropis*, very common in the plains and occasionally met with in the lower valleys, are better suited for the purpose and are well described by Müller.

- Stems erect.
  - Corolla-tube very short.
    - Flowers $\frac{3}{4}$–1 in. diam., pink, spotted with purple . . . 2. *Calotropis.*
    - Flowers less than $\frac{1}{4}$ in. diam., yellow . . . . . 5. *Cynanchum.*[1]
  - Corolla-tube $\frac{3}{4}$–1 in. long. Flowers dark red-purple . 10. *Ceropegia.*
- Stems twining or climbing.
  - Flowers orange, $\frac{1}{3}$ in. diam. . . . . 6. *Marsdenia.*
  - Flowers purple.
    - Leaves $1\frac{1}{2}$–3 in. broad. Flowers 1–$1\frac{1}{2}$ in. diam., silvery white outside . . . . 4. *Holostemma.*
    - Leaves $\frac{1}{10}$–$\frac{1}{4}$ in. broad. Flowers $\frac{1}{3}$ in. diam. . . . 8. *Tylophora.*[2]
  - Flowers waxy white, tinged with pink, $\frac{3}{4}$–1 in. diam. Leaves fleshy, 2–5 × $\frac{1}{2}$–1 in. . . . . 9. *Hoya.*
  - Flowers yellow, pale green or green-yellow.
    - Coronal scales attached to the corolla-tube closing its mouth. Filaments free . . . . 1. *Cryptolepis.*
    - Coronal scales attached to the staminal tube. Filaments united.
      - Corolla-tube $\frac{1}{4}$ in. long, dilated at the base . . . 7. *Pergularia.*
      - Corolla-tube very short, not dilated.
        - Corona longer than the staminal tube.
          - Leaves 2–3 in. broad. Corolla fringed. . . . 3. *Dæmia.*

[1] *C. Vincetoxicum* and *C. glaucum*. [2] *T. tenerrima* only.

Leaves $\frac{1}{2}$–1 in. broad. Corolla not fringed	5. *Cynanchum Dalhousieæ.*
Corona not longer than the staminal tube.	
Leaves glabrous, 2–5 in. broad; stalks with basal lobes . .	5. *Cynanchum auriculatum.*
Leaves hairy, $1\frac{1}{2}$–2 in. broad; basal lobes none . . .	8. *Tylophora hirsuta.*

1. CRYPTOLEPIS. From the Greek *cryptos*, hidden, and *lepis*, a scale; the coronal scales close the mouth of the corolla-tube and hide the anthers and stigma.—Tropical Asia and Africa.

Cryptolepis Buchanani, *Roem. & Schult.*; *Fl. Br. Ind.* iv. 5. A glabrous, twining shrub; juice milky. Leaves shortly stalked, oblong-ovate, 3–6 × 1–$2\frac{1}{2}$ in.; lower surface nearly white. Flowers $\frac{1}{2}$–$\frac{3}{4}$ in. diam., yellow-green, in axillary, paniculate cymes. Corolla-tube short; lobes narrowly oblong. Coronal scales 5, club-shaped, attached at the top of the corolla-tube, closing its mouth. Stamens at the base of the corolla-tube, filaments very short, free; anther-bases adhering to the stigma, tips long, converging over it; pollen masses granular. Stigma conical. Follicles 2–4 in., smooth, straight, terete, tapering.

Giri valley; May, June.—Throughout India, ascending to 4000 ft.

2. CALOTROPIS. From the Greek *kalos*, beautiful, and *tropis*, the keel of a boat; referring to the shape of the coronal scales.—Tropical Asia and Africa.

Calotropis procera, *R. Br.*; *Fl. Br. Ind.* iv. 18. An erect, white, downy shrub; juice milky. Leaves sessile, cordate, ovate-oblong, 4–9 × 1–4 in. Flowers $\frac{3}{4}$–1 in. diam., pink, spotted with purple, in lateral, umbellate cymes. Corolla thick, cup-shaped; tube very short; lobes triangular, acute. Coronal scales 5, fleshy, smooth, white, laterally flattened, adnate to the staminal tube, base upcurved. Filaments united, anther-tips inflexed; pollen masses waxy. Stigma flat, 5-angled. Follicles 4–5 in., thick, wrinkled, covered with white woolly pubescence.

Sutlej valley; February–May.—Throughout India, ascending to 4000 ft.—Tropical Asia and Africa.

C. gigantea, *R. Br.*; *Fl. Br. Ind.* iv. 17, is also common in the plains, occasionally ascending to 2000 ft. Flowers 1–2 in. diam. Coronal scales hairy. The powdered roots of both species are used in native medicine. The acrid juice is poisonous for human beings, but the leaves are eaten by goats with impunity. Native name *Mudár.*

3. DÆMIA. An alteration of the vernacular Arabic name of *D. extensa* or an allied species.

Dæmia extensa, *R. Br.*; *Fl. Br. Ind.* iv. 20. A slender, twining, hairy shrub; juice milky. Leaves long-stalked, deeply cordate, broadly ovate, 2–3 in. across, acute. Flowers fœtid, $\frac{1}{2}$–$\frac{3}{4}$ in. diam., pale yellow-green, tinged with pink at the base, long-stalked, in axillary, umbellate cymes. Corolla-tube very short; lobes broad, fringed. Coronal scales in two series; outer 10 minute, affixed to the base of the staminal tube; inner 5 white, laterally flattened, adnate to the staminal tube, spurred on the back, tips long, linear, spirally incurved over the stigma. Filaments united; anther-tips inflexed; pollen masses waxy. Stigma flat, obscurely 5-angled. Follicles $1\frac{1}{2}$–2 in., lanceolate, long-pointed, covered with long, soft prickles.

Valleys below Simla; April–July.—Throughout India, ascending to 3000 ft. —Burmah, Afghanistan.

4. HOLOSTEMMA. From the Greek *holos*, whole, entire, and *stemma*, a chaplet, wreath; referring to the ring-shaped corona.—India.

Holostemma Rheedei, *Wall.*; *Fl. Br. Ind.* iv. 21. A glabrous, twining shrub; juice milky. Leaves long-stalked, deeply cordate, ovate, $2\frac{1}{2}$–$4 \times 1\frac{1}{2}$–3 in., acute or long-pointed; midrib minutely glandular at its base; nerves red. Flowers 1–$1\frac{1}{2}$ in. diam., purple, outer surface silvery-white, in axillary, umbellate cymes. Corolla thick, cup-shaped; tube very short; lobes broad, acute. Corona a short, fleshy ring affixed to and encircling the base of the staminal tube. Filaments united, tube 10-winged; anther-tips small, inflexed; pollen masses waxy. Stigma small, 5-angled, convex. Follicles short, thick, smooth, acute.

Valleys below Simla; July–September.—Simla to Sikkim, 3000–5000 ft.; hilly districts throughout India.—Burmah.

5. CYNANCHUM. From the Greek *kuon*, a dog, and *ancho*, to strangle; referring to the poisonous properties of some species. —Tropical and temperate regions.

Erect or twining shrubs. Flowers small, in axillary, umbellate cymes. Calyx nearly as long as or much shorter than the corolla. Corolla-tube very short. Corona thin, affixed to the base of the staminal tube, erect, 5-lobed or bell-shaped, sometimes bearing small scales within. Filaments united, tube very short; anther-tips inflexed; pollen masses waxy. Stigma small, convex. Follicles 2–4 in., smooth, slender, tapering in a long point.

Stems erect.
- Corolla glabrous . . . . 1. *C. Vincetoxicum.*
- Corolla hairy . . . . 2. *C. glaucum.*

Stems twining.
- Leaves $\frac{1}{2}$–1 in. broad. Corona nearly as long as the corolla, bell-shaped, toothed . . . . . . 3. *C. Dalhousieæ.*
- Leaves 2–5 in. broad. Corona much shorter than the corolla, deeply 5-lobed . . . . 4. *C. auriculatum.*

1. **Cynanchum Vincetoxicum,** *Pers.*; *Fl. Br. Ind.* iv. 22. Pubescent; stems erect, 6–18 in. Leaves shortly stalked, ovate, $2 \times 1\frac{1}{2}$ in., acute. Cymes stalked. Flowers $\frac{1}{5}$ in. diam., yellow. Calyx nearly as long as the corolla. Corolla glabrous. Corona deeply 5-lobed.

Shali, Sungree, Patarnala; June.—Temperate Himalaya, 7000–11,000 ft. —W. Asia, Europe.

2. **Cynanchum glaucum,** *Wall.*; *Fl. Br. Ind.* iv. 22. Pubescent or hairy; stems erect, 6–24 in. Leaves pale green, ovate-lanceolate, $3 \times \frac{3}{4}$ in., acute. Cymes shortly stalked or nearly sessile. Flowers $\frac{1}{6}$ in. diam., yellow. Calyx about half as long as the corolla. Corolla hairy on the inner surface. Corona deeply 5-lobed.

Simla, Mushobra, in woods; May–July.—Temperate Himalaya, 5000–9000 ft.

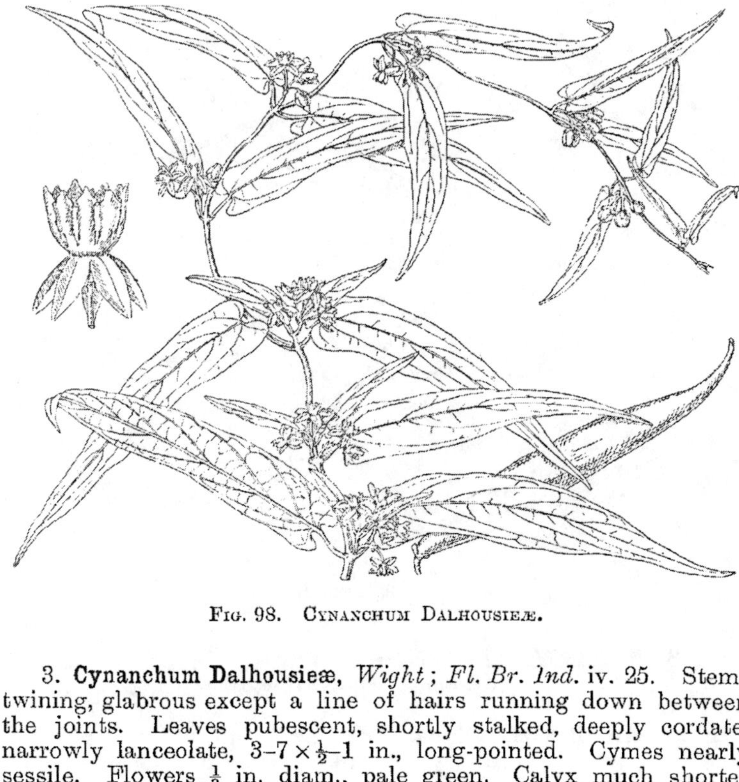

FIG. 98. CYNANCHUM DALHOUSIEÆ.

3. **Cynanchum Dalhousieæ,** *Wight*; *Fl. Br. Ind.* iv. 25. Stems twining, glabrous except a line of hairs running down between the joints. Leaves pubescent, shortly stalked, deeply cordate, narrowly lanceolate, $3\text{–}7 \times \frac{1}{2}\text{–}1$ in., long-pointed. Cymes nearly sessile. Flowers $\frac{1}{3}$ in. diam., pale green. Calyx much shorter than the corolla. Corolla glabrous; lobes reflexed. Corona bell-

shaped, 10-toothed, nearly as long as the corolla, bearing 10 small scales near the base within. (Fig. 98.)

Simla; July, August.—Simla to Mussoorie, 5000–7000 ft.

4. **Cynanchum auriculatum,** *Wight*; *Fl. Br. Ind.* iv. 25. Stems twining, glabrous except a line of hairs running down between the joints. Leaves glabrous or nearly so, deeply cordate, ovate or ovate-lanceolate, $3\frac{1}{2}$–7×2–5 in., acute; stalks with a pair of leaf-like, basal lobes. Cymes long-stalked. Flowers $\frac{1}{3}$–$\frac{1}{2}$ in. diam., yellow-green. Calyx much shorter than the corolla. Corolla pubescent within. Corona much shorter than the corolla, cup-shaped, bearing 5 small scales near the base within, deeply 5-lobed, lobes free.

Mushobra, Mahasu; June–August.—Temperate Himalaya, 6000–12,000 ft.

FIG. 99. MARSDENIA ROYLEI.

6. **MARSDENIA.** In honour of W. Marsden, traveller and botanist of the eighteenth century.—Nearly all warm regions.

Marsdenia Roylei, *Wight*; *Fl. Br. Ind.* iv. 35. A softly tomentose, twining shrub; juice milky. Leaves stalked, cordate, ovate-lanceolate, 3–$5 \times 1\frac{1}{2}$–3 in., acute. Flowers $\frac{1}{3}$ in. diam., orange, crowded in axillary, umbellate cymes. Calyx hairy, about half as long as the corolla. Corolla fleshy; tube short; lobes pubescent within. Coronal scales 5, attached at the base of the staminal tube, flat, linear, erect, much longer than the tube, tips free, converging. Filaments united, tube short; anther-tips inflexed; pollen masses waxy. Stigma convex. Follicles hairy, deeply wrinkled, about 3×1 in., shortly pointed. (Fig. 99.)

Simla, Jako, Annandale; June–August.—Simla to Sikkim, 3000–7000 ft.

7. PERGULARIA. From the Latin *pergula*, an arbour, referring to the twining habit of the plants.—Tropical regions of Asia and Africa.

***Pergularia pallida,** *Wight & Arn.*; *Fl. Br. Ind.* iv. 38. A twining shrub; young parts and inflorescence more or less hairy, otherwise glabrous. Leaves stalked, cordate, ovate, $2–4 \times 1\frac{1}{2}–3$ in., acute. Flowers yellow-green, $\frac{3}{4}$ in. diam., in axillary, umbellate cymes. Corolla glabrous; tube $\frac{1}{4}$ in. long, dilated near the base, constricted at the throat; lobes narrow, much longer than the tube. Coronal scales 5, membranous, flat, oblong, adnate to the staminal tube; tips acute, free, each bearing on the inner side a short, linear appendage projecting beyond the scales and converging over the stigma. Filaments united, tube short; anther-tips inflexed; pollen masses waxy. Stigma convex. Follicles glabrous, smooth, tapering, $3 \times \frac{3}{4}$ in.

Throughout India, ascending to 5000 ft.
The closely allied *P. odoratissima*, a native of China, is cultivated throughout India on account of its highly fragrant, orange or green-yellow flowers. The throat of the corolla is hairy.

8. TYLOPHORA. From the Greek *tylos*, a swelling or protuberance, and *phorein*, to bear; referring to the coronal scales.—Tropical regions of the Old World.

Twining shrubs. Leaves ovate or very narrow. Flowers small, in axillary, umbellate cymes. Corolla-tube very short; lobes long. Coronal scales fleshy, adnate to the staminal tube, base much dilated, tips narrow. Filaments united, tube very short; anther-tips inflexed; pollen masses waxy. Stigma conical. Follicles smooth, nearly glabrous, tapering, long-pointed, about $2 \times \frac{1}{3}$ in.

Leaves $1\frac{1}{2}$–2 in. broad. Flowers white or pale green . . 1. *T. hirsuta*.
Leaves not more than $\frac{1}{4}$ in. broad. Flowers dark purple . 2. *T. tenerrima*.

*1. **Tylophora hirsuta,** *Wight*; *Fl. Br. Ind.* iv. 43. Stems softly tomentose or hairy. Leaves hairy, ovate or ovate-lanceolate, $2\frac{1}{2}–4 \times 1\frac{1}{2}–2$ in., acute. Flowers white or pale green, $\frac{1}{6}–\frac{1}{4}$ in.

diam. Coronal scales not longer than the staminal tube, wholly adnate to it.

Throughout N. India, ascending to 5000 ft.

2. **Tylophora tenerrima,** *Wight*; *Fl. Br. Ind.* iv. 44. Glabrous or pubescent; stems very slender. Leaves linear or narrowly lanceolate, 1–4 × $\frac{1}{10}$–$\frac{1}{4}$ in., acute. Flowers few, dark purple, $\frac{1}{3}$ in. diam. Coronal scales longer than the staminal tube, tips free, acute, incurved.

Simla, the Glen ; July, August.—Simla to Sikkim, 3000–6000 ft.

9. **HOYA.** In honour of Thomas Hoy, once gardener to the Duke of Northumberland at Sion House, near Kew.—Tropical and subtropical regions of Asia and Australasia.

Hoya longifolia, *Wall.*; *Fl. Br. Ind.* iv. 56. A glabrous shrub; stems rooting and climbing over trees and rocks; branches pendulous. Leaves fleshy, thick, narrowly lanceolate, 2–5 × $\frac{1}{2}$–1 in., acute; stalks short, thick. Flowers waxy white, tinged with pink, $\frac{3}{4}$–1 in. diam., in axillary, shortly stalked, umbellate cymes. Corolla fleshy; tube very short; lobes triangular. Coronal scales thick, fleshy, adnate to the staminal tube, flattened, stellately spreading, inner angle produced in a short tooth, back rounded. Filaments united, tube short; anther-tips inflexed; pollen masses waxy. Stigma flat. Follicles smooth, slender, terete, straight, 4–5 in.

Below Chota Simla ; July, August.—Eastward to Sikkim and Khasia, 1000–4500 ft.

10. **CEROPEGIA.** From the Greek *ceros*, wax, and *pege*, a fountain ; referring to the waxy appearance of the inflorescence.—Tropical and subtropical regions of the Old World.

Ceropegia Wallichii, *Wight*; *Fl. Br. Ind.* iv. 67. A pubescent herb; stems erect, 8–12 in. Leaves shortly stalked, ovate or oblong, 1$\frac{3}{4}$ × 1 in., obtuse or acute. Flowers dark red-purple, axillary, solitary or in small clusters. Corolla-tube $\frac{3}{4}$–1 in. long, base dilated; mouth funnel-shaped, 5-angled; lobes $\frac{1}{3}$ in. long, narrow, erect, hairy within, tips cohering. Coronal scales 10, in 2 series, outer united in a short, 10-lobed cup adnate to the staminal tube; inner longer, linear, erect, free. Filaments united, tube very short; anther-tips obtuse, not produced; pollen masses waxy. Follicles smooth, tapering, long-pointed, 2$\frac{1}{2}$ × 1 in.

Simla, Prospect and Elysium hills, Shali, in woods, rare ; June, July.—Simla to Nepal, 4000 8000 ft.

LXIII. LOGANIACEÆ

A SMALL Order widely distributed throughout nearly all tropical and subtropical regions, represented in the N.W. Himalaya by only one genus.—Named in honour of James Logan, a British botanical author of the eighteenth century.

The poison, strychnine, is prepared from the seeds of *Strychnos Nux-vomica*, a small tree belonging to this Order, common in S. India.

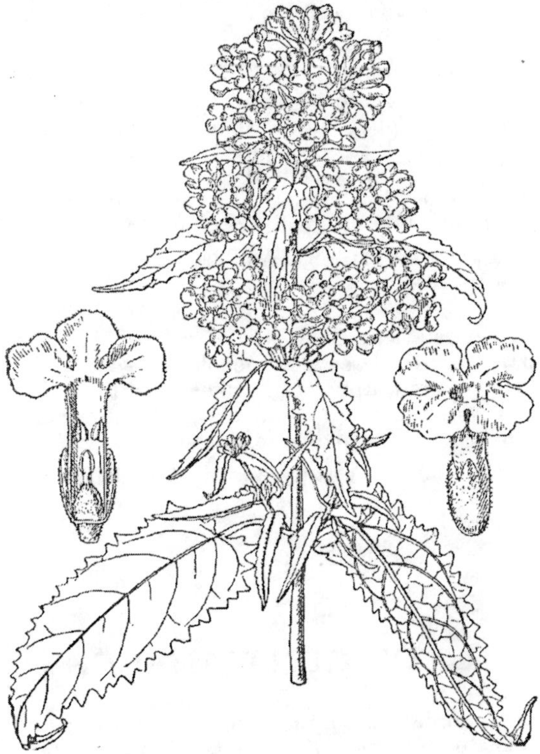

FIG. 100. BUDDLEIA PANICULATA.

BUDDLEIA. In honour of the Rev. Adam Buddle, a British botanical author of the eighteenth century.—Tropical and subtropical regions of Asia, Africa and America.

Tall, erect shrubs; young branches, leaves and inflorescence more or less tomentose. Leaves stalked, opposite, simple, the bases of the stalks connected by a raised, stipular line. Flowers small, fragrant, regular, 2-sexual, nearly sessile, crowded in heads, whorls or spikes. Calyx free, bell-shaped, much shorter than the corolla-tube, 4-lobed, persistent. Corolla hypogynous; tube nearly cylindric; lobes 4, spreading, rounded, minutely toothed. Stamens 4, inserted on the corolla-tube, alternate with the lobes; anthers nearly sessile. Ovary superior, 2-celled; style short, stigma terminal, 2-lobed; ovules numerous in each cell. Capsule ovoid, opening by 2 valves; seeds numerous, minute.

Flowers nearly ½ in. long, in heads or whorls . . . 1. *B. paniculata.*
Flowers hardly ¼ in. long, in slender spikes . . . . 2. *B. asiatica.*

1. **Buddleia paniculata,** *Wall.*; *Fl. Br. Ind.* iv. 81. Tomentum red-brown. Leaves ovate or oblong, about 5×2 in., crenate or sharply toothed, upper ones usually lanceolate and entire. Flowers nearly ½ in. long, crowded in leafy heads or whorls on the short branches of terminal panicles. Corolla-tube pink throat orange; lobes lavender-blue; sometimes the whole corolla varies to white or pink. Capsule tomentose. (Fig. 100.)

Simla, Fagoo, Matiana; March, April.—Temperate Himalaya, 4000-7500 ft. —Afghanistan, Burmah.

2. **Buddleia asiatica,** *Lour.*; *Fl. Br. Ind.* iv. 82. Tomentum white or pale yellow. Leaves lanceolate, 3–6×½–1¼ in., minutely toothed, long-pointed, upper ones usually entire. Flowers hardly ¼ in. long, crowded in long, slender, usually drooping spikes, often combined in terminal panicles. Corolla white. Capsule glabrous.

Valleys below Simla; February–April.—Throughout India ascending to 5000 ft.—E. Asia.

LXIV. GENTIANACEÆ

Annual or perennial herbs, more or less bitter, usually glabrous. Leaves opposite, very rarely alternate, simple, entire, often united at the base or connected by a raised line; stipules none. Flowers regular, except in *Canscora*, 2-sexual, in terminal, forking, paniculate or corymbose cymes. Calyx free, tubular or deeply lobed. Corolla hypogynous; tube long or short; limb 3–5-lobed, spreading. Stamens as many as the corolla-lobes, except in *Canscora*, and alternate with them, inserted in the tube or near the base of the corolla; anthers 2-celled. Ovary superior, usually 1-celled; style linear, stigma terminal, usually 2-lobed; ovules several or many, attached to the cell-walls. Capsule opening by two valves; seeds several or many, small.—A rather large Order extending nearly all over the world but chiefly in temperate and mountainous regions, some species ascending to the utmost limits of vegetation.

Corolla-tube shorter than the lobes.
  Ovary 2-celled. Stigma entire. Corolla-lobes without glands or spurs . . . . 1. *Exacum.*
  Ovary 1-celled. Stigma 2-lobed. Corolla-lobes glandular or spurred
    Corolla-lobes glandular near the base . . . . . 4. *Swertia.*
    Corolla-lobes spurred at the base . . . . . . 5. *Halenia.*
Corolla-tube longer than the lobes.
  Corolla 3 lobed . . . . 2. *Canscora.*
  Corolla 5- or 4-lobed . . . . 3. *Gentiana.*

1. **EXACUM.** Name of classical origin; etymology obscure.—Asia, Africa.

***Exacum tetragonum,** *Roxb.*; *Fl. Br. Ind.* iv. 95. Stems erect, 1–4 ft., 4-sided, branching. Leaves opposite, stem-clasping, broadly lanceolate, $1\frac{1}{2}$–$5 \times \frac{1}{2}$–$1\frac{1}{2}$ in., acute. Flowers blue, $1\frac{1}{4}$ in. diam., in terminal panicles. Calyx deeply 4-lobed; lobes ovate, keeled, long-pointed. Corolla-tube inflated, much shorter than the 4 ovate, acute lobes. Stamens 4, filaments short; anthers narrowly oblong, opening by two terminal pores. Ovary 2-celled; style long, stigma capitate, entire; ovules numerous. Capsule globose.

N. India, in grassy places, ascending to 5000 ft.; July–September.

2. **CANSCORA.** Adapted from *Cansjancora*, the native name of *C. perfoliata*, as given in Rheede, *Hort. Mal.* x. 103.—Asia, Australia, tropical Africa.

Canscora decussata, *Roem. & Schult.*; *Fl. Br. Ind.* iv. 104. Stems erect, 6–18 in., 4-sided, the angles winged. Leaves opposite, sessile, oblong-lanceolate, $1 \times \frac{1}{3}$ in. Flowers irregular, white, $\frac{1}{4}$ in. diam., in forked cymes forming terminal panicles. Calyx tubular, inflated, 4-winged, 4-toothed. Corolla-tube as long as the calyx, cylindric, much longer than the 3 obtuse lobes, one of which is notched. Stamens 4, one perfect, the others smaller, imperfect; filaments short. Ovary 1-celled; style short, stigma 2-lobed. Capsule oblong.

Valleys below Simla; August, September.—Throughout India, ascending to 5000 ft.—Burmah, tropical Africa.

Canscora diffusa, *R. Br.*; *Fl. Br. Ind.* iv. 103, is distinguished from the above by its pale pink flowers, and by the angles of the stem and calyx not being winged. It is common throughout India, and ascends in Kumaon to 2000 ft.

3. **GENTIANA.** The classical name of *G. lutea*; etymology uncertain.—Chiefly temperate and mountainous regions of the N. Hemisphere; a few species in southern latitudes.

Glabrous or nearly glabrous herbs; stems usually erect. Leaves opposite, sessile. Flowers in racemes, heads or paniculate cymes. Calyx tubular, 5- rarely 4-lobed, persistent. Corolla-tube nearly cylindric, much longer than the lobes; lobes 4 or 5, usually with a fold at the angles. Stamens as many as the corolla-lobes, attached to the tube, included. Ovary 1-celled, narrowed upwards into the persistent style; stigma 2-lobed; ovules several or many. Capsule sessile or stalked, more or less included in the calyx.

Flowers less than half an inch long.
  Flowers stalked, in cymes. Calyx about half as long as the corolla.
    Leaves green. . . . . 1. *G. quadrifaria.*
    Leaves silvery shining . . . . 2. *G. aprica.*
  Flowers sessile, in heads. Calyx nearly as long as the corolla.
    Leaves silvery shining, narrowly lanceolate. Stems leafy . . . . 3. *G. argentea.*
    Leaves green, broadly ovate. Stems usually naked 4. *G. capitata.*
Flowers one to two inches long.
  Stems decumbent. Corolla 5-lobed . . . . 5. *G. Kurroo.*
  Stems erect. Corolla 4-lobed . . . . . . 6. *G. contorta.*

1. **Gentiana quadrifaria,** *Blume*; *Fl. Br. Ind.* iv. 111. Stems erect, 4–10 in., branching from the base. Leaves green; radical rosulate, $1–1\frac{1}{2}$ in.; upper smaller. Flowers blue, $\frac{1}{3}$ in. long, in terminal cymes. Calyx about half as long as the corolla including the broad, acute lobes. Capsule ovoid.

Simla, Matiana, in meadows; July.—Temperate Himalaya, 3000–10,000 ft. —Burmah, China.

2. **Gentiana aprica,** *Decaisne*; *Fl. Br. Ind.* iv. 112, *under G. decemfida.* Stems erect, 2–6 in., usually much branched. Leaves silvery-shining; radical rosulate, broadly ovate, $\frac{1}{2}$ in.; stem-leaves narrowly lanceolate, $\frac{1}{4}$ in. Flowers blue, $\frac{1}{3}$ in. long, in terminal cymes. Calyx about half as long as the corolla; lobes narrow, finely pointed. Capsule ovoid.

Sutlej valley, Suni; April.—N. India, ascending to 3000 ft.

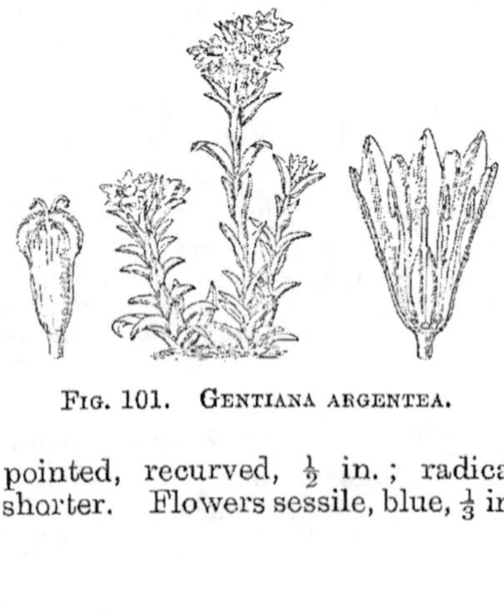

FIG. 101. GENTIANA ARGENTEA.

3. **Gentiana argentea,** *Royle*; *Fl. Br. Ind.* iv. 112. Stems leafy, erect, 1–4 in., simple or branched. Leaves silvery-shining, lanceolate, finely pointed, recurved, $\frac{1}{2}$ in.; radical rosulate; stem-leaves rather shorter. Flowers sessile, blue, $\frac{1}{3}$ in. long, crowded in terminal, leafy

heads. Calyx nearly as long as the corolla; lobes finely pointed. Capsule ovoid. (Fig. 101.)

Simla on banks, common; April, May.—W. Himalaya, 7000-12,000 ft.

4. **Gentiana capitata,** *Buch.-Ham.*; *Fl. Br. Ind.* iv. 113. Stems erect, 1–4 in., simple or branching. Leaves green, broadly obovate, $\frac{1}{4}\times\frac{1}{3}$ in., crowded close under the flowers; radical soon disappearing; stem-leaves few or none. Flowers sessile, blue or white, $\frac{1}{4}$ in. long, crowded in terminal, leafy heads $\frac{1}{2}$–$\frac{3}{4}$ in. diam. Calyx nearly as long as the corolla; lobes oblong, acute. Capsule globose.

Simla; September.—Simla to Bhotan, 4000–12,000 ft.

5. **Gentiana Kurroo,** *Boyle*; *Fl. Br. Ind.* iv. 117. Rootstock thick; stems tufted, decumbent, 4–12 in. Leaves narrowly oblong; radical rosulate, 3–5 $\times\frac{1}{4}$–$\frac{1}{2}$ in.; stem-leaves 1 in., narrower. Flowers blue, spotted with white, $1\frac{3}{4}$–2 in. long, $\frac{3}{4}$ in. diam., solitary or racemose. Calyx about half as long as the corolla; lobes 5, linear. Corolla 5-lobed. Capsule oblong.

Shali, near the top; September.—W. Himalaya, 5000–11,000 ft.

6. **Gentiana contorta,** *Royle*; *Fl. Br. Ind.* iv. 118. Stems erect, 4–10 in., branching. Leaves ovate, $1\times\frac{1}{3}$ in. Flowers blue, 1–$1\frac{1}{4}$ in. long, racemed. Calyx about half as long as the corolla; lobes 4, lanceolate. Corolla 4-lobed. Capsule oblong.

Simla, Summer Hill, not common; August-October.—W. Himalaya, 5000-8000 ft.

4. SWERTIA. In honour of Emanuel Swert, a Dutch botanical author of the seventeenth century.—Asia, Africa, Europe; chiefly in mountainous regions.

Erect herbs; stems more or less 4-sided, usually branching. Leaves opposite, except in *S. alternifolia*, sessile or narrowed in a stalk-like base. Flowers about $\frac{1}{2}$ in. diam., in paniculate or corymbose cymes. Calyx 4- or 5-parted; segments lanceolate, acute. Corolla 4- or 5-lobed nearly to the base; lobes acute, each furnished near the base with 1 or 2 honey-secreting glands. Stamens as many as the corolla-lobes, attached at the base of the corolla. Ovary 1-celled; style short or almost none, stigma 2-lobed; ovules several or many. Capsule sessile, oblong.

The following larger flowered species occur on the Chor, but have not been found nearer Simla; they all flower in the autumn:—

Swertia speciosa, *Wall.*; *Fl. Br. Ind.* iv. 128. Stems robust, 2-4 ft., hollow. Radical leaves long-stalked. Stem-leaves opposite, sessile, ovate, 5 × 2 in., long-pointed, bases united, stem-clasping. Flowers lurid grey, $1\frac{1}{2}$ in diam. Corolla 5-lobed, glands 2 on each lobe, long-fringed.

Swertia alternifolia, *Royle*; *Fl. Br. Ind.* iv. 128. Resembles *S. speciosa*, but the leaves are alternate.

Swertia cuneata, *Wall.*; *Fl. Br. Ind.* iv. 129. Stems 6–18 in., hollow. Leaves opposite, spathulate, $1\frac{1}{2}$–3 × $\frac{1}{4}$–$\frac{1}{2}$ in., lower long-stalked, upper sessile. Flowers lurid blue, $1\frac{1}{2}$ in. diam. Corolla 5-lobed; glands 2 on each lobe, linear, fringed.

Calyx and corolla 5-lobed.
  One gland on each corolla-lobe.
    Corolla pale red purple, a complete ring of darker purple at its base . . . . 1. *S. purpurascens.*
    Corolla white, a broken, purple ring at its base . 2. *S. paniculata.*
    Corolla yellow-white; margins marked with short, pale purple streaks . . . . 4. *S. cordata.*
  Two glands on each corolla-lobe . . . . . 3. *S. tetragona.*
Calyx and corolla 4-lobed.
  One gland on each corolla lobe.
    Leaves ovate, $\frac{3}{4}$ in. broad. Glands fringed . . 6. *S. alata.*
    Leaves linear-lanceolate, $\frac{1}{4}$ in. broad. Glands not fringed . . . . 7. *S. angustifolia.*
  Two glands on each corolla-lobe, long-fringed . . 5. *S. Chirata.*

1. **Swertia purpurascens,** *Wall.*; *Fl. Br. Ind.* iv. 121. Stems 1–3 ft.; branches spreading. Leaves oblong or lanceolate, $1\frac{1}{2} \times \frac{1}{3}$ in. Calyx and corolla 5-lobed. Corolla pale red-purple, a darker complete ring at its base; lobes reflexed; one gland on each lobe, horse-shoe shaped, naked. (Fig. 102.)

Simla, Mushobra, common; September.—N.W. Himalaya, 5000–12,000 ft.

2. **Swertia paniculata,** *Wall.*; *Fl. Br. Ind.* iv. 122. Stems 1–3 ft.; branches spreading. Leaves oblong or lanceolate, $1\frac{1}{2} \times \frac{1}{3}$ in. Calyx and corolla 5-lobed. Corolla white in the upper half with two purple blotches at the base forming an interrupted ring; one gland on each lobe, ovate, naked.

Simla, Mushobra; September, October.—Temperate Himalaya, 5000–8000 ft.

3. **Swertia tetragona,** *C. B. Clarke*; *Fl. Br. Ind.* iv. 122. Stems 6–24 in., usually branching. Leaves lanceolate, $\frac{3}{4}$–1 in. Calyx and corolla 5-lobed. Corolla nearly white; two glands on each lobe, oblong, hairy.

Simla, Mushobra; September, October.—W. Himalaya, 5000–8000 ft.

4. **Swertia cordata,** *Wall.*; *Fl. Br. Ind.* iv. 123. Stems 1–3 ft., usually branching. Leaves broadly ovate, $1–2 \times \frac{3}{4}–1\frac{1}{4}$ in., acute. Calyx and corolla 5-lobed. Corolla yellow-white; margins marked with short, pale purple streaks; one gland on each lobe, circular, naked.

Simla, Mushobra, common; August, September.—Temperate Himalaya, 4000–10,000 ft.

5. **Swertia Chirata,** *Buch.-Ham.*; *Fl. Br. Ind.* iv. 124. Stems robust, 2–5 ft., branching, terete except near the top. Leaves broadly lanceolate, 4 × 1½ in., acute. Calyx and corolla 4-lobed. Corolla green-yellow, tinged with purple; two glands on each lobe, green, fringed with long hairs.

Simla, Chadwick Falls, Mushobra, Matiana; September–November.—Temperate Himalaya, 5000–10,000 ft.

The medicine *Chiretta* is obtained from the roots and stems of this species.

FIG. 102. SWERTIA PURPURASCENS.

6. **Swertia alata,** *Royle*; *Fl. Br. Ind.* iv. 125. Stems 1–2 ft., branching, angles winged. Leaves ovate, 1¾ × ¾ in., acute. Calyx and corolla 4-lobed. Corolla lurid green-yellow, dotted and veined with purple; one gland on each lobe, fringed.

Simla, below Bishop Cotton's school, Naldera; September.—W. Himalaya, 4000–6000 ft.

7. **Swertia angustifolia,** *Buch.-Ham.*; *Fl. Br. Ind.* iv. 125. Stems 1–3 ft., branching, angles narrowly winged. Leaves linear-lanceolate, 2¼ × ¼ in., acute. Calyx and corolla 4-lobed. Corolla white or pale blue, darker dotted; one gland on each lobe, green, circular, naked.

Simla, Mushobra; September.—Temperate Himalaya, 2000–7000 ft.

5. **HALENIA.** In honour of J. Halen, a Swedish botanical author of the eighteenth century.—Mountainous regions of Asia and America.

Halenia elliptica, *D. Don*; *Fl. Br. Ind.* iv. 130. An erect, glabrous herb; stems 4-sided, angles narrowly winged. Leaves opposite, sessile, ovate, 1–2 × $\frac{3}{4}$–$1\frac{1}{4}$ in., obtuse. Flowers pale blue,

FIG. 103. HALENIA ELLIPTICA.

$\frac{1}{3}$ in. diam., in axillary cymes. Calyx 4-parted; segments ovate-lanceolate. Corolla bell-shaped, deeply 4-lobed; each lobe produced downwards in a slender, straight spur longer than the calyx. Stamens 4, attached near the base of the corolla. Ovary 1-celled; style short, stigma 2-lobed; ovules many. Capsule ovoid. (Fig. 103.)

Mushobra, Mahasu, in woods; July–September.—Temperate Himalaya, 6000–12,000 ft.

LXV. BORAGINACEÆ

TREES, shrubs or herbs, usually roughly hairy; stems terete. Leaves alternate, rarely opposite, simple, entire, rarely toothed; stipules none. Flowers regular, 2-sexual, rarely polygamous, often changing in colour with age, usually in long, simple or branched, one-sided racemes, inrolled from the tip when young. Calyx free, 5-toothed or 5-lobed, persistent, often enlarged in fruit. Corolla hypogynous; tube cylindric, usually short, mouth naked or furnished with 5 small scales; limb spreading, 5-lobed. Stamens 5, attached in the corolla-tube, alternate with the lobes; filaments very short; anthers 2-celled, usually included. Ovary ovoid or 4-lobed, 4-, rarely 2-celled; style linear, simple or branched, terminal or inserted between the lobes of the ovary, stigma small, terminal; ovules 1, rarely 2 in each cell. Fruit a drupe or consisting of 4 one-seeded nutlets ultimately separating from the receptacle.—A large Order dispersed over nearly the whole world. —Named from *Borago*, a genus not represented in India; etymology obscure.

Mouth of corolla-tube without scales.
  Trees or shrubs.
    Ovary 4-celled. Style 4-branched . . . . . 1. *Cordia.*
    Ovary 2-celled. Style 2-branched . . . . . 2. *Ehretia.*
  Herbs.
    Leaves $\frac{1}{4}$–$\frac{1}{2}$ in. Flowers $\frac{1}{16}$ in. diam.. . . . . 3. *Heliotropium.*
    Leaves 1–4 in. Flowers $\frac{3}{4}$–1 in. diam. . . . . 4. *Trichodesma.*
Mouth of corolla-tube furnished with 5 scales.
  Nutlets bristly.
    Ovary flattened. Bristles of nutlets minute . . 5. *Cynoglossum.*
    Ovary conical. Bristles of nutlets $\frac{1}{4}$ in. long . . 6. *Paracaryum.*
  Nutlets smooth.
    Flowers white. Corolla-tube longer than the calyx . 7. *Mertensia.*
    Flowers blue. Corolla-tube shorter than the calyx . 8. *Myosotis.*

1. CORDIA. In honour of E. Cordus, a German physician and writer on medicinal plants in the sixteenth century.—Nearly all warm regions, but chiefly America.

Cordia Myxa, *Linn.*; *Fl. Br. Ind.* iv. 136. A tree. Leaves alternate, stalked, ovate or orbicular, 3–6 in., entire; upper surface glabrous, lower pubescent. Flowers white, $\frac{1}{4}$ in. diam., often polygamous, in open, usually terminal panicles; bracts none or minute. Calyx irregularly lobed. Corolla-tube as long as the calyx; lobes narrowly oblong, recurved. Stamens protruding, filaments hairy. Ovary ovoid, 4-celled; style terminal, cleft about half-way up into 4 long, linear branches; ovule one in each cell. Drupe pale brown or pink, nearly black when ripe, ovoid, $\frac{3}{4}$–1$\frac{1}{4}$ in.

long, girt at the base by the enlarged, cup-shaped calyx; stone wrinkled, containing 1–4 seeds.

Valleys below Simla; March, April.—Throughout India, ascending to 5000 ft.—Tropical regions of the Old World; often cultivated.

C. vestita, *Hook. f. & Thoms.*; *Fl. Br. Ind.* iv. 139, a small tree, extends from the Jhelum to Oudh, and may occur in the outer hills. The buds and young shoots are thickly clothed with long, red brown hairs, and the flowers are pale yellow.

2. EHRETIA. In honour of G. D. Ehret, a German botanical artist of the eighteenth century, much of whose work was done in England. He married a sister of the celebrated Philip Miller.—Tropical and subtropical regions of the Old World.

Ehretia lævis, *Roxb.*; *Fl. Br. Ind.* iv. 141. A tree. Leaves alternate, stalked, ovate or orbicular, 2–5 in., entire; upper surface glabrous, lower roughly pubescent. Flowers white, nearly $\frac{1}{4}$ in. diam., in one-sided, slender spikes forming terminal or axillary corymbs. Calyx pubescent, 5-lobed. Corolla-tube very short; lobes long, spreading. Stamens protruding. Ovary ovoid, 2 celled; style terminal, cleft near the top into 2 branches; ovules 2 in each cell. Drupe red, globose, $\frac{1}{6}$ in. diam., containing 3 or 4 small, 1-seeded stones.

Sutlej valley, Basantpur; January–April.—Throughout India, ascending to 3000 ft.—Tropical and subtropical regions of the Old World.

E. acuminata, *R. Br.*; *Fl. Br. Ind.* iv. 141, a tree, extends from the Indus to Sikkim, and may occur in the outer hills; it differs from the above in having ovate-oblong, sharply toothed leaves, and in the drupe containing only two stones.

3. HELIOTROPIUM. The classical name of *H. europæum*, from the Greek *helios*, the sun, and *tropeo*, to turn towards.—Nearly all tropical and temperate regions.

Heliotropium strigosum, *Willd.*; *Fl. Br. Ind.* iv. 151. A small, perennial, usually procumbent herb, clothed with short, white, appressed hairs; stems tufted, spreading, much branched, 1–6 in. long. Leaves alternate, nearly sessile, linear-lanceolate, $\frac{1}{4}$–$\frac{1}{2}$ in., entire, acute. Flowers pale blue or white, $\frac{1}{10}$ in. diam., in terminal, bracteate spikes 1–3 in. long, lower flowers often shortly stalked. Calyx 5-lobed. Corolla-tube cylindric, about twice as long as the calyx; lobes spreading. Stamens included. Ovary ovoid, 4-celled; style terminal, short, stigma conical; ovule one in each cell. Fruit of 4 more or less united, minute, 1-seeded nutlets.

Valleys below Simla; July–September.—Throughout India, ascending to 5000 ft.—Tropical Asia, Australia.

4. TRICHODESMA. From the Greek *thrix, trichos*, hair, and *desmos*, a band or fastening; the anthers are united by hairs.—Tropical and subtropical regions of the Old World.

Trichodesma indicum, *R. Br.*; *Fl. Br. Ind.* iv. 153. An annual herb, rough with appressed, bulbous-based hairs; stems 6–18 in., erect or diffuse. Leaves stem-clasping, lower opposite, upper often alternate, lanceolate, 1–4 in., acute. Flowers pale blue, turning to pink and ultimately to white, $\frac{3}{4}$–1 in. diam., single on drooping, axillary stalks. Calyx conical, prolonged below the divisions in 5 recurved tails; lobes lanceolate, finely pointed. Corolla-tube nearly as long as the calyx; lobes ovate, abruptly tapering into a narrow point, a glandular, yellow spot at the base of each. Anthers lanceolate, cohering in a woolly, projecting cone, tips naked, twisted. Ovary 4 lobed, 4-celled; style terminal, simple; ovule one in each cell. Fruit enclosed in the enlarged calyx; nutlets 4, smooth, oblong-ovoid, 1-seeded, ultimately separating from the conical receptacle.

Valleys below Simla; September, October.—Throughout India, ascending to 5000 ft.—W. Asia.

5. CYNOGLOSSUM. From the Greek *cyon*, a dog, and *glossa*, a tongue; referring to the rough leaves of some species.—Most temperate and subtropical regions; abundant in Asia.

Erect, hairy or pubescent herbs, hairs often bulbous-based. Leaves entire, rarely toothed; radical stalked, spreading, often disappearing before flowering-time; stem-leaves alternate, sessile or nearly so. Flowers in long, simple or forked, 1-sided racemes; bracts none. Calyx deeply lobed, persistent. Corolla-tube as long as the calyx, furnished at the mouth with 5 small, obtuse scales; lobes spreading, obtuse. Stamens included in the corolla-tube. Ovary flattened, 4-lobed, 4-celled; style simple, inserted between the lobes; ovule one in each cell. Nutlets 4, small, 1-seeded, more or less covered with minute, hooked bristles, ultimately separating from the convex receptacle.

Flowers $\frac{1}{5}$ in. diam., or less.
  Flowers pale blue or white. Nutlets uniformly bristly.
    Leaves densely clothed with short, soft, appressed hairs. Flowers $\frac{1}{5}$ in. diam. . . . . . 1. *C. furcatum.*
    Leaves covered with long, white, conspicuously bulbous-based hairs. Flowers hardly $\frac{1}{10}$ in. diam. 2. *C. micranthum.*
  Flowers dark blue. Leaves covered with long, white, mostly bulbous based hairs. Nutlets bristly on the margins, faces nearly naked . . . . 3. *C. Wallichii.*
Flowers $\frac{1}{2}$ in. diam., dark blue. Upper surface of leaves covered with bulbous based hairs, lower softly pubescent . . . . 4. *C. microglochin.*

1. **Cynoglossum furcatum,** *Wall.*; *Fl. Br. Ind.* iv. 155. Stems and leaves densely clothed with short, soft, brown, appressed hairs

often tawny or yellow on the young parts; hairs often bulbous-based. Leaves narrowly lanceolate, about $3 \times \frac{1}{2}$ in. Flowers pale blue or white, $\frac{1}{5}$ in. diam. Nutlets uniformly bristly. (Fig. 104.)

Simla, Mushobra, common; June-September.—Throughout India, ascending to 9000 ft.

FIG. 104. CYNOGLOSSUM FURCATUM.

2. **Cynoglossum micranthum,** *Desf.*; *Fl. Br. Ind.* iv. 156. Stems and leaves rough with long, white, bulbous-based hairs sometimes mingled with short, white pubescence. Leaves narrowly lanceolate, $1\frac{1}{2}$-$3\frac{1}{2} \times \frac{1}{4}$-$\frac{1}{2}$ in., hairs most conspicuous on the upper surface. Flowers pale blue or white, hardly $\frac{1}{10}$ in. diam. Nutlets uniformly bristly.

Simla, common; June-August.—N. India, ascending to 8000 ft.

3. **Cynoglossum Wallichii,** *G. Don*; *Fl. Br. Ind.* iv. 157, including *C. denticulatum*, *A. DC.* Stems and leaves rough with long, white hairs mostly bulbous-based. Leaves ovate-lanceolate, 1-$4 \times \frac{1}{2}$-1 in., often more or less toothed, sometimes

narrowed in a short stalk, hairs most conspicuous on the upper surface. Flowers dark blue, $\frac{1}{5}$ in. diam. Nutlets bordered with a line of broad-based, united bristles, faces nearly naked.

Simla, Mahasu, common; July–October.—Temperate Himalaya, 4000–10,000 ft.

*4. **Cynoglossum microglochin,** *Benth.*; *Fl. Br. Ind.* iv. 158. Stems softly pubescent. Leaves ovate-lanceolate, about 4 × 2 in., acute, upper surface covered with long, white, bulbous-based hairs, lower with soft, white pubescence. Flowers dark blue, $\frac{1}{2}$ in. diam. Nutlets bristly on the margins, faces nearly naked.

Kashmir to Kumaon, 7000–11,000 ft.; July–October. — Common at Dalhousie.

The closely allied *C. nervosum*, Benth., occurs on the Chor and on the Jalaori Pass; it differs from the above in having narrowly lanceolate leaves about 4 × 1 in.

6. **PARACARYUM.** From the Greek *para*, alongside, and *caryon*, a nut; referring to the position of the nutlets as regards the receptacle.—W. and Central Asia, N. Europe.

Paracaryum glochidiatum, *Benth.*; *Fl. Br. Ind.* iv. 161. A softly pubescent herb; stems 2–3 ft., erect. Radical leaves long-stalked, cordate, ovate, 3–6 × 2–4 in., entire, finely pointed; stem-leaves alternate, smaller, shortly stalked, uppermost sessile. Flowers pale blue, $\frac{1}{3}$ in. diam., in long, usually forked racemes. Calyx deeply lobed. Corolla-tube very short, mouth furnished with 5 small, obtuse scales; lobes spreading, rounded. Stamens included. Ovary conical, 4-lobed, 4-celled; style simple, inserted between the lobes; ovule one in each cell. Nutlets 4, small, ovate, ultimately separating from the conical receptacle, margins beset with tapering, hooked bristles nearly $\frac{1}{4}$ in. long, faces smooth.

Matiana hill, Huttoo; July, August.—Temperate Himalaya, 9000–12,000 ft.

7. **MERTENSIA.** In honour of F. C. Mertens, a German botanical author of the nineteenth century.—Temperate Asia, E. Europe, N. America.

Mertensia racemosa, *Benth.*; *Fl. Br. Ind.* iv. 171. A softly hairy herb; stems weak, diffuse or nearly erect, 4–8 in. Leaves alternate, entire; radical long-stalked, ovate, $\frac{3}{4}$–1 in.; upper shortly stalked or sessile, oblong-lanceolate, 1–2 in. Flowers white, $\frac{1}{2}$ in. diam., in terminal racemes. Calyx deeply lobed; segments linear. Corolla-tube longer than the calyx, mouth furnished with 5 short, blunt scales; lobes spreading, obtuse. Stamens included, anther-tips protruding. Ovary 4-lobed, 4-celled; style simple, inserted between the lobes; ovule one in each cell.

Fruit of 4 small, smooth nutlets ultimately separating from the flat receptacle. (Fig. 105.)

Simla, Mushobra, on damp rocks; March, April.—Simla to Kumaon, 7000–10,000 ft.

FIG. 105. MERTENSIA RACEMOSA.

8. MYOSOTIS. From the Greek *mys*, a mouse, and *ous*, *otos*, the ear; referring to the leaves.—N. temperate regions, New Zealand, Australia.

Hairy herbs. Leaves alternate, entire. Flowers small, in terminal racemes; bracts usually none. Calyx lobed to about the middle or nearly to the base. Corolla-tube shorter than the calyx; mouth furnished with 5 short, blunt scales; lobes spreading, obtuse. Stamens included. Ovary 4-lobed, 4-celled; style short, inserted between the lobes; ovule one in each cell. Fruit of 4 small, smooth, 1-seeded nutlets, ultimately separating from the flat receptacle.

Calyx not lobed below the middle, covered with appressed, straight hairs. Corolla $\frac{1}{6}$ in. diam. . . . . 1. *M. cæspitosa.*
Calyx lobed nearly to the base, covered with spreading, hooked hairs. Corolla $\frac{1}{4}$–$\frac{1}{3}$ in. diam. . . . . 2. *M. sylvatica.*

*1. **Myosotis cæspitosa,** *Schultz*; *Fl. Br. Ind.* iv. 173. Stems weak, ascending, 6–18 in., covered with appressed hairs or nearly glabrous. Leaves sessile, oblong, $1\frac{1}{2} \times \frac{1}{2}$ in. Calyx lobed to the middle, hairs appressed, straight. Corolla $\frac{1}{6}$ in. diam., bright blue with a yellow centre.

Kunawar to Kashmir, in wet ditches or on the banks of streams, 9000–12,000 ft.; August-October.—W. Asia, N. Africa, Europe (Britain, Forget-me-not), N. America.

2. **Myosotis sylvatica,** *Hoffm.*; *Fl. Br. Ind.* iv. 173. Stems tufted, erect or decumbent, 6–18 in., covered with spreading hairs. Leaves oblong, $1\frac{1}{2} \times \frac{1}{4}$ in., lower stalked, upper sessile. Calyx lobed nearly to the base, hairs spreading, hooked. Corolla $\frac{1}{4}$–$\frac{1}{3}$ in. diam., bright blue with a yellow centre.

Simla, Fagoo, in pastures and shady places; July-October.—W. Himalaya, 7000–12,000 ft.—W. Asia, Europe (Britain, Wood Forget-me-not).

LXVI. CONVOLVULACEÆ

Herbs or shrubs; stems usually twining. Leaves alternate, simple, entire or lobed, none in *Cuscuta*; stipules none. Flowers regular, 2-sexual, often showy. Calyx free, deeply 5-lobed; lobes overlapping, persistent, sometimes enlarged in fruit. Corolla hypogynous, usually bell-shaped or funnel-shaped; limb 5-lobed, often folding at the angles. Stamens 5, equal or unequal, inserted on the corolla-tube, alternate with the lobes, filaments usually dilated at the base; anthers 2-celled. Ovary free, sessile, often encircled at the base by a ring-shaped disk, 2- rarely 3-celled; styles one or two, simple or branching, stigma globose or linear. Capsule globose, usually more or less enclosed by the persistent calyx; seeds usually 4.—A large Order widely dispersed over nearly the whole world, most abundant in warm regions.

Leaf-bearing shrubs or herbs.
  Style single.
    Style not branching. Stigma capitate.
      Stamens unequal. Style long, slender . . . . 1. *Ipomœa.*
      Stamens equal. Style short, thick . . . . . 4. *Porana.*
    Style branching. Stigmas linear. . . . . . . 2. *Convolvulus.*
  Styles 2, each branching in two linear stigmas . . . 3. *Evolvulus.*
Leafless, parasitic herbs. Flowers very small. . . . . 5. *Cuscuta.*

1. **IPOMŒA.** From the Greek *ips*, bindweed, and *omoios*, similar; referring to the climbing habit of most of the species of

this genus, and closely resembling *Convolvulus.*—Nearly all warm countries, absent from Europe.

Twining or rarely procumbent herbs. Leaves stalked, usually entire, sometimes lobed. Flowers large or small, axillary, in clusters, heads or racemes, sometimes solitary. Corolla-tube long or short; limb spreading, more or less distinctly 5-lobed, folding at the angles. Stamens unequal, attached near the top of the tube. Ovary 2- or 3-celled; style single, long, stigma terminal, globose or 2-lobed; ovules 2 in each cell. Capsule opening from the top by 4 valves; seeds 4 or 6, sometimes fewer, large, glabrous or hairy.

The American Sweet Potato, *Ipomœa Batatas*, having tuberous, edible roots and large, purple flowers, is occasionally cultivated in the plains. In the *Fl. Br. Ind.* iv. 215, Simla is given as a locality for *I. dasysperma*, Jacq.; but there is no specimen from the Himalaya in the Kew Herbarium.

Flowers pink, purple or blue.
  Flowers large. Corolla $1\frac{1}{2}$–3 in. long.
    Calyx glabrous. Corolla-tube long, cylindric . . . 1. *I. muricata.*
    Calyx hairy. Corolla-tube very short.
      Leaves 3-lobed. . . . . 2. *I. hederacea.*
      Leaves ovate . . . . 3. *I. purpurea.*
  Flowers small. Corolla $\frac{1}{4}$–1 in. long.
    Lower surface of leaves green, thinly hairy. Flowers in sessile heads . . . . 4. *I. eriocarpa.*
    Lower surface of leaves silvery-tomentose. Flowers in stalked clusters or racemes . . . . . . 6. *I. pilosa.*
Flowers yellow. Corolla $\frac{1}{2}$–$\frac{3}{4}$ in. long . . . . . . 5. *I. chryseides.*

*1. **Ipomœa muricata,** *Jacq.*; *Fl. Br. Ind.* iv. 197. Glabrous; stems rough with small, tubercular outgrowths. Leaves ovate, 2–4 in., cordate, abruptly tapering into a narrow point. Flowers large, pale purple, in small, stalked clusters, sometimes solitary. Sepals glabrous, broad, abruptly pointed. Corolla funnel-shaped, $2\frac{1}{2}$–3 in. long; tube 1–2 in., narrowly cylindric, much longer than the calyx, hairy within. Ovary 2-celled. Capsule $\frac{1}{2}$ in. diam.; stalk thickened in fruit.

Temperate Himalaya, 1000–5000 ft.; August–October.—Hilly districts throughout India; often cultivated.

2. **Ipomœa hederacea,** *Jacq.*; *Fl. Br. Ind.* iv. 199. Hairy. Leaves ovate, 2–5 in., cordate, more or less deeply 3-lobed. Flowers large, pale blue, often tinged with pink, in small, stalked clusters, sometimes solitary. Sepals linear, hairy near the base. Corolla funnel-shaped, $1\frac{1}{2}$–$2\frac{1}{2}$ in. long; tube very short. Ovary 3-celled. Capsule $\frac{1}{3}$ in. diam.

Simla, Shali; August, September.—Throughout India, ascending to 6000 ft.; often cultivated.—Nearly all warm countries.

3. **Ipomœa purpurea,** *Lam.*; *Fl. Br. Ind.* iv. 200. Hairy. Leaves ovate, 1–2 in., cordate, acute. Flowers large, pink, in

small, stalked clusters, sometimes solitary. Sepals hairy at the base, lanceolate. Corolla funnel-shaped, $1\frac{1}{2}$–2 in. long; tube very short. Ovary 3-celled. Capsule $\frac{1}{4}$ in. diam.

Valleys below Simla; August, September.—Throughout India, ascending to 7000 ft.; doubtfully indigenous, often cultivated.—Tropical America and cultivated in nearly all warm countries.

FIG. 106. IPOMŒA HEDERACEA.

4. **Ipomœa eriocarpa,** *R. Br.*; *Fl. Br. Ind.* iv. 204. Hairy. Leaves lanceolate, $2\text{–}3 \times \frac{1}{3}\text{–}1\frac{1}{4}$ in., deeply cordate, long-pointed. Flowers small, pink, in sessile or nearly sessile heads. Sepals hairy, long-pointed. Corolla bell-shaped, $\frac{1}{4}$–$\frac{3}{4}$ in. long. Ovary 2-celled. Capsule $\frac{1}{4}$ in. diam.

Valleys below Simla; August, September.—Throughout India, ascending to 4000 ft.—Tropical regions of the Old World.

5. **Ipomœa chryseides,** *Ker*; *Fl. Br. Ind.* iv. 206. Glabrous; stems usually rough with small, tubercular outgrowths, sometimes procumbent. Leaves broadly ovate, $1\frac{1}{2} \times 1\frac{1}{4}$ in., cordate, sinuously toothed, long-pointed. Flowers small, yellow, in stalked clusters.

Sepals broadly oblong, abruptly pointed. Corolla salver-shaped, $\frac{1}{2}$–$\frac{3}{4}$ in. long. Ovary 2-celled. Capsule $\frac{1}{4}$ in. diam.

Valleys below Simla; August, September.—Throughout India, ascending to 4000 ft.—Tropical Asia, Africa, Australia.

6. **Ipomœa pilosa,** *Sweet*; *Fl. Br. Ind.* iv. 213. Softly hairy. Leaves broadly ovate, 3 × 4 in., cordate, sometimes 3-lobed, acute; upper surface thinly hairy, lower silvery-tomentose. Flowers small, pink, in stalked clusters or racemes. Sepals hairy, narrowly lanceolate, long-pointed. Corolla funnel-shaped, $\frac{1}{2}$–1 in. long. Ovary 2-celled. Capsule $\frac{1}{4}$ in. diam.

Valleys below Simla, Subathoo; August–October.—Throughout India, ascending to 3000 ft.—Tropical Africa.

2. CONVOLVULUS. The classical name of the Bindweed, *C. sepium*, derived from *convolvo*, to roll up; referring to the twining habit.—Temperate and tropical regions.

Convolvulus arvensis, *Linn.*; *Fl. Br. Ind.* iv. 219. A glabrous or pubescent herb; rootstock creeping; stems slender, prostrate, twining, 6–24 in. Leaves stalked, ovate or lanceolate, 1–3 × $\frac{1}{4}$–1 in., entire, base sagittate; lobes spreading, acute. Flowers purple, with white or pale yellow centre, solitary or 2–3 on an axillary stalk. Sepals ovate, obtuse. Corolla $\frac{3}{4}$–1 in. long; tube very short; limb spreading, 1 in. diam., obscurely 5-lobed, folding at the angles. Stamens unequal, attached near the bottom of the tube. Ovary 2-celled; style single, branching near the top in 2 short, linear stigmas; ovules 2 in each cell. Capsule $\frac{1}{4}$ in. diam., opening by 4 valves; seeds 4.

Simla, in fields; April–October.—Throughout India, ascending to 7000 ft.—A weed of cultivation in nearly all temperate and subtropical regions.—Britain, Field Bindweed.

3. EVOLVULUS. From the Latin *evolvo*, to unroll, in opposition to *convolvo*; the stems and branches do not twine.—Nearly all warm countries, most numerous in America.

Evolvulus alsinoides, *Linn.*; *Fl. Br. Ind.* iv. 220. A softly hairy, perennial herb; branches numerous, slender, 4–12 in., diffuse or procumbent. Leaves sessile or nearly so, lanceolate or ovate, $\frac{1}{4}$–$\frac{1}{2}$ in., entire, acute. Flowers small, blue or white, axillary, stalked, solitary or 2 or 3 together, forming terminal racemes. Sepals narrowly lanceolate. Corolla funnel-shaped; tube very short; limb spreading, $\frac{1}{4}$ in. diam., obscurely 5-lobed, folding at the angles. Stamens attached near the bottom of the tube. Ovary 2-celled; styles 2, each branching in 2 long, linear stigmas; ovules 2 in each cell. Capsule globose; seeds 4, smooth.

Valleys below Simla, Syree; March–October.—Throughout India, ascending to 6000 ft.—Nearly all tropical and subtropical regions.

4. PORANA. Supposed to be derived from the Javanese name of *P. volubilis*.—India, Malaya, Australia, N. America.

***Porana paniculata,** *Roxb.*; *Fl. Br. Ind.* iv. 223. A twining, softly tomentose shrub; lateral branches often very long, drooping. Leaves stalked, ovate, 3–5 × 2–3 in., cordate, entire, long-pointed; upper surface pubescent, lower tomentose. Flowers very numerous, small, white, in terminal, pendulous panicles. Calyx-segments oblong, unequal, 3 becoming membranous and greatly enlarged in fruit. Corolla funnel-shaped, $\frac{1}{4}$ in. long; tube s·ort; limb spreading, obscurely 5-lobed, folding at the angles. Stamens equal, attached near the top of the tube; filaments short. Ovary 2-celled; style thick, very short, stigma globose, 2-lobed; ovules 2 in each cell. Capsule hairy, $\frac{1}{5}$ in. diam.; enlarged sepals $\frac{3}{4}$ in. long; seed one, glabrous.

Throughout India, ascending to 3000 ft.—Burmah, Java.

P. racemosa, *Roxb.*; *Fl. Br. Ind.* iv. 222, is of similar habit to the above but the flowers are in long racemes; the deeply lobed corolla is nearly $\frac{1}{3}$ in. long; the style is slender; and all 5 sepals become membranous and enlarged in fruit. The species is common in the E. Himalaya from 2000 to 6000 ft. extending to Kumaon and perhaps further west.

5. CUSCUTA. Etymology doubtful.—Widely dispersed in nearly all temperate and warm regions.

Annual, parasitic, leafless herbs; stems twining, thread-like, attached to the plants on which they grow by minute, adhesive disks. Flowers small, in clusters or racemes. Calyx coloured, shorter than the corolla. Corolla tubular; lobes short, triangular. Stamens attached near the mouth of the tube which has 5 small, fringed scales at the base. Ovary 2-celled; stigmas 2, sessile or terminal on short, diverging styles; ovules 2 in each cell. Capsule globose, opening by a horizontal line near the base; seeds 4.

Corolla $\frac{1}{4}$–$\frac{1}{3}$ in. long; lobes reflexed. Stigmas sessile . . . 1. *C. reflexa.*
Corolla hardly $\frac{1}{10}$ in. long; lobes erect. Styles nearly as long as the stigmas . . . . 2. *C. europæa.*

1. **Cuscuta reflexa,** *Roxb.*; *Fl. Br. Ind.* iv. 225. Stems succulent, yellow, densely interlaced over small trees or shrubs. Flowers fragrant, waxy white, shortly stalked, crowded in numerous, small clusters or racemes. Corolla-tube $\frac{1}{4}$–$\frac{1}{3}$ in. long; lobes reflexed. Stigmas sessile, diverging, acute. (Fig. 107.)

Mushobra, Fagoo, Matiana; July–October.—Throughout India, ascending to 6000 ft.—Malaya.

*2. **Cuscuta europæa,** *Linn.*; *Fl. Br. Ind.* iv. 227. Stems pale yellow or pink. Flowers waxy white, often tinged with pink, sessile in numerous, small, globose clusters. Corolla-tube hardly

$\frac{1}{10}$ in. long, cylindric, becoming globose in fruit; lobes erect. Styles distinct, diverging, nearly as long as the linear stigmas.

Temperate Himalaya, 5000–12,000 ft.—Central and W. Asia, Europe (Britain, Greater Dodder).

FIG. 107. CUSCUTA REFLEXA.

LXVII. SOLANACEÆ

HERBS or shrubs, usually erect. Leaves alternate, simple; stipules none. Flowers axillary or lateral, 2-sexual, regular. Calyx free, 5-lobed or 5-toothed, sometimes 5-parted almost to the base, persistent, often enlarged in fruit. Corolla hypogynous; tube short or long; limb usually spreading, 5-angled or 5-lobed, often folding at the angles. Stamens 5, alternate with the corolla-lobes, attached to the tube; filaments free; anthers 2-celled, usually free, coherent in *Solanum*. Ovary free, 2- rarely 5-celled; style terminal, slender, undivided, stigma usually capitate; ovules numerous in each cell. Fruit an indehiscent berry or a capsule opening by 4 valves or by a transverse slit; seeds numerous, usually flattened.—A large Order widely dispersed through all warm and temperate regions.

Many useful and some poisonous plants belong to this Order. In addition to the species described and mentioned the following are commonly cultivated and may occasionally appear as escapes: the Tomato, *Lycopersicum esculentum*, flowers yellow; the Tobacco, *Nicotiana Tabacum*, flowers white or pink; the Chilly, *Capsicum frutescens*, flowers white, fruit pungent.

Flowers distinctly stalked.
  Flowers in clusters, racemes or irregular umbels.
    Anthers coherent, opening by terminal pores . . . 1. *Solanum.*
    Anthers free, opening by lateral slits . . . . . 3. *Withania.*
  Flowers solitary, usually axillary.
    Flowers $\frac{3}{4}$ in. diam. or less.
      Leaves 2 in. Fruiting calyx globose, enclosing the berry . . . . 2. *Physalis.*
      Leaves 4-8 in. Fruiting calyx spreading. Berry free . . . . 5. *Atropa.*
    Flowers 1-3 in. diam.
      Flowers blue. Calyx lobed nearly to the base . 4. *Nicandra.*
      Flowers white or purple. Calyx tubular . . . 6. *Datura.*
Flowers sessile, crowded in a leafy spike. Corolla purple-veined . . . . 7. *Hyoscyamus.*

1. SOLANUM. The classical name of *S. nigrum*; etymology doubtful.—Chiefly tropical and subtropical regions; most numerous in America.

Shrubs or herbs. Leaves stalked. Flowers in lateral cymes, racemes or irregular umbels, sometimes solitary. Calyx small. Corolla-tube very short; limb spreading, 5-lobed, folding at the angles. Filaments very short; anthers oblong, acute, coherent in a projecting cone, opening by pores at the top. Ovary 2-celled; style long, stigma small. Berry globose.

The Potato, *S. tuberosum*, belongs to this genus; its cultivation at Simla has caused the destruction of much fine forest, notably between Mahasu and Fagoo. The Brinjal, *S. Melongena*, is also commonly cultivated; it has prickly, lobed, woolly leaves and blue flowers 1 in. diam.

Leaves smooth.
  Flowers white.
    Leaves glabrous or nearly so . . . . . 1. *S. nigrum.*
    Leaves stellately tomentose . . . . . 3. *S. verbascifolium.*
  Flowers purple . . . . 2. *S. Dulcamara.*
Leaves prickly.
  Leaves ovate, sinuate; lower surface tomentose . 4. *S. indicum.*
  Leaves oblong, pinnatifid; lower surface glabrous or nearly so . . . . 5. *S. xanthocarpum.*

1. **Solanum nigrum,** *Linn.*; *Fl. Br. Ind.* iv. 229. An erect, nearly glabrous, branching herb, 12–18 in. Leaves ovate or oblong, $1\frac{1}{2}$–4 in., with coarse, angular teeth. Flowers white, $\frac{1}{4}$–$\frac{1}{2}$ in. diam., on slender, drooping stalks forming irregular, umbel-like clusters. Calyx-teeth obtuse. Berry $\frac{1}{4}$ in. diam., red, yellow or black.

Simla, in woods, common; June–October.—Throughout India, ascending to 7000 ft.—Nearly all temperate and tropical regions (Britain, Black Nightshade).

2. **Solanum Dulcamara,** *Linn.*; *Fl. Br. Ind.* iv. 229. A pubescent herb; stems shrubby at the base; branches long, climbing or trailing. Leaves ovate or oblong, 1–3 in., long-pointed, entire or sometimes lobed at the base. Flowers purple, $\frac{1}{2}$–$\frac{3}{4}$ in. diam., in loose, drooping cymes. Calyx-teeth obtuse. Corolla-lobes recurved. Berry $\frac{1}{4}$ in. diam., red when ripe.

Narkunda; August.—W. Himalaya, 4000–8000 ft.—Temperate Asia, Europe (Britain, Woody Nightshade or Bittersweet).

3. **Solanum verbascifolium,** *Linn.*; *Fl. Br. Ind.* iv. 230. An erect shrub, 10–20 ft., covered with dense, stellate tomentum. Leaves broadly lanceolate, 5–10 × 3–5 in., entire, long-pointed. Flowers white, $\frac{1}{2}$–$\frac{3}{4}$ in. diam., crowded in stalked, compound cymes. Calyx-teeth broad, acute. Corolla woolly outside. Berry $\frac{1}{3}$ in. diam., yellow.

Valleys below Simla; September, October.—Throughout India, ascending to 5000 ft.—Tropical Asia, Australia, America.

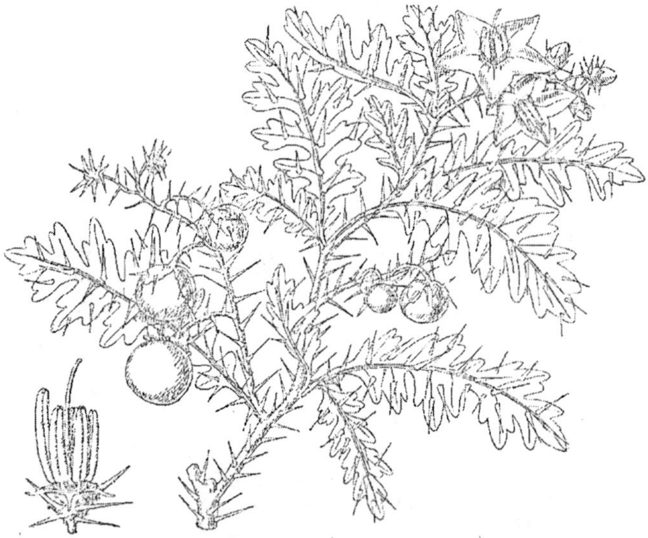

FIG. 108. SOLANUM XANTHOCARPUM.

4. **Solanum indicum,** *Linn.*; *Fl. Br. Ind.* iv. 234. A small shrub or perennial herb, 1–6 ft.; stems prickly, branching. Leaves ovate, 3–6 × 1–4 in., sinuate; upper surface stellately hairy, lower tomentose; nerves on both surfaces prickly. Flowers blue, $\frac{3}{4}$–1 in. diam., in racemes, rarely solitary. Calyx tomentose, usually prickly. Corolla tomentose outside. Berry glabrous, $\frac{1}{3}$ in. diam., yellow.

Valleys below Simla; May-October.—Throughout India, ascending to 5000 ft.—Tropical Asia.

5. **Solanum xanthocarpum**, *Schrad & Wendl.*; *Fl. Br. Ind.* iv. 236. A low, diffuse herb, more or less rough with scattered, stellate hairs; stems prickly, procumbent, branching. Leaves ultimately glabrous, oblong, 2–4 in., pinnatifid, nerves on both surfaces armed with numerous, long, straight prickles. Flowers blue, 1 in. diam., solitary or in small cymes. Calyx prickly. Corolla stellately pubescent outside. Berry glabrous, $\frac{1}{2}$ in. diam., yellow, often blotched with green. (Fig. 108.)

Simla, common; May–October.—Throughout India, ascending to 7000 ft.—Tropical Asia and Australia.

2. **PHYSALIS.** From the Greek *physa*, a bladder, referring to the fruiting calyx.—Chiefly tropical America; several species introduced in the Old World.

Physalis minima, *Linn.*; *Fl. Br. Ind.* iv. 238. An annual, erect or diffuse, pubescent herb, 1–3 ft. Leaves stalked, ovate, $2 \times 1\frac{1}{2}$ in., sinuately angular, acute. Flowers yellow or blue, $\frac{1}{4}$ in. diam., single on axillary stalks. Calyx 5-lobed. Corolla broadly bell-shaped, obscurely 5-lobed, folding at the angles. Ovary 2-celled. Berry green, globose, $\frac{1}{2}$ in. diam., loosely enclosed in the much enlarged, inflated, 5-angled calyx.

Simla, on waste ground near houses; July–November.—Throughout India, ascending to 7000 ft.

The Cape Gooseberry, *P. peruviana*, is cultivated throughout India; the corolla has 5 large purple spots near the base, and the ripe fruit is yellow.

3. **WITHANIA.** Supposed to be in honour of H. Witham, a British geologist and writer on fossil botany in the nineteenth century.—Mediterranean region, W. Asia.

Withania coagulans, *Dunal*; *Fl. Br. Ind.* iv. 240. An erect shrub, 1–3 ft., densely clothed with minute, ashy-grey, stellate hairs. Leaves stalked, thick, oblong-ovate, 1–2 in., entire, obtuse. Flowers yellow, nearly $\frac{1}{2}$ in. diam., often 1-sexual, on short, drooping stalks in axillary clusters. Calyx tomentose, 5-toothed. Corolla bell-shaped, stellately hairy outside; lobes recurved. Anthers free. Ovary 2-celled. Berry globose, $\frac{1}{4}$ in. diam., nearly enclosed by the enlarged calyx.

Sutlej valley; November–April.—Punjab, ascending to 3000 ft.—Sind, Baluchistan, Afghanistan.

The powdered seeds are used to coagulate milk preparatory to the manufacture of cheese. Native name *Punirband*, cheese-maker.

4. **NICANDRA.** In honour of Nicander, a Greek writer on medicine and the properties of plants, about A.D. 150.—A single species, native of Peru, cultivated in nearly all warm regions.

Nicandra physaloides, *Gaertn.*; *Fl. Br. Ind.* iv. 240. An annual, erect, glabrous herb, 1–3 ft. Leaves stalked, ovate-lanceolate, 4–8 in., irregularly, sinuately lobed and toothed. Flowers blue, 1–1½ in. diam., single on recurved, usually axillary stalks. Calyx lobed nearly to the base; segments ovate, cordate, acute. Corolla bell-shaped; limb spreading, 5-lobed. Filaments hairy, bases dilated, covering the ovary. Ovary 5-celled; style linear, stigma 5-lobed, lobes cohering. Berry globose, ½ in. diam., loosely enclosed by the enlarged, membranous, net-veined, 5-angled calyx.

Simla, roadsides, common; July–September.—Temperate Himalaya, 3000–6000 ft.; introduced.

5. ATROPA. From the Greek *Atropos*, the Fate who was fabled to cut the thread of life; referring to the poisonous properties of the plants.—W. Asia, Europe.

Atropa Belladonna, *Linn.*; *Fl. Br. Ind.* iv. 241. An erect, glandular-pubescent or nearly glabrous herb, 2–3 ft. Leaves stalked, ovate-lanceolate, 4–8 in., entire, long-pointed; upper ones usually with a much smaller leaf springing from the same point. Flowers pale purple, tinged with yellow or green, ¾ in. diam., single on drooping, usually axillary stalks. Calyx lobed nearly to the base; segments leaf-like. Corolla bell-shaped; lobes 5, short, broad, spreading. Bases of filaments hairy, dilated, covering the ovary. Ovary 2-celled; style longer than the corolla, stigma green. Berry globose, ¾ in. diam., purple-black, surrounded at the base by the enlarged, spreading calyx.

Narkunda, in forest; August, September.—W. Himalaya, 6000–11,000 ft.—W. Asia, Europe (Britain, Dwale, Belladonna, Deadly Nightshade).

6. DATURA. From *Dhatura*, the Oriental name of *D. fastuosa*.—Temperate and tropical regions.

Datura Stramonium, *Linn.*; *Fl. Br. Ind.* iv. 242. An annual, erect, nearly glabrous herb, 2–4 ft. Leaves stalked, ovate, about 7 × 4 in., coarsely and irregularly lobed and toothed. Flowers white, single on short, usually axillary stalks. Calyx tubular, 1–1¾ in., 5-toothed, 5-ribbed. Corolla funnel-shaped, 3–6 in. long; limb spreading, 1–3 in. across, 5-lobed, folding at the angles, lobes ending in long, narrow points. Stamens included. Ovary 4-lobed, 2-celled, covered with short, soft points; stigma 2-lobed, oblong. Capsule ovoid, about 1½ × 1 in., covered with rigid, sharp prickles, surrounded at the base by the enlarged, reflexed, lower part of the calyx, ultimately 4-celled in the lower portion, opening nearly to the base by 4 valves; seeds wrinkled.

Simla, on waste ground; June–October.—Temperate Himalaya, 3000–8000 ft.—Nearly all temperate and warm regions (Britain, a casual weed, Thorn Apple). Var. *Tatula* with purple flowers also occurs at Simla.

D. fastuosa, Linn.; is the species common in the plains; it has larger flowers than *D. Stramonium*.

7. HYOSCYAMUS. The classical name, signifying hog-bean. —Temperate Asia, Europe.

Hyoscyamus niger, *Linn.*; *Fl. Br. Ind.* iv. 244. An erect, more or less hairy and viscid herb with a disagreeable, heavy odour; stems robust, 1–3 ft. Radical leaves spreading, stalked, oblong-ovate, 6–8 in., coarsely sinuate-toothed. Stem-leaves smaller, sessile, ovate, irregularly pinnatifid, passing into bracts. Flowers pale yellow-green, veined with purple, darker in the centre, nearly sessile, lower ones in the forks of the branches, upper solitary in the axils of leaf-like bracts, forming long, 1-sided spikes rolled back at the top before flowering, ultimately becoming elongated and straight. Calyx $\frac{3}{4}$ in.; tube ovoid; limb funnel-shaped, 5-toothed. Corolla funnel-shaped; limb spreading, 1–1$\frac{1}{4}$ in. across, lobes 5, broad, short, slightly unequal. Stamens protruding. Ovary 2-celled; style longer than the stamens. Capsule $\frac{1}{2}$ in. diam., enclosed in the globose tube of the enlarged calyx, lower part membranous, top hard, rigid, opening transversely along the constriction between the two portions.

Narkunda; July–September.—W. Himalaya, 8000–11,000 ft.—Temperate Asia, Europe (Britain, Henbane).

LXVIII. SCROPHULARIACEÆ

Herbs. Leaves simple or pinnatifid, lower opposite, upper usually alternate, often passing into floral bracts, rarely all alternate; stipules none. Flowers 2-sexual, more or less irregular, solitary in the axils of leaves or bracts, usually forming racemes or spikes. Calyx free, persistent; tube long or short; limb 5- sometimes 4-lobed or -toothed. Corolla gamopetalous; tube long or short; limb 5- or 4-lobed, distinctly 2-lipped or spreading. Stamens 4, 2 or 5, attached to the corolla-tube, alternate with the lobes; anthers often cohering, 2- rarely 1-celled, cells sometimes separated. Disk more or less prominent, ring-shaped, encircling the base of the ovary, sometimes obsolete. Ovary free, entire, sessile, 2-celled, in *Lathræa* 1-celled; style simple, stigma terminal, usually 2-cleft or -lobed; ovules numerous in each cell, rarely few. Fruit a capsule, berry-like in *Hemiphragma*, usually opening by 2 valves which separate from the seed-bearing axis; seeds small, numerous, rarely few.—A very large Order, distributed in nearly all parts of the world.

A. Stamens 2 (*Bonnaya* has also two staminodes).

Calyx 4-lobed. Corolla-tube very short . . . . . . 16. *Veronica.*
Calyx 5-lobed. Corolla-tube longer than the calyx.
  Leaves 3–6 in., all basal, coarsely toothed. Flowers blue-purple . . . . 15. *Wulfenia.*

Leaves ½–1½ in., opposite; teeth finely pointed. Flowers white, spotted or tinged with pink . . 13. *Bonnaya.*

B. Stamens 4.

*Corolla distinctly 2-lipped.

Flowers yellow.
- Corolla-tube spurred at the base . . . . . 3. *Linaria.*
- Corolla-tube not spurred.
  - Leaves simple.
    - Leaves stalked. Anthers 2-celled; cells separated 8. *Lindenbergia.*
    - Leaves sessile. Anthers 1-celled . . . . 18. *Striga.*
  - Leaves pinnatifid. Upper lip of corolla long-beaked . . . . 23. *Pedicularis.*[1]

Flowers blue, purple or pink, never yellow.
- Calyx 4-lobed.
  - Stems aerial, leafy. Upper lip of corolla 2-lobed 22. *Euphrasia.*
  - Stems subterranean, scaly. Upper lip of corolla entire . . . . 24. *Lathræa.*
- Calyx 5-lobed
  - Calyx-tube prominently keeled on the ribs. Leaves sessile, entire . . . . 6. *Mimulus.*
  - Calyx-tube not keeled.
    - Mouth of corolla closed; tube bulged at the base 4. *Antirrhinum.*
    - Lower lip of corolla 2-ridged at the base . . 7. *Mazus.*
    - Leaves gland-dotted. Anther-cells widely separated . . . . 9. *Limnophila.*
    - Filaments of the longer pair of stamens spurred near the base . . . . 12. *Vandellia.*
    - Upper lip of corolla laterally flattened, abruptly bent, extremity beak-like . . . . . 23. *Pedicularis.*[2]

**Corolla not 2-lipped.

Stems prostrate.
- Leaves all oblong or spathulate. Corolla 4-lobed . 10. *Herpestis.*
- Leaves of 2 kinds, orbicular and linear. Corolla 5-lobed . . . . 14. *Hemiphragma.*

Stems erect.
- Flowers yellow.
  - Leaves 1–2 in. broad, radical pinnatifid, upper oblong-ovate . . . . 2. *Celsia.*
  - Leaves all linear, mostly 3-fid . . . . . 20. *Sopubia.*
- Flowers purple or pink, never yellow.
  - Calyx-tube prominently keeled on the ribs . . 11. *Torenia.*
  - Calyx-tube not keeled on the ribs.
    - Leaves less than ¼ in. broad.
      - Leaves simple. Calyx ovate, inflated . . 19. *Centranthera.*
      - Leaves pinnatisect. Calyx bell-shaped . . 21. *Leptorhabdos.*
    - Leaves ¾ in. or more broad.
      - Calyx 5-parted. Corolla-tube globose . . 5. *Scrophularia.*
      - Calyx tubular. Corolla-tube cylindric . . 17. *Buchnera.*

C. Stamens 5.

Tomentose. Flowers yellow. Corolla-limb spreading . 1. *Verbascum.*

1. VERBASCUM. The classical name of *V. Thapsus*; etymology obscure.—W. Asia, Mountains of tropical Africa, Europe.

[1] *P. megalantha* only. [2] Excluding *P. megalantha.*

Verbascum Thapsus, *Linn.*; *Fl. Br. Ind.* iv. 250. An erect herb densely clothed with soft, yellow-grey, stellate hairs; stems robust, 3–6 ft., winged with the prolonged leaf-bases. Leaves entire or nearly so; radical and lower stalked, ovate, 4–12 in.; upper sessile, oblong-lanceolate, 6–18 in. Flowers nearly sessile, yellow, $\frac{3}{4}$–1 in. diam., crowded in terminal spikes. Calyx 5-lobed. Corolla concave, woolly outside; tube very short; lobes 5, spreading, nearly equal, broad, obtuse. Stamens 5; filaments 3 short and hairy, 2 longer and glabrous. Stigma capitate. Capsule tomentose, ovoid.

Simla, Mushobra; May–September.—Temperate Himalaya, 6000–11,000 ft. —W. Asia, Europe (Britain, Great Mullein).

2. CELSIA. In honour of Olaus Celsius, a Swedish botanist of the eighteenth century.—Asia, Africa, Europe.

Celsia coromandeliana, *Vahl*; *Fl. Br. Ind.* iv. 251. An erect, pubescent herb, 2–3 ft. Leaves 1–2 in., broad toothed; radical crowded, stalked, pinnatifid, 6 in., end lobe much the largest; upper alternate, sessile, oblong-ovate, 2–4 in. Flowers yellow, $\frac{1}{3}$ in. diam., in simple or branched racemes 1–2 ft. long, often forming a large, terminal panicle. Calyx 5-parted. Corolla-tube very short; lobes 5, spreading, obtuse. Stamens 4, equal; filaments hairy. Stigma capitate. Capsule globose.

Sutlej valley; January–May.—Throughout India, ascending to 5000 ft.—Afghanistan, Burmah, China.

3. LINARIA. From the Latin *linum*, flax, referring to the shape of the leaves of *L. vulgaris*, the Toad Flax of Britain.—W. Asia, Europe.

Perennial herbs; branches numerous, slender, prostrate, 6–24 in., spreading from the base. Leaves alternate, stalked, variable in shape and size. Flowers yellow, single on long, slender, axillary stalks. Calyx 5-parted. Corolla 2-lipped; tube produced at the base in a hollow spur; upper lip erect, 2-lobed; lower spreading, 3-lobed, base dilated, closing the mouth. Stamens 4, in unequal pairs, included. Style thread-like; stigma minute. Capsule ovoid, opening by pores at the top.

Glabrous. Leaves long-stalked. Spur short, straight, obtuse . . . . 1. *L. ramosissima.*
Softly hairy. Leaves shortly stalked. Spur long, curved, acute . . . . 2. *L. incana.*

1. **Linaria ramosissima,** *Wall.*; *Fl. Br. Ind.* iv. 251. Glabrous or slightly pubescent. Leaves long-stalked; lower ovate, $\frac{1}{2}$–2 in., deeply cordate, angularly lobed; upper narrowly lanceolate, sagittate, basal lobes long, acute, diverging. Calyx-segments

linear. Spur straight, obtuse, about one quarter the length of the tube.

Theog; May, June.—Throughout India on rocks and stony places, ascending to 7000 ft.—Afghanistan, Burmah.

2. **Linaria incana,** *Wall.*; *Fl. Br. Ind.* iv. 252. Covered with long, soft, white, spreading hairs. Leaves shortly stalked; lower ovate or ovate-lanceolate, ½–1 in. across, entire or angularly lobed; upper similar but smaller. Calyx-segments lanceolate. Corolla pubescent, dotted with purple; spur curved, acute, about half the length of the tube.

Sutlej valley, Suni; April.—Temperate Himalaya, 2000–8000 ft.

4. **ANTIRRHINUM.**—From the Greek *anti*, in comparison, and *rin*, a snout; referring to the flowers.—W. Asia, Europe.

Antirrhinum Orontium, *Linn.*; *Fl. Br. Ind.* iv. 253. An erect herb, 6–18 in., more or less glandular-hairy on the upper parts. Leaves sessile, narrowly oblong, 1–2 in., entire, lower opposite, upper alternate. Flowers pale pink, streaked with purple, ½ in. long, solitary and nearly sessile in the axils of the upper leaves. Calyx 5-parted; segments linear, spreading, overtopping the corolla. Corolla 2-lipped; tube slightly bulged at the base; upper lip erect, 2-lobed; lower spreading, 3-lobed, base dilated, closing the mouth. Stamens 4, in unequal pairs, included. Stigma 2-lobed. Capsule ovoid, opening by pores at the top.

Simla, in fields; April–October.—N.W. India, ascending to 6000 ft.—W. Asia, N. Africa, Europe (Britain, Corn Snapdragon).

5. **SCROPHULARIA.** Name refers to a former use of the plants as a remedy for scrofula.—N. temperate regions (Britain, Figwort).

Erect herbs; stems robust, angular, glabrous towards the base, viscidly glandular on the upper parts. Leaves stalked, opposite or the upper alternate, ovate or ovate-lanceolate, crenate or sharply toothed. Flowers small, dingy green-purple, in opposite, stalked cymes forming terminal panicles. Calyx 5-parted. Corolla-tube very short, globose; lobes 5, short, broad, flat, the upper 4 erect, lowest spreading or recurved. Stamens 4, in unequal pairs, turned downwards; anthers 1-celled. Style long; stigma minute. Capsule ovoid or globose; seeds usually several.

Sepals acute. Upper corolla-lobes equal. Stamens included . . 1. *S. calycina.*
Sepals rounded. Upper corolla-lobes unequal. Stamens protruding . . . . 2. *S. himalensis.*

1. **Scrophularia calycina,** *Benth.*; *Fl. Br. Ind.* iv. 253. Stems 1–2 ft. Leaves ovate or ovate-lanceolate, 1–4 in., usually cordate, acute. Cymes shortly stalked, forming an erect, stiff, narrow panicle; flowers numerous, crowded. Sepals lanceolate, long-pointed, acute. Upper corolla-lobes equal. Stamens included. Capsule ovoid, acute.

Narkunda, Huttoo, the Chor; July–September.—Temperate Himalaya, 9000–12,000 ft.

FIG. 109. SCROPHULARIA HIMALENSIS.

2. **Scrophularia himalensis,** *Royle*; *Fl. Br. Ind.* iv. 255; including *S. polyantha.* Stems 3–4 ft. Leaves ovate or lanceolate, $3–5 \times 1\frac{1}{4}–2\frac{1}{2}$ in., often cordate, sometimes lobed at the base, acute. Cymes long-stalked, few-flowered, loosely spreading, sometimes forming a large panicle. Sepals rounded, margins scarious. The two upper corolla-lobes much longer than the two lateral. Stamens far protruding. Capsule globose. (Fig. 109.)

Simla, Mushobra, Theog, common June–September.—Temperate Himalaya, 4000–10,000 ft.

6. MIMULUS. From the Greek *mimo*, an ape, referring to the shape of the flower; commonly known as the Monkey Flower.—Most temperate and tropical regions.

***Mimulus gracilis,** *R. Br.*; *Fl. Br. Ind.* iv. 259. An erect, glabrous herb; stems 6–12 in., 4-angled, often branching from the base. Leaves opposite, stem-clasping, narrowly oblong, $1\frac{1}{2}$–$2\frac{1}{2}$ in., entire. Flowers nearly white, spotted with yellow, single on long, axillary stalks. Calyx tubular, ribs prominently keeled, teeth 5. Corolla 2-lipped, $\frac{1}{2}$ in. long; tube cylindric; upper lip erect, 2-lobed; lower spreading, 3-lobed, 2-ridged at the base. Stamens 4, in unequal pairs, included. Stigma flat, 2-lobed.

N. India, ascending to 3000 ft.; common on riversides and in moist, shady places; April, May.—China, Australia, Tropical and S. Africa.

FIG. 110. MAZUS RUGOSUS.

7. MAZUS. From the Greek *mazos*, a teat; referring to the two nipple-like warts at the mouth of the corolla-tube.—Asia, Australia.

Small, erect, nearly glabrous herbs, 2–12 in. Leaves mostly rosulate or opposite and crowded near the base of the stem; upper alternate, few or none. Flowers small, in terminal racemes.

Calyx bell-shaped, 5-lobed or 5-toothed. Corolla 2-lipped, $\frac{1}{4}$–$\frac{1}{2}$ in. long; tube short; upper lip erect, 2-lobed; lower much larger, spreading, 3-lobed, with 2 prominent, glandular ridges at the base. Stamens 4, in unequal pairs, included. Stigma flat, 2-lobed. Capsule globose.

Calyx lobed half-way down. Runners none . . . . 1. *M. rugosus.*
Calyx shortly toothed. Runners long, leafy . . . . 2. *M. surculosus.*

1. **Mazus rugosus**, *Lour.*; *Fl. Br. Ind.* iv. 259. Stems tufted. Runners none. Radical leaves oblong or obovate, 1–3 in., narrowed to a stalk-like base, coarsely, irregularly toothed. Stem-leaves spathulate, $\frac{1}{2}$–$1\frac{1}{2}$ in. Flowers pale blue or white, streaked with blue, upper lip darker. Calyx lobed half-way down. (Fig. 110.)

Simla, common; May–October.—N. India, ascending to 7000 ft.—Tropical Asia.

2. **Mazus surculosus**, *Don*; *Fl. Br. Ind.* iv. 260. Stems often tufted. Runners several, long, leafy, rooting at the joints. Radical leaves broadly obovate, 1–3 in., narrowed to a stalk-like base, coarsely and irregularly toothed, often pinnatifid near the base. Stem-leaves similar but smaller. Flowers pale blue or white. Calyx shortly 5-toothed.

Simla, the Glen; May–October.—Temperate Himalaya, 3000–7000 ft.

8. **LINDENBERGIA.** In honour of J. B. Lindenberg, a German botanical author of the nineteenth century.—Asia, Africa.

Perennial or annual herbs. Leaves opposite, stalked, toothed. Flowers nearly sessile, yellow, usually forming spikes or racemes. Calyx bell-shaped, 5-lobed. Corolla 2-lipped; tube cylindric, short; upper lip recurved, 2-lobed; lower much larger, spreading, 3-lobed, with 2 prominent folds at the base. Stamens 4, in unequal pairs, included; anthers 2 celled, cells separated from one another. Ovary hairy; style slender, stigma 2-lobed. Capsule ovoid.

L. grandiflora, *Benth.*; *Fl. Br. Ind.* iv. 261, is common in the E. Himalaya, extending to Kumaon; it is a softly hairy, half climbing, rambling herb, bearing numerous, bright yellow flowers 1 in. long.

Stems 2–3 ft. Flowers crowded in 1-sided spikes . . 1. *L. macrostachya.*
Stems 4–12 in. Flowers axillary, solitary or in small clusters . . . . 2. *L. urticæfolia.*

1. **Lindenbergia macrostachya**, *Benth.*; *Fl. Br. Ind.* iv. 262. Glabrous or nearly so; stems robust, erect, 2–3 ft. Leaves ovate or oblong-lanceolate, 1–3 × $\frac{1}{2}$–1 in., long-pointed. Flowers $\frac{1}{2}$ in. long, crowded in terminal or axillary, 1-sided, rigid spikes.

Sutlej valley, Suni; April.—N. India, ascending to 4000 ft.—Siam, China.

2. **Lindenbergia urticæfolia,** *Lehm.*; *Fl. Br. Ind.* iv. 262. Glandular hairy; stems often tufted, 4–12 in., erect or ascending. Leaves broadly ovate, about $\frac{1}{2}$–$1\frac{1}{2}\times\frac{1}{2}$–1 in. Flowers $\frac{1}{3}$ in. long, axillary, solitary or in small clusters, sometimes forming long, leafy racemes. Corolla-tube tinged with red.

Simla, Mushobra, common on walls; April-October.—Throughout India, ascending to 6000 ft.—Afghanistan, Burmah.

9. **LIMNOPHILA.** From the Greek *limne*, a marsh, and *phileo*, I love, in allusion to the habitat of most species.—Asia, Africa, Australia.

Herbs growing in water or marshy places; stems erect or ascending; leaves and inflorescence covered with glandular dots. Leaves opposite, the submerged, basal leaves sometimes pinnatifid or divided into thread-like segments. Flowers sessile, in heads or leafy spikes. Calyx 5-lobed nearly to the base; segments nearly equal, lanceolate, acute. Corolla 2-lipped; tube cylindric; upper lip erect, 2-lobed; lower spreading, 3-lobed. Stamens 4, in unequal pairs, included; anther-cells stalked, widely separated from one another. Style bent at the top; stigma flat, 2-lobed. Capsule ovoid.

Leaves shortly stalked. Flowers in sessile or stalked, axillary heads . . . . 1. *L. Roxburghii.*
Leaves stem-clasping. Flowers axillary, forming leafy spikes . . . . 2. *L. hypericifolia.*

*1. **Limnophila Roxburghii,** *G. Don*; *Fl. Br. Ind.* iv. 265. Glabrous or nearly so, aromatic; stems tufted, 1–2 ft. Leaves shortly stalked, ovate or lanceolate, $1\frac{1}{2}$–$3\times\frac{1}{2}$–$1\frac{1}{2}$ in., crenate; lateral nerves about 6 pairs, pinnate, curved. Flowers $\frac{1}{3}$ in. long, blue, mouth yellow, in sessile or stalked, axillary heads.

Throughout India, ascending to 6000 ft.; flowers in the cold season.—Tropical Asia, Pacific islands.

*2. **Limnophila hypericifolia,** *Benth.*; *Fl. Br. Ind.* iv. 269. Glabrous; stems 1–2 ft. Leaves sessile, stem-clasping, oblong-ovate, 1–$1\frac{3}{4}\times\frac{1}{2}$–1 in., entire or crenate; nerves 3-5, basal, straight, nearly parallel. Flowers pink-purple, $\frac{3}{4}$ in. long, solitary, axillary, forming leafy spikes.

Throughout India, ascending to 5000 ft.; flowers in the cold season.

10. **HERPESTIS.** From the Greek *herpestes*, a creeper.—All warm countries.

Herpestis Monnieria, *Kunth*; *Fl. Br. Ind.* iv. 272. A glabrous, creeping, succulent herb growing in marshes; stems several, 6–12 in., much branched, rooting at the joints. Leaves opposite, sessile, fleshy, oblong or spathulate, $\frac{1}{4}$–1 in., entire, obtuse, lower surface dotted. Flowers pale blue, purple-veined, nearly $\frac{1}{2}$ in. diam., single on alternate, axillary stalks. Calyx 5-parted; segments unequal, acute. Corolla-tube cylindric, longer than the calyx; limb spreading, lobes 4, nearly equal, upper one notched. Stamens 4, in unequal pairs, included. Style linear, dilated upwards; stigma capitate, 2-lobed. Capsule ovoid, acute.

Sutlej valley, Suni; April.—Throughout India, ascending to 4000 ft.—All warm countries.

Herpestis Hamiltoniana, *Benth.*; *Fl. Br. Ind.* iv. 272, is common in marshy places throughout N. India and may occur in the outer hills. It differs from the above in its erect stem, linear-lanceolate, acute leaves and opposite, sessile flowers.

11. TORENIA. In honour of Olaf Toren, a Swedish traveller of the eighteenth century.—Tropical Asia and Africa.

Torenia cordifolia, *Roxb.*; *Fl. Br. Ind.* iv. 276. An erect, slightly hairy herb, 4–10 in.; stems and branches 4-angled. Leaves

FIG. 111. TORENIA CORDIFOLIA.

opposite, stalked, ovate, $1 \times \frac{1}{2}$ in., sharply toothed. Flowers pale lilac or blue-purple, the limb darker than the tube, $\frac{3}{4}$ in. long, single on axillary stalks, crowded towards the end of branches. Calyx tubular, 2-lipped, 5-toothed, ribs prominently keeled. Corolla-tube curved, longer than the calyx, dilated upwards; limb spreading, 4-lobed, one lobe notched, the others entire. Stamens 4,

A A

in unequal pairs ; filaments arching, anthers cohering. Style linear, curved ; stigma flat, 2-lobed. Capsule oblong, acute. (Fig. 111.)

Valleys below Simla, on grassy slopes ; July-September.—Throughout India, ascending to 6000 ft.—China, Java.

12. VANDELLIA. In honour of Domenico Vandelli, a Portuguese botanist of the eighteenth century.—Chiefly tropical Asia.

Erect or diffusely branching herbs. Leaves opposite, toothed Flowers small, single on axillary stalks, often crowded towards the end of branches. Calyx 5-lobed. Corolla 2-lipped ; tube cylindric, longer than the calyx ; upper lip erect, notched ; lower broader, spreading, 3-lobed. Stamens 4, in unequal pairs ; filaments of the longer pair spurred near the base ; anthers cohering in pairs. Style curved ; stigma flat, 2-lobed. Capsule ovoid.

Stems diffuse. Flowers pale purple . . . . . 1. *V. crustacea.*
Stems erect. Flowers red-purple. Lateral lobes of lower lip white . . . . 2. *V. nummularifolia.*

1. **Vandellia crustacea,** *Benth.* ; *Fl. Br. Ind.* iv. 279. Glabrous ; stems 4–18 in., diffusely branched from the base. Leaves shortly stalked, ovate, ½–1 in. Flowers pale purple, ½ in. long. Capsule obtuse, shorter than the calyx.

Sutlej valley ; October.—Throughout India, ascending to 3000 ft.—Tropical regions of the Old World.

2. **Vandellia nummularifolia,** *Don* ; *Fl. Br. Ind.* iv. 282. Stems 2–6 in., erect, minutely hairy along the angles. Leaves sessile, broadly ovate, ¼–½ in. Flowers ¼ in. long, red-purple. Lateral lobes of lower lip white. Capsule acute, longer than the calyx.

Valleys below Simla ; July, August.—Temperate Himalaya, 2000–7000 ft.

13. BONNAYA. In honour of the Marquis de Bonnay, French ambassador at Copenhagen in the nineteenth century.—Tropical Asia, Africa, Australia.

Bonnaya brachiata, *Link & Otto* ; *Fl. Br. Ind.* iv. 284. An erect or diffusely branching, glabrous herb, 4–10 in. Leaves opposite, sessile, oblong, ½–1½ in. ; teeth closely set, finely pointed. Flowers white, spotted or tinged with pink, single on short, axillary stalks forming terminal racemes. Calyx 5-lobed ; segments linear, acute. Corolla 2-lipped ; tube cylindric, longer than the calyx ; upper lip erect, entire ; lower spreading, 3-lobed. Stamens 2, the upper pair being reduced to staminodes ; filaments curved, anthers cohering. Stigma flat, 2-lobed. Capsule narrowly cylindric, much longer than the calyx.

Valleys below Simla ; July-October.—Throughout India, ascending to 5000 ft.—Java, China.

14. HEMIPHRAGMA. From the Greek *hemi*, half, and *phragma*, a partition; referring to the valves of the capsule.—Himalaya, China.—A single species.

Hemiphragma heterophyllum, *Wall.*; *Fl. Br. Ind.* iv. 289. A hairy herb; stems several, slender, prostrate. Leaves of two forms: opposite, shortly stalked, cordate, orbicular, $\frac{1}{3}$–$\frac{2}{3}$ in. across, crenate, on the main stems; and tufted, sessile, linear, less than $\frac{1}{2}$ in., acute, on the branches. Flowers pink, $\frac{1}{3}$ in.

FIG. 112. WULFENIA AMHERSTIANA.

diam., solitary, axillary, usually sessile in the leaf-tufts on the branches, sometimes stalked in the axils of the stem-leaves. Calyx 5-parted; segments narrow. Corolla-tube short; limb 5-lobed, spreading, lobes broad, nearly equal. Stamens 4, equal;

anther-tips cohering. Style short. Capsule berry-like, globose, $\frac{1}{3}$ in. diam., red, shining, ultimately opening by two valves.

Huttoo; May–October.—Simla to Bhotan, 6000–12,000 ft.—China.

15. WULFENIA. In honour of F. X. Wulfen, an Austrian botanical author of the nineteenth century.—Asia, Europe.

Wulfenia Amherstiana, *Benth.*; *Fl. Br. Ind.* iv. 291. A perennial, nearly glabrous herb; scapes 6–12 in., erect, slender. Leaves basal, crowded, obovate-oblong, 3–6 × 1–2 in., coarsely and irregularly crenate or sharply toothed, narrowed into the stalk. Flowers drooping, blue-purple, varying to white, crowded in bracteate, 1-sided, spike-like racemes 3–6 in. long. Calyx 5-parted; segments acute. Corolla $\frac{1}{3}$ in. long; tube cylindric, longer than the calyx; lobes 4, nearly erect, acute, upper one minutely notched. Stamens 2. Style long, protruding; stigma minute, capitate. Capsule oblong, 2-lobed, as long as the calyx. (Fig. 112.)

Mahasu, Theog, Narkunda, on damp rocks in shady forest; July, August.—W. Himalaya, 7000–11,000 ft.—Afghanistan.

16. VERONICA. A mediæval name of doubtful derivation.—Most temperate regions, rare in the tropics.

Perennial or annual herbs. Leaves, at least the lower ones, opposite, usually passing into alternate, floral leaves or bracts. Flowers small, blue, white or tinged with purple, in axillary or terminal racemes. Calyx 4-parted; segments unequal. Corolla-tube very short; limb 4-lobed, spreading, lobes unequal, obtuse, entire. Stamens 2. Style linear; stigma minute. Capsule flattened, notched or deeply 2-lobed, opening along the edges in 2 valves; seeds few.

Racemes axillary.
  Leaves sessile. Racemes 3–6 in. long.
    Leaves 2–6 in., entire or nearly so . . . . . 1. *V. Anagallis.*
    Leaves 1–2 in., coarsely toothed . . . . . 4. *V. laxa.*
  Leaves stalked. Racemes $\frac{1}{2}$–3 in. long.
    Perennial. Root-stock creeping. Capsule triangular, broadest at the base . . . . 5. *V. cana.*
    Annual. Root fibrous. Capsule heart-shaped, narrowed to the base . . . . 6. *V. javanica.*
Racemes terminal.
  Flowers drooping, long-stalked.
    Leaves stalked, ovate. Sepals obtuse. Capsule notched . . . . 2. *V. agrestis.*
    Leaves sessile, lanceolate. Sepals acute. Capsule deeply lobed. . . . . 3. *V. biloba.*
  Flowers erect, shortly stalked.
    Leaves crenate. Flowers minute . . . . . 7. *V. arvensis.*
    Leaves entire. Flowers $\frac{1}{4}$ in. diam. . . . . . . 8. *V. serpyllifolia.*

1. **Veronica Anagallis,** *Linn.*; *Fl. Br. Ind.* iv. 293. Perennial, glabrous or nearly so; stems succulent, hollow, erect or

ascending, 6–24 in. Leaves stem-clasping, oblong-ovate or oblong-lanceolate, 2–6 × $\frac{1}{3}$–$\frac{2}{3}$ in., entire or nearly so. Flowers pale purple or white, $\frac{1}{6}$–$\frac{1}{3}$ in. diam., in axillary racemes 3–6 in. long; bracts shorter than the flower-stalks. Capsule notched.

Valleys below Simla, Mushobra, in wet ditches; March–October.—Throughout India, ascending to 9000 ft.—Asia, Africa, Europe (Britain), N. America.

2. **Veronica agrestis,** *Linn.*; *Fl. Br. Ind.* iv. 294. Annual, pubescent; stems procumbent, spreading, 6–18 in., much branched. Leaves shortly stalked, broadly ovate, $\frac{1}{3}$–1 in., toothed; the lowest opposite, without flowers; upper alternate, gradually becoming smaller, each bearing in its axil a single flower. Flowers blue or white, $\frac{1}{6}$–$\frac{1}{3}$ in. diam., on slender, drooping stalks usually shorter than the leaves, forming terminal racemes. Sepals obtuse. Capsule notched.

Valleys below Simla, in fields; March–October.—N. India, ascending to 6000 ft.—Temperate Asia, Europe (Britain), N. Africa.

3. **Veronica biloba,** *Linn.*; *Fl. Br. Ind.* iv. 294. Annual, pubescent; stems erect or ascending, diffusely branched from the base, 6–18 in. Leaves sessile, lanceolate, $\frac{1}{2}$–1 in., more or less toothed; the lowest opposite, without flowers; upper alternate, gradually passing into short, entire bracts, each bearing in its axil a single flower. Flowers blue, $\frac{1}{4}$ in. diam., on slender, drooping stalks longer than the leaves or bracts, forming terminal racemes. Sepals acute. Capsule deeply lobed.

Simla, in fields, common; April–October.—W. Himalaya, 5000–10,000 ft.—Asia Minor.

4. **Veronica laxa,** *Benth.*; *Fl. Br. Ind.* iv. 295. Perennial, pubescent; stems weak, ascending, 10–20 in. Leaves sessile, ovate, 1–2 × $\frac{3}{4}$–1$\frac{1}{4}$ in., coarsely toothed. Flowers blue, $\frac{1}{4}$–$\frac{1}{3}$ in. diam., in axillary racemes 3–6 in. long; bracts as long as the flower-stalks. Capsule notched.

Narkunda; June–August.—W. Himalaya, 5000–11,000 ft.—Japan.

5. **Veronica cana,** *Wall.*; *Fl. Br. Ind.* iv. 295. Perennial, grey-pubescent; rootstock woody, creeping; stems erect, 4–10 in., usually unbranched. Leaves stalked, ovate, 1–2 in., crenate. Flowers blue, $\frac{1}{2}$ in. diam., in axillary racemes 2–3 in. long; bracts longer than the flower-stalks. Capsule triangular, broadest at the base, $\frac{1}{4}$–$\frac{1}{3}$ in. across, notched.

Huttoo; June–August.—Temperate Himalaya, 9000–13,000 ft.—Japan.

6. **Veronica javanica,** *Blume*; *Fl. Br. Ind.* iv. 296. Annual, pubescent; root fibrous; stems ascending, 6–18 in., much branched. Leaves shortly stalked, ovate, $\frac{3}{4}$–1 in., toothed. Flowers blue, $\frac{1}{4}$ in. diam., in axillary racemes $\frac{1}{2}$–1 in. long; bracts longer than

the flower-stalks. Capsule heart-shaped, narrowed to the base, $\frac{1}{8}$ in. broad, notched.

Simla June.—Simla to Bhotan, 3000–7000 ft.—Java, Luchu archipelago.

7. **Veronica arvensis,** *Linn.*; *Fl. Br. Ind.* iv. 296. Annual, pubescent, hairy or glandular hairy; stems erect or ascending, 2–6 in., often branching from the base. Leaves sessile or the lowest shortly stalked, ovate, $\frac{1}{4}$–$\frac{1}{2}$ in., crenate; lower opposite, without flowers, gradually passing into small, alternate, entire bracts each bearing in its axil a single flower. Flowers minute, pale blue, nearly sessile, forming terminal, spike-like racemes. Capsule glandular hairy, notched.

Mushobra, in grass; April–October.—W. Himalaya, 7000-9000 ft.—Temperate Asia, N. Africa, Europe (Britain).

8. **Veronica serpyllifolia,** *Linn.*; *Fl. Br. Ind.* iv. 296. Perennial, glabrous or pubescent, often glandular; stems ascending, 4–12 in. Leaves sessile or the lowest shortly stalked, oblong-ovate, $\frac{1}{2}$–$\frac{3}{4}$ in., entire, obtuse; lower opposite, without flowers, gradually passing into small, alternate bracts each bearing in its axil a single flower. Flowers white or lilac, $\frac{1}{4}$ in. diam., shortly stalked, forming terminal racemes. Capsule pubescent, notched.

Narkunda; May–July.—W. Himalaya, 8000–13,000 ft.—Temperate Asia, N. Africa, Europe (Britain), America.

17. **BUCHNERA.** In honour of J. G. Buchner, a German naturalist of the eighteenth century.—Nearly all warm countries.

Buchnera hispida, *Buch.-Ham.*; *Fl. Br. Ind.* iv. 298. A slender, erect, rigid, roughly bristly herb, 6–18 in. Leaves opposite, sessile or narrowed into a stalk-like base; lower crowded, obovate or oblong, $1–2 \times \frac{3}{4}–1\frac{1}{2}$ in.; upper narrower, lanceolate or linear, passing into alternate, narrow, floral bracts. Flowers white or pale purple, $\frac{1}{3}$ in. long, solitary, axillary, sessile, forming terminal spikes. Calyx tubular, 5-toothed. Corolla-tube slender, cylindric, longer than the calyx; limb spreading, $\frac{1}{4}$ in. across, lobes 5, nearly equal. Stamens 4, in unequal pairs, included; anthers 1-celled. Style short, thickened upwards; stigma capitate. Capsule oblong, shorter than the calyx.

Valleys below Simla, in grassy places; July–October.—Throughout India, ascending to 9000 ft.

18. **STRIGA.** From the Latin *striga*, a furrow, referring to the grooved capsule.—Tropical regions of the Old World, Australia.

Striga lutea, *Lour.*; *Fl. Br. Ind.* iv. 299. A slender, erect, roughly bristly herb, 4–12 in. Leaves sessile, linear, $\frac{1}{2}$–1 in.;

lower opposite, passing into smaller, alternate, floral bracts. Flowers yellow, ½ in. long, solitary, axillary, sessile, forming terminal spikes. Calyx tubular, 5-ribbed, 5-toothed. Corolla 2-lipped; tube cylindric, slender, curved, much longer than the calyx; upper lip reflexed, notched; lower much larger, 3-lobed, spreading. Stamens 4, in unequal pairs, included; anthers 1-celled. Style shorter than the corolla-tube; stigma capitate. Capsule oblong, grooved, shorter than the calyx.

Valleys below Simla, in grassy places; May–September.—Throughout India, ascending to 6000 ft.—Tropical Asia and Africa.

19. CENTRANTHERA. From the Greek *centron*, a spur, referring to the anthers.—Asia, Australia.

Centranthera hispida, *R. Br.*; *Fl. Br. Ind.* iv. 301. An erect, rigid, roughly bristly herb, 1–2 ft. Leaves sessile, narrowly oblong, ½–1 × ¼ in.; lower opposite, passing into smaller, alternate, floral bracts. Flowers pale purple or white, ½ in. long, solitary, axillary, nearly sessile, forming terminal spikes. Calyx ovate, inflated, narrowed to the mouth, ultimately splitting nearly to the base in 2 segments. Corolla funnel-shaped; tube curved, much longer than the calyx; limb spreading, ½ in. diam., lobes 5, nearly equal, rounded, minutely crenate. Stamens 4, in unequal pairs, included; filaments hairy; anthers coherent in pairs, cells spurred, one imperfect. Style shorter than the corolla-tube; stigma flat, dilated, acute. Capsule ovoid, grooved, as long as the calyx.

Valleys below Simla, in damp, grassy places; July–October.—Throughout India, ascending to 3000 ft.—Tropical Asia, Australia.

20. SOPUBIA. Adapted from *Sopubi Swa*, the Goorkha name of *S. trifida*.—Asia, Africa, Australia.

Sopubia trifida, *Buch.-Ham.*; *Fl. Br. Ind.* iv. 302. A slender, roughly pubescent herb; stems erect, 1–2 ft.; branches ascending. Leaves sessile, linear, ½–1½ in., toothed or entire, mostly 3-fid; lower opposite or clustered; upper alternate, undivided. Flowers yellow, ½ in. diam., in numerous, terminal, bracteate racemes. Calyx bell-shaped, woolly inside, 5-toothed. Corolla-tube short; limb 5-lobed, spreading, lobes nearly equal. Stamens 4, in unequal pairs; anthers cohering, one cell of each imperfect. Style long, thickened upwards into a broad, flat stigma. Capsule ovoid, longer than the calyx. (Fig. 113.)

Simla, Jako, common on grassy slopes; June–October.—Simla to Sikkim, 3000–7000 ft.—Hilly districts throughout India.—Ceylon.

21. LEPTORHABDOS. From the Greek *leptos*, slender, and *rhabdos*, a rod, referring to the stems.—Central Asia, N. India.

Leptorhabdos Benthamiana, *Walp.*; *Fl. Br. Ind.* iv. 303. An erect, nearly glabrous herb; stems 1–3 ft., branching. Leaves sessile, pinnatisect, 1–3 in.; segments linear, toothed or entire; lower leaves opposite or clustered, upper alternate. Flowers pale pink, $\frac{1}{5}$ in. diam., in slender, bracteate, minutely glandular racemes. Calyx bell-shaped, 5-toothed. Corolla-tube short; limb 5-lobed, spreading, lobes nearly equal. Stamens 4, in unequal pairs; anthers free, cells perfect. Style long; stigma minute; ovules only 2 in each cell. Capsule oblong, flattened, enclosed in the calyx; seeds 2–4.

Simla, Mushobra, Matiana; August–October.—W. Himalaya, 5000–11,000 ft.—Afghanistan, Persia.

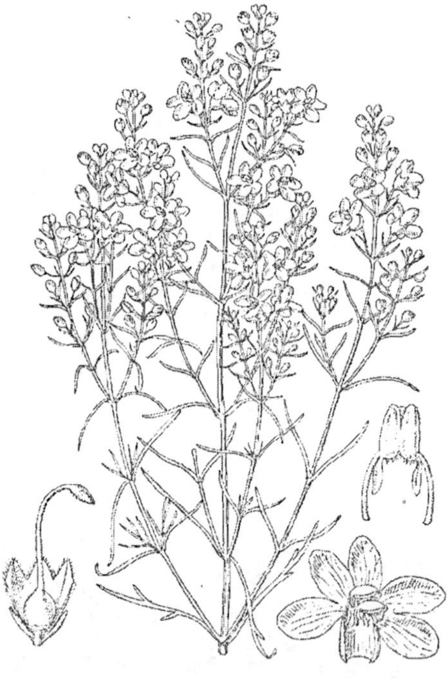

FIG. 113. SOPUBIA TRIFIDA.

22. EUPHRASIA. From the Greek *euphrasia*, joy, gladness, referring to a reputed power of restoring impaired vision.—Most temperate regions.

Euphrasia officinalis, *Linn.*; *Fl. Br. Ind.* iv. 305. An erect, pubescent, often glandular herb; stems 6–18 in., slender, branching. Leaves opposite, sessile, ovate, $\frac{1}{4}$–$\frac{1}{2}$ in., sharply and deeply toothed. Flowers white or lilac, purple-veined, usually tinged with yellow in the throat, in terminal spikes; bracts leaf-like. Calyx tubular, 4-lobed. Corolla 2-lipped, $\frac{1}{6}$–$\frac{1}{2}$ in. long; tube cylindric, longer than the calyx; upper lip erect, 2-lobed; lower spreading, 3-lobed, lobes usually all notched. Stamens 4, in unequal pairs; anthers hairy, cohering in pairs under the upper lip, lower pair long-spurred. Style long; stigma small, capitate. Capsule oblong, flattened, as long as the calyx.

Mahasu, Fagoo, Huttoo, on grassy slopes.—Temperate Himalaya, 7000–13,000 ft.—N. temperate regions (Britain, Eyebright).

23. PEDICULARIS. From the Latin *pediculus*, a louse; the application variously explained. N. temperate regions.

Erect herbs. Leaves alternate or whorled, pinnatifid or crenate. Flowers yellow or pink, in bracteate spikes or racemes. Calyx tubular. Corolla 2-lipped; tube nearly cylindric; upper lip erect, laterally flattened, enclosing the stamens and style, abruptly bent and prolonged in a straight or curved, beak-like extremity; lower spreading, 3-lobed. Stamens 4, in unequal pairs, anthers cohering in pairs. Style long, slender; stigma capitate, often protruding from the tip of the beak. Capsule longer than the calyx; seeds sometimes only few.

The arrangement of the species in this genus has been adapted from Major D. Prain's *Monograph of the Indian Pedicularis* in the *Annals of the Royal Botanic Garden*, Calcutta, vol. iii.

Flowers yellow . . . . 1. *P. megalantha.*
Flowers purple or pink.
  Leaves whorled, pinnatifid.
    Calyx-teeth regular, entire. Tip of corolla recurved 2. *P. pectinata.*
    Calyx irregularly toothed. Tip of corolla straight . 3. *P. gracilis.*
  Leaves alternate, oblong, crenate . . . . . 4. *P. carnosa.*

1. **Pedicularis megalantha,** *Don*; *Fl. Br. Ind.* iv. 312. Pubescent, 1–2 ft. Leaves alternate, long-stalked, oblong-lanceolate, 2–10 × 1–3 in., pinnatifid; segments oblong, crenate. Flowers bright yellow, racemed. Calyx hairy; teeth 5, irregularly jagged. Corolla $2\frac{1}{4}$ in. long; tube twice as long as the calyx; beak long, incurved, tip toothed. Stamens attached at the top of the tube, filaments of the longer pair hairy. Capsule 1 in., oblong, acute.

Matiana, Huttoo, Baghi; July–September.—Temperate Himalaya, 7000–14,000 ft.

2. **Pedicularis pectinata,** *Wall.*; *Fl. Br. Ind.* iv. 306. Nearly glabrous, $\frac{1}{2}$–$2\frac{1}{2}$ ft. Radical leaves persistent, long-stalked, lanceolate, 3–5 × 2–3 in., pinnatifid; segments toothed, sometimes again pinnatifid. Stem-leaves whorled, stalked, lanceolate, 3 × 2 in., pinnatifid; segments toothed. Flowers pink, spicate. Calyx-teeth 5, entire, acute. Corolla $\frac{3}{4}$ in. long; tube as long as the calyx;

beak sickle-shaped, tip recurved. Stamens attached at the bottom of the tube ; filaments hairy. Capsule $\frac{1}{2}$ in., ovoid, acute.

Theog, Narkunda ; August, September.—W. Himalaya, 7000-11,000 ft.—Afghanistan.

3. **Pedicularis gracilis,** *Wall* ; *Fl. Br. Ind.* iv. 307. Stems much branched, with 4 lines of hairs running down. Leaves glabrous, shortly stalked, whorled, oblong-lanceolate, $1-2 \times \frac{3}{4}-1\frac{1}{2}$ in., pinnatifid ; segments crenate, sometimes again pinnatifid. Flowers pink-purple, racemed. Calyx irregularly 5-toothed. Corolla $\frac{1}{2}$ in. long ; tube slightly longer than the calyx ; beak nearly straight,

Fig. 114. Pedicularis carnosa.

entire. Stamens attached at the middle of the tube, filaments glabrous. Capsule $\frac{1}{2}$ in., oblong, acute.

Mahasu, Narkunda ; August, September.—Temperate Himalaya, 6000-10,000 ft.

4. **Pedicularis carnosa,** *Wall.* ; *Fl. Br. Ind.* iv. 313. Roughly pubescent, $\frac{1}{2}-1\frac{1}{2}$ ft. Leaves alternate, stalked, ovate or oblong, $1-3 \times \frac{1}{2}-\frac{2}{3}$ in. ; radical persistent. Flowers bright pink-purple, racemed. Calyx irregularly jagged, split half-way down in front. Corolla 1 in. long ; tube twice as long as the calyx ; beak straight,

obtuse. Stamens attached near the top of the tube, filaments glabrous. Capsule $\frac{3}{4}$ in., broadly oblong. (Fig. 114.)

Simla, Mushobra, common; July–September.—Temperate Himalaya, 5000–9000 ft.

24. LATHRÆA. From the Greek *lathraios*, hidden; the greater part of the plant is subterranean.—Himalaya, Northern Asia, Europe.

Lathræa squamosa, *Linn.*; *Fl. Br. Ind.* iv. 318. A pale pink, leafless, perennial herb, parasitic on roots of trees; stems subterranean, much branched, creeping, fleshy, covered with closely set, short, thick scales. Flowering branches aerial, erect, 4–12 in., bearing a few thin scales. Flowers cream-white, tipped with pink-purple, horizontal, nearly $\frac{3}{4}$ in. long, crowded in terminal, bracteate racemes, bent in bud, elongating and straightening as the flowers expand. Calyx hairy, tubular, 4-lobed. Corolla 2-lipped; tube as long as the calyx; upper lip entire, margins inflexed at the tip; lower 3-lobed; both-lips nearly erect. Stamens 4, in unequal pairs, attached near the top of the tube, anthers hairy, slightly cohering. Ovary 1-celled; style curved, stigma capitate, protruding. Capsule ovoid.

Baghi forest; April–June.—W. Himalaya, 6000–9000 ft.—Northern Asia, Europe (Britain, Toothwort).

LXIX. OROBANCHACEÆ

A SMALL Order of leafless, parasitic herbs spread over nearly all temperate and tropical regions; represented in the neighbourhood of Simla by only one species.

OROBANCHE. From the Greek *orobus*, a vetch, and *ancho*, to strangle; some species are parasitic on vetches.—Chiefly northern and subtropical regions of the Old World.

Orobanche Epithymum, *DC.*; *Fl. Br. Ind.* iv. 325. A glandular-pubescent, red- or purple-brown herb; stems erect, unbranched, scaly, 3–12 in., thickened at the base. Scales alternate, lanceolate, $\frac{1}{2}$–1 in. Flowers red-brown, irregular, 2-sexual, each in the axil of a bract, forming a terminal spike. Calyx free, deeply divided in 4 unequal, lanceolate lobes. Corolla hypogynous, 2-lipped, $\frac{2}{3}$ in. long; tube cylindric, curved; upper lip erect, arched, notched; lower spreading, 3-lobed, margins wavy, minutely toothed. Stamens 4, included, in unequal pairs, attached near the base of the tube; filaments hairy, anthers cohering. Ovary ovoid, 1-celled, the numerous ovules inserted on 4 parietal placentas meeting in the centre; style long, linear, curved; stigma broad, peltate, obscurely 2-lobed. Capsule opening by 2 valves; seeds numerous, minute.

Simla, Mahasu, parasitic on the roots of thyme, grass, etc., common; July-October.—W. Himalaya, 7000-13,000 ft.—W. and Central Asia, Europe (Britain, Red Broom-rape). *O. rubra*, Linn., of most authors.

LXX. LENTIBULARIACEÆ

An Order containing a few genera of marsh or aquatic plants dispersed over the greater part of the globe; represented in the neighbourhood of Simla by only one very small and rare species.

UTRICULARIA. From the Latin *utriculus*, a small bladder, referring to the bladder-like vessels borne on the leaves of most species.—Nearly all regions.

Utricularia orbiculata, *Wall.*; *Fl. Br. Ind.* iv. 334. A small, delicate herb; stems creeping, thread-like, leafy. Leaves rosulate or alternate, crowded, orbicular or obovate, about $\frac{1}{8}$ in. across, interspersed with minute, bladder-like vessels. Flowers few, lilac, irregular, 2-sexual, $\frac{1}{4}$ in. long, forming terminal racemes on very slender, erect, naked scapes 2-6 in. high, springing from leafy rosettes. Calyx free, divided nearly to the base in 2 very unequal, rounded segments. Corolla hypogynous, 2-lipped, base prolonged backwards in a tubular, curved, pointed spur; upper lip very short, erect or recurved, notched; lower much larger, spreading, obscurely 3-lobed, base convex, closing the mouth of the spur. Stamens 2, included, attached at the base of the upper lip; filaments curved. Ovary 1-celled; style very short; stigma 2-lipped. Capsule globose, surrounded by the enlarged calyx; seeds numerous, minute.

On wet rocks in a stream below Chota Simla; August, September.—Hilly districts throughout India, ascending to 8000 ft.—Burmah, Malaya, S. China.

The minute, bladder-like vessels among the leaves serve to capture and utilise as food various animalculæ. See Darwin's *Insectivorous Plants*, chap. xvii.; and Kerner's *Nat. Hist. of Plants*, i. 120.

LXXI. GESNERACEÆ

Herbs; stems or flowering scapes erect. Leaves simple. Flowers irregular, 2-sexual, blue or purple, rarely white. Calyx free, 5-lobed, persistent. Corolla hypogynous; tube long or short; limb 2-lipped or spreading. Stamens 4 in unequal pairs or only 2, the other pair being reduced to staminodes, attached to the corolla-tube, alternate with the lobes; filaments curved, anthers cohering in pairs. Ovary free, 1-celled; style simple, usually rather long, stigma small, terminal; ovules very numerous, attached to the walls of the ovary. Capsule narrowly oblong, splitting nearly to the base in 2 valves; seeds numerous, minute. —A large Order widely dispersed through nearly all tropical and subtropical regions.—Named in honour of Conrad Gesner, a Swiss naturalist of the sixteenth century.

Stamens 4; staminodes none.
Leaves numerous, stalked, all radical. Flowers pale purple or white . . . . 1. *Didissandra.*
Leaf solitary, sessile at the top of the short stem. Flowers dark blue . . . . 3. *Platystemma.*
Stamens 2; staminodes 2. Leaves opposite, unequal . 2. *Chirita.*

1. DIDISSANDRA. From the Greek *di* or *dis*, twice, and *aner*, *andros*, a man; referring to the two pairs of perfect stamens as compared with the single pair in the allied genus *Didymocarpus*. —India, China, Malaya.

Didissandra lanuginosa, *C. B. Clarke*; *Fl. Br. Ind.* iv. 355. A stemless herb. Leaves all radical, stalked, spreading, ovate, $1 \times \frac{3}{4}$ in., crenate; upper surface wrinkled, nearly glabrous; lower densely hairy. Scapes tufted, erect, 3–6 in., hairy near the base. Flowers few, $\frac{1}{3}$ in. long, pale purple or white, in a terminal cyme. Calyx-lobes acute. Corolla 2-lipped; tube cylindric; upper lip erect, notched; lower larger, spreading, 3-lobed. Stamens 4. Stigma flat, 2-lobed. Capsule $\frac{3}{4}$ in., erect, curved, acute.

Valleys below Simla, on rocks, not common; August, September.—Simla to Bhotan, 4000–6000 ft.—Khasia hills.

2. CHIRITA. From *Cherayta*, the Hindustani name of *Swertia Chirata*; the plants are supposed to possess similar properties.—E. Asia.

Small, hairy, erect herbs. Leaves thin, opposite, unequal, often reduced to a single pair. Flowers purple, solitary or in small, axillary cymes. Calyx-lobes acute. Corolla funnel-shaped; lobes 5, rounded, spreading. Perfect stamens 2, staminodes 2; filaments flattened. Ovary narrowly oblong; style very short; stigma 2-lobed. Capsule 3–4 in., curved, finely pointed.

Leaves broadly ovate. Flowers deep blue-purple . . . 1. *C. bifolia.*
Leaves lanceolate, acute. Flowers pale purple . . . 2. *C. pumila.*

1. **Chirita bifolia,** *Don*; *Fl. Br. Ind.* iv. 357. Stems 3–6 in. Leaves 2, sessile, cordate, broadly ovate, toothed, the larger leaf about 3×2½ in., the other much smaller. Flowers one to three, 1½–2 in. long, deep purple-blue, tinged with yellow about the mouth. (Fig. 115.)

Valleys below Simla, in damp, shady places; July–September.—Simla to Nepal, 5000–6000 ft.

Fig. 115. Chirita bifolia.

2. **Chirita pumila,** *Don*; *Fl. Br. Ind.* iv. 357. Stems 2–6 in., often branching. Leaves 2–6, stalked, lanceolate, acute, toothed, the larger leaf 2½–6×1–2 in., the other smaller. Flowers one to six, 1–¾ in. long, pale purple, tinged with yellow.

Valleys below Simla; July–September.—Simla to Bhotan, 1500–6000 ft.

3. **PLATYSTEMMA.** From the Greek *platys*, broad, and *stemma*, a wreath; referring to the corolla.—Himalaya.

Platystemma violoides, *Wall.*; *Fl. Br. Ind.* iv. 361. A slender, pubescent, erect herb; stems 2–6 in. Leaf terminal, solitary, rarely with a much smaller one opposite to it, hairy, sessile, broadly ovate, 1–2½ in. across, cordate, toothed. Scape 1–2 in., rising from the base of the leaf, bearing a small, terminal cyme of 1–4 dark blue flowers. Calyx-lobes acute. Corolla-tube very short; limb flat, ⅓ in. across, lobes 4, oblong, rounded, one lobe

FIG 116. PLATYSTEMMA VIOLOIDES.

notched, the others entire. Stamens 4; filaments very short, curved; anthers 1-celled. Ovary ovoid; stigma truncate. (Fig. 116.)

Simla, the Glen, on wet rocks; July, August.—Simla to Nepal, 6000–9000 ft.

LXXII. BIGNONIACEÆ

TREES or perennial herbs. Leaves opposite or alternate, odd-pinnate. Flowers showy, nearly regular, 2-sexual, in terminal racemes. Calyx free, bell-shaped, persistent. Corolla hypognous, bell-shaped or funnel-shaped; limb spreading, lobes 5, nearly equal, toothed or entire. Stamens 5 or 4, attached to the corolla-tube, alternate with the lobes; filaments thickened and hairy near the base; anthers 2-celled. Disk conspicuous, fleshy, encircling the base of the ovary. Ovary free, 2-celled; style long, simple; stigma terminal, flattened, 2-lobed; ovules numerous in each cell. Capsule long, narrow, flat or terete, opening by 2 valves; seeds numerous, large, flattened, surrounded by a membranous, nearly transparent wing, entire or divided into linear segments.—Widely dispersed in nearly all tropical regions; rare in temperate.—Name in honour of the Abbé Bignon, a French savant of the eighteenth century.

A tree. Leaves opposite; leaflets entire . . . . . 1. *Oroxylum.*
Herbs. Leaves alternate; leaflets toothed . . . . . 2. *Amphicome.*

1. OROXYLUM. From the Greek *oros*, a mountain, and *xylon*, wood; referring to the habitat of this, the only species.—India, Malay archipelago.

FIG. 117. AMPHICOME ARGUTA.

Oroxylum indicum, *Vent.*; *Fl. Br. Ind.* iv. 378. A tree. Leaves glabrous, opposite, 2-pinnate, 4–6 ft.; leaflets stalked, broadly ovate, about 6×3 in., entire, long-pointed. Flowers fœtid, dark red; racemes erect. Calyx leathery, 1 in. long, obscurely toothed. Corolla fleshy, 2–3 in. long, bell-shaped; lobes irregularly toothed. Stamens 5, four nearly equal, the fifth shorter; anthers protruding. Disk broad, obscurely 5-angled. Capsule flat, 15–30×2–4 in.; wing of seeds entire.

Valleys below Simla, rare; May–July.—Throughout India, ascending to 4000 ft.—Burmah, Malay Archipelago.

The long, sword-like capsules often remain hanging on the tree for months.

2. **AMPHICOME.** From the Greek *amphi*, on both sides or ends, and *come*, hair; the membranous wing of the seeds is divided at each end into hair-like segments.—India, Afghanistan.

Perennial, glabrous, erect herbs; stems 12–24 in., sometimes thick and woody at the base. Leaves alternate, pinnate; leaflets toothed. Flowers pink; racemes erect or drooping. Calyx $\frac{1}{3}$ in. long. Corolla funnel-shaped; tube curved; lobes entire. Stamens 4, in unequal pairs; anthers cohering. Disk ring-shaped. Capsule slender, terete, 4–8 in.; wing of seeds divided at each end into numerous, linear segments.

Leaflets 5–7, lanceolate. Calyx-teeth linear, acute . . . 1. *A. arguta.*
Leaflets 9–15, ovate. Calyx-teeth none or obscure . . . 2. *A. Emodi.*

1. **Amphicome arguta,** *Lindl.*; *Fl. Br. Ind.* iv. 385. Leaves 3–5 in.; leaflets 5–7, lanceolate, end one longest, sometimes lobed. Calyx-teeth distinct, linear, acute. Corolla $1\frac{1}{2}$–2 in. long, $\frac{1}{2}$–$\frac{3}{4}$ in. wide at the mouth. (Fig. 117.)

Road between Theog and Matiana on rocks; July, August.—N.W. Himalaya, 7000–8000 ft.

2. **Amphicome Emodi,** *Lindl.*; *Fl. Br. Ind.* iv. 385. Leaves 5–8 in.; leaflets 9–15, ovate, end one usually the longest, sometimes lobed. Calyx entire or obscurely toothed. Corolla $1\frac{1}{2}$–$2\frac{1}{2}$ in. long, $\frac{1}{2}$–$1\frac{1}{4}$ in. wide at the mouth; tube tinged with yellow.

Sutlej valley, on rocks, Subathoo; July, August.—Temperate Himalaya, 2000–9000 ft.

LXXIII. ACANTHACEÆ

HERBS or shrubs. Leaves simple, opposite; stipules none. Flowers 2-sexual, more or less irregular, usually in spikes or clusters often forming terminal panicles, rarely solitary or whorled, each flower usually in the axil of a bract and furnished with 2 bracteoles; bracts frequently overlapping. Calyx free, 4- or 5-parted or lobed. Corolla hypogynous; tube cylindric or dilated upwards; limb spreading or 2-lipped. Stamens 4 in unequal pairs or 2, one pair being imperfect or wanting, attached to the corolla-tube, alternate with the lobes; filaments free or united near the base; anthers 2-celled, cells contiguous or separated, one cell sometimes abortive. Disk fleshy, more or less surrounding the base of the ovary, inconspicuous. Ovary free, 2-celled; style simple, usually long and threadlike, tip 2-lobed, one lobe often minute or wanting; ovules 2–4 in each cell, rarely many. Capsule oblong or linear, opening by two valves; seeds few; seed-stalks hardened, incurved.—A large Order, widely distributed, chiefly in tropical regions.—Named from the genus *Acanthus* which is remarkable for its beautiful leaves.

Perfect stamens 4.

Corolla-limb spreading.
  Anther-bases bristle-tipped . . . . . 2. *Petalidium.*
  Anther-bases blunt.
    Ovules 4–6 in each cell. Capsule linear. Seeds 6–8 . . . . 4. *Æchmanthera.*
    Ovules 2 in each cell. Capsule oblong. Seeds 4 or fewer . . . . . 5. *Strobilanthes.*
Corolla-limb 2-lipped.
  Flowers in axillary, spinous whorls . . 1. *Hygrophila spinosa.*
  Flowers in unarmed spikes . . . . . 7. *Lepidagathis.*

Perfect stamens 2.

Corolla-limb spreading.
  Flowers deep blue. Calyx equally 5-lobed . 3. *Dædalacanthus.*
  Flowers lilac or pink. Calyx unequally 4-parted . . . . 6. *Barleria.*[1]
Corolla-limb 2-lipped.
  Flowers purple or pink.
    Corolla-tube straight. Lower anther-cell spurred . . . . 8. *Justicia.*
    Corolla-tube twisted. Anther-cells not spurred . . . . 10. *Dicliptera.*
  Flowers pale blue or white, sometimes dotted and streaked with pink.
    A creeping herb. Flowers $\frac{1}{3}$ in. long, pale blue or white . . . . 1. *Hygrophila polysperma.*[1]
    An erect shrub. Flowers $1\frac{1}{4}$ in. long, white, dotted and streaked with pink . . 9. *Adhatoda.*

1. HYGROPHILA. From the Greek *hygros*, wet, moist, and *phileo*, to love; referring to the habitat of the plants.—Most tropical and subtropical regions.

Erect or procumbent herbs, growing in marshy places, unarmed or furnished with axillary spines. Leaves sessile, entire. Flowers nearly sessile, crowded in spikes or axillary whorls; bracts lanceolate; bracteoles linear. Calyx 5-lobed or 4-parted; lobes or segments narrowly lanceolate. Corolla-tube dilated near the mouth; limb 2-lipped, upper lip erect, concave, notched or 2-lobed, lower spreading, 3-lobed. Stamens 4 or 2. Style-tip linear, recurved, the upper lobe reduced to a minute tooth; ovules 2–4 or many in each cell. Capsule linear-oblong; seeds 4–8 or numerous.

Procumbent, unarmed. Flowers in spikes. Calyx 5-lobed 1. *H. polysperma.*
Erect, spinous. Flowers in whorls. Calyx 4-parted . 2. *H. spinosa.*

[1] *Barleria* and *Hygrophila polysperma* have 2 very short imperfect stamens in addition to the 2 long perfect ones.

*1. **Hygrophila polysperma,** *T. Anders.*; *Fl. Br. Ind.* iv. 406. Procumbent, pubescent; branches spreading, 6–12 in., rooting at the joints. Leaves lanceolate, ½–1½ in. Flowers pale blue or white, in axillary and terminal spikes. Calyx 5-lobed. Corolla ⅓ in. long, upper lip notched. Stamens 4, upper pair rudimentary. Capsule ¼ in. long; seeds 20–30.

Throughout India, ascending to 5000 ft.; May, June.—Tropical Asia.

*2. **Hygrophila spinosa,** *T. Anders.*; *Fl. Br. Ind.* iv. 408. Erect, 2–5 ft., roughly hairy. Leaves lanceolate or oblong-lanceolate, 3–6 × ½–1 in. Flowers pale or bright blue, sometimes tinged with pink, in axillary, spinous whorls; spines ½–1½ in., straight, sharp. Calyx 4-parted, upper segment largest. Corolla 1 in. long; upper lip 2-lobed. Stamens 4. Capsule ⅓ in. long; seeds 4–8.

Throughout India, common in ditches, ascending to 3000 ft.; January–March.

2. PETALIDIUM. From the Greek *petalos*, broad, flat; referring to the conspicuous bracteoles.—India, Africa.

***Petalidium barlerioides,** *Nees*; *Fl. Br. Ind.* iv. 416. An erect, finely pubescent shrub, 2–3 ft. Leaves shortly stalked, broadly ovate, 2–4 in., toothed, acute. Flowers pale blue or white, nearly sessile, axillary, solitary or in small clusters; bracts none; bracteoles ovate, 1 in. long, net-veined, acute, enclosing the lower part of the flowers. Calyx deeply 5-lobed; lobes linear. Corolla 1¼–1½ in. long; tube cylindric, hairy on the throat within; limb spreading, 1½ in. across, 5-lobed, lobes nearly equal, rounded. minutely crenate. Stamens 4; base of anther-cells bristle-tipped. Style unequally 2-lobed; ovules 2 in each cell. Capsule shortly stalked, ovoid, ½ in.; seeds usually only 2.

Throughout India, chiefly in hilly districts, ascending to 3000 ft.; January–April.

3. DÆDALACANTHUS. From the Greek *dædaleos*, variegated, referring to the bracts, and *Acanthus*, an allied genus.—India, Malaya.

Dædalacanthus nervosus, *T. Anders.*; *Fl. Br. Ind.* iv. 418. An erect, roughly pubescent shrub, 2–6 ft. Leaves shortly stalked, ovate, about 6 × 3 in., entire, long-pointed. Flowers deep blue, crowded in numerous spikes 1–3 in. long, forming close, erect panicles; bracts leaf-like, variegated green and white, oblong-ovate, long-pointed, enclosing the lower part of the flower; bracteoles shorter than the calyx. Calyx equally 5-lobed. Corolla 1¼ in. long; tube elongate, cylindric, dilated near the top; limb oblique, spreading, ¾ in. across, lobes 5, nearly equal, rounded.

Stamens 2; anthers blunt. Style 2-lobed; ovules 2 in each cell. Capsule shortly stalked, oblong, $\frac{1}{2}$ in.; seeds 4.

Sutlej valley, in damp places; March.—Outer Himalaya from the Punjab to Bhotan, ascending to 3000 ft., usually in forest undergrowth.

4. ÆCHMANTHERA. From the Greek *aichme*, the point of a spear, and *anther*; referring to the minutely pointed anther-cells. —India.

Æchmanthera tomentosa, *Nees*; *Fl. Br. Ind.* iv. 428. An erect shrub, 1–3 ft.; stems white-tomentose. Leaves stalked, lanceolate, 2–4 × 1–2 in., crenate, acute; upper surface hairy, lower white-tomentose. Flowers pale blue, in small clusters sessile along the spreading branches of a terminal panicle; bracts glandular-hairy, linear, as long as the calyx; bracteoles similar, smaller. Calyx glandular-hairy, 5-parted; segments linear. Corolla 1 in. long; tube cylindric at the base, dilated upwards; limb spreading, $\frac{1}{2}$ in. across, lobes 5, rounded. Stamens 4, included; anther-bases blunt, tips minutely pointed. Style linear, upper lobe obsolete or nearly so; ovules 4–6 in each cell. Capsule linear, hardly longer than the calyx, splitting to the base; seeds 6–8.

Valleys below Simla, Subathoo; August–October.—Temperate Himalaya, 3000–5000 ft.

5. STROBILANTHES. From the Greek *strobilos*, a fir-cone, and *anthos*, a flower; referring to the appearance of the young inflorescence.—Asia, Africa.

Erect shrubs. Leaves often unequal, crenate or sharply toothed. Flowers blue, solitary in the axils of bracts, arranged in spikes or heads often forming terminal panicles; bracts leaf-like or very small, persistent or falling off before the flowers expand; bracteoles linear. Calyx 5-parted; segments linear. Corolla-tube usually curved, more or less cylindric in its lower portion, dilated upwards; limb spreading, 5-lobed, lobes nearly equal, rounded. Stamens 4; anther-bases blunt. Style-tip linear, recurved, upper lobe obsolete; ovules 2 in each cell. Capsule pubescent, often viscid, oblong, about $\frac{3}{4}$ in.; seeds 4 or fewer, pubescent.

Some species of *Strobilanthes* are gregarious as undergrowth in mountain forests, flowering only at intervals of sometimes several years; at these seasons the plants die down after flowering, and permit the seedlings of forest trees to grow up which had been impossible while the *Strobilanthes* occupied the ground.

Bracts persistent.
- Stems terete. Leaves hairy. Corolla-tube cylindric for half its length . . . . 1. *S. glutinosus.*
- Stems 4-angled or deeply furrowed. Leaves glabrous or nearly so. Corolla-tube cylindric only at the base . . . . 4. *S. atropurpureus.*

Bracts falling off before the flowers expand.
Leaves nearly sessile or tapering into a winged stalk. Flowers in heads or very short spikes . 2. *S. Dalhousianus.*
Leaves stalked, cordate. Flowers in interrupted, usually panicled spikes . . . . . . 3. *S. alatus.*

1. **Strobilanthes glutinosus,** *Nees*; *Fl. Br. Ind.* iv. 458. Stems 2–5 ft., pubescent, terete. Leaves stalked, hairy on both surfaces, ovate, about 3 × 1¼ in., crenate or sharply toothed. Flowers pale blue, in short, often interrupted spikes; bracts leaf-like, ovate,

FIG. 118. STROBILANTHES DALHOUSIANUS

persistent. Calyx glandular-hairy. Corolla 1½–2 in. long; lower half of tube cylindric, upper half dilated; limb 1–1½ in. across.

Valleys below Simla, usually in forest undergrowth; October, November.—Temperate Himalaya, 3000–6000 ft.
Flowers annually.

2. **Strobilanthes Dalhousianus,** *C. B. Clarke*; *Fl. Br. Ind.* iv. 460. Stems 2–3 ft., hairy, at least when young. Leaves hairy on both surfaces, nearly sessile or tapering into a winged stalk, ovate,

3–6 × $1\frac{1}{4}$–$2\frac{1}{2}$ in., toothed, long-pointed. Flowers dark blue, in heads or very short spikes; bracts small, concave, soon falling off. Calyx usually glandular-pubescent. Corolla $1\frac{1}{2}$–2 in. long; tube curved, gradually dilated from near the base; limb $\frac{1}{2}$–$\frac{3}{4}$ in. across. (Fig. 118.)

Simla, Mahasu, common; July–September.—W. Himalaya, 6000–8000 ft.
Sometimes gregarious in forests of the Karshu oak, *Quercus semecarpifolia*; flowers annually.

3. **Strobilanthes alatus,** *Nees*; *Fl. Br. Ind.* iv. 464, including *S. angustifrons, C. B. Clarke.* Stems 2–4 ft., pubescent. Leaves hairy, mostly long-stalked, ovate, $2\frac{1}{2}$–9 × $1\frac{3}{4}$–4 in., cordate, sharply toothed, long-pointed; stalks winged, at least near the top. Flowers dark blue, in interrupted, glandular-pubescent, usually panicled spikes; bracts small, narrowly oblong, soon falling off. Calyx glandular-pubescent. Corolla $1\frac{1}{4}$ in. long; tube curved, gradually dilated from near the base, bulging in the middle; limb $\frac{3}{4}$ in. across.

Simla, Mushobra, common in woods; August–October.—W. Himalaya, 6000–10,000 ft.—Afghanistan.
Flowers annually.

4. **Strobilanthes atropurpureus,** *Nees*; *Fl. Br. Ind.* iv. 472, including *S. Wallichii, Nees*, var. *microphyllus*. Stems 6–24 in., pubescent, sometimes viscid, 4-angled or deeply furrowed. Leaves glabrous or nearly so, ovate or ovate-lanceolate, usually 2–4 × $1\frac{1}{2}$–2 in., sometimes smaller, crenate or sharply toothed, tapering into a winged stalk. Flowers blue, in interrupted spikes; bracts leaf-like, persistent. Calyx glandular-hairy. Corolla 1–$1\frac{3}{4}$ in. long; tube pale blue or nearly white, curved, broadly dilated from a short, cylindric base; limb dark blue, $\frac{1}{2}$–$\frac{3}{4}$ in. across.

Simla, Matiana, Huttoo; June–October.—Temperate Himalaya, 7000–10,000 ft.
Gregarious in forests of the Indian spruce-fir, *Abies Smithiana*, and silver fir, *Abies Webbiana*; flowers at intervals of often several years.

6. **BARLERIA.** In honour of J. Barrelier, a French botanist of the seventeenth century.—Tropical regions, chiefly of the Old World.

Barleria cristata, *Linn.*; *Fl. Br. Ind.* iv. 488. An erect, bairy, perennial herb; stems 2–4 ft., branching. Leaves shortly stalked, ovate-lanceolate, 2–4 in., entire, acute. Flowers lilac or pink, crowded in short, head-like, nearly sessile, axillary spikes; bracts none; bracteoles linear, hairy. Calyx 4-parted; segments hairy, outer pair lanceolate, $\frac{3}{4}$ in., spinous-toothed, acute, inner narrow, $\frac{1}{4}$ in., entire. Corolla $1\frac{1}{4}$–$1\frac{1}{2}$ in. long; lower half of tube cylindric, upper half dilated upwards; limb spreading, 1 in. across, lobes 5, ovate, nearly equal. Stamens 2, as long as the corolla-tube and 2 imperfect, much shorter; anther-cells blunt. Ovules 2 in each cell; style minutely capitate. Capsule oblong, $\frac{1}{2}$ in., acute; seeds 4 or fewer, silky.

Valleys below Simla; July–October.—Throughout India, ascending to 6000 ft.—China, Malaya.

7. LEPIDAGATHIS. From the Greek *lepis*, a scale, and *agathis*, a ball; referring to the inflorescence of some species.—Most tropical regions.

***Lepidagathis hyalina,** *Nees*; *Fl. Br. Ind.* iv. 521. A pubescent, perennial herb; stems erect or ascending, 6–24 in., branching from the base. Leaves glandular-pubescent, nearly sessile, ovate, 1–3 in., entire, acute. Flowers white, spotted with brown, crowded in oblong or ovoid, 1-sided, terminal or axillary, nearly cylindric spikes $\frac{1}{2}$–$1\frac{1}{2}$ in. long; bracts hairy, lanceolate, long-pointed, scarious; bracteoles narrower, scarious. Calyx scarious, 5-parted; segments hairy, lanceolate, upper one broader, 2 lower more or less united. Corolla $\frac{1}{4}$ in. long; tube as long as the calyx, dilated from the base; limb 2-lipped, upper lip erect, notched, lower longer, recurved, 3-lobed. Stamens 4, included; anther-cells blunt. Style-tip recurved, obtuse, entire; ovules 2 in each cell. Capsule oblong, hardly $\frac{1}{4}$ in.; seeds 4, hairy.

Throughout N. India, ascending to 4000 ft.—Burmah, S. China.

8. JUSTICIA. In honour of J. Justice, a Scotch horticulturalist of the eighteenth century.—Nearly all warm regions.

Herbs or shrubs. Leaves entire. Flowers in loose, axillary cymes or crowded in erect spikes; bracts linear or lanceolate; bracteoles linear or minute or wanting. Calyx 4- or 5-parted; segments linear, nearly equal. Corolla-tube nearly cylindric, straight, not twisted; limb 2-lipped, upper lip erect, notched, lower recurved, 3-lobed. Stamens 2; anther-cells distinct, upper one blunt, lower with a small, white spur at the base. Style minutely 2-lobed; ovules 2 in each cell. Capsule stalked, oblong; seeds 4 or fewer.

Flowers in loosely panicled cymes. Corolla $\frac{2}{3}$ in. long . . . 1. *J. pubigera.*
Flowers crowded in erect spikes. Corolla $\frac{1}{5}$ in. long . . . 2. *J. simplex.*

1. **Justicia pubigera,** *Wall.*; *Fl. Br. Ind.* iv. 536. An erect shrub; stems 1–4 ft., terete, hairy. Leaves hairy, stalked, ovate-lanceolate, about $3 \times 1\frac{1}{4}$ in., long-pointed. Flowers purple-red, in loose, axillary cymes forming terminal, leafy panicles; bracts linear; bracteoles minute or none. Calyx 5-parted. Corolla $\frac{2}{3}$ in. long. Capsule $\frac{1}{2}$ in.

Simla, not common; August–October.—N.W. Himalaya, 4000–7000 ft.

2. **Justicia simplex,** *Don*; *Fl. Br. Ind.* iv. 539. A herb; stems 6–12 in., erect or ascending, grooved, much branched. Leaves

hairy, shortly stalked, ovate or lanceolate, 1–1¼ in., acute. Flowers pale purple, crowded in erect spikes ¾–1 in. long; bracts hairy, lanceolate; bracteoles hairy, linear. Calyx hairy, 4-parted. Corolla ⅕ in. long. Capsule ⅛ in. (Fig. 119.)

Simla, very common; June–October.—Throughout India, chiefly in hilly districts, ascending to 7000 ft.

FIG. 119. JUSTICIA SIMPLEX.

9. ADHATODA. Probably derived from the Cingalese name. —Most tropical regions.

Adhatoda vasica, *Nees*; *Fl. Br. Ind.* iv. 540. A glabrous shrub, 4–8 ft. Leaves shortly stalked, ovate-lanceolate, 5–6 × 1½–2 in., entire. Flowers white, streaked and dotted with pink, crowded in stalked, axillary, erect spikes 1–3 in. long, usually clustered toward the end of branches; bracts leaf-like, ovate; bracteoles narrowly lanceolate. Calyx 5-parted; segments lanceolate. Corolla 1¼ in. long; tube short, broad; limb incurved, 2-lipped, upper lip notched, lower 3-lobed. Stamens 2; anther-cells blunt.

Ovary hairy; style obtuse, tip minutely hairy. Capsule $\frac{3}{4}$ in.; seeds usually 4.

Valleys below Simla; December–March.—Throughout India, ascending to 3000 ft.—S.E. Asia, Malaya.

Goats do not eat this shrub, so it often escapes destruction when other species succumb.

10. DICLIPTERA. From the Greek *diclis*, folding doors, and *pteron*, a wing, referring to the 2-celled, winged capsule.—Most tropical regions.

Dicliptera bupleuroides, *Nees*; *Fl. Br. Ind.* iv. 554, *under D. Roxburghiana.* A hairy, diffuse herb; stems 6–24 in., grooved. Leaves stalked, ovate-lanceolate, usually about $2 \times \frac{3}{4}$ in., sometimes in moist, shady places up to $5 \times 2\frac{3}{4}$ in., entire, long-pointed.

Fig. 120. Dicliptera bupleuroides.

Flowers pink, spotted with purple, crowded in axillary cymes clustered towards the end of branches; bracts and bracteoles linear. Calyx 5-parted; segments linear. Corolla pubescent, $\frac{3}{4}$ in. long; tube cylindric, twisted; limb 2-lipped, upper lip erect, notched, lower recurved, 3-toothed. Stamens 2; anther-cells blunt. Style minutely 2-lobed. Capsule $\frac{1}{4}$ in.; seeds 4. (Fig. 120.)

Simla, common; May–December.—Throughout India in hilly districts, ascending to 7000 ft.—Afghanistan.

LXXIV. VERBENACEÆ

Herbs or shrubs. Leaves opposite, usually simple; stipules none. Flowers 2-sexual, more or less irregular, in spikes, racemes or cymes. Calyx free, persistent, often enlarged in fruit; tube bell-shaped or tubular, sometimes very short; limb 4- or 5-lobed or toothed, rarely entire and spreading. Corolla hypogynous; tube usually nearly cylindric, often curved; limb 5- or 4-lobed, sometimes 2-lipped, lobes spreading or erect, usually unequal. Stamens 4, usually in unequal pairs, attached to the corolla-tube, alternate with the lobes; filaments free, anthers 2-celled, never cohering in pairs. Disk inconspicuous. Ovary free, sessile, 1-celled when young, usually becoming 2- or 4-celled when mature; style terminal, simple, tip 2-lobed or entire; ovules 4, rarely 2 or 1. Fruit usually drupe-like, sometimes dry, rarely capsular, more or less enclosed by the calyx-tube, usually containing 4 one-seeded nutlets.—An Order widely dispersed in nearly all warm and temperate regions.

Flowers in long, slender spikes or racemes.
  Flowers stalked. Calyx-teeth unequal, 3 lower long, 2 upper minute . . . . 1. *Phryma.*
  Flowers sessile. Calyx-teeth equal . . . . . 4. *Verbena.*
Flowers in ovoid or oblong heads.
  An erect shrub. Flowers $\frac{1}{3}$ in. long . . . . . 2. *Lantana.*
  A creeping herb. Flowers $\frac{1}{10}$ in. long . . . . . 3. *Lippia.*
Flowers in cymes.
  Cymes axillary.
    Leaves tomentose. Flowers hardly $\frac{1}{5}$ in. long. Calyx-limb erect, 4-toothed . . . . 5. *Callicarpa.*
    Leaves glabrous. Flowers $\frac{3}{4}$ in. long. Calyx limb spreading, entire, very large . . . . . . 7. *Holmskioldia.*
  Cymes aggregated in narrow, terminal panicles.
    Leaves digitate; leaflets 3–5 . . . . 6. *Vitex.*
    Leaves simple, lanceolate . . . . 8. *Caryopteris.*

1. PHRYMA. Etymology obscure.—Central and E. Asia, N. America.—A single species.

Phryma leptostachya, *Linn.*; *Fl. Br. Ind.* iv. 562. A thinly hairy, erect herb, 1–2 ft. Leaves stalked, ovate-lanceolate, 2–4 in., toothed. Flowers $\frac{1}{4}$–$\frac{1}{3}$ in. long, pale pink, in long, slender racemes. Calyx tubular, prominently 5-ribbed; teeth 5, unequal, 3 lower long, linear, becoming hooked in fruit, 2 upper minute. Corolla-tube cylindric; limb 2-lipped, upper lip erect, concave, notched, lower larger, somewhat spreading, 3-lobed. Stamens in unequal pairs, included. Ovary 1-celled; style 2-lobed. Fruit dry, oblong, enclosed in the reflexed calyx; seed solitary, loose within the membranous pericarp.

Valleys below Simla; August, September.—Temperate Himalaya, 3000–7000 ft.

2. LANTANA. Name adopted from *Viburnum Lantana*, the Wayfaring tree, on account of resemblances in the foliage and fruit.—Most tropical regions.

Lantana indica, *Roxb.*; *Fl. Br. Ind.* iv. 562. A roughly hairy shrub; branches long, rambling, 4-sided. Leaves shortly stalked, ovate, 1–3 in., crenate. Flowers $\frac{1}{3}$ in. long, white, pale purple or yellow, crowded in axillary, long-stalked, bracteate, ovoid heads. Calyx very small, obscurely 4-toothed. Corolla hairy; tube long, curved, cylindric; limb spreading, usually 4-lobed. Stamens in unequal pairs, included. Ovary 2-celled, narrowed upwards into a short style; stigma terminal, oblique. Drupe smooth, purple, globose, containing a 2-celled stone; seeds 1 in each cell.

Valleys below Simla; April–June.—Throughout India, ascending to 3000 ft.—Tropical Africa.

3. LIPPIA. In honour of Augustus Lippi, a French traveller of the seventeenth century.—Most tropical regions.

Lippia nodiflora, *Rich.*; *Fl. Br. Ind.* iv. 563. A roughly pubescent herb; stems prostrate, 6–30 in., rooting at the joints. Leaves obovate or spathulate, 1 in., narrowed to the sessile base, toothed near the top. Flowers $\frac{1}{10}$ in. long, pink or white, crowded in axillary, long-stalked, oblong-ovoid, bracteate heads. Calyx minute, 2-parted. Corolla-tube cylindric; limb obscurely 2-lipped, upper lip 2-lobed, lower rather longer, 3-lobed. Stamens in unequal pairs, included. Ovary 2-celled; style short, stigma capitate. Fruit dry, minute, separating in two 1-seeded nutlets.

Sutlej valley, Suni; April–June.—Throughout India, ascending to 3000 ft.—Nearly all warm regions.

4. VERBENA. The classical name of *V. officinalis*.—Most tropical and temperate regions; chiefly America.

Verbena officinalis, *Linn.*; *Fl. Br. Ind.* iv. 565. An erect, nearly glabrous, perennial herb; stems 1–3 ft., 4-sided, branching. Lower leaves stalked, oblong or ovate, pinnatifid or coarsely toothed; upper sessile, usually 3-parted. Flowers $\frac{1}{4}$ in. long, lilac, sessile in long, slender, bracteate spikes. Calyx glandular-hairy, tubular, 5-toothed. Corolla hairy; tube nearly cylindric, longer than the calyx; limb spreading, unequally 5-lobed. Stamens in unequal pairs, included. Ovary 4-lobed, 1- or 4-celled; style short, stigma capitate. Fruit dry, ultimately separating into 4 one-seeded nutlets.

Simla; April–June.—Throughout India, ascending to 7000 ft.—Nearly all temperate and subtropical regions (Britain, Vervein).

5. CALLICARPA. From the Greek *callos*, beauty, and *carpos*, fruit.—Chiefly E. Asia and N. Australia.

Callicarpa macrophylla, *Vahl.*; *Fl. Br. Ind.* iv. 568. An erect shrub, 4–8 ft.; branches, leaf-stalks and inflorescence densely clothed with tawny, wool-like tomentum. Leaves shortly stalked, lanceolate, 6–9 × 2–3 in., crenate or sharply toothed, long-pointed; upper surface wrinkled, stellately pubescent; lower tomentose. Flowers hardly $\frac{1}{5}$ in. long, pink, crowded in axillary, stalked cymes. Calyx bell-shaped, 4-toothed. Corolla-tube short; limb 4-lobed, lobes nearly equal, spreading. Stamens equal, far-protruding. Ovary 2- or 4-celled; style long, stigma minutely capitate. Fruit succulent, globose, white, containing 4 one-seeded nutlets.

Valleys below Simla; July–November.—Throughout N. and E. India, ascending to 6000 ft.

6. VITEX. The classical name of *V. Agnus-castus*, a South European shrub.—Most tropical and warm regions.

Vitex Negundo, *Linn.*; *Fl. Br. Ind.* iv. 583. A shrub or small tree; branchlets, leaf-stalks and inflorescence densely grey-pubescent. Leaves stalked, digitately compound; leaflets 3–5, lanceolate, unequal, largest about 4 × $1\frac{1}{4}$ in., entire, long-pointed; upper surface glabrous or nearly so, lower densely grey-pubescent. Flowers $\frac{1}{3}$ in. long, blue-purple, crowded in short cymes forming erect, narrow, tapering, terminal panicles. Calyx bell-shaped, 5-toothed. Corolla-tube not longer than the calyx; limb obscurely 2-lipped, lobes 5, unequal, lowest much the largest. Stamens in unequal pairs, protruding. Ovary 2- or 4-celled; style long, tip 2-lobed. Fruit succulent, black, ovoid, $\frac{1}{4}$ in. long, containing 4 one-seeded nutlets.

Valleys below Simla; March–June.—Throughout India, ascending to 5000 ft.—Nearly all tropical regions.

7. HOLMSKIOLDIA. In honour of Theodor Holmskiold, a Danish botanical author of the eighteenth century.—India, Africa.

Holmskioldia sanguinea, *Retz*; *Fl. Br. Ind.* iv. 596. A nearly glabrous, straggling shrub, 10–30 ft. Leaves stalked, cordate, ovate, about 3 × 2 in., toothed or entire. Flowers scarlet, tinged with orange, crowded in axillary, stalked cymes. Calyx coloured like the corolla; tube very short; limb membranous, circular, entire, spreading, 1 in. diam. Corolla $\frac{3}{4}$ in. long; tube nearly cylindric, curved; limb short, obscurely 2-lipped, lobes 5, unequal, lowest the longest. Stamens in unequal pairs, protruding. Ovary 4-celled; style long, tip 2-lobed. Fruit 4-lobed, nearly dry, containing 4 one-seeded nutlets.

Valleys below Simla, Subathoo; October–December.—Outer Himalaya, from the Sutlej to Assam and Burmah, ascending to 3000 ft.

8. CARYOPTERIS. From the Greek *caryon*, a nut, and *pteron*, a wing, referring to the winged capsule-valves.—E. Asia.

Caryopteris Wallichiana, *Schauer*; *Fl. Br. Ind.* iv. 597. An erect, nearly glabrous shrub, 4–10 ft. Leaves shortly stalked, lanceolate, about 4 × 1 in., toothed or nearly entire, long-pointed. Flowers fragrant, white, tinged with blue, lowest corolla-lobe darker, crowded in short cymes forming narrow, terminal panicles.

FIG. 121. CARYOPTERIS WALLICHIANA.

Calyx pubescent, bell-shaped, deeply 5-lobed. Corolla pubescent, $\frac{1}{2}$ in. long; tube cylindric, slightly longer than the calyx; limb spreading, $\frac{3}{4}$ in. diam., 5-lobed, 4 upper lobes oblong, nearly equal, lowest larger, notched. Stamens in unequal pairs, protruding. Ovary imperfectly 4-celled; style long, tip 2-lobed. Fruit pubescent, nearly dry, dark blue, globose, 4-lobed, ultimately separating into 4 concave valves each winged along one margin and carrying a single seed. (Fig. 121.)

Valleys below Simla; March, April.—Outer Himalaya, ascending to 5000 ft.

LXXV. LABIATÆ

HERBS or shrubs; stems and branches usually 4-sided. Leaves simple, lobed only in *Leonurus*, opposite, rarely whorled, often more or less covered with aromatic glands; stipules none. Flowers irregular, regular or nearly so, usually 2-sexual, in opposite, axillary cymes composed of many or few, rarely only one or two flowers; each pair of cymes constituting a whorl. Whorls sometimes placed one above the other at the extremity of the branches forming simple or paniculate racemes or spikes. Sepals 5, free from the ovary, more or less united in a 5- or 4- rarely 10-toothed, tubular or sometimes 2-lipped calyx. Corolla hypogynous; tube distinct; limb 4- or 5-toothed or lobed, regular or nearly so, or distinctly 2-lipped, the upper lip usually erect and 2-lobed or notched, the lower spreading and 3-lobed, rarely entire. Stamens usually 4, in unequal pairs, rarely all equal, sometimes only 2, attached to the corolla-tube and alternate with the lobes; filaments free from one another, very rarely united near the base. Anthers 2- or 1-celled, cells widely separated in *Salvia*. Disk hypogynous, usually thick and fleshy, often lobed. Ovary free, 4-lobed to the base, lobes 1-celled; style simple, slender, inserted in the centre of the ovary between the lobes, tip 2-lobed, stigmas minute; ovules solitary in each cell. Fruit included within the persistent calyx, 4-lobed or by abortion 3- to 1-lobed, the lobes ultimately separating into as many indehiscent, 1-seeded, usually smooth nutlets.—A very large Order spread over nearly the whole globe, rare in arctic regions.—Name from the Latin *labium*, a lip, referring to the shape of the flowers.

The leaves at the base of a whorl are termed floral leaves, and often have the appearance of bracts. In compound forms of inflorescence the bracts are placed at the base of the branches of a cyme or of the flower-stalks, but are always small and often wanting; when the cyme is contracted into a head the bracts form an involucre outside. If the corolla of a 2-lipped flower having 4 stamens in unequal pairs is slit up along the front through the lower lip and laid out flat, the outer or anterior pair of stamens will be found to overtop the inner or posterior pair in all the genera except *Nepeta*, in which alone the inner pair project above the outer.

For details regarding the fertilisation of the flowers see Müller's *Fertilisation of Flowers*, p. 469; Kerner's *Natural History of Plants*, ii. p. 247.

A. Corolla regular or nearly so, not 2-lipped.

I. Stamens 2.

A herb. Leaves glabrous. Flowers in axillary whorls . . 10. *Lycopus*.
A shrub. Leaves tomentose beneath. Flowers in spikes . 15. *Meriandra*.

II. Stamens 4.

Corolla 4-lobed.
Filaments bearded.
Leaves stalked, in pairs . . . . 4. *Pogostemon*.
Leaves sessile, whorled . . . . 5. *Dysophylla*.

Filaments naked.
  Calyx 5-lobed; lobes linear, elongated and feathery in fruit . . . . 6. *Colebrookea.*
  Calyx 5-toothed, bell-shaped.
    Flowers white, purple or yellow. Stamens in unequal pairs . . . . 7. *Elsholtzia.*
    Flowers lilac. Stamens all equal . . . . . 9. *Mentha.*
Corolla 5-lobed.
  Flowers pale purple, in terminal heads. . . . . 1. *Acrocephalus.*
  Flowers white, in racemes . . . . 8. *Perilla.*

B. Corolla irregular, limb 2-lipped.[1]

I. Stamens 2.

Filaments very short, anther-cells widely separated . . 16. *Salvia.*

II. Stamens 4.

* Lower lip of corolla boat-shaped, entire.

Filaments free. Flowers about $\frac{1}{4}$ in. long . . . . . 2. *Plectranthus.*
Filaments united near the base. Flowers $\frac{3}{4}$–1 in. long . 3. *Coleus.*

* * Lower lip of corolla distinctly 3-lobed.[2]

† Calyx not 2-lipped, teeth equal or nearly so.

Upper lip of corolla flat or nearly so.[1]
  Leaves 1 in. or more long.
    Flowers pink, in short spikes . . . . 11. *Origanum.*
    Flowers blue or lilac, in axillary whorls . . . . 29. *Ajuga.*
  Leaves $\frac{1}{4}$ in. long. Whorls axillary, 1–4-flowered. . 13. *Micromeria.*
Upper lip of corolla concave or hood-like.
  Inner or upper pair of stamens longer than the outer . 17. *Nepeta.*
  Outer or lower pair of stamens longer than the inner.
    Flowers about $\frac{1}{5}$ in. long . . . . 20. *Craniotome.*
    Flowers $\frac{1}{2}$ in. or more long.
      Calyx 10-toothed . . . . 26. *Leucas.*
      Calyx 5-toothed or lobed.
        Leaves deeply lobed . . . . 23. *Leonurus.*
        Leaves undivided.
          Calyx nearly as long as the corolla . . . 25. *Roylea.*
          Calyx not longer than the corolla-tube.
            Flowers white except mid-lobe of lower lip. 21. *Anisomeles.*
            Flowers pink, spotted with purple . . 22. *Stachys.*
            Flowers dull blue-purple . . . . . 27. *Phlomis.*

† † Calyx 2-lipped.

Calyx-mouth remaining open after flowering.[3]
  Leaves $\frac{1}{3}$ in. long . . . . 12. *Thymus.*
  Leaves $\frac{3}{4}$ in. or more long . . . . 14. *Calamintha.*
Calyx-mouth closing after flowering.
  Calyx-lips entire . . . . 18. *Scutellaria.*
  Calyx-lips toothed or lobed . . . . 19. *Brunella.*

[1] Upper lip very short in *Ajuga.* [2] Middle lobe often notched. [3] In *Thymus* the mouth of the calyx is closed by hairs.

*** Lower lip of corolla 3-lobed, but the lateral lobes very small or wanting. . . . . 24. *Lamium.*

C. Corolla irregular, limb 1-lipped, upper lip wanting.

Flowers in pairs, forming erect racemes. Lip of corolla 5-lobed . . . . 28. *Teucrium.*

1. ACROCEPHALUS. From the Greek *acros*, the top, and *cephale*, a head, referring to the terminal inflorescence.—Tropical and subtropical regions in Asia and Africa.

***Acrocephalus capitatus,** *Benth.*; *Fl. Br. Ind.* iv. 611. An annual, pubescent herb; stems 6–12 in., decumbent or ascending, usually branching from near the base. Leaves ovate or lanceolate, ½–1 in., coarsely toothed, narrowed into a nearly sessile base. Flowers small, pale purple, crowded in stalked, terminal, globose heads about ½ in. diam.; floral leaves usually spreading. Calyx ovoid in flowering time, elongated and tubular in fruit, 2-lipped; upper lip flat, entire, lower shorter, 4-toothed. Corolla nearly regular; tube longer than the calyx; limb 5-lobed, lobes nearly equal. Stamens 4, nearly equal, included.

Throughout India, ascending to 5000 ft., common in moist situations; flowers during the cold season.

2. PLECTRANTHUS. From the Greek *plectron*, a spur, and *anthos*, a flower, referring to the unequally dilated base of the corolla-tube in some species.—Tropical and subtropical regions of the Old World.

Erect shrubs or undershrubs. Leaves opposite or whorled, stalked or the upper sessile. Flowers about ¼ in. long, in small cymes forming racemes or panicles. Calyx bell-shaped in flowering time, enlarging and becoming 2-lipped or tubular in fruit; teeth 5, nearly equal or very unequal. Corolla-tube usually longer than the calyx; limb 2-lipped, upper lip short, broad, recurved, 3- or 4-lobed, lower longer, boat-shaped, entire. Stamens 4, in unequal pairs, lying along the lower lip of the corolla; filaments free.

Leaves opposite.
  Calyx-teeth equal or nearly so at least in flower.
    Lower surface of leaves glabrous or nearly so.
      Corolla-tube straight.
        Corolla white, mid-lobes of upper lip spotted with purple . . . . 1. *P. Gerardianus.*
        Corolla white . . . . 2. *P. striatus.*
      Corolla-tube abruptly decurved . . . . . 3. *P. Coetsa.*
    Lower surface of leaves white-tomentose. . . . 4. *P. rugosus.*
  Calyx-teeth very unequal, uppermost ovate, obtuse, others narrowly lanceolate, acute . . . . . 6. *P. incanus.*
Leaves in whorls of three . . . . 5. *P. ternifolius.*

1. **Plectranthus Gerardianus,** *Benth.*; *Fl. Br. Ind.* iv. 617. Nearly glabrous, 4–6 ft. Leaves opposite, ovate or ovate-lanceolate, 2–6 × 1–2½ in., crenate or sharply toothed, long-pointed; lower surface gland-dotted. Cymes forming narrow, tapering, axillary panicles, the upper ones usually combined in a spreading, terminal inflorescence. Calyx gland-dotted; tube bell-shaped at flowering time, elongated and curved in fruit; teeth nearly equal, obtuse. Corolla white, the two mid-lobes of upper lip purple-spotted; tube straight, much longer than the calyx.

Simla, common; August–October.—Temperate Himalaya, 3000–9000 ft.

FIG. 122. PLECTRANTHUS COETSA.

2. **Plectranthus striatus,** *Benth.*; *Fl. Br. Ind.* iv. 618. Roughly pubescent or shortly hairy, 6–24 in. Leaves opposite, ovate, 1–4 × 1–2½ in., crenate; lower surface gland-dotted. Cymes forming narrow, tapering, axillary panicles, the upper ones usually combined in a spreading, terminal inflorescence. Calyx gland-dotted; tube bell-shaped at flowering time, elongated and curved in fruit; teeth nearly equal, obtuse. Corolla white; tube straight, much longer than the calyx.

Simla; August–October.—Temperate Himalaya, 4000–8000 ft.

Closely allied to *P. Gerardianus*; distinguished by its smaller size and rough pubescence.

3. **Plectranthus Coetsa,** *Buch.-Ham.*; *Fl. Br. Ind.* iv. 619. Pubescent, 3–6 ft. Leaves opposite, ovate or ovate-lanceolate, 2–4 × 1–2

in., crenate or sharply toothed. Cymes forming narrow, tapering, axillary panicles, the upper ones usually combined in a spreading, terminal inflorescence. Calyx bristly; tube bell-shaped at flowering time, enlarged and curved in fruit; teeth nearly equal, acute. Corolla lavender-blue; tube abruptly decurved, much longer than the calyx. (Fig. 122.)

Simla, common; September, October.—Temperate Himalaya, 3000–8000 ft. —Burmah.

4. **Plectranthus rugosus,** *Wall.*; *Fl. Br. Ind.* iv. 620. Stellately pubescent, 2–6 ft. Leaves opposite, ovate or oblong, usually 1–1½ in., often reduced in dry situations to ¼ in. or less, crenate or sharply toothed, obtuse; upper surface pubescent, closely wrinkled; lower white- or grey-tomentose. Cymes forming narrow, leafy, axillary or terminal racemes. Calyx tomentose; tube bell-shaped at flowering time, elongated and curved in fruit; teeth nearly equal, acute. Corolla white, upper lip spotted and streaked with purple; tube straight, longer than the calyx.

Simla, common in stony places; March–October.—Temperate Himalaya, 3000–8000 ft.—Afghanistan.

5. **Plectranthus ternifolius,** *Don*; *Fl. Br. Ind.* iv. 621. White-tomentose, 3–5 ft. Leaves in whorls of three, nearly sessile, lanceolate, 2–6 in., toothed; upper surface hairy, wrinkled; lower tomentose. Cymes shortly stalked, crowded in erect, cylindric racemes forming terminal panicles. Calyx tomentose; tube bell-shaped at flowering time, elongated and tubular in fruit; teeth nearly equal, acute. Corolla white, the upper lip pink-spotted at the base; tube curved, longer than the calyx.

Valleys below Simla; August–October.—N. India, ascending to 5000 ft.—Burmah, S. China.

6. **Plectranthus incanus,** *Link*; *Fl. Br. Ind.* iv. 621. Pubescent, 1–3 ft. Leaves opposite, cordate, broadly ovate, 2–4 in., crenate. Cymes forming long, narrow, erect, axillary and terminal racemes. Calyx pubescent; tube bell-shaped at flowering time, elongated and 2-lipped in fruit; teeth very unequal, uppermost ovate, obtuse, reflexed in fruit, other 4 narrowly lanceolate, acute, the 2 lowest the longest. Corolla pale lavender-blue; tube straight, hardly longer than the calyx.

Valleys below Simla; August, September.—Hilly districts throughout India, ascending to 6000 ft.

3. COLEUS. From the Greek *coleos*, a sheath, referring to the united filaments.—Chiefly tropical Asia and Africa.

Coleus barbatus, *Benth.*; *Fl. Br. Ind.* iv. 625. An erect, hairy herb, 1–3 ft. Leaves stalked, ovate or oblong, about 2½×1 in., crenate, obtuse; upper surface hairy; lower tomentose. Flowers

¾–1 in. long, pale blue, in whorls of 6–8 forming long, leafless, interrupted, spike-like racemes. Calyx hairy; tube bell-shaped, deflexed and slightly enlarged in fruit; teeth 5, acute, upper one ovate, others narrowly lanceolate. Corolla-tube deflexed, longer than the calyx; limb 2-lipped, upper lip reflexed, 3-lobed, lower much longer, boat-shaped, entire, acute. Stamens 4, in unequal pairs, lying along the lower lip of the corolla, filaments united near the base, sheathing the style.

Valleys below Simla; September.—Simla to Nepal, 2000–7000 ft.—S. India. —Africa.

Cultivated in S. India for the edible, tuberous roots.

C. aromaticus, Benth., a native of the Moluccas, is cultivated in gardens throughout India, the fragrant leaves being used in domestic economy.

4. POGOSTEMON. From the Greek *pogon*, a beard, and *stemon*, thread; referring to the hairy filaments.—India, Central Asia.

Pogostemon plectranthoides, *Desf.*; *Fl. Br. Ind.* iv. 632. A strongly scented, pubescent shrub; young parts tomentose. Leaves opposite, stalked, ovate, 3–6 in., coarsely and irregularly toothed, long-pointed. Flowers hardly ¼ in. long, white, tinged with pink, in large whorls crowded in numerous, cylindric spikes forming terminal, erect panicles; floral leaves bract-like, hairy, glandular, ovate, acute. Calyx tubular, 5-toothed; teeth nearly equal. Corolla-tube curved, longer than the calyx; limb spreading, 4-lobed, lobes nearly equal, obtuse. Stamens 4, nearly equal, far protruding, filaments lilac, bearded with long, lilac, beaded hairs.

Sutlej valley, Suni; April–October.—Throughout India, ascending to 5000 ft.

The perfume patchouli is obtained from *P. Patchouli*, a native of tropical Asia, cultivated for export in the Straits Settlements.

5. DYSOPHYLLA. From the Greek *dysodes*, fetid, and *phyllon*, a leaf; referring to the strong odour of the leaves.—Tropical Asia and Australia.

***Dysophylla crassicaulis,** *Benth.*; *Fl. Br. Ind.* iv. 640. A glabrous, erect or ascending herb, 6–24 in. Leaves 4–6 in a whorl, sessile, narrowly oblong or lanceolate, 1–2 in., toothed, obtuse. Flowers minute, blue-purple, in large whorls crowded in slender, cylindric, terminal spikes 1–4 in. long. Calyx hairy, ovoid, 5-toothed. Corolla tubular; limb 4-lobed, erect or slightly spreading. Stamens 4, nearly equal, far protruding, filaments bearded with blue-purple, beaded hairs.

N. India, in swamps, ascending to 4000 ft.

6. COLEBROOKEA. In honour of H. T. Colebrooke, Chief Judge of the Supreme Court at Calcutta, and a botanical author of the eighteenth century.—India.—A single species.

Colebrookea oppositifolia, *Sm.*; *Fl. Br. Ind.* iv. 642. An erect, tomentose shrub, 5–10 ft. Leaves opposite or in threes, shortly stalked, lanceolate, 4–8 in., crenate, long-pointed; upper surface pubescent, wrinkled, lower grey-tomentose. Flowers minute, white, 2- or 1-sexual, the male and female often on different plants, in large whorls crowded in long, cylindric, erect spikes, axillary or paniculate at the end of branches. Calyx deeply 5-lobed; lobes linear, hairy, becoming much elongated and feathery in fruit when the tips often turn purple. Corolla pubescent; tube as long as the calyx; limb spreading, 4-lobed, lobes unequal. Stamens 4, equal, protruding in the male flowers, included in the female, filaments naked. Style protruding in the female flowers, wanting in the male. Nutlet usually only one, tip hairy.

Valleys below Simla, Dharmpur, Suni; flowers in the cold season.—Throughout India, ascending to 4000 ft.

7. ELSHOLTZIA. In honour of J. S. Elsholtz, a German botanist of the seventeenth century.—Chiefly temperate Asia.

Erect herbs or undershrubs. Flowers very small, in large whorls crowded in cylindric or flat spikes often clustered towards the end of branches; bracts small or conspicuous. Calyx bell-shaped, 5-toothed, small at flowering time, enlarged in fruit. Corolla-tube usually longer than the calyx; limb 4-lobed, upper lobe nearly erect, notched, the others spreading, entire. Stamens 4 in unequal pairs, protruding, filaments naked.

Spikes cylindric, bearing flowers all round. Flowers white or pale yellow.
- Spikes 2–6 in. Floral leaves bract-like, very small.
  - Shrubby, 3–6 ft. Leaves nearly sessile, lanceolate, 3–5 in. . . . . 1. *E. polystachya.*
  - Herbaceous, 1–3 ft. Leaves long-stalked, ovate, 1–2 in. . . . . 2. *E. incisa.*
- Spikes $\frac{1}{2}$–$1\frac{1}{2}$ in. Floral leaves conspicuous, forming broad, overlapping involucres nearly concealing the purple flowers . . . . 3. *E. strobilifera.*

Spikes flat, bearing flowers only on one side. Flowers purple . . . . 4. *E. cristata.*

1. **Elsholtzia polystachya,** *Benth.*; *Fl. Br. Ind.* iv. 643. A pubescent shrub, 3–6 ft. Leaves nearly sessile, lanceolate, 3–5 in., toothed, acute. Spikes slender, cylindric, 4–6 in. Flowers white or pale yellow; floral leaves bract-like, minute. Fruiting calyx elongated, tubular, curved. (Fig. 123.)

Simla, common; June-October.—Temperate Himalaya, 7000–9000 ft.

2. **Elsholtzia incisa,** *Benth.*; *Fl. Br. Ind.* iv. 644. A pubescent, slender herb, 1–3 ft. Leaves fragrant, long-stalked, ovate, 1–2 in., coarsely toothed, base tapering, entire, lower surface gland-dotted. Spikes very slender, cylindric, 2–4 in.

Flowers white; floral leaves bract-like, small, linear. Calyx glandular.

Valleys below Simla, fields and roadsides, common; July–October.—Temperate Himalaya, 3000–5000 ft.—Burmah.

3. **Elsholtzia strobilifera,** *Benth.*; *Fl. Br. Ind.* iv. 645. A herb, 4–12 in. Leaves stalked, ovate, ½–1 in., crenate. Spikes cone-like, cylindric, ½–1½ in. Floral leaves bract-like, mem-

FIG. 123. ELSHOLTZIA POLYSTACHYA.

branous, persistent, united, forming broad, fringed, overlapping involucres nearly concealing the pale purple flowers. Fruiting calyx elongated, tubular.

Simla, fields and roadsides, common; June–October.—Temperate Himalaya 5000–10,000 ft.

4. **Elsholtzia cristata,** *Willd.*; *Fl. Br. Ind.* iv. 645. A pubescent herb, 1–2 ft. Leaves fragrant, long-stalked, lanceolate, 1–4 in.,

coarsely toothed, base tapering, entire, lower surface gland-dotted. Spikes flat, bearing flowers only on one side, 1–2½ in. Flowers purple; floral leaves bract-like, conspicuous, orbicular, abruptly pointed.

Simla and valleys below, fields and roadsides; September, October.—Himalaya, 1000–9000 ft.—China, Japan, N. Europe.

8. **PERILLA.** Name of doubtful origin.—Eastern Asia.

Perilla ocimoides, *Linn.*; *Fl. Br. Ind.* iv. 646. An annual, erect, aromatic, hairy herb, 2–4 ft. Leaves stalked, ovate or orbicular, 3–5 in., coarsely toothed. Flowers small, white, in whorls of 2, forming long, erect, axillary and terminal racemes; floral leaves bract-like, lanceolate, as long as the flowers. Calyx bell-shaped, 5-toothed, becoming much enlarged and 2-lipped in fruit. Corolla-tube included in the calyx; limb spreading, 5-lobed, lower lobe slightly the larger. Stamens 4, as long as the corolla.

Valleys below Simla; April-October.—Himalaya, 2000–5000 ft.—Burmah, China, Japan.

Frequently cultivated in the Himalaya; the seeds yield an aromatic oil. Native name *Bhanjiri*.

9. **MENTHA.** The classical name of a species of Mint.—Nearly all temperate regions.

Mentha sylvestris, *Linn.*; *Fl. Br. Ind.* iv. 647. A strongly scented, erect or diffuse herb; root-stock creeping; stems 1–3 ft., hoary-pubescent. Leaves nearly sessile, lanceolate, ovate or oblong, 1–3 in., sharply toothed, acute; upper surface hoary-pubescent, lower white-tomentose. Flowers small, lilac, in large whorls crowded in axillary and terminal, cylindric, tapering spikes; lower floral leaves leaflike, upper smaller, lanceolate. Calyx hairy, bell-shaped, acutely 5-toothed. Corolla-tube included in the calyx; limb erect, 4-lobed, lobes nearly equal. Stamens 4, equal, protruding, filaments naked.

Simla, common in wet places; July–October.—W. Himalaya, 4000–12,000 ft.—Temperate Asia, Europe (Britain, Horse mint).

The variety, *incana*, having the stems and upper surface of the leaves white-tomentose also occurs, usually at lower elevations.

10. **LYCOPUS.** From the Greek *lycos*, a wolf, and *pous*, a foot; referring probably to the leaves.—N. temperate regions, Australia.

Lycopus europæus, *Linn.*; *Fl. Br. Ind.* iv. 648. An erect, nearly glabrous herb, 1–3 ft.; rootstock creeping. Leaves nearly sessile, lanceolate, 2–4 in., deeply and sharply toothed. Flowers small, white, dotted with purple, crowded in sessile, axillary whorls. Calyx bell-shaped, deeply 5-toothed; teeth equal, narrowly lanceolate, acute. Corolla bell-shaped, slightly longer than the calyx, 4-lobed. Stamens 2, slightly protruding.

Matiana, in marshy ground; July.—Punjab plains, ascending to 7000 ft.—Temperate Asia, Europe (Britain, Gipsywort).

11. ORIGANUM. The classical name of a species of wild Marjoram.—N. temperate regions.

Origanum vulgare, *Linn.*; *Fl. Br. Ind.* iv. 648. An erect herb, 1–3 ft., more or less clothed with short hairs. Leaves stalked, ovate, about $1 \times \frac{3}{4}$ in., entire. Flowers small, pink, crowded in numerous, 4-sided spikes $\frac{1}{4}$–1 in. long in clusters or heads at the end of branches, sometimes forming terminal panicles; floral leaves bract-like, lanceolate, longer than the calyx, overlapping, often tinged with purple. Calyx bell-shaped, enlarged in fruit, 5-toothed, mouth hairy within. Corolla-tube longer than the calyx; limb 2-lipped, upper lip erect, nearly flat, notched, lower spreading, 3-lobed. Stamens 4 in unequal pairs, slightly protruding.

Simla, common; August, September.—Temperate Asia, N. Africa, Europe (Britain, Wild Marjoram).

The Sweet Marjoram, *O. Marjorana*, is cultivated in gardens throughout India; an oil is obtained from the seeds.

12. THYMUS. The classical name of the common Thyme, *T. vulgaris.*—Temperate regions of the Old World.

Thymus Serpyllum, *Linn.*; *Fl. Br. Ind.* iv. 649. An aromatic, hairy, more or less procumbent, often tufted shrub, usually about 6–12 in. Leaves nearly sessile, gland-dotted, oblong-ovate, about $\frac{1}{3}$ in., entire, obtuse. Flowers small, purple, sometimes 1-sexual, in small whorls crowded in short, terminal spikes. Calyx hairy, gland-dotted, 2-lipped, mouth hairy within; upper lip broad, 3-toothed, lower 2-parted, segments linear. Corolla-tube as long as the calyx; limb 2-lipped, upper lip nearly erect, flat, notched, lower spreading, 3-lobed. Stamens 4, nearly equal, protruding.

Simla, common on the downs; May-October.—W. Himalaya, 5000–10,000 ft.—Temperate Asia, N. Africa, Europe (Britain, Wild Thyme).

13. MICROMERIA. From the Greek *micros*, small, and *meros*, a part; referring to the small flowers.—Most temperate and warm regions; absent from Australia.

Micromeria biflora, *Benth.*; *Fl. Br. Ind.* iv. 650. A hairy, usually tufted, nearly erect shrub, 6–12 in., somewhat resembling Thyme. Leaves sessile, gland-dotted, ovate, $\frac{1}{4}$ in., acute. Flowers stalked, small, pink or nearly white, in axillary whorls of 1–4. Calyx hairy, tubular, prominently 13-nerved, equally 5-toothed.

Corolla-tube slightly longer than the calyx; limb 2-lipped, upper lip erect, nearly flat, notched, lower spreading, 3-lobed. Stamens 4, in unequal pairs. (Fig. 124.)

Simla, common; April–October.—Temperate Himalaya, 1000–7000 ft.—W. Asia, Africa.

14. CALAMINTHA. The classical name of an aromatic plant of this affinity; from the Greek *calos*, beautiful, and *mentha*, mint.—N. temperate regions.

Softly hairy herbs, 1–3 ft. Leaves distant, shortly stalked. Flowers small, pink or purple, in axillary or terminal whorls sometimes forming short, interrupted spikes; floral leaves linear.

FIG. 124. MICROMERIA BIFLORA.

Calyx tubular, 13-nerved, 2-lipped; upper lip 3-toothed, lower 2-toothed, lower teeth longer and narrower than the upper; mouth remaining open after flowering. Corolla-tube longer than the calyx; limb 2-lipped, upper lip erect, nearly flat, notched, lower spreading, 3-lobed. Stamens 4, in unequal pairs.

Whorls many-flowered, crowded, compact, surrounded by an involucre of numerous, long bracts . . . 1. *C. Clinopodium*.
Whorls few-flowered, loose. Bracts few, short, not forming an involucre . . . . 2. *C. umbrosa*.

1. **Calamintha Clinopodium**, *Benth.*; *Fl. Br. Ind.* iv. 650. Stems erect. Leaves ovate, 1–$1\frac{3}{4}$ in., entire or toothed. Flowers in

large, crowded, compact whorls each surrounded by an involucre of numerous, long, linear, hairy bracts. Calyx $\frac{1}{3}$ in. long.

Simla, Mushobra; July–September.—W. Himalaya, 4000–12,000 ft.—Temperate Asia, N. Africa, Europe (Britain, Wild Basil), Canada.

2. **Calamintha umbrosa,** *Benth.*; *Fl. Br. Ind.* iv. 650. Stems ascending, often rooting near the base. Leaves ovate, $\frac{3}{4}$–$1\frac{1}{2}$ in., sharply toothed. Flowers in loose, small whorls; bracts few, short, not forming an involucre. Calyx $\frac{1}{4}$ in. long.

Simla, Mahasu, common; July–September.—Temperate Himalaya, 4000–12,000 ft., S. India.—Temperate Asia.

FIG. 125. MERIANDRA STROBILIFERA.

15. MERIANDRA. From the Greek *meros*, a part, and *aner*, *andros*, a man; referring to the distinct anther-cells.—India, E. Africa.

Meriandra strobilifera, *Benth.*; *Fl. Br. Ind.* iv. 652. An erect, tomentose shrub, 2–5 ft. Leaves thick, shortly stalked, oblong or lanceolate, 2–4 × $\frac{3}{4}$–$1\frac{1}{2}$ in., crenate, base prolonged downwards in 2 pointed lobes; upper surface pubescent, closely wrinkled; lower white-tomentose. Flowers small, white, in large whorls crowded in erect, tomentose, 4-sided, often paniculate spikes; floral leaves small, bract-like, sessile, ovate, overlapping. Calyx tubular-ovoid, 2-lipped; upper lip concave, entire, lower 2-toothed. Corolla-tube as long as the calyx; limb spreading, 4-lobed. Stamens 2, anthers protruding. (Fig. 125.)

Valleys below Simla, common; April–October.—W. Himalaya, 5000–6000 ft.

16. SALVIA. From the Latin *salveo*, to be in good health; referring to the healing properties of the Sage, *S. officinalis*.—Most temperate and tropical regions.

Erect herbs. Flowers in small whorls forming erect, often panicled racemes. Calyx bell-shaped, enlarged in fruit, 2-lipped; upper lip entire or 3-toothed, lower 2-toothed. Corolla-tube dilated upwards; limb 2-lipped, upper lip erect, usually long, arching, concave, flattened, lower spreading, 3-lobed. Stamens 2; filaments very short; anther-cells widely separated, one at each end of a slender, curved connective jointed to the top of the filament, upper cell perfect, enclosed within the upper lip of the corolla, lower imperfect.

For the action of the stamens in connection with insect visitors, see Lubbock's *British Wild Flowers* p. 149 and Müller's *Fertilisation of Flowers* p. 478.

Flowers $\frac{3}{4}$–$1\frac{1}{2}$ in. long. Upper lip of corolla long, arching.
  Flowers yellow . . . . 1. *S. glutinosa.*
  Flowers blue, lilac or nearly white.
    Stems $1\frac{1}{2}$–3 ft. Leaves long-stalked. Corolla-tube much longer than the calyx . . . . 2. *S. Moorcroftiana.*
    Stem 1–$1\frac{1}{2}$ ft. Leaves sessile. Corolla-tube not longer than the calyx . . . . . . 3. *S. lanata.*
Flowers hardly $\frac{1}{4}$ in. long. Upper lip of corolla short, nearly straight. . . . . 4. *S. plebeia.*

1. **Salvia glutinosa,** *Linn.*; *Fl. Br. Ind.* iv. 653. Viscidly hairy, strongly scented; stems 2–3 ft. Leaves stalked, ovate-oblong, 3–8 × $1\frac{1}{2}$–4 in., crenate or sharply toothed, base usually prolonged outwards in 2 pointed lobes, rarely cordate or tapering downwards. Flowers 1–$1\frac{1}{2}$ in. long, yellow, upper lip purple-dotted, in distant whorls; bracts small, leaf-like. Calyx broadly bell-shaped, upper lip entire. Corolla-tube longer than the calyx, upper lip long, curved, flattened, concave.

Simla, common; July–October.—Temperate Himalaya, 6000–9000 ft.—W. Asia, S. Europe.

2. **Salvia Moorcroftiana,** *Wall.*; *Fl. Br. Ind.* iv. 654. Clothed with white, usually woolly or cottony hairs; stems $1\frac{1}{2}$–3 ft. Leaves thick, long-stalked, ovate or oblong, 5–8 × $2\frac{1}{2}$–6 in., sinuately and irregularly lobed, crenate or sharply toothed; upper surface nearly glabrous or cottony-tomentose, closely wrinkled; lower white-

tomentose. Flowers 1 in. long, pale blue, lilac or nearly white, in distant whorls ; bracts large, pale, green-veined, orbicular, abruptly pointed. Calyx bristly, bell-shaped ; teeth spinous ; upper lip 3-toothed. Corolla-tube much longer than the calyx ; upper lip long, curved, flattened, concave.

Shali, Solan ; June.—W. Himalaya, 6000–9000 ft.

3. **Salvia lanata,** *Roxb.* ; *Fl. Br. Ind.* iv. 654. White woolly-tomentose ; stems 1–1½ ft. Leaves mostly radical, sessile, oblong-lanceolate, 3–6 × ¾–1½ in., toothed ; upper surface tomentose or nearly glabrous, closely wrinkled ; lower tomentose. Flowers

FIG. 126. SALVIA LANATA.

¾ in. long, blue-grey, in distant whorls ; bracts viscidly hairy, large, orbicular, abruptly pointed. Calyx viscidly hairy, bell-shaped ; teeth spinous ; upper lip 3-toothed. Corolla-tube not longer than the calyx ; upper lip long, curved, flattened, concave. (Fig. 126.)

Simla, common ; April–July.—W. Himalaya, 5000–8000 ft.

4. **Salvia plebeia,** *R. Br.* ; *Fl. Br. Ind.* iv. 655. Roughly pubescent ; inflorescence glandular ; stems 6–18 in. Leaves stalked, ovate or oblong, 1–3 in., toothed, obtuse. Flowers hardly ¼ in. long, lilac or nearly white in small whorls in numerous

slender, panicled racemes; bracts small, lower leaf-like, upper lanceolate. Calyx bell-shaped, upper lip entire. Corolla-tube included; upper lip short, nearly straight, slightly flattened, concave.

Sutlej valley, Suni, common in fields; April–July.—Throughout India, ascending to 5000 ft.—China, Malaya, Australia.

17. NEPETA. The classical name of a plant of the *Labiatæ*, probably a Mint.—Asia, chiefly in mountains, N. Africa, Europe (Britain).

Erect or ascending herbs. Whorls few- or many-flowered, sessile or stalked, crowded in terminal heads or spikes or more or less distant, sometimes axillary, rarely paniculate. Calyx tubular, 15-nerved, enlarging in fruit, usually incurved, 5-toothed, mouth oblique, upper teeth usually longer than the others. Corolla-tube slender near the base, dilated towards the mouth, usually longer than the calyx; limb 2-lipped, upper lip erect, concave, notched, lower spreading, 3-lobed, lateral lobes small, usually reflexed, mid-lobe much larger, narrow at the base, concave, entire or minutely crenate. Stamens 4, in unequal pairs, ascending under the upper lip, the inner or posterior pair longer than the outer or anterior.

Leaves sessile.

Stems glabrous or nearly so.
  Leaves linear, entire . . . . 1. *N. linearis.*
  Leaves oblong-lanceolate, toothed . . . . . 2. *N. campestris.*
Stems densely hairy. Leaves ovate-oblong; teeth close-set, regular, acute . . . . 3. *N. elliptica.*

Leaves stalked.

Flowers not more than ½ in. long.
  Whorls sessile, crowded, distant only near the base of the spike.
    Lower surface of leaves glabrous or nearly so . 4. *N. spicata.*
    Lower surface of leaves tomentose.
      Calyx glabrous or nearly so . . . . . 5. *N. distans.*
      Calyx covered with long hairs . . . . . 6. *N. ciliaris.*
  Whorls, at least the lower ones, distinctly stalked, distant nearly throughout the spike.
    Flowers sessile or nearly so.
      Flowers ¼ in. long. Corolla only slightly longer than the calyx . . . . 7. *N. ruderalis.*
      Flowers ½ in. long. Corolla twice as long as the calyx . . . . 8. *N. leucophylla.*
    Flowers on long, slender stalks . . . . . 9. *N. graciliflora.*
Flowers ¾–1¼ in. long.
  Flowers yellow . . . . 10. *N. Govaniana.*
  Flowers blue . . . . 11. *N. erecta.*

*1. **Nepeta linearis,** *Royle*; *Fl. Br. Ind.* iv. 657. Pubescent; rootstock tuberous; stems ascending, 6–18 in. Leaves sessile, linear, 1–3 × ⅛ in., entire. Whorls sessile, crowded in small heads or terminal spikes up to 2 in. long, often interrupted near the base. Flowers $\frac{1}{2}$–$\frac{3}{4}$ in. long, blue. Calyx hairy; teeth linear-lanceolate, spinous, shorter than the tube. Corolla-tube twice as long as the calyx.

W. Himalaya, 7000–11,000 ft.; May–August.

2. **Nepeta campestris,** *Benth.*; *Fl. Br. Ind.* iv. 658. Pubescent; stems erect, 1–3 ft. Leaves sessile, oblong-lanceolate, 1–2 × $\frac{1}{2}$–$\frac{3}{4}$ in., toothed. Whorls sessile, crowded in terminal or axillary spikes often interrupted near the base. Flowers $\frac{1}{2}$ in. long, blue. Calyx hairy; teeth linear-lanceolate, nearly as long as the tube, acute. Corolla-tube longer than the calyx, widely dilated near the mouth.

Simla; May–August.—W. Himalaya, 7000–9000 ft.

3. **Nepeta elliptica,** *Royle*; *Fl. Br. Ind.* iv. 658. Stems densely hairy, ascending. Leaves sessile, hairy or pubescent, ovate-oblong, $\frac{1}{2}$–1$\frac{1}{2}$ in.; teeth small, close-set, regular, acute. Whorls sessile, crowded in terminal spikes up to 3 in. long, usually interrupted at the base. Flowers about $\frac{1}{3}$ in. long, pale blue or nearly white. Calyx hairy; teeth linear-lanceolate, as long as the tube, acute. Corolla-tube hardly longer than the calyx.

Simla, Mushobra, on grassy downs; July–October.—W. Himalaya, 5000–8000 ft.

4. **Nepeta spicata,** *Benth.*; *Fl. Br. Ind.* iv. 659. Glabrous or pubescent; stems erect, 1–3 ft. Leaves stalked, usually cordate, ovate or triangular, 1–3 × 1–1$\frac{1}{2}$ in., crenate or sharply toothed. Whorls sessile, crowded in terminal spikes up to 4 in. long, sometimes interrupted near the base. Flowers $\frac{1}{2}$ in. long, purple-blue. Calyx-teeth linear-lanceolate, acute, as long as the tube. Corolla-tube much longer than the calyx.

Simla, common; July–October.—W. Himalaya, 6000–10,000 ft.

5. **Nepeta distans,** *Benth.*; *Fl. Br. Ind.* iv. 660. Softly tomentose; stems erect, 6–18 in., often tufted. Leaves few, stalked, oblong or lanceolate, 1–1$\frac{1}{2}$ in., crenate. Whorls sessile, crowded in terminal spikes more or less interrupted near the base. Flowers $\frac{1}{3}$ in. long, pale pink, spotted with purple. Calyx glabrous or nearly so, curved; teeth linear-lanceolate, acute, much shorter than the tube. Corolla-tube much longer than the calyx.

Simla, common; April–October.—W. Himalaya, 6000–9000 ft.

6. **Nepeta ciliaris,** *Benth.*; *Fl. Br. Ind.* iv. 661. Softly tomentose; stems erect, 2–3 ft. Leaves stalked, cordate, broadly ovate, 1–1$\frac{1}{2}$ in., crenate, obtuse. Whorls sessile, crowded in

terminal spikes more or less interrupted near the base. Flowers $\frac{1}{3}$ in. long, lilac; bracts often tinged with purple. Calyx densely covered with long hairs; teeth linear-lanceolate, shorter than the tube, often tinged with purple. Corolla hairy; tube longer than the calyx.

Simla, Mahasu; July–October.—W. Himalaya, 6000–8000 ft.

7. **Nepeta ruderalis,** *Buch.-Ham.*; *Fl. Br. Ind.* iv. 661. Pubescent; stems erect or ascending, 6–18 in. Leaves stalked, cordate, broadly ovate or orbicular, $\frac{3}{4}$–2 in., crenate, obtuse. Whorls, at least the lower ones, distinctly stalked, distant nearly throughout

FIG. 127. NEPETA LEUCOPHYLLA.

the spike. Flowers $\frac{1}{4}$ in. long, blue or purple, minutely darker dotted. Calyx hairy; teeth linear-lanceolate, shorter than the tube. Corolla pubescent, slightly longer than the calyx.

Valleys below Simla; July–October.—Throughout India, common on roadsides, ascending to 4000 ft.

8. **Nepeta leucophylla,** *Benth.*; *Fl. Br. Ind.* iv. 662. Hoary-tomentose; stems erect, 2–3 ft. Leaves stalked, cordate, ovate, $\frac{3}{4}$–$1\frac{1}{2} \times \frac{1}{2}$–$\frac{3}{4}$ in., crenate, obtuse, lower surface silvery white. Whorls, at least the lower ones, distinctly stalked and distant, interrupted nearly throughout the spike. Flowers $\frac{1}{2}$ in. long,

lilac or blue. Calyx hairy; teeth linear-lanceolate, shorter than the tube. Corolla hairy, twice as long as the calyx. (Fig. 127.)

Simla, common on stony ground; July–October.—W. Himalaya, 4000–8000 ft.

9. **Nepeta graciliflora,** *Benth.*; *Fl. Br. Ind.* iv. 663. Pubescent or nearly glabrous; stems slender, 1–3 ft., erect or ascending. Leaves stalked, cordate, ovate, 1–1¾ × ¾–1½ in., crenate or sharply toothed. Whorls, except the uppermost, distinctly stalked; lower ones axillary; upper more or less distant. Flowers ⅓ in. long, pale lilac, on long, slender stalks, forming narrow, loose, often drooping panicles; bracts linear. Calyx-teeth linear-lanceolate, shorter than the tube. Corolla pubescent; tube hardly longer than the calyx.

Valleys below Simla; flowers during the cold season.—Central and Northern India, ascending to 4000 ft.

10. **Nepeta Govaniana,** *Benth.*; *Fl. Br. Ind.* iv. 663. Pubescent; stems erect, 2–4 ft. Leaves stalked, ovate or ovate-oblong, 3–6 × 1½–3 in., crenate. Whorls distant, lower ones stalked. Flowers 1–1¼ in. long, yellow. Calyx straight, tubular, 2-lipped in fruit; teeth triangular, much shorter than the tube. Corolla-tube much longer than the calyx, curved, widely dilated towards the mouth.

Narkunda, in forest; September.—W. Himalaya, 8000–10,000 ft.

11. **Nepeta erecta,** *Benth.*; *Fl. Br. Ind.* iv. 663. Pubescent; stems erect, 1–3 ft. Leaves stalked, cordate, ovate or oblong, 2–3 × 1¼–1½ in., crenate, obtuse or acute. Whorls distant, sessile or nearly so, lower ones axillary. Flowers ¾–1 in. long, blue. Calyx tubular, curved; teeth triangular, much shorter than the tube. Corolla-tube much longer than the calyx, curved, widely dilated towards the mouth.

Mushobra, Narkunda, in forest; June–September.—W. Himalaya, 6000–10,000 ft.

18. **SCUTELLARIA.** From the Latin *scutella*, a small cup, referring to the shape of the calyx.—N. temperate and tropical regions, New Zealand, the Andes (Britain, Skullcap).

Perennial often shrub-like herbs; stems decumbent or ascending, usually diffuse, branching. Flowers solitary, axillary, forming terminal racemes; floral leaves often bract-like. Calyx broadly bell-shaped, 2-lipped; lips short, broad, entire, closing after flowering time, upper lip bearing on its back a small, transverse, scale-like protuberance; in fruit the upper lip falls off and the lower lip closes the calyx-mouth. Corolla-tube much longer than the calyx, sharply upcurved near the base, dilated upwards; limb small, 2-lipped, upper lip erect, hood-like, notched, lower spreading, 3-lobed. Stamens 4, in unequal pairs, ascending under the upper lip; anthers hairy.

Leaves lanceolate, $\frac{1}{3}$–$1\frac{1}{2}$ in. broad.
  Flowers $\frac{3}{4}$ in. long.
    Stems nearly terete. Flowers dark blue . . . 1. *S. grossa.*
    Branches 4-angled. Flowers pale yellow or nearly white . . . . 2. *S. angulosa.*
  Flowers $\frac{1}{3}$–$\frac{1}{2}$ in. long, dull yellow . . . . . . 3. *S. repens.*
Leaves linear, $\frac{1}{10}$–$\frac{1}{5}$ in. broad. Flowers pale purple with yellow tips . . . . 4. *S. linearis.*

1. **Scutellaria grossa,** *Wall.*; *Fl. Br. Ind.* iv. 669. Pubescent; stems slender, ascending, 1–2 ft., nearly terete. Leaves stalked, cordate or truncate, triangular or lanceolate, 1–3 × $\frac{3}{4}$–2 in., coarsely crenate, acute or obtuse. Flowers $\frac{3}{4}$ in. long, dark blue, lip partly white.

Simla, Mushobra; June–October.—W. Himalaya, 4000–8000 ft.

2. **Scutellaria angulosa,** *Benth.*; *Fl. Br. Ind.* iv. 669. Pubescent or thinly hairy; branches long, diffuse, acutely 4-angled. Leaves stalked, ovate or lanceolate, 1–2 in., coarsely crenate, acute; lower surface often purple. Racemes glandular. Flowers $\frac{3}{4}$–1 in. long, pale yellow or nearly white, tip tinged with purple.

Simla, common; April, May.—Temperate Himalaya, 4000–9000 ft.

3. **Scutellaria repens,** *Buch.-Ham.*; *Fl. Br. Ind.* iv. 669. Pubescent; branches long, diffuse, ascending, obtusely 4-angled. Leaves stalked, ovate, $\frac{1}{4}$–$1\frac{1}{2}$ in., lower ones usually toothed, upper entire. Racemes glandular. Flowers $\frac{1}{3}$–$\frac{1}{2}$ in. long, dull yellow, sometimes tinged with purple.

Valleys below Simla, in stony places; April–July.—Temperate Himalaya, 1000–6000 ft.

4. **Scutellaria linearis,** *Benth.*; *Fl. Br. Ind.* iv. 669. Pubescent; stems numerous, tufted, slender, terete, 6–18 in., procumbent or ascending. Leaves nearly sessile, linear, $\frac{1}{2}$–$1\frac{1}{2}$ × $\frac{1}{10}$–$\frac{1}{5}$ in., entire; margins recurved. Racemes hairy, often glandular. Flowers $\frac{3}{4}$–1 in. long, pale purple, tip of lower lip yellow.

Simla, Naldera; April–June.—W. Himalaya, 3000–8000 ft.

19. BRUNELLA. Etymology obscure.—Most temperate regions.

Brunella vulgaris, *Linn.*; *Fl. Br. Ind.* iv. 670. A thinly hairy, erect or ascending herb, 4–12 in. Leaves stalked, ovate or oblong, 1–2 in., entire or toothed, acute or obtuse. Flowers $\frac{1}{2}$–$\frac{3}{4}$ in. long, violet-purple, in whorls of 6 crowded in erect, terminal spikes 1–2 in. long and bearing a pair of sessile leaves at the base; floral leaves bract-like, hairy, purple-margined, broadly ovate, acute, overlapping. Calyx tinged with purple, bell-shaped, 2-lipped; upper lip broad, 3-toothed; lower deeply 2-lobed; mouth closed after flowering time. Corolla-tube broad, slightly longer than the calyx; limb 2-lipped, upper lip erect, hood-like, notched, lower spreading, 3-lobed, mid-lobe largest, minutely toothed. Stamens 4, in unequal pairs, ascending under the upper lip; filaments bearing a small tooth below the anthers.

Simla, roadsides, common; March-October.—Hilly districts throughout India, ascending to 10,000 ft.—Most temperate regions (Britain, Self-heal).

FIG. 128. CRANIOTOME VERSICOLOR.

20. CRANIOTOME. From the Greek *cranion*, the skull, and *tome*, a section; referring to the almost truncate limb of the corolla.—Himalaya; a single species.

Craniotome versicolor, *Reichb.*; *Fl. Br. Ind.* iv. 671. A softly hairy, erect, branching herb, 1–3 ft. Leaves stalked, cordate, broadly ovate, about 3×2 in., toothed. Flowers very numerous, minute, white, pink or yellow, crowded in small, stalked cymes forming narrow, terminal panicles. Calyx ovoid, equally 5-toothed, enlarged in fruit. Corolla-tube much longer than the calyx; limb 2-lipped, upper lip very short, erect, hood-like, lower longer, spreading, 3-lobed, mid-lobe largest. Stamens 4, in unequal pairs, ascending under the upper lip, outer or anterior pair longer than the inner. (Fig. 128.)

Simla, in woods; August–October.—Temperate Himalaya, 5000–7000 ft.

21. ANISOMELES. From the Greek *anisos*, unequal, and *melos*, a member, limb; referring to the anthers of the longer stamens.—Warm regions of Asia and Australia.

Anisomeles ovata, *R. Br.*; *Fl. Br. Ind.* iv. 672. An erect, hairy herb, 3–6 ft. Leaves stalked, ovate, 1–3 in., crenate. Flowers ½ in. long, white except the purple mid-lobe of the lower lip, crowded in axillary whorls forming more or less interrupted, terminal spikes. Calyx ovoid; teeth 5, lanceolate, acute. Corolla-tube hardly longer than the calyx; limb 2-lipped, upper lip short, erect, concave, entire, lower 3-lobed, spreading, mid-lobe much longer than the lateral, deeply notched. Stamens 4, in unequal pairs, protruding from under the upper lip, outer or anterior pair longer than the inner.

Valleys below Simla, Sipi; August–October.—Throughout India, ascending to 5000 ft.—Tropical Asia.

22. STACHYS. The Greek for an ear or spike of corn, and the classical name of *S. palestina*; referring to the inflorescence.—Most temperate regions; absent from Australia and New Zealand (Britain, Woundwort).

Stachys sericea, *Wall.*; *Fl. Br. Ind.* iv. 675. An erect herb covered with long, silky hairs; stems 2–4 ft., usually unbranched. Leaves stalked, cordate, ovate or oblong, $2\frac{1}{2}$–$4 \times 1\frac{1}{4}$–$2\frac{1}{4}$ in., crenate or sharply toothed. Flowers $\frac{1}{2}$–$\frac{3}{4}$ in. long, pink, spotted with purple, crowded in axillary whorls forming more or less interrupted, long, terminal spikes. Calyx bell-shaped, 10-nerved; teeth 5, lanceolate, spine-tipped, often tinged with pink. Corolla hairy; tube cylindric, hardly longer than the calyx; limb 2-lipped, upper lip erect, hood-like, entire, lower spreading, 3-lobed, mid-lobe broad, much longer than the lateral, notched. Stamens 4, in unequal pairs, ascending under the upper lip, outer or anterior pair longer than the inner.

Simla, Mushobra, common; July–October.—Temperate Himalaya, 6000–9000 ft.—W. Asia.

23. LEONURUS. From the Greek *leon*, a lion, and *oura*, a tail; referring to the inflorescence.—Temperate Asia, N. America, Europe.

Leonurus Cardiaca, *Linn.*; *Fl. Br. Ind.* iv. 678. A pubescent, erect herb, 2–4 ft. Leaves stalked; lower ovate-lanceolate, about 5 × 3 in., deeply and irregularly cut into several coarsely toothed lobes; upper narrow, lobed or nearly entire. Flowers

$\frac{1}{2}$ in. long, pink, crowded in axillary whorls forming more or less interrupted, long, terminal spikes; bracts spinous. Calyx shortly tubular; teeth 5, triangular, spine-tipped, spreading. Corolla hairy, especially the upper lip; tube hardly longer than the calyx-tube; limb 2-lipped, upper lip erect, hoodlike, entire, lower spreading, 3-lobed, mid-lobe longest, entire. Stamens 4, in unequal pairs, ascending under the upper lip, outer or anterior pair longer than the inner.

Narkunda, in forest; July.—W. Himalaya, 6000–10,000 ft.—W. Asia, Europe (Britain, Motherwort).

24. LAMIUM. The Latin name of the Deadnettle, *L. maculatum*.—Temperate Asia, N. Africa, Europe.

Hairy, decumbent or ascending herbs. Flowers in axillary whorls; lower whorls distant; uppermost often crowded in a leafy head. Calyx bell-shaped, 10-nerved; teeth 5, narrow, acute. Corolla hairy; tube slender at the base, much widened to the mouth, longer than the calyx; limb 2-lipped, upper lip erect, arching, hood-like, lateral lobes of lower lip small or obsolete, terminal lobe broadly orbicular, notched or 2-lobed, abruptly contracted at the base. Stamens 4, in unequal pairs, ascending under the upper lip. Nutlets 3-angled.

Floral leaves sessile, orbicular. Flowers $\frac{1}{2}$–$\frac{3}{4}$ in. long, purple-red . . . . 1. *L. amplexicaule.*
Floral leaves stalked, ovate. Flowers $\frac{3}{4}$–1 in. long, white or pale pink . . . . 2. *L. album.*

1. **Lamium amplexicaule,** *Linn.*; *Fl. Br. Ind.* iv. 679. A decumbent, much branched annual, 4–12 in. Leaves orbicular; lower long-stalked, $\frac{1}{4}$–$\frac{3}{4}$ in. across, crenate. Flowers $\frac{1}{2}$–$\frac{3}{4}$ in. long, purple-red; floral leaves sessile, larger than the stem leaves, deeply crenate. Calyx-teeth as long as the tube, converging in fruit. Lateral lobes of corolla obsolete or minute.

Simla, common on borders of fields; April–October.—N. India, ascending to 10,000 ft.—W. Asia, N. Africa, Europe (Britain, Henbit).

2. **Lamium album,** *Linn.*; *Fl. Br. Ind.* iv. 679. A decumbent or ascending perennial, 6–18 in.; rootstock creeping. Leaves all stalked, cordate, ovate, $1\frac{1}{2}$–3 in., coarsely and sharply toothed. Flowers $\frac{3}{4}$–1 in. long, white or pale pink. Calyx-teeth longer than the tube, spreading in fruit. Lateral lobes of corolla narrow, reflexed, sometimes furnished with a small tooth.

Simla, roadsides, common; April–October.—W. Himalaya, 5000–10,000 ft. —W. Asia, N. Africa, Europe (Britain, White Deadnettle).

25. ROYLEA. In honour of Dr. J. F. Royle, Bengal Army, a distinguished botanist of the nineteenth century.—W. Himalaya; a single species.

Roylea elegans, *Wall.*; *Fl. Br. Ind.* iv. 679. An erect shrub, 3–5 ft.; branches terete, pale brown, finely tomentose. Leaves shortly stalked, hairy, ovate, 1–1½ in., crenate, acute. Flowers ½ in. long, white, tinged with pink, in axillary whorls. Calyx-tube cylindric, 10-nerved; lobes 5, erect, oblong, net-veined, obtuse. Corolla hairy, hardly longer than the calyx; tube cylindric; limb 2-lipped, upper lip erect, hood-like, entire, lower 3-lobed, spreading, midlobe longest, entire. Stamens 4, in unequal pairs, ascending under the upper lip, outer or anterior pair longer than the inner.

Sutlej and Giri valleys; May–October.—W. Himalaya, 2000–5000 ft.

FIG. 129. LEUCAS LANATA.

26. LEUCAS. From the Greek *leucos*, white; referring to the flowers.—Warm regions of Asia, Africa and Australia.

Erect, woolly or hairy herbs. Flowers white, in axillary or terminal whorls. Calyx tubular; teeth 10, short, erect, equal or slightly unequal. Corolla-tube cylindric, included; limb 2-lipped, upper lip erect, hood-like, very hairy, lower much longer, spreading, 3-lobed, mid-lobe the largest, entire. Stamens 4, in unequal pairs, ascending under the upper lip, outer or anterior pair longer than the inner

Leaves $\frac{1}{2}$–1 in. broad, toothed.
  Leaves softly woolly. Whorls axillary . . . . 1. *L. lanata.*
  Leaves roughly hairy. Whorls crowded in globose, terminal heads . . . . 2. *L. Cephalotes.*
Leaves less than $\frac{1}{4}$ in. broad, entire . . . . . . 3. *L. hyssopifolia.*

1. **Leucas lanata,** *Benth.*; *Fl. Br. Ind.* iv. 681. Perennial, 12–18 in., clothed with soft, white, woolly tomentum. Leaves shortly stalked or nearly sessile, ovate or oblong, 1–2 × $\frac{1}{2}$–1 in., crenate or sharply toothed. Flowers $\frac{1}{2}$ in. long, in numerous, small, axillary whorls. Calyx woolly. (Fig. 129.)

Simla, common on stony ground; June–October.—Throughout India on dry hills, ascending to 8000 ft.—Burmah, S. China.

2. **Leucas Cephalotes,** *Spreng.*; *Fl. Br. Ind.* iv. 689. Annual, 1–3 ft., roughly hairy. Leaves shortly stalked, ovate-lanceolate, 2–4 × $\frac{1}{2}$–1 in., toothed. Flowers 1 in. long, crowded in globose, terminal whorls 1–2 in. diam., surrounded by numerous, lanceolate, hairy bracts. Calyx hairy near the top, otherwise glabrous.

Valleys below Simla, common in fields; July–October.—Throughout India, ascending to 6000 ft.

3. **Leucas hyssopifolia,** *Benth.*; *Fl. Br. Ind.* iv. 690. Perennial, 4–8 in., roughly hairy. Leaves sessile, linear, 1–2 × $\frac{1}{8}$–$\frac{1}{4}$ in., entire. Flowers $\frac{3}{4}$ in. long, in small, axillary and terminal whorls. Calyx glabrous.

Valleys below Simla in grassy places; flowers during the cold season.—N. India, ascending to 3000 ft.

27. **PHLOMIS.** A Greek plant-name, probably of a *Verbascum.*—Temperate Asia, N. Africa, E. Europe.

Phlomis bracteosa, *Royle*; *Fl. Br. Ind.* iv. 693. An erect, hairy herb, 1–3 ft. Leaves cordate, ovate, 2–4 in., crenate. Flowers nearly 1 in. long, dull blue-purple, crowded in large, axillary whorls 1–1$\frac{1}{2}$ in. across. Calyx tubular; teeth 5, linear-lanceolate, acute. Corolla-tube included; limb 2-lipped, upper lip erect, hood-like, very hairy, lower spreading, 3-lobed, midlobe the longest. Stamens 4, in unequal pairs, ascending under the upper lip, outer or anterior pair longer than the inner pair.

Simla, on Jako, Mushobra, in forest; August–October.—W. Himalaya, 5000–11,000 ft.—W. Asia.

28. **TEUCRIUM.** From *teucrion*, the Greek name of a species of this genus.—Most temperate and warm regions (Britain, Germander).

Erect or ascending herbs. Leaves ovate or oblong-ovate. Flowers in pairs, forming erect racemes. Calyx bell-shaped,

10-nerved; teeth 5, unequal, upper one broadest. Corolla-tube dilated upwards; limb 1-lipped, upper lip wanting, lower lip long, spreading, 5-lobed, lateral lobes tooth-like, acute, terminal lobe broad, concave. Stamens 4, in unequal pairs, protruding from the back of the corolla-mouth.

Flowers white or yellow-white. Corolla-tube twice as long as the calyx . . . . 1. *T. Royleanum.*
Flowers pink or purple. Corolla-tube hardly longer than the calyx . . . . 2. *T. quadrifarium.*

1. **Teucrium Royleanum,** *Wall.*; *Fl. Br. Ind.* iv. 700. Tomentose or hairy; stems 10–18 in., ascending. Leaves stalked, cordate, ovate or oblong-ovate, 1½–2½ in., crenate or sharply toothed, acute. Racemes seldom more than 2–3 in. Flowers nearly ½ in. long, white or yellow-white; floral leaves bract-like, narrowly lanceolate, less than ¼ in. long, inconspicuous. Corolla-tube twice as long as the calyx.

Mahasu; July.—W. Himalaya, 3000–6000 ft.—W. Asia.

2. **Teucrium quadrifarium,** *Buch.-Ham.*; *Fl. Br. Ind.* iv. 170. Tomentose or hairy; stems 2–4 ft., erect. Leaves shortly stalked, cordate, ovate or oblong-ovate, 1½–3 in., toothed, acute or obtuse. Racemes up to 6 in. long, 4-sided in bud. Flowers ½ in. long, pink or purple, almost concealed by the conspicuous bracts; floral leaves bract-like, red-purple, broadly ovate, abruptly pointed, ⅓ in. long, overlapping in bud. Corolla-tube hardly longer than the calyx.

Simla, common; August–October.—Temperate Himalaya, 4000–8000 ft.—Burmah, China.

29. **AJUGA.** Origin of name obscure.—Temperate regions of the Old World (Britain, Bugle).

Softly hairy herbs; stems 4–12 in., erect or ascending. Leaves ovate or oblong. Flowers small, crowded in axillary whorls forming leafy spikes, more or less interrupted near the base. Calyx ovoid; teeth 5, acute, nearly equal. Corolla-tube slightly dilated at the mouth; limb 2-lipped, upper lip very short, erect, flat, -lobed, lower much longer, spreading, 3-lobed, lateral lobes oblong, midlobe longer, broader, notched. Stamens 4, in unequal pairs, protruding from under the upper lip or included in the tube.

Flowers nearly ⅓ in. long. Stamens protruding . . . 1. *A. bracteosa.*
Flowers hardly ¼ in. long. Stamens included . . . 2. *A. parviflora.*

1. **Ajuga bracteosa,** *Wall.*; *Fl. Br. Ind.* iv. 702. Stems erect or ascending, usually diffusely branching from the base. Leaves ovate, 1–4 in., toothed or nearly entire, lower ones stalked, upper sessile. Flowers nearly ⅓ in. long, pale blue or lilac; floral leaves

smaller. Corolla-tube nearly twice as long as the calyx. Stamens protruding from under the upper lip.

Simla; April–October.—N. India, ascending to 7000 ft.—Temperate Asia, Africa.

2. **Ajuga parviflora,** *Benth.*; *Fl. Br. Ind.* iv. 703. Stems ascending, diffusely branched from the base. Leaves sessile or shortly stalked, ovate or oblong, 2–6 in., toothed or nearly entire, lower surface often tinged with purple; radical leaves spreading. Flowers hardly ¼ in. long, blue; floral leaves smaller. Corolla-tube hardly longer than the calyx. Stamens included within the tube.

Simla, common; March–October.—W. Himalaya, 2000–7000 ft.—W. Asia.

LXXVI. PLANTAGINACEÆ

A SMALL Order widely spread over the globe, but most abundant in the temperate regions of the Old World.

PLANTAGO. The classical name of the common species of Plantain, *P. major*.—Distribution of the Order.

Perennial, glabrous or pubescent, stemless herbs. Leaves radical, tufted or spreading, simple, prominently ribbed. Scapes nearly erect, naked, furrowed. Flowers numerous, small, green, regular, usually 2-sexual, crowded in terminal, cylindric or ovoid spikes. Calyx free, 4-parted; segments nearly equal, usually distinct. Corolla hypogynous, scarious; tube cylindric, about as long as the calyx; limb 4-lobed. Stamens 4, attached to the corolla-tube, alternate with the lobes; anthers large, pendulous, versatile. Ovary free, 2-celled; style thread-like, undivided; ovules one or more in each cell. Capsule small, membranous, enclosed in the persistent calyx, opening transversely near the base; seeds 2–16, small, black.

Capsule containing 8–16 seeds. Spike cylindric, 3–15 in. long . . . . 1. *P. major*.
Capsule containing 2–4 seeds.
  Spikes ovoid or shortly cylindric, 1–1½ in. long . . . 2. *P. lanceolata*.
  Spikes cylindric, 3–4 in. long . . . . 3. *P. tibetica*.

1. **Plantago major,** *Linn.*; *Fl. Br. Ind.* iv. 705. Leaves distinctly stalked, broadly ovate or oblong-ovate, about $5 \times 2\frac{1}{2}$ in., usually 7-ribbed, entire or sinuate. Scapes 3–8 in. Spikes cylindric, seldom less than 3, sometimes attaining 15 in. in length. Stamens protruding. Capsule containing 8–16 minute seeds.

Simla, roadsides; April–October.—Hilly districts throughout India, ascending to 10,000 ft.—Westward to the Atlantic (Britain).

2. **Plantago lanceolata,** *Linn.*; *Fl. Br. Ind.* iv. 706. Leaves lanceolate, 3–8 × $\frac{3}{4}$–1 in., 3–5-ribbed, nearly or quite entire, tapering downwards in a short stalk. Scapes 12–18 in., deeply furrowed. Spikes ovoid or shortly cylindric, 1–1$\frac{1}{2}$ in. long. Two lower sepals usually united. Stamens far protruding. Capsule containing 2–4 oblong seeds.

Simla, roadsides; April–October.—W. Himalaya, 5000–8000 ft.—N. Asia, Europe (Britain).

FIG. 130. PLANTAGO TIBETICA.

3. **Plantago tibetica,** *Hook. f. & Thoms.*; *Fl. Br. Ind.* iv. 706. Leaves ovate or ovate-lanceolate, 2–3 × $\frac{3}{4}$–1 in., usually 5-ribbed, toothed, tapering downwards in a short stalk. Scapes 2–6 in. Spikes cylindric, 3–4 in. Stamens protruding. Capsule containing 2–4 ovoid seeds. (Fig. 130.)

Simla, roadsides; April–October.—W. Himalaya, 4000–10,000 ft.

LXXVII. NYCTAGINACEÆ

PERENNIAL herbs. Leaves opposite, simple, entire or sinuate; stipules none. Flowers small or minute, in *Oxybaphus* enclosed by a bell-shaped involucre, 2-sexual, regular, solitary or in small heads at the end of axillary stalks, usually forming loose, terminal panicles. Perianth hypogynous, pink or red, tubular, contracted

FIG. 131. BOERHAAVIA REPENS.

above the ovary; limb spreading, falling off after flowering; tube persistent. Stamens 2–4, hypogynous. Ovary free, 1-celled; style simple, stigma small, terminal; ovule solitary. Fruit consisting of the hardened perianth-tube adherent to an indehiscent, membranous, 1-seeded utricle.—Name derived from the Greek *nux*, night, the flowers of some species open in the evening and fall off at sunrise.—Chiefly tropical America.

The Marvel of Peru, *Mirabilis Jalapa*, is a common escape from gardens; it bears a profusion of red, white, yellow or variegated flowers, scarcely differing in structure from *Boerhaavia*.

Flowers solitary, each enclosed by a bell-shaped involucre . . 1. *Oxybaphus*.
Flowers in small heads. Involucre none. . . . . . 2. *Boerhaavia*.

1. OXYBAPHUS. From the Greek *oxybaphon*, a saucer; referring to the involucre.—America; and this one Himalayan species.

***Oxybaphus himalaicus,** *Edgew.*; *Fl. Br. Ind.* iv. 708. Glandular-hairy; stems 2–4 ft., ascending, branched. Leaves stalked, ovate, $1\frac{1}{2}$–$2\frac{1}{2}$ × 1–2 in., cordate, acute. Flowers solitary on long, slender, axillary stalks forming a loose panicle, each enclosed in a persistent, bell-shaped, 5-toothed involucre $\frac{1}{4}$ in. long. Perianth pink. Stamens 4, included. Fruit rough, black, ovoid, 5 in. long.

Kulu to Garhwal, 6000–9000 ft.; July–September.

2. BOERHAAVIA. In honour of Herman Boerhaave, a famous Dutch physician of the eighteenth century.—Nearly all warm regions.

Boerhaavia repens, *Linn.*; *Fl. Br. Ind.* iv. 709. Pubescent or nearly glabrous; stems 6–24 in., ascending, diffusely branched. Leaves stalked, one in each pair alternately smaller than the opposite one, ovate, $\frac{1}{2}$–2 in., cordate, entire or sinuate, obtuse; upper surface rough, green; lower smooth, silvery-white. Flowers minute, crowded in small, bracteate heads at the end of long, slender, axillary stalks often forming loose, terminal panicles. Perianth red; limb 5-lobed. Stamens 2 or 3, anthers protruding. Fruit $\frac{1}{8}$ in., 5-ribbed, viscidly glandular. (Fig. 131.)

Valleys below Simla; January–December.—Throughout India, ascending to 6000 ft.—Tropical and subtropical Asia, Africa and America.

LXXVIII. ILLECEBRACEÆ

A small Order, widely diffused except in cold regions, represented in the Himalaya by a single species.—Name of doubtful origin.

HERNIARIA. From the Latin *hernia*, a rupture; referring to its supposed curative properties.—W. and Central Asia, N. Africa, Europe (Britain).

***Herniaria hirsuta,** *Linn.*; *Fl. Br. Ind.* iv. 712. A small, perennial, prostrate, hairy herb; branches numerous, 2–8 in., spreading from the base. Leaves opposite, shortly stalked, narrowly ovate, $\frac{1}{10}$–$\frac{1}{3}$ in.; stipules scarious. Flowers minute, 2-sexual, regular, nearly sessile in axillary clusters. Perianth green, hairy outside, smooth within, 5-parted; segments ovate, acute, spreading. Stamens 5, opposite to and shorter than the perianth-lobes, alternate with 5 staminodes. Ovary free, globose, 1-celled; styles 2, short, diverging; ovule solitary. Fruit an ovoid, indehiscent, smooth, 1-seeded utricle enclosed in the persistent perianth.

Kashmir to Kumaon; May–October.—N.W. India, ascending to 8000 ft.—Westward to the Atlantic.

LXXIX. AMARANTACEÆ

HERBS or undershrubs. Leaves opposite or alternate, simple, entire or nearly so. Flowers small or minute, with a bract and 2 bracteoles at the base of each, 2-sexual, rarely polygamous, spicate, racemose or paniculate; bracts and bracteoles scarious. Perianth herbaceous or dry, persistent, 5- rarely 4-parted; segments imbricate, nearly equal, usually erect. Stamens 5, rarely fewer, hypogynous, opposite the perianth-segments, united at or near the base, often with interposed staminodes. Ovary usually ovoid, free, 1-celled; style simple, stigma usually capitate; ovules few or solitary. Fruit berry-like or a dry, membranous utricle usually enclosed in the persistent perianth, breaking up irregularly or opening by a horizontal line; seeds few or solitary, usually black, shining and kidney-shaped.—Name derived from the Greek *a*, not, and *maraino*, to wither; the flowers last a long time.—Tropical and subtropical regions.

Amarantus paniculatus, *Linn.*; *Fl. Br. Ind.* iv. 718, is a common rainy season crop in the hills, conspicuous from afar by reason of its tall stems and numerous, long, erect spikes of red or yellow flowers. It is cultivated throughout India and up to 9000 ft. in the Himalaya. Native name *Bathu*.

A. caudatus, *Linn.*; *Fl. Br. Ind.* iv. 719, the Love-lies-bleeding of English gardens, is occasionally cultivated; it resembles the preceding except that the long, tail-like spikes are drooping.

Perianth herbaceous. Fruit succulent.	
Perianth-segments spreading or reflexed . . .	1. *Deeringia*.
Perianth-segments erect.	3. *Bosia*.
Perianth scarious. Fruit dry.	
Flowers in long, terminal, simple spikes.	
Spikes silvery-shining. Flowers erect . . .	2. *Celosia*.
Spikes dull green, often tinged with purple. Flowers soon deflexed	6. *Achyranthes*.
Flowers in short spikes, axillary or paniculate.	
Spikes very short, head-like, all axillary. Perianth glabrous.	7. *Alternanthera*.
Spikes ¼–1 in. long, axillary or paniculate. Perianth hairy	5. *Ærua*.
Flowers in globose whorls containing numerous, hooked perianth-lobes and aggregated in terminal or panicled spikes.	4. *Cyathula*.

1. DEERINGIA. In honour of G. C. Deering, a botanist of the eighteenth century.—Most warm regions of the Old World.

Deeringia celosioides, *R. Br.*; *Fl. Br. Ind.* iv. 714. A climbing undershrub with long, arching branches. Leaves alternate, stalked, ovate or broadly lanceolate, 2–5 in., long-pointed. Flowers shortly stalked, pale yellow-green, in simple or branched racemes 4–10 in. long, forming terminal panicles. Perianth herbaceous, 5-parted; segments ovate, concave, spreading or reflexed. Stamens 5, united at the base. Ovary ovoid; style short, 3-parted. Fruit berry-like, red, globose, nearly $\frac{1}{4}$ in. diam., seated on the persistent perianth and containing usually 3 small seeds at the base of the cavity.

Sutlej valley; July–October.—N. India, ascending to 5000 ft.—Tropica Asia, Australia.

2. CELOSIA. Etymology doubtful.—Most tropical regions.

Celosia argentea, *Linn.*; *Fl. Br. Ind.* iv. 714. An erect, annual, glabrous herb, 1–3 ft. Leaves alternate, stalked or nearly sessile, linear or narrowly lanceolate, 1–6 in. Flowers white, shining, crowded in ovoid or cylindric, terminal, simple spikes 1–8 in. long, resembling the inflorescence of a grass, often pink at the tip. Perianth scarious, 5-parted; segments lanceolate, acute. Stamens 5, united at the base in a short tube. Ovary ovoid; style long, tip 2-lobed. Fruit dry, membranous, ovoid, enclosed by the perianth and containing several small seeds at the base of the cavity.

Valleys below Simla, common in fields and hedges; May–October.—Throughout India, ascending to 4000 ft.—Most tropical regions.

3. BOSIA. In honour of E. G. Bose, a German botanist of the eighteenth century.—N.W. India, S. Europe, Canary Islands.

Bosia Amherstiana, *Hook. f.*; *Fl. Br. Ind.* iv. 716. A glabrous, erect shrub. Leaves alternate, shortly stalked, ovate-lanceolate, $2\frac{1}{2}$–$5 \times 1\frac{1}{2}$–3 in., acute. Flowers green, nearly sessile, crowded in axillary, simple or compound spikes, erect or forming a spreading, terminal panicle. Perianth herbaceous, 5- or 4-parted; segments erect, ovate, concave, margins membranous. Stamens 5 or 4; filaments long, protruding, united at the base. Ovary oblong; style short, stigmas 2, thick, persistent. Fruit berry-like, red, globose, $\frac{1}{5}$ in. diam.

Simla, common, ascending to 6500 ft.; May–October.—Kashmir to Yarkand.

4. CYATHULA. The Greek for a small cup; referring to the flower.—Warm regions of Asia, Africa and America.

Straggling undershrubs. Leaves opposite, shortly stalked, broadly ovate, long-pointed. Flowers white, shining, in small clusters crowded in globose whorls forming terminal, often panicled spikes, each cluster containing 1 or 2 perfect flowers and several imperfect ones which are reduced to a single, hooked perianth-segment. Perfect flowers: perianth scarious, 5-parted, segments narrowly lanceolate, acute; stamens 5, alternate with 5 oblong, fringed staminodes and united with them at the base; ovary ovoid,

FIG. 132. CYATHULA TOMENTOSA.

style slender, stigma capitate. Fruit a dry, ovoid utricle enclosed by the perianth and containing a single seed.

Leaves thick, tomentose. Spikes long . . . . . . 1. *C. tomentosa.*
Leaves thin, nearly glabrous. Spikes globose . . . . 2. *C. capitata.*

1. **Cyathula tomentosa,** *Moq.*; *Fl. Br. Ind.* iv. 722. Densely woolly. Leaves lanceolate to orbicular, 2–10 in. long, acute, shortly stalked. Spikes 2–6 in. long, stalked; clusters of flowers crowded or separated. Sepals linear-lanceolate, 2 or all ending in hooked awns, lengthening with age. (Fig. 132.)

Simla, common; August-October.—Kashmir to Sikkim and Khasia, 2000–7000 ft.

2. **Cyathula capitata,** *Moq.*; *Fl. Br. Ind.* iv. 722. Less hairy than *C. tomentosa*. Leaves shortly stalked, oval, acuminate, 2–5 in. long. Heads about 1 in. in diam., white, glistening.

Simla, common; August, September.—Kashmir to Sikkim, 6000–9000 ft.

5. **ÆRUA.** From *arua*, the Arabic name of this or an allied plant.—Warm regions of Asia and Africa.

Ærua scandens, *Wall.*; *Fl. Br. Ind.* iv. 727. A grey-tomentose, climbing undershrub. Leaves alternate or opposite, shortly stalked, hairy, ovate, 1–4 in., acute. Flowers polygamous, silvery white, crowded in shining, ovoid or oblong, sessile, axillary or paniculate spikes $\frac{1}{4}$–1 in. long. Perianth scarious, hairy outside, 5-parted; segments lanceolate, finely pointed. Stamens 5 or 4, usually unequal, alternate with 5 or 4 linear, short or long staminodes and united with them at the base. Ovary ovoid; style short, stigma capitate. Fruit a dry, ovoid utricle enclosed by the perianth and containing a single seed.

Valleys below Simla, common; July–October.—Throughout India, ascending to 6000 ft.—Tropical Asia and Africa.

6. **ACHYRANTHES.** From the Greek *achyron*, chaff, and *anthos*, a flower; referring to the scarious inflorescence.—Nearly all tropical and subtropical regions.

Straggling, more or less hairy undershrubs; stems usually dividing into long, rambling branches. Leaves opposite, shortly stalked. Flowers shining, dull green or tinged with purple, soon deflexed, crowded in long, terminal, simple spikes elongating as the fruit forms; bracts and bracteoles spinescent. Perianth stiff, scarious, 5-parted; segments lanceolate, acute. Stamens 5, alternate with 5 oblong staminodes and united with them at the base. Ovary oblong; style long, stigma capitate. Fruit an oblong utricle enclosed by the perianth and containing a single seed.

Leaves thick, leathery, not long-pointed. Spikes robust, up to 18 in. long . . . . 1. *A. aspera*.
Leaves thin, membranous, narrowed in a long, slender point. Spikes slender, rarely more than 4–5 in. long . . . 2. *A. bidentata*.

1. **Achyranthes aspera,** *Linn.*; *Fl. Br. Ind.* iv. 730. Leaves usually thick, leathery, broadly ovate or orbicular, 3–5 × 2–3 in. Spikes robust, up to 18 in. long.

Simla, common; May–October.—Throughout India, ascending to 7000 ft.—Most tropical regions.

2. **Achyranthes bidentata,** *Bl.*; *Fl. Br. Ind.* iv. 730. Leaves thin, membranous, ovate-lanceolate, 3–6 × 1$\frac{1}{2}$–3 in., narrowed upwards in a long, slender point. Spikes slender, rarely more than 4–5 in. long. Staminodes minutely toothed at the tip.

Simla, common; May-October.—Hilly districts throughout India, ascending to 7000 ft.—Tropical Asia.

7. ALTERNANTHERA. Of Latin origin, referring to the stamens.—Tropical and subtropical regions.

Alternanthera sessilis, *R. Br.*; *Fl. Br. Ind.* iv. 731. A prostrate or ascending, nearly glabrous herb, branching from the base, 6–18 in. Leaves opposite, nearly sessile, narrowly oblong or ovate, 1–3 in., obtuse. Flowers minute, white, crowded in shining, very short, head-like, sessile, axillary spikes. Perianth scarious, 5-parted; segments ovate, acute. Stamens 5, the alternate ones sometimes without anthers; filaments united at the base, anthers 1-celled. Ovary ovoid, notched at the top; style very short, stigma capitate. Fruit a dry, flattened utricle enclosed by the perianth and containing a single seed.

Valleys below Simla, in ricefields or ditches; July-October.—Throughout India, ascending to 4000 ft.—Most warm countries.

LXXX. CHENOPODIACEÆ

Erect or diffuse herbs, often with a meal-like covering. Leaves alternate, more or less lobed and toothed; stipules none. Flowers minute, green, usually 2-sexual, sessile, single or arranged in small clusters. Perianth-segments hypogynous, 5, rarely 3 or none, more or less united at the base. Stamens 5, rarely fewer, hypogynous, opposite the segments, anthers 2-celled. Ovary free, ovoid or flattened, 1-celled; stigmas 2 or 3. Fruit a utricle seated on or enclosed by the more or less thickened perianth or bracts; seed solitary, usually kidney-shaped, with a black, brittle, shell-like coat.—Spread over the whole world; specially abundant in Central Asian and African deserts.

The cultivated Beetroot, *Beta vulgaris*, and the Spinach, *Spinacia oleracea*, belong to this Order.

Flowers 2-sexual.
- Inflorescence spiny. Fruit exposed . . . . . 1. *Acroglochin.*
- Inflorescence smooth. Fruit enclosed in the persistent perianth . . . . 2. *Chenopodium.*

Flowers sexual. Fruit enclosed in 2 bracts . . . . 3. *Atriplex.*

1. ACROGLOCHIN. From the Greek *akros*, summit, and *glochin*, a point, referring to the spiny infloresence.—N. India, W. China.

***Acroglochin chenopodioides,** *Schrad.*; *Fl. Br. Ind.* v. 2. An erect, glabrous, branched herb, 1–2 ft. Leaves stalked, ovate,

1–2½ in., acute; margins irregularly lobed; teeth numerous, sharp, unequal. Flowers 2-sexual, clustered in short, axillary cymes bearing numerous, needle-like, barren branchlets. Perianth-segments 5, acute, persistent. Stamens 1–3. Stigmas 2. Utricle flattened, discoid, exposed, opening transversely.

Kashmir to Kumaon; July, August.—W. Himalaya, 5000–8000 ft.—China.

2. CHENOPODIUM. From the Greek *chen*, a goose, and *pous*, a foot; referring to the shape of the leaves.—Nearly the whole globe; (Britain, Goosefoot).

Erect herbs, glabrous, mealy or glandular-pubescent; stems angled and grooved. Leaves more or less sinuately lobed. Flowers 2-sexual, in small clusters sessile on short, axillary spikes or panicles, which are sometimes combined to form a large, terminal panicle. Perianth-segments 5, equal. Styles 2 or 3. Utricle enclosed in the slightly thickened perianth-segments.

Scentless or slightly fetid herbs. Flower-clusters in spikes.
  Leaves ovate or oblong, upper ones entire. Seeds smooth . . . . 1. *C. album.*
  Leaves broadly triangular, upper ones lobed. Seeds minutely dotted . . . . 2. *C. opulifolium.*
Strongly aromatic herbs. Flower-clusters in short, axillary panicles . . . . 3. *C. Botrys.*

1. **Chenopodium album,** *Linn.*; *Fl. Br. Ind.* v. 3. Often mealy-white especially on the flowers and under side of the leaves, sometimes pale green; stems 1–3 ft. Leaves stalked, extremely variable; lower ones ovate or oblong, 1–2 in., margins more or less sinuate, sometimes angular or toothed; upper usually narrow and entire. Flower-clusters in axillary spikes, often tinged with purple, the upper ones forming a long panicle leafy at the base. Utricle entirely covered by the persistent perianth; seeds smooth.

Simla, common in waste places; May–October.—Throughout India, ascending to 12,000 ft.—All regions (Britain, White Goosefoot).

Cultivated in the hills as a rainy season crop for its leaves and seeds. The cultivated plants are often 10 ft. high with leaves 4–6 in. long.

*2. **Chenopodium opulifolium,** *Schrad.*; *Fl. Br. Ind.* v. 3. Habit of and closely allied to *C. album.* Usually mealy. Leaves long-stalked, broadly triangular, about 1½ in. each way, margins sinuate or irregularly lobed; upper leaves similar to the lower. Utricle only partially covered by the persistent perianth; seeds minutely dotted.

Kashmir to Nepal; May–October.—N. India, ascending to 8000 ft.—N. and W. Asia, Europe.

3. **Chenopodium Botrys,** *Linn.*; *Fl. Br. Ind.* v. 3. Strongly aromatic, glandular-pubescent; stems 6–18 in.; branches numerous,

spreading and recurved. Leaves stalked, oblong, 1–3 in., pinnately lobed, the upper ones nearly entire. Flower-clusters in numerous, short, axillary panicles forming large, terminal panicles. Perianth glandular-pubescent. Seed smooth. (Fig. 133.)

Simla, May–October.—N.W. India ascending to 10,000 ft.—N. and W. Asia, N. Africa, Europe.

3. ATRIPLEX. Derivation obscure.—Temperate and tropical regions.

Fig. 133. Chenopodium Botrys.

***Atriplex crassifolia,** *C. A. Mey.*; *Fl. Br. Ind.* v. 5. An erect or diffuse herb, 1-2 ft., usually mealy; stems and branches white. Leaves stalked, oblong or ovate, 1–1½ in., entire or the margins sinuate, tip pointed or obtuse, base wedge-shaped or sagittate. Flowers 1-sexual, male and female on the same plant. Male flowers: bracts 2; perianth-segments and stamens 3 or 5; flower-clusters in long, terminal, slender, interrupted spikes. Female flowers: bracts 2; perianth none; stigmas 2; flower-clusters small, axillary, on the lower parts of the branches. Utricle enclosed by the much enlarged, leaf-like bracts each bearing a thick, white, convex, smooth disk on its base.

Plains of N.W. India, ascending to 8000 ft.; June–October.—Central and W. Asia.

The name *crassifolia*, thick-leaved, is not appropriate.

LXXXI. PHYTOLACCACEÆ

DIFFERS from *Chenopodiaceæ* in the larger number of stamens, and the compound ovary.

PHYTOLACCA. From the Greek *phyton*, a plant, and the French *lac*, lake-colour, referring to the crimson juice of the fruit.—Tropical and subtropical regions.

Phytolacca acinosa, *Roxb.*; *Fl. Br. Ind.* v. 21. A nearly glabrous, erect herb; stems 3–5 ft., robust, succulent. Leaves alternate, broadly lanceolate, 6–10 in., entire long-pointed, narrowed into a short stalk; stipules none. Flowers $\frac{1}{3}$ in. diam., pale green, 2-sexual, in leaf-opposed, cylindrical racemes 2–6 in. long; bracts linear. Perianth of 5 nearly separate segments. Stamens 8–10; filaments united at the base, anthers 2-celled, soon falling off. Ovary composed of 6–8 carpels arranged in a whorl, each with a short, recurved stigma. Fruit dark purple, succulent, crowded in an erect, thick raceme 4–8 in. long; carpels separating when ripe and each containing a single black, shining, kidney-shaped seed.

Cultivated and often seen as an escape near villages, 4000–9000 ft.; May, June.—China, Japan.

An introduced Chinese plant having poisonous properties, but the leaves are cooked and eaten.

LXXXII. POLYGONACEÆ

HERBS, rarely shrubs; stem and branches thickened at the joints. Leaves alternate, simple, rarely lobed; stipules membranous, more or less sheathing the stem. Flowers 2-, rarely 1-sexual, in racemes or panicles. Perianth of 5 or 6, rarely fewer segments. Stamens 5–8, rarely fewer; anthers 2-celled. Ovary free, flattened or 3-angled; styles 2 or 3, stigmas capitate or fringed; ovule 1. Nut hard, more or less covered by the persistent perianth; seed one.—A large Order inhabiting all temperate and cold regions.

A wild Rhubarb, *Rheum Emodi*, Wall., grows on the Chor and on Marali at 11,000–12,000 ft. It is 5–6 ft. high, with large leaves often 2 ft. diam., and an erect panicle 2–3 ft. long of small flowers.

Perianth 4- or 5-parted. Stigmas capitate.
  Nut enclosed in the perianth-segments . . . . . 1. *Polygonum*.
  Nut only partially enclosed in the perianth-segments . 2. *Fagopyrum*.
Perianth 6-parted. Stigmas fringed . . . . . . 3. *Rumex*.

1. POLYGONUM. From the Greek *polus*, many, and *gonu*, the knee, referring to the stem being often enlarged and bent at the joints.—Nearly all regions.

Herbs, rarely of shrubby habit; stems erect or prostrate. Leaves entire; stipules sheathing the stem, often fringed at the edge, usually becoming torn and jagged, minute and 2-partite only in *P. filicaule*. Flowers 2-sexual, small, shortly stalked, rarely sessile, usually pink or white, in bracteate clusters, axillary or forming racemes, heads or panicles; bracts flat or tubular, each containing usually 2–4 flowers. Perianth sometimes glandular, 4- or 5-cleft, the 2 outer segments usually the smaller. Stamens 4–8, rarely fewer, alternating with small, honey-secreting glands, except species 2 to 5; anthers attached by the centre. Ovary flattened or 3-angled; styles 2 or 3, free or more or less united, stigmas capitate. Nut 3-angled or flattened like a lens with convex faces, usually smooth and black, enclosed in and not longer than the perianth.

Stipules 2-parted, minute.

Stems straw-like, very slender. Flowers minute . . 1. *P. filicaule*.

Stipules tubular.

Stems erect or prostrate.
  Flowers axillary.
    Nerves of stipules prominent.
      Stems rough. Leaves ovate . . . . . 2. *P. recumbens*.
      Stems smooth. Leaves narrowly lanceolate . 3. *P. aviculare*.
    Nerves of stipules none or very faint.
      Perianth shortly toothed . . . . . . 4. *P. tubulosum*.
      Perianth deeply toothed . . . . . . 5. *P. plebejum*.
  Flowers in terminal racemes.
    Bracts flat.
      Bracts hairy. Styles 2. Nut flattened . . 6. *P. orientale*.
      Bracts glabrous. Styles 3. Nut 3-angled.
        Leaves ovate, cordate . . . . . . 7. *P. amplexicaule*.
        Leaves linear-lanceolate . . . . . 8. *P. Emodi*.
    Bracts tubular.
      Stipules not fringed at the margin.
        Leaves glabrous . . . . 9. *P. glabrum*.
        Leaves minutely hairy on the margins, mid-rib and nerves . . . . 10. *P. simlense*.
      Stipules fringed at the margin.
        Stipules hairy.
          Styles 2. Nut flattened . . . . . 11. *P. minus*.
          Styles 3. Nut 3-angled . . . . . 12. *P. Donii*.

Stipules glabrous or only minutely hairy on the nerves . . . . 13. *P. Hydropiper.*
Flowers in heads or short spikes.
Stems terete, not prickly.
Heads solitary or 2 together.
Leaf-stalks $\frac{1}{3}$–1 in., winged . . . . 14. *P. alatum.*
Leaf-stalks less than $\frac{1}{4}$ in., not winged . . 15. *P. capitatum.*
Heads in clusters or corymbs . . . . 16. *P. chinense.*
Stems square, prickly along the angles . . 17. *P. sagittatum.*
Flowers in large, erect panicles . . . . 18. *P. polystachyum.*
Stems twining. Nut enclosed in the 3 winged segments of the perianth . . . . 19. *P. pterocarpum.*

1. **Polygonum filicaule,** *Wall.*; *Fl. Br. Ind.* v. 25. Stems nearly erect, straw-like, tufted, 4–18 in., hairy below the joints and on the upper parts, glabrous elsewhere. Leaves distant, shortly stalked, hairy, ovate or broadly lanceolate, $\frac{1}{3}$–1 in.; stipules minute, 2-parted, hairy. Flowers very small, white, shortly stalked, in axillary and terminal clusters. Perianth 5-parted. Stamens 3 or 4; filaments very short. Styles 3, free, minute. Nut 3-angled.

Huttoo; August.—Temperate Himalaya, 9000–16,000 ft.

2. **Polygonum recumbens,** *Royle*; *Fl. Br. Ind.* v. 25. Stems and branches prostrate, 1–2 ft., grooved, rough, leafy, flowering throughout their length or sometimes barren. Leaves shortly stalked, rough especially on the edges and lower surface, broadly ovate, $\frac{1}{2}$–1 in., usually acute; stipules tubular, with 2 long bristles. Flowers small, white or pink, in axillary clusters. Perianth 4- or 5-parted. Stamens 4 or 5. Styles 3, free, minute. Nut 3-angled, smooth and shining.

Simla, common; July–September.—W. Himalaya, 4000–8000 ft.

3. **Polygonum aviculare,** *Linn.*; *Fl. Br. Ind.* v. 26, including *P. Roylei, Bab.*; *Trans. Linn. Soc.* xviii. p. 115. Stems and branches prostrate, 1–2 ft., smooth, leafy, finely grooved, flowering throughout their length or sometimes barren. Leaves nearly sessile, narrowly lanceolate, $\frac{1}{2}$–1 in., sometimes glandular-dotted; stipules tubular, long, nerves several, strong, straight, the tips more or less projecting. Flowers small, green, tipped with white or red, in axillary clusters. Perianth 4- or 5-parted. Stamens 4 or 5. Styles 3, free, minute. Nut 3-angled, minutely wrinkled.

Simla; June–October.—W. Himalaya, 6000–10,000 ft.—N. Asia, Europe including Britain (Knot-grass).

A very variable plant.

*4. **Polygonum tubulosum,** *Boiss.*; *Fl. Br. Ind.* v. 27. Stems and branches prostrate, wiry, rarely more than 6 in., leafy, angled, not grooved, flowering throughout their length. Leaves sessile, linear, less than $\frac{1}{2}$ in., crowded; stipules conspicuous, tubular, long, white, transparent, nerves none or very faint. Flowers very small, white or pink, sessile, in axillary clusters. Perianth shortly 4- or 5-toothed. Stamens usually 4 or 5. Styles 3, free, mimute. Nut 3-angled, smooth, shining.

N.W. Himalaya, 6000–7000 ft.; June–September.—W. Asia.

5. **Polygonum plebejum,** *R. Br.*; *Fl. Br. Ind.* v. 27. Stems and branches prostrate, 6–24 in., leafy, terete, finely grooved, smooth, flowering throughout their length. Leaves linear or narrowly obovate, rarely more than $\frac{1}{2}$ in.; stipules tubular, short, transparent, nerves none or faint Flowers minute, white or pale pink, in axillary clusters half concealed among the stipules. Perianth 4- or 5-parted. Stamens 4 or 5. Styles 3, free, minute. Nut 3-angled, smooth, shining.

Valleys below Simla; April–October.—Throughout India, ascending to 5000 ft.—Asia, Africa, Australia.

A variable plant.

6. **Polygonum orientale,** *Linn.*; *Fl. Br. Ind.* v. 30. An erect, softly hairy herb; stems robust, 3–10 ft., grooved, branched. Leaves pubescent, long-stalked, ovate, $6–9 \times 2\frac{1}{2}–5$ in., acute; stipules tubular, mouth truncate, dilated, margin often green and lobed. Flowers red or white, in dense, erect or drooping racemes 2–4 in. long forming terminal panicles; bracts flat, ovate, densely hairy, each containing 3–6 flowers. Perianth 4- or 5-parted. Stamens 7 or 8. Styles 2, united for half their length. Nut round, flattened.

In swamps; April–November.—N. India, ascending to 5000 ft.—Tropical Asia, often cultivated.

7. **Polygonum amplexicaule,** *Don*; *Fl. Br. Ind.* v. 32. A nearly glabrous, erect herb; stems tufted, 2–3 ft., slender. Leaves few, distant, lower long-stalked, upper stem-clasping, ovate, 3–6 in., cordate, long-pointed, minutely crenate; stipules tubular, 1–2 in. Flowers pink or deep red, varying to white, $\frac{1}{6}–\frac{1}{3}$ in. diam., crowded in one or two erect racemes 2–6 in. long; bracts flat, scarious, glabrous, ovate, acute. Perianth 5-parted. Stamens 8. Styles 3, free, long. Nut 3-angled, smooth, shining.

Simla, Mahasu, common; June–October.—Temperate Himalaya, 6000–10,000 ft.

In the *Fl. Br. Ind.* this species is divided into the type, having flowers $\frac{1}{6}–\frac{1}{4}$ in. diam., and var. *speciosum* with broader leaves, shorter spikes and deep red flowers $\frac{1}{3}$ in. diam. Both forms occur at Simla, the latter variety usually at higher elevations.

8. **Polygonum Emodi,** *Meissn.*; *Fl. Br. Ind.* v. 33. Glabrous; stems woody, prostrate, rooting at the joints; branches 6–10 in., leafy, ascending. Leaves nearly sessile, stiff, linear-lanceolate, $1\frac{1}{2}–2$ in., acute; stipules tubular, 1 in., long-pointed, more or less divided from the tip, nerves many. Flowers red, in erect, terminal racemes $1–1\frac{1}{2}$ in., solitary or two together; bracts flat, ovate, acute.

glabrous, scarious. Perianth 5-parted. Stamens 8. Styles 3, united for half their length. Nut 3-angled, smooth, shining.

Jako, Matiana, Narkunda, on dry rocks; July–September.—Temperate Himalaya, 8000–11,000 ft.

9. **Polygonum glabrum,** *Willd.*; *Fl. Br. Ind.* v. 34. Glabrous; stems 2–4 ft., erect, branched. Leaves shortly stalked, broadly or narrowly lanceolate, 4–7 in., finely pointed, minutely glandular; stipules tubular, $\frac{3}{4}$ in., not fringed. Flowers pink or white, varying much in size, in erect, slender racemes 2–4 in. long, forming a terminal panicle; bracts tubular, glabrous. Perianth usually 5-parted. Stamens 6–8. Styles usually 2, sometimes 3, united below the middle. Nut usually rounded and flattened, 3-angled in the 3-styled flowers.

Simla, in ditches, etc.; May–October.—Throughout India, ascending to 6000 ft.—Tropical Asia, Africa, America.

10. **Polygonum simlense,** *Royle*; *Bab. in Trans. Linn. Soc.* xviii. (1841) 102, including var. *nodosum* and var. *laxum* of *P. lapathifolium, Linn.*; *Fl. Br. Ind.* v. 35. Stems 1–2 ft., glabrous on the lower parts, rough with minute glands upwards. Leaves gland-dotted, on short, narrowly winged stalks, the uppermost sessile, lanceolate, 3–6 in., finely pointed, narrowed to the base, the margins, midrib and nerves more or less covered with small, coarse, appressed hairs pointing upwards; stipules tubular, not fringed. Flower red, $\frac{1}{16}$–$\frac{1}{8}$ in. long, in erect or half-drooping racemes $1\frac{1}{4}$–2 in. long, axillary or forming terminal panicles; bracts tubular, short. Perianth 4-parted. Stamens 6. Styles 2, united close to the base. Nut round, flattened, minutely dotted.

Near Matiana and in marshes near Theog.—N. India, ascending to 7000 ft.

*11. **Polygonum minus,** *Huds.*; *Fl. Br. Ind.* v. 36. Stems glabrous, 6–12 in., slender, angled and creeping at the base, then ascending. Leaves sessile, glabrous, linear or lanceolate, 1–2 in., pointed; stipules tubular, $\frac{1}{3}$ in., thinly hairy, truncate, fringed with short bristles. Flowers minute, pink or red, in slender, erect, terminal racemes $\frac{1}{2}$–1 in. long; bracts tubular, short, fringed with bristles. Perianth 5-parted. Stamens 5. Styles 2, united for half their length. Nut round, flattened, smooth, shining.

Throughout India, ascending to 6000 ft., common in ditches; January–December.—Asia, Europe, including Britain.

12. **Polygonum Donii,** *Meissn.*; *Fl. Br. Ind.* v. 38, *under P. serratulum*. Stems glabrous, 1–3 ft., procumbent and rooting at the joints, then ascending. Leaves variable, sessile, lanceolate, narrowed to both ends or nearly linear, 2–5 in., both surfaces rough with minute points, margins and midrib more or less covered with small, appressed hairs pointing upwards, otherwise

glabrous; stipules tubular, thinly hairy, fringed with the long points of the projecting nerves. Flowers pink or white, $\frac{1}{8}$ in. long, in slender, erect or drooping racemes 1–2 in. long; bracts tubular, fringed with long, needle-like points. Perianth 5-parted, sometimes glandular. Stamens 8. Styles 3, united for half their length. Nut 3-angled, smooth.

Simla, Tara Devi, Narkunda, usually near water; July–October.—N.W. Himalaya, 6000–10,000 ft.

13. **Polygonum Hydropiper,** *Linn.*; *Fl. Br. Ind.* v. 39. Stems 12–18 in., prostrate and rooting at the lower joints, then ascending, minutely glandular, glabrous, much-branched, swollen at the joints. Leaves shortly stalked, lanceolate, 2–3 in., narrowed to the base, glandular-dotted, midrib minutely hairy; stipules tubular, about $\frac{1}{3}$ in., inflated near the middle, glabrous or minutely hairy on the nerves, fringed with unequal bristles. Flowers pink or red, in slender, interrupted racemes 2–3 in. long, tips drooping; bracts tubular, shortly fringed. Perianth 5-parted, glandular. Stamens usually 6. Styles 2 or 3, free nearly to the base. Nuts finely dotted, of the 2-styled flowers flattened and circular, of the 3-styled 3-angled.

Simla, Nal Dehra, usually near water; July–October.—Throughout India, ascending to 7000 ft.—N. temperate and tropical regions, including Britain (Water-pepper).—Australia.

The leaves have an acrid taste.

14. **Polygonum alatum,** *Buch.-Ham.*; *Fl. Br. Ind.* v. 41. A very variable plant. Stems erect, glabrous or thinly hairy; in the smaller forms 3–6 in., slender and unbranched; in the larger 6–18 in., robust and branched. Leaves glabrous, rarely hairy, gland-dotted, rough with minute points, ovate, obtuse or acute, abruptly or gradually narrowed into a winged stalk sometimes eared at its base; in the smaller forms $\frac{1}{4}$–$\frac{1}{2}$ in.; in the larger 1–3 in.; stipules tubular, hairy or glandular towards the base, not fringed. Flowers white, purple or red, in heads $\frac{1}{5}$–$\frac{1}{2}$ in. diam., usually with a sessile involucral leaf; stalks glandular-hairy near the top; bracts flat, glabrous. Perianth 4- or 5-parted. Stamens 6 or 8. Styles 2 or 3, united to near the top. Nut quite enclosed in the perianth, 3-angled, or flattened and circular, minutely dotted.

Simla, abundant in damp places; January–December.—Hilly districts throughout India, up to 10,000 ft.—W. Asia, Africa.

In the *Fl. Br. Ind.* this species is divided into six varieties, four of which, viz. *nepalense*, *parviflorum*, *Metzianum*, and *rigidulum*, are found at Simla; these are included in the above description. Their differences do not appear constant.

15. **Polygonum capitatum,** *Buch.-Ham.*; *Fl. Br. Ind.* v. 44. Rootstock woody; stems many, leafy, 6–10 in., trailing and rooting, red-brown, hairy. Leaves in 2 rows, broadly ovate, $\frac{3}{4}$–$1\frac{1}{2}$ in.,

acute, more or less downy on both surfaces, margins fringed; stalks very short, usually with 2 rounded ears at their base; stipules tubular, $\frac{1}{4}$–$\frac{1}{2}$ in., glandular-hairy. Flowers pink, in dense heads $\frac{1}{4}$–$\frac{1}{2}$ in. diam., on hairy and glandular stalks, usually 2 together, one being often nearly sessile; bracts flat, acute. Perianth 5-parted. Stamens 8. Styles 3, united for $\frac{2}{3}$ of their length. Nut 3-angled, dull black, enclosed in the adherent perianth. (Fig. 134.)

Simla, very common on rocks, walls, etc.; June–November.—Temperate Himalaya, 4000–6000 ft.

FIG. 134. POLYGONUM CAPITATUM.

16. **Polygonum chinense,** *Linn.*; *Fl. Br. Ind.* v. 44. A nearly erect shrub, 3–5 ft.; stems glabrous, angled, finely grooved. Leaves rough with minute prickles, oblong-lanceolate, $5 \times 1\frac{1}{2}$ in., long-pointed; stalks shortly winged near the top, sometimes 2-eared at the base; stipules tubular, white, very long, nerves numerous, parallel, base glandular. Flowers white or pink, in heads $\frac{1}{4}$–$\frac{1}{2}$ in. diam., on glandular stalks forming a corymb; bracts flat, ovate. Perianth 5-parted. Stamens 8. Styles 3, united for about half their length. Nut 3-angled, dull black.

Simla, the Glen; September, October.—Hilly districts throughout India, up to 8000 ft.—Tropical Asia on hills and mountains.

In the *Fl. Br. Ind.* this species is divided into five varieties, of which only one, *corymbosum*, occurs at Simla.

*17. **Polygonum sagittatum,** *Linn.*; *Fl. Br. Ind.* v. 47. Stems glabrous, 1–3 ft., nearly erect or prostrate, square, with small, sharp, recurved prickles along the angles. Leaves thinly hairy, stalked or the upper nearly sessile, linear-oblong, 1–2 in., pointed, arrowhead-shaped, the stalks and midrib prickly; stipules tubular, short. Flowers pink, in small, long-stalked heads; bracts flat.

FIG. 135. POLYGONUM POLYSTACHYUM.

Perianth 5-parted. Stamens 6 or 8. Styles 3, free nearly to the base. Nut 3-angled.

Kulu to Assam, 4000–8000 ft.; May–October.—W. Himalaya, 7000–8000 ft.—N. Asia, N. America.

Common in rice fields and wet places, sometimes growing in dense masses.

18. **Polygonum polystachyum,** *Wall.*; *Fl. Br. Ind.* v. 50. Shrubby, erect, 3–6 ft.; stems angled, hairy, becoming tomentose

in the upper parts. Leaves stalked or the upper nearly sessile, oblong-lanceolate, $4–9 \times 1\frac{1}{4}–3\frac{1}{2}$ in., long-pointed, upper surface glabrous or thinly hairy, the lower softly and densely hairy especially on the midrib and nerves; stipules tubular, very long, hairy, strongly nerved, pointed. Flowers white or tinged with pink, in terminal, usually erect panicles 6–18 in. long; bracts flat. Perianth 5-parted, $\frac{1}{4}$ in. diam.; segments spreading, the 2 outer narrow, the 3 inner much broader. Stamens 8. Styles 3, free nearly to the base. Nut 3-angled, pale brown. (Fig. 135.)

Matiana, Narkunda, abundant in forest; July–October.—Temperate Himalaya, 7000–12,000 ft.—W. Asia.
The leaves are used as a potherb.

19. **Polygonum pterocarpum,** *Wall.*; *Fl. Br. Ind.* v. 54. Glabrous; stems twining, grooved, minutely rough on the ribs. Leaves stalked, cordate, ovate, 3×2 in., long-pointed, basal lobes rounded; stipules tubular, short. Flowers green or tinged with pink, on curved stalks in short, axillary racemes or clusters; bracts flat. Perianth 5-parted, margins of segments white. Stamens 8. Styles 3, united for half their length. Nut 3-angled, acute at both ends, enclosed in the three enlarged and broadly winged outer segments of the perianth; stalk more or less winged, sometimes to its base.

Simla, Annandale; June–October.—Temperate Himalaya, 5000–9000 ft.

2. **FAGOPYRUM.** From the Greek *phagein*, to eat, and *pyros*, wheat; referring to the edible seeds.—Temperate Asia, Europe (Buckwheat).

The flowers of *Fagopyrum* are sometimes dimorphic, that is, short-styled with long stamens, or long-styled with short stamens, as in *Lythrum*, *Reinwardtia*, *Primula* and other genera belonging to different orders.

Fagopyrum cymosum, *Meissn.*; *Fl. Br. Ind.* v. 55. A pubescent, erect, branching herb, 1–3 ft. Leaves long-stalked, entire, broadly triangular, 2–4 in. across, acutely pointed, cordate, the uppermost narrower and stem-clasping; stipules tubular. Flowers 2-sexual, small, white, in racemes 2–5 in. long forming long-stalked panicles; flower-stalks jointed near the middle. Perianth 5-parted; segments nearly equal, blunt. Stamens 8, alternating with honey-secreting glands. Styles 3, long, free; stigmas capitate. Nut ovate, acutely 3-cornered, more than twice as long as the perianth enclosing its base.

Simla, usually in woods; July–September.—Temperate Himalaya, 5000–11,000 ft.—China.
Two species of *Fagopyrum* are cultivated in the hills, and may often be found as escapes, namely:—*F. esculentum*, Mœnch, glabrous, flower-stalks not jointed; and *F. tataricum*, Gærtn., glabrous, faces of the nut deeply grooved, angles rounded.

3. RUMEX. The classical name of Sheep's Sorrel, *Rumex Acetosella.*—Most temperate regions.

Erect, glabrous herbs; stems and branches grooved. Leaves oblong, ovate or hastate; stipules tubular, not fringed, soon torn and disappearing. Flowers 2-sexual or polygamous, small, green, often turning red, in whorl-like, distant clusters forming terminal or axillary racemes or branching into panicles. Perianth 6-parted. Stamens 6; anthers basifixed. Ovary 3-sided; styles 3, stigmas fringed. Nut brown, acutely 3-angled, enclosed in the

FIG. 136. RUMEX HASTATUS.

three, enlarged and finely net-veined inner segments of the perianth or fruiting sepals.

The absence of honey-secreting glands and the fringed stigmas point to the cross-fertilisation of the flowers being effected by the wind instead of by insects.

Fruiting sepals entire.
  Lower leaves stalked, oblong; upper sessile, lanceolate . 1. *R. orientalis.*
  Leaves all stalked, broadly triangular or 3-lobed . . 3. *R. hastatus.*
Fruiting sepals fringed . . . . 2. *R. nepalensis.*

*1. **Rumex orientalis,** *Bernh.*; *Fl. Br. Ind.* v. 58. Stems 3–4 ft., often very thick. Leaves entire, pointed; lower ones long-stalked, oblong, 1–2 ft., cordate; upper sessile, smaller, lanceolate. Flowers 2-sexual, in crowded whorls forming leafy panicles, 12–18 in. long, often very dense in fruit. Fruiting sepals orbicular, entire, cordate, the mid-vein usually thickened and forming a small tubercle like a grain of wheat.

Kashmir to Kumaon; July–October.—W. Himalaya, 6000–9000 ft.—W. Asia, S. Europe.

2. **Rumex nepalensis,** *Spreng.*; *Fl. Br. Ind.* v. 60. Stems $1\frac{1}{2}$–4 ft., robust; branches stiff, spreading. Leaves entire, pointed; lower ones long-stalked, oblong-ovate, 6×3 in. or larger, cordate; upper nearly sessile, smaller, narrowed to the base; uppermost sessile, lanceolate. Flowers 2-sexual, in whorls forming long, nearly leafless racemes. Fruiting sepals broadly ovate, fringed with comb-like, hooked teeth, the mid-vein of one thickened and forming an oblong tubercle.

Simla, common on roadsides; May–October.—Temperate Himalaya, 4000–9000 ft.—Hills in S.E. India.—W. Asia, S. Africa.
Habit of *R. obtusifolius, Linn.* Common on waste ground in England.

3. **Rumex hastatus,** *Don*; *Fl. Br. Ind.* v. 60, including *R. scutatus, Linn.*; *Fl. Br. Ind.* v. 60. Stems 1–2 ft.; branches numerous, slender, erect. Leaves stalked, entire, broadly triangular, long-pointed, $1\text{–}2\frac{1}{2} \times \frac{3}{4}\text{–}2$ in.; or hastately 3-lobed, the lobes narrow or almost linear. Flowers polygamous, in small whorls racemed and forming terminal panicles, often dense in fruit. Fruiting sepals orbicular, pink, not fringed, notched at both ends. (Fig. 136.)

Simla, common in fields; May–October.—W. Himalaya, 1000–8000 ft.—W. Asia, S. Europe.
R. vesicarius, Linn., a pale green herb with stalked, ovate leaves, and orbicular fruiting sepals $\frac{1}{2}$ in. diam., is common as an escape near houses.

LXXXIII. PIPERACEÆ

Aromatic herbs or shrubs. Leaves alternate or whorled, undivided, entire, dotted. Flowers minute, 1- or 2-sexual, crowded in stalked, catkin-like spikes, each flower in the axil of a very small bract. Perianth none. Stamens 2 or 3, hypogynous; anthers 2-celled. Ovary of 3 carpels united towards the base, each containing many ovules, or 1-celled and 1-ovuled; styles free and erect or the stigmas sessile. Fruit of 3 many-seeded follicles, or a spike of 1-seeded berries.—A small Order confined to tropical regions, most abundant in America.

Flowers 2-sexual.
  Leaves alternate. Spikes with an involucre of large bracts . . . . 1. *Houttuynia.*
  Leaves whorled. Spikes without an involucre. . . . 3. *Peperomia.*
Flowers 1-sexual . . . . 2. *Piper.*

1. HOUTTUYNIA. In honour of Martin Houttuyn, a Dutch physician and author of a treatise on timber-trees.—E. Asia, California.

Houttuynia cordata, *Thunb.*; *Fl. Br. Ind.* v. 78. A pubescent herb; stems 4–12 in., sometimes more, erect, angular. Leaves alternate, stalked, broadly ovate, sometimes cordate, $1\frac{1}{2}$–$2\frac{1}{2}$ in., long-pointed; base of stalks dilated and sheathing; stipules long.

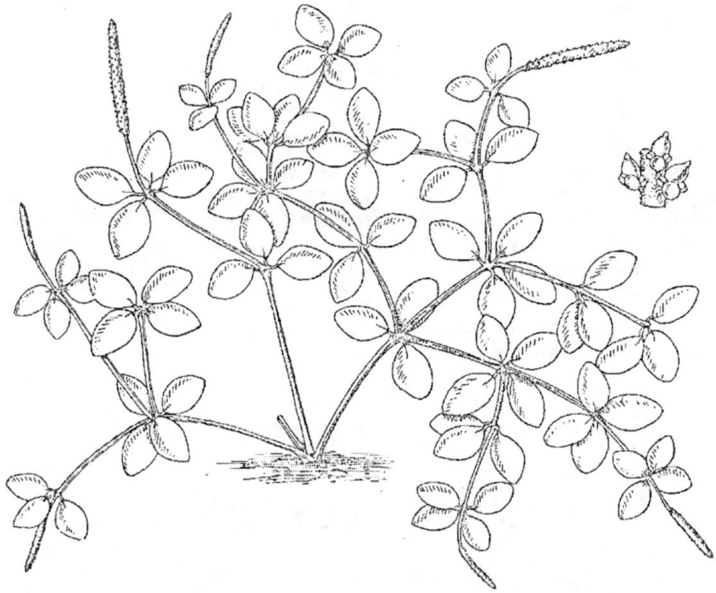

FIG. 137. PEPEROMIA REFLEXA.

Spikes stalked, erect, $\frac{1}{2}$ in., with a basal involucre of 4–6 large, spreading, white, petal-like bracts. Flowers green, 2-sexual. Stamens 3; filaments adnate at the base to the ovary. Ovary of 3 many-ovuled carpels united towards the base; styles 3, free, erect, tips recurved. Fruit globose, consisting of 3 many-seeded follicles; fruiting spike 1–2 in.

Sutlej valley, below Narkunda, on marshy ground; June–September.—Tropical Himalaya, 1000–5000 ft.—E. Asia.

2. PIPER. The Latin name for Pepper.—Tropical and subtropical regions.

Piper brachystachyum, *Wall.*; *Fl. Br. Ind.* v. 87. A rambling shrub: stems often very long, climbing on trees or rocks, pubescent or hairy, swollen and rooting at the joints; flowering shoots glabrous, free, spreading, 1–3 ft. or more. Leaves of the climbing stem orbicular, 1–2 in., pointed, pale on the lower surface; those of the free shoots ovate, 2–5 × 1–2 in., long-pointed, narrowed to the base. Flowers purple, 1-sexual, the male and female on different plants. Male spikes 2–3 in., slender, drooping: stamens 2. Female spikes ovoid, $\frac{1}{4}$ in. long; stigmas 3, sessile, spreading over the 1-celled, 1-ovuled ovary. Fruiting spike globose; berries $\frac{1}{10}$ in. diam., 1-seeded, crowded.

Valley below Chota Simla, 4500 ft.; May.—Subtropical Himalaya, 2000–5000 ft.—Nilghiris.

3. PEPEROMIA. From the Greek *peperi*, pepper, and *homoios*, similar.—Tropical regions.

Peperomia reflexa, *A. Dietr.*; *Fl. Br. Ind.* v. 99. A succulent, pubescent herb, 3–10 in.; branches tufted, rooting at the joints, creeping on trees or rocks. Leaves whorled in fours, nearly sessile, broadly ovate, $\frac{1}{3}$ in. Spikes stalked, erect, $\frac{1}{2}$–1 in. Flowers green, 2-sexual, half sunk in the rachis of the spike. Perianth none. Stamens 2. Stigma sessile, minutely 2-lobed. Berries indehiscent, one-seeded. (Fig. 137.)

Simla, below Annandale; November.—Subtropical Himalaya, 4000–6000 ft. —Tropical Asia, Africa, and America.

LXXXIV. LAURACEÆ

EVERGREEN trees or shrubs, more or less aromatic. Leaf-buds large, enveloped in imbricate scales. Leaves entire; stipules none. Flowers small, 1- or 2-sexual, in panicles or densely clustered in small umbels. Perianth regular, 4–6-parted; segments in 2 series. Stamens 6–13, usually in 2 series, the inner series often partly consisting of staminodes; anthers 4-celled, the cells opening by upturned, often deciduous lids. Ovary free, sessile, 1-celled, 1-ovuled; style linear, stigma terminal, dilated and sometimes lobed. Drupe 1-seeded, seated on or clasped by the persistent perianth-segments or their bases.—From the Latin *Laurus*, the classical name of *L. nobilis*, a European and Oriental species.—Nearly all tropical and subtropical regions; rare in temperate regions.

Flowers in panicles, usually 2-sexual.
  Leaves opposite, 3-nerved from the base . . . . 1. *Cinnamomum.*
  Leaves alternate.
    Perianth-segments spreading or reflexed in fruit . 2. *Machilus.*
    Perianth-segments erect and clasping the base of the fruit . . . . 3. *Phœbe.*
Flowers in densely clustered umbels, 1-sexual . . . 4. *Litsea.*

1. CINNAMOMUM. The Greek name, derived from the Arabic *Kinamon.*—Asia, Australia, Pacific islands.

***Cinnamomum Tamala,** *Nees*; *Fl. Br. Ind.* v. 128. Leaves glabrous, opposite or nearly so, leathery, shortly stalked, ovate-oblong, 3–6 in., 3-nerved from the base, long-pointed. Flowers often 1-sexual, numerous, white, in pubescent panicles 3–6 in. long. Perianth 6-parted. Perfect stamens 9, in 2 series; the outer of 6 stamens, the inner of 3; inner ones alternate with 3 short staminodes, and each bearing 2 glands at its base. Drupe ovoid, $\frac{1}{2}$ in., seated on the persistent bases of the perianth-segments, black when ripe.

Himalaya, 3000–7000 ft., from the Indus to Bhootan; rare west of the Jumna; February–May.

The Cinnamon tree of commerce, *C. zeylanica*, is indigenous in the forests of Ceylon, and closely allied to this species.

2. MACHILUS. Origin of name obscure.—E. Asia.

Trees. Leaves alternate, glabrous, leathery, ovate-lanceolate, long-pointed, lower surface covered with a pale bloom, nerves lateral. Flowers $\frac{1}{4}$–$\frac{1}{3}$ in. diam., 2-sexual, pale yellow, fragrant, in panicles. Perianth 6-parted, lobes obtuse. Perfect stamens 9, in two series; the outer series of 6 stamens, the inner of 3; the latter alternating with 3 short staminodes and each furnished with two glands at its base. Drupe seated on the persistent perianth, dark purple when ripe.

Perianth glabrous. Drupe oblong . . . . . . 1. *M. odoratissima.*
Perianth pubescent. Drupe globose . . . . . . 2. *M. Duthiei.*

1. **Machilus odoratissima,** *Nees*; *Fl. Br. Ind.* v. 139 and 859. Leaves 4–6 in. Panicles usually about 3 in. long, shortly stalked and compact. Perianth glabrous. Drupe oblong, $\frac{1}{2}$–$\frac{3}{4}$ in.

Sutlej valley, Suni; April.—Temperate Himalaya up to 5000 ft.

2. **Machilus Duthiei,** *King*; *Fl. Br. Ind.* v. 861. Leaves 5–10 in. Panicles usually about 6 in. long, long-stalked, spreading. Perianth pubescent outside. Drupe globose, $\frac{1}{2}$ in. diam. (Fig. 138.)

Simla, the Glen, and below Annandale; April.—Temperate Himalaya, 4000–9000 ft.

3. PHŒBE. From *Phœbus*, a name given to Apollo to whom the Bay Laurel was sacred; the genus was formerly included in *Laurus.*—India, Malay peninsula.

Phœbe lanceolata, *Nees*; *Fl. Br. Ind.* v. 141. Glabrous; branchlets white or pale yellow. Leaves alternate, shortly stalked, often crowded towards the ends of the branches, lanceolate, 6–9 × 1–2 in., long-pointed, narrowed to the base. Flowers pale yellow, 2-sexual, in axillary panicles 2–4 in. long; bracts soon falling off. Perianth 6-parted, hairy inside. Perfect stamens 9, in 2 series; the outer series of 6 stamens, the inner of 3; the latter alternating with 3 short staminodes, and each furnished with

FIG. 138. MACHILUS DUTHIEI.

2 glands at its base. Drupe narrowly oblong, about ½ in., clasped at the base by the hardened perianth, black when ripe.

Bhajji, Sutlej valley; February–June.—Subtropical Himalaya ascending to 6000 ft.—S. India, Burmah.

4. LITSEA. From the Japanese name of the genus.—Asia, Australia, the Pacific islands; rare in Africa and America.

Leaves alternate or crowded, shortly stalked. Flowers white or pale yellow, stalked, 1-sexual, the male and female on different trees. Umbels 4–6-flowered, stalked, enclosed when in bud by 4–5 concave, overlapping bracts, and crowded in sessile, axillary or lateral clusters. Perianth 4–6-parted. Male flowers: stamens 6–7 or 9–13, the inner ones 2-glandular near the base; pistil rudimentary. Female flowers: stamens none; stigma dilated and lobed. Drupe seated on the persistent bases of the perianth-segments.

Perianth 5- or 6- parted. Stamens 9–13, not protruding . 1. *L. polyantha.*
Perianth 4-parted. Stamens 6 or 7, far protruding
 Leaves 6–12 in., 3-nerved from the base. Glands of the inner stamens stalked . . . . 2. *L. lanuginosa.*
 Leaves 3–6 in.; nerves lateral. Glands of the inner stamens sessile . . . . 3. *L. consimilis.*

FIG. 139. LITSEA CONSIMILIS.

*1. **Litsea polyantha,** *Juss.*; *Fl. Br. Ind.* v. 162. Leaves alternate, broadly oblong-ovate, 3–7 × 2–4 in., base rounded or cordate; upper surface glabrous, lower tomentose; stalks tomentose. Flowers white; bracts 5, persistent in flower. Umbels forming clusters ½–1 in. diam. in the axils of leaves or fallen leaves. Perianth 5–6-parted. Stamens 9–13, not longer than the perianth, the 3 or 4 inner ones shorter than the outer, each with a pair of glands near its base. Drupe ovoid, ¼ in. long, black when ripe.

Burmah to the Ravi, ascending to 3000 ft., rare; March–May.—Java, China.

2. **Litsea lanuginosa,** *Nees*; *Fl. Br. Ind.* v. 178. Leaves usually crowded, sometimes alternate, tomentose on the lower surface, sometimes glabrous, lanceolate, 6–12 × 2–4 in., 3-nerved from the

base. Leaf-buds conspicuous, 1 in. long, enclosed by softly pubescent scales. Flowers white, hairy; bracts 4, hairy, soon falling off. Umbels forming dense, lateral clusters $\frac{1}{2}$–1 in. diam. Perianth 4-parted; segments fringed, hairy outside. Stamens 6 or 7, much longer than the perianth, the two inner ones each with a pair of stalked glands near its base. Drupe oblong, $\frac{1}{2}$ in., narrowed to both ends.

Sutlej valley; June.—Outer Himalaya, ascending to 3000 ft.

3. **Litsea consimilis,** *Nees*; *Fl. Br. Ind.* v. 179, *under L. umbrosa.* Glabrous except the leaf-buds and flowers. Leaves alternate, lower surface covered with white bloom, lanceolate, 3–6 × 1–2 in., long-pointed, nerves lateral. Leaf-buds softly pubescent, $\frac{1}{3}$ in. long. Flowers pale yellow or white; bracts 4, soon falling off. Umbels forming lateral clusters $\frac{1}{3}$ in. diam. Perianth 4-parted; segments fringed, pubescent outside. Stamens 6, much longer than the perianth, the 2 inner ones each with a pair of sessile, kidney-shaped glands near its base. Drupe globose, $\frac{1}{3}$ in. diam. (Fig. 139.)

Mahasu, Narkunda; March–May.—W. Himalaya, 3000–9000 ft.

LXXXV. THYMELÆACEÆ

Erect shrubs; bark usually tough and fibrous. Leaves simple, entire; stipules none. Flowers 2-sexual, in heads or spikes, sometimes forming terminal panicles. Perianth regular, tubular, 4-lobed. Stamens 8, inserted on the perianth-tube in 2 series of 4 each; anthers 2-celled. Disk none or represented by erect scales. Ovary free, 1-celled; ovule one; style none or short, stigma capitate. Drupe ovoid, 1-seeded.—Most temperate and tropical regions.—From the Greek *thymos*, thyme, and *elaia*, the olive, referring to the foliage and fruit of the genus *Thymelæa*.

Perianth-lobes acute. Disk none . . . . 1. *Daphne.*
Perianth-lobes obtuse. Disk of 4–5 erect scales . . . 2. *Wikstrœmia.*

1. DAPHNE. The Greek name of the Bay-tree, *Laurus nobilis.*—Europe, N. Africa, temperate Asia.

Leaves alternate, leathery. Flowers in terminal heads of 3–12. Perianth-lobes acute. Anthers nearly sessile. Disk none. Stigma nearly sessile. Drupe about $\frac{1}{3}$ in., red or orange when ripe.

Leaves $1\frac{1}{2}$ in., acute. Heads without bracts . . . 1. *D. oleoides.*
Leaves 3–5 in., obtuse. Heads surrounded by numerous bracts 2. *D. cannabina.*

1. **Daphne oleoides,** *Schreb.*; *Fl. Br. Ind.* v. 193. More or less pubescent, 4–8 ft. Leaves sessile, narrowly lanceolate, rarely oblong or ovate, $1\frac{1}{2}$ in., acute. Flowers white, tinged with pink; bracts none or small and soon falling off. Perianth-tube $\frac{1}{3}$–$\frac{1}{2}$ in., grey-tomentose outside.

Simla; September, October.—W. Himalaya, 3000–9000 ft.—W. Asia, S. Europe.

2. **Daphne cannabina,** *Wall.*; *Fl. Br. Ind.* v. 193. Glabrous except the young shoots, 5–8 ft. Leaves shortly stalked, crowded near the end of branches, lanceolate, 3–5 in., obtuse. Flowers

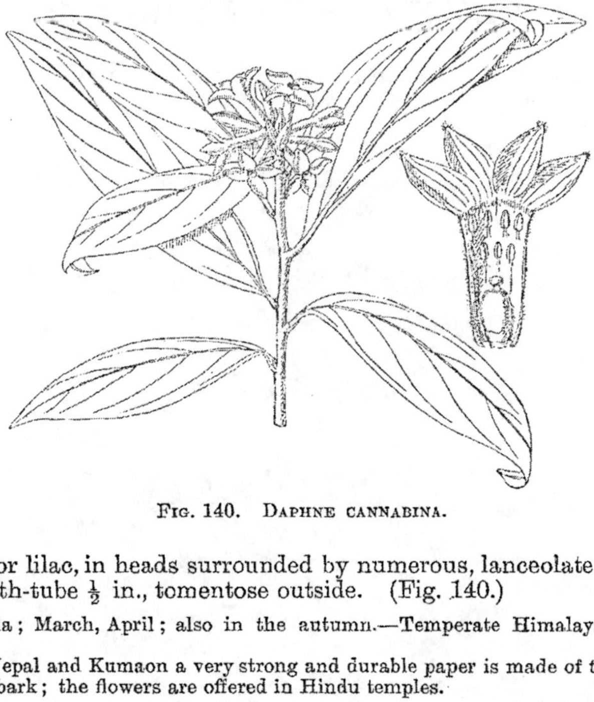

Fig. 140. Daphne cannabina.

white or lilac, in heads surrounded by numerous, lanceolate bracts. Perianth-tube $\frac{1}{2}$ in., tomentose outside. (Fig. 140.)

Simla; March, April; also in the autumn.—Temperate Himalaya, 5000–7000 ft.

In Nepal and Kumaon a very strong and durable paper is made of the inner fibrous bark; the flowers are offered in Hindu temples.

2. **WIKSTRŒMIA.** In honour of J. E. Wikström, a Swedish botanist of the nineteenth century.—Tropical and E. Asia, Australia, Pacific islands.

Wikstrœmia canescens, *Meissn.*; *Fl. Br. Ind.* v. 195. Silky pubescent, 1–3 ft. Leaves alternate or nearly opposite, shortly stalked, thin, oblong-lanceolate, 1–2 in., often with a minute, white bud in the axils. Flowers yellow or white, in heads or spikes forming terminal panicles. Perianth-tube $\frac{1}{4}$ in., slender, pubescent outside ; lobes small, obtuse. Filaments short. Disk of 4 or 5 erect, linear scales. Ovary hairy ; style short, stigma large, globose. Drupe $\frac{1}{4}$ in., enclosed at first in the perianth which ultimately splits and falls off, black when ripe.

Narkunda, Patarnala ; June, July.—Temperate Himalaya, 5000–9000 ft.—N. Asia.

Common about Mussoorie and in Kumaon. It furnishes a useful fibre.

LXXXVI. ELÆAGNACEÆ

Erect shrubs, more or less covered with minute, silvery or brown, scurfy, peltate scales. Leaves alternate, shortly stalked, simple,

Fig. 141. Elæagnus umbellata.

entire ; stipules none. Flowers small, 2- or 1-sexual, usually in axillary clusters. Perianth tubular, with 4 deciduous lobes or in the male flowers of *Hippophae* of 2 opposite, leaf-like segments. Stamens 4 ; anthers nearly sessile. Ovary free, 1-celled, 1-ovuled ; style linear, stigma lateral. Nut 1-seeded, enclosed in the succulent perianth-tube.—A small Order inhabiting N. temperate or tropical regions.

Leaves oblong-lanceolate, $\frac{1}{2}$–1 in. broad. Flowers 2-sexual . 1. *Elæagnus.*
Leaves linear-lanceolate, $\frac{3}{8}$ in. broad. Flowers 1-sexual . . 2. *Hippophae.*

1. ELÆAGNUS. A name applied by classical authors to the Wild Olive and also to a Common Willow, *Salix fragilis*.—N. temperate regions.

Elæagnus umbellata, *Thunb.*; *Fl. Br. Ind.* v. 201. Usually thorny; stems 2–6 ft. Leaves oblong-lanceolate, 1–3 × ½–1 in., obtuse, glabrous or stellately hairy on the upper surface, silvery-scaly on the lower. Flowers fragrant, white, stalked, in axillary clusters, appearing with the leaves. Perianth nearly ½ in., densely scaly; tube constricted above the ovary. Stamens on the mouth of the perianth and alternate with the triangular, acute lobes. Style included, tip curved. Fruit ovoid, ⅓ in. long; nut bony, ribbed, covered on the inside with white hairs. (Fig. 141.)

Simla, Mushobra; April, May.—Temperate Himalaya, 3000–10,000 ft.—N. Asia.—Fruit edible.

2. HIPPOPHAE. From *hippophaes*, the Greek name of the Prickly Spurge, *Euphorbia spinosa*; its application here is unexplainable.—N. Asia, Europe.

***Hippophae salicifolia,** *Don*; *Fl. Br. Ind.* v. 203. Thorny; stems 10–20 ft. Leaves linear-lanceolate, 2–3 × ⅜ in., glabrous or stellately pubescent on the upper surface, softly white-tomentose on the lower except the rusty red midrib, edges recurved. Flowers scaly, less than ¼ in., 1-sexual, the male and female on different plants. Male flowers sessile, clustered in the axils of usually fallen leaves: perianth of 2 opposite, concave, rounded, leaf-like segments; stamens 4. Female flowers stalked, axillary, solitary or clustered: perianth tubular, minutely 2-toothed; stigma protruding. Fruit ovoid, ¼ in., orange or scarlet when ripe, the seed contained in a membranous utricle.

Sutlej valley; June, July.—Temperate Himalaya, 5000–10,000 ft.
Nearly allied to the British Sea Buckthorn, *H. rhamnoides*.

LXXXVII. LORANTHACEÆ

Small shrubs, parasitic on the trunk or branches of trees. Leaves usually opposite, simple, entire, sometimes none. Flowers regular, 2- or 1-sexual, in clusters or racemes, in *Loranthus* composed of both calyx and corolla, in *Viscum* of only a single perianth. Tube of calyx or perianth adnate to the ovary; limb in *Loranthus* none or short, in *Viscum* 4- or 3-parted. Corolla in *Loranthus* tubular, 4- or 5-lobed; lobes valvate in bud. Stamens as many as the corolla- or perianth-lobes, opposite, or in *Viscum* adnate to them. Ovary inferior, 1-celled; style linear or none; stigma terminal or sessile; ovule solitary. Berry containing a single seed.—A small Order inhabiting temperate and tropical regions.

Flowers coloured, $\frac{3}{4}$–2 in. long, 2-sexual . . . . . 1. *Loranthus.*
Flowers green, less than $\frac{1}{4}$ in. long, 1-sexual . . . . . 2. *Viscum.*

1. LORANTHUS. From the Greek *loron*, a thong, and *anthos*, a flower, referring to the narrow corolla-lobes.—Tropical and temperate regions.

Robust shrubs, the Simla species usually growing on oaks. Leaves thick, opposite, rarely alternate. Flowers 2-sexual, shortly

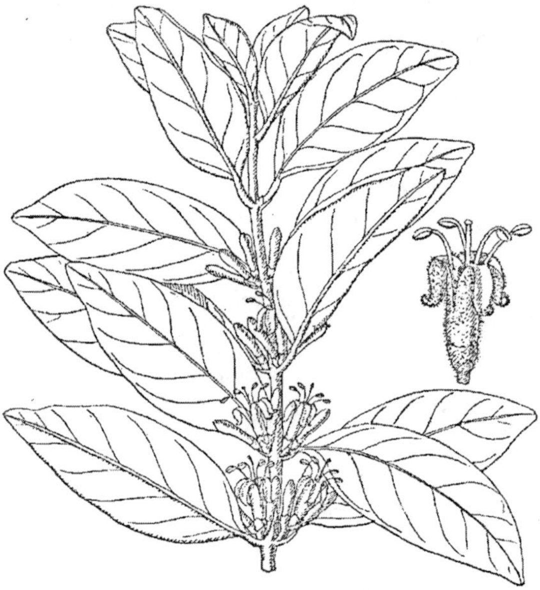

FIG. 142. LORANTHUS VESTITUS.

stalked, in clusters or racemes. Calyx-limb short, truncate. Corolla slender, tubular, curved, 4- or 5-lobed. Stamens attached near the mouth of the corolla-tube. Style long; stigma terminal.

Flowers tomentose.
- Buds sharply pointed . . . . 1. *L. cordifolius.*
- Buds globose . . . . 3. *L. vestitus.*

Flowers glabrous.
- Corolla 4-lobed . . . . 2. *L. elatus.*
- Corolla 5-lobed . . . . 4. *L. longiflorus.*

1. **Loranthus cordifolius,** *Wall.*; *Fl. Br. Ind.* v. 209. Young parts tomentose. Leaves opposite, stalked, usually cordate, broadly ovate, 2–3 in., both surfaces tomentose or the upper nearly glabrous.

Flowers $\frac{3}{4}$–1 in. long, in axillary clusters; buds sharply pointed. Calyx-limb none or very short. Corolla brown-tomentose outside, pink or pale yellow within; lobes 4, acute. Stigma club-shaped, tip conical. Berry $\frac{1}{3}$ in., top-shaped.

Abundant on the oak, *Quercus dilatata*, below Daha in the Giri valley; July–October.—Temperate Himalaya, 1000–5000 ft.—Central India, Nilghiris.

2. **Loranthus elatus,** *Edgew.*; *Fl. Br. Ind.* v. 212. Glabrous except the rusty, pubescent buds. Leaves opposite, stalked, broadly ovate, 3–6 in. Flowers 1–1$\frac{1}{2}$ in. long, in axillary clusters. Calyx-limb short, obscurely 4-toothed. Corolla red in the lower part, green towards the top; lobes 4, linear, reflexed. Stigma minute. Berry $\frac{1}{3}$ in., broadly top-shaped.

Theog; July.—Temperate Himalaya, 5000–10,000 ft.

3. **Loranthus vestitus,** *Wall.*; *Fl. Br. Ind.* v. 212. Young parts tomentose. Leaves opposite, stalked, ovate-oblong or ovate-lanceolate, 2–3 in., upper surface glabrous, lower tomentose. Flowers $\frac{3}{4}$ in. long, in axillary clusters; buds globose. Calyx-limb very short, obscurely toothed. Corolla brown-tomentose outside, smooth and purple within; lobes 4. Stigma capitate. Berry ovoid, $\frac{1}{3}$–$\frac{1}{2}$ in., tomentose, ultimately glabrous. (Fig. 142.)

Simla, the Glen; September–January.—W. Himalaya, 5000–10,000 ft.

4. **Loranthus longiflorus,** *Desrouss.*; *Fl. Br. Ind.* v. 214. Glabrous. Leaves opposite, rarely alternate, nearly sessile, variable in shape and size, usually oblong-ovate, about $5 \times 2\frac{1}{2}$ in. Flowers 1$\frac{1}{2}$–2 in. long, in racemes. Calyx-limb shortly tubular, entire. Corolla red in the lower part, yellow-green towards the top; lobes 5, linear, reflexed. Berry oblong, $\frac{1}{3}$–$\frac{1}{2}$ in., crowned with the cup-shaped calyx-limb.

Sutlej valley, near Basantpur; December.—Throughout India, ascending to 7000 ft.

2. VISCUM. The classical name of the Mistletoe, *V. album*, derived from the Greek.—Tropical and temperate regions.

Glabrous shrubs; branches repeatedly forking. Leaves opposite or none. Flowers small or minute, green, 1-sexual, sessile in groups of usually 3 within a cup-shaped, fleshy, lobed bract, solitary or clustered in the forks or at the joints of the branches. Male flowers: perianth 4- or 3-parted; anthers sessile, adnate to the perianth-lobes, opening by numerous surface-pores. Female flowers: perianth-tube adnate to the ovary, limb 4- or 3-parted; stigma sessile. Berry viscidly juicy.

Leaves 1–2 in. Branches terete . . . . . . 1. *V. album.*
Leaves none. Branches flat.
Joints 1–2 in., grooved. . . . . 2. *V. articulatum.*
Joints $\frac{1}{5}$–$\frac{3}{4}$ in., not grooved . . . . 3. *V. japonicum.*

1. **Viscum album,** *Linn.*; *Fl. Br. Ind.* v. 223. A yellow-green, tufted, erect bush 2–3 ft. diam.; branches terete, jointed. Leaves leathery, sessile, flat, oblong or obovate, 1–2 in., obtuse. Flowers clustered in the forks of the branches; male nearly $\frac{1}{4}$ in. long, female smaller, the two sexes on different plants. Perianth-lobes not persistent in fruit. Berry globose, $\frac{1}{4}$ in. diam., white, almost translucent.

Simla, Mahasu, usually on apricot trees; March–May; berries ripen in November.—Temperate Himalaya, 3000–7000 ft.—N. and W. Asia, Europe (Britain, Mistletoe).

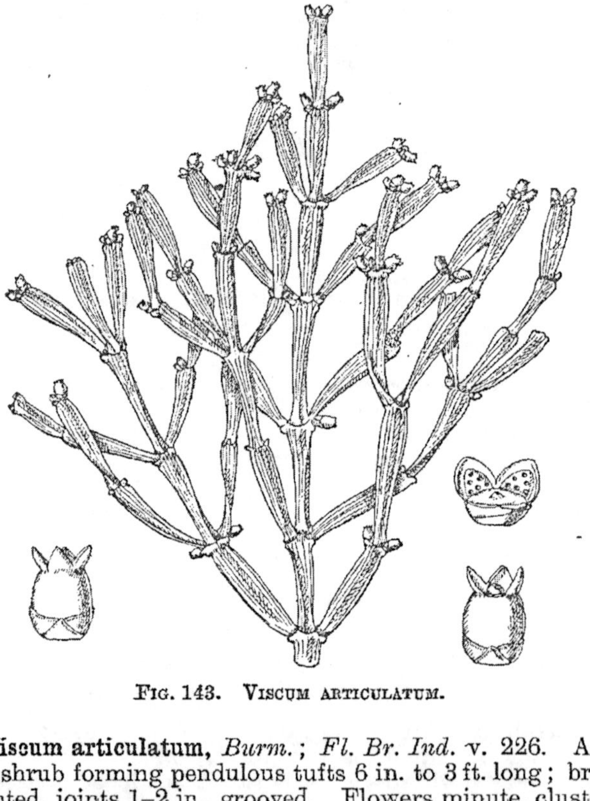

FIG. 143. VISCUM ARTICULATUM.

2. **Viscum articulatum,** *Burm.*; *Fl. Br. Ind.* v. 226. A green, leafless shrub forming pendulous tufts 6 in. to 3 ft. long; branches flat, jointed, joints 1–2 in., grooved. Flowers minute, clustered at the tops of the joints, male and female in the same cluster. Perianth-lobes not persistent in fruit. Berry globose, $\frac{1}{6}$ in. diam., yellow. (Fig. 143.)

Simla, the Glen; June–October.—Throughout India, ascending to 5000 ft. —Malay archipelago.

3. **Viscum japonicum,** *Thunb.*; *Fl. Br. Ind.* v. 226. A green, leafless shrub forming nearly erect tufts rarely more than 6 in.

long; branches fleshy, flat, jointed, joints $\frac{1}{3}$–$\frac{3}{4}$ in., not grooved. Flowers minute, clustered at the tops of the joints, male and female in the same cluster. Berry ovoid, $\frac{1}{10}$ in., crowned with the persistent perianth-lobes.

Simla, the Glen, usually on *Quercus incana*; May–July.—Temperate Himalaya, 5000–7000 ft.—China, Japan, Australia.

LXXXVIII. SANTALACEÆ

SHRUBS or herbs, glabrous. Leaves alternate, simple, entire; stipules none. Flowers small, 1- or 2-sexual. Perianth 3–5-lobed. Stamens 3–5, short, inserted on the lobes; anthers 2-celled. Ovary inferior, 1-celled; ovules 2–4. Fruit a one-seeded nut or drupe.—Temperate and tropical regions.—From the Persian or Arabic *Shandal*, supposed to be derived from the Sanskrit name of the Sandal-wood tree.

The strongly scented sandal-wood, used for carved work and incense, is obtained from *Santalum album*, indigenous in S. India, and cultivated as far north as Saharunpore.

A herb. Leaves linear . . . . 1. *Thesium.*
A shrub. Leaves oblong-ovate . . . . 2. *Osyris.*

1. THESIUM. Origin of name obscure. *Thesseon* is a name used by Theophrastus for a plant not identified by modern botanists.—Temperate and tropical regions.

***Thesium himalense,** *Royle*; *Fl. Br. Ind.* v. 229. A straggling, often much branched herb, parasitic on the roots of other plants; stems 6–18 in., slender, procumbent or nearly erect. Leaves sessile, linear, 1–2 in. Flowers small, 2-sexual, yellow or pale green, stalked, axillary, forming terminal racemes or panicles; bracts 3, leaf-like, one much longer than the others. Perianth-lobes 5, obtuse. Stamens 5. Style short, linear; stigma capitate. Nut ovoid, $\frac{1}{6}$ in., wrinkled, crowned with the remains of the perianth.

From the Chenab to Kumaon, on open stony ground, 5000–10,000 ft.; June, July.

Habit of *Thesium linophyllum*, the Bastard Toadflax of S. England.

The reference given in the *Fl. Br. Ind.* for the authorship of this species, 'Royle, *Illustr.* 322,' contains no description of the plant; for description, see Edgeworth in *Trans. Linn. Soc.* xx. 88.

2. OSYRIS. The Greek name of a plant supposed to have been dedicated to the deity *Osiris*.—Europe, Africa, India.

Osyris arborea, *Wall.*; *Fl. Br. Ind.* v. 232. A shrub, 5–10 ft.; young shoots sharply 3-angled. Leaves nearly sessile, oblong-ovate, 1–1½ in., tip acute. Flowers minute, 2- or 1-sexual, yellow-green, shortly stalked. Perianth 3–4-lobed. Male flowers in small, stalked, axillary clusters, often forming short panicles: stamens 3–4. Female or 2-sexual flowers, solitary on axillary

Fig. 144. Osyris arborea.

stalks, lengthening in fruit: style short, thick, stigmas 3–4, recurved. Drupe globose, ¼ in., red when ripe. (Fig. 144.)

Simla; August–April.—Subtropical Himalaya, 1000–6000 ft.—S. India.

LXXXIX. BALANOPHORACEÆ

Flowers small, 1-sexual. Perianth of male flowers usually 3-parted, of female none; stamens usually 3, filaments united; ovary 1-celled, ovule 1. Fruit minute, nut-like.—A small Order consisting of fleshy, leafless herbs parasitic on roots; tropical and subtropical regions.

BALANOPHORA. From the Greek *balanos*, an acorn, and *pherein*, to bear; referring to the shape of the heads of flowers.—E. Asia, Australia.

Balanophora involucrata, *Hook. f.*; *Fl. Br. Ind.* v. 237. A glabrous, fleshy, fungus-like herb parasitic on the roots of trees; stems erect, 1–6 in., the base sheathed in the tuberous rootstock and bearing about the middle an involucre of 2–4 partially united scales. Flowers minute, 1-sexual, crowded in an ovoid or globose, red or yellow head about 1 in. long. Female heads sometimes bear a few male flowers at their base or their summit; more rarely the male heads contain also a few imperfect female flowers. Male flowers: perianth half sunk in the rachis, limb usually 3-parted; stamens usually 3, filaments very short, united, anthers oblong, opening by a slit along the top. Female flowers often clustered round a club-shaped bracteole: perianth none; ovary ovoid, shortly stalked, produced upwards in a slender style; stigma terminal, ovule 1. Nut minute, hard, one-seeded.

Near Kotgurh in forest, 6000 ft.—July, August.—Temperate Himalaya, 6000–10,000 ft.

This curious plant grows in shady forests, and was collected by Dr. T. Thomson on August 6, 1847, when on the march from Narkunda to Kotgurh, apparently near where the road crosses a stream before commencing the ascent to Kotgurh, see his *Western Himalaya and Thibet*, p. 47. The species is common in the moist forests near Darjeeling, but has not, to my knowledge, been again collected so far west.

XC. EUPHORBIACEÆ

Trees, shrubs or herbs, often with acrid, milky juice. Leaves usually alternate and entire. Inflorescence of various forms, usually axillary. Flowers small, often minute, always 1-sexual. In *Euphorbia* the male and female flowers are within the same involucre, and thus have the appearance of being a single flower; in the other genera the flowers are distinct. Perianth in *Euphorbia* none, in the other genera the calyx is usually 3–5-parted. Corolla rarely present. Disk of varied form, sometimes absent. Stamens 1 in *Euphorbia*, in the other genera 2–5 or many; anthers 2-celled. Ovary free, usually 3-celled, 1 or 2 ovules in each cell; styles usually 3, often branched. A rudimentary pistil is sometimes present in the male flowers. Fruit a capsule, usually containing 3 small, 1- or 2-seeded nuts or cocci separating from a persistent axis, or a drupe containing 1–3 stones.—A very large Order, abundant and widely distributed in tropical regions, much rarer in cold climates.

The Castor Oil plant, *Ricinus communis*, is cultivated throughout India, and is common on waste ground in the hills. It has peltate, palmately 8–10-lobed leaves 1–2 ft. across, and panicled flowers, the sexes being on separate plants. Capsule about 1 in. long, prickly, containing three spotted seeds.

The following species are recorded in the *Fl. Br. Ind.* from the Simla region, but it is doubtful whether they occur:—

Cleistanthus collinus, *Benth.*; *Fl. Br. Ind.* v. 274. The locality rests on a MS. quotation by Wallich from Hamilton's Herbarium; the specimen is not at Kew. Brandis, *For. Fl.* 450, and Gamble, *Man. Ind. Timb. Trees*, 358, both give Bundelkhand as the northern limit of this species.

Antidesma Ghaesembilla, *Gaertn.*; *Fl. Br. Ind.* v. 357. The locality rests on a specimen of Thomson's ticketed 'Simla, foot of hills.' This tree inhabits the plains.

Male and female flowers contained in a calyx-like involucre . 1. *Euphorbia.*
Male and female flowers distinct.
  Trees or shrubs, small and herb-like in *Phyllanthus.*
    Stamens 2. Flowers on thick, erect spikes . . . 12. *Sapium.*
    Stamens 3.
      Styles recurved, linear, deeply 2-branched . . 6. *Phyllanthus.*
      Styles united in an erect column . . . . . 7. *Glochidion.*
      Styles spreading, dilated in crescent-shaped, lobed stigmas . . . . 9. *Putranjiva.*
    Stamens 4.
      Leaves alternate . . . . 2. *Sarcococca.*
      Leaves opposite . . . . 3. *Buxus.*
    Stamens 5.
      Flowers with petals.
        A tree. Flowers nearly sessile. Styles 2 . . 4. *Bridelia.*
        A shrub. Flowers long-stalked. Styles 3 . 5. *Andrachne.*
      Flowers without petals, male with a rudimentary ovary of 3 linear, erect styles . . . . 8. *Flueggia.*
    Stamens numerous. A tree . . . . . . 11. *Mallotus.*
  Herbs. Female flowers sessile in the axils of conspicuous bracts . . . . 10. *Acalypha.*

1. EUPHORBIA. The Greek name for certain species of the genus.—All regions except the very cold (Britain, Spurge).

Herbs or shrubs, abounding in milky juice. Leaves alternate or opposite, undivided. Inflorescence axillary or terminal, cymose or umbellate. In the umbellate form the stem or branches terminate in a whorl of several leaves placed under a compound umbel of 5–9 primary rays, each ray ending in a whorl of 3 bracts and branching in 3 secondary rays, which sometimes again divide, bearing 2 bracts at the forks. Flowers small, both sexes contained in a cup-shaped, 4–5-toothed or lobed involucre, thus having the appearance of a single flower; teeth or lobes almost concealed by 5 horizontal glands placed in their angles; glands smooth, fleshy, usually yellow-green or purple, sometimes conspicuous from a petal-like border; margins rounded and entire, or crescent-shaped with projecting horns. Male flowers numerous, each consisting of a single stalked stamen without any perianth, a joint marking the division between stalk and filament, with minute, linear, hairy scales interspersed among them: anther-cells globose. Female flowers: one placed in the centre of each involucre and surrounded by the male flowers: perianth none; ovary 3-celled, stalked, protruding from the involucre; styles 3, usually branched, the tips spreading or recurved. Capsule globose, 3-lobed, splitting into 3 two-valved, one-seeded cocci.

Leaves opposite. Involucral glands with a petal-like border.
Glands green. Styles short.
Leaves $\frac{1}{2}$–1 in. long . . . . 1. *E. hypericifolia.*
Leaves $\frac{1}{4}$ in. long . . . . 3. *E. thymifolia.*
Glands purple. Styles long . . . . 2. *E. Emodi.*
Leaves alternate. Involucral glands not bordered.
A cactus-like shrub. Branches 5-angled. Involucres in cymes . . . . 4. *E. Royleana.*
Herbs. Branches round. Involucres usually in umbels.
Glands rounded, entire.
Styles united for about half their length . . 5. *E. pilosa.*
Styles free to the base . . . . . . 6. *E. Helioscopia.*
Glands crescent-shaped.
Leaves obovate-spathulate . . . . . . 7. *E. Maddeni.*
Leaves linear or oblong . . . . . . 8. *E. prolifera.*

1. **Euphorbia hypericifolia,** *Linn.*; *Fl. Br. Ind.* v. 249. A glabrous or slightly pubescent, annual herb; stems 6–16 in., erect or ascending, sometimes decumbent. Leaves opposite, shortly stalked, oblong, $\frac{1}{2}$–1 × $\frac{1}{4}$–$\frac{1}{2}$ in., tip rounded, base rounded or cordate, margins toothed except near the bottom. Involucres minute, in terminal or axillary cymes often with 2 floral leaves at their base; teeth 4; glands green, conspicuously bordered by a white or pale pink, rounded limb. Styles very short. Capsule pubescent; seeds smooth. (Fig. 145.)

Simla; April–October.—Throughout India, ascending to 4000 ft.—All tropical regions except Australia and the Pacific islands.

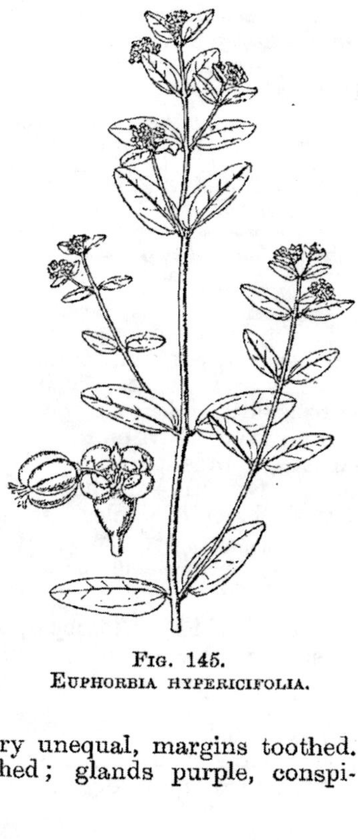

FIG. 145.
EUPHORBIA HYPERICIFOLIA.

2. **Euphorbia Emodi,** *Hook. f.*; *Fl. Br. Ind.* v. 250 An annual herb, usually hairy; stems 4–10 in., straggling from the base, ascending or decumbent, often purple. Leaves opposite, nearly sessile, oblong, $\frac{1}{4}$–$\frac{3}{4}$ in., tip obtuse, base very unequal, margins toothed. Involucres minute, axillary, 4-toothed; glands purple, conspi-

cuously bordered with a broad, white or pink, rounded limb. Styles long. Capsule glabrous; seeds rough with minute points.

Valleys below Simla; April–October.—W. Himalaya, 1500–4000 ft.—W. Asia.

3. **Euphorbia thymifolia,** *Burm.*; *Fl. Br. Ind.* v. 252. A pubescent, much branched, annual herb; stems 4–12 in., spreading flat on the ground. Leaves opposite, oblong, $\frac{1}{4}$ in., obtuse; teeth acute or rounded. Involucres minute, axillary; teeth 4; glands green, narrowly bordered with a white, rounded limb. Styles short. Capsule pubescent; seeds wrinkled.

Valleys below Simla, on roads and in waste places; April–October.—Throughout India, ascending to 4000 ft.—All hot countries except Australia.

4. **Euphorbia Royleana,** *Boiss.*; *Fl. Br. Ind.* v. 257. An erect, glabrous, fleshy shrub of cactus-like aspect, attaining 15 ft.; stems sometimes 2–3 ft. or more in girth; branches straight, ascending, prominently 5- or sometimes 6- or 7-angled. Leaves 4–6 in., inserted along the angles of the branches, soon falling off, alternate, sessile, spathulate, entire; stipules thorny, persistent. Involucres $\frac{1}{2}$ in. diam., yellow, in sessile, axillary cymes; lobes 4, spathulate, fringed; glands brown, rounded. Styles long. Capsule $\frac{3}{4}$ in. diam., glabrous.

Common on dry hills below 6000 ft.; June, July.—W. Himalaya.

This plant is usually called a cactus, but the Cactaceæ, with the exception of the genus *Rhipsalis*, found in S. Africa, the Mauritius and Ceylon, are indigenous only in America. The genus *Opuntia*, Prickly Pear, has been introduced into nearly all warm countries, and *O. Dillenii* has been naturalised in India, and may sometimes be seen as a hedge-plant near Simla. It is easily recognised by the thick, flat, fleshy joints of its branches dotted with hairy tufts of short, spinescent bristles, and its large, orange-red, many-petalled flowers.

5. **Euphorbia pilosa,** *Linn.*; *Fl. Br. Ind.* v. 260. A glabrous or pubescent, perennial herb; stems 1–3 ft., erect, branched at the top. Leaves alternate, sessile, oblong, $\frac{3}{4}$–$2\frac{1}{2}$ in., entire, narrowed to the base or rounded, tip rounded. Inflorescence umbellate; bracts yellow-green. Involucres $\frac{1}{8}$ in. diam., 5-toothed; glands yellow, margins rounded, entire. Styles long, united about half their length. Capsule $\frac{1}{4}$ in. diam., more or less covered with small, often minutely hairy tubercles; seeds smooth.

Simla, common; May–July.—W. Himalaya, ascending to 8000 ft.—N. and W. Asia, Europe, including Britain.

6. **Euphorbia Helioscopia,** *Linn.*; *Fl. Br. Ind.* v. 262. A glabrous, erect, annual herb; stems 6–18 in., usually much branched at the top. Stem-leaves alternate, shortly stalked, obovate or spathulate, $\frac{1}{2}$–2 in.; lower ones smaller, tip finely toothed. Inflorescence umbellate, rays often very short. Involucres 4-toothed; glands yellow, rounded, entire. Styles free. Capsule $\frac{1}{8}$ in. diam., smooth; seeds minutely net-veined.

Simla, common; March–November.—Punjab and W. Himalaya, up to 8000 ft., in fields.—W. Asia, Europe, including Britain (Sun Spurge); widely colonised in other countries.

7. **Euphorbia Maddeni,** *Boiss.*; *Fl. Br. Ind.* v. 263. A glabrous, erect, annual herb; stems 6–24 in., usually much branched. Stem-leaves alternate, sessile, obovate-spathulate, $2 \times \frac{1}{2}$ in. or smaller, narrowed to the base, tip rounded. Involucres solitary in the forks of the branches or in the axils of the opposite leaves on the flowering branches or sometimes in umbels; teeth 4 or 5; glands

FIG. 146. SARCOCOCCA PRUNIFORMIS.

yellow, crescent-shaped, horns long and slender. Styles free nearly to the base. Capsule $\frac{1}{8}$ in. diam., smooth; seeds smooth.

Mushobra, Mahasu; May–July.—W. Himalaya, 5000–9000 ft.
Aspect of *E. Peplus*, a common weed in Britain.

8. **Euphorbia prolifera,** *Buch.-Ham.*; *Fl. Br. Ind.* v. 264. Perennial, glabrous; rootstock thick and woody; stems 6–24 in., erect, often emitting barren, densely leafy, rooting shoots from near the base. Stem-leaves alternate, sessile, thick, usually linear, $1\text{–}3 \times \frac{1}{6}$ in., sometimes oblong, $1\frac{1}{2} \times \frac{1}{3}$ in., entire, tips acute or obtuse. Inflorescence umbellate. Involucres $\frac{1}{8}$ in. diam.; teeth 4–5; glands yellow, crescent-shaped, horns usually short and blunt, the margins

between them entire or toothed. Styles united about half their length. Capsule $\frac{1}{6}$–$\frac{1}{4}$ in. diam., smooth; seeds smooth.

Valleys below Simla; April–June.—N. India, ascending to 6000 ft.

2. SARCOCOCCA. From the Greek *sarx, sarkos*, flesh, and *kokkos*, a berry; alluding to the fleshy fruit.—Asia.

Sarcococca pruniformis, *Lindl.*; *Fl. Br. Ind.* v. 266. A glabrous shrub, 2–4 ft. Leaves alternate, shortly stalked, narrowly lanceolate, 3–4 × $\frac{1}{2}$–1 in., long-pointed, entire. Flowers pale yellow, $\frac{1}{3}$ in. long, in short, erect, axillary racemes, a few female towards the base, the rest male. Male flowers: sepals 4, oblong, obtuse; stamens 4, free, opposite the sepals, protruding. Female flowers: sepals reduced to several small, overlapping scales; ovary 2–3-celled, terminating in 2 long, recurved, flattened styles. Drupe dark purple, ovoid, about $\frac{1}{3}$ in. long, containing 2–3 stones. (Fig. 146.)

Simla, the Glen, common; March–May.—Temperate Himalaya, 5000–9000 ft.; hills in S. India.—W. Asia.

3. BUXUS. Name of Greek origin; application uncertain.—Asia, Africa, Europe, W. Indies.

Buxus sempervirens, *Linn.*; *Fl. Br. Ind.* v. 267. A much branched shrub or small tree. Leaves nearly sessile, opposite, narrowly lanceolate or ovate, 1–3 in., entire, usually obtuse. Flowers small, yellow-green, strongly scented, in small, axillary heads or spikes; the terminal flower usually female, the rest male. Male flowers: sepals 4; stamens 4, opposite to the sepals, far protruding; ovary rudimentary. Female flowers: sepals 6; ovary triangular, 3-celled, top flat, the 3 corners ending in thick, short styles. Capsule ovoid, $\frac{1}{2}$ in. long, 3-horned; seeds 3–6, small.

Simla, Mushobra, Mahasu; March–May.—Temperate Himalaya, 5000–9000 ft.—W. Asia, N. Africa, Europe, including Britain (Common Box).

4. BRIDELIA. In honour of S. E. Bridel-Brideri, a Swiss botanist of the eighteenth century.—Tropical regions of Asia, Africa and Australia.

***Bridelia montana,** *Willd.*; *Fl. Br. Ind.* v. 269. A glabrous tree. Leaves alternate, shortly stalked, entire, ovate or obovate, 3–6 × 2–4 in. Flowers minute, pale green, nearly sessile, in small, dense, axillary clusters, male and female together; bracts small, numerous, pubescent. Calyx 5-parted; segments broadly lanceolate, acute. Petals 5, orbicular, shortly clawed. Male flowers: stamens 5, the lower portion of the filaments united in an erect column rising from a flat, sinuately margined disk; pistil rudimentary enclosed by the staminal column, tip protruding. Female flowers: ovary ovoid, 2- sometimes 3-celled, nearly enclosed in the fleshy disk ; styles 2, terminal, 2-branched. Drupe ovoid, $\frac{1}{4}$ in. long, seated on the persistent calyx; stones usually 2.

Lower hills from Assam to the Jheelam, ascending to 3500 ft. ; April, May.

5. ANDRACHNE. Origin of name obscure.—Asia, S. Europe, N. America.

Andrachne cordifolia, *Muell. Arg.* ; *Fl. Br. Ind.* v. 283. A small shrub; branches round, glabrous, slender. Leaves alternate, long-stalked, thin, entire, ovate-oblong, $1\text{–}3\frac{1}{2} \times \frac{1}{3}\text{–}1\frac{1}{2}$ in., base

FIG. 147. ANDRACHNE CORDIFOLIA.

rounded or narrowed into the stalk, rarely cordate, upper surface glabrous, lower pale and thinly hairy. Flowers $\frac{1}{6}$ in. diam., green, on long, slender, axillary stalks, the males usually in clusters of 3–6, the female solitary, both sexes on the same plant. Male flowers : calyx 5-parted, segments ovate ; petals 5, spathulate ; disk 10-toothed, star-like ; stamens 5, surrounding a small, rudimentary pistil, filaments incurved. Female flowers : calyx as in the male but enlarging in fruit to $\frac{1}{2}$ in. diam. ; petals reduced to minute glands ; disk a fleshy ring encircling the base of the globose, 3-celled ovary ; styles 3, deeply divided in 2 long branches. Capsule globose $\frac{1}{4}$ in. diam., 6-valved ; seeds 6, triangular. (Fig. 147.)

Simla, the Glen, Mushobra ; May–September.—Temperate Himalaya, 5000–8000 ft.—W. Asia.

6. PHYLLANTHUS. From the Greek *phyllon*, a leaf, and *anthos*, a flower; the flowering branches having, in some species, the appearance of pinnate leaves bearing flowers.—All warm countries.

Trees or small shrubs, often herb-like. Leaves alternate, in two rows, sessile or nearly so, glabrous, entire. Flowers small, clustered or solitary, male and female on the same plant. Sepals 6, oblong, obtuse. Male flowers: disk obsolete or of minute glands; stamens 3, rarely 5, filaments short, more or less united at the base, rarely free. Female flowers: ovary globose, 3-celled, styles 3, reflexed, each deeply divided in two branches. Fruit globose, succulent or dry, obscurely 6-lobed; seeds 6.

A tree. Flowers densely clustered along the branches. Fruit succulent . . . . 1. *P. Emblica.*
Small, herb-like shrubs. Flowers axillary, solitary or 2–3 together. Fruit a capsule
 Leaves ovate, $\frac{1}{8}$–$\frac{1}{2}$ in. Seeds smooth . . . . 2. *P. parvifolius.*
 Leaves narrowly oblong, $\frac{1}{2}$–$1\frac{1}{2}$ in. Seeds rough . . 3. *P. simplex.*

1 **Phyllanthus Emblica,** *Linn.*; *Fl. Br. Ind.* v. 239. A small tree; foliage light green, feathery. Leaves narrowly oblong, $\frac{1}{2}$ in., closely set on pubescent branchlets having the appearance of pinnate leaves. Flowers green-yellow, densely clustered along the branchlets; male numerous, female few, both sexes on the same branchlets. Male flowers: stalks short; filaments united in a short column; disk obsolete. Female flowers nearly sessile: disk a fringed cup enclosing the ovary; style-branches flattened and lobed at the tips. Fruit succulent, globose, $\frac{2}{3}$ in. diam., green or pale yellow, often tinged with red when ripe, very acid and astringent, enclosing 3 two-seeded cocci.

Sutlej valley, in dry forest; March–May.—Throughout India, ascending to 4500 ft.—China, Malay islands.

The bark, leaves and fruit are used for tanning; the fruit is also employed in medicine and pickled for eating. Native name *aoula*.

2. **Phyllanthus parvifolius,** *Buch.-Ham.*; *Fl. Br. Ind.* v. 294. A small shrub, 1–4 ft., rarely larger; stems sometimes half-prostrate; branches slender, often pendulous, minutely pubescent in lines. Leaves ovate or oblong-ovate, $\frac{1}{3}$–$\frac{1}{2}$ in., pale on the lower surface. Flowers minute, brown-purple, stalked, axillary, mostly solitary. Male flowers: filaments united at the base, disk represented by glands. Female flowers: ovary encircled at its base by the ring-like disk; style-branches undivided. Capsule $\frac{1}{8}$ in. diam.; seeds smooth.

Naldera, Theog, often growing in crevices of rocks.—September, October.—Temperate Himalaya, 5000–7000 ft.

3. **Phyllanthus simplex,** *Retz.*; *Fl. Br. Ind.* v. 295. A small, glabrous shrub, 1–3 ft.; branches slender, erect. Leaves narrowly oblong, $\frac{1}{2}$–$1\frac{1}{2}$ in., pale on the lower surface. Flowers minute,

brown-purple, stalked, axillary, solitary or 2–3 together, the female overtopping the male. Male flowers: stamens 3, filaments free; disk represented by glands. Female flowers: sepals reflexed in fruit; ovary encircled at the base by the ring-like disk; style-branches undivided. Capsule $\frac{1}{10}$ in. diam.; seeds minutely rough.

Valleys below Simla; July–October.—Throughout India, ascending to 6000 ft.—China, Pacific islands.

7. GLOCHIDION. From the Greek *glochis*, a point; referring to the pointed anthers.—Tropical regions, chiefly Asia.

Glochidion velutinum, *Wight*; *Fl. Br. Ind.* v. 322. A small tree; young branches softly tomentose. Leaves alternate, in two rows, shortly stalked, pubescent, entire, ovate or oblong-ovate, 2–3 in., pointed. Flowers small, green-yellow, in axillary clusters, the male and female usually in the same cluster. Disk none. Male flowers stalked: sepals 6, lanceolate, spreading, hairy outside; stamens 3, filaments very short, united, anthers oblong, cohering, pointed by the prolonged connective. Female flowers nearly sessile: sepals 5 or 6, ovate, erect, hairy outside; ovary globose; styles 3, united in a thick, cylindric column 4–5-lobed at the top and projecting above the sepals. Capsule $\frac{1}{3}$ in. diam., globose, more or less flattened, 4–6-celled, 8–12-lobed, crowned by the persistent styles; seeds 8–12, red.

Sutlej valley; May, June.—Outer Himalaya up to 5000 ft.—S. India.

8. FLUEGGIA. In honour of J. Flügge, a German botanist and author of a monograph of the grasses in 1810.—Tropical regions of the Old World.

Flueggia microcarpa, *Bl.*; *Fl. Br. Ind.* v. 328. A glabrous shrub. Leaves alternate, in two rows, shortly stalked, ovate or orbicular, 1–2 in. entire. Flowers minute, yellow-green, in axillary clusters, the male and female on separate plants. Calyx 5-cleft. Male flowers numerous, long-stalked, in rounded, dense clusters: sepals spreading; stamens 5, opposite the sepals, surrounding a rudimentary ovary consisting of 3 long, linear, erect styles, filaments free, long, far-exserted; disk represented by 5 glands alternating with the stamens. Female flowers shortly stalked, in clusters of 3–6: sepals erect; ovary ovoid, encircled at the base by the ring-shaped, toothed disk; styles 3 or 4, shortly united at the base, reflexed and each deeply divided into 2 or 3 narrow, pointed lobes. Fruit globose, crowned by the star-like stigma, of two kinds, usually dry, 6-lobed, and about $\frac{1}{6}$ in. diam., sometimes white and fleshy, $\frac{1}{3}$ in. diam.; seeds 3–6, minutely dotted.

Valleys below Simla; May–July.—Throughout India, ascending to 5000 ft. —China, Australia, Africa.

9. PUTRANJIVA. From two Sanskrit words signifying the life of the child, referring to the stones of the fruit being worn as necklaces by children to preserve them from harm.—India.

***Putranjiva Roxburghii,** *Wall.*; *Fl. Br. Ind.* v. 336. A tree; young shoots and flowers pubescent, otherwise glabrous; branches drooping. Leaves alternate, shortly stalked, dark green, oblong-ovate, 3–5 in., entire or toothed, base unequal, margins crimped, tip obtuse, acute or long-pointed. Flowers small, axillary, stalked, yellow, the male and female usually on different trees. Male flowers numerous, in dense, rounded clusters: calyx 3–5-parted, segments unequal; stamens 3, filaments short, united at the base. Female flowers solitary or in pairs: calyx 5–6-parted, segments minute; ovary 3-celled; styles 3, short, spreading, dilated into broad, crescent-shaped, lobed stigmas. Drupe ovoid, ⅔ in. long, pointed, white-tomentose, 1-celled; stone hard, deeply wrinkled.

Valleys of the outer hills; March–May.—Throughout India, ascending to 2500 ft.—Often cultivated.

10. ACALYPHA. From the Greek name of the common nettle.—All tropical and subtropical regions.

Weak, straggling, more or less pubescent herbs, having the aspect of nettles. Leaves alternate, long-stalked, ovate, pointed. Flowers minute, in short, axillary spikes, both sexes on the same spike. Male flowers few, in small, sessile clusters towards the end of the spike, the summit being occupied by 1 or 2 abortive ones: sepals 4; disk none; stamens usually 8, filaments free, short, anther-cells distinct, diverging, linear, often twisted; rudimentary pistil none. Female flowers 1–3, rarely all fertile, sessile in the axils of conspicuous bracts placed below the male flowers: sepals 3–4; ovary 3-celled; styles free, long, threadlike. Capsule concealed in the bracts; cocci 3, seeds 3.

Bracts of female flowers cut into 3 linear, entire segments . 1. *A. brachystachya.*
Bracts of female flowers orbicular, deeply fringed . . 2. *A. ciliata.*

1. **Acalypha brachystachya,** *Hornem.*; *Fl. Br. Ind.* v. 416. Stems 6–12 in. Leaves 1–3 in. crenate, base often cordate. Spikes ½ in., male portion very short. Bracts of the female flowers green, usually only 2 or 3, cut into 3 linear, entire, 1-nerved, obtuse, spreading lobes. Capsule roughly hairy.

Simla; July–October.—Temperate Himalaya, 4000–8000 ft.—S. India.—Java, Africa.

2. **Acalypha ciliata,** *Forsk.*; *Fl. Br. Ind.* v. 417. Stems 1–2 ft. Leaves 2–3 in., sharply toothed, often long-pointed. Spikes ¾ in. Bracts of the female flowers pale coloured, usually 6–10, orbicular;

nerves many, radiating and projecting in a long, marginal fringe. Capsule glabrous.

Valleys below Simla, Subathoo; July–October.—Throughout India, ascending to 6000 ft.—Arabia, Africa.

11. MALLOTUS. From the Greek *mallotos*, woolly; referring to the tomentose leaves and branches of many species.—Tropical regions of the Old World.

Mallotus philippinensis, *Muell. Arg.*; *Fl. Br. Ind.* v. 442. A small tree; young branches and inflorescence rusty-pubescent. Leaves alternate, long-stalked, variable in form, usually ovate or ovate-lanceolate, 3–6 in., entire or sinuate, upper surface glabrous, lower rusty-tomentose, minutely scarlet-dotted. Flowers small, in panicled racemes or spikes, the male and female on different trees. Male flowers yellow, shortly stalked, usually 3 together, in slender, drooping racemes 3–6 in. long: sepals 3–4, reflexed; stamens numerous, filaments free. Female flowers sessile, solitary, in stiff, nearly erect spikes 2–3 in. long: sepals usually 2, half-enclosing the scarlet, 3-celled ovary; styles 3, free, $\frac{1}{4}$ in. long, green, spreading. Capsule globose, $\frac{1}{3}$ in. diam., 3-lobed, covered with a bright red powder; seeds 3, black, smooth.

Sutlej and Giri valleys; October–January.—Throughout India, ascending to 4500 ft.—China, Australia.

The powder on the ripe fruit is collected in some parts of India for export; it is used for dyeing silk and in medicine.

12. SAPIUM. From the Latin *sapo*, soap, referring to the milky juice, containing caoutchouc, in which the trees of this genus abound.—Tropical regions.

Sapium insigne, *Benth.*; *Fl. Br. Ind.* v. 471. A glabrous shrub or small tree; branches thick, soft, leafy towards the end. Leaves alternate, bright green, toothed, ovate or oblong-lanceolate, 6–12 in.; stalks 1–2 in. bearing two large glands near the top. Flowers appearing before the leaves, small, yellow-green, on thick, erect, terminal, solitary spikes 3–10 in. long, male and female on the same plant but on different spikes. Male flowers in circular clusters $\frac{1}{4}$ in. diam., central ones soon falling off and leaving their short stalks, outer ones sessile: calyx membranous, deeply 2-lipped, segments concave, rounded; stamens 2, filaments very short, free, anthers scarlet. Female flowers solitary, shortly stalked: spike much thickened in fruit; sepals 2–3, ovate, long-pointed; ovary globose, 3-celled; styles 3, free, short, recurved. Capsule $\frac{1}{4}$ in. long, obscurely 3-lobed, fleshy when young; seeds 3.

Valleys below Simla; January–March.—Subtropical Himalaya, up to 6000 ft.—Burmah.

In the hot valleys of the outer hills this species is a tree 50 ft. high with a trunk 3 ft. in girth. Near Simla it rarely exceeds 10 or 12 ft., and is often killed by the frost.

XCI. URTICACEÆ

Trees, shrubs or herbs of various habit. Leaves stipulate, usually alternate and undivided, never pinnate. Flowers small, inconspicuous, usually 1-sexual, in panicles, spikes, cymes or clusters, or sometimes crowded on a fleshy receptacle either open and saucerlike as in *Lecanthus* and *Elatostemma* or closed and flasklike as in *Ficus*. Corolla none. Male flowers: perianth usually 4–5-lobed or parted; stamens as many as and opposite to the perianth-segments, rarely fewer, filaments free, sometimes corrugated and inflexed in bud, suddenly straightening and scattering the pollen as the flower opens, anthers 2-celled; rudimentary pistil small or none. Female flowers: perianth lobed or tubular, usually enclosing, rarely adnate to the one-celled ovary, often persistent; style entire, 2-branched, very short or absent; stigma often resembling a sessile tuft of hairs. Fruit various; seed 1.—A very large Order, chiefly tropical but more or less represented in nearly all regions.

The flowers are mostly anemophilous, the pollen being conveyed from the male to the female flowers by the wind; but the agency of insects appears to be indispensable in the fertilisation of the Figs, *Ficus*.

The Hop, *Humulus Lupulus*, cultivated in Kashmir &c., and the Jackfruit, *Artocarpus integrifolia*, and *A. Lakoocha*, sometimes seen in cultivation in the plains of the North West, belong to this Order.

Trees or shrubs.	
Fruit the product of one flower.	
A samara	1. *Ulmus*.
A drupe	
Leaves smooth	2. *Celtis*.
Leaves rough	3. *Trema*.
An achene enclosed in a dry perianth	
Flowers in long spikes	12. *Bœhmeria*.
Flowers in axillary clusters[1]	13. *Pouzolzia*.[1]
Fruit the product of numerous flowers.	
A short, globose spike of numerous, succulent perianths	5. *Morus*.
A head of numerous small drupes	15. *Debregeasia*.
A closed, flasklike receptacle containing numerous, minute achenes	6. *Ficus*.
An open, flat receptacle with numerous, minute achenes partially immersed in it	14. *Villebrunea*.
Herbs.	
Leaves alternate.	
Plants with stinging hairs	8. *Girardinia*.
Plants without stinging hairs.	
Stigma of 2 linear branches	4. *Cannabis*.
Stigma resembling a tuft of hairs.	
Flowers on a saucerlike receptacle	11. *Elatostemma*.[2]
Flowers in cymose clusters	16. *Parietaria*.

[1] *P. viminea* only; the other species are herbs. [2] The ordinary leaves sometimes have a minute leaf opposite to them.

Leaves opposite.
  Plants with stinging hairs . . . . 7. *Urtica.*
  Plants without stinging hairs.
    Flowers on a saucerlike receptacle . . . . . 10. *Lecanthus.*
    Flowers panicled . . . . 9. *Pilea.*
    Flowers in axillary clusters . . . . 13. *Pouzolzia.*[1]

1. ULMUS. The classical name of the Elm-tree.—N. temperate regions, including Britain (Wych-Elm, *U. montana*).

Ulmus Wallichiana, *Planch.*; *Fl. Br. Ind.* v. 480. A tree, often 80–90 ft. high. Leaves alternate, shortly stalked, ovate, 4–8 in., long-pointed, base unequal, cordate or tapering, margins sharply, often doubly toothed. Flowers red-brown, appearing before the leaves, 2-sexual, clustered in racemes about 1 in. long. Perianth persistent; lobes 5–6, obtuse, fringed. Stamens 5–6, longer than the perianth, inserted on the tube, anthers purple. Ovary 2-celled; style-arms 2, long, slender. Fruit a winged nut or samara, $\frac{1}{2}$–$\frac{2}{3}$ in. diam., stalk very slender, wings rounded, membranous; nut central, containing a single seed.

Narkunda, in forest; common; March, April.—W. Himalaya, 4000–10,000 ft. The wood is used for making furniture.

2. CELTIS. From the Greek *celtis*, a whip; referring to the use of the wood for whip handles.—Temperate and tropical regions, chiefly in the Northern Hemisphere.

Celtis australis, *Linn.*; *Fl. Br. Ind.* v. 482. A tree. Leaves alternate, shortly stalked, nearly glabrous, ovate, 3–5 in., long-pointed, sharply toothed, base very unequal. Flowers pale yellow, appearing before or with the leaves, polygamous; the male in clusters or short racemes towards the base of the shoots; the female and 2-sexual in the axils of the upper leaves. Perianth soon falling off, 4–5-parted; segments obtuse. Male flowers: stamens 4–5, surrounding a woolly disk. Female: ovary ovoid, seated on a hairy disk; style-arms 2, broad, sessile, spreading. Fruit a long-stalked, ovoid, usually solitary drupe, about $\frac{1}{3}$ in. long, more or less woolly at the base or sometimes all over; stone wrinkled.

Simla, Boileaugunge; April, May.—Temperate Himalaya, 4000–8000 ft.—Westward to Spain.

Often planted near villages; commonly lopped for fodder.

The variety with a woolly drupe, *C. eriocarpa*, has been collected at Barmu, north of Simla.

3. TREMA. From the Greek *trema*, a hole; the nut is minutely pitted.—Tropical and subtropical regions.

[1] The uppermost floral leaves in *P. pentandra* are alternate; *P. viminea* is a shrub.

***Trema politoria**, *Planch.*; *Fl. Br. Ind.* v. 484. A small tree; branchlets roughly hairy. Leaves alternate, shortly stalked, hard and very rough, oblong- or ovate-lanceolate, 2–5 in., often long-pointed, base rounded, nearly equal; teeth small, sharp, regular. Flowers 1-sexual, in small, axillary cymes, the male and female on the same tree. Male flowers: perianth 5-parted; stamens 5. Female flowers: perianth 5-parted, persistent; ovary globose; styles 2, short, linear. Fruit a small, globose drupe seated on the perianth and crowned by the styles.

Valleys of the outer Himalaya, on roadsides in hedges and on waste ground; April–June.—Throughout N. India, up to 3000 ft.

The leaves are as hard as sandpaper, and are used to polish wood and horn. Rough ropes are made from the fibre.

4. CANNABIS. The classical name of the Hemp. The genus contains only one species.—N.W. Himalaya, Central Asia; cultivated and naturalised elsewhere.

Cannabis sativa, *Linn.*; *Fl. Br. Ind.* v. 487. An erect herb; stems grooved, finely tomentose, 3–10 ft. or taller in cultivation; branches few, slender. Leaves stalked, palmate, alternate or the lower opposite; lobes 1–5 in the upper leaves, 5–11 in the lower, linear-lanceolate, 2–8 in., the middle one longest, coarsely and sharply toothed, long-pointed, narrowed to the base, upper surface dark green, rough, lower pale downy. Flowers pale yellow-green, 1-sexual, the male and female on separate and dissimilar plants. Male flowers clustered in short, axillary, drooping panicles: perianth 5-parted, segments boat-shaped; stamens 5, filaments long, threadlike. Female flowers axillary, sessile, erect: perianth a single entire leaf enclosing the ovary; style-arms 2, threadlike, protruding. Fruit an achene, about $\frac{1}{12}$ in., enclosed in the persistent perianth.

Simla, common, especially near houses; July, August.

The intoxicating drugs *gánjá* and *charas* are prepared from a resinous exudation of the stem, young leaves and flowers. *Bhang* consists of the larger leaves dried and mixed with a few achenes. The fibrous stems furnish hemp. The seeds are used as food for cage-birds.

5. MORUS. The classical name of the Mulberry.—Tropical and temperate regions.

Trees or shrubs. Leaves alternate, stalked, ovate, often lobed, toothed, base 3-nerved. Flowers 1-sexual, in shortly stalked spikes, male and female on the same or on different trees. Male flower-spikes 1–2 in., falling off after flowering: perianth 4-parted; stamens 4, filaments flattened at the base. Female flower-spikes about $\frac{1}{2}$ in.: perianth-segments 4 or 3, rarely 2, enclosing the ovary and becoming succulent in fruit; style-arms 2. Fruit a short, globose, fleshy spike resulting from the union of the numerous perianths, each enclosing a small achene.

Leaves with small and nearly uniform teeth.
Style-arms glabrous or nearly so, short, free to the base . 1. *M. alba.*
Style-arms hairy, long, united for about one quarter of their length . . . . 2. *M. indica.*
Leaves with large and very unequal teeth . . . . . . 3. *M. serrata.*

1. **Morus alba,** *Linn.*; *Fl. Br. Ind.* v. 492. A middle-sized tree. Leaves 2–3 in., acute, often cordate; teeth small, nearly uniform; stalk $\frac{1}{2}$–1 in. Male and female flowers on the same tree. Female flowers: perianth-segments 4, glabrous or shortly fringed; style-arms glabrous or nearly so, short, free to the base. Fruit white or red, sweet.

Simla: cultivated throughout N. India, and up to 11,000 ft. in the Himalaya; March, April.—An introduced tree: believed to be wild in N. Asia and Afghanistan.

2. **Morus indica,** *Linn.*; *Fl. Br. Ind.* v. 492. A shrub or small tree. Leaves rough, 2–5 in., long-pointed, frequently deeply lobed, often cordate; teeth small, nearly uniform; stalk $\frac{1}{2}$–1$\frac{1}{2}$ in. Female flowers: perianth-segments 4, with broad, white edges; style-arms hairy, long, united for about one quarter of their length. Fruit black when ripe.

Simla, usually below 5000 ft.; February.—Temperate Himalaya, ascending to 7000 ft.

Cultivated in Bengal and elsewhere for its leaves which are used as food for silkworms. Closely allied to *M. alba* and not easily distinguished from it.

3. **Morus serrata,** *Roxb.*; *Fl. Br. Ind.* v. 492. A tree, sometimes 60 ft. high. Leaves broadly ovate, 2–8 in., long-pointed, usually cordate; teeth large and very unequal; stalk 1–2 in. Male and female flowers usually on different trees. Female flowers: perianth-segments 3, rarely 2 or 4; style-arms long, very hairy, united near the base. Fruit purple.

Simla, often planted near villages; April, May.—W. Himalaya, 4000–9000 ft.

6. **FICUS.** The classical name of the Common Fig.—A very large genus mostly inhabiting tropical countries.

Erect or climbing trees or shrubs; juice milky. Leaves alternate, opposite in *F. hispida*, undivided, sometimes lobed in *F. palmata*. Flowers minute, crowded on the inner surface of a hollow, globose or ovoid receptacle, usually 3-bracteate at the base, and more or less completely closed at the mouth by numerous, overlapping scales; receptacle or fig axillary or borne on special fruiting branches produced from the stem or boughs. Flowers often mixed with bracteoles, and, in the species here described, of three kinds, male, fertile female and imperfect, barren female or so-called gall-flowers. Male flowers usually placed near the mouth of the fig: perianth of 3–5 segments, free or sometimes united, thin and colourless, or sometimes opaque and red or brown; stamens usually one, sometimes two, rarely three, filaments short, rarely long, often united when more than one. Fertile female flowers: perianth usually as in the male, often very minute; ovary ovoid, style distinct, usually lateral, stigma various; ripe achenes seed-like, pale yellow. Gall-flowers more or less resembling the fertile female, but the style and stigma are rudimentary, and the ovary is empty, or contains the egg or pupa of an insect, never an ovule or seed.

The figs of the Banyan, *F. bengalensis*, of the Pipal, *F. religiosa*, and of *F. Rumphii*, contain all three kinds of flowers; in the other species the male and the gall-flowers are borne in one set of figs, and the fertile female in another set, the figs being externally quite similar. We thus see one set of figs containing barren female flowers associated with a number of pollen-producing males, while a different set contains only fertile female flowers, and yet these females all produce fertile seeds. In what manner the pollen is conveyed from the male flowers into the almost completely closed figs containing the female flowers has not yet been satisfactorily explained. That the flowers of the common edible fig, *F. Carica*, are unisexual was known to Linnæus, and had, indeed, in a vague way, been suspected since the time of Aristotle, but it is only within recent years that the existence and nature of gall-flowers have been demonstrated. Further details will be found in King's *Monograph of the Indo-Malayan and Chinese Figs*, published in the *Annals of the Royal Botanic Garden, Calcutta*, vol. i.

Most of the species have fruits which are eaten by birds, and their seeds thus become widely disseminated.

The India-rubber tree, *F. elastica*, wild in the Sikkim Himalaya and eastward, is sometimes planted in gardens in the lower hills. In its native country it is a large tree towering above the surrounding forest. Leaves leathery, shining, entire, oblong, 3–12 in., abruptly pointed; nerves closely parallel, stipules very large.

Figs borne on ordinary leafy branches, axillary.[1]
  Leaves entire.
    Leaf-stalks more than 2 in.
      Tail-like tip of leaf about $\frac{1}{6}$ of its total length . 2. *F. Rumphii.*
      Tail-like tip of leaf about $\frac{1}{3}$ of its total length . 3. *F. religiosa.*
    Leaf-stalks less than 1 in.
      A climbing or creeping shrub . . . . 7. *F. foveolata.*
      Erect shrubs or trees
        Leaves obtuse . . . . 1. *F. bengalensis.*
        Leaves long-pointed . . . . 9. *F. nemoralis.*
  Leaves toothed, at least in the upper half.
    Leaves oblong-lanceolate, 4–7 in.; stalks $\frac{1}{5}$ in. . 4. *F. clavata.*
    Leaves broadly ovate or lobed, 2–5 in.; stalks 1–2 in. . . . . 8. *F. palmata.*
Figs borne on special leafless branches.[1]
  Leaves opposite . . . . 5. *F. hispida.*

[1] *F. hispida* generally bears its figs on special leafless branches, but sometimes in axillary pairs on ordinary branches; it may always be known by its opposite leaves.

Leaves alternate.
 Leaves lanceolate; basal lobes very unequal. Figs $\frac{1}{2}$ in. diam. . . . . 6. *F. Cunia.*
 Leaves broadly ovate; basal lobes equal. Figs 2–3 in. diam. . . . . 10. *F. Roxburghii.*

1. **Ficus bengalensis,** *Linn.*; *Fl. Br. Ind.* v. 499. A large, spreading tree producing numerous, aerial roots which enter the ground and form trunks, thus indefinitely extending the growth of the tree; young parts pubescent, otherwise nearly or quite glabrous. Leaves leathery, ovate, 4–8 × 2–5 in., obtuse, entire; stalks $\frac{1}{2}$–2 in., thick. Figs pubescent, axillary, sessile in pairs, globose, $\frac{1}{2}$–$\frac{3}{4}$ in. diam., red when ripe.

Valleys below Simla; figs ripen April, May, and remain long on the tree.—Wild only in the sub-Himalayan forests and on the hills of Southern India; planted throughout the plains and up to 4000 ft. in the Himalaya. The Banyan.

The Banyan in the Calcutta Botanic Gardens began life as an epiphyte on a wild date-tree of which all trace has long disappeared. Dr. (now Sir George) King gave the following details regarding this famous tree in 1886. 'The tree is now about a hundred years old; it has 232 aerial roots all reaching the ground and forming trunks from a few inches to 12 ft. in girth. The main trunk girths 42 ft., the circumference of its leafy crown is 857 ft. It is still growing vigorously.'

*2. **Ficus Rumphii,** *Bl.*; *Fl. Br. Ind.* v. 512. A large tree, glabrous, often epiphytal, having the aspect of the Pipal, *F. religiosa,* to which it is closely allied. Leaves leathery, broadly ovate, 4–6 in., upper surface shining, base rounded, margins entire, slightly undulate, tip narrowed into a tail-like point about one-sixth of the total length of the leaf; stalks $2\frac{1}{2}$–$3\frac{1}{2}$ in. Figs axillary, sessile in pairs, globose, $\frac{1}{2}$ in. diam., pale with dark spots when young, nearly black when ripe; basal bracts 3, small, rounded.

Throughout India, ascending to 5000 ft., not common; figs ripen May, June.—Malay islands.

3. **Ficus religiosa,** *Linn.*; *Fl. Br. Ind.* v. 513. A large tree, glabrous, usually epiphytal. Leaves leathery, broadly ovate, $4\frac{1}{2}$–7 × 3–$4\frac{1}{2}$ in., upper surface shining, base rounded, margins entire, undulate, tip narrowed into a linear, tail-like point, about one third of the total length of the leaf; stalks 3–4 in., slender; young foliage flushed with pink. Figs axillary, sessile in pairs, globose, slightly vertically flattened, $\frac{1}{2}$ in. diam., dark purple when ripe; basal bracts 3, broad.

Valleys below Simla; figs ripen April, May.—Wild in the sub-Himalayan forests, in Bengal and in Central India; planted throughout the plains, and up to 5000 ft. in the Himalaya. The Pipal.

4. **Ficus clavata,** *Wall.*; *Fl. Br. Ind.* v. 520. An erect shrub; young branches rough. Leaves glabrous, rough, oblong-lanceolate, 4–7 in.; margins irregularly and sinuately toothed in the upper half, tip narrowed into a long point; stalks about $\frac{1}{3}$ in. Figs shortly

stalked, axillary, solitary or rarely in pairs, ovoid or globose, about ½ in., rough or wrinkled, yellow when ripe.

Sutlej valley, Basantpur, usually in forest undergrowth; figs ripen May, June.—Outer Himalaya, ascending to 4500 ft.—Burmah, Malacca.

*5. **Ficus hispida,** *Linn. f.*; *Fl. Br. Ind.* v. 522. A shrub or small tree, roughly pubescent all over. Leaves opposite, stalked, broadly ovate or ovate-oblong, 4–9 in., base rounded or slightly cordate or wedge-shaped, margins toothed, tip sometimes shortly and abruptly pointed. Figs shortly stalked, globose or slightly flattened, ½–1 in. diam., sometimes warty and bearing small, brown scales on the surface, usually clustered on short or long, leafless branches issuing from the stem or boughs, but sometimes in axillary pairs, pale yellow when ripe.

Common in the plains throughout India, ascending to 3500 ft.; figs ripen April, May.—Malay islands, China, Australia.

6. **Ficus Cunia,** *Buch.-Ham.*; *Fl. Br. Ind.* v. 523. A small tree. Leaves rough, especially when young, shortly stalked, oblong-lanceolate or ovate, 6–12 in., very unequally 2-lobed at the base, the lower lobe rounded, projecting, margins toothed at least in the upper half, tip long-pointed. Figs shortly stalked, globose, about ½ in. diam., rough and wrinkled, often scaly, borne on numerous, long, scaly, usually leafless branches issuing from the boughs and lower parts of the stem.

Valleys below Simla, Sutlej valley; figs ripen August, September and often at other seasons.—N. and Central India, ascending to 4000 ft.—Burmah.

7. **Ficus foveolata,** *Wall.*; *Fl. Br. Ind.* v. 528. A climbing or creeping shrub; stems, when young or when growing in damp, shady places, pubescent or hairy, creeping on rocks or trunks of trees, and rooting at the nodes; when older or when growing on open ground, nearly or quite glabrous, climbing, but without adventitious roots. Leaves usually glabrous, lanceolate or ovate-lanceolate, those on the creeping stems thin, rarely exceeding 2 in.; but on fruiting branches, and in open situations, leathery, 3-6 in., base rounded, cordate or wedge-shaped, margins always entire, tip acute, often long-pointed; stalks ½ in. or less, pubescent. Figs axillary, sessile or shortly stalked, solitary, globose, ⅓–½ in. diam., hairy, often warty and wrinkled. Fruit rarely or never produced in the creeping state.

Simla, the Glen, etc., the creeping form; the climbing form is not uncommon below Elysium, and on trees or on steep banks elsewhere; figs ripen June, July.—Outer Himalaya, 2000–7000 ft.—Burmah, China.

8. **Ficus palmata,** *Forsk.*; *Fl. Br. Ind.* v. 530. A shrub or small tree; young branches tomentose or pubescent, often becoming glabrous. Leaves thick, usually broadly ovate, 2–5 in., sometimes deeply 3–5-lobed, base cordate or wedge-shaped.

margins toothed, tip usually acute, upper surface rough, lower pubescent; stalk 1–2 in. Figs axillary, stalked, solitary, globose or pear-shaped, ½–1 in. diam., narrowed to the base, usually tomentose, purple when ripe. (Fig. 148.)

Simla, the Glen; figs edible, ripen June–October.—Central and N.W. India, ascending to 5000 ft., often cultivated.—Westward to Egypt and Abyssinia. The Indian representative of the common European edible fig, *F. Carica*.

9. **Ficus nemoralis,** *Wall.*; *Fl. Br. Ind.* v. 534. A glabrous shrub or small tree. Leaves lanceolate or ovate-lanceolate, 4–6

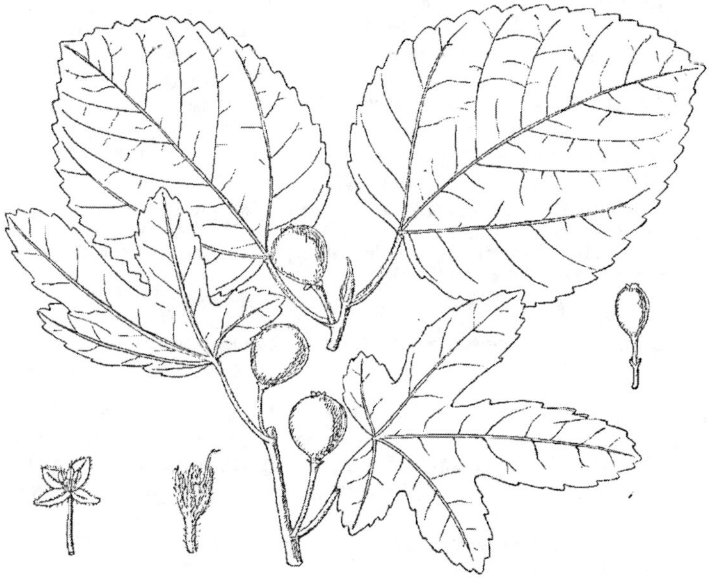

Fig. 148. Ficus palmata.

in., base wedge-shaped, often much narrowed, margins entire, tip narrowed into a long point; stalk ½–1 in. Figs axillary, sessile or shortly stalked, often crowded, globose, about ¼ in. diam., quite glabrous.

Simla, below Annandale, Shah; figs ripen August, September.—Temperate Himalaya, 1500–7000 ft.—Assam.

10. **Ficus Roxburghii,** *Wall.*; *Fl. Br. Ind.* v. 534. A spreading tree; young branches pubescent. Leaves stalked, broadly ovate, 6–12 × 5–9 in., sometimes even larger, deeply cordate, entire or toothed, usually shortly pointed. Figs stalked, clustered on short, thick, leafless branches issuing from the boughs or stem, some-

times close to the ground, broadly top-shaped, 1–2 in. long, 2–3 in. diam., strongly ridged, pubescent when young, becoming glabrous afterwards, russet-brown, tinged with red or dull purple when ripe.

Sutlej valley; figs ripen March–May.—Outer Himalaya, ascending to 5000 ft.—Burmah.

7. URTICA. From the Latin *uro*, to burn; referring to the pain caused by the stings.—Temperate and subtropical regions.

Erect herbs, more or less clothed with stinging hairs; inner bark containing tough fibres. Leaves opposite, long-stalked, thin, toothed. Flowers small, green, 1-sexual, clustered on the branches of loosely spreading, axillary panicles 1–3 in. long. Perianth 4-parted. Male flowers: perianth-segments concave; stamens 4, filaments rolled up in bud, straightening with a jerk when the flower opens. Female flowers: perianth-segments unequal, flat; stigma resembling a small tuft of hairs. Achene flattened, embraced by the persistent perianth.

The Roman nettle, *U. pilulifera*, a weed of waste places in England, occurs occasionally near houses in Simla. Leaves ovate, 1–3 in.; teeth very long, often linear, acute. Male flowers in slender, panicled spikes; female in globose heads; both sexes on the same plant.

Plants bearing flowers of both sexes. Leaves with small, irregular teeth . . . . 1. *U. parviflora.*
Plants bearing either male or female flowers. Leaves with large, regular teeth . . . . 2. *U. dioica.*

1. **Urtica parviflora,** *Roxb.*; *Fl. Br. Ind.* v. 548. Stems 3–5 ft., slender, obtusely angled. Leaves ovate or lanceolate, usually cordate, 2–4 × 1–2½ in., long-pointed; teeth small, acute, irregularly jagged; stipules united. Male and female flowers on the same plant.

Simla, common; flowers throughout the summer.—Temperate Himalaya, 5000–12,000 ft.—Nilghiris.

2. **Urtica dioica,** *Linn.*; *Fl. Br. Ind.* v. 548. Stems 3–5 ft., often robust, grooved. Leaves ovate or lanceolate, usually cordate, 2–4 in., long-pointed; teeth large, coarse, regular, acute; stipules usually free. Male and female flowers on separate plants.

Simla, Huttoo; June, July.—W. Himalaya, 7000–10,000 ft.—Westward to the Atlantic, including Britain (Common Nettle). Widely spread in other countries, but often introduced.

8. GIRARDINIA. In honour of Girardin, a French botanist, joint author of a Manual of Botany in 1827.—Tropical Asia and Africa.

Girardinia heterophylla, *Decne.*; *Fl. Br. Ind.* v. 550. A robust, coarse, erect herb, 4–6 ft., covered with rigid, sharp, stinging bristles. Leaves 4–12 in., alternate, stalked, 3-nerved from the base, broadly ovate, often deeply lobed, usually cordate, margins sharply toothed. Flowers small, green, 1-sexual, sessile, densely crowded. Male flowers in long, slender, often paniculately branched spikes: perianth 4-parted; stamens 4. Female flowers in short, oblong spikes becoming thick, densely bristly and often over 6 in. long in fruit: perianth tubular, narrowed upwards in a small 3-toothed mouth, splitting when the fruit ripens; style

FIG. 149. GIRARDINIA HETEROPHYLLA.

long, threadlike, persistent, stigma minute. Achenes flattened, ovate, black. (Fig. 149.)

Simla, common in forest; July, August.—Himalaya, S. India.—Java.

Roxburgh, *Fl. Ind.* p. 655, calls this 'a most ferocious looking plant.' The stings produce acute pain, but it is of short duration. The stems furnish a fine silky fibre, used in Sikkim for ropes, twine and coarse cloth.

9. PILEA. From the Latin *pileus*, a cap; the perianth-segments are connate and thrown off in the form of a cap.—Tropical regions.

Erect herbs. Leaves stalked, opposite, often unequal, toothed, 3-nerved from the base. Flowers minute, green, 1-sexual, sessile in clusters on the slender branches of stalked, spreading, axillary panicles 2–4 in. long, the male and female on the same or on different plants. Male flowers: perianth 4-parted; stamens 4, anthers white. Female flowers: perianth 3-parted, segments unequal; stigma resembling a small, sessile tuft of hairs. Achene flattened, embraced at the base by the persistent perianth.

Hairy. Leaves ovate; teeth large . . . . 1. *P. umbrosa.*
Glabrous. Leaves lanceolate; teeth small . . . . . 2. *P. scripta.*

1. **Pilea umbrosa**, *Wedd.*; *Fl. Br. Ind.* v. 556. More or less hairy; stems 1–4 ft. Leaves ovate, 3–5 × 2–3½ in., base wedge-

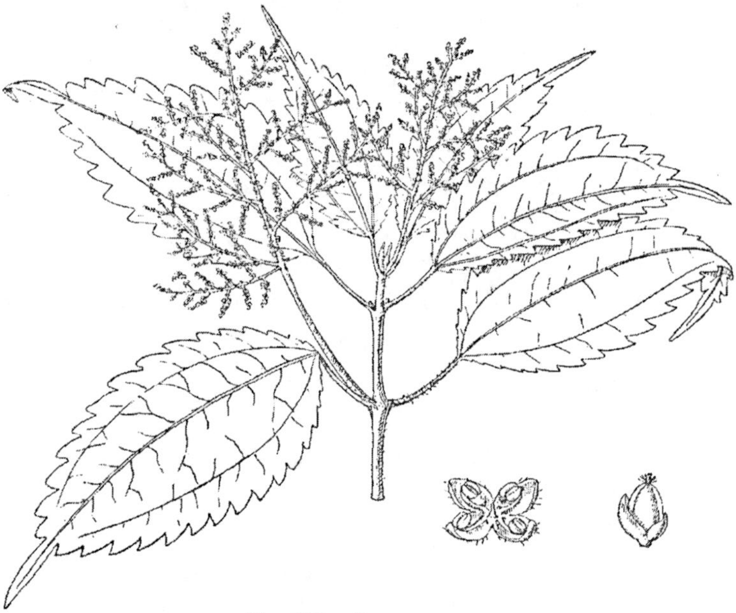

FIG. 150. PILEA UMBROSA.

shaped, rounded or cordate; tip tail-like, acute; teeth large, coarse, sharp; stalks 1–3 in. Achenes smooth. (Fig. 150.)

Simla, common in shady places; June-September.—Temperate Himalaya, 4000–9000 ft.

2. **Pilea scripta,** *Wedd.*; *Fl. Br. Ind.* v. 556. Glabrous; stems 1–4 ft. Leaves lanceolate, 3–8 × 1–2½ in., narrowed to both ends, long-pointed; teeth small, shallow; stalks ½–2 in. Achenes rough.

Simla, common in shady place ; June-September.—Temperate Himalaya, 4000–7000 ft.

10. LECANTHUS. From the Greek *lekane*, a dish, and *anthos*, a flower, referring to the shape of the floral receptacles.—India, China, Java, Africa.

Succulent, pubescent herbs; stems ascending, base decumbent and often rooting. Leaves opposite, stalked, unequal, ovate, toothed, 3-nerved from the oblique base; stipules united. Flowers minute, pink, 1-sexual, bracteolate, crowded on axillary, stalked, saucer-like receptacles bordered with involucral bracts; male and female on separate receptacles borne on the same or on different plants. Male flowers: perianth 4- or 5-parted, segments nearly equal; stamens 4 or 5. Female flowers: perianth 3- or 4-parted, segments nearly equal or very unequal, persistent; ovary straight; stigma divided into a tuft of hair-like branches, not persistent. Achenes rough with microscopic tufts of white hairs.

Stems 1–4 in. Receptacles $\frac{1}{4}$–$\frac{1}{3}$ in. diam. . . . . . 1. *L. Wightii.*
Stems 12–24 in. Receptacles $\frac{1}{2}$–$1\frac{1}{2}$ in. diam. . . . 2. *L. Wallichii.*

1. **Lecanthus Wightii,** *Wedd.*; *Fl. Br. Ind.* v. 559, in part Stems 1–4 in., weak. Leaves $\frac{1}{2}$–1 in. Receptacles $\frac{1}{4}$–$\frac{1}{3}$ in. diam., on stalks barely 1 in. long. Perianth of female flowers 3-parted; segments very unequal, one larger, hooded at the top, the other two flat. Achenes narrowly oblong, longer than the perianth, red.

Simla, on old walls, etc.; July-September.—Throughout India, ascending to 10,000 ft.—Africa.

2. **Lecanthus Wallichii,** *Wedd.*; *Fl. Br. Ind.* v. 559, under *L. Wightii* in part. Stems 12-24 in., robust. Leaves 2–4 in., tip long, tail-like. Receptacles $\frac{1}{2}$–$1\frac{1}{2}$ in. diam., on stalks 2–12 in. long. Perianth of female flowers 4-parted; segments nearly equal, hooded at the tip. Achenes ovoid, shorter than the perianth, purple-brown.

Simla, the Glen; July–September.—Throughout India, ascending to 10,000 ft.—Ceylon, China.

11. ELATOSTEMMA. From the Greek *elatos*, elastic, and *stemon*, a stamen; referring to the stamens unrolling with a jerk as the flowers open.—Tropical and subtropical regions of the Old World.

Pubescent or glabrous herbs; stems unbranched. Leaves alternate or sometimes opposite and very unequal in size. Flowers minute, green, 1-sexual, and interspersed with minute bracteoles, crowded on the surface of axillary, fleshy, saucer-like receptacles usually bordered with an involucre of bracts; male and female borne on the same or on different plants. Male flowers: perianth 4–5-parted; stamens 4–5. Female flowers: perianth 3-parted, segments unequal, persistent; stigma resembling a sessile tuft of hairs. Achenes ovoid, flattened.

Stems 1–2 ft. Leaves toothed from base to tip . . . . 1. *E. sessile.*
Stems 1–8 in.
Leaves all entire . . . . 2. *E. pusillum.*
Upper leaves toothed towards the tip . . . . . 3. *E. surculosum.*

1. **Elatostemma sessile,** *Forst.*; *Fl. Br. Ind.* v. 563. Stems 1–2 ft., often bent at the joints, prostrate, usually rooting towards the base. Leaves sessile or nearly so, ovate-lanceolate, about 6 × 3 in., sides very unequal, coarsely and sharply toothed, tip narrowed into a slender, tail-like point. Heads $\frac{1}{4}$–$\frac{1}{2}$ in. diam., sometimes 2 or 3 together; the male sessile, the female shortly stalked and without involucral bracts.

Simla, the Glen; June–September.—Temperate Himalaya, 4000–8000 ft., Assam, Nilghiris.—China, Malay and Pacific islands, tropical Africa.

2. **Elatostemma pusillum,** *C. B. Clarke*; *Fl. Br. Ind.* v. 568. Stems 1–6 in., nearly erect, slender, weak. Leaves few, sessile, ovate, $\frac{1}{3}$ in., entire, sometimes with a small, opposite leaf. Heads sessile, about $\frac{1}{10}$ in. diam.

Simla, on damp rocks in shady places, often growing in moss; August, September.—Temperate Himalaya, 7000–8000 ft.

3. **Elatostemma surculosum,** *Wight*; *Fl. Br. Ind.* v. 572. Stems 2–8 in., tufted, slender, erect. Leaves few, sessile, lanceolate, $\frac{1}{2}$–1 in., the lower ones entire, the upper toothed towards the tip, each leaf having a small one opposite to it. Heads sessile, about $\frac{1}{10}$ in. diam.

Simla, on damp rocks; August, September.—Temperate Himalaya, 4000–7000 ft., Assam.—Ceylon.
The Simla plant is the variety *elegans* of the *Fl. Br. Ind.*

12. **BŒHMERIA.** In honour of G. R. Bœhmer, a German botanist of the eighteenth century, who wrote a '*Flora Lipsiæ,*' etc.—Chiefly tropical regions.

Bœhmeria platyphylla, *Don*; *Fl. Br. Ind.* v. 578. A variable shrub, all parts covered with a rough or sometimes smooth pubescence; stems and branches 4-sided. Leaves stalked, opposite or alternate, broadly ovate or orbicular, 3–9 in., roughly wrinkled or nearly smooth, base 3-nerved, usually cordate, margins toothed, tip acute, sometimes abruptly narrowed into a tail-like point; leaves when opposite often unequal. Flowers small, 1-sexual, nearly white, sessile, clustered in axillary, interrupted spikes; the male and female in separate spikes borne on the same or on different plants. Male spikes 3–6 in., nearly erect, often branched: perianth 4-lobed; stamens 4. Female spikes 6–12 in., pendulous: perianth tubular, mouth small, 4-toothed; style long, thread-like, hairy, persistent. Achene enclosed in the dry perianth.

Valleys below Simla; April–August.—Nearly throughout India, ascending to 5000 ft.—Tropical Asia and Africa.

In the *Fl. Br. Ind.* this species is divided into nine varieties, of which the following two may be distinguished in Simla:—

B. platyphylla proper. Leaves ovate, roughly wrinkled, tip pointed or narrowed in a short, tail-like point; teeth small and uniform.

Var. rotundifolia. Leaves orbicular, nearly smooth, tip abruptly narrowed into a tail-like point sometimes an inch long; teeth large, often unequal.

The Rhea and 'China grass' fibres are obtained from varieties of *B. nivea*, a native of China and the Malay islands, believed to have been introduced into India in very early times. The cultivation of this plant, and the extraction of the fibre, have formed the subject of numerous experiments during recent years, but up to the present time without marked commercial success.

13. POUZOLZIA. In honour of P. M. C. de Pouzolz, a French botanical author of the nineteenth century.—All tropical regions.

Shrubs or herbs, very variable in habit and size, usually more or less roughly pubescent. Leaves undivided, 3-nerved from the base. Flowers small, 1-sexual, pale green, in axillary clusters; the male and female in the same or in distinct clusters borne on the same or on different plants. Male flowers short-stalked: perianth 4- or 5-parted; stamens 4 or 5. Female flowers sessile: perianth tubular, enclosing the ovary; style long, linear, protruding, soon falling off. Fruit an achene, enclosed in the persistent, ribbed or winged perianth.

Perianth of male flowers usually 4-parted. Stamens 4.
- Leaves alternate, toothed . . . . 1. *P. viminea.*
- Leaves opposite, entire . . . . 2. *P. indica.*

Perianth of male flowers usually 5-parted. Stamens 5.
- Lower leaves opposite, the upper alternate and crowded 3. *P. pentandra.*
- Leaves all opposite, the upper not crowded . . . 4. *P. hirta.*

*1. **Pouzolzia viminea,** *Wedd.*; *Fl. Br. Ind.* v. 581. An erect shrub; branches slender, straight. Leaves alternate, shortly stalked, lanceolate, 2–5 in., toothed, long-pointed, lower surface usually pale or white-tomentose. Flowers in small, dense, rounded clusters. Male perianth usually 4-parted; stamens 4. Fruit angled and obscurely margined

Valleys below 5000 ft., from Chamba to Assam; June–September.—Subtropical Himalaya, Assam.—Malay islands.

2. **Pouzolzia indica,** *Gaud.*; *Fl. Br. Ind.* v. 581. A small herb, rarely exceeding 1 ft.; stems half-prostrate; branches slender, spreading. Leaves opposite, shortly stalked, ovate, ½–1 in., entire, pointed. Flowers in small clusters. Male perianth usually 4-parted; stamens 4. Fruit ribbed, sometimes winged.

Valleys below Simla, usually on dry, rocky slopes; June–September.—Throughout tropical and subtropical India, ascending to 5000 ft.—Tropical Asia.

*3. **Pouzolzia pentandra,** *Benn.*; *Fl. Br. Ind.* v. 583. A nearly glabrous, annual, erect herb, 2–3 ft.; stems robust; branches long and slender. Leaves sessile or shortly stalked, oblong-lanceolate, entire, pointed; the lower ones 1–4 in., opposite; the upper alternate, crowded, gradually decreasing in size upwards. Flowers in small clusters, sometimes of only 2 or 3 flowers. Male perianth usually 5-parted; stamens 5. Fruit 3-winged.

Valleys below 3000 ft., from Kangra to Assam; June–September.—Subtropical and tropical India.—China, Java.

*4. **Pouzolzia hirta,** *Hassk.*; *Fl. Br. Ind.* v. 586. A decumbent or half-erect herb; stems slender, 6 in. to 3 ft. Leaves opposite, sessile or nearly so, ovate or lanceolate, 1–4 in., entire, pointed. Flowers in small, rounded, dense clusters. Male perianth usually 5-parted; stamens 5. Fruit strongly ribbed, sometimes winged.

Valleys below 5000 ft., from Chamba to Assam; June–September.—Tropical and subtropical Himalaya.—China, Malay islands, Australia.

14. VILLEBRUNEA. A commemorative name, unexplained.—India, Malay islands, China, Japan.

Villebrunea frutescens, *Blume*; *Fl. Br. Ind.* v. 590. A shrub; branches slender, pubescent. Leaves alternate, ovate, 2–5 in., 3-nerved from the base, tip narrowed into a long, tail-like point, margins sharply toothed, except near the base; upper surface rough, the lower usually pale, sometimes white-tomentose; stalks slender, 1–2 in. Flowers 1-sexual, crowded in small, sessile or nearly sessile clusters inserted on the stem and branches between or below the leaves; the male and female on different plants. Male perianth 5- sometimes 4-parted; stamens 5 or 4. Female perianth tubular, ovoid, narrowed to a minute mouth, adnate to the enclosed ovary; stigma resembling a small, sessile tuft of hairs. Achenes numerous, minute, black, partially immersed in a white, gelatinous receptacle.

Valleys below Simla; May–July.—Tropical and subtropical Himalaya, ascending to 5000 ft.—China, Japan.

15. DEBREGEASIA. A commemorative name, unexplained.—Tropical Asia and Africa, eastward to Japan.

Debregeasia hypoleuca, *Wedd.*; *Fl. Br. Ind.* v. 591. A softly pubescent shrub. Leaves alternate, short-stalked, broadly or narrowly lanceolate, 3–7 in., long-pointed, base 3-nerved; teeth numerous, regular, sharp; upper surface rough, lower white-tomentose; stipules 2-parted. Flowers 1-sexual, interspersed with numerous bracteoles, in rounded, sessile, axillary clusters; the male and female on different plants. Male flowers: perianth tomentose, 4-parted; stamens 4. Female flowers: perianth tubular, narrowed to a minute, 4-toothed mouth, more or less adnate to the enclosed ovary; stigma resembling a sessile tuft of hairs. Drupes small, yellow, aggregated in a head.

Simla, Mahasu; March, April.—Temperate Himalaya, ascending to 6000 ft. —W. Asia, Abyssinia.

Twine and ropes are made from the fibre.

16. PARIETARIA. From the Latin *paries*, a wall, referring to the habitat of some species.—Temperate and tropical regions.

Parietaria debilis, *Forst.*; *Fl. Br. Ind.* v. 593. A diffuse, pubescent herb; stems numerous, 6–12 in., very slender, straggling, often matted. Leaves alternate, thin, entire, 3-nerved from the base, variable in shape, usually ovate or orbicular, $\frac{1}{2}$–$1\frac{1}{2}$ in., obtuse; stalks long. Flowers minute, polygamous, in axillary clusters; bracts linear, united at the base. Male flowers few: perianth 4-parted; stamens 4. Female flowers numerous: perianth tubular, 4-lobed, enclosing the ovary; stigma resembling a sessile tuft of hairs. Bisexual flowers few. Achene enclosed in the ovoid, persistent perianth.

Simla, on rocks &c., in shady places; January–December.—Temperate Himalaya, 7000–12,000 ft., mountains in S. India.—Many temperate and tropical regions, extending to Australia and Chili.

Allied to the British Pellitory of the wall, *P. officinalis*.

XCII. JUGLANDACEÆ

Trees. Leaves alternate, odd-pinnate. Flowers small, 1-sexual, both sexes on the same tree. Male flowers numerous, in long, pendulous catkins: perianth narrow, margins irregularly 5-lobed; stamens 10–20, nearly sessile, free. Female flowers few, in small, terminal clusters: ovary 1-celled, enclosed in an adnate, ovoid involucre; perianth-lobes 4. Fruit a drupe, rind thick, fleshy, enclosing a woody nut. Seed one, cotyledons large, lobed.—N. temperate regions.

Engelhardtia Colebrookiana, *Lindl.*; *Fl. Br. Ind.* v. 596. A small tree belonging to this Order is common in Kumaon and Garhwal, but rare West of the Jumna and is not recorded from Simla. The female flowers are in drooping spikes 6 in. long; the fruiting bracts 1–$1\frac{1}{2}$ in., unequally 4-lobed, each enclosing a small, hairy nut. Flowers in March or April.

JUGLANS. The classical name, a contraction of *Jovis glans*, the nut of Jupiter.—N. temperate regions.

Juglans regia, *Linn.*; *Fl. Br. Ind.* v. 595. A large tree, nearly glabrous. Leaves 6–12 in., alternate, odd-pinnate; leaflets

7–9, rarely more, end one the largest, stalked, side ones opposite, sessile, ovate-oblong, 3–8 in., pointed, entire. Flowers green, male and female on the same tree, appearing with the leaves. Male flowers numerous, in pendulous, lateral catkins 2–5 in. long: perianth narrow, nearly flat, irregularly 5-lobed, combined with the bract the free tip of which appears on its under side; stamens 15–20, nearly sessile. Female flowers 1–3, clustered on the end of branches, the bracts combined in a pubescent, ovoid involucre adnate to the ovary, its narrow mouth obscurely 4-toothed: perianth of 4 linear-lanceolate lobes inserted on the mouth of the involucre alternate with its teeth; ovary 1-celled, ovule 1, style-arms 2, short, broad, recurved, roughly wrinkled. Drupe ovoid, 2 in. long, the green, thick, fleshy rind enclosing a woody, wrinkled, 2-valved nut, the edible part consisting of the large, corrugated, 4-lobed cotyledons of the single seed.

Bagi, wild, 7000–10,000 ft., cultivated down to 3000 ft.; February–April.—Himalaya, N. Persia, the Caucasus.—The Common Walnut.

XCIII. MYRICACEÆ

AROMATIC trees or shrubs. Leaves undivided, entire, alternate, crowded. Flowers minute, 1-sexual, in spikes. Perianth none. Stamens 3–6. Ovary with 2–4 scale-like bracts at the base, 1-celled, 1-ovuled. Fruit a succulent, scaly drupe.—Nearly all temperate and warm regions except Australia.

MYRICA. The Greek name of the Tamarisk, transferred to this genus by Linnæus.—The only genus; distribution of the Order.

Myrica Nagi, *Thunb.*; *Fl. Br. Ind.* v. 597. A small tree, nearly glabrous. Leaves crowded towards the ends of branches, lanceolate, 3–5 in., acute or obtuse, entire, the lower surface pale or rust-coloured, minutely gland-dotted, aromatic, stalks short, pubescent; the leaves of young shoots sometimes 5–8 in. and toothed. Flowers minute, 1-sexual, glandular, the male and female on different trees. Male flowers in catkins $\frac{1}{4}$–1 in. long, solitary in the leaf-axils or sessile on a common, drooping, axillary stalk 1–3 in. long: bracts orbicular, often with 2 or 3 smaller ones; perianth none; stamens 3–6, filaments free except at the base. Female flowers in axillary, erect spikes $\frac{1}{2}$–1 in. long: bracts 2–4; perianth none; ovary 1-celled, style-arms 2, long, incurved, red. Drupe sessile, scaly, ovoid, $\frac{1}{2}$–$\frac{3}{4}$ in., flesh red, stone wrinkled and pitted. (Fig. 151.)

Simla, below 6000 ft., the Glen &c.; October–December, sometimes in the spring.—Himalaya and Khasia.—Malaya, China and Japan.

The fruit commonly known as *Kaiphal* is eaten, and the bark is used in medicine.

The Sweet Gale, *M. Gale*, is common in bogs and on wet moors in Britain.

Fig. 151. Myrica Nagi.

XCIV. CUPULIFERÆ

Trees or shrubs. Leaves alternate, undivided or rarely slightly lobed, usually toothed; stipules soon falling off. Flowers small or minute, 1-sexual, the male in catkins, the female in spikes, both sexes on the same tree. Male catkins usually cylindric and drooping; female spikes cylindric or ovoid, usually erect at least when young. Male flowers: perianth membranous or none; stamens 3–16, filaments free, sometimes minutely forked, anthers usually 2-celled. Female flowers: perianth none or tubular, more or less adnate to the ovary, the limb if present minute and toothed; ovary 2- or 3-celled, cells not distinct until after fertilisation, ovules 1–2 in each cell, all but one usually abortive; styles as many as the cells, usually more or less united at the base. Fruit a nut, the nuts either large and solitary or in small clusters or minute and numerous in cones or spikes.—Europe, mountains of Asia and America, and S. temperate regions.—From the Latin *cupula*, a little cup; referring to the shape of the involucre in the fruit of *Quercus*.

In the flowers of this Order the pollen is conveyed to the stigmas by the wind.

Nuts small, seed-like, numerous, in cones or spikes.
  Nuts flattened.
    Stamens 2. Bracts of cone thin, ultimately falling off . . 1. *Betula*.
    Stamens 4. Bracts of cone thick, woody, persistent . . 2. *Alnus*.
  Nuts globose, ribbed. Bracteoles much enlarged, lobed and leaf-like in fruit . . . . 5. *Carpinus*.
Nuts large, solitary or in clusters of 2–3.
  Nuts or acorns more or less enclosed in a cup . . . . 3. *Quercus*.
  Nuts more or less enclosed in the enlarged inner bract . . 4. *Corylus*.

1. BETULA. The Latin name of the Birch.—N. temperate and Arctic regions.

Trees; bark smooth and paper-like, peeling off in thin sheets. Leaves stalked, ovate, long-pointed, sharply and irregularly toothed. Male catkins drooping: flowers bracteate, in groups of usually three; perianth 4-parted, segments sometimes fewer by abortion; stamens 2, filaments minutely forked, anther-cells separated. Female cones drooping or nearly erect: flowers bracteate, in groups of usually three; perianth none; ovary 2-celled; style long, slender. Nuts minute, flattened, winged on both sides; bracts 3-lobed, ultimately falling off.

The bark of *B. utilis*, and of some other species, is used as paper for writing and packing, also for making umbrellas. The 'twig bridges' of the inner Himalaya are made of the branches.

Female cones usually solitary. Lobes of fruiting bract nearly equal . . . . 1. *B. utilis*.
Female cones usually in clusters. Mid-lobe of fruiting bract much the longest . . . . 2. *B. alnoides*.

1. **Betula utilis,** *Don*; *Fl. Br. Ind.* v. 599. Outer bark white, inner layers pink. Leaves 2–3 in. Female cones usually single: lobes of fruiting bract nearly equal.

The Chor, and perhaps Huttoo, not under 10,000 ft.; April, May.—Temperate Himalaya, from Kashmir to Sikkim and Bhotan, 7000–14,000 ft.—Afghanistan, Japan.

2. **Betula alnoides,** *Buch.-Ham.*; *Fl. Br. Ind.* v. 599. Leaves 3–6 in. Female cones usually in clusters; mid-lobe of fruiting bract much the longest.

Simla, Narkunda, 6000–9000 ft.; April–June, and sometimes in the autumn.—Temperate and sub-tropical Himalaya, Khasia and Martaban Hills.

2. ALNUS. The Latin name of the genus.—N. temperate regions; the Andes.

Trees. Leaves stalked, glabrous, ovate, 4–6 in. Male catkins drooping, in terminal panicles or racemes: flowers 3 to a bract; bracts closely imbricate in bud, opening in flower, with usually 4 adnate bracteoles to each bract; perianth sessile, 4-parted; stamens 4, filaments very short, anther-cells distinct. Female cones short, erect: flowers minute, 2 to each bract; perianth none; ovary 2-celled; styles 2, red, diverging, ovules 1 in each cell. Fruiting cones woody, remaining long on the trees; bracts woody, persistent; nutlets flattened, narrowly winged.

Leaves with 14–18 pairs of lateral nerves. Wings of nutlet thin, membranous . . . . 1. *A. nepalensis.*
Leaves with 8–12 pairs of lateral nerves. Wings of nutlet thick, leathery . . . . 2. *A. nitida.*

1. **Alnus nepalensis,** *Don*; *Fl. Br. Ind.* v. 600. Branchlets glabrous. Leaves shortly pointed, entire or obscurely toothed; lateral nerves 14–18 pairs. Male catkins, 4–10 in., numerous, panicled. Female cones $\frac{1}{4}$ in. Fruiting cones $\frac{1}{2}$–1 in., numerous, in erect panicles; wings of nutlet thin, membranous.

Simla, the Glen &c., 3000–9000 ft.; October–December.—Temperate Himalaya and Khasia.—Burmah, China.

2. **Alnus nitida,** *Endl.*; *Fl. Br. Ind.* v. 600. Branchlets pubescent. Leaves long-pointed, more or less distinctly toothed; lateral nerves 8–12 pairs. Male catkins 2–4 in., rarely more than 6, in erect, sometimes leafy racemes. Female cones $\frac{1}{2}$–$\frac{3}{4}$ in. Fruiting cones $\frac{3}{4}$–$1\frac{1}{2}$ in., solitary or 2–5 in short, erect racemes; wings of nutlet thick, leathery.

Giri valley, Synj; September, October.—W. Temperate Himalaya.

3. **QUERCUS.** The Latin name of the Oak.—Chiefly temperate regions of the N. Hemisphere, extending to the mountains of the tropics, except in Africa.

Trees. Male catkins 2–4 in., drooping, usually clustered: perianth bell-shaped, more or less 4–6-lobed; stamens 3–16, filaments free, anther-cells contiguous. Female catkins short, erect, few-flowered, each flower enclosed by an involucre of scales: perianth tubular, the lower part adnate to the ovary, limb minute; ovary commonly 3-celled, occasionally 4–5-celled; styles of the same number as cells, linear, recurved, protruding; ovules 2 in each cell, all but one usually abortive. Fruit an acorn or nut, more or less enclosed by the enlarged and hardened, involucral scales.

Scales of acorn-cup imbricate.
Leaves brown-tomentose on the lower surface . . 1. *Q. semecarpifolia*
Leaves glabrous . . . . 2. *Q. dilatata.*
Leaves white-tomentose on the lower surface . . 3. *Q. incana.*
Scales of acorn-cup united in rings . . . . . 4. *Q. glauca.*

1. **Quercus semecarpifolia,** *Sm.*; *Fl. Br. Ind.* v. 601. Leaves nearly sessile, oblong-ovate, 2–5 × 1¼–2½ in., entire, undulate or spinous-toothed, obtuse; upper surface glabrous, lower brown-tomentose, sometimes nearly glabrous in old leaves. Male flowers:

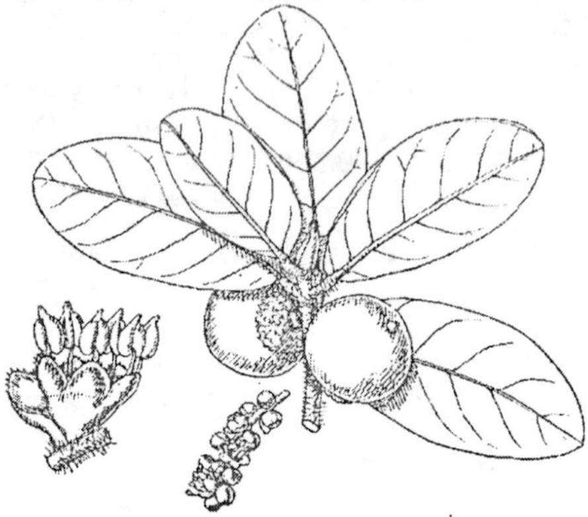

FIG. 152. QUERCUS SEMECARPIFOLIA.

stamens 8–16. Female flowers: styles 3–5. Acorns solitary; cup covering only the base of the nut; scales imbricate, thin; nut globose, smooth, dark brown. (Fig. 152.)

Mahasu, Narkunda, 8500–12,000 ft.; June.—Temperate Himalaya.—Afghanistan.

The Kharshu oak. It is common in the higher mountain forests and is distinguished by its rusty-brown foliage.

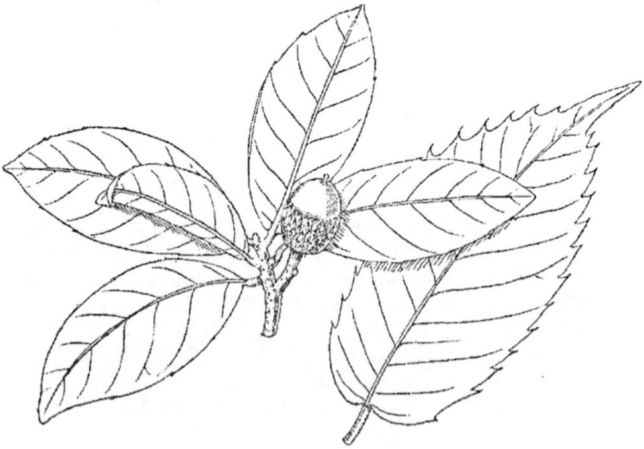

FIG. 153. QUERCUS DILATATA.

2. **Quercus dilatata,** *Lindl.*; *Fl. Br. Ind.* v. 602. Leaves shortly stalked, glabrous, oblong-lanceolate or ovate, 2–3 × 1–1½ in., spinous-

toothed or entire, acute or obtuse. Male flowers distant from each other: stamens 4–8. Female flowers: styles 3-5. Acorns usually solitary; cup covering about half the nut; scales imbricate; nut ovoid, pointed, smooth, brown. (Fig. 153.)

Simla, rare, Mahasu to Narkunda, common, Daha in the Giri valley; April, May.—W. Temperate Himalaya.—Afghanistan.

The Moru oak. It is found from 6000 to 9000 ft. and is distinguished by its green foliage.

3. **Quercus incana,** *Roxb.*; *Fl. Br. Ind.* v. 603. Leaves stalked, ovate-lanceolate, 3–5 × 1¼–2 in., spinous-toothed towards the tip; upper surface glabrous, lower white-tomentose. Male flowers: stamens 3–5. Female flowers: styles 3. Acorns single or in pairs; cup at first almost covering the nut, but only about half of it

Fig. 154. Quercus incana.

when mature; scales imbricate; nut ovoid, white-tomentose when young, ultimately glabrous, brown. (Fig. 154.)

Simla, common; April, May.—Temperate Himalaya.—Upper Burmah.

The Ban oak. It grows on dry, grassy hillsides from 5000 to 8000 ft., rarely lower and is distinguished by its grey foliage, appearing white when the leaves are turned back by the wind.

4. **Quercus glauca,** *Thunb.*; *Fl. Br. Ind.* v. 604. Leaves stalked, pubescent when young, ultimately glabrous, oblong- or ovate-lanceolate, 3–5½ × 1–2 in., long-pointed, more or less spinous-toothed towards the tip. Male catkins interrupted: flowers crowded in small clusters; stamens 4–5. Female flowers: styles 4. Acorns single or in pairs; cup covering about two-thirds of the nut; scales united, forming 4–8 tomentose, concentric belts; nut ovoid, pointed, smooth, brown. (Fig. 155.)

Simla, below 5000 ft.; March–June.—Subtropical Himalaya, 2000–6000 ft.—China, Japan.

This oak occurs only as scattered trees, not in forests as the other three species; distinguished by the belted acorn-cup.

4. **CORYLUS.** The classical name, from *corys*, a helmet, in allusion to the involucre.—N. temperate regions.

Corylus Colurna, *Linn.*; *Fl. Br. Ind.* v. 625. A shrub. Leaves stalked, glabrous or nearly so, ovate, 3–6 × 2–4 in., cordate, irregularly lobed and toothed, long-pointed; the buds and base of leaf-stalks covered with tawny, glandular hairs. Male catkins 2–3 in., drooping, clustered: flowers single; bracts small, hairy, 3; perianth none; stamens 8, filaments short, often more or less united, anthers 1-celled. Female cones ovoid, very small: flowers in pairs in the axils of the upper bracts, each enclosed by a 3–4-cleft, hairy bracteole; bracts imbricate; perianth tubular, the lower part adnate to the ovary, limb free, minutely toothed; ovary 2-celled, 1 ovule in each cell; styles 2, long, linear, red, protruding from the tip of the bud-like cone. Fruit in clusters of 2–3, consisting of a hard, ovoid

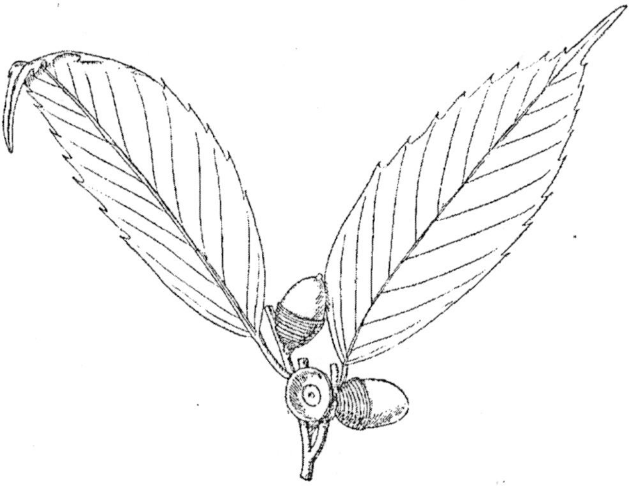

FIG. 155. QUERCUS GLAUCA.

nut sheathed by the much-enlarged, lobed and toothed, glandular-hairy bracteole, with the withered outer bracts at its base.

Simla, rare, Narkunda, common; April, May.—W. Temperate Himalaya.—S.E. Europe.

The kernels are as good as English Hazel-nuts.

5. CARPINUS. The classical name.—N. temperate regions.

Carpinus viminea, *Wall.*; *Fl. Br. Ind.* v. 626. A tree; branches slender, drooping. Leaves stalked, glabrous, ovate-lanceolate, 3–5 in., teeth unequal, sharp, tip very long, tail-like. Male catkins appearing before the leaves, drooping, $1\frac{1}{2}$ in.: flowers solitary; bracts small, hairy; perianth none; stamens about 12, filaments free, minutely forked, anther-cells separated, their tips hairy.

Female spikes short, appearing with the leaves, at first nearly erect, afterwards drooping: flowers in pairs, in the axils of deciduous, linear-lanceolate bracts, each flower within a narrow, unequal-sided, inner bract, the broad side toothed, the narrow entire, base 2-lobed ; the 2 inner bracts sessile on a common stalk ; perianth tubular, the lower part adnate to the ovary, limb toothed ; ovary 2-celled, 1 ovule in each cell ; styles 2, long, linear, erect. Fruiting spike 2–3 in. ; bracts leaf-like, about 1 in., each enclosing at its base a small, globose, ribbed nut crowned by the minute perianth-lobes.

Sipi, below Mushobra on the banks of a stream ; February–April ; the fruit ripens June–September.—Temperate Himalaya, Khasia and Martaban Hills.

Carpinus faginea, *Lindl.* Occurs in Garhwal but has not been found near Simla. It differs from the species described above in having ovate-oblong leaves with uniform teeth and without the tail-like point ; the fruiting bracts are broadly triangular.

XCV. SALICACEÆ

Trees or shrubs. Leaves alternate, undivided, stalked ; stipules usually soon falling off. Flowers small, 1-sexual, in catkins, the male and female on separate plants ; perianth in *Salix* reduced to a small scale or glands, in *Populus* bell-shaped. Male flowers : stamens 2 or 5–10 or many, filaments free or partially united, anthers 2-celled. Female flowers : ovary 1-celled. Fruiting catkins often much-elongated ; capsule conical or ovoid, opening by 2–4 valves ; seeds several or many, minute, each enveloped in a tuft of long, white, silky hairs.—Chiefly N. temperate regions.

Leaf-stalks $\frac{1}{4}$–$\frac{1}{3}$ in. Capsule opening by 2 valves. Stamens 2 or 5–10 . . . . 1. *Salix*.
Leaf-stalks 2–4 in. Capsule opening by 2–4 valves. Stamens many. . . . . 2. *Populus*.

1. SALIX. The classical name ; of disputed origin.—Chiefly N. temperate regions ; rare in South Africa and South America.

Leaves on young, barren shoots sometimes abnormally large ; stalks not exceeding $\frac{1}{3}$ in. Flowers in catkins, solitary in the axils of the bracts. Male flowers : perianth reduced to a small scale or glands ; stamens 2 or 5–10, filaments long, free or partially united, protruding. Female flowers : style forked, stigmas notched or entire, ovules at the base of the ovary. Capsule conical, opening by 2 recurved valves.

Stamens 5–10. Capsule long-stalked	1. *S. tetrasperma.*
Stamens 2.	
Filaments free.	
Flowers appearing before the leaves. Catkins sessile or nearly so.	
Leaves usually entire; lower surface silky, pubescent	2. *S. Wallichiana.*
Leaves toothed; lower surface glabrous, glaucous .	7. *S. daphnoides.*
Flowers appearing with or after the leaves. Catkins on leafy shoots.	
Leaves narrowly lanceolate.	
Leaves silky at least on the lower surface . .	3. *S. alba.*
Leaves glabrous	4. *S. babylonica.*
Leaves ovate or oblong.	
Lower surface of leaves covered with a pale bloom	5. *S. elegans.*
Lower surface of leaves green	6. *S. hastata.*
Filaments united to about the middle. Leaves narrowed to both ends	8. *S. oxycarpa.*

1. **Salix tetrasperma,** *Roxb.*; *Fl. Br. Ind.* v. 626. A small tree, very variable; young branches silky, becoming glabrous. Leaves ovate-lanceolate, 4–6 in., acute or long-pointed, more or less silky when young, afterwards glabrous, lower surface covered with a white or pale bloom; teeth small, often obscure. Flowers appearing after the leaves. Catkins hairy, drooping, terminating short, leafy, lateral branchlets. Male catkins 2–3 in., sweet-scented: stamens 5–10, filaments free. Female catkins 3–4 in.: style short, stigmas usually entire. Fruiting catkins sometimes 5 in.; capsule glabrous, long-stalked; seeds 4–6.

Sutlej and Giri valleys, below 4000 ft.; March, April.—Common on river banks &c. nearly throughout India.—Malaya.

2. **Salix Wallichiana,** *Anderss.*; *Fl. Br. Ind.* v. 628. A shrub or small tree; young branches pubescent or tomentose, ultimately nearly glabrous. Leaves lanceolate or ovate-lanceolate, 2½–5 in., on young shoots sometimes 8 in., usually entire, sometimes with a few teeth, long-pointed or acute, upper surface green, hairy when young, nearly glabrous afterwards, lower surface covered with a white, silky pubescence. Flowers appearing before the leaves. Male catkins 1–2 in., densely silky, nearly sessile, with 2 or 3 small leaves at the base, erect, thick: bracts black; stamens 2, filaments free, hairy. Female catkins 3–5 in., hairy, drooping, slender: bracts usually brown. Capsule silky, pubescent, shortly stalked.

Simla, Mahasu, Fagoo, 6000–9000 ft.; March, April.—Temperate Himalaya.—Afghanistan.

3. **Salix alba,** *Linn.*; *Fl. Br. Ind.* v. 629. A tree. Leaves narrowly lanceolate, 2–4 in., long-pointed, minutely toothed, white-silky on both surfaces when young, the upper becoming glabrous when older. Flowers appearing after the leaves. Catkins terminating short, lateral, leafy shoots, drooping. Male catkins

$1-1\frac{1}{2}$ in.: stamens 2, filaments free. Female catkins 2–3 in.: stigmas deeply notched. Capsule nearly sessile, pubescent.

Simla, introduced and often planted along watercourses; April.—Europe, N. Asia.
The White Willow of Britain.

4. **Salix babylonica**, *Linn.*; *Fl. Br. Ind.* v. 629. A tree; branches drooping. Leaves narrowly lanceolate, $3-6 \times \frac{1}{2}$ in., finely toothed, glabrous. Flowers appearing with the leaves. Catkins very slender, terminating short, lateral, leafy branchlets. Male catkins

FIG. 156. SALIX ELEGANS.

$\frac{1}{2}-1$ in.: stamens 2, filaments free. Female catkins 1 in., drooping: stigmas entire. Capsule glabrous, sessile.

Simla, introduced and often planted in gardens and along watercourses; February–May.—Europe, N. and W. Asia.
The Weeping Willow of Britain.

5. **Salix elegans**, *Wall.*; *Fl. Br. Ind.* v. 630. A shrub or small tree; branches pubescent when young, glabrous afterwards. Leaves ovate or oblong, 1–2 in., acute or obtuse, upper surface green, lower covered with a white or pale bloom, margins finely toothed or nearly entire. Flowers appearing after the leaves. Catkins slender, pubescent, terminating short, leafy branchlets; bracts yellow or pale brown. Male catkins $1-1\frac{1}{2}$ in., nearly erect: stamens 2, filaments free, hairy. Female catkins 3–5 in., drooping, scales

minute : style very short, stigmas deeply notched. Capsule glabrous, shortly stalked. (Fig. 156.)

Simla, on Jako &c., 6000–11,000 ft., very common ; March, April.—W. Himalaya.—Turkestan.

Catkins consisting partly of male and partly of female flowers are occasionally found.

6. **Salix hastata.** *Linn.* ; *Fl. Br. Ind.* v. 630. A shrub ; young shoots and leaves silky, becoming glabrous. Leaves ovate or oblong, 1–3 × $\frac{3}{4}$–2 in., green, acute or abruptly pointed, teeth very small. Flowers appearing with the leaves. Catkins densely silky, terminating short, leafy branchlets ; bracts oblong, obtuse, almost concealed in the long, silky hairs. Male catkins 1–1$\frac{1}{2}$ in., erect : bracts black ; stamens 2, filaments free. Female catkins 2–2$\frac{1}{2}$ in., nearly erect, thick : bracts brown ; style long, stigmas notched. Fruiting catkins attaining 6 in. ; capsule glabrous, nearly sessile.

Huttoo, Marali, rare ; June–August.—Himalaya, 9000–15,000 ft.—N. Asia, Subalpine Europe.

7. **Salix daphnoides,** *Villars* ; *Fl. Br. Ind.* v. 631. A tree or large shrub ; young shoots pubescent or tomentose ; branches glabrous, often covered with a grey bloom. Leaves ovate lanceolate, 3–6 × 1–2 in., acute, toothed, upper surface nearly glabrous, lower covered with a white or pale bloom. Flowers appearing before the leaves. Male catkins 1–1$\frac{1}{2}$ in., sessile, erect, with a few small leaves at their base, densely silky : bracts black-tipped, fringed with long hairs ; stamens 2, filaments free. Female catkins 2–4 in., terminating short, usually leafy branchlets, drooping, tomentose : ovary pubescent ; style short, stigmas entire. Fruiting catkins attaining 9 in. ; capsule glabrous.

Simla, Elysium hill, Mahasu, Narkunda ; March–May. Temperate Himalaya.— N. Asia, Europe.

8. **Salix oxycarpa.** *Anderss.* ; *Fl. Br. Ind.* v. 636. A shrub or small tree ; young shoots pubescent, becoming glabrous. Leaves lanceolate, 2–4 × $\frac{3}{4}$–1$\frac{1}{4}$ in., pointed ; teeth small, gland-tipped, close-set or distant, sometimes only near the tip of the leaf, sometimes altogether absent (all variations may be seen on the same branch) ; upper surface nearly glabrous, lower covered with a pale or white bloom. Flowers appearing with or a little before the leaves. Male catkins 2–2$\frac{1}{2}$ in., terminating short, leafy branchlets, nearly erect, densely hairy : bracts black ; stamens 2, filaments united to about the middle. Female catkins 2–3 in., shortly stalked, drooping : bracts brown ; style very short, stigmas minutely notched. Fruiting catkins 3–5 in. ; capsule glabrous, shortly stalked. In the fruiting state this species closely resembles *S. daphnoides.*

Simla, Narkunda, &c. ; May.– W. Himalaya, 6000–11,000 ft. —Afghanistan. The Simla plant is var. *serrata,* Anderss., having very lax catkins 4–5 in.

2. POPULUS. The classical name.—N. temperate regions.

Populus ciliata, *Wall.*; *Fl. Br. Ind.* v. 638. A tree. Leaf-buds sticky. Leaves ovate-lanceolate, 3–6 × $2\frac{1}{2}$–$4\frac{1}{2}$ in., cordate, acute, minutely pubescent along the edges; teeth small, often unequal; stalks 2–$4\frac{1}{2}$ in. Flowers in drooping, raceme-like catkins appearing before or with the young leaves. Male flowers: perianth bell-shaped, margins undulate; stamens numerous, filaments free; bracts fringed. Female catkins 6–12 in.: perianth bell-shaped, bluntly toothed; ovary conical, ovules along the centre of the valves; stigmas 3–4, nearly sessile, spreading, 2-lobed. Capsule ovoid, $\frac{1}{4}$–$\frac{1}{3}$ in., opening by 3–4 valves, rarely by 2; seeds numerous. The female tree is common, the male apparently rare.

Simla; February–April.—Temperate Himalaya.

The Lombardy Poplar, *P. pyramidalis*, and the White Poplar or Abele *P. alba*, are planted at Simla as they are in Britain.

XCVI. GNETACEÆ

EPHEDRA. The classical name.—Europe, temperate Asia, S. America.

Ephedra gerardiana, *Wall.*; *Fl. Br. Ind.* v. 640, *and* 863. A shrub, 1–2 ft., rigid, nearly erect, glabrous; branches slender, green, finely grooved, often curved. Leaves reduced to opposite, membranous scales sheathing the joints of the branches. Flowers minute, 1-sexual, in the axils of the uppermost bracts of small, cone-like spikes; bracts opposite, united, the lower ones empty. Male and female spikes on separate plants. Male spikes solitary or in pairs, rarely in whorls of three: flowers 3–4 pairs; perianth shortly tubular, membranous, flattened, mouth 2-lobed; filaments united in a column protruding from the perianth and carrying a head of 5–8 globose, 2-celled anthers opening by pores. Female spike solitary: bracts 2–3 pairs; flowers 1 or 2, each consisting of a single, erect, sessile, naked ovule with 2 coats, the outer one thick and perforated at the tip, the inner thin and prolonged upwards into a style-like tube which protrudes through the outer coat and is persistent in fruit. Fruit ovoid, $\frac{1}{4}$ in. long, sweet, edible, pink or red when ripe, consisting of 1 or 2 hard seeds more or less enclosed by the succulent bracts.

Top of Shali; May, June.—Himalaya.—Tibet.

The Shali plant is var. *saxatilis*, Stapf, *Die Arten der Gattung Ephedra*, Wien, 1889, p. 75.

XCVII. CONIFERÆ

TREES or shrubs; the bark, wood and leaves more or less charged with turpentine. Leaves usually lasting for several years, alternate or whorled or clustered or spirally scattered, needle-shaped or scale-like, spreading or closely imbricate. Flowers minute, in 1-sexual cones, the male and female usually on the same plant. Perianth none. Male cones falling off after flowering: bracts often coloured red when young, usually all basal, the floral axis being prolonged above them and bearing numerous stamens of peculiar form, each consisting of a stalk with a small, flat limb usually bent upwards and imbricating with the others; anther single, 2–6-celled, sessile, pollen grains usually buoyant and easily dispersed by currents of air. Female cones of structure differing in the several genera: in *Cupressus* a few of the uppermost bracts bear 4–6 seeds on their base; in *Juniperus* 3–6 of the uppermost bracts each enclose a single seed; in *Taxus* the two uppermost bracts together enclose a single seed; in *Pinus*, *Cedrus*, *Picea* and *Abies* the bracts are minute and each produces in its axil a seed-bearing scale often coloured red when young; the bracts, except in *Abies*, disappear or are at least completely hidden before the fruit arrives at maturity, while the scales become greatly enlarged and woody, ultimately forming the chief part of the cone. When the cones are in flower the scales separate so as to leave a passage for the pollen to reach the two minute, naked ovules borne near the base of each scale. After fertilisation the seeds harden and acquire a flat, membranous wing, the scales close and the whole cone becomes much larger. In the mature cone the hard, brown scales again open and the winged seeds drop out or are carried away by the wind. The genera of the Coniferæ likewise differ widely in the structure of their fruit: in *Cupressus* it is a globose cone composed of woody, peltate scales, their margins being opposed, not imbricating; in *Juniperus* it is succulent and berry-like; in *Taxus* a red, fleshy cup; while in *Pinus*, *Cedrus*, *Picea* and *Abies* the fruit is a cone with imbricating scales. The seeds in all the genera are hard and usually winged.—Chiefly in cold regions; in India only in the mountains.

The flowers of Coniferæ are dependent on the wind for the transfer of the pollen.

Trees.
- Leaves very short, scale-like, imbricate . . . . . . 1. *Cupressus*
- Leaves needle-like, spreading.
  - Leaves in clusters.
    - Leaves 1–1½ in., many in a cluster . . . . . . 5. *Cedrus.*
    - Leaves more than 5 in., few in a cluster . . . . . 4. *Pinus.*
  - Leaves single.
    - Leaves 4-sided . . . . 6. *Picea.*
    - Leaves flattened.
      - Leaves stiff; lower surface white . . . . . . 7. *Abies.*
      - Leaves flexible; lower surface green . . . . . 3. *Taxus.*

Shrubs. Leaves linear, spreading, acute . . . . . . 2. *Juniperus.*

1. CUPRESSUS. The classical name.—South-east Europe, temperate Asia and America.

Cupressus torulosa, *Don*; *Fl. Br. Ind.* v. 645. A tree; branches spreading, ends drooping; general outline narrowly conical; young foliage blue-green, becoming much darker with age. Leaves opposite, scale-like, triangular, $\frac{1}{16}$ in., closely imbricate, margins white. Cones $\frac{1}{8}$ in., terminal on branchlets, male and female on the same tree; the stamens of the male bearing 3–4 globose anther-cells on the edge of the limb; the few uppermost bracts of the female cones bearing 4–6 ovules at their base. Fruit a globose head $\frac{1}{2}$ in. diam., consisting of woody, peltate scales tightly closed along their edges at first, opening when mature; seeds numerous, small, winged. The sessile clustered fruits ripen in October and November of the year after flowering.

Simla, road to Pumping Station, beyond the Tunnel, Shali, north side, at 8000–9000 ft.; January, February.—W. Himalaya, 5500–8000 ft.

Deodar is the native name of this tree, which is sometimes planted in Simla gardens and the wood is burned as incense in Hindu temples. It is usually found on limestone, and is common near Chakrata and at Naini Tal.

The Weeping Cypress, *C. funebris*, native of China, is occasionally planted in India.

2. JUNIPERUS. The classical name.—Temperate and cold regions of the N. Hemisphere.

Shrubs, usually decumbent and growing in patches. Leaves linear, in threes or pairs, spreading or erect, crowded, acute. Male and female cones on the same or on separate shrubs. Male cones numerous, ovoid, $\frac{1}{8}$ in.: limb of stamens broadly triangular, pointed, bearing a single, 3–6-celled anther. Female cones minute, bud-like: lower bracts empty, the 3–6 uppermost each enclosing a single ovule. Fruit compound, berry-like, blue or blue-black and covered with bloom when ripe, formed by the few fertile bracts cohering and becoming fleshy as they mature, their tips usually remaining visible on the surface; seeds minute, hard, embedded in the fleshy bracts of the fruit.

Leaves $\frac{1}{4}$–$\frac{3}{4}$ in., straight. Male cones axillary . . . 1. *J. communis.*
Leaves $\frac{1}{8}$ in., curved. Male cones terminal . . . . . 2. *J. recurva.*

1. **Juniperus communis,** *Linn.*; *Fl. Br. Ind.* v. 646. A dense, diffuse shrub. Leaves $\frac{1}{4}$–$\frac{3}{4}$ in., straight, spreading or erect, base narrowed, upper surface pale or white, concave, lower green, convex. Catkins axillary. Fruit globose, $\frac{1}{4}$–$\frac{1}{3}$ in., very fleshy, ripening in August and September of the year after flowering; seeds usually 3.

Huttoo; March, April.—W. Himalaya.—N. temperate and sub-arctic regions and N. Africa.

The Common Juniper of Europe.

2. **Juniperus recurva,** *Buch.-Ham.*; *Fl. Br. Ind.* v. 647. A decumbent or prostrate shrub. Leaves $\frac{1}{3}$ in., sometimes in pairs, curved, spreading or erect, both surfaces green, the upper concave, the lower convex. Cones terminal, the female on short branchlets. Fruit ovoid, $\frac{1}{3}$–$\frac{1}{2}$ in., ripening July–October of the year after flowering; seed usually one.

The Chor (var. *squamosa*), and perhaps Huttoo; June, July.—Temperate and alpine Himalaya, 7500–15,000 ft.—Afghanistan.

3. TAXUS. The classical name of the Yew.—N. temperate regions; only one species which varies widely in habit and foliage in different countries.

Taxus baccata, *Linn.*; *Fl. Br. Ind.* v. 648. A tree; trunk short; branches horizontal; foliage dark green. Leaves flattened, flexible, linear, 1–1$\frac{1}{2}$ in., spreading, in two opposite ranks, acute, narrowed into a short stalk, upper surface shining, lower pale or rusty red. Cones axillary, sessile, the male and female usually on separate trees. Male cones $\frac{1}{4}$ in.: bracts empty, the axis ending in a rounded cluster of stamens; anthers 3–6-celled. Female cones minute, bud-like: lower bracts empty, the two uppermost enclosing a single ovule surrounded at the base by a membranous disk. As the young fruit matures the disk enlarges, becomes succulent and finally forms a bright red, fleshy cup about $\frac{1}{3}$ in. long, in which the olive-green seed is partially embedded; the fruit ripens September and November of the year after flowering.

Mahasu, Narkunda, &c.; March–May.—Temperate Himalaya.—Khasia, Upper Burmah.—Temperate Europe, Asia, N. Africa and N. America.

The Yew of Britain. In the Himalaya it sometimes attains 100 ft. in height, with a girth of 15 ft.

Some botanists regard the N. American Yew as a distinct species.

4. PINUS. The classical name of the genus.—Chiefly northern regions; rare in the north tropics.

Large trees; bark divided by furrows into irregularly shaped plates. Leaves needle-like, in clusters of 3 or 5. Male and female cones on the same tree. Male cones densely clustered round the branches just below the current year's shoot: anther-cells 2. Female cones usually at the end of the young shoots, solitary or clustered, erect. Scales of the mature cones more or less thickened towards the tip.

Pinus Gerardiana furnishes the oily, edible seeds, *Chilghoza*, sold in bazaars. It is common in Afghanistan, and occurs near Chini; the leaves are in threes, 3–5 in. long.

Leaves in clusters of 5. Cones cylindric . . . . . 1. *P. excelsa*.
Leaves in clusters of 3. Cones ovoid-conical . . . . 2. *P. longifolia*.

1. **Pinus excelsa,** *Wall.*; *Fl. Br. Ind.* v. 651. Foliage blue- or grey-green. Leaves 5–8 in., in clusters of 5, drooping, except

when quite young. Male cones ovoid, about $\frac{1}{3}$ in. Mature cones cylindric, 6–10 in., erect when young, pendulous afterwards, tip of scales slightly thickened, beak obtuse. Seed, including the wing, $1\frac{1}{4}$ in. The cones ripen in the autumn of the year after flowering, and remain on the branches long after the seeds have been shed. (Fig. 157.)

Simla, 6000–10,000 ft; April-June.—Temperate Himalaya.—Afghanistan. Local name *Kail.*

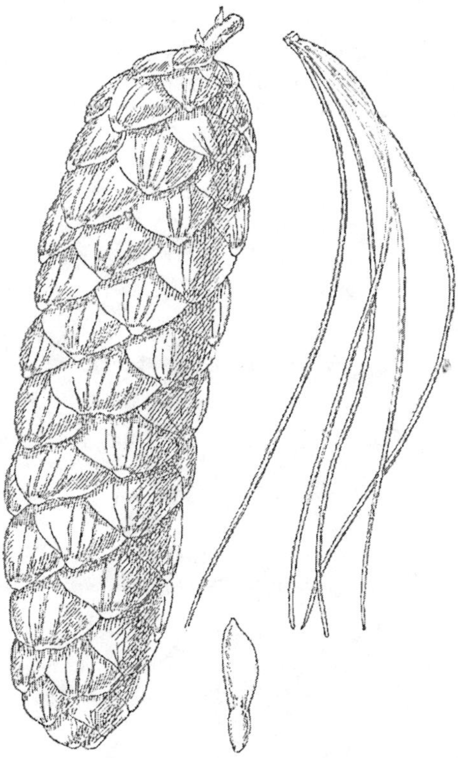

FIG. 157. PINUS EXCELSA.

2. **Pinus longifolia,** *Roxb.*; *Fl. Br. Ind.* v. 652. Trunk tall and straight, but sometimes stunted and gnarled; foliage light green when young, darker afterwards. Leaves 9–12 in., sometimes longer, in clusters of 3. Male cones cylindric, $\frac{3}{4}$ in. Mature cones ovoid, conical, 4–7 in., solitary or clustered, erect or the stalks recurved; tip of scales much thickened, lobed, beak pointed. Seed, including the wing, $\frac{1}{2}$–1 in. The cones ripen in the summer or autumn of the second year after flowering and

remain on the branches long after the seeds have been shed. (Fig. 158.)

Simla, 1500–7000 ft.; February–April.—Himalaya, eastward to Bhotan, 1500–7500 ft.—Afghanistan.
Local name *Chil.*

5. CEDRUS. The Latin name of the Cedar of Lebanon.—A single species comprising three well-marked forms, the Deodar, the Cedar of Lebanon and the Atlas Cedar of North Africa.

Cedrus Libani, *Barrel.*, var. *Deodara, Hook. f.*; *Fl. Br. Ind.* v. 653. Bark dark, smooth, fissures vertical, close; branches horizontal; foliage light green when young, becoming very dark with

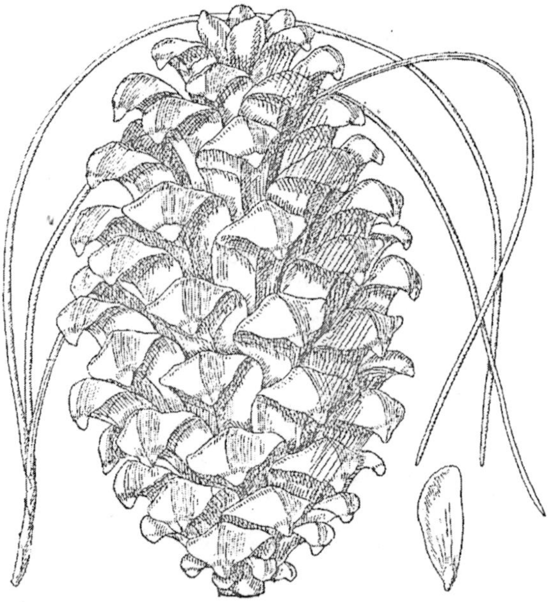

FIG. 158. PINUS LONGIFOLIA.

age. Leaves needle-like, 1–1½ in., 3-sided, clustered at the end of short branchlets. Male and female cones on the same tree. Male cones numerous, erect, solitary at the end of leaf-bearing branchlets, cylindric, 1¾ in. when mature; anther-cells 2. Female cones few, erect, solitary at the end of leaf-bearing branchlets. Mature cones ovoid or ovoid-cylindric, 4–5 × 3–4 in., dark brown when ripe, top rounded; scales thin at the tip, thickened towards the base. Seeds ¼ in. long, wing 1 in. across, triangular rounded. The young cones appear in July and the male ones ripen in

October shedding their yellow pollen in great profusion. The female cones at this season are ½ in. long and scarcely increase in size until the following April when they are about 1¼ in. The cones ripen in October and November of the year after flowering and the scales fall off with the seeds, leaving the naked axis of the cone remaining on the branches. (Fig. 159.)

Simla, common.—N.W. Himalaya.—Afghanistan, 3500–12,000 ft. Local name *Kelu*.

6. PICEA. From the Latin *pix*, pitch; the trees produce abundance of resin.—N. temperate and arctic regions.

Picea Morinda, *Link*; *Fl. Br. Ind.* v. 653. A tall tree; general outline conical; branches horizontal, with hanging, tassel-like branchlets; bark grey, divided by shallow cracks into small,

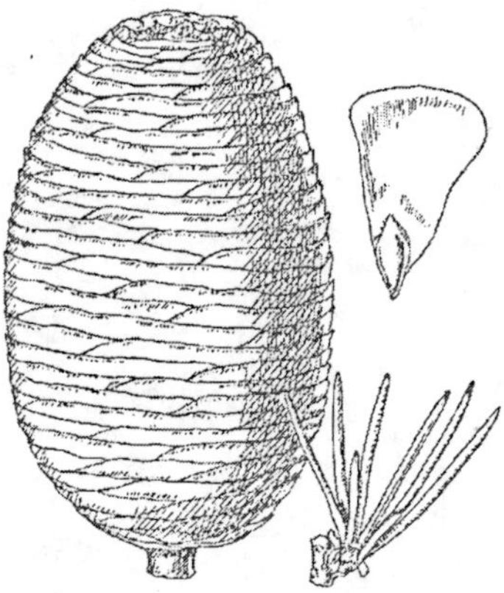

FIG. 159. CEDRUS LIBANI, var. DEODARA.

irregularly 4-sided scales; foliage blue- or grey-green; in April the old bud-scales may often be seen capping the end of the young shoots. Leaves 1–1½ in., needle-like, green, 4-sided, scattered round the branches. Male and female cones on the same tree. Male cones 1 in. when mature, single, erect, nearly sessile in the axils of the upper leaves; anther-cells 2. Female cones terminal, single, ovoid-oblong, erect. Mature cones cylindric, 4–6 × 1–2 in., obtuse, pendent from the end of branches, dark brown when ripe; scales thin and rounded at the tip, slightly thickened towards the base. Seed ⅙ in., wing spathulate, nearly ½ in. long. The cones ripen in October and November of the year after flowering, the scales remaining on the axis after the seeds have been shed. (Fig. 160.)

Simla, a few trees, Mahasu, Narkunda, common; April.—Temperate Himalaya, 6000–11,000 ft.—Afghanistan.
Local name *Rau*.

7. ABIES. The Latin name for some kind of Fir.—N. temperate and arctic regions.

Abies Pindrow, *Spach*; *Fl. Br. Ind.* v. 655. A large tree, in general outline resembling the Cypress; bark dark grey, divided into long, narrow scales by deep, vertical grooves; foliage very dark. Leaves flattened, linear, 1–3 in., stiff, single, spirally arranged round the branches but spreading more or less in one plane, narrowed into a short, twisted stalk, tip-notched, upper surface dark green, shining, the lower with a silvery-white line along each side of the midrib. Male and female cones on the same tree. Male cones

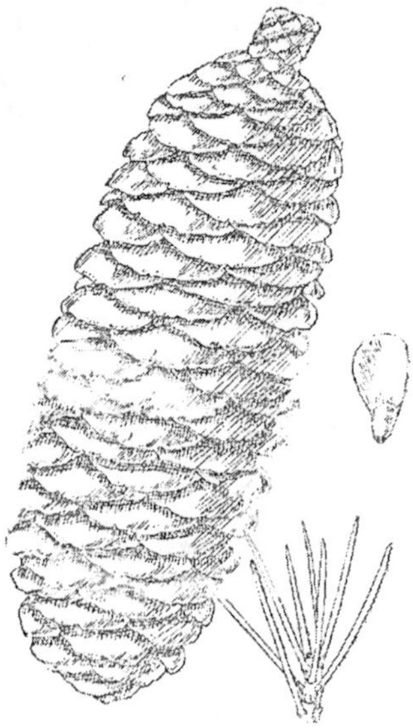

FIG. 160. PICEA MORINDA.

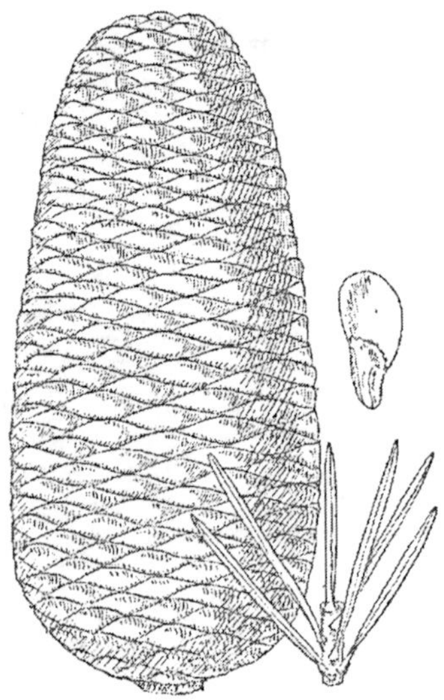

FIG. 161. ABIES PINDROW.

$\frac{3}{4}$ in., sessile, usually clustered; stamens bearing 2 pocket-like receptacles each containing an anther-cell. Female cones terminal, solitary, ovoid; bracts fringed, pointed, persistent. Mature cones ovoid, 4–6 × $1\frac{1}{2}$–3 in., obtuse, nearly sessile, erect, dark purple when ripe; scales thin, slightly thickened along the rounded margins between which the points of the bracts just appear. Seed $\frac{1}{3}$ in., wing $\frac{1}{2}$ in., broad, rounded. The cones ripen in September and October of the year after flowering; the bracts and scales fall off with the seeds leaving the naked axis of the cone remaining on the branches. (Fig. 161.)

Mahasu, a few trees, Narkunda, common; April.—N.W. Himalaya.

Reduced in the *Fl. Br. Ind.* to a variety of *A. Webbiana*, Spach, a tree that grows at higher elevations.—The foliage from a distance is almost black, whence the name *Kala ban*, black forest, which is applied to several localities in the N.W. Himalaya.

XCVIII. ORCHIDACEÆ

TERRESTRIAL, usually succulent, scapose herbs; roots fibrous or tuberous, annually producing erect flowering-stems. Leaves simple, entire, sometimes reduced to scales, alternate or crowded, base usually sheathing. Flowers of peculiar shape and structure, in a terminal, spike-like raceme. Perianth superior, usually fleshy; segments 6, in two series, free or variously combined; the three outer or sepals nearly alike, usually green; the three inner or petals dissimilar, coloured, the two side ones similar, the third or lip very differently shaped and sometimes extended downwards in a hollow spur. Functional stamen one, except in *Cypripedium*, united with the style in a fleshy column; neither stamen nor style is differentiated or externally visible. Anther one, except in *Cypripedium*, situated on the column, cells 2, except in *Oreorchis*, contiguous or widely separated, parallel or divergent; pollen, except in *Cypripedium*, cohering in 1, 2 or 4 pairs of minute, waxy or powdery, usually club-shaped masses or pollinia, either free or attached at the base or by a thread-like stalk or caudicle to a viscid gland naked or sometimes covered by a small pouch. Ovary 1-celled, usually linear and twisted, placed below the flower; stigma, except in *Cypripedium*, a small, more or less concave portion of the face of the column, or, as in most species of *Habenaria*, consisting of two linear, projecting arms. Capsule cylindrical or ovoid, generally ribbed; seeds minute, very numerous. In *Cypripedium* there are two functional stamens; the pollen is granular and glutinous; and the stigma is borne on a very short style.—One of the largest Natural Orders, generally spread over nearly the whole globe; most numerous in subtropical climates but extending into the arctic regions nearly to the limits of vegetation; rare in remote islands.

Most of the tropical Orchids are epiphytes, growing on trees; some grow on rocks; but those in Simla and its neighbourhood are almost all terrestrial.

The fact that the peculiar structure of the flowers of Orchids renders them in most cases entirely dependent on insect agency for the transference of the pollen to the stigma has been known in a general way for more than a hundred years, but it was not until 1862, when Darwin published his famous work on *The various Contrivances by which Orchids are fertilised (pollenised) by Insects*, that our knowledge of the subject became in any degree either accurate or complete. It is not within the scope of this book to repeat Darwin's ingenious explanations of the complex contrivances exhibited in these flowers, but the action of the essential parts may, perhaps, with advantage, be briefly summarised.

The honey, secreted in the spur or sometimes on the surface of the lip, offers an attractive food for insects, and the lip serves as a convenient resting place. The viscid drop or gland, placed directly in the path of an insect seeking to obtain the honey, glues the pollinia so firmly to its head that, when the insect flies off, they are dragged out of the anther, and are carried in such a position that the pollen comes in contact with the stigma of the next flower visited. The structural details by which this transference of pollen is facilitated differ in the several genera, and in some cases they are of a wonderful mechanical complexity.

A reference is given to the second edition of Darwin's work whenever the species or an allied species is therein described.

Anther one. Pollen cohering in pollinia.
  Perianth-segments united in a tube . . . . . 9. *Gastrodia.*
  Perianth-segments distinct or only united near the base
    Lip not spurred.
      Lip flat at the base.
        Lip short, broad, flat.
          Lip without glands at the base . . . . 1. *Microstylis.*
          Lip with 2 small glands or glandular spots at the base . . . . 2. *Liparis.*
        Lip long, deeply 3-lobed, mid-lobe large.
          Leaves 1 or 2, stalked. Column long, curved 3. *Oreorchis.*
          Leaves usually several, base sheathing. Column short, thick . . . . 4. *Calanthe.*[1]
        Lip long, narrow, 2-lobed at the tip . . . 7. *Neottia.*
      Lip concave at the base.
        Flowers sessile.
          Root fibrous.
            Spike spirally twisted . . . . . . 6. *Spiranthes.*
            Spike straight, one-sided . . . . . 8. *Goodyera.*
          Root tuberous . . . . 14. *Herminium.*
        Flowers shortly stalked.
          Sepals and petals erect, tips converging . . 11. *Cephalanthera.*
          Sepals and petals spreading . . . . . 12. *Epipactis.*
    Lip spurred.
      Root fibrous.
        Height 6–10 in. Leaves ovate, netted with yellow veins . . . . 5. *Anœctochilus.*
        Height 12–24 in. Leaves narrowly lanceolate, not netted . . . . 4. *Calanthe.*[2]
      Root creeping, producing a number of short, thick branches. Leaves none . . . . 10. *Epipogum.*
      Root tuberous.
        Glands of pollinia enclosed in a pouch . . . 13. *Orchis.*
        Glands of pollinia naked.
          Stem bearing a single bract and one basal leaf 16. *Hemipilia.*
          Stem leafy, at least at the base.
            Spur one . . . . 15. *Habenaria.*
            Spurs two . . . . 17. *Satyrium.*
Anthers two. Pollen-grains not cohering in pollinia.
  Lip folded, forming an inflated pouch . . . . . 18. *Cypripedium.*

1. MICROSTYLIS. From the Greek *micros*, small, and *stylon*, a column; referring to the short column.—Temperate and tropical regions, absent from S. Africa and Australia.

Root fibrous. Flowering-stem 6–18 in., erect, swollen at the base. Leaves 1 or 2 or 2–4, base sheathing. Flowers small or minute; bracts lanceolate, shorter than the ovary. Sepals and

[1] Except *C. plantaginea*. [2] *C. plantaginea* only.

petals spreading. Lip sessile, ovate, flat; spur none. Column very short. Anther sessile on its top; pollinia 4, free, ovoid; in buds and very young flowers the tips of the pollinia cohere by a minute, viscid drop. Stigma concave, placed just below the anther.

Flowers $\frac{1}{2}$ in. Leaves 2–4 . . . . 1. *M. Wallichii.*
Flowers $\frac{1}{8}$ in.
  Leaves two . . . . 2. *M. muscifera.*
  Leaf one . . . . 3. *M. cylindrostachya.*

1. **Microstylis Wallichii,** *Lindl.*; *Fl. Br. Ind.* v. 686. Flowering-stem 6–10 in., ribbed. Leaves 2–4, usually 3, ovate-lanceolate, 4×2 in., acute. Flowers shortly stalked, about $\frac{1}{2}$ in. long, pale

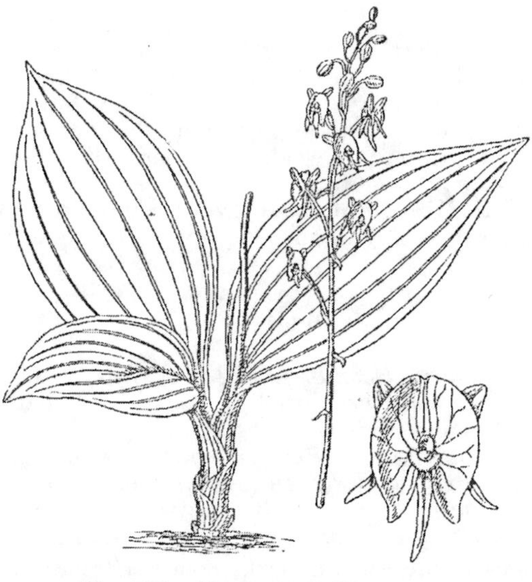

FIG. 162. MICROSTYLIS WALLICHII.

yellow-green, more or less marked or tinged with purple especially near the centre. Sepals oblong, 2 lateral rather shorter than the dorsal, margins recurved. Petals linear, longer than the sepals, margins recurved. Lip shield-like, broadly ovate, tip notched, basal lobes straight, acute, sometimes slightly overlapping. (Fig. 162.)

Simla, the Glen, Boileaugunge, Elysium Hill, in woods, 6000–6500 ft.; July, August.—Himalaya, Khasia.—Travancore, Andaman islands.

2. **Microstylis muscifera,** *Ridley*; *Fl. Br. Ind.* v. 689. Flowering-stem 6–18 in. Leaves 2, oblong or ovate, 3×2 in., obtuse.

Flowers $\frac{1}{8}$ in. long, pale yellow-green. Sepals broadly lanceolate. Petals linear. Lip ovate, abruptly pointed, margins thickened.

Mushobra, Fagoo, Huttoo, in woods; July.—Himalaya eastward to Sikkim. —Afghanistan.

3. **Microstylis cylindrostachya,** *Reichb. f.*; *Fl. Br. Ind.* v. 689. Flowering-stem 6–18 in. Leaf one, oblong $2\frac{1}{2} \times 1\frac{1}{4}$ in., or ovate $2\frac{1}{4} \times 1\frac{1}{2}$ in. Flowers $\frac{1}{8}$ in. long, pale yellow-green, crowded. Sepals broadly lanceolate. Petals linear, shorter than the sepals. Lip ovate, abruptly pointed, margins thickened.

Simla; July, August.—Himalaya, eastward to Sikkim.

2. **LIPARIS.** Etymology obscure.—Temperate and tropical regions.

Root fibrous. Stem erect, swollen at the base. Leaves 2–5, base sheathing. Flowers about $\frac{3}{4}$ in. across. Sepals and petals free, spreading. Lip adnate to the foot of the column, flat, broad, reflexed, bearing 2 minute glands or glandular spots at its base; spur none. Column long, curved, the upper half winged. Anther hinged at the back to the top of the column, pointed in front; pollinia 4, free, the tips in buds and young flowers cohering by a minute, viscid drop. Stigma on the top of the column, between the wings.

Stem 3–6 in. Leaves 2. Lip yellow-green . . . . . 1. *L. rostrata.*
Stem 6–18 in. Leaves 3–5. Lip purple . . . . . 2. *L. paradoxa.*

1. **Liparis rostrata,** *Reichb. f.*; *Fl. Br. Ind.* v. 694. Flowering-stem 3–6 in., usually tufted. Leaves 2, nearly opposite, ovate, $3 \times 1\frac{1}{2}$ in., sometimes only $1 \times \frac{1}{2}$ in., acute. Flowers about $\frac{1}{3}$ in. across; bracts $\frac{1}{10}$ in. Sepals lanceolate, margins reflexed. Petals linear, nearly as long as the sepals. Lip yellow-green, 2-lobed, with a short, acute point between the lobes, margins minutely toothed, 2 glandular spots at the base.

Simla, Annandale, the Glen, on rocks or mossy trunks of trees; June–September.—W. Himalaya, 5000–8000 ft.

2. **Liparis paradoxa,** *Reichb. f.*; *Fl. Br. Ind.* v. 697. Flowering-stem, 6–18 in. Leaves 3–5, broadly lanceolate, $5 \times 2\frac{1}{2}$ in. Flowers about $\frac{1}{3}$ in. across; bracts triangular, of the lower flowers $\frac{1}{2}$ in., decreasing to $\frac{1}{6}$ in. in the upper. Sepals linear, yellow-green, margins reflexed, tip membranous, acute. Petals oblong, striped yellow and purple, shorter than the sepals, tip inrolled. Lip dull purple, 2 small, conical glands on its base, tip broad, flat, notched.

Mahasu, 8000 ft., in woods; August.—Himalaya, Kumaon to Khasia.—Deccan, Ceylon.—S.E. Asia.

3. **OREORCHIS.** Derived from the Greek *oros*, a mountain, and *orchis*, referring to their habitat.—Siberia to Japan.

Root tuberous. Flowering-stem erect. Leaves 1 or 2, long, narrow, stalked. Flowers small. Sepals and petals distinct, nearly similar, oblong, erect. Lip attached to the foot of the column by a narrow, recurved claw, limb 3-lobed; side-lobes short, turned up; mid-lobe large, spreading; spur none. Column long, curved. Anther 1-celled, sessile on the top of the column; pollinia 4, globose, distinct. Caudicle short, attached to a viscid gland.

Leaf one.
- Flowering-stem slender. Flowers $\frac{1}{2}$ in. . . . . . 1. *O. foliosa.*
- Flowering-stem robust. Flowers nearly 1 in. . . . . 2. *O. indica.*

Leaves two. Lip notched and crumpled at the tip . . . 3. *O. micrantha.*

1. **Oreorchis foliosa,** *Lindl.*; *Fl. Br. Ind.* v. 709. Flowering-stem 10–12 in., slender. Leaf 1, narrowly lanceolate, $6 \times \frac{3}{4}$ in., narrowed downwards into a stalk; nerves prominent. Flowers $\frac{1}{2}$ in. long, red, shortly stalked; bracts lanceolate, $\frac{1}{4}$ in. Sepals linear-oblong, the upper one straight, obtuse, the side ones curved, pointed. Petals broadly oblong, obtuse. Mid-lobe of lip notched.

Mushobra, Mahasu, on rocks near the Retreat; June. July.—Himalaya, Gahrwal to Sikkim.

2. **Oreorchis indica,** *Hook. f.*; *Fl. Br. Ind.* v. 709. Flowering-stem 12–18 in., robust. Leaf 1, narrowly lanceolate, about 6×1 in., narrowed downwards into a stalk. Flowers nearly 1 in. across; bracts lanceolate, nearly $\frac{1}{3}$ in. Sepals linear-lanceolate, the upper one straight, the side ones curved. Petals oblong, curved. Mid-lobe of lip notched at the tip.

Huttoo; August.—W. Himalaya, 8000–9000 ft.

3. **Oreorchis micrantha,** *Lindl.*; *Fl. Br. Ind.* v. 709. Flowering-stem 12 in. Leaves 2, about $12 \times \frac{1}{2}$ in., prominently ribbed. Flowers white, more or less spotted with purple, $\frac{1}{3}$ in. across, shortly stalked; bracts lanceolate, $\frac{1}{5}$ in. Sepals oblong, upper one straight, obtuse, side ones curved, acute. Petals broadly oblong. Side-lobes of lip small, mid-lobe notched, tip crumpled.

Mushobra, Mahasu, 8000 ft.; July.—W. Himalaya, 8000–10,000 ft.

4. CALANTHE. From the Greek *calos*, beautiful, and *anthos*, a flower.—Most temperate and subtropical regions.

Root fibrous. Flowering-stem erect, swollen at the base. Leaves usually several, the blade narrowed into a sheathing stalk. Flowers about 1 in. across. Sepals and petals nearly equal, lanceolate, spreading. Base of lip adnate to the sides of the column, limb 3-lobed; side-lobes small, rounded; mid-lobe large, broad, spreading, narrowed to a hinge-like base; spur either long or none. Column short, thick, obliquely truncate at the top.

Anther conical, sessile on the top of the column; pollinia 8, cohering in 4 pairs by their viscid tips.

Spur none.
  Mid-lobe of lip rounded at the end . . . . . . 1. *C. tricarinata.*
  Mid-lobe of lip narrowly pointed at the end . . . 2. *C. puberula.*
Spur long. Mid-lobe of lip truncate at the end . . . 3. *C. plantaginea.*

1. **Calanthe tricarinata,** *Lindl.*; *Fl. Br. Ind.* v. 847. Flowering-stem 1–2 ft. Leaves 2 or 3, ovate, narrowed downwards, 8–15 × 2–3 in. Flowers $\frac{3}{4}$ in. across; bracts shorter than the flower-stalk. Sepals and petals green outside, edged with white, pale yellow-green inside. Lip of the same colour; side-lobes erect; mid-lobe with 3 large, purple, fleshy ridges along the middle, margin crumpled, tip rounded; spur none. Anther purple.

Mahasu, Narkunda, in forest; July.—Sikkim to Kashmir.

2. **Calanthe puberula,** *Lindl.*; *Fl. Br. Ind.* v. 848. Flowering-stem 1–2 ft. Leaves 5–7, very unequal, the lower hardly more than a sheath, ovate-lanceolate, 4–6 × $1\frac{3}{4}$–2 in., narrowly pointed. Flowers about 1 in. across, pale lavender; bracts $\frac{1}{2}$–1 in. Mid-lobe of lip with 2 ridges at the base between the flat side-lobes, margin irregularly toothed, tip pointed; spur none. Anther lavender.

Below Narkunda, 5000 ft.; August.—Himalaya, eastward to Khasia and Naga hills.

3. **Calanthe plantaginea,** *Lindl.*; *Fl. Br. Ind.* v. 853. Flowering-stem 1–2 ft. Leaves several, narrowly lanceolate, 10 × 2 in. Flowers $1\frac{1}{4}$ in. across, pale pink; bracts $\frac{1}{4}$–$\frac{1}{3}$ in. Mid-lobe of lip with three small ridges near the base, tip broadly wedge-shaped, truncate; spur long, slender.

Simla, the waterfall below Elysium House, 6000 ft.; April.—Himalaya, eastward to Bhotan.

5. **ANŒCTOCHILUS.** Derived from the Greek *anoiktos*, open, and *cheilos*, a lip; referring to the spreading lip.—India, Malaya.

Anœctochilus Roxburghii, *Lindl.*; *Fl. Br. Ind.* vi. 95. Root a few fleshy fibres. Flowering-stem decumbent at the base, 6–10 in., glandular-pubescent, bracteate. Leaves several, near the base of the stem, spreading, ovate, $1\frac{1}{4}$–$2\frac{1}{2}$ × $\frac{3}{4}$–1 in., short-stalked, acute, velvety purple-red, with yellow and pink centre and netted with yellow veins. Flowers 2, glandular-hairy, about $1\frac{1}{2}$ in. long, including the ovary. Sepals pale pink, ovate-lanceolate, the 2 side ones spreading, the upper one erect, and with the pale pink or nearly white, glabrous petals forming a hood arching over the column. Lip about $\frac{2}{3}$ in. long, adnate to the bottom of the column, base furnished with 2 fleshy protuberances and lateral fringes, tip broadly 2-lobed; spur nearly half as long as the ovary, conical, having 2 wart-like glands inside, tip minutely 2-lobed. Column short, winged on the sides, prolonged upwards in a beak-like process, the anther lying above it; pollinia 4, in 2 pairs united at their base, and both attached to a viscid gland.

Simla, on mossy banks below 5000 ft.; July, August.—Himalaya, eastward to Assam and Sylhet.—China.

6. SPIRANTHES. From the Greek *speira*, a spiral, and *anthos*, a flower, referring to the twisted flower-spike—Temperate and tropical regions; the most widely dispersed genus in the Order.

Spiranthes australis, *Lindl.*; *Fl. Br. Ind.* vi. 102. Pubescent. Roots cylindrical, fleshy. Flowering-stem 6–15 in., leafy near the base. Leaves linear-lanceolate, 2–4 in., base sheathing. Flowers very small, pink, sometimes white, crowded in a spiral, slender spike 2–6 in. long; bracts ovate-lanceolate, longer than the ovary. Sepals lanceolate, the two side ones spreading, the upper one combined with the petals to form a 3-lobed hood enclosing the column, tips recurved. Lip oblong, adnate to the foot of the column, base dilated, concave, having 2 small glands within, limb crisped along the margins, tip dilated, recurved; spur none. Column short, prolonged upwards in a flat, pointed process overhanging the circular, green stigma, the anther lying above it; pollinia 4, united in pairs, sessile on a single, minute, linear gland embedded in the viscid process, the two sides of which, after the pollinia have been removed, remain projecting upwards.

Simla, common on pastures; September.—Temperate Himalaya.—China, Australia, New Zealand.

A plant of the plains, ascending to 8000 ft. There are 2 or 3 British specie s called Lady's Tresses. See Darwin, p. 106.

7. NEOTTIA. The Greek name for a bird's nest; referring to the matted, fibrous roots.—Temperate Europe and Asia.

Neottia listeroides, *Lindl.*; *Fl. Br. Ind.* vi. 103. Root a dense mass of fleshy fibres. Flowering-stem 6–15 in., brown, glabrous near the base, glandular-pubescent upwards. Leaves reduced to brown scales. Flowers small, green-brown; bracts ovate-lanceolate, as long as or longer than the ovary. Sepals free, ovate-lanceolate, concave, erect at first, afterwards spreading. Petals smaller, free, linear, obtuse, ultimately spreading. Lip adnate to the foot of the column, flat, narrowly oblong, pendulous, 2–3 times as long as the sepals, broader towards the 2-lobed tip, mid-rib broad, dark green; spur none. Column short, incurved, prolonged in a pointed process overhanging the stigma, the anther lying above it; pollinia 4, in 2 pairs; in young flowers, the ends of the pollinia become united to a viscid drop exuded by the pointed process on being touched by an insect. Ovary prominently ribbed.

Simla, in forest, growing on decaying vegetable matter; August, September.—Himalaya, Kashmir to Sikkim.

I have seen a specimen from Elysium Hill with the lip hardly longer than the sepals, and the tip nearly entire; this might perhaps be regarded as distinct, but the species appears to vary in the length and shape of the lip. See Darwin, p. 125.

8. GOODYERA. Named in honour of John Goodyer, an English botanist of the seventeenth century.—Europe, Asia, America.

Root fibrous. Flowering-stem decumbent near the base, then erect, scaly or leafy. Leaves stalked. Flower-spike one-sided. Sepals and petals free, nearly equal; the upper sepal and the 2 petals forming a hood over the column. Lip adnate to the foot of the column, base concave; spur none. Column short, erect, prolonged upwards in a rounded or beaked process overhanging the stigma, the anther lying above it; pollinia 2, club-shaped, sessile on a membranous, linear gland embedded in the viscid process, the two sides of which after the removal of the pollinia remain projecting upwards.

Leaves white, net-veined. Base of lip bowl-shaped, smooth within . . . . 1. *G. repens.*
Leaves golden, net-veined. Base of lip boat-shaped, hairy within . . . . 2. *G. biflora.*

1. **Goodyera repens,** *R. Br.*; *Fl. Br. Ind.* vi. 113. Rootstock creeping; fibres few, thick. Flowering-stem 4–9 in., leafy near the base, scaly on the upper part. Leaves ovate or lanceolate, $\frac{1}{2}$–$1\frac{1}{2}$ in., shortly stalked, netted with white veins. Flowers numerous, $\frac{1}{7}$ in. diam., white, tinged with brown or pink, globose, pointed; spike $1\frac{1}{2}$–3 in.; bracts linear-lanceolate, longer than the ovary. Lateral sepals ovate, pointed, erect at first, spreading afterwards, upper sepal narrow, erect, forming with the 2 petals a hood enclosing the column. Lip bowl-shaped, smooth within, bearing a short, recurved, terminal lobe. Column prolonged upwards in a short, rounded process containing the linear gland. Anther oblong.

Simla, Observatory and Prospect Hills, Fagoo, not common; August, September.—Himalaya, eastward to Sikkim.—Europe, N. Asia, N. America.
A British plant, rare in the Highlands of Scotland.

2. **Goodyera biflora,** *Hook. f.*; *Fl. Br. Ind.* vi. 114. Root a few long, thick fibres. Flowering-stem 3–4 in., leafy. Leaves ovate-lanceolate, 1–2 in., acute, netted with golden veins; stalks short, sheathing. Flowers 2–4, yellow, about $1\frac{1}{3}$ in. long; spike $1\frac{1}{2}$ in.; bracts linear-lanceolate, shorter than the flowers. Lateral sepals 1 in. long, erect, narrowly lanceolate, united at the base, tip of the upper sepal recurved; petals linear, obtuse; sepals and petals enclosing the column and covering the basal part of the lip. Lip long, boat-shaped, hairy within, tip recurved. Column prolonged upwards in a narrow, pointed process containing the linear gland. Anther very long and slender.

Simla, Elysium Hill, in woods, not common; August.—W. Himalaya, 4000–6000 ft.

9. GASTRODIA. Derived from the Greek *gaster*, belly; referring to the thick, swollen column.—Asia, Australia.

Gastrodia orobanchoides, *Benth.*; *Fl. Br. Ind.* vi. 122. Root a large, oblong-ovoid, scaly tuber. Flowering-stem 10–24 in., erect, pale yellow-brown, smooth and shining. Leaves reduced to a few scales. Flowers about $\frac{1}{2}$ in. long, numerous, yellow; spike short and nodding at first, elongated and erect afterwards; bracts nearly as long as the flowers. Perianth-segments united in a tube, their obtuse tips free, that of the lip slightly longer than the others, and recurved. Column erect, nearly as long as the perianth-tube. Anther terminal; pollinia 2. Stigma prominent.

Mahasu, Fagoo, in woods, rare, usually growing among decaying leaves; June–September.—W. Himalaya, 7000–8000 ft.

I can find no published account of the method of fertilisation in this curious Orchid.

10. EPIPOGUM. Derived from the Greek *epi*, upon, and *pogon*, a beard; possibly in allusion to the glandular hairs on the lip.—Asia, Africa, Europe, Australia.

Epipogum aphyllum, *Swartz*; *Fl. Br. Ind.* vi. 124. Rootstock creeping, producing a number of short, thick, fleshy branches. Flowering-stem 4–8 in., erect, pale brown, smooth. Leaves reduced to a few scales. Flowers 3–6, about $\frac{3}{4}$ in. long, yellow-pink; bracts shorter than the flowers. Sepals and petals $\frac{1}{2}$–$\frac{3}{4}$ in., nearly equal, free, narrowly lanceolate. Lip uppermost, adnate to the base of the column, 3-lobed; mid-lobe much the largest, pointed, recurved, concave in the centre and bearing a few rows of small, red glands; spur large, blunt. Column short, thick. Anther terminal; pollinia 2, tapering into slender caudicles, the ends attached to a single, white, triangular, viscid gland placed on the top of the column.

Fagoo, the Chor, growing in forest among decaying leaves, rare; July–October.—W. and temperate Himalaya, 6000–8500 ft.—Europe, N. Asia.

A very rare British plant.

11. CEPHALANTHERA. Derived from the Greek *cephale*, the head, and *anther*, referring to the position of the anther.—N. temperate regions.

Cephalanthera ensifolia, *Rich.*; *Fl. Br. Ind.* vi. 125. Nearly or quite glabrous. Rootstock creeping; fibres long, numerous, thick. Flowering-stem 6–18 in., erect, grooved, leafy throughout or the lower portion bearing long, sheathing scales. Leaves sessile, acute, the lower lanceolate, 2–6 in., the upper longer and narrower. Flowers white, nearly erect; bracts ovate, acute, variable, the lower usually long, the upper much shorter, sometimes minute. Sepals and petals $\frac{1}{2}$–$\frac{3}{4}$ in. long, nearly equal, their tips converging; sepals lanceolate, acute; petals ovate, obtuse. Lip erect, included, deeply 3-lobed, the base concave, adnate to and embracing the bottom of the column; side-lobes erect, rounded; mid-lobe broadly triangular, conspicuously ridged and often marked with a yellow spot, tip bluntly toothed, recurved; spur none. Column as long as the lip. Anther terminal; pollinia 2, each 2-lobed. Stigma broad, situated below the anther.

Mahasu, Fagoo, Matiana, growing in shady forests; May–July.—Temperate Himalaya, Kashmir to Bhotan.—Europe, N. Africa, Central Asia.
A British plant. See Darwin, p. 80.

12. EPIPACTIS. The classical name of a plant of this affinity. —N. temperate regions.

Rootstock creeping, fibrous. Flowering-stem erect, leafy throughout or the lower portion bearing sheathing scales. Leaves orbicular or lanceolate, stem-clasping, acute. Flower-spike 4–10 in.; bracts lanceolate, acute, the lower 2–2½ in., the upper ½–1 in. Sepals and petals nearly equal, ultimately spreading. Lip adnate to the base of the column, narrowed near the middle in a hinge-like joint, basal part concave, terminal part flat, petal-like; spur none. Column short. Anther terminal; pollinia 2, each 2-lobed, the tips attached to a small, globose, viscid gland seated on the head of the column and overhanging the broad stigma.

Flowers crowded. Basal portion of lip bowl-shaped . . 1. *E. latifolia.*
Flowers distant.
 Lower leaves orbicular. Basal portion of lip narrow, canoe-shaped . . . . 2. *E. consimilis.*
 Lower leaves lanceolate. Basal portion of lip relatively large, the sides broad, rounded . . . . . . 3. *E. Royleana.*

1. **Epipactis latifolia,** *Swartz*; *Fl. Br. Ind.* vi. 125. Flowering-stem 1–3 ft., robust, glabrous, except for the pubescent inflorescence. Lower leaves orbicular, 2½–6 × 2–3 in., the upper ovate-lanceolate, 4 × 2 in., nerves curved. Flowers about ½ in. diam., dingy purple, crowded; bracts leafy. Sepals and petals ⅜ in., lanceolate, acute, glabrous or nearly so. Lip ¼ in. long, basal part bowl-shaped, margins rounded, terminal part shorter, flat, broadly triangular, bearing 2 protuberances at its base, margins crumpled, obscurely toothed.

Simla, Jako, &c., common, up to about 9500 ft.; July, August.—Himalaya, Kashmir to Sikkim.—Europe, N. Africa, N. Asia to Japan.
The Helleborine of Britain. See Darwin, p. 101.

2. **Epipactis consimilis,** *Wall.*; *Fl. Br. Ind.* vi. 126. Flowering-stem 1–2 ft., slender. Leaves narrow, lanceolate, 6 × 1¼ in., long-pointed, nerves nearly straight. Flowers about 1 in. diam., distant, orange-green, sometimes spotted, lip paler. Sepals and petals about ½ in., pubescent. Lip as long as the sepals, basal

part narrow, canoe-shaped, terminal part 3-lobed, the side-lobes turned up, the tip lanceolate, spreading.

Sutlej valley, near Suni, in marshy ground; April.—Himalaya, Kashmir to Nepal.—Westward to Syria.

3. **Epipactis Royleana,** *Lindl.*; *Fl. Br. Ind.* vi. 126. Flowering-stem 1–2 ft., robust, glabrous or pubescent on the upper parts. Lower leaves orbicular, $3 \times 1\frac{3}{4}$ in., the upper lanceolate, nerves nearly straight. Flowers about 1 in. diam., distant, red with yellow centre. Sepals and petals about $\frac{1}{2}$ in., glabrous or nearly so. Lip longer than the sepals, basal part relatively large, with prominent nerves, the sides broad, rounded, erect, terminal part shorter, flat, lanceolate.

Kashmir to Sikkim, 7000–12,000 ft.—Central Asia, N. America.

There is a specimen collected by Edgeworth in the Kew Herbarium, marked 'Synj, 3000 ft.' This may be the village of that name in the Giri valley below Fagoo. I have seen no other specimen from near Simla.

13. ORCHIS. The Greek name of various ground orchids.—N. temperate regions.

Orchis latifolia, *Linn.*; *Fl. Br. Ind.* vi. 127. Glabrous. Root tuberous, slightly flattened and divided into 2 or 3 finger-like lobes. Flowering-stem 1–3 ft., robust, erect, hollow, leafy throughout or the lower portion bearing a few sheathing scales. Leaves erect, oblong-lanceolate, $2\frac{1}{2}$–6 in., obtuse, base sheathing. Flowers about $\frac{2}{3}$ in. long, crowded, dull purple, the lip darker spotted; bracts green, narrowly lanceolate, the lower much longer than the flowers, the upper slightly so or shorter. Sepals and petals nearly equal, the lateral sepals spreading, the dorsal one forming with the petals a hood over the column. Lip adnate to the column, turned downwards, orbicular, obscurely 3-lobed, margins minutely toothed; spur straight, cylindric, nearly as long as the ovary. Column very short. Anther adnate to its face, cells diverging; pollinia 2, caudicles attached to 2 small, globose, viscid glands enclosed in a minute pouch overhanging the broad, 2-lobed stigma.

Huttoo, on wet ground; June, July.—Himalaya, Kashmir to Nepal to 16,000 ft.—Westward to the Atlantic and in N. Asia.

The Marsh Orchis of Britain. See Darwin, p. 15.

14. HERMINIUM. Derivation obscure.—Europe, N. Asia.

Herminium angustifolium, *Benth.*; *Fl. Br. Ind.* vi. 129. Glabrous. Root of 2 small, ovoid tubers. Flowering-stem 1–$2\frac{1}{2}$ ft., slender, erect, leafy. Leaves few, linear, 4–8 in., acute, base sheathing. Flowers small, green, crowded; spike 4–8 in.; bracts about as long as the ovary. Perianth about $\frac{1}{4}$ in. long, spreading. Sepals oblong. Petals linear. Lip continuous with the base of the column, longer than the sepals, linear, base minutely concave, tip divided into 3 pointed lobes, the side ones much the longer, curved; spur none. Column very short, bearing 2 ear-like processes. Anther adnate to the face of the column; pollinia 2, caudicles attached to 2 globose, viscid glands which in young flowers are concealed in a minute pouch. (Fig. 163.)

Simla, common in grass; August.—Himalaya to Khasia.—Tenasserim, China, Japan.

FIG. 163. HERMINIUM ANGUSTIFOLIUM.

15. HABENARIA. Derived from the Latin *habena*, a thong or rein, referring to the linear, projecting, stigmatic arms of most species.—Temperate and tropical regions.

Root tuberous. Flowering-stem erect, usually leafy. Sepals and petals nearly equal; the upper sepal concave, erect, the lateral ones flat and usually spreading or reflexed; petals erect. Lip continuous with the base of the column, 3-lobed or undivided, spurred at the base. Anther adnate to the short column, cells usually diverging and produced into tubes; pollinia 2, caudicles thread-like, attached to 2 small, globose, naked, viscid glands. Stigma in *H. Susannæ* and *H. galeandra* on the column below the anther, in the other species consisting of 2 projecting arms.

Lip 3-lobed.
Side-lobes of lip fringed.
Spur 4–5 in. Flowers 3–4 in. across, white . . 1. *H. Susannæ.*
Spur 1–1½ in. Flowers 1–2 in. across.
Petals glabrous, linear, narrower than the dorsal sepal, sides nearly parallel . . . . . 2. *H. pectinata.*
Petals pubescent, broader than the dorsal sepal, the outer margin rounded, projecting . . 3. *H. arietina.*
Spur 2¼ in. Flowers 2 in. across . . . . . 4. *H. intermedia.*
Side-lobes of lip entire.
Lip lobed nearly to the base.
Flowers white . . . . 5. *H. ensifolia.*
Flowers yellow . . . . 6. *H. marginata.*
Lip lobed at the tip only.
Leaves clustered about the middle of the stem, ovate, acute. Flowers white . . . . . 9. *H. goodyeroides.*
Leaves scattered, chiefly below the middle of the stem, lanceolate, acuminate. Flowers green . 10. *H. Elisabethæ.*
Lip undivided.
Lip narrow, strap-like. Flowers green-yellow.
Spur longer than the ovary . . . . . . 7. *H. Edgeworthii.*
Spur shorter than the ovary . . . . . . 8. *H. densa.*
Lip broadly triangular. Flowers purple . . . . 11. *H. galeandra.*

1. **Habenaria Susannæ,** *R. Br.*; *Fl. Br. Ind.* vi. 137. Glabrous. Flowering-stem 2–4 ft., robust, leafy. Leaves overlapping, ovate-oblong, 2–6 in., base sheathing. Flowers 2–4, pure white, 3–4 in. across, nearly sessile, erect, fragrant; bracts leaf-like, nearly 3 in. long. Petals linear, falcate, acute. Lip 3-lobed nearly to the base; side-lobes broad, the margins cut into a comb-like fringe, the segments unequal and often forked; mid-lobe narrowly lanceolate, entire; spur green, slender, 4–5 in. long. Stigma on the front of the column.

Simla, on pastures below 6000 ft.; July–September.—Tropical Himalaya.—Deccan.—Burmah, China, Malay Archipelago.

This fine Orchid was formerly abundant on the spur below Bishop Cotton's School; it is now nearly extirpated near Simla, but in 1886 it was still common about Khyree-ghat and Syree.

2. **Habenaria pectinata,** *Don*; *Fl. Br. Ind.* vi. 137. Glabrous. Flowering-stem 1–2 ft., robust, leafy. Leaves narrowly sword-shaped, 6×1 in., 3-nerved, base sheathing. Flowers about 1 in. across, pale yellow-green or white, crowded; spike 3–8 in.; bracts leaf-like, the lower ones longer than the ovary, the upper about as long. Sepals green. Petals glabrous, narrower than the upper sepal, sides slightly curved, nearly parallel. Lip 3-lobed nearly to the base; side-lobes fringed, comb-like, the segments variable in length; mid-lobe linear, entire, rather longer than the side-lobes; spur green, ¾ in. long, swollen at the tip. Stigmatic arms dilated in the upper half, curving outwards.

Simla, common; July–September.—Simla to Sikkim.

The comb-segments vary so much in length that I suspect two species may be confused here.

3. **Habenaria arietina,** *Hook. f.*; *Fl. Br. Ind.* vi. 138. Habit and appearance of *H. pectinata*. Leaves ovate-lanceolate, 4 × 1½ in. Petals pubescent, broader than the upper sepal, inner margin straight, outer strongly curved. Lip lobed only for about three-fourths of its length, segments of the fringe very long and slender; mid-lobe rather shorter than the side-lobes; spur 1½ in., hardly swollen at the tip.

Simla; July, August.—Himalaya, eastward to Khasia.
Usually confounded with *H. pectinata*.

Fig. 164. Habenaria intermedia.

4. **Habenaria intermedia,** *Don*; *Fl. Br. Ind.* vi. 138. Glabrous. Flowering-stem 10–24 in., robust, leafy. Leaves rarely overlapping, usually 5-nerved, ovate-lanceolate, 2–4 in., narrowed to an acute point, base sheathing. Flowers 2 in. across, green-white, few, distant; bracts leaf-like, the lower ones usually longer

than the flowers, the upper as long as the ovary. Sepals green, lateral spreading, tips reflexed, upper one white inside. Petals white. Lip 3-lobed to about two-thirds of its length, green or yellow-green, except the narrow, white base; side-lobes deeply

FIG. 165. HABENARIA ENSIFOLIA.

fringed, the segments long and narrow; mid-lobe linear, entire, as long as the side lobes; spur $2\frac{1}{4}$ in., pale green, curved, swollen towards the tip. Stigmatic arms spreading, tips recurved. (Fig. 164.)

Simla, common on banks or grassy slopes; July, August.—Himalaya, Kashmir to Sikkim.

5. **Habenaria ensifolia,** *Lindl.*; *Fl. Br. Ind.* vi. 137, *under H. pectinata*. Glabrous. Flowering-stem 2–3 ft., sometimes more, robust, leafy. Leaves oblong-lanceolate, 3–6 in., conspicuously white-margined, pointed, base sheathing. Flowers $\frac{1}{2}$–$\frac{3}{4}$ in. across, white: bracts narrow, long-pointed, ciliolate along the edges, as long as the flowers. Lip about $1\frac{1}{4}$ in. long, 3-lobed nearly to the base, lobes spreading, linear, entire; mid-lobe the shortest and thickest, with recurved edges forming a groove on its under side; spur $1\frac{1}{2}$ in., sometimes longer, green, curved, swollen towards the tip. Stigmatic arms long, incurved. (Fig. 165.)

Syree; August.—Himalaya, eastward to Khasia.
Incorrectly associated with *H. pectinata* in *Fl. Br. Ind.*

6. **Habenaria marginata,** *Colebr.*; *Fl. Br. Ind.* vi. 150. Glabrous. Flowering-stem 4–8 in., bearing 2 or 3 sheathing, pointed scales. Leaves 3 or 4, near the base of the stem, ovate, $1\frac{1}{2}$ in., margins yellow, base sheathing. Flowers $\frac{1}{2}$ in. across, crowded, yellow; spike $1\frac{1}{2}$–2 in.; bracts lanceolate, acute, ciliolate, slightly longer than the ovary. Sepals green. Petals yellow. Lip longer than the sepals, 3-lobed nearly to the base, lobes linear, entire, spreading; side-lobes having filiform points, mid-lobe the shortest and broadest; spur about as long as the ovary, swollen below the middle. Stigmatic arms long.

Simla, on grassy slopes near the fifth waterfall, 5000 ft.; August.—W. Himalaya, 5000–7000 ft.—Throughout India.

7. **Habenaria Edgeworthii,** *Hook. f. in Herb. Kew.* Glabrous, except the sepals. Flowering-stem $\frac{1}{2}$–$2\frac{1}{2}$ ft., leafy. Leaves ovate or oblong-lanceolate, the lower $1\frac{1}{2}$–$4\frac{1}{2}$ in., the upper gradually smaller, acute, nerves 5 or 7, sometimes 3, base sheathing. Flowers $\frac{1}{3}$–$\frac{1}{2}$ in. across, erect, yellow-green, not crowded; spike 3–10 in.; bracts lanceolate, acute, the lower shorter, the upper longer than the ovary. Sepals green, pubescent, the margins minutely fringed. Petals yellow, thick, erect. Lip yellow, longer than the sepals, strap-shaped, undivided, broadest at the base and abruptly narrowed; spur yellow-green, much longer than the ovary, slender, turned upwards, tip curved. Caudicles very short. Stigmatic arms oblong. (Fig. 166.)

Simla, common; July, August.
This plant is included in the *Fl. Br. Ind.* vi. 153 under *H. latilabris*, *Hook. f.*, but it differs from the Sikkim species described and figured under that name in the *Annals of the Roy. Bot. Gard. Calcutta*, vol. v. part i. 66 t. 100. In the Kew Herbarium there is a specimen of the Simla plant named *H. Edgeworthii* by Sir J. D. Hooker; therefore I have adopted the name.

8. **Habenaria densa,** *Wall.*; *Fl. Br. Ind.* vi. 153. Glabrous. Flowering-stem 1–2 ft., leafy. Leaves lanceolate, lower ones $2\frac{1}{2}$–4 in., the upper gradually smaller, acute, base sheathing. Flowers hardly $\frac{1}{4}$ in. across, erect, rather crowded; spike 4–10 in.; bracts narrowly lanceolate, long-pointed, the lower much longer than the

ovary, the upper equal to it. Sepals green, thick. Petals yellow-green, fleshy. Lip green, slightly longer than the sepals, undivided, linear, thick; spur green, turned downwards, much shorter than the ovary, lower half dilated, tip rounded. Caudicles very short. Stigmatic arms large, oblong.

Simla, common; August, September.—Himalaya, eastward to Sikkim.

9. **Habenaria goodyeroides,** *Don*; *Fl. Br. Ind.* vi. 161. Glabrous. Flowering-stem 1–2 ft., robust. Leaves about 4, placed close

FIG. 166. HABENARIA EDGEWORTHII.

together near the middle of the stem, ovate, $3\frac{1}{2} \times 3$ in. or larger, base sheathing; below the leaves are a few scales, above them sessile bracts. Flowers $\frac{1}{3}$ in. across, yellow-green, crowded; spike 6–10 in.; bracts lanceolate, as long as the ovary. Lip broad, recurved, longer than the sepals, tip 3-lobed, mid-lobe the broadest; spur small, bag-like, narrowed at the mouth. Stigmatic arms short, oblong.

Simla, 6000 ft.; August.—Himalaya.—Throughout India and Malaya.

10. **Habenaria Elisabethæ,** *Duthie, n. sp.* Tubers ovoid, $1\frac{3}{4}$ in. long. Flowering-stem sulcate, glabrous. Leaves $2\frac{1}{2}$–4 in. by $\frac{1}{3}$–$\frac{2}{3}$

in., amplexicaul, narrowly lanceolate, acuminate or obtuse, 7–9-veined, mid-rib prominent beneath. Flowers very small, green, rather crowded, sessile; spike slender, about 4 in. long; bracts lanceolate, acuminate, equalling or exceeding the ovaries. Sepals erect; dorsal concave, ovate, obtuse; lateral obliquely ovate. Petals a little longer than the sepals, obliquely ovate-lanceolate, obtuse. Lip 3-cleft, fleshy, longer than the sepals, claw concave; side-lobes linear, spreading, gibbous on their basal edges, mid-lobe broader but not longer than the lateral, straight; spur short, obovate, one-fifth the length of the ovary.

Near Simla, 9000–10,000 ft. (Lady Elizabeth Babington Smith); near Mussoorie, 8000–9000 ft.; Western Himalaya, 8000–10,000 ft.

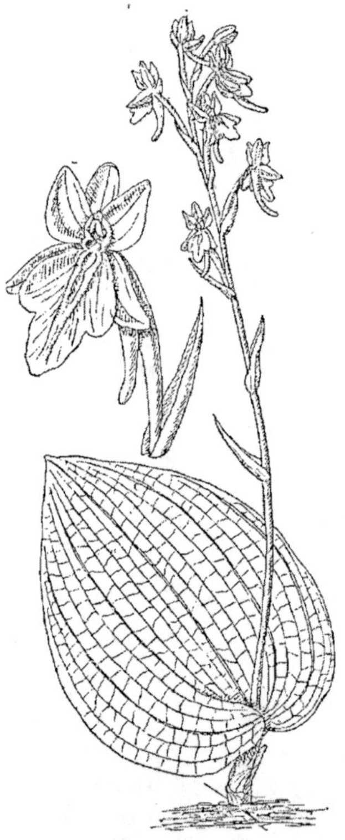

FIG. 167.
HEMIPILIA CORDIFOLIA.

11. **Habenaria galeandra,** *Benth.*; *Fl. Br. Ind.* vi. 163. Glabrous or nearly so. Flowering-stem 6–10 in., slender, leafy. Leaves oblong-lanceolate, 1–2 in., sessile. Flowers $\frac{1}{2}$ in. across, purple; spike 2–4 in.; bracts leaf-like, the lower much longer than the flowers, the upper shorter. Dorsal sepal narrowly lanceolate, erect; lateral about as long, falcately lanceolate, acuminate and spreading. Petals a little shorter than the sepals, falcately lanceolate, obtuse. Lip broadly triangular, spreading or the sides recurved, base shortly clawed, terminal margin notched; spur short, conical, blunt. Stigma on the column below the anther.

Simla, in grass, on sunny slopes, 6000 ft.; August. — W. Himalaya. — Central India, China.

16. **HEMIPILIA.** Derivation obscure.—Himalaya, Burmah.

Hemipilia cordifolia, *Lindl.*; *Fl. Br. Ind.* vi. 167. Glabrous. Root tuberous. Flowering-stem 6–12 in., erect, bearing a single leaf near its base. Leaf fleshy, stem-clasping, broadly ovate, $2–4 \times 1\frac{1}{4}–2\frac{1}{2}$ in., acute, net-veined, dotted with purple, lateral nerves arching. Flowers $\frac{1}{2}–\frac{3}{4}$ in. across, carmine-purple; bracts lanceolate, acute, shorter than the ovary. Sepals equal, obtuse, lateral ones broadly sickle-shaped, spreading, upper one erect. Petals erect, forming a hood. Lip continuous with the column, broad, spreading, obscurely 3-lobed; spur curved, longer than the sepals, shorter than the ovary, tip 2-lobed, upturned. Column very short, prolonged upwards in a broad, thin process folded in the middle and projecting from between the anther-cells. Anther-cells separated, diverging; pollinia 2, caudicles long, attached to 2 naked, viscid glands. Stigma on the column below the anther. (Fig. 167.)

Simla, Elysium Hill, Mushobra, Mahasu, on rocks; August.—Himalaya, eastward to Nepal.

17. SATYRIUM. From the Greek *Satyrion*, a name said to have been applied by Dioscorides to another orchid, *Aceras anthropophora*.—India; Africa, chiefly south.

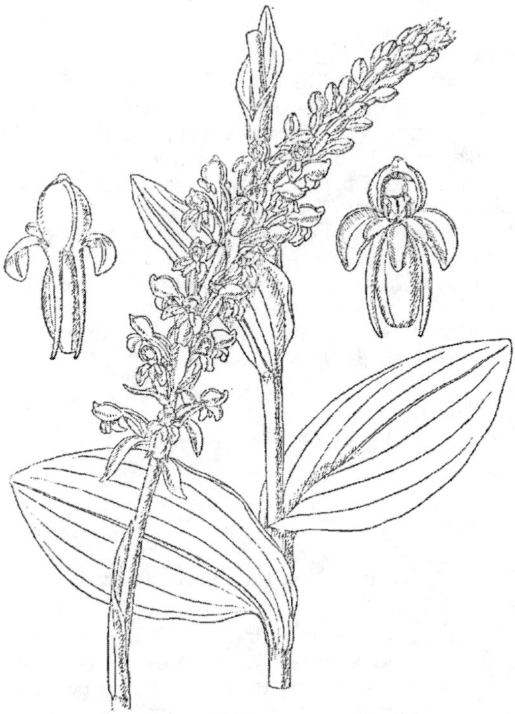

FIG. 168. SATYRIUM NEPALENSE.

Satyrium nepalense, *Don*; *Fl. Br. Ind.* vi. 168. Glabrous. Root tuberous. Flowering-stem 6–24 in., erect. Leaves usually 2, near the base of the stem, lanceolate, $3–6 \times \frac{3}{4}–2\frac{1}{2}$ in., or ovate 3×2 in., base sheathing, a few leaf-like bracts above them. Flowers $\frac{1}{3}–\frac{3}{4}$ in. across, fragrant, pink, crowded; bracts tinged with pink, larger than the flowers. Sepals narrowly oblong, lateral ones spreading, upper one recurved. Petals smaller than the sepals, recurved. Lip uppermost, sessile on the base of the column, erect, hoodlike, margins turned back ; spurs 2, pointing downwards, usually slender and about as long as the ovary, sometimes stout and not half as long. Column short, bearing 2 ear-like processes. Anther pendant from the top of the column, cells contiguous ; pollinia 2, caudicles recurved, glands large, exposed, ivory-white. Stigma broad, concave. (Fig. 168.)

Simla, common ; July–September.—Himalaya.—Throughout India.

18. CYPRIPEDIUM. From *Cypris*, the Greek for Venus, and *pedilon*, a slipper ; referring to the shape of the lip.—Europe, Asia, America.

Cypripedium cordigerum, *Don* ; *Fl. Br. Ind.* vi. 170. Glabrous or nearly so. Root fibrous. Flowering-stem 1–2 ft., erect, leafy. Leaves spreading, ovate or lanceolate, 5×3 in., acute. Flower solitary, terminal ; bract large, leaf-like. Sepals green, ovate-lanceolate, $1\frac{1}{2}$–2 in., long-pointed, the 2 lateral united and placed under the lip, the third erect and above it. Petals green or white, spreading, lanceolate. Lip 1–$1\frac{1}{4}$ in. long, white, sessile, folded to form an oblong, inflated, open-mouthed pouch. Column short, curved over and nearly closing the posterior portion of the mouth and bearing a shield-like process at its end. Anthers 2, globose, one on each side of the base of the column ; pollen-grains glutinous. Ovary straight ; style very short, stigma oblong, its face turned downwards.

Mushobra, 7500–8000 ft., Mahasu, Fagoo, Narkunda ; May, June.—W. Himalaya, 7000–11,000 ft.

Lady's Slipper. See Darwin, p. 226.

XCIX. SCITAMINEÆ

GLABROUS herbs ; roots cylindrical, fleshy ; stems erect, unbranched. Leaves alternate, sometimes only one, lanceolate, entire, sessile or stalked, veins numerous, parallel. Flowers showy, irregular, 2-sexual, in terminal spikes ; one or several in the axil of each bract. Perianth superior. Calyx tubular, toothed. Corolla-tube short or long and slender, slightly dilated towards the top and expanding in a 3-lobed limb, the upper lobe usually erect and concave ; within the corolla there is a second whorl of 3 petal-like segments or staminodes, the two lateral usually erect, the lower broader, spreading and usually lobed. Fertile stamen 1, filament short, erect, grooved, inserted on the mouth of the corolla-tube ; anther linear-oblong, curved, versatile, cells 2, contiguous, the connective sometimes produced at the base in a fork. Ovary inferior, 3-celled, bearing at the top 2 short, linear, erect glands; style terminal, very long, thread-like, the upper portion more or less adnate to or enclosed by the filament; stigma globose, resting on the top of the anther. Capsule 3-valved; seeds many, more or less enclosed in a white or coloured, outer coat or aril.—India, E. Asia, America.—From the Latin *scitamentum*, delicate food, dainties, referring perhaps to some products of the Order which comprises the Gingers, Arrowroot, &c.

Anther-connective produced in a fork.
  Flowers purple . . . . 1. *Roscoea.*
  Flowers yellow.
    Bracts 1-flowered. Lip deeply 2-lobed . . . . . 2. *Cautleya.*
    Bracts several-flowered. Lip notched . . . . . 3. *Curcuma.*
Anther-connective not produced . . . . 4. *Hedychium.*

1. ROSCOEA. In honour of William Roscoe, author of a work on this Order.—Himalaya; one species in Cochin China.

Stems leafy. Leaves sessile. Bracts small, persistent, 1-flowered. Flowers purple, in terminal spikes, only one flower in the spike expanding at a time. Calyx-tube more or less slit on one side, 2-toothed. Corolla-tube long, slender; upper lobe erect, more or less concave and hood-like; lateral lobes narrow, recurved. Lateral staminodes erect, more or less united, covering the anther; the lower large, broad, spreading; anther notched at the top, the connective produced at the base in a fork. Ovary cylindrical, slender. Capsule oblong-ovoid, ultimately opening by 3 valves; seeds many, small.

The fork at the base of the anther in this genus and in the next, on being pushed by an insect in its efforts to obtain the honey secreted in the base of the flower, causes the anther to descend on its back, the action being similar to the pushing of the short arm in the stamens of *Salvia*, see Labiatæ, page 394. It is worthy of note that the same mechanical adaptation secures the same end in Orders so different in floral structure.

Flowers dark purple. Corolla-tube much longer than the calyx 1. *R. alpina.*
Flowers lilac. Corolla-tube hardly longer than the calyx . . 2. *R. procera.*

1. **Roscoea alpina,** *Royle*; *Fl. Br. Ind.* vi. 207. Stems 4–8 in., slender. Leaves 2–4, often not developed at the flowering time, oblong-lanceolate, 3–6 in. Flowers few, dark purple. Corolla-tube much longer than the calyx; upper lobe $\frac{1}{2}$–$\frac{3}{4}$ in., orbicular, slightly concave; lateral lobes linear-oblong. Lower staminode $\frac{1}{2}$–$\frac{3}{4}$ in. long, 2-lobed. (Fig. 169.)

Simla, common on banks; July.—W. Himalaya, up to 11,000 ft.

2. **Roscoea procera,** *Wall.*; *Fl. Br. Ind.* vi. 208. Stems 12–24 in., robust. Leaves 3–6, lanceolate, $6 \times 1\frac{1}{2}$ in. Flowers several, lilac,

faintly streaked and tinged with pink. Corolla-tube hardly longer than the calyx; upper lobe $1\frac{3}{4}$ in. long, the margin inflexed, forming a narrow, flattened, pointed hood; lateral lobes linear-lanceolate. Lower staminode $1\frac{3}{4} \times 1\frac{1}{2}$ in., obscurely 3-lobed, spreading, notched at the tip.

Simla, Mahasu; August.—W. Himalaya, up to 10,000 ft.

The Simla plant is certainly that represented in Hooker's *Exot. Flor.* tab. 144, under the name of *R. purpurea*, Smith. But the true *R. purpurea*, Smith, figured in his *Exot. Bot.* ii. t. 108, and in the *Bot. Mag.* t. 4630, has dark purple flowers and a deeply-lobed lower staminode. It is apparently an Eastern Himalayan form, and does not occur at Simla. A name is therefore required for the Simla species, and I have taken *R. procera*, Wallich, figured in his *Pl. As. Rar.* t. 242, and reduced in the *Fl. Br. Ind.* to a variety of *R. purpurea*.

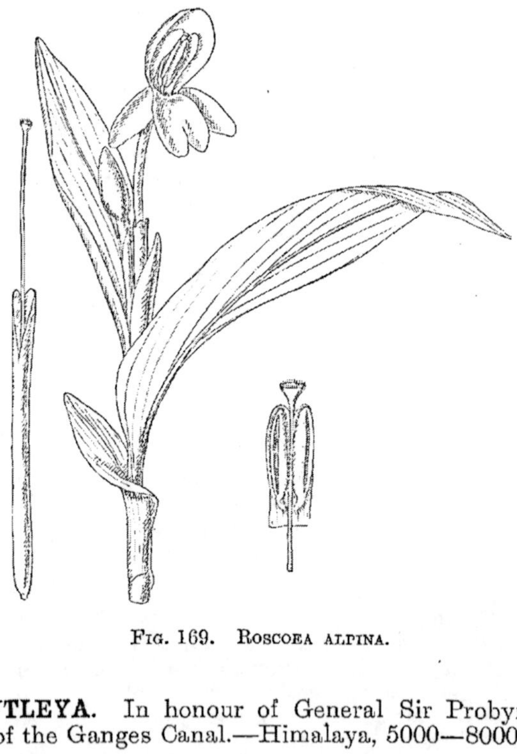

FIG. 169. ROSCOEA ALPINA.

2. CAUTLEYA. In honour of General Sir Probyn Cautley, Engineer of the Ganges Canal.—Himalaya, 5000—8000 ft.

Stems leafy. Leaves sessile. Bracts 1-flowered. Flowers yellow, in terminal spikes. Calyx red, slit on one side, minutely toothed. Corolla-tube long, slender; upper lobe erect, narrow, concave; the 2 lateral lobes broader and reflexed. Lateral staminodes nearly as long as the corolla-lobes, erect, tips incurved, forming a hood over the anther; the lower deeply 2-lobed, reflexed; anther notched at the top, the connective produced at the base in a fork. Ovary globose. Capsule red; when ripe the 3 valves are reflexed exposing their red lining and numerous small seeds.

Leaves narrow. Flowers few, distant. Bracts green, shorter than the calyx . . . . 1. *C. lutea.*
Leaves broad. Flowers many, crowded. Bracts red, as long as the calyx . . . . 2. *C. spicata.*

FIG. 170. CAUTLEYA SPICATA.

1. **Cautleya lutea,** *Royle*; *Fl. Br. Ind.* vi. 208. Stems 1–$1\frac{1}{2}$ ft. Leaves 5–10 × 1–$1\frac{1}{2}$ in., long-pointed, upper surface green, lower tinged with red. Sheaths red-striped. Spike 4–8 in., drooping; bracts green, shorter than the calyx. Flowers few, distant. Corolla-tube longer than the calyx; upper lobe $\frac{1}{2}$–$\frac{3}{4}$ in. Seeds black, angular, partially enclosed in a white aril.

Simla, on Jako, Mahasu; July, August.—Temperate Himalaya.

2. **Cautleya spicata,** *Baker*; *Fl. Br. Ind.* vi. 209. Stems 1–2 ft. Leaves 10–15 × 2–3 in., long-pointed. Spike 5–9 in., erect; bracts red, as long as the calyx. Flowers many, crowded. Corolla-tube hardly longer than the calyx. Seeds black, ovoid, enclosed in a white aril. (Fig. 170.)

Simla, on Jako, Mahasu; August, September.—Temperate Himalaya.

3. **CURCUMA.** From the Arabic name, *Kurkum*, for a plant of this affinity.—India, Siam, Malay Islands, N. Australia.

Curcuma angustifolia, *Roxb.*; *Fl. Br. Ind.* vi. 210. Rootstock globose; tubers many, oblong, at the end of long fibres. Leaves appearing about the same time as the flowers, sometimes solitary, 6–12 × 2–3 in.; stalks 6 in. Spike stalked, 3–6 in. long, crowned by several enlarged, empty, pink bracts; lower bracts green, ovate. Flowers yellow, crowded, several in the axil of each bract, opening in succession, quickly fading. Calyx short, 3-toothed. Corolla-tube ½ in.; upper lobe erect, concave, ovate; the 2 lateral lobes shorter, oblong. Lateral staminodes oblong, united to the short filament; lower large, broad, spreading, notched; connective of the anther produced at the base in a fork. Capsule ovoid, ultimately opening by 3 valves; seeds many, small, oblong.

Valleys below 4000 ft., rare; June-October.—An East Himalayan plant, hardly extending so far westwards as Simla.

4. **HEDYCHIUM.** From the Greek *hedys*, sweet, and *chion*, snow; referring to the fragrant white flowers of some species.—India and the Malay Islands.

Hedychium acuminatum, *Wall.*; *Fl. Br. Ind.* vi. 227, *under H. spicatum*. Root horizontal. Stems 3–5 ft., robust, leafy. Leaves sessile, broadly lanceolate, 1–2 ft. × 3–4 in., ending in a tail-like tip. Spike 6–10 in.; bracts 1-flowered, green, oblong, obtuse; inner bract shorter, membranous. Flowers fragrant. Calyx membranous, slit on one side, 3-toothed. Corolla-tube 2–2½ in., longer than the calyx; lobes 1½ in., linear, spreading, pale yellow. Lateral staminodes 1¾ in., linear-spathulate, spreading, white, except the orange-red bases, lower 2 in., spreading, the blade 1 in. broad, white, deeply divided in 2 ovate, pointed lobes, and narrowed downwards in an orange-red claw; filament red, curved, the margins inrolled over the style; anther red. Ovary short, thick. Capsule globose; when ripe the 3 valves are reflexed, exposing their orange-red lining and numerous small seeds enclosed in a red aril.

Simla, on Jako, Mahasu; August.—Temperate Himalaya.

C. HÆMODORACEÆ

PERENNIAL herbs; stems very short or none. Leaves sessile, long, narrow. Flowers small, regular, 2-sexual, in racemes terminating slender scapes. Perianth corolla-like, bell-shaped,

FIG. 171. OPHIOPOGON INTERMEDIUS.

6-lobed, persistent. Stamens 6, opposite the perianth-lobes and inserted at their base; filaments very short, anthers 2-celled. Ovary wholly or only half adnate to the perianth-tube, 3-celled; ovules many or only 2 in each cell; style linear. Fruit a capsule or consisting of about 6 exposed, brightly coloured seeds.—America, Asia, Africa and Australia where they are most numerous.—From the Greek *haima*, blood, and *doron*, a gift; application obscure.

Perianth-lobes short, recurved. Ovules many in each cell . 1. *Aletris*.
Perianth-lobes long, spreading. Ovules 2 in each cell . . 2. *Ophiopogon*.

1. ALETRIS. From the Greek *aletron*, meal; referring to the powdery appearance of some species.—Asia, N. America.

Aletris nepalensis, *Hook. f.*; *Fl. Br. Ind.* vi. 264. A small, scapose herb. Leaves radical, grass-like, $3–8 \times \frac{1}{8}–\frac{1}{4}$ in., nerves prominent. Scapes 4–12 in., tomentose on the upper half and bearing 1 or 2 short leaves near the top; raceme short; bracts linear, erect. Flowers white or pale pink. Perianth $\frac{1}{5}$ in. long; lobes short, obtuse, recurved. Lower half of ovary adnate to the perianth-tube; ovules many in each cell; style shorter than the stamens, 3-parted at the top. Racemes lengthening to 4 in. or more in fruit; capsule globose, opening by 3 valves; seeds many, minute.

The Chor, Marali and perhaps Huttoo; June-August.—Temperate and alpine Himalaya.

2. OPHIOPOGON. From the Greek *ophis*, a serpent, and *pogon*, a beard: application obscure.—Central and East Asia.

Ophiopogon intermedius, *Don*; *Fl. Br. Ind.* vi. 269. Stems very short, the base usually clothed with the remains of old leaves. Leaves tufted, linear, $6–24 \times \frac{1}{6}–\frac{1}{2}$ in., margins very minutely toothed. Scapes glabrous, leafless, about as long as the leaves; raceme 2–5 in.; bracts lanceolate. Flowers white, usually tinged with lilac, often in pairs. Perianth $\frac{1}{4}$ in. long, lobed to the base; lobes in 2 series, obtuse, spreading. Ovary wholly adnate to the perianth-tube; ovules 2 in each cell; style longer than the stamens, minutely 3-lobed at the top. The fruit is peculiar in that the seeds burst through the ovary before they mature; when ripe the fruit consists of about 6 berry-like, bright blue seeds resting on the base of the withered perianth. (Fig. 171.)

Simla, common; June-August.—Temperate Himalaya.—Khasia, Deccan, Ceylon.

A variable plant as regards the size of the leaves and flowers. Often called the Lily of the Valley in India.

CI. IRIDACEÆ

Perennial herbs. Leaves narrow, folded lengthwise and alternately overlapping, blade flat, sword-like. Flowers 2-sexual, showy. Perianth superior, base tubular; limb 6-parted, petal-like, the segments in two dissimilar, imbricate series. Stamens 3, opposite the outer segments. Ovary inferior, 3-celled; ovules many; style simple, bearing 3 large, petal-like, recurved, stigmatic lobes. Capsule 3-valved; seeds numerous.—Chiefly temperate regions.

IRIS. The Greek name for the rainbow, referring to the hues of the flowers.—N. temperate regions.

Roots cylindric, fleshy; stems erect, sheathed by alternate, lanceolate, shortened leaves. Leaves chiefly radical, linear, entire, in 2 opposite rows, bases stem-sheathing and folded lengthwise, the outermost covering the edges of the next and so on, blade flat, sword-like. Flowers showy, in pairs or sometimes

Fig. 172. Iris nepalensis.

solitary. Inflorescence sheathed in a leaf-like spathe, deeply divided into 2 long, narrow, lanceolate segments; each flower has also 2 much shorter, narrow, membranous bracts; flower-stalks short. Perianth superior, base tubular; limb 6-parted, segments all petal-like, in 2 series, the outer reflexed, crested or bearded inside, the inner rather shorter, erect. Stamens 3, at the base of the outer segments; filaments distinct, anthers 2-celled, linear, basifixed. Ovary inferior, 3-celled; ovules many; style linear, stigmas 3, petal-like, with 2 lobes reflexed over the stamens. Capsule 3-sided, ribbed, enclosed in the persistent spathe, opening by 3 valves; seeds numerous, globose or flattened.

Flowers pale lilac. Outer perianth-segments crested . 1. *I. nepalensis.*
Flowers bright lilac. Outer perianth-segments mottled, bearded . . . . 2. *I. kumaonensis.*

1. **Iris nepalensis,** *Don*; *Fl. Br. Ind.* vi. 273. Stems 6–12 in. Leaves 6–12 in. long at the time of flowering, lengthening afterwards, $\frac{1}{4}$ in. broad. Spathe $1\frac{1}{2}$–2 in. Perianth-tube $1\frac{1}{2}$ in.; segments pale lilac, 1–$1\frac{1}{2}$ in., outer ones $\frac{1}{2}$ in. broad, a yellow, ridge-like crest along the centre, inner ones $\frac{1}{3}$ in. broad. Stigmas 1 in. long, deeply 2-lobed, margins toothed. Capsule 1–$1\frac{1}{2}$ in., oblong. (Fig. 172.)

Simla, common; April-June.—Temperate Himalaya.

2. **Iris kumaonensis,** *Wall.*; *Fl. Br. Ind.* vi. 274. Rootstock thick, creeping; stems 4–12 in., usually tufted. Leaves 4–12 in. long at the time of flowering, lengthening afterwards, $\frac{1}{3}$ in. broad. Spathe 3 in., often enveloped by the uppermost leaf. Perianth-tube 2–$2\frac{1}{2}$ in.; segments bright lilac, $1\frac{1}{2}$–2 in. long, outer ones mottled and bearded with a central line of yellow-tipped hairs, inner ones $\frac{1}{2}$ in. broad. Stigmas $\frac{3}{4}$ in. long, margins entire, the tip deeply 2-lobed and toothed. Capsule 1–2 in., ovoid, ends pointed.

Marali, 10,000 ft., and perhaps on Huttoo; June.—W. Himalaya.

CII. HYPOXIDACEÆ

RHIZOME tuberous, globose, coated with fibres. Leaves radical, grass-like. Flowers 2-sexual, regular, usually solitary on slender, axillary scapes. Perianth sessile on the top of the ovary, 6-parted; segments in two series, lanceolate, spreading. Stamens 6, at the base of the segments. Ovary inferior, 3-celled; ovules many; style short, thick, stigmas 3, erect. Capsule 3-valved; seeds many.—Asia, Africa, Australia, America.

HYPOXIS. From the Greek *hypo*, beneath, and *oxys*, sharp; referring to the base of the capsule.—Asia, S. Africa.

Hypoxis aurea, *Lour.*; *Fl. Br. Ind.* vi. 277. A stemless, perennial, hairy herb; tuber globose or oblong, clothed with black fibres, and emitting several pale, fleshy roots. Leaves radical, sheathing at the base, linear, usually 3–6 in., sometimes 16 in. long, $\frac{1}{8}$ in.

broad, nerves prominent. Flowers 2-sexual, regular, yellow, single or in pairs on thread-like, sometimes branched, axillary scapes shorter than the leaves. Perianth sessile on the top of the ovary, 6-parted nearly to the base; segments in two series, lanceolate, $\frac{1}{3}$ in., spreading, green on the back. Stamens 6, at the base of the segments and shorter than them. Ovary 3-celled; ovules many; style short, column-like, stigmas 3, erect. Capsule $\frac{1}{4}$ in., oblong, crowned by the withered perianth, 3-valved; seeds many, small, black, rough. (Fig. 173.)

Simla, in grass; common.—June-August.—Subtropical Himalaya.—Khasia, Deccan.—Java, China, Japan.

FIG. 173. HYPOXIS AUREA.

CIII. DIOSCOREACEÆ

CLIMBING shrubs; stems annual. Leaves simple or digitately 3–5-foliolate, basal nerves prominent, curving outwards. Flowers minute, 1-sexual, in spikes or racemes. Perianth superior, 6-parted; segments petal-like, in two series. Stamens 6, at the base of the segments, sometimes only 3 perfect. Ovary inferior, 3-celled; ovules two in each cell; styles 3. Capsule hard, 3-valved, 3-winged; seeds flattened.—Tropical and subtropical regions.

DIOSCOREA. From *Dioscorides*, the classical author.—Warmer regions of both Hemispheres.

Climbing plants; root tuberous; tubers large, especially in the cultivated species; stems leafy, sometimes prickly, twining to the left. Leaves usually alternate, stalked, digitately 3–5-foliolate or lobed or simple; margins entire; basal nerves 5–9, prominent, curving outwards, veins netted. Flowers minute, bracteate, 1-sexual, in slender, axillary spikes or racemes, the male and female usually on different plants. Perianth persistent, regular, 6-parted; segments nearly equal, in 2 series. Male flowers: stamens 6, at the base of the segments, sometimes only 3 bearing anthers, filaments free. Female flowers: perianth on the top of the ovary; ovary 3-sided, 3-celled, ovules 2 in each cell, styles 3, short. Capsule hard, leathery, 3-winged, opening by 3 valves; seeds flattened, winged.

The plants are often propagated by small, scaly buds or bulbils borne in the axils of the leaves or flower-bracts, which fall to the ground, strike root and grow into independent plants. The leaves of some species closely resemble those of *Smilax*, but their flowers are in spikes or racemes, not in umbels, and the fruit is capsular not berried.

Two species are commonly cultivated in the N.W.P. for their tubers called yams: *D. sativa* and *D. globosa*.

Leaves digitately divided. Male flowers racemed . . 1. *D. kumaonensis.*
Leaves undivided. Male flowers spiked.
  Male spikes solitary . . . . 2. *D. deltoidea.*
  Male spikes clustered.
    Spikes 1–1½ in. Perianth-segments ovate . . 3. *D. glabra.*
    Spikes 3–6 in. Perianth-segments linear . . . 4. *D. sativa.*

1. **Dioscorea kumaonensis,** *Kunth*; *Fl. Br. Ind.* vi. 290. Leaves glabrous or nearly so, usually alternate, 3–5-foliolate; leaflets narrowly lanceolate, 1–3 × ¼–¾ in., tip finely acute. Inflorescence pubescent. Male flowers in racemes 1–2½ in. long: anther-bearing stamens 3, staminodes 3; pistillode erect, club-shaped. Female flowers in spikes 2–6 in. long. Capsule ¾ in., oblong, ends rounded; seeds winged at the top. (Fig. 174.)

Simla, below Sipi, 5000 ft.; July.—Temperate Himalaya, 4000–8000 ft.

The bulbils of this plant are peculiar in structure; the outer coat is black and coriaceous or crustaceous, and inside is a flat body having the appearance of a seed; the whole simulating a fruit.

2. **Dioscorea deltoidea,** *Wall.*; *Fl. Br. Ind.* vi. 291. Glabrous or nearly so. Leaves usually alternate, variable in shape and size, general outline ovate-lanceolate, 2–6 × 1½–4½ in., long-pointed, widely cordate, the basal lobes often rounded and projecting; stalks sometimes 10 in. Spikes solitary. Perianth-segments broadly oblong. Male spikes 3–15 in., very slender: flowers in small, distant clusters; stamens all anther-bearing. Female spikes 6 in. Capsule ¾–1 in., wings broadly rounded; seeds usually winged all round, but sometimes only on one side.

Simla, Narkunda; May–July.—Temperate Himalaya, 6000–10,000 ft.—Afghanistan.

3. **Dioscorea glabra,** *Roxb.*; *Fl. Br. Ind.* vi. 294. Glabrous. Leaves usually opposite, oblong-ovate, 3–81–4 × $\frac{1}{2}$ in., deeply cordate, tip prolonged into a narrow, tail-like point. Flowers in spikes. Perianth-segments ovate. Male spikes 1–1$\frac{1}{2}$ in., numerous, clustered, spreading: flowers globose, single or in small clusters; stamens all anther-bearing. Female spikes 6–8 in., usually solitary. Capsule 1 in., wings broadly rounded; seeds winged all round.

Simla, below 5000 ft., Fifth waterfall; August.—Subtropical Himalaya, up to 5000 ft., and southwards over the plains.—Deccan.—Burma, Malay Peninsula.

FIG. 174. DIOSCOREA KUMAONENSIS.

4. **Dioscorea sativa,** *Linn.*; *Fl. Br. Ind.* vi. 295. Glabrous; stems bearing numerous bulbils. Leaves usually alternate, broadly ovate-cordate, about 4 × 3 in., sometimes larger, the tip prolonged into a narrow, tail-like point. Flowers in drooping, clustered spikes. Perianth-segments linear. Male spikes 3–6 in.: flowers rather crowded; stamens much shorter than the perianth, all anther-bearing. Female spikes 4–10 in. Capsule $\frac{3}{4}$ in.; seeds winged at the base.

Simla, below 5000 ft.; July, August.—Cultivated throughout N. India and in various other countries.

CIV. LILIACEÆ

Herbs or shrubs, usually bulbous or tuberous, sometimes having a creeping rootstock; roots often thick and fleshy. Leaves simple, entire, except sometimes in *Smilax*. Flowers 2-sexual or 1-sexual in *Smilax*. Perianth inferior; segments 6, rarely 8–12, in two more or less distinct series, usually all similar and petal-like, free or rarely partially united. Stamens 6, rarely 8–12, opposite the perianth-segments, affixed to their bases or hypogynous; filaments free, anthers versatile or basifixed. Ovary free, 3-celled or in *Paris* 4–5-celled; style short or long, entire or 3-lobed or 3-branched; ovules 1, 2 or many in each cell. Fruit a capsule or a berry; seeds few or many.—A large Order comprising plants of very different appearance dispersed throughout both Hemispheres, but most abundant in temperate and subtropical regions.

Rootstock creeping or many-branched, often tuberous and fleshy.

Leaves alternate or in numerous whorls.	
Flowers in umbels.	
Shrubs. Flowers small, 1-sexual	1. *Smilax*.
Herbs. Flowers 1 in. long, 2-sexual	16. *Disporum*.
Flowers in axillary, drooping racemes	3. *Polygonatum*.
Flowers in an erect, terminal raceme	4. *Smilacina*.
Flowers solitary, axillary, very large	15. *Gloriosa*.
Leaves in a single, terminal whorl. Flower solitary.	
Leaves 3. Perianth-segments all similar	17. *Trillium*.
Leaves 4–9. Perianth-segments in two very dissimilar series	18. *Paris*.
Leaves all radical, linear. Flowers in erect racemes	5. *Asphodelus*.
Pseudo-leaves in tufts. Flowers axillary	2. *Asparagus*.

Bulbous herbs; in *Allium* the bulbs sometimes small and clustered.

Stems scape-like. Leaves radical.	
Flowers in umbels or cymes.	
Flowers white, pink or purple	6. *Allium*.
Flowers yellow	13. *Gagea*.
Flowers in racemes.	
Perianth lobed $\frac{1}{3}$ of its length	7. *Dipcadi*.
Perianth lobed to the base	8. *Urginea*.
Stems leafy, often very short.	
Anthers versatile.	
Flowers $1\frac{1}{2}$–6 in. long. Perianth-segments broad	9. *Lilium*.
Flowers $\frac{1}{2}$–$\frac{3}{4}$ in. long. Perianth-segments linear	14. *Iphigenia*.
Anthers basifixed.	
Flowers yellow-green, chequered with dull purple	10. *Fritillaria*.
Flowers white. Perianth-lobes spreading	11. *Lloydia*.
Flowers white, tinged with red. Perianth bell-shaped	12. *Tulipa*.

1. SMILAX. The classical name.—Temperate and tropical regions of both Hemispheres.

Climbing shrubs; rootstock creeping, often thick. Leaves alternate, entire or rarely toothed, usually 3- or 5-nerved from the base, veins netted; stalks more or less sheathing, usually tendril-bearing and disarticulating above the tendrils. Flowers small, 1-sexual, in umbels, the male and female on different plants; umbels solitary or in spikes. Perianth-segments 6, free, narrow. Male flowers: stamens 6, at the base of the segments. Female flowers: staminodes 3 or 6; ovary 3-celled, stigmas 3, sessile, recurved, ovules 1 or 2 in each cell. Berry globose; seeds usually 2, sometimes 1, rarely 3.

The leaves of *Smilax* resemble those of *Dioscorea* but the flowers are in umbels and the fruit is a berry and superior.

The drug Sarsaparilla is prepared from the roots of several species of *Smilax*.

Umbels solitary. Flowers purple.
 Leaf-stalks tendril-bearing. Umbels bracteate . . . 1. *S. parvifolia.*
 Leaf-stalks without tendrils. Umbels without bracts . 2. *S. vaginata.*
Umbels in spikes. Flowers white . . . . 3. *S. aspera.*

1. **Smilax parvifolia,** *Wall.*; *Fl. Br. Ind.* vi. 304. Branches round, smooth, unarmed, often zigzag, the younger ones grooved. Leaves broadly lanceolate, $2\frac{1}{2}$–$3\frac{1}{2}$ × $1\frac{1}{4}$–$1\frac{3}{4}$ in., cordate, usually long-pointed, glaucous on the lower surface, nerves 3 or 5, sometimes 7, sheaths of the leaf-stalks bearing a pair of tendrils at the top. Umbels axillary, solitary, stalked. Bracts numerous, small, lanceolate. Flowers minute, purple. Male flowers: stamens much shorter than the perianth. Female flowers: staminodes 3. Berry $\frac{1}{3}$ in. diam., blue-black.

Simla, common; May.—Temperate Himalaya.

The Simla form is typical *S. glaucophylla*, Klotzsch, reduced to *S. parvifolia*, Wall. in the *Fl. Br. Ind.* It is common in the N. W. Himalaya and Kashmir. Wallich's type has much smaller leaves, green on both sides, and is not recorded west of Sikkim.

There is also a variety common in the neighbourhood of Simla, which may conveniently be distinguished as *angustifolia*. Leaves linear-lanceolate, $1\frac{3}{4}$–$3\frac{1}{2}$ × $\frac{1}{3}$–$\frac{3}{4}$ in., tapering to an acute point from a rounded base.

2. **Smilax vaginata,** *Decne.*; *Fl. Br. Ind.* vi. 305. Branches round, smooth, unarmed, often mottled. Leaves without tendrils, ovate, $2\frac{1}{4}$ × $1\frac{1}{2}$ in., or nearly orbicular, $2\frac{1}{2}$ × $2\frac{1}{2}$ in., generally more nearly round on female plants, lower surface pale, tip shortly and often abruptly pointed, base slightly cordate or rounded, main nerves usually 3, sometimes 5, blade often aborted. Umbels axillary, solitary, stalked. Bracts none. Flowers minute, purple. Male flowers: stamens much shorter than the perianth. Female flowers: staminodes 6. Berry $\frac{1}{3}$ in. diam., blue-black.

Simla, on Jako, Mahasu, Narkunda; May.—W. Himalaya, Assam.

3. **Smilax aspera,** *Linn.*; *Fl. Br. Ind.* vi. 306. Branches grooved, zigzag, more or less prickly. Leaves linear-lanceolate, ovate-lanceolate or orbicular, 3-4 × 1–3 in., margins entire or sometimes

with prickly teeth, base round or cordate, or the basal lobes projecting and rounded; stalks short, usually prickly, bearing near the base a pair of long, slender tendrils. Umbels numerous, in axillary and terminal spikes 1–6 in. long. Bracts minute. Flowers small, white, fragrant. Male flowers: stamens $\frac{2}{3}$ the length of the perianth. Female flowers rather smaller than the male: staminodes 6. Berry $\frac{1}{4}$–$\frac{1}{3}$ in. diam., red at first, blue-black when ripe. (Fig. 175.)

Simla, the Glen, common below 6000 ft.; September-November.—Hilly regions throughout India.—N. Africa, S. Europe.

The Simla plant is var. *maculata* of A. De Candolle's *Monogr. Smilax*, 163.

FIG. 175. SMILAX ASPERA.

2. ASPARAGUS. From the Greek *sparasso*, to tear, referring to the spines of some species.—Europe, Asia, Africa.

Erect or climbing, often straggling, much-branched, prickly or unarmed shrubs or herbs; rootstock thick, creeping, with cylindrical, fleshy branches or sometimes tuberous. Leaves reduced to minute, sometimes spinescent scales bearing in their axils tufts of unequal, needle-like branchlets or cladodes having the appearance of linear leaves. Flowers axillary, small, white, drooping, usually 2-sexual, solitary or in clusters or racemes, the stalks jointed near the middle. Perianth bell-shaped, 6-parted. Stamens 6, at the base of the segments. Ovary 3-celled; style single, stigmas 3; ovules usually 2 in each cell. Berry globose, about $\frac{1}{4}$ in. diam., usually red when ripe; seeds 2–6, black.

Flowers solitary or in small clusters.
  Cladodes flat, curved . . . . 1. *A. filicinus.*
  Cladodes terete, straight . . . . 2. *A. gracilis.*
Flowers in racemes.
  Cladodes spreading, 2–6 in each tuft. Prickles recurved 3. *A. racemosus.*
  Cladodes erect, 6–20 in each tuft. Prickles straight . 4. *A. adscendens.*

1. **Asparagus filicinus,** *Buch.-Ham.*; *Fl. Br. Ind.* vi. 314. Stems often tall, erect, hollow, unarmed. Cladodes $\frac{1}{8}$–$\frac{1}{3}$ in., flat, curved, in tufts of 2–5. Flowers polygamous, single or in pairs; stalks about $\frac{1}{2}$ in., very slender.

Mushobra, in woods; June.—Temperate Himalaya.—Burmah, China.

2. **Asparagus gracilis,** *Royle*; *Fl. Br. Ind.* vi. 315. Stems tall, slender, erect, prickly on the lower branches. Cladodes $\frac{1}{8}$–$\frac{1}{3}$ in., straight, stiff, in tufts of 2–5. Flowers in clusters of 3–4, sometimes in pairs, rarely solitary, very shortly stalked.

Valleys below 6000 ft.; July, August.—Plains of the Punjab.—Baluchistan.

3. **Asparagus racemosus,** *Willd.*; *Fl. Br. Ind.* vi. 316. Stems tall, climbing; prickles about $\frac{1}{4}$ in., more or less recurved. Cladodes $\frac{1}{2}$–1 in., curved, terete, spreading, in tufts of 2–6. Flowers in racemes 1–4 in. long; stalks $\frac{1}{5}$ in., very slender.

Valleys below 4000 ft.; July–October.—Throughout India.—Tropical Africa and Australia.

4. **Asparagus adscendens,** *Roxb.*; *Fl. Br. Ind.* vi. 317. Stems tall, straggling or half-climbing; spines $\frac{1}{2}$–$\frac{3}{4}$ in., straight; branches grooved, rough. Cladodes $\frac{1}{2}$–$\frac{1}{3}$ in., straight or slightly curved, terete, erect, in crowded tufts of 6–20. Flowers in numerous racemes 1–3 in. long; stalks very short.

Syree, 6000 ft.; November.—Plains of the Punjab.—Afghanistan.

3. POLYGONATUM. From the Greek *polu*, many, and *gonu*, a knee; referring to the zigzag stem.—N. temperate regions.

Herbs, glabrous or nearly so; rootstock thick, creeping; stems unbranched, the upper part leafy and zigzag. Leaves alternate or whorled, veins parallel. Flowers drooping, in axillary, single or whorled, short, loose, corymbose racemes, the flower-stalks jointed near the top. Perianth tubular, 6-lobed. Stamens 6, inserted in the tube; filaments very short. Ovary 3-celled; style linear, straight, stigma small, terminal; ovules usually 2 in each cell. Berry globose, blue-black, more or less enclosed at first in the withered perianth; seeds few.

Leaves alternate . . . . 1. *P. multiflorum.*
Leaves whorled
  Tips of leaves straight . . . . 2. *P. verticillatum.*
  Tips of leaves tendril-like . . . . 3. *P. cirrifolium.*

1. **Polygonatum multiflorum,** *Allioni*; *Fl. Br. Ind.* vi. 319. Stems 2–3 ft., round, arching. Leaves alternate, oblong-ovate, $3\frac{1}{2} \times 1\frac{1}{2}$ in., nearly sessile, pointed, lower surface glaucous. Racemes solitary, axillary, 2–5-flowered. Perianth $\frac{1}{2}$–$\frac{3}{4}$ in., tube white, lobes green. Berry $\frac{1}{2}$ in. diam.

Mahasu, Narkunda, in woods; May, June.—W. Temperate Himalaya, 6000–9000 ft.—Europe, including Britain (Solomon's Seal).

2. **Polygonatum verticillatum,** *Allioni*; *Fl. Br. Ind.* vi. 321. Stems 2–4 ft., erect, angled and grooved, sometimes mottled. Leaves in whorls of 4–8, sessile, linear, $4\text{–}8 \times \frac{1}{4}$–$\frac{1}{2}$ in., or lanceolate, $3\frac{1}{2} \times \frac{3}{4}$ in., tips usually acute, sometimes obtuse or slightly inrolled, lower surface glaucous. Racemes whorled, 2–3-flowered. Perianth $\frac{1}{3}$ in., white, tinged with green. Berry $\frac{1}{4}$ in. diam.

Simla, Mahasu, Narkunda; June, July.—Temperate Himalaya, 6000–12,000 ft.—Central Asia, Europe.

3. **Polygonatum cirrifolium,** *Royle*; *Fl. Br. Ind.* vi. 322. Stems 2–4 ft., terete, round or grooved, climbing by means of the tendril-like tips of the leaves. Leaves in whorls of 3–6, sessile, linear, 2–3 in., lower surface glaucous, the margins often inrolled to the midrib. Racemes whorled, 2–4-flowered. Perianth $\frac{1}{5}$ in., white, often tinged with green or purple. Berry $\frac{1}{4}$ in. diam.

Simla, Matiana, Narkunda; June.—Temperate Himalaya.—N. Asia.

4. **SMILACINA.** Diminutive of *Smilax*, from the similar leaves.—Europe, temperate Asia and America.

Smilacina pallida, *Royle*; *Fl. Br. Ind.* vi. 323. A herb; rootstock creeping; stems $1\frac{1}{2}$–3 ft., erect, the upper part leafy. Leaves alternate, parallel-veined, nearly sessile, oblong-lanceolate, $4\text{–}9 \times 1\frac{1}{2}\text{–}3$ in., pointed, lower surface pubescent, pale. Flowers $\frac{1}{6}$ in. long, white, in terminal, pubescent, more or less crowded, simple or branched racemes 2–6 in. long. Perianth 6-parted; segments nearly equal, spreading. Stamens 6, at the base of the segments. Ovary 3-celled; style straight, short; stigma small, terminal; ovules 2 in each cell. Berry globose, $\frac{1}{4}$ in. diam., blue-black; seeds few.

Huttoo, 9000 ft.; May, June.—Temperate Himalaya, 8000–11,000 ft.

5. **ASPHODELUS.** The classical name.—S. Europe, Canary Islands and eastward to India.

Asphodelus tenuifolius, *Cav.*; *Fl. Br. Ind.* vi. 332. An erect, glabrous herb. Leaves radical, linear, 6–12 in., terete, hollow. Scapes 6–24 in., often much branched. Flowers bracteate, racemed. Perianth 6-parted, $\frac{1}{4}$ in. long; segments spreading, white, with a central red-brown streak. Stamens 6, hypogynous, bases of filaments dilated, concave, closely covering the ovary, upper portion spindle-shaped. Ovary 3-celled; style straight, stigma 3-lobed, terminal; ovules 2 in each cell. Capsule globose, $\frac{1}{6}$ in. diam., horizontally wrinkled; seeds usually 3, 3-sided.

Simla; July–October.—The plains and occasionally ascending to 7000 ft.—Westward to the Canary Islands.

Eremurus himalaicus, *Baker*; *Fl. Br. Ind.* vi. 332. A stately, scapose herb 2–5 ft. high, with flat leaves and a dense raceme 1–2 ft. long of white flowers 1 in. across, occurs in the drier regions of the inner hills, Rogi Cliffs. The genus differs from *Asphodelus* in having 4–6 ovules in each cell. It flowers in June.

6. ALLIUM. The Latin name of Garlic, *Allium sativum.*—N. temperate regions.

Glabrous, bulbous herbs mostly possessing a strong, pungent odour. Leaves radical, but sometimes sheathing the scape to a considerable height. Scapes erect, bearing a terminal umbel of small flowers surrounded by an involucre of 2 or 3 thin, membranous bracts sometimes united forming a spathe. Perianth bell-shaped or rotate, 6-parted. Stamens 6, at the base of the segments. Ovary 3-angled, 3-celled; style straight, stigma minute, terminal; ovules few. Capsule 3-valved; seeds 1 or 2 in each cell, black.

The following species are commonly cultivated in the hills:—*A. Cepa*, the Onion; *A. Ascalonicum*, the Shallot; *A. porrum*, the Leek; and *A. sativum*, the Garlic.

Leaves and scape terete or nearly so.
  Stamens shorter than the perianth . . . . . 1. *A. rubellum.*
  Stamens longer than the perianth . . . . . . 2. *A. lilacinum.*
Leaves flat. Flowering-stem angled.
  Flowers purple . . . . 3. *A. Wallichii.*
  Flowers white . . . . 4. *A. Govanianum.*

*1. **Allium rubellum,** *Bieb.*; *Fl. Br. Ind.* vi. 339. Bulb free, solitary. Leaves 4–6, narrow, terete or nearly so, 6–20 in. Scapes 8–18 in., terete. Umbel $\frac{2}{3}$–1 in. diam.; stalks $\frac{1}{2}$–$\frac{3}{4}$ in. Perianth $\frac{1}{6}$ in. long, bell-shaped, pink. Stamens half the length of the perianth-segments.

Kashmir to Kumaon, 1500–8000 ft.; May.—Westward to the Ural and Caucasus and in Siberia.

2. **Allium lilacinum,** *Royle*; *Fl. Br. Ind.* vi. 339. Bulb free, solitary. Leaves 2–3, narrow, terete or nearly so, 4–16 in. Scapes 6–12 in., terete. Umbel 1–1$\frac{1}{2}$ in. diam.; stalks $\frac{1}{4}$–$\frac{1}{3}$ in. Perianth $\frac{1}{4}$ in. long, bell-shaped, pale red. Stamens longer than the perianth-segments.

Mahasu, Shali; July.—Western Himalaya.

3. **Allium Wallichii,** *Kunth*; *Fl. Br. Ind.* vi. 341. Bulbs small, clustered. Stem-base clothed with leaf-sheaths. Leaves 4–6, narrowly sword-shaped, 2–3 ft. × $\frac{1}{3}$–$\frac{2}{3}$ in. Scapes 1–2$\frac{1}{2}$ ft., robust, acutely 3-angled. Umbel 2–3 in. diam.; stalks 1–1$\frac{1}{2}$ in. Perianth rotate, purple; segments $\frac{1}{2}$ in. long, ultimately reflexed. Stamens shorter than the segments.

Huttoo; July, August.—Temperate Himalaya.—Turkestan.

4. **Allium Govanianum,** *Wall.*; *Fl. Br. Ind.* vi. 344. Bulbs clustered. Stem-base clothed with leaf-sheaths. Leaves many, narrow, 6 × $\frac{1}{4}$ in., flat, obtuse. Scapes 4–12 in., acutely angled. Umbel 1–1$\frac{1}{2}$ in. diam.; stalks $\frac{1}{2}$ in. Perianth rotate, white; segments $\frac{1}{3}$ in. long, ultimately reflexed. Stamens much shorter than the segments.

The Chor and perhaps Huttoo; June.—Temperate Himalaya, 8000–12,000 ft.

7. **DIPCADI.** Derivation unexplained.—South Europe, Africa, Western Asia.

Dipcadi hydsuricum, *Baker*; *Fl. Br. Ind.* vi. 347. A glabrous, bulbous herb. Leaves 3–4, radical, narrow, 6–12 in. Scapes 1–2 ft., erect. Flowers many, bracteate, rather distant, racemose. Perianth $\frac{1}{2}$ in. long, nearly cylindrical, white, green-ribbed; segments 6, in 2 series, the outer 3-parted, reflexed, the inner erect, less deeply divided, tips diverging, Stamens 6, attached to the middle of and shorter than the segments. Ovary shortly stalked, oblong, 3-celled; style straight, thick, 3-grooved; ovules many in each cell. Capsule about $\frac{1}{2}$ in., 3-angled, 3-valved; seeds many, black.

Simla, on grassy slopes below 5000 ft.; July.—Western Himalaya.—Punjab.

8. **URGINEA.** From the Latin *urgere*, to squeeze, referring to the flattened seeds.—S. Europe, Africa, W. Asia.

Urginea indica, *Kunth*; *Fl. Br. Ind.* vi. 347. A glabrous herb. Bulb $\frac{1}{2}$ in. diam. or more. Leaves radical 6–18 × $\frac{1}{2}$ in. Scapes 12–18 in., erect; bracts soon disappearing; stalks 1–1$\frac{1}{2}$ in., slender. Flowers appearing before the leaves, drooping or spreading, distant in a terminal raceme 6–12 in. long. Perianth $\frac{1}{3}$ in. long, bell-shaped, 6-parted; segments white, with 3 green ribs in the centre, tip rounded. Stamens 6, at the base of the segments and shorter. Ovary 3-celled, 3-grooved; style shorter than the ovary, straight, tapering downwards; ovules several in each cell. Capsule $\frac{1}{2}$–$\frac{3}{4}$ in., oblong, 3-valved; seeds many, flat, black.

Simla, below 5000 ft., Subathoo; May.—W. Himalaya.—Deccan.—Burmah, Tropical Africa.

9. **LILIUM.** Derivation variously explained; perhaps from the Greek *leirion*, a lily.—N. temperate regions.

Bulbous herbs; stems leafy, erect, rarely branched. Leaves usually alternate. Flowers large, nodding, fragrant, terminal or racemose. Perianth funnel-shaped or bell-shaped; segments 6, distinct. Stamens hypogynous, nearly as long as the perianth; anthers large, linear-oblong, versatile, ultimately curved. Ovary narrowly oblong, grooved, 3-celled; style long, slender, straight, stigma capitate, often 3-lobed; ovules many in each cell. Capsule oblong, obtusely angled, 3-valved; seeds very many, flattened.

The locality, Simla, given for *L. nepalense*, Don, in *Fl. Br. Ind.* vi. 351, rests on a specimen so named in the Kew Herbarium, gathered by Jacquemont in 'shady woods, Simla.' But this appears to be *L. polyphyllum*, the perianth being only 3 in. long.

Flowers 4–6 in., white; tube dark purple inside . 1. *L. giganteum.*
Flowers $2\frac{1}{2}$–3 in., green-white, the inside purple-dotted 2. *L. polyphyllum.*
Flowers $1\frac{1}{2}$–2 in., pink . . . . 3. *L. Thomsonianum.*

1. **Lilium giganteum,** *Wall.*; *Fl. Br. Ind.* vi. 349. Stems 6–12 ft., tapering upwards, hollow. Leaves alternate, cordate, broadly ovate, 5–11 × 4–10 in., lower leaves the largest. Bracts ovate, soon falling off. Flowers shortly stalked, in a terminal raceme. Perianth 4–6 in. long, white; tube purple inside, tips of segments rounded, recurved. Stigma obscurely 3-lobed. Capsule 2–3 in.

Narkunda, 9000 ft., in damp, shady forest; May, June.—Temperate Himalaya.—Khasia.
The hill-people use the stem to make musical pipes.

2. **Lilium polyphyllum,** *Don*; *Fl. Br. Ind.* vi. 351. Stems 1–3 ft. Leaves sessile, alternate or nearly opposite or whorled, narrowly lanceolate or linear, 3–5 × $\frac{1}{5}$–$\frac{1}{2}$ in. Bracts leaf-like, often whorled. Flowers solitary or whorled or racemed; stalks $1\frac{1}{2}$–4 in. Perianth $2\frac{1}{2}$–3 in. long, green-white with purple dots inside; segments obtuse, recurved when fully expanded. Stigma obscurely 3-lobed. Capsule 1–$1\frac{1}{4}$ in. (See Frontispiece.)

Simla, in woods, common; June, July.—Himalaya.—Afghanistan.

3. **Lilium Thomsonianum,** *Royle*; *Fl. Br. Ind.* vi. 352. Stems 1–3 ft. Leaves thin, sessile, alternate, 2–8 × $\frac{1}{4}$–$\frac{1}{3}$ in., narrowed to a fine point. Bracts leaf-like. Flowers often numerous, in a terminal raceme 4–18 in. long; stalks $\frac{1}{4}$–$\frac{1}{2}$ in. Perianth $1\frac{1}{2}$–2 in. long, pale pink, tips of segments rounded, recurved. Stigma 3-lobed. Capsule $\frac{1}{2}$–$\frac{3}{4}$ in.

Simla, 5000 ft.; April.—W. Himalaya.—Afghanistan.

10. **FRITILLARIA.** From the Latin *fritillus*, a dice-box; referring to the six glands within the perianth.—N. temperate regions.

Fritillaria Roylei, *Hook.*; *Fl. Br. Ind.* vi. 353. A glabrous, bulbous herb; stems 6–24 in., erect, unbranched, leafy except on the lower portion. Leaves 3–6 in a whorl, or the upper ones sometimes opposite, linear-lanceolate, 2–5 × $\frac{1}{8}$–$\frac{1}{2}$ in., the lowest ones sometimes 1–1$\frac{1}{2}$ in. broad; tips of the upper leaves often linear and hooked. Flowers nodding, terminal, solitary or 2–4 in a short raceme. Perianth 1–1$\frac{1}{2}$ in. long, bell-shaped; segments 6, distinct, yellow-green, chequered with dull purple, each bearing a large, viscid gland at the base, tips rounded, not recurved. Stamens 6, at the base of the perianth-segments and much shorter; anthers linear-oblong, attached at the base. Ovary oblong, 3-celled; style thick, straight, divided at the top in 3 short, pointed lobes; ovules many in each cell. Capsule obovoid, $\frac{1}{2}$–$\frac{3}{4}$ in., obtusely 6-angled, 3-valved; seeds many, small, flattened, minutely winged.

Huttoo; May, June.—W. Himalaya.

11. LLOYDIA. In honour of Edward Lloyd, an antiquary of the eighteenth century, who discovered the following species in Wales.—Mountains of Europe, Asia, N. America.

Lloydia serotina, *Reichb.*; *Fl. Br. Ind.* vi. 354. A small, glabrous herb; root bulbous; stems 3–6 in., slender, bearing a few small leaves and 1 or 2 nearly erect flowers. Radical leaves 1–3, linear, 4–10 in. Perianth bell-shaped, $\frac{1}{3}$–$\frac{2}{3}$ in. long; segments 6, distinct, ultimately spreading, white with violet veins, tips rounded. Stamens 6, at the base of the segments and much shorter; anthers attached at the base. Ovary oblong, 3-celled; style thick, straight, tip minutely 3-lobed; ovules many in each cell. Capsule globose, $\frac{1}{4}$ in. diam., 3-valved; seeds numerous, small, flattened.

Huttoo, on rocks; May, June.—High mountains of Asia, N. America, Europe, including Snowdon in Britain.

12. TULIPA. From the Persian *tuliban* or *thoulyban*, a turban; referring to the shape of the flowers.—Temperate regions of Europe, N. Asia, N. Africa.

Tulipa stellata, *Hook.*; *Fl. Br. Ind.* vi. 355. A glabrous, bulbous herb; stems 12–18 in., erect. Leaves 4–6, alternate on the lower part of the stem, linear, 9–12 in., acute, channelled and sheathing towards the base. Flowers terminal, usually only one. Perianth 1$\frac{1}{2}$–2 in. long; segments 6, oblanceolate, distinct, spreading when fully expanded, white, tinged with red, the bases yellow inside. Stamens 6, hypogynous, much shorter than the perianth; anthers oblong, attached at the base. Ovary oblong, 3-celled; style very short, stigma 3-lobed; ovules many in each cell. Capsule 1 in., oblong; seeds numerous, small, flat.

Simla, in fields near Boileaugunge, 6000 ft.; April, May.—W. Himalaya.—Afghanistan.

13. GAGEA. In honour of Sir Thomas Gage, a British amateur botanist of the last century.—N. temperate regions.

Small, glabrous, bulbous herbs; stems short, erect, having only one leaf usually overtopping the flowers. Inflorescence umbellate or cymose, terminating the stem. Flowers yellow, stalked, star-like when fully expanded. Perianth persistent; segments 6, nearly equal, distinct, green on the back. Stamens 6, at the base and shorter than the segments; anthers adnate to the base. Ovary small, 3-sided, 3-celled; style straight, thick, tapering downwards, stigma entire; ovules many in each cell. Capsule oblong, 3-grooved; seeds numerous, flat.

Inflorescence umbellate.
  Leaf $\frac{1}{4}$–$\frac{1}{2}$ in. broad . . . . 1. *G. lutea.*
  Leaf grass-like . . . . 3. *G. reticulata.*
Inflorescence cymose . . . . 2. *G. persica.*

1. **Gagea lutea,** *Schult.*; *Fl. Br. Ind.* vi. 355. Stems 2–4 in. Leaf lanceolate, 4–6 × $\frac{1}{4}$–$\frac{1}{2}$ in. Inflorescence umbellate. Bracts 2, unequal, leaf-like, usually nearly opposite. Flowers 3–6. Perianth $\frac{1}{2}$ in. long, yellow; segments linear-oblong, usually acute.

Narkunda, in damp meadows; April–June.—W. Himalaya, 6000–13,000 ft. —N. Asia, N. Africa, Europe, including Britain (Star of Bethlehem).

*2. **Gagea persica,** *Boiss.*; *Fl. Br. Ind.* vi. 355. Stems 2–6 in. Leaf narrowly lanceolate, 4–6 × $\frac{1}{4}$–$\frac{1}{3}$ in. Inflorescence cymose. Bracts numerous, very short, linear, each bearing a flower or a bulbil in its axil. Flowers many. Perianth $\frac{1}{4}$–$\frac{1}{3}$ in. long; segments linear, obtuse.

Kashmir to Kunawar, 5000–8000 ft., frequent on the inner, dry hills; April–June.—Persia and Central Asia.

*3. **Gagea reticulata,** *Schult.*; *Fl. Br. Ind.* vi. 356. Stems 2–3 in. Leaf 4–8 in., grass-like. Inflorescence umbellate. Bracts several, leaf-like, very unequal, whorled. Flowers several. Perianth $\frac{1}{2}$–$\frac{3}{4}$ in. long; segments linear, finely pointed.

Kashmir to Almora, below 6000 ft.; February–April.—Punjab plains.—Turkestan, westward to N. Africa, Greece.

14. IPHIGENIA. Name of classical origin.—India, Africa, Australasia.

Iphigenia indica, *Kunth.*; *Fl. Br. Ind.* vi. 357. A herb having a solid bulb or corm; stems 3–10 in., erect, leafy. Leaves alternate, sessile, linear, 6–8 in., finely pointed, the lower the larger. Bracts leaf-like. Flowers purple, erect, solitary and terminal or corymbose and axillary; stalks 1–2 in. Perianth $\frac{1}{2}$–$\frac{3}{4}$ in. long, soon falling off; segments 6, linear, distinct, nearly equal, acute, spreading or reflexed. Stamens 6, hypogynous, much shorter than the perianth; anthers versatile. Ovary 3-celled; styles 3, minute, united at the base, recurved. Capsule oblong, $\frac{1}{2}$–$\frac{3}{4}$ in., 3-grooved, obtuse; seeds many, globose.

Simla, Mahasu, in fields; June–August.—Throughout India.—Australia, Malaya.

15. GLORIOSA. From the Latin *gloria*, splendour; referring to the beauty of the flowers.—Tropical Asia and Africa.

Gloriosa superba, *Linn.*; *Fl. Br. Ind.* vi. 358. A herb climbing by means of its leaves; rootstock creeping, fleshy; stems 5–10 ft. or more, leafy. Leaves alternate or opposite or in whorls of 3–4 on different parts of the stem, sessile, oblong-lanceolate, 5–8 in., tips linear, spirally twisting. Flowers solitary in the leaf-axils, nodding; stalks 4–6 in. Perianth 3–4 in. across when fully expanded, persistent; segments 6, distinct, spreading at first, reflexed afterwards, narrowly lanceolate, 2–3 in., margins curled and wavy, yellow when young, changing to bright red. Stamens 6, hypogynous, slightly shorter than the perianth, filaments at first green, then yellow, finally red; anthers versatile, connective green, pollen orange. Ovary oblong, 3-celled; style long, linear, green, turning to red, abruptly bent upwards at the base, tip shortly 3-branched; ovules many in each cell. Capsule oblong, $1\frac{1}{2}$–2 in., obtuse; seeds numerous, globose.

Sutlej valley, Subathoo; August, September.—Himalaya, up to 5000 ft.—Tropical Asia and Africa.

16. DISPORUM. From the Greek *dis*, double, and *spora*, a seed, referring to the two seeds in each cell of the berry.—Asia, N. America.

Disporum pullum, *Salisb.*; *Fl. Br. Ind.* vi. 360. A glabrous herb; rootstock creeping, branches long, thick; stems $1\frac{1}{2}$–4 ft., erect, branched, upper part leafy, lower scaly. Leaves alternate, sessile, narrowly lanceolate, 2–6 in., long-pointed, nerves prominent. Flowers white, tinged with green, drooping in shortly stalked, axillary umbels. Perianth 1 in., narrowly bell-shaped; segments 6, distinct, lanceolate, acute, base dilated. Stamens 6, at the base of the segments and shorter than them, filaments tapering upwards; anthers attached near the base. Ovary ovoid, 3-celled; style straight, thick, tip shortly 3-branched; ovules 2 in each cell. Berry globose, $\frac{1}{4}$ in. diam., black; seeds ovoid, normally 6.

Simla, below Annandale, in forest, 6000 ft.; May.—Temperate Himalaya.—Java, China.

In Sikkim the flowers are dull purple

17. TRILLIUM. From the Latin *trilix*, a tissue of three threads, referring to the parts of the flower being in threes.—N. America, N. Asia.

Trillium Govanianum, *Wall.*; *Fl. Br. Ind.* vi. 361. A glabrous herb; rootstock short, thick, creeping; stems 6–10 in., erect, unbranched. Leaves 3, shortly stalked, broadly ovate, $1\frac{1}{2}$–$4\frac{1}{4} \times 1\frac{1}{4}$–4 in., acute, arranged in a whorl at the summit of the stem with a solitary, stalked flower in the centre. Perianth lurid purple, persistent; segments 6, distinct, narrowly lanceolate, $\frac{3}{4}$–1 in., spreading in flower, reflexed in fruit. Stamens 6, attached to the base and erect, much shorter than the perianth; anthers basifixed. Ovary 3-celled; style purple, divided to the base in 3 long, linear arms; ovules many in each cell. Berry globose, $\frac{1}{2}$–$\frac{3}{4}$ in. diam.; seeds numerous, ovoid, having a pulpy, lateral appendage.

Narkunda, Huttoo; May, June.—Temperate Himalaya, 8000–11,000 ft.

18. PARIS. From the Latin *par*, equal, referring to the parts of *P. quadrifolia* being disposed symmetrically in fours.—Temperate Asia, Europe.

Paris polyphylla, *Smith*; *Fl. Br. Ind.* vi. 362. A glabrous herb, curiously variable in the number and dimensions of its parts; rootstock thick, creeping; stems usually 12–18 in., erect, unbranched. Leaves 4–9, shortly stalked, lanceolate, 3–6 in., long-pointed, arranged in a whorl at the summit of the stem with a solitary, stalked flower in the centre. Perianth persistent; segments 8–12, in two dissimilar series, the outer green, leaf-like, 1–4 in., the inner usually shorter, sometimes longer, yellow or yellow-green, linear. Stamens as many as the segments, attached to their base, erect, slightly overtopping the style-arms; anthers narrow, longer than the filaments, basifixed. Ovary globose, imperfectly 4–5-celled owing to the cell-divisions not meeting in the centre; style divided almost to the base into 4–5 short, erect arms with curved tips; ovules many in each cell. Capsule globose, yellow-brown when ripe, 1 in. diam., 4–5-valved; seeds numerous, ovoid, scarlet.

Simla, 6000 ft., in shady forest; April, May.—Temperate Himalaya.—W. China.

Closely allied to the British Herb Paris, *P. quadrifolia*.

CV. COMMELINACEÆ

Succulent herbs. Leaves alternate, undivided, entire, the bases sheathing, nerves parallel. Flowers small, 2-sexual, usually slightly irregular. Perianth inferior, 6-parted, in two series clearly distinguishable as calyx and corolla; the 3 outer segments or sepals green or membranous, free or united at the base, persistent; the 3 inner or petals coloured, free or the claws united to form a tube. Stamens 6, inserted at the base of the segments, all or only 3 anther-bearing; anthers 2-celled, those of the sterile stamens or staminodes linear, variously curved, containing little or no pollen, filaments naked or hairy. Ovary free, 3-celled; style thread-like, stigma small; ovules one or few in each cell. Capsule 3-valved or 2-valved by abortion; seeds few, small, usually angular and wrinkled.—Tropical and warm regions.

The bright yellow, deformed anthers of the staminodes attract and afford food to insects, thus aiding in cross-fertilisation.

Fertile stamens 3. Staminodes 3.
  Flowers sky-blue. Filaments naked . . . . . . 1. *Commelina.*
  Flowers red-blue. Filaments hairy . . . . . . 2. *Aneilema.*
Fertile stamens 6 . . . . 3. *Cyanotis.*

1. COMMELINA. In honour of K. and J. Commelin, Dutch botanists.—Tropical and warm regions.

Stems slender, creeping and rooting towards the base. Flowers blue, in a small cluster or cyme enclosed in a leaf-like, folded bract or spathe from which the flowers successively issue as they expand. Spathe broadly ovate, $\frac{1}{4}$–$\frac{3}{4}$ in. long, cordate, pointed. Sepals membranous, sometimes united at the base. Petals free, longer than the sepals, one larger than the others, claw long, limb orbicular, spreading. Fertile stamens 3, staminodes 3, filaments naked. Ovules 1 or 2 in each cell. Seeds 3 or 5, small, oblong.

C. cœlestis, a Mexican species known as the Spider-wort, $1\frac{1}{2}$ ft. high, with large, sky-blue flowers, is cultivated at Simla, and may occasionally be found as an escape. For an account of the self-fertilisation of this plant by means of the spirally coiled style, see Kerner's *Natural History of Plants*, ii. 357.

Leaves ovate; tip obtuse or rounded. Capsule 5-seeded . 1. *C. benghalensis.*
Leaves lanceolate; tip acute. Capsule 3-seeded . . 2. *C. obliqua.*

1. **Commelina benghalensis,** *Linn.*; *Fl. Br. Ind.* vi. 370. Stems several, 6–18 in., sometimes longer, pubescent or glabrous. Leaves sessile or stalked, finely pubescent, broadly ovate, $1–3 \times \frac{1}{2}–1\frac{1}{2}$ in., tip obtuse or rounded; sheaths hairy, fringed. Spathes 1–3 together, axillary or terminal. Petals pale blue, one of them nearly white. Ovary 3-celled, 2 cells with 2 ovules in each, the third with 1. Capsule 5-seeded; seeds wrinkled.

Valleys below 6000 ft.; July–October.—Throughout India.—Tropical Asia and Africa.

2. **Commelina obliqua,** *Buch.-Ham.*; *Fl. Br. Ind.* vi. 372. Stems 2–3 ft., branched, pubescent or glabrous. Leaves sessile, lanceolate, $1\frac{1}{2}–4 \times \frac{3}{4}–1$ in., acute or long-pointed; sheaths fringed. Spathes in a terminal head partially enclosed by a pair of opposite leaves usually filled with a clear, glutinous substance. Petals pale blue, one of them nearly white. Ovary 3-celled, 1 ovule in each cell. Capsule 3-seeded; seeds minutely dotted. (Fig. 176.)

Simla, common; July, August.—Throughout India.—Tropical Asia.

2. ANEILEMA. From the Greek *a*, not, and *eilema*, a covering, referring to the flowers not being enclosed in a spathe.—Warm regions, chiefly Asia.

Stems erect, leafy. Leaves few, distant. Bracts small, not sheathing. Flowers red-blue, panicled. Sepals free, membranous. Petals free, obovate, equal. Fertile stamens 3, staminodes 4, filaments hairy. Ovules 2–6 in each cell. Seeds several, wrinkled and minutely pitted.

Stems $1\frac{1}{2}$–3 ft., simple. Capsule $\frac{1}{3}$ in. Seeds 9–12 . . 1. *A. divergens.*
Stems $\frac{1}{2}$–$1\frac{1}{2}$ ft., branched from the base. Capsule $\frac{1}{6}$ in. Seeds usually not more than 6 . . . . . . 2. *A. nudiflorum.*

FIG. 176. COMMELINA OBLIQUA.

1. **Aneilema divergens,** *C. B. Clarke*; *Fl. Br. Ind.* vi. 376. Nearly glabrous; stems $1\frac{1}{2}$–3 ft., simple. Leaves linear-lanceolate, the lower about $5 \times \frac{3}{4}$ in., upper ones gradually smaller; sheaths fringed. Panicle terminal, branches spreading, usually opposite or the upper ones whorled; bracts persistent. Capsule $\frac{1}{3}$ in., oblong-ovate, 3-angled; seeds 3–6, usually 4 in each cell.

Simla, below 6000 ft.; July, August.—Himalaya, up to 6000 ft.

2. **Aneilema nudiflorum,** *R. Br.*; *Fl. Br. Ind.* vi. 378. Stems 6–18 in., branched from the base, some of the branches often decumbent and rooting. Leaves linear or linear-lanceolate, 2-5 in., glabrous or nearly so; sheaths hairy, fringed. Panicles usually terminal, small, compact, branches short; bracts soon falling off. Flowers crowded. Anther of one of the fertile stamens smaller than the other two and nearly sterile. Capsule $\frac{1}{6}$ in., oblong, pointed; seeds 2 in each cell.

Valleys below 5000 ft., Simla, 5th Waterfall; July, August.—Throughout India.—Tropical Asia.

3. CYANOTIS. From the Greek *cyanos*, blue, and *ous*, an ear, referring to the petals.—Warm regions of the Old World.

Stems slender, erect, branched, leafy, the lower part creeping and rooting. Leaves sessile. Flowers blue, in short clusters or scorpioid cymes enclosed within two series of overlapping, green, sickle-shaped bracts, the petals and stamens protruding; clusters nearly sessile, terminal or axillary, usually 2 or 3 together. Sepals lanceolate, nearly equal, united at the base. Petals nearly equal, the claws united in a tube, limb orbicular, spreading. Stamens 6, all perfect, filaments hairy. Ovary 3-celled; ovules 2 in each cell; style swollen towards the top. Capsule 3-valved; seeds normally 6, small, wrinkled.

Leaves ovate-oblong . . . . 1. *C. cristata.*
Leaves linear-lanceolate . . . . 2. *C. barbata.*

1. **Cyanotis cristata,** *Schult. f.*; *Fl. Br. Ind.* vi. 385. Stems 6-18 in., glabrous or hairy. Leaves ovate-oblong, 2-4 × $\frac{1}{3}$–$\frac{2}{3}$ in., pubescent. Flower-clusters usually terminal.

Sutlej valley, below 4000 ft.; July, August.—Widely spread in hilly districts in tropical Asia and Africa.

2. **Cyanotis barbata,** *Don*; *Fl. Br. Ind.* vi. 385. Stems 6–18 in., often tufted, hairy. Leaves linear-lanceolate, $1\frac{1}{2}$–3 × $\frac{1}{8}$–$\frac{1}{4}$ in. Flowers dark blue; clusters hairy, terminal and in the axils of the stem-leaves.

Simla, common; July–September.—Himalaya, up to 8000 ft.—Burmah, China.

CVI. JUNCACEÆ

ERECT or procumbent, trailing, usually perennial herbs; rootstock scaly and fibrous, often creeping. Leaves linear, flat or cylindrical, often hollow and jointed, the upper surface sometimes channelled, base sheathing. Flowers solitary or in clusters, often panicled, small, regular, 2-sexual, usually green or brown; clusters or panicles usually bearing at their base a leaf-like bract; floral bracts short, scarious. Perianth inferior, dry, membranous or scarious, persistent; segments 6, distinct, in two series, nearly equal, lanceolate, pointed. Stamens 6 or 3, hypogynous or at the base of the segments, filaments free; anthers basifixed. Ovary free, 1- or 3-celled; ovules many or few; style straight, 3-branched at the top. Capsule 1- or 3-celled, enclosed in the perianth; seeds minute, many or few.—Spread over nearly the whole world, but less abundant in tropical regions.

Glabrous herbs. Capsule 3-celled. Seeds numerous . . . . 1. *Juncus.*
Hairy herbs. Capsule 1-celled. Seeds 3 . . . . 2. *Luzula.*

1. JUNCUS. From the Latin *jungo*, to tie, referring to the use made of the stems and leaves.—Temperate and Arctic regions.

Glabrous, usually perennial herbs, growing in damp or wet ground; stems often tufted, usually unbranched, leafless in *J. glaucus*. Flowers green, white or brown, shortly stalked, sometimes solitary, usually in small clusters on the branches of a panicle. Mid-rib of the 3 outer perianth-segments prominent. Stamens 6, in *J. prismatocarpus* only 3. Ovary 3-celled; ovules many. Capsule 3-celled, usually 3-sided, 3-valved; seeds numerous.

The inflorescence of *Juncus* is sometimes viviparous, that is, buds are formed in the place of flowers, finally becoming detached and growing into independent plants.

Stamens 6.
  Stamens shorter than the perianth.
    Stems leafy.
      Leaves flat . . . . 1. *J. bufonius.*
      Leaves cylindrical . . . . 3. *J. lamprocarpus.*
    Stems leafless . . . . 2. *J. glaucus.*
  Stamens longer than the perianth.
    Flowers dark brown . . . . 5. *J. himalensis.*
    Flowers white . . . . 6. *J. concinnus.*
Stamens 3 . . . . 4. *J. prismatocarpus.*

*** 1. Juncus bufonius,** *Linn.*; *Fl. Br. Ind.* vi. 392. A small, pale-coloured, tufted herb; stems 1–10 in., slender, branching from near the base. Leaves few, chiefly radical, stem-leaves shorter. Flowers solitary or in small clusters, sessile on the stem or branches. Stamens 6, half the length of the perianth. Capsule oblong, minutely pointed, shorter than the perianth.

In wet places; March–October.—Plains of N. India, and up to 13,000 ft. in the Himalaya.—N. temperate regions, including Britain (Toad Rush).

2. **Juncus glaucus,** *Ehrh.*; *Fl. Br. Ind.* vi. 393. Stems 1–3 ft., many, tufted, pale green, stiff, cylindric, finely grooved, leafless; the barren stems look like leaves, the others bear on one side near the top an erect or drooping panicle of small, brown flowers. Flowers sessile, solitary. Stamens 6, shorter than the perianth. Capsule ovoid, pointed, equal to or rather longer than the perianth.

Matiana, Theog. on damp ground; May–September.—N. Asia, N. Africa, Europe, including Britain (Hard Rush).

3. **Juncus lamprocarpus,** *Ehrh.*; *Fl. Br. Ind.* vi. 395. Stems 6–12 in., tufted, cylindric. Leaves terete, pointed, hollow, the interior divided by transverse partitions of pith. Flowers brown, in small clusters sessile in the angles and at the ends of the straight branches of a terminal, forking panicle. Stamens 6, much shorter than the perianth. Capsule oblong-ovoid, pointed, longer than the perianth.

Simla, damp ground; June–September.—Plains of the Punjab and up to 14,000 ft. in the Himalaya.—N. temperate regions, including Britain (Jointed Rush).

4. **Juncus prismatocarpus,** *R. Br.*; *Fl. Br. Ind.* vi. 395. Stems 18–24 in., sometimes less, tufted. Leaves 2–10 in., few, flat. Flowers green or brown, in small clusters sessile in the angles and at the ends of the unequal branches of an erect, terminal panicle. Stamens 3, much shorter than the perianth. Capsule 3-sided, pointed, equal to or slightly longer than the perianth.

Sutlej valley, Rampore; June–September.—Plains of N. India and up to 10,000 ft. in the Himalaya.—E. Asia, Australia.

5. **Juncus himalensis,** *Klotzsch*; *Fl. Br. Ind.* vi. 398. Stems 8–20 in., tufted, cylindric, hollow, bearing a single leaf near the middle; basal leaves numerous, linear, variable in length. Flowers dark brown, in sessile clusters ½ in. across, sometimes solitary, more often crowded on the branches of a short, erect, terminal panicle. Stamens 6, nearly as long as the perianth. Capsule ovoid, 3-angled, dark brown, shining, much longer than the perianth, beaked with the persistent style.

Huttoo; July, August.—Himalaya above 7000 ft.
Near the British *J. castaneus*, L., of which it may be considered a large form.

6. **Juncus concinnus,** *Don*; *Fl. Br. Ind.* vi. 399. Stems 6–18 in., slender, leafy, cylindric, usually single. Leaves 2–4, linear, shorter than the stems; sheaths membranous. Flowers white, 10–12

in sessile clusters $\frac{1}{3}$ in. across, sometimes solitary, more often 2–5 in the fork and at the ends of 1 or 2 short branches spreading from the top of the stem. Stamens 6, slightly longer than the perianth; anthers protruding. Capsule ovoid, 3-sided,

FIG. 177. JUNCUS CONCINNUS.

hardly longer than the perianth, beaked with the persistent style. (Fig. 177.)

Simla, common; July–September.

The specimens in the Kew Herbarium of this common Simla Rush are named *J. concinnus*, but in the typical form of that species the stems rarely exceed 6–8 in., the clusters contain only 4–6 flowers and the stamens are at least twice the length of the perianth; this form occurs on rocks near the top of Huttoo, flowering September–October. The Simla specimens appear more nearly allied to *J. membranaceus*, Royle, *Fl. Br. Ind.* vi. 397, except that the clusters are rarely solitary.

2. LUZULA. From the Latin *luciola*, a glow-worm, referring to the shining flower-clusters.—Temperate and cold regions.

***Luzula campestris,** *DC.*; *Fl. Br. Ind.* vi. 401. A small, hairy herb; rootstock creeping; stems 6–12 in., slender, tufted. Leaves 2–3 in., chiefly near the base of the stem, grass-like, fringed with long, white hairs. Flowers dark brown, sessile in several stalked, ovoid clusters ¼ in. long in the forks and at the ends of the very unequal branches of a short, erect, terminal panicle. Perianth-segments 6, scarious. Stamens 6, shorter than the perianth. Ovary 1-celled; style-branches very long; ovules 3. Capsule slightly shorter than the perianth, ovoid-oblong, pointed; seeds 3.

Himalaya, in grass, 10,000–14,000 ft.; July, August.—Hilly districts throughout India.—Temperate and cold regions (Britain, Wood Rush).

CVII. ARACEÆ

PERENNIAL herbs; rootstock tuberous or thick and creeping. Leaves various, radical or alternate, margins entire or nearly so. Inflorescence of numerous, small, 1-sexual flowers, sessile and usually crowded on a fleshy, erect column or spadix terminating the stem and more or less enclosed in a large bract or spathe. The lower portion of the spathe, called the spathe-tube, is folded round the spadix, while the upper portion or spathe-limb is open and spreading, rarely having its margins inrolled. Male and female flowers on the same or on different plants; if a spadix bears flowers of both sexes they are in distinct zones, the female always below the male and usually the two are separated by a zone of neutral organs. In some genera the spadix is prolonged above the flowers in a barren, tail-like, rarely club-shaped appendage. Male flowers: perianth none; anthers 2–5, sessile. Female flowers: perianth none; ovary globose or ovoid, 1-celled, ovules 1 or 2, sometimes several, stigma sessile. Two-sexual flowers: perianth 6-parted; stamens 6; ovary 3-celled, ovules many, stigma sessile. Fruit a spike or head of berries, sometimes enveloped in the persistent spathe-tube.—Temperate and tropical regions, chiefly the latter.

Acorus is exceptional in having bisexual flowers and in the spadix not being enclosed by the spathe.

Flowers 1-sexual.
  Spadix prolonged above the flowers.
    Margins of spathe-tube not united.
      Male and female flowers usually on different plants, if on the same, the two sexes contiguous . . . 1. *Arisæma.*
      Male and female flowers always on the same plant, the two sexes separated . . . . 3. *Typhonium.*
    Margins of spathe-tube united . . . . . . 2. *Sauromatum.*
  Spadix not prolonged above the flowers.
    Spathe-tube ovoid, not constricted, straight . . . 4. *Remusatia.*
    Spathe-tube constricted and abruptly bent at the middle 5. *Gonatanthus.*
Flowers 2-sexual. Spadix not prolonged nor enclosed in the spathe. Leaves like those of an *Iris* . . . . . 6. *Acorus.*

1. **ARISÆMA**. From the Greek *arisamos*, conspicuous, distinguished.—Temperate and tropical Asia, N. America.

Erect herbs; root tuberous, usually globose; stems sheathed at the base by membranous scales. Leaves one or two, digitately or pedately compound, base of stalk sheathing. Margins of spathe-tube free, overlapping; limb open, arching over the mouth of the tube. Spadix prolonged above the flowers into a short or long, usually tail-like appendage, club-shaped in *A. flavum*. Flowers 1-sexual, the male and female usually on different plants, if on the same spadix the sexes are contiguous and not separated by a barren interval. Male flowers more or less scattered, consisting of a shortly stalked head of about 3 anthers, except in *A. flavum* where the anthers are sessile and united. Female flowers crowded, ovary 1-celled, ovules usually 2. Neutral organs none, or, if present, few, awl-shaped and placed above the flowers of either sex. Fruiting spike naked; berries red, usually 1-seeded.

The tuberous roots are poisonous in the raw state.

Leaves digitately compound; leaflets 3.
  Spathe gradually narrowed into a long, acute point . 1. *A. intermedium.*
  Spathe abruptly contracted into a short, tail-like tip . 2. *A. Wallichianum.*
Leaves digitately compound; leaflets 5–7. Spathe gradually narrowed into a thread-like tail . . . . 6. *A. Jacquemontii.*
Leaves pedately compound.
  Spadix prolonged in a tail-like appendage protruding from the spathe.
    Leaflets linear-lanceolate, sessile. Anthers blue or purple . . . . 3. *A. curvatum.*
    Leaflets ovate-lanceolate, mostly stalked. Anthers white or pale yellow . . . . 4. *A. helleborifolium.*
  Spadix prolonged in a club-like appendage enclosed within the spathe . . . . 5. *A. flavum.*

1. **Arisæma intermedium,** *Bl.*; *Fl. Br. Ind.* vi. 500. Stems $1\frac{1}{2}$ ft. Leaf usually single, sometimes two, digitately compound; leaflets 3, sessile, ovate, long-pointed, the side ones oblique, $6–10 \times 3\frac{1}{2}–4$ in., the middle one $6–9 \times 3–5$ in. Spathe green, striped with purple and white; limb gradually narrowed into a long, acute point. Spadix prolonged in a very slender, far-protruding,

tail-like appendage, green, except the purple base. Male and female flowers on different plants.

Simla, Mushobra, Mahasu, common ; June, July.—W. Himalaya.

2. **Arisæma Wallichianum,** *Hook. f.* ; *Fl. Br. Ind.* vi. 500. Stems $1\frac{1}{2}$–2 ft. Leaf single, digitately compound ; leaflets 3, sessile, broadly ovate, shortly pointed, the side ones oblique, $3\frac{1}{2}$–$10 \times 2\frac{1}{2}$–7 in., the middle one orbicular, 3–$7\frac{1}{2} \times 2\frac{3}{4}$–9 in. Spathe-tube ribbed, dark green on a pale ground ; limb broad, abruptly contracted in a short, tail-like tip, the centre dark purple-striped, the margins chequered with pale green veins. Spadix prolonged in a very slender, far-protruding, purple, tail-like appendage. Male and female flowers on different plants.

Mushobra, Mahasu ; June, July.—Himalaya.
Commonly known as the Cobra or Snake plant.

3. **Arisæma curvatum,** *Kunth* ; *Fl. Br. Ind.* vi. 502. Stems $1\frac{1}{2}$–3 ft. Leaves 2, pedately compound ; leaflets 7 up to 13, unequal, sessile, linear-lanceolate, 5–$7 \times \frac{1}{4}$–$\frac{1}{3}$ in. Spathe pale green, finely ribbed ; tube narrow, mouth contracted ; limb broad, ending in a long-pointed tip. Spadix prolonged into a far-protruding, tail-like appendage, abruptly and strongly curved near the base, then turning upwards, green, except the purple base. Male and female flowers on different or on the same plants. Anthers blue or purple.

Simla, common ; July, August.—Temperate Himalaya.
This species rarely comes into flower before the middle of July ; it is included in the *Fl. Br. Ind.* under *A. tortuosum*, Schott.

4. **Arisæma helleborifolium,** *Schott* ; *Fl. Br. Ind.* vi. 502. Stems 1–5 ft., mottled with purple. Leaves 2, pedately compound ; leaflets 9 up to 15, unequal, most of them stalked, ovate-lanceolate, $1\frac{1}{2}$–$4 \times \frac{1}{2}$–$1\frac{1}{4}$ in., long-pointed. Spathe green, finely ribbed ; tube narrow, mouth contracted ; limb broad, ending in a long-pointed tip. Spadix prolonged into a far-protruding, tail-like appendage, curved near the base, then turning upwards, purple or the tip green. Male and female flowers usually on the same plant but in very unequal numbers. Anthers white or pale yellow. (Fig. 178.)

Simla, common ; June, July.—Temperate Himalaya.
This species is the first to appear ; it is sometimes in flower before the rains commence. Included in the *Fl. Br. Ind.* under *A. tortuosum*, Schott.

5. **Arisæma flavum,** *Schott* ; *Fl. Br. Ind.* vi. 503. Stems 6–18 in. Leaves usually 2, sometimes only one, pedately compound ; leaflets 9 up to 11, unequal, sessile or nearly so, lanceolate, 3–$6 \times \frac{1}{2}$–$1\frac{1}{2}$ in., long-pointed. Spathe purple inside ; tube very short, green ; limb pointed, yellow. Spadix short, thick, conical, prolonged into a

yellow, club-shaped appendage included within the spathe. Male and female flowers on the same plant; the male sessile, the anthers united and forming a continuous layer.

Simla, Mushobra, not common; June, July.—Temperate Himalaya.—Afghanistan, Arabia.

6. **Arisæma Jacquemontii,** *Bl.*; *Fl. Br. Ind.* vi. 505. Stems 1–2 ft., sometimes mottled. Leaves usually 2, digitately com-

Fig. 178. Arisæma helleborifolium.

pound; leaflets 5–7, unequal, lanceolate, 3–8 × 1–2 in. Spathe green, striped with white; tube long, narrow; limb broad, gradually narrowed into a long, green or purple, thread-like tail. Spadix prolonged into a slender, tapering appendage, much shorter than the spathe, the tip curved forwards and protruding to one side. Male and female flowers on different plants.

Simla, common; June, July.—Temperate Himalaya.

2. SAUROMATUM. From the Greek *sauros*, a lizard, referring to the spotted spathe.—Tropical Asia and Africa.

Sauromatum guttatum, *Schott*; *Fl. Br. Ind.* vi. 508. Root tuberous, large, globose; stems 2–4 in., spotted with purple, sheathed at the base by membranous, spotted scales. Leaf solitary, appearing after the flowers, radical, pedately compound; stalk 12–18 in., spotted; leaflets 9–11, oblong-lanceolate, unequal, more or less united at the base, very variable in size and shape, the central one 6–13 × 1½–4 in., outer ones gradually smaller. Spathe 12–24 in., green-purple outside; tube 3–4 in., cylindric or globosely inflated, margins united, the inner surface speckled purple on yellow ground, the base deep purple; limb lanceolate, narrowed into a long, linear, curved tip, the inside irregularly blotched with purple and white, the margins purple. Spadix prolonged into a tapering, dark purple appendage 6–10 in. long. Male and female flowers on the same plant. Female flowers crowded round the base of the spadix with a few club-shaped, neutral organs above them; ovary obovate, ovules 1–2. Male flowers crowded in a ring 2 or 3 in. above the female. Berries scarlet, 1-seeded, in a globose head more or less enveloped in the withered base of the spathe.

Simla, in woods, Dhobis ghat, Annandale.—Himalaya.—The evil-smelling flowers appear in April–May, the leaf in July–September.

3. TYPHONIUM. Name of mythological origin applied to some Aroid.—Tropics of the Old World.

***Typhonium diversifolium,** *Schott*; *Fl. Br. Ind.* vi. 510. Root tuberous, globose; stems 3–9 in., slender. Leaf solitary, rarely 2, appearing with the flowers, very variable in shape and size, usually about 3–6 in. long and as much across, hastate or sagittate or pedately divided into 5 broadly lanceolate or narrow lobes; stalk 3–12 in., slender. Spathe 2–8 in., erect, green, striped and tinged with purple; tube short, margins free, overlapping; limb lanceolate, finely pointed. Spadix terminating in a terete, obtuse, dark purple appendage 1½ in. long, protruding or enclosed. Male and female flowers on the same plant. Female flowers purple, crowded round the base of the spadix, having a few club-shaped, neutral organs above them: ovary 1-celled. Male flowers sessile, crowded in a ring about ¾ in. above the female, the interposed, neutral organs being flat scales. Berries ovoid, 1- or 2-seeded.

Sutlej valley, 6000–8000 ft., Rampore, common in Kumaon; June–August.—W. Himalaya.—The flowers have a highly unpleasant smell.

4. REMUSATIA. In honour of Abel Remusat, orientalist and physician.—Himalaya, Burmah, Java.

Remusatia Hookeriana, *Schott*; *Fl. Br. Ind.* vi. 522. Rootstock tuberous, emitting long, slender branches bearing small bulbils covered with fibres; stems 2–3 in., erect, slender. Leaf radical, solitary, peltate, entire, ovate-oblong, about $4\frac{1}{2} \times 2\frac{1}{4}$ in., cordate, long-pointed, the upper surface glabrous, often variegated with pale and dark green, lower surface pubescent on the nerves; stalk about 5 in. Spathe $1\frac{1}{2}$–2 in.; tube ovoid, green, margins overlapping; limb erect, yellow, ovate-lanceolate, pointed, the margins overlapping near the top and often twisted, but open below exposing the top of the spadix. Spadix not prolonged. Flowers fragrant, male and female on the same plant; female on the lower part of the short spadix, male on the top, a few narrow, scale-like, neutral organs separating them. Ovary ovoid, 1-celled, ovules many, inserted on the walls of the ovary. Berries small, in a head enclosed in the persistent spathe-tube.

Simla, on shady rocks below 6000 ft., Mushobra.—Temperate Himalaya.

This plant is believed to be propagated chiefly by the bubil-bearing shoots. I have seen no specimens of either flowers or fruit from Simla.

Remusatia vivipara, Schott, may perhaps also occur in valleys below 5000 ft., it differs from the foregoing in its larger leaves and in the limb of the spathe being reflexed, not erect.

5. GONATANTHUS. From the Greek *gonu*, a knee, and *anthos*, a flower, referring to the bent spathe.—India.

Gonatanthus sarmentosus, *Klotzsch*; *Fl. Br. Ind.* vi. 522. Rootstock tuberous, usually emitting long, slender branches bearing small bulbils covered with fibres; stems $1\frac{1}{2}$–3 in., erect, slender. Leaves 1–3, radical, peltate, entire, ovate-oblong, 3–6 × 2–4 in., cordate, acute, upper surface glabrous, dark green, lower pale, pubescent on the nerves; stalk 4–6 in. Spathe 6–10 in. long; tube about $\frac{3}{4}$ in., green, inflated, constricted and abruptly bent at the middle, margins overlapping but gaping in the upper half and exposing the top of the spadix; limb yellow, narrow, erect, tip drooping, margins overlapping throughout. Spadix 1–$1\frac{1}{2}$ in., not prolonged. Flowers fragrant, the male and female on the same plant. Female flowers on the lower part of the spadix with a row of imperfect ovaries at their base. Male flowers dark purple, on the club-shaped top, a few scale-like, neutral organs separating them. Ovary ovoid, 1-celled; ovules many, inserted on the base of the ovary. Berries small, yellow, in a head enclosed in the persistent spathe-tube.

Simla, in shady valleys, 5000 ft.; June.—Temperate Himalaya, 2000–6000 ft. —Khasia.

6. ACORUS. The classical name.—Europe, temperate Asia, N. America.

***Acorus Calamus,** *Linn.*; *Fl. Br. Ind.* vi. 555. An aromatic, erect herb; rootstock thick, creeping; stems 6–12 in., flat. Leaves radical, tufted, 2–3 ft. by about $\frac{1}{2}$ in. broad, resembling those of an *Iris*, margins crimped. Spathe leaf-like, long, narrow, not enclosing the spadix. Spadix $1\frac{1}{2}$–3 in., tapering, not prolonged, destitute of neutral organs, covered with small, yellow-green, 2-sexual flowers. Perianth-segments 6, free, persistent. Stamens 6, at the base of the segments. Ovary free, oblong, 3-celled, top conical; ovules many. Berries yellow-green, angular from mutual compression, 1–3-seeded.

Throughout India, in marshes or on river banks, ascending to 8000 ft.; June, July.—Temperate and warm regions of the North Hemisphere. (Britain, Sweet Flag.)

CVIII. LEMNACEÆ

MINUTE, floating plants growing in colonies, consisting of leaf-like fronds, either separate or cohering two or three together by their edges and usually emitting one or several root-fibres from their lower surface. Flowers 1-sexual, male and female on the same plant, issuing from a fissure in the edge or on the upper surface of the frond, usually at first enclosed in a minute, membranous bract or spathe. Perianth none. Stamens 1 or 2. Ovary 1-celled; style short; ovules 1–7. Fruit a bottle-shaped utricle containing one or more seeds.—In stagnant water over nearly the whole world.

The propagation of these plants is effected usually by means of new fronds growing out of the margins of the old ones or by bulbils. Flowers are rarely produced.

Fronds with roots. Flowers in marginal clefts . . . . . 1. *Lemna.*
Fronds exceedingly small, without roots. Flowers bursting through the upper surface . . . . 2. *Wolffia.*

1. LEMNA. The classical name.—Nearly all temperate and tropical regions.

Fronds bearing root-fibres. Flowers in marginal clefts of the fronds, at first enclosed in a minute spathe. Stamens 1–2, filaments slender; anthers 2-celled. Ovules 1–7.

Root-fibre single.
Fronds $\frac{1}{8}$–$\frac{1}{4}$ in.; lower surface nearly flat . . . . 1. *L. minor.*
Fronds $\frac{1}{8}$–$\frac{1}{2}$ in.; lower surface much swollen . . . 2. *L. gibba.*
Root-fibres several . . . . 3. *L. polyrhiza.*

1. **Lemna minor,** *Linn.*; *Fl. Br. Ind.* vi. 556. Root-fibre single. Fronds $\frac{1}{8}$–$\frac{1}{4}$ in. long, broadly ovate or oblong, both surfaces nearly flat. Stamens 2. Ovule 1.

Common throughout India, ascending to 9000 ft.—All regions (Britain, Lesser Duckweed).

2. **Lemna gibba,** *Linn.*; *Fl. Br. Ind.* vi. 556. Root-fibre single. Fronds $\frac{1}{3}$–$\frac{1}{2}$ in. diam., orbicular, upper surface flat, lower swollen, almost hemispherical. Stamens 2. Ovules 2–7.

Still waters throughout India, ascending to 7000 ft.—All regions (Britain, Gibbous Duckweed).

3. **Lemna polyrhiza,** *Linn.*; *Fl. Br. Ind.* vi. 557. Root-fibres several, clustered. Fronds $\frac{1}{4}$–$\frac{1}{3}$ in. diam., broadly ovate or orbicular, both surfaces nearly flat. Stamens 2. Ovules 1 or 2.

Common throughout India, ascending to 5000 ft.—Temperate and tropical regions (Britain, Greater Duckweed).

2. **WOLFFIA.** In honour of J. F. Wolff, a writer on *Lemna*.—Inhabits nearly all regions.

Wolffia arrhiza, *Wimm.*; *Fl. Br. Ind.* vi. 557. Root-fibres none. Fronds less than $\frac{1}{12}$ in. diam., upper surface flat, lower swollen. Flowers bursting through the upper surface; spathe none. Anther 1, sessile. Ovule 1.

Common, probably throughout India.—Europe (Britain, Rootless Duckweed). The smallest flowering plant in Britain.

CIX. ALISMACEÆ

MARSH or aquatic herbs; stems erect. Leaves radical, undivided. Flowers small, 2-sexual, paniculate. Perianth inferior; segments 6, free, in two series, the outer green, the inner petal-like. Stamens 6, hypogynous. Ovaries numerous, free, 1-celled, 1-ovuled, arranged in a ring or head. Achenes surrounded by the persistent, outer perianth-segments.—Nearly all parts of the world.

ALISMA. Origin of name doubtful.—Temperate and tropical regions.

Alisma Plantago, *Linn.*; *Fl. Br. Ind.* vi. 559. A scapose, aquatic herb; root fibrous; stems $1\frac{1}{2}$–3 ft., base swollen. Leaves radical, undivided, entire, ovate-lanceolate, about $3\frac{1}{2} \times 1\frac{1}{2}$ in., base tapering or slightly cordate; stalks $1\frac{1}{2}$–10 in. Flowers small, 2-sexual, on long, slender, unequal stalks in bracteate whorls forming a large, terminal, pyramidal panicle. Perianth inferior; segments 6, free, in two series; the outer small, green, persistent; the inner larger, petal-like, pale pink, with yellow claws. Stamens 6. Ovaries numerous, small, free, arranged in a ring; stigmas terminal; ovules single. Fruit a ring of achenes surrounded by the persistent, outer perianth-segments.

In ditches and ponds, below 4500 ft.; June–September.—Lower Himalaya. —N. and S. temperate regions (Britain, Water Plantain).

A. reniforme is common in the plains, and may perhaps occur in the hills below 3000 ft.; it has orbicular, cordate or kidney-shaped leaves and only 5–8 achenes forming an irregular head, not in a ring.

CX. NAIADACEÆ

WATER-PLANTS, entirely submerged or the upper leaves floating; stems branching, usually long and slender. Leaves undivided, sheathing at the base or provided with sheathing stipules. Flowers small or minute, usually green, 1- or 2-sexual, on stalked, axillary spikes or sessile and solitary or clustered in the leaf-axils. Perianth of 4 scale-like segments or tubular or none. Stamens 1 or 4. Ovary of 4 distinct carpels each with a single ovule and a separate stigma or of a single carpel with 1 ovule and 3 stigmas. Fruit of 1-seeded drupelets or achenes.—Spread over temperate and tropical regions, in the sea as well as in fresh water.

Flowers in stalked spikes . . . . 1. *Potamogeton.*
Flowers sessile in the leaf-axils.
  Leaves entire . . . . 2. *Zannichellia.*
  Leaves variously toothed . . . . 3. *Naias.*

1. POTAMOGETON. From the Greek *potamos*, a river, and *geiton*, a neighbour, referring to the usual habitat of the plants.—Spread over nearly the whole world.

Water-plants, submerged or the upper leaves floating; rootstock creeping; stems long, usually forking. Leaves stipulate, often translucent, alternate or the upper ones opposite, stalked or sessile, entire or finely toothed. Flowers small, 2-sexual, in stalked, axillary spikes rising above the water. Perianth hypogynous; segments 4, concave, green. Anthers 4, sessile on the perianth-segments. Ovary of 4 distinct, sessile, 1-celled, 1-ovuled carpels, each with a nearly sessile stigma. Drupelets small, more or less beaked, becoming dry and seed-like.

Though the flowers of *Potamogeton* are 2-sexual, the pistil usually matures before the anthers of the same flower are ripe and self-fertilisation therefore rarely occurs. The plants are dependent on the wind for the transference of the pollen. *P. crispus* produces in the autumn thick shoots which are detached from the stem, sink to the bottom and pass the winter in the mud, safe from the frost, reproducing the plant in the following spring. See Kerner's *Nat. Hist. of Plants*, i. 552, ii. 739, and Müller's *Fertilisation of Flowers*, p. 567.

Leaves ovate, oblong or lanceolate.
Leaves entire.
Leaves stalked.
Leaves 4–5 in. long . . . . 1. *P. natans.*
Leaves $\frac{1}{2}$–1 in. long . . . . 2. *P. javanicus.*
Leaves stem-clasping . . . . 3. *P. perfoliatus.*
Leaves finely toothed.
Flower-spikes $\frac{1}{3}$ in. long . . . . 4. *P. crispus.*
Flower-spikes $1\frac{1}{2}$–2 in. long . . . . 5. *P. lucens.*
Leaves very narrow, grass-like . . . . 6. *P. pectinatus.*

*1. **Potamogeton natans,** *Linn.*; *Fl. Br. Ind.* vi. 565. Leaves alternate or the upper ones opposite, stalked, ovate-oblong, 2–6 in., pointed at both ends, entire. Spike 1–2 in.; flowers crowded.

Plains of the Punjab, ascending to 5000 ft.; May–October.—Most temperate climates, including Britain.

FIG. 179. POTAMOGETON JAVANICUS.

2. **Potamogeton javanicus,** *Hassk.*; *Fl. Br. Ind.* vi. 566. Stems very slender. Leaves alternate or the upper ones opposite, stalked, ovate-oblong, $\frac{3}{4}$–$1\frac{1}{2}$ in., pointed at both ends, entire. Spike $\frac{1}{3}$–$\frac{1}{2}$ in., interrupted; flowers very small. (Fig. 179.)

Simla; May–October.—Plains of India, ascending to 7000 ft.—Tropical Asia, Africa and Australia.

*3. **Potamogeton perfoliatus,** *Linn.*; *Fl. Br. Ind.* vi. 566. Stems robust. Leaves alternate or the upper ones opposite, broadly ovate, 1–4 in., entire, stem-clasping. Spike $\frac{3}{4}$ in.; flowers crowded.

Kashmir–Kumaon, 4000–8000 ft.; May–October.—N. temperate regions, including Britain, Australia.

*4. **Potamogeton crispus,** *Linn.*; *Fl. Br. Ind.* vi. 566. Stems slender. Leaves alternate and sessile or the upper ones opposite and stem-clasping, linear-oblong, 1–3 in., margins very wavy, having the appearance of being lobed, finely toothed. Spike $\frac{1}{3}$ in.; flowers from 3–6.

Kashmir–Bhootan, 4000–6000 ft.; May–October.—Plains of India.—N. and S. tropical and temperate regions, including Britain.

*5. **Potamogeton lucens,** *Linn.*; *Fl. Br. Ind.* vi. 567. Stems robust. Leaves alternate or the upper ones opposite, lanceolate, 4–10 in., sessile, margins very slightly wavy, finely toothed. Spike $1\frac{1}{2}$–2 in., thick; flowers crowded.

Kashmir–Kumaon, 5000–7000 ft.; May–October.—N. temperate regions, including Britain, Australia.

*6. **Potamogeton pectinatus,** *Linn.*; *Fl. Br. Ind.* vi. 567. Stems thread-like, much-branched. Leaves alternate, very narrow, grass-like, 3–8 in., base sheathing; stipules appearing as very small lobes on the margin of the leaf-sheath. Flowers in small, separate clusters forming an interrupted spike.

Common in the plains, ascending to 12,000 ft.; May–October.—Spread over most regions, including Britain.

2. **ZANNICHELLIA.** In honour of Zannichelli, a Venetian botanist.—Temperate and tropical regions.

***Zannichellia palustris,** *Linn.*; *Fl. Br. Ind.* vi. 568. A very slender, submerged plant; stems 3–6 in., branched. Leaves linear, 1–3 in., opposite or in threes; stipules small, sheathing, membranous Flowers minute, 1-sexual, a male and a female sessile in the leaf-axils within the stipules. Perianth none. Male flower: a single stamen, filament long, anther 2-celled. Female flower: ovary of 4 distinct carpels each 1-celled and 1-ovuled, style long, stigma terminal, disk-shaped. Achenes 2–4, curved, flattened, usually wrinkled or tubercled, sometimes shortly stalked, tipped by the withered style.

Common in marshes and ponds throughout India, ascending to 15,000 ft.; May–October.—Spread over nearly all regions (Britain, Horned Pondweed).

3. **NAIAS.** From the Greek *naias*, a water nymph.—Temperate and tropical regions.

***Naias major,** *Allioni*; *Fl. Br. Ind.* vi. 569. A slender, submerged herb; stems often long-branched and interlacing, rough with short outgrowths. Leaves opposite or whorled, linear, $\frac{1}{2}$–$1\frac{1}{2}$ in., deeply and sharply toothed, base sheathing. Flowers minute, axillary, sessile, 1-sexual, the male and female on different plants. Male flowers: perianth tubular, 2–3-toothed; anther 1, sessile, 4-celled, enclosed in and adnate to the perianth. Female flowers:

perianth none; ovary of a single, 1-celled, 1-ovuled carpel, stigmas 3, thread-like. Achene oblong, smooth.

Marshes and ponds throughout India, ascending to 8000 ft.; May-October. —Almost cosmopolitan, except frigid zones.

Naias flexilis is a British plant.

CXI. ERIOCAULACEÆ

Dwarf, scapose, perennial, rarely annual herbs, growing on the margins of lakes and ponds. Leaves radical, narrow, entire. Scapes erect, naked. Flowers minute, 1-sexual, male and female intermixed in globose, dense, terminal heads. Perianth hypogynous, scarious, number of segments variable. Stamens usually 6. Ovary free, 3-celled; ovule one in each cell; style 3-branched. Capsule 3-lobed; seeds 3.—Chiefly tropical regions.—The Order is represented in Europe by a single American species, *Eriocaulon septangulare,* found only in the Hebrides and on the west coast of Ireland.

ERIOCAULON. From the Greek *erion,* wool, and *caulos,* a stem, referring to the woolly scapes of some species.—Chiefly tropical regions.

Rootstock creeping, fibrous. Leaves radical, crowded, narrow, glabrous, entire, base sheathing. Scapes many, erect, naked, slender, terminating in globose or ovoid heads of minute, 1-sexual flowers. Receptacle convex or columnar. Central flowers chiefly male, the outer chiefly female intermixed with small bracts; the outer bracts larger and forming an involucre round the base of the head. Perianth very thin, hypogynous, of 4–6 segments in two series; the outer or sepals free; the inner or petals free in the female flowers, but in the males united in a tube. Stamens usually 6, inserted on the perianth-tube; anthers versatile. Ovary free, 3-celled; ovule one in each cell; style straight, 3-branched at the top. Capsule 3-lobed; seeds 3.

Receptacle glabrous. Scapes 2–9 in.
  Leaves rarely $\frac{1}{10}$ in. broad . . . . 1. *E. Sieboldianum.*
  Leaves $\frac{1}{8}$–$\frac{1}{4}$ in. broad . . . . 3. *E. nepalense.*
Receptacle hairy. Scapes 8–18 in. . . . . . . 2. *E. oryzetorum.*

*1. **Eriocaulon Sieboldianum,** *Sieb. & Zucc.*; *Fl. Br. Ind.* vi. 577. Annual. Leaves 2–4 in., rarely $\frac{1}{10}$ in. broad. Scapes 2–6 in. Heads $\frac{1}{8}$ in. diam., pale grey or tinged with purple; involucral bracts glabrous, oblong, obtuse; receptacle glabrous; floral bracts glabrous, oblong-lanceolate. Male flowers: sepals 3; stamens 1–6. Female flowers: sepals 1–2 or none; petal 1; ovary stalked. Seeds red-brown, smooth. (Fig. 180.)

Common throughout India, ascending to 4000 ft.; August–October.—China, Japan.

*2. **Eriocaulon oryzetorum,** *Mart.; Fl. Br. Ind.* vi. 579. Perennial. Leaves $1–3 \times \frac{1}{6}–\frac{1}{4}$ in. Scapes 8–18 in. Heads $\frac{1}{4}–\frac{1}{3}$ in. diam., pale yellow; involucral bracts glabrous, oblong, obtuse; receptacle densely hairy; floral bracts glabrous, wedge-shaped,

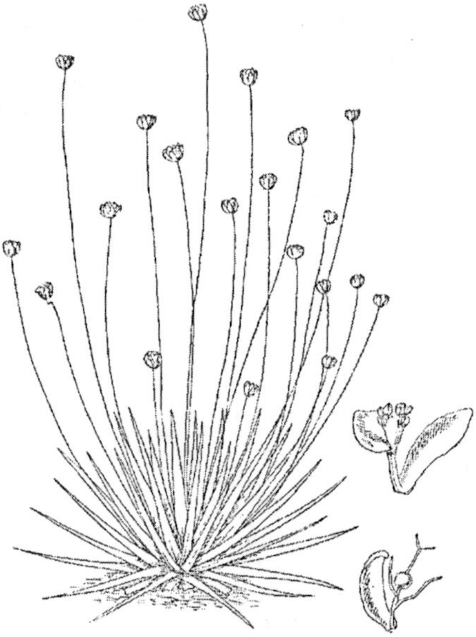

FIG. 180. ERIOCAULON SIEBOLDIANUM.

shortly pointed. Male flowers: sepals 2; stamens 6. Female flowers: sepals 3; petals 3; the petals and ovary carried up on a stalk above the sepals. Seeds pale yellow, smooth.

Garhwal to Sikkim, below 6000 ft.; August–October.—Tropical Asia.

3. **Eriocaulon nepalense,** *Prescott*; *Fl. Br. Ind.* vi. 581. Leaves $2–3 \times \frac{1}{6}–\frac{1}{4}$ in. Scapes 4–9 in. Heads $\frac{1}{5}$ in. diam., blue-grey; involucral bracts glabrous, obovate; receptacle glabrous; floral bracts minutely hairy, narrow. Male flowers: sepals 3, linear; stamens 6. Female flowers: sepals 3, concave, tip fringed, back hairy; petals 3, narrow, tip hairy; ovary sessile. Seeds ribbed.

Kangra to Sikkim, 4000–6000 ft.; August–October.—Khasia.

CXII. CYPERACEÆ

PERENNIAL, rarely annual herbs with the aspect of Grasses but usually more rigid, sometimes rush-like; stems solid, terete or angled. Leaves narrow, pointed, often sharply edged; sheaths tubular, not split down one side as in the true grasses. Flowers male, female or 2-sexual. Nut-bearing flowers 2-sexual in all genera, except *Kobresia* and *Carex*, in which they are female. Perfect perianth none, but in some genera represented by a few hypogynous bristles or scales. Male flowers in all the genera consisting of 1–3 stamens, filaments free, thread-like; anthers linear, 2-celled, basifixed. Female and 2-sexual flowers: stamens, if present, as in the male flowers; ovary 1-celled, flattened and having 2-branched styles or 3-sided and having 3-branched styles; ovule solitary, basal. In *Kobresia* the ovary is enclosed in a bract or utricle split nearly to its base on one side; in *Carex*, in a bag-like bract or utricle; in all other genera it is in the axil of a bract. Fruit a small, flattened or 3-sided nut; embryo minute, at the very base of the nut, its position not indicated externally by a scar or spot as in the Grasses. Flowers solitary in the axils of small bracts or glumes combined in spikelets. Spikelets having the glumes arranged spirally round the axis or in two opposite rows, solitary or several or many, forming spikes, panicles, simple or compound umbels, corymbs or heads with a few spreading, rarely erect, leaf-like bracts at the base. —Nearly all regions, usually growing in damp or marshy ground.

Plants of this Order and of the *Gramineæ* flower at almost all seasons. They mostly inhabit swamps and wet pastures, and several of the annual species of *Cyperus* form a conspicuous feature among the weeds of the rice-fields in the plains.

A. Nut-bearing flowers containing perfect stamens

* Glumes in two opposite rows

Axis of fruiting spikelet disarticulating and falling off.
  Style 2-branched . . . . 1. *Kyllinga*.
  Style 3-branched . . . . 4. *Mariscus*.
Axis of fruiting spikelet persistent.
  Style 2-branched . . . . 2. *Pycreus*.
  Style 3-branched . . . . 3. *Cyperus*.

* * Glumes imbricated all round the axis

Flowers with bristles or scales.
  Bristles 6–9, not longer than the glumes.
    Nut crowned by the swollen style-base . . . . . 5. *Eleocharis*.
    Nut pointed; style-base not swollen . . . . . 8. *Scirpus*.[1]

[1] In some species of *Scirpus* bristles are present, in others they are absent.

Bristles divided into numerous segments longer than the glumes . . . . 9. *Eriophorum.*
Scales 2, relatively long, narrow, thin . . . . . 10. *Lipocarpha.*
Flowers without bristles or scales.
Style swollen at the base.
Nut pointed; style-base falling off . . . . . 6. *Fimbristylis.*
Nut obtuse with the persistent style-base . . . . 7. *Bulbostylis.*
Style not swollen at the base; nut pointed . . . . 8. *Scirpus.*[1]

B. Nut-bearing flowers without stamens

Nut partially enclosed in a bract or utricle split nearly to its base on one side . . . . 11. *Kobresia.*
Nut wholly enclosed in a bag-like bract or utricle . . . 12. *Carex.*

1. KYLLINGA. In honour of P. Kylling, a Dutch botanist of the seventeenth century.—All hot and temperate climates, except Europe.

***Kyllinga squamulata,** *Vahl; Fl. Br. Ind.* vi. 589. A nearly glabrous herb; root fibrous; stems tufted, erect, 2–12 in. Leaves mostly radical, often longer than the stem, $\frac{1}{8}$ in. broad. Spikelets many, crowded in a green or brown, ovoid, terminal head $\frac{1}{4}$ in. diam.; bracts 3, unequal, spreading. Glumes 4, in 2 opposite series; 2 lower minute, empty; 2 upper large, acute, keels toothed, one containing a 2-sexual, fertile flower, the other empty or containing a male flower. Stamens 3. Style 2-branched. Nut flat, circular. The axis of the spikelet disarticulates in fruit just above the 2 lower glumes and falls off.

Dalhousie to Garhwal, below 6000 ft.—Western India, Canara.—N. tropical Africa.

2. PYCREUS. An anagram of *Cyperus*, in which genus the species are placed by most botanists.—Warm and temperate regions.

Glabrous herbs; stems erect or decumbent, leafy only near the base, except in *P. sanguinolentus*. Leaves not longer than the stem nor more than $\frac{1}{6}$ in. broad. Spikelets usually numerous, linear, flattened, in clusters or short spikes at the end of the unequal rays of a terminal umbel, or sometimes the rays are suppressed when the inflorescence becomes capitate; axis persistent in fruit; bracts 3 or 4, unequal, spreading. Glumes green or brown, often streaked with red, in two opposite rows, two lowest empty, succeeding ones 2-sexual, uppermost 1–3 male or empty. Stamens 1–3. Ovary tapering gradually into the 2-branched style. Nut flattened, circular or compressed-ovoid.

Stems decumbent, lower third leafy . . . . . 1. *P. sanguinolentus.*
Stems erect, leafy only at the base.
Height less than 6 in. Stamen usually one . . 2. *P. nitens.*
Height 10–18 in. Stamens usually 2 . . . . 3. *P. capillaris.*

[1] In some species of *Scirpus* bristles are present, in others they are absent.

1. **Pycreus sanguinolentus,** *Nees*; *Fl. Br. Ind.* vi. 590. Perennial; stems 10–20 in., decumbent near the base, the lower third covered by leaf-sheaths. Spikelets $\frac{1}{4}$–$\frac{3}{4}$ in. Glumes 12–24, obtuse, margins red. Stamens usually 3. Nut slightly compressed, both surfaces slightly convex.

Throughout India, ascending to 10,000 ft.; May–October.—Warm regions of the Old World.

2. **Pycreus nitens,** *Nees*; *Fl. Br. Ind.* vi. 591. Annual; stems usually less than 6 in., very slender, erect, leafless, tufted. Spikelets $\frac{1}{4}$–$\frac{3}{4}$ in. Glumes 10–40, acute or obtuse, pale. Stamen usually one. Nut minute, ovoid. (Fig. 181.)

Throughout India, ascending to 6000 ft.; May-October.—Warm regions of the Old World.

FIG. 181. PYCREUS NITENS.

3. **Pycreus capillaris,** *Nees*; *Fl. Br. Ind.* vi. 591. Annual; stems tufted, 10–18 in., slender, erect, leafless. Spikelets $\frac{1}{2}$–$\frac{3}{4}$ in. Glumes about 40, obtuse, pale yellow or dark brown. Stamens usually two. Nut small, ovoid.

N. India, ascending to 6000 ft.; May–October.—Temperate and tropical regions of the Old World.

3. **CYPERUS.** The Greek name for one or more species of this genus.—All warm and temperate regions.

Erect, annual or perennial herbs, usually growing in damp or wet places; stems often tufted. Leaves crowded near the base of the stem or sometimes none. Umbels simple or compound, one or two of the central rays usually suppressed so that the point of forking is occupied with a sessile cluster of spikes or spikelets; sometimes the rays are altogether suppressed when the spikelets become capitate. Bracts unequal, spreading. Spikelets linear, more or less flattened, in clusters or spikes. Glumes 8–50, in two opposite rows, usually imbricate, the two lowest empty, the uppermost 1–3 empty or containing male flowers, the intermediate containing 2-sexual flowers. Axis of spikelets persistent in fruit, the intermediate glumes falling off successively from the base of the spikelets. Ovary passing gradually into the 3-branched style. Nut 3-sided.

Spikelets clustered, not spicate.
  Spikelets red-brown.
    Stems 6 in. or less. Glumes long-pointed . . . 1. *C. uncinatus.*
    Stems 6–30 in. Glumes obtuse or minutely pointed.
      Nut nearly as long as the glume . . . . . 2. *C. difformis.*
      Nut less than half the glume . . . . . . 3. *C. Haspan.*
  Spikelets white or very pale brown.
    Spikelets in a single head . . . . 4. *C. niveus.*
    Spikelets in an umbel . . . . 5. *C. Atkinsoni.*
Spikelets in spikes.
  Annuals. Root fibrous. Stems usually slender.
    Spikelets $\frac{1}{2}$–1 in. Glumes 20–30 . . . . . 6. *C. compressus.*
    Spikelets $\frac{1}{4}$–$\frac{1}{2}$ in. Glumes 8–20.
      Spikes ovoid, $\frac{1}{4}$–$\frac{3}{4}$ in. . . . . 7. *C. aristatus.*
      Spikes linear, 1–2 in. . . . . 8. *C. Iria.*
  Perennials.[1] Rootstock creeping. Stems usually robust.
    Spikelets $\frac{1}{2}$ in. or less.
      Axis of spike hairy . . . . 10. *C. pilosus.*
      Axis of spike glabrous . . . . 13. *C. exaltatus.*
    Spikelets $\frac{3}{4}$–$1\frac{1}{2}$ in.
      Glumes distant, not imbricate . . . . . . 9. *C. distans.*
      Glumes closely imbricate.
        Stems 3–6 ft. Leaves short or none . . . 11. *C. tegetum.*
        Stems $\frac{1}{2}$–$2\frac{1}{2}$ ft. Leaves long . . . . . 12. *C. rotundus.*

1. **Cyperus uncinatus**, *Poir.*; *Encyc.* vii. 247. Annual, glabrous; stems tufted, 2–6 in., very slender. Leaves not longer than the stem, linear. Umbel-rays slender. Spikelets $\frac{1}{4}$–$\frac{1}{2}$ in., red-brown, in globose clusters. Glumes about 20, 3-nerved, tip long, linear, recurved. Stamens usually 2. Nut less than half the length of the glume, ovoid, pale brown.

Throughout India, ascending to 5000 ft.—All warm regions.

Described in the *Fl. Br. Ind.* vi. 598 as *C. cuspidatus*, H.B. & K., but Mr. C. B. Clarke now considers it as identical with *C. uncinatus*, Poir., which is the older name.

2. **Cyperus difformis**, *Linn.*; *Fl. Br. Ind.* vi. 599. Annual, glabrous; stems tufted, 6–18 in., acutely 3-angled near the top.

[1] Individuals of this section occasionally flower during their first season before the creeping rootstock has developed.

Leaves usually shorter than the stem, flaccid. Umbel-rays rarely more than 2 in. Spikelets $\frac{1}{8}$–$\frac{1}{4}$ in., red-brown, crowded in globose clusters. Glumes 10–30, closely imbricate, obtuse. Stamen usually 1. Nut nearly as long as the glume, ovoid, pale brown.

Throughout India, in rice-fields and elsewhere, up to 8000 ft.—Common in all warm regions.

3. **Cyperus Haspan,** *Linn.*; *Fl. Br. Ind.* vi. 600. Biennial, glabrous; rhizome long with stems rising singly and far apart or short and the stems tufted; stems 6–30 in., 3-angled or almost 3-winged near the top. Leaves short or long, sometimes none. Umbel-rays usually long and slender. Spikelets $\frac{1}{4}$ in., red-brown, in clusters. Glumes 10–40, closely imbricate, obtuse or sometimes minutely pointed. Stamens 3 or 2. Nut less than half the length of the glume, ovoid, pale brown.

Throughout India, common in rice-fields up to 3000 ft.—All warm regions.
This species often flowers in its first season before the creeping rootstock is developed, in which state it is with difficulty distinguished from the annual *C. flavidus*, Retz.; but the latter has usually only one stamen and the ripe nut is white. *C. flavidus* is abundant in rice-fields throughout India and is likely to occur in low, hot valleys.

4. **Cyperus niveus,** *Retz.*; *Fl. Br. Ind.* vi. 601. Perennial, glabrous; stems 8–16 in., slender, closely arranged in a single row, the thickened bases touching and forming a woody rhizome with wiry rootlets. Leaves half as long as the stem. Inflorescence capitate. Umbel-rays almost suppressed. Spikelets $\frac{1}{2}$–$\frac{3}{4}$ in., much flattened, white, in a single, terminal head. Glumes 20–40, closely imbricate, strongly keeled, pointed. Stamens 1–3. Nut one third the length of the glume, ovoid, black. (Fig. 182.)

Simla, common in forest undergrowth.—N. India, ascending to 6000 ft.—S. Europe.

5. **Cyperus Atkinsoni,** *C. B. Clarke*; *Fl. Br. Ind.* vi. 603. Perennial, glabrous; rhizome short, creeping; stems crowded, 2–8 in., thickened at the base. Leaves usually shorter than the stem. Umbel-rays short. Spikelets $\frac{1}{4}$–$\frac{3}{4}$ in., much flattened, pale brown, in clusters. Glumes 20–30, closely imbricate, keeled, acute. Stamens 1–3. Nut half the length of the glume, ovoid, pale brown.

Kotgurh.—N.W. India, ascending to 6000 ft.

6. **Cyperus compressus,** *Linn.*; *Fl. Br. Ind.* vi. 605. Annual, glabrous; stems tufted, 6–12 in. Leaves shorter than the stem. Umbel simple; rays up to 6 in. Spikelets $\frac{1}{2}$–1 in., green, much flattened, in short spikes. Glumes 20–30, closely imbricate, streaked with brown, acutely keeled, tip linear, slightly recurved.

Stamens 3. Nut one third the length of the glume, broadly ovoid, black or dark brown, faces concave.

Abundant throughout India, ascending to 4000 ft.—All warm regions.

7. **Cyperus aristatus,** *Rottb.*; *Fl. Br. Ind.* vi. 606. Annual, glabrous; stems tufted, 2–6 in., very slender. Leaves often longer than the stem. Umbel simple; rays few, usually less than ½ in., sometimes contracted in a single, dense head. Spikelets

FIG. 182. CYPERUS NIVEUS.

¼ in., red-brown, crowded in ovoid spikes ¼–¾ in. Glumes 8–12, nerves 5 or more, tip long, bristle-like, recurved. Stamens 3 or 2. Nut one third the length of the glume, narrowly obovoid, pale brown.

Throughout India, ascending to 8000 ft.—Most warm and temperate regions.

8. **Cyperus Iria,** *Linn.*; *Fl. Br. Ind.* vi. 606. Annual, glabrous; stems tufted, 6–24 in. Leaves ⅕ in. broad, often nearly as long as the stem. Umbel simple or compound, varying much in size,

sometimes 20 in. diam.; primary rays 3–5, up to 12 in. long. Spikelets $\frac{1}{4}$–$\frac{1}{2}$ in., yellow-brown, in loosely arranged, linear spikes 1–2 in. Glumes 10–20, slightly imbricate in fruit, strongly keeled, acute, margins nerveless. Stamens 2 or 3. Nut nearly as long as the glume, narrowly ovoid, pale brown.

Common in rice-fields throughout India, ascending to 5000 ft.—Warm regions of the Old World.

9. **Cyperus distans,** *Linn. f.*; *Fl. Br. Ind.* vi. 607. Perennial, glabrous, frequently producing stolons; stems 1–3 ft. Leaves often as long as the stem, $\frac{1}{4}$–$\frac{1}{3}$ in. broad. Umbel compound; primary rays usually 2–6 in., sometimes much longer. Bracts longer than the umbel. Spikelets $\frac{3}{4}$–1 in., very narrow, red-brown, nodding when young, spreading at right angles when mature, in spikes $\frac{1}{2}$–2 in. Glumes 10–20, not imbricated, obtuse. Stamens 3. Nut nearly as long as the glume, narrowly oblong, pale brown.

Throughout India, ascending to 5000 ft.—All warm regions.

10. **Cyperus pilosus,** *Vahl*; *Fl. Br. Ind.* vi. 609. Perennial, producing stolons, glabrous except the rhachis of the spikes; stems 1–3 ft., acutely 3-angled at the top. Leaves about three quarters the length of the stem, $\frac{1}{5}$–$\frac{1}{2}$ in. broad. Umbel compound, sometimes 16 in. diam.; primary rays 2–6 in. Spikelets nearly $\frac{1}{2}$ in., red-brown, nodding when young, spreading at right angles when mature, in spikes $\frac{1}{2}$–2 in.; rhachis hairy. Glumes 10–20, imbricate, obtuse, margins white. Stamens 3. Nut two thirds the length of the glume, narrowly ovoid, pointed, black, faces concave.

Abundant throughout India, ascending to 5000 ft.—Most tropical regions.

11. **Cyperus tegetum,** *Roxb.*; *Fl. Br. Ind.* vi. 613. Perennial, glabrous; rhizome horizontal, thick; stems 3–6 ft., robust, 3-angled at the top. Leaves usually few, sometimes none, much shorter than the stem, $\frac{1}{3}$ in. broad. Umbel usually compound, 4–12 in. diam.; primary rays usually numerous, slender. Spikelets $\frac{3}{4}$ in., red-brown, in numerous, short spikes. Glumes 10–20, oblong, obtuse, slightly imbricate, spreading obliquely in fruit. Stamens 3. Nut half the length of the glume, oblong, dark brown.

Throughout India, ascending to 6000 ft., sometimes cultivated. Calcutta matting is made from the stems of this species.

12. **Cyperus rotundus,** *Linn.*; *Fl. Br. Ind.* vi. 614. Perennial, glabrous; rhizome wiry, often thickened into ovoid, black, woody tubers; stems 6–30 in., 3-angled at the top. Leaves nearly as long as the stem, sometimes longer, $\frac{1}{5}$–$\frac{1}{3}$ in. broad. Umbels simple or compound, 1–4 in. diam. or more; primary rays 2–8 in. Spikelets $\frac{3}{4}$–$1\frac{1}{2}$ in., red-brown, in short spikes. Glumes 20–50, obtuse,

margins narrowly scarious. Stamens 3. Nut one third the length of the glume, narrowly ovoid, pale brown.

Throughout India, ascending to 6000 ft.—All warm regions.

13. **Cyperus exaltatus**, *Retz.*; *Fl. Br. Ind.* vi. 617. Annual or sometimes biennial, glabrous; stems 3–6 ft. Leaves about half as long as the stem, $\frac{1}{3}$ in. broad. Umbels compound, 6–12 in. diam. Spikelets $\frac{1}{5}$–$\frac{1}{4}$ in., very numerous, red-brown, in linear-oblong spikes 1–2 in. long. Glumes 10–15, acute, closely imbricate. Nut barely half the length of the glume, ovoid, white or pale brown.

Throughout India, ascending to 3000 ft., common in rice-fields.—S. Europe, N. Africa.

4. **MARISCUS**. From the Celtic *mar*, a bog, swamp; referring to the habitat of most species.—Warm and temperate regions.

Perennial, glabrous herbs having the general aspect and characters of *Cyperus*, usually growing on grassy hill-sides. Umbels simple; rays 5–10, short. Bracts long. Spikelets $\frac{1}{4}$ in. or rather less, linear, not flattened, crowded in terminal spikes. Glumes 4–5, in 2 opposite series, persistent, the two lowest and the uppermost minute, empty, the intermediate 1 or 2 containing 2-sexual flowers. Axis of spikelet disarticulating and falling off in fruit just above the 2 lowest glumes. Bristles none. Style 3-branched. Nut two thirds the length of the glume, ovoid-oblong, 3-sided.

The three species described below are closely allied, and were considered by Bentham as varieties of *M. umbellatus*.

Rootstock producing stolons . . . . 1. *M. paniceus*.
Rootstock without stolons.
  Length of spikes less than twice their breadth. Fruiting spikelets pointing upwards . . . . 2. *M. cyperinus*.
  Length of spikes nearly thrice their breadth. Fruiting spikelets spreading horizontally . . . . . 3. *M. Sieberianus*.

1. **Mariscus paniceus**, *Vahl*; *Fl. Br. Ind.* vi. 620. Rootstock producing long stolons; stems $\frac{1}{2}$–2 ft. Leaves $\frac{1}{6}$ in. broad, flaccid. Umbel-rays $\frac{1}{2}$ in. or less. Spikes $\frac{1}{2}$ in. Fertile flower 1. Nut black.

Throughout India, ascending to 6000 ft.—Tropical Asia.

2. **Mariscus cyperinus**, *Vahl*; *Fl. Br. Ind.* vi. 621. Rootstock hardly $\frac{1}{4}$ in., not producing stolons; stems 1–2 ft. Leaves $\frac{1}{4}$ in. broad. Umbel-rays $\frac{1}{2}$–1 in., usually curved, acutely 3-angled. Spikes short, less than twice their breadth. Fruiting spikelets pointing upwards. Fertile flowers usually 2.

Throughout India, ascending to 6000 ft.—Tropical Asia.

3. **Mariscus Sieberianus,** *Nees* ; *Fl. Br. Ind.* vi. 622. Rootstock short, not producing stolons ; stems 1–2½ ft. Leaves $\frac{1}{8}$–$\frac{1}{6}$ in. broad. Umbel-rays ½–4 in., straight. Spikes long, nearly 3 times their breadth. Fruiting spikelets spreading horizontally. Fertile flowers 1 or 2. Nut chestnut-brown.

Throughout India, ascending to 6000 ft.—Warm regions of the Old World.

5. **ELEOCHARIS.** From the Greek *helos*, a marsh, and *charis*, delight, referring to the habitat of the plants.—Nearly all regions except tropical plains, most abundant in temperate climates.

Glabrous, leafless herbs growing in marshy ground; stems tufted, erect, base sheathed by scales. Spikelets solitary, terminal, rarely more. Glumes many, obtuse, densely imbricate all round the axis, the one or two lowest rather larger than the others, usually empty; the others all containing a 2-sexual flower, but the uppermost soon withering. Bristles 4–7, usually 6, rough with minute, barb-like hairs. Stamens 3. Style 2- or 3-branched, base swollen. Nut about half the length of the glume, crowned by the persistent style-base.

Style 2-branched. Nut flattened . . . . . . 1. *E. palustris.*
Style 3-branched. Nut 3 sided.
  Stems terete . . . . 2. *E. congesta.*
  Stems 4-angled . . . . 3. *E. tetraquetra.*

1. **Eleocharis palustris,** *R. Br.* ; *Fl. Br. Ind.* vi. 628. Rhizome creeping ; stems 6–20 in. Spikelet ⅓–1 in. Bristles as long as the nut. Style 2-branched. Nut pale yellow-brown, smooth, flattened, faces slightly convex.

Marshes near Theog.—N. India, ascending to 12,000 ft.—Cosmopolitan.

2. **Eleocharis congesta,** *Don* ; *Fl. Br. Ind.* vi. 630. Root fibrous ; stems 3–12 in., terete, finely grooved. Spikelet ⅕–½ in. Bristles as long as the nut. Style 3-branched. Nut pale yellow-brown, smooth, 3-sided.

Throughout India, ascending to 6000 ft.—Ceylon.

3. **Eleocharis tetraquetra,** *Nees* ; *Fl. Br. Ind.* vi. 630. Rhizome short, usually descending, often producing stolons ; stems ½–3 ft., nearly square. Bristles rather longer than the nut, hairy. Style 3-branched. Nut pale yellow, smooth, 3-sided.

Hills throughout India, 1500–11,000 ft.—Tropical Asia, S. Australia.

6. **FIMBRISTYLIS.** From the Latin *fimbria*, a fringe, and *stylus*, style, referring to the hairy style of some species.—All warm regions.

Herbs, growing on dry pastures, along hedges and in rice-fields ; stems erect, usually tufted, leafy only near the base.

Leaves narrow. Umbels sometimes reduced to a single head or even spikelet, usually simple or compound up to the third degree; rays unequal, one or two of the central rays occasionally suppressed so that the point of forking is occupied by a sessile cluster of spikelets. Bracts usually short, often erect. Spikelets few or many, in *F. monostachya* and frequently in *F. schœnoides* there is only one, in pairs or in clusters. Glumes many, ovate, imbricate all round the axis, falling off successively from below; the lowest 1 or 2 empty, the others containing a 2-sexual flower, but the uppermost soon withering. Stamens 3, sometimes 2 or 1. Style long, frequently hairy, 2- or 3-branched, swollen towards the base but abruptly constricted just above the nut, at which point it ultimately falls off. Nut obtuse, narrowed towards the base.

Style 2-branched. Nut flattened.
  Stems terminating in 1–3 spikelets . . . . 1. *F. schœnoides.*
  Stems terminating in more than three spikelets.
    Style fringed at the base . . . . . . 2. *F. squarrosa.*
    Style-base not fringed.
      Nut longitudinally striped.
        Spikelets angular. Stems 2–10 in. . . 3. *F. dichotoma.*
        Spikelets cylindric. Stems 6–24 in. . . 4. *F. diphylla.*
      Nut not striped. Spikelets globose . . 5. *F. rigidula.*
Style 3-branched. Nut 3-sided.
  Stems terminating in more than one spikelet.
    Spikelets nearly all solitary, not clustered.
      Spikelets 5–20. Stems stoloniferous . . 6. *F. Pierotii.*
      Spikelets numerous. Stems without stolons.
        Stems 4–5-angled at the top . . . . 7. *F. quinquangularis.*
        Stems flattened at the top . . . . . 8. *F. complanata.*
    Spikelets in clusters of 2–5 . . . . . 9. *F. junciformis.*
  Stems terminating in a single spikelet . . . 10. *F. monostachya.*

1. **Fimbristylis schœnoides,** *Vahl*; *Fl. Br. Ind.* vi. 634. Glabrous; rhizome none or very short; stems tufted, 4–12 in., slender, grooved, base often thickened. Leaves about three quarters the length of the stem. Spikelets $\frac{1}{3}$–$\frac{2}{3}$ in., ovoid, rusty-brown, 1–3 in a single head. Glumes obtuse. Style hairy nearly to the base, 2-branched. Nut one third to half the length of the glume, flattened, smooth.

Throughout India, ascending to 6500 ft.—China, Australia.

2. **Fimbristylis squarrosa,** *Vahl*; *Fl. Br. Ind.* vi. 635. Annual; stems tufted, 2–8 in., slender, grooved. Leaves half to three quarters the length of the stem, usually pubescent. Umbels compound, often 2–4 in. diam. Spikelets many, $\frac{1}{5}$–$\frac{1}{4}$ in., narrowly oblong, red-brown. Mid-rib of glumes running out at the top in a tail-like point nearly as long as the glume itself. Style minutely hairy, 2-branched, fringed at the base with 10–18 white hairs. Nut one third the length of the glume, flattened, smooth.

Common in rice-fields throughout India, ascending to 3000 ft.—All warm regions.

3. **Fimbristylis dichotoma,** *Vahl*; *Fl. Br. Ind.* vi. 635. Annual; stems tufted, 2–10 in., grooved. Leaves nearly as long as the stem, pubescent. Umbels compound, often 2–4 in. diam. Spikelets many, $\frac{1}{6}$–$\frac{1}{3}$ in., oblong, angular, red-brown. Glumes acute, keel prominent. Style hairy nearly to the base, 2-branched. Nut half the length of the glume, flattened, each face longitudinally striped.

Common in rice-fields, throughout India, ascending to 4000 ft.—Warm regions of the Old World.

4. **Fimbristylis diphylla,** *Vahl*; *Fl. Br. Ind.* vi. 636. Annual; stems tufted, 6–24 in., grooved, angled at the top. Leaves about one third the length of the stem, usually glabrous in the Himalayan form. Umbels compound, 1–8 in. diam., but sometimes reduced to a head of a few spikelets or even one. Spikelets usually many, $\frac{1}{5}$–$\frac{1}{3}$ in., ovoid to nearly cylindric, brown. Glumes acute. Style hairy, 2-branched. Nut one third the length of the glume, flattened, each face longitudinally striped.

Throughout India, ascending to 6000 ft.—All warm regions.

5. **Fimbristylis rigidula,** *Nees*; *Fl. Br. Ind.* vi. 640. Perennial; rhizome horizontal, short, woody; stems 4–16 in., base thickened, closely arranged in a single row. Leaves half the length of the stem or less, glabrous or pubescent. Umbel compound, 1–5 in. diam. Spikelets many, solitary or in pairs, $\frac{1}{5}$–$\frac{1}{2}$ in., almost globose, brown. Glumes obtuse. Style hairy, at least on the upper half, 2-branched. Nut one third the length of the glume, flattened, faces not striped.

Simla.—N. India, ascending to 6000 ft.—China.

6. **Fimbristylis Pierotii,** *Miq.*; *Fl. Br. Ind.* vi. 642. Glabrous; stolons short, hardening into a woody rhizome; stems tufted, 6–12 in., slender. Leaves about half the length of the stem. Umbels simple or compound, 1–3 in. diam. Spikelets 5–20, broadly lanceolate, $\frac{1}{3}$ in., chestnut-brown. Glumes acute. Style glabrous; branches 3, minutely hairy. Nut one third the length of the glume, 3-sided, smooth or obscurely tuberculate. (Fig. 183.)

Simla.—W. Himalaya, from 4000 up to 9000 ft.—Japan.

7. **Fimbristylis quinquangularis,** *Kunth*; *Fl. Br. Ind.* vi. 644. Annual, glabrous, very variable in size; stems tufted, 4–24 in., base flattened, top 4–5-angled. Leaves usually half the length of the stem, very variable in development, sometimes none. Umbels sometimes compound to the fourth degree, 4–8 in. diam. or much smaller. Spikelets usually numerous, rarely few, $\frac{1}{8}$–$\frac{1}{5}$ in., linear-lanceolate, pale brown. Glumes pointed. Style slightly hairy near the top, 3-branched. Nut half the length of the glume, 3-sided, reticulate or obscurely tuberculate.

Throughout India, ascending to 6000 ft.—Tropical Asia.—Australia.

8. **Fimbristylis complanata,** *Link*; *Fl. Br. Ind.* vi. 646. Perennial, glabrous; rhizome very short, horizontal, without stolons; stems tufted, 8–24 in., flattened near the top. Leaves about three fourths the length of the stem, sometimes nearly $\frac{1}{4}$ in. broad. Umbels sometimes compound to the third degree, often 4 in. diam. Lower bract nearly erect, flattened, the tip abruptly obtuse. Spikelets usually numerous, $\frac{1}{4}$ in., linear, dark brown. Glumes acute. Style glabrous; branches 3, minutely hairy. Nut hardly one third the length of the glume, 3-sided, more or less tuberculate.

FIG. 183. FIMBRISTYLIS PIEROTII.

Narkunda.—Throughout India, ascending to 8000 ft.—All warm regions.

9. **Fimbristylis junciformis,** *Kunth*; *Fl. Br. Ind.* vi. 647. Glabrous; rhizome woody, usually short; stems tufted, 4–16 in.,

rigid, angular or somewhat flattened. Leaves usually short, sometimes half the length of the stem, stiff, obtuse. Umbel sometimes compound to the second degree, 1–4 in. diam. Spikelets usually in clusters of 2–5 or a few solitary, $\frac{1}{6}$–$\frac{1}{4}$ in., linear, red-brown. Glumes acute. Style nearly glabrous, branches 3, hairy. Nut hardly one third the length of the glume, 3-sided, nearly smooth.

Throughout India, ascending to 5000 ft.—Madagascar.

10. **Fimbristylis monostachya,** *Hassk.*; *Fl. Br. Ind.* vi. 649. Perennial, glabrous; rhizome none or very short; stems tufted, 4–16 in., slender, angular. Leaves half the length of the stem. Spikelet solitary, terminal, $\frac{1}{4}$–$\frac{1}{2}$ in., flattened, pale yellow. Bracts shorter than the spikelet. Glumes apparently in 2 opposite series, acute, keel green. Style hairy, branches 3. Nut about half the length of the glume, obtusely 3-sided, minutely tuberculate, base much contracted.

Throughout India, ascending to 3000 ft., common in pastures.—All warm regions.

7. BULBOSTYLIS. From the Greek *bolbos*, a bulb, and *stylos*, a style, referring to the swollen style-base.—Most warm regions, abundant in Africa.

Annual herbs; stems tufted, erect, very slender, glabrous, leafy only at the base. Leaves very narrow, the sheaths covered with fine, needle-like hairs. Spikelets in a head. Glumes many, ovate, brown, minutely hairy on the back, keel green; the lowest 1 or 2 empty, the others all containing a 2-sexual flower, but the uppermost soon withering. Stamens 1–3, usually 2. Style glabrous, 3-branched, the base swollen in a button-like expansion, which becomes discoloured and is persistent in fruit. Nut small, 3-sided, obtuse, smooth.

Spikelets in a globose head . . . . 1. *B. barbata.*
Spikelets in an umbel . . . . 2. *B. capillaris.*

1. **Bulbostylis barbata,** *Kunth*; *Fl. Br. Ind.* vi. 651 Stems 2–10 in. Leaves half the length of the stem. Spikelets $\frac{1}{8}$–$\frac{1}{3}$ in., oblong-lanceolate, sessile in a globose head of 3–20. Glumes acute, margins minutely fringed.

Throughout India, ascending to 4000 ft.—Most warm regions.

2. **Bulbostylis capillaris,** *Kunth*; *Fl. Br. Ind.* vi. 652. Stems 4–10 in. Leaves half to two thirds the length of the stem. Spikelets $\frac{1}{5}$ in., narrowly oblong, nearly all solitary on the spreading rays of a simple or compound umbel. Glumes obtuse.

Simla, Charaog.—Himalaya, up to 8000 ft.—All warm regions.
The Himalayan form is var. *trifida* of Kunth.

8. SCIRPUS. The old Latin name for a Rush.—Inhabits nearly all regions.

Herbs, glabrous or nearly so; stems erect, tall and robust, except in *S. squarrosus*. Leaves few, none or many. Spikelets in a single head or in an umbel. Glumes many, ovate, imbricated all round the axis; the lowest 1 or 2 empty, the others all containing a 2-sexual flower, but the uppermost soon withering. Bristles usually 3–6, sometimes none. Stamens 1–3. Style not swollen at the base, 2- or 3-branched. Nut about half the length of the glume, 3-sided or flattened.

Spikelets in a single head.
 Stems 3-sided, robust. Tip of glumes not prolonged . 1. *S. mucronatus.*
 Stems terete, slender. Tip of glumes prolonged, tail-like 4. *S. squarrosus.*
Spikelets in an umbel.
 Upper part of stems naked. Glumes notched at the tip. Style 3-branched . . . . 2. *S. lacustris.*
 Upper part of stems leafy. Glumes entire. Style 2-branched . . . . 3. *S. chinensis.*

1. **Scirpus mucronatus,** *Linn.*; *Fl. Br. Ind.* vi. 657. Perennial; stems tufted, 1–2½ ft., robust, 3-sided, leafless or nearly so. Spikelets ⅓–½ in., in a single, dense, lateral head. Lowest bract ½–4 in., looking like a continuation of the stem. Glumes acute. Bristles 5–6, rough with recurved hairs. Stamens 3. Style 3-branched. Nut 3-sided, dark brown or black, rough.

Throughout India, ascending to 6000 ft.—Warm regions of Europe, Asia, Australia.

2. **Scirpus lacustris,** *Linn.*; *Fl. Br. Ind.* vi. 658. Perennial stems 1½–4 ft., robust, terete or nearly so. Leaves none or 1–2 near the base of the stem. Spikelets ½ in., in small clusters or solitary on the rays of a simple or compound umbel, rarely reduced to a single cluster. Lowest bract short, erect. Glumes notched at the tip, a small point in the notch. Bristles 5–6, sometimes very short, rough with recurved hairs. Stamens 3. Style 3-branched. Nut 3-sided, pale brown, finally black, smooth.

Kashmir to Kumaon, 4000–5000 ft., usually grows in lakes or ponds.—Africa, Australia, N. America, Europe (Britain, Bulrush).

3. **Scirpus chinensis,** *Munro*; *Fl. Br. Ind.* vi. 662. Perennial; stems 2–7 ft., solitary, leafy on the upper part. Leaves long, ⅓ in. broad. Spikelets ⅙ in., in clusters of 3–15 on the rays of a large, spreading, compound umbel 4–8 in. across. Bracts several, the lowest sometimes 20 in. Glumes obtuse. Bristles none or 3–5, smooth. Stamens 2, rarely 3. Style 2-branched. Nut flattened, pale coloured.

Chumba to Kumaon, ascending to 5000 ft.—China.

4. **Scirpus squarrosus,** *Linn.*; *Fl. Br. Ind.* vi. 663. Annual; stems tufted, 2–12 in., slender, terete. Leaves few, 1–2 in., linear,

all basal. Spikelets $\frac{1}{5}$ in., in heads of usually 2–4. Bracts $\frac{1}{2}$–1 in., leaf-like. Glumes abruptly narrowed into a long, recurved, tail-like tip. Bristles none. Stamen 1, sometimes 2. Style 3-branched. Nut 3-sided.

N. India, ascending to 6000 ft.—Tropical Asia, Africa.

9. **ERIOPHORUM**. From the Greek *erion*, wool, and *phero*, to bear; referring to the fruit.—Europe, temperate Asia, N. America.

Eriophorum comosum, *Wall.*; *Fl. Br. Ind.* vi. 664. A glabrous herb; stems tufted, 4–20 in., erect, slender, leafy only near the base. Leaves numerous, linear, often overtopping the stem, rough, edges minutely toothed. Spikelets numerous, $\frac{1}{4}$–$\frac{1}{3}$ in., brown, narrowly ovoid, mostly solitary on the rays of a compound umbel 2–8 in. diam. Bracts longer than the umbel. Glumes many, spirally imbricate, acute, the lower 1 or 2 empty, the others all containing a 2-sexual flower. Bristles 6, longer than the glume, divided into numerous, linear, flat segments elongating in fruit, when they form a tangle of glistening, white hairs at the tip of the spikelets. Stamens 3, anthers red-pointed. Style shorter than the nut, 3-branched. Nut slender, 3-sided, pointed.

Simla, common on dry hill-sides; August–October.—Throughout India, ascending to 10,000 ft.—China.

This plant is often confused with the Bhabar grass, *Ischæmum angustifolium*, which is very woolly at the base of the stem.

E. polystachion is common in bogs in Britain and is known as Cotton-grass.

10. **LIPOCARPHA**. From the Greek *leipo*, to let go, release, and *carpe*, a glume, referring to the glumes soon falling off.—Most warm regions.

***Lipocarpha argentea,** *R. Br.*; *Fl. Br. Ind.* vi. 667. A glabrous herb; stems erect, 6–24 in., obtusely 3-sided, leafy only near the base. Leaves long or short, $\frac{1}{8}$ in. broad or less. Spikelets $\frac{1}{5}$–$\frac{1}{3}$ in., ovoid, in a single terminal cluster of 3–8. Bracts $\frac{1}{2}$–2 in. Glumes many, crowded, membranous, obovate, imbricated all round the axis, each containing a 2-sexual flower, the uppermost soon withering. Scales 2, thin, transparent, nearly twice as long as the nut, narrowly oblong. Stamens 3. Nut obscurely 3-sided, oblong-ovoid. Style 3-branched, base not swollen.

W. Himalaya, on grassy hill-sides up to 6000 ft.—Tropical and subtropical regions of the Old World.

11. **KOBRESIA**. In honour of Von Kobres, a collector of objects of natural history, whose collections were purchased by Ludwig, King of Bavaria, in 1811.—N. temperate regions, chiefly at high levels.

Kobresia filicina, *C. B. Clarke*; *Fl. Br. Ind.* vi. 696. A glabrous, perennial herb; stems 2–10 in., erect. Leaves shorter than the stem, very narrow, all basal. Glumes $\frac{1}{8}$ in., in a single terminal, very slender spike, $\frac{3}{4}$–$1\frac{1}{3}$ in. long; upper ones containing male flowers, the lower a spikelet of one female and one male or a female only. Bristles none. Stamens 1–3. Style 3-branched. Nut narrowly oblong, partially enclosed in the persistent glume; beak long, protruding, often ultimately recurved.

Fagoo.—N.W. Himalaya, 8000–10,000 ft.

12. CAREX. From the Greek *keiro*, to cut; the leaves of many species having sharp, saw-like edges.—A genus of about 1,400 species inhabiting nearly all regions.

Herbs, mostly perennial, usually glabrous except the utricles; stems tufted, erect or nearly so, more or less angular. Leaves usually crowded at the base of the stem. Bracts long or short. Spikelets short, usually several combined in a terminal spike, if in more than one spike the lower ones stalked and often distant forming an interrupted spike or sometimes a loose or dense panicle; both spikelets and spikes may consist wholly of male or wholly of female flowers or partially of both. Glumes imbricate all round the axis, the mid-rib frequently projecting as a bristle-like point. Flowers 1-sexual, male and female always in separate glumes. Male flowers: stamens 3, rarely fewer. Female flowers: ovary enclosed in a bag-like bract or utricle with an opening in its contracted top through which the 2- or 3-branched style protrudes. Nut flattened or 3-sided, enclosed within the persistent utricle.

Style 2-branched. Nut flattened.
  Spikes ovoid, $\frac{1}{5}$ in. long, sessile.
    Utricle winged on the upper half . . . . . 5. *C. Rochebruni.*
    Utricle not winged.
      Nerves of utricle many, prominent . . . 1. *C. nubigena.*
      Nerves of utricle none or few and obscure . . 2. *C. foliosa.*
  Spikes linear, 1–2 in. long, stalked.
    Beak of utricle much shorter than the body. Glume ovate . . . . 3. *C. brunnea.*
    Beak of utricle about as long as the body. Glume lanceolate, long-pointed . . . . . . 4. *C. longicruris.*
Style 3-branched. Nut 3-sided.
  Spikes numerous, in a large panicle, the uppermost ones male at the top.
    Spikes oblong, crowded . . . . 6. *C. condensata.*
    Spikes linear, distant . . . . 7. *C. meiogyna.*
  Spikes 2–8.
    Uppermost spike female at the top, male at the base, rarely wholly male . . . . . . 8. *C. psycrophila.*
    Uppermost spike wholly male.
      Leaves linear.
        Margins of female glumes brown or chestnut.
          Mid-rib of glume prolonged.
            Tip of glume acute . . . . . . 9. *C. setigera.*
            Tip of glume notched or truncate . . . 11. *C. cardiolepis.*

Mid-rib of glume not prolonged . . . . 10. *C. hæmatostoma.*
Margins of female glumes white, transparent . 12. *C. breviculmis.*
Leaves $\frac{1}{4}$–$\frac{1}{3}$ in. broad.
Flowering stems naked . . . . . . 13. *C. Wallichiana.*
Flowering stems leafy . . . . . . 14. *C. ligulata.*

1. **Carex nubigena,** *D. Don*; *Fl. Br. Ind.* vi. 702. Stems 6–30 in., slender. Leaves long, $\frac{1}{8}$ in. broad or less. Spikes $\frac{1}{5}$ in., ovoid, sessile, male at the top, pale coloured, forming an interrupted spike 1–5 in. long or sometimes contracted into an ovoid head. Glumes containing female flowers ovate; midrib prominent,

FIG. 184. CAREX NUBIGENA.

hardly prolonged; margins white, transparent. Utricle ovoid, glabrous; nerves many, prominent; beak oblong, linear, usually smooth. Style 2-branched. Nut hardly half the length of the utricle, flattened. (Fig. 184.)

Simla, Naldera, Matiana.—Hilly districts throughout India, 5000–12,000 ft. —Malaya, China, Japan.

2. **Carex foliosa,** *D. Don*; *Fl. Br. Ind.* vi. 703, *under C. muricata, Linn.* Stems 12–24 in., slender, rough towards the top.

Leaves long, $\frac{1}{5}$ in. broad. Spikes $\frac{1}{5}$ in., ovoid, sessile, male at the top, pale coloured, forming an interrupted spike $1\frac{1}{2}$–3 in. long. Glumes containing female flowers ovate, usually long-pointed; midrib prominent, hardly prolonged; margins white, transparent. Utricle ovoid, glabrous; nerves none or few and obscure; beak linear, rough on the margins. Style 2-branched. Nut hardly half the length of the utricle, flattened.

Simla, Mushobra, Matiana.—Himalaya, 6000–9000 ft.—Nilghiris.
Closely allied to the British *C. muricata.*

*3. **Carex brunnea,** *Thunb.*; *Fl. Br. Ind.* vi. 705. Stems 1–3 ft., slender. Leaves nearly as long as the stem, $\frac{1}{6}$ in. broad or less. Spikes 1–2 in., linear, stalked, nodding, red-brown, the uppermost male at the top, forming a long, lax panicle. Glumes containing female flowers ovate. Utricle ovoid; nerves many on each face, minutely hairy; margins smooth, brown, flat; beak straight, much shorter than the body. Style 2-branched; arms very long, brown. Nut ovoid, flattened.

Hilly districts throughout India, 3000–6000 ft.—Madagascar, Australia.

4. **Carex longicruris,** *Nees*; *Fl. Br. Ind.* vi. 705. Stems 2–4 ft., slender. Leaves nearly as long as the stem, $\frac{1}{5}$ in. broad. Spikes 1–2 in., linear, stalked, nodding, red-brown, the uppermost male at the top, forming a long, lax panicle. Glumes containing female flowers lanceolate, long-pointed. Utricle ovoid, red-brown, glabrous; nerves several on each face; margins rough, green, incurved; beak straight, about as long as the body. Style 2-branched; arms very long, brown. Nut ovoid, flattened.

Simla.—W. Himalaya, 4000–8000 ft.—Ceylon.

5. **Carex Rochebruni,** *Franch. & Sav.*; *Fl. Br. Ind.* vi. 706, *under C. remota.* Stems 1–$2\frac{1}{2}$ ft., slender. Leaves nearly as long as the stem, $\frac{1}{8}$ in. broad or less. Spikes $\frac{1}{5}$ in., ovoid, sessile, pale green, the uppermost male at the top, lower ones 1 in. or more apart, upper more or less crowded, the whole forming a much interrupted spike often half the length of the plant. Glumes containing female flowers ovate, acute. Utricle glabrous, ovoid; margins of the upper half winged, minutely toothed; nerves few and weak; beak short. Style 2-branched. Nut ovoid, flattened.

Simla.—Temperate Himalaya, 7000–12,000 ft.
Closely allied to *C. remota*, a British plant from which it differs in the utricle being winged.

6. **Carex condensata,** *Nees*; *Fl. Br. Ind.* vi. 716. Stems 2–3 ft., robust. Leaves nearly as long as the stem, $\frac{1}{3}$–$\frac{1}{2}$ in. broad. Spikes 50–200, oblong, $\frac{1}{4}$–$\frac{1}{2}$ in., crowded, red-brown, male at the top or the terminal ones sometimes wholly male, nearly sessile on the rough branches of dense, erect, lateral panicles 1–3 in. long, the

whole forming a composite panicle often a foot long. Glumes containing female flowers ovate, glabrous, except the rough, prolonged midrib. Utricle narrowly ovoid, 3-sided, minutely hairy; nerves few, distinct; beak long, straight, deeply bifid. Style 3-branched. Nut 3-sided.

Simla, Mahasu, common in pastures.—Temperate Himalaya, 1000-10,000 ft.

7. **Carex meiogyna,** *Strachey*; *Fl. Br. Ind.* vi. 718, *under C. filicina.* Stems 1–3 ft. Leaves long, $\frac{1}{3}$–$\frac{1}{2}$ in. broad. Spikes 50–200, linear, up to 1 in., lengthening in fruit, not crowded, red-brown, male at the top, the lower utricles distant, forming an oblong panicle usually more than half the length of the plant. Glumes containing female flowers ovate, acute. Utricle glabrous, narrowly lanceolate, more or less 3-sided; nerves few, distinct; beak straight, shortly bifid. Style 3-branched. Nut 3-sided.

Simla, common.—Temperate Himalaya, 3000–9000 ft.

8. **Carex psycrophila,** *Nees*; *Fl. Br. Ind.* vi. 732. Stems 1–2 ft., slender. Leaves nearly as long as the stem, narrow. Spikes 3–5, rather close, oblong, $\frac{1}{2}$–$\frac{3}{4}$ in., the lowest one stalked; terminal spike female at the top, male at the base, rarely wholly male, the others female. Glumes containing female flowers ovate, pointed. Utricle glabrous, lanceolate, 3-sided; nerves obscure; beak short, straight. Style 3-branched. Nut 3-sided.

Narkunda.—Temperate Himalaya, 8000–12,000 ft.

9. **Carex setigera,** *D. Don*; *Fl. Br. Ind.* vi. 743. Stems varying from 4 in. to 2 ft. Leaves long, linear. Spikes usually 4–8, cylindric, erect, varying much in length and thickness, the terminal 1–3 male, the lower female, usually stalked and rather distant from the others. Glumes containing female flowers ovate; margins pale brown; midrib prolonged as a short or long bristle. Utricle ovoid, more or less 3-sided, minutely hairy; nerves obscure; beak short, oblong. Style 3-branched. Nut 3-sided.

Simla, Fagoo, common.—Temperate Himalaya, 7000–10,000 ft.

As here described this species includes *C. Schlagintweitiana* and *C. inanis* of the *Fl. Br. Ind.*

10. **Carex hæmatostoma,** *Nees*; *Fl. Br. Ind.* vi. 744. Stems 8–30 in., nearly terete. Leaves long or short, linear. Spikes 2–6, chestnut-brown, linear-cylindric, $\frac{1}{2}$–1 in., the terminal 1–3 male, the lower female, erect, shortly stalked, rather distant from the others. Glumes containing female flowers ovate, acute; margins chestnut-brown. Utricle ovoid, more or less 3-sided, chestnut-purple towards the top, minutely hairy; nerves few, obscure. Style 3-branched. Nut stalked, oblong-ovoid, obscurely 3-sided.

Narkunda.—Temperate Himalaya, 9000–17,000 ft.—Tibet

11. **Carex cardiolepis,** *Nees*; *Fl. Br. Ind.* vi. 744. Stems 6–18 in. Leaves short or long, linear. Spikes 3–5, cylindric, $\frac{1}{2}$–1 in., erect, the terminal one male, the others female, often rather distant from each other. Glumes containing female flowers oblong-ovate; margins chestnut-brown; tip truncate or notched; midrib prolonged as a rough bristle. Utricle ovoid, 3-sided, minutely hairy; nerves numerous, rather prominent; beak very short. Style 3-branched. Nut 3-sided.

Simla.—W. Himalaya, 6000–11,000 ft.—Afghanistan.

12. **Carex breviculmis,** *R. Br.*; *Fl. Br. Ind.* vi. 746. Stems 4–16 in., slender. Leaves short or long, linear. Spikes 2–5, cylindric, $\frac{1}{4}$–$\frac{1}{2}$ in., pale coloured, nearly sessile, usually close together or the lowest one distant, terminal spike male, the others female. Glumes containing female flowers ovate; margins white, transparent; midrib prolonged as a long, rough bristle. Utricle ovoid, 3-sided, minutely hairy; nerves few, obscure; beak very short. Style 3-branched. Nut 3-sided, usually crowned with the dilated base of the style.

Simla, Baghi.—Hilly districts throughout India, 6000–10,000 ft.—China, Australia.

13. **Carex Wallichiana,** *Prescott*; *Fl. Br. Ind.* vi. 747. Stems 6–30 in., robust. Leaves all basal, nearly as long as the stem, $\frac{1}{4}$ in. broad; sheaths fringed with long hairs. Spikes 4–8, cylindric, $\frac{3}{4}$–1$\frac{1}{2}$ in., the upper 1–3 male, close together, the lower female, erect, stalked, distant. Glumes containing female flowers ovate, white, acute; midrib often prolonged as a long, rough bristle. Utricle ovoid, 3-sided, densely covered with minute hairs; nerves few, obscure; beak short, deeply bifid. Style 3-branched. Nut shortly stalked, 3-sided.

Sainj, Giri valley.—Throughout N. India, ascending to 6000 ft.—Afghanistan.

*14. **Carex ligulata,** *Nees*; *Fl. Br. Ind.* vi. 747. Stems 12–30 in., leafy. Leaves 6–12 × $\frac{1}{4}$–$\frac{1}{3}$ in. Spikes 6–8, cylindric, 1–1$\frac{1}{4}$ in., grey or pale brown, terminal one male, the others female, distant, erect, shortly stalked. Glumes containing female flowers ovate, acute; margins white; midrib usually prolonged as a short, rough bristle. Utricle ovoid, 3-sided, densely covered with minute hairs; nerves obscure; beak oblong, notched. Style 3-branched. Nut 3-sided.

Kashmir to Nepal, 5000–7000 ft.—China, Japan.

CXIII. GRAMINEÆ

ANNUAL or perennial herbs, shrubs or trees in *Bambuseæ*, often having underground, creeping stems or rhizomes; roots fibrous or occasionally tuberous; stems erect or decumbent, often tufted, terete or slightly flattened, usually hollow between the joints. Leaves mostly crowded near the base of the stem, the upper ones alternate, sheathing; sheath split longitudinally and usually furnished at the top with a short appendage or ligule, which is membranous or scarious or reduced to a ring of hairs; blade narrow, usually flat and entire, parallel-veined, the margins often inrolled especially when dry. Flowers generally 2-sexual, in spikelets arranged in terminal spikes, racemes or panicles. Panicle-branches often spreading only when in flower or fruit and sometimes so short as to form a compact or even cylindric panicle. The axis of the whole inflorescence is called the rhachis and that of a spikelet the rhachilla. Each spikelet consists of 3 or several or sometimes many scale-like, keeled bracts or glumes arranged alternately on opposite sides of the spikelet, their concave faces towards its axis, and the midrib frequently prolonged as a bristle or awn. Usually the 2 lowest or outermost glumes are nearly opposite and enclose the flower or flowers constituting the spikelet. In a few genera there are more than 2 empty glumes, rarely only one. Each flower usually consists of a flowering glume enclosing a rather smaller, flat, 2-nerved bract or glume, called the pale, placed with its back to the rhachilla or axis of the spikelet. Between the flowering glume and the pale is the flower proper consisting usually of 2, rarely more, minute, hypogynous scales called lodicules representing the perianth in other Orders, the stamens and the ovary. Stamens 3, rarely more or fewer; filaments long, hair-like, usually free; anthers linear, versatile, cells 2, parallel or more or less diverging at both ends. Ovary 1-celled, 1-ovuled, crowned by 2, rarely 3 or 1, feathery styles. Fruit or grain seed-like, with the very thin pericarp inseparable from the seed, free as in *Triticum* or adhering to the pale as in *Avena* or to both pale and flowering glume as in *Hordeum*. At the base of the grain is a scar indicating the position and shape of the usually very minute embryo. It is often convenient to refer to the empty and flowering glumes collectively as glumes; thus a spikelet containing two empty and three flowering glumes is described as 5-glumed. When a spikelet contains more than three glumes above the empty ones the uppermost or the lowermost may enclose a male or only a rudimentary flower. In some genera the rhachilla is prolonged above the terminal flower and naked or bearing 1–3 rudimentary glumes. In the following keys and descriptions the spikelets are often described as awned or awnless, because it is easier to put it this way than to particularise the glume or glumes bearing the awns. Particulars on this point are given in the descriptions of the genera and species.—This natural Order, although not the most numerous in genera and species, is the most generally dispersed, almost reaching the altitudinal and latitudinal limits of flowering plants and covering more of the surface of the earth than any other class of plants. Moreover, it stands first in importance in the dietary of man and beast.

The following conspectus and key are mainly adapted from Bentham and Hooker's *Genera Plantarum* and Hooker's *Flora of British India.*

CONSPECTUS OF THE TRIBES (exceptions omitted).

SERIES A. PANICACEÆ. Spikelets 1- or 2-flowered, if 2-flowered the upper flower fertile, the lower male or rudimentary. Stalk of spikelet jointed below the empty glumes.

TRIBE I. **Paniceæ.** Spikelets usually hermaphrodite, spicate or paniculate. Rhachis of the inflorescence not jointed. Flowering glume not awned, hardened in the fruiting stage or at least stiffer than the outer ones.

TRIBE II. **Zoysieæ.** Spikelets hermaphrodite or some imperfect. Rhachis not jointed. Spikes simple, solitary or in clusters. Flowering glume membranous, usually smaller than the empty ones and transparent.

TRIBE III. **Andropogoneæ.** Spikelets in pairs or the terminal in threes, along the rhachis of a spike or the branches of a panicle. Flowers homogamous or heterogamous in each pair. Flowering glume smaller than the empty ones, transparent and often awned.

SERIES B. POACEÆ. Stalk of spikelet not jointed below the empty glumes. Rhachilla often jointed above the persistent lower glumes, produced beyond the fertile flowers in the form of a stalk or bearing empty glumes or imperfect flowers; or sometimes, as in the *Panicaceæ,* bearing one terminal fertile flower, but which eventually disarticulates above the persistent empty glumes.

TRIBE IV. **Phalarideæ.** Spikelets bearing one terminal, hermaphrodite flower. Glumes 6, or 5 and a pale, 1-nerved or keeled.

TRIBE V. **Agrostideæ.** Spikelets 1-flowered. Rhachilla naked above the flower or produced in the form of a bristle or stalk.

Sub-tribe 1. **Stipeæ.** Panicle loose or spike-like. Flowering glume usually terminating in an awn, closely covering the grain in fruit. Rhachilla not produced beyond the flower.

Sub-tribe 2. **Phleoideæ.** Panicle spike-like, dense, cylindrical or subglobose. Flowering glume awnless or 1–3-awned, loosely enclosing the grain in fruit. Rhachilla sometimes produced.

Sub-tribe 3. **Sporoboleæ.** Panicle loose or reduced to a simple raceme. Flowering glume awnless. Grain with more or less open glumes. Rhachilla not produced beyond the flower.

Sub-tribe 4. **Euagrosteæ.** Panicle various, usually loose. Flowering glume usually furnished with a dorsal awn. Grain loosely included in the glumes.

Tribe VI. **Aveneæ.** Spikelets 2- or rarely many-flowered, mostly paniculate. Flowering glume furnished with a dorsal or terminal awn or in the equally 2-flowered genera awnless. Rhachilla often produced above the flowers.

Tribe VII. **Chlorideæ.** Spikelets 1- to many-flowered, arranged in two sessile rows along one side of the rhachis.

Tribe VIII. **Festuceæ.** Spikelets 2- to many-flowered, variously panicled, rarely racemose. Flowering glume awnless or furnished with one or more, sometimes numerous, terminal awns.

Tribe IX. **Hordeæ.** Spikelets 1- to many-flowered, sessile in the hollows of the rhachis of simple spikes.

Tribe X. **Bambuseæ.** Shrubby or arboreous. Leaves flat, almost always jointed to the sheath. Spikelets 1- to many-flowered. Lodicules often 3. Stamens usually exceeding 3.

Key to the Genera.

SERIES A. PANICACEÆ. Spikelets 1- or 2-flowered; if 2-flowered the upper flower only fertile, the lower male or rudimentary, except in *Isachne*, where both are sometimes fertile; stalk of spikelet jointed below the empty glumes, except in *Isachne* and *Arundinella* (see also *Pennisetum*), the joint often not obvious, except in the fruiting spikelet.

Tribe I. **Paniceæ.** Spikelets usually 2-flowered; terminal flower 2-sexual, fertile; lower male or rudimentary, rarely both fertile; in *Paspalum* the lowest glume wanting or minute.

Spikelets awnless, except in *Panicum Crus-galli*, and not surrounded by an involucre of bristles.

Spikelets crowded on the straight, spike-like branches of the panicle.

Lower empty glume minute or wanting. Lower flowering glume empty or sometimes containing a rudimentary flower . . . . 1. *Paspalum*.

Lower empty glume shorter than the upper, but obvious. Lower flowering glume containing a rudimentary or male flower or empty . . . 3. *Panicum.*
Spikelets scattered on hair-like, drooping branches, 2-flowered, both flowers often fertile. Rhachilla jointed above the 2 equal, empty glumes . . . 2. *Isachne.*

Spikelets awned, but not surrounded by an involucre of bristles.

Spikelets 1-flowered. Empty glumes 3, nearly equal, the lowest long-awned. Flowering glume not awned 4. *Oplismenus.*
Spikelets 2-flowered, not jointed. Empty glumes 2, unequal, acute. Flowering glume awned . . . 5. *Arundinella.*

Spikelets awnless and surrounded by an involucre of bristles.

Spikelets in spikes or in a cylindric, tapering panicle; stalks bearing an involucre of long bristles and not jointed at the base . . . . 6. *Setaria.*
Spikelets in a dense raceme; stalks bearing an involucre of long, sometimes fringed bristles and jointed at the base . . . . 7. *Pennisetum.*

TRIBE II. **Zoysieæ.** Spikelets in a slender raceme, 1-flowered, very narrow, falling off with their stalks. Empty glumes 2, long-awned . . . . 8. *Perotis.*

TRIBE III. **Andropogoneæ.** Spikelets in spikes or panicles, rarely in racemes, 1-flowered (except in *Ischæmum* and the sessile spikelets of *Pogonatherum, Apluda* and *Rottboellia*), hairy, rarely glabrous, usually in pairs, one sessile, the other stalked, alike or dissimilar, sometimes in threes, one sessile, two stalked, rarely solitary. Empty glumes 2 or 3, of firmer texture and longer than the flowering glumes. Flowering glumes small, very thin, usually bifid, with a long awn.

Spikelets in simple spikes. Spikes clustered, rarely solitary.

Spikelets in pairs, both alike.
Spikes not jointed, very many. Spikelets 1-flowered, partially enveloped in a tuft of long, yellow hairs . 9. *Miscanthus.*
Spikes jointed, soon breaking up, 2–10. Spikelets 1-flowered, nearly glabrous or more or less enveloped in brown or white hairs . . . . 11. *Pollinia.*
Spikes one to several. Spikelets 2-flowered, each with a tuft of short hairs at its base . . . . 14. *Ischæmum.*
Spikes several, rarely only one, thick, cylindric, jointed. Spikelets 2-flowered, sometimes dissimilar, adpressed against or partially sunk in the rhachis . . . . 18. *Rottboellia.*
Spikelets in pairs, dissimilar (see also *Rottboellia*).
Spikes solitary, slender. Sessile spikelet 2-flowered; stalked spikelet 1-flowered . . . . . . 15. *Pogonatherum.*
Spikes digitately or umbellately clustered or in pairs, rarely solitary, sheathed in a spathe-like bract . 19. *Andropogon.*[1]
Spikelets solitary, sessile, usually accompanied by the stalk of a second abortive spikelet. Spikes 2 or more, clustered . . . . 16. *Arthraxon.*

[1] Species 1, 2 and 8–14.

Spikelets in panicles.

Spikelets in pairs, the terminal ones sometimes in threes.
- Spikelets dissimilar, unawned, each spikelet enveloped in a tuft of long hairs . . . . 12. *Saccharum.*
- Spikelets dissimilar, awned, terminal spikelets usually in threes . . . . 19. *Andropogon.*[1]
- Spikelets similar, awned, each spikelet more or less enveloped in a tuft of hairs . . . . . . 13. *Erianthus.*
- Spikelets 7–9 in a spike, only 1–3 of the upper ones fertile, awned, terminal spikelets in threes. Spikes in clusters of 2–8, each cluster and each spike sheathed in a spathe-like bract . . . . 20. *Anthistiria.*

Spikelets all in threes.
- Spikelets awned, all 1-flowered, sessile spikelet male, stalked ones 2-sexual. The otherwise naked panicle-branches bearing at the tip 3 spikelets . . . . 10. *Spodiopogon.*
- Sessile spikelet 2-flowered; one of the stalked spikelets reduced to an empty glume, the other containing a male flower. Naked panicle-branches bearing at the tip 3 spikelets sheathed in a pointed bract . . . . 17. *Apluda.*
- Spikelets awned, all 1-flowered, sessile spikelet 2-sexual, stalked ones male or rudimentary. Naked panicle-branches bearing at the dilated tip 1–4 groups of 3 spikelets each . . . . 19. *Andropogon.*[2]

SERIES B. POACEÆ. Spikelets not jointed below the empty glumes, the joint or joints, if present, always above them, one- to many-flowered; if more than one, the lower flower or flowers fertile, the upper often male or rudimentary, except in *Phragmites.* Rhachilla often prolonged above the uppermost flowering glume.

TRIBE IV. **Phalarideæ.** Spikelets $\frac{1}{5}$ in., in ovoid or cylindric, spike-like panicles, flattened, 1-flowered. Empty glumes 2, nearly equal, longer than the flowering glume, keels winged. Rhachilla not prolonged . . . . 21. *Phalaris.*

TRIBE V. **Agrostideæ.** Spikelets in dense, spike-like or more or less spreading panicles, 1-flowered or occasionally 2-flowered in *Agrostis Royleana.* Rhachilla rarely prolonged.

Spikelets in dense, ovoid or cylindric, spike-like panicles. Flowering glume thin, transparent.

- Empty glumes equal, their keels terminating in short points . . . . 26. *Phleum.*
- Empty glumes awnless, united near the base . . . . 27. *Alopecurus.*
- Empty glumes awned on the back below the tip . . . 28. *Polypogon.*

[1] Species 3, 4 and 5.

[2] Species 6 and 7.

Spikelets in more or less spreading, loose panicles. Rhachilla not prolonged, except in *Deyeuxia*.

Spikelets awned.

- Spikelets $\frac{1}{3}$–$\frac{1}{2}$ in. Empty glumes unequal. Flowering glume rigid, tip produced in a long, 3-branched awn . . . . 22. *Aristida.*
- Spikelets $\frac{1}{3}$ in. Empty glumes nearly equal. Fruiting glume narrow, acuminate, tip produced in a long, simple awn . . . . 23. *Stipa.*
- Spikelets $\frac{1}{4}$ in. Empty glumes nearly equal. Fruiting glume obovoid or rather broad, tip narrowed into a long, simple awn . . . . 24. *Oryzopsis.*
- Spikelets minute. Flowering glume shorter than the empty glumes, hairy, thin, shortly awned on the back, tip truncate, minutely jagged . . . . 30. *Agrostis.*[1]
- Spikelets minute. Flowering glume stiff, hairy on the lower half, narrowed into a long, slender awn . 31. *Muehlenbergia.*
- Spikelets $\frac{1}{4}$ in., narrow. Empty glumes unequal, long-pointed. Flowering glume much shorter, awned, enveloped in a tuft of long, silky hairs . 32. *Calamagrostis.*
- Spikelets $\frac{1}{8}$ in. Rhachilla terminating in a tuft of hairs. Flowering glume thin, tip 2-lobed, awned in the cleft . . . . 33. *Deyeuxia.*

Spikelets awnless.

- Spikelets $\frac{1}{6}$ in. Empty glumes nearly equal, thin. Flowering glume thick, smooth, hard, shining . 25. *Milium.*
- Spikelets minute. Glumes thin. Empty glumes unequal. Flowering glume acute. Grain free from the glumes; pericarp loose . . . . . 29. *Sporobolus.*
- Spikelets minute. Flowering glume shorter than the empty glume, thin, glabrous, tip truncate, minutely jagged . . . . 30. *Agrostis.*[2]

Tribe VI. **Aveneæ.** Spikelets $\frac{1}{2}$–1 in., in panicles, narrow, terete, 2–5-flowered. Flowering glume long-awned.

- Flowering glume 2–4-lobed at the tip, awned on the back. Grain adherent to the pale . . . . . 34. *Avena.*
- Flowering glume produced in 2 long points, awned in the cleft. Grain free . . . . 35. *Danthonia.*

Tribe VII. **Chlorideæ.** Spikelets small or minute, sessile in 2 rows along one side of the usually digitately arranged spikes.

- Spike solitary. Spikelets 3–10-flowered. Empty glumes very unequal. Flowering glume toothed and awned at the tip . . . . 36. *Tripogon.*
- Spikes 2–5 in a cluster. Spikelets 1-flowered, not awned. Empty glumes nearly equal . . . . 37. *Cynodon.*
- Spikes 4–7 in a cluster. Spikelets 3–6-flowered, not awned. Empty glumes unequal . . . . . 38. *Eleusine.*

Tribe VIII. **Festuceæ.** Spikelets in spreading or contracted panicles, rarely in spikes, 3- to many-flowered or sometimes only 2-flowered in *Koeleria* and in *Eragrostis interrupta,* stalked or rarely sessile. Rhachilla usually jointed below each fertile flowering glume, often prolonged, tip naked or bearing 1–3 rudimentary glumes.

[1] Species 1 and 2. [2] Species 3 and 4.

Stems 6-10 ft., erect. Leaves 1–2 ft., flat, broad. Spikelets $\frac{1}{4}$–$\frac{3}{4}$ in., hairy, 3–8-flowered, forming large, dense, erect, shining, silky panicles.

Rhachilla glabrous. Lowest flower 2-sexual. Empty glumes as long as the spikelet, nearly equal. Flowering glume covered on the lower half with long hairs, tip 2-lobed, shortly awned . . . . . . 39. *Arundo.*

Rhachilla densely hairy. Lowest flower male. Empty glumes shorter than the spikelet, very unequal. Flowering glume of fertile flowers narrowed into a long point . . . . 40. *Phragmites.*

Empty glumes much shorter than the lowest flowering glume, very unequal. Flowering glume bearded at the base, fringed, tip bifid, shortly awned. Lowest flower 2 sexual . . . . 41. *Neyraudia.*

Stems 1–4 ft. Spikelets glabrous or nearly so, in panicles or spicate in *Brachypodium* and *Erugrostis nardoides.*

Spikelets awned.

Spikelets $\frac{1}{4}$ in.. 3–5-flowered, flattened, in one-sided, ovoid clusters. Flowering glume rigid, 5-nerved, shortly awned. Ovary glabrous . . . . 45. *Dactylis.*

Spikelets $\frac{1}{3}$–$\frac{3}{4}$ in., 3–8-flowered. Flowering glume ending in an awn, tip not notched. Ovary glabrous or slightly hairy on the top . . . . . 48. *Festuca.*[1]

Spikelets $\frac{1}{2}$–$1\frac{1}{2}$ in., 7–14-flowered. Tip of flowering glume notched, awned. Ovary densely hairy on the top . . . . 49. *Bromus.*

Spikelets $\frac{3}{4}$–2 in., 6–18-flowered. Tip of flowering glume narrowed nto a slender awn. Ovary densely hairy on the top . . . . 50. *Brachypodium.*

Spikelets awnless.

Flowering glume 3-nerved.

Spikelets minute or rarely $\frac{1}{2}$ in., several- or many-flowered. Rhachilla not prolonged . . . 43. *Eragrostis.*

Flowering glume more than 3-nerved.

Spikelets $\frac{1}{6}$–$\frac{1}{4}$ in., 2–4-flowered, crowded. Rhachilla prolonged, tip naked. Flowering glume 5-nerved at the base. Ovary glabrous . . . . 42. *Koeleria.*

Spikelets $\frac{1}{4}$–$\frac{1}{2}$ in., 3–5-flowered. Rhachilla-tip bearing two or three rudimentary glumes. Flowering glume acute, 7-9-nerved. Ovary glabrous . . . . 44. *Melica.*

Spikelets $\frac{1}{7}$–$\frac{1}{4}$ in., 2–7-flowered. Rhachilla prolonged, tip naked. Flowering glume acute, usually hairy near the base. Ovary glabrous . 46. *Poa.*

Spikelets $\frac{1}{4}$ in., usually 4-flowered. Rhachilla prolonged, tip naked. Flowering glume blunt, 7-nerved. Ovary glabrous . . . . . 47. *Glyceria.*

Spikelets $\frac{1}{2}$ in., 3–4-flowered. Flowering glume acute, 5–7-nerved. Ovary hairy on the top . 48. *Festuca.*[2]

TRIBE IX. **Hordeæ.** Spikelets three- to many-flowered, flattened; solitary, sessile in notch-like grooves and alternate on the rhachis of a simple spike.

Spikelets $\frac{1}{3}$–$\frac{1}{2}$ in., placed edgewise to the rhachis. Empty glume only one, except in the terminal spikelet. Ovary glabrous . . . . 51. *Lolium.*

[1] Except *F. modesta.* [2] *F. modesta* only.

Spikelets $\frac{1}{3}$–1 in., placed broadside to the rhachis.
  Empty glumes 2. Ovary hairy on the top . . . 52. *Agropyron.*

TRIBE X. **Bambuseæ.** Shrub-like or arborescent. Stem-joints furnished with caducous sheaths. Leaves flat, the blade abruptly narrowed into a very short stalk.

Spikelets spineless, 2- to many-flowered, in short
  racemes. Stamens 3 . . . . 53. *Arundinaria.*
Spikelets spinous, 2–3-flowered, crowded in globose
  clusters. Stamens 6 . . . . 54. *Dendrocalamus.*

SERIES A. PANICACEÆ.

TRIBE I. Paniceæ.

1. **PASPALUM.** From *paspalos*, one of the Greek names of Millet.—All warm regions.

Annual or perennial; stems erect or ascending. Leaves usually glabrous except the mouth of the sheath. Ligule short, truncate or jagged. Spikelets unequally stalked, in clusters of 2–4 on straight spikes digitately spreading from near the top of the stem or distributed at intervals along the rhachis, $\frac{1}{8}$ in. or less, 1-flowered or with a second rudimentary flower, flattened, jointed below the empty glumes. Glumes normally 4, often only 3; lowest minute or wanting; second distinct, membranous, empty; third membranous, usually empty, sometimes containing a rudimentary flower; fourth thick, smooth, containing a 2-sexual, fertile flower. Pale nearly as long as the fourth glume. Stamens 3. Styles 2, free nearly to the base. Grain free within the hardened glume and pale.

Spikelets $\frac{1}{10}$–$\frac{1}{8}$ in.
  Margin of rhachis minutely toothed . . . . . 1. *P. sanguinale.*
  Margin of rhachis entire . . . . 2. *P. ambiguum.*
Spikelets less than $\frac{1}{12}$ in.
  Stalks of spikelets smooth . . . . 3. *P. longiflorum.*
  Stalks of spikelets rough . . . . 4. *P. Royleanum.*

1. **Paspalum sanguinale**, *Lamk.*; *Fl. Br. Ind.* vii. 13. Stems 6 in. to 3 ft., erect or ascending from a decumbent, branched base, often rooting at the joints. Leaves 1–12 × $\frac{1}{6}$–$\frac{1}{3}$ in., flat, glabrous or the sheath hairy. Spikes usually 4–8, sometimes more, 3–6 in., margins minutely toothed. Spikelets $\frac{1}{10}$–$\frac{1}{8}$ in. Lowest glume minute; second about half the length of the third and fourth, which are nearly equal. (Fig. 185.)

Simla.—Throughout India, ascending the Himalaya to 6000 ft.—All warm countries.

Panicum sanguinale and *Digitaria sanguinalis* are synonyms.

In the *Fl. Br. Ind.* this species is divided into nine varieties, of which the following four occur or may be expected to occur at Simla:—

Var. 1. **cruciatum.** Spikes 2–3 in. Spikelets glabrous, purple. Flowering glume suddenly narrowed at the tip into a short point.—Simla and below Kotgurh.

Var. 2. **commutatum.** Spikes 3–6 in. Second and third glumes glabrous or pubescent or shortly fringed. Flowering glume tapering into a point.—Simla, very common.

*Var. 3. **ciliare.** Spikes 3–6 in. Second and third glumes fringed with long hairs.—Common in the plains, ascending to 6000 ft.

FIG. 185. PASPALUM SANGUINALE.

*Var. 4. **Rottleri.** Stems 4–10 in., much-branched from the tufted, prostrate or creeping base. Spikes 2–5, rarely more than 1–3 in. Second and third glumes pubescent or shortly fringed.—Common in the plains, ascending to 6000 ft.—An introduced weed of cultivation in S. England.

2. **Paspalum ambiguum,** *DC.*; *Fl. Br. Ind.* vii. 17. Stems 6–12 in., diffusely spreading or ascending from a decumbent base.

Leaves 1–2 in., glabrous except the mouth of the sheath. Spikes 2–6, 1–2 in. long, margins entire. Spikelets $\frac{1}{10}$ in., minutely hairy. Lowest glume often absent; second acute, as long as the two upper ones.

Simla.—W. Himalaya, 5000–10,000 ft.—N. Asia, Europe, including Britain. *Panicum glabrum* and *Digitaria humifusa* are synonyms.

*3. **Paspalum longiflorum,** *Retz*; *Fl. Br. Ind.* vii. 17. Stems 6–18 in., tufted, more or less procumbent and rooting at the joints. Leaves usually $\frac{1}{2}$–2 in., glabrous except the mouth of the sheath. Spikes 2–5, very slender, 1–4 in., silvery white. Spikelets less than $\frac{1}{12}$ in., glabrous or minutely hairy; stalks smooth. Lowest glume absent; second nearly as long as the two upper ones.

Throughout India, ascending to 6000 ft.—Tropical and subtropical regions of the Old World.

4. **Paspalum Royleanum,** *Nees*; *Fl. Br. Ind.* vii. 18. Stems 12–18 in., tufted, erect. Leaves 2–6 in., erect, glabrous except the mouth of the sheath. Spikes 2–5, very slender, 1–4 in., silvery white. Spikelets less than $\frac{1}{12}$ in., densely and minutely hairy; stalks rough with minute points. Lowest glume absent; second nearly as long as the two upper ones.

Simla.—Hilly districts throughout India, ascending to 7000 ft.

2. **ISACHNE.** From the Greek *isos*, equal, and *achne*, a glume, referring to the equal glumes.—Tropical and subtropical regions.

Perennial; stems erect or ascending. Leaves flat, rough, narrowly lanceolate; sheaths hairy along the margins. Ligule a fringe of hairs. Spikelets numerous, globose, glabrous or minutely pubescent, $\frac{1}{20}$ in., 2-flowered, stalked, not jointed at the base, scattered along the very slender branches of a loose, spreading panicle. Glumes 4, nearly equal, hemispheric; second empty; third sessile, containing a male, female or 2-sexual flower; fourth minutely stalked, jointed at the base, containing a 2-sexual flower. Stamens 3. Styles 2, free nearly to the base. Grain free within the hardened glume and pale.

Leaves $\frac{1}{4}$–$\frac{3}{4}$ in. broad. Panicle 6–14 in. . . . . . . 1. *I. albens*.
Leaves $\frac{1}{6}$–$\frac{1}{3}$ in. broad. Panicle 2–4 in. . . . . . . 2. *I. himalaica*.

1. **Isachne albens,** *Trin.*; *Fl. Br. Ind.* vii. 22. Stems 1–4 ft., erect, often branched. Leaves 2–12 × $\frac{1}{4}$–$\frac{3}{4}$ in. Spikelets pale green or nearly white. Panicle 6–14 in.

Simla.—Occasional in the plains and ascending to 6000 ft.—China, Malaya.

*2. **Isachne himalaica,** *Hook. f.*; *Fl. Br. Ind.* vii. 23. Stems 1–2 ft., often ascending from a decumbent base. Leaves 2–12 × $\frac{1}{6}$–$\frac{1}{3}$ in. Spikelets green or pale purple. Panicle 2–4 in.

Occasional in the plains, ascending to 6000 ft. and usually growing in wet places.—Temperate and subtropical Himalaya.

3. PANICUM. The classical name.—A vast genus represented in all warm countries, but most abundant in the Tropics; it includes most of the cultivated Millets.

Annual or perennial; stems erect or more or less decumbent, sometimes rooting at the lower joints. Leaves flat; sheaths hairy at the mouth and often along the margins. Ligule none or a ring of hairs. Spikelets ovoid, $\frac{1}{10}$–$\frac{1}{8}$ in., 2-flowered, stalked or sessile, jointed below the empty glumes, more or less crowded on straight spikes distributed along the rhachis or combined in a panicle. Glumes 4; 2 lower membranous, empty, lowest small but always obvious, the next longer; third membranous, nearly equal to the fourth, containing a male or a rudimentary flower; fourth of firmer texture containing a 2-sexual, fertile flower. Stamens 3. Styles 2, free nearly to the base. Grain free, enclosed within the shining, hardened glume and pale.

Spikelets glabrous.
Spikelets nearly or quite sessile.
Spikes alternate on the rhachis . . . . . 1. *P. flavidum.*
Spikes crowded in a panicle.
Stems 6–18 in. Annual . . . . . . 6. *P. plicatum.*
Stems 2–6 ft. Perennial . . . . . . 7. *P. rhachitrichum.*
Spikelets long-stalked . . . . 5. *P. psilopodium.*
Spikelets hairy.
Spikelets in clusters of three. Leaves long.
Spikelets awned . . . . 2. *P. Crus-galli.*
Spikelets awnless. Leaves $\frac{1}{5}$ in. broad . . . . 3. *P. colonum.*
Spikelets alternate. Leaves short, 1–2 in.. . . . 4. *P. villosum.*

*1. **Panicum flavidum,** *Retz.*; *Fl. Br. Ind.* vii. 28. Annual; stems branching from near the base, 1–2 ft., erect, leafy. Leaves glabrous except near the top of the sheath, 3–5 × $\frac{1}{6}$–$\frac{1}{4}$ in. Spikelets glabrous, sessile, crowded in 2 rows on several erect spikes $\frac{1}{2}$–1 in. long, alternate on the rhachis. Lower empty glume half the length of the upper; uppermost glume minutely dotted, abruptly pointed.

Common in watery places on the plains throughout India, ascending to 5000 ft.—Tropical Asia and Africa.

2. **Panicum Crus-galli,** *Linn.*; *Fl. Br. Ind.* vii. 30. Annual; stems 2–3 ft., ascending from a decumbent base. Leaves long, $\frac{1}{2}$–1 in. broad, glabrous or hairy. Spikelets about $\frac{1}{10}$ in., excluding the awns, minutely bristly, in clusters of 3, one nearly sessile, the other two unequally stalked, crowded on the numerous branches of a close, erect, narrow panicle; branches $\frac{1}{2}$–4 in. Lower empty glume broad, about one third the length of the shortly awned, upper one. Lower flowering glume long-awned, awns very variable in length

Common in watery places on the plains throughout India, ascending to 6000 ft.—All warm countries; occurs occasionally as a weed of cultivation in S. England.

A variety, *frumentaceum*, is cultivated under the name of *sawan* in the lower hills as a rainy season crop; in 1877 there were some fields of it below Merlin Park, Simla. The spikelets are without awns, crowded on numerous, incurved branches about 1 in. long.

*3. **Panicum colonum,** *Linn.*; *Fl. Br. Ind.* vii. 32. Annual; stems 2 ft. or more, erect or ascending. Leaves glabrous, long, ⅛ in. broad. Spikelets minutely hairy, in clusters of 3, one nearly sessile, the other two unequally stalked, crowded on the ½–1 in. long branches of an erect panicle. Lower empty glume ⅓ the length of the upper, both acute; uppermost glume hard and white in fruit.

Common in the plains throughout India, ascending to 5000 ft.; sometimes cultivated.—All warm countries.

The typical forms of *P. Crus-galli* and *P. colonum* are connected by intermediates and the variety *frumentaceum* has been referred to both species. Some botanists regard *P. colonum* as a variety of *P. Crus-galli.*

4. **Panicum villosum,** *Lamk.*; *Fl. Br. Ind.* vii. 34. Annual; stems hairy, 6–18 in., ascending. Leaves hairy, 1–2 in. long, up to ¾ in. broad, base stem-clasping. Spikelets hairy, nearly sessile, closely alternate on the several erect branches, often 1 in. long, of a narrow panicle. Lower empty glume about one third the length of the upper, both pointed; uppermost glume abruptly narrowed at the lip into an acute point.

Simla, near Kairi, 6500 ft.—Tropical and subtropical Himalaya, 3000–6000 ft.—China.

5. **Panicum psilopodium,** *Trin.*; *Fl. Br. Ind.* vii. 46. Annual; stems many, erect, 2-3 ft. Leaves glabrous, 4–12 × ⅕–⅓ in., tapering to a fine point. Ligule a ring of hairs. Spikelets glabrous, in pairs or alternate, with long, unequal stalks on the numerous, very slender, rough branches of a narrow, erect panicle; branches drooping in fruit. Lower empty glume broad, one third the length of the upper, shortly pointed; uppermost glume white, shining.

Simla.—Common in the plains, ascends to 6000 ft.—Tropical Asia.

A variety, *coloratum*, having a violet or purple tinged panicle is the form usually seen in the hills.

6. **Panicum plicatum,** *Lamk.*; *Fl. Br. Ind.* vii. 55. Perennial; stems 2–6 ft., erect or ascending from a woody, branched stock. Leaves hairy, narrowly lanceolate, 6–12 × ½–1 in., tapering to a long, fine point, flat but more or less corrugated between the prominent nerves; mouth of sheath fringed. Spikelets glabrous, nearly sessile, alternate on the short branches of a narrow, erect or drooping panicle 6–12 in. long; branches often tinged with purple and usually ending in a stiff bristle. Empty glumes much

shorter than the flowering; lower one obtuse; uppermost one and the pale hard, minutely wrinkled. (Fig. 186.)

Simla.—Hilly districts throughout India, ascending to 7000 ft.—China, Malay Islands.

The Simla form is typical *P. excurrens*, Trin.

FIG. 186. PANICUM PLICATUM.

*7. **Panicum rhachitrichum**, *Hochst.*; *Fl. Br. Ind.* vii. 56. Annual; stems tufted, 6–18 in., erect, leafy. Leaves hairy, lanceolate, pointed, 6–8 × 1–1¼ in., more or less longitudinally folded, nerves prominent; mouth of sheath fringed. Spikelets glabrous, nearly sessile, alternate, often with a short bristle near the base on the branches of an erect, narrow or spreading panicle 2–6 in. long; branches hairy, ending in a long, stiff, awn-like bristle. Lower empty glume broad, rounded, one fourth the length of the upper; uppermost glume hard, minutely wrinkled in fruit.

Throughout N. India, ascending to 6000 ft.—Tropical Africa.

4. OPLISMENUS. From the Greek *oplismenos*, armed, referring to the awns of the empty glumes.—Tropical and subtropical regions.

Annual, hairy; stems leafy, usually slender, weak and ascending, often rooting at the lower joints. Leaves thin, flat, lanceolate, tapering to a fine point. Ligule a line of hairs. Spikelets narrowly ovoid, nearly sessile, jointed at the base, about $\frac{1}{7}$ in. excluding the awns, 1-flowered, solitary or in pairs or small clusters arranged in a single spike or on several short, spike-like branches distributed along the rhachis. Empty glumes 3, nearly equal, green, membranous; the lowest fringed, long-awned; second the shortest, with a shorter awn or sometimes acute; uppermost longest, with a still shorter awn or acute, occasionally enclosing a narrow pale; awns variable in length but in paired spikelets the awns of the upper spikelet are always longer than those of the lower one. Flowering glume 1, awnless, acute, white, of firmer texture than the empty glumes; flower 2-sexual. Stamens 3. Styles 2, free to the base. Grain free within the hardened glume and pale.

Spikelets in a single, unbranched spike . . . . 1. *O. undulatifolius*.
Spikelets on several short branches distributed along the rhachis . . . . 2. *O. compositus*.

1. **Oplismenus undulatifolius,** *Beauv.*; *Fl. Br. Ind.* vii. 66. Stems 1–2 ft. Leaves 2–6 × $\frac{1}{2}$–$\frac{3}{4}$ in. Spikelets in pairs or clusters or occasionally solitary in a single, unbranched, often interrupted spike. (Fig. 187.)

Simla, common.—Temperate Himalaya, 6000–9000 ft.—Most warm regions.

2. **Oplismenus compositus,** *Beauv.*; *Fl. Br. Ind.* vii. 66. Stems 1–3 ft. Leaves 2–6 × $\frac{1}{2}$–1 in. Spikelets in pairs or clusters or occasionally solitary on few or many spike-like branches $\frac{1}{2}$–3 in. long distributed along the rhachis.

Simla, common.—Throughout India, ascending to 8000 ft.—Most tropical regions except Australia.

5. ARUNDINELLA. Diminutive of the Latin *arundo*, a reed.—Tropical and subtropical regions.

Perennial, with a creeping, woody rootstock; stems tufted, tall, erect, leafy. Leaves narrowly lanceolate, long-pointed, margins often inrolled; sheaths fringed with long hairs at the mouth and along the edges. Ligule none. Spikelets numerous, ovoid, $\frac{1}{4}$ in. or less excluding the awn, 2-flowered, not jointed at the base, in pairs or small clusters, rarely solitary, on the branches of an erect panicle; stalks unequal. Glumes membranous. Empty glumes 2, unequal, long-pointed, awnless; lower smaller; upper the longest in the spikelet. Flowering glumes 2, the lower nearly as long as the upper empty one, oblong, blunt, containing a male or a rudimentary flower ; upper glume the shortest in the spikelet, lanceolate, awned, containing a 2-sexual, fertile flower.

FIG. 187. OPLISMENUS UNDULATIFOLIUS.

Stamens 3. Styles 2, free to the base. Grain free within the hardened glume and pale.

Awn long, bent in the middle, protruding.
  Flowering glume 3-awned . . . . . . 1. *A. setosa.*
  Flowering glume 1-awned . . . . . . 2. *A. brasiliensis.*
Awn short, straight, barely protruding . . . . 3. *A. Wallichii.*

1. **Arundinella setosa,** *Trin.*; *Fl. Br. Ind.* vii. 70. Hairy; stems slender, 1–3 ft. Leaves 6–10 in. Spikelets narrowly ovoid, $\frac{1}{4}$ in. excluding the awn, usually in pairs. Panicle narrow, 2–6 in.; branches slender, erect. Empty glumes hairy, tinged with purple. Flowering glumes glabrous, the fertile one 3-awned; central awn as long as the spikelet, protruding, bent in the middle and twisted in the lower half; lateral awns very short, bristle-like.

Simla.—Throughout India, ascending to 8000 ft.—China, Philippines.

2. **Arundinella brasiliensis,** *Raddi*; *Fl. Br. Ind.* vii. 73. Glabrous or nearly so; stems 1–5 ft. Leaves 6–12 in. Spikelets nearly glabrous, purple-tipped, narrowly ovoid, $\frac{1}{7}$ in. excluding the awns, usually in pairs. Panicle narrow, 4–12 in.; branches slender, rough, erect. Lower empty glume minutely bristly along the keel, with 3 prominent nerves. Flowering glume with a basal tuft of silky hairs, terminating in a single awn as long as the spikelet bent at the middle and twisted in the lower half.

Simla.—Hilly districts throughout India.—China, Australia, S. Africa, S. Europe, tropical America.

3. **Arundinella Wallichii,** *Nees*; *Fl. Br. Ind.* vii. 75. Usually hairy, but sometimes nearly glabrous; stems 1–3 ft. Leaves 12–18 in. Spikelets hairy, tinged with pink at the base, ovoid, $\frac{1}{10}$ in. excluding the awn, usually in crowded clusters. Panicle narrow, contracted, 6–12 in.; branches rough, $\frac{1}{2}$–1 in., stiffly erect. Empty glumes bristly. Flowering glume tipped with a very short, straight, barely protruding awn.

Simla, on dry banks.—E. Himalaya, 1000–6000 ft., Bengal plains.—China. I have seen no specimen, but it is recorded from Simla in the *Fl. Br. Ind.*

6. SETARIA. From the Latin *seta*, a bristle, referring to the bristly involucre surrounding the flowers.—Most temperate and tropical regions.

Annual; stems erect. Leaves flat, lanceolate, long-pointed. Ligule a fringe of hairs. Spikelets numerous, glabrous, usually 1-flowered, ovoid, about $\frac{1}{10}$ in., jointed on very short stalks bearing an involucre of long, minutely barbed bristles, in spike-like or close, cylindric, tapering panicles. Empty glumes usually 3, membranous; lowest small; second and third nearly equal; uppermost sometimes containing a male or rudimentary flower. Flowering glume 1, of a firmer texture and smaller than the uppermost empty glume, deeply concave, containing a 2-sexual flower. Stamens 3. Styles 2, long, free to the base. Grain free, enclosed within the hardened glume and pale.

Spikelets in a narrow, spike-like panicle.
  Fruiting glume wrinkled . . . . 2. *S. glauca.*
  Fruiting glume smooth . . . . 5. *S. viridis.*

Spikelets in a looser, cylindric panicle.
Barbs of the bristles pointing upwards.
Panicle cylindric, very dense. Fruiting glume smooth . . . 1. *S. italica.*
Panicle tapering, interrupted. Fruiting glume wrinkled . . . 3. *S. intermedia.*
Barbs of the bristles pointing downwards . . . . 4. *S. verticillata.*

1. **Setaria italica,** *Beauv.*; *Fl. Br. Ind.* vii. 78. Stems tufted, smooth, 2–5 ft., sometimes decumbent near the base and rooting at the lower joints. Leaves $1\frac{1}{2}$–2 ft. by about 1 in., rough; sheaths softly hairy. Spikelets on branches about 1 in. long, crowded in a compact, nearly cylindrical, interrupted, nodding panicle 4–10 in. long and $\frac{1}{2}$–1 in. diam. Bristles variable in length. Fruiting glume smooth.

Simla, below Merlin Park, Sutlej valley.—Cultivated throughout India, and up to 6000 ft.—Most warm and temperate regions.

Italian millet; native name *kâkun*. One of the most ancient of cultivated plants, having been found in the Swiss lake-dwellings of the Stone Age. Stunted forms often occur in a wild state.

2. **Setaria glauca,** *Beauv.*; *Fl. Br. Ind.* vii. 78. Stems 1–3 ft. Leaves about 1 ft. by $\frac{1}{3}$ in., usually pale green, glabrous or with a few scattered hairs, margins rough. Spikelets nearly sessile, crowded in dense, spike-like panicles 1–6 in. long and about $\frac{1}{4}$ in. diam. excluding the bristles. Bristles unequal, from twice to four times as long as the spikelet, pale brown or tinged with purple. Fruiting glume coarsely wrinkled.

Simla.—Throughout India, especially in cultivated ground, ascending to 6000 ft.—Most warm and temperate regions.

3. **Setaria intermedia,** *Roem. & Schult.*; *Fl. Br. Ind.* vii. 79. Stems 1–3 ft. Leaves hairy, about $12 \times \frac{1}{3}$ in. Spikelets crowded on the short branches of a narrow, interrupted, tapering panicle 1–6 in. long and $\frac{1}{4}$–$\frac{3}{4}$ in. diam. Barbs of bristles pointing upwards. Fruiting glume finely wrinkled.

Below Kotgurh.—Throughout India, ascending to 4000 ft., but not common.—Temperate and tropical regions.

*4. **Setaria verticillata,** *Beauv.*; *Fl. Br. Ind.* vii. 80. Stems, leaves and inflorescence of *S. intermedia*, but the barbs of the bristles point downwards.

Throughout India, in shady places, ascending to 6000 ft., not very common. —Temperate and tropical regions.

*5. **Setaria viridis,** *Beauv.*; *Fl. Br. Ind.* vii. 80. Stems, leaves and inflorescence of *S. glauca*, but the fruiting glume is smooth and the bristles green or tinged with red.

Throughout India, ascending to 11,000 ft., rare in the plains.—Temperate and subtropical regions, but colonised in many countries.

7. PENNISETUM. From the Latin *penna*, a feather, and *seta*, a bristle, referring to the nature of the involucre surrounding the flowers.—All warm countries.

Perennial; rootstock creeping, often thick; stems tufted, leafy, erect or ascending. Leaves flat, narrowly lanceolate or linear. Ligule a fringe of hairs. Spikelets numerous, crowded in

FIG. 188. PENNISETUM FLACCIDUM.

a dense, spike-like raceme, glabrous or roughly pubescent, usually 1-flowered, ovoid, about $\frac{1}{4}$ in.; stalks jointed to the rhachis at their base and bearing near the top an involucre of long, rough bristles, simple or branched, naked or fringed with silky hairs and usually tinged with purple. Empty glumes 3, membranous; lowest small; second shorter than the uppermost, obtuse or acute; uppermost acute or needle-tipped, sometimes containing a male or a rudimentary flower. Flowering glume of firmer texture, acute or needle-tipped, slightly longer than the uppermost empty glume, containing a 2-sexual flower. Stamens 3. Styles 2, long, united near the base, fringe long. Grain free within the more or less hardened, persistent glumes.

Bajra or spiked millet, *P. typhoideum*, is cultivated throughout India and up to about 3000 ft. in the outer hills. It has compact, cylindric spikes 6–9 in. long and about 1 in. diam.; inner bristles of the involucre fringed.

Involucral bristles branched . . . . 1. *P. lanatum.*
Involucral bristles unbranched.
Spikelets only one on a stalk. Bristles not fringed . . 2. *P. flaccidum.*
Spikelets 1–5 on a stalk. Bristles fringed . . . . . 3. *P. orientale.*

*1. **Pennisetum lanatum,** *Klotzsch*; *Fl. Br. Ind.* vii. 84. Stems 1–3 ft. Leaves 6–18 × $\frac{1}{6}$–$\frac{1}{2}$ in., densely hairy. Spikes 2–5 in., by $\frac{1}{2}$–$\frac{2}{3}$ in. diam. Spikelets only one on a stalk. Bristles branched, fringed, hardly longer than the spikelets. Uppermost empty glume and flowering glumes acute, but not needle-tipped.

W. Himalaya, 7000–9000 ft.

2. **Pennisetum flaccidum,** *Griseb.*; *Fl. Br. Ind.* vii. 84. Stems 6–24 in., decumbent and creeping near the base. Leaves 5–10 × $\frac{1}{6}$–$\frac{1}{4}$ in., glabrous or thinly hairy. Spikes 2–6 in. Spikelets one on a stalk. Bristles not branched, naked, except sometimes near the base, much longer than the spikelets. Uppermost empty glume and flowering glumes needle-tipped. (Fig. 188.)

Simla.—Temperate Himalaya, 5000–11,000 ft.

3. **Pennisetum orientale,** *Rich.*; *Fl. Br. Ind.* vii. 86. Stems 2–6 ft., erect or decumbent at the base. Leaves 1–2 ft. × $\frac{1}{6}$–$\frac{1}{2}$ in. Spikes 6–12 in. Spikelets usually 2–5 on a stalk, occasionally only one; outer spikelets often containing only a male flower. Bristles not branched, fringed, inner ones much longer than the spikelets. Uppermost empty glume and the flowering glumes needle-tipped.

Simla.—W. Himalaya, 3000–7000 ft.—Westward through Asia Minor to North Africa.

Tribe II. Zoysieæ.

8. **PEROTIS.** From the Greek *peros*, maimed, deficient, referring to the minute, awnless flowering glume.—Asia, Africa.

***Perotis latifolia,** *Ait.*; *Fl. Br. Ind.* vii. 98. Annual; stems leafy, 6–18 in., ascending. Leaves usually hairy, cordate, lanceolate, $\frac{1}{2}$–1 in., minutely toothed. Ligule a fringe of hairs. Spikelets numerous, shortly stalked, tinged with purple, very narrow, about $\frac{1}{10}$ in. excluding the awns, 1-flowered, crowded in a slender raceme 1–8 in. long, falling off with their stalks, not jointed below the glumes. Empty glumes 2, nearly equal, very narrow, rigid, pubescent, tapering into long, straight awns; awn of the lower glume the longer. Flowering glume minute, glabrous, membranous, containing a 2-sexual flower. Stamens 3. Styles 2, short, united at the base. Grain linear, much longer than its glume, free within the outer glumes. (Fig. 189.)

Throughout India, ascending to 8000 ft., common on barren, sandy soil.—Tropical Asia and Africa.

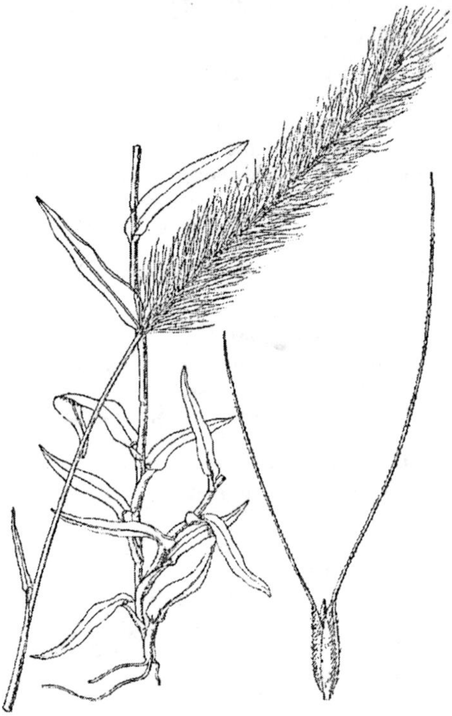

FIG. 189. PEROTIS LATIFOLIA.

TRIBE III. **Andropogoneæ.**

9. MISCANTHUS. From the Greek *mischos*, a stalk, and *anthos*, a flower, referring probably to the stalked spikelets.—Asia, Pacific Islands.

Miscanthus nepalensis, *Hack.*; *Fl. Br. Ind.* vii. 107. Perennial; stems erect, 3–6 ft. Leaves 6–18 × $\frac{1}{3}$–$\frac{1}{2}$ in. Ligule rounded. Spikelets similar, narrowly ovoid, $\frac{1}{10}$ in. excluding the awn, 1-flowered, partially enveloped in a tuft of long, silky, shining, golden-yellow hairs springing from its base, in pairs, unequally stalked, on very many slender, spike-like, unjointed branches 3–7 in. long and spreading fan-wise from near the top of the stems. Empty glumes 3; two lower nearly equal, red-brown, concave; uppermost flat, thin, white. Flowering glume 1, rather smaller than the uppermost empty glume, membranous, deeply notched, with a long, slender awn in the cleft. Stamens 3. Styles 2, free. Grain linear-oblong, free, enclosed within the glumes.

Daha, Giri valley.—Temperate Himalaya, 5000–8000 ft.—Khasia and Naga hills.

10. SPODIOPOGON. From the Greek *spodios*, ash-coloured, and *pogon*, a beard, referring to the grey, hairy spikelets of some species.—Temperate Asia.

Perennial; stems erect, tall, robust, leafy, solid. Leaves flat, long, finely pointed, narrowed into a stalk-like base. Ligule a fringe of hairs. Spikelets numerous, borne at the tips of the otherwise naked, jointed branches of a panicle, occasionally with a pair of spikelets inserted laterally, 1-flowered, narrowly ovoid, about $\frac{1}{5}$ in., in clusters of three; 1 sessile, containing a male flower; 2 stalked, each containing a 2-sexual flower. Empty glumes 3; 2 lower nearly equal, stiff, concave, 7–9-nerved; uppermost rather smaller, transparent, sometimes containing a minute pale. Flowering glume 1, transparent, deeply notched, with a long awn in the notch. Stamens 3. Styles 2, free, fringed about half way down. Grain free, enclosed within the glumes.

Panicle oblong, dense; branches short. Spikelets silky hairy . 1. *S. dubius.*
Panicle pyramidal; branches long, spreading. Spikelets bristly with a tuft of hairs at the base . . . . 2. *S. cotulifer.*

1. **Spodiopogon dubius,** *Hack.*; *Fl. Br. Ind.* vii. 108. Stems 2–4 ft. Leaves 12–18 × $\frac{1}{4}$–$\frac{1}{3}$ in., densely hairy. Panicle narrowly oblong, 6–18 in., pale silvery brown; branches short, nearly erect, densely crowded. Spikelets and stalks silky hairy. Two outer glumes pale brown; awn as long as the spikelet.

Simla, one of the commonest grasses on sunny hill-sides at high levels.—Temperate Himalaya, 6000–8000 ft.

*2. **Spodiopogon cotulifer,** *Hack.*; *Fl. Br. Ind.* vii. 108. Stems 3–8 ft. or more. Leaves 2–3 ft. by $\frac{1}{2}$–$\frac{2}{3}$ in., thinly hairy. Panicle pyramidal, 6–12 in.; branches long, very slender, whorled, spreading. Spikelets minutely bristly, with a tuft of hairs at the base; stalks glabrous, dilated upwards into a cup-like expansion. The 3 empty glumes very shortly awned. Awn of the flowering glume twice as long as the spikelet.

Kashmir to Garhwal, 4000–6000 ft.—China, Japan.

11. POLLINIA. Named after Ciro Pollini, an Italian physician and professor of botany, author of 'Elementi di Botanica' and other works, who died in 1833.—Tropical and subtropical regions of the Old World.

Annual or perennial; stems erect or decumbent near the base. Leaves narrow, long-pointed. Ligule very short, fringed. Spikelets 1-flowered, similar, in pairs, one sessile, the other stalked, each more or less enveloped in a basal tuft of hairs, narrowly ovoid, about $\frac{1}{8}$ in., on 2–10 simple, jointed, spike-like branches spreading from near the top of the stems. Empty glumes 3; uppermost smaller, thin, transparent, sometimes wanting; 2 lower nearly equal, coloured; lowest membranous, hairy or glabrous, stiff, tip usually truncate; second rather thinner, acute. Flowering glume much the smallest, sometimes reduced to a mere rudiment, transparent, tip bifid, with an awn in the cleft usually long and slender, sometimes hairy, often bent near the middle, the base more or less twisted. Stamens usually 3, rarely 2. Styles 2, long, distinct, the upper portion fringed. Grain narrowly oblong, free within the outer glumes.

Stems erect. Spikes distinctly hairy.
- Stems 2–3 ft., robust. Spikes 3–8 in. Hairs red-brown or tinged with violet . . . . 1. *P. quadrinervis.*
- Stems 1–2 ft., slender. Spikes 1–3 in. Hairs white or silvery.
  - Perennial. Hairs silvery, longer than the spikelets, almost concealing them . . . . 2. *P. mollis.*
  - Annual. Hairs white, much shorter than the spikelets, only fringing them . . . . 3. *P. fimbriata.*

Stems decumbent and much-branched near the base. Spikes nearly glabrous.
- Stamens 3. Stalks of spikelets minutely fringed . . 4. *P. imberbis.*
- Stamens 2. Stalks of spikelets glabrous . . . . 5. *P. nuda.*

1. **Pollinia quadrinervis,** *Hack.*; *Fl. Br. Ind.* vii. 110. Stems 2–3 ft., erect, robust, leafy. Leaves 8–18 in., narrow, finely pointed, hairy on both surfaces or nearly glabrous. Spikes 3–8 in each cluster, densely hairy, rather thick, 2–8 in.; hairs red-brown, sometimes tinged with violet. Spikelets pale yellow-brown. Empty glumes 3. Awn rather thick, three or four times as long as the spikelet. Stamens 3.

Simla.—Subtropical Himalaya, 3000–5000 ft.—China.

This includes *P. hirtifolia, Hack.*; *Fl. Br. Ind.* vii. 111. Huegel's specimen, recorded from Simla, on which this species was founded, is not available for examination. The two specimens named *hirtifolia* in Kew Herbarium cannot be distinguished from *quadrinervis.*

2. **Pollinia mollis,** *Hack.*; *Fl. Br. Ind.* vii. 111. Perennial; stems 10–12 in., erect, slender, leafy chiefly at the base. Leaves 2–3 in., narrowly lanceolate, nearly glabrous. Spikes 3–10 in each cluster, slender, 1–2 in.; hairs silvery, silky, much longer than the pale brown spikelets and so dense as almost to conceal them. Empty glumes 3. Awn slender, three or four times as long as the spikelet. Stamens 3.

Simla.—Temperate Himalaya, 5000–8000 ft.

3. **Pollinia fimbriata,** *Hack.*; *Fl. Br. Ind.* vii. 112. Annual; stems erect, slender, 1–2 ft., leafy, shining. Leaves 6–10 in., very narrow, glabrous or thinly hairy. Spikes 2–4 in each cluster, hairy, slender, 1–3 in.; hairs white, much shorter than the light, yellow-brown spikelets and only fringing them. Empty glumes 3.

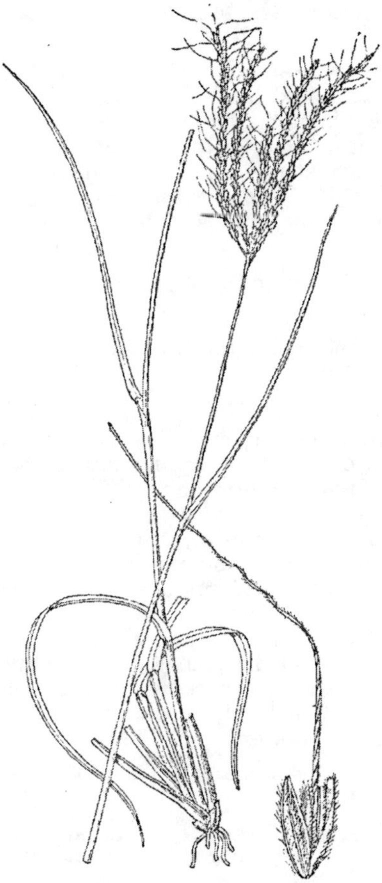

FIG. 190. POLLINIA FIMBRIATA.

Awn slender, three or four times as long as the spikelet, hairy towards the base. Stamens 3. (Fig. 190.)

Simla, Mahasu.—W. Himalaya.—Burmah.

4. **Pollinia imberbis,** *Nees*; *Fl. Br. Ind.* vii. 117. Stems 2–4 ft., slender, decumbent and much branched near the base. Leaves lanceolate, about $3 \times \frac{1}{3}$ in., narrowed to a stalk-like base, flaccid,

hairy or nearly glabrous, mid-rib prominent. Spikes 2–6 in each cluster, nearly glabrous, slender, 1–3 in. Spikelets pale green; nerves minutely bristly; stalks fringed. Empty glumes 2, the uppermost wanting. Awn slender, usually shorter than the spikelet. Stamens 3.

Simla.—Temperate Himalaya, 4000–7000 ft.—China, Japan.

5. **Pollinia nuda,** *Trin.*; *Fl. Br. Ind.* vii. 117. Stems 2–3 ft., very slender, decumbent and much branched near the base. Leaves lanceolate, about $3 \times \frac{1}{8}$ in., glabrous or nearly so, narrowed into a stalk-like base, finely pointed. Spikes 2–8 in each cluster, nearly glabrous, very slender, 1–4 in. Spikelets pale green, glabrous except the basal tuft; stalks glabrous. Empty glumes 3 or 2, the uppermost being sometimes absent. Awn hair-like, short or long. Stamens 2.

Simla, the Glen.—Temperate Himalaya, 4000–7000 ft.—China, S. Africa.

12. SACCHARUM. From the Latin *saccharum*, sugar.—Tropical regions, chiefly in Asia.

Saccharum spontaneum, *Linn.*; *Fl. Br. Ind.* vii. 118. Perennial; stems 5–15 ft., erect, densely silky just below the panicle. Leaves erect, very long and narrow; margins smooth or rough; mouth of sheath woolly. Ligule short, hairy. Spikelets very numerous, awnless, narrowly ovoid, $\frac{1}{7}$ in., 1-flowered, in pairs or threes at the end of branches, dissimilar, one sessile, 2-sexual, the other stalked, female, both fertile and enveloped in a basal tuft of long, white, silky hairs, arranged along the straight, spike-like, whorled branches of a narrow, dense, erect, silky panicle 1–2 ft. long. Empty glumes 3; two lower nearly equal, concave, pointed; uppermost rather smaller, flat, lanceolate, transparent. Flowering glume 1, smaller; the others transparent, sometimes wanting. Stamens 3. Styles 2, distinct, purple-fringed. Grain oblong, free within the persistent glumes.

Simla.—Throughout India, ascending to 6000 ft.—S. Europe and warm regions of the Old World.

Native name *Kans.*

The sugar-cane, *S. officinarum*, is occasionally cultivated in the lower valleys, but it rarely, if ever, produces seed and is propagated by cuttings or layers. Native name *Ukh.*

13. ERIANTHUS. From the Greek *erion*, wool, and *anthos*, a flower, in allusion to the hairy spikelets.—Temperate and tropical regions.

Perennial; stems erect, usually tall. Leaves long, narrow. Ligule short, hairy. Spikelets small, very numerous, awned, narrowly ovoid, 1-flowered, borne on the hairy branches of a dense, silky panicle, in pairs or in threes at the end of branches, similar, one sessile, the other stalked, each containing a 2-sexual, fertile flower and more or less enveloped in a basal tuft of silky hairs. Empty glumes 3; two lower nearly equal, concave, pointed, opaque towards the base; uppermost flat, lanceolate, transparent. Flowering glume 1, smaller than the others, transparent, awned. Stamens 3. Styles 2, distinct, purple-fringed. Grain oblong, free within the persistent glumes.

Basal hairs three or four times as long as the spikelet . . 2. *E. fulvus.*
Basal hairs only slightly longer than the spikelet, sometimes shorter.
Panicle 1–3 ft. Awn less than twice as long as the spikelet . . . . 1. *E. Ravennæ.*
Panicle 6–8 in. Awn three to five times as long as the spikelet . . . . 3. *E. filifolius.*

*1. **Erianthus Ravennæ,** *Beauv.*; *Fl. Br. Ind.* vii. 121. Stems 6–10 ft., glabrous. Leaves 2–3 ft., by 1–1½ in., rough, hairy near the base. Panicle 1–3 ft., grey-white or purple. Spikelets about ¼ in.; basal hairs hardly longer, sometimes shorter. Awn very slender, usually less than twice as long as the spikelet.

Kashmir to Kumaon, 6000–9000 ft.—Plains of N. India.—W. Asia, S. Europe.

2. **Erianthus fulvus,** *Nees*; *Fl. Br. Ind.* vii. 123. Stems 6–8 ft., silky hairy just below the panicle. Leaves 2–3 ft., by ¼–1 in., slightly rough; margins of sheath hairy. Panicle 8–18 in., grey-white or tinged with purple. Spikelets about $\frac{1}{10}$ in.; basal hairs three or four times as long, white, dense, concealing the spikelets. Awn about four times as long as the spikelet.

Simla.—Temperate Himalaya, 5000–7000 ft.

3. **Erianthus filifolius,** *Nees*; *Fl. Br. Ind.* vii. 123. Stems 2–3 ft., downy just below the panicle. Leaves 8–12 in., very narrow, tip hair-like; sheath glabrous. Panicle 6–8 in., red-purple. Spikelets about ⅕ in.; basal hairs hardly longer, sometimes shorter. Awn three to five times as long as the spikelet.

Simla.—Temperate Himalaya, 5000–8000 ft.

14. ISCHÆMUM. From the Greek *ischo*, to hinder, stop, and *haima*, blood, perhaps referring to its reputed styptic qualities.—Chiefly tropical regions.

Annual or perennial; stems erect. Leaves long, usually narrow. Spikelets arranged on one to several, simple, jointed, spike-like branches erect or spreading from near the top of the stem, awned, each with a tuft of short hairs at its base, narrowly ovoid, ⅙–⅓ in., 2-flowered, in pairs, one sessile, the other stalked, similar and fertile or both flowers of the stalked spikelet sometimes male. Empty glumes 2, nearly equal, opaque at least towards the base; upper sometimes shortly awned. Flowering glumes 2; in both spikelets the lower transparent and containing a male flower; upper very narrow, awned and containing a 2-sexual flower or sometimes awnless in the stalked spikelet and containing a male flower. Stamens 3. Styles 2, long, distinct, purple-fringed. Grain oblong, free within the persistent glumes.

Spikelets hairy. Spikes 2–4 in a cluster . . . . . 1. *I. angustifolium.*
Spikelets glabrous.
  Spike solitary . . . . 2. *I. notatum.*
  Spikes 8–20 in a cluster . . . . 3. *I. petiolare.*

*1. **Ischæmum angustifolium,** *Hack.*; *Fl. Br. Ind.* vii. 129. Stems 2–3 ft., woolly at the base. Leaves 1–2 ft., very narrow, rigid, sharply pointed. Ligule a line of hairs. Spikes 1–2 in., in clusters of 2–4. Spikelets $\frac{1}{6}$ in., in pairs, similar, the base of the outer glumes thickly covered with long, golden or brown hairs. Upper empty glume shortly awned. Awn of the fertile glume twice or thrice as long as the spikelet.

Lower Himalaya, from Kashmir to Sikkim, ascending to 7000 ft. in Garhwal. —Throughout India.—China.

This is the *Bhabar* grass, often confounded with *Eriophorum comosum*, used for thatching, the manufacture of coarse string and for paper-making.

*2. **Ischæmum notatum,** *Hack.*; *Fl. Br. Ind.* vii. 138. Stems 2–5 ft. Leaves 6–12 in., very narrow, rigid, rough; sheath hairy near the top. Ligule a line of long hairs. Spike solitary, 3–8 in., erect, shortly fringed at the joints and on the stalks of the spikelets. Spikelets $\frac{1}{3}$ in., glabrous; nerves of outer glumes rough. Upper flowering glume of the sessile spikelet having an awn $\frac{3}{4}$–1 in.; that of the stalked spikelet awnless and often containing a male flower.

W. Himalaya, from Chamba to Kumaon, 4000–7000 ft.

*3. **Ischæmum petiolare,** *Hack.*; *Fl. Br. Ind.* vii. 138. Stems 2–3 ft. Leaves 8–12 × $\frac{3}{4}$–$1\frac{1}{4}$ in., narrowed into a hair-like tip; margins rough. Ligule stiff, oblong, truncate. Spikes 8–20 in a cluster, crowded, more or less digitately spreading, $\frac{1}{2}$–$1\frac{1}{2}$ in., shortly fringed at the joints and on the stalks of the spikelets. Spikelets $\frac{1}{5}$ in., glabrous. Upper flowering glume of the sessile spikelet deeply bifid, shortly awned; that of the stalked spikelet awnless and often containing a male flower.

Garhwal to Nepal, 5000–8000 ft.—Hilly districts throughout India.—Burmah.

15. **POGONATHERUM.** From the Greek *pogon*, a beard, and *ather*, an awn, referring to the awned spikelets.—India, China, Japan.

Pogonatherum saccharoideum, *Beauv.*; *Fl. Br. Ind.* vii. 141. Stems tufted, 6–18 in., slender, erect. Leaves very narrow, 1–3 in. Ligule short, truncate, fringed with long, soft hairs. Spikelets awned, about $\frac{1}{10}$ in., in pairs, one sessile, 2-flowered, the other stalked, 1-flowered, both fertile or the stalked spikelet barren, imbricate on the fragile, hairy, jointed rhachis of a solitary, terminal, slender spike $\frac{1}{2}$–1 in. long. Glumes all thin and transparent; empty glumes 2, tip of the lower fringed, obtuse; upper one longer, tip notched, long-awned; flowering glumes in the sessile spikelet 2, the lower containing a male flower, the upper a 2-sexual flower, tip bifid, long-awned; flowering glume in the stalked spikelet 1, containing a female flower or empty, tip bifid, long-awned. Stamens 2, rarely 1. Styles long, distinct, fringed. Grain minute, free within the persistent glumes.

Simla.—Hilly districts throughout India, ascending to 8000 ft.—China.

16. ARTHRAXON. From the Greek *arthron*, a joint, and *axon*, an axis, referring to the jointed rhachis.—Tropical regions of the Old World.

Annual or perennial; stems usually tufted, slender, weak, decumbent and branched near the base, seldom erect. Leaves cordate, lanceolate or ovate, flat, hairy, fringed. Ligule short, hairy. Spikelets awned, except in *A. submuticus*, small, solitary but usually accompanied by the stalk of a second abortive spikelet often bearing rudimentary glumes, 1-flowered, sessile along 2 or more simple, jointed, spike-like branches clustered near the top of the stem. Empty glumes usually 3; lowest opaque, acute, nerves minutely spinous or rough; second nearly equalling it, keeled, long-pointed, margins transparent; uppermost minute, transparent, sometimes wanting. Flowering glume 1, shorter than the empty glumes, transparent, containing a 2-sexual flower, usually long-awned from near the base.

Stamens 3; anthers more than half the length of the flowering glume.
- Awn far-projecting . . . . 1. *A. lanceolatus.*
- Awn included or wanting . . . . 2. *A. submuticus.*

Stamens 2, rarely 3; anthers less than half the length of the flowering glume.
- Spikelets $\frac{1}{8}$–$\frac{1}{5}$ in. Stalks glabrous below the spikes . 3. *A. ciliaris.*
- Spikelets $\frac{1}{10}$–$\frac{1}{8}$ in. Stalks hairy below the spikes . . 4. *A. microphyllus.*

1. Arthraxon lanceolatus, *Hochst.*; *Fl. Br. Ind.* vii. 143. Stems 1–3 ft., ascending or half-climbing. Leaves $2–3 \times \frac{1}{4}–\frac{1}{2}$ in. minutely toothed or fringed with stiff hairs. Spikes few or many, $\frac{1}{2}$–2 in.; rhachis and joints hairy. Spikelets $\frac{1}{3}$ in., with the stalk of a second usually bearing rudimentary glumes. Lowest empty glume narrowly oblong, its marginal nerves fringed with curved, prickly teeth. Awn about 1 in. Stamens 3; anthers about three quarters the length of the flowering glume.

Simla, the Glen.—N. India, ascending to 8000 ft.—China, Africa.

***2. Arthraxon submuticus,** *Hochst.*; *Fl. Br. Ind.* vii. 144. Stems 6–12 in., rarely more. Leaves broadly ovate, $\frac{1}{2}$–$1\frac{1}{2}$ in., fringed with stiff hairs, finely pointed. Spikes 3–5, $\frac{1}{2}$–1 in.;

rhachis and joints glabrous. Spikelets $\frac{1}{8}$ in., solitary, without the stalk of a second. Stamens 3; anthers nearly as long as the flowering glume. Awn minute, included, sometimes wanting.

W. Himalaya, 2000–6000 ft.—China.

A specimen from Bussahar in the Kew Herbarium has a stem 3 ft. long, bearing several spikes in the axils of the upper leaves in addition to the terminal spike.

3. **Arthraxon ciliaris,** *Beauv.*; *Fl. Br. Ind.* vii. 145. Stems 6–12 in., glabrous throughout. Leaves ovate or lanceolate, about 1 in.; margins and sheaths fringed. Spikes 2 or 3, rarely more, $\frac{1}{2}$–$\frac{3}{4}$ in., usually tinged with purple; rhachis glabrous or nearly so, joints minutely fringed. Spikelets $\frac{1}{5}$ in., with the stalk of a second rarely bearing rudimentary glumes. Nerves of the lowest empty glume minutely prickly. Stamens 2, rarely 3; anthers less than half the length of the flowering glume.

Simla.—Hilly districts throughout India, ascending to 5500 ft.

The Simla plant is var. *muriculatus* of the *Fl. Br. Ind.*, very closely allied to *A. microphyllus*.

4. **Arthraxon microphyllus,** *Hochst.*; *Fl. Br. Ind.* vii. 147. Stems 6–12 in., hairy just below the inflorescence. Leaves oblong-lanceolate, about 1 in., acute. Spikes 2–8, often tinged with purple, $\frac{1}{2}$–$\frac{3}{4}$ in.; rhachis and joints hairy. Spikelets $\frac{1}{10}$ in., with the stalk of a second spikelet usually bearing rudimentary glumes. Nerves of the lowest empty glume rough but not prickly. Stamens 2, rarely 3; anthers less than half the length of the flowering glume.

Simla.—Temperate Himalaya, 4000–5000 ft.—Burmah, China, Africa.

17. **APLUDA.** A name used by Pliny for a small, slender grass.—Tropical Asia, Pacific Islands.

Apluda aristata, *Hack.*; *Fl. Br. Ind.* vii. 150, *under A. varia.* Perennial; stems solid, leafy, branched, 1–5 ft., decumbent near the base, bent at the joints. Leaves flat, rough, narrow, 4–18 in., finely pointed, the sheaths of those on the panicle dilated, spathe-like, the blade being often much reduced. Ligule short, rounded. Spikelets in numerous, short, sheathed spikes terminal on the branches of a long, leafy panicle and containing 3 spikelets, one sessile, the second rudimentary, the third stalked. Each spike about $\frac{1}{3}$ in., enclosed within a rather shorter, narrowly ovoid, pointed bract and borne on the dilated extremity of a slender, glabrous stalk. Sessile spikelet 2-flowered, about $\frac{1}{5}$ in.; glumes nearly equal, transparent; empty glumes 2, the lower oblong-lanceolate, obtuse, the upper dilated, tip bifid; flowering glumes 2, the lower containing a male flower, the upper the shortest, deeply bifid, long-awned, containing a 2-sexual flower. Rudimentary spikelet consisting of a single, nearly sessile, oblong-lanceolate glume. Stalked spikelet 1-flowered; stalk flattened; empty glumes

2, nearly equal; flowering glume smaller, awnless, containing a male flower. Stamens 3. Styles 2, long, distinct, fringed. Grain oblong, free within the hardened, persistent, outer glumes.

Simla, Mahasu.—Common throughout India, ascending to 7000 ft.

This species constitutes a large portion of the undergrowth on forest lands. In hedges and bushes it often assumes a climbing habit.

18. ROTTBOELLIA. In honour of G. F. Rottboell, a Danish botanist and author, who died in 1797.—Temperate and tropical regions.

Annual or perennial; stems erect, usually tall and robust, leafy, filled with pith. Leaves flat, roughly hairy, narrowly lanceolate, finely pointed, margins minutely prickly. Ligule very short, fringed. Spikelets awnless, in pairs, one sessile, the other stalked, appressed against or partially sunk in the rhachis of several, rarely only one, cylindric, jointed spikes digitately spreading from near the top of the stems. Spikes readily breaking up into joints which are flattened or excavated on one side for the reception of the spikelets. Sessile spikelet: empty glumes 2, hard and stiff; flowering glumes 2, thin, transparent, the lower containing a male, the upper a 2-sexual flower. Stalked spikelet rather smaller, 2-flowered or sometimes containing only a male or a rudimentary flower; stalk flattened. Stamens 3. Styles long, free, fringed. Grain oblong, free within the persistent glumes.

Joints of spike flattened on one side, shorter than the spikelets 1. *R. speciosa.*
Joints of spike excavated on one side, longer than the spikelets 2. *R. exaltata.*

1. **Rottboellia speciosa,** *Hack.*; *Fl. Br. Ind.* vii. 152. Perennial; stems 1–4 ft. Leaves 6–12 × $\frac{1}{4}$–$\frac{1}{2}$ in. Spikes 2–8 in a cluster, rarely solitary, 3–7 in., pale green or tinged with purple; joints flattened on one side, shorter than the spikelets. Sessile spikelet $\frac{1}{4}$ in. Both spikelets usually 2-flowered.

Simla.—W. Himalaya, 5000–9000 ft.

*2. **Rottboellia exaltata,** *Linn. f.*; *Fl. Br. Ind.* vii. 156. Annual; stems 4–10 ft. Leaves 6–24 × $\frac{1}{4}$–1 in. Spikes 2–4 in a cluster, sometimes only one, terete, narrowed upwards, 3–6 in., pale green; joints excavated on one side, rather longer than the spikelets. Sessile spikelet $\frac{1}{5}$ in. Stalked spikelet rarely 2-flowered, often containing only a male or a rudimentary flower.

Throughout India, ascending to 7000 ft. in Garhwal.—China, Australia, Africa.

19. ANDROPOGON. From the Greek *aner*, *andros*, a man, and *pogon*, a beard, referring to the hairy spikes.—Chiefly tropical regions.

Usually perennial; rootstock often aromatic; stems tufted, often tall, erect or decumbent near the base. Leaves flat, long, usually narrow, tapering to a fine point, edges often rough. Ligule short, hairy. Spikelets awned, 1-flowered, all in pairs, one sessile, the other stalked; or all in threes, one sessile, two stalked; or the terminal spikelets of a spike are in threes and the others in pairs. Spikes in pairs or in clusters near the top of the stems or distributed along the branches of a spreading panicle, usually bearing many spikelets, sometimes few, rarely only three. In some species the lower spikelets in a spike contain only male or rudimentary flowers. Sessile spikelets: empty glumes 3, the lowest usually with prominent, marginal keels, the next nearly as long, the uppermost smaller, thin; flowering glume 1, narrow, thin, tip bifid, awned, sometimes reduced to the awn alone, containing a female or 2-sexual flower. Stalked spikelets: empty glumes 2 or 3; flowering glume 1, awnless, containing a male or a rudimentary flower; stalk short, usually hairy. Stamens 3. Styles 2, distinct, fringed. Grain free within the hardened, persistent glumes.

It was the author's intention to rewrite this genus and restore *Heteropogon*, *Chrysopogon*, *Sorghum*, etc. to generic rank, on the lines of Bentham and Hooker's *Genera Plantarum*; but indisposition prevented it from being carried out. The classification is Hackel's, which is also adopted in the *Flora of British India*.

Spikes in a digitate, terminal or axillary cluster.
  Flowering glume of sessile spikelet membranous, bifid . . . 1. *A. tristis*.
  Flowering glume of sessile spikelet reduced to an awn.
    Lower empty glume of sessile spikelet acute . . . 2. *A. Ischæmum*.
    Lower empty glume of sessile spikelet obtuse . . . 8. *A. annulatus*.
Spikes long-stalked, umbellately clustered in a leaf-axil, rarely solitary . . . . 9. *A. contortus*.
Spikes in pairs, terminal on a slender stalk, sheathed in a spathe-like bract.
  Spikes woolly with long, white hairs . . . . . 10. *A. Iwarancusa*.
  Spikes thinly and shortly hairy.
    Spikes $\frac{1}{4}$–$\frac{1}{2}$ in. Bracts numerous, red-brown.
      Leaves $\frac{1}{2}$–$\frac{3}{4}$ in. broad; base stem-clasping . . 11. *A. Schœnanthus*.
      Leaves less than $\frac{1}{3}$ in. broad; base not stem-clasping 12. *A. Nardus*.
    Spikes $\frac{1}{2}$–$1\frac{1}{2}$ in. Bracts solitary or few.
      Spikes 1–$1\frac{1}{2}$ in. Lowest empty glume flat-backed 13. *A. distans*.
      Spikes $\frac{1}{2}$–1 in. Lowest empty glume concave on back . . . . 14. *A. Gidarba*.
Spikes on the branches of a panicle, not sheathed.
  Spikelets in pairs
    Spikes of many pairs of spikelets. Lower empty glume of sessile spikelet pitted on the back . . 3. *A. intermedius*.
    Spikes of few, rarely more than 3 pairs of spikelets.
      Leaves less than $\frac{1}{4}$ in. broad. Spikelets $\frac{1}{10}$ in., with a basal tuft of hairs . . . . . . 4. *A. micranthus*.[1]
      Leaves $\frac{1}{4}$–$1\frac{1}{2}$ in. broad. Spikelets $\frac{1}{5}$ in., naked at the base . . . . 5. *A. halepensis*.[1]
  Spikelets in threes.
    Sessile spikelets $\frac{1}{4}$ in. Keels of the lower empty glume minutely prickly-toothed . . . . . 6. *A. Gryllus*.
    Sessile spikelets $\frac{1}{10}$ in. Keels of the lower empty glume smooth . . . . 7. *A. monticola*.

[1] A few of the spikes are occasionally reduced to a single group of 3 spikelets.

1. **Andropogon tristis,** *Nees*; *Fl. Br. Ind.* vii. 169. Stems 2–3 ft., erect, branching. Leaves very narrow, 6–12 in., slightly hairy or glabrous. Spikelets in pairs, loosely imbricate on 2–6 unequal, minutely hairy spikes 1–3 in. long and forming a digitate cluster at the end of an axillary stalk often partially enclosed in the dilated leaf-sheath. Sessile spikelet $\frac{1}{4}$ in.; flowering glume membranous, narrow, bifid; awn about twice the length of the spikelet.

Simla.—W. Himalaya, 5000–10,000 ft.

2. **Andropogon Ischæmum,** *Linn.*; *Fl. Br. Ind.* vii. 171. Stems 2–3 ft., erect, usually simple. Leaves mostly basal, 1–6 × $\frac{1}{8}$ in., hairy. Spikelets in pairs, on 3–20 unequal spikes 1$\frac{1}{2}$–3 in. long and forming a digitate cluster at the top of the stem; stalk and rhachis of spikelets covered with long, white, silky hairs. Sessile spikelet $\frac{1}{5}$ in., nearly glabrous; lower empty glume acute; flowering glume reduced to a naked awn three or four times the length of the rest of the spikelet.

Simla.—N.W. India, ascending the Himalaya to 12,000 ft.

3. **Andropogon intermedius,** *R. Br.*; *Fl. Br. Ind.* vii. 175. Stems 3–5 ft., erect. Leaves narrow, 6–12 in., more or less hairy. Spikelets pale green or tinged with purple, in numerous pairs, on spikes about 1–2 in. long and arranged on the very slender, glabrous, whorled, spreading branches of a terminal panicle 3–6 in. long. Sessile spikelet $\frac{1}{7}$ in.; lower empty glume hairy, pitted on the back; flowering glume reduced to an awn $\frac{3}{4}$–1$\frac{1}{2}$ in. long.

Simla.—Throughout India, ascending to 8000 ft.
The Simla plant is the variety *punctatus* of the *Fl. Br. Ind.* vii. 176.

4. **Andropogon micranthus,** *Kunth*; *Fl. Br. Ind.* vii. 178. Stems 2–3 ft., erect. Leaves 4–12 in., less than $\frac{1}{4}$ in. broad, roughly hairy. Spikelets $\frac{1}{10}$ in., with a basal tuft of short, spreading, white hairs, in spikes containing only 2 or 3 pairs arranged on the very slender, glabrous, whorled, spreading branches of a terminal panicle 3–8 in. long. Awn of sessile spikelet $\frac{1}{3}$–$\frac{2}{3}$ in.

Simla.—Hilly districts throughout India, 4000–6000 ft.—Australia, S. Africa.
The Simla plant is the variety *villosulus*, Hack.

A. assimilis, *Steud.*; *Fl. Br. Ind.* vii. 179 may perhaps occur below 5000 ft.; it can only be distinguished from the above by its taller, thicker, much-branched stems creeping at the base.

*5. **Andropogon halepensis,** *Brot.*; *Fl. Br. Ind.* vii. 182. Stems many, 3–12 ft., erect. Leaves 6–18 × $\frac{1}{4}$–1$\frac{1}{2}$ in. or more, smooth except the rough edges. Spikelets $\frac{1}{5}$ in., without a basal tuft of hairs, in spikes containing only 1–3 pairs, rarely 5–7 pairs, sometimes only 3 spikelets and arranged on the very slender, whorled, spreading or drooping branches of a terminal panicle 6–24 in. long, the branches hairy at the joints and axils. Sessile spikelet : lower empty glume hairy ; flowering glume minute, awn twice to four times the length of the rest of the spikelet or sometimes wanting.

Common throughout India, ascending to 5000 ft.
The wild form of the cultivated Juar, *A. Sorghum*.

FIG. 191. ANDROPOGON GRYLLUS.

6. **Andropogon Gryllus,** *Linn.* ; *Fl. Br. Ind.* vii. 187. Stems 1–5 ft., simple, erect, forming dense, hard tufts. Leaves 6–18 in., very narrow, usually hairy, edges minutely spinous-toothed ; sheaths hairy. Spikelets in threes, on 2–4 (rarely only one) spikes

each containing only 3 spikelets and clustered on the dilated, hairy tips of the very slender, whorled, spreading branches of a terminal panicle 4–8 in. long, Sessile spikelet $\frac{1}{4}$ in.; keels of the lower empty glume minutely prickly-toothed; flowering glume containing a 2-sexual flower, tip toothed, awn nearly $\frac{3}{4}$ in. Stalked spikelets each containing a male or a rudimentary flower; stalks glabrous or nearly so. (Fig. 191.)

Simla, Jako, common.—W. Himalaya, 4000–8000 ft.—S. Europe, N. Africa, Australia.

The Simla plant is the variety *echinulatus*, Hack. of the *Fl. Br. Ind.* vii. 188.

7. **Andropogon monticola,** *Schult.*; *Fl. Br. Ind.* vii. 192. Stems 1–3 ft., slender, erect or decumbent at the base. Leaves 6–18 in., very narrow. Spikelets in threes, on solitary, rarely geminate spikes each containing only 3 spikelets and borne on the dilated, hairy tips of the very slender, whorled, spreading branches of a terminal panicle 2–6 in. long. Sessile spikelet $\frac{1}{10}$ in.; keels of the lower empty glume smooth; flowering glume containing a 2-sexual flower, tip toothed, awn about $\frac{1}{2}$ in. Stalked spikelets each containing a male or a rudimentary flower; stalks hairy.

Simla, Annandale.—Hilly districts throughout India, ascending to 6000 ft. —W. Asia, S. Africa.

8. **Andropogon annulatus,** *Forsk.*; *Fl. Br. Ind.* vii. 196. Stems $\frac{1}{2}$–3 ft., branching, often half-climbing, bent at the lower joints, then ascending. Leaves mostly basal, 6–12 in., narrow, rigid, upper surface hairy. Spikelets in pairs, on 5–8 unequal spikes 1–2$\frac{1}{2}$ in. long and forming a digitate cluster at the top of the stem; rhachis and spikelet-stalks hairy. Sessile spikelet $\frac{1}{8}$–$\frac{1}{5}$ in.; lower empty glume hairy, truncate or obtuse; flowering glume reduced to a simple awn $\frac{1}{2}$–1 in. long. Stalked spikelet hairy.

Simla.—Throughout India, ascending to 6000 ft.—China, tropical Africa, Australia.

9. **Andropogon contortus,** *Linn.*; *Fl. Br. Ind.* vii. 199. Stems densely tufted, 1–2 ft., erect or decumbent near the base. Leaves 6–18 in., narrow, rigid, acute, upper surface thinly hairy. Spikelets in pairs, crowded on 3–4 (rarely only 1) spikes, excluding the awns, 1–2 in. long and forming an umbellate cluster in the axil of an upper leaf. On the lower part of the spikes the sessile spikelets are without awns and contain only a male flower; on the upper part they are long-awned and contain a 2-sexual, fertile flower. The stalked spikelets all contain a male or a rudimentary flower. Sessile lower spikelets male, $\frac{1}{3}$–$\frac{1}{2}$ in.; lower empty glume lanceolate, many-nerved, studded with long, bulbous-based bristles, margins transparent. Sessile upper spikelets fertile, $\frac{1}{4}$ in.; lower empty glume thick, cylindric, minutely pubescent, the base prolonged downwards in a hard, sharp, slightly curved point bearded with stiff,

brown hairs pointing upwards; the point at first attached to the similar point of the next lower spikelet from which it separates when the grain ripens. Flowering glume reduced to a bent, hairy awn $1\frac{1}{2}$–3 in. long and attenuated towards the base. In the upper fertile portion of the spike the rhachis is undeveloped and when the grain is ripe the twisting of the awns, caused by varying hygroscopic conditions, pulls away the narrow, cylindric fruits and this part of the spike breaks up leaving only the lower male portion on the stem.

Simla.—Throughout India, ascending to 5000 ft.—Mediterranean region and the Tropics generally (Common Spear-grass).

The grain of this grass, having sharp points, barbs of stiff hairs and long awns, is curiously adapted to obtain a firm hold when it falls on the ground, and its power of adhering to and penetrating one's clothes needs no description. The Burmese name for the Spear-grass is Monkey's Tail, which is very appropriate in the young state.

*10. **Andropogon Iwarancusa,** *Jones*; *Fl. Br. Ind.* vii. 203. Rootstock aromatic; stems smooth, 1–3 ft., sometimes more. Leaves glabrous, 6–12 in., very narrow. Spikelets in 3–6 pairs, on spikes $\frac{1}{4}$–$\frac{3}{4}$ in. long and paired at the end of a slender stalk sheathed in a pointed, spathe-like bract $\frac{1}{2}$–$\frac{3}{4}$ in., the spikes arranged on the smooth branches of a narrow, erect panicle 6–12 in.; joints of the spikes and the spikelet-stalks woolly, the long, white hairs nearly concealing the sessile spikelets. Sessile spikelet $\frac{1}{5}$ in., lowest one or two usually containing only a male or a rudimentary flower; second or intermediate empty glume boat-shaped; flowering glume narrow, bifid, awn nearly twice the length of the spikelet. Stalked spikelets tinged with purple.

Throughout N. India, ascending to 5000 ft.—W. Asia, N. Africa.

The roots of this grass are often used to make tatties or screens. The true *khaskhas*, *A. squarrosus*, does not grow in the hills.

11. **Andropogon Schœnanthus,** *Linn.*; *Fl. Br. Ind.* vii. 204. Rootstock aromatic; stems smooth, 3–6 ft., erect. Leaves glabrous, long, $\frac{1}{2}$–$\frac{3}{4}$ in. broad, cordate, stem-clasping; sheaths loose. Spikelets in 3–6 pairs on spikes $\frac{1}{4}$–$\frac{1}{2}$ in. long and paired at the end of a slender stalk sheathed in a pointed, spathe-like bract $\frac{1}{2}$–$\frac{2}{3}$ in., the spikes crowded on the smooth branches of a narrow, erect panicle 6–24 in.; joints of the spikes and the spikelet-stalks fringed with short, white hairs; bracts and glumes tinged with red-brown. Sessile spikelets $\frac{1}{7}$ in., nearly glabrous, lowest one or two usually containing only a male or a rudimentary flower; second or intermediate empty glume boat-shaped; flowering glume narrow, bifid, awn rather thick, usually more than thrice the length of the spikelet.

Simla.—Throughout India, ascending to 5000 ft.—W. Asia, Tropical Africa.

*12. **Andropogon Nardus,** *Linn.*; *Fl. Br. Ind.* vii. 205. Characters of *A. Schœnanthus* except that the leaves are less than

$\frac{1}{3}$ in. broad with a straight, not cordate and stem-clasping base. The panicle rarely exceeds 18 in., and the sessile spikelets are $\frac{1}{6}$–$\frac{1}{5}$ in.

Throughout India, ascending to 3000 ft.—Tropical Asia, Africa, Australia.

FIG. 192. ANDROPOGON DISTANS.

13. **Andropogon distans,** *Nees*; *Fl. Br. Ind.* vii. 207. Rootstock aromatic; stems glabrous, 1–5 ft., erect; branches few or none. Leaves mostly basal, glabrous, 6–12 in., very narrow. Spikelets in 4–8 pairs on spikes 1–1$\frac{1}{2}$ in. long and paired at the end of a slender stalk sheathed in a pointed, spathe-like bract $\frac{3}{4}$–1$\frac{3}{4}$ in., the spikes deflexed and solitary, rarely in a

cluster of 2 or 3 on the few and distant branches of a narrow, erect panicle; joints of the spikes and the spikelet-stalks fringed with short, white hairs. Sessile spikelets $\frac{1}{4}$ in., pubescent, lowest one or two usually containing only a male or a rudimentary flower; lowest empty glume flat-backed, strongly 2-keeled, 2-pointed; second or intermediate empty glume boat-shaped; flowering glume narrow, bifid, awn two or three times the length of the spikelet. (Fig. 192.)

Simla, common.—W. Himalaya, 4000–9000 ft.

14. **Andropogon Gidarba,** *Buch.-Ham.*; *Fl. Br. Ind.* vii. 208. Characters of *A. distans* except that the leaves are broader and the branches of the panicle closer, each bearing 2 or several sheathing bracts with their enclosed spikes. Spikes $\frac{1}{2}$–1 in. Sessile spikelets about $\frac{1}{7}$ in.; lowest empty glume having a deep impression on the lower half of the back.

Simla.—W. Himalaya, 7000–8000 ft.

20. **ANTHISTIRIA.** Supposed to be from the Greek *anthistemi*, to withstand or oppose, referring to the stiff, tough stems.—Warm regions of the Old World, and especially characteristic in Australian grass vegetation.

Perennial; stems leafy, erect, 1–4 ft. Leaves long, narrow, flat. Ligule short, oblong. Spikelets 7 or 9 in a spike, 1-flowered, the lower 4 or 6 in pairs, three terminal; spikes in clusters of 2–8, each spike and each cluster more or less sheathed in a spathe-like, long-pointed bract, the clusters disposed on the branches of a panicle; only 1 or 2, sometimes 3 spikelets in a spike fertile. Fertile spikelets: empty glumes 3, the lowest prolonged downwards in a hard, curved tip, the second or intermediate nearly equal, the upper much smaller, membranous; flowering glume narrow, membranous, awned or awnless, containing a 2-sexual flower. Stamens 3. Styles distinct, fringed. Grain free within the hardened, persistent glumes. Barren spikelets: empty glumes 2; flowering glume 1, containing a male or a rudimentary flower or wanting.

Spikes usually bearing 7 spikelets. Rhachis hairy. Fertile spikelet 1, awned . . . . 1. *A. imberbis.*
Spikes usually bearing 9 spikelets. Rhachis glabrous. Fertile spikelets 2 or 3, awnless . . . . 2. *A. anathera.*

1. **Anthistiria imberbis,** *Retz.*; *Fl. Br. Ind.* vii. 211. Stems 2–3 ft. Leaves 3–12 in. Clusters of flower-spikes fan-shaped; sheathing-bract $1\frac{1}{2}$–$3\frac{1}{2}$ in. Spikes 2–6 in a cluster, crowded; rhachis very short, densely hairy; sheathing-bract $\frac{3}{4}$–1 in. Spikelets usually 7 in a spike, thinly hairy; the 4 lower $\frac{1}{3}$ in., sessile round the base of the rhachis, barren; terminal sessile spikelet $\frac{1}{4}$ in., fertile, flowering glume long-awned; terminal stalked spikelets $\frac{1}{3}$ in., long-pointed, barren.

Simla, near the tunnel.—Throughout India, ascending to 7000 ft.—Warm regions of the Old World.

The Simla plant is the variety *Roylei* of the *Fl. Br. Ind.*

2. **Anthistiria anathera,** *Nees*; *Fl. Br. Ind.* vii. 215. Stems 1–4 ft. Leaves 3–12 in. Clusters of flower-spikes usually elongated; sheathing-bract 1–2½ in. Spikes 2–8 in a cluster, usually distant; rhachis rather long, zigzag, glabrous; sheathing-bract ½–¾ in. Spikelets usually 9 in a spike, the 6 lower in pairs, one in each pair very shortly stalked; the sessile spikelet of the upper pair, rarely both fertile; the others barren; terminal sessile spikelet fertile; terminal stalked spikelets barren. Fertile spikelets ⅕ in., lower empty glume minutely fringed, flowering glume awnless; barren spikelets ⅙ in., lower empty glume fringed with long, white hairs.

Simla, near the Sanjoli bazaar.—W. Himalaya, 4000–7000 ft.

SERIES B. POACEÆ.

TRIBE IV. Phalarideæ.

21. **PHALARIS.** From the Greek *phalaros*, white, shining, referring to the spikelets.—Temperate and tropical regions.—Some of the species widely colonised.

Phalaris minor, *Retz.*; *Fl. Br. Ind.* vii. 221. Annual; stems 6–18 in., erect or decumbent near the base. Leaves glabrous, long, flat, finely pointed. Ligule oblong, blunt. Spikelets ⅕ in., shortly stalked, flattened, shining, 1-flowered but with 1 or 2 minute scales or imperfect glumes below the flowering glume, crowded in an ovoid or cylindric, green, spike-like panicle ½–1½ × ¼–¾ in. Rhachilla jointed above the empty glumes, not prolonged. Empty glumes 2, boat-shaped, nearly equal, pointed, prominently 3-nerved, keel broadly winged; flowering glume about one third the length of the empty glumes and enclosed by them, containing a 2-sexual flower. Stamens 3. Styles 2, distinct. Grain free within the persistent glumes. (Fig. 193.)

Simla, common.—Himalaya and plains of Western India, ascending to 5000 ft.—W. Asia, S. Africa, Australia.

Allied to *P. canariensis*, Canary Grass, naturalised in Britain.

TRIBE V. Agrostideæ.

22. **ARISTIDA.** From the Latin *arista*, an awn, referring to the awned spikelets.—Most warm countries.

Annual or perennial; stems tufted, slender, erect, smooth. Leaves long, very narrow. Ligule composed of a row of hairs. Spikelets long, narrow, terete, pointed, 1-flowered, arranged in a thin, feathery, spreading panicle. Rhachilla not prolonged. Empty glumes 2, the lower the shorter. Flowering glume rigid, closely enwrapping a 2-sexual flower, the tip produced in a long, rough awn

3-branched from the base, the middle branch the longest ; base of flowering glume stalk-like, jointed above the empty glumes. Stamens 3. Styles 2, distinct, feathered. Grain cylindric, free, but closely embraced by the persistent glumes.

Panicle-branches short, erect. Awns about $\frac{3}{4}$ in. . . 1. *A. Adscenscionis.*
Panicle-branches long, drooping. Awns 2–$2\frac{1}{2}$ in. . . 2. *A. cyanantha.*

*1. **Aristida Adscensionis,** *Linn.* ; *Fl. Br. Ind.* vii. 224. Annual or perennial ; stems 1–3 ft. Panicle green or brown, 4–12 in., narrow ; branches short, erect. Spikelets $\frac{1}{3}$ in., excluding

FIG. 193. PHALARIS MINOR.

the awn. Empty glumes pointed, awnless, the upper one about as long as the flowering glume. Awn about $\frac{3}{4}$ in.

Throughout India, in dry, sandy soil, ascending to 4000 ft.—Widely dispersed in warm countries of the Old World.

*2. **Aristida cyanantha,** *Steud.* ; *Fl. Br. Ind.* vii. 225. Perennial ; stems 3–6 ft. Panicle purple, 12–18 in. ; branches very long, widely spreading, drooping. Spikelets $\frac{1}{2}$ in., excluding the awns. Empty glumes shortly awned, the upper one much longer than the flowering glume. Awn 2–$2\frac{1}{2}$ in.

W. Himalaya, 3000–5000 ft.—Low hills in the Punjab.—Afghanistan.

23. STIPA. From the Greek *stupe*, tow, referring to the long, entangled awns.—Temperate and tropical regions.

Perennial; stems tufted, smooth, 1–3 ft., erect. Leaves glabrous, long, narrow, flat. Ligule short, oblong. Spikelets green, narrow, $\frac{1}{3}$ in., terete, pointed, 1-flowered, arranged on the rough, erect branches of a long, very narrow, loose panicle. Rhachilla not prolonged. Empty glumes 2, oblong-lanceolate, glabrous, upper one slightly longer. Flowering glume nearly as long, hairy, hard, closely enwrapping a 2-sexual flower, the tip produced in a rough, pubescent, rather thick, long, simple awn. Stamens 3. Styles 2, distinct, feathery. Grain cylindric, free, but closely embraced by the persistent glumes.

Awn twice as long as the spikelet. Anther-tips bearded 1. *S. sibirica.*
Awn 4–6 times as long as the spikelet. Anther-tips naked 2. *S. Orthoraphium*

1. **Stipa sibirica,** *Lam.*; *Fl. Br. Ind.* vii. 231. Stems 2–3 ft. Leaves 1–2 ft., about $\frac{1}{4}$ in. broad. Panicle 6–12 in. Spikelets $\frac{1}{3}$ in. Flowering glume densely hairy; awn twice as long as the spikelet, lower half twisted. Anther-tips bearded.

Simla.—W. Himalaya, 7000–9000 ft.—Central Asia, eastward to Corea.

2. **Stipa Orthoraphium,** *Steud.*; *Fl. Br. Ind.* vii. 233. Stems 1–2 ft. Leaves 6–12 in., about $\frac{1}{8}$ in. broad. Panicle 6–12 in. Spikelets $\frac{1}{3}$ in. Flowering glume thinly hairy, furnished on the back just below the base of the awn with 2 or 3 pairs of straight, downward-pointing, diverging, short spines; awn four to six times as long as the spikelet, not twisted. Anther-tips naked.

Fagoo.—Temperate Himalaya, eastward to Sikkim, 7000–11,000 ft.—Naga Hills.

24. ORYZOPSIS. From the Greek *oryza*, rice, and *opsis*, appearance.—N. temperate regions.

Oryzopsis æquiglumis, *Duthie*; *Fl. Br. Ind.* vii. 234. Perennial; stems tufted, smooth, 2–4 ft., erect. Leaves smooth or the margins slightly rough 6–12 in., narrow, flat, finely pointed. Ligule long, oblong. Spikelets green or tinged with purple, about $\frac{1}{4}$ in., slightly flattened, pointed, 1-flowered, arranged on the rough, very slender, paired or whorled branches of a loose panicle 6–12 in. long; lower branches long, naked for about half their length. Rhachilla not prolonged. Empty glumes 2, persistent, thin, glabrous, nearly equal, lanceolate, long-pointed. Flowering glume about three-quarters the length of the empty glumes, red-brown, pubescent, stiff, jointed at the base, narrowed into a slender, rough awn as long as or slightly longer than the spikelet. Stamens 3, anthers tipped with a tuft of minute hairs. Styles 2, free, feathery. Grain oblong, flattened, free, but closely embraced by the hardened, persistent glumes.

Simla, Mahasu.—Temperate Himalaya, 6000–10,000 ft.

25. MILIUM. A name taken by Linnæus from classical authors, but applied by them to a kind of Millet.—N. temperate regions.

Milium effusum, *Linn.*; *Fl. Br. Ind.* vii. 235. Perennial; stems tufted, 2–4 ft., erect, smooth, shining. Leaves nearly glabrous, flat, 6–12 in., up to $\frac{1}{2}$ in. broad. Ligule oblong, truncate, torn. Spikelets green, glabrous, awnless, ovoid, $\frac{1}{6}$ in., slightly flattened, 1-flowered, arranged on the rough, slender, whorled branches of a loose panicle 6–10 in. long; branches naked towards the base, sometimes deflexed in flower. Rhachilla not prolonged. Empty glumes 2, thin, nearly equal, acute. Flowering glume nearly as long, thick, smooth, acute, hard and shining in fruit. Stamens 3. Styles 2, free, short, feathery. Grain ovoid, free, but closely embraced by the persistent glumes.

Mushobra, Mahasu, in shady places.—W. Himalaya, 7000–11,000 ft.—N. temperate and arctic regions, including Britain (Millet Grass).

26. PHLEUM. A modification of the Greek *phleos*, a name applied to different plants including *Imperata arundinacea.*—Temperate, arctic and antarctic regions.

Annual or perennial; stems erect, sometimes decumbent near the base. Leaves flat; upper sheaths loose. Ligule membranous. Spikelets green, flattened, $\frac{1}{8}$–$\frac{1}{6}$ in., 1-flowered, crowded on the very short branches of a dense, ovoid or cylindric, spike-like panicle. Rhachilla sometimes prolonged beyond the flower. Empty glumes 2, equal, boat-shaped, the keels terminating in short points. Flowering glume much shorter, transparent, tip pointed, entire. Stamens 3. Styles 2, very feathery. Grain flattened, free, loosely enclosed within the persistent glumes.

P. pratense, the common Timothy Grass of Britain, is said to occur on the Chor, but authentic specimens are wanting.

Empty glumes fringed.
- Empty glumes truncate. Panicle usually ovoid . . . 1. *P. alpinum.*
- Empty glumes tapering. Panicle cylindric . . . . 2. *P. arenarium.*

Empty glumes not fringed. Panicle cylindric, long . . 3. *P. asperum.*

1. **Phleum alpinum,** *Linn.*; *Fl. Br. Ind.* vii. 236. Perennial; stems solitary, 6–18 in. Leaves spreading, 1–6 in., up to $\frac{1}{3}$ in. broad. Panicle $\frac{1}{2}$–1 in., rarely up to 2 in., ovoid or cylindric, usually tinged with purple. Empty glumes with broad, scarious margins, truncate, keel fringed, terminating in a short, stiff point.

Huttoo.—Temperate Himalaya, 10,000–13,000 ft.—Arctic and Alpine regions, including the higher mountains of Scotland.

2. **Phleum arenarium,** *Linn.*; *Fl. Br. Ind.* vii. 237. Annual; stems tufted, 6–12 in. Leaves 1–3 in., about $\frac{1}{8}$ in. broad. Panicle

cylindric, $\frac{3}{4}$–$1\frac{1}{2}$ in. Empty glumes lanceolate, tapering into a short point, the upper part of the keel fringed with stiff hairs.

Sutlej valley, Suni.—W. Himalaya, 2000–9000 ft., in sandy soil.—The Punjab.—W. Asia, Europe (Britain).

*3. **Phleum asperum,** *Jacq.*; *Fl. Br. Ind.* vii. 237. Annual; stems tufted, 6–18 in. Leaves 2–4 in., up to $\frac{1}{4}$ in. broad. Panicle cylindric, 1–3 in. Empty glumes rough, lanceolate, rather suddenly contracted into a short, stiff point, keel not fringed.

W. Himalaya, 5000–6000 ft.—W. Asia, Europe.

27. **ALOPECURUS.** From the Greek *alopex*, a fox, and *oura*, a tail, referring to the inflorescence.—Temperate and cold regions.

***Alopecurus geniculatus,** *Linn.*; *Fl. Br. Ind.* vii. 239. Perennial; stems 6–18 in., erect or the base decumbent. Leaves 3–6 in., $\frac{1}{5}$ in. broad, flat; upper sheaths inflated. Ligule membranous, short. Spikelets pubescent, yellow-green, oblong, flattened, $\frac{1}{7}$ in., 1-flowered, crowded on the very short branches of a dense, cylindric, spike-like panicle 1–3 in. long. Rhachilla not prolonged. Empty glumes 2, boat-shaped, nearly equal, united near the base, pointed, keels fringed. Flowering glume as long, transparent, margins united near the base, tip truncate, minutely jagged, a rough, straight, shortly projecting awn inserted on the back near the base. Stamens 2 or 3. Styles 2, long, distinct, feathery. Grain ovate, flattened, loosely enclosed within the persistent glumes.

Temperate Himalaya, 3000–7000 ft.—Most temperate regions, including Britain (Fox-tail Grass).

28. **POLYPOGON.** From the Greek *polys*, many, and *pogon*, a beard, referring to the numerous awns.—Most warm and some temperate regions.

Annual or perennial; stems tufted, erect, usually decumbent near the base. Leaves flat. Ligule membranous. Spikelets flattened, less than $\frac{1}{10}$ in., 1-flowered, crowded on the very short branches of a dense, cylindric or lobed, spike-like panicle. Rhachilla not prolonged. Empty glumes 2, pubescent, oblong, equal, boat-shaped, a slender awn inserted on the back just below the tip, keels rough. Flowering glume much smaller, transparent, usually shortly awned. Stamens 1–3, anthers minute. Styles 2, short, distinct. Grain minute, free, enclosed within the persistent glumes.

Panicle cylindric or slightly lobed. Margins of empty glumes fringed; awns long . . . . 1. *P. monspeliensis.*
Panicle interrupted or conspicuously lobed. Margins of empty glumes not fringed; awns short . . . 2. *P. littoralis.*

1. **Polypogon monspeliensis,** *Desf.*; *Fl. Br. Ind.* vii. 245. Annual; stems 1–2 ft. Leaves 3–6 in., up to $\frac{1}{4}$ in. broad. Panicle pale, shining, yellow-green, usually cylindric, sometimes slightly lobed. Empty glumes: margins fringed; awns usually two to four times as long as the glumes, rarely only slightly longer.

Sutlej valley below Kotgurh, in rice-fields.—Throughout India, ascending to 9000 ft.—Tropical and temperate regions, including Britain (Beard Grass).

2. **Polypogon littoralis,** *Sm.*; *Fl. Br. Ind.* vii. 246. Usually perennial; stems $\frac{1}{2}$–$1\frac{1}{2}$ ft. Leaves 2–4 in., up to $\frac{1}{8}$ in. broad. Panicle green or tinged with purple, 1–3 in., interrupted or lobed, rarely cylindric. Empty glumes: margins pubescent, not fringed; awns usually about as long as the glumes, rarely twice as long.

Simla, Theog, below Kotgurh in rice-fields.—Temperate Himalaya, 4000–10,000 ft.—Subtropical and temperate regions, including Britain (Beard Grass).

29. SPOROBOLUS. From the Greek *spora*, a seed, and *ballo*, to cast forth, referring to the ripe grain dropping out.—Chiefly tropical regions.

Perennial, rarely annual. Leaves mostly basal, narrow, flat or the margins inrolled. Ligule reduced to a few hairs. Spikelets numerous, less than $\frac{1}{10}$ in., awnless, 1-flowered, arranged on the branches of a narrow or pyramidal panicle. Rhachilla not prolonged. Glumes all membranous. Empty glumes 2, the lower the shorter. Flowering glume acute. Stamens 2 or 3. Styles 2, short, distinct, feathery. Grain ovoid, loosely enclosed within the persistent glumes, ultimately exposed and soon dropping out, outer coat loose.

Upper empty glume much shorter than the flowering glume.
  Leaf-margins entire.
    Panicle pyramidal, 4–10 in. . . . . 1. *S. diander.*
    Panicle narrow, 6–18 in. . . . . 2. *S. indicus.*
Upper empty glume as long as the flowering glume. Leaf-margins toothed . . . . 3. *S. piliferus.*

1. **Sporobolus diander,** *Beauv.*; *Fl. Br. Ind.* vii. 247. Perennial; stems 1–3 ft. Leaves 3–10 in., glabrous; margins entire. Panicle pyramidal, 4–10 in.; branches spreading, the lower 1–2 in. Spikelets $\frac{1}{20}$ in., pale brown. Upper empty glume much shorter than the flowering glume.

Below Kotgurh.—Throughout India, ascending to 5000 ft.—Tropical Asia and Australia.

2. **Sporobolus indicus,** *R. Br.*; *Fl. Br. Ind.* vii. 247. Perennial; stems 2–3 ft. Leaves 8–24 in., glabrous; margins entire. Panicle very narrow, 6–18 in., tapering to a fine point; branches erect, the

lower 1–2 in. Spikelets $\frac{1}{12}$ in., green, crowded. Upper empty glume much shorter than the flowering glume.

Simla.—Throughout India, ascending to 5000 ft.—All warm countries.

3. **Sporobolus piliferus,** *Kunth*; *Fl. Br. Ind.* vii. 251. Annual; stems 3–12. Leaves hairy; margins minutely toothed. Panicle very narrow, almost cylindric, 1–3 in.; branches erect, the lower $\frac{1}{2}$ in. or less. Spikelets $\frac{1}{15}$ in., brown. Empty glumes very unequal, the upper as long as the flowering glume.

Simla, Syree.—W. Himalaya, 3000–8000 ft.—Malacca.

30. AGROSTIS. The Greek name for all Grasses; derived from *agros*, a field.—Chiefly temperate regions.

Perennial, rarely annual; stems tufted, smooth, usually erect. Leaves glabrous, entire, flat or the margins inrolled. Ligule membranous, usually short. Spikelets numerous, slightly flattened, about $\frac{1}{10}$ in., 1-flowered, occasionally 2-flowered in *A. Royleana*, arranged on the whorled branches of a pyramidal or narrow panicle. Rhachilla not prolonged. Empty glumes 2, boat-shaped, equal or nearly so, awnless, acute. Flowering glume shorter, transparent, glabrous or hairy, awned or not, tip truncate, minutely jagged. Stamens 3. Styles 2, very short, distinct, feathery. Grain oblong, free within the persistent glumes.

Flowering glume hairy, awned.
  Awn protruding. Pale much shorter than the flowering glume . . . . 1. *A. Royleana*.
  Awn included. Pale nearly as long as the flowering glume . . . . 2. *A. Munroana*.
Flowering glume glabrous, awnless.
  Panicle pyramidal, 4–10 in.; branches spreading . . 3. *A. alba*.
  Panicle oblong, $1\frac{1}{2}$–3 in.; branches nearly erect . . 4. *A. verticillata*.

1. **Agrostis Royleana,** *Trin.*; *Fl. Br. Ind.* vii. 264, *under Calamagrostis pilosula, Hook. f. var. scabra.* Annual; stems 1–3 ft., erect. Leaves smooth, 6–12 in. long, up to $\frac{1}{4}$ in. broad. Panicle spreading at least in flower, 4–12 in.; branches roughly pubescent, $1\frac{1}{2}$–$3\frac{1}{2}$ in., naked for about half their length. Spikelets shining, pale yellow or green or tinged with purple, narrowly lanceolate, pointed, sometimes $\frac{1}{7}$ in., occasionally 2-flowered. Lower empty glumes slightly the longer, keel rough. Flowering glume hairy, about three fourths the length of the empty glume, base with a tuft of minute hairs, a slender, protruding awn below the middle of its back; pale much shorter than the glume. (Fig. 194.)

Simla, Mahasu, common.—W. Himalaya, 7000–10,000 ft.

2. **Agrostis Munroana,** *Aitch. & Hemsl.*; *Fl. Br. Ind.* vii. 263, *under Calamagrostis Munroana, Boiss.* Annual; stems tufted, 6–18 in., erect. Leaves smooth, 2–8 in., by $\frac{1}{8}$ in. Panicle spreading

at least in flower, 2–5 in.; branches smooth, 1–2 in., naked near the base. Spikelets shining, green or tinged with purple, ovate-lanceolate, hardly $\frac{1}{10}$ in. Lower empty glume slightly the longer. Flowering glume hairy, about three fourths the length of the empty glume, base with a tuft of minute hairs, a very short, slender, included awn below the middle of its back; pale nearly as long as the glume.

Simla.—W. Himalaya, 8000–12,000 ft.

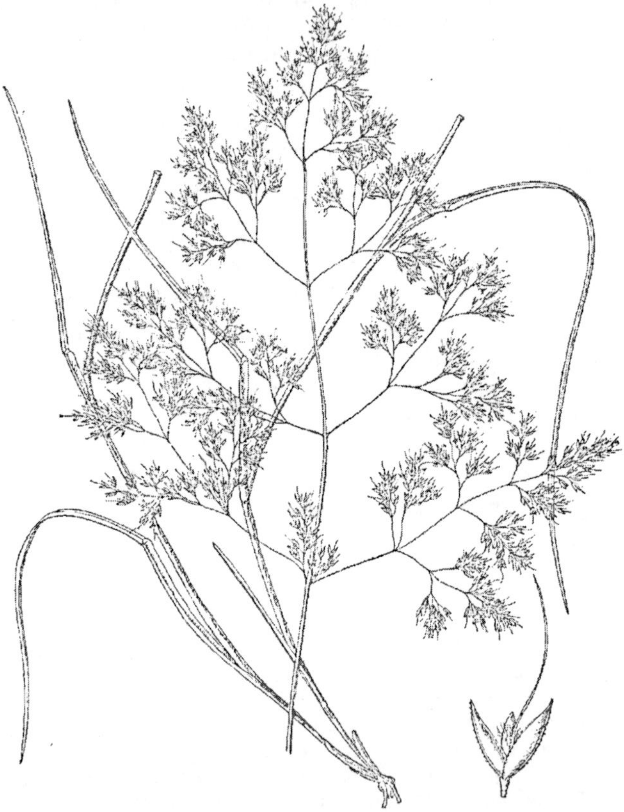

FIG. 194. AGROSTIS ROYLEANA.

*3. **Agrostis alba**, *Linn.*; *Fl. Br. Ind.* vii. 254. Perennial; stems 1–3 ft., erect. Leaves slightly rough, 4–10 in., up to $\frac{1}{4}$ in. broad. Panicle spreading at least in flower; branches smooth, $1\frac{1}{2}$–$2\frac{1}{2}$ in., naked towards the base. Spikelets shining, green or tinged with purple, narrowly ovoid. Empty glumes equal, keel of the lower rough. Flowering glume glabrous, awnless, nearly as long as the empty glumes; pale nearly half as long as the glume.

Temperate Himalaya 6000–11,000 ft.—N. temperate regions, including Britain.

*4. **Agrostis verticillata,** *Vill.*; *Fl. Br. Ind.* vii. 254. Perennial; stems 12–24 in., creeping near the base. Leaves rough, 2–6 in., up to $\frac{1}{3}$ in. broad. Panicle oblong, dense, $1\frac{1}{2}$–3 in.; branches smooth, nearly erect, rarely more than 1 in., flower-bearing to the base. Spikelets crowded, not shining, green, narrowly ovoid. Empty glumes equal, roughly pubescent. Flowering glume glabrous, awnless, about two thirds the length of the empty glumes; pale nearly as long as the glume.

W. Himalaya, 2000–4000 ft.—N. temperate regions.

The Simla locality given in the *Fl. Br. Ind.* is quoted from a paper by Dr. A. Grisebach on the 'Grasses of High Asia,' dated 1868, published in his *Gesammelte Abhandlungen*, Leipzig, 1880. The specimen is not at Kew.

31. **MUEHLENBERGIA.** In honour of H. Muehlenberg, an American clergyman and botanical author.—Temperate regions, chiefly America.

Perennial, rarely annual; stems tufted, slender, ascending, creeping near the base. Leaves rough, flat, narrow. Ligule membranous, short, jagged. Spikelets numerous, terete, pointed, $\frac{1}{10}$–$\frac{1}{7}$ in., 1-flowered, arranged on the rough, whorled branches of a narrow, erect or drooping panicle. Rhachilla not prolonged. Empty glumes 2, glabrous, thin, concave, acute, keel rough. Flowering glume stiff, hairy on the lower half, narrowed upwards in a slender, straight, rough, far-protruding awn; pale hairy near the base. Stamens usually 3. Styles 2, distinct, feathery. Grain cylindric, free but enclosed within the persistent glumes.

Panicle contracted, erect. Empty glumes equal, about as long as the flowering glume. Awn $\frac{1}{6}$–$\frac{1}{2}$ in. . . . 1. *M. sylvatica.*
Panicle loose, drooping. Awn $\frac{1}{4}$–1 in.
  Panicle 4–12 in., bright green. Spikelets $\frac{1}{10}$ in. Empty glumes very variable, usually unequal . . . . 2. *M. viridissima.*
  Panicle 3–6 in., pale green or tinged with violet. Spikelets $\frac{1}{7}$ in. Empty glumes equal . . . . 3. *M. himalayensis.*

1. **Muehlenbergia sylvatica,** *Torr. & Gray*; *Fl. Br. Ind.* vii. 259. Stems 1–2 ft. Leaves 3–6 in., up to $\frac{1}{6}$ in. broad. Panicle pale green or violet, contracted, erect, 4–6 in.; branches erect, $\frac{1}{2}$–1 in., flower-bearing to the base. Spikelets crowded, $\frac{1}{10}$ in. Empty glumes equal, narrowly lanceolate, finely pointed. Flowering glume about as long; awn $\frac{1}{6}$–$\frac{1}{2}$ in.

Simla, Fagoo.—W. Himalaya, 4000–9000 ft.—Japan, N. America.

2. **Muehlenbergia viridissima,** *Nees*; *Fl. Br. Ind.* vii. 259. Stems 1–3 ft. Leaves 4–12 in., up to $\frac{1}{4}$ in. broad. Panicle bright green, loose, drooping, 4–12 in.; branches drooping, 1–4 in., flower-bearing to the base. Spikelets crowded, $\frac{1}{10}$ in. Empty

glumes ovate-lanceolate, very variable in length, slightly or very unequal, both very small or one small and the other nearly as long as the flowering glume or both long. Flowering glume longer, sometimes much longer than the empty glumes; awn $\frac{1}{4}$–1 in.

Simla, Narkunda, common.—Temperate Himalaya, 3000–9000 ft.

3. **Muehlenbergia himalayensis,** *Hack.*; *Fl. Br. Ind.* vii. 259. Stems 12–24 in. Leaves 4–12 in., up to $\frac{1}{8}$ in. broad. Panicle pale green, often tinged with violet, narrow, loose, drooping, 3–6 in.; branches drooping, 1–2 in., usually naked near the base. Spikelets not crowded, $\frac{1}{7}$ in. Empty glumes equal, lanceolate, acute. Flowering glume about one third or slightly longer than the empty glumes; awn $\frac{1}{2}$–1 in.

Simla.—W. Himalaya, 6000–7000 ft.

32. CALAMAGROSTIS. From the Greek *calamos*, a reed, and *agrostis*, a grass.—Cold and temperate regions.

Perennial; stems tufted, 2–5 ft., erect, usually robust. Leaves glabrous, slightly rough, long, flat. Ligule membranous, oblong. Spikelets numerous, narrow, $\frac{1}{4}$ in., 1-flowered, crowded on the rough, whorled branches of a dense, silky, shining, nearly erect panicle often nearly a foot long; branches 2–3 in., more or less spreading, naked towards the base. Rhachilla not prolonged. Empty glumes 2, the lower the longer, concave, narrowly lanceolate, long-pointed, keeled. Flowering glume much shorter, transparent, glabrous but enveloped in a basal tuft of long, silky hairs, tip 2-lobed, a slender, straight awn in the cleft. Stamens 3. Styles 2, short, distinct, feathery. Grain obovate, free but enclosed within the persistent glumes.

Awn protruding . . . . 1. *C. emodensis.*
Awn included . . . . 2. *C. littorea.*

*1. **Calamagrostis emodensis,** *Griseb.*; *Fl. Br. Ind.* vii. 261. Stems 3–5 ft. Leaves 12–18 in., by $\frac{1}{2}$–$\frac{3}{4}$ in.; lower surface glaucous. Panicle 6–10 in., pale grey. Awn protruding.

Temperate Himalaya, 7000–12,000 ft.

2. **Calamagrostis littorea,** *DC.*; *Fl. Br. Ind.* vii. 261. Stems 2–5 ft. Leaves 12–18 in., up to $\frac{1}{6}$ in. broad. Panicle 6–10 in., purple when young, turning pale yellow in fruit. Empty glumes tinged with purple at the base. Awn included.

Simla.—Temperate Himalaya, 6000–10,000 ft.—W. Asia, Europe.

33. DEYEUXIA. In honour of Nicolas Deyeux, a French botanist.—Most temperate and mountainous regions.

Deyeuxia scabrescens, *Munro*; *Fl. Br. Ind.* vii. 267. Perennial; stems tufted, 2–5 ft., erect. Leaves rough, 6–18 in., up to $\frac{1}{8}$ in. broad. Ligule membranous, long. Spikelets numerous, green or tinged with purple, roughly pubescent, $\frac{1}{6}$ in., slightly flattened, 1-flowered, crowded on the rough, slender, whorled branches of a narrow, erect panicle 3–6 in. long; branches spreading at least in flower, 1–2 in., flower-bearing nearly to the base. Rhachilla prolonged as a tuft of silky hairs as long as the flowering glume. Empty glumes 2, nearly equal, concave, lanceolate, keels rough. Flowering glume shorter, transparent, tip 2-lobed, a straight, shortly protruding awn in the cleft, tips of lobes truncate, jagged. Stamens 3. Styles 2, short, distinct, feathery. Grain narrowly oblong, free within the persistent glumes.

Simla.—Temperate Himalaya, 8000–13,000 ft.

TRIBE VI. **Aveneæ.**

34. AVENA. The Latin name of the Oat.—Temperate and cold regions.

Annual or perennial; stems robust, erect. Leaves flat, 6–12 in., up to $\frac{1}{3}$ in. broad, long-pointed. Ligule membranous, short, oblong, truncate or jagged. Spikelets stalked, $\frac{1}{2}$–1 in., narrow, terete, 2–4-flowered (the uppermost flower usually rudimentary), arranged on the whorled branches of a loose, spreading panicle. Rhachilla densely silky, prolonged. Glumes concave, acute; nerves prominent. Empty glumes 2, glabrous, thin, lanceolate, the margins and tip scarious. Flowering glumes rather shorter, firmer, oblong-lanceolate, the tip split into 2, sometimes 3 or 4 finely pointed lobes, rarely nearly entire, a long, thick, bent and twisted awn inserted on the back. Stamens 3. Ovary hairy on the top; styles 2, short, distinct, feathery. Grain oblong, furrowed, hairy on the top, enclosed within the persistent glumes and more or less adherent to the pale.

The Common Oat, *A. sativa*, is cultivated in N.W. India, principally as green fodder for horses.

Spikelets 1 in., drooping. Empty glumes nearly equal . . . 1. *A. fatua*.
Spikelets $\frac{1}{2}$ in., erect. Empty glumes very unequal . . . 2. *A. aspera*.

1. **Avena fatua,** *Linn.*; *Fl. Br. Ind.* vii. 275. Annual; stems 1–3 ft. Leaves rough; sheaths smooth. Panicle 6–10 in.; branches spreading; rhachis and branches nearly smooth. Spikelets about 1 in., 3- or 2-flowered, pendulous; stalks rough, unequal. Empty glumes nearly equal, 9-nerved. Flowering glumes thinly hairy, tip 2-lobed, awn nearly three times the length of the glume, inserted below the middle; lowest flowering glume with a tuft of bristle-like hairs at its base.

Simla, in fields.—Punjab, N.W. Himalaya, up to 9000 ft.—N. Asia, N. Africa, Europe, including Britain (Wild Oat).

2. **Avena aspera,** *Munro*; *Fl. Br. Ind.* vii. 277. Perennial; stems 2–4 ft. Leaves nearly smooth; sheaths softly pubescent. Panicle narrow, nodding, 6–12 in.; branches nearly erect; rhachis and branches rough. Spikelets pale green, erect, about ½ in., 3–4-flowered, glistening. Empty glumes very unequal, 3–5-nerved. Flowering glume glabrous, tip 2-lobed or irregularly split into 3–4 bristle-like lobes, rarely nearly entire; awn 1½–3 times as long as the glume, inserted rather above its middle. (Fig. 195.)

Simla, Mahasu, common.—Temperate Himalaya, 6000–12,000 ft. The Simla plant is var. *Roylei* of the *Fl. Br. Ind.*

Fig. 195. Avena aspera.

35. DANTHONIA. In honour of Etienne Danthoine, a French botanist.—Most warm and temperate regions.

Danthonia cachemyriana, *Jaub. & Spach*; *Fl. Br. Ind.* vii. 281. Perennial; rootstock often creeping, fibres fleshy; stems tufted, 1–2 ft., erect or decumbent near the base. Leaves glabrous, as long as the stem or longer, very narrow, flat; sheaths hairy. Ligule very short, pubescent. Spikelets shining, narrow, terete, $\frac{1}{2}$–$\frac{3}{4}$ in., 2–5-flowered (uppermost flower male or rudimentary), arranged on the branches of a narrow, erect panicle 4–5 in. long. Rhachilla hairy, jointed between the flowers, prolonged. Empty glumes 2, nearly equal, glabrous, thin, lanceolate, as long as the whole spikelet, often tinged with purple, keeled, 3–5-nerved. Flowering glumes concave, thin, hairy, fringed, lanceolate, 7–9-nerved, the tip deeply 2-lobed; lobes prolonged as awn-like points, much longer than the glume but shorter than the rigid, twisted awn inserted in the cleft, the glume thus appearing as 3-awned. Stamens 3. Style, 2, distinct, feathery. Grain oblong, free, enclosed within the persistent glumes.

Huttoo.—Temperate Himalaya, 10,000–14,000 ft.

Tribe VII. **Chlorideæ.**

36. TRIPOGON. From the Greek *tri*, three, and *pogon*, a beard, referring to the 3-awned flowering glumes of some species.—Tropical and warm regions in Asia and Africa.

Perennial, glabrous; stems tufted, slender. Leaves as long as the stem or longer, very narrow, flat. Ligule minutely hairy. Spikelets flattened, $\frac{1}{6}$–$\frac{1}{4}$ in., 3–10-flowered (the upper 1 or 2 flowers usually male), sessile in 2 opposite rows along one side of a solitary, slender spike. Empty glumes very unequal, the lower the shorter, stiff, pointed, keeled, 1-nerved. Flowering glumes thin, ovate, concave, base minutely hairy, tip 2-toothed or jagged, 3-awned or with a single very minute awn. Stamens 3. Styles 2, short, distinct, feathery. Grain narrowly oblong, free within the persistent glumes.

Flowering glume 1-awned; awn very minute . . . 1. *T. abyssinicus.*
Flowering glume 3-awned; awns long . . . . 2. *T. filiformis.*

1. **Tripogon abyssinicus,** *Nees*; *Fl. Br. Ind.* vii. 287. Stems 6–24 in. Spike 1–10 in. Spikelets rather distant, 3–6-flowered. Empty glumes narrowly lanceolate. Flowering glumes: tip irregularly 2-toothed or 2-lobed or jagged, with a very minute awn hardly projecting beyond the lobes or teeth.

Simla.—W. Himalaya, 5000–7000 ft.—W. Asia, Tropical Africa.

2. **Tripogon filiformis,** *Nees*; *Fl. Br. Ind.* vii. 288. Stems 4–16 in. Spike 1$\frac{1}{2}$–8 in. Spikelets crowded, 4–10-flowered. Lower empty glume ovate, broadly lobed on one side; upper narrowly lanceolate, sharply toothed on one or both margins near the top. Flowering glumes: tip 2-toothed, teeth acute or jagged, a long awn inserted in the cleft and a shorter awn on the outer side of each tooth, the glume thus being 3-awned, middle awn twice as long as the glume or longer. (Fig. 196.)

Simla, common.—Temperate Himalaya, 5000–10,000 ft.

37. CYNODON. From the Greek *kyon*, a dog, and *odous*, a tooth, said to refer to the sharp teeth of the glumes.—Warm and temperate regions, most abundant in Australia.

Cynodon dactylon, *Pers.*; *Fl. Br. Ind.* vii. 288. Perennial, glabrous; stems prostrate, often widely creeping and forming

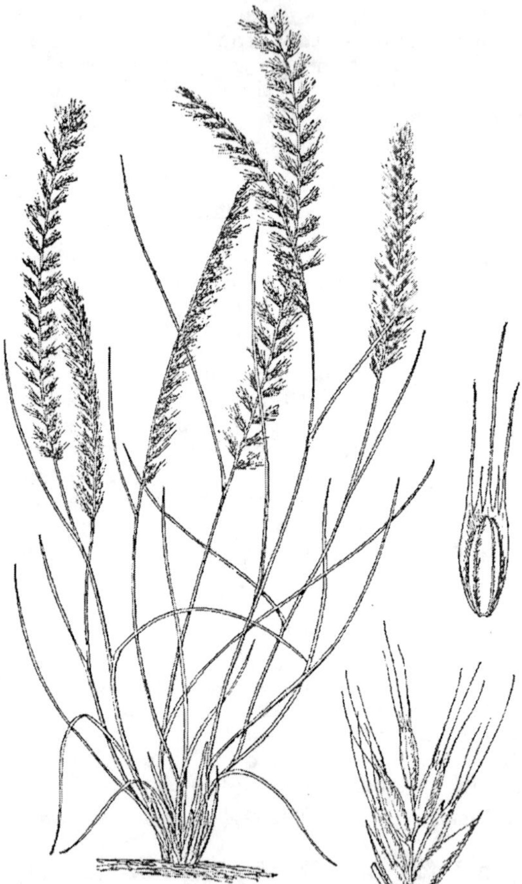

FIG. 196. TRIPOGON FILIFORMIS.

matted tufts with short, ascending branches. Leaves flat, 1–4 in., up to $\frac{1}{4}$ in. broad. Ligule very short, hairy. Spikelets green or purple, awnless, $\frac{1}{12}$ in., 1-flowered, alternate, not in clusters or pairs as in *Paspalum*, sessile along one side of 2–5 simple, straight, flattened branches 1–2 in. long and digitately spreading from near the top of the stem. Empty glumes 2, nearly equal, shorter than the flowering glume, keeled, acute, often falling off separately. Flowering glume broadly boat-shaped, keel hairy. Pale nearly as long, the prolonged rhachilla appearing at its base as a minute bristle. Stamens 3. Styles 2, distinct, feathery. Grain oblong, free within the persistent glumes.

Simla.—Throughout India, ascending to 5000 ft.—Most warm countries; commonly cultivated.

The Doob Grass of the plains. It forms the chief pasture in many dry climates.

38. ELEUSINE. From *Eleusis*, an ancient city of Greece, famous for the worship of Ceres, the goddess of agriculture.—Most warm regions.

***Eleusine indica,** *Gærtn.*; *Fl. Br. Ind.* vii. 293. Annual, glabrous; stems tufted, 1–2 ft., erect, soft. Leaves flat, 3–12 in., up to $\frac{1}{4}$ in. broad; sheaths hairy at the mouth. Ligule obsolete. Spikelets green or tinged with purple, awnless, about $\frac{1}{7}$ in., 3–5-flowered, alternate, not opposite as in *Panicum*, sessile, crowded in 2 series along one side of 4–7 simple, straight, flattened branches 2–5 in. long and digitately spreading from near the top of the stem Glumes thin, boat-shaped. Empty glumes 2, shorter than the lowest flowering glumes, unequal, the lower the smaller, keels roughly hairy. Flowering glumes glabrous, acute. Stamens 3. Styles 2, short, distinct, feathery. Grain oblong, free within the persistent glumes, outer coat loose; seed wrinkled.

Throughout India, ascending to 5000 ft.—Tropical regions of the Old World.

E. Coracana, a cultivated form of this species, is a common crop in N. India and in the lower hills. Native name *Mandwa*; it is the *Ragi* of S. India.

TRIBE VIII. **Festuceæ.**

39. ARUNDO. The Latin name for a reed.—Temperate and tropical regions.

Arundo Donax, *Linn.*; *Fl. Br. Ind.* vii. 302. Perennial; stems 6–10 ft., erect or creeping near the base. Leaves smooth, flat, 1–2 ft., in 2 opposite series, drooping, tapering from a stem-clasping base $\frac{1}{2}$–$1\frac{1}{2}$ in. broad to a fine point. Ligule very short, hairy. Spikelets slightly flattened, $\frac{1}{3}$–$\frac{1}{2}$ in., 3–4-flowered (flowers all 2-sexual except sometimes the uppermost), in a dense, erect, shining, silky panicle 1–2 ft. long; branches erect or drooping, in half-whorls. Rhachilla glabrous, jointed between the flowers, prolonged. Glumes thin, narrowly lanceolate, concave. Empty glumes 2, glabrous, as long as the spikelet, slightly unequal, acute. Flowering glumes: lower half covered with long, white, silky hairs; tip 2-lobed, lobes acute, a short, straight awn in the cleft. Stamens 3.

Styles 2, distinct, feathery. Grain oblong, free within the persistent glumes.

Charaog, near Simla.—Plains of N. India, ascending to 6000 ft.—W. Asia, N. Africa, Europe.

40. PHRAGMITES. From the Greek *phragma*, a fence, hedge, referring to a common use made of the stems.—Temperate and tropical regions.

***Phragmites communis,** *Trin.*; *Fl. Br. Ind.* vii. 303. Perennial; rootstock thick, creeping; stems erect, 6–10 ft., leafy throughout. Leaves in 2 series, smooth, flat, lanceolate, 18–24 × $\frac{1}{2}$–1$\frac{1}{2}$ in., tapering into a long, fine point, base rounded, not stem-clasping. Ligule very short, hairy. Spikelets purple-brown, narrow, slightly flattened, $\frac{1}{2}$–$\frac{3}{4}$ in., 3–7-flowered, crowded on the more or less drooping branches of a dense, erect, shining, silky panicle 6–18 in. long, hairy at the base; branches in half-whorls; lowest flower of the spikelets male, naked, the others 2-sexual or the uppermost male or rudimentary, enveloped in the long, silky hairs clothing the rhachilla. Rhachilla prolonged. Glumes glabrous, thin, keeled. Empty glumes 2, lanceolate, much shorter than the spikelet, very unequal, the lower the shorter. Flowering glumes $\frac{1}{2}$–$\frac{3}{4}$ in., oblong-lanceolate, the fertile ones narrowed into an awn-like point. Stamens 3, except in the lowest flower which sometimes has 2 or only 1. Styles 2, distinct, feathery. Grain oblong, free within the persistent glumes.

In lakes and marshes throughout N.W. India, ascending to 10,000 ft.—N. and S. temperate regions, including Britain (Common Reed), the *Arundo Phragmites* of Bentham's *British Flora*.

The silky hairs clothing the rhachilla lengthen as the grain ripens, giving a beautiful silvery appearance to the panicle.

41. NEYRAUDIA. In honour of M. Reynaud, a French botanist.—Tropical and temperate regions of Asia and Africa.

***Neyraudia madagascariensis,** *Hook. f.*; *Fl. Br. Ind.* vii. 305. Perennial; stems 6–10 ft., solid, leafy. Leaves flat, 1–2 ft., up to 1 in. broad, base stem-clasping. Ligule very short, hairy. Spikelets purple-brown, narrow, slightly flattened, $\frac{1}{4}$–$\frac{1}{3}$ in., 4–8-flowered (flowers all fertile except sometimes the uppermost), in a shining, silky, erect panicle 1–3 ft. long; branches in half whorls, more or less spreading. Rhachilla prolonged. Glumes thin, lanceolate. Empty glumes 2, glabrous, acute, much shorter than the lowest flowering glume, very unequal, the lower the shorter. Flowering glumes narrow, base hairy, margins fringed with long, white, silky hairs, tip divided in 2 bristle-like lobes, a short, straight, rough awn in the cleft. Stamens 3. Styles 2, distinct, feathery. Grains oblong, free within the persistent glumes.

Plains of N. India, ascending to 5000 ft.—Tropical Asia and Africa, Madagascar.

42. KOELERIA. In honour of G. L. Koeler, a German botanist of the eighteenth century, author of a work on the Grasses of France and Germany.—N. temperate regions.

Koeleria cristata, *Pers.*; *Fl. Br. Ind.* vii. 308. Perennial; stems tufted, 8–24 in., erect. Leaves flat, pubescent or hairy, 2–5 in., less than $\frac{1}{8}$ in. broad. Ligule very short, hairy. Spikelets green or tinged with purple, shining, flattened, awnless, $\frac{1}{6}$–$\frac{1}{4}$ in., 2–4-flowered (the uppermost flower often male or rudimentary), crowded on the short, rough branches of a narrowly oblong, interrupted or lobed panicle $2\frac{1}{2}$–5 in. long; branches in half-whorls, nearly erect or the lower longer and somewhat spreading. Rhachilla glabrous, prolonged. Glumes thin, boat-shaped, acute, keels rough, sides transparent. Empty glumes 2, shorter than the lowest flowering glume, nearly equal. Flowering glumes entire, 5-nerved at the base. Stamens 3. Ovary glabrous; styles 2, short, distinct, feathery. Grain narrowly oblong, free within the persistent glumes.

Simla, common.—Temperate Himalaya, 5000–13,000 ft.—N. temperate regions, including Britain.

43. ERAGROSTIS. From the Greek *eri*, very, much, and *agrostis*, grass, referring to the many-flowered spikelets of some species.—Most warm countries.

Annual or perennial, usually glabrous; stems erect or ascending from a zigzag, more or less decumbent base. Leaves usually flat, narrow; mouth of sheath hairy. Ligule obsolete. Spikelets flattened, minute or up to $\frac{1}{2}$ in., awnless, 2–50-flowered (very rarely only 2, usually several or many flowers, the uppermost often male), arranged on the branches of an erect or nodding panicle, spreading at least when in flower or, in *E. nardoides* only, sessile in a simple, terminal spike. Rhachilla not prolonged as a naked point. Glumes boat-shaped, usually acute, glabrous or nearly so, keeled. Empty glumes 2, shorter than the lowest flowering glume, unequal. Flowering glumes broadly ovate, membranous, overlapping, 3-nerved, ultimately falling off. Pale nearly as long, falling off with its glume or persistent. Stamens 3, rarely 2. Styles 2, distinct, feathery. Grain minute, oblong or globose, loosely enclosed within the glumes.

Spikelets stalked, in panicles.
  Spikes minute, $\frac{1}{20}$ in., numerous, 2–5-flowered . . . . 1. *E. interrupta.*
  Spikelets ovate, $\frac{1}{6}$–$\frac{1}{2}$ in., 20–50-flowered . . . . . 2. *E. amabilis.*
  Spikelets narrowly oblong, $\frac{1}{10}$–$\frac{1}{3}$ in.
    Leaves with glandular edges. Grain globose.
      Spikelets $\frac{1}{10}$–$\frac{2}{10}$ in. broad, 10–40-flowered . . . 4. *E. major.*
      Spikelets less than $\frac{1}{10}$ in. broad, 6–12-flowered . . 5. *E. minor.*
    Leaves not glandular. Grain oblong-ovoid.
      Spikelets light green or tinged with purple.
        Branches of panicle solitary. Spikelets $\frac{1}{10}$ in. broad, 8–30-flowered . . . . 3. *E. elegantula.*

Branches of panicle clustered. Spikelets $\frac{1}{20}$ in. broad, 5–12-flowered . . . . 6. *E. pilosa.*
Spikelets dark olive-green, usually few, scattered . 7. *E. nigra.*
Spikelets sessile in a spike . . . . 8. *E. nardoides.*

1. **Eragrostis interrupta,** *Beauv.*; *Fl. Br. Ind.* vii. 316. Annual; stems tufted, 6–24 in., erect. Leaves flat, 6–12 in., up to $\frac{1}{4}$ in. broad. Panicle loose, narrow, 4–12 in., tapering; branches $\frac{1}{2}$–2 in., clustered; branchlets hair-like. Spikelets very numerous, minute. Flowers 3–5, sometimes only 2. Flowering glumes obtuse.

Simla.—Throughout India, ascending to 7000 ft.—Africa.
The Simla plant is var. *tenuissima*, Stapf, of the *Fl. Br. Ind.*

2. **Eragrostis amabilis,** *Wight & Arn.*; *Fl. Br. Ind.* vii. 317. Annual; stems 6–18 in., erect. Leaves flat, 1–4 in., up to $\frac{1}{4}$ in. broad, tapering in a fine point. Panicle oblong, 1$\frac{1}{2}$–4 in.; branches solitary, $\frac{1}{2}$–2 in., rarely longer. Spikelets ovate, $\frac{1}{6}$–$\frac{1}{2}$ in., much flattened, tinged with purple, 20–50-flowered. Flowering glumes crowded, transparent, broadly ovate, acute, nerves prominent.

Simla.—Throughout India, ascending to 6000 ft.—Tropical Asia.

*3. **Eragrostis elegantula,** *Steud.*; *Fl. Br. Ind.* vii. 318. Perennial; stems 1–3 ft., erect or ascending. Leaves 2–10 in., up to $\frac{1}{10}$ in. broad, margins not glandular, often inrolled. Panicle oblong, 2–6 in., nodding; branches solitary, $\frac{1}{2}$–4 in., sometimes so short that the spikelets appear clustered. Spikelets narrowly oblong, $\frac{1}{7}$–$\frac{1}{3}$ in. by $\frac{1}{10}$ in. broad, green or tinged with purple, 8–30-flowered. Flowering glumes acute, keels rough. Grain oblong-ovoid.

Throughout India, ascending to 4000 ft.

*4. **Eragrostis major,** *Host.*; *Fl. Br. Ind.* vii. 320. Annual; stems 1–2 ft., erect or ascending. Leaves flat, 4–10 in., up to $\frac{1}{4}$ in. broad, glandular along the edges. Panicle oblong or pyramidal, 2–8 in.; branches 1–4 in. Spikelets narrowly oblong, tapering, $\frac{1}{5}$–$\frac{1}{3}$ in., by $\frac{1}{10}$–$\frac{2}{10}$ in. broad, 10–40-flowered, dark olive-green at first. Flowering glumes acute. Grain globose.

Throughout India, ascending to 5000 ft.—W. Asia, S. Europe.

*5. **Eragrostis minor,** *Host.*; *Fl. Br. Ind.* vii. 321. Annual; stems tufted, 6–18 in., erect. Leaves flat, 1–4 in., up to $\frac{1}{5}$ in. broad, glandular along the edges. Panicle oblong, 2–8 in.; branches $\frac{1}{2}$–2 in. Spikelets narrowly oblong, $\frac{1}{6}$–$\frac{1}{3}$ in., by less than $\frac{1}{10}$ in. broad, 6–12-flowered, pale green or tinged with purple, glistening. Flowering glumes obtuse. Grain globose.

Plains of N. India, ascending to 8000 ft.—W. Asia, S. Europe.

*6. **Eragrostis pilosa,** *Beauv.*; *Fl. Br. Ind.* vii. 323. Annual; stems tufted, varying from 3 in. to 3 ft., erect. Leaves flat, 2-6 in., up to $\frac{1}{8}$ in. broad, edges not glandular. Panicle oblong or pyramidal, erect or nodding, $1\frac{1}{2}$–8 in., hairy at the base and usually at the joints; branches 1-6 in., clustered. Spikelets narrowly oblong, $\frac{1}{6}$–$\frac{1}{4}$ in., by $\frac{1}{20}$ in. broad, 5–12 flowered, usually pale green, tipped with purple. Flowering glumes acute. Grain oblong-ovoid.

Throughout India, ascending to 4000 ft.—Most hot countries, S. Europe.

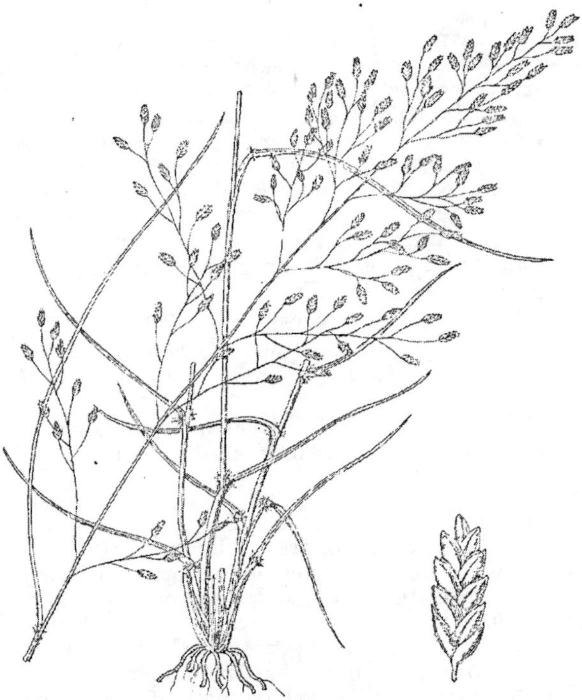

FIG. 197. ERAGROSTIS NIGRA.

7. **Eragrostis nigra,** *Nees*; *Fl. Br. Ind.* vii. 324. Perennial; stems $\frac{1}{2}$–3 ft., erect. Leaves flat, usually narrow or up to $\frac{1}{4}$ in. broad, edges not glandular. Panicle oblong or pyramidal, 3–12 in., loose; branches $1\frac{1}{2}$–5 in. Spikelets dark olive-green, usually few, scattered, narrowly oblong, $\frac{1}{10}$–$\frac{1}{6}$ in., 3–9-flowered. Grain oblong-ovoid. (Fig. 197.)

Simla, common.—Throughout India, ascending to 9000 ft.

*8. **Eragrostis nardoides,** *Trin.*; *Fl. Br. Ind.* vii. 326. Perennial; stems tufted, very slender, 12–18 in., erect. Leaves hairy, very narrow, 3–9 in., margins inrolled. Spikelets narrowly oblong, $\frac{1}{3}$–$\frac{1}{2}$ in., 13–30-flowered, sessile, crowded in two ranks in a simple, slender spike 6–12 in. long.

Throughout N. India, on sandy and rocky ground, ascending to 5000 ft.

44. MELICA. From the Greek *meli*, honey, referring to the sweet properties of this Grass.—Temperate and subtropical regions.

Melica scaberrima, *Hook. f.*; *Fl. Br. Ind.* vii. 330. Perennial; stems rough, 3–5 ft., erect. Leaves rough, 6–10 in., up to $\frac{1}{3}$ in. broad. Ligule membranous, short, jagged. Spikelets awnless, pale green, shortly stalked, slightly flattened, $\frac{1}{4}$–$\frac{1}{2}$ in., 3–5-flowered, irregularly disposed on the 2–6 in. long branches of a spreading, variable panicle 6–18 in. long, sometimes reduced to a nearly simple raceme. Rhachilla terminated by a cluster of 2 or 3 barren glumes. Glumes membranous, lanceolate, margins and tip transparent. Empty glumes 2, shorter than the lowest flowering glume, the lower the shorter. Flowering glumes distant, acute, strongly 7–9-nerved. Stamens 3. Ovary glabrous; styles 2, distinct, feathery. Grain oblong, free within the persistent glumes.

Mahasu, in forest.—W. Himalaya, 6000–10,000 ft.

45. DACTYLIS. From the Greek *dactulos*, a finger; supposed to refer to the division of the inflorescence.—Cold and temperate regions.

Dactylis glomerata, *Linn.*; *Fl. Br. Ind.* vii. 335. Perennial; stems tufted, smooth, 2–4 ft., erect. Leaves flat, 6–12 in.; sheaths flattened. Ligule membranous, long, torn. Spikelets green or tinged with purple, shortly stalked, flattened, $\frac{1}{4}$ in., 3–5-flowered, crowded in one-sided, ovoid clusters in an erect panicle 1–6 in. long; branches rough, the upper ones short, erect, crowded, the lower $\frac{1}{2}$–$2\frac{1}{2}$ in., spreading, distant, naked towards the base. Rhachilla prolonged, tip naked or bearing 1–2 barren glumes. Glumes lanceolate, boat-shaped, keeled. Empty glumes 2, slightly unequal, long-pointed, shorter than the lowest flowering glume. Flowering glumes stiff, tip shortly awned, 5-nerved, keel rough. Stamens 3. Ovary glabrous; styles 2, distinct, feathery. Grain oblong, 3-sided, grooved, loosely enclosed within the persistent glumes.

Simla, Mahasu, common.—N.W. Himalaya, 8000–10,000 ft.—W. Asia, N. Africa, Europe, including Britain (Cock's-foot Grass).
Introduced into North America and many other countries.

46. POA. From the Greek *poa*, fodder.—Temperate and cold regions, rarely tropical.

Annual or perennial; stems tufted, smooth, erect, leafy. Leaves flat. Ligule membranous. Spikelets green or tinged with purple, flattened, $\frac{1}{7}$–$\frac{1}{4}$ in., 2–7-flowered (uppermost flower sometimes male), in an erect, usually pyramidal panicle; branches whorled, rarely solitary, spreading in flower or at least in fruit. Rhachilla prolonged, tip naked. Glumes lanceolate, boat-shaped, keeled, acute, margins and tip scarious. Empty glumes 2, nearly opposite, shorter than the lowest flowering glume, the outer the shorter. Flowering glumes usually with web-like hairs at the base and on the lower half of the back; nerves more than 3. Stamens 3. Ovary glabrous; styles 2, distinct, short, feathery. Grain enclosed within the persistent glumes, free or adherent to the pale.

Stems robust, usually tall. Leaves rather broad. Outer empty glume 1-nerved . . . . 1. *P. pratensis.*
Stems slender, usually less than 12 in. Leaves narrow.
 Outer empty glume 3-nerved . . . . 2. *P. nemoralis.*
 Outer empty glume 1-nerved.
  Anthers $\frac{1}{12}$ in. . . . . 3. *P. polycolea.*
  Anthers $\frac{1}{30}$ in.
   Panicle 2–6 in., very loose and flaccid . . . 4. *P. himalayana.*
   Panicle 1–3 in., rarely 4 in., stiff . . . . 5. *P. annua.*

1. **Poa pratensis,** *Linn.*; *Fl. Br. Ind.* vii. 339. Perennial; rootstock producing stolons; stems robust, 6–24 in., usually tall. Leaves 1–6 in., chiefly basal, rather broad. Ligule short, blunt. Panicle stiff, $2\frac{1}{2}$–$4\frac{1}{2}$ in.; lower branches usually in whorls of 5, naked for at least half their length. Spikelets numerous, $\frac{1}{6}$ in., 3–5-flowered. Outer empty glume 1-nerved. Flowering glumes hairy.

Simla, Matiana.—W. Himalaya, above 5000 ft.—N. temperate regions, including Britain.

2. **Poa nemoralis,** *Linn.*; *Fl. Br. Ind.* vii. 341. Perennial; stems slender, 1–2 ft. Leaves 2–12 in., about $\frac{1}{12}$ in. broad. Ligule very short. Panicle narrow, 2–6 in., loose, often drooping; branches mostly erect, solitary or in whorls of 2 or 3. Spikelets $\frac{1}{6}$ in., 2–4-flowered. Outer empty glume 3-nerved. Flowering glumes hairy, nerves obscure.

Simla, wet rocks on old Mahasu road.—W. Himalaya, above 5000 ft.—N. temperate regions, including Britain.

*3. **Poa polycolea,** *Stapf*; *Fl. Br. Ind.* vii. 342. Perennial; stems slender, 6–12 in. Leaves 2–8 in., very narrow, flat or wiry. Ligule very short. Panicle diffuse, $2\frac{1}{2}$–4 in.; branches naked for more than half their length, the lower ones in whorls of 2–5. Spikelets few, $\frac{1}{7}$ in., 3-flowered, crowded towards the end of the branches. Glumes very thin. Outer empty glume 1-nerved. Flowering glumes glabrous except a few minute hairs at the base. Anthers $\frac{1}{12}$ in.

W. Himalaya, 8000–12,000 ft.

4. **Poa himalayana,** *Nees*; *Fl. Br. Ind.* vii. 344. Perennial or annual; stems slender, 12–18 in., sometimes ascending. Leaves $1\frac{1}{2}$–6 in., up to $\frac{1}{10}$ in. broad. Panicle diffuse, flaccid, 2–6 in.; branches naked for more than half their length, the lower ones in whorls of 2–4. Spikelets few, $\frac{1}{7}$ in., 2–4-flowered, crowded towards the end of the branches. Glumes thin. Outer empty glume 1-nerved. Flowering glumes hairy, 5-nerved. Anthers $\frac{1}{30}$ in.

Simla.—Temperate Himalaya, 7000–13,000 ft.

5. **Poa annua,** *Linn.*; *Fl. Br. Ind.* vii. 345. Annual or perennial; stems slender, 6–12 in., often zigzag near the base. Leaves flaccid, 2–6 in., up to $\frac{1}{6}$ in. broad. Ligule oblong, pointed. Panicle stiff, 1–3 in., rarely 4 in.; lower branches in whorls of 2 or 3, flower-bearing from near the base, usually ultimately deflexed. Spikelets numerous, $\frac{1}{8}$–$\frac{1}{5}$ in., shining, 3–6-flowered. Outer empty glume 1-nerved. Flowering glumes 5-nerved, hairy or nearly glabrous. Anthers $\frac{1}{30}$ in.

Simla, common on roadsides.—N. India, ascending to 9000 ft.—N. temperate regions, including Britain.

47. GLYCERIA. From the Greek *glukeros*, sweet, referring to the grain.—Temperate and cold regions.

***Glyceria tonglensis,** *C. B. Clarke*; *Fl. Br. Ind.* vii. 346. Perennial, aquatic; stems slender, 6–18 in., ascending, the base procumbent and creeping in wet ground, often tufted and nearly erect in drier places. Leaves 4–8 in., up to $\frac{1}{6}$ in. broad, floating if growing in water. Ligule membranous, short, blunt, eared at the base. Spikelets few, awnless, green or tinged with purple, glabrous, $\frac{1}{4}$ in., usually 4-flowered (uppermost flower often male), on the few short, rigid, spreading branches of a narrow, erect panicle 4–8 in. long. Rhachilla prolonged, tip naked. Empty glumes 2, shorter than the lowest flowering glume, the lower much the shorter, lanceolate, thin, transparent. Flowering glumes stiff, margins and tip transparent, often torn, ovate-oblong, concave, blunt, prominently 7-nerved. Stamens 3. Ovary glabrous; styles 2, distinct, short, feathery. Grain oblong, grooved, free within the persistent glumes.

Temperate Himalaya, 4000–9000 ft., usually growing in ponds or ditches. Allied to and resembling the British *Glyceria* or *Poa fluitans*.

48. FESTUCA. A classical name of uncertain derivation applied to various herbs.—Generally spread in cold and temperate regions.

Perennial, rarely annual; stems usually tufted, smooth, erect. Leaves flat or the margins inrolled. Ligule membranous, short, truncate. Spikelets awned except in *F. modesta*, green or tinged with purple, glabrous, $\frac{1}{3}$–$\frac{3}{4}$ in., 3–8-flowered (uppermost flower often male or rudimentary), on the roughly pubescent, ultimately spreading branches of a pyramidal or narrow, erect panicle. Rhachilla not prolonged. Glumes thin, membranous. Empty glumes 2, narrowly lanceolate, keeled, acute, shorter than the lowest flowering glume, the lower the shorter, in *F. Myuros* rudimentary. Flowering glumes stiff, concave, oblong-lanceolate, margins scarious, tip not notched; awn terminal, rough. Stamens 3, sometimes 1 or 2 in *F. Myuros.* Ovary glabrous or slightly hairy on the top; styles 2, distinct, very short, feathery. Grain narrowly oblong, grooved, enclosed within the persistent glumes, free or adherent to the pale.

Spikelets awned.
  Panicle pyramidal. Lower empty glume about half the length of the upper.
    Leaves $\frac{1}{10}$ in. broad. Stem-joints 1 or 2. Awn shorter than the flowering glume . . . . 1. *F. kashmiriana.*
    Leaves $\frac{1}{5}$–$\frac{1}{2}$ in. broad. Stem-joints 3–5. Awn longer than the flowering glume . . . . 2. *F. gigantea.*
  Panicle narrow. Lower empty glume reduced to a minute rudiment . . . . 4. *F. Myuros.*
Spikelets awnless. Panicle pyramidal, very loose and open . . . . 3. *F. modesta.*

1. **Festuca kashmiriana,** *Stapf; Fl. Br. Ind.* vii. 351. Perennial; stems 1–3 ft.; joints only 1 or 2, the uppermost below the middle of the stem. Leaves 4–12 in., about $\frac{1}{10}$ in. broad, margins often inrolled. Panicle pyramidal, 6–12 in.; lower branches long. Spikelets green or tinged with purple, $\frac{1}{2}$–$\frac{3}{4}$ in., 3–5-flowered. Lower empty glume about half the length of the upper. Flowering glumes prominently 5-nerved; awn straight, rather shorter than the glume. Ovary hairy on the top. Grain slightly adherent to the pale.

Simla, Mahasu, common.—Temperate Himalaya, 7000–14,000 ft.
Closely allied to and resembling the British *F. ovina* var. *duriuscula.*

F. rubra, *Linn.; Fl. Br. Ind.* vii. 352, differs only in the awn being somewhat shorter, and the ovary glabrous or minutely hairy. It occurs at Simla.

2. **Festuca gigantea,** *Vill.; Fl. Br. Ind.* vii. 353. Perennial; stems 2–4 ft.; joints 3–5. Leaves flat, 6–12 in., $\frac{1}{5}$–$\frac{1}{2}$ in. broad, base stem-clasping. Panicle pyramidal, 6–16 in., very loose, nodding; branches long, undivided to near the middle. Spikelets pale green, few, crowded towards the end of the branches, about $\frac{1}{2}$ in., 2–3-flowered, the uppermost flower often reduced to a long-awned rudiment. Lower empty glume about half the length of the upper. Flowering glumes faintly 5-nerved; awn longer than the glume, slender, often bending. Ovary glabrous. Grain closely adherent to the pale.

Simla, Jako, Mahasu.—W. Himalaya, 5000–9000 ft.—N. Asia, Europe, including Britain.

*3. **Festuca modesta,** *Steud.*; *Fl. Br. Ind.* vii. 354. Perennial; stems robust, 4–5 ft.; joints 2 or 3. Leaves flat, the lower ones up to 2 ft., by ½–⅔ in., the upper 4–6 in., by about ¼ in. Panicle pyramidal or ovate, 6–12 in., loose, open; lower branches often 8 in. long. Spikelets green, about ½ in., 3–4-flowered. Empty glumes nearly equal. Flowering glumes 5–7-nerved, acute, not awned. Ovary hairy on the top. Grain free.

W. Himalaya, 7000–9000 ft.

4. **Festuca Myuros,** *Linn.*; *Fl. Br. Ind.* vii. 356. Annual; stems slender, 6–18 in. Leaves ½–2 in., very narrow; sheath of the uppermost dilated, often enclosing the base of the panicle. Panicle narrow, one-sided, 4–10 in.; branches short. Spikelets pale green, narrow, about ⅓ in., 5–8-flowered, crowded. Lower empty glume reduced to a minute rudiment. Awn of flowering glume about half as long again as the glume. Stamens 1–3. Ovary glabrous. Grain adherent to the pale.

Simla.—W. Himalaya, 5000–9000 ft.– N. Asia, Europe, including Britain.

49. BROMUS. From *bromos,* the Greek name for the Wild Oat.—Temperate and cold regions.

Annual or perennial; stems erect. Leaves hairy, narrow, flat. Ligule membranous, short. Spikelets awned, green, oblong, flattened, ½–1½ in., 7–14-flowered (uppermost flower male or rudimentary), on the rough, more or less drooping branches of a panicle; branches in clusters of 2–5, rarely solitary, naked for about half their length. Rhachilla not prolonged. Glumes stiff, margins and tip scarious. Empty glumes 2, nearly opposite, lanceolate, shorter than the lowest flowering glume, the outer one the shorter. Flowering glumes oblong-lanceolate, nearly cylindric, tip notched, a straight, stiff, rough awn in the cleft. Stamens 3. Styles 2, lateral, inserted below the top of the hairy ovary, feathery. Grain nearly as long as the pale, narrow, keeled, usually free.

Stems 2–6 ft. Lower empty glume 1-nerved; upper 3-nerved . 1. *B. asper.*
Stems 1–2 ft. Lower empty glume 3-nerved; upper 7-nerved . 2. *B. patulus.*

1. **Bromus asper,** *Murray*; *Fl. Br. Ind.* vii. 358. Perennial; stems smooth, 2–6 ft. Leaves and sheaths hairy, 1–1½ ft., by ⅛–½ in. broad; margins rough. Panicle pyramidal, 4–12 in.; branches drooping. Spikelets ½–1½ in., 7–10-flowered. Glumes hairy. Lower empty glume 1-nerved, upper 3-nerved. Flowering glume 5-nerved; awn from half the length to as long as the glume.

Simla, Mahasu.—Temperate Himalaya, 6000–11,000 ft.—W. Asia, N. Africa, Europe, including Britain.

2. **Bromus patulus,** *Mert. & Koch*; *Fl. Br. Ind.* vii. 361. Annual; stems smooth, 1–2 ft., sometimes decumbent near the

base. Leaves 2–8 in., by $\frac{1}{8}$–$\frac{1}{4}$ in. broad; sheath pubescent; blade hairy. Panicle oblong, 4–8 in.; branches nearly erect, often turned to one side. Spikelets pale green, $\frac{3}{4}$–$1\frac{1}{2}$ in., 7–14-flowered. Glumes roughly pubescent. Lower empty glume 3-nerved, upper 7-nerved. Flowering glume 7-nerved; awn from half the length to longer than the glume.

Simla, Mahasu.—W. Himalaya, 6000–14,000 ft.—N. Asia, Europe.

50. BRACHYPODIUM. From the Greek *brachys*, short, and *pous, podos*, a foot, referring to the very short spikelet-stalks.—N. temperate regions and mountains in the Tropics.

Brachypodium sylvaticum, *Beauv.*; *Fl. Br. Ind.* vii. 362. Perennial; stems tufted, slender, 2–4 ft., erect or bent and decumbent near the base. Leaves flat, flaccid, hairy, 6–12 in., by $\frac{1}{5}$–$\frac{2}{3}$ in. broad, finely pointed. Ligule membranous, short, obtuse. Spikelets few, green, pubescent or hairy, $\frac{3}{4}$–2 in., 6–18-flowered (uppermost flower often male or rudimentary), nearly sessile in a loose, drooping spike 4–10 in. long. Rhachilla jointed below each flower, tip not prolonged. Empty glumes 2, strongly nerved, the lower the shorter, lanceolate, shorter than the lowest flowering glume. Flowering glumes stiff, hairy or pubescent, oblong-lanceolate, about $\frac{1}{2}$ in., 7-nerved, nearly cylindric, the tip narrowed into a slender, straight awn variable in length, longer or shorter than the glume. Stamens 3, sometimes 2. Styles 2, lateral, inserted below the top of the hairy ovary, feathery. Grain oblong, usually free, enclosed within the persistent glumes.

Simla, Mahasu, common.—Temperate Himalaya, 6000–12,000 ft.—N. Asia, Europe, including Britain.

Tribe IX. **Hordeæ.**

51. LOLIUM. The classical name.—North temperate regions.

Annual or perennial; stems usually erect. Leaves flat, long-pointed. Ligule membranous, short. Spikelets green or tinged with purple, flattened, $\frac{1}{3}$–$\frac{1}{2}$ in., 3–11-flowered (uppermost flower often male or rudimentary), singly sessile in notch-like grooves alternate in the rhachis of a simple spike; spikelets placed edgewise to the rhachis, not broadside. Rhachilla not prolonged. Empty glume one, except the terminal spikelet which has two, nearly equal. Flowering glumes awned or not. Stamens 3. Ovary glabrous; styles 2, terminal, distant, feathery nearly to the base. Grain oblong, adherent to the glume and pale.

Empty glume as long as or longer than the spikelet. Flowering glume usually awned . . . . . . 1. *L. temulentum.*
Empty glume shorter than the spikelet. Flowering glume usually awnless . . . . 2. *L. perenne.*

*1. **Lolium temulentum,** *Linn.*; *Fl. Br. Ind.* vii. 364. Annual; stems erect, 6–24 in. Leaves 4–10 in., base stem-clasping. Spike 6–12 in. Spikelets $\frac{1}{3}$–$\frac{1}{2}$ in., sometimes more, 3–8-flowered. Empty glume as long as or longer than the spikelet, oblong-lanceolate, many-nerved. Flowering glumes ovate-oblong, concave, obtuse, usually awned near the top; awn straight, about as long as the glume.

N. India, in fields, ascending to 6000 ft.—N. Asia, Europe, including Britain (Darnel).

The grains are poisonous.

2. **Lolium perenne,** *Linn.*; *Fl. Br. Ind.* vii. 365. Perennial; stems 1–2 ft., erect or decumbent near the base, leafy only on the lower part. Leaves 4–8 in., very narrow. Spike 4–10 in. Spikelets $\frac{1}{3}$–$\frac{1}{2}$ in., smooth, shining, 3–11-flowered. Empty glume oblong-lanceolate, shorter than the spikelet. Flowering glume oblong-lanceolate, obtuse, rarely shortly awned.

Simla, introduced.—N. Asia, Europe, including Britain (Rye Grass).

The cultivated form known as Italian Rye Grass has much longer spikelets.

52. **AGROPYRON.** From the Greek *agros*, a field, and *pyros*, wheat.—All temperate regions.

Annual or perennial; stems tufted, leafy, erect or ascending. Leaves flat or the margins inrolled, more or less hairy. Ligule membranous, short. Spikelets green, flattened, $\frac{1}{2}$–1 in., 3- to many-flowered (uppermost flower usually male or rudimentary), singly sessile in notch-like grooves alternate in the rhachis of a simple spike; spikelets placed broadside to the rhachis, not edgewise. Rhachilla not prolonged. Glumes stiff. Empty glumes 2, opposite, unequal, shorter than the lowest flowering glume. Flowering glumes oblong-lanceolate, concave, gradually narrowed upwards into a rough, slender awn; nerves 5, indistinct at the base, meeting near the tip. Stamens 3. Ovary hairy at the top; styles 2, terminal, distant, feathery nearly to the base. Grain narrowly oblong, flattened, grooved, tip hairy, free or adherent to the pale.

Empty glumes 3–5-nerved. Spikelets spreading. Awn usually 1–1$\frac{1}{2}$ in., recurved . . . . 1. *A. longearistatum.*
Empty glumes 5–7-ribbed. Spikelets appressed. Awn less than 1 in., straight . . . . 2. *A. semicostatum.*

1. **Agropyron longearistatum,** *Boiss.*; *Fl. Br. Ind.* vii. 368. Stems 1–3 ft. Leaves 6–12 in., up to $\frac{1}{6}$ in. broad. Spike 4–6 in., nodding. Spikelets $\frac{1}{2}$–$\frac{3}{4}$ in., spreading. Empty glumes narrowly lanceolate, finely pointed, 3–5-nerved, much shorter than or nearly as long as the flowering glume. Flowering glume spreading; awn 1–1$\frac{1}{2}$ in., rarely less, recurved. (Fig. 198.)

Simla, Mahasu.—W. Himalaya, 5000–12,000 ft.—W. Asia, N. Africa.

2. **Agropyron semicostatum,** *Nees*; *Fl. Br. Ind.* vii. 369. Stems usually 2–3 ft., sometimes up to 8 ft. Leaves 4–12 in., up to $\frac{1}{4}$ in. broad. Spike 3–8 in., erect. Spikelets $\frac{3}{4}$–1 in., erect, appressed to the rhachis. Empty glumes oblong-lanceolate, usually

FIG. 198. AGROPYRON LONGEARISTATUM.

nearly as long as the flowering glume, 5–7-ribbed. Flowering glume erect, appressed to the rhachilla; awn less than 1 in., straight.

Simla, Mahasu.—Temperate Himalaya, 4000–11,000 ft.—W. Asia. Closely allied to the British *A. caninum*.

Tribe X. Bambuseæ.

53. **ARUNDINARIA.** Used as a diminutive of the Latin *arundo*, a reed, on account of its appearance.—Asia, Africa, America.

Shrub-like bamboos growing gregariously; rootstock perennial; stems annual, numerous, tufted, erect, smooth, cylindric, less than 1 in. diam.; joints prominent, bearing thin, papery, straw-coloured, very deciduous stem-sheaths with short ligule and rudimentary blade; branches short, clustered at the nodes. Leaves flat, narrowly lanceolate, constricted at the base. Flowers borne on the leafless branches of separate stems. Spikelets flattened, 1- to many-flowered (the uppermost flower sometimes male or rudimentary), solitary or in short racemes in the axils of more or less sheathing bracts which are crowded along the clustered branches of a racemose or paniculate inflorescence. Rhachilla prolonged as a short, hairy point. Glumes stiff. Empty glumes 2, lanceolate, unequal, shorter than the lowest flowering glume. Flowering glumes ovate-lanceolate, concave, acute. Stamens 3. Ovary glabrous; styles 2 or 3, distinct, feathery nearly to the base. Grain narrowly oblong, grooved, free within the persistent glumes.

Leaves not net-veined. Stem-sheaths tapering upwards.
  Bracts less than 1 in. . . . . 1. *A. falcata*.
Leaves net-veined. Stem-sheaths oblong, tip rounded.
  Bracts 3 in. . . . . 2. *A. spathiflora*.

1. **Arundinaria falcata,** *Nees*; *Fl. Br. Ind.* vii. 381. Stems 6–10 ft., $\frac{1}{3}$–$\frac{1}{2}$ in. diam.; joints much swollen; stem-sheaths tapering upwards, blade $\frac{1}{2}$–2 in., recurved, ligule up to $\frac{1}{2}$ in., toothed; branches slender, many-jointed. Leaves not net-veined, usually about 3–4 × $\frac{1}{3}$–$\frac{1}{3}$ in., sometimes on young shoots up to 12 × 1 in., tapering into a long, fine, often twisted tip; sheath glabrous. Ligule long. Bracts linear or lanceolate, less than 1 in. long. Spikelets $\frac{1}{2}$–$\frac{2}{3}$ in., usually 2-, sometimes 1-flowered, crowded in numerous, simple or branched, spreading, curved racemes 4–10 in. long. Glumes minutely hairy at the tip. Ovary narrowly oblong, tapering upwards; styles 2. Grain tipped with the persistent style-base. (Fig. 199.)

Simla, 5000 ft.—W. Himalaya, 4000–7000 ft.

Common in forest undergrowth, usually on northern slopes or in ravines. Flowers gregariously, but a few clumps may be found in flower almost any year. Native name *Ringal*. The stems are used for pipes, basket work, &c.

2 **Arundinaria spathiflora,** *Trin.*; *Fl. Br. Ind.* vii. 382. Stems 12–20 ft., $\frac{1}{2}$–$\frac{3}{4}$ in. diam.; stem-sheaths oblong, tip rounded, blade 2–4 × $\frac{1}{3}$ in., ligule very short; branches chiefly from the upper joints, many-jointed. Leaves net-veined, 3–5 × $\frac{1}{3}$–$\frac{1}{2}$ in.; sheath 2–3 in., a few purple bristles at the mouth. Ligule long, dark-coloured. Bracts 3 in. long, oblong, stem-clasping, usually

bearing a rudimentary blade and ligule, tip truncate. Spikelets 1–2½ in., 4–8-flowered, crowded in numerous, drooping, raceme-like branches 10–18 in. long. Lower empty glume obtuse, upper finely pointed. Styles 3.

Huttoo.—W. Himalaya, 7000–9000 ft.

Common in the undergrowth of deodar and fir forest in moist localities. Usually flowers gregariously. Native name *Ringal*. The stems are used for pipes, basket work, &c.

FIG. 199. ARUNDINARIA FALCATA.

54. DENDROCALAMUS. From the Greek *dendron*, a tree, and *calamos*, a reed, referring to the tree-like habit of this Grass.—Tropical and subtropical Asia.

Dendrocalamus strictus, *Nees*; *Fl. Br. Ind.* vii. 404. An arborescent bamboo; rootstock much branched; stems perennial, 20–40 ft., 1–3 in. diam., erect or bent and rooting at the joints near the base, occasionally solid or with only a small cavity; joints swollen, bearing stiff, shining, papery, very deciduous, stem-sheaths, 3–12 in. long, narrowed upwards to a rounded top, blade triangular, ligule short, narrow; branches clustered, horizontal or curving downwards. Leaves not net-veined, narrowly lanceolate, 1–2 in. in dry localities, up to 10 in. in moist, $\frac{1}{5}$–2 in. broad, finely pointed, abruptly constricted at the base; upper surface rough, lower softly hairy; sheaths hairy, mouth bristly. Ligule narrow, toothed. Spikelets spinous, $\frac{1}{4}$–$\frac{1}{2}$ in. (fertile and smaller sterile ones intermixed), 2–3-flowered, crowded in large, globose, sessile heads disposed at intervals along the branches of a panicle. Glumes boat-shaped, hairy near the tip. Empty glumes 2, sometimes more, acute. Flowering glumes spine-tipped. Stamens 6, far-protruding. Style single or branching near the feathery tip, thread-like, very long. Grain free within the persistent glumes, ovoid, hairy, beaked with the persistent style-base.

Sutlej valley &c.—Throughout India, on dry hills, ascending to 3500 ft.

Usually known as the Male Bamboo. Flowers gregariously at intervals of several years, but a clump may here and there be found in flower during the cold season of almost any year. Native name *Bans* or *Bans kaban*. Highly valued for building purposes, lance-shafts, sticks, mat and basket manufacture.

D. Hamiltonii, *Nees & Arn.*; *Fl. Br. Ind.* vii. 405.—A common bamboo in the E. Himalaya and Assam and sometimes cultivated near villages in the lower hills. It has broader leaves than *D. strictus* and the globose heads of purple spikelets are not spinous.

Corrigenda.

p. 28,	eighth line from	bottom,	*for*	'khol'	*read*	'kohl.'
p. 43,	sixth ,,	top,	,,	'speies'	,,	'species.'
p. 70,	eleventh ,,	bottom,	,,	'Wad'	,,	'Road.'

GENERAL INDEX

Vernacular names, synonyms and species incidentally mentioned are in italics